# BATTLES AND LEADERS OF THE CIVIL WAR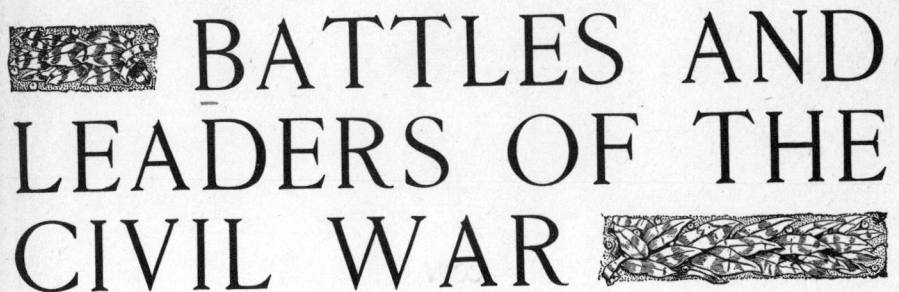

## VOLUME II

BEING FOR THE MOST PART CONTRIBUTIONS BY UNION AND CONFEDERATE OFFICERS. BASED UPON "THE CENTURY WAR SERIES." EDITED BY ROBERT UNDERWOOD JOHNSON AND CLARENCE CLOUGH BUEL, OF THE EDITORIAL STAFF OF "THE CENTURY MAGAZINE."

  D75887

NEW YORK: THOMAS YOSELOFF, INC.

The Special Contents of this Edition Copyright 1956
By THOMAS YOSELOFF, INC.
Manufactured in the United States of America

# CONTENTS OF VOLUME TWO.

PAGE

FRONTISPIECE, "THE DISPATCH BEARER." From the painting by Gilbert Gaul .......... VI
LIST OF MAPS ............................................................................ XVIII
LIST OF ARTISTS ......................................................................... XIX
LIST OF DRAUGHTSMEN ................................................................. XIX
LIST OF ENGRAVERS ..................................................................... XIX

## FORT PULASKI.

SIEGE AND CAPTURE OF FORT PULASKI ........ *GENERAL Q. A. GILLMORE* .......... 1

    ILLUSTRATIONS: Fort Pulaski after the Surrender (*Xanthus Smith*) — Map of the Siege of Fort Pulaski (*Jacob Wells*) — Martello Tower and Lighthouse, Tybee Island (*Xanthus Smith*) — Brigadier-General Egbert L. Vielé, from Brady photo. — Fort Pulaski from Turtle Island (*Theo. R. Davis*) — Brevet Brigadier-General Horace Porter, from photo. — Brevet Brigadier-General Charles G. Halpine, from photo. by C. D. Fredericks & Co. (*F. H. Schell*) — Views of Fort Pulaski after the Surrender, from Gardner photos. (*C. A. Vanderhoof*).

## THE CAPTURE OF NEW ORLEANS.

EARLY OPERATIONS IN THE GULF ............. *PROFESSOR J. RUSSELL SOLEY* ...... 13
NEW ORLEANS BEFORE THE CAPTURE .......... *GEORGE W. CABLE* ............... 14

    ILLUSTRATIONS: The Confederate Cruiser "Sumter" leaving New Orleans (*Theo. R. Davis*) — Major-General Mansfield Lovell, C. S. A., from Anderson-Cook photo. — The Union Fleet arriving at New Orleans (*J. O. Davidson*).

THE OPENING OF THE LOWER MISSISSIPPI ...... *ADMIRAL DAVID D. PORTER* ........ 22

    ILLUSTRATIONS: Farragut's Flag-ship, the "Hartford," from photo. by J. W. Black (*J. O. Davidson*) — Maps of the Lower Mississippi (*Jacob Wells*) — Confederate Sharp-shooters and Swamp Hunters attacking Mortar-boats (*A. C. Redwood*) — Mortar-schooners engaged against Fort Jackson (*J. O. Davidson*) — Plan of Fort Jackson, showing the Effect of the Bombardment (*W. L. Lathrop*) — Brigadier-General Johnson K. Duncan, C. S. A., from photo. lent by J. J. Duncan — Map showing the Defenses of the Mississippi and the Positions of the Mortar-fleet at the Opening of the Bombardment, from drawing lent by Commander J. R. Bartlett — Rear-Admiral Henry H. Bell, from photo. lent by Mrs. Margaret C. Bell (*I. R. Wiles*) — Commander John K. Mitchell, C. S. N., from Anderson photo. — Lieutenant Thomas B. Huger, C. S. N., from a photo. lent by W. H. Huger — Birds-eye View of the Passage of the Forts below New Orleans (*J. O. Davidson*) — Captain Theodorus Bailey, in the "Cayuga," breaking through the Confederate Fleet (*J. O. Davidson*) — Rear-Admiral Theodorus Bailey, from Brady photo. — Rear-Admiral Melancton Smith, from photo. (*I. R. Wiles*) — The course of the United States Screw-sloop "Mississippi" in the Passage of the Forts, from drawing lent by Commander J. R. Bartlett — The United States Steamer "Mississippi" attempting to run down the Confederate Ram "Manassas" (*J. O. Davidson*) — The Confederate Iron-clad "Louisiana" on the way to Fort St. Philip (*W. Taber*) — Plan of the "Louisiana," after a war-time sketch (*W. Taber*) — Mortar-steamers attacking the Water-battery of Fort Jackson (*J. O. Davidson*) — Commander Porter receiving Confederate Officers on the "Harriet Lane" (*J. O. Davidson*) — Commander Charles F. McIntosh, C. S. N., from photo. lent by William C. Whittle — Explosion of the Confederate Ram "Louisiana" (*J. O. Davidson*) — The Confederate "River Defense" Ram "Stonewall Jackson," from a sketch by Captain Beverley Kennon (*J. O. Davidson*) — Major-General Benjamin F. Butler, from Brady photo.

THE "BROOKLYN" AT THE PASSAGE OF THE FORTS ........................... } .... *COM. JOHN RUSSELL BARTLETT* ..... 56

    ILLUSTRATIONS: Fort Jackson in 1885 (*W. L. Lathrop*) — Admiral D. G. Farragut, from Brady photo., with Autograph — Section of Chain Armor placed on the side of the "Brooklyn" to protect her boilers, from sketch lent by Commander J. R. Bartlett — Admiral David D. Porter, from Brady photo. — Rear-

---

☆ In order to save much repetition, particular credit is here given to the Massachusetts Commandery of the Loyal Legion, to Colonel Arnold A. Rand, General Albert Ordway, and Charles B. Hall for the use of photographs and drawings. War-time photographers whose work is of the greatest historical value, and has been freely drawn upon in the preparation of the illustrations, are M. B. Brady, Alexander Gardner, and Captain A. J. Russell in the North; and D. H. Anderson of Richmond. Va., and George S. Cook of Charleston, S.C. — the latter, since the war, having succeeded to the ownership of the Anderson negatives.

ix

## CONTENTS OF VOLUME TWO.

Admiral Thomas T. Craven, from photo lent by H. S. Craven — The Course of the "Brooklyn" in the Passage of the Forts, from drawing lent by Commander J. R. Bartlett — Stand to hold Grape, called "Lampposts" by the Confederates, from sketch lent by Commander J. R. Bartlett — Flag-Ship "Hartford" attacked by a Fire-raft *(J. O. Davidson)* — Section of Fort St. Philip during the Engagement *(J. O. Davidson)* — The "Brooklyn" attacked by the Confederate Ram "Manassas" *(J. O. Davidson)* — Rear-Admiral Charles S. Boggs, from Brady photo.

FARRAGUT'S CAPTURE OF NEW ORLEANS...... *WILLIAM T. MEREDITH*.............. 70

THE OPPOSING FORCES IN THE OPERATIONS AT NEW ORLEANS, LA. Composition, Losses, and Strength ................................................................. 73

FIGHTING FARRAGUT BELOW NEW ORLEANS.... *CAPTAIN BEVERLEY KENNON* ....... 76

ILLUSTRATIONS: River side Interior of Fort St. Philip, from photo. *(E. J. Meeker)* — Captain Beverley Kennon, Louisiana State Navy, from tintype — Map showing Final Disposition of the Confederate Fleet, from drawing lent by Commander J. R. Bartlett — Firing at the "Varuna" through the bow of the "Governor Moore." *(J. O. Davidson)* — The "Stonewall Jackson" ramming the "Varuna" *(J. O. Davidson)* — The "Pensacola" disabling the "Governor Moore" — *(J. O. Davidson)* — The "Governor Moore" at the end of the Fight *(J. O. Davidson)* — The "Governor Moore" in Flames *(J. O. Davidson)* — Entrance to Fort St. Philip, from photo. *(W. L. Lathrop).*

THE RAM "MANASSAS" AT THE PASSAGE OF THE NEW ORLEANS FORTS....... } .... *CAPTAIN A. F. WARLEY*............. 89

INCIDENTS OF THE OCCUPATION OF NEW ORLEANS........................... } ....*CAPTAIN ALBERT KAUTZ*............ 91

ILLUSTRATIONS: The Maintop of the "Hartford" with Howitzer *(W. Taber)* — Captain Theodorus Bailey and Lieutenant George H. Perkins on their way to Demand the Surrender of New Orleans *(T. de Thulstrup)* — Scene at the City Hall — Hauling down the State Flag *(T. de Thulstrup)*.

FARRAGUT'S DEMANDS FOR THE SURRENDER OF NEW ORLEANS..................... } .. *MARION A. BAKER* ................. 95

ILLUSTRATION: Pierre Soulé, from daguerreotype.

THE WATER-BATTERY AT FORT JACKSON....... *CAPTAIN WILLIAM B. ROBERTSON*... 99

CONFEDERATE RESPONSIBILITIES FOR FARRAGUT'S SUCCESS.... ...... } ........1. *JAMES GRIMSHAW DUNCAN*......101
........2. *COMMODORE JOHN K. MITCHELL*..102

## OPERATIONS IN THE FAR SOUTH-WEST.

THE CONFEDERATE INVASION OF NEW MEXICO AND ARIZONA .......... } ........*CAPTAIN GEORGE H. PETTIS*.......103

ILLUSTRATIONS: Cavalry Orderly, from photo. *(W. Taber)* — Map of the Campaign and of Sibley's Retreat, and Map of Fort Craig and Valverde *(Jacob Wells)* — Major-General Edward R. S. Canby, from Brady photo. — Brigadier-General Henry H. Sibley, C. S. A., from photo.

CANBY'S SERVICES IN THE NEW MEXICAN CAMPAIGN ............................. } .. *BREVET BRIG.-GENERAL LATHAM ANDERSON*......................697

CANBY AT VALVERDE........................... *LIEUT.-COLONEL A. W. EVANS*......699

SIBLEY'S NEW MEXICAN CAMPAIGN. Its Objects and the Causes of its Failure.............. } .. *MAJOR T. T. TEEL*..................700

## EVENTS OF 1861-2.

McCLELLAN ORGANIZING THE GRAND ARMY..... *PHILIPPE, COMTE DE PARIS* ........112

ILLUSTRATIONS: Provost Guard, Washington *(Winslow Homer)* — Confederate Works on Munson's Hill, from sketch by Robert K. Sneden *(E. J. Meeker)* — Mt. Olivet Church on the old Fairfax Road, and "Claremont," the residence of Commodore French Forrest, C. S. N., from sketches by Robert K. Sneden *(E. J. Meeker)* — Edwin M. Stanton, from photo., with Autograph — The North Front of the War Department, Washington, from photo. *(E. J. Meeker).*

## CONTENTS OF VOLUME TWO.

PAGE

BALL'S BLUFF AND THE ARREST OF GENERAL STONE .............................. } ..*COLONEL RICHARD B. IRWIN* ........123

    ILLUSTRATIONS: Map of the Upper Potomac *(Jacob Wells)* — Map of Ball's Bluff *(Jacob Wells)* — The Cliff at Ball's Bluff, from photo. *(E. J. Meeker)* — Colonel Edward D. Baker, from Brady photo. — Governor John A. Andrew, from Brady photo.

CAPTAIN WILKES'S SEIZURE OF MASON AND SLIDELL ..................... } ..*REAR-ADMIRAL D. MᴀcN. FAIRFAX* ..135

    ILLUSTRATIONS: James M. Mason, from daguerreotype — John Slidell, from photo. — Captain Charles Wilkes, from Anthony photo. — William H. Seward, from daguerreotype.

EARLY OPERATIONS ON THE POTOMAC RIVER... *PROFESSOR J. RUSSELL SOLEY* ......143

OPERATIONS OF 1861 ABOUT FORT MONROE.... *GENERAL JOSEPH B. CARR* .........144

    ILLUSTRATIONS: Fort Monroe in 1860, from lithograph lent by General John C. Tidball *(W. Taber)* — Light-house, Fort Monroe — Chesapeake Hospital, Hampton, Va., and Sallyport, Fort Monroe, from Gardner photos. *(H. C. Edwards)* — Arrival of the Original "Contraband" *(Theo. R. Davis)* — Camp of Duryea's Zouaves, near Fort Monroe *(Frank H. Schell)* — Uniform of Duryea's Zouaves *(H. A. Ogden)* — The 4th Massachusetts Regiment Fortifying Camp Butler, Newport News *(Frank H. Schell)* — Confederate Earthworks at Big Bethel, from sketch by R. K. Sneden *(E. J. Meeker)* — Major Theodore Winthrop, from a portrait by Rowse — Ruins of Hampton, Va., from sketch by R. K. Sneden *(E. J. Meeker)*.

CAMPAIGNING TO NO PURPOSE (Recollections of a Private — II.)...................... } ..*WARREN LEE GOSS* ................153

    ILLUSTRATIONS: Inspection *(Winslow Homer)* — A Sutler's Tent, from photo. *(W. H. Shelton)* — Harper's Ferry in 1862, from the North, from Gardner photo. *(E. J. Meeker)* — Confederate Prisoners, from Gardner photo. *(W. H. Shelton)* — A Camp Oven, from sketch by F. H. Schell *(Thomas Hogan)* — Transports on the Potomac, from photo. *(W. H. Shelton)*.

## MCCLELLAN BEFORE RICHMOND.

THE PENINSULAR CAMPAIGN ..................... *GENERAL GEORGE B. MᶜCLELLAN* ...160

    ILLUSTRATIONS: Fort Monroe — Parade of the 3d Pennsylvania Artillery, from Gardner photo. *(W. Taber)* — Major-General John E. Wool, from Brady photo. — View of Alexandria from the Camp of the 40th New York Volunteers, from sketch by R. K. Sneden *(E. J. Meeker)* — Headquarters of Brigadier-General John Sedgwick, on the Leesburg Turnpike near Washington, from sketch by R. K. Sneden *(E. J. Meeker)* — Map of the Virginia Campaigns *(Jacob Wells)* — Quartermaster's Dock, Fort Monroe *(Theo. R. Davis)* — Map of the Peninsula Campaign *(Jacob Wells)* — Heintzelman's Headquarters at Howe's Sawmill before Yorktown, from sketch by R. K. Sneden *(E. J. Meeker)* — View from Mortar-battery No. 4, from sketch by R. K. Sneden *(E. J. Meeker)* — Clark's House, near Howe's Saw-mill, from sketch by R. K. Sneden *(E. J. Meeker)* — View of Main Street, Yorktown, the Union Troops Marching In, from sketch by R. K. Sneden *(E. J. Meeker)* — Union Water-battery in Front of Yorktown, Exploded Gun, Confederate Fortifications at Yorktown, Confederate Water-battery, and an Angle of the Confederate Fortifications at Yorktown, from Gardner photos. *(W. Taber)* — St. Peter's Church near New Kent Court-house, and New Kent Court-house, from sketches by R. K. Sneden *(C. A. Vanderhoof)* — Section of the Encampment of the Army of the Potomac near White House, Va., process reproduction of Gardner photo. — White House, the Home of General W. H. F. Lee, and Ruins of the White House *(A. R. Waud)* — The Orleans Princes and Suite at Dinner, from Gardner photo. — Confederate Battery at Mathias Point, or Budd's Ferry, from sketch by R. K. Sneden *(E. J. Meeker)*.

YORKTOWN AND WILLIAMSBURG (Recollections of a Private — III.)........................ } ..*WARREN LEE GOSS* ................189

    ILLUSTRATIONS: Map of the fight at Big Bethel, Siege of Yorktown, and of the Battle of Williamsburg *(Jacob Wells)* — On to Richmond *(W. Taber)* — Mrs. T———'s Exodus *(W. H. Shelton)* — Confederate Battery on the Terraced Magazine, Gosport Navy-Yard *(F. H. Schell)* — "Get that Team out of the Mud!" *(W. H. Shelton)* — Skirmish at Lee's Mills *(Winslow Homer)* — Union Mortar-battery before Yorktown, from Gardner photo. *(W. Taber)* — The 61st New York Regiment in Camp at Ship Point *(Winslow Homer)* — A Tempting Breastwork *(W. H. Shelton)* — Camp of the Union Army near White House, from Gardner photo. *(W. Taber)* — Union Camp at Cumberland Landing, from Gardner photo. *(W. Taber)*.

THE OPPOSING FORCES AT WILLIAMSBURG, VA. Composition, Strength, and Losses ......200

CONFEDERATE USE OF SUBTERRANEAN SHELLS ON THE PENINSULA..................... } .........................................201

xii                    CONTENTS OF VOLUME TWO.

PAGE
MANASSAS TO SEVEN PINES ................... GENERAL JOSEPH E. JOHNSTON .... 202
    ILLUSTRATIONS: Confederate Sharp-shooter (*W. Taber*) — Map of the Region between Washington and Richmond (*Jacob Wells*) — Fort Magruder and other Confederate Earth-works, and William and Mary College, from sketches by R. K. Sneden (*C. A. Vanderhoof*) — Major-General John B. Magruder, C. S. A., from photo. — Major-General Benjamin Huger, C. S. A., from photo. — Lieutenant-General Daniel H. Hill, C. S. A., from Cook photo. — Burying the Dead, and Burning Horses at the Twin Houses, near Casey's Redoubt, Seven Pines (*A. R. Waud*) — Major-General Gustavus W. Smith, C. S. A., from photo. by Gurney & Son.

THE OPPOSING FORCES AT SEVEN PINES. Composition, Strength, and Losses ............. 218

TWO DAYS OF BATTLE AT SEVEN PINES }
(Fair Oaks) ........................ } ...... GENERAL GUSTAVUS W. SMITH ..... 220
    ILLUSTRATIONS: The Seven Pines, looking East, from sketch by G. L. Frankenstein (*W. Taber*) — Major-General S. P. Heintzelman, from Brady photo. — Major-General Erasmus D. Keyes, from Brady photo. — Map showing Positions Preliminary to the Battle of Seven Pines, after sketch map by General G. W. Smith, C. S. A. (*Jacob Wells*) — Major-General W. H. C. Whiting, C. S. A., from photo. lent by Colonel Charles C. Jones, Jr. — The Twin Farm-houses behind Casey's Redoubt, and the Twin Farm-houses as seen from Casey's Redoubt, from Gardner photos. (*Harry Fenn*) — Major-General Silas Casey, from Brady photo. — Brigadier-General Henry M. Naglee, from Brady photo. — Major-General David B. Birney, from Brady photo. — Allen's Farm House near the Williamsburg Road (*W. L. Sheppard*) — Map of the Battle of Seven Pines, compiled by General G. W. Smith (*Jacob Wells*) — Line of Battle of General Devens's Brigade (*Julian Scott*) — Major-General Darius N. Couch, from Brady photo. — Sumner's Corps crossing the Overflowed "Grapevine" Bridge (*A. R. Waud*) — Major-General E. V. Sumner, from Brady photo. — Sumner's March to Reënforce Couch at Fair Oaks Station (*W. Taber*) — Houses on the Battle-field used as Union Hospitals, from Gardner photos. (*W. Taber*) — Major-General O. O. Howard, from Brady photo. — Farmhouse near Fair Oaks used as a Union Hospital, Hyer's House, near Fair Oaks, used as a Union Hospital, and House near Fair Oaks, used after the Battle as Quarters for the Officers of the 1st Minnesota, from sketches by R. K. Sneden (*C. A. Vanderhoof*) — Second Line of the Union Works at the Twin Houses (*A. R. Waud*) — Pettit's Battery in Fort Richardson, in front of Fair Oaks Station, from Gardner photo. (*A. C. Redwood*) — Putting the Wounded on Cars (*A. R. Waud*).

THE NAVY IN THE PENINSULAR CAMPAIGN ...... PROFESSOR J. RUSSELL SOLEY ...... 264
    ILLUSTRATIONS: On the Gun-deck of the Confederate Iron-clad "Merrimac" (*W. Taber*) — Maps of the "Monitor" and "Merrimac" Fight (*Jacob Wells*) — In the Turret of the "Monitor" (*Henry Sandham*) — Fort Darling, from photo. (*W. Taber*) — Rear-Admiral John Rodgers, from Brady photo. — Fort Darling, Looking Down the James, and Sunken Steamboats and other Obstructions in the James River near Fort Darling, from photos. (*Harry Fenn*).

STUART'S RIDE AROUND McCLELLAN ........... COLONEL W. T. ROBINS ............. 271
    ILLUSTRATIONS: Trooper of the Virginia Cavalry (*A. C. Redwood*) — Map of Stuart's Ride around McClellan (*Jacob Wells*) — Duel between a Union Cavalryman and a Confederate Trooper (*W. T. Trego*).

ANECDOTES OF THE PENINSULAR CAMPAIGN ..................................... 275
    I. General Johnston to the Rescue — *F. Y. Dabney.* II. Hood "Feeling the Enemy" — *J. H. L.* III. Characteristics of General Wise — *J. H. L.* IV. Origin of the Lee Tomatoes — *W. Roy Mason.*

## THE SHENANDOAH VALLEY IN '62.

WEST VIRGINIA OPERATIONS UNDER FRÉMONT .. GENERAL JACOB D. COX ............ 278
    ILLUSTRATION: Map of West Virginia (*Jacob Wells*).

STONEWALL JACKSON IN THE SHENANDOAH ..... GENERAL JOHN D. IMBODEN ......... 282
    ILLUSTRATIONS: A Confederate of 1862 (*A. C. Redwood*) — Brigadier-General John D. Imboden, C. S. A., from photo. — Map of Jackson's Campaign in the Shenandoah Valley (*Jacob Wells*) — Map of Battle of McDowell, from map by Major Jed. Hotchkiss — Union Camp at Front Royal (*Edwin Forbes*) — Brevet Major-General John R. Kenly, from photo. by J. H. Young — View from Banks's Fort, near Strasburg, from photo. by W. G. Reed (*E. J. Meeker*) — Arrival of Frémont's Vanguard above Strasburg (*Edwin Forbes*) — Map of the Battle of Cross Keys, from map by Major Jed. Hotchkiss — View of the Battle of Cross Keys (*Edwin Forbes*) — Map of the Battle of Port Republic, from map by Major Jed. Hotchkiss — The First Maryland (Confederate) Regiment at Harrisonburg and the Death of Ashby, lent by General Bradley T. Johnson (*W. L. Sheppard*) — Brigadier-General Turner Ashby, C. S. A., from photo.

NOTES ON THE BATTLE OF McDOWELL ............................................. 298
    I. General Robert C. Schenck. II. Extracts from the Report of General R. H. Milroy.

# CONTENTS OF VOLUME TWO. xiii

PAGE

THE OPPOSING FORCES IN THE VALLEY CAMPAIGNS. Composition, Losses and Strength..299

FIGHTING JACKSON AT KERNSTOWN............ *GENERAL NATHAN KIMBALL*........302
    ILLUSTRATIONS: Brigadier-General Frederick W. Lander, from Brady photo.—Brigadier-General James Shields, from photo. lent by David Delany — Map of the Battle of Kernstown, based upon maps in the "Official Records" *(J. S. Kemp)* — Battle-field of Kernstown, Va., from photo. by W. G. Reed *(E. J. Meeker)* — Brevet Major-General Nathan Kimball, from photo. by Adams.

## THE SEVEN DAYS' FIGHTING.

THE OPPOSING FORCES IN THE SEVEN DAYS' BATTLES. Composition, Losses, and Strength..313

HANOVER COURT HOUSE AND GAINES'S MILL.... *GENERAL FITZ JOHN PORTER*.......319
    ILLUSTRATIONS: George B. McClellan, from photo. by G. C. Cox — Rush's Lancers, 6th Pennsylvania Cavalry *(Winslow Homer)* — Map of the Upper Chickahominy and Neighboring Country *(Jacob Wells)* — Replenishing the Gas of Professor Lowe's Military Balloon "Intrepid," and Professor Lowe observing the Battle of Seven Pines, from photos. *(W. Taber)* — Confederate Retreat through Mechanicsville before the Advance of McClellan's Artillery *(A. R. Waud)* — Union Artillery at Mechanicsville Shelling the Confederate Works, from sketch by A. R. Waud *(W. L. Sheppard)* — Union Defenses at Ellerson's Mill, from sketch by A. R. Waud *(Charles Kendrick)* — Map of the Battle of Beaver Dam Creek *(Jacob Wells)* — Battle of Gaines's Mill, from a photo. of the painting by the Prince de Joinville, lent by General Fitz John Porter — Major-General Fitz John Porter, from Brady photo.— Map of the Battle-field of Gaines's Mill *(Jacob Wells)* — Uniform of the 83d Pennsylvania *(H. A. Ogden)* — Capture of abandoned Union Guns at Gaines's Mill *(A. R. Waud)* — Ruins of Gaines's Mill, from photo. *(Harry Fenn)* — Brevet Major-General Philip St. George Cooke, from photo. by Whitehurst.

THE CHARGE OF COOKE'S CAVALRY AT }....... *GENERAL P. ST. GEORGE COOKE*....344
GAINES'S MILL ................... }

RECOLLECTIONS OF A PARTICIPANT IN THE } ..*REV. W. H. HITCHCOCK*........346
CHARGE ........................ }

LEE'S ATTACKS NORTH OF THE CHICKAHOMINY.*GENERAL DANIEL H. HILL*..........347
    ILLUSTRATIONS: "W'at war dey Fightin' 'bout?" *(W. Taber)* — Confederate Skirmish-line driven in by the Union Advance *(W. L. Sheppard)* — Exterior Line of Defenses of Richmond *(W. L. Sheppard)* — Mechanicsville from the North-west, from photo. *(Harry Fenn)* — Charge of Confederates under Ripley and Pender at Beaver Dam Creek *(A. C. Redwood)* — Old Cold Harbor Tavern, from photo. *(W. Taber)* — Battle-field of Beaver Dam Creek, from photo. *(Harry Fenn)* — Charge of a Sutler upon G. B. Anderson's Brigade at Gaines's Mill *(T. de Thulstrup)* — "Captured by Stonewall Jackson himself!" *(A. C. Redwood.)*

ON THE CONFEDERATE RIGHT AT GAINES'S MILL.*GENERAL E. M. LAW*..............363

THE CAUSE OF A SILENT BATTLE.............*PROFESSOR JOHN B. DeMOTTE*......365

REAR-GUARD FIGHTING DURING THE CHANGE } ..*GENERAL W. B. FRANKLIN*.........366
OF BASE..................... }
    ILLUSTRATIONS: Uniform of the 72d Pennsylvania *(H. A. Ogden)* — Union Troops Building the Corduroy Approaches to Grapevine Bridge, from Gardner photo. *(R. F. Zogbaum)* — The Retreat from the Chickahominy *(A. R. Waud)* — Dr. Trent's Farm-house, McClellan's Headquarters, from photo. *(W. L. Sheppard)* — Battle of Savage's Station *(A. R. Waud)* — Running Ammunition Trains into the Chickahominy *(A. R. Waud)* — View of Savage's Station from the North Side of the Railroad, from sketch by R. K. Sneden *(H. C. Edwards)* — Map of the Plan of the Battle at Savage's Station *(Jacob Wells)* — Major-General William B. Franklin, from photo.— The Rear-Guard at White Oak Swamp, showing General William F. Smith's division, from the painting owned by the Union League Club, New York *(Julian Scott)*.

McCLELLAN'S CHANGE OF BASE AND MAL- } ..*GENERAL DANIEL H. HILL*...........383
VERN HILL ........................ }
    ILLUSTRATIONS: Woodbury's Bridge across the Chickahominy, from Gardner photo. *(W. Taber)* — Map of the Region of the Seven Days' Fighting *(Jacob Wells)* — A Sample of the Chickahominy Swamp, from Brady photo. *(J. D. Woodward)* — Union Field-Hospital at Savage's Station, after the Battle of Gaines's Mill, from Gardner photo. *(T. de Thulstrup)* — The Artillery Engagement at White Oak Bridge *(A. R. Waud)* — Sketch Map of the Vicinity of Malvern Hill *(Jacob Wells)* — Willis Church, on the Quaker Road, near Glendale *(E. J. Meeker)* — George W. Randolph, Secretary of War of the Confederacy from March 17th, 1862, until November 17th, 1862, from a photo.

## CONTENTS OF VOLUME TWO.

"THE SEVEN DAYS," INCLUDING FRAYSER'S FARM .................................. } ..GENERAL JAMES LONGSTREET ......396

 ILLUSTRATIONS: "Gin'l Longstreet's Body-Sarvant, Sah, endu'in de Wah!" *(W. L. Sheppard)* — Map of the Battle of Frayser's Farm *(Jacob Wells)* — Frayser's Farm-House, from photo. *(Harry Fenn)* — Uniform of a Non-Commissioned Officer of the 1st New-York *(H. A. Ogden)* — Opening of the Battle of Frayser's Farm *(A. R. Waud)* — Charge of Confederates upon Randol's Battery at Frayser's Farm *(A. C. Redwood)* — General George A. McCall, from Brady photo. — General Heintzelman's Headquarters at Nelson's House, during the Battle of Glendale, from sketch by R. K. Sneden *(C. A. Vanderhoof).*

THE BATTLE OF MALVERN HILL ................GENERAL FITZ JOHN PORTER........406

 ILLUSTRATIONS: An Orderly at Headquarters *(W. H. Shelton)* — The Parsonage, near Malvern Hill, after photo. taken in 1885 *(Harry Fenn)* — Major-General George W. Morell, from Brady photo. — The Crew House of war time, from sketch by G. L. Frankenstein, and the new Crew House, from photo. *(Harry Fenn)* — Map of the Battle of Malvern Hill *(Jacob Wells)* — Berdan's Sharp-shooters Skirmishing in the Meadow Wheat-Field *(A. C. Redwood)* — The West House, from photo. *(Harry Fenn)* — View from the Meadow west of the Crew House, from photo. *(Harry Fenn)* — Scene of the Confederate Attack on the west side of Crew's Hill, from photo. *(Harry Fenn)* — Repulse of the Confederates on the Slope of Crew's Hill *(T. de Thulstrup)* — The Main Battle-field, Views of the Union and Confederate Positions, from photo's *(Harry Fenn)* — Malvern Hill, from the direction of Turkey Island Bridge, from sketch by G. L. Frankenstein — View from Malvern Hill, looking toward the James, from photo. *(Harry Fenn)* — Brevet Brigadier-General James McQuade, from Brady photo. — The Malvern House, from photo. *(Harry Fenn)* — Headquarters of General Heintzelman on the River Side of Malvern Hill, and Turkey Bridge, under Malvern Hill, from sketches by R. K. Sneden *(C. A. Vanderhoof)* — General Fitz John Porter's Headquarters in the Westover Mansion, Camp at Harrison's Landing *(A. R. Waud)* — Supplying the Hungry Army at Harrison's Landing, from sketch by A. R. Waud *(W. L. Sheppard)* — Berkeley, Harrison's Landing *(A. R. Waud).*

THE ARMY OF THE POTOMAC AT HARRISON'S LANDING ........................ } ..GEORGE L. KILMER..... ...........427

 ILLUSTRATION: Dummies and Quaker Guns left in the Works at Harrison's Landing on the Evacuation by the Army of the Potomac *(A. R. Waud).*

WITH THE CAVALRY ON THE PENINSULA .......GENERAL WILLIAM W. AVERELL ....429

 ILLUSTRATIONS: A Part of the Fortified Camp at Harrison's Landing, from sketch by A. R. Waud *(J. D. Woodward)* — Roll-Book of Co. D, 27th New-York Regiment, from the "History of the 27th New-York Volunteers."

THE REAR-GUARD AT MALVERN HILL ...... { I. BREVET-MAJOR HENRY E. SMITH.. <br> II. GENERAL ERASMUS D. KEYES..... } 434

THE ADMINISTRATION IN THE PENINSULAR CAMPAIGN .......................... } ....LIEUT.-COLONEL RICHARD B. IRWIN.435

RICHMOND SCENES IN '62.........................MRS. BURTON HARRISON...........439

 ILLUSTRATIONS: The Old Clifton Hotel *(W. L. Sheppard)* — Front and Rear Views of the Virginia Armory, Richmond *(W. L. Sheppard)* — Richmond, from the Manchester Side of the James *(Fortier Concklin)* — Food for the Confederate Wounded *(E. W. Kemble)* — In the Streets of Richmond — Wounded from the Battle of Seven Pines *(W. L. Sheppard)* — View of Washington Monument, in Capitol Square, Richmond *(Thomas Moran).*

## LEE'S CAMPAIGN AGAINST POPE.

THE SECOND BATTLE OF BULL RUN ............GENERAL JOHN POPE................449

 ILLUSTRATIONS: Picketing the Rapidan *(R. F. Zogbaum)* — Outline Map of the Campaign *(Jacob Wells)* — View in Culpeper during the occupation by Pope, from Gardner photo. *(W. Taber)* — Major-General John Pope, from photo., with Autograph — Retreat of the Union Troops across the Rappahannock at Rappahannock Station *(Edwin Forbes)* — The Battle of Cedar Mountain, View from the Union Line *(Edwin Forbes)* — Brigadier-General Charles S. Winder, C. S. A., from photo. lent by his widow — House on the Battle-field of Cedar Mountain where General Winder died, from Gardner photo. *(W. Taber)* — Map of the Battle-field of Cedar Mountain *(Jacob Wells)* — Charge of Union Cavalry upon the Confederate Advance near Brandy Station *(Edwin Forbes)* — Brevet Major-General John W. Geary, from photo. lent by Dr. H. E. Goodman — Map of Relative Positions of Forces at Sunset, August 26th, 1862 *(Jacob Wells)* — The Rear of the Column *(Edwin Forbes)* — Map of Relative Positions of Forces at Sunset, August 27th, 1862 *(Jacob Wells)* — Collision on Thursday, August 28th, between Reynolds's Division and Jackson's Right Wing *(Edwin Forbes)* — Map of Relative Positions of Forces at Sunset, August 28th, 1862 *(Jacob Wells)* — Map of Battle-field of the Second Bull Run, showing Relative Positions at Noon, August 29th, reproduction of a drawing lent by General John Pope — Map of Relative Positions at Sunset, August 29th *(Jacob Wells)* — The Battle of Groveton, August 29th, as seen from Centreville *(Edwin Forbes)* — Major-

## CONTENTS OF VOLUME TWO.

PAGE

General Cuvier Grover, from Brady photo.— The Halt on the Line of Battle (*Edwin Forbes*) — Collecting the Wounded (*R. F. Zogbaum*) — Map of First and Last Positions of the Fighting of August 30th (*Jacob Wells*) — Major-General George Sykes, from Brady photo.— Monument to the Union Soldiers who fell at Groveton, from Gardner photo. (*W. Taber*) — The Retreat Over the Stone Bridge (*R. F. Zogbaum*) — Major-General Robert C. Schenck, from photo.— Major-General Philip Kearny, from photo. lent by General J. Watts De Peyster — Major-General Isaac I. Stevens, from Gardner photo.

IN VINDICATION OF GENERAL RUFUS KING ..... *CAPTAIN CHARLES KING* .......... 495

THE OPPOSING FORCES AT CEDAR (SLAUGHTER) MOUNTAIN, VA. Composition, Strength, and Losses .................................................................. } 495

THE OPPOSING FORCES AT THE SECOND BULL RUN. Composition, Strength and Losses ... 497

JACKSON'S RAID AROUND POPE ................ *GENERAL W. B. TALIAFERRO* ....... 501

ILLUSTRATIONS: Raid upon a Union Baggage Train by Stuart's Cavalry, from sketch lent by George Haven Putnam (*W. Taber*) — Map of Relative Positions of Forces at Sunset, August 26th (*Jacob Wells*) — Supper after a Hard March (*A. C. Redwood*) — Maps of Relative Positions of Forces at Sunset, August 27th and 28th (*Jacob Wells*) — The Stone Bridge, Bull Run (*Joseph Pennell*) — The Union Monument near the "Deep Cut," Groveton (*Joseph Pennell*) — The "Deep Cut," Groveton (*Joseph Pennell*) — Map of Jackson's Line on the Afternoon of August 30th (*Jacob Wells*) — Sudley Church, from Gardner photo. (*J. D. Woodward*) — Ruins of the Henry House, from Gardner photo. (*E. J. Meeker*).

OUR MARCH AGAINST POPE .................. *GENERAL JAMES LONGSTREET* ...... 512

ILLUSTRATIONS: "Our March against Pope" (*A. C. Redwood*) — Longstreet's March through Thoroughfare Gap (*Edwin Forbes*) — A Straggler on the Line of March (*A. C. Redwood*) — View of Jackson's Position, near Groveton, from photo. by J. E. Barr (*W. Taber*) — Colonel W. S. H. Baylor, C. S. A., from photo. lent by Major Jed. Hotchkiss — View from the Henry Hill during the Attack upon Jackson, August 30th, (*Edwin Forbes*) — Major-General Robert H. Milroy, from Brady photo. — Colonel Fletcher Webster, from Brady photo.— Map showing the Marches of the 12th Massachusetts Regiment, 1861-64.

THE TIME OF LONGSTREET'S ARRIVAL AT GROVETON .............................. 527

MARCHING ON MANASSAS ..................... *MAJOR W. ROY MASON* ............ 528

JACKSON'S "FOOT-CAVALRY" AT THE SECOND BULL RUN ..................... } .. *ALLEN C. REDWOOD* ................ 530

ILLUSTRATIONS: Route Step (*A. C. Redwood*) — Confederate Camp-Servant on the March (*W. L. Sheppard*) — Jackson's Troops Pillaging the Union Depot of Supplies at Manassas Junction (*A. C. Redwood*) — Starke's Brigade Fighting with Stones near the "Deep Cut," Groveton (*A. C. Redwood*) — Death of General Philip Kearny (*A. C. Redwood*).

THE SIXTH CORPS AT THE SECOND BULL RUN .. *GENERAL WILLIAM B. FRANKLIN* .... 539

ILLUSTRATION: Heintzelman's Headquarters at Alexandria, from sketch by R. K. Sneden (*C. A. Vanderhoof*).

WASHINGTON UNDER BANKS ............. ........ *LIEUT.-COLONEL RICHARD B. IRWIN* . 541

ILLUSTRATIONS: Major-General W. F. Barry, from Brady photo. — Map of the Defenses of Washington during the Antietam Campaign (*Jacob Wells*).

[See also The Fitz John Porter Case, p. xvii.]

## LEE'S INVASION OF MARYLAND.

FROM THE PENINSULA TO ANTIETAM ........... *GENERAL GEORGE B. M<sup>C</sup>CLELLAN* ... 545

ILLUSTRATIONS: The National Cemetery at Sharpsburg, from photo. (*W. Taber*) — Fac-simile of a part of General McClellan's Last MS. — Map of the Maryland Campaign (*Jacob Wells*) — Rostrum in the National Cemetery at Sharpsburg, from photo. (*J. D. Woodward*).

IN THE RANKS TO THE ANTIETAM .............. *DAVID L. THOMPSON* ................ 556

ILLUSTRATION: A Disorganized Private, from photo. (*W. Taber*).

THE BATTLE OF SOUTH MOUNTAIN, OR BOONSBORO' ..................... } ..... *GENERAL DANIEL H. HILL* ........... 559

ILLUSTRATIONS: Rations from the Stalk (*A. C. Redwood*) — Brigadier-General Samuel Garland, Jr., C. S. A., from photo. - Map of the Battle of South Mountain, showing positions at Fox's and Turner's

## CONTENTS OF VOLUME TWO.

Gaps *(Jacob Wells)*—Fox's Gap, The Approach to Wise's Field, and Wise's Field as seen from the Pasture north of the Road, from photos. taken in 1885 *(J. D. Woodward)*—View from Turner's Gap, looking south-east, from a photo. taken in 1886 *(John A. Fraser)*—Brigadier-General George B. Anderson, C. S. A., from oil portrait lent by Colonel W. E. Anderson—Major-General R. E. Rodes, C. S. A., from photo.—Major-General J. E. B. Stuart, from Anderson-Cook photo.; and autograph, lent by Col. C. C. Jones, Jr.

FORCING FOX'S GAP AND TURNER'S GAP........*GENERAL JACOB D. COX*............583
  ILLUSTRATIONS: Confederate Dead at the Cross-Roads by Wise's House at Fox's Gap, from sketch by James E. Taylor *(W. Taber)*—Major-General Jesse L. Reno, from Brady photo.—The Washington Monument on South Mountain, from photos. by E. M. Recher *(W. Taber)*.

NOTES ON CRAMPTON'S GAP AND ANTIETAM...*GENERAL WILLIAM B. FRANKLIN*....591
  ILLUSTRATIONS: Cavalry Skirmishers *(Edwin Forbes)*—Map of the Battle of Crampton's Gap *(Jacob Wells)*—A Battery going into Action *(Edwin Forbes)*—Major-General E. V. Sumner, from photo. taken before the war.

THE OPPOSING FORCES IN THE MARYLAND CAMPAIGN. Composition, Strength, and Losses ...................................................................... ..598

THE FINDING OF LEE'S LOST ORDER............*GENERAL SILAS COLGROVE*........603

JACKSON'S CAPTURE OF HARPER'S FERRY.......*GENERAL JOHN G. WALKER*........604
  ILLUSTRATIONS: Map of the Defenses and Approaches of Harper's Ferry *(Jacob Wells)*—View from Walker's Position on Loudoun Heights of the Union Position on Maryland Heights *(F. H. Schell)*.

THE CAPITULATION OF HARPER'S FERRY.......*GENERAL JULIUS WHITE*............612
  ILLUSTRATION: Army Water-cart, from war-time photo. *(W. Taber)*.

STONEWALL JACKSON'S INTENTIONS AT   { I. *GENERAL BRADLEY T. JOHNSON*..
HARPER'S FERRY......................  { II. *COLONEL HENRY KYD DOUGLAS*.. } 615

THE OPPOSING FORCES AT HARPER'S FERRY, VA. Composition, Strength, and Losses.....618

THE HISTORICAL BASIS OF WHITTIER'S }
  "BARBARA FRIETCHIE"............ } ......*GEORGE O. SEILHEIMER*............618
  ILLUSTRATION: Union Hospital in a Barn near Antietam Creek *(Edwin Forbes)*.

STONEWALL JACKSON IN MARYLAND............*COLONEL HENRY KYD DOUGLAS*....620
  ILLUSTRATIONS: Roasting Green Corn at the Camp-fire *(A. C. Redwood)*—Jackson's Men Wading the Potomac at White's Ford *(A. C. Redwood)*—A Glimpse of Stonewall Jackson *(A. C. Redwood)*—Lieut.-Gen. A. P. Hill, C. S. A., from Anderson-Cook photo.—Brig.-Gen. W. E. Starke, C. S. A., from tintype.

THE BATTLE OF ANTIETAM....................*GENERAL JACOB D. COX*............630
  ILLUSTRATIONS: North of the Dunker Church, A Union Charge through the Corn-field *(W. Taber)*—Union Signal Station on Elk Mountain, from Gardner photo. *(W. Taber)*—Doubleday's Division of Hooker's Corps Crossing the Upper Fords of the Antietam *(Edwin Forbes)*—The Sharpsburg Bridge over the Antietam, from Gardner photo. *(John A. Fraser)*—German Reformed Church in Keedysville, used as a Union Hospital, from photo. taken in 1886 *(W. H. Drake)*—Map of the Field of Antietam *(Jacob Wells)*—The Pry House, General McClellan's Headquarters at the Battle of Antietam, from photo. taken in 1886 *(J. D. Woodward)*—Major-General Joseph K. F. Mansfield, from Brady photo.—Sumner's Advance—French's Division closing in upon Roulette's Barns and House—Richardson's Division continuing the Line far to the Left *(F. H. Schell)*—Major-General Israel B. Richardson, from Brady photo.—Scene at the Ruins of Mumma's House and Barns *(F. H. Schell)*—Charge of Irwin's Brigade (Smith's Division) at the Dunker Church *(Edwin Forbes)*—General View of the Battle of Antietam *(Edwin Forbes)*—General McClellan Riding the Line at Battle of Antietam *(Edwin Forbes)*—Brigadier-General Isaac P. Rodman, from Brady photo.—The Charge Across the Burnside Bridge *(Edwin Forbes)*—Burnside's Attack upon Sharpsburg *(Edwin Forbes)*—President Lincoln in General McClellan's Tent at Antietam after the Battle, and General McClellan and President Lincoln at Antietam, from Gardner photos. *(W. Taber)*.

WITH BURNSIDE AT ANTIETAM ................*DAVID L. THOMPSON*................660
  ILLUSTRATIONS: On the Line of a Scattered Fence at Antietam, from Gardner photo. *(W. Taber)*—Major-General John G. Walker, C. S. A., from photo. by Blessing.

THE INVASION OF MARYLAND ..................*GENERAL JAMES LONGSTREET*.......663
  ILLUSTRATIONS: The Old Lutheran Church, Sharpsburg, from Gardner photo. *(W. Taber)*—Lee's Headquarters in Sharpsburg, from photo. taken in 1885 *(E. J. Meeker)*—South-eastern Stretch of the Sunken Road, or "Bloody Lane," from photo. by J. E. Barr—The Sunken Road, from photo. by E. M. Recher *(W. Taber)*—The Sunken Road Looking East from Roulette's Lane, from photo. lent by L. K. Graves

## CONTENTS OF VOLUME TWO.    xvii

*(W. Taber)* — Confederate Dead (of D. H. Hill's Division) in the Sunken Road, from Gardner photo. *(W. Taber).* — Views of Buildings on Roulette's Farm, from photos. *(W. H. Drake)* — After the Battle, Position of the Confederate Batteries in Front of Dunker Church, from Gardner photo. *(W. Taber)* — Field-Hospitals of French's Division, at Antietam, from Gardner photos. *(W. Taber)* — Blackford's (or Boteler's) Ford from the Maryland Side, from photo. taken in 1885 *(J. D. Woodward).*

SHARPSBURG .................................... GENERAL JOHN G. WALKER ........ 675

    ILLUSTRATIONS: Rallying Behind the Turnpike Fence *(W. Taber)* — Two Views of Burnside's Bridge, from photos. taken in 1885 *(Harry Fenn)* — Brigadier-General Roswell S. Ripley, C. S. A., from photo. lent by the Rev. John Johnson — Confederate Dead on the West Side of the Hagerstown Road, from Gardner photo. *(W. Taber)* — North-west Angle of the "East Wood" and the Corn-field *(Frank H. Schell).*

ANTIETAM SCENES ........................... CHARLES CARLETON COFFIN ........ 682

    ILLUSTRATION: Union Burial Party at Antietam, from Gardner photo. *(W. Taber).*

A WOMAN'S RECOLLECTIONS OF ANTIETAM ..... MARY BEDINGER MITCHELL ......... 686

    ILLUSTRATIONS: In the Wake of Battle *(W. Taber)* — Shepherdstown, and View to the Ford below, from photos. *(W. Taber)* — Confederate Monument at Shepherdstown, from photo. by J. E. Barr *(E. J. Meeker).*

THE CASE OF FITZ JOHN PORTER ........ ...... LIEUT.-COLONEL RICHARD B. IRWIN .695

[For titles relating to the New Mexican Campaign see chapter-heading " Operations in the Far South-west," p. x. of this Table of Contents.]

## IUKA AND CORINTH.

OPERATIONS IN NORTH ALABAMA .............. GENERAL DON CARLOS BUELL ...... 701

    ILLUSTRATIONS: Map of Kentucky and Tennessee *(Jacob Wells)* — Major-General Ormsby M. Mitchel, from Brady photo.

THE LOCOMOTIVE CHASE IN GEORGIA ........... REV. WILLIAM PITTENGER .......... 709

    ILLUSTRATIONS: Confederates in Pursuit, and Beginning of the Pursuit *(W. Taber)* — James J. Andrews, from photo. lent by Miss Elvira Layton — Big Shanty (now Kenesaw) Station *(Theo. R. Davis)* — Map of the Railroad from Marietta to Chattanooga *(Jacob Wells)* — Captain William A. Fuller, C. S. A., from ambrotype lent by the Rev. William Pittenger — Plan of the Blockade at Kingston Station *(Jacob Wells)* — Pursuers Off the Track *(W. Taber)* — The Pursuers Pushing the Burning Car from the Bridge *(W. Taber)* — End of the Run; The Stolen Engine, "The General," Abandoned *(W. Taber)* — Memorial Day at Chattanooga, 1883, showing Graves of Andrews and His Companions *(Theo. R. Davis).*

NOTES ON THE LOCOMOTIVE CHASE ............ GENERAL JAMES B. FRY ............ 716

WITH PRICE EAST OF THE MISSISSIPPI .......... COLONEL THOMAS L. SNEAD ........ 717

    ILLUSTRATIONS: Halleck's Army on the March to Corinth; The 31st Ohio Volunteers Building Breastworks before Corinth in May, 1862; General Pope's Encampment before Corinth in May, 1862; three pictures from lithographs of sketches by A. E. Mathews *(E. J. Meeker)* — Map of the Corinth and Iuka Region, from a Government Map — Dwellings in Iuka, from photographs taken in 1884 *(W. Taber)* — Map of Iuka *(F. E. Sitts)* — Brigadier-General Henry Little, C. S. A., from photo. lent by Colonel Thomas L. Snead — Major-General C. S. Hamilton, from Brady photo.

THE BATTLE OF IUKA ......................... GENERAL CHARLES S. HAMILTON ... 734

THE OPPOSING FORCES AT IUKA, MISS. Composition, Strength, and Losses ....... ........ 736

THE BATTLE OF CORINTH ..................... GENERAL WILLIAM S. ROSECRANS .. 737

    ILLUSTRATIONS: Fillmore Street, Corinth, from photo. taken in 1884 *(Harry Fenn)* — Provost Marshal's Office, Corinth, from photo. by Armstead *(Harry Fenn)* — Corona College, Corinth, from photo. by Armstead *(W. Taber)* — Major-General Thomas A. Davies, from Brady photo. — Railway Depot and Tishomingo Hotel, Corinth, from photo. by Armstead *(Harry Fenn)* — Map of the Battle of Corinth *(Jacob Wells)* — View on the Railway, Looking North-west from the Corinth Depot, from photo. by Armstead *(W. Taber)* — Memphis and Charleston Railroad, Looking Towards Corinth, Remains of Fort Williams on the Right, from photo. taken in 1884 *(J. D. Woodward)* — Brigadier-General Pleasant A. Hackleman, from a steel engraving — The Defense of Battery Robinett, from lithograph of sketch by D. Auld, lent by Robert Hunter *(F. H. Schell)* — The Ground in Front of Battery Robinett, from photo. lent by Matt Morgan *(W. Taber)* — Grave of Colonel William P. Rogers, from photo. taken in 1884 *(J. D. Woodward)* — Colonel William P. Rogers, C. S. A., from photo. lent by Colonel Charles C. Jones, Jr. — Group of Union Soldiers at Corinth, from photo. by Armstead *(W. Taber)* — Quarters at Corinth Occupied by the 52d, Illinois Volunteers during the Winter of 1862-63, from photo. by Armstead *(W. H. Drake)* — Camp of the 57th Illinois Infantry at Corinth, from photo. by Armstead *(W. Taber).*

## CONTENTS OF VOLUME TWO.

| | PAGE |
|---|---|
| HAMILTON'S DIVISON AT CORINTH............*GENERAL CHARLES S. HAMILTON*...757 | |
| AN ORDER TO CHARGE AT CORINTH..........*GENERAL DAVID S. STANLEY*......758 | |
| THE OPPOSING FORCES AT CORINTH. Composition, Strength, and Losses................759 | |
| ILLUSTRATION: Monument in the National Cemetery, Corinth, from photo. taken in 1884 (*W. Taber*). | |

## MAPS.

| | |
|---|---|
| SIEGE OF FORT PULASKI, GEORGIA | 3 |
| THE LOWER MISSISSIPPI | 25 |
| PLAN OF FORT JACKSON, LOUISIANA | 34 |
| DEFENSES OF THE MISSISSIPPI AND POSITIONS OF THE MORTAR-FLEET | 36 |
| COURSE OF THE U. S. SCREW-SLOOP "MISSISSIPPI" IN THE PASSAGE OF THE FORTS. | 46 |
| COURSE OF THE "BROOKLYN" IN THE PASSAGE OF THE FORTS | 62 |
| FINAL DISPOSITION OF THE CONFEDERATE FLEET BELOW NEW ORLEANS | 78 |
| SIBLEY'S CAMPAIGN IN NEW MEXICO AND ARIZONA | 105 |
| THE UPPER POTOMAC | 124 |
| BATTLE OF BALL'S BLUFF, VIRGINIA | 126 |
| OUTLINE MAP OF THE VIRGINIA CAMPAIGNS | 164 |
| THE PENINSULAR CAMPAIGN | 167 |
| BIG BETHEL—SIEGE OF YORKTOWN—BATTLE OF WILLIAMSBURG, VIRGINIA | 188 |
| POSITIONS OF FORCES PRELIMINARY TO THE BATTLE OF SEVEN PINES | 227 |
| BATTLE OF SEVEN PINES, OR FAIR OAKS, VIRGINIA | 240 |
| THE "MONITOR" FIGHT, AND OPERATIONS IN THE YORK AND JAMES RIVERS | 265 |
| STUART'S RIDE AROUND McCLELLAN ON THE PENINSULA | 272 |
| WEST VIRGINIA | 279 |
| JACKSON'S CAMPAIGN IN THE SHENANDOAH VALLEY | 284 |
| BATTLE OF McDOWELL, VIRGINIA | 286 |
| BATTLE OF CROSS KEYS, VIRGINIA | 291 |
| BATTLE OF PORT REPUBLIC, VIRGINIA | 293 |
| BATTLE OF KERNSTOWN, VIRGINIA | 307 |
| THE UPPER CHICKAHOMINY AND NEIGHBORING COUNTRY | 320 |
| BATTLE OF BEAVER DAM CREEK, VIRGINIA | 328 |
| BATTLE OF GAINES'S MILL, VIRGINIA | 334 |
| BATTLE AT SAVAGE'S STATION, VIRGINIA | 374 |
| REGION OF THE SEVEN DAYS' FIGHTING | 384 |
| SKETCH MAP OF THE VICINITY OF MALVERN HILL, VIRGINIA | 392 |
| BATTLE OF FRAYSER'S FARM (CHARLES CITY CROSS-ROADS, OR GLENDALE), VIRGINIA | 397 |
| BATTLE OF MALVERN HILL, VIRGINIA | 412 |
| OUTLINE MAP OF THE SECOND BULL RUN CAMPAIGN | 450 |
| BATTLE OF CEDAR MOUNTAIN, VIRGINIA | 459 |
| SECOND BULL RUN—RELATIVE POSITIONS OF FORCES AT SUNSET, AUGUST 26TH...464, | 503 |
| RELATIVE POSITIONS OF FORCES AT SUNSET, AUGUST 27TH ....................467, | 505 |
| RELATIVE POSITIONS OF FORCES AT SUNSET, AUGUST 28TH ....................469, | 505 |
| RELATIVE POSITIONS AT NOON, FRIDAY, AUGUST 29TH | 472 |
| RELATIVE POSITIONS AT SUNSET, FRIDAY, AUGUST 29TH | 473 |
| FIRST AND LAST POSITIONS IN THE FIGHTING OF AUGUST 30TH | 482 |

## CONTENTS OF VOLUME TWO. xix

| | PAGE |
|---|---|
| JACKSON'S LINE ON THE AFTERNOON OF THE LAST DAY, AUGUST 30TH | 509 |
| MARCHES OF THE WEBSTER REGIMENT, 12TH MASS. VOLS., JULY, 1861, TO JUNE, 1864 | 525 |
| DEFENSES OF WASHINGTON DURING THE ANTIETAM CAMPAIGN, SEPTEMBER 1-20, 1862 | 543 |
| THE MARYLAND CAMPAIGN | 553 |
| BATTLE OF SOUTH MOUNTAIN, MARYLAND | 568 |
| BATTLE OF CRAMPTON'S GAP, MARYLAND | 593 |
| DEFENSES AND APPROACHES OF HARPER'S FERRY | 606 |
| BATTLE OF ANTIETAM, MARYLAND | 636 |
| KENTUCKY AND TENNESSEE | 702 |
| RAILROAD FROM MARIETTA, GEORGIA, TO CHATTANOOGA, TENNESSEE | 711 |
| PLAN OF THE BLOCKADE AT KINGSTON STATION, GEORGIA | 712 |
| MAP OF THE CORINTH AND IUKA REGION | 727 |
| BATTLE OF IUKA, MISSISSIPPI | 730 |
| BATTLE OF CORINTH, MISSISSIPPI | 744 |

## ARTISTS.

| | | | |
|---|---|---|---|
| CONCKLIN, FORTIER | GAUL, GILBERT | OGDEN, HENRY A. | SMITH, XANTHUS |
| DAVIDSON, J. O. | HOGAN, THOMAS | PENNELL, JOSEPH | TABER, WALTON |
| DAVIS, THEO. R. | HOMER, WINSLOW | REDWOOD, ALLEN C. | THULSTRUP, T. DE |
| DRAKE, WILL. H | KEMBLE, E. W. | SANDHAM, HENRY | TREGO, W. T. |
| EDWARDS, H. C. | KENDRICK, CHARLES | SCHELL, FRANK H. | VANDERHOOF, C. A. |
| FENN, HARRY | LATHROP, W. L. | SCOTT, JULIAN | WAUD, ALFRED R. |
| FORBES, EDWIN | MEEKER, EDWIN J. | SHELTON, W. H. | WILES, IRVING R. |
| FRASER, JOHN A. | MORAN, THOMAS | SHEPPARD, W. L. | WOODWARD, J. D. |
| | ZOGBAUM, RUFUS F. | | |

## DRAUGHTSMEN.

KEMP, J. S.      SITTS, FRED. E.      WELLS, JACOB

## ENGRAVERS.

| | | | |
|---|---|---|---|
| AIKEN, PETER | DE LORME, E. H. | JOHNSON, THOMAS | SCHWARTZBURGER, C. |
| ATWOOD, K. C. | ERTZ, EDWARD | KLASEN, W. | SPEER, J. T. |
| BABCOCK, H. E. | EVANS, J. W. | KRUELL, G. | SPIEGLE, CHARLES |
| BARTLE, G. P. | FAY, GASTON | LOCKHARDT, A. | SUGDEN, T. D. |
| BOGERT, J. A. | GAMM, ANTHONY | MOLLIER, WILLIAM | SUTHERLAND, F. W. |
| BOOKHOUT, E. | HALL, ELIZABETH | MORSE, WILLIAM H. | SYLVESTER, H. E. |
| BUTLER, C. I. | HAYMAN, ARTHUR | NAYLOR, JESSIE | TIETZE, R. G. |
| BUTLER, T. A. | HEARD, T. H. | NAYLOR, OLIVIA | TYNAN, JAMES |
| CLEMENT, E. | HEINEMANN, E. | NICHOLS, DAVID | VELTEN, H. |
| COLE, TIMOTHY | HELD, E. C. | OWENS, MARY L. | WALDEYER, A. |
| COLLINS, R. C. | HIRSCHMANN, W. A. | POWELL, C. A. | WHITNEY, A. J. |
| DANA, W. J. | HOGE, J. E. | PUTNAM, S. G. | WHITNEY, J. H. E. |
| DAVIS, JOHN P. | IRWIN, ALLEN | SCHUSSLER, T. | |

FORT PULASKI AFTER THE SURRENDER. FROM A SKETCH MADE AT THE TIME.

## SIEGE AND CAPTURE OF FORT PULASKI.

BY Q. A. GILLMORE, MAJOR-GENERAL, U. S. V.

THE capture of the forts at Port Royal was promptly followed by the abandonment by the Confederates of the entire coast and all the coast towns south of Charleston except Savannah, which was defended by Fort Pulaski, at the mouth of the Savannah River.

This work is of brick, with five faces, casemated on all sides, and has a wet ditch. The walls are seven and a half feet thick, and rise twenty-five feet above high water, mounting one tier of guns in casemates and one *en barbette*. The gorge face is covered by a demi-lune of good relief, arranged for one tier of guns *en barbette*. This also has a wet ditch.

The fort is situated on Cockspur Island, a marshy formation, surrounded by broad channels of deep water. The nearest approach to it on tolerably firm ground is from one to two miles distant, to the south-east, along a narrow strip of shifting sands formed on Tybee Island by the action of wind and waves. In the light of subsequent events it is of interest to recall the fact that before operations for investing the place were begun the fort was visited by several Confederate officers of rank, formerly of the regular army, who freely expressed the opinion that the isolated position of the work, and the nature of its environs, rendered any successful siege operations against it absolutely impracticable. The Confederate commander, Colonel Charles H. Olmstead, appears quite naturally to have been governed by the opinions of his superior officers;↓ and the measures adopted for adding strength and safety to the work were of the most meager character. Moreover, General Joseph G. Totten, Chief Engineer United States Army, wrote, in reply to a letter requesting his views on the subject, that "the work could not be reduced in a month's firing with any number of guns of manageable calibers."

↓ The officer in command of the department was Brigadier-General A. R. Lawton, C. S. A.— EDITORS.

I had been appointed chief engineer of the Expeditionary Corps, and in that capacity was directed by General T. W. Sherman, on the 29th of November, to make an examination of Tybee Island and Fort Pulaski, and to report upon the propriety of holding the island, and upon the practicability, and, if practicable, on the best method, of reducing the fort. I reported that I deemed the reduction of the work practicable with batteries of mortars and rifled guns established on Tybee Island, and recommended the occupation of the island, adding some details concerning the disposition of the batteries, the precautions to be observed in their construction, and the intensity of the fire to be delivered by them. This project having been approved by General Sherman and by the higher authorities, the 46th New York Infantry, Colonel Rosa commanding, took possession of the island early in December. In February, 1862, they were reënforced by the addition of the 7th Connecticut Infantry, two companies of New York Volunteer Engineers, and two companies of the 3d Rhode Island Artillery, and all were placed under command of Colonel (now Major-General) A. H. Terry, of the 7th Connecticut. By the labor of these troops eleven batteries were constructed, at distances from the fort varying from 1650 to 3400 yards.‡

Tybee Island is mostly a mud marsh, like other marsh islands on this coast, varied, however, by ridges and hummocks of firm ground. The distance along the north shore, from the landing-place to the advanced batteries, on the sand ridge above mentioned, is about two and a half miles. Over the last mile, which is low and marshy, and within effective range of the guns of Fort Pulaski, was constructed a causeway of fascines and brushwood.

The work of unloading on the open beach the ordnance, implements, and equipments, and of transporting them to the batteries, was in charge of Lieutenant (afterward General) Horace Porter, and is thus described by him:

"The heavy guns were landed by lowering them from the vessels into lighters having a strong decking built across their gunwales. They were towed ashore by row-boats at high tide, often in a heavy surf, and careened by means of a rope from shore, manned by soldiers, until the piece rolled off. At low tide this was dragged above high-water mark.

"For the purpose of transporting the 13-inch mortars, weighing 17,000 pounds, a pair of skids was constructed of timber ten inches square and twenty feet long, held together by three cross-pieces, notched on. One end of the skids was lashed close under the axle of a large sling-cart, with the other end resting on the ground. The mortar was rolled up by means of ropes until it reached the middle of the skids and chocked. Another large sling-cart was run over the other end of the skids, which was raised by the screw, forming a temporary four-wheeled wagon. Two hundred and fifty men were required to move it over the difficult roads by which the batteries were reached.

"I can pay no greater tribute to the patriotism of the 7th Connecticut Volunteers, the troops generally furnished me for this duty, than to say that, when the sling-carts frequently sank to their hubs in the marshes, and had to be extricated by unloading the mortar, rolling it upon

‡ No. 1, 3 heavy 13-inch mortars.3400 yards.
" 2, 3   "      "      "   .3200  "
" 3, 3 10-inch Columbiads . 3100  "
" 4, 3 8-inch      "     ...3045  "
" 5, 1 heavy 13-inch mortar .2790 "
" 6, 3   "      "      "   .2600  "
" 7, 2   "      "      "   .2400  "
" 8, 3 10-in.Col'b'ds and 1 8-in.1740 "

No. 9, 5 30-pounder Parrott rifles
       and 1 48-pounder James
       rifle (old 24-pounder) 1670 yards.
" 10, 2 84-pounder James rifles
       (old 42-pounders), and
       2 64-pounder James
       rifles (old 32-pounders)1650  "
" 11, 4 10-inch siege mortars . 1650  "

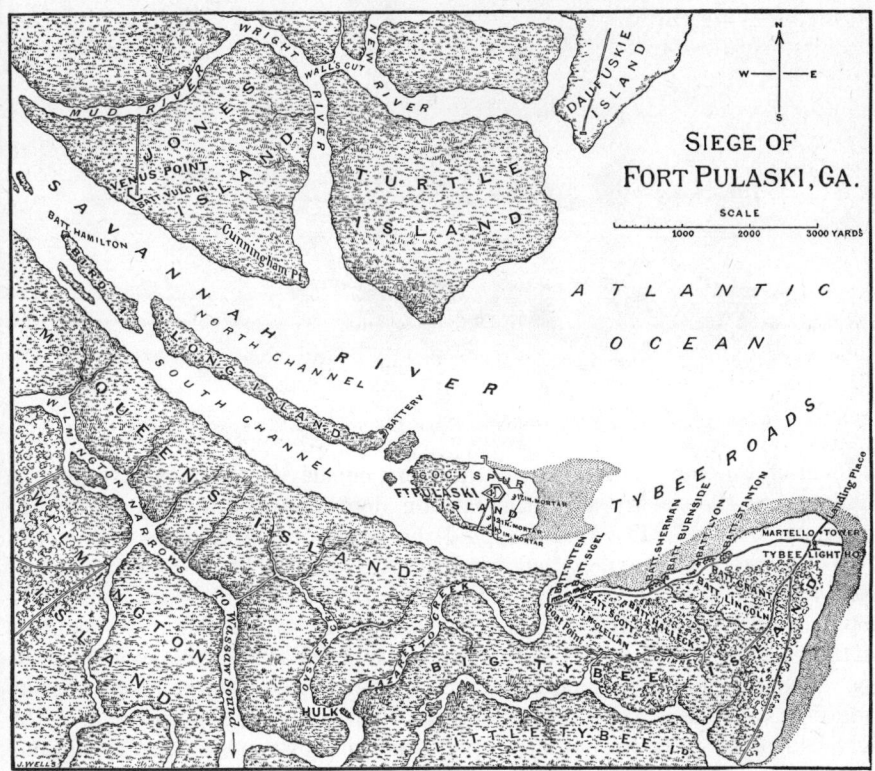

planks until harder ground could be found, and then reloading it, they toiled night after night, often in a drenching rain, under the guns of the fort, speaking only in whispers, and directed entirely by the sound of a whistle, without uttering a murmur. When drilling the same men in the mortar-batteries, they exhibited an intelligence equaled only by their former physical endurance."

In constructing the batteries, as well as in transporting their armament, the greater part of the work was, of necessity, done under cover of night, and with the greatest caution. The positions selected for the five advanced batteries were artificially screened from the view of the fort by almost imperceptible changes, made little by little each night, in the condition and distribution of the brushwood and bushes in front of them. No sudden alteration in the outline of the landscape was permitted. After the concealment had been perfected to such a degree as to permit a safe parapet behind it, less care was taken, and some of the work requiring mechanical skill was done in the daytime, the fatigue parties going to their labor before break of day and returning to camp after nightfall. The garrison of the fort was either unsuspicious or indifferent; at any rate, the natural difficulties of our task received no increment through interference from that quarter. The ability of their guns to punish impertinent intrusion had been already shown. Two soldiers of the 46th New York, which had occupied the island as a precautionary measure before the siege operations began, having strolled out to

MARTELLO TOWER AND LIGHT-HOUSE, TYBEE ISLAND. FROM A WAR-TIME SKETCH.

the end of the sand point nearest the fort, conceived the idea of issuing a challenge to the enemy after the fashion described in the "Adventures of Robinson Crusoe." The fort accepted the situation and replied with a shot from a Blakely gun which had recently run the blockade at Wilmington. One of the men was cut in two; the other retreated in disorder, and could not be induced to return and pay the last offices to his ill-starred comrade till after dark. It was said that the gun was sighted by the colonel commanding. The experiment was encouraging, but the garrison did not seem to take the hint. Sometime after they dropped a shell near my headquarters at the light-house, but as it did not accord with our policy to exhibit any symptoms of annoyance, the attention was not repeated.

Meanwhile, in another quarter, operations for the investment of the fort, as complete as the peculiar topography of the region would permit, had been substantially completed by the establishment of two batteries of six guns each, about four miles above the fort,—one at Venus Point, on Jones Island, on the north bank of the Savannah River, and the other on Bird Island, nearly opposite. This latter point had been fixed upon after a reconnoissance made by Lieutenant P. H. O'Rorke, of the Engineers, who, with Major Oliver T. Beard, of the 48th New York, had gone in a small boat up the river as far as the west end of Elba Island, within two miles of Fort Jackson. In addition, two companies of infantry, with three pieces of artillery, were placed on a hulk anchored in Lazaretto Creek, about two and a quarter miles south of the fort, to intercept communication from the direction of Wassaw Sound. After all, even with the efficient aid of the vessels on the station, it was found impossible to isolate perfectly a place lying, as Fort Pulaski does, in a wilderness of low marsh islands submerged by spring-tides, intersected by numerous tortuous channels, and covered with a rank growth of reeds and tall grass. With light boats, small parties familiar with the locality could easily make their way from creek to creek and over the marshes by night, avoiding guards and pickets. It was known that messengers frequently passed in this way to and from the fort, and some of them were captured.

The construction of the Venus Point battery and the transportation of its armament had been effected in the face of difficulties of the same sort as were met with on Tybee Island, but much more discouraging. Jones Island is nothing but a mud marsh, whose general surface is about on the level of ordinary high tide, with a few spots of limited area which are submerged only by spring-tides or when the ordinary tide is favored by the wind. Even in the most elevated places the partly dry crust is only three or four inches in depth, the substratum being a semi-fluid mud, quivering like jelly at every slight blow. A pole or an oar can be forced into it with ease to a depth of twelve or fifteen feet, and the resistance seems to diminish with increase of penetration. The roots of reeds and grasses partly sustain the weight of a man, so that he will sink only a few inches; but when these give way, he goes down two feet or more.

Over this unpromising tract all the materials, sand-bags, planks, etc., used in constructing the battery were carried,—about three hundred yards on a causeway of poles, and for the remaining distance by a wheel-barrow track made of planks laid end to end. On the night of February 10th, Lieutenant O'Rorke, of the Engineers, began the construction of the magazine and gun platforms, while Lieutenant Horace Porter, assisted by Major Beard, 48th New York, and Lieutenant James H. Wilson, Topographical Engineers, undertook the task of bringing up the guns. A wharf of poles and sand-bags had been made in Mud River, about 1300 yards from the battery, to which all the materials were brought in boats from Daufuskie Island, the nearest dry land, four miles away.

It had been intended to carry the guns and ammunition for the Venus Point battery on flats through New River and Wall's Cut into Wright River, and thence by Mud River into the Savannah, under convoy of the gun-boats; but the delay threatened by tide and weather, and the probability of encountering torpedoes, for which the vessels were not prepared, determined a change of plan; and it was decided, without depending on the gun-boats, to tow the flats to the Mud River wharf, and haul the guns across the marsh. The landing was made without accident; and the pieces, mounted on their carriages and limbered

BRIGADIER-GENERAL EGBERT L. VIELE, AT THE SIEGE OF FORT PULASKI COMMANDER OF THE UNION FORCES ON DAUFUSKIE ISLAND. FROM A PHOTOGRAPH.

up, were moved forward on shifting runways of 3-inch planks laid end to end. Lieutenant Wilson, with thirty-five men, took charge of the two pieces in advance, and Major Beard and Lieutenant Porter, with a somewhat larger force, of the four other pieces. Each party had two planks in excess of the number required for the guns and limbers when closed together. This extra

FORT PULASKI FROM TURTLE ISLAND (SEE MAP, PAGE 3), TYBEE LIGHT-HOUSE IN THE LEFT DISTANCE. FROM A WAR-TIME SKETCH.

pair of planks was successively taken up from the rear and laid down in front as the guns were moved forward.

By some mistake the men detailed for this work had already been on duty for twenty-four hours, and were in no condition for such fatiguing service. They sank to their knees at every step. The planks soon became slippery with mud, and were hauled forward with drag-ropes; the wheels frequently slipped off, sinking to the hubs, to be replaced only by the greatest exertions. The last gun had been landed at 10 o'clock, and by 2 A. M. two pieces had crossed about one-fourth of the marsh, and the men were utterly exhausted. The guns were concealed by reeds and grass and left until the next night, when a fresh detail carried them through to their position, crossing the worst part of the marsh and repeating all the experiences of the previous night. By half-past 8 on the morning of the 12th the battery was ready for service.

The Bird Island battery was established eight days later, the crossing being made on the night of the 20th.

The Venus Point battery was tested on the morning of the 13th, when the rebel steamer *Ida* passed down under full steam. In firing nine shots at her, all the guns but one recoiled off the platforms. These were at once enlarged to double their former size. The *Ida* was unhurt, but preferred to return to Savannah by another route. On the next day three gun-boats engaged the battery for a short time, withdrawing after one of them was struck.‡

The first vessel, with ordnance and ordnance stores for the siege, had arrived in Tybee Roads on the 21st of February, and on the 9th of April the batteries were ready to open fire. Lieutenant Horace Porter says:

"So much were the preparations hurried for opening the bombardment, that we could not wait for many of the ordnance stores that had been ordered from the North. Powder-measures

‡ The 48th New York, which furnished the guard for the battery, had not a reputation for conspicuous sanctity, but it is doubtful whether one story told of them would not suffer in point by contact with hard facts.

There was an iron-clad at Savannah named the *Atlanta*, but commonly known as the "Ladies' gun-boat," from the fact that means for building it had been largely supplied by contributions of jewelry from the ladies of the city. Some time after our occupation of Jones Island, it was reported that the *Atlanta* was coming down to shell us out. The thoughts of the battery-guard naturally turned toward measures for meeting such an attack, and it was resolved to fire shot connected by chains, and so tangle her up and haul her ashore. When the question arose how they should get into their iron-bound prize, the officer in command of the detachment was ready with his solution: "I've got the men to do it." Then he paraded his men, and informed them of the facts. "Now," said he, "you've been in this cursed swamp for two weeks, up to your ears in mud,—no fun, no glory, and blessed poor pay. Here's a chance. Let every one of you who has had experience as a cracksman or a safe-blower step to the front." It is said that the whole detachment stepped off its two paces with perfect unanimity. The *Atlanta* did not, in fact, make any demonstration on the Savannah, but went, some time later, to Wassaw Sound, only to be captured by Commander John Rodgers with the monitor *Weehawken*.— Q. A. G.

were made out of copper from the metallic cases in which the desiccated vegetables are received. Columbiad shells were strapped with strips of old tents, rough blocks being used for sabots. A large party was kept working day and night, during the bombardment, making 10-inch Columbiad cartridge-bags, and wooden fuse-plugs for 10-inch mortars, in which paper fuses were used."

The men engaged in making the fuse-plugs were mostly Connecticut Yankees, and it was interesting to observe, in the expression of supreme content that settled upon their countenances, the manifest relief afforded by the change from the day and night toil of moving and mounting guns to the congenial employment of whittling. ♭ Once, in passing, Lieutenant Porter asked how they were getting along. "Thank ye, Leftenant; we're undergoin' a consid'able degree o' comfort."

General orders were issued on the afternoon of the 9th, prescribing for each battery its point of attack, the rate of firing, and the charges and elevation of the pieces. The mortars were to drop their shells over and within the faces of the work; the fire of the guns should be directed partly against the barbette guns of the fort, and to take the gorge and north walls in reverse, but mainly upon the pan-coupé joining the south and south-east faces, with the double view of opening a practicable breach for assault and of exposing to a reverse fire the magazine in the opposite angle. With one or two exceptions, it was not found necessary to change these orders during the whole course of the bombardment. One officer, a German, commanding a battery, so far failed to imbibe the spirit of the order, that when the moment for opening fire came, he mounted the parapet on the flank of his battery, drew his sword with a melodramatic clash and flourish, and let off all his guns in one volley. The effect was grievously marred by the fact that in his enthusiasm he had overlooked instructions which he had personally received, to open embrasures through the sand ridge forming his parapet as the last thing before firing. Naturally the shot, glancing from the slope, took any direction but the one intended, part of them landing as far from the fort as they were when they left the pieces. The same officer, by the way, afterward expressed the hope that the methods pursued in the siege of Fort Pulaski would not become known in military circles in Europe, lest, being in violation of all the rules laid down in the books, they should bring discredit upon American military engineering.

Just after sunrise on the morning of the 10th, Major-General David Hunter, commanding the department (of the South), sent a flag under Lieutenant James H. Wilson to the fort, with a summons to surrender. Colonel Olm-

♭ "At the 10-inch mortar battery, fuse-plugs were still wanting, and the ordnance officer [Horace Porter] was in despair. He had brought out a specimen of one prepared for another piece, in hopes it might serve. . . . Here were these four pieces, at this most advanced position, rendered entirely useless. Not one could be fired. Finally, a happy thought struck him: there was a Yankee regiment on the island; all Yankees are whittlers; if this regiment could be turned out to-night, they might whittle enough fuse-plugs before morning to fire a thousand rounds. So we put spurs to our horses, and rode (in the darkness) . . . back to camp. The 6th Connecticut was ordered out to whittle, and did whittle to advantage, providing all the plugs that were used in Battery Totten on the two succeeding days." [Correspondence of the "New York Times."] — EDITORS.

stead briefly declined to comply with the demand, saying that he was there "to defend the fort, not to surrender it."

The first shell was fired at a quarter-past 8 o'clock A. M., from Battery Halleck, about the middle of the line, and by half-past 9 all the batteries were in operation, each mortar firing at fifteen-minute intervals, and the guns from two to three times as rapidly. The enemy replied vigorously, though at first not very accurately, with his barbette and casemate guns, following up our line as the batteries successively disclosed their position. It appeared subsequently that he knew the exact position of only two of our batteries— Nos. 5 and 6, which had been established with no special attempt at concealment.

By 1 o'clock in the afternoon it became evident that, unless our guns should suffer seriously from the enemy's fire, a breach would be effected: with a glass it could be seen that the rifled projectiles were surely eating their way into the scarp of the pan-coupé and adjacent south-east face. When the firing ceased for the night, after nine and a half hours' duration, the commencement of a breach was plainly visible. It was equally manifest, to the surprise and disappointment of all experienced officers present, that the 13-inch mor-

BREVET BRIGADIER-GENERAL HORACE PORTER.
FROM A PHOTOGRAPH.

General Horace Porter, in a letter to the editors, records the subjoined incidents of the siege:

"One of the regiments which was assigned to duty on Tybee Island, and participated prominently in the siege operations, was the 46th New York, composed entirely of Germans. There was the savor of German cooking in their mess, the sound of German songs in their camp; all the commands were given in German at drill, and the various calls, such as reveille and tattoo, were the same as those used in the German army. We were at this time very anxious to get some information about the construction of the interior arrangements for the defense of the fort, and one morning a strapping fellow in the regiment, who looked as if he might have been a lineal descendant of a member of Frederick the Great's Potsdam Guards, became enthusiastic in the belief that if there was any son of Germany in the fort the playing of the strains of the Vaterland within hearing of the enemy would bring him promptly into camp. The plan was put into execution, and, sure enough, one dark night a German came floating over on a log from Cockspur to Tybee Island. We got from him some very useful information.

"When the white flag went up, General Gillmore, with a number of officers, started for the fort in a whale-boat to receive the surrender. The boat was loaded to the gunwales, as everybody was anxious to go on this mission and get a first sight of the captured work. There was a sea running which threatened at times to swamp the craft, and the rowers could make little headway against the wind and tide. In fact, the parties made such slow progress in pulling for the fort that the effort became rather ludicrous, and it looked for a time as if even the patience of a garrison waiting to surrender might become exhausted, and they be tempted to open fire again on their dilatory captors.

"Among the visitors to the fort was George W. Smalley, the correspondent of the 'New York Tribune,' and now the well-known London representative of that journal.

"One of the captured officers asked me who was the person in citizen's dress, and when I replied that he was a war correspondent of the 'Tribune,' exclaimed, 'What! that old abolition sheet?' 'Yes.' 'Edited by old man Greeley?' 'Yes.' 'And we're going to be written up by his gang?' 'Yes.' 'Well, I could have stood the surrender, but this humiliation is too much!'"

tars, though carefully and fairly well served, were from some cause practically inefficient, not more than one-tenth of the shells falling within the fort. It was clear that for the reduction of the work we should have to depend on breaching alone, ending, perhaps, in an assault. An assault was really impracticable, owing to the lack of boats to carry the troops, although these could have been procured from the navy after considerable delay.

To increase the security of our advanced batteries, a constant fire against the barbette guns of the fort had been kept up through the day. Two of these guns were disabled and three casemate guns silenced. During the night two or three pieces were kept at work to prevent the enemy from repairing the damage he had sustained.

Shortly after sunrise on the 11th our batteries again opened with vigor and accuracy, the enemy returning a resolute and well-directed fire. A detachment of seamen, furnished by Captain C. R. P. Rodgers, of the *Wabash*, who personally superintended their service, had been assigned to one of the most important batteries, where their skill and experience were applied with telling effect. By noon the first two casemates in the south-east face were opened to their full width, our shots passing through the timber blindage in their rear and reaching the magazine at the north-west angle of the fort.

It was plain that a few hours' work of this kind would clear away the scarp wall to a greater width than the small garrison could defend against assault, and preparations for storming were ordered. Meanwhile our guns were pounding at the next casemate, which was fast crumbling away, puffs of yellow dust marking the effect of shot and shell, when, at 2 o'clock, a white flag was shown, and the colors, fluttering for a few minutes at half-mast, came slowly down.

I was directed to receive the surrender, and crossed to the fort for that purpose. The articles were signed that afternoon, and the place occupied by our troops, between whom and the late garrison the best of feeling prevailed. ☆ Many a jest and repartee passed between them. One Georgian, of a sarcastic bent, recalled the ancient myth of wooden nutmegs. "We don't make them

---

☆ "At the entrance [of Fort Pulaski] stood Colonel Olmstead, the commandant. He showed the way to his own quarters, having previously requested that several National officers who were approaching might, as a matter of courtesy, be desired to remain outside until the preliminaries were adjusted. This was accorded him, and an interview of an hour took place, at which only himself and General Gillmore were present. The terms of the capitulation having been settled, General Gillmore was shown over the fort by the colonel, and then took his leave, accompanied by Colonel Rust. Messengers from General Hunter had meantime arrived. These, together with General Gillmore's aide, made the rounds of the fort under the escort of Colonel Olmstead, who introduced us to his officers, and were the only persons present when the swords were delivered. Major Halpine, as the representative of General Hunter, received the weapons. The ceremony was performed in the colonel's headquarters, all standing. It was just at dark, and the candles gave only a half-light. The weapons were laid on a table, each officer advancing in turn, according to his rank, and mentioning his name and title. Nearly every one added some remark. The colonel's was dignified: 'I yield my sword, but I trust I have not disgraced it.' . . . . Major Halpine, in reply, spoke gracefully of the painfulness of the duty he had been called upon to perform — to receive the swords of men who had shown by their bravery that they deserved to wear them. . . . As soon as the surrender was complete, Colonel Olmstead turned to his officers and began making some remarks to them, upon which his captors withdrew. The American flag was then raised on the ramparts." [Correspondence of the "New York Times" in Moore's "Rebellion Record."] EDITORS.

of wood any longer," retorted a Connecticut man, pointing to a 10-inch shot that one of our Columbiads had sent through the wall.

Among the articles of capitulation was one providing that the sick and wounded should be sent under a flag of truce to the Confederate lines. This article General Hunter declined to ratify, and the whole garrison were sent as prisoners to the forts in New York harbor.

The garrison was found to consist of 385 men, including a full complement of officers. Several of them were severely, and one fatally, wounded. Our own loss was limited to one man, killed through his own neglect of the proper precautions.

The full armament of the fort was 140 guns. At the time of the siege it contained 48, of which 20 bore on Tybee Island. After the position of our several batteries became known to the enemy, each of these guns was trained on a particular point, and was served unvaryingly in that direction. Our men soon learned the point of attack of each gun, and were warned by the cry of "Cover!" when a shot was coming. They took great satisfaction in seeing visitors to the batteries dodge at false alarms, in their pursuit of amusement, not always respecting even high rank. In all, 16 of these 20 guns were silenced by our fire, while not one of our pieces was struck.

During the siege our batteries fired 5275 shots, of which 3543 were from the 20 guns and 1732 from the 16 mortars. We were provided with ammunition for a week's firing, of which about one-fifth was expended.

BREVET BRIG.-GENERAL CHARLES G. HALPINE.
FROM A PHOTOGRAPH.

The photograph was evidently intended to show General Halpine in his literary character of "Private Miles O'Reilly," whose war poems were among the most popular of that period. At Fort Pulaski, Major Halpine was Assistant Adjutant-General on the staff of General David Hunter, commanding the Department of the South, which included South Carolina, Georgia, and Florida. He died August 3d, 1868.

The effect of our fire upon the walls of the fort is interesting, as the first example, in actual warfare, of the breaching power of rifled ordnance at long

THE OPPOSING LAND FORCES AT FORT PULASKI, GA.

UNION FORCES.

Maj.-Gen. David Hunter, department commander. Brig.-Gen. Henry W. Benham, division commander.
*Daufuskie Island*, Brig.-Gen. Egbert L. Viele: 6th Conn., Col. John L. Chatfield; 8th Me. (5 co's), Lieut.-Col. Ephraim W. Woodman; 48th N. Y., Col. James H. Perry. *Jones Island* (K, 1st N. Y. Engineers, Capt. H. L. Southard, and G, 3d R. I. Artillery, Capt. John H. Gould), Lieut.-Col. William B. Barton. *Bird Island* (E, 3d R. I. Artillery, Capt. James E. Bailey, and E, 1st N.Y. Engineers, Capt. James E. Place), Maj. Oliver T. Beard.

## SIEGE AND CAPTURE OF FORT PULASKI.

range. Not only were the two casemates opened to an aggregate width of thirty feet, but the scarp wall was battered down in front of three casemate piers, and the adjacent wall on each side was so badly shattered that a few hours' firing would have doubled the width of practicable breach, a ramp of débris reaching to the foot of the counterscarp. In repairing the work subsequently, one hundred linear feet of wall had to be rebuilt.

A messenger who escaped from the fort just before the surrender succeeded in making his way over the creeks and marshes, and carried to Savannah, fifteen miles up the river, the news that the fort had fallen.‡ The consternation was supreme. All hope of saving

VIEWS OF FORT PULASKI AFTER THE SURRENDER. FROM PHOTOGRAPHS.

the city seemed lost, and the citizens began to secure themselves by sending their families and property into the interior. Their confidence in the ability

*Tybee Island*, Acting Brig.-Gen. Q. A. Gillmore: 7th Conn., Col. Alfred H. Terry; 8th Mich., Col. William M. Fenton; 46th N. Y., Col. Rudolph Rosa; 1st N. Y. Engineers, (Co's A and D, Lieut. Thomas B. Brooks and Capt. Frederick E. Graef), Lieut.-Col. James F. Hall; B, F, and H, 3d R. I. Artillery, Capts. L. C. Tourtellot, Pardon Mason, and Horatio Rogers, Jr.; detachment A, U. S. Engineers, Sergeant James E. Wilson.

CONFEDERATE FORCES.

Col. Charles H. Olmstead: Montgomery Guard, Capt. L. J. Gilmartin; German Volunteers, Capt. John H. Steigen; Oglethorpe Light Infantry, Capt. T. W. Sims; Wise Guard, Capt. M. J. McMullan; Washington Volunteers, Capt. John McMahon.

Of the garrison and armament of Fort Pulaski, General A. R. Lawton said in his report: "As there have been no returns received from Fort Pulaski for some time, I cannot give you the precise strength of the garrison. It consisted, however, of five companies, numbering a little over 400 men, and commanded by Colonel C. H. Olmstead. The armament consisted of five 10-inch Columbiads, nine 8-inch Columbiads, three 42-pounders, three 10-inch mortars, one 12-inch mortar, one 24-pounder howitzer, two 12-pounder howitzers, twenty 32-pounders, and two 4½-inch (Blakely) rifled guns, with 130 rounds of ammunition per gun."

‡ "Corporal Law [who carried the news of the surrender to the Confederates] arrived in the fort in company with the signal man, whom he went to pilot, at 5 o'clock Friday morning, the day of the surrender. He remained inside the works during

of Fort Pulaski to sustain a siege had been absolute. General Henry C. Wayne, of the Confederate army, who was in Savannah at the time, was one of the first to doubt, and met with the usual fortune of prophets of evil in times of intense popular feeling. He had been an officer in the regular army, and his experience had taught him to distinguish the sound of guns at different distances and fired in opposite directions. As his trained ear noted how, from hour to hour, the guns pointed toward the city kept up their steady volume, while the intervals of reply grew longer and longer, he told the citizens on the second day that the guns of the fort were being gradually silenced, and that it could not hold out. Out of incredulity grew a suspicion that "the wish was father to the thought," and indignation was fast tending toward personal violence, when the truth became known, and the wrath of the people was lost in their fears.

The result of this victory was to close the Savannah River entirely to blockade-runners, and to set free for service elsewhere the naval force which had been employed there.

the whole of the bombardment on that day, and left as the flag was lowered [not being a member of the garrison], making his way to the south wharf as the enemy's steamer was approaching the north landing. When the bombardment commenced on Thursday none of the enemy's batteries on Tybee were visible, except from the smoke which pointed out the different localities to our garrison. . . . The firing of the enemy on Thursday was not so effective as to create an apprehension that the work would fall. The enemy were obtaining the range of their guns for the operations of night and the day following. . . . The north-east casemates were all in which the garrison could bunk with any security whatever through Thursday night, though but little sleep was enjoyed, as the enemy threw twelve shells per hour into the fort until daylight. . . . Corporal Law witnessed the whole of Friday's fight for himself, mingling freely with the garrison throughout the terrible scene. . . . At the close of the fight all the parapet guns were dismounted except three — two 10-inch Columbiads, known as 'Beauregard' and 'Jeff Davis,' but one of which bore on the island, and a rifle-cannon. Every casemate gun in the south-east section of the fort, from No. 7 to No. 13, including all that could be brought to bear upon the enemy's batteries except one, were dismounted, and the casemate walls breached, in almost every instance, to the top of the arch — say between five and six feet in width. The moat outside was so filled with brick and mortar that one could have passed over dry-shod. The officers' quarters were torn to pieces, the bomb-proof timbers scattered in every direction over the yard, and the gates to the entrance knocked off. The parapet walls on the Tybee side were all gone, in many places down to the level of the earth on the casemates. The protection to the magazine in the north-west angle of the fort had all been shot away; the entire corner of the magazine next to the passage-way was shot off, and the powder exposed, while three shots had actually penetrated the chamber. Of this, Corporal Law is positive, for he examined it for himself before leaving. Such was the condition of affairs when Colonel Olmstead called a council of officers in a casemate; and, without a dissenting voice, they acquiesced in the necessity of a capitulation, in order to save the garrison from utter destruction by an explosion, which was momentarily threatened. Accordingly, at 2 o'clock, P. M., the men were called from the guns and the flag was lowered. Early in the day Colonel Olmstead had no doubt of his ability to silence every battery on the island, and to this end he determined, when night came and the enemy's fire slackened, to change the position of all his heavy guns, so as to bring them to bear on the enemy. As the day progressed, however, his situation became desperate. . . . Every man did his duty with alacrity, and, there being few guns that bore on the enemy, there was a continued contest as to who should man them. When volunteers were called for to perform any laborious duty, there was a rush of the men from every company in the fort. . . . Among the last guns fired were those on the parapet, and the men stood there exposed to a storm of iron hail to the last." [Correspondence of the Savannah "Republican" of April 23d, 1862.]     EDITORS.

# EARLY OPERATIONS IN THE GULF.

### BY PROFESSOR J. R. SOLEY, U. S. N.

AFTER the seizure of the Pensacola Navy Yard and the movements connected with the relief of Fort Pickens (Vol. I., p. 32), the Gulf Coast remained comparatively quiet until the establishment of the blockade. Hitherto the vessels in this quarter had formed a part of the Home Squadron, under Flag-Officer Pendergrast; but on June 8th, 1861, Flag-Officer William Mervine assumed command of the station, his vessels constituting the Gulf Blockading Squadron. Already the blockade had been set on foot by the *Powhatan*, at Mobile, and by the *Brooklyn*, at New Orleans; and soon after Mervine arrived in the steamer *Mississippi*, he had twenty vessels in his fleet. On July 2d, Galveston, the third port of importance in the Gulf, was blockaded by the *South Carolina*.

The first collision occurred in August, when one of the tenders of the *South Carolina*, blockading Galveston, was fired on by a battery on the shore. Commander Alden, commanding the *South Carolina*, laid his ship close to the shore and returned the fire. A few shells were accidentally discharged into the town, but the affair was in no sense a bombardment of Galveston.

In September Flag-Officer William W. McKean replaced Mervine in command of the squadron. Shortly after, the blockading vessels off the mouths of the Mississippi, commanded by Captain John Pope, moved up to the Head of the Passes. Early on the morning of the 12th of October this squadron, consisting of the *Richmond*, *Vincennes*, *Preble*, and *Water Witch*, was attacked by the iron-clad ram *Manassas*, under Lieutenant A. F. Warley. The *Manassas* rammed the *Richmond* without inflicting serious injury, and, being herself damaged by the blow, withdrew up the river. At the same time, the *Richmond* and her consorts turned their heads down-stream, and retreated as fast as possible to the mouth of South-west Pass. The *Preble* got over the bar, but the *Vincennes* and the *Richmond* grounded. In this position they were attacked by a small flotilla of converted river boats under Commodore G. N. Hollins. Notwithstanding the evident panic that prevailed in the fleet, the Confederate attack was not sustained with any great spirit, and the result was indecisive, neither party obtaining an advantage. The *Water Witch* was skillfully and boldly commanded by Lieutenant Francis Winslow; while the action of the captain of the *Vincennes* in abandoning his vessel while she was ashore, but under cover of the *Richmond's* heavy battery, was a subject of well-merited reproach.

On the night of the 13th of September occurred the destruction of the Confederate privateer *Judah*, in Pensacola harbor (see Vol. I., p. 32).

A similar exploit was performed at Galveston early in November. The attacking party, under Lieutenant James E. Jouett, set out in two launches from the frigate *Santee*, Captain Henry Eagle, on the night of the 7th, and captured and burnt the privateer schooner *Royal Yacht*, carrying one 32-pounder. Thirteen prisoners were taken. The casualties in the Union force were 2 killed and 7 wounded.

On the 16th of September, Ship Island, an important point commanding the passage of Mississippi Sound, which formed the water connection between New Orleans and Mobile, was evacuated by the Confederate forces. On the next day the steamer *Massachusetts*, under Captain Melancton Smith, landed a force and took possession of the island. The fort was strengthened by a formidable armament of rifles and 9-inch Dahlgren guns. Occasional attempts were made to recover the island, but without success. On the 19th of October the Confederate steamer *Florida* (Captain George N. Hollins) made a demonstration, and an encounter took place between that vessel and the *Massachusetts*. The *Florida*, having the advantage of higher speed and less draught, was able to choose her distance, and exploded a 68-pounder rifle shell in the *Massachusetts*, but without doing serious damage. The engagement was indecisive. In December a detachment of 2500 troops under Brigadier-General John W. Phelps was posted on the island, which had up to this time been held by the navy.

According to Secretary Welles (in "The Galaxy" for Nov., 1871), the Navy Department first conceived the idea of an attack on New Orleans in September, 1861, and the plan took definite shape about the middle of November, ‡ from which time the department was busily engaged in preparation for the expedition. As a part of the plan, it was decided to divide the Gulf Squadron into two commands, and when, on the 23d of December, Farragut received his preparatory orders, they directed him to hold himself in readiness to take command of the West Gulf Squadron and the expedition to New Orleans. Farragut received his full orders as flag-officer on the 20th of January, 1862, and sailed from Hampton Roads in the *Hartford* on the 3d of February, arriving at Ship Island on the 20th.

The East Gulf Squadron, comprising the vessels on the west coast of Florida, remained under the command of Flag-Officer McKean. On May 10th, 1862, Pensacola was evacuated, and came once more into the possession of the United States. A month later, on June 4th, Flag-Officer McKean was relieved by Captain J. L. Lardner, who was followed by Commodores Theodorus Bailey and C. K. Stribling. Operations in this quarter during the remainder of the war consisted chiefly of boat expeditions, encounters with blockade-runners or armed schooners, attacks upon guerrillas in the neighborhood of the coast, raids upon salt-works, and other small affairs of like character.

---

‡ Commander D. D. Porter undoubtedly had the scheme in mind as early as June, 1861, when he was off the Passes in the *Powhatan*.—J. R. S.

THE CONFEDERATE CRUISER "SUMTER," CAPTAIN SEMMES, LEAVING NEW ORLEANS, JUNE 18, 1861. FROM A SKETCH MADE AT THE TIME.

## NEW ORLEANS BEFORE THE CAPTURE.

### BY GEORGE W. CABLE, CO. 1, 4TH MISSISSIPPI CAVALRY.

IN the spring of 1862, we boys of Race, Orange, Magazine, Camp, Constance, Annunciation, Prytania, and other streets had no game. Nothing was "in"; none of the old playground sports that commonly fill the school-boy's calendar. We were even tired of drilling. Not one of us between seven and seventeen but could beat the drum, knew every bugle-call, and could go through the manual of arms and the facings like a drill-sergeant. We were *blasé* old soldiers—military critics.

Who could tell us anything? I recall but one trivial admission of ignorance on the part of any lad. On a certain day of grand review, when the city's entire defensive force was marching through Canal street, there came along, among the endless variety of good and bad uniforms, a stately body of tall, stalwart Germans, clad from head to foot in velveteen of a peculiarly vociferous fragrance, and a boy, spelling out the name upon their banner, said:

"H-u-s-s-a-r-s: what's them?"

"Aw, you fool!" cried a dozen urchins at once, "them's the Hoosiers. Don't you smell 'em?"

But that was earlier. The day of grand reviews was past. Hussars, Zouaves, and numberless other bodies of outlandish name had gone to the front in Tennessee and Virginia. Our cultivated eyes were satisfied now with one uniform that we saw daily. Every afternoon found us around in Coliseum Place, standing or lying on the grass watching the dress parade of the "Confederate Guards." Most of us had fathers or uncles in the long, spotless, gray, white-gloved ranks that stretched in such faultless alignment down the hard, harsh turf of our old ball-ground.

This was the flower of the home guard. The merchants, bankers, underwriters, judges, real-estate owners, and capitalists of the Anglo-American part of the city were "all present or accounted for" in that long line. Gray heads, hoar heads, high heads, bald heads. Hands flashed to breast and waist with a martinet's precision at the command of "Present arms,"—hands that had ruled by the pen—the pen and the dollar—since long before any of us young spectators was born, and had done no harder muscular work than carve roasts and turkeys these twenty, thirty, forty years. Here and there among them were individuals who, unaided, had clothed and armed companies, squadrons, battalions, and sent them to the Cumberland and the Potomac. A good three-fourths of them had sons on distant battle-fields, some living, some dead.

We boys saw nothing pathetic in this array of old men. To us there was only rich enjoyment in the scene. If there was anything solemn about it, why did the band play polkas? Why was the strain every day the same gay

Tra la la, tra la la, tra la la la la ......................

Away down to the far end of the line and back again, the short, stout German drum-major—holding his gaudy office in this case by virtue of his girth, not height (as he had himself explained)—flourished his big stick majestically, bursting with rage at us for casually reiterating at short intervals in his hearing that "he kot it mit his size."

In those beautiful spring afternoons there was scarcely a man to be found, anywhere, out of uniform. Down on the steamboat landing, our famous Levee, a superb body of Creoles drilled and paraded in dark-blue uniform. The orders were given in French; the manual was French; the movements were quick, short, nervy. Their "about march" was four sharp stamps of their neatly shod feet — *un, deux, trois, quatre* — that brought them face about and sent them back, tramp, tramp, tramp, over the smooth white pavement of powdered oyster-shells. Ah, the nakedness of that once crowded and roaring mart!

And there was a "Foreign Legion." Of course, the city had always been full of foreigners; but now it was a subject of amazement, not unmixed with satire, to see how many whom every one had supposed to be Americans or "citizens of Louisiana" bloomed out as British, or French, or Spanish subjects. But, even so, the tremendous pressure of popular sentiment crowded them into the ranks and forced them to make every show of readiness to "hurl back the foe," as we used to call it. And they really served for much. Merely as a gendarmerie they relieved just so many Confederate soldiers of police duty in a city under martial law, and enabled them to man forts and breastworks at short notice whenever that call should come.

That call, the gray heads knew, was coming. They confessed the conviction softly to one another in the counting-room and idle store-fronts when they thought no one was listening. I used to hear them — standing with my back turned, pretending to be looking at something down street, but with both ears turned backward and stretched wide. They said under their breath that there was not a single measure of defense that was not behindhand. And they spoke truly. In family councils a new domestic art began to be studied and discussed — the art of hiding valuables.

There had come a great silence upon trade. Long ago the custom-warehouses had begun to show first a growing roominess, then emptiness, and then had remained shut, and the iron bolts and cross-bars of their doors were gray with cobwebs. One of them, in which I had earned my first wages as a self-supporting lad, had been turned into a sword-bayonet factory, and I had been turned out. For some time later the Levee had kept busy; but its stir and noise had gradually declined, faltered, turned into the commerce of war and the clatter of calkers and ship-carpenters, and faded out. Both receipts and orders from the interior country had shrunk and shrunk, and the brave, steady fellows, who at entry and shipping and cash and account desks could no longer keep a show of occupation, had laid down the pen, taken up the sword and musket, and followed after the earlier and more eager volunteers. There had been one new, tremendous sport for moneyed men for a while, with spoils to make it interesting. The sea-going tow-boats of New Orleans were long, slender side-wheelers, all naked power and speed, without either freight or passenger room, each with a single tall, slim chimney and hurrying walking-beam, their low, taper hulls trailing behind scarcely above the water, and perpetually drenched with the yeast of the wheels. Some merchants of the more audacious sort, restless under the strange new quiet of Tchoupitoulas street, had got letters of mark and reprisal, and let slip these sharp-nosed deerhounds upon the tardy, unsuspecting ships that came sailing up to the Passes unaware of the declaration of war. But that game too was up. The blockade had closed in like a prison-gate: the lighter tow-boats, draped with tarpaulins, were huddled together under Slaughterhouse Point, with their cold boilers and motionless machinery yielding to rust; the more powerful ones had been moored at the long wharf vacated by Morgan's Texas steamships; there had been a great hammering, and making of chips, and clatter of railroad iron, turning these tow-boats into iron-clad cotton gunboats, and these had crawled away, some up and some down the river, to be seen in that harbor no more. At length only the foundries, the dry-docks across the river, and the ship-yard in suburb Jefferson, where the great ram *Mississippi* was being too slowly built, were active, and the queen of Southern commerce, the city that had once believed it was to be the greatest in the world, was absolutely out of employment.

There was, true, some movement of the sugar and rice crops into the hands of merchants who had advanced the money to grow them; and the cotton-presses and cotton-yards were full of cotton, but there it all stuck; and when one counts in a feeble exchange of city for country supplies, there was nothing more. Except — yes — that the merchants had turned upon each other, and were now engaged in a mere passing back and forth among themselves in speculation the daily diminishing supply of goods and food. Some were too noble to take part in this, and dealt only with consumers. I remember one odd little old man, an extensive wholesale grocer, who used to get tipsy all by himself every day, and go home so, but who would not speculate on the food of a distressed city. He had not got down to that.

Gold and silver had long ago disappeared. Confederate money was the currency; and not merely was the price of food and raiment rising, but the value of the money was going down. The State, too, had a paper issue, and the city had another. Yet with all these there was first a famine of small change, and then a deluge of "shinplasters." Pah! What a mess it was! The boss butchers and the keepers of drinking-houses actually took the lead in issuing "money." The current joke was that you could pass the label of an olive-oil bottle, because it was greasy, smelt bad, and bore an autograph — Plagniol Frères, if I remember rightly. I did my first work as a cashier in those days, and I can remember the smell of my cash-drawer yet. Instead of five-cent pieces we had car-tickets. How the grimy little things used to stick together! They would pass and pass until they were so soft and illegible with grocers' and butchers' handling that you could tell only by some faint show of their original color what company had issued them. Rogues did a lively business in "split tickets," literally splitting them and making one ticket serve for two.

Decay had come in. In that warm, moist climate it is always hungry, and wherever it is allowed to feed, eats with a greed that is strange to see. With the wharves, always expensive and difficult to maintain, it made havoc. The occasional idle, weather-stained ship moored beside them, and resting on the water almost as light and void as an empty peascod, could hardly find a place to fasten to. The streets fell into sad neglect, but the litter of commerce was not in them, and some of their round-stone pavements after a shower would have the melancholy cleanness of weather-bleached bones. How quiet and lonely the harbor grew! The big dry-docks against the farther shore were all empty. Now and then a tug fussed about, with the yellow river all to itself; and one or two steamboats came and went each day, but they moved drowsily, and, across on the other side of the river, a whole fleet of their dingy white sisters laid tied up to the bank, *sine die*. My favorite of all the sea-steamers, the little *Habana*, that had been wont to arrive twice a month from Cuba, disgorge her Spanish-American cargo, and bustle away again, and that I had watched the shipwrights, at their very elbows, razee and fit with three big, raking masts in place of her two small ones, had long ago slipped down the river and through the blockaders, and was now no longer the *Habana*, but the far-famed and dreaded *Sumter*.

The movements of military and naval defense lent some stir. The old revenue-cutter *Washington*, a graceful craft, all wings, no steam, came and went from the foot of Canal street. She was lying there when Farragut's topmasts hove in sight across the low land at English Turn. Near by, on her starboard side, lay a gun-boat, moored near the spot where the "lower coast" packet landed daily, to which spot the crowd used to rush sometimes to see the commanding officer, Major-General Mansfield Lovell, ride aboard, bound down the river to the forts. Lovell was a lithe, brown-haired man of forty-odd, a very attractive figure, giving the eye, at first glance, a promise of much activity. He was a showy horseman, visibly fond of his horse. He rode with so long a stirrup-leather that he simply stood astride the saddle, as straight as a spear; and the idlers of the landing loved to see him keep the saddle and pass from the wharf to the steamboat's deck on her long, narrow stage-plank without dismounting.

Such petty breaks in the dreariness got to be scarce and precious toward the last. Not that the town seemed so desolate then as it does now, as one tells of it; but the times were grim. Opposite the rear of the store where I was now employed,— for it fronted in Common street and stretched through to Canal,— the huge, unfinished custom-house reared its lofty granite walls, and I used to go up to its top now and then to cast my eye over the broad city and harbor below. When I did so, I looked down upon a town that had never been really glad again after the awful day of Shiloh. She had sent so many gallant fellows to help Beauregard, and some of them so young,— her last gleaning,— that when, on the day of their departure, they marched with solid column and firm-set, unsmiling mouths down the long gray lane made by the open ranks of those old Confederate Guards, and their escort broke into cheers and tears and waved their gray shakoes on the tops of their bayonets and seized the dear lads' hands as they passed in mute self-devotion and steady tread, while the trumpets sang "Listen to the Mocking-bird," that was the last time; the town never cheered with elation afterward; and when the people next uncovered it was in silence, to let the body of Albert Sidney Johnston, their great chevalier, pass slowly up St. Charles street behind the muffled drums, while on their quivering hearts was written as with a knife the death-roll of that lost battle. One of those—a former school-mate of mine—who had brought that precious body walked beside the bier, with the stains of camp and battle on him from head to foot. The war was coming very near.

Many of the town's old forms and habits of peace held fast. The city, I have said, was under martial law; yet the city management still went through its old routines. The volunteer fire department was as voluntary and as redundantly riotous as ever. The police courts, too, were as cheerful as of old. The public schools had merely substituted "Dixie," the "Marseillaise," and the "Bonnie Blue Flag" for "Hail Columbia" and the "Star-Spangled Banner," and were running straight along. There was one thing besides, of which many of us knew nothing at the time,— a system of espionage, secret, diligent, and fierce, that marked down every man suspected of sympathy with the enemy in a book whose name was too vile to find place on any page. This was not the military secret service,— that is to be expected wherever there is war,— nor any authorized police, but the scheme of some of the worst of the villains who had ruled New Orleans with the rod of terror for many years—the "Thugs."

But the public mind was at a transparent heat. Everybody wanted to know of everybody else, "Why don't you go to the front?" Even the gentle maidens demanded tartly, one of another, why their brothers or lovers had not gone long ago, though, in truth, the laggards were few indeed. The very children were fierce. For now even we, the uninformed, the lads and women, knew the enemy was closing down upon us. Of course we confronted the fact very valorously, we boys and mothers and sisters — and the newspapers. Had we not inspected the fortifications ourselves? Was not every man in town ready to rush into them at the twelve taps of the fire-alarm bells? Were we not ready to man them if the men gave out? Nothing afloat could pass the forts. Nothing that walked could get through our swamps. The *Mississippi*—and, in fact, she was a majestically terrible structure, only let us *complete* her—would sweep the river clean!

MAJOR-GENERAL MANSFIELD LOVELL, COMMANDER OF CONFEDERATE DEPARTMENT NO. 1, WITH HEADQUARTERS AT NEW ORLEANS. FROM A PHOTOGRAPH.

But there was little laughter. Food was dear; the destitute poor were multiplying terribly; the market men and women, mainly Germans, Gascon-French, and Sicilians, had lately refused to take the shinplaster currency, and the city authority had forced them to accept it. There was little to laugh at. The Mississippi was gnawing its levees and threatening to plunge in upon us. The city was believed to be full of spies.

I shall not try to describe the day the alarm-bells told us the city was in danger and called every man to his mustering-point. The children poured out from the school-gates and ran crying to their homes, meeting their sobbing mothers at their thresholds. The men fell into ranks. I was left entirely alone in charge of the store in which I was employed. Late in the afternoon, receiving orders to close it, I did so, and went home. But I did not stay. I went to the river-side. There until far into the night I saw hundreds of drays carrying cotton out of the presses and yards to the wharves, where it was fired. The glare of those sinuous miles of flame set men and women weeping and wailing thirty miles away on the farther shore of Lake Pontchartrain. But the next day was the day of terrors. During the night fear, wrath, and sense of betrayal had run through the people as the fire had run through the cotton. You have seen, perhaps, a family fleeing with lamentations and wringing of hands out of a burning house: multiply it by thousands upon thousands; that was New Orleans, though the houses were not burning. The firemen were out; but they cast fire on the waters, putting the torch to the empty ships and cutting them loose to float down the river.

Whoever could go was going. The great mass, that had no place to go to or means to go with, was beside itself. "Betrayed! betrayed!" it cried, and ran in throngs from street to street, seeking some vent, some victim for its wrath. I saw a crowd catch a poor fellow at the corner of Magazine and Common streets, whose crime was that he looked like a stranger and might be a spy. He was the palest living man I ever saw. They swung him to a neighboring lamp-post, but the Foreign Legion was patroling the town in strong squads, and one of its lieutenants, all green and gold, leaped with drawn sword, cut the rope, and saved the man. This was but one occurrence: there were many like it. I stood in the rear door of our store, Canal street, soon after reopening it. The junior of the firm was within. I called him to look toward the river. The masts of the cutter *Washington* were slowly tipping, declining, sinking — down she went. The gun-boat moored next to her began to smoke all over and then to blaze. My employers fell into ranks and left the city — left their goods and their affairs in the hands of one mere lad (no stranger would have thought I had reached fourteen) and one big German porter. I closed the doors, sent the porter to his place in the Foreign Legion, and ran to the levee to see the sights.

What a gathering! The riff-raff of the wharves, the town, the gutters. Such women — such wrecks of women! And all the juvenile rag-tag. The lower steamboat landing, well covered with sugar, rice, and molasses, was being rifled. The men smashed; the women scooped up the smashings. The river was overflowing the top of the levee. A rain-storm began to threaten. "Are the Yankee ships in sight?" I asked of an idler. He pointed out the tops of their naked masts as they showed up across the huge bend of the river. They were engaging the batteries at Camp Chalmette — the old field of Jackson's renown. Presently that was over. Ah, me! I see them now as they come slowly round Slaughterhouse Point into full view, silent, grim, and terrible; black with men, heavy with deadly portent; the long-banished Stars and Stripes flying against the frowning sky. Oh, for the *Mississippi!* the *Mississippi!* Just then she came down upon them. But how? Drifting helplessly, a mass of flames.

The crowds on the levee howled and screamed with rage. The swarming decks answered never a word; but one old tar on the *Hartford*, standing with lanyard in hand beside a great pivot-gun, so plain to view that you could see him smile, silently patted its big black breech and blandly grinned.

And now the rain came down in sheets. About 1 or 2 o'clock in the afternoon (as I remember), I being again in the store with but one door ajar, came a roar of shoutings and imprecations and crowding feet down Common street. "Hurrah for Jeff Davis! Hurrah for Jeff Davis! Shoot them! Kill them! Hang them!" I locked the door on the outside, and ran to the front of the mob, bawling with the rest, "Hurrah for Jeff Davis!" About every third man there had a weapon out. Two officers of the United States navy were walking abreast, unguarded and alone, looking not to right or left, never frowning, never flinching, while the mob screamed in their ears, shook cocked pistols in their faces, cursed and crowded, and gnashed upon them. So through the gates of death those two men walked to the City Hall to demand the town's surrender. It was one of the bravest deeds I ever saw done.

Later events, except one, I leave to other pens. An officer from the fleet stood on the City Hall roof about to lower the flag of Louisiana. In the street beneath gleamed the bayonets of a body of marines. A howitzer pointed up and another down the street. All around swarmed the mob. Just then Mayor Monroe — lest the officer above should be fired upon, and the howitzers open upon the crowd — came out alone and stood just before one of the howitzers, tall, slender, with folded arms, eying the gunner. Down sank the flag. Captain Bell, tall and stiff, marched off with the flag rolled under his arm, and the howitzers clanking behind. Then cheer after cheer rang out for Monroe. And now, I dare say, every one is well pleased that, after all, New Orleans never lowered her colors with her own hands.

THE UNION FLEET ARRIVING AT NEW ORLEANS.

FARRAGUT'S FLAG-SHIP THE "HARTFORD."

# THE OPENING OF THE LOWER MISSISSIPPI.

### BY DAVID D. PORTER, ADMIRAL, U. S. N.

THE most important event of the War of the Rebellion, with the exception of the fall of Richmond, was the capture of New Orleans and the forts Jackson and St. Philip, guarding the approach to that city. To appreciate the nature of this victory, it is necessary to have been an actor in it, and to be able to comprehend not only the immediate results to the Union cause, but the whole bearing of the fall of New Orleans on the Civil War, which at that time had attained its most formidable proportions.

Previous to fitting out the expedition against New Orleans, there were eleven Southern States in open rebellion against the Government of the United States, or, as it was termed by the Southern people, in a state of secession. Their harbors were all more or less closed against our ships-of-war, either by the heavy forts built originally by the General Government for their protection, or by torpedoes and sunken vessels. Through four of these seceding States ran the great river Mississippi, and both of its banks, from Memphis to its mouth, were lined with powerful batteries. On the west side of the river were three important States, Louisiana, Arkansas, and Texas, with their great tributaries to the Mississippi,— the White, the Arkansas, and the Red,— which were in a great measure secure from the attacks of the Union forces. These States could not only raise half a million soldiers, but could furnish the Confederacy with provisions of all kinds, and cotton enough to supply the Rebel Government with the sinews of war. New Orleans was the largest Southern city, and contained all the resources of modern warfare, having great workshops where machinery of the most powerful kind could be built, and having artisans capable of building ships in wood or iron, casting heavy guns, or making small arms. The people of the city were in no way behind the most zealous secessionists in energy of purpose and in hostility to the Government of the United States.

The Mississippi is thus seen to have been the backbone of the Rebellion, which it should have been the first duty of the Federal Government to break. At the very outset of the war it should have been attacked at both ends at the same time, before the Confederates had time to fortify its banks or to turn the guns in the Government forts against the Union forces. A dozen improvised gun-boats would have held the entire length of the river if they had been sent there in time. The efficient fleet with which Du Pont, in November, 1861, attacked and captured the works at Port Royal could at that time have steamed up to New Orleans and captured the city without difficulty. Any three vessels could have passed Forts Jackson and St. Philip a month after the commencement of the war, and could have gone on to Cairo, if necessary, without any trouble. But the Federal Government neglected to approach the mouth of the Mississippi until a year after hostilities had commenced, except to blockade. The Confederates made good use of this interval, putting forth all their resources and fortifying not only the approaches to New Orleans, but both banks of the river as far north as Memphis.

WHILE in command of the *Powhatan*, engaged in the blockade of the southwest Pass of the Mississippi,—a period of seventy-six days,—I took pains to obtain all possible information concerning the defenses of the river. I learned from the fishermen who supplied the city with oysters and fish that very little progress had been made in strengthening the forts, and that no vessel of any importance was being built except the ram *Manassas*, which had not much strength and but a single gun. The only Confederate vessel then in commission was a small river-boat, the *Ivy*, mounting one 4-pounder rifled gun. Had I been able to cross the bar with my ship, I would have felt justified in going up to the city and calling on the authorities to surrender. I could easily have passed the forts under cover of the night without the aid of a pilot, as I had been up and down the river some thirty times in a large mail steamer. But the *Powhatan* drew three feet too much water, and there was no use thinking about such an adventure.

This was the position of affairs on May 31st, 1861, only forty-nine days after Fort Sumter had been fired on.

On the 9th of November, 1861, I arrived at New York with the *Powhatan* and was ordered to report to the Navy Department at Washington, which I did on the 12th. In those days it was not an easy matter for an officer, except one of high rank, to obtain access to the Secretary of the Navy, and I had been waiting nearly all the morning at the door of his office when Senators Grimes and Hale came along and entered into conversation with me concerning my service on the Gulf Coast. During this interview I told the senators of a plan I had formed for the capture of New Orleans, and when I had explained to them how easily it could be accomplished, they expressed surprise that no action had been taken in the matter, and took me in with them at once to see Secretary Welles. I then gave the Secretary, in as few words as possible, my opinion on the importance of capturing New Orleans, and my plan for doing so. Mr. Welles listened to me attentively, and when I had finished what I had to say he remarked that the matter should be laid before the President at once; and we all went forthwith to the Executive Mansion, where we were received by Mr. Lincoln.

My plan, which I then stated, was as follows: To fit out a fleet of vessels-of-war with which to attack the city, fast steamers drawing not more than 18 feet of water, and carrying about 250 heavy guns; also a flotilla of mortar-vessels, to be used in case it should be necessary to bombard Forts Jackson and St. Philip before the fleet should attempt to pass them. I also proposed that a body of troops should be sent along in transports to take possession of the city after it had been surrendered to the navy. When I had outlined the proposed movement the President remarked:

"This should have been done sooner. The Mississippi is the backbone of the Rebellion; it is the key to the whole situation. While the Confederates hold it they can obtain supplies of all kinds, and it is a barrier against our forces. Come, let us go and see General McClellan."

At that time General McClellan commanded all of the military forces, and was in the zenith of his power. He held the confidence of the President and the country, and was engaged in organizing a large army with which to guarantee the safety of the Federal seat of Government, and to march upon Richmond.

Our party was now joined by Mr. Seward, the Secretary of State, and we proceeded to McClellan's headquarters, where we found that officer diligently engaged in the duties of his responsible position. He came to meet the President with that cheery manner which always distinguished him, and, seeing me, shook me warmly by the hand. We had known each other for some years, and I always had the highest opinion of his military abilities.

"Oh," said the President, "you two know each other! Then half the work is done."

He then explained to the general the object of his calling at that time, saying:

"This is a most important expedition. What troops can you spare to accompany it and take possession of New Orleans after the navy has effected its capture? It is not only necessary to have troops enough to hold New Orleans, but we must be able to proceed at once toward Vicksburg, which is the key to all that country watered by the Mississippi and its tributaries. If the Confederates once fortify the neighboring hills, they will be able to hold that point for an indefinite time, and it will require a large force to dislodge them."

In all his remarks the President showed a remarkable familiarity with the state of affairs. Before leaving us, he said:

⸺⸺⸺⸺⸺⸺⸺⸺⸺⸺⸺⸺⸺⸺⸺⸺⸺⸺⸺⸺⸺⸺⸺⸺⸺⸺⸺⸺⸺⸺⸺⸺⸺⸺⸺⸺⸺⸺

⸹ Secretary Welles, in a paper printed in "The Galaxy" for November, 1871, says: "The President, General McClellan, and the two gentlemen named [Assistant-Secretary Fox and Commander D. D. Porter] with myself, were the only persons present at the conference."—EDITORS.

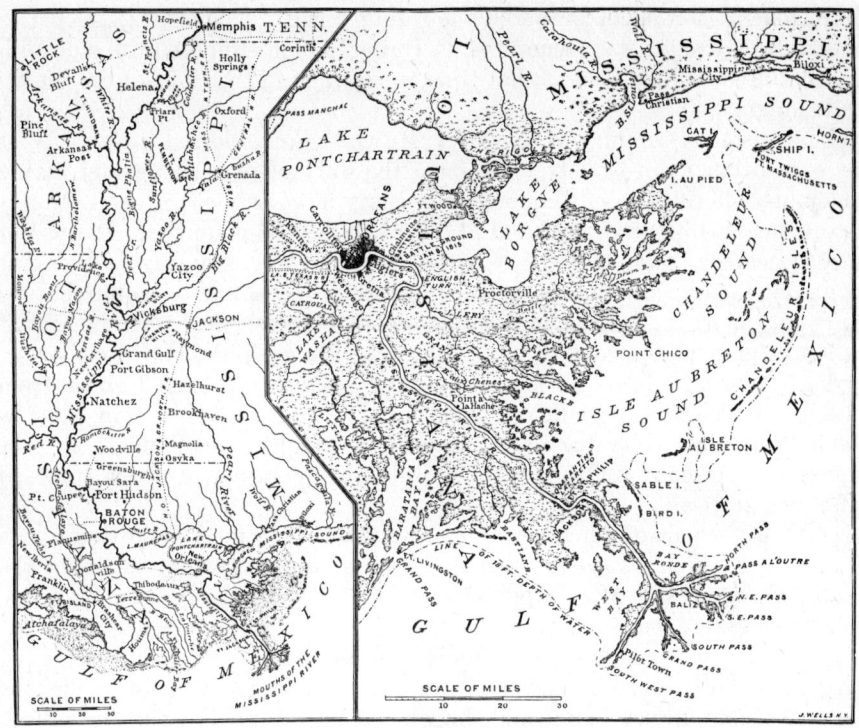

MAPS OF THE LOWER MISSISSIPPI.

"We will leave this matter in the hands of you two gentlemen. Make your plans, and let me have your report as soon as possible."

General McClellan and myself were then left to talk the matter over and draw up the plan of operations. With a man of McClellan's energy, it did not take long to come to a conclusion; and, although he had some difficulty in finding a sufficient number of troops without interfering with other important projects, he settled the matter in two days, and reported that his men would be ready to embark on the 15th of January, 1862.

The plan of the campaign submitted to the President was as follows: A naval expedition was to be fitted out, composed of vessels mounting not fewer than two hundred guns, with a powerful mortar-flotilla, and with steam transports to keep the fleet supplied. The army was to furnish twenty thousand troops, not only for the purpose of occupying New Orleans after its capture, but to fortify and hold the heights about Vicksburg. The navy and army were to push on up the river as soon as New Orleans was occupied by our troops, and call upon the authorities of Vicksburg to surrender. Orders were to be issued to Flag-Officer Foote, who commanded the iron-clad fleet on the upper Mississippi, to join the fleet above Vicksburg with his vessels and mortar-boats.

The above plans were all approved by the President, and the Navy Department immediately set to work to prepare the naval part of the expedition, while General McClellan prepared the military part. The officer selected to command the troops was General B. F. Butler, a man supposed to be of high administrative ability, and at that time one of the most zealous of the Union commanders.

The Assistant-Secretary of the Navy, Mr. G. V. Fox, selected the vessels for this expedition, and to me was assigned the duty of purchasing and fitting out a mortar-flotilla, to be composed of twenty large schooners, each mounting one heavy 13-inch mortar and at least two long 32-pounders. It was not until December, 1861, that the Navy Department got seriously to work at fitting out the expedition. Some of the mortar-vessels had to be purchased; the twenty mortars, with their thirty thousand bomb-shells, had to be cast at Pittsburg and transported to New York and Philadelphia, and the mortar-carriages made in New York. It was also necessary to recall ships from stations on the coast and fit them out; also to select officers from the few available at that time to fill the various positions where efficiency was required — especially for the mortar-flotilla, the operation of which imposed unfamiliar duties.

By the latter part of January the mortar-flotilla got off. In addition to the schooners, it included seven steamers (which were necessary to move the vessels about in the Mississippi River) and a store-ship. Seven hundred picked men were enlisted, and twenty-one officers were selected from the merchant marine to command the mortar-schooners.

An important duty now devolved on the Secretary of the Navy, viz., the selection of an officer to command the whole expedition. Mr. Fox and myself had often discussed the matter. He had had in his mind several officers of high standing and unimpeachable loyalty; but, as I knew the officers of the navy better than he did, my advice was listened to, and the selection fell upon Captain David Glasgow Farragut.

I had known Farragut ever since I was five years old. He stood high in the navy as an officer and seaman, and possessed such undoubted courage and energy that no possible objection could be made to him. On the first sign of war Farragut, though a Southerner by birth and residence, had shown his loyalty in an outspoken manner. The Southern officers had used every argument to induce him to desert his flag, even going so far as to threaten to detain him by force. His answer to them has become historical: "Mind what I tell you: You fellows will catch the devil before you get through with this business." ‡ Having thus expressed himself in a manner not to be misunderstood, he left Norfolk with his family and took a house on the Hudson River, whence he reported to the Navy Department as ready for duty. I knew Farragut better than most other officers of the navy knew him; and as he is here to appear as the central figure of the greatest naval achievement of our war, I will give a brief sketch of his early naval life.

Farragut was born in Tennessee, from which State his family moved to New

---

‡ It is worthy of note that in 1833, during the nullification troubles, Farragut was sent by Andrew Jackson to South Carolina to support his mandate that "the Union must and shall be preserved."— EDITORS.

Orleans. His father was not a man of affluence, and had a large family to support. In 1807 Captain David Porter, United States Navy, was appointed to the command of the New Orleans station. His father, David Porter, senior (who had been appointed by General Washington a sailing-master in the navy, for services performed during the Revolution), accompanied him to this post and served under his command. Being eighty-four years of age, his services were nominal, and he only lived in New Orleans for the sake of being near his son. One day, while fishing on Lake Pontchartrain, the old gentleman fell over with a sunstroke, and Farragut's father took him to his house near by, and treated him with the most assiduous attention. Mr. Porter died at the residence of Mr. and Mrs. Farragut, it being considered dangerous to move him. Captain Porter then, in order to show his gratitude to the Farraguts for their kindness to his father, offered to adopt their son Glasgow. This offer was gladly accepted, and from that time young Farragut became a member of Captain Porter's family, and was recognized as his adoptive son. The boy was placed at school when he was eight years old, and on the 17th of December, 1810, he was appointed an acting midshipman in the navy. He accompanied Captain Porter in the cruise of the *Essex* around Cape Horn, and was with him at the memorable capture of that frigate, on which occasion he showed the spirit of a brave boy. He remained with his adopted father some years, and served under him in the "mosquito fleet" of the West India squadron. In whatever position he was placed, Farragut maintained his reputation as a fine officer and genial, cheery companion. He was esteemed by all who knew him, and no one in the navy had more personal friends or fewer enemies. At the time of his appointment to the command of the New Orleans expedition, he was over sixty years of age; but he was as active as a man of fifty, with an unimpaired constitution, and a mind as bright as ever.

On his return to the North with his family, he had been assigned to duty by the department as president of a board for the examination of officers, and he accepted it as an acknowledgment on the part of the Government that he was a loyal man. The department hesitated for some time, however, when his name was proposed for commander of the important expedition against New Orleans. A wide-spread feeling prevailed at that time that Southern officers should not be given active duty afloat; for, although their loyalty was not doubted, it was naturally thought that they would find no duty congenial that would compel them to act offensively against their friends and relations. It was afterward proved that this opinion was unjust, for among the officers who hailed from the South were some of the most zealous and energetic defenders of the Union flag — men who did their duty faithfully. When Farragut came North he simply reported himself to the department as ready for duty, without applying for active service against the enemy. It was owing to this fact that the department was so long in coming to a conclusion, and this explains why the commander of the expedition was not (as he ought to have been) the very first man selected.

I continually urged Farragut's appointment, and finally the department directed me to go on to New York, and ascertain in a personal interview

CONFEDERATE SHARP-SHOOTERS AND SWAMP HUNTERS ATTACKING MORTAR-BOATS.

whether he would accept the command and enter warmly into the views of the Government. I found him, as I had expected, loyal to the utmost extent; and, although he did not at that time know the destination of the expedition, he authorized me to accept for him the Secretary's offer, and I telegraphed the department: "Farragut accepts the command, as I was sure he would."

In consequence of this answer he was called to Washington, and on the 20th of January, 1862, he received orders to command the expedition against New Orleans. In the orders are included these passages: "There will be attached to your squadron a fleet of bomb-vessels, and armed steamers enough to manage them, all under command of Commander D. D. Porter, who will be directed to report to you. As fast as these vessels are got ready they will be sent to Key West to await the arrival of all and the commanding officers, who will be permitted to organize and practice with them at that port.

"When these formidable mortars arrive, and you are completely ready, you will collect such vessels as can be spared from the blockade, and proceed up the Mississippi River, and reduce the defenses which guard the approaches to New Orleans, when you will appear off that city and take possession of it under the guns of your squadron, and hoist the American flag therein, keeping possession until troops can be sent to you. If the Mississippi expedition from Cairo shall not have descended the river, you will take advantage of the panic to push a strong force up the river to take all their defenses in the rear."

As soon as possible Farragut proceeded to his station and took command of the West Gulf Blockading Squadron. In the meantime the Confederates had not been idle. They had early been made acquainted with the destination of the expedition, and had put forth all their energies in strengthening Forts Jackson and St. Philip, obstructing the river, and preparing a naval force with which to meet the invaders. The ram *Manassas* was finished and placed in commission, and the iron-clad *Louisiana*, mounting sixteen heavy guns and heavily armored, was hurried toward completion. Besides these vessels there was another powerful iron-clad, building at New Orleans, which was expected to sweep the whole Southern coast clear of Union vessels. Two iron-clad rams, the *Arkansas* and *Tennessee*, were building at Memphis, and several other iron-clad vessels were under construction at different points on the tributaries.

This energy and forethought displayed by the South seems marvelous when compared with what was done by the North during the same period of time; for among all the ships that were sent to Farragut there was not one whose sides could resist a twelve-pound shot. Considering the great resources of the Northern States, this supineness of the Government appears inexcusable. Up to the time of the sailing of the expedition, only three iron-clads, the *Monitor*, *Galena*, and *New Ironsides*, had been commenced, in addition to the gun-boats on the Upper Mississippi; and it was only after the encounter of the *Monitor* with the *Merrimac* that it was seen how useful vessels of this class would be for the attack on New Orleans, particularly in contending with the forts on the banks of the Mississippi.

Flag-Officer Farragut did not arrive at Ship Island with the *Hartford* until the 20th of February, 1862, having been detained for some time at Key West, where he began to arrange his squadron for the difficult task that lay before him.

The vessels which had been assigned to his command soon began to arrive, and by the middle of March all had reported, together with six steamers belonging to the mortar-flotilla: the *Harriet Lane*, *Owasco*, *Clifton*, *Westfield*, *Miami*, *Jackson*; besides the mortar-schooners. The frigate *Colorado*, mounting fifty guns, had arrived, but Flag-Officer Farragut and Captain Bailey both came to the conclusion that she could not be lightened sufficiently to cross the bar.

On the 18th of March all the mortar-schooners crossed the bar at Pass à l'Outre, towed by the steamers *Harriet Lane*, *Owasco*, *Westfield*, and *Clifton*. They were ordered by Farragut to proceed to South-west Pass.

As yet the only ships that had crossed the bar were the *Hartford* and *Brooklyn*. The Navy Department had made a mistake in sending vessels of too great draught of water, such as the *Colorado*, *Pensacola*, and *Mississippi*. The two latter succeeded in crossing with great difficulty, but the whole fleet was delayed at least twelve days.

The first act of Farragut was to send Captain Henry H. Bell, his chief-of-staff, up the river with the steamers *Kennebec* and *Wissahickon*, to ascertain, if possible, what preparations had been made by the enemy to prevent the passage of the forts. This officer reported that the obstructions seemed formidable. Eight hulks were moored in line across the river, with heavy chains extending from one to the other. Rafts of logs were also used, and the passage between the forts was thus entirely closed.

The Confederates had lost no time in strengthening their defenses. They had been working night and day ever since the expedition was planned by the Federal Government. Forts Jackson and St. Philip were strong defenses, the former on the west and the latter on the east bank of the Mississippi. As they are to hold an important place in the following narration of events, it will be well to give a description of them.

Fort Jackson was built in the shape of a star, of stone and mortar, with heavy bomb-proofs. [See page 34.] It was back about one hundred yards from the levee, with its casemates just rising above it. I am told that the masonry had settled somewhat since it was first built, but it was still in a good state of preservation. Its armament consisted of 42 heavy guns in barbette, and 24 in casemates; also 2 pieces of light artillery and 6 guns in water-battery—in all, 74 guns. The last was a very formidable part of the defenses, its heavy guns having a commanding range down the river. The main work had been strengthened by covering its bomb-proofs and vulnerable parts with bags of sand piled five or six feet deep, making it proof against the projectiles of ordinary guns carried by ships-of-war in those days. The fort was also well supplied with provisions and munitions of war, which were stowed away in a heavily built citadel of masonry situated in the center of the works. Altogether, it was in a very good condition to withstand either attack or siege. Fort Jackson was under the immediate command of Lieutenant-Colonel Edward Higgins, formerly an officer of the United States navy, and a very gallant and intelligent man.

Fort St. Philip was situated on the other side of the river, about half a mile above Fort Jackson, and, in my opinion, was the more formidable of the two works. It covered a large extent of ground, and although it was open, without casemates, its walls were strongly built of brick and stone, covered with sod. The guns were mounted in barbette, and could be brought to bear on any vessel going up or down the river. There were in all 52 pieces of ordnance. One heavy rifled gun bore on the position of the mortar-fleet, and caused us considerable disturbance until the second or third day after the bombardment commenced, when it burst.

Each of the forts held a garrison of about seven hundred men, some of whom were from the Northern States, besides many foreigners (Germans or

Irish). The Northern men had applied for duty in the forts to avoid suspicion, and in the hope that they would not be called upon to fight against the Federal Government. In this hope they had been encouraged by their officers, all of whom, including the colonel in command, were of the opinion that no naval officer would have the hardihood to attack such strong positions.

All of the land defenses were under Brigadier-General Johnson K. Duncan, who showed himself to be an able and gallant commander.

The best passage up the river was near the west bank close under the guns of Fort Jackson, where the current was not very rapid and few eddies existed. Across this channel the Confederates had placed a raft of logs, extending from the shore to the commencement of a line of hulks which reached to the other side of the river. These hulks were anchored and connected to each other by chains. The raft was so arranged that it could be hauled out of the way of passing vessels, and closed when danger threatened. Although this plan of blocking the river was better than the first one tried by the Confederates, viz., to float a heavy chain across on rafts, it was not very formidable or ingenious.

In addition to the defenses at the forts, the Confederates worked with great diligence to improvise a fleet of men-of-war, using for this purpose a number of heavy tugs that had been employed in towing vessels up and down the river, and some merchant steamers. These, with the ram *Manassas* and the iron-clad *Louisiana*, made in all twelve vessels. The whole naval force was nominally under the control of Commander John K. Mitchell, C. S. N.♭

The iron-clad *Louisiana*, mounting 16 heavy guns, with a crew of 200 men, was a powerful vessel, almost impervious to shot, and was fitted with a shot-proof gallery from which her sharp-shooters could fire at an enemy with great effect. Her machinery was not completed, however, and during the passage of the Union fleet she was secured to the river-bank and could only use one broadside and three of her bow guns. At this time she was under the immediate command of Commander Charles F. McIntosh, formerly of the United States navy. The *McRae*, Lieutenant Thomas B. Huger, was a sea-going steamer mounting 6 32-pounders and 1 9-inch shell-gun; the steamer *Jackson*, Lieutenant F. B. Renshaw, mounting 2 32-pounders; the iron-clad ram *Manassas*, Lieutenant A. F. Warley, mounting 1 32-pounder (in the bow); and two launches, mounting each one howitzer. Two steamers had been converted into Louisiana State gun-boats, with pine and cotton barricades to protect the machinery and boilers: the *Governor Moore*, Commander Beverley Kennon, and the *General Quitman*, Captain Grant. "All the above steamers, being converted vessels," says Commander Mitchell, "were too slightly built for war purposes."

The River Defense gun-boats, consisting of six converted tow-boats under the command of a merchant captain named Stephenson, were also ordered to report to Commander Mitchell; but they proved of little assistance to

♭ The finding of the Confederate Court of Inquiry, December 5th, 1863, states that Commander Mitchell assumed command of the *Louisiana* at New Orleans, April 20th.— EDITORS.

MORTAR-SCHOONERS ENGAGED AGAINST FORT JACKSON.
Distance of leading schooner from the fort, 2850 yards. Duration of fire, six days. Total number of shells fired, 16,800.

him owing to the insubordination of their commander. "All of the above vessels," says Commander Mitchell, "mounted from one to two pivot 32-pounders each, some of them rifled. Their boilers and machinery were all more or less protected by thick, double pine barricades, filled in with compressed cotton." They were also prepared for ramming by flat bar-iron casings around their bows.

The Confederate fleet mounted, all told, 40 guns, of which 25 were 32-pounders, and one-fourth of them rifled.

It is thus seen that our wooden vessels, which passed the forts carrying 192 guns, had arrayed against them 126 guns in strongly built works, and 40 guns on board of partly armored vessels.↓

In addition to the above-mentioned defenses, Commodore Mitchell had at his command a number of fire-rafts (long flat-boats filled with pine-knots,

↓ To the 192 guns of the vessels making the passage should be added those on board the mortar-flotilla, 110 in number (including 9 howitzers), which performed their part in the reduction of the forts, thus making the aggregate of guns on the Union side 302.— EDITORS.

etc.), which were expected to do good service, either by throwing the Union fleet into confusion or by furnishing light to the gunners in the forts. On comparing the Confederate defenses with the attacking force of the Union fleet, it will be seen that the odds were strongly in favor of the former. It is generally conceded by military men that one gun in a fort is about equal to five on board of a wooden ship, especially when, as in this case, the forces afloat are obliged to contend against a three-and-a-half knot current in a channel obstructed by chains and fire-rafts. [See p. 75.] Our enemies were well aware of their strength, and although they hardly expected us to make so hazardous an attack, they waited impatiently for Farragut to "come on," resting in the assurance that he would meet with a disastrous defeat. They did not neglect, however, to add daily to the strength of their works during the time that our ships were delayed in crossing the bar and ascending the river.

Farragut experienced great difficulty in getting the larger vessels over the bar. The *Hartford* and *Brooklyn* were the only two that could pass without lightening. The *Richmond* stuck fast in the mud every time she attempted to cross. The *Mississippi* drew two feet too much water, and the *Pensacola*, after trying several times to get over, ran on a wreck a hundred yards away from the channel. There she lay, with her propeller half out of water, thumping on the wreck as she was driven in by the wind and sea. Pilots had been procured at Pilot Town, near by; but they were either treacherous or nervous, and all their attempts to get the heavy ships over the bar were failures. Farragut felt extremely uncomfortable at the prospect before him, but I convinced him that I could get the vessels over if he would place them under my control, and he consented to do so. I first tried with the *Richmond* (Commander Alden), and, although she had grounded seven times when in charge of a pilot, I succeeded at the first attempt, crossed the bar, and anchored off Pilot Town. The next trial was with the frigate *Mississippi*. The vessel was lightened as much as possible by taking out her spars, sails, guns, provisions, and coal. All the steamers of the mortar-fleet were then sent to her assistance, and after eight days' hard work they succeeded in pulling the *Mississippi* through. To get the *Pensacola* over looked even more difficult. I asked Captain Bailey to lend me the *Colorado* for a short time, and with this vessel I went as close as possible to the *Pensacola*, ran out a stream-cable to her stern, and, by backing hard on the *Colorado*, soon released her from her disagreeable position. The next day at 12 o'clock I passed her over the bar and anchored her off Pilot Town.

The U. S. Coast Survey steamer *Sachem*, commanded by a very competent officer, Mr. F. H. Gerdes, had been added to the expedition for the purpose of sounding the bar and river channel, and also to establish points and distances which should serve as guides to the commander of the mortar-flotilla. Mr. Gerdes and his assistants selected the positions of the bomb-vessels, furnished all the commanders of vessels with reliable charts, triangulated the river for eight miles below the forts, and planted small poles with white flags on the banks opposite the positions of the different vessels, each flag marked with the

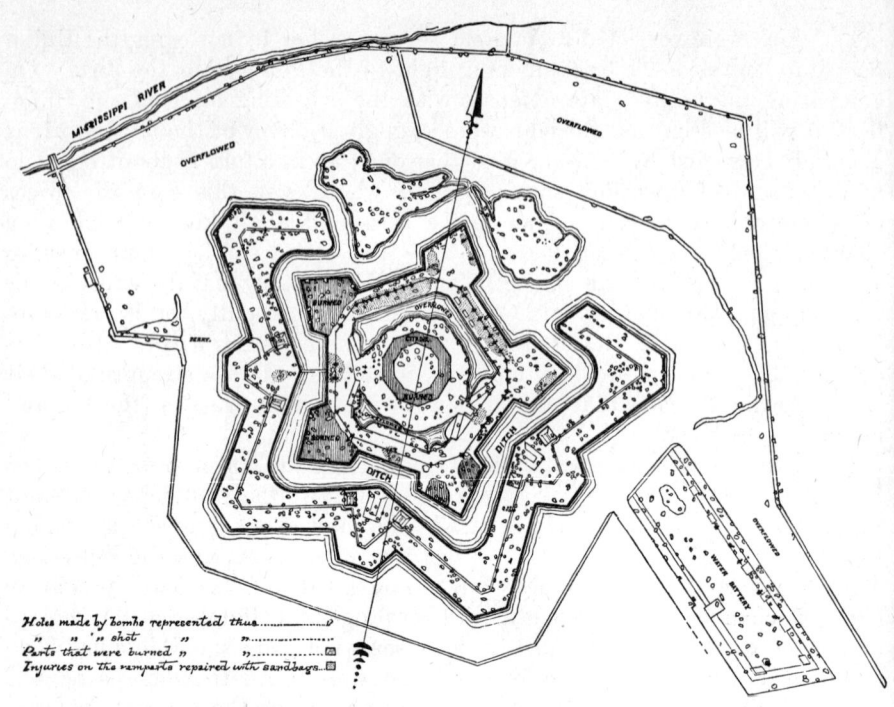

PLAN OF FORT JACKSON, SHOWING THE EFFECT OF THE BOMBARDMENT, APRIL 18TH TO 24TH. FROM THE GOVERNMENT MAP SURVEYED BY J. S. HARRIS UNDER THE DIRECTION OF F. H. GERDES, U. S. COAST SURVEY.

"All the scows and boats near the fort except three small ones were sunk. The drawbridge, hot-shot furnaces, and fresh-water cisterns were destroyed. The floors of the casemates were flooded, the levee having been broken.

"All the platforms for pitching tents on were destroyed by fire or shells. All the casemates were cracked (the roof in some places being entirely broken through) and masses of brick dislodged in numerous instances. The outer walls of the fort were cracked from top to bottom, admitting daylight freely."—Inscription on the original plan.

name of a vessel and the distance from the mouth of its mortar to the center of the fort. The boats of the surveyors were frequently attacked by sharpshooters, who fired from concealed positions among the bushes of the river bank. During the bombardment the Coast Survey officers were employed day and night in watching that the vessels did not move an inch from their places, and the good effect of all this care was shown in the final result of the mortar practice.

Having finished the preliminary work, on the 16th of April Farragut moved up with his fleet to within three miles of the forts, and informed me that I might commence the bombardment as soon as I was ready. The ships all anchored as they came up, but not in very good order, which led to some complications.

The place which I had selected for the first and third divisions of the mortar-vessels was under the lee of a thick wood on the right bank of the river, which presented in the direction of the fort an almost impenetrable mass. The forts could be plainly seen from the mast-heads of the mortar-schooners, which had been so covered with brush that the Confederate gunners could not distinguish them from the trees. The leading vessel of the first division, of seven vessels, under Lieutenant-Commanding Watson Smith, was placed at a point distant 2850 yards from Fort Jackson and 3680 yards from Fort St. Philip. The third division, commanded by Lieutenant Breese, came next in order, and the second division, under Lieutenant Queen, I placed on the east side of the river, the head of the line being 3680 yards from Fort Jackson.

The vessels now being in position, the signal was given to open fire; and on the morning of the 18th of April the bombardment fairly commenced, each mortar-vessel having orders to fire once in ten minutes.

The moment that the mortars belched forth their shells, both Jackson and St. Philip replied with great fury; but it was some time before they could obtain our range, as we were well concealed behind our natural rampart. The enemy's fire was rapid, and, finding that it was becoming rather hot, I sent Lieutenant Guest up to the head of the line to open fire on the forts with his 11-inch pivot. This position he maintained for one hour and fifty minutes, and only abandoned it to fill up with ammunition. In the meantime the mortars on the left bank (Queen's division) were doing splendid work, though suffering considerably from the enemy's fire.

I went on board the vessels of this division to see how they were getting on, and found them so cut up that I considered it necessary to remove them, with Farragut's permission, to the opposite shore, under cover of the trees, near the other vessels, which had suffered but little. They held their position, however, until sundown, when the enemy ceased firing.

BRIGADIER-GENERAL JOHNSON K. DUNCAN, C. S. A., IN COMMAND OF FORTS JACKSON AND ST. PHILIP. FROM A PHOTOGRAPH.

At 5 o'clock in the evening Fort Jackson was seen to be on fire, and, as the flames spread rapidly, the Confederates soon left their guns. There were many conjectures among the officers of the fleet as to what was burning. Some thought that it was a fire-raft, and I was inclined to that opinion myself until I had pulled up the river in a boat and, by the aid of a night-glass, convinced myself that the fort itself was in flames. This fact I at once reported to Farragut.

At nightfall the crews of the mortar-vessels were completely exhausted; but when it became known that every shell was falling inside of the fort, they redoubled their exertions and increased the rapidity of their fire to a shell every five minutes, or in all two hundred and forty shells an hour. During the night, in order to allow the men to rest, we slackened our fire, and only sent a shell once every half hour. Thus ended the first day's bombardment, which was more effective than that of any other day during the siege.

Next morning the bombardment was renewed and continued night and day until the end, with a result that is thus described in a letter from Colonel Edward Higgins, dated April 4th, 1872, which I received in answer to my inquiry on the subject:

"Your mortar-vessels were placed in position on the afternoon of the 17th of April, 1862, and opened fire at once upon Fort Jackson, where my headquarters were established. The practice was excellent from the commencement of the fire to the end, and continued without intermission until the morning of the 24th of April, when the fleet passed at about 4 o'clock. Nearly every shell of the many thousand fired at the fort lodged inside of the works. On the first night of the attack the citadel and all buildings in rear of the fort were fired by bursting shell, and also the sand-bag walls that had been thrown around the magazine doors. The fire, as you are aware, raged with great fury, and no effort of ours could subdue it. At this time, and nearly all this night, Fort Jackson was helpless; its magazines were inaccessible, and we could have offered no resistance to a passing fleet. The next morning a terrible scene of destruction presented itself. The wood-work of the citadel being all destroyed, and the crumbling walls being knocked about the fort by the bursting shells, made matters still worse for the garrison. The work of destruction from now until the morning of the 24th, when the fleet passed, was incessant.

"I was obliged to confine the men most rigidly to the casemates, or we should have lost the best part of the garrison. A shell, striking the parapet over one of the magazines, the wall of which was seven feet thick, penetrated five feet and failed to burst. If that shell had exploded, your work would have ended. Another burst near the magazine door, opening the earth and burying the sentinel and another man five feet in the same grave. The parapets and interior of the fort were completely honeycombed, and the large number of sand-bags with which we were supplied alone saved us from being blown to pieces a hundred times, our magazine doors being much exposed.

"On the morning of the 24th, when the fleet passed, the terrible precision with which your formidable vessels hailed down their tons of bursting shell upon the devoted fort made it impossible for us to obtain either rapidity or accuracy of fire, and thus rendered the passage comparatively easy. There was no very considerable damage done to our batteries, but few of the guns being dismounted by your fire; everything else in and around the fort was destroyed."

I was not ignorant of the state of affairs in the fort; for, on the third day of the bombardment, a deserter presented himself and gave us an account of the

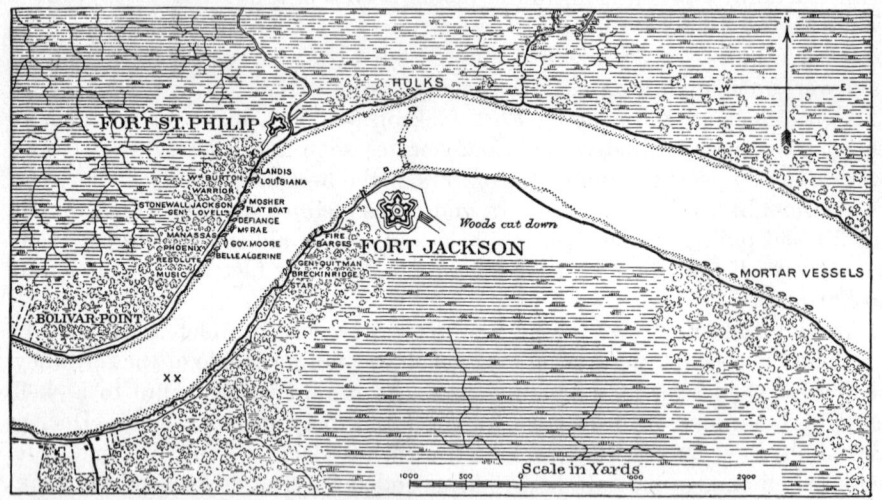

MAP SHOWING THE DEFENSES OF THE MISSISSIPPI AND THE POSITIONS OF THE MORTAR-FLEET AT THE OPENING OF THE BOMBARDMENT.

havoc created by our shells, although I had doubts of the entire truth of his statements. He represented that hundreds of shells had fallen into the fort, breaking in the bomb-proofs, setting fire to the citadel, and flooding the interior by cutting the levees. He also stated that the soldiers were in a desperate

REAR-ADMIRAL HENRY H. BELL, AT NEW ORLEANS FARRAGUT'S CHIEF-OF-STAFF.

and demoralized condition. This was all very encouraging to us, and so stimulated the crews of the mortar-boats that they worked with unflagging zeal and energy. I took the deserter to Farragut, who, although impressed by his statement, was not quite prepared to take advantage of the opportunity; for at this time the line of hulks across the river was considered an insurmountable obstruction, and it was determined to examine and, if possible, remove it before the advance of the fleet.

On the night of the 20th an expedition was fitted out for the purpose of breaking the chain which was supposed to extend from one shore to the other. Two steamers, the *Pinola*, Lieutenant Crosby, and *Itasca*, Lieutenant Caldwell, were detailed for the purpose and placed under the direction of Captain Bell, chief-of-staff. Although the attempt was made under cover of darkness, the sharp eyes of the Confederate gunners soon discovered their enemies, and the whole fire of Fort Jackson was concentrated upon them. I had been informed of the intended movement by Farragut, so was ready to redouble the fire of the mortars at the proper time with good effect. In Farragut's words: "Commander Porter, however, kept up such a tremendous fire on them from the mortars that the enemy's shot did the gun-boats no injury, and the cable was separated and their connection broken sufficiently to pass through on the left bank of the river."

COMMANDER JOHN K. MITCHELL, IN COMMAND OF THE CONFEDERATE STATES NAVAL FORCES AT NEW ORLEANS. FROM A PHOTOGRAPH.

The work of the mortar-fleet was now almost over. We had kept up a heavy fire night and day for nearly 5 days — about 2800 shells every 24 hours; in all about 16,800 shells. The men were nearly worn out for want of sleep and rest. The ammunition was giving out, one of the schooners was sunk, and although the rest had received little actual damage from the enemy's shot, they were badly shaken up by the concussion of the mortars.

On the 23d instant I represented the state of affairs to the flag-officer [see p. 72], and he concluded to move on past the works, which I felt sure he could do with but little loss to his squadron. He recognized the importance of making an immediate attack, and called a council of the commanders of vessels, which resulted in a determination to pass the forts that night. The movement was postponed, however, until the next morning, for the reason that the carpenters of one of the larger ships were at work down the river, and the commander did not wish to proceed without them. The iron-clad *Louisiana* had now made her appearance, and her commander was being strongly urged by General Duncan to drop down below the forts [see the map, p. 36] and open fire upon the fleet with his heavy rifle-guns. On the 22d General Duncan wrote to Commander Mitchell from Fort Jackson:

"It is of vital importance that the present fire of the enemy should be withdrawn from us, which you alone can do. This can be done in the manner suggested this morning under the cover of our guns, while your work on the boat can be carried on in safety and security. Our position is a critical one, dependent entirely on the powers of endurance of our casemates, many of which have been completely shattered, and are crumbling away by repeated shocks; and, therefore, I respectfully but earnestly again urge my suggestion of this morning on your notice. Our magazines are also in danger."

Fortunately for us, Commander Mitchell was not equal to the occasion, and the *Louisiana* remained tied up to the bank, where she could not obstruct the river or throw the Union fleet into confusion while passing the forts.

While Farragut was making his preparations, the enemy left no means untried to drive the mortar-boats from their position. A couple of heavy guns in Fort St. Philip kept up a continual fire on the head of the mortar column, and the Confederates used their mortars at intervals, but only succeeded in sinking one mortar-schooner and damaging a few others. A body of riflemen was once sent out against us from the forts, but it was met by a heavy fire and soon repulsed.

Two o'clock on the morning of the 24th instant was fixed upon as the time for the fleet to start, and Farragut had previously given the necessary orders to the commanders of vessels, instructing them to prepare their ships for action by sending down their light spars, painting their hulls mud-color, etc.; also to hang their chain-cables over the sides abreast the engines, as a protection against the enemy's shot. He issued the following "General Order":

UNITED STATES FLAG-SHIP *Hartford*, MISSISSIPPI RIVER, April 20th, 1862.

The flag-officer, having heard all the opinions expressed by the different commanders, is of the opinion that whatever is to be done will have to be done quickly, or we shall be again reduced to a blockading squadron, without the means of carrying on the bombardment, as we have nearly expended all the shells and fuses, and material for making cartridges. He has always entertained the same opinions which are expressed by Commander Porter; that is, there are three modes of attack, and the question is, which is the one to be adopted? His own opinion is that a combination of two should be made, viz.: the forts should be run, and when a force is once above the forts, to protect the troops, they should be landed at quarantine from the gulf side by bringing them through the bayou, and then our forces should move up the river, mutually aiding each other as it can be done to advantage.

When, in the opinion of the flag-officer, the propitious time has arrived, the signal will be made to weigh and advance to the conflict. If, in his opinion, at the time of arriving at the respective positions of the different divisions of the fleet, we have the advantage, he will make the signal for close action, No. 8, and abide the result, conquer or to be conquered, drop anchor or keep under way, as in his opinion is best.

Unless the signal above mentioned is made, it will be understood that the first order of sailing will be formed after leaving Fort St. Philip, and we will proceed up the river in accordance with the original opinion expressed. The programme of the order of sailing accompanies this general order, and the commanders will hold themselves in readiness for the service as indicated.\ Very respectfully, your obedient servant, D. G. FARRAGUT. Flag-Officer West Gulf Blockading Squadron.

LIEUTENANT THOMAS B. HUGER, C. S. N., IN COMMAND OF THE "MCRAE." FROM A PHOTOGRAPH.

\ The order of battle for the fleet was inclosed with this, but as it was not adopted and contained errors afterward officially corrected by Farragut, it is here omitted.— EDITORS.

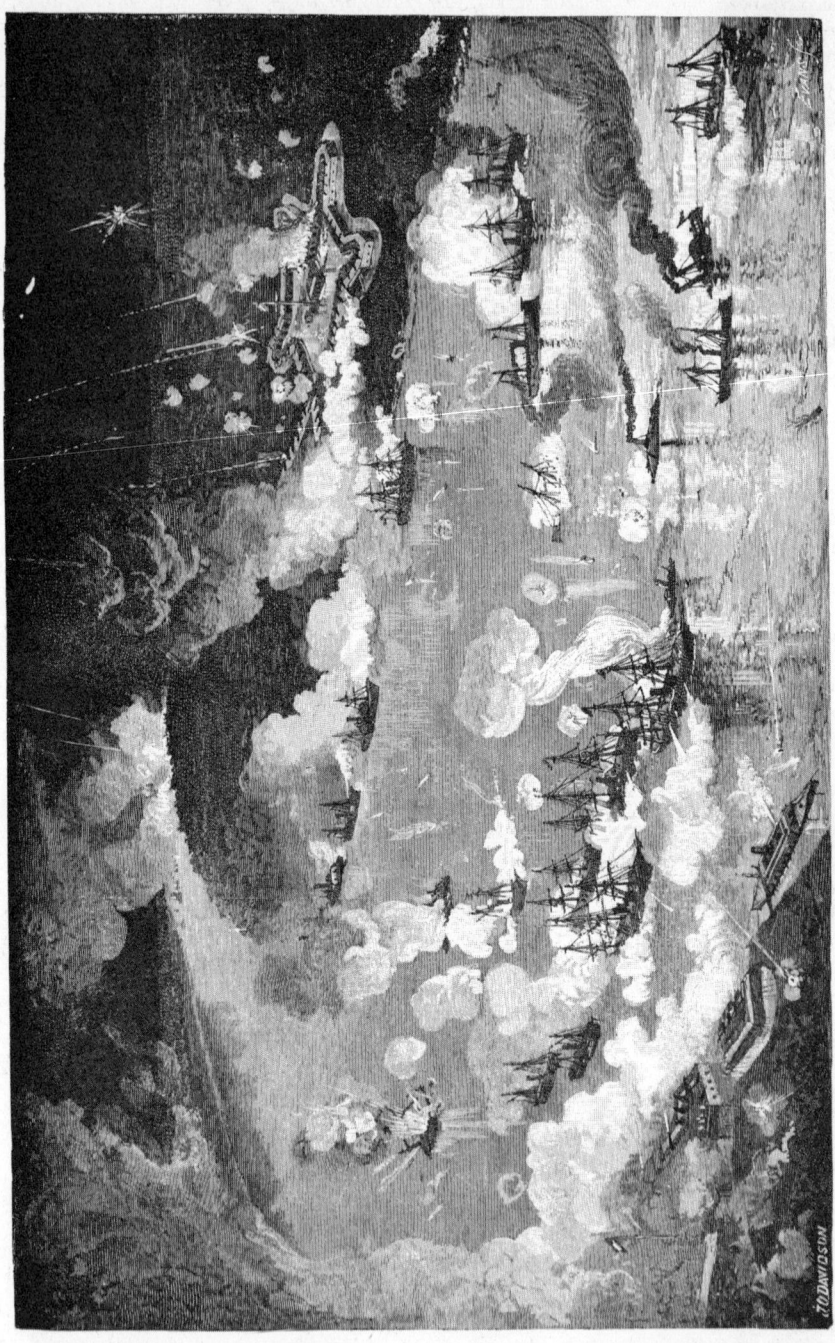

WRECKS OF CONFEDERATE RIVER FLEET. MORTAR-FLEET IN THE DISTANCE. "RICHMOND." "McRAE," CONFEDERATE.
FORT ST. PHILIP AND CONFEDERATE IRON-CLAD "LOUISIANA." MORTAR-STEAMERS ATTACKING WATER-BATTERY, FORT JACKSON. "MANASSAS," CONFEDERATE. "IROQUOIS." REAR VESSEL OF BAILEY'S DIVISION.
FARRAGUT'S DIVISION OF THE FLEET, LED BY THE "HARTFORD." CONFEDERATE RAMS AND SINKING VESSELS.

BIRD'S-EYE VIEW OF THE PASSAGE OF THE FORTS BELOW NEW ORLEANS, APRIL 24, 1862. THE SECOND DIVISION IN ACTION, 4:15 A. M.

Farragut's first plan was to lead the fleet with his flag-ship, the *Hartford*, to be closely followed by the *Brooklyn, Richmond, Pensacola*, and *Mississippi*, thinking it well to have his heavy vessels in the van, where they could immediately crush any naval force that might appear against them. This plan was a better one than that afterward adopted; but he was induced to change the order of his column by the senior commanders of the fleet, who represented to him that it was unwise for the commander-in-chief to take the brunt of the battle. They finally obtained his reluctant consent to an arrangement by which Captain Bailey was to lead in the gun-boat *Cayuga*, commanded by Lieutenant N. B. Harrison,— a good selection, as it afterward proved, for these officers were gallant and competent men, well qualified for the position. Captain Bailey had volunteered for the service, and left nothing undone to overcome Farragut's reluctance to give up what was then considered the post of danger, though it turned out to be less hazardous than the places in the rear.

The mortar-flotilla steamers under my command were directed to move up before the fleet weighed anchor, and to be ready to engage the water-batteries of Fort Jackson as the fleet passed. These batteries mounted some of the heaviest guns in the defenses, and were depended upon to do efficient work.

The commanders of vessels were informed of the change of plan, and instructed to follow in line according to the subjoined order of attack:

At 2 o'clock on the morning of April 24th all of the Union vessels began to heave up their anchors. It was a still, clear night, and the click of the capstans, with the grating of the chain-cables as they passed through the hawse-holes, made a great noise, which we feared would serve as a warning to our enemies. This conjecture proved to be correct, for the Confederates were on the alert in both forts and steamers to meet the invaders. One fact only was in our favor, and that was the division of their forces under three different heads, which prevented unanimity of action. In every other respect the odds were against us.

Before Farragut ascended the river, the French admiral and Captain Preedy, of the English frigate *Mersey*, had both been up as far as the forts and had communicated with the military commanders. On their return, they gave discouraging accounts of the defenses, and pronounced it impossible for our fleet to pass them. This, of course, did not tend to cheer our sailors. There were some in the fleet who were doubtful of success, and there was not that confidence on our side that should have existed on such an occasion; but when it was seen that the river obstructions and rafts had been washed away by the currents, and that there appeared to be an open way up the river, every one became more hopeful.

ORDER OF ATTACK.
First Division,
CAPTAIN BAILEY.

⚓ *Cayuga.*
⚓ *Pensacola.*
⚓ *Mississippi.*
⚓ *Oneida.*
⚓ *Varuna.*
⚓ *Katahdin.*
⚓ *Kineo.*
⚓ *Wissahickon.*

Center Division,
FLAG-OFFICER FARRAGUT.

⚓ *Hartford.*
⚓ *Brooklyn.*
⚓ *Richmond.*

Third Division,
CAPTAIN H. H. BELL.

⚓ *Sciota.*
⚓ *Iroquois.*
⚓ *Kennebec.*
⚓ *Pinola.*
⚓ *Itasca.*
⚓ *Winona.*

CAPTAIN THEODORUS BAILEY, IN THE "CAYUGA," BREAKING THROUGH THE CONFEDERATE FLEET.

The entire fleet did not get fully under way until half-past 2 A. M. The current was strong, and although the ships proceeded as rapidly as their steam-power would permit, our leading vessel, the *Cayuga*, did not get under fire until a quarter of 3 o'clock, when both Jackson and St. Philip opened on her at the same moment. Five steamers of the mortar-flotilla took their position below the water-battery of Fort Jackson, at a distance of less than two hundred yards, and, pouring in grape, canister, and shrapnel, kept down the fire of that battery. The mortars opened at the same moment with great fury, and the action commenced in earnest.

Captain Bailey, in the *Cayuga*, followed by the other vessels of his division in compact order, passed the line of obstructions without difficulty. He had no sooner attained this point, however, than he was obliged to face the guns of Fort St. Philip, which did him some damage before he was able to fire a shot in return. He kept steadily on, however, and, as soon as his guns could be brought to bear, poured in grape and canister with good effect and passed safe above. He was here met by the enemy's gun-boats, and, although he was beset by several large steamers at the same time, he succeeded in driving them off. The *Oneida* and *Varuna* came to the support of their leader, and by the rapid fire of their heavy guns soon dispersed the enemy's flotilla. This was more congenial work for our men and officers than that through which they had just passed, and it was soon evident that the coolness and discipline of our navy gave it a great advantage over the fleet of the enemy. Bailey dashed on up the river, followed by his division, firing into everything they met; and soon after the head of the flag-officer's division had passed the forts, most of the river craft were disabled, and the battle was virtually won. This was evident even to Lieutenant-Colonel Higgins, who, when he saw our large ships pass by, exclaimed, "Better go to cover, boys; our cake is all dough!"

In the meantime the *Varuna*, being a swift vessel, passed ahead of the other ships in the division, and pushed on up the river after the fleeing enemy, until she found herself right in the midst of them. The Confederates, supposing in the dark that the *Varuna* was one of their own vessels, did not attack her until Commander Boggs made himself known by delivering his fire right and left. One shot exploded the boiler of a large steamer crowded with troops, and she drifted ashore; three other vessels were driven ashore in flames. At daylight the *Varuna* was attacked by the *Governor Moore*, a powerful steamer, fitted as a ram, and commanded by Lieutenant Beverley Kennon, late of the U. S. Navy. This vessel raked the *Varuna* with her bow-gun along the port gangway, killing 5 or 6 men; and while the Union vessel was gallantly returning this fire, her side was pierced twice by the iron prow of the ram. The Confederate ram *Stonewall Jackson* also attacked the *Varuna*, ramming her twice about amidships; the *Varuna* at the same moment punished her severely with grape and canister from her 8-inch guns, and finally drove her out of action in a disabled condition and in flames.☆ But the career of the *Varuna* was ended; she began to fill rapidly, and her gallant commander was obliged to run her into shoal water, where she soon went to the bottom. Captain Lee, of the *Oneida*, seeing that his companion needed assistance, went to his relief, and rescued the officers and men of the *Varuna*. The two Confederate rams were set on fire by their crews and abandoned. Great gallantry was displayed on both sides during the conflict of these smaller steamers, which really bore the brunt of the battle, and the Union commanders showed great skill in managing their vessels.

Bailey's division may be said to have swept everything before it. The *Pensacola*, with her heavy batteries, drove the men from the guns at Fort St. Philip, and made it easier for the ships astern to get by. Fort St. Philip had not been at all damaged by the mortars, as it was virtually beyond their reach, and it was from the guns of that work that our ships received the greatest injury.

As most of the vessels of Bailey's division swept past the turn above the forts, Farragut came upon the scene with the *Hartford* and *Brooklyn*. The other ship of Farragut's division, the *Richmond*, Commander James Alden, got out of the line and passed up on the west side of the river, near where I was engaged with the mortar-steamers in silencing the water-batteries of Fort Jackson. At this moment the Confederates in Fort Jackson had nearly all been driven from their guns by bombs from the mortar-boats and the grape and canister from the steamers. I hailed Alden, and told him to pass close to the fort and in the eddy, and he would receive little damage. He followed this advice, and passed by very comfortably.

By this time the river had been illuminated by two fire-rafts, and everything could be seen as by the light of day. I could see every ship and gun-boat as she passed up as plainly as possible, and noted all their positions.

It would be a difficult undertaking at any time to keep a long line of vessels in compact order when ascending a crooked channel against a three-and-a-half-knot current, and our commanders found it to be especially so under the present trying circumstances. The *Iroquois*, Commander De Camp, as gallant an officer as ever lived, got out of line and passed up ahead of her

---

☆ According to the testimony of Captain Philips, of the *Stonewall Jackson*, the shock which she received in striking the *Varuna* shifted the boiler and broke the steam-pipe connections, thus disabling the vessel. — EDITORS.

REAR-ADMIRAL THEODORUS BAILEY, AT NEW ORLEANS IN COMMAND OF THE FIRST DIVISION OF THE FLEET.
FROM A PHOTOGRAPH.

consorts; but De Camp made good use of his opportunity by engaging and driving off a ram and the gun-boat *McRae*, which attacked him as soon as he had passed Fort Jackson. The *McRae* was disabled and her commander (Huger) mortally wounded. The *Iroquois* was much cut up by Fort St. Philip and the gun-boats, but did not receive a single shot from Fort Jackson, although passing within fifty yards of it.

While the events above mentioned were taking place, Farragut had engaged Fort St. Philip at close quarters with his heavy ships, and had driven the men from their guns. He was passing on up the river, when his flag-ship was threatened by a new and formidable adversary. A fire-raft in full blaze was seen coming down the river, guided toward the *Hartford* by a tug-boat, the *Mosher*. It seemed impossible to avoid this danger, and as the helm was put to port in the attempt to do so, the flag-ship ran upon a shoal. While in this position the fire-raft was pushed against her, and in a minute she was enveloped in flames half-way up to her tops, and was in a condition of great peril. The fire department was at once called away, and while the *Hartford's* batteries kept up the fight with Fort St. Philip, the flames were extinguished and the vessel backed off the shoal into deep water,— a result due to the coolness of her commander and the good discipline of the officers and men. While the *Hartford* was in this perilous position, and her entire destruction was threatened, Farragut showed all the qualities of a great commander. He walked up and down the poop as coolly as though on dress-parade, while Commander Wainwright directed the firemen in putting out the flames. At times the fire would rush through the ports and almost drive the men from the guns.

"Don't flinch from that fire, boys," sang out Farragut; "there's a hotter fire than that for those who don't do their duty! Give that rascally little tug a shot, and don't let her go off with a whole coat!" The *Mosher* was sunk.

While passing the forts the *Hartford* was struck thirty-two times in hull and rigging, and had 3 men killed and 10 wounded.

The *Brooklyn*, Captain Thomas T. Craven, followed as close after the flag-ship as the blinding smoke from guns and fire-rafts would admit, and the garrison of the fort was again driven to cover by the fire of her heavy battery. She passed on with severe punishment, and was immediately attacked by the most powerful vessel in the Confederate fleet, excepting the *Louisiana* — the ram *Manassas*, commanded by Lieutenant Warley, a gallant young officer of the old service. The blow that the *Manassas* struck the *Brooklyn* did but little apparent injury, ♭ and the ram slid off in the dark to seek other prey. (It must be remembered that these scenes were being enacted on a dark night, and in an atmosphere filled with dense smoke, through which our commanders had to grope their way, guided only by the flashes of the guns in the forts and the fitful light of burning vessels and rafts.)

REAR-ADMIRAL MELANCTON SMITH, AT NEW ORLEANS IN COMMAND OF THE "MISSISSIPPI." DRAWN FROM A PHOTOGRAPH.

The *Brooklyn* was next attacked by a large steamer, which received her broadside at the distance of twenty yards, and drifted out of action in flames. Notwithstanding the heavy fire which the *Brooklyn* had gone through, she was only struck seventeen times in the hull. She lost 9 men killed and 26 wounded.

When our large ships had passed the forts, the affair was virtually over. Had they all been near the head of the column, the enemy would have been crushed at once, and the flag-ship would have passed up almost unhurt. As it was, the *Hartford* was more exposed and imperiled than any of her consorts, and that at a time when, if anything had happened to the commander-in-chief, the fleet would have been thrown into confusion.

♭ Owing to the chain armor and to the full coal-bunker; but when the bunker was emptied later, the wound was found to be serious. See Commander Bartlett's article, page 56.— EDITORS.

The forts had been so thoroughly silenced by the ships' guns and mortars that when Captain Bell came along in the little *Sciota*, at the head of the third division, he passed by nearly unharmed. All the other vessels succeeded in getting by, except the *Itasca*, Lieutenant Caldwell, the *Winona*, Lieutenant Nichols, and the *Kennebec*, Lieutenant Russell. The first two vessels, having kept in line, were caught at daylight below the forts without support, and, as the current was swift and they were slow steamers, they became mere targets for the Confederates, who now turned all that was left of their fighting power upon them. Seeing their helpless condition, I signaled them to retire, which they did after being seriously cut up. The *Itasca* had a shot through her boiler, and was so completely riddled that her commander was obliged to run her ashore just below the mortar-fleet in order to prevent her sinking. She had received fourteen shot and shell through her hull, but her list of killed and wounded was small. Had not the people in the forts been completely demoralized, they would have sunk these two vessels in ten minutes.

While these events were taking place, the mortar-steamers had driven the men from the water-batteries and had kept up a steady fire on the walls of Fort Jackson. Although at first sight my position in front of these batteries, which mounted six of the heaviest guns in the Confederate works (1 10-inch and 2 8-inch Columbiads, 1 10-inch sea-coast mortar, and 2 rifled 32-pounders), seemed a very perilous one, it was not at all so. I ran the steamers close alongside of the levee just below the water-batteries, and thus protected their hulls below the firing-decks. I got in my first broadside just as the middle of Bailey's column was opened upon by Fort Jackson. The enemy responded quickly, but our fire was so rapid and accurate that in ten minutes the water-battery was deserted. I had 25 8-inch and 32-pounders on one side and 2 11-inch pivot-guns. During the remainder of the action I devoted most of

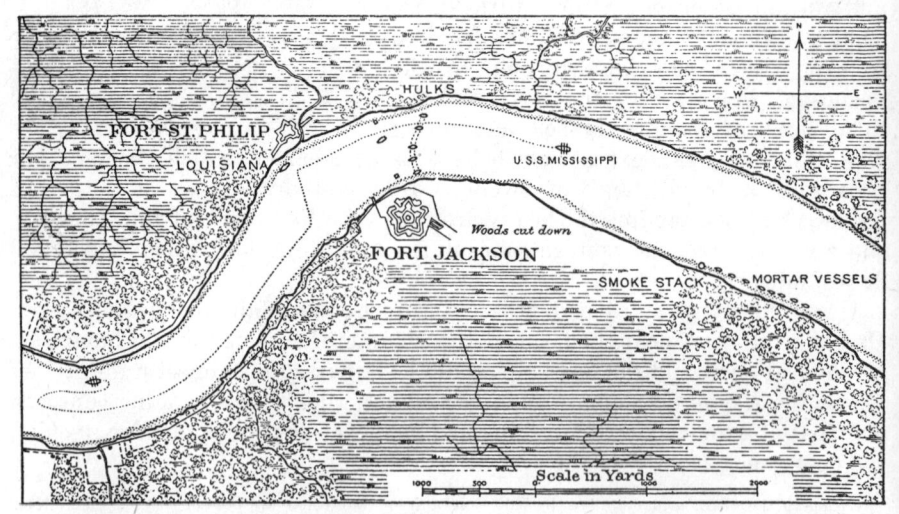

THE COURSE OF THE UNITED STATES SCREW-SLOOP "MISSISSIPPI" IN THE PASSAGE OF THE FORTS.

THE UNITED STATES STEAMER "MISSISSIPPI" ATTEMPTING TO RUN DOWN THE CONFEDERATE RAM "MANASSAS."

my attention to the battlements of the main fort, firing an occasional shot at the water-battery. The *Harriet Lane* had two men killed, but the only damage done to the vessels was to their masts and rigging, their hulls having been well protected by the levees.

While engaged on this duty I had an excellent opportunity of witnessing the movements of Farragut's fleet, and, by the aid of powerful night-glasses, I could almost distinguish persons on the vessels. The whole scene looked like a beautiful panorama. From almost perfect silence — the steamers moving slowly through the water like phantom ships — one incessant roar of heavy cannon commenced, the Confederate forts and gun-boats opening together on the head of our line as it came within range. The Union vessels returned the fire as they came up, and soon the guns of our fleet joined in the thunder, which seemed to shake the very earth. A lurid glare was thrown over the scene by the burning rafts, and, as the bomb-shells crossed each other and exploded in the air, it seemed as if a battle were taking place in the heavens as well as on the earth. It all ended as suddenly as it had commenced. In one hour and ten minutes after the vessels of the fleet had weighed anchor, the affair was virtually over, and Farragut was pushing on toward New Orleans, where he was soon to crush the last hope of Rebellion in that quarter by opening the way for the advance of the Union army.

From what I had seen of the conflict I did not greatly fear for the safety of our ships. Now and then a wreck came floating by, all charred and disabled, but I noted that these were side-wheel vessels, and none of ours.

I must refer here to a gallant affair which took place between the *Mississippi* and the ram *Manassas*. The latter vessel proved the most troublesome of the Confederate fleet. She had rammed the *Brooklyn* and the *Mississippi* at different times during the action.

At early daylight, as the vessels approached the quarantine above the forts, the *Manassas* was seen coming up the river as rapidly as her steam would allow.

THE CONFEDERATE IRON-CLAD "LOUISIANA" ON THE WAY TO FORT ST. PHILIP.

As she approached the fleet, Flag-Officer Farragut directed Commander Smith in the *Mississippi* to turn and run her down. The order was instantly obeyed by the *Mississippi* turning and going at the ram at full speed; but when it was expected to see the *Manassas* annihilated, the vessels being within fifty yards of each other, the ram put her helm hard-a-port, dodged the *Mississippi*, and ran ashore, where her crew deserted her. Commander Smith set fire to her, and then so riddled her with shot that she was dislodged from the bank and drifted below the forts, where she blew up and sank.

Previous to this a kind of guerrilla warfare had been carried on, and most of the enemy's river boats had been run ashore or otherwise destroyed, while the *Varuna* lay sunk at the bank with two of her adversaries wrecked beside her, a monument to the gallantry of Commander Boggs.

When the fleet had passed the forts, and there was no longer any necessity for me to hold my position, I dropped down the river with the steamers to where the mortar-boats were anchored, and gave the signal to cease firing. I knew that our squadron had failed to destroy all of the enemy's fleet. The iron-clad *Louisiana* lay at the bank apparently uninjured, the *McRae* was at anchor close to Fort Jackson, and three other vessels whose character I could not make out were moving back and forth from one shore to the other.

Mr. William C. Whittle, who was third lieutenant on the *Louisiana* during the contest against Farragut's fleet in the Mississippi, has sent to the Editors the following statement concerning her armament:

"The hull of the *Louisiana* was almost entirely submerged. Upon this were built her heavy upper works, intended to contain her battery, machinery, etc. This extended to within about twenty-five feet of her stem and stern, leaving a little deck forward and aft, nearly even with the water, and surrounded by a slight bulwark. The structure on the hull had its ends and sides inclined inward and upward from the hull, at an angle of about forty-five degrees, and covered with T railroad iron, the lower layer being firmly bolted to the woodwork, and the upper layer driven into it from the end so as to form a nearly solid plate and a somewhat smooth surface. This plating resisted the projectiles of Farragut's fleet (none of which perforated our side), although one of his largest ships lay across and touching our stem, and in that position fired her heavy guns. Above this structure was an open deck which was surrounded by a sheet-iron bulwark about four feet high, which was intended as a protection against sharp-shooters and small arms, but was entirely inefficient, as the death of our gallant commander, McIntosh, and those who fell around him, goes to prove. The plan for propelling the *Louisiana* was novel and abortive. She had two propellers aft, which we never had an opportunity of testing. The novel conception, which proved entirely inefficient, was that right in the center section of the vessel there was a large well in which worked the two wheels, one immediately forward of the other. I suppose they were so placed to be protected from the enemy's fire. The machinery of these two wheels was in order when my father, Commodore W. C. Whittle, the naval commanding officer at New Orleans, against his better judgment, was compelled to send the vessel down to the forts. The vessel left New Orleans on the 20th of April, I think. The work on the propellers was incomplete, the machinists and mechanics being still on board, and most of the guns were not mounted. The center wheels were started, but were entirely inefficient, and, as we were drifting helplessly down the stream, tow-boats had to be called to take us down to the point about half a mile above Fort St. Philip, on the left side of the river, where we tied up to the bank with our bow down-stream. Thus, as Farragut's fleet came up and passed, we could only use our bow-guns and the starboard broadside. Moreover, the port-holes for our guns were entirely faulty, not allowing room to train the guns either laterally or in elevation. I had practical experience of this fact, for I had immediate charge of the bow division when a vessel of Admiral Farragut's fleet got across our stem, and I could only fire through and through her at point-blank instead of depressing my guns and sinking her."

This looked serious, for such a force, if properly handled, was superior to mine; and I had to provide immediately against contingencies. There were now seven efficient gun-boats under my command, and I at once prepared them to meet the enemy. My plan was to get as many of my vessels as possible alongside of the *Louisiana*, each one to make fast to her, let go two anchors, and then "fight it out on that line."

Meantime Farragut was speeding on his way up the river with all his fleet except the *Mississippi* ☆ and one or two small gun-boats, which were left to guard the lazaretto. On his way up the flag-officer encountered more Confederate batteries at Chalmette, the place made famous by the battle of January 8th, 1815.

The Chalmette batteries on both sides of the river mounted twenty heavy guns, and were all ready to meet our fleet, which was advancing toward them in two lines as rapidly as the swift current would permit. Farragut made short work of them, however, and our fleet, meeting with no further resistance, passed on and anchored before New Orleans. The Queen City of the South lay at the conqueror's feet, unable to do anything in the way of defense, as the Confederate General Lovell had retreated, leaving the city in the hands of the civil authorities.

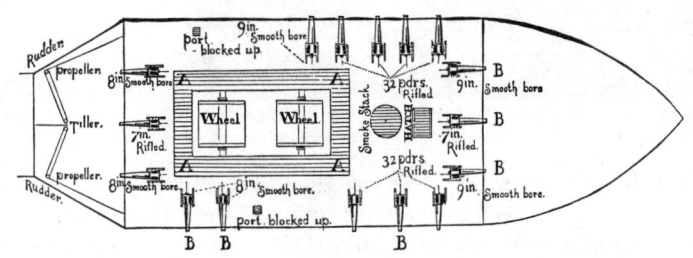

THE PLAN OF THE "LOUISIANA." AFTER A SKETCH MADE BY COMMANDER J. K. MITCHELL ABOUT THE TIME OF THE ENGAGEMENT.

A A, Bulkhead around wheels.   B B, Guns used in action.

AT noon of the 25th instant I sent Lieutenant-Commanding Guest with a flag of truce to Fort Jackson, to call on the commanding officer to surrender the two forts and what was left of the Confederate navy into the possession of the United States, telling him that it was useless to have any more bloodshed, as Farragut had passed up the river with very little damage to his fleet, and was now probably in possession of New Orleans. I also took advantage of the occasion to compliment the enemy on his gallant resistance, and further to inform him that, if his answer was unfavorable, I would renew the bombardment. General Duncan sent me a very civil reply, but declined to surrender until he should hear from New Orleans; whereupon I immediately opened a very rapid fire on Fort Jackson with all the mortars, and with such good effect that a mutiny soon broke out among the Confederate gunners, many of whom, refusing to stay in the fort and be slaughtered uselessly, left

---

☆ In a letter to the Editors, Rear-Admiral Melancton Smith, who commanded the *Mississippi*, says: "The *Mississippi* proceeded with the fleet up the river and was present at the engagement with the Chalmette batteries. At 3 P. M. the same day, when at anchor off New Orleans, I was ordered to return to the quarantine station (just above Fort St. Philip) to look after the *Louisiana* and to cover the landing of the troops under General Butler. Admiral Porter, seeing the *Mississippi* the morning after the fleet passed up, doubtless supposed it had remained at anchor below."—EDITORS.

"CLIFTON" AND "WESTFIELD," ALTERED NEW YORK CITY FERRY BOATS.   "OWASCO."   "HARRIET LANE."

MORTAR-STEAMERS ATTACKING THE WATER-BATTERY OF FORT JACKSON.

their posts and went up the bank out of range of our shell. Those who remained declined to fight any longer. They had borne without flinching a terrible bombardment, and their officers had exposed themselves throughout the trying ordeal with great courage; but it was now the opinion of all that the fort should be surrendered without further loss of life. The mortars kept up their fire until late in the evening, when their bomb-shells were all expended. On the 26th instant I ordered the schooners to get under way, proceed to Pilot Town, and fill up with ammunition. Six of them were ordered to cross the bar and proceed to the rear of Fort Jackson, and be ready to open fire when signaled.

In the meantime we kept an eye upon the *Louisiana* and the Confederate gun-boats. On the 27th instant five mortar-vessels appeared in the rear of Fort Jackson, and the U. S. steamer *Miami* commenced landing troops close to Fort St. Philip. The garrison of Jackson was still mutinous, refusing to do duty, and General Duncan at midnight of the 28th sent an officer on board the *Harriet Lane* to inform me of his readiness to capitulate. On the following day I proceeded with nine gun-boats up to Fort Jackson, under a flag of truce, and upon arrival sent a boat for the commanding officer of the river defenses, and such others as he might think proper to bring with him.

I received these officers at the gangway, and treated them as brave men who had defended their trusts with a courage worthy of all praise; and though I knew that they felt mortified at having to surrender to what they must have known was in some respects an inferior force, their bearing was that of men who had gained a victory, instead of undergoing defeat.

I knew nothing of the mutiny in the forts, or the inconvenience to which the people there were subjected; I was in total ignorance of what was happening up the river, whether Farragut had sustained much damage in passing the forts, or whether he had been able to get by the formidable batteries at English Turn. In any case I knew that it was important to obtain possession of the forts as quickly as possible, and had prepared terms of capitulation, which were accepted by General Duncan and Lieutenant-Colonel Higgins As we were about to sign the articles, I was quite surprised to find that it was not expected that the vessels of war were to be included in the terms agreed to by the Confederate officers.✧ General Duncan told me that he had no authority whatever over the naval vessels, and that, in fact, Commander Mitchell, of the regular naval forces, had set the military authorities at defiance. So I waived the point, being determined in my own mind what I would do when the forts were in our possession.

We were all sitting at the table on board the *Harriet Lane*, with the terms of capitulation before us; I had signed the paper, as had also Commander Renshaw, of the *Westfield;* and Lieutenant-Commanding Wainwright, of the *Harriet Lane*, was about to follow our example, when he was suddenly called on deck by one of his officers. He returned immediately, and informed me that the iron-clad *Louisiana* was in flames and was drifting down the river toward the mortar-flotilla (steamers), through which there was not room for her to pass, as our vessels were anchored within thirty yards of each other.

"This is sharp practice," I said to the Confederate officers, "but if *you* can stand the explosion when it comes, we can. We will go on and finish the capitulation." At the same time I gave Lieutenant Wainwright orders to hail the vessel next to him and pass the word to each of the others to veer to the end of their chains and be ready, by using steam, to sheer out of the way of the *Louisiana* if necessary, but not to leave their anchorage. Then I handed the pen to General Duncan and Colonel Higgins, who coolly signed their names in as bold a hand as if they were not momentarily in danger of being blown up. Then we all sat quietly awaiting the result. In a few moments an explosion took place that fairly shook us all out of our seats and threw the *Harriet Lane* over on her side, but we finished the terms of capitulation. The *Louisiana* had blown up before reaching the flotilla. The Confederate officers severely condemned this performance, and assured us that they did not feel responsible for anything that the navy did, as it was entirely under Commander Mitchell's control.

When I went on deck the *Louisiana* was nowhere to be seen, and not even a ripple showed where she had gone down. Thus we lost a powerful vessel, which would have been of much use to us in our future operations.

---

✧ Mention is made in Commander Porter's letter of April 26th to Lieut.-Colonel Higgins of the Confederate vessels of war, for he says: "And the vessels lying near the forts will be surrendered to the United States Government." Lieut.-Colonel Higgins replied on April 27th that he could then entertain no proposition for a surrender; he did not allude to the Confederate war vessels. The next day he wrote as follows:

"HEADQUARTERS, FORTS JACKSON and ST. PHILIP, April 28th, 1862.— COMMODORE DAVID D. PORTER, United States Navy, Commanding Mortar Fleet.—*Sir:*

Upon mature deliberation, it has been decided to accept the terms of surrender of these forts, under the conditions offered by you in your letter of the 26th inst., viz., that the officers and men shall be paroled — officers retiring with their side-arms. We have no control over the vessels afloat. Very respectfully, your obedient servant, EDWARD HIGGINS, Lieutenant-Colonel Commanding.

Admiral Porter says in a recent note [November, 1887] that he never received this letter. In his official report, dated April 30th, 1862, he says: "On the 28th a flag of truce came on board the *Harriet Lane* proposing to surrender Jackson and St. Philip on the terms offered." EDITORS.

COMMANDER PORTER RECEIVING CONFEDERATE OFFICERS ON THE "HARRIET LANE."

General Duncan and his companions now left the *Harriet Lane* and went on shore. In less than ten minutes afterward the Confederate flags were hauled down, and both forts were delivered over to the officers appointed to take possession of them. Our victory was not yet complete, however, for the enemy's flag still floated on the river, and my next duty lay in this direction. When Commander Mitchell set fire to the *Louisiana*, he transferred his officers and men to a river steamer and ran over to the opposite shore, a mile above the forts. His movements had been reported to me, and as soon as General Duncan had left the ship I gave orders for the *Harriet Lane* to weigh anchor and beat to quarters. We steered directly for the vessel carrying Mitchell's flag, and the order was given to fire at the flag-pole; but the smoke was not out of the gun before the Confederate flag was hauled down. Lieutenant Wainwright was sent on board the enemy to take possession, and was met by Commander Mitchell, who demanded the same terms as the officers of the forts had received.‡ Wainwright informed him that no terms

‡ Commander Mitchell, in a communication to the Editors, states that "no such demand was made, but . . . the right to be treated as prisoners of war was claimed."— EDITORS.

would be granted him or his officers, that he and they would be held as close prisoners to answer for violating the sanctity of a flag of truce, and that they would all be sent to the North. Mitchell at once wrote me a letter relieving all the officers (except three or four) from the odium of having set fire to the *Louisiana*, and thus endangering the Union vessels while under a flag of truce.

I sent the prisoners up to Flag-Officer Farragut, to be disposed of as he thought best, and that was the end of the affair. The forts were ours, the city was ours, and the river was open and free all the way up to New Orleans.

After the battle the officers of the Confederate army complained greatly of Commander Mitchell's behavior, saying, first, that he had failed to coöperate heartily with the land forces; secondly, that he had not made good use of the *Louisiana* (as far as I can learn she was not ready for action when the fleet passed up, and I am of the opinion that had she been properly managed, she might have thrown our fleet into confusion); thirdly, that he had failed to ignite and send down all the fire-rafts that were under his charge, at the proper time to meet our fleet as it came up the river. He had quite a number of these tied up to the bank, and it can well be imagined what the effect of millions of burning pine-knots on thirty or forty rafts would have been, when it is remembered how seriously the *Hartford* was endangered by one of those which were actually sent.↓

After all the defenses were in our power, I sent a steamer down to the bar and brought up one of General Butler's ships, on board of which was General Phelps with one or two regiments of infantry, who took possession of the forts.

CHARLES F. McINTOSH, COMMANDER OF THE "LOUISIANA." FROM A PHOTOGRAPH.

↓ It is but just to say that Commander Mitchell and the other Confederate naval officers denied that they had any intention of endangering the Union vessels, or that they were guilty of any "sharp practice" in destroying the *Louisiana*. They were put in close confinement at Fort Warren, Boston harbor; but on making the above representations to the Secretary of the Navy they were treated as ordinary prisoners of war. A Confederate naval court of inquiry afterward investigated and approved the conduct of Commander Mitchell. The following extract from the letter from Lieutenant Whittle, quoted on page 48, bears on the point in question: "On the morning of the 24th, when Farragut's fleet passed, the work on the propellers was still incomplete, and so our vessel was only an immovable floating battery. When, on the morning of April 28th, the work was finished, and we were about to test the efficiency of the motive power, we were notified by General Duncan, commanding Forts Jackson and St. Philip, that he had accepted the terms of capitulation offered by Commander Porter and before rejected. As the *Louisiana* was not included in the surrender, and Commander Porter's fleet was coming up under a flag of truce, in answer to a flag of truce from the forts, a council of war decided to destroy the *Louisiana*, and I was dispatched by Commander Mitchell to notify Commander Porter that although we had done what we could to drown the magazine and the charges in the guns, our hawsers might burn, and the *Louisiana* drift down among his vessels. While on my way to deliver this message the *Louisiana* blew up. I continued, however, and delivered the message in person to Commander D. D. Porter on board his flag-ship, the *Harriet Lane*." — EDITORS.

EXPLOSION OF THE CONFEDERATE RAM, "LOUISIANA."

Farragut's vessels were only struck twenty-three times in their hulls by shots from Fort Jackson, while they received their great damage from Fort St. Philip, as appears from the official reports. This shows how difficult it was for the Confederate gunners in the former work to fight while enduring the terrible pounding of the mortars. There can be no doubt that their fire prevented a greater loss of life in the Federal fleet and materially assisted toward the final result. Our total loss in the fleet was—killed, 37; wounded, 147. The ships which suffered most were the *Pensacola*, 37; *Brooklyn*, 35; and *Iroquois*, 28.

When the sun rose on the Federal fleet the morning after the fight, it shone on smiling faces, even among those who were suffering from their wounds. Farragut received the congratulations of his officers with the same imperturbability that he had exhibited all through the eventful battle; and while he showed great feeling for those of his men who had been killed or wounded, he did not waste time in vain regrets, but made the signal, "Push on to New Orleans." The fact that he had won imperishable fame did not seem to occur to him, so intent were his thoughts on following up his great victory to the end.

THE CONFEDERATE "RIVER DEFENSE" RAM "STONEWALL JACKSON."

FROM A PHOTOGRAPH TAKEN IN VIRGINIA IN 1864.

MAJOR-GENERAL BENJAMIN F. BUTLER, COMMANDER OF THE MILITARY FORCES OF THE NEW ORLEANS EXPEDITION.

ASPECT OF FORT JACKSON IN 1885. FROM THE SUMMIT OF THE LEVEE LOOKING SOUTH FROM THE RIVER.

## THE "BROOKLYN" AT THE PASSAGE OF THE FORTS.

### BY COMMANDER JOHN RUSSELL BARTLETT, U. S. N.

FROM February 2d to March 7th, 1862, the United States steamer *Brooklyn*, Captain Thomas T. Craven, was engaged in blockading Pass à l'Outre, one of the mouths of the Mississippi River. It is impossible to describe the monotony of the life on board ship during this period. Most of the time there was a dense fog, so thick that we could not see the length of the ship. The fog collected in the rigging, and there was a constant dripping from aloft like rain, which kept the decks wet and made things generally uncomfortable. No news was received from the North, and our waiting and watching seemed endless. We had our routine of drill each day, but nothing to talk about. Our only excitement was the lookout at the main-topgallant cross-tree, who was above the fog-bank, shouting "Smoke h-oo!" It was a great relief to shout through the deck-trumpet, " Where away ?" but the answer was always the same,—" Up the river, sir!" Days and weeks went by, and the smoke came no nearer. Once only, on February 24th, it came out of the river, and we had an exciting chase of a blockade-runner, following her for miles, with an officer aloft conning the ship by the smoke seen above the fog; we captured the chase, which proved to be the steamer *Magnolia* with 1200 bales of cotton.

At last the spell was broken, for on the 7th of March the *Hartford* and *Pensacola* arrived with Captain D. G. Farragut, then flag-officer commanding the West Gulf Blockading Squadron, and we learned that we were going to open the Mississippi River.

I had never met Farragut, but had heard of him from officers who were with him in the *Brooklyn* on her previous cruise. He had been represented as a man of most determined will and character—a man who would assume any responsibility to accomplish necessary ends. I saw a great deal of him at the Head of the Passes and after we passed the forts. Often, when I came on board the *Hartford* with a message from the captain of the *Brooklyn*, Farragut sent me somewhere to carry an order or to do certain duty. I was much impressed with his energy and activity and his promptness of decision and action. He had a winning smile and a most charming manner and was jovial and talkative. He prided himself on his agility, and I remember his telling

FROM A PHOTOGRAPH.

me once that he always turned a handspring on his birthday, and should not consider that he was getting old until he was unable to do it. The officers who had the good fortune to be immediately associated with him seemed to worship him. He had determination and dash in execution, but in planning and organizing he appeared to want method. He showed me one day an old envelope containing memoranda, and said that that was all the record or books that he kept. He had, however, the good fortune to have on his staff two of the best organizers and administrators of detail in the service,—Captains Henry H. Bell at New Orleans and Percival Drayton at Mobile.

On the 15th of March we began to congregate at the Head of the Passes, and at this time the energy and activity of the flag-officer made themselves felt. We lay here several weeks preparing our ships for the coming action, drilling the crews, firing at targets, and getting in provisions and coal. Farragut was about the fleet from early dawn until dark, and if any officers or men had not spontaneous enthusiasm he certainly infused it into them. I have been on the morning watch, from 4 to 8, when he would row alongside the ship at 6 o'clock, either hailing to ask how we were getting along, or, perhaps, climbing over the side to see for himself. One of the preparations that we made at the Head of the Passes was to hang the chain-cables along each side, abreast of the engine and boilers. A jack-stay, or iron rod, was fastened by means of eye-bolts to the ship's side about eight feet above the water, and one of the chain-cables in bights was suspended to it and fastened with spun yarn. The links of the cable were of iron an inch and a half in diameter, and each strand, or bight, was lapped over the next, the links fitting between each other so that it made an almost continuous coat of mail. It extended about two feet below the water-line. Around the steam-drum, which rose five feet above the berth-deck, sand-bags were piled, and the sick-bay, in the bow, was filled solid with hawsers and rigging, taken from the hold, which had been cleared to form a hospital for the surgeon. Everything was arranged for the convenience of the surgeon in attending the wounded. At the main hatch a cot-frame was rigged and slung from two davits so that the wounded men could be lowered to the berth-deck and thence carried to the surgeon in the forehold. A howitzer was placed in the foretop and one in the maintop. A large kedge-anchor was hung to the main brace bumkin on each quarter, with a hawser attached, to be used whenever it became necessary to turn the ship suddenly.

There was considerable delay in getting the larger vessels over the bar and in filling up with ammunition and coal. At last, on April 16th, Farragut steamed up with the fleet and anchored just below the point where Porter's mortar-

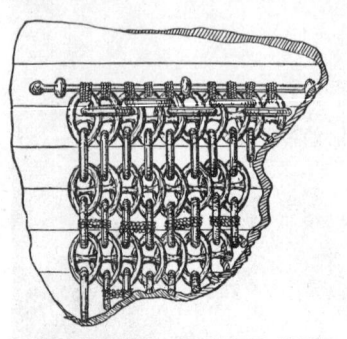

SECTION OF CHAIN ARMOR PLACED ON THE SIDE OF THE "BROOKLYN" TO PROTECT HER BOILERS. FROM A SKETCH LENT BY COMMANDER BARTLETT.

ADMIRAL DAVID D. PORTER, IN COMMAND OF THE MORTAR-FLEET AT FORTS JACKSON AND ST. PHILIP. FROM A PHOTOGRAPH.

vessels, or, as the sailors used to call them, the "bummers," had taken their position and had made ready to open fire upon the forts. Admiral Porter has described in this work the part taken by these vessels in the opening of the lower Mississippi. I can vouch for the accuracy of their aim, for I used to sit on the cross-trees all day, when not on duty, seeing the shells fall into the fort and witnessing the havoc they made in it.

We had plenty of occupation while anchored below the forts, and as an accompaniment one of the mortars was fired every half minute all day. It was trying work for the poor fellows on the mortar-schooners, for when their mortar was fired, all of them were obliged to go aft and stand on tiptoe with open mouths to receive the concussion. The powder blackened everything.

and the men looked like negroes. At intervals fire-rafts came down. The first one caused much alarm, and we prepared to slip our cable and get out of the way. The rafts were immense flat-boats with wood piled loosely twenty feet high and saturated with tar and resin, and the flame from them would rise a hundred feet into the air. They certainly looked dangerous, but they were set adrift only one at a time and otherwise were so badly managed that in a little while they merely served to amuse us. The fleet lay under the point on the right bank, and the rafts would tend to the left bank with the strength of the current, and so pass harmlessly by or ground on the bank. Others caught in the obstructions and failed to come down. Sometimes boats from the ships were sent to help tow them away. If there had been any one man to direct the enemy's operations, and so secure concert of action, we should have fared badly; for half a dozen rafts chained together and pushed into position by their gun-boats would have made havoc with the fleet. One night five rafts were sent down, one of which had been towed over to the right bank and came almost directly into the fleet; the *Westfield* made for it and pushed it out into the stream; but it came so near that even with hose playing on the side and rigging the *Brooklyn's* paint was badly blistered.

The forts kept up a continual fire from their rifle-guns, and now and then a shell would pass uncomfortably near the ship. To keep down this fire as much as possible, and thus protect the mortar-vessels, one of the smaller sloops or two of the gun-boats were kept under way. They would steam up to the west bank under cover of the trees and suddenly shoot out into the stream and open fire with their 11-inch pivots, and then drift down-stream. As they were always in rapid motion, it was difficult for the gunners in the forts to hit them; still, a number of men were wounded.⁆

On the 23d, after five days of continual firing, Commander Porter informed the flag-officer that his men were worn out from want of sleep and rest, and that his ammunition was nearly expended. The obstructions, which had formed an apparently impassable barrier, had now been overcome. The opening of a passage through the hulks [see p. 38] was one of the most daring feats of the war, and here again the want of concert among the independent floating commands of the enemy led him to neglect the protection of what was really his main reliance for defense. The only cause for delay was now removed. Councils of war were held on board the *Hartford* every day during the bombardment, and the plan of running by the forts was fully discussed. Some of the captains thought it suicidal and believed that the whole fleet would be annihilated; others, that perhaps one or two vessels might get by, but they would be sunk by the rams. All this time Farragut maintained that it must and should be done, even if half the ships were lost. A final council was called on the afternoon of the 23d, and it was decided to attempt the passage that night. ‡

⁆ There were none killed in the sloops or gun-boats in the bombardment preceding the battle. Twenty-four men were wounded, including one on board the schooner *Norfolk Packet*. Two deaths are reported April 18th–24th, one of them on board the mortar-schooner *Arletta*, and one by a fall from the mast-head on board the *Katahdin*.— J. R. B.

‡ In July, 1861, I was on board the steam frigate *Mississippi* when she made a visit to the Southwest Pass, and having been sent to the *Powhatan*, commanded by Lieutenant D. D. Porter, near by, I

The present article is intended merely as a personal narrative of the passage of the forts as seen from the deck of the *Brooklyn*. This vessel was a flush-deck sloop-of-war, carrying 22 9-inch guns, 1 80-pounder Dahlgren rifle, and 1 30-pounder Parrott rifle. A small poop-deck extended about fifteen feet from the taffrail, and under this were the steering-wheel and binnacles. I was a midshipman on board doing lieutenant's duty, having charge of a regular watch and in command of a division of guns. My division consisted of 4 guns (2 guns' crews) at the after end of the ship. The guns were numbered in pairs 10 and 11. The No. 11 gun on the starboard side was shifted over to the port side under the poop-deck, and both the No. 11 guns were manned by the marines. It was expected that our principal work would be with our port battery directed against Fort Jackson on the right bank. My two crews manned the No. 10 gun on each side, and also prepared to man the 30-pounder on the poop if occasion should require. On each side of the poop there was a ladder to the main deck. While steaming up to the hulks and until it was necessary for me to be at my guns, I stood on the port ladder with my head above the rail, where I could watch our approach to the forts, and I mounted this ladder several times to see what was going on as we advanced.

REAR-ADMIRAL THOMAS T. CRAVEN, IN COMMAND OF THE "BROOKLYN" AT NEW ORLEANS. FROM A PHOTOGRAPH.

On the poop were Captain Craven, Midshipman John Anderson, who had volunteered a few days before from the *Montgomery*, which did not take part in the action, Captain's Clerk J. G. Swift, afterward a graduate of West Point and a lieutenant in the army, and two quartermasters. There was a small piece of ratline stuff carried around the poop, about waist-high. Captain Craven stood at the forward edge of the poop with his hands on this line, and did not move during the whole passage. I had the good fortune during the war to serve with many brave commanders, but I have never met in the service, or out of it, a man of such consummate coolness, such perfect apparent indifference to danger as Admiral Craven. As I write, I hear the sad news of his death.

At 2 o'clock on the morning of the 24th two red lights were hoisted at the peak of the flag-ship as a signal to get under way. All hands had been on deck since midnight to see that everything about the deck and guns was

walked up and down the quarter-deck with the commanding officer. He was very much exasperated that the department at Washington delayed sending vessels of proper draught to enter the river, and said that if he had half a dozen good vessels he would undertake to run by the forts and capture New Orleans. Admiral Porter has already recounted in this work the prominent part that he took in the opening of the Mississippi, and I therefore omit further reference to it.— J. R. B.

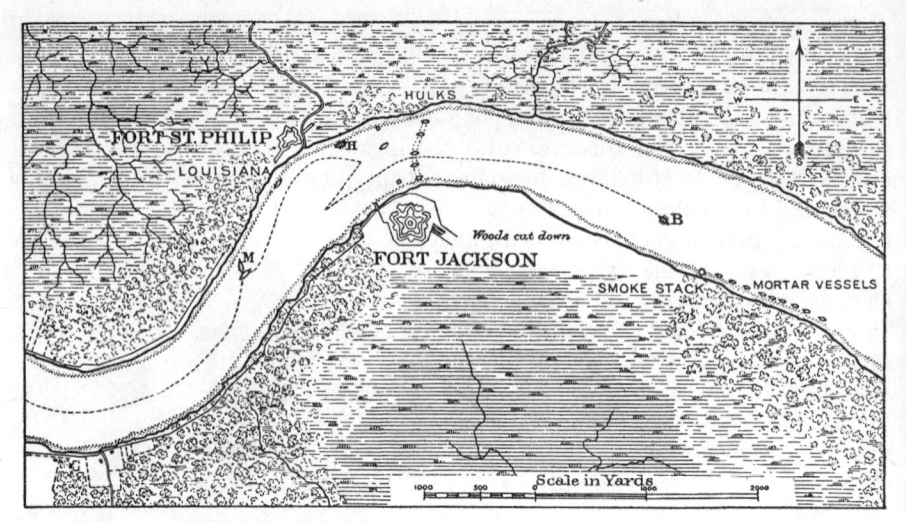

THE COURSE OF THE "BROOKLYN" IN THE PASSAGE OF THE FORTS.
FROM A DRAWING LENT BY COMMANDER J. R. BARTLETT.

B—*Brooklyn*, and course taken.  H—*Hartford* aground.  M—*Manassas* ramming the *Brooklyn*.

ready for action, and when the decks were wet down and sanded, it really began to look as if we were going to have some pretty hot business on our hands. The anchor was hove up with as little noise as possible, and at half-past 2 we steamed off, following the *Hartford* toward the entrance to the opening which had been made in the obstructions. The Confederates opened fire about 3 o'clock, when the advance division came in sight and range of the forts, and as we passed ahead of the mortar-vessels we also came in range; but the forts were so far ahead that we could not bring our broadside guns to bear. For twenty minutes we stood silent beside the guns, with the shot and shell from Forts St. Philip and Jackson passing over us and bursting everywhere in the air. As we came to the obstruction the water-battery on the Fort Jackson side opened a most destructive fire, and here the *Brooklyn* received her first shot. We gave the water-battery a broadside of grape. With our own smoke and the smoke from the vessels immediately ahead, it was impossible to direct the ship, so that we missed the opening between the hulks and brought up on the chain. We dropped back and tried again; this time the chain broke, but we swung alongside of one of the hulks, and the stream-anchor, hanging on the starboard quarter, caught, tore along the hulk, and then parted its lashings. The cable secured us just where the Confederates had the range of their guns, but somebody ran up with an axe and cut the hawser, and we began to steam up the river.‡ A few moments later there was a sudden jar, and the engines stopped. The propeller had no doubt struck some hard object, but no one knew the cause of the stoppage; and as Craven called out, "Stand by the starboard anchor," and a fatal pause under

‡ I went on the poop to help clear the hawser, and looked around for my classmate Anderson. He must have been knocked overboard by a shot when we first came to the obstructions. The anchor on the port quarter was broken off close to the stock at this point by a shot from Fort Jackson.—J. R. B.

the enemy's fire seemed imminent, a thrill of alarm ran through the ship. The alarm was groundless, however, as no injury was done, and presently the engines started again, and the ship moved on.

There were many fire-rafts, and these and the flashing of the guns and bursting shells made it almost as light as day, but the smoke from the passing fleet was so thick that at times one could see nothing ten feet from the ship. While entangled with the rafts, the *Brooklyn* was hulled a number of times; one shot from Fort Jackson struck the rail just at the break of the poop and went nearly across, plowing out the deck in its course. Another struck Barney Sands, the signal quartermaster, and cut his body almost in two. The first lieutenant, Lowry, coming along at the time, inquired who it was, and understanding the response to be "Bartlett," instead of "Barney," he passed the word that he had sent down "all that was left of poor Bartlett." As he came on deck and was about in all parts of the ship during the fight, he gave the men news of the progress of the fight and of the casualties, and for once I was completely out of existence.

The ship was now clear of the hulks and steamed up the river, throwing shells and shrapnel into Fort Jackson as fast as the guns could be loaded and fired. When just abreast of the fort a shot struck the side of the port of No. 9 gun on the port side, and at the same time a shell burst directly over the gun. The first captain's head was cut off and nine of the gun's crew were wounded. I was standing amidships between the two No. 10 guns, and was struck on the back by the splinters and thrown to the deck. I was on my feet in a moment and turned to my port gun. There were only two men standing at it, the first loader and the first sponger, who were leaning against the side of the ship: the others were all flat on deck, one of them directly in the rear of the gun. The gun had just been loaded, and I pulled this man to one side, clear of the recoil, and fired the gun. It was a time when every one felt that he must do something. After the discharge of the gun the men on the deck got up and came to their places. None of them were seriously hurt. The captain of the gun found a piece of shell inside his cap, which did not even scratch his head; another piece went through my coat-sleeve.

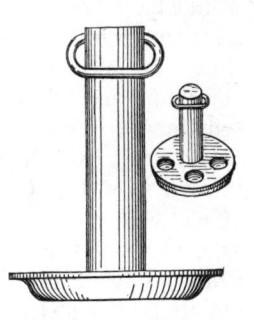

STAND TO HOLD GRAPE,— CALLED "LAMP-POSTS" BY THE CONFEDERATES. (SEE P. 65.)

Just after passing Fort Jackson we saw a bright glare on the starboard quarter, and a moment after Captain Craven said, in his deep bass voice, "One bell!" (to slow down), and then, "Two bells!" (to stop her). I went up the poop ladder, and there in plain sight on the left bank, just below Fort St. Philip, was the *Hartford*, with a fire-raft alongside and with flames running up the rigging on the tarred rope to the mast-head. The tug *Mosher* was near by, but I did not see the ram *Manassas*. It was evidently Craven's intention when he saw Farragut's trouble to go to his rescue. As the engine stopped, the *Brooklyn* dropped down, her head swinging to starboard, until she was on a line between Fort Jackson and the *Hartford*. The

FLAG-SHIP "HARTFORD" ATTACKED BY A FIRE-RAFT, PUSHED BY THE CONFEDERATE TUG-BOAT "MOSHER." ♭

fort immediately opened fire on the *Brooklyn* with renewed energy, and she would have been blown out of the water had not the enemy aimed too high and sent the shot through the rigging, boats, and hammock-nettings, many of them just clearing the rail. The port battery was manned, and shell and shrapnel were fired as fast as the guns could be loaded. The *Brooklyn* remained under the fire of Fort Jackson until Craven saw Farragut free from the fire-raft, and then she steamed ahead. This was one of the coolest and bravest acts that I saw during the war, but it was not mentioned in any official report or newspaper account at the time. In fact, the *Brooklyn's* passage of the forts was hardly noticed by the newspaper correspondents, as Craven had old-fashioned ideas and would allow no reporters on board. I am glad, even at this late date, that I can put on record this act of heroism.

As the *Hartford* lay aground with the fire-raft alongside, her crew were at their work, and I saw the flag-officer distinctly on the port side of the poop looking toward us. From this point the *Brooklyn* steamed ahead, toward Fort St.

♭ Commander Albert Kautz, who was at this time lieutenant on the *Hartford*, in a letter to the Editors thus describes this memorable scene:

"No sooner had Farragut given the order 'Hard-a-port,' than the current gave the ship a broad sheer, and her bows went hard up on a mud bank. As the fire-raft came against the port side of the ship, it became enveloped in flames. We were so near to the shore that from the bowsprit we could reach the tops of the bushes, and such a short distance above Fort St. Philip that we could distinctly hear the gunners in the casemates give their orders; and as they saw Farragut's flag at the mizzen, by the bright light, they fired with frightful rapidity. Fortunately they did not make sufficient allowance for our close proximity, and the iron hail passed over our bulwarks, doing but little damage. On the deck of the ship it was bright as noonday, but out over the majestic river, where the smoke of many guns was intensified by that of the pine-knots of the fire-rafts, it was dark as the blackest midnight. For a moment it looked as though the flag-ship was indeed doomed, but the firemen were called away, and with the energy of despair rushed aft to the quarter-deck. The flames, like so many forked tongues of hissing serpents, were piercing the air in a frightful manner that struck terror to all hearts. As I crossed from the starboard to the port side of the deck, I passed close to Farragut, who, as he looked forward and took in the situation, clasped his hands high in air, and exclaimed, 'My God, is it to end in this way!' Fortunately it was not to end as it at that instant seemed, for just then Master's Mate Allen, with the hose in his hand, jumped into the mizzen rigging, and the sheet of flame succumbed to a sheet of water. It was but the dry paint on the ship's side that made the threatening flame, which went down before the fierce attack of the firemen as rapidly as it had sprung up. As the flames died away the engines were backed 'hard,' and, as if providentially, the ram *Manassas* [mistake: see p. 90] struck the ship a blow under the counter, which shoved her stern in against the bank, causing her bow to slip off. The ship was again free; and a loud, spontaneous cheer rent the air, as the crew rushed to their guns with renewed energy." EDITORS.

Philip, and passed close to the fort, firing grape from the starboard battery. When she first came abreast of the fort there was a long blaze of musketry from the parapet, but it soon stopped when she got to work.⸱ We were at this time less than one hundred feet from the bank, and the *Hartford* had passed ahead. The barbette guns of the fort not being depressed sufficiently, we received no damage while passing, but we were so close that the powder scorched the faces and clothes of the men. A bullet entered the port of No. 1 gun and struck Lieutenant James O'Kane, who had charge of the first division, in the leg. He fell to the deck, but would not allow himself to be carried below until he had himself fired two of the broadside guns into Fort St. Philip. But the most uncomfortable position on board the ship, during this part of the engagement, was that of the quartermaster, Thomas Hollins, who stood in the starboard main chains, heaving the lead and calling out the soundings. The outside of the ship near him was completely peppered with bullets, and the flames from the enemy's guns seemed almost to reach him; still he stood coolly at his post, and when abreast of the fort he was heard calling out, "Only thirteen feet, sir."

As we passed clear of Fort St. Philip, Captain Craven gave orders to load the starboard battery with solid shot. He had seen the iron-clad *Louisiana*, moored just above the fort. She gave us one or two shots, but when we came directly abeam of her, she closed her port shutters and received our broadside. We could hear our shot strike against her iron sides. We gave but one broadside and then sheered out into the river. A 9-inch shell, fired by the *Louisiana*, struck the *Brooklyn* about a foot above the water-line, on the starboard side of the cutwater, near the wood ends, forced its way for three feet through the dead-wood and timbers, and remained there. At New Orleans this shot was cut out, and it was found that in their hurry the gunners had neglected to remove the lead patch from the fuse, so that the shell did not explode. Had it done so it would have blown the whole bow off, and the *Brooklyn* would have gone to the bottom.

As we swung out into the current and steamed up the river, we began to see the vessels ahead fighting with the Confederate gun-boats, and a few moments later the cry came aft, "A steamer coming down on our port bow." We could see two smoke-stacks and the black smoke from them. I took a look from the poop ladder, and saw a good-sized river steamer coming down on us, crowded with men on her forward deck, as if ready to board. The order had

SECTION OF FORT ST. PHILIP DURING THE ENGAGEMENT. THE DETAILS OF THE FORT DRAWN FROM A PHOTOGRAPH.

---

⸱ I was afterward in charge of a boat from the *Brooklyn* which landed the paroled Confederate prisoners at New Orleans, and they said that the grape came like rain, but that the worst of all were the "infernal lamp-posts" that we fired; that the fort was full of them. These were the stands that held the grape — cylinders attached to a cast-iron base, around which the grape-shot are secured.— J. R. B.

THE "BROOKLYN" ATTACKED BY THE CONFEDERATE RAM "MANASSAS."

The *Manassas* was described by her commander, Lieutenant Warley, as "a tug-boat that had been converted into a ram, covered with half-inch iron, and had a 32-pounder carronade; her crew consisted of thirty-five persons, officers and men. She was perforated in the fight by shot and shell as if she had been made of paper."

Admiral Melancton Smith thus describes his encounter with the ram: "Having discovered the *Manassas* stealing up along the St. Philip side of the river behind me, I signaled Farragut for permission to attack, which was given. The *Mississippi* turned in mid-stream and tried to run down the ram, barely missing her, but driving her ashore, when her crew escaped, fired at by the *Kineo*, which had not yet anchored. The ram's engines were found to be still in motion, but the approach of a burning wreck compelled me to abandon the idea of attaching a hawser. Her machinery was destroyed by my boats, and after receiving a broadside or two from the *Mississippi*, she floated down the river in flames and blew up."

already been given, "Stand by to repel boarders," and to load with shrapnel; the fuses were cut to burn one second. As she approached, Craven gave the vessel a sheer to starboard, and we began with No. 1 gun, the guns aft following in quick succession, the shells bursting almost immediately as they left the guns. There was a rush of steam, shrieks from the people on board the steamer, and, when it came time for my No. 10 gun to fire, the steamer was lost in the smoke. This was the only one of the river flotilla which we encountered or fired into. Just after our engagement with this steamer, a column of black smoke, which came from the dreaded *Manassas*, was seen on the starboard side, and the cry was passed along by men who were looking out of the ports, "The ram, the ram!" Craven called out, "Give her four bells! Put your helm hard-a-starboard!" Then I saw the smoke-stacks of the *Manassas* and the flash from her gun, and the next moment I was nearly thrown on the deck by the concussion, caused by her striking us just amidships. The ram was going full speed but against the current, and, with our helm to starboard, the blow was not at right angles to our keel, though nearly so. I ran to the No. 10 port, the gun being in, and looked out, and saw her almost directly alongside. A man came out of her little hatch aft, and ran forward along the port side of the deck, as far as the smoke-stacks, placed his hand against one, and looked to see what damage the ram had done. I saw him turn, fall over, and tumble into the water, but did not know at the moment what caused his sudden disappearance, until I asked the quartermaster, who was leadsman in the chains, if he had seen him fall.

"Why, yes, sir," said he, "I saw him fall overboard,— in fact, I helped him; for I hit him alongside of the head with my hand-lead."

No guns were fired at the ram from the starboard battery; all the crews a moment before had been at the port guns. As the *Manassas* drifted by I ran up on the poop, calling the gun's crew with me, to see if I could hit her with the 30-pounder Parrott, but we were unable to depress it sufficiently, at its high elevation, to bring it to bear before she was lost to sight in the smoke. The shot which she had fired came through the chain and planking, above the berth-deck, through a pile of rigging placed against the ship's side, and just entered the sand-bags placed to protect the steam-drum.

A few moments after this incident a vessel passed on our starboard side, not ten feet from us, and I could see through the port the men loading a pivot gun. She was directly abreast of No. 10 gun and I took the lock-string to fire, when a cry came from on board the vessel, "Don't fire, it is the *Iroquois!*" At the same moment, Lieutenant Lowry also shouted from near the mainmast, "Don't fire!" Seeing the black smoke pouring from her stack, and noticing that it was abaft the mainmast, I called to Captain Craven, "It can't be the *Iroquois!* It is not one of our vessels, for her smoke-stack is abaft her mainmast!" Captain Craven, however, repeated the order, "Don't fire!" and I obeyed. I was sure it was one of the Confederate gun-boats, but it was my duty to obey orders, and thus the Confederate gun-boat *McRae* escaped being sunk by the *Brooklyn;* for the gun had been depressed, and a 9-inch shell would have gone through her deck and out below the water-line.

Just after leaving Fort St. Philip a shot came in on the starboard quarter and went across the deck, taking off a marine's head and wounding three other men. Lieutenant Lowry came along about this time, and I heard him report to Captain Craven that Lieutenant O'Kane had been wounded. Craven directed him to put me in charge of the First Division, to which Lowry answered:

"I sent poor Bartlett down below half an hour ago cut in two."

"Oh, no, you did not," said Craven; "he is on deck close to you."

Lowry turned and was as much surprised as if he had seen a ghost, and told me to run forward and take charge of the First Division. There had been terrible havoc here. The powder-man of the pivot gun had been struck by a shell, which exploded and blew him literally to atoms, and parts of his body were scattered all over the forecastle. The gun was disabled, a primer having broken off in the vent; but there was nothing to fire at, as all the vessels that we passed had been run on the bank and either set on fire or deserted. It was now almost daylight, and we could see the crews of the deserted boats running for cover to the woods a little way back. Shortly after, the *Brooklyn* came up with the other vessels and anchored near a point where there had been an encampment of troops. They only remained long enough to land and bury the dead. The commanding officers assembled on board the *Hartford* to offer their congratulations to the flag-officer.

About the time that the *Brooklyn* arrived at quarantine the *Manassas* was seen steaming up the river, and Farragut made signal to the *Mississippi* to attack her. [See note, p. 66.] She ran down toward her, but the *Manassas* sheered toward the left bank and ran her nose ashore. When the *Mississippi* opened fire upon her, the crew poured out of the little hatch aft, ran along the deck, and jumped on shore and over the levee into the swamp beyond.

REAR-ADMIRAL CHARLES S. BOGGS, AT NEW ORLEANS IN COMMAND OF THE "VARUNA." FROM A PHOTOGRAPH.

The fleet steamed up the river during the afternoon of the 24th until dark, and then came to anchor. Nothing of importance occurred during the passage. Soon after midnight a great blaze of light was seen up the river, and fearing fire-rafts, all the vessels got under way, and remained so until daylight, when they proceeded up the river toward New Orleans. At 6 o'clock we passed a large vessel loaded with cotton on fire, and at 7:30 passed two more in the same condition. Arrived at Chalmette, four miles below the city, we found that batteries had been erected on both banks, armed with field-pieces. A few broadsides made the troops leave their guns and disperse into the country. The *Brooklyn* fired 21 shells from the 80-pound Dahlgren into the battery on the left bank and a couple of broadsides into that on the right.

The fleet steamed on to the city, passing close to the levees, which were swarming with people. They were simply a howling mob. The Confederate flags were flying about the city, and we passed so close—not more than two hundred feet from the bank—that the people called out abusive names and shouted at us in derision. In the French quarter there was apparently some disturbance, and a body of troops was seen firing a volley into the crowd. As the ship arrived abreast of the Custom-house and anchored off Canal street, a pouring rain came down, but even this did not seem to reduce the crowd.

Soon after we had anchored, burning steamers, barges, and other vessels loaded with cotton came drifting down on fire. Among the burning vessels was the Confederate iron-clad *Mississippi*. It seemed the purpose of the mob to destroy everything. During the night the city was set on fire in a dozen different places, and there was a continual ringing of fire-alarm bells.

The next day we steamed up the river, as obstructions and batteries had been reported above the city. All the fortifications were deserted, but an immense raft was found lying along the left bank. This was made of four logs lashed together side by side, with a heavy chain extending their whole length. It had been the intention of the Confederates to stretch this boom across the river to prevent Foote and his flotilla from reaching New Orleans. The barrier looked formidable as it lay under the river-bank, but when the Confederates had finished their work they could not get the raft across the river on account of the current. They made the lower end fast to the bank, and with three steamboats took the upper end and endeavored to reach the opposite bank, but the huge structure was more than they could manage, and the current swept it down the river with such force that it broke, drifted from the steamers, and swung around against the bank and so proved a failure. ☆

On the day after the passage of the forts, it was noticed that the *Brooklyn* leaked more than usual, but not enough to give any alarm, as the steam-pumps were able to keep her free, and in the course of a few days the leak diminished. It was not until the coal in the starboard bunker had been used up and the side of the ship was uncovered that we realized what a blow she had received from the *Manassas*. On the outside the chain had been driven its depth into the planking, and on the inside, for a length of five feet or more, the planking was splintered and crushed in. The only thing that prevented the prow of the *Manassas* from sinking us was the fact that the bunker was full of coal.

The wound gave no trouble so long as we remained in the river, as the mud held in suspension in the river water filled up all the interstices between the fibers of the wood. When we went out to sea and rolled about a little, and the ship began to work, it was found that she leaked very badly, and she was obliged to go to Pensacola, heave down, and bolt on a large patch of plank to cover the spot where the ram had struck.

☆ The river, when we arrived at New Orleans, was higher than it ever had been known to be before, and the levees had been added to, to prevent the water from overflowing. As we found it, the water was within a few inches of the top of the levee.— J. R. B.

NOTE.— Since writing the above article, I have compared it carefully with letters I wrote to my father from New Orleans. In some instances I do not agree with the official reports in the sequence of events, but I hold to my own account. Craven says he encountered the *Manassas* a few minutes after passing the obstructions. I place this event well above the forts, and this is corroborated by Captain Warley of the *Manassas*. Farragut, in his official report, does not state exactly where he encountered the fire-raft, but says: "The fire was extinguished. In the meantime our battery was never silent, but poured its missiles of death into Fort St. Philip, opposite to which we had got by this time." I place the *Hartford* at this time just below the fort, or abreast of the lower flanking battery, as the iron-clad *Louisiana* was moored to the bank immediately above. When the *Manassas* rammed the *Brooklyn* she had two smoke-stacks, but she lost one before she drifted down the river.— J. R. B.

## FARRAGUT'S CAPTURE OF NEW ORLEANS.

BY WILLIAM T. MEREDITH, LATE U. S. N., AND SECRETARY TO ADMIRAL FARRAGUT.

IT has astonished a great many people to learn from Admiral Porter's article in "The Century" magazine [reprinted in the present work] that he was the first man to propose the opening of the Mississippi. Montgomery Blair, in the "United Service Magazine" for January, 1881, and ex-Secretary Welles, in "The Galaxy" for November, 1871, both fix the time when the discussion of the question was begun by the naval authorities, which was before the appearance of Porter on the scene at Washington. And, indeed, the importance of the great river to the South was so evident to any one who studied our coast and the South-west, that it is safe to say that the eyes of the whole nation were bent on New Orleans as a point of attack just about the time that Porter imagines he suggested it.

Why was Farragut chosen flag-officer of the squadron to attack New Orleans? The answer is that he was known as an experienced and capable officer, who was on record as having plans to capture forts with ships. He was one of the few officers of sufficient rank to command a squadron who also had the strength and vigor necessary to bear the strain of arduous duty. These were the main reasons that Mr. Welles, the Secretary, and Mr. Fox, the Assistant Secretary, had for selecting him. Besides this, his appointment met the approval of Porter, who, when consulted by the Secretary, gave his voice for Farragut. It is easy now to understand how with the lapse of time Admiral Porter has learned to think that he chose the commander of the expedition. That he could have defeated Farragut's appointment is probably true, but that he chose him is a mistake; he simply assented to the previous choice of Mr. Welles and Mr. Fox. (See articles by Welles and Blair, above referred to.)

Ex-Secretary Welles relates that the armament of the fleet had been determined, *before Farragut's appointment to the command*, after consultation with the War Department and with General McClellan, who detailed General Butler to command the land forces of the expedition. Porter, whose advice was listened to, insisted on the importance of a fleet of schooners carrying 13-inch mortars, and asserted that a bombardment of forty-eight hours would reduce Forts Jackson and St. Philip to a heap of ruins. Mr. Welles says that Mr. Fox, who was a trained naval officer, at first objected to the mortars, and advocated running by the forts with the fleet, but finally was won over by the forcible arguments of Porter, whose plan the Department fully adopted. There is evidence, given by Commander Porter himself, that he advocated bombarding the forts till they surrendered or could be captured by assault, and that he was opposed to running the fire with the fleet leaving an enemy in the rear. (See his letter on p. 71.)

The forces to attack New Orleans were fixed, measures were taken to cast thirty thousand mortar-shells, collect the fleet and transport the soldiers, before Farragut was summoned to Washington from New York. Mr. Blair says positively that he was not to be given the command until he had been subjected to a critical overhauling by the authorities. We hear of Farragut at breakfast with Mr. Blair and Mr. Fox, probably on the morning of his arrival at the capital. Mr. Fox then showed him the point of attack, the plans, and the force to be employed. Farragut said he would engage to capture New Orleans with two-thirds the naval force. Mr. Blair tells us that he was so enthusiastic and confident of success that when he went away Mr. Fox thought him over-sanguine, and was a little inclined to distrust his ability. Mr. Welles relates that after this interview Farragut was brought to him, and they entered at once into all the plans of the expedition. When they came to the mortar-flotilla, Farragut said that he placed little reliance on mortars, and that they would not have been part of his plan and advisement, but that he would take the mortar-fleet with him, as it had been adopted as part of the equipment of the fleet and might prove of more advantage than he anticipated.

At 10 o'clock on the 20th of April, while the bombardment by the mortars was at its height, the flag-ship made signal that Farragut wanted to hold a conference of commanding officers. In an hour they had all arrived excepting three, who commanded vessels detailed that day for guard duty above the fleet, and Commander Porter, who was probably too much occupied with the mortars to leave his command.

Thirteen boats trailed at the stern of the *Hartford*, while the captains waited anxiously in the cabin to hear what the flag-officer would say. A private journal kept by Commodore Bell, who led the 2d division of gun-boats in the attack, describes as follows what took place at the conference:

"The flag-officer [Farragut] unfolded his plan of operations. Some discussion ensued, and Commander Alden read a written communication to Farragut from Porter, expressing his views as to the operations against the forts. Having read them, Alden folded up the paper and returned it to his pocket, whereupon I [Commodore Bell] suggested the propriety of the document's being left with Farragut, and the paper was accordingly placed in his hands. It was therein stated that the boom, being a protection to the mortars against attack from above, should not be destroyed, upon which Farragut remarked that Porter had that morning assented to the boom's being broken, and again (it was stated in the communication) that the fleet should not go above the forts, as the mortar-vessels would be left unprotected. Farragut said he thought the mortars would be as well protected (with the fleet) above as below the forts, and that the coöperation of the army, which entered into the plans of both parties, could not be effectual unless some of the troops were introduced above the forts at the same time that they were below. He intended to cover their landing at the Quarantine, five miles above, they coming to the river through the bayou. Once above, the forts cut off, and his propellers intact for ascending the river to the city, if he found his ships able to cope with the enemy he would fight it out. Some of the officers considered it a hazardous thing to go above out of the reach of supplies. Farragut remarked that our ammunition was being rapidly exhausted, without a supply at hand, and that something must be done immediately. He believed in celerity."

Farragut "believed in celerity." He saw that while the ammunition was being exhausted but little impression had been made on the forts, and he felt sure that the time had come to carry out his plan of dashing boldly up the river through the fire of the forts.

The communication from Commander Porter containing his plans of attack, to which I have already alluded, and which was referred to by Commodore Bell, is as follows:

"When the ships are over the bar, guns mounted, coal-bunkers filled, sick on shore, hospital arrangements made for the wounded, the fleet should move up, mortar-fleet all in tow; the chain across the river to remain untouched for the present, or until after the mortars get their position and open their fire. It is a good defense on our side against fire-ships and rams which may be sent down the river, and our ships can so command the opening that nothing can pass down. As the mortar-vessels are somewhat helpless, they should be protected at all points by vessels of war, which should be ready at a moment's notice to repel an attack on them by rams, floating torpedoes, or fire-ships; the two latter to be towed out of the way, the rams to be run down by the heavy ships, while such vessels as the *Westfield* and *Clifton* attack them end on with cannon, while gun-boats try to force them to the shore. When everything is ready for the assault, a demand for surrender should be made in language least calculated to exasperate, and of such a nature as to encourage those who might be disposed to return to their allegiance. There is evidence of a strong Union feeling in New Orleans, and everything should be done without losing by delay to prevent a counter-feeling.

"When it is evident that no surrender of the forts will be made, the mortars should open deliberate fire, keeping two shells in the air all the time, or each mortar-vessel should fire once in every ten minutes. Fort Jackson, being casemated, should receive the largest share of the bombardment, three or four vessels being employed against Fort St. Philip, firing as often as they can coolly and conveniently load and point. In the meantime preparations should be made to destroy at a moment's notice the vessels holding up the chain, or the chain itself, which can be done by applying a petard to the bobstays of the vessels or to the chain, all of which petards are prepared, and a man accustomed to the business with a galvanic battery will accompany the expedition.

"In my opinion there are two methods of attack,—one is for the vessel to run the gauntlet of the batteries by night or in a fog; the other is to attack the forts by laying the big ships close alongside of them, avoiding the casemates, firing shells, grape, and canister into the barbette, clearing the ramparts with boat-guns from the tops, while smaller and more agile vessels throw in shrapnel at shrapnel distance, clearing the parapets, and dismounting the guns in barbette.

"The larger ships should anchor with forty-five fathoms of chain with slip-ropes; the smaller vessels to keep under way and be constantly moving about, some to get above and open a cross-fire; the mortars to keep up a rapid and continuous fire, and to move up to a short range.

"The objections to running by the forts are these: It is not likely that any intelligent enemy would fail to place a chain across above the forts, and to raise such batteries as would protect them against our ships.

"Did we run the forts we should leave an enemy in our rear, and the mortar-vessels would have to be left behind. We could not return to bring them up without going through a heavy and destructive fire. If the forts are run, part of the mortars should be towed along, which would render the progress of the vessels slow against the strong current at that point. If the forts are first captured, the moral effect would be to close the batteries on the river and open the way to New Orleans, whereas, if we don't succeed in taking them, we will have to fight our way up the river. Once having possession of the forts, New Orleans would be hermetically sealed, and we could repair damages and go up on our own terms and our own time.

"Nature points out the English Turn as the position to be strongly fortified, and it is there the enemy will most likely make his strongest stand and last effort to prevent our getting up. If this point is impassable there is solid ground there, and troops can be brought up and landed below the forts and attack them in the rear while the ships assail them in front. The result will doubtless be a victory for us. If the ships can get by the forts, and there are no obstructions above, then the plan should be to push on to New Orleans every ship that can get there, taking up as many of the mortar-fleet as can be rapidly towed. An accurate reconnoissance should be made, and every kind of attainable information provided before any movement is made.

"Nothing has been said about a combined attack of army and navy. Such a thing is not only practicable, but, if time permitted, could be adopted. Fort St. Philip can be taken with three thousand men covered by the ships; the ditch can be filled with fascines, and the walls can be easily scaled with ladders. It can be easily attacked in front and rear."—D. D. PORTER.

Farragut stood facing his destiny, imperishable fame or failure. He was determined to run by the forts with his ships. It was plain to him that nothing more would be accomplished by the mortars. He would not cumber his fleet during the passage by towing the mortars as Porter desired him to do. Once above the defenses, and the enemy's fleet overcome, he would either push on to New Orleans past the batteries, which he knew were at Chalmette, or cover with his guns the landing of the army through the bayou in the rear of the forts. In his heart he was determined, if events favored him, to push right on seventy-five miles up the river to New Orleans without waiting for the army. Porter's views expressed in his letter to the conference gave no support to these plans. He speaks of three methods of attack: *First*, by running the forts; *second*, bombardment by the whole fleet, mortars included, with a view to the reduction of the defenses; and *third*, a combined attack of the navy and army. The first method, which was Farragut's plan and the plan that succeeded, he strongly condemns. He feared the result of leaving an enemy in the rear. Some of the commanding officers agreed with him.

On the next day Farragut issued a General Order [see p. 39], which bears date one day earlier than its issuance, and is at once a reply to Porter's communication to the conference of officers and an announcement of the flag-officer's determination to challenge all objections, run the forts, conquer or be conquered.

No one can read Commodore Bell's journal and Flag-Officer Farragut's general order without seeing that there was cause for disappointment in the fleet. After a bombardment of three days the defense was still vigorous and the Confederates were undismayed. As a consequence of this Farragut had lost the little faith he ever had in mortars, and was prepared to carry out his own plans, differ as they might from the instructions of the Navy Department.

Farragut had a stupendous undertaking before him. A river with a current of three and a half miles an hour against the line of attack; two forts on opposite sides of the stream mounting 126 guns, and above them the Confederate steamers carrying 40 guns, while in the river, both above and below the forts, rafts were floating ready to be fired and cut loose on the first sign of an attempt to pass the boom. His fleet consisted of 8 steam sloops-of-war, 15 gun-boats, 1 sailing sloop, and 19 mortar-schooners. The 17 vessels which were to attempt the passage carried 166 guns and 26 howitzers. It is true that the mortar-shells were of assistance to Farragut in the passage, as they helped his own guns to distract the fire of the enemy and added to the confusion and distress in Fort Jackson. But that the passage would have been made in the darkness without the assistance of the mortars has never been seriously questioned, and is proved by Farragut's successful passage of Fort Morgan at the battle of Mobile Bay in broad daylight, which involved exactly the same principles of attack and was achieved without the use of a single mortar. The protraction of the bombardment gave the Confederates just six days more to push forward the work on the iron-clad and the fleet. Mr. Welles, in "The Galaxy," quotes a dispatch from Porter himself which shows his recognition of the fact that the Confederates were strengthening their defenses during this period. Porter says, speaking of the siege, that the enemy was "daily adding to his defense and strengthening his naval forces with iron-clad batteries."

What was the situation of affairs in Fort Jackson and Fort St. Philip about this time—the 22d of April—as shown by the testimony before the Confederate Court of Inquiry? In the two garrisons of 1100 men, 4 soldiers had been killed and 14 wounded—7 guns of the armament of 126 had been disabled. The barracks and citadel of Fort Jackson had been destroyed by fire.

There was nothing more to burn. Whenever the gun-boats approached the defenses a vigorous fire was opened on them by both forts, but when they retired the soldiers withdrew to the casemates out of reach of the mortar-fire.

And up to this time the mortar-flotilla had fired more than 13,500 shells. Porter had expected to reduce the forts to a heap of ruins in forty-eight hours, but at the end of ninety-six hours the defense was as vigorous as ever.

Did Porter believe that Farragut's passage of the forts and appearance before New Orleans would result in a speedy downfall of the defenses and the capture of the river and city? He did not, and he was very uneasy about the fleet after it passed the forts. He wondered how Farragut would return down the river to the mortar-fleet and to the army. He could not appreciate the fact that it was not necessary for him to come back; that all the defenses must soon fall, Forts Jackson and St. Philip among them, as the effect of the occupation of the river and New Orleans. He feared that Farragut was caught in a trap. He thought he would find the forts harder to take than ever, and that he would have to fight his way down the river and attack them again. All this appears in the letter of Commander Porter, which is given below. It was written to Farragut from below the forts on the morning after the passage, three days before they surrendered. The italics are not in the original:

"MORTAR-FLOTILLA, April 25th, 1862.

"DEAR SIR: Captain Boggs has arrived. I congratulate you on your victory. I witnessed your passage with great pleasure. My hopes and predictions were at last realized. You left at the forts four steamers and the famous iron-clad battery; they are mounting guns on it, and one thousand men are at work on it. She is unhurt and moves about with the stream. How fast she is I don't know. One of the steamers is iron-clad on the bow. The McRae is also at the fort. I sent a summons to surrender, but it was politely declined. As we have used up all the shells in the schooners, and wishing to be unhampered with the mortar-vessels, sent everything down and collected boats and spars. . . .

"They are moving all their heavy guns upon the riverside. *You will find the forts harder to take now than before unless their ammunition gives out.* I threw bombs at them all day, and tantalized them with rifle-shot, but they never fired a gun. *I hope you will open your way down, no matter what it costs.* I am sending some of the schooners down to blockade back of Fort Jackson to prevent their escaping by way of Barataria.

"D. D. PORTER."

Porter overlooks the difference between his hopes and his predictions, as shown by his communication to the conference of officers, which he says are realized in this letter, and Farragut's achievement. He had opposed the plan of attack by which Farragut succeeded.

Porter's letter to the Secretary of the Navy, written before the surrender, also shows his distrust of the result of Farragut's bold ascent of the river, leaving an enemy in his rear. He says, speaking of the Confederate iron-clad below Farragut's fleet at the forts, "She mounts sixteen guns, and is almost as formidable as the *Merrimac*. This is one of the ill effects of leaving an enemy in the rear." And again, "These forts can hold out still for some time. I would suggest that the *Mystic* and *Monitor*, if they can be spared, be sent here without a moment's delay to settle the question."

On the 28th of April, three days later, the forts surrendered, and Farragut, who was then in possession of New Orleans, did not find it necessary to open his way down the river as advised by Porter, to whom the surrender must have been a surprise.

What was the immediate cause of the surrender of the forts? This is exactly the question that was asked of Colonel Edward Higgins, who had commanded Fort Jackson, by the Confederate Court of Inquiry, and his reply was: "The mutiny of the garrison." But what was the cause of the mutiny? General Duncan, who had commanded the lower defenses, including the forts, answered this in his report: "The garrison mutinied on the night of the 27th of April, giving as a reason that the city had surrendered and there was no further use in fighting." And why did the city surrender? Was it because Porter bombarded Fort Jackson 75 miles below the city, for six days, disabling, up to the night of the passage of the fleet, only 9 guns of the armament of 128, with a loss to the Confederates of less than 40 men in both garrisons? ☆ Or was it because Farragut dashed through the fire of the forts, destroyed the Confederate fleet, and then pushed on past the Chalmette batteries 75 miles up the river, cutting off all communication, till he anchored before the city with his torn fleet?

☆ The following official statements made by Confederate and Union officers are given to show the condition of Fort Jackson and the garrison after the bombardment. On the 30th of April, 1862, in a letter to Adjutant-General Bridges, Colonel Edward Higgins says: "I have the honor to report that on the morning of the 27th of April a formal demand for the surrender of Forts Jackson and St. Philip was made by Commander Porter; the terms which were offered were liberal, but so strong was I in the belief that we could resist successfully any attack, either by land or by water, that the terms were at once refused. Our fort was still strong."

General Duncan, commanding all the lower Confederate defenses, says after the passage: "We are just as capable of repelling the enemy to-day as we were before the bombardment."

General Weitzel, of the United States Engineer Corps, in a report of the condition of Fort Jackson dated in May, 1862, says: "Fort St. Philip, with one or two slight exceptions, is to-day without a scratch. Fort Jackson was subjected to a torrent of 13-inch and 11-inch shells during 140 hours. To an inexperienced eye it seems as if this work were badly cut up. It is as strong to-day as when the first shell was fired at it."

Captain Harris, of the Coast Survey, whose map of the forts is published in Porter's article, says in his report after the surrender that of the "75 guns in Fort Jackson 4 guns were dismounted and 11 carriages were struck." But this was not done by the mortars alone.

The fleet did its share in the passage. Granting that the injury of 11 gun-carriages permanently disabled 6 guns, the disablement of 10 guns in 75 is scarcely worth considering, with 116 guns in both forts still intact.

Comparing the losses on both sides during the bombardment and the passage of the forts, it will be seen that Farragut's loss, nearly all of which occurred in the passage of the lower defenses on the night of the final attack, was four times the Confederate list of killed and wounded at the forts during the entire siege. Does this look as if Fort Jackson had been disabled by the mortars before the final attack?

Colonel Edward Higgins on the 27th of April says: "Orders had been issued to the officers and men to retire to the casemates of the fort the moment the bombardment began; but when it became necessary to repel the attack our batteries were instantly in readiness and were at once engaged in a most terrific conflict with the enemy."

I have taken no notice in this article of a letter written to Admiral Porter by the above-mentioned Colonel Higgins dated April 4th, 1872, ten years after the occurrence of the events which he professes to describe. This letter is useless as evidence, because it contradicts Colonel Higgins's own report to the Confederate authorities quoted here. Surely the official evidence of a man fresh from the scene of action is to be believed in preference to an account given by him ten years afterward in a letter.

W. T. M.

## THE OPPOSING FORCES IN THE OPERATIONS AT NEW ORLEANS, LA.

The composition, losses, and strength of each force as here stated give the gist of all the data obtainable in the Official Records. K stands for killed; w for wounded; m w for mortally wounded; m for captured or missing; c for captured.

### THE UNION FORCES.

UNION FLEET: West Gulf Blockading Squadron, Flag-Officer D. G. Farragut.

FIRST DIVISION OF GUN-BOATS, Captain Theodorus Bailey.
SECOND DIVISION OF GUN-BOATS, Fleet-Captain Henry H. Bell.

| UNION CASUALTIES. | PRIOR TO THE ACTION OF APR. 24th. Killed. | Wounded. | Total. | DURING THE ACTION OF APR. 24th. Killed. | Wounded. | Total. | Total Casualties. |
|---|---|---|---|---|---|---|---|
| Hartford | .. | 5 | 5 | 3 | 10 | 13 | 18 |
| Brooklyn | .. | .. | .. | 9 | 26 | 35 | 35 |
| Richmond | .. | .. | .. | 2 | 4 | 6 | 6 |
| Pensacola | .. | .. | .. | 4 | 33 | 37 | 37 |
| Mississippi | .. | .. | .. | 2 | 6 | 8 | 8 |
| Oneida | .. | 15 | 15 | .. | 3 | 3 | 18 |
| Varuna | .. | .. | .. | 3 | 9 | 12 | 12 |
| Iroquois | .. | 3 | 3 | 6 | 22 | 28 | 31 |
| Cayuga | .. | .. | .. | .. | 6 | 6 | 6 |
| Itasca | .. | .. | .. | .. | 4 | 4 | 4 |
| Katahdin | 1 | .. | 1 | .. | .. | .. | 1 |
| Kineo | .. | .. | .. | 1 | 8 | 9 | 9 |
| Pinola | .. | .. | .. | 3 | 7 | 10 | 10 |
| Sciota | .. | .. | .. | .. | 2 | 2 | 2 |
| Winona | .. | .. | .. | 3 | 5 | 8 | 8 |
| Portsmouth | .. | .. | .. | .. | 1 | 1 | 1 |
| Harriet Lane | .. | .. | .. | 1 | 1 | 2 | 2 |
| Norfolk Packet | .. | 1 | 1 | .. | .. | .. | 1 |
| Arletta | 1 | .. | 1 | .. | .. | .. | 1 |
| Total | 2 | 24 | 26 | 37 | 147 | 184 | 210 |

FIRST-CLASS SCREW SLOOPS: Flag-ship *Hartford*, Commander Richard Wainwright; *Brooklyn*, Captain Thomas T. Craven; *Richmond*, Commander James Alden; *Pensacola*, Captain Henry W. Morris. Side-wheel steamer: *Mississippi*, Commander Melancton Smith. Second-class screw sloops: *Oneida*, Commander S. Phillips Lee; *Varuna*, Commander Charles S. Boggs; *Iroquois*, Commander John De Camp. Screw gun-boats: *Cayuga*, Lieutenant N. B. Harrison; *Itasca*, Lieutenant C. H. B. Caldwell; *Katahdin*, Lieutenant George H. Preble; *Kennebec*, Lieutenant John H. Russell; *Kineo*, Lieutenant George M. Ransom; *Pinola*, Lieutenant Pierce Crosby; *Sciota*, Lieutenant Edward Donaldson; *Winona*, Lieutenant Edward T. Nichols; *Wissahickon*, Lieutenant A. N. Smith. Sailing sloop (stationed with mortar division): *Portsmouth*, Commander Samuel Swartwout.

MORTAR DIVISION: Commander David D. Porter. Flag-ship: *Harriet Lane*, Lieutenant J. M. Wainwright. Gun-boat: *Owasco*, Lieutenant John Guest. Side-wheel steamers (ferry-boats): *Clifton*, Lieutenant C. H. Baldwin; *John P. Jackson*, Lieutenant Selim E. Woodworth; *Westfield*, Commander W. B. Renshaw. Side-wheel steamer (double-ender): *Miami*, Lieutenant A. D. Harrell. First division of schooners, Lieutenant Watson Smith, commanding: *Norfolk Packet*, Lieutenant Watson Smith; *Oliver H. Lee*, Acting Master Washington Godfrey; *Para*, Acting Master Edward G. Furber; *C. P. Williams*, Acting Master Amos R. Langthorne; *Arletta*,

## ARMAMENTS OF UNION FLEET.

| VESSELS. | 13-in. mortar. | 11-in. S. B. | 10-in. S. B. | 9-in. S. B. | 8-in. S. B. | 32-pdr. S. B. | 100-pdr. R. | 80-pdr. R. | 50-pdr. R. | 30-pdr. R. | 20-pdr. R. | 6-in. Sawyer Rifle, 87 cwt. | Total guns. | HOWITZERS 24-pdr. | HOWITZERS 12-pdr. | HOWITZERS Total. | Total including Howitzers. |
|---|---|---|---|---|---|---|---|---|---|---|---|---|---|---|---|---|---|
| Hartford | | | | 24[1] | | | | | 1 | | | 2 | 26 | | 2 | 2 | 28 |
| Brooklyn | | | | 22 | | | 1 | | 1 | | | | 24 | | 2 | 2 | 26 |
| Richmond | | | | 20 | | | 1 | | 1 | | | | 22 | | | | 22 |
| Pensacola | | 1 | | 20 | | | 1 | 1 | | | | | 23 | | 2 | 2 | 25 |
| Mississippi | | | 1 | | 19[2] | | | | | 3 | | 1 | 21 | | 1 | 1 | 22 |
| Oneida | | 2 | | | 4 | | | | | 2 | | | 9 | | 1 | 1 | 10 |
| Varuna | | | | 8 | | | | | | 2 | | | 10 | | | | 10 |
| Iroquois | | 2 | | 2 | 4 | | | | 1 | | | 14 | 10 | | 1 | 1 | 11 |
| Cayuga | | 1 | | | | | | | 1 | | | | 2 | 2 | | 2 | 4 |
| Itasca | | | 1 | | 2 | | | | | 1 | | | 2 | 2 | | 2 | 4 |
| Katahdin | | 1 | | | | | | | 1 | | | | 2 | 2 | | 2 | 4 |
| Kennebec | | 1 | | | | | | | 1 | | | | 2 | 2 | | 2 | 4 |
| Kineo | | 1 | | | | | | | 2 | | | | 3 | 2 | | 2 | 5 |
| Pinola | | 1 | | | | | | | 1 | | | | 2 | 3[5] | | 3 | 5 |
| Sciota | | 1 | | | | | | | 1 | | | | 2 | 2 | | 2 | 4 |
| Winona | | 1 | | | | | | | 1 | | | | 2 | 2 | | 2 | 4 |
| Wissahickon | | 1 | | | | | | | | | | | | | | | |
| Total | | 13 | 2 | 88 | 27 | 10 | 1 | 3 | 1 | 8 | 12 | 1 | 166 | 17 | 9 | 26 | 192 |

### MORTAR DIVISION.

| VESSELS. | 13-in. mortar. | 11-in. S. B. | 10-in. S. B. | 9-in. S. B. | 8-in. S. B. | 32-pdr. S. B. | 100-pdr. R. | 80-pdr. R. | 50-pdr. R. | 30-pdr. R. | 20-pdr. R. | 6-in. Sawyer Rifle. | Total guns. | HOWITZERS 24-pdr. | HOWITZERS 12-pdr. | HOWITZERS Total. | Total including Howitzers. |
|---|---|---|---|---|---|---|---|---|---|---|---|---|---|---|---|---|---|
| Harriet Lane | | | | 3 | | | | | | | | | 3 | 2 | | 2 | 5 |
| Owasco | | 1 | | | | | | | 1 | | | | 2 | 2 | | 2 | 4 |
| Clifton | | | | 2 | | 4 | | | 1 | | | | 7 | | | | 7 |
| John P. Jackson | | | | 1 | | 4 | | | | | | 1 | 6 | | | | 6 |
| Westfield | | | | 1 | 4 | | 1 | | | | | | 6 | | | | 6 |
| Miami | | | | 2[6] | | | | | 1 | | | | 3 | 4 | | 4 | 7 |
| Portsmouth | | | | | | 16 | | | | | | 1 | 17 | | 1 | 1 | 18 |
| Nineteen Mortar Schooners | 19 | | | | | 38 | | | | | | | 57 | | | | 57 |
| Total mortar division | 19 | 1 | | 9 | 20 | 46 | 1 | 1 | | 1 | 2 | 1 | 101 | 8 | 1 | 9 | 110 |
| Total ships and gun-boats | | 13 | 2 | 88 | 27 | 10 | 1 | 3 | 1 | 8 | 12 | 1 | 166 | 17 | 9 | 26 | 192 |
| Total fleet | 19 | 14 | 2 | 97 | 47 | 56 | 2 | 4 | 1 | 9 | 14 | 2 | 267 | 25 | 10 | 35 | 302 |

NOTES.
[1] 2 of these were transferred from the Colorado.
[2] 14 of these were transferred from the Colorado.
[3] Transferred from the Colorado.
[4] Transferred from the army.
[5] One of these was transferred from the Colorado.
[6] One of these was transferred from the Colorado.

The Colorado supplied altogether:
2 9-inch to the Hartford.
2 9-inch to the Iroquois.
1 9-inch to the Miami.
14 8-inch to the Mississippi.
1 24-pounder howitzer to the Sciota.
—
20 guns.

Acting Master Thomas E. Smith; *William Bacon*, Acting Master William P. Rogers; *Sophronia*, Acting Master Lyman Bartholomew. Second division of schooners, Lieutenant W. W. Queen, commanding: *T. A. Ward*, Lieutenant W. W. Queen; *Maria J. Carlton*, Acting Master Charles E. Jack; *Matthew Vassar*, Acting Master Hugh H. Savage; *George Mangham*, Acting Master John Collins; *Orvetta*, Acting Master Francis E. Blanchard; *Sidney C. Jones*, Acting Master J. D. Graham. Third division of schooners, Lieutenant K. Randolph Breese, commanding: *John Griffith*, Acting Master Henry Brown; *Sarah Bruen*, Acting Master Abraham Christian; *Racer*, Acting Master Alvin Phinney; *Sea Foam*, Acting Master Henry E. Williams; *Henry Janes*, Acting Master Lewis W. Pennington; *Dan Smith*, Acting Master George W. Brown.

UNION ARMY. ☆
Major-General Benjamin F. Butler.
BRIGADE COMMANDERS, Brig.-Gen'ls John W. Phelps and Thomas Williams.
*Infantry:* 9th Conn., Col. Thomas W. Cahill; 12th Conn., Col. Henry C. Deming; 21st Ind., Col. James W. McMillan; 26th Mass., Col. Edward F. Jones; 30th Mass., Col. N. A. M. Dudley; 31st Mass., Col. Oliver P. Gooding; 6th Mich., Col. Frederick W. Curtenius; 4th Wis., Col. Halbert E. Paine. *Cavalry:* 2d Mass. Battalion (2 cos.), Capts. S. Tyler Read and Henry A. Durivage. *Artillery:* 4th Mass. Battery, Capt. Charles H. Manning; 6th Mass. Battery, Capt. Charles Everett; 2d Vt. Battery, Capt. P. E. Holcomb.
The strength of this command is reported at 6000 ("Official Records," Vol. VI., p. 708).

☆ Not engaged.

# OPERATIONS AT NEW ORLEANS, LA.

## THE CONFEDERATE FORCES.

**FORCE AFLOAT** — COMMANDER JOHN K. MITCHELL.

| NAME. | 7-in. R. | 9-in. S. B. | 8-in. S. B. | 32-pdr. S. B. | 32-pdr. | 24-pdr. | 9-pdr. | Howitzers. | Total including Howitzers. |
|---|---|---|---|---|---|---|---|---|---|
| **NAVAL VESSELS.** | | | | | | | | | |
| Louisiana, Comr. Charles F. McIntosh (m w) | | 2 | 3 | 4 | 7 | .. | .. | .. | 16 |
| McRae, Lieut. Thos. B. Huger (m w) | | .. | 1 | .. | .. | 6 | .. | 1[1] | .. | 8 |
| Jackson (at Quarantine), Lieut. F. B. Renshaw | | .. | .. | .. | .. | 2 | .. | .. | .. | 2 |
| Manassas, Lieut. A. F. Warley | | .. | .. | .. | .. | 1[2] | .. | .. | .. | 1 |
| Launch No. 3, Acting Master Telford | | .. | .. | .. | .. | .. | .. | 1 | 1 |
| Launch No. 6, Acting Master Fairbanks | | .. | .. | .. | .. | .. | .. | 1 | 1 |
| **Louisiana State Gun-boats** | | | | | | | | | |
| Governor Moore, Lieut. Beverley Kennon | | .. | .. | .. | 2 | .. | .. | .. | 2 |
| General Quitman, Capt. Alexander Grant | | .. | .. | .. | .. | 2 | .. | .. | .. | 2 |
| **River Defense Boats.** | | | | | | | | | |
| Warrior, Capt. John A. Stephenson | | .. | .. | .. | .. | 1 | .. | .. | .. | 1 |
| Stonewall Jackson, Capt. Geo. W. Philips | | .. | .. | .. | .. | .. | 1 | .. | .. | 1 |
| Defiance, Capt. Joseph D. McCoy | | .. | .. | .. | .. | 1 | .. | .. | .. | 1 |
| Resolute, Capt. Isaac Hooper | | .. | .. | .. | 1 | 1 | .. | .. | .. | 2 |
| General Lovell, Capt. Burdett Paris | | .. | .. | .. | .. | 1 | .. | .. | .. | 1 |
| R. J. Breckinridge, Capt. James Smith | | .. | .. | .. | .. | .. | 1 | .. | .. | 1 |
| **Total** | | 2 | 4 | 4 | 10 | 15 | 2 | 1 | 2 | 40 |

[1] Experimental gun.    [2] Carronade.

UNARMED TUGS. *Landis*, Captain Davis, and *W. Burton*, Captain Hammond (tenders to the *Louisiana*); *Phœnix*, Captain James Brown (tender to the *Manassas*); *Mosher*, Captain Sherman, and *Belle Algerine*, Captain Jackson (k); *Music*, Captain McClellan (tender to the forts); *Star*, Captain Laplace (telegraph boat). The last four were chartered by the army.

Grand total of Confederate guns, 166.

General Lovell reports that the city of New Orleans "was only garrisoned by about 3000 ninety-day troops." The strength of the garrisons of the two forts is stated by Col. Higgins, in his testimony before the Court of Inquiry, as 1100 men. The loss at Forts Jackson and St. Philip was 11 killed and 39 wounded; and at the upper batteries 1 killed and 1 wounded. At Fort Jackson 121 officers and men were surrendered; number at other points not fully reported.

**CONFEDERATE ARMY.**
Major-General Mansfield Lovell.

COAST DEFENSES, Brig.-Gen. Johnson K. Duncan.
FORTS JACKSON AND ST. PHILIP, Lieut.-Col. Edward Higgins.

*Fort Jackson:* La. Scouts and Sharp-shooters, Capt. W. G. Mullen; St. Mary's (La.) Cannoneers, Capt. F. O. Cornay; other company and battery commanders, Capt. James Ryan (detached on the *Louisiana*), Capt. J. B. Anderson (w), Lieut. William M. Bridges, Capt. W. B. Robertson, Capt. R. J. Bruce, Lieut. Eugene W. Baylor, Lieut. A. N. Ogden, Lieut. Beverly C. Kennedy, Lieut. William T. Mumford, Lieut. J. W. Gaines, Capt. S. Jones, Capt. F. Peter, and Lieut. Thomas K. Pierson (k).

*Fort St. Philip,* Capt. M. T. Squires: La. Scouts and Sharp-shooters, Capt. Armand Lartigue; other company and battery commanders, Capt. R. C. Bond, Capt. J. H. Lamon, Lieut. Lewis B. Taylor, Lieut. J. K. Dixon (detached on the *Louisiana*), Lieut. A. J. Quigley, Capt. Charles Assenheimer, and Capt. Massicott. *Quarantine:* Chalmette (La.) Regt., Col. Ignatius Szymanski.

**BATTERIES OF THE FORTS.**

*Fort Jackson.* Barbette: 2 10-inch Columbiads; 3 8-inch Columbiads; 1 7-inch rifle; 2 8-inch mortars; 6 42-pounders; 15 32-pounders, of which 2 were dismounted in the action; 11 24-pounders, of which 2 were dismounted in the action; 1 8-inch howitzer, dismounted; 1 7⅜-inch howitzer. Casemates: 10 24-pounder howitzers (flank); 14 24-pounder guns. Parade: 1 6-pounder; 1 12-pounder howitzer. Water-battery: 1 10-inch Columbiad; 2 8-inch Columbiads; 1 10-inch sea-coast mortar; 2 32-pounders, rifled. Total, 74 guns.

*Fort St. Philip.* On face 8 : 4 8-inch Columbiads. On salient: 1 24-pounder. On covered way: 1 8-inch mortar; 1 10-inch siege mortar; 1 13-inch sea-coast mortar (disabled: bed broke in two at thirteenth round). In upper battery: 16 24-pounders (of the 16, 2 were disabled — 1 broken in two by a shot, and one platform undermined). In lower battery: 9 32-pounders; 6 42-pounders; 1 7-inch rifle (burst by shell exploding in bore); 1 8-inch Columbiad (dismounted); 4 24-pounders. In north-east battery (field-work): 4 10-inch sea-coast mortars. On parade: 1 6-pounder; 1 12-pounder; 1 24-pounder field howitzer. Total, 52 guns.

CHALMETTE AND McGEHEE LINES, Brig.-Gen. Martin L. Smith. *Subordinate Commanders:* Brig.-Gen. Benjamin Buisson, Lieut.-Col William E. Pinkney, Capt. Patton, Lieut-Butler, *et al.*

## RELATIVE STRENGTH OF THE OPPOSING FORCES.

IN a letter to the Editors, Professor J. R. Soley, U. S. N. says: "In discussing the question of the relative force of the two sides (see p. 33), it should be borne in mind that of the Confederate total of 166 guns, 117 were 32-pounders or smaller; while out of the Union total of 302 guns, only 114 were 32-pounders and smaller. In other words, 70 per cent. of the Confederate batteries were 32-pounders or below, while only 37 per cent. of the Union batteries were 32-pounders or below. This difference in the caliber of the guns goes a great way to offset the advantage of fort guns over ship guns, where the ships are trying to reduce the forts. But in this case it was not a question of reducing the forts, but of running by the forts. In such an action the advantage of guns in forts over guns on shipboard may be regarded as very much reduced; indeed, if the passage is open, so that the ships are not kept under fire for a long time (as later at Port Hudson) by natural or artificial obstructions, and especially if made at night, it may be said to be zero.

"On the other hand, the value of the Confederate fleet, at New Orleans, made up as it was chiefly of fast tow-boats, with plated bows, cannot be estimated alone in guns. It was essentially a ram fleet, and, if it had been handled efficiently, might have thrown Farragut's advance into confusion. As Commander Bartlett suggests also, the fire-rafts, with attendant tugs, might have been put to formidable use. This was shown in the case of the *Hartford*. Doubtless the Confederate flotilla, however efficiently handled, would have had hard work to check such an impetuous onset as that of Farragut.

"Out of a nominal total of 14 vessels (9 of them rams and 2 of them iron-clad) and 40 guns, Commander Mitchell had practically only 4 vessels and 12 guns — the *McRae*, *Manassas*, *Governor Moore*, and perhaps the *Stonewall Jackson*. For this Mitchell was in no way responsible. It was due to the delays in completing the *Louisiana*, to the absurd organization of the River Defense Fleet, to the want of seamen, and to the bungling of the civil administration at Richmond. The materials of Mitchell's force, if they had been completed and properly officered and manned, would have made a very pretty force for the purpose; but no commander taking hold of them four days before the fight could have made much out of them."

EDITORS.

# FIGHTING FARRAGUT BELOW NEW ORLEANS.

### BY BEVERLEY KENNON, CAPTAIN, LA. S. N., COMMANDER OF THE "GOVERNOR MOORE."

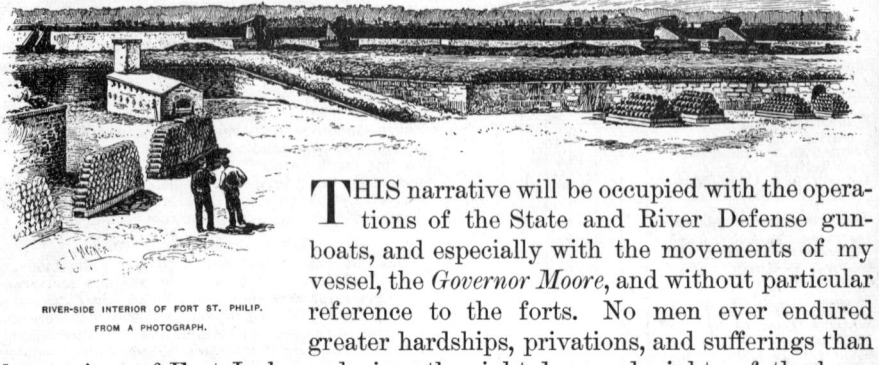

RIVER-SIDE INTERIOR OF FORT ST. PHILIP.
FROM A PHOTOGRAPH.

THIS narrative will be occupied with the operations of the State and River Defense gun-boats, and especially with the movements of my vessel, the *Governor Moore*, and without particular reference to the forts. No men ever endured greater hardships, privations, and sufferings than the garrison of Fort Jackson during the eight days and nights of the bombardment, when more than fourteen hundred 13-inch shells struck within their fort. When the "run by" took place, the garrisons of both forts left no stone unturned to stem the tide of battle, but to no purpose.

Nor shall I refer especially to the *Louisiana, Manassas,* and *McRae,* of the regular C. S. Navy. Of these I saw nothing after the battle began. I did see and do know of the movements of all the other gun-boats, which, to avoid confounding with the regular navy vessels, I will refer to as "rams."

The *Louisiana* was simply an iron floating battery. She was in an unfinished state, and although officered from the regular navy, her crew was composed exclusively of volunteer soldiers, totally unused to ships and the handling of heavy guns. Her ports were too small to admit of the elevation or depression of her guns, thereby almost entirely destroying their efficiency. The responsibility for this was long since placed with Secretary Mallory, who did not order the construction of the *Louisiana* until four months before New Orleans fell, and *after* Stephenson had fashioned that "pigmy monster" the *Manassas*, and in a measure had tested her power. The *Louisiana* was decked over, roofed, iron-plated, armed, and given engines which never propelled her. Commander McIntosh, her "fighting captain," was mortally wounded early in the action, and was succeeded by Lieutenant John Wilkinson, and his brave officers and men did all in their power to beat back the enemy, but to little purpose, as fourteen of the enemy's seventeen vessels passed their vessel and the forts.

The *McRae*, a small vessel mounting a battery of 1 9-inch and 6 32-pounders, lost her commander, T. B. Huger, early in the battle, and as it happened, he was killed by a shot fired from the *Iroquois*, the vessel on which he was serving when he resigned his commission in the United States Navy. He was succeeded by Lieutenant Read, who fought the ship gallantly until the end.

The *Manassas*, commanded by Lieutenant Warley, had previously done good service, and this time came to grief after two hours' fighting, because every ship that neared her selected her thin, half-inch-iron roof and sides for a target. In considering the responsibility for the fall of New Orleans, it should be remembered that Messrs. Benjamin and Mallory were better fitted for the law than to preside over the War and Navy departments of a newly fledged government.

The vessel which I commanded was formerly the ocean-built wooden paddle steamship *Charles Morgan*, of about nine hundred tons, and having a walking-beam engine. When armed by the State of Louisiana, she was named the *Governor Moore*, and received 2 rifled 32-pounders (not banded and not sighted) and a complement of 93 persons. She was not iron-plated in any manner whatever. Her stem was like that of hundreds of other vessels, being faced its length on its edges above water, with two strips of old-fashioned flat railroad iron, held in place by short straps of like kind at the top, at the water-line, and at three intermediate points. These straps extended about two feet abaft the face of the stem, on each side, where they were bolted in place. The other "rams" had their "noses" hardened in like manner. All had the usual-shaped stems. Not one had an iron beak or projecting prow under water. All of them had their boiler-houses, engines, and boilers protected by a bulkhead of cotton bales which extended from the floor of the hold to five feet or more above the spar-deck. These and other such vessels were fitted out by the State and the city of New Orleans after the regular navy neglected to take them, and to Lieutenant-Colonel W. S. Lovell (ex-lieutenant United States Navy) is due the credit of their novel construction.

CAPTAIN BEVERLEY KENNON, LA. S. N., COMMANDER OF THE "GOVERNOR MOORE." FROM A TINTYPE.

Of the other seven "rams" the *General Quitman* was like my ship, but smaller. The remaining six had been tug-boats, and were of wood, with walking-beam engines. Each of them mounted one or two guns, had about 35 men, and measured not far from 150 tons.

These six "rams" were an independent command, and recognized no outside authority unless it suited their convenience; and it was expected that this "fleet" and its branch at Memphis "would defend the upper and lower Mississippi, without aid from the regular navy." We lay at the head of the turn in the river just above the forts, the place of all others for all the Confederate vessels to have been. Here they would have been less liable to be surprised; they would have been clear of the cross-fire from the forts and not exposed to the broadsides of the enemy when passing them, while both guns of each ram could have raked the enemy for over a mile as they approached; they would have been out of the smoke, and would have had extra time to raise steam, to prepare to fire and to ram; moreover, they would have been at a great advantage in ramming, since the advancing vessels

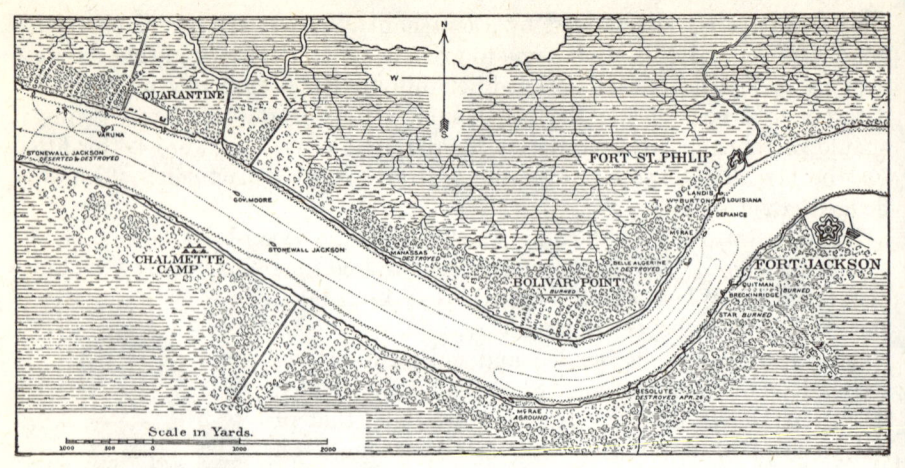

MAP SHOWING FINAL DISPOSITION OF THE CONFEDERATE FLEET. FROM A DRAWING LENT BY COMMANDER J. R. BARTLETT.

1.—The *Governor Moore* ramming the *Varuna*. 2.—The *Stonewall Jackson* ramming the *Varuna*.

would have had to incline to the eastward on reaching them. Not one of them to my knowledge, nor was it ever reported, availed itself of one of these advantages, for when they saw the enemy approaching, those having steam tried to escape, whilst others that did not have it were set afire where they lay, as I myself witnessed. Not one of them made the feeblest offensive or defensive movement, excepting in the case of the *Stonewall Jackson* nearly three hours after, as I shall relate. Had they done their duty simply in firing, what might they not have accomplished! Nearly every United States ship reports firing into them, but not a single one reports having been rammed or fired at by one of them, with the exception of the *Stonewall Jackson* and my ship.

As an act of fairness to the people on board the "rams" who so signally failed to coöperate with the forts and the regular war-ships, I must say it was attributable to their commander, Captain Stephenson. On the purchase by the Confederate Government of the *Manassas* (which was his creation from the tug-boat *Enoch Train*), the command of her was refused him; hence his insubordination and its evil results. None of the men on the rams were wanting in courage. They simply needed competent officers to command, lead, and instruct them, for they were totally "at sea" in their new vocation. After the war, one of them said to me, "If the forts and you fellows could not prevent the enemy from reaching you, how could you expect us with a dozen guns to check their further advance? I saw there was no use risking life for nothing, so I fired the vessel and skipped." The fault rests with those who kept them there. Had regular naval officers, instead of being kept in the mud forts on the creeks in Virginia, and in the woods of the Carolinas cutting timber to build iron-clads, been sent to these vessels, even at the eleventh hour, they would have proven very formidable.

The Confederates had in all thirteen vessels, and but fourteen of Farragut's vessels passed the forts. The former lost a fine opportunity here. Richmond, in the minds of some officials, bore the same relation to the Confederacy that Paris has ever done to France; hence the delay for several months to prepare for the defense of New Orleans, whilst Richmond was being fortified, and the mistake in not sending Commander John K. Mitchell to the "three fleets," near the forts, until three and a half days before the fight, and then with a vessel (the *Louisiana*) which could simply float, but nothing more!

The *Governor Moore*, which was anchored near Fort St. Philip opposite Fort Jackson, could not have been surprised at any time. I slept for the most part only during the day, and but rarely at night. At 8 P. M. four sentinels were always posted on the spar-deck and wheel-houses, and a quartermaster in the pilot-house; an anchor and engine-room watch was set; the chain was unshackled and the fires were banked; both guns were carefully pointed at the opening in the obstructions through which the enemy had to pass to reach us. The vessel being secured as firmly as if at a dock, effective firing of her guns was assured. Every opening in the vessel's side through which a light might be seen was kept closed. At dark the vessel's holds and decks and magazines were brightly lighted to save delay in the event of a sudden call to quarters. Two guns' crews were ready for service, and the officer of the deck and myself were always at hand.

The evening previous to the battle I reported to General Duncan, the commander of the two forts, my observations on the enemy's movements as seen by myself from the mast-head. Yet to my knowledge no picket boat was sent down by us, or any means adopted to watch the enemy and guard against surprise. ┆ The result was they were abreast the forts before some of our vessels fired a shot. In a few moments this space was filled with smoke from the guns and exploded shells, intensifying the darkness of the night. A slackening of the fire on both sides was necessary, since neither could distinguish friend from foe. In some places no object was distinguishable until directly upon it, when it was as soon lost to view, yet the United States squadron steamed ahead, blindfolded, as it were, through the darkness and confusion, soon to find themselves in places of absolute safety and with comparatively few casualties.

At about 3:30 A. M. (April 24th, 1862) an unusual noise down the river attracted my attention. As we expected to be attacked at any moment I descended the ladder to near the water, where I distinctly heard the paddles of a steamer (the *Mississippi*). I saw nothing on reaching the deck, but instantly fired the after gun, the one forward being fired by the sentry there; at the same moment the water-batteries of Fort Jackson and Fort St. Philip let drive, followed in an instant by a general discharge from all the available guns in the forts, and both batteries of the advancing fleet, mounting 192 guns, and Commander Porter's squadron of 7 vessels, mounting 53 guns,

┆ Commander Mitchell, in his testimony before the Confederate Court of Inquiry, states that launch No. 6 was stationed below St. Philip as a guard-boat, but on the enemy's approach deserted her station.—EDITORS.

which attacked Fort Jackson's flank below the obstructions. There was also a splendid practice from 19 Federal mortars, which fired their 13-inch shells at intervals (between the vessels) of 10 seconds.

The bursting of every description of shells quickly following their discharge, increased a hundred-fold the terrific noise and fearfully grand and magnificent pyrotechnic display which centered in a space of about 1200 yards in width. The ball had not more than fairly opened before the enemy's ships were between the forts, and the Uncle Sam of my earlier days had the key to the valley of the Mississippi again in his breeches-pocket, for which he had to thank his gallant navy and the stupidity, tardiness, ignorance, and neglect of the authorities in Richmond.

The first gun fired brought my crew to their stations. We had steam within 3 minutes, it having been ordered by that hour; the cable was slipped, when we delayed a moment for Lieutenant Warley to spring the *Manassas*, then inside of us, across the channel. A little tug-boat, the *Belle Algerine*, now fouled us — to her mortal injury. By the time we started, the space between the forts was filling up with the enemy's vessels, which fired upon us as they approached, giving us grape, canister, and shell. My vessel being a large one, we had too little steam and elbow-room in the now limited and crowded space to gather sufficient headway to strike a mortal blow on ramming. So rather than simply "squeeze" my adversary, I made haste slowly by moving close under the east bank to reach the bend above, where I would be able to turn down-stream ready for work. I took this course also, to avoid being fired and run into by the Confederate rams moored above me; but the ground for this fear was soon removed, as, on getting near them, I saw that one had started for New Orleans, while the telegraph steamer *Star*, ram *Quitman*, and one other had been set afire at their berths on the right bank, and deserted before any of the enemy had reached them, and were burning brightly. They being in a clear space were in full view, and I was close to them. Another reason for leaving our berth directly under Fort St. Philip, where the *Louisiana*, *McRae*, and *Manassas* also lay, was to get clear of the cross-fire of the forts, and that of each ship of the enemy as they passed up close to us, for we sustained considerable damage and losses as we moved out into the stream.

When we were turning at the head of the reach we found ourselves close to the United States steamer *Oneida*, 10 guns, with the United States steamer *Cayuga*, 4 guns, on our port beam. On being hailed with "What ship is that?" I replied, "United States steamer *Mississippi*," to deceive, she being a side-wheel vessel also, but, seeing our distinguishing light, the *Oneida* raked with her starboard broadside at a few feet distance; the *Cayuga* delivered her fire thirty yards distant; the *Pensacola*, 25 guns, a little farther from us, at one fire with shrapnel from the howitzers in her tops cleared out 12 men at our bow-gun. Beyond her the firing of single guns in quick succession, as some vessel, unseen to any one, was moving rapidly up-stream, attracted my attention. At the same instant the United States steamer *Pinola*, 5 guns, close to on our port quarter, delivered her fire,

FIRING AT THE "VARUNA" THROUGH THE BOW OF THE "GOVERNOR MOORE."

killing 5 men in our bunkers. This combined attack killed and wounded a large number of men, and cut the vessel up terribly. Suddenly two, then one Confederate ram darted through the thick smoke from the right to the left bank of the river, passing close to all of us. They missed the channel for New Orleans, grounded on and around the point next above and close to Fort St. Philip; one was fired and deserted, and blew up soon after as we passed her; the others were disabled and were soon after abandoned by their crews. One (the *Resolute*) was taken possession of later by men from the Confederate steamer *McRae*. I do not know what became of the other, the smoke was so dense. All this passed in a few moments. Suddenly I saw between my vessel and the burning *Quitman*, close to us on the west bank, a large, two-masted steamer rushing up-stream like a racer, belching "black smoke," firing on each burning vessel as she passed, and flying her distinguishing white light at the mast-head and red light at the peak. I thought of General Lovell, not far ahead of her on board the passenger steamer *Doubloon*, and quickly made a movement to follow this stranger in the hope of being able to delay or destroy her. Besides, the four or even more large ships so close to us, but obscured from view, needed but a little more room, and one good chance and a fair view of us, quickly to annihilate my old "tinder-box" of a ship. I therefore slipped out in the smoke and darkness around us after the advancing stranger, which proved to be the *Varuna*, Captain Charles S. Boggs, mounting 8 8-inch guns and 2 30-pounder rifles, with a complement of about 200 persons. My whereabouts remained unknown to my former adversaries until all of them came to the *Varuna's* assistance at 6:20 A. M., nine miles above, where she sank, and where parts of her wreck are yet to be seen (1885).

When I started after the *Varuna*, I shot away our blue distinguishing light at the mast-head with a musket, as to have hauled it down would have attracted notice. We could see her, as she was in a clear space, and her lights showed her position. But she soon lost sight of us, for, besides being somewhat in the smoke, there were back of us at this location moderately high trees thickly placed, the spaces filled with a luxuriant undergrowth, making a high dark wall or background on both sides of the river. Until we got clear of this, there was nothing to attract attention toward us, the *Varuna* being half a mile ahead, as shown by her lights. Her engines were working finely and driving her rapidly on her "spurt."⸸ We too, by using oil on our coal, had all the steam we needed. My old ship, shaking all over and fairly dancing through the water, was rapidly lessening the distance between us.

As soon as we reached an open space we hoisted a white light at our mast-head and a red light at the peak. This ruse worked successfully, as the sequel proves. Since our existence depended upon closing with her before she made us out, I urged the men to resist the temptation to fire, and to be quiet and patient, otherwise we would soon be put under water from the effects of her broadsides. We were now one and a half miles from the forts, and one mile from where we gave chase. On our port bow and the *Varuna's* port beam, close under the land, I saw the runaway ram *Stonewall Jackson* making slow progress for want of steam, but working hard to get out of danger. She did not notice us. The *Varuna* could not have seen her or would have fired at her. We soon left the *Stonewall Jackson* astern. Four miles more and we were nearly abreast of Szymanski's regiment at Chalmette camp. Still the *Varuna* had not recognized us. I wanted assistance from that regiment, for I could now see that I had a far superior vessel to mine on my hands. I hoped also for assistance from the ram *Stonewall Jackson*, now a mile or two on our quarter, and from the Confederate States gun-boat *Jackson*, over one mile above us, serving as guard-boat at the quarantine station. To secure all this assistance I had but to show our colors and make ourselves known. The day was just dawning, and there was no smoke about us; so as a bid for help from the sources named, we hauled down the enemy's distinguishing lights and opened fire for the first time upon the *Varuna*, distant about one hundred yards, and with a surprise to her people plainly to be seen. This shot missed her! She replied quickly with one or more guns, when a running fight commenced, she raking us with such guns as she could bring to bear, but not daring the risk of a sheer to deliver her broadside, as we were too close upon her. Her former great superiority was now reduced to a lower figure than that of our two guns, for we, having assumed the offensive, had the advantage and maintained it until she sank.

⸸ Lieutenant C. H. Swasey, of the *Varuna*, remarks in his report upon the slowness of the *Varuna* at this point: "Owing to the small amount of steam we then had (17 pounds), he [Kennon] soon began to come up with us."—EDITORS.

THE "STONEWALL JACKSON" RAMMING THE "VARUNA."

Our hoped-for and expected aid never came from any source. So far from it the gun-boat *Jackson*, lying at quarantine, slipped her cable when the fight commenced, firing two shots at both of us, believing us both enemies (one striking our foremast), and started with all haste for the head-waters of the Mississippi, delaying at New Orleans long enough for her people with their baggage to be landed, when Lieutenant F. B. Renshaw, her commander, burnt her at the levee! The infantry at Chalmette camp could not help us, and the "ram" *Stonewall Jackson*, as it then seemed to us, would not!

Then I saw that we had to fight the *Varuna* alone. On finding our bow gun useless because it was mounted too far abaft the knight-heads to admit of sufficient depression to hull the enemy, then close under our bows, and noting that every shell from the enemy struck us fair, raking the decks, killing former wounded and well men, and wounding others, I realized that something had to be done and that quickly. I then depressed the bow-gun to a point *inside our bow* and fired it, hoping to throw its shell into the engine-room or boiler of the chase. It went through our deck all right but struck the hawse-pipe, was deflected and passed through the *Varuna's* smoke-stack. It was soon fired again through this hole in our bows, the shell striking the *Varuna's* pivot-gun, where it broke or burst, and killed and wounded several men. Until we had finished reloading, the *Varuna* was undecided what to do, when suddenly and to my surprise she ported her helm.

Not wishing to avoid her fire any longer, being quite near to her, we put our helm to port and received the fire from her pivot-gun and rifles in our port bow, but as her shot struck us, under the cover of the smoke our helm was put hard to starboard,— she not righting hers quickly enough,— and before she could recover herself, we rammed her near the starboard gangway, receiving her starboard broadside and delivering our one shot as we struck her.

Her engines stopped suddenly. We backed clear, gathered headway again, and rammed her a second time as near the same place as possible.✠ Before separating, the two vessels dropped alongside each other for a couple of minutes and exchanged musket and pistol shots to some injury to their respective crews, but neither vessel fired a large gun. I expected to be boarded at this time and had had the after gun loaded with a light charge and three stand of canister, and pointed fore and aft ready for either gangway. It was an opportunity for the *Varuna's* two hundred men to make a second Paul Jones of their commander, but it was not embraced. As for ourselves, we had neither the men to board nor to repel boarders. The vessels soon parted, hostilities between them ceased, and the *Varuna* was beached to prevent her sinking in deep water. Then and not until then did the *Varuna's* people know that any other Confederate vessel than mine was within several miles of her. Suddenly the ram *Stonewall Jackson*, having to pass the *Varuna* to reach New Orleans, rammed deep into the latter's port gangway.↓ When close upon her, the *Varuna* delivered such of her port broadside guns as could be brought to bear. The *Stonewall Jackson* backed clear, steamed about four miles up the river, and was beached on the opposite bank, fired, and deserted. Her wreck is there now. Having but one gun, and that mounted aft, she did not fire it. Soon after the *Stonewall Jackson* struck the *Varuna* the latter finished sinking, leaving her topgallant forecastle out of the water, and upon it her crew took refuge.

The United States ships *Oneida, Iroquois,* ▷*Pensacola, Pinola,* ◁ and *Cayuga* were now rapidly approaching and near at hand. I started down-stream to meet and try to ram one of them. On passing abreast the *Varuna* some thoughtless man, knowing her forecastle rifle was loaded, fired it and killed and wounded five of our men, one officer included. Had I returned the fire with our after gun, which was loaded with canister, at the crowd of people closely packed upon and near that little shelf, the damage to life and limb would have been fearful. But not a shot did we fire at her after she was disabled.

We had proceeded down-stream but a short distance when Mr. Duke, the first lieutenant, then at the conn,⸸ where, though wounded, he had remained throughout the fight doing his duty like a brave man, exclaimed, "Why do this? We have no men left; I'll be —— if I stand here to be murdered," so he slapped the helm hard-a-starboard. As we came round, the enemy's ships, being near, fired a shower of heavy projectiles which struck the vessel in every part. One gun was dismounted. The boats had already been destroyed. The wheel-ropes, the head of the rudder, the slide of the engine, and a large piece of the walking-beam were shot away; the latter fell on the cylinder-

---

✠ The first instance of a wooden vessel ramming her adversary in battle as her principal means of offensive-defensive action.— B. K.

↓ Commander Boggs and Lieutenant Swasey, of the *Varuna*, and Captain Philips, commanding the *Stonewall Jackson*, agree in saying that the *Stonewall Jackson* rammed the *Varuna* while she was afloat, and that it was *in consequence* of this blow that the *Varuna* was disabled and beached. Boggs says both vessels rammed the *Varuna* twice.— EDITORS.

▷ As the *Iroquois* and *Pinola* were the last vessels to pass the forts, it is difficult to see how they could have been up with the other three vessels at this time.— EDITORS.

⸸ The person who stands at the compass in a man-of-war, to see that the correct course is steered, is "at the conn."— EDITORS.

THE "PENSACOLA" DISABLING THE "GOVERNOR MOORE."

Captain H. W. Morris of the *Pensacola* says, in his report: "The ram [*Governor Moore*], after having struck the *Varuna* gun-boat, and forced her to run on shore to prevent sinking, advanced to attack this ship, coming down on us right ahead. She was perceived by Lieutenant F. A. Roe just in time to avoid her by sheering the ship, and she passed close on our starboard side, receiving, as she went by, a broadside from us." Until I read this, I thought the vessel that did us most damage was the *Oneida*, the other vessels being astern of her. Captain Lee of the *Oneida* in his report speaks of firing into the *Governor Moore*.— B. K.

head and cracked it and filled the engine-room with steam, driving every man out of it. The head of the jib was now hoisted, and with a strong current on the port bow, assisted by the headway left on the vessel, we succeeded in reaching the river-bank just above the *Varuna's* wreck, where the anchor was let go to prevent drifting into deep water to sink, the last heavy firing having struck the vessel on and under her water-line. At this place she was destroyed by fire, her colors burning at her peak. The vessel was not disabled until this last attack upon her, although much cut up. By it no one on the *Governor Moore* outside the cotton bulkhead protection to the engine, excepting those in the magazine and shell-room, escaped being struck by shot, bullets, or splinters. Additional men were killed, several more of the wounded were killed, and others wounded. It should be remembered that my vessel had been under a terrific fire for 3 hours, in a narrow river with unruffled surface, and at close quarters, from vessels [the *Oneida*, *Cayuga*, *Pensacola*, and *Varuna*] mounting in the aggregate over 30 of the heaviest guns afloat. Out of 93 all told we lost 57 killed and 17 wounded, of whom 4 died in the hospital.☆

Twenty-four years have now passed without any Confederate account of this fight being made public. Now that "the fictions of hastily compiled histories of partisan writers" are being corrected, I add my mite as an act of justice to all interested, and to the gallant dead and those living, of the *Governor Moore*.↲

The burning of my ship has ever been a source of regret to me, as it was done by my order, and by me individually, simply because I did not wish to

☆ My officers were merchant mates, so were the quartermasters; the gunner had been to sea as a sailor on a man-of-war. My crew consisted of artillery and infantry detachments, and of 'longshoremen, cotton-pressers, and river boatmen.— B. K.

↲ When the *Governor Moore* was destroyed she was four miles from any Confederate vessel under water, and nine miles from any on the water, and surrounded on the water front by five United States ships.— B. K.

surrender her. Finding that the boats of the United States ships were picking up the *Varuna's* people, I ordered the uninjured of my crew to assist our wounded to our boat, and to the shore. Many took hold, others did not. I saw several wounded men landed. I aided several to leave the vessel, and called to men then standing in the water to help them, which they did. I placed life-preservers on others. One man who was wounded in the arm was afraid to jump; he had on two life-preservers. I shoved him overboard and saw him assisted to the shore. When the boats reached the ship I tried to save my servant, he having had his leg shot clean off; but we had to leave him, because on moving him to the gangway his body broke open near the shattered thigh. These two cases, in part, led to my being put in solitary confinement on board the *Colorado*, and in close confinement on board the *Rhode Island*, and at Fort Warren—in all, three months. Some one had reported that "I had killed my steward because he had failed to call me at 3 o'clock in the morning, and that then I had thrown his half-dead body overboard." I did not depend upon any one to call me. Moreover, the steward and his eight-year-old boy, who was on a visit to him (and who was to have returned on the steamer *Doubloon*), being in the magazine, were not touched. They were made prisoners.

I set fire to the ladders leading to the magazine and shell-room, first pouring oil over them and over clothing hanging in some of the state-rooms to insure the ship's destruction. I went then to the gangway, expecting to find what remained of one of our boats, into which I had ordered Lieutenants Haynes and Henderson (both wounded slightly) to place such of the wounded as were unable to move themselves. I found those two had taken it *alone*, and left the vessel. As they were quite near, I "persuaded" the return of the boat, which the latter brought back, the former jumping overboard and being picked up by the *Oneida's* boat. He was taken to Fort Warren. Into our boat I was preparing to lower some wounded men when the boats of the squadron came alongside, and took them and myself off the burning ship. When I

THE "GOVERNOR MOORE," AT THE END OF THE FIGHT.

THE "GOVERNOR MOORE" IN FLAMES.

The Union ships in their order, beginning with the left, are the *Oneida*, the *Pinola*, the sunken *Varuna*, the *Iroquois*, and, in the foreground, the *Pensacola*. [See note concerning the *Pinola* and the *Iroquois*, p. 84.] — EDITORS.

went to the gangway to see if any wounded had been placed in our boat, for I expected the boilers and the magazines to explode at any moment, I found the wounded men referred to, in the gangway. They said, "Captain, we stood by you; do not desert us now." I told them I would not, and I remained with them until they left the vessel, and then I left in the *Oneida's* boat, and not half a second too soon. I was too much bruised to help any one overmuch, but I did all I could. Had no uninjured man left the vessel until the wounded had been cared for, I could have escaped capture, like Lieutenants Duke and Frame and the purser, the two former being wounded.

When the *Oneida's* boat approached the *Governor Moore*, one of its crew recognized me. The officer of the boat wished to know if there was danger of an explosion. I replied, "You surely can come where I can stay; come and take off these wounded men." In a moment it was done. One of the boat's crew asked, pointing to a room close by, "Is that your trunk?" I no sooner said it was than he had it in the boat.

We soon reached the *Oneida*, whose captain, S. P. Lee, having known me from a child, received me kindly and entertained me most hospitably. The wounded of my vessel were attentively cared for on the *Oneida* and other United States ships. They ultimately went to the city hospital. The uninjured prisoners of my crew (eighteen men) were transferred to the *Hartford*, where I saw them. I do not think any of my wounded were burned. If they were, it was because they were stowed out of sight, and I was left alone (as is well known) to care for them.

As to the fate of the thirteen Confederate vessels, Commander Porter in his official report states that "the *Louisiana, McRae*, and ram *Defiance*, with the *Burton* and *Landis*, both river passenger boats, which had been used by the *Louisiana*, close to which they lay, to berth her officers and crew, were still at the forts flying their colors two days after the battle." The *Jackson*, 2 guns, escaped before daylight to New Orleans from Quarantine Station, 6 miles above the forts, without being seen by any other United States vessel than the *Varuna*. The *Manassas*, disabled by the *Mississippi*, aided by other vessels, was destroyed by her commander, who swam to the *Louisiana* with his crew and was made prisoner with her people two days after. The *Stonewall Jackson*, seen in the distance only, excepting by the *Varuna's* and *Governor Moore's* people, was destroyed by her officers about 13 miles above the forts, and out of gun-shot of the enemy; and my ship was destroyed by my own hand about 9 miles above them. The *Quitman* and another gun-boat, with the telegraph steamer *Star*, were fired on the report of the first gun. They were blazing when my ship reached them. I have already described the fate of the *Resolute* and one other ram. The passenger boat *Doubloon* reached New Orleans all right. My vessel ran over the little tug *Belle Algerine*. The *Mosher* was destroyed when taking a fire-raft alongside the *Hartford*. Of the little tug *Music* and three of the rams I know nothing beyond seeing them burn and explode their magazines after being deserted.

My old classmates and messmates among the officers, and shipmates among the crews of the United States ships at New Orleans, treated me with great kindness. To mention a few, Captain Lee shared his cabin with me; Lieutenant J. S. Thornton gave me his room on board the *Hartford*, and with Lieutenant Albert Kautz made it possible for me to extend some hospitality to friends who called upon me. Lieutenant-Commanding Crosby on receiving me on board the *Pinola* gave me the freedom of the cabin. When taking me to the *Colorado* Lieutenants Kidder Breese and Phil Johnson, both my classmates, came with offers of money and clothes, as did Acting Master Furber. When on board the *Oneida*, anchored close to the levee at the city, I slept from choice under a shelter aft — not a poop deck exactly — which was under the orderly's eye. Near daylight something called him away. An old sailor who had been on several ships with me, and who by my evidence in his favor was once rescued from much discomfort and trouble, suddenly jumped to my cot, saying, "The preparations are made, lose no time, out of the port by the line there ready for you," and, handing a paper inclosing several gold pieces, was off as suddenly as he came. I watched my opportunity and returned his money to him rolled up in a tobacco wrapper, saying in as few words as possible why I would not betray the confidence placed in me.

When General Butler came on board the *Cayuga* he asked of Lieutenant-Commanding Harrison, pointing with his thumb over his shoulder at me as he walked aft, "Where did you catch him?" Loud enough for Butler to hear I replied, "Where you were not on hand, or your army either."

I was to have been paroled, but the burning of my vessel and the reported killing of the steward and reported burning of my wounded, changed my destination to Fort Warren, where, although I was denied the freedom enjoyed by the other prisoners, I was treated with much consideration by Colonel Justin Dimick, who made fast friends of every prisoner under his charge for his kindness to them.

The war has long been over with me, and the most "uncompromising" on both sides must acknowledge the creation of a new, richer, happier, and better South and mightier common country as the result of the unhappy strife.

My old antagonists have ever been kind to me, and to many others of their old ante-bellum companions and friends. In 1867 a Union man gave me the command of a vessel he owned. In 1868 a Boston company offered me the position of first mate of one of their new iron steamships. In 1869 the colonel of a New York regiment and a rear-admiral of the United States Navy secured my appointment as Colonel of Coast Defenses in the Egyptian Army; and I am now holding positions for which I was recommended by an officer whose ship fought mine below New Orleans.

ENTRANCE TO FORT ST. PHILIP. FROM A PHOTOGRAPH TAKEN IN 1884.

## THE RAM "MANASSAS" AT THE PASSAGE OF THE NEW ORLEANS FORTS.

BY A. F. WARLEY, CAPTAIN, C. S. N.

JUST after the war I thought "bygones" had better be "bygones" and the stirring up of bitter memories was a thing to be avoided; now that so many years have passed, it seems to me almost impossible for one who was observant, and had good opportunities to observe, to tell all he believed he witnessed without in some way reflecting upon one or another of those in position who have gone to their rest and are no longer able to meet criticism.

But from the day of the veracious historian Pollard to the present one of Captain Kennon, no mention has been made of the vessel under my command on the night Admiral Farragut passed "the Forts," except in slighting, sneering, or untruthful statements.

There are only a few of those who were with me left, and I think it due to them and to the memory of those gone that I tell in as few words as I can what the *Manassas* did on the night in question.

The *Manassas* was made fast to the bank on the Fort St. Philip side above the forts, and had alongside of her a heavy steam-tug to enable her to be turned promptly down the river. On the evening before the attack I went on board of the Confederate steamer *McRae*, carrying some letters to put in the hands of my friend Captain Huger, and found him just starting to call on me, on the same errand. Both of us — judging from the character of the officers in the enemy's fleet, most of whom we knew — believed the attack was at hand, and neither of us expected support from the vessels that had been sent down to help oppose the fleet.

Before night all necessary orders had been given, and when at 3:30 A. M. the flash of the first gun was seen on the river below the forts, the *Manassas* was cut away from the bank, turned downstream, cast off from the tug, and was steaming down to the fleet in quicker time than I had believed to be possible.

The first vessel seen was one of the armed Confederate steamers. She dashed up the river, passing only a few feet from me, and no notice was taken of my hail and request for her to join me. The next vessel that loomed up was the United States steamer *Mississippi*. She was slanting across the river when the *Manassas* was run into her starboard quarter, our little gun being fired at short range through her cabin or ward-room. What injury she received must be told by *her* people. She fired over the *Manassas*, tore away, and went into the dark. While this was going on other vessels no doubt passed up, but the first I saw was a large ship (since known to have been the *Pensacola*). As the *Manassas* dashed at her quarter, she shifted her helm, avoided the collision beautifully, and fired her stern pivot-gun close into our faces, cutting away the flag-staff.

By that time the *Manassas* was getting between the forts, and I told Captain Levin, the pilot, that we could do nothing with the vessels which had passed, but we could go down to the mortar-fleet; but no sooner had we got in *seeing range* than both forts opened on us, Fort Jackson striking the vessel several times on the bend with the lighter guns. I knew the vessel must be sunk if once under the 10-inch guns, so I turned up the river again, and very soon saw a large ship, the *Hartford* ☆ [meaning the *Brooklyn*], lying across-stream. As

I was not fired upon by her I thought then that her crew were busy fending off what I think now to have been a burning pile-driver, and could not see the *Manassas* coming out of the dark. The *Manassas* was driven at her with everything open, resin being piled into the furnaces. The gun was discharged when close on board. We struck her fairly amidship; the gun recoiled and turned over and remained there, the boiler started, slightly jamming the Chief Engineer, Dearning, but settled back as the vessel backed off. Just then another steamer came up through the fire of the forts. I thought her the *Iroquois*, and tried to run into her, but she passed as if the *Manassas* had been at anchor.

Steaming slowly up the river,— very slow was our best,— we discovered the Confederate States steamer *McRae*, head up-stream, receiving the fire of three men-of-war. As the *Manassas* forged by, the three men-of-war steamed up the river, and were followed, to allow the *McRae* to turn and get down to the forts, as she was very badly used up.

Day was getting broader, and with the first ray of the sun we saw the fleet above us; and a splendid sight it was, or rather would have been under other circumstances. Signals were being rapidly exchanged, and two men-of-war steamed down, one on either side of the river. The *Manassas* was helpless. She had nothing to fight with, and no speed to run with. I ordered her to be run into the

---

☆ Professor J. Russell Soley, U. S. N., in a communication to the Editors, gives the following discussion of the question, Did the *Manassas* ram the *Hartford* at the battle of New Orleans? "In the affirmative is the following testimony: (1) 'Captain Kautz, a lieutenant on board the *Hartford*, says that immediately after the *Hartford* went ashore she was struck by the fire-raft which was pushed up by the tug *Mosher*, and immediately after that event the *Manassas* struck her and turned her round so that she slid off the shoal. (2) Lieutenant Warley, commanding the *Manassas*, states that she struck the *Hartford*. He does not state that she struck the *Brooklyn*.' In the negative is the following testimony: (1) Admiral Farragut makes no mention of being struck by a ram. His report says: 'I discovered a fire-raft coming down upon us, and in attempting to avoid it ran the ship on shore, and the ram *Manassas*, which I had not seen, lay on the opposite side of it and pushed it down upon us.' Farragut evidently mistook the *Mosher* for the *Manassas*, as it is a well-established fact that the *Mosher* shoved the raft against the *Hartford*. (2) Commander Richard Wainwright, commanding the *Hartford*, makes no mention in his detailed report of having been struck by any ram. He describes the incident of the fire-raft thus: 'At 4:15 grounded on shoal near Fort St. Philip, in the endeavor to clear a fire-raft which was propelled by a ram on our port quarter, setting fire to the ship.' Wainwright also makes the mistake of calling the *Mosher* a ram, but this only bears out the general opinion among the Union officers as to the character of all the Confederate vessels. (3) The report of James H. Conley, carpenter of the *Hartford*, stating in detail the damages sustained by the ship in the action, makes no mention of any injury which could have been inflicted by a ram. (4) It seems impossible that the *Manassas* should have struck such a blow to the *Hartford* as Warley describes and have left no traceable injury. (5) It is exceedingly improbable that the *Manassas* would have struck the *Hartford* under such advantageous circumstances as Captain Kautz describes (when the *Hartford* was ashore) and have had no effect other than to turn the *Hartford* round so that she slid off the shoal. (6) Commander Watson informs me that he thinks it is a mistake to suppose that the *Manassas* touched the *Hartford* at any time. He goes on to say: 'Farragut thought it was the *Manassas* which pushed the fire-raft against the *Hartford's* port side, while the Confederate reports state that this was done by a certain tug-boat. The admiral never, to my knowledge, entertained the idea that such a blow' as the *Manassas* is supposed to have given 'would have released the *Hartford's* bow. I believe he ascribed her release to the backing of the screw as I did; I always understood him that way.' (7) Mr. Herbert B. Tyson says, in a recent letter (Mr. Tyson was a midshipman and the navigator of the *Hartford* at this time, but has since left the service): 'I am satisfied the *Hartford* was never rammed at the battle of New Orleans. The nearest approach to her being rammed was when a Confederate craft pushed a fire-raft under her port quarter while she was aground under Fort St. Philip.' (8) Lieutenant Warley mentions only one vessel rammed by him in this way, and his description certainly answers for what happened in the attack on the *Brooklyn*. (9) In reference to the *Brooklyn* there is no possible question. Captain Craven's and Commander Bartlett's testimony is absolutely conclusive. (10) Commander A. T. Mahan, U. S. N., in his book, 'The Gulf and Inland Waters' [pp. 76 and 77], does not mention any ramming of the *Hartford* by the *Manassas*. His statements are such that if he had supposed the *Manassas* rammed the *Hartford* he could not have omitted it. He says of the *Hartford*: 'She took the ground close under St. Philip, the raft lying on her port quarter, against which it was pushed by the tug *Mosher*,' adding in a foot-note, 'As this feat has been usually ascribed to the *Manassas*, it may be well to say that the statement in the text rests on the testimony of the commander of the ram, as well as other evidence.' He closes his description of this episode by saying: 'Then working herself clear, the *Hartford* passed from under their fire.' Finally he gives a minute description of the ramming of the *Brooklyn* by the *Manassas*."

NOTE.— Captain Warley, since the appearance of the first edition, writes to say that his conviction that the *Manassas* struck the *Hartford* was based upon an incorrect reading of a letter from Captain Mahan.

EDITORS.

bank on the Fort St. Philip side, her delivery-pipes to be cut, and the crew to be sent into the swamp through the elongated port forward, through which the gun had been used. The first officer, gallant Frank Harris, reported all the men on shore. We examined the vessel, found all orders had been obeyed, and we also took to the swamp.

I think our two attendants ran into each other. Harris said such was the case. At any rate I soon heard heavy firing,— some for our benefit, but most, I think, for the abandoned *Manassas*. I heard afterward that she was boarded, but, filling astern, floated off, on fire, and blew up somewhere below in the neighborhood of the mortar-fleet.

I have confined my remarks to the *Manassas*, and it is just that I should tell what the *Manassas* was,— a tow-boat *boarded* over with five-inch timber and armored with one thickness of flat railroad iron, with a complement of thirty-four persons and an armament of one light carronade and four double-barreled guns. She was very slow. I do not think she made at any time that night more than five miles an hour.

NEW ORLEANS, July 30th, 1886.

If on that occasion she was made to do less than she should have done, if she omitted any possible chance of putting greater obstructions in the track of the fleet, the fault was mine,— for I was trammeled by no orders from superior authority; I labored under no difficulty of divided counsel; I had not to guard against possible disaffection or be jealous about obedience to my orders.

I have finished, having endeavored to avoid personality even to omitting much in praise I could say of brother officers in the same fight, but not in any way connected with the *Manassas*.

Captain Squires, who commanded Fort St. Philip, informed me that his fort had fired seventy-five times at the *Manassas*, mistaking her for a disabled vessel of the enemy's floating down-stream. The *Manassas* was not struck once by Fort St. Philip.

The following are the only officers living, as far as I know, who were with me on the night referred to: Engineers George W. Weaver and T. A. Menzies, and Pilots Robert Levin and Robert Wilson.

## INCIDENTS OF THE OCCUPATION OF NEW ORLEANS.

### BY ALBERT KAUTZ, CAPTAIN, U. S. N.

AT 1 o'clock P. M. of the 25th of April, 1862, Farragut's squadron, having completed its memorable passage of Forts Jackson and St. Philip, and having silenced the Chalmette batteries, anchored in front of the city of New Orleans in a drenching rain.

Captain Theodorus Bailey, being second in command, claimed the privilege of carrying ashore the demand for the surrender of the city.

THE MAINTOP OF THE "HARTFORD," WITH HOWITZER.

This was accorded him by the flag-officer, and the captain, accompanied by Lieutenant George H. Perkins (now captain), at once proceeded to the City Hall. Mayor Monroe took the ground that as General Lovell had not yet left the city, the demand should be made on him. At the captain's request the mayor sent for the general, who in a few moments appeared with his staff. General Lovell said he would not surrender the city, adding that he had already withdrawn his soldiers, and that at the close of the interview he intended to join his command. Captain Bailey had to return and report to Farragut that there was no one on shore willing to surrender the city. Two or three gentlemen had accompanied Captain Bailey and Lieutenant Perkins to the City Hall, and after the interview Colonel W. S. Lovell and one other of the general's staff escorted them to the landing.

The mob, overawed by the frowning batteries of the ships, really seemed dazed and did not offer to assault the Union officers. On the following morning, however, the people in the streets began to wonder whether anything more was going to be done, and became more violent and boisterous.

Farragut determined to make a formal demand for the surrender on Mayor Monroe, and at 10 o'clock on the morning of the 26th he sent me ashore, with instructions to deliver the official demand to the mayor. My little force on leaving the *Hartford* consisted of Midshipman John H. Read and a marine guard of twenty men under command of Second Lieutenant George Heisler. We landed on the levee in front of a howling mob, which thronged the river-front as far as the eye could reach. It was expected that I would take the marines with me to the City Hall, as a body-guard, and Farragut informed me that if a shot was fired at us by the mob, he would open fire from all the ships and level the town. The marines were drawn up in line, and I attempted to reason with the mob, but soon found this impossible. I then thought to clear the way by bringing the marines to an aim, but women and children were shoved to the front, while the angry mob behind them shouted: "Shoot, you ——

CAPTAIN THEODORUS BAILEY AND LIEUTENANT GEORGE H. PERKINS ON THEIR WAY TO DEMAND THE SURRENDER OF NEW ORLEANS.

Yankees, shoot!" The provocation was certainly very great, and nothing but the utter absence of respectability in the faces of the people caused me to refrain from giving the order to fire.

Fortunately at this critical moment I discovered an officer of the City Guards, whom I hailed and told that I wished to communicate with the mayor. He begged me to leave the marines on the levee, for he felt sure that to march them through the streets at this time would provoke a conflict. As my object was to communicate with the mayor without unnecessary shedding of blood, I sent the marine guard back to the ship, retaining only one non-commissioned officer, with a musket.

I tied my handkerchief on the bayonet, and with Midshipman Read and this man took up the march for the City Hall. We were cursed and jostled by the mob which filled the streets, but no actual violence was offered us. We found the mayor in the City Hall with his council. The Hon. Pierre Soulé was also there, having doubtless been called in as an adviser. The mayor declined to surrender the city formally, but said as we had the force we could take possession.

While we were in the City Hall a mob came up from the lower part of the city with an American ensign, and when they saw us they tore the flag to shreds and threw them into the open window at us. I did not comprehend the meaning of this singular and wild demonstration at the time, but afterward learned that on the morning of this same day Farragut had instructed Captain H. W. Morris of the *Pensacola*, then at anchor abreast of the United States Mint, to hoist a flag on that building, it being United States property. Captain Morris accordingly sent Lieutenant Stillwell with some officers and men from the ship, and the flag was hoisted. It was up only a short time when Mumford hauled it down. It was seized by the mob, which paraded it through the streets with fife and drum until they reached the City Hall, where it was destroyed, as above described. I afterward happened to be present when Farragut reported the hauling down of this flag to General Butler, and I heard the latter say, "I will make an example of that fellow by hanging him." Farragut smiled and remarked, "You know, General, you will have to catch him before you can hang him." General Butler said, "I know that, but I will catch him, and then hang him." History attests how well he kept his word, and there is no doubt but that this hanging proved a wholesome lesson.

The mob soon appeared to be growing more violent, and above the general din was heard an occasional invitation to "the —— Yankees" to "come out and be run up to lamp-posts." At this time Mr. Soulé suggested to me that it would save much trouble to all concerned if I would take my party in a carriage from the rear exit of the hall, the mayor's secretary, Mr. Marion Baker, going with us, while he addressed the mob. He did not hope to have the mob obey him, he only expected to hold it long enough to give us time to get to the landing; and he accomplished his undertaking admirably. Few people ever knew what an important service Mr. Soulé thus rendered to New Orleans.

Farragut fully approved my action. I was not expected to bring a satisfactory answer from the mayor, for he was really helpless and had no control over the city. All he could say was, "Come and take the city; we are powerless."

The 27th and 28th passed in rather a fruitless negotiation, but time did an important work. The mob tired itself out, and no longer threatened such violence as on the 26th.

On the 29th Farragut decided that the time had come for him to take formal possession of the city; he felt that this was a duty he owed to the navy, and he accordingly sent an expedition on shore under command of Fleet Captain H. H. Bell, and of this party I was second in command. I had a detachment of sailors and two boat-howitzers, and was assisted by Midshipmen John H. Read and E. C. Hazeltine. ‡ A battalion of marines made part of our expedition; this was under the command of Captain John L. Broome. We landed at the foot of Canal street and proceeded to a position in front of the Custom-house, where the marines were drawn up in line, with loaded pieces, and flanked by the howitzers loaded with shrapnel. The people made no demonstration, but looked on in sullen silence. Captain Bell and I, with a boatswain's mate carrying our ensign, entered the Custom-house, where the postmaster received us cordially, remarking, "Thank God that you are here. I have been a Union man all the time. I was appointed by Buchanan, not by Jeff Davis; he only allowed me to remain." The postmaster showed us to the roof of the building, where we found a flag-staff with halliards. The boatswain's mate bent on the flag and I reported all ready, when Captain Bell gave the order, "Hoist away!" and the boatswain's mate and I put our hands to the halliards, and "the Stars and Stripes rose into the sky and swelled on the breeze." A guard with the lieutenant of marines was left in charge of the flag at the Custom-house, and the landing party moved on to the City Hall, the crowd increasing as that small body of Union men approached the "State flag." There the marines were again drawn up in line, and the howitzers commanded the streets; thousands of spectators filled the open spaces. That immense assemblage had the will to annihilate the small force of sailors and marines, but they had begun to think, and the impression that resistance to United States authority would invoke the wrath of the squadron had gone abroad; still no one knew but that one or two desperate men were ready to fire the train that would lead to the magazine.

Captain Bell gave Mayor Monroe the privilege of hauling down the State flag, but he indignantly declined. Captain Bell then directed me to go to the roof of the building and haul the flag down, he remaining on the top floor at the foot of the ladder. An ordinary ladder led to the roof, through a small covered hatchway. The boatswain's mate ascended first, shoved the hatch cover to one side, and gained the roof. I followed him, and finding the halliards knotted, I drew my sword and cut them; we then hauled the flag down, took it to the floor below and handed it to Captain Bell, who on our return to the ship delivered it to Farragut. Before we ascended to the roof, the mayor informed Captain Bell, in the presence of his officers, that the men who attempted to haul down the flag might be shot by

---

| Of the occurrences of the 28th, Captain H. H. Bell says in his diary: "Apr. 28th, Delivered Flag-Officer's letter to the Mayor and Council, who in an address from the Mayor repeated all that was in their letters to [the] Flag-Officer, and nothing more; only wanting me to explain the last clause of Flag-Officer's last letter to them. I replied that I could say nothing that could add to or take away from the clause in question — that the language was very clear. It was suggested that the populace in front of the hall was violent, and that they would furnish me a guard for escort to boat, which I respectfully declined as unnecessary. They then ordered a hack, and, accompanied by Chief of Police McClelland, and Mayor's Clerk, and Master Tyson, U. S. N., passing out through a private way, drove to the landing without meeting mob. Mr. Soulé was present and seated on the right hand of Mayor — the only man seated in the chamber. Their countenances expressed consternation. They repeated that 'the man lived not in the city who dared to haul down the flag from over the City Hall.' The people — boys generally — were perfectly quiet until near the City Hall, when they began to give vent to their feelings by 'Hurrah for Jeff Davis!' 'Hurrah for Beauregard!' and the use of some angry language." — EDITORS.

‡ It is a strange fact that the three officers of the line with whom I went on shore on this occasion were all afterward drowned. Bell, who was then rear-admiral, and Read, who was lieutenant-commander, were swamped in a boat while going ashore from the *Hartford*, at Osaka, Japan, and Hazeltine as an ensign went down in the *Housatonic*. — A. K.

SCENE AT THE CITY HALL — HAULING DOWN THE STATE FLAG.

The local papers spoke of the State flag on the City Hall at the time as the "Lone Star flag." General Beauregard, in a letter to Admiral Preble, in 1872, says this flag was adopted in 1861 by the State Convention of Louisiana. It had thirteen stripes, four blue, six white, and three red, commencing at the top, with the colors as written. The Union was red, with its sides equal to the width of seven stripes. In its center was a single pale-yellow five-pointed star.— A. K.

the indignant populace assembled on the surrounding house-tops, and he expressed his fears in the hope that he would not be held responsible for the act, in case it should be perpetrated. Fortunately for the peace of the city of New Orleans, the vast crowd looked on in sullen silence as the flag came down. There was no flag hoisted on the City Hall in place of the State flag, for the reason that it had not covered United States property. The mission of the landing party having been accomplished, the officers and men returned to the levee in marching order, where they took boats for their respective vessels. The flag on the Custom-house was guarded by the marines of the *Hartford*, until the arrival of General Butler with his troops [May 1st].

On the morning of May 2d Farragut sent me with the keys of the Custom-house to the St. Charles Hotel, where I delivered them to General Butler, remarking as I did so, "General, I fear you are going to have rather a lawless party to govern, from what I have seen in the past three or four days." The general replied, "No doubt of that, but I think I understand these people, and can govern them." The general took the reins in his hands at once, and held them until December 23d, 1862, when he was relieved of the command of the Department of the Gulf by General N. P. Banks.

## FARRAGUT'S DEMANDS FOR THE SURRENDER OF NEW ORLEANS.

### BY MARION A. BAKER, THE MAYOR'S PRIVATE SECRETARY.

ON the morning of the 25th of April, 1862, there being no longer any doubt as to the approach of the Federal fleet, Mayor Monroe determined to hoist the flag of Louisiana over the City Hall. At his request, I ascended to the roof of the building prepared to execute his design, but with instructions to await the issue of the possible contest at Chalmette, some four miles below the center of the city where our last line of defense was established. I waited accordingly with the flag bent on to the halliards, and my gaze fixed eagerly upon the approaching steamers. Suddenly quick flashes leaping from their dark sides indicated that they were abreast of the redoubts, but their fire was delivered without check to their speed, and in hardly more time than I take to tell of it, they were dark and silent once more.

I reported to Mr. Monroe, who was standing in the street below, that it was all over, and at a signal from him I ran up the flag whose lowering was to be the occasion of so much angry controversy.

There was now nothing left to do but to wait and speculate upon the probable course of the enemy, and we were not long kept in suspense. At half-past 1 came two officers, wearing the uniform of the United States Navy. Mr. Monroe received them courteously and presented them to the Hon. Pierre Soulé and a number of other gentlemen who chanced to be present, chiefly councilmen and members of the Committee of Public Safety. The senior officer, Captain Bailey, second in command of the fleet, then stated that he came as the bearer of a demand from Flag-Officer Farragut, for the surrender of the city, the lowering of the State flag on the City Hall, and the hoisting of the United States flag over the Post-office, Custom-house, and Mint.

The interview took the form of an informal, open conference between Captain Bailey and the mayor, Mr. Soulé, and the other gentlemen whose connection with public affairs gave them the right to engage in it. The mayor's advisers agreed with him that he had no authority to surrender the city, and that General Lovell was the proper person to receive and reply to that demand. To the second clause, relating to the lowering of the State flag, an unqualified refusal was returned. Mr. Monroe then sent for General Lovell, and while they waited for his coming, conversation turned upon other subjects.

General Lovell appeared promptly, and Captain Bailey repeated his demand to him, prefacing it with the statement that his mission was to the mayor and common council. The general refused to surrender the city or his forces, but stated that he would retire with his troops, and leave the civil authorities to act as they saw fit. The question of the surrender being thus referred back to him, the mayor said that he would submit the matter to the council, and send a formal reply as soon as their advice could be obtained, whereupon the officers withdrew, being furnished with an escort by General Lovell.

The council met at 6:30 that evening, and received a message from the mayor. As a civil magistrate, he held that he was incompetent to the performance of a military act, and thought it would be proper to say that the withdrawal of the troops rendering resistance impossible, no obstruction could be offered to the occupation of the place by the enemy; but that all acts involving a transfer of authority must be performed by the invading force themselves. "We yield to physical force alone," said the mayor, "and maintain our allegiance to the Government of the Confederate States. Beyond this a due respect for our dignity, our rights, and the flag of our country does not, I think, permit us to go."

The council, unwilling to act hastily in so important a matter, simply listened to the reading of this message, and adjourned to meet again at 10 A. M. of the next day. I saw the mayor at his own house that evening, and he requested me to go off to the *Hartford* as early as possible the next morning, and explain to Flag-Officer Farragut that the council would meet at 10 that morning, and that a written answer to his demands would be returned as soon as possible after that hour. Mr. Monroe took this step entirely upon his own responsibility, fearing probably that the delay in the official reply might in some way be construed to our disadvantage. About 6 o'clock the next morning, Mr. McClelland, chief of police, and myself took a boat at the foot of Lafayette street, and hoisting a handkerchief upon a walking-stick by way of a flag of truce, were pulled out to the flag-ship. Having made myself known as the bearer of a message from the mayor of the city to Captain Farragut, we were invited on board, and shown to the flag-officer's cabin, where we found assembled the three commanders, Farragut, Bailey, and Bell.

Captain Farragut, who had known me from my boyhood, received me with the utmost kindness, and when my errand was disposed of readily answered my inquiries about the battle at the forts. He took me over the ship and showed me with almost boyish interest the manner in which the boilers were defended, and the scars upon the ship's sides where the shots had taken effect. Then making me stand beside him upon the very spot where he had stood during the passage of the forts, he described in eloquent terms the conflict, perhaps the most terrific that had ever been withstood. "I seemed to be breathing flame," said the captain. It was still quite early when we reached the wharf on our return, and the levee appeared deserted, but, though we saw nobody, we were seen. We went at 8 o'clock to the mayor's office to make our report. While still with him Mr. Soulé entered, accompanied by his son, and with much excitement made known the fact that two persons, traitors beyond doubt, had that very morning been seen to leave one of the enemy's ships and land at the levee. He strongly urged the arrest and punishment of the guilty persons, and the mayor blandly promised that it should be attended to, while the guilty persons silently enjoyed the little joke.

The council met at the appointed hour, and, having listened to a second reading of the mayor's message, unanimously resolved, that being "informed by the military authorities that the city was indefensible" no resistance would be made to the forces of the United States. Also that the "council and the entire population of this metropolis concurred in the sentiments expressed by the mayor, and that he be respectfully requested to act in the spirit manifested in said message." In anticipation of such a result, a letter had already been prepared embodying the views contained in the message, and reiterating the determination neither to hoist the United States flag nor lower that of our own adoption.

Mr. Monroe, though a man of much energy and decision of character, was entirely a "self-made" man, and his secretary was very young. Both were inexperienced in diplomatic correspondence; indeed, the emergency was one quite unexampled in the experience of the chief magistrate of an American city. We had, therefore, called to our assistance Mr. Durant da Ponte, at that time one of the editors and proprietors of the New Orleans "Delta," with which paper I had been connected previous to my appointment as private secretary to the mayor. At the invitation of the council I appeared before them and read the letter we had prepared. It was well received, and from expressions let fall by some of the members I retired with the impression that it was entirely satisfactory. Shortly afterward, however, a message was brought the mayor, requesting his presence in the council chamber. The object of this summons was to gain his consent to the substitution of a letter written by Mr. Soulé, and submitted to their consideration by one of the members.

The relations between the mayor and the council had not been of the most harmonious character, and he, wishing to conciliate them at this unfortunate juncture, yielded to their wish.

Before a copy of this letter could be made ready for transmission to the fleet, two officers, Lieutenant Albert Kautz and Midshipman John H. Read, appeared bearing a written demand, couched in the most peremptory terms, for the "unqualified surrender of the city," the hoisting of "the emblem of the sovereignty of the United States" over the Mint, Custom-house, and City Hall by meridian of that day (Saturday, April 26th), and the removal of all emblems of sovereignty other than that of the United States from all public buildings by that hour.

Mr. Monroe added a paragraph to the letter acknowledging the receipt of this last communication and promising a reply before 2 o'clock, if possible. I set out at once to convey it to Captain Farragut. As a matter of fact, the United States flag had already been raised on the Mint, and I called the attention of the Federal commander to the fact that a flag had been raised while negotiations were still pending. Captain Farragut replied that the flag had been placed there without his knowledge, but he could not now order it down. His men, he said, were flushed with victory, and much excited by the taunts and gibes of the crowd on the levee. Pointing to the "tops" where a number of men were stationed, some armed with muskets, others nervously clutching the strings of the howitzers, he called my attention to their excited appearance, and remarked that it was as much as he could do to restrain them from firing on the crowd, and should he attempt to haul that flag down, it would be impossible to keep them within bounds.

I returned to the City Hall before Lieutenant Kautz and Midshipman Read had concluded their visit. A large and excited crowd were outside. Some of them pressed their way up the front steps, and seemed intent upon entering the building. In order to prevent their forcing an entrance, the mayor ordered the heavy doors to be closed. Upon

---

⸗ This conversation, which was quite informal, did not at the time assume in my estimation the importance lent to it by subsequent events which occurred after I left the city as bearer of dispatches to President Davis at Richmond. In the excitement of the next few hours and the anomalous multiplication of my duties, it is possible that I may have even neglected to report it to the mayor, but it is certain that the impression obtained at the City Hall that the act was entirely unauthorized. Parton, whose account of the capture of the city is, in some respects, very incorrect, and who makes the tearing down of the United States flag from the Mint occur on Sunday the 27th, instead of Saturday the 26th, as shown by the record, says that General Butler arrived a few hours after that event, to share in the exasperation of the fleet and the councils of its chief. It was Butler, according to this historian, who advised the threat to bombard, and the order for the removal of the women and children. It may have been by his advice, also, that Captain Farragut assumed the placing of the flag on the Mint as his act, wishing to give it sufficient weight to make the tearing of it down a punishable offense.— M. A. B.

It will be noted that on page 92 Commander Kautz says the flag was raised over the Mint on the morning of April 26th in accordance with instructions from Farragut to Captain Morris of the *Pensacola*. But in a letter to the Assistant Secretary of the Navy, dated April 27th, Farragut himself says: "This morning at 6 A. M. I sent to Captain Morris, whose ship commanded the Mint, to take possession of it and hoist the American flag thereon, which was done and the people cheered it."

The apparent contradictions of these various statements cannot be disposed of by a study of the "Official Records." Neither do military and naval histories shed clear light on the subject. But the facts, half-truths, and explainable misapprehensions that can be sifted from the mass, indicate that early on the morning of the 26th a boat's crew from the fleet, without orders from Farragut, raised a flag over the Mint. This flag was hauled down by Mumford on April 27th, as related above by Farragut, and another flag was raised over the Mint in accordance with the flag-officer's instructions to Captain Morris. Before the first flag had been hauled down, the flag-officer, as intimated in his conversation with Mr. Baker, had decided to assume responsibility for the raising of it; this he did officially in a communication to the mayor dated April 28th. Apparently, therefore, Kautz has made the mistake of connecting the first flag with the order for the raising of the second flag.— EDITORS.

PIERRE SOULÉ. FROM A DAGUERREOTYPE TAKEN ABOUT 1851.

my arrival, I learned that the United States flag had just been torn down from the Mint.

Mr. Monroe, thinking it unwise for the officers to attempt to return openly to their boat, proposed to send them back under military escort. Lieutenant Kautz thought that quite unnecessary, but the mayor persisting that there was danger, a carriage was sent for and was stationed at the corner of Carondelet and Lafayette streets. Aided by two special officers of the police, I conducted them through a rear entrance while the mayor occupied the crowd in front, and got them into the carriage, but we were discovered as we drove away, and some of the crowd started up St. Charles street with the evident expectation of heading us off. I ordered the driver to whip up his horses and turn into Julia street, the second street above, and drive post-haste to the river. Many of our pursuers were armed, and I expected that we would be fired at as we crossed St. Charles street, but we went by so rapidly that they had no opportunity to fire, even had they so intended. They kept up the chase for some distance, but we so outstripped them that the most enduring finally gave it up. The officers' boat was found lying some little distance off in the stream, and the coxswain explained that he had been compelled to push out from the landing to prevent his tiller-ropes from being cut. No violence was offered to our party. As we took our places in the boat a shot was fired from the bow-gun of the *Hartford*, and for a moment I fancied that the fleet was about to bombard the city, but the officers explained that it was the signal recalling them to the ship.

The police force being clearly inadequate for the preservation of order, the mayor now called to his assistance the European Brigade, an organization made up of foreign residents, and commanded by General Paul Juge, *fils*. This general issued a proclamation assuming command of all foreign troops "by order of his Honor John T. Monroe," and asking the aid of all good citizens in the preservation of order.

The mayor was thus constituted commander-in-chief of an army, as well as of the civil forces, and the City Hall became a sort of military headquarters. Officers in gorgeous uniforms glittering with gold lace clanked their swords across the marble-paved halls, and from one to half a dozen mounted orderlies were constantly in waiting in the street, while I and the whole clerical force of the office were kept busy issuing requisitions for arms, horses, forage, and provisions for the home brigade, and orders for transportation, by steamboat and rail, for Confederate troops, en route from the outlying fortifications to General Lovell's headquarters, at Camp Moore. Martial law reigned, and a countersign was communicated to the patrol every night, without which no citizen was allowed to pass after 9 o'clock. A dispute arising between two officers of the French Legion as to precedence in rank, the matter was referred to the mayor for decision. Mr. Monroe improvised a military court, before which the disputants appeared, represented by learned counsel. Mr. Soulé was advocate for one side, and under the threatening guns of the fleet the momentous question was gravely argued and decided. I have still before me the dramatic figure of the victor as he issued from the tribunal, waving his cap in triumph, closely followed by the gorgeously equipped members of his staff.

Sunday passed without intercourse with the fleet, but Monday brought a still more vivid excitement in the shape of a communication from Flag-Officer Farragut, reciting all the evidences of insubordination and contumacy on the part of the citizens and authorities, and admonishing us that the fire of the fleet might be drawn upon the city at any moment. "The election is with you," says the flag-officer, "but it becomes my duty to notify you to remove the women and children within forty-eight hours if I have rightly understood your determination."

This communication was brought to the City Hall by Commander Henry H. Bell, who was accompanied by Acting Master Herbert B. Tyson. After reading it Mr. Monroe said: "As I consider this a threat to bombard the city, and as it is a matter about which the notice should be clear and specific, I desire to know when the forty-eight hours began to run."

"It begins from the time you receive this notice," replied the captain.

"Then," said the mayor, taking out his watch and showing it to the captain, "you see it is fifteen minutes past 12 o'clock."

Commander Bell acknowledged the correctness of the mayor's time, and went on to say that he was further charged to call attention to the "bad faith" of the commander of the *McRae*, the steamer which had brought up the wounded and dead from the forts under a flag of truce, in either sinking or allowing his steamer to sink without reporting to the flag-officer his inability to keep his pledge and take it back to the forts.

The council was convoked for the consideration of Captain Farragut's letter, and the mayor appeared before them and gave his views regarding the answer to be returned. Captain Farragut had assumed as his own act the raising of the flag on the Mint and alluded to an attempt having been made by him to place one upon the Custom-house. The mayor's reply, which was drafted by Mr. Soulé, renews his refusal to lower the flag of Louisiana.

"This satisfaction," he says, "you cannot obtain at our hands. We will stand your bombardment, unarmed and undefended as we are."

Accompanied by Mr. Soulé I conveyed this reply to the *Hartford* early on the morning of the 29th. On our arrival Mr. Soulé at once entered upon a discussion of international law, which was listened to patiently by the flag-officer and Commanders Bailey and Bell. When Mr. Soulé had concluded, Captain Farragut replied that he was a plain sailor and it was not expected that he should understand the nice points of international usage; that he was simply there as the commander of the fleet and aimed only to do his duty in that capacity.

Mr. Soulé, having apparently fulfilled his mission, now asked to be set on shore, as he had an engagement at 9 o'clock. This engagement was to meet the mayor and some others, including, if I remember aright, General Lovell (who had come down to the city from Camp Moore), with a view of urging upon them a scheme for making a combined night attack, by means of a flotilla of ferry-boats, upon the fleet, whose ammunition it was generally believed had been exhausted. There had been an informal conference at the mayor's residence the evening previous, at which I was present, when Mr. Soulé unfolded his plan of the contemplated night attack and urged it strongly upon the mayor's attention. The meeting at 9 o'clock the following morning was for the purpose of discussing this matter more freely. It was, however, too late for such an undertaking, even had the plan been a much more feasible one. The forts had surrendered! Captain Farragut had already dispatched a message to the mayor notifying him of that event, and adding that he was about to raise the United States flag on the Mint and Custom-house. He still insisted that the lowering of the flag over the City Hall should be the work of those who had raised it, but before I left the ship he had yielded that point also, and I reported to my chief that there would be no bombardment and that the ungrateful task of lowering our flag would be performed by those who demanded its removal.

Mayor Monroe at once issued a proclamation requesting all citizens "to retire to their homes during these acts of authority which it would be folly to resist," and impressing upon them the melancholy consolation that the flag was not to be removed by their authorities, "but by those who had the power and the will to exercise it." I carried a copy of this proclamation on board the flag-ship.

The duty of raising and removing the flags was intrusted to Captain Bell. I left the ship in advance of his force, and returned to the City Hall to report their coming. The stage was now set for the last act, and soon the officers, marines, and sailors appeared in Lafayette square with bayonets and two brass howitzers glittering in the sunlight. The marines were formed in line on the St. Charles street side of the square near the iron railing which at that time inclosed it, while the guns were drawn through the gates out into the middle of the street, and placed so as to command the thoroughfare either way.

The crowd flowed in from every direction and filled the street in a compact mass both above and below the square. They were silent, but angry and threatening. Many openly displayed their arms. An open way was left in front of the hall, and their force being stationed, Captain Bell and Lieutenant Kautz passed across the street, mounted the hall steps, and entered the mayor's parlor. Approaching the mayor, Captain Bell said: "I have come in obedience to orders to haul down the State flag from this building."

Mr. Monroe replied, his voice trembling with restrained emotion, "Very well, sir, you can do it; but I wish to say that there is not in my entire constituency so wretched a renegade as would be willing to exchange places with you."

He emphasized this speech in a manner which must have been very offensive to the officers. Captain Bell visibly restrained himself from reply and asked at once that he might be shown the way to the roof. The mayor replied by referring him to the janitor, whom he would find outside.

As soon as the two officers left the room, Mr. Monroe also went out and placed himself immediately in front of the howitzer pointing down St. Charles street. There, folding his arms, he fixed his eyes upon the gunner who stood lanyard in hand ready for action. Here he remained until the flag had been hauled down and Lieutenant Kautz and Captain Bell had reappeared. At an order from the officers the sailors drew their howitzers back into the square, the marines fell into marching order behind them, and retired as they had come. As they passed out through the Camp street gate, Mr. Monroe turned toward the hall, and the people who had hitherto preserved the silence he had asked from them broke into cheers for their mayor.

## THE WATER-BATTERY AT FORT JACKSON.

### BY WILLIAM B. ROBERTSON, CAPTAIN, 1ST LOUISIANA ARTILLERY, C. S. A.

ON the 15th of April, 1862, I was directed by Lieutenant-Colonel Edward Higgins, commanding Forts Jackson and St. Philip, to take command of the water-battery. [See map, p. 34.] This was an outwork of Fort Jackson, separated from it by two moats. It was quadrilateral in shape, inclosed on three sides by a breastwork made of earth, the side next to the fort being open. The battery had no casemates or covered ways. It had been hastily prepared for use just previous to the appearance of the enemy's fleet in our front. During the siege it was directly in the line of fire from the mortar-boats, or very nearly so.

The battery was manned by a detachment of Company D, 1st Louisiana Artillery, under First Lieutenant R. J. Bruce, a detachment of the St. Mary's Cannoneers, under First Lieutenant George O. Foot, and a detachment of my company, "B," 1st Louisiana Artillery, under Sergeant Henry Herman, numbering, all told, about 100 men. There were mounted in the work 8 guns, viz., 2 rifled 32-pounders (old smooth-bores rifled), 1 10-inch Columbiad, 1 9-inch Columbiad, 3 smooth-bore 32-pounders, and 1 10-inch sea-coast mortar.♭ In the battery there were two magazines which had been hurriedly constructed. They were built of old flat-boat gunwales (pieces of timber about 12×24 inches square) placed close together, resting at one end on the edge of the parapet, and at the other on the *terre-plein* of the battery. These gunwales were laid on their flat sides and were covered with several courses of bags filled with sand to a depth of two or three feet. There were also two temporary hovels intended for shelter for the men while sleeping. They were so low that it was impossible to stand erect in them, and the men could not lie down at full length.

On the 18th of April the enemy commenced the bombardment of Fort Jackson and the water-battery with all his mortar-boats. The fort and the water-battery replied vigorously, but finding it impossible to reach them with any of my guns, owing chiefly to the inferiority of our powder, I was ordered to use my mortar only. This was the nearest piece in the fortifications to the enemy, and whenever it happened that the charge of powder was of good quality the shells from this mortar made it hot for the mortar-boats, though we could see that many of them fell short. During the first days of the bombardment the enemy's gun-boats appeared occasionally above the point of woods, but were soon driven to seek cover in every instance by the combined fire of Forts Jackson and St. Philip and the water-battery. On April 19th the bombardment was renewed with increased fury, and several of the enemy's gun-boats endeavored to maintain positions above the point of woods, about three miles below Fort Jackson, and behind which the mortar-boats lay concealed from view and in comparative safety, owing to the inferiority of our ordnance and ammunition,— but they were unable to withstand the fire from the forts and the water-battery, and soon retired. In these engagements I used only the rifle guns and Columbiads. That day the enemy's mortar fire was very accurate, and disabled both of the 32-pounder rifle guns in the water-battery. We patched them up as well as we could afterward, and made them serviceable.

On the 20th the bombardment continued, hav-

---

♭ Captain Robertson's enumeration of guns in the water-battery differs from that given on page 75. The latter, which was made up before the receipt of Captain Robertson's account, was based on the following facts: Admiral Porter, in his report of April 30th, 1862, written after a visit to the fort, states that the water-battery at Jackson contained 6 guns. The plan [see p. 34] made by Messrs. Harris and Gerdes of the coast survey gives 6 pieces, viz., 5 guns and 1 mortar. Lieutenant (now General) John C. Palfrey, being ordered by Lieutenant Weitzel to make a list of the ordnance in the fort, gives the armament of the outer battery as follows: "Two 32-pounders rifled, one 10-inch Columbiad, two 8-inch Columbiads, and one 10-inch sea-mortar,— total, 6."— EDITORS.

ing been maintained uninterruptedly all the previous night. The Federal gun-boats several times poked their noses cautiously around the point, delivered shots, and dodged back quickly.

Some time during the first days of the bombardment, the Confederate States steamer *McRae*, lying about the fort and in its rear, commenced firing at the mortar-fleet, with the good intention of aiding us. The projectiles from her guns passed directly over the water-battery, and many sabots from them fell in and around it. Seeing that her shot were falling far short of the enemy, and that it would be but a waste of ammunition for her to continue firing, I notified Colonel Higgins of the facts, and he requested her commander to cease firing, which he promptly did. This was the only attempt, according to my recollection, on the part of the navy, after the first day of the bombardment, to render us any assistance, until they were forced into action by Farragut's advance.

After the 20th of April the enemy's mortar-boats continued to rain shell incessantly, night and day, upon Fort Jackson and the water-battery, until nearly sundown on the 24th. During all this trying period the officers and men who served under me in the water-battery never wavered, *and not a single one was ever driven from his post.*

On the afternoon of the 23d I received a communication from Colonel Higgins, notifying me that the enemy were planting signals along the river-bank, just above the position of the mortar-fleet, and that this and other movements among them indicated that they would make an attempt that night to rush by our works, with their steamers, and ordering me to prepare to resist their passage. He also notified me that the river would be lit up by fire-rafts. I was very watchful all that night, hardly sleeping an instant. Every gun in the battery was loaded and pointed toward the river, and the men were kept at their posts.

At 3:30 the bombardment was redoubled, and soon afterward Sergeant Herman called my attention to several black, shapeless masses, barely distinguishable from the surrounding darkness, moving silently, but steadily, up the river. Not a light was visible anywhere; not a torch had been applied to a single fire-raft, and not one of them had been started from its moorings. As soon as I caught sight of the moving objects, I knew they were the enemy's vessels, and I ordered the guns to be trained upon the two which were in the lead, and to open a rapid fire upon them. Only a moment sufficed for the gunners to sight the guns, so thoroughly was everything prepared, and the water-battery thundered its greeting to the enemy. Fort Jackson followed instantly with a grand crash of artillery from the guns under Anderson and Ogden, Baylor and Agar along the lower and river fronts, and from those of Mumford in the mortar bastion and Kennedy in the flag-staff bastion. Fort St. Philip echoed with the boom of its guns. The Federal vessels replied with broadsides. The flashes of the guns, from both sides, lit up the river with a lurid light that revealed the outlines of the Federal steamers more distinctly.

I do not believe there ever was a grander spectacle witnessed before in the world than that displayed during the great artillery duel which then followed. The mortar-shells shot upward from the mortar-boats, rushed to the apexes of their flight, flashing the lights of their fuses as they revolved, paused an instant, and then descended upon our works like hundreds of meteors, or burst in mid-air, hurling their jagged fragments in every direction. The guns on both sides kept up a continual roar for nearly an hour, without a moment's intermission, and produced a shimmering illumination, which, though beautiful and grand, was illusive in its effect upon the eye, and made it impossible to judge accurately of the distance of the moving vessels from us; and this fact, taken in connection with their rapid and constant change of positions, as they speeded up the river, rendered it very difficult to hit them with our projectiles. On the other hand, our positions being stationary, they operated at no such disadvantage, though moving themselves. All the shore guns were served with great rapidity, until the vessels had passed beyond our range. As the vessels were masked by Fort Jackson from our view as they passed up the river, our attention was turned to those following, in succession; and no vessel stood in front of Fort Jackson and the water-battery many moments without receiving their compliments in the shape of iron missiles. *No guns were silenced in either Fort Jackson or the water-battery at any time during this engagement. Not a man was driven from his post at the guns in the water-battery, much less from the battery itself,* as is asserted by Admiral Porter. [See p. 43.]

After Farragut passed with most of his steamers there was a slackening of the fire in the forts and the water-battery, simply for the reason that it would have been madness to have wasted any more ammunition than was necessary to drive away Admiral Porter and all the vessels which had failed to pass the forts under cover of darkness. But as soon as it was light enough to see them plainly *we silenced* and drove rapidly down the river *all the vessels, including Admiral Porter's, that remained below the forts.* As soon as Farragut's vessels could, they pushed up the river out of our range.

The passage of the forts by Farragut and his fleet was an act of grand heroism that should forever shed luster on the American navy, and Porter and his mortar-fleet did splendid work, and contributed very materially to the success which the Federal navy achieved over us. I have no doubt he fought his flotilla in front of the water-battery with great courage. But some things he *did not* accomplish, and among them the silencing of Fort Jackson and the water-battery. I think it could be proven that it was a physical impossibility for him to have gotten as near the water-battery as he claims to have done, as I think the water-battery is farther from the *river-bank itself.* But to Farragut belongs the great glory of the capture.

In reference to the mutiny, I have only to say this, that there was no indication that any of the men in the water-battery were implicated in it. No officers and I believe no native Southerners were involved in this disgraceful affair.

# CONFEDERATE RESPONSIBILITIES FOR FARRAGUT'S SUCCESS.

### I.— BY JAMES GRIMSHAW DUNCAN, SON OF THE COMMANDER OF FORTS JACKSON AND ST. PHILIP.

ON the 22d of April, by order of Major-General Lovell, everything afloat, including the tow-boats and the entire control of the fire-barges formerly under General J. K. Duncan, was turned over to Captain J. K. Mitchell, commanding the Confederate States naval forces on the lower Mississippi River; and 150 men from both forts were given him as gunners and sharp-shooters for the *Louisiana*.

In an interview with Captain Mitchell on the morning of this date, General Duncan learned that the motive power of the *Louisiana* was not likely to be completed in time to bring her, as an aggressive steamer, into the pending action. As an iron-clad floating battery, mounting sixteen guns of the heaviest caliber, she was then as complete as she would ever be. Under these circumstances General Duncan considered that her best possible position would be below the raft, close in on the Fort St. Philip shore. This position would give us three direct and cross fires upon the enemy's approach, and at the same time insure the *Louisiana* against a direct assault. Accordingly, General Duncan urged these views upon Captain Mitchell in the following letter:

"It is of vital importance that the present fire of the enemy should be withdrawn from us, which you alone can do. This can be done in the manner suggested this morning, under cover of our guns, while your work on the boat can be carried on in safety and security. Our position is a critical one, dependent entirely on the powers of endurance of our casemates, many of which have been completely shattered and are crumbling away by repeated shocks; and therefore I respectfully but earnestly again urge my suggestion of this morning on your notice. Our magazines are also in danger."

Captain Mitchell replied:

"I have the honor to acknowledge the receipt of yours of this date, asking me to place the *Louisiana* in position below the raft this evening, if possible. This vessel was hurried away from New Orleans before her steam power and batteries were ready for service, without a crew, and in many other respects very incomplete, and this condition of things is but partially remedied now. She is not yet prepared to offer battle to the enemy, but should he attempt to pass the forts, we will do all we can to prevent it; and it was for this purpose only that she was placed in position where necessity might force her into action, inadequately prepared as she is at this moment. We have now at work on board about fifty mechanics, as well as her own crew and those from other vessels doing work essential to the preparation of the vessel for battle. Under these circumstances it would, in my estimation, be hazarding too much to place her under the fire of the enemy. Every effort is being made to prepare her for the relief of Fort Jackson, the condition of which is fully felt by me; and the very moment I can venture to face our enemy with any reasonable chance of success, be assured, General, I will do it, and trust that the result will show you that I am now pursuing the right course."

On the 23d, Captain Mitchell replied to another urgent request from General Duncan:

"I know the importance to the safety of Forts Jackson and St. Philip and the city of New Orleans of having this vessel in proper condition before seeking an encounter with the enemy. If he seeks one or attempts the passage of the forts before this vessel is ready, I shall meet him, however unprepared I may be. We have an additional force of mechanics from the city this morning, and I hope that by to-morrow night the motive power of the *Louisiana* will be ready, and that in the meantime her battery will be in place and other preparations will be completed, so as to enable her to act against the enemy. When ready, you will be immediately advised."

In this refusal Captain Mitchell was supported by Captains McIntosh, Huger, and Warley. Two other notes were also addressed him this day, requesting that fire-barges be sent down and a vigilant outlook kept from all his vessels, and asking his coöperation should the enemy attempt to pass during the night. This was promised, but no success attended the attempts at sending down fire-barges, for which there was no excuse; for, although the tugs were not in working order, there were six boats of the river fleet available, and fire-barges were plentiful. No immediate relief being looked for from our fleet, the entire command of Fort Jackson was turned out to repair damages under a very heavy fire. The bombardment continued without intermission throughout the 23d, but slackened off about 12 o'clock M., at which time there was every indication of exhaustion on the part of the mortar-flotilla. The following letter was sent to Captain Mitchell by General Duncan:

"I am of the opinion that the mortar practice of the enemy against Fort Jackson must be nearly exhausted, and that there is every indication that the enemy, as the next plan of attack, is about to move up his large vessels to the point of woods, and open upon us with his broadsides. One of the large vessels has already been brought up and placed in position. Should the above prove to be the case, it is imperatively necessary that the batteries of the *Louisiana* should be brought into action at all hazards, as well as those of Forts Jackson and St. Philip. A proper position for the *Louisiana* would be on the Fort St. Philip side, a short distance below the raft and close to the shore, which will give us three direct and cross fires upon the point of attack."

To this Captain Mitchell replied as before. Nothing now could be expected of the *Louisiana*; the only position which offered every possible chance of success had been repeatedly refused. Still Captain Mitchell had other duties to perform, and at sundown General Duncan wrote to him:

"The enemy has just sent up a small boat, and planted a series of white flags on the Fort St. Philip side, commencing about 350 yards above the lone tree. It is the probable position of his ships in the new line of attack which, in my opinion, he contemplates for attacking Fort Jackson with his large vessels. As you may not have seen this operation, I furnish you with the information. Please keep the river well lit up with fire-rafts to-night, as the attack may be made at any time."

The flags referred to were planted under cover of a perfect hail of shells. At about 9 P. M., Lieutenant Shryock, C. S. N., Captain Mitchell's aide, came ashore to inform General Duncan that the *Louisiana* would be ready for service by the next evening (the 24th). General Duncan informed him "that time was everything to us, and that to-morrow would in all probability prove too late." Lieutenant-Colonel Higgins warmly seconded this opinion, and warned Lieutenant Shryock that the final battle was imminent within a few hours. In regard to lighting the river, Lieutenant Shryock stated that fire-barges would be sent down regularly every two hours throughout the night, and as none had been sent up to that hour (9:30 P. M.), he left, informing these officers that the matter would be attended to as soon as he arrived on board. Hour after hour passed, and not a barge was lighted. In consequence of this neglect, the river remained in complete darkness the entire night. The bombardment continued all night, and toward morning grew furious. At 3:30 A. M. the large vessels of the enemy were observed in motion. General Duncan then made this, his last and final appeal to Captain Mitchell:

"FORT JACKSON, La., 3:30 A. M., April 24th, 1862.— CAPTAIN: As I anticipated, and informed you yesterday, the enemy are taking up their positions at the present moment, with their large ships, on the St. Philip shore, to operate against Fort Jackson. They are placing themselves boldly, with their lights at their mast-heads. You are assuming a fearful responsibility if you do not come at once to our assistance with the *Louisiana* and the fleet. I can say no more."

Mitchell did not come, but Farragut did.

## II.— BY JOHN K. MITCHELL, COMMODORE, C. S. N.

THE article by Admiral D. D. Porter, entitled "The Opening of the Lower Mississippi," published in "The Century" magazine for April, 1885, is open to adverse criticism, and particularly where he indulges in personal reflections upon the officers of my command. He claims that "one fact only was in our [Farragut's] favor, and that was the division of their [the Confederate] forces under three different heads, which prevented unanimity of action. In every other respect the odds were against us."

But taking Admiral Porter's own showing of the armaments, it appears that the weight of one entire round of projectiles was approximately: Confederate, 7139 pounds; Union, 20,224; making a difference in favor of the Union force of 13,085 pounds, or nearly 3 to 1 in weight of projectiles.

The weight of one entire round of all the Confederate forces *afloat* (including the 10 guns of the *Louisiana* that could not be used) was 1760 pounds, and did not equal one round of any one of 4 of the first class United States sloops of war, as, for instance, the *Pensacola*, which was 1860 pounds. The ordnance of the United States fleet was the heaviest known to any navy of that day; her vessels were inferior to those of no other nation in construction, equipment, and speed, and were manned by officers and crews of unsurpassed courage, skill, training, and discipline. The Confederate armament was composed of the old discarded guns of the United States army and navy, many of which were old smooth bores, rifled or reamed out to a larger caliber; or, if newly cast, made from scrap iron, insufficiently tested and inspected, and so, with good reason, distrusted by the crews that worked them. Admiral Porter further says:

"It is generally conceded by military men that 1 gun in a fort is about equal to 5 on board of a wooden ship, especially when, as in this case, the forces afloat are obliged to contend against a 3½-knot current in a channel obstructed by chains and fire-rafts." [See note, p. 75.]

Nowhere is it shown that any obstructions were encountered by the fleet in its passage by the forts, and it appears that the *Hartford* was the only vessel that got foul of a fire-raft. As to the *Louisiana*, Admiral Porter states:

"The *Louisiana* remained tied up to the bank, where she could not obstruct the river or throw the Union fleet into confusion while passing the forts."

The fact is that the *Louisiana*, being immovable, could use only her 3 bow guns and 3 of her starboard broadside guns, and those only as the vessels of the enemy passed directly in front of them, for they could be trained but 5 degrees either way. Her heterogeneous crew was sent on board in less than four days before the action; there was no time for the men even to know each other at the same gun, no time for training or practice, but they were occupied during this brief period in mounting or remounting their guns, few of them having ever seen a cannon fired.

In his account of the capitulation in the cabin of the *Harriet Lane*, Admiral Porter says:

"As we were about to sign the terms, I was quite surprised to find that it was not expected that the vessels of war were to be included in the terms agreed to by the Confederate officers."

"Surprised," indeed! when that very morning Colonel Higgins had sent his letter of the same day (April 28th), offering the "*surrender of these forts*" (Jackson and St. Philip), which he commanded; and closing with the words, "*we have no control over the vessels afloat.*" [See note, p. 51.] Moreover, in the terms presented to Duncan when he went on board, which the Admiral says he had prepared before, *nothing is said of the surrender of the naval forces*. Such a contradictory statement, however, has its parallel in the assertion as to the effect of the explosion of the *Louisiana*, that it

"fairly shook us all out of our seats and threw the *Harriet Lane* over on her side, but we finished the terms. . . . The *Louisiana* was blown up *just before* reaching the flotilla."

Lieutenant William M. Bridges, Adjutant of Fort Jackson, now (1887) a resident of Richmond, Va., was present in the cabin at the signing of the capitulation, and he denies, most emphatically, that such an effect was produced on the *Harriet Lane* and on those seated in her cabin.

My belligerent rights were not impaired or suspended by the surrender of General Duncan and the flying of a flag of truce, to which I was not a party; and had the effect of the explosion been to destroy the *Harriet Lane* and the entire Federal force, the laws of war would have justified it.

As to my difference of opinion with General Duncan: naval officers ought surely to be considered better judges of how the forces and appliances at their command should be managed than army officers. The conduct of the naval forces, by the finding of a Confederate court of inquiry, was fully sustained, and the court prolonged its session two months, vainly waiting for the appearance of General Lovell and Lieut.-Colonel Higgins, who were summoned to testify before the court at my instance, they being the most prominent complainants against the Navy, General Duncan having died.

# THE CONFEDERATE INVASION OF NEW MEXICO AND ARIZONA.

BY GEORGE H. PETTIS, BREVET CAPT., U. S. V., LATE LIEUTENANT COMMANDING CO. K 1st CALIFORNIA INFANTRY, AND LIEUTENANT AND ADJUTANT 1st NEW MEXICO INFANTRY.

THE buffalo hunt of Captain John R. Baylor culminated on his reaching El Paso (Franklin), Texas, on the border of New Mexico, in the first week in July, 1861, with about three hundred men of his regiment, the 2d Texas Mounted Rifles, C. S. A., and occupying Fort Bliss, across the river, which had been abandoned by the regular troops. He was warmly welcomed by the few secessionists in that neighborhood, prominent among whom were Colonel B. Magoffin, Judge Simeon Hart, and Judge J. F. Crosby, who were the wealthiest persons in that vicinity. On the 23d of July Captain Baylor, with about two hundred and fifty men, advanced up the Rio Grande, crossing to the west side of the river at San Tomas, and proceeding to La Mesilla. On the afternoon of the 25th Major Isaac Lynde, 7th U. S. Infantry, who was in command at Fort Fillmore, a post about four miles distant from Mesilla, proceeded against the rebels with about four hundred men,—artillery, cavalry, and infantry,—and after a desultory attack on the town, involving a loss of three men killed and two officers and four men wounded, he cowardly returned to the adobe walls of Fort Fillmore. On the morning of the 27th Lynde evacuated the fort without reason, and commenced a retreat for Fort Stanton, having about five hundred men. When near San Augustine Springs, Baylor appeared in his rear with less than three hundred men; and without a shot on either side Lynde surrendered his entire force, which consisted of seven companies of the 7th Regular Infantry and three companies of Mounted Rifles.‡

In the meantime, Fort Buchanan, situated near Tubac, and Fort Breckinridge, on the north side of the San Pedro River and above its confluence with the Gila, had been abandoned, and the troops ordered to Fort Fillmore. Upon reaching Cook's Cañon, this command, consisting of Captain Isaiah N. Moore, 1st Dragoons, with four companies, were informed of Major Lynde's disgraceful surrender, whereupon they destroyed a large amount of Government stores which they had in charge, as well as private property at the eastern end of the cañon, and fled precipitately to Fort Craig. On the 1st of August Captain Baylor issued a proclamation organizing all that part of the Territory of New Mexico lying south of the thirty-fourth parallel

---

↓ See Mrs. Caroline B. Darrow's "Recollections of the Twiggs Surrender," Vol. I., p. 33; also map on p. 8 of that volume.—EDITORS.

‡ On November 25th, 1861, for this conduct Major Lynde was dropped from the army. This action was revoked November 27th, 1866, by general orders, restoring him to his commission and placing him on the retired list of the army.— G. H. P.

of north latitude as the Confederate territory of Arizona, the seat of government being at Mesilla, and the authority of governor being assumed by himself. August 2d, Fort Stanton, under the command of Lieutenant-Colonel Benjamin S. Roberts, 3d U. S. Cavalry, was abandoned, all the public stores that could not be carried away being destroyed. During the month of September Baylor sent several small parties northerly toward Fort Craig, who had a number of skirmishes with the Union troops, in which the latter were usually worsted.

On the 8th of July, 1861, the Confederate Government at Richmond authorized General H. H. Sibley (who had formerly been a major in the army, and had recently served in New Mexico) to proceed to Texas and organize a brigade of troops for the conquest of New Mexico. On the 18th of November Sibley was ready to move from San Antonio, Texas. His brigade consisted of Colonel John R. Baylor's regiment of Texas Mounted Rifles (then in New Mexico), Reily's 4th Regiment, Green's 5th, and Steele's 7th Regiment of Texas mounted troops, and he arrived at Fort Bliss on the 14th of December, and assumed command of all the "forces of the Confederate States on the Rio Grande at and above Fort Quitman, and all in the territory of New Mexico and Arizona," and his command was designated as the "Army of New Mexico."

By General Orders, No. 97, November 9th, 1861, the United States Department of New Mexico was reëstablished and placed under the command of Colonel E. R. S. Canby, 19th U. S. Infantry, who had previously relieved Colonel W. W. Loring, commanding the regiment of Mounted Rifles, who had tendered his resignation to the President, and had left his station before its acceptance. After Lynde's surrender, New Mexico, south of the *Jornado del Muerto*, was in possession of the rebels, and Canby set about enlisting and reorganizing the militia of the Territory. He also caused Fort Craig to be strengthened by throwing up earth-works, while Fort Union, in the northeastern part of the Territory, was changed from its old location under the mesa, and moved about a mile into the plains, and converted into a fieldwork, all the quarters, both officers' and men's, being made bomb-proof. The Indians in the meantime were causing much trouble to both the Union and rebel commanders in their respective districts. The Mescalero Apaches, Kiowas, Comanches, and Navajoes were constantly making forays on Canby's district, while in the southern district the Gila River and Chiricahua Apaches were causing trouble for Baylor.

During the first week in January, 1862, Sibley commenced the march up the Rio Grande with his command, and arrived at Fort Thorn. On the 7th of February he left Fort Thorn for Fort Craig. On the 16th a reconnoissance in force was made to within two miles of the post, which was met by the dispatch of a force of cavalry, whereupon the Confederates withdrew a short distance down the river, and on the 19th crossed over to the eastern bank. On the 20th a considerable force of Union troops left the fort, and, crossing the river, made a feint of attack on the Confederate camp near the river crossing. The Confederates immediately placed all their artillery in

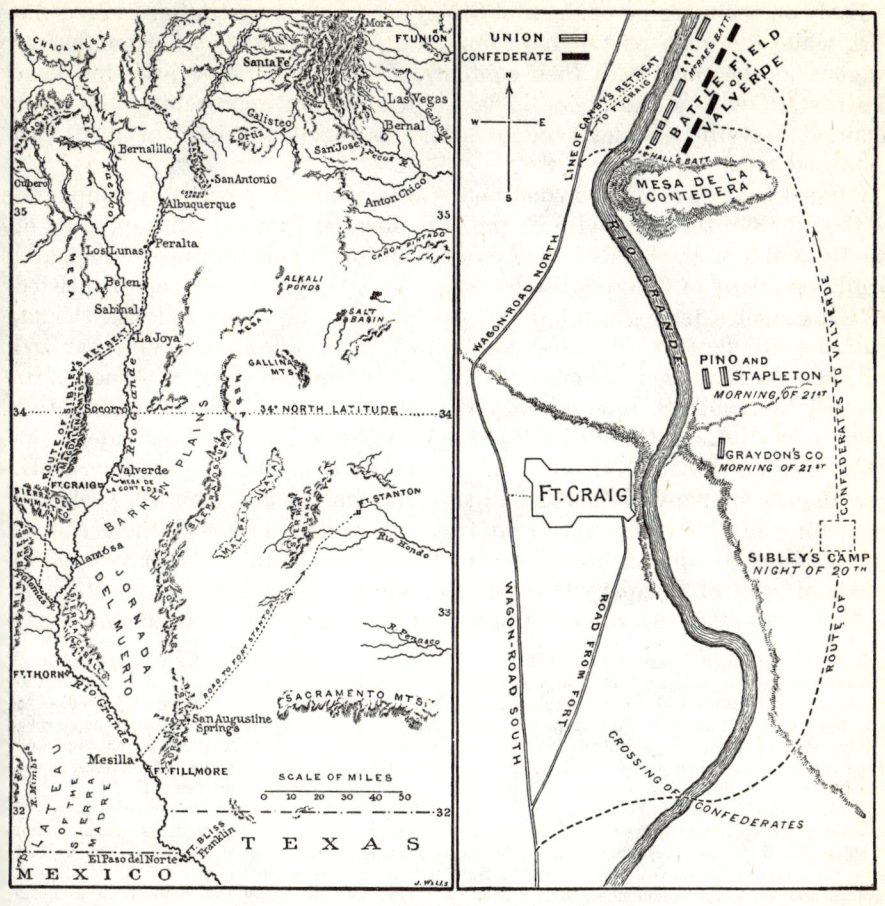

MAP OF THE CAMPAIGN AND OF SIBLEY'S RETREAT.   MAP OF FORT CRAIG AND VALVERDE.

battery and commenced firing, whereupon the Union artillery and cavalry returned to the fort, leaving the infantry to watch the enemy, who that night made a "dry camp" in the sand-hills directly opposite to and within sight of Fort Craig, at a distance of less than two miles. No operations were attempted by either party during the night, with the exception of "Paddy" Graydon's mule attack upon the Confederate camp.‡

‡ Captain James Graydon (familiarly known as "Paddy" Graydon) had been a soldier in the regular army, and on the approach of the Confederates had been authorized to organize an independent spy company, and as such it was mustered into the service of the United States. As its name implies, it was truly an "independent" company. It was seldom under the restraint of a superior officer, as it was nearly all the time on the road, its captain not liking the monotony of garrison life. Captain Graydon was a brave man, and no undertaking was too hazardous for him to attempt. His company were nearly all natives of New Mexico, and they would go anywhere their captain would lead them. On the evening of February 20th, when the enemy were encamped opposite Fort Craig, Graydon was allowed to make a night attack upon them. Without explaining the details of his plan, he had prepared a couple of wooden boxes, in each of which half a dozen 24-pounder howitzer shells were placed, with the fuses cut. These boxes were securely lashed on the backs of two old mules,

Early on the morning of the 21st Sibley made a demonstration toward the fort, while the main part of his command, having abandoned a number of wagons at the camp with their contents, proceeded northerly, passing near the eastern end of the Mesa de la Contedera, and approaching the river again at Valverde. Sibley's command in this region consisted of about two thousand men.

Colonel Canby's command consisted of 3810 men, composed of 5 companies of the 5th, 3 of the 7th, and 3 of the 10th Regular Infantry; 2 companies of the 1st and 5 of the 3d Regular Cavalry; McRae's and Hall's batteries; and Ford's company of Colorado Volunteers. The New Mexico troops consisted of Kit Carson's 1st regiment, 7 companies of the 2d, 7 companies of the 3d, 1 of the 4th, 2 of the 5th, Graydon's Spy Company, and some unorganized militia. As the enemy commenced its movements at about 8 o'clock A. M., Colonel Benjamin S. Roberts with the regular and volunteer cavalry, two sections of McRae's (provisional) battery, Hall's section of 24-pounder howitzers, Captain David H. Brotherton's company of the 5th, Captain Charles H. Ingraham's company of the 7th, and two (Mortimore's and Hubbell's) selected companies of volunteers were sent from the fort to intercept them should they attempt to approach the river at Valverde. McRae's battery was composed of men of Company G of the 2d, and Company I of the 3d Regular Cavalry. Captain Alexander McRae, 3d Cavalry, was in command, with

and the captain with three or four of his men crossed the river just below the fort and proceeded in the darkness toward the Confederate camp. Graydon's project was to get the torpedo mules within sight of the enemy's picket-line without being discovered, when he was to light the fuses, and the mules being directed toward the picket-line, would move in the direction of the animals there. He finally arrived within 150 yards of the picket-line, and everything being in readiness, the fuses of the boxes were fired, and the captain and his party commenced their retreat, when to their consternation they found that the mules, instead of going toward the enemy, were following themselves; the shells soon began to explode, the Confederate camp was quickly under arms, and Graydon's party made its way back to Fort Craig without the mules.

On another occasion, when the enemy were on their retreat, Graydon, with one man, arrived late at night at the village of Socorro, when he was informed that there were seven Confederates in town, quartered in a house not far away. With his army of one soldier, Graydon approached the house, and commenced giving orders in a stentorian voice: "Captain Adams, move your company to the north side of the house, and commence firing as soon as you see a man move out of the building! Captain Brown, you proceed to the rear of the house with one platoon of your company, and send your second platoon to the south side, and observe the same orders that I have given Captain Adams!" Then, after much ordering of his own imaginary company, he called upon the enemy to surrender, which they soon proceeded to do by coming out of the house, without their arms, which were secured by the gallant captain, and the next day the seven men were delivered to the commanding officer at Fort Craig.‡

Although the captain was in the service several months with his company, the same men and the same number were mustered out as had been originally mustered in, when in fact, *unofficially*, he had really lost more than a dozen men in action, and as many more by desertion. This was brought about as follows: When his first sergeant reported to him of a morning that private "Juan Chacon" or "José de Dios Montoyn y Armijo" had deserted during the previous night, no record was made, as the first Mexican peon he would chance to see that day would be pounced upon, and the captain would say, in Spanish: "Here Juan Chacon, get into your place. I have a great mind to shoot you for desertion." Whereupon the poor peon would probably answer: "No, señor; yo soy Jesus Garcia, y no estoy soldado" (No, sir; I am Jesus Garcia, and I am not a soldier). "Callo la boca, chevato" (Close your mouth, you brute). "Here, sergeant, give this man a uniform, and give him a horse, as I'll excuse him this time." At the next camp the recruit would get a suit of clothes and a good meal. The men picked up in this manner often became the best of soldiers.— G. H. P.

‡ Major Teel writes that the Confederate party consisted of four men under Lieutenant Simmons, and that they were surprised by Captain Graydon and his whole company, one Confederate being killed by Graydon's men in the attempt to escape.— EDITORS.

Lyman Mishler, 5th Infantry, and I. McBell, 2d New Mexico Volunteers, as lieutenants. Graydon's Spy Company, and five hundred mounted militia under Colonels Pino and Robert H. Stapleton, had already been sent to the eastern side of the river to watch the movements of the enemy. Colonel Roberts was too late to prevent the Confederates from reaching the river: when he arrived at the ford at the foot of the Mesa de la Contedera he found them already there. The action was immediately begun by sending Major Duncan with his regular cavalry across the river, who were dismounted and skirmished on foot. The enemy were soon driven back, the batteries were established on the western bank, and Roberts crossed his command to the eastern side. The action commenced at 10 o'clock A. M., and consisted of artillery firing on both sides, charging and countercharging, and by 12 o'clock the Confederates had been driven from all the positions they had taken, and were forced to move their heavy guns to a position higher up the river.

During these hours the Confederates kept coming upon the field in companies and parts of companies, being strung out on their march. At 12 o'clock Colonel Roberts was reënforced by Captain Dick Selden's battalion of regular infantry and Colonel Carson's regiment of New Mexico Volunteers. These new troops were soon placed in position by Colonel Roberts, and every movement made by him up to this time was successful. Several parties of the enemy had been driven from their positions, to take up new ones farther away, and the superior service of the Union guns, under the skill and conduct of Captain McRae and Lieutenant Hall, silenced the Confederate batteries and seemed to assure victory to the Union forces. Thus matters stood when Colonel Canby reached the field and assumed command at 2:45 P. M. The enemy had been driven by Colonel Roberts from all their positions, and had retired behind a high drift of sand, where they re-formed undiscovered, and prepared to storm the two Union batteries. After a short lull in the action, the two storming parties, armed with shot-guns, squirrel rifles, revolvers, and lances, and on foot, made a charge with great fury. The force that charged on Hall's battery, on the Union right, met with such a gallant resistance from the battery's support, consisting of Captain Brotherton's company, Major Duncan's dismounted cavalry, Captain Wingate's battalion of regular infantry, and Kit Carson's regiment of volunteers, that they were repulsed with great slaughter, and fled from the field. But the result was different on the Union left. McRae's battery, though held with heroic determination, with the loss of every horse, and more than one-half the gunners

MAJOR-GENERAL EDWARD R. S. CANBY.
FROM A PHOTOGRAPH.

killed or disabled, was taken by the enemy. Captain McRae and Lieutenant Mishler were both killed at the guns. The Confederate charge was made on foot, and was led by the gallant Major S. A. Lockridge, of Colonel Green's 5th Regiment, who was the foremost to reach the battery. As he approached the battery Captain McRae was standing at one of the guns, with his left hand upon the knob of the cascabel. Lockridge placed his left hand upon the muzzle of the same piece and demanded McRae's surrender. Both raised their revolvers, which were not more than three feet apart, and fired together, and both dropped dead in their tracks.‡ After the enemy reached the battery, there was a short hand-to-hand fight, in which revolvers, clubbed rifles, and sponge staffs were used, but the support soon fell back and crossed the river in retreat. A panic now ensued among the New Mexicans, but the regulars and the Colorado Volunteers were all withdrawn across the river in comparatively good order. The captured guns of McRae's battery were manned by the Confederates, turned to the rear, and assisted in producing the disorder that ensued Canby retreated to the adobe walls of Fort Craig, having sustained a loss on the field of 3 officers and 65 men killed, 3 officers and 157 men wounded, and 1 officer and 34 men prisoners. The enemy's loss was about 40 killed and 200 wounded. It will be observed that while Colonel Roberts was in command of the Union troops everything was moving in their favor, but when Canby assumed command the tide of battle turned, until finally the Union forces were beaten and in retreat. It was the almost unanimous opinion of the officers engaged at Valverde, that if Canby had remained at Fort Craig the Confederates would have commenced their retreat for Texas.

After remaining two days at Valverde, to bury the dead and give needed rest to his men, Sibley moved up the river to Albuquerque, leaving his sick and wounded at Socorro. Sibley found, upon his arrival at Albuquerque, that Captain Herbert M. Enos, assistant-quartermaster, U. S. A. who was in command there, had destroyed the larger part of the Government stores at that place and had retreated with his command toward Santa Fe On the 4th of March, Major J. L. Donaldson, U. S. A., commanding at Santa Fe, destroyed the Government stores at that place, and retreated with his command to Fort Union. The enemy soon after occupied Santa Fe.

In the first week in March, 1862, Colonel John P. Slough, commanding the 1st Regiment Colorado Volunteers, arrived at Fort Union, having made some extraordinary marches, and relieved Colonel G. R. Paul, 4th Regiment New Mexico Volunteers, of the command of the Northern District of New Mexico. Colonel Slough, who was a thorough fighting-man, proceeded to form a command, composed of his own regiment, with what regulars and New Mexico Volunteers he found at Fort Union, for the purpose of operating against the Confederates, whose next movement was supposed to be toward Fort Union; or of forming a junction with Canby's force, which was supposed to have left Fort Craig. His command numbered 1342 officers and men, with a battery of 4 guns, under command of Captain J. F. Ritter, 15th

‡ Major T. T. Teel, C. S. A., who was in the engagement, writes: "There was no duel or fight between Major Lockridge and Captain McRae. . . . Captain McRae's pistol was not discharged; the chambers were loaded."—EDITORS.

Infantry, and a battery of 4 mountain howitzers commanded by Captain Ira W. Claflin, 3d Cavalry. Slough left Fort Union on March 22d. On the 26th, when at Bernal Springs, he dispatched Major Chivington, of the 1st Colorado Volunteers, with 200 cavalry and 180 infantry, toward Santa Fe. The enemy were encountered at Johnson's Ranch, in Apache Cañon, about fifteen miles from Santa Fe. An engagement followed, in which both sides claimed the victory: the Union loss was 5 killed and 14 wounded, while the Confederate loss was 32 killed, 43 wounded, and 71 prisoners. Chivington fell back to Pigeon's Ranch, and Major Pyron, who had commanded the Confederates, was reënforced during the night by Colonel W. R. Scurry and his command, who had been encamped at Galisteo. On the 27th Colonel Slough arrived at Koslowski's Ranch; on the 28th he moved toward Apache Cañon, and at 11 o'clock A. M. the enemy's pickets were encountered. This was a terrible place for an engagement—a deep gorge, with a narrow wagon-track running along the bottom, the ground rising precipitously on each side, with huge bowlders and clumps of stunted cedars interspersed. The batteries on both sides were brought forward, the infantry thrown out upon the flanks, and the firing soon became general. Colonel Slough had been informed that the entire baggage and ammunition train of the Confederates was at Johnson's Ranch, and before the action began Major Chivington's command was sent direct over the mountain, unobserved by the enemy, came down upon their camp, which was guarded by some two hundred men, and fell upon their train, consisting of sixty wagons, which, with their entire contents and a 6-pounder gun, were completely destroyed. Two Confederate officers and fifteen men were taken prisoners. This loss was the most serious that the enemy had met with in the whole of their campaign, as all their ammunition, baggage, and provisions—of which they were already short—were destroyed, and it was accomplished without the loss of a single Union man. The fight in the cañon continued until late in the afternoon, when Colonel Slough moved back to Koslowski's Ranch. This engagement is known in Union reports as "Apache Cañon," and at the South as the "battle of Glorieta." The Union loss was 1 officer and 28 men killed, 2 officers and 40 men wounded, and 15 prisoners; the Confederate, 36 killed, 60 wounded, and 17 prisoners. Colonel Scurry returned to Santa Fe in a completely demoralized condition, while Colonel Slough, having accomplished all that was desired, returned to Fort Union.

On April 1st Colonel Canby, who still remained at Fort Craig, left that post with a force consisting of 860 regulars and 350 volunteers, and arrived

BRIGADIER-GENERAL HENRY H. SIBLEY, C. S. A. FROM A PHOTOGRAPH.

at or near Albuquerque on the afternoon of the 8th. His intention was to effect a junction with the Fort Union troops. He made a feint of attack on Albuquerque by sending in Paddy Graydon's company, supported by a few regular cavalry under Major Duncan. The Confederates were ready to receive them, and fired a few rounds, when Canby retired and passed through Carnuel Cañon to the little adobe village of San Antonio on the east side of the Sandia Mountain, where he soon was joined by Colonel G. R. Paul and his command from that post. When news was received at Santa Fe that Canby had attacked Albuquerque, Colonel Scurry with his entire force started for that town.

General Sibley was now in straitened circumstances. Forts Union and Craig contained all the subsistence stores in the territory, with the exception of what was in the hands of the people, all of which was *cachéd*, or hidden away. He had no money to purchase with, except Confederate bills, which were valueless. He could not advance to Fort Union, as Colonel Slough could withstand any force that he could send in that direction, and he was not strong enough to attack Fort Craig. Accordingly, he determined upon retreating from the territory if Canby would allow him to do so. On the morning of April 12th, the evacuation of Albuquerque commenced by the crossing to the west side of the river of Scurry's and Steele's regiments, Pyron's battalion, and a part of the artillery. Green's regiment moved down on the east side of the river to Peralta, where it crossed over, after a serious skirmish with some of Canby's troops, in which the Confederates lost 6 killed, 3 wounded, and 22 prisoners. On the 15th and 16th the two commands moved down the river, on either side, in view of each other, and most of the time within easy cannon-range. Although Canby's force was double that of the enemy, he would not cross over the river and capture Sibley's forces, as he easily could have done, for he considered it more expedient to allow them to retreat out of the territory and through the wilderness to San Antonio, Texas, than to capture the entire party and be forced to subsist them. This action of Canby caused great discontent in his command, and the Union men of the territory never forgave him. On the evening of the 16th both forces went into camp on the river between Sabinal and La Joya. On the morning of the 17th reveille was sounded in Canby's camp, but no move could be observed in the enemy's, although their camp-fires were burning brightly. After waiting a long time for them to commence their march, Canby sent some scouts across, who soon returned with the information that the Confederate camp was vacant, and that it had been abandoned during the night. It was soon ascertained that Sibley had left the river, leaving behind all his wagons, thirty-eight in number, with their contents, and had proceeded to the westward in the direction of the northern end of the Sierra Madelena.

Canby now proceeded leisurely down the river, and arrived at Fort Craig on the afternoon of the 22d. Sibley's retreat was a most desperate one. He passed on the west side of the Sierra Madelena, through the Sierra de San Mateo, until he reached the dry bed of the Rio Palomas, down which he continued until he reached the Rio Grande, where supplies had been sent from Mesilla to meet him. His command was entirely worn out, and nearly famished. The distance from where he left the Rio Grande until he reached it again was over one hundred miles, and the Confederates were ten days accomplishing this distance with five days of poor rations. The route was through the worst country in that territory, with no guides, trail, or road. What artillery they got through with was dragged uphill and lowered by the men, who used long ropes for that purpose. The undergrowth and brush were so dense that for several miles they were forced to cut their way through with axes and bowie-knives. Nearly all the ammunition was abandoned on the way, as was nearly everything else, except what the men carried upon their persons. On passing over the route of these unfortunate men, nearly a year after, I not infrequently found a piece of a gun-carriage, or part of a harness, or some piece of camp or garrison equipage, with occasionally a white, dry skeleton of a man. At some points it seemed impossible for men to have made their way. During this retreat the Confederates were unmolested by the Union troops, with the exception of the ubiquitous Captain Graydon,‡ who, with his company, followed them alone for a long distance, picking up a large amount of serviceable articles which they had abandoned on their way.

Sibley himself arrived at Fort Bliss in the first week of May, while his command was strung out for fifty miles to the rear. He remained here but a few days, and upon hearing that the "California Column," under the command of Colonel James H. Carleton, was rapidly approaching from Southern California, he commenced his farther retreat for San Antonio, Texas. His force was entirely demoralized, and moved on its way without discipline or command, every man for himself, until all finally arrived. Sibley's command, when he reached Fort Bliss, in 1861, numbered nearly or quite 3700 men; when he returned it was less than 2000, making a loss of over 1700 men, the bones of a large number of whom were left on the arid plains of Arizona, New Mexico, and Texas.

‡ Captain James Graydon's laconic report of the pursuit is dated Polvadera, N. M., May 14th, 1862. He says:

"Last night I reached here from Salada. On the 8th I reached Nugales Spring. From there the road ran between the hills for about 15 miles, then took toward the Magdalene Mountain, where they found water; distance from Nugales about 29 miles; road very rough. On the road they deserted 1 wagon and a camp and left 3 dead bodies half buried. . . . I had all buried. From there the road took to Feather Springs,— I called it so on account of feather-beds being strewed around; distance from Dead Man's Spring seventeen miles. They encamped there. From there they took the road to Ojo del Pueblo; distance fifteen miles; road very rough. Here they blew up a caisson, burned three wagons, hospital department, medicines, etc.; left a few shell and round shot. From there they took to the Salada; distance from Ojo del Pueblo about thirty miles; road very rough. On this road, near and at Salada, they blew up and burned 6 caissons, 1 12-pounder howitzer and 2 mountain-howitzer carriages. I found out where they had buried some 40 shell, loaded, in one place, and 38 in another: 78 in all. I took them up and hid them in another place. To-morrow the quartermaster from here sends for them. They burned up about 19 wagons, 10 ambulances, 6 caissons, and 3 carriages. I think they left 3 howitzers, 1 12-pounder and 2 mountain. I had with me a man who came with them, who saw them leave the howitzers. I believe the Mexicans have the large one buried, and by offering a reward we could find out. They destroyed six 100-pound barrels of powder at Salada, and a great deal of camp-equipage. The road from Ojo del Pueblo is strewn with old harness, iron ovens, and in fact everything but small ammunition. It seems they destroyed very little if any, of that. It appears that the Mexicans have carried off a great deal. There is nothing worth sending for in the shape of ammunition except the shell. The distance from Nugales to Rio Puerco is about 109 miles; road very bad. Sibley's command made it in five days. Left dead on the road about 60 or 70 mules and horses."

EDITORS.

PROVOST GUARD, WASHINGTON. FROM A SKETCH MADE IN 1862.

## McCLELLAN ORGANIZING THE GRAND ARMY.

### BY PHILIPPE, COMTE DE PARIS, AIDE-DE-CAMP TO GENERAL McCLELLAN.

NO one has denied that McClellan was a marvelous organizer. Every veteran of the Army of the Potomac will be able to recall that extraordinary time when the people of the North devoted all their native energy and spirit of initiative to the raising of enormous levies of future combatants and their military equipment, and when infantry battalions, squadrons of cavalry, and batteries of artillery sprung, as it were, from the earth in a night, and poured in from all sides upon the barren wastes of vacant building-lots that then went to the making up of fully three-quarters of the Federal capital.

It was in the midst of this herculean task of organization that two French aides-de-camp were assigned to duty as military attachés on McClellan's staff. His brilliant operations in Western Virginia against Lee,— who had not yet revealed the full extent of his military genius, and whom McClellan was destined to find again in his front but a year later,— the successes of Laurel Hill and Rich Mountain, gave evidence of what might be expected of the inexperienced troops placed in McClellan's hands. ☆ He had already shown rare strategic ability, and the President had confided to him the task of creating the Army of the Potomac from the disorganized bands who had fallen back on Washington under the brave and unfortunate McDowell. Surrounded for the most part by young officers, he was himself the most youthful of us all, not only by reason of his physical vigor, the vivacity of his impressions, the noble candor of his character, and his glowing patriotism, but also, I may add, by his inexperience of men. His military bearing breathed a spirit of frankness, benevolence, and firmness. His look was piercing, his voice gentle, his temper equable, his word of command clear and definite. His

☆ See "McClellan in West Virginia," by General J. D. Cox, Vol. I., p. 126.—EDITORS.

encouragement was most affectionate, his reprimand couched in terms of perfect politeness. Discreet, as a military or political chief should be, he was slow in bestowing his confidence; but, once given, it was never withdrawn. Himself perfectly loyal to his friends, he knew how to inspire others with an absolute devotion.

Unfortunately for himself, McClellan succeeded too quickly and too soon to the command of the principal army of the republic. His lieutenants were as new to the work as he — they had not been tested. Public opinion in the army itself — a judge all the more relentless for the very reason that discipline gives it no opportunity to express itself — had as yet been able neither to pronounce on them, nor to ratify the preferences of the general-in-chief. Paradoxical as it may seem, would it not really have been better could McClellan have received a check at first, as Grant did at Belmont, rather than to have begun with the brilliant campaign in West Virginia which won for him the *sobriquet* of "The Young Napoleon"? Just at the time when I joined his staff the exacting confidence of the people and the Government was laying on him an almost superhuman task. In forging the puissant weapon which, later, snatched from his grasp, was destined, in the hands of the Great Hammerer, to bray the army of Lee, he acquired an imperishable title to the gratitude of his compatriots. He wrought, will it be said, for the glory of his successors? No! He labored for his country, even as a private soldier who dies for her, with no thought of fame. In order to give to his weapon every perfection, he soon learned to resist the impatient solicitations of both the people and the Government.

At the end of September, 1861, while yet under the orders of General Scott, McClellan represented the ardent and impatient spirit of men chafing at the slowness of a chief whose faculties had been chilled by the infirmities of age.

Nevertheless, McClellan's first care was to place the capital beyond all peradventure of being carried by sudden attack: on the one hand, for the sake of reassuring the inhabitants and the political organism within its limits; and, on the other, that the army might be at liberty to act independently when it should be called to the field, leaving a sufficient garrison only to secure the defense of the city. He knew that an army tied up about a place it has to protect is virtually paralyzed. The events of 1870 have only too fully confirmed this view. An engineer of distinction, McClellan himself devised in all its details the system of defensive works from Alexandria to Georgetown. He gave his daily personal supervision to the execution of this work, alternating outdoor activity with office business. Tireless in the saddle, he was equally indefatigable with the pen. Possessed of a methodical and exact mind, he comprehended the organization of his army in every minute detail. The creation of all the material of war necessary to its existence and action was extraordinary proof of the wonderful readiness of the Americans in an emergency. . . .

But the season advanced. The army was being formed. At the end of September the enemy had fallen back on Fairfax Court House, leaving to us at Munson's Hill a few Quaker guns of logs and pasteboard. The time for action seemed to have come. The rigors of winter in Virginia hardly make themselves felt before the beginning of December. By the 17th of October the enemy had again retreated. The Army of the Potomac replied with a commensurate advance. But this was a *faux pas*. The blunder was consummated at Ball's Bluff [see p. 123]. McClellan's orders had been given in entire ignorance of the topography of the environs of Edwards's Ferry (all the maps being inexact) and of the force of the enemy in front of Leesburg. In fact, at that time the organization of the secret service was entirely insufficient to the occasion, in spite of the praiseworthy efforts of Mr. Allen Pinkerton.[ McClellan, who was established beyond Dranesville with McCall's division, believed himself to be within supporting distance of Baker's brigade. The latter was crushed on the 21st, before any one on the right bank of the Potomac knew of his fate. This disaster, of comparatively little moment by itself, led to the most acrimonious recriminations. It proved, above all, how slight and imperfect were the connections between the head of the army and the parts he was called on to manœuvre. On that day a fatal hesitation took possession of McClellan. If he did not then decide to postpone the campaign till the following spring, his conduct of affairs was such as soon to leave him no alternative but recourse to this lamentable necessity. Shortly thereafter a great change came over the military situation: a change which should have encouraged him to the promptest offensive action, but which, unfortunately for him, produced only a directly contrary result.

On the evening of November 1st the whole political world of Washington was in a flutter of agitation. It labored still under the effects of the displacement of General Frémont, guilty of having intruded upon political ground by the issue of an abolitionist proclamation [see Vol. I., p. 278]. The disgrace of "The Pathfinder," so popular with the Western Republicans, had caused some friction in Congress, and had provoked rejoicing among his numerous political enemies in the Army of the Potomac; and now it was learned that a measure of still graver importance had been forced on the Government: Scott had resigned his commission as commander-in-chief of the Federal armies,‡ the natural inference being that McClellan would be designated his successor. Of great stature and of a martial figure, General Scott

---

[ Usually mentioned in the Official Records under the assumed name of E. J. Allen.— EDITORS.

‡ Early in August, 1861, General Scott had asked to be relieved. His request grew out of the irritation caused by a letter McClellan had addressed to him on August 8th, in which the junior officer gave his opinion that the enemy had at least 100,000 men in front of Washington, or in the vicinity, and put himself on record as to the measures (including an enlargement of his own command) deemed by him necessary for the safety of Washington. On the following day, August 9th, General Scott addressed the following letter to the Secretary of War:

"SIR: I received yesterday from Major-General McClellan a letter of that date, to which I design this as my only reply. Had Major-General McClellan presented the same views in person, they would have been freely entertained and discussed. All my military views and opinions had been so presented to him, without eliciting much remark, in our few meetings, which I have in vain sought to multiply. He has stood on his guard, and now places himself on record. Let him make the most of his unenvied advantages. Major-General McClellan has propagated in high quarters the idea expressed in the letter before me, that Washington was not only 'insecure,' but in 'imminent danger.' Relying on our numbers, our forts, and the Potomac River, I am confident in the opposite opinion; and considering the stream of new regiments that is pouring in upon us (before this alarm could have reached their homes), I have not the slightest apprehension for the safety of the Government here.

"Having now been long unable to mount a horse, or to walk more than a few paces at a time, and consequently being unable to review troops, much less to direct them in battle,— in short, being broken down by many particular hurts, besides the general infirmities of age,— I feel that I have become an incumbrance to the army as well as to myself, and that I ought, giving way to a younger commander, to seek the palliatives of physical pain and exhaustion. Accordingly, I must beg the President, at

CONFEDERATE WORKS ON MUNSON'S HILL, AS SEEN FROM THE UNION ADVANCE POST AT BAILEY'S CROSS-ROADS. [SEE MAP, VOL. I., P. 172.] FROM A SKETCH MADE IN SEPTEMBER, 1861.

joined to his physical advantages rare military and diplomatic attainments. He had known how to conquer Mexico without suffering a check; he had been able to establish a government that would warrant evacuation of the country, capable of maintaining itself without extraneous assistance, and he had secured a treaty with leonine conditions for the Americans. But age had attacked him physically and mentally. Obese and impotent, the brilliant Scott was in 1861 but the shadow of his former self. While recognizing the services rendered by him to the republic at the outbreak of the civil war, by his fidelity to the Stars and Stripes in spite of his Virginion origin, the young generals reproached him with paralyzing their ardor and interfering with their projects. The President and his Secretary of State, Mr. Seward, who, through political habitude, was also a temporizer, regretted the resignation of Scott, and augured ill of the youth and rashness of

the earliest moment, to allow me to be placed on the officers' retired list, and then quietly to lay myself up — probably forever — somewhere in or about New York. But, wherever I may spend my little remainder of life, my frequent and latest prayer will be, 'God save the Union.'"

On August 10th, at the request of the President, General McClellan gave the latter authority to withdraw this letter of August 8th, which, as he said, "was designed to be a plain and respectful expression" of his views. President Lincoln went with this letter to General Scott, and requested him to withdraw his reply. On August 12th General Scott wrote again to the Secretary of War, to say that he could not withdraw his letter, for three reasons; the third relating to his physical infirmities, and the first two being the following:

"1. The original offense given to me by Major-General McClellan (see his letter of the 8th inst.) seems to have been the result of deliberation between him and some of the members of the Cabinet, by whom all the greater war questions are to be settled, without resort to or consultation with me, the nominal General-in-Chief of the army. In further proof of this neglect,— although it is unofficially known that in the last week (or six days) many regiments have arrived and others have changed their positions; some to a considerable distance,— not one of these movements has been reported to me (or anything else) by Major-General McClellan; while it is believed, and, I may add, known, that he is in frequent communication with portions of the Cabinet and on matters appertaining to me. That freedom of access and consultation have, very naturally, deluded the junior general into a feeling of indifference toward his senior.

"2. With such supports on his part, it would be as idle for me as it would be against the dignity of my years, to be filing daily complaints against an ambitious junior, who, independent of the extrinsic advantages alluded to, has, unquestionably, very high qualifications for military command. I trust they may achieve crowning victories in behalf of the Union."

EDITORS.

McClellan. The latter, on the other hand, seemed to imagine that the withdrawal of the old warrior removed the last remaining obstacle to the realization of his vast strategic conceptions. But, as is not seldom the case in the course of human events, both these expectations were mistaken. In brief, McClellan, once invested with supreme command, proved himself more of a temporizer than his predecessor, and, as will soon be seen, his premature promotion to this post was the cause of all his subsequent mortification and misfortune.

The next day (November 2d), at 4 o'clock in the morning, we were at his side, mounted, to accompany to the railway station the commander whose place McClellan was about to occupy. As we went along every one chatted about the matter, and sought to penetrate the future and to divine the fortunes and rôle of the young general in the terrible crisis through which the republic was passing. It would have been easier to pierce the night and fog which enveloped us. An hour later McClellan was at his office. A new task of enormous proportions, whose difficulty he had not, perhaps, paused to contemplate, stared him in the face, and threatened him with destruction. Without giving him the full rank enjoyed by Scott, the President had given him full command of the armies of the republic. It should be said that he had the right to this position as the oldest major-general of the regular army. In assuming his new function he did not give up his own personal and particular direction of the Army of the Potomac. Here he was right; for he could neither have found any one to whom he might safely confide his own proper work of organization, nor could he have left the command of the first army of the republic without condemning himself to perpetual prison in the bureau at Washington.

It must be admitted, however, that his two functions were incompatible. As an old French proverb has it, "*Qui trop embrasse, mal étreint.*" When, two years later, Grant himself undertook to conduct the decisive campaign against Richmond, at the same time continuing the direction in chief of all the armies of the Union, he was not only surrounded by the aureole of his splendid victories and incontestable military authority, and not only had a cruel experience proved to the people the necessity for concentrating the military power in the hands of one man, but the different armies which he controlled were confided to approved chiefs whom he could trust with perfect liberty of action, while, in case of need, he might leave at the head of the Army of the Potomac the conqueror of Gettysburg. In Washington, Halleck presided as chief of staff, reduced by Grant to a subordinate function, it is true, but a function for which he possessed special aptitude. The situation of McClellan was different. He perceived this on the day when, entering on the campaign, he placed himself at the head of the Army of the Potomac. At first he was equal to the emergency by dint of incessant work; but he was obliged to renounce the daily routine which had served to maintain his relations with all his divisions, and had contributed to facilitate and hasten forward his schemes of organization. McClellan, confined to his office, undertook the orderly and methodical concentration of the immense number of men enrolled in the service of the republic, in the formation of his armies, and in constructing a scheme for their concerted action. General Halleck, but just then arrived in Washington, was sent to the West with extensive powers [see Vol. I., p. 315]. McClellan assigned to him one of his best lieutenants, General Buell [see Vol. I., p. 385]. Finally, he prepared the great naval expeditions which should give to the Federal arms Port Royal, Roanoke, and New Orleans. Scarcely had he begun the work when the fact was borne in on him that the armies of the West were, as regarded material, less well prepared for the offensive than those of the East, and as it seemed requisite that they should act together, it may be inferred that from the first days of his assuming command, the scheme of post-

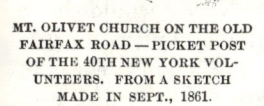

MT. OLIVET CHURCH ON THE OLD FAIRFAX ROAD — PICKET POST OF THE 40TH NEW YORK VOLUNTEERS. FROM A SKETCH MADE IN SEPT., 1861.

poning till spring the operations of the Army of the Potomac was explicitly determined on. McClellan wisely concealed from every one this resolution, the objections to which he understood better than any one.

"CLAREMONT," THE RESIDENCE OF COMMODORE FRENCH FORREST, C. S. N.— PICKET POST OF THE 40TH NEW YORK VOLUNTEERS. FROM A SKETCH MADE SEPT. 26, 1861.

But his soldiers were not slow to comprehend; often the crowd has sagacious instincts, and may divine the calculations of even the most wary statesman. The army proved it in this case by constructing, with all the ready skill of American backwoodsmen, log-huts to protect them from the inclemencies of the season. They did well. When the snow and ice rendered military operations impossible, veritable pioneers' villages had grown up everywhere in the midst of the timber, and afforded the soldiers excellent shelter. The army had coolly taken the liberty of going into winter quarters, without consulting anybody.

The complications of foreign politics contributed their share to restrain McClellan, at a period when the season would yet have permitted him to act on the offensive. It was the 16th of November when the news reached

Washington of the incident afterward known as the *Trent* affair [see p. 134].
... The capture of the Confederate Commissioners on the high seas under a neutral flag, in flagrant violation of the law of nations,— a violation brutal in its method and useless in its results, most dangerous in its consequences,— was hailed by public opinion as a splendid victory for the Stars and Stripes.
... Two men at Washington comprehended from the first the danger to their country of the inconsiderate act of Wilkes: these were Seward and McClellan. The former, burdened with an immense responsibility, patriotically dissimulated his opinion with extraordinary *finesse;* he permitted the excitement to spend itself, and, thanks to the slowness of communication with England, gained time enough ▯ to extricate his Government at the critical juncture, by enveloping the decision he had succeeded in extorting from "the powers that be" in a specious web of plausibilities, calculated to sweeten the bitterness caused at home by England's exactions, and at the same time to satisfy her just demands. He succeeded in sparing his country and the world the horrors of a war the results of which could hardly be imagined. ...

It was not for McClellan to implicate himself in questions of a purely political character, but he probably foresaw the consequences of a war in which England, mistress of the seas, would have inundated the Southern States with arms and munitions of war, with money and volunteers, blockading the Federal ports, and in the spring making Canada the base of operations for her regular army. The States of the North would have found themselves hemmed in along a vast line of boundary by two hostile powers, extending from the Atlantic to the Pacific. McClellan's care, in view of such an emergency, was to perfect and strengthen his army; but, above all, not to compromise the safety of his forces by any attempt at operations on the other side of the Potomac. Grand reviews established, to the satisfaction of the inexperienced, the fact of progress in the equipment, instruction, and drill of the troops. At Bailey's Cross-roads might have been seen a rendezvous of 50,000 men, with all the paraphernalia of a campaign, a large number of cavalry, and a formidable array of artillery. No such spectacle had ever been seen in the United States; the novelty of the display caused the liveliest interest among the inhabitants of Washington. But to a European, not the least curious part of the pageant was the President, with his entire Cabinet, in citizens' dress, boldly caracoling at the head of a brilliant military *cortége*, and riding down the long lines of troops to the rattle of drums, the flourish of trumpets, and the loud huzzas of the whole army. While his aides-de-camp were engaged in the field, McClellan worked ceaselessly with the Secretaries of War and of the Navy, Simon Cameron and Gideon Welles, preparing great expeditions, half military and half naval, that should plant the national flag on the principal points of the enemy's coast, and secure convenient bases for future operations. The success won at Port Royal encouraged the Federal Government in these projects. McClellan himself had brought back from the Crimea a personal experience which enabled him, better than any one else, to preside over the details of preparation.

▯ Seward's letter consenting to the return of the Commissioners bears date of Dec. 26, 1861.— EDITORS.

FROM A PHOTOGRAPH.

*Edwin M Stanton*

Mr. Seward, having courageously ended the *Trent* affair to the satisfaction of the public, now recovered from its first attack of folly, the only obstacle to be feared—the danger of a maritime war—was finally removed. Burnside embarked at New York, during the early days of 1862, with the little army that should seize Roanoke and march on the interior of North Carolina [see Vol. I., p. 632]. The troops destined for the attack on New Orleans were sent to Ship Island in detail. But an unusually severe winter followed. While the naval expeditions intended to land troops on the coasts of the Southern States might still have been fitted out, though the severe gales of the season would have subjected them to serious danger, deep snows and intense cold made movements on the part of the Army of the Potomac next to impossible. Even had it been desirable to expose raw troops to the rigors of a winter campaign, it would have been impracticable to provision an advancing army, on account of the impassable condition of the roads. This set McClellan, as well as many of his subordinates, to thinking of transportation by water, down the Western rivers, or through the deep estuaries of Eastern Virginia.

One day, I think it was the 20th of December, General McClellan, ordinarily so assiduous, did not appear at headquarters. The next day it was learned that he was ill. Three days later his life was in danger. Exhausted with work, his robust physique was seized with a typhoid of the most serious type. . . . His absence paralyzed work at headquarters. He had not regularly delegated his powers. His father-in-law and chief of staff, General Marcy, did not dare to act definitively in his name. McClellan had made the mistake of not creating a general field-staff service, with a duly appointed chief of staff. This might have aided him in securing a consistent *ensemble* of military operations. . . . On his return to the duties of his office [January 13], he realized that during his absence important changes had been arranged. On the 15th of January, Mr. Cameron was superseded by Mr. Stanton, a celebrated lawyer, who was spoken of as one of the coming men of the Democratic party. McClellan, who knew and appreciated him, had, before his illness, contributed materially to Stanton's nomination by recommending him earnestly to the President. But he was not slow to regret this. Mr. Stanton, endowed with a remarkable faculty for work, rendered incontestable service in the organization of the armies; but, fearing the growing importance of those who commanded them, and wishing to impose his authority, he was instrumental, more than any one else, in developing in Mr. Lincoln's mind the idea of directing military operations in person, from the depths of the White House itself. The personal intervention of the President, provoked by the inconsiderate impatience of the public and the precipitate solicitations of McClellan's political adversaries, first declared itself in a singular order, kept a secret as regards the public at the time, but given to the press on March 11th. This order ["President's General War Order No. 1"], dated the 27th of January, directed all the armies of the republic to take the field on the same day, that is, on the 22d of February, in honor of Washington's birthday! In the West, where the rivers

THE NORTH FRONT OF THE WAR DEPARTMENT, WASHINGTON. FROM A WAR-TIME PHOTOGRAPH.

were open, everything was in readiness. Moreover, the order of the President was not necessary to warrant Grant, already under orders from McClellan, in beginning the campaign, and Grant anticipated that order. His début was as a lightning-stroke. His victory at Fort Donelson, followed by the capitulation of 15,000 Confederates, was the return for Bull Run. The impression created throughout the whole army was profound. The Federal volunteers took heart again. The confidence of the Army of the Potomac was redoubled. The general was now restored to health. The weather had moderated. The time had at last come for this army to act. . . . But the immense flotilla which should transport it to Urbana, near the mouth of the Rappahannock [see map, p. 164], or to Fort Monroe, another point of debarkation equally considered with the other, was not yet ready, and no one more than McClellan regretted the delay. It is well known that he was obliged to fight many objections in order to secure the adoption of his favorite plan. He was obliged to exhibit the details of his projects before numerous councils of war, some of them political and some of them military, some of the members of which were, perhaps, not possessed of absolute discretion. He was obliged to reassure and convince all those who feared lest Washington should be left without sufficient protection. He finally obtained the Government's approval.

At the very moment when all seemed ready for the realization of his grand design, two unforeseen circumstances arose to thwart the calculations of McClellan. The first was the sudden evacuation of Manassas by the Confederates. I do not believe that this could be attributed to indiscretions following the councils of war at Washington. I prefer, rather, to ascribe it to the military sagacity of the great soldier who then commanded the Army of Northern Virginia. His positions at Manassas were protected only by the snow and ice which paralyzed the Federals. With the opening of the season he would be obliged to withdraw behind the Rappahannock. This movement brought the Southern army nearer to Richmond, at the same time placing it on the Urbana route, thus making a landing there impossible for us, and permitting Lee to anticipate McClellan on the Virginia peninsula. McClellan would not give up his plan of approaching Richmond from the south-east. Fort Monroe, occupied by the Federals, was chosen as the new point of debarkation, and the pursuit of the enemy on the road from Manassas to Fredericksburg had no other object than to deceive him as to the intentions of the Federals. The army, after having feigned pursuit, was ordered to concentrate near Alexandria, the rendezvous of the grand flotilla which McClellan awaited with so much impatience.

But on the 12th of March another unexpected event again caused consternation among the officers of the staff. The indefatigable newsdealers, who followed the army almost to the very line of battle, had brought papers from Washington, in which we read a decree [" President's War Order No. 3 "], dated March 11th, in effect relieving McClellan from the direction in chief of the armies of the United States, the pretext being that McClellan had not taken the field on the 22d of February [see p. 167]. It was recalled to mind that on that very day, McClellan, on going upon the floor of the House of Representatives, had been greeted by a triple salvo of applause, a demonstration flattering enough, but damaging to a general, whose functions forbid even the suspicion of political partisanship. The measure in question was inept, since it virtually restricted McClellan within the Department of the Potomac, excluding West Virginia, then assigned to Frémont. The measure was especially disastrous in suppressing all general direction of military operations, and disintegrating the *ensemble*. It had been decided that Scott was too superannuated to attend to this general direction; it was not for the purpose of abolishing it entirely that command had been confided to younger and more energetic hands. Unfortunately, at this moment Mr. Lincoln had the weakness to think that he himself could effectively exercise the supreme control, assigned him in form, it is true, by a figment of the national Constitution. As for McClellan, the President's decision was mortifying in its method, Lincoln having delayed its promulgation till after the departure of his general, and having left it to be communicated to the latter by the daily papers. Yet McClellan would have consoled himself, had not this measure been followed by others still more harassing, and of a nature to completely cripple intelligent action. But he was relieved of an immense responsibility; he was left at the head of an army eager to follow his lead, eager for battle, and confident of victory under his orders. He alone seemed to preserve his *sang-froid* in the midst of officers of all grades who flocked to his headquarters at Fairfax Court House as the news spread rapidly from camp-fire to camp-fire. Among these officers were stanch supporters, secret foes, those jealous of his fame, would-be worshipers of the rising sun, and, last but not least, indiscreet and compromising friends. In this evil hour McClellan felt how sternly patriotic duty demanded of him that he should hide the mortification he felt at this wound to his feelings as an officer and a man. He sought for consolation only in the sympathy and confidence of his soldiers.

# BALL'S BLUFF AND THE ARREST OF GENERAL STONE.

### BY RICHARD B. IRWIN, LIEUT.-COLONEL AND ASSISTANT ADJUTANT-GENERAL, U. S. V.

ABOUT 1 o'clock on the morning of the 9th of February, 1862, General Charles P. Stone, a native of Massachusetts, a graduate with honors of the United States Military Academy, a distinguished officer of the ordnance corps during the Mexican war, colonel of the 14th regular infantry, and brigadier-general of volunteers, commanding a division of ten thousand men in the Army of the Potomac, was arrested in Washington, by the commander of the provost guard, and sent, in custody of a lieutenant and two policemen, to Fort Lafayette, in New York harbor. There, and at Fort Hamilton, he was kept in close and solitary confinement, his pockets being emptied and his letters examined, until the 16th of August, when, after the lapse of 189 days, he was set at liberty, under the peremptory requirements of an act of Congress, approved July 17th, 1862, forbidding the detention of any officer or soldier more than thirty days without charges.

It will be observed that he was held for a fresh period of thirty days before this law was allowed to operate, and it is also worth remarking that a law as old as the Government, known as the Articles of War, the fundamental law of the army of the United States, contained substantially the same provision, the only essential difference being that the new law, in effect, lengthened the time for preferring charges from eight days to thirty.

Though promptly and often asked for, and repeatedly promised, no statement of the charges was ever furnished to General Stone. In truth, no charges were ever preferred against him. No cause for his arrest has ever been shown. It has even been disputed upon whose initiative it was ordered. The vague and loose "evidence," and the floating suspicions engendered by it, that formed the groundwork for his arrest, never admitted of being condensed into an accusation, simply because there was nothing in them to condense. The real cause must be sought for amid the tangled mesh of a net-work of circumstances, such as is occasionally the despair of men who read history by the light of human sympathy.

Before trying to trace its threads, it may be well to recall how for weeks the safety, not only of Washington but of the President and his cabinet, had depended mainly upon the loyalty, the prudence, and the vigilance of Colonel Stone and his District of Columbia volunteers.╎ Well might Mr. Lincoln exclaim, with his smile, "Oh! I could never believe General Stone would be disloyal!"

In the autumn of 1861 Stone's division, comprising the brigades of Gorman, Lander, and Baker,‡ was observing the ferries or fords of the Potomac in front of Poolesville. On the 20th of October, McCall's division being at Dranesville, General McClellan telegraphed to General Stone directing

╎ See General Stone's article, "Washington on the Eve of the War," Vol. I., p. 7.—EDITORS.
‡ Afterward Sedgwick's division, Second Corps, brigade commanders Gorman, Dana, and Burns.—R. B. I.

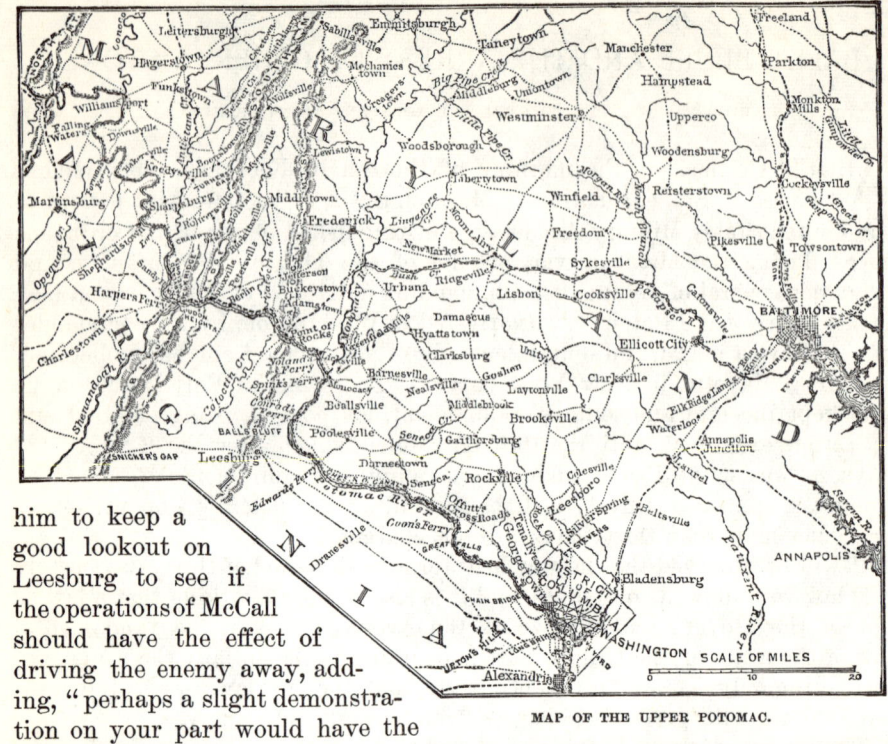

him to keep a good lookout on Leesburg to see if the operations of McCall should have the effect of driving the enemy away, adding, "perhaps a slight demonstration on your part would have the effect to move them." This slight demonstration resulted in the battle of Ball's Bluff.

MAP OF THE UPPER POTOMAC.

On the morning of the 21st of October General Stone gave Colonel Baker discretionary authority to retire the small detachment then at Ball's Bluff, or to send over his brigade to support it. Colonel Baker at once, without further information, without visiting the Virginia shore, and without organizing the boat service, gave the order to cross. Early in the afternoon he crossed himself and posted his command. In support of this movement, and to hold the enemy's attention, Stone sent Gorman's brigade across at Edwards Ferry, where the principal force of the enemy had been seen.

The Confederate Commander, General Evans,‡ early discovering both movements and having the advantage of a shorter line, concealed, moreover, by the nature of the ground, gradually withdrew all his force, save one regiment, from Gorman's front, concentrated it against Baker, and about 3 o'clock attacked with vigor. Each side numbered about seventeen hundred; our troops had three light guns, soon disabled, the Confederates none; but their men moved to the attack from commanding ground, well covered by trees and bushes, while ours, badly posted and badly arranged, were held to the bluff without room to retire, or means of retreat.

We find the opening events described as follows, by Colonel Charles

‡ Colonel N. G. Evans, who distinguished himself at the first Bull Run.— EDITORS.

Devens, commanding the 15th Massachusetts Regiment, afterwards major-general of volunteers, and, under President Hayes, attorney-general of the United States:

"About 12 o'clock Sunday night, October 20th, I crossed the Potomac by your [Stone's] order from Harrison's Island to the Virginia shore with five companies, numbering about 300 men, of my regiment, with the intention of taking a rebel camp, reported by scouts to be situated at the distance of about a mile from the river, of destroying the same, of observing the country around, and of returning to the river, or of waiting and reporting if I thought myself able to remain for reënforcements, or if I found a position capable of being defended against a largely superior force. Having only three boats, which together conveyed about thirty men, it was nearly 4 o'clock when all the force was transferred to the opposite shore. We passed down the river about sixty rods by a path discovered by the scouts, and then up the bluff known as Ball's Bluff, where we found an open field surrounded by woods. At this point we halted until daybreak, being joined here by a company of one hundred men from the 20th Massachusetts, accompanied by Colonel Lee, who were to protect our return.

"At daybreak we pushed forward our reconnoissance toward Leesburg to the distance of about a mile from the river, to a spot supposed to be the site of the rebel encampment, but found on passing through the woods that the scouts had been deceived by a line of trees on the brow of the slope, the opening through which presented, in an uncertain light, somewhat the appearance of a line of tents. Leaving the detachment in the woods, I proceeded with Captain Philbrick and two or three scouts across the slope and along the other line of it, observing Leesburg, which was in full view, and the country about it, as carefully as possible, and seeing but four tents of the enemy. My force being well concealed by the woods, and having no reason to believe my presence was discovered, and no large number of the enemy's tents being in sight, I determined not to return at once, but to report to yourself, which I did, by directing Quartermaster Howe to repair at once to Edwards Ferry to state these facts, and to say that in my opinion I could remain until I was reënforced.

"The means of transportation between the island and the Virginia shore had been strengthened, I knew, at daybreak, by a large boat, which would convey 60 or 70 men at once, and as the boat could cross and recross every ten minutes, I had no reason to suppose there would be any difficulty in sending over 500 men in an hour, as it was known there were two large boats between the island and the Maryland shore, which would convey to the island all the troops that could be conveyed from it to the Virginia shore.

"Mr. Howe left me with his instructions at about 6:30 A. M. . . . I was rejoined at 8 A. M. by Quartermaster Howe, who reported to me that I was to remain where I was, and would be reënforced, and that Lieutenant-Colonel Ward would proceed to Smart's Mill ♭ with the remainder of the regiment, that a communication should be kept up between us, and that 10 cavalry would report to me for the purpose of reconnoitering. For some reason they never appeared or reported to me, but I have since learned they came as far as the bluff. ⸕ If they had reported to me, they could have rendered excellent service. I directed Quartermaster Howe to return at once and report the skirmish that had taken place. . . .

"At about 10 o'clock Quartermaster Howe returned and stated that he had reported the skirmish of the morning, and that Colonel Baker would shortly arrive with his brigade and take command. Between 9 and 11 o'clock I was joined by Lieutenant-Colonel Ward with the remainder of my regiment, making in all, a force of 625 men, with 28 officers, from my regiment, as reported to me by the adjutant, many of the men of the regiment being at this time on other duty.

"About 12 o'clock it was reported to me a force was gathering on my left, and about 12:30 o'clock a strong attack was made on my left by a body of infantry concealed in the woods, and

---

♭ According to General Stone, he directed "five companies to be thrown into a strong mill on the right of Ball's Bluff. Colonel Baker allowed these companies to be directed to the front."— EDITORS.

⸕ According to General Stone, he "sent cavalry scouts to be thrown out in advance of the infantry on the right. Colonel Baker allowed this cavalry to return without scouting, and did not replace it although he had plenty at his disposition."— EDITORS.

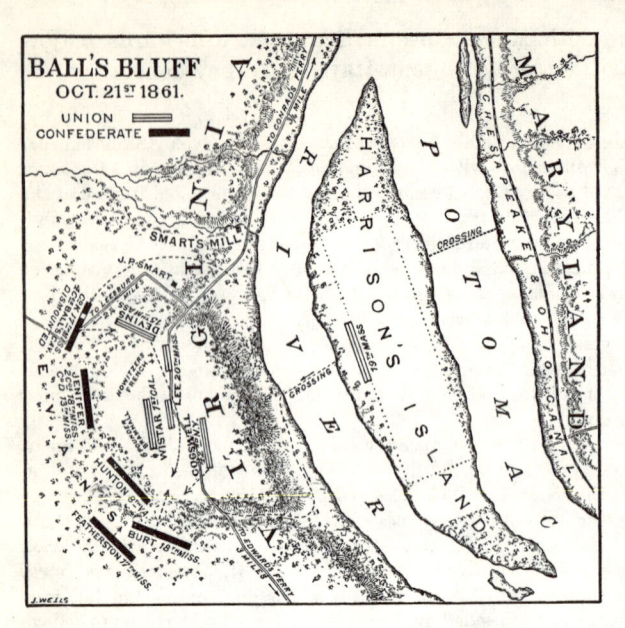

upon the skirmishers in front by a body of cavalry. The fire of the enemy was resolutely returned by the regiment, which maintained its ground with entire determination. Reënforcements not yet having arrived, and the attempts of the enemy to outflank us being very vigorous, I directed the regiment to retire about 60 paces into an open space in the wood, and prepare to receive any attack that might be made, while I called in my skirmishers. When this was done I returned to the bluff, where Colonel Baker had already arrived. This was at 2:15 P. M. He directed me to form my regiment at the right of the position he proposed to occupy, which was done by eight companies, the center and left being composed of a detachment of the 20th Massachusetts, numbering about 300 men, under command of Colonel Lee. A battalion of the California Regiment, numbering about 600 men, Lieutenant-Colonel Wistar commanding; 2 howitzers, commanded by Lieutenant French, and a 6-pounder, commanded by Lieutenant Bramhall, were planted in front, supported by Company D, Captain Studley, and Company F, Captain Sloan, of the 15th Massachusetts."

Himself remaining with Gorman at Edwards Ferry to direct the crossing there, General Stone placed Colonel E. D. Baker, of the 71st Pennsylvania Regiment (also called the "1st California," in compliment to Colonel Baker), in command of the movement by Harrison's Island and Ball's Bluff, under the following orders:

HEADQUARTERS CORPS OF OBSERVATION, EDWARDS FERRY, October 21st — 11:50.— COLONEL E. D. BAKER, Commanding Brigade. COLONEL: I am informed that the force of the enemy is about 4000, all told. If you can push them, you may do so as far as to have a strong position near Leesburg, if you can keep them before you, avoiding their batteries. If they pass Leesburg and take the Gun Spring road you will not follow far, but seize the first good position to cover that road. Their design is to draw us on, if they are obliged to retreat, as far as Goose Creek, where they can be reënforced from Manassas and have a strong position. Report

THE OPPOSING FORCES AT BALL'S BLUFF, VA.— OCTOBER 21ST, 1861.

*Union Forces:* Colonel Edward D. Baker ⸸ (k); Colonel Milton Cogswell (w and c): 15th Mass., Col. Charles Devens; 20th Mass., Col. William R. Lee (c); 42d New York (called "Tammany regiment"), Col. Milton Cogswell; 71st Pa. (also called 1st California), Lieut.-Col. Isaac J. Wistar (w). *Artillery:* B, 1st R. I. (one gun), Lieut. Walter M. Bramhall (w); I, 1st U. S. (two guns), Lieut. Frank S. French.

The casualties in the Union forces were 49 killed, 158 wounded, and 714 captured or missing = 921.

*Confederate Forces:* Brigadier-General Nathan G. Evans: 17th Miss., Col. W. S. Featherston; 18th Miss., Col. E. R. Burt (m w), Lieut.-Col. Thomas M. Griffin; 8th Va., Col. Eppa Hunton; Co. D, 13th Miss., Capt. L. D. Fletcher; Va. Cavalry (3 co's), Col. Walter H. Jenifer.

The Confederate loss was 33 killed, 115 wounded, and 1 missing = 149.

⸸ Colonel Baker received the appointment of Brigadier-General, U. S. Volunteers, August 6th, 1861, to rank from May 17th, 1861. This he declined, August 31st, 1861. On September 21st, 1861, he was appointed Major-General, U. S. Volunteers, but at the date of his death he had neither accepted nor declined the appointment. General McClellan was then the only other officer in the Army of the Potomac holding that rank.— EDITORS.

frequently, so that when they are pushed, Gorman [at Edwards Ferry] can come in on their flank. Yours respectfully and truly, CHAS. P. STONE, Brigadier-General, Commanding.

HEADQUARTERS CORPS OF OBSERVATION. EDWARDS FERRY, October 21st, 1861.—COLONEL E. D. BAKER, Commanding Brigade. COLONEL: In case of heavy firing in front of Harrison's Island, you will advance the California regiment of your brigade, or retire the regiments under Colonels Lee and Devens upon the Virginia side of the river, at your discretion, assuming command on arrival. Very respectfully, Colonel, your most obedient servant, CHAS. P. STONE, Brigadier-General, Commanding.

Captain Francis J. Young, assistant quartermaster of Colonel Baker's staff, says that as soon as the latter order had been received

"Colonel Baker immediately sent for three regiments and a squadron of cavalry from his brigade and for Colonel Cogswell and the rest of his Tammany regiment.

"Proceeding to the crossing at Harrison's Island, we found the means of transportation to consist of two flat-boats of the capacity of 25 to 40 men, and a small skiff, which would carry but 3 or 4 men. The river was swollen and the current rapid, and there was much labor and delay in making use of the boats. Another flat-boat was found in the canal one mile distant, and, being towed down to the crossing, was with much difficulty got into the Potomac.⁂ Colonel Baker immediately crossed with me and as many men as could be got into the boats to the island, and reaching the opposite side of the island found one flat-boat and a small metallic boat. He crossed to the Virginia shore without delay with Adjutant-General Harvey, sending me back with an order for Colonel Cogswell to bring over the artillery.

"It was now 2 o'clock P. M., and Colonel Cogswell coming over from the Maryland side with 2 pieces of artillery, horses, and men, we carried with us the 2 howitzers of the Rhode Island Battery and crossed to the Virginia side. The bank is of a miry clay, and the heights almost precipitous, with fallen trees and rocks, making it very difficult to get up the artillery. Arriving by circuitous routes on the summit, we found an open field of six acres, covered with wild grass, scrub oak, and locust trees, and forming a segment of a circle, the arc of which was surrounded with trees. Colonel Baker apprised Colonel Devens that he had been placed in command, and learned that the 15th Massachusetts, after having advanced for a mile in the direction of Leesburg, had been attacked and fallen back to the position which they then occupied, just in the edge of the woods on the right. The other forces were lying under the brow of the hill; and with the exception of an occasional rifle shot all was quiet, and no sight of an enemy. The 2 howitzers and 1 piece of artillery were drawn by the men out into the open field, pointing to the woods in front, the artillery horses not being brought up the steep."

Occurrences at Harrison's Island and at the bluff, during the arrival of reënforcements, are described by Colonel Milton Cogswell, of the "Tammany" or 42d New York regiment, whose report is dated New York, September 22d, 1862, after his return from captivity. At 2 o'clock on the 21st he received orders to cross the Potomac at Harrison's Island:

"Arrived at the landing opposite Harrison's Island, I found the greatest confusion existing. No one seemed to be in charge, nor any one superintending the passage of the troops, and no order was maintained in their crossing. The eight companies of my regiment on picket were rapidly concentrated at the crossing, and I moved with one company of my regiment and two pieces of artillery belonging to the 6th New York Battery to the island, leaving verbal orders with Major Bowe, who remained in charge, to push the remainder of my regiment on as soon as possible. I immediately crossed the island to make the passage of the second branch of the river, and there found still greater confusion existing than at the first landing. . . .

"I ascended the bluff (about 70 feet high) and reported myself to Colonel Baker. I found

---

⁂ General Stone says in a report dated December 2d, 1861, that "Colonel Baker spent more than an hour in personally superintending the lifting of a boat from the canal to the river, when a junior officer or sergeant would have done as well, the meantime neglecting to visit or give orders to the advanced force in the face of the enemy."—EDITORS.

THE CLIFF AT BALL'S BLUFF. FROM A PHOTOGRAPH.

him near the bluff, on the edge of an open field of about 8 or 10 acres' extent, trapezoidal in form, the acute angle being on the left front, the shortest parallel side near the edge of the bluff, and along this line was the 1st California Regiment, while the 15th Massachusetts Regiment was formed in line in the open woods, forming the right-hand boundary of the field, its line being nearly perpendicular to that of the California regiment Two mountain howitzers, under Lieutenant French, of the United States artillery, were posted in front of the angle formed by these two regiments. A deep ravine, having its mouth on the left of the point where we landed, extended along the left of the open field and wound around in front of it, forming nearly a semicircle, bounded by wooded hills commanding the whole open space. Some companies of the 20th Massachusetts Regiment were posted in reserve behind the line of the California regiment.

"Colonel Baker welcomed me on the field, seemed in good spirits, and very confident of a successful day. He requested me to look at his line of battle, and with him I passed along the whole front. He asked my opinion of his disposition of troops, and I told him frankly that I deemed them very defective, as the wooded hills beyond the ravine commanded the whole so perfectly, that should they be occupied by the enemy he would be destroyed, and I advised an immediate advance of the whole force to occupy the hills, which were not then occupied by the enemy. I told him that the whole action must be on our left, and that we must occupy those hills. No attention was apparently paid to this advice, and Colonel Baker ordered me to take charge of the artillery, but without any definite instructions as to its service. About twenty minutes afterward the hills on the left front to which I had called attention were occupied by the enemy's skirmishers, who immediately opened a sharp fire on our left. I immediately directed the artillery to open fire on those skirmishers, but soon perceived that the fire was ineffectual, as the enemy was under cover of the trees, shooting down the artillerists at easy musket range.☆ Soon Lieutenant Bramhall and nearly all the artillerymen had been shot

☆ Captain William F. Bartlett, of the 20th Massachusetts, says of this attack: "The enemy now opened on us from the woods in front with a heavy fire of musketry, which was very effective. They fired low, the balls all going within from one to four feet of the ground. Three companies of the 20th were kept in reserve, but on the open ground, exposed to a destructive fire. It was a continual fire now, with occasional pauses of one or two minutes, until the last. The rifled cannon was on the left in the open ground, in front of a part of Baker's regiment, exposed to a hot fire. It was not discharged more than eight times. The gunners were shot down in the first of

## BALL'S BLUFF AND THE ARREST OF GENERAL STONE. 129

down, and the pieces were worked for a time by Colonel Baker in person, his assistant adjutant-general (Captain Harvey), Captain Stewart, assistant adjutant-general of the division, a few other officers, and myself.

"Leaving the pieces, as I saw the whole strength of the enemy was being thrown on the left, I proceeded to the extreme left, where I found Lieutenant-Colonel Wistar had been badly wounded, and that the left wing, without a commander, was becoming disorganized. I then ordered Captain Markoe, of the 1st California Regiment, to move his company to the left, and hold the hill at all hazards. Captain Markoe moved as directed, engaged the enemy's skirmishers, and held his ground for some time, but could gain no advantage over the enemy. About half an hour afterward Colonel Baker came from the right of the line and passed in front of the line of skirmishers, when he was instantly killed by the fire of the enemy's sharp-shooters.

"By this time the hills on the left front were fully occupied by the enemy. Two companies of my regiment, under Captain Alden, arrived on the field, cheering most heartily, and with this fresh force we pushed the enemy some fifty yards back, but they had now obtained too strong possession of the hills to be dislodged. An unequal contest was maintained for about half an hour, when Captain Harvey, assistant adjutant-general, reported to me that Colonel Baker having been killed, I was in command of the field, and that a council of war was being held by the remaining colonels. I repaired to the point occupied by Colonels Lee and Devens, and found that they had decided on making a retreat. I informed them I was in command of the field; that a retreat across the river was impossible, and the only movement to be made was to cut our way through to Edwards Ferry, and that a column of attack must be at once formed for that purpose. At the same time I directed Captain Harvey, assistant adjutant-general, to form the whole force into column of attack, faced to the left.

COLONEL EDWARD D. BAKER. FROM A PHOTOGRAPH.

"Having given these orders, I proceeded to the front, and finding our lines pressed severely, I ordered an advance of the whole force on the right of the enemy's line. I was followed by the remnants of my two companies and a portion of the California regiment, but, for some reasons unknown to me, was not joined by either the 15th or the 20th Massachusetts regiments. We were overpowered and forced back to our original position, and again driven from that position to the river-bank by overwhelming numbers. On the river-bank I found the whole force in a state of great disorder. As I arrived, two companies of my own regiment [42d New York], under Captains Gerety and O'Meara, landed from the large boat. I ordered these fresh companies up the bluff, and they instantly ascended and deployed as skirmishers to cover the passage to the island, while I took about a dozen men and moved to the left to check a heavy fire of the enemy which had opened on us from the mouth of the ravine near. We were almost immediately surrounded and captured. This took place shortly after dark."

the engagement, and I saw Colonel Lee carry a charge to the gun with his own hands. The last time that it was fired the recoil carried it down the rise to the edge of the bank." Colonel Eppa Hunton, of the 8th Virginia, who made the attack, says: "At the first fire from my regiment nearly every man at the enemy's cannon was shot down, and so incessant and galling was the fire we kept up that there were only three discharges of cannon after the first fire from the 8th."— EDITORS.

✠ Colonel Cogswell says in conclusion: "I deem it my duty as commander of the field during the last part of the action to state my convictions as to the principal causes of the untoward results of the day: First. The transportation of troops across the two branches of the river was in no way guarded or organized. There were no guards at any of the landings. No boats' crews had been detailed, and each command as it arrived was obliged to organize its own. No guns were placed in position either on the Maryland side or on the island to protect the passage, although several

Colonel Devens thus describes the closing events as observed by him:

"The action commenced about 3 P. M., and at about 4 P. M. I was ordered to detach two companies from the left of my regiment to the support of the left of the line, and to draw in, proportionately, the right flank, which was done, Companies G and H, Captains Forehand and Philbrick, being detached for that purpose. By this time it had become painfully evident, by the volume and rapidity of the enemy's fire and the persistency of his attacks, that he was in much larger force than we. The two howitzers were silent and the 6-pounder also. Their commanders came from the field wounded.

"Soon after, I was called from the right of my regiment, there being at this time a comparative cessation of the enemy's fire, to the center of the line, and learned for the first time that Colonel Baker had been killed and that Lieutenant-Colonel Ward, of the 15th Massachusetts, had been carried from the field severely wounded. Colonel Lee supposing it his duty to take command, I reported myself ready to execute his orders. He expressed his opinion that the only thing to be done was to retreat to the river, and that the battle was utterly lost. It soon appeared that Colonel Cogswell was entitled to the command, who expressed his determination to make the attempt to cut our way to Edwards Ferry, and ordered me, as a preliminary movement, to form the 15th Regiment in line toward the left. The 15th Regiment accordingly moved across from the right to the left of the original line. Two or three companies of the Tammany [42d New York] Regiment, just then arrived, formed also on his left. While endeavoring to make the necessary dispositions to retreat, confusion was created by the appearance of an officer of the enemy's force in front of the Tammany Regiment, who called on them to charge on the enemy, who were now in strong force along the wood occupied formerly by the 15th Massachusetts during the former portion of the action. The detachment of the Tammany Regiment, probably mistaking this for an order from their own officers, rushed forward to the charge, and the 15th Massachusetts, supposing that an order had been given for the advance of the whole line, rushed with eagerness, but was promptly recalled by their officers, who had received no such order. The detachment of the Tammany Regiment was received with a shower of bullets, and suffered severely. In the disturbance caused by their repulse the line was broken, but was promptly re-formed.

"After this, however, although several volleys were given and returned and the troops fought vigorously, it seemed impossible to preserve the order necessary for a combined military movement, and Colonel Cogswell reluctantly gave the order to retreat to the river-bank. The troops descended the bluff, and reached the bank of the river, where there is a narrow plateau between the river and the ascent of the bluff, both the plateau and the bluff being heavily wooded. As I descended upon this plateau, in company with Colonel Cogswell, I saw the large boat, upon which we depended as the means of crossing the river, swamped by the number of men who rushed upon it.

"For the purpose of retarding as much as possible the approach of the enemy, by direction of Colonel Cogswell I ordered the 15th Regiment to deploy as skirmishers over the bank of the river, which order was executed, and several volleys were given and returned between them and others of our forces and the enemy, who were now pressing upon us in great numbers and forcing down furious volleys on this plateau and into the river to prevent any escape. It was impossible longer to continue to resist, and I should have had no doubt, if we had been contending with the troops of a foreign nation, in justice to the lives of men, it would have been our duty to surrender; I had no hesitation in advising men to escape as they could, ordering them in all cases to throw their arms into the river rather than give them up to the enemy. This order was generally obeyed, although several of the men swam the river with their muskets on their backs, and others have returned to camp, bringing with them their muskets, who had remained on the Virginia shore for two nights rather than to part with their weapons in order to facilitate their escape. Having passed up along the line of that portion of the river occupied by my regiment, I returned to the lower end of it, and at dark myself swam the river by the aid of three of the soldiers of my regiment."

pieces were disposable on the Maryland shore near the landing. Had the full capacity of the boats been employed, more than twice as many men might have crossed in time to take part in the action. Second. The dispositions on the field were faulty, according to my judgment."— EDITORS.

The final effect of not looking after the boat service was seen in the presence of the fifteen companies at Harrison's Island on their way to the scene of action at the moment of defeat. This error, like the others, was the result of Colonel Baker's inexperience. No one has ever sought to blame him. The whole load was at once thrown upon General Stone, though not, indeed, by those who knew the facts and were capable of judging.

With the light we have to-day, it would, indeed, be easy to admit that, even with forces outnumbering the enemy as four to one, to cross a rapid river in a few boats at two points practically four miles apart, climb a steep bank, and thence advance against an enemy centrally posted within two miles of either landing, is too delicate an operation to be undertaken by inexperienced troops, without that knowledge of individual qualities which can only be gained by the test of actual warfare, and, moreover, without a positive command or an object adequate to the risk.

If we are to judge by the light of '61, then it must be remembered that General Stone supposed himself to be carrying out the wishes of his commanding general‡ in regard to dislodging the enemy from Leesburg, that the scouting parties found no large force of Confederates, that he had no reason to apprehend any one of the negligences and ignorances which followed, that the main body of the Confederates seemed to be in Gorman's front; finally, that he believed McCall to be still reconnoitering beyond Dranesville.♭

It was thus that General McClellan, no less just than generous to his subordinates, judged in vindicating Stone from reproach, and retaining him in command when self-interest would in any case have suggested his retirement, and duty would have demanded it if he were to blame.¶ So, too, judged the leading officers who took part in the battle, including those who suffered wounds and long imprisonment.

But with the cry of grief that went up all over the land at the untimely death of the brave and eloquent Baker, who had left the Senate to take the field, was mingled the cry of rage of a few men among his personal followers. They filled the public ear with misrepresentations, to which Stone and his officers, restrained by discipline, were unable to reply. ☆

---

‡ Although the strict letter of his instructions was admittedly exhausted. But this was not the only communication that had passed. Observe, that although surprised by the movement, and greatly distressed by the disaster, General McClellan uttered not a word of censure. He even telegraphed, "Take Leesburg." Curiously enough, this dispatch, being in cipher, could not be read by General Stone, who replied, "*I have the box, but not the key.*" At first this was supposed to refer to a box, and I was sent to General Stone's family for the key; of course, to no purpose.— R. B. I.

♭ General McClellan says he thinks notice was sent to General Stone of McCall's withdrawal from Dranesville. He had a right to think so; but the fact remains that *no such notice was sent.* I state this of my own knowledge.— R. B. I.

¶ In "McClellan's Own Story," the general writes of Stone: "He was a most charming and amiable gentleman; honest, brave, a good soldier, though occasionally carried away by his chivalrous ideas. He was very unfortunate, and was as far as possible from meriting the sad fate and cruel treatment he met with."— EDITORS.

☆ The following extract denotes the substance of such irresponsible accusations against General Stone as reached the public at the time: "Brigadier-General Charles P. Stone was arrested in Washington this morning, at 2 o'clock, by a posse of the Provost Marshal's force, and sent to Fort Lafayette, New York harbor. The charges against General Stone are: First, for misbehavior at the battle of Ball's Bluff; second, for holding correspondence with the enemy before and since the battle of Ball's Bluff, and receiving visits from rebel officers in his camp; third, for treacherously suffering the enemy to build a fort or strong work, since the battle of Ball's Bluff, under his guns with-

General Stone asked his commanding general for a court of inquiry; it was refused as unnecessary and inexpedient.

Congress met and promptly called on the Executive for information and an investigation. Both requests were denied as contrary to the public interests, but the demand being repeated, the President so far yielded as to promise an immediate inquiry. This was not enough to satisfy Congress, which appointed the Joint Committee on the Conduct of the War, and began the investigation for itself, and in a mood which may be inferred from the denunciation of the affair, in advance, as "the most atrocious military murder in history."

In the meantime, a series of incidents had taken place, of a character tending to give point to the vague suspicions entertained against General Stone in some quarters. In September, two alleged fugitive slaves were returned to their master, under General Stone's orders, by a subaltern of the 20th Massachusetts regiment of his division. Not knowing, or perhaps ignoring, the fact that General Stone's action was in exact accord with the orders, and was sustained by the approval of his superiors, including the President, as well as in conformity with the policy of the Government, as then declared by Congress, Governor Andrew, upon the first information received, wrote a letter to the regimental commander, reprimanding the lieutenant.

JOHN A. ANDREW, WAR-GOVERNOR OF MASSACHUSETTS. FROM A PHOTOGRAPH.

A warm correspondence followed, in which, on the one hand, Governor Andrew maintained the correctness of his own action, and severely criticised General Stone's, while, on the other hand, General McClellan and General Stone protested against the governor's course as an unwarranted interference with the discipline of the armies of the United States.

Governor Andrew sent the correspondence to Senator Sumner, who laid it before the Senate, and denounced Stone in unmeasured terms.

Stung to the quick, Stone instantly replied in a letter to Mr. Sumner, for which I need seek no better description or criticism than is contained in Mr.

out molestation; fourth, for a treacherous design to expose his force to capture and destruction by the enemy, under pretense of orders for a movement from the commanding general, which had not been given."—["Diary of Events" for February 9th, 1862, in Vol. IV. of Moore's "Rebellion Record," published in 1862.] These few lines involve nine distinct misstatements or perversions, only the single fact embodied in the first paragraph being correctly set forth.— R. B. I.

Lincoln's remark, after reading the letter and patiently hearing the whole story, while it was still hot: "I don't know that I should have written such a letter; but if I had wanted to, I think, under the circumstances,— under the circumstances, mind you,— I would have had a right to do so."♦

These circumstances, imperfectly known or understood, have caused many to suppose that Mr. Sumner was in some way the originator of General Stone's arrest; it is, however, as certain as any fact can be upon negative evidence, that Mr. Sumner had nothing whatever to do with the subsequent proceedings.

The Committee on the Conduct of the War proceeded to investigate Ball's Bluff by the methods common to nearly all similar bodies. Witnesses were summoned and examined without order; there was no cross-examination; the accused was not confronted with the witnesses nor told their names, nor the charge upon which he had been already tried, condemned, and sentenced before he was even allowed to appear. No one was responsible. Of many important details there was no record. The secrets of a committee may not be divulged even to the authority from which its existence is derived. On behalf of the committee, the responsibility has been sought to be avoided. It cannot avail. General McClellan's statement is explicit, that Mr. Stanton informed him, when ordering the arrest, that he did so "at the solicitation of the committee." General McClellan was one of the most truthful of men. Mr. Stanton, unfriendly as he had then become, did not deny it; but he explicitly denied the authorship of the arrest. On the part of the committee no such explicit denial was ever made. As a matter of fact, some, at least, of its members hailed the arrest with demonstrations of delight. In April, in the Senate, the committee vehemently opposed a resolution calling on the President for the evidence taken before the committee. The chairman, Mr. Wade, admitted that the committee had done something, and had suggested something, but his language, elsewhere so violent, was guarded when he came to tell what this was. A sub-committee laid the evidence, which the Senate was not to be allowed to see, before the President and his cabinet, and "left it pretty much to them," in Mr. Wade's words. The resolution was supported by Mr. Sumner, and was passed against the opposition of the committee. Nine days later the President declined to lay the evidence before the Senate in a message, which, as Mr. Blaine points out, bears marks of having been written in the War Office; but the fact that the information withheld consisted of the evidence taken by its own committee was not revealed to the Senate.

Mr. Stanton's order for Stone's arrest was issued on the 28th of January. It was not executed until the morning of the 9th of February. What happened in the interval has never been told. It is soon done. General McClellan asked that General Stone might be heard in his defense. The committee assented, and General Stone was examined on the 31st. Meantime, the

♦ Adjutant-General Schouler ("Massachusetts in the War") says, "Mr. Sumner took no notice" of Stone's letter. General Schouler was evidently not aware that Mr. Sumner took the letter at once to Mr. Lincoln, with the above result.— R. B. I.

execution of the order was informally suspended in deference to General McClellan's express statement to the Secretary, that he did not see how any charges could be framed on the testimony. ☆

In a few days the missing link was supplied by a surprising occurrence. A refugee came into General W. W. Burns's lines from Leesburg, with a vague and utterly groundless story of mysterious flags of truce and of how much the Confederates thought of their friend Stone.‡ General McClellan was now placed in a cruel dilemma. He had either to show the refugee's story to the Secretary, or withhold it. The course he chose was that which seemed to him his duty. Mr. Stanton instantly renewed the order, and Stone's ruin was accomplished.

Not only were no charges ever preferred, but no acknowledgment of error was ever made, unless Stone's retention in the service and his restoration to duty, long subsequently, and under secret surveillance, be so considered. General McClellan in vain applied for him. General Hooker's first act on taking command was to ask for him as chief-of-staff. At last, in May, 1863, upon the earnest request of General Banks, commanding the Department of the Gulf, Stone was ordered to report to him. He arrived during the siege of Port Hudson, and rendered valuable service, though without assignment. Immediately afterward, General Banks appointed him chief-of-staff, in which capacity he served until April 16th, 1864, when, coincidently with the disaster on the Red River, but under orders previously issued at Washington, he was deprived of his commission as brigadier-general, and ordered to "report by letter" as colonel of the 14th infantry. In the following August, Lieutenant-General Grant assigned him to the command of a brigade in the Fifth Army Corps. A month later, worn out at last by the strain of the unmerited suffering he had so long endured in silence, he resigned.

And thus it was that this most gallant, accomplished, and faithful soldier was, upon no charges, without a hearing, upon "evidence" on which no humane or fair-minded man would punish a pet terrier, condemned not merely to long and rigorous imprisonment, but to a punishment so much worse than death that in all ages men have sought death because they have lacked the courage to endure it.

☆ The Joint Committee on the Conduct of the War, appointed in December, 1861, during the second session of the 37th Congress, consisted of Senators Benjamin F. Wade, of Ohio; Zachariah Chandler, of Michigan, and Andrew Johnson, of Tennessee; and Representatives D. W. Gooch, of Massachusetts; John Covode, of Pennsylvania; George W. Julian, of Indiana, and M. F. Odell, of New York. On the appointment of Andrew Johnson as Military Governor of Tennessee, March 4th, 1862, his place on the committee was filled, temporarily, by Joseph A. Wright, of Indiana. Only six names appear in the report, submitted April 6th, 1863, with respect to the First Bull Run, Ball's Bluff, the Western Department of Missouri, and other subjects.— EDITORS.

‡ General McClellan informed General Stone that he had last seen the written statement at the War Office on the 8th of February, 1862. I saw it at his headquarters in Washington in September, 1862, in a wardrobe full of papers turned over to me when I, as Acting Assistant Adjutant-General, was detached "to prevent the tail of the army from being again cut off," and it was among a double handful which I delivered back to General Seth Williams after Antietam. I suggest that the name of this refugee, and all the facts regarding him, and all the statements made by him, will probably turn up in the archives of the "Secret Service." I know the man was turned over to "Colonel E. J. Allen" (Allen Pinkerton) and examined by him.— R. B. I.

# CAPTAIN WILKES'S SEIZURE OF MASON AND SLIDELL.

BY D. MACNEILL FAIRFAX, REAR-ADMIRAL, U. S. N., EXECUTIVE OFFICER OF THE "SAN JACINTO."

IN October, 1861, the United States screw-sloop *San Jacinto*, of which Captain Charles Wilkes was commander and the writer was executive officer, on her return from the west coast of Africa, touched at the island of St. Thomas to coal ship. Here for the first time we learned of the presence in those waters of the Confederate cruiser *Sumter* (Captain Raphael Semmes).↓ Captain Wilkes immediately determined to search for the enemy. At Cienfuegos, on the south coast of Cuba, he learned from the United States consul-general at Havana that Messrs. Mason and Slidell, Confederate commissioners to Europe, and their secretaries and families had recently reached that port from Charleston en route to England. He immediately put to sea, October 26th, with the purpose of intercepting the blockade runner which had brought them out. The commissioners were to have left Charleston by the cruiser *Nashville*, but their plans had been changed, and the steamer *Gordon*, otherwise known as the *Theodora* (Captain Lockwood), had been substituted. They had run the Union blockade successfully during a storm on the night of October 11th, and had arrived at Nassau on the 13th, and at Havana on the 17th. There we ascertained that their plan was to leave on the 7th of November in the English steamer *Trent* for St. Thomas on their way to England, and readily calculated when and where in the Bahama Channel we might intercept them. Meanwhile, on the 2d of November, Captain Wilkes continued his cruise after the *Sumter* along the north coast of Cuba, also running over to Key West in the hope of finding the *Powhatan* or some other steamer to accompany him to the Bahama Channel to guard against the possibility of the escape of the commissioners. But the *Powhatan* had left the day before, and the *San Jacinto* therefore returned alone to the channel to await the *Trent*. Here, 240 miles from Havana, and 90 miles from Sagua la Grande, where the channel contracts to the width of 15 miles, at noon on the 8th of November the *Trent* was sighted.

On our way from St. Thomas to Havana we had stopped at the Caymans, an English possession, to procure fresh provisions for the crew. The natives had not many days before received a visit from the *Sumter*, and were loud

↓ The *Sumter*, one of the first, if not the very first, of the regularly commissioned vessels of the Confederate navy, left New Orleans on the 18th of June, 1861 (see cut, p. 14), and, running the blockade, almost immediately began privateering operations. She was a screw steamer of 500 tons, and was armed with 5 guns — an 8-inch pivot, and 4 24-pound howitzers. She cruised for two months in the Caribbean Sea and along the coast of South America, receiving friendly treatment and coaling without hindrance in the neutral ports. During the succeeding two months she cruised in the Atlantic. On the night of the 23d of November, she ran out of the port of St. Pierre, Island of Martinique, eluding the *Iroquois* (Captain Palmer), which had been sent to search for her. At Gibraltar, having been effectually blockaded by the *Tuscarora*, she was sold, afterward becoming a blockade runner. Among the vessels sent in search of her were the *Niagara, Powhatan, Keystone State, Richmond,* and *San Jacinto*.

In his volume, "The Blockade and the Cruisers" (Charles Scribner's Sons), Professor J. R. Soley sums up her career thus:

"During her cruise she had made 17 prizes, of which 2 were ransomed, 7 were released in Cuban ports by order of the Captain-General, and 2 were recaptured. Apart from the delays caused by interrupted voyages, the total injury inflicted by the *Sumter* upon American commerce consisted in the burning of six vessels with their cargoes." — EDITORS.

JAMES M. MASON, CONFEDERATE COMMISSIONER TO GREAT BRITAIN. FROM A PHOTOGRAPH.

in praise of the Confederate cruiser. They had in times past shown great pleasure in selling turtle and fresh beef and vegetables to the United States war vessels, but now their sympathy for the Southern cause was uppermost, and they really showed indifference to selling us provisions. This feeling had displayed itself wherever we had stopped either at St. Thomas or on the southern coast of Cuba, and when we reached Havana it was still more apparent. It was evident, even at that early day, that the South had the sympathy of nearly all Europe — particularly of England and France. When Captain Wilkes first took me into his confidence, and told me what he purposed to do, I earnestly reminded him of the great risk of a war with these two Governments, supported as they were by powerful navies; and when we reached Key West I suggested that he consult with Judge Marvin, one of the ablest maritime lawyers. I soon saw, however, that he had made up his mind to intercept and capture the *Trent* as well as to take possession of the commissioners, and I therefore ceased to discuss the affair. As the next in rank to Captain Wilkes, I claimed the right to board the mail-packet. Captain Wilkes fully expected that I would tender my services for this "delicate duty," and rather left to me the plan of carrying out his instructions. I was impressed with the gravity of my position, and I made up my mind not to do anything unnecessary in the arrest of these gentlemen, or anything that would irritate the captain of the *Trent*, or any of his passengers, particularly the commissioners — lest it might occur to them to throw the steamer on my hands, which would necessitate my taking her as a prize.

⚓ Following is the text of Captain Wilkes's instructions, which, as will be seen from the narrative, were not literally observed by Lieutenant Fairfax:

"U. S. STEAMER *San Jacinto*. At sea, Nov. 8th, 1861. SIR: You will have the second and third cutters of this ship fully manned and armed, and be in all respects prepared to board the steamer *Trent*, now hove to under our guns.

"On boarding her you will demand the papers of the steamer, her clearance from Havana, with the list of passengers and crew.

"Should Mr. Mason, Mr. Slidell, Mr. Eustis, and Mr. McFarland be on board, you will make them prisoners and send them on board this ship immediately, and take possession of her as a prize.

"I do not deem it will be necessary to use force, that the prisoners will have the good sense to avoid any necessity for using it; but if they should they must be made to understand that it is their own fault.

"*They must be brought on board.*

"All trunks, cases, packages, and bags belonging to them you will take possession of, and send on board this ship; any dispatches found on the persons of the prisoners, or in possession of those on board the steamer,

## CAPTAIN WILKES'S SEIZURE OF MASO[N]

As the *Trent* approached she hoisted Englis[h] sign was hoisted and a shot was fired across her b[ow] speed and showed no disposition to heave to, a shel[l] bow which brought her to. Captain Wilkes hailed that he [wanted] a boat on board, and I then left with the second cutter.

The manner of heaving the *Trent* to evidently was galling to [Captain] Moir. When he did stop his steamer, he showed how provoked he [was] by impatiently singing out through his trumpet, "What do you mean [by] heaving my vessel to in this manner?" I felt that I must in every way conciliate him when I should get on board. Two boats had been equipped ready to lower and the officers and crews detailed to jump into them. These were not employed until later. The boat I took was a third one, and as the sea was smooth, but a few minutes elapsed before we reached the *Trent*. I instructed the boat's crew to remain alongside for orders, and, boarding the vessel, I was escorted by one of her officers to the upper or promenade deck and was introduced to Captain Moir, who, though very gentlemanly in his way of receiving me, was also very dignified and manifested no little indignation as he spoke of the unusual treatment received at our hands. I immediately asked if I might

JOHN SLIDELL, CONFEDERATE COMMISSIONER TO FRANCE.
FROM A PHOTOGRAPH.

see his passenger-list, saying that I had information that Messrs. Mason and Slidell were on board. The mention of Mr. Slidell's name caused that gentleman to come up and say, "I am Mr. Slidell; do you want to see me?" Mr. Mason, whom I knew very well, also came up at the same time, thus relieving me from Captain Moir's refusal, which was very polite but very

will be taken possession of, examined, and retained if necessary.

"I have understood that the families of these gentlemen may be with them; if so, I beg you will offer some of them in my name a passage in this ship to the United States, and that all the attention and comforts we can command are tendered them and will be placed in their service.

"In the event of their acceptance, should there be anything which the captain of the steamer can spare to increase the comforts in the way of necessaries or stores, of which a war vessel is deficient, you will please to procure them; the amount will be paid for by the paymaster.

"Lieutenant James A. Greer will take charge of the third cutter which accompanies you, and assist you in these duties. I trust that all those under your command in executing this important and delicate duty will conduct themselves with all the delicacy and kindness which become the character of our Naval Service.

"I am, very respectfully, your obedient servant,
CHARLES WILKES, Captain.

"To Lieutenant D. M. FAIRFAX, U. S. N., Executive Officer, *San Jacinto*."

could not under such circumstances be shown any list of passengers... asked where their secretaries, Mr. McFarland and Mr. Eustis, ... wanted to see them also, and Mr. Mason pointed them out to ...ing near. In the briefest time I had the four gentlemen before me, ...n I informed Captain Moir that I had been sent by my commander to ... Mr. Mason and Mr. Slidell and their secretaries, and send them prisoners on board the United States war vessel near by.

As may readily be understood, when it was known why I had boarded the *Trent*, there was an outburst of rage and indignation from the passengers, who numbered nearly one hundred, many of them Southerners. The captain and the four gentlemen bore themselves with great composure, but the irresponsible lookers-on sang out, "Throw the d—— fellow overboard!" I called on Captain Moir to preserve order, but, for the benefit of the excited passengers, I reminded them that our every move was closely observed from the *San Jacinto* by spy-glasses (she was within hailing distance), that a heavy battery was bearing upon them, and that any indignity to any of her officers or crew then on board might lead to dreadful consequences. This, together with Captain Moir's excellent commanding manner, had a quieting effect. During this uproar among the passengers, the officer in charge of the *San Jacinto's* boat, not knowing what it meant, and fearing some ill-treatment of me, hurried up with six or eight of the crew. Captain Moir was the first to see this body of armed men, and remonstrated with me at their appearance on the promenade-deck among his passengers, there being many ladies and children among them. I immediately directed the officer to return to his boat and await my orders. I assured him, amidst the noise of his passengers, that the men had come contrary to my instructions. I was really pleased to find the captain so tenacious of his command, for my mind was possessed with the idea that Mr. Mason or Mr. Slidell, or both, would urge Captain Moir to relinquish his command, making it necessary for me to assume it, as in such event my instructions left no opening for me to decline it. After order had been restored, we discussed the affair more generally, Captain Moir, however, scarcely joining in the conversation—always dignified and punctilious. The mail-agent, Commander Williams, an officer of the Royal Navy, on the retired list, was more officious, for he scarcely left me, and more than once reminded me that he represented Her Majesty's Service, and that I must refer things to him. Of course, I knew what was due to him, but I also knew that Captain Moir was the only person with whom I could have any official relations. I carefully avoided giving offense, and confined myself strictly to the duty which had taken me on board. I was anxious that Mr. Slidell and Mr. Mason should not leave any of their luggage behind. Mrs. Slidell having asked me who commanded the *San Jacinto*, I replied, "Your old acquaintance, Captain Wilkes"; whereupon she expressed surprise that he should do the very thing the Confederates were hoping for—something to arouse England; and she also spoke of our having run down a French brig, a short time before, saying that two French men-of-war were at Havana when the brig came in with jury-masts, almost a wreck, as the captain of the brig reported to them, and adding that their commanders had expressed great indignation, and would make the most of our treatment of one of their merchantmen. "Really," she added, "Captain Wilkes is playing into our hands!" Mr. Mason here suggested that it would be just as well not to discuss these matters at such a time. Captain Wilkes's offer of his cabin was conveyed by me to Mrs. Slidell and Mrs. Eustis, and declined by both ladies.

After the first uproar had subsided, I sent the boat to Captain Wilkes to say that these gentlemen were all on board, and had objected to being sent to the *San Jacinto*, and that I must use force to accomplish my orders; I asked for a boat to carry them comfortably on board, another for their baggage, and a third to carry stores, which the paymaster's clerk, at Captain Wilkes's order, had already purchased from the steward of the *Trent*, to add to the comfort of the new guests.

When all was ready and the boats were in waiting, I notified both Mr. Mason and Mr. Slidell that the time had come to send them to the *San Jacinto*. They came quietly down to the main-deck, and there repeated that they would not go unless force was used—whereupon two officers, previously instructed, escorted each commissioner to the side, and assisted them into the comfortable cutter sent especially for them.

REAR-ADMIRAL CHARLES WILKES. FROM A PHOTOGRAPH.

The two secretaries followed them into the boat without making opposition. At this stage of the proceedings another outcry was raised by the passengers—noise enough to cause Lieutenant Greer, who was waiting for these gentlemen to accompany them on board, to send a corporal's guard inside of the main-deck cabin. This produced considerable consternation among the ladies near by, but it was soon allayed by Captain Moir, and the marines were sent back outside. They had been sent in one of the boats by Captain Wilkes's order, under the impression that they might be required. Some machinists also came, in the event of the *Trent* being taken as a prize; they were not needed, and were sent back to their ship a little while before I returned to make my report. Commander Williams was reported as saying when he went to England that I had caused marines to charge upon defenseless women and children with fixed bayonets. The men, of course, had their muskets at "carry" or "shoulder," and moved into the cabin with quick step—but there was no other foundation for the statement. Again he represented, and it was pictured in one of the London illustrated papers, that Miss Slidell, for some cause or other, had struck me in the face. This was based on the fact that she accidentally touched my shoulder while I was talking to Mrs. Slidell at the door of Mr. Slidell's state-room. While I was standing there, Miss Slidell, then a girl of 15 or 17 years, was protesting against my taking her father from her, when a little roll of the steamer caused her to lose her balance, and thus she touched me slightly. Mrs. Slidell, writing afterward from Paris to her near relative, and a friend of mine, expressed her mortification that such a story should have been circulated. But Commander Williams bade me good-bye pleasantly when I left the *Trent*, saying that he was very much pleased at my moderate and gentlemanly manner throughout this very embarrassing and perplexing duty, and that he would report the same to his Government, for which I thanked him, mentioning his language afterward to Captain Wilkes. The truth is that much was made of Williams in England, and he evidently lost his head.

Once while the transfer of luggage and stores delayed us, Captain Moir, seeing his vessel drifting out of channel and in sight of shoal water, said to me, "If you do not hurry and get out of my vessel, I will not be responsible for her safety." I immediately hailed the *San Jacinto* and requested that she be kept more to windward and in mid-channel, and then said to Captain Moir, "Now you can move up nearer to the *San Jacinto*," which he did. I speak of this to show how watchful I was to keep him in an amiable frame of mind, and so to lessen the chance of his throwing the *Trent* on my hands. When all was finished I went on board the *San Jacinto* and reported to Captain Wilkes that I had not taken the *Trent* as a prize, as he had instructed me to do, giving certain reasons, which satisfied him; for he replied, "inasmuch as you have not taken her, you will let her go" or "proceed on her voyage." To make clear one of these reasons, I should before have mentioned that Captain Wilkes, while at Havana, had learned more definitely of the character of Du Pont's fleet, from which he inferred its destination, for of the Southern ports the larger vessels could enter only Port Royal. He directed me "to refit our battery and get the *San Jacinto* ready in all respects for battle," adding that he would "join Du Pont in time to coöperate with him." (As it was, Port Royal fell the day before we boarded the *Trent*, as we learned on our arrival off Charleston.) The reasons I assigned to Captain Wilkes for my action were: First, that the capture of the *Trent* would make it necessary to put a large prize crew (officers and men) on board, and thus materially weaken our battery for use at Port Royal; secondly, that as there were a large number of women and children and mails and specie bound to various ports, the capture would seriously inconvenience innocent persons and merchants; so that I had determined, before taking her, to lay these matters before him for more serious consideration.↓

I returned immediately to the *Trent* and informed Captain Moir that Cap-

---

↓I gave my real reasons some weeks afterward to Secretary Chase, whom I met by chance at the Treasury Department, he having asked me to explain why I had not literally obeyed Captain Wilkes's instructions. I told him that it was because I was impressed with England's sympathy for the South, and felt that she would be glad to have so good a ground to declare war against the United States. Mr. Chase seemed surprised, and exclaimed, "You have certainly relieved the Government from great embarrassment, to say the least."— D. M. F.

WILLIAM H. SEWARD, SECRETARY OF STATE. FROM A DAGUERREOTYPE TAKEN ABOUT 1851.

tain Wilkes would not longer detain him, and he might proceed on his voyage. The steamers soon separated, and thus ended one of the most critical events of our civil war. We went up the coast from St. Augustine to the blockading fleet off Charleston, and thence to Fort Monroe, from which point we were ordered first to New York and afterward to Boston, with the prisoners. When we reached the outer roads of Boston I escorted the four gentlemen to Fort Warren, and parted from them with expressions of the most pleasant character; for everything had been done by Captain Wilkes and his officers to make them feel at home while on board the vessel. Mr. Eustis and myself had several conversations as to the probable reception of the news in England and on the Continent. He maintained from the first, that England would immediately demand their release, and that our Government would be obliged to accede to this demand. When Mr. Slidell was leaving the side of the *Trent*, he said to his wife, "Good-bye, my dear, we shall meet in Paris in 60 days." If I remember aright, he was but 20 days longer in rejoining her.

After the war I had a conversation with Captain Moir, in the presence of an English chaplain, at St. Thomas. Captain Moir was there in command of a large steamer running between Liverpool and Aspinwall, and I was in command of the *Susquehanna*. Captain Moir invited the chaplain and myself to lunch, and after we were relieved from the presence of the waiters, only we three in the cabin, he then reverted to an interview he had with the British Admiralty on his return to England, whither he had been called from St. Thomas. They were very much disappointed and displeased with him for not having thrown the *Trent* on our hands, to which he replied (so he said to me) that it never had occurred to him; that, in fact, the officer who boarded the *Trent* was so civil, and had so closely occupied him in conversation about foreign matters, that he had failed to see what afterward was very plain. He recounted the excitement on 'Change over the affair, and expressed the conviction that all England would have demanded speedy redress, had I taken the *Trent*. He had seen the reports in print in our newspapers, and had read my orders to take possession and wondered that I had not.

Although Captain Wilkes and I viewed the seizure of the commissioners from different points of view, I cannot close this narrative without saying that Wilkes was one of our very best officers, a man of strong will-power, brave and intelligent, and I always entertained the highest respect for his abilities and worth.

After parting from the *Trent*, the *San Jacinto* proceeded to the Florida coast, and thence, by way of the blockading fleet off Charleston, to Fort Monroe. Here report of the seizure was made, and the vessel was ordered to New York, and thence, by order of Secretary Seward, to Fort Warren, Boston harbor, where the prisoners were confined during the diplomatic correspondence which followed. The commissioners expressed their satisfaction at the considerate treatment which they received, both from Captain Wilkes during the voyage and from Colonel Justin Dimick, the commander at Fort Warren.

On the 30th of November, Earl Russell, the British minister for foreign affairs, having received the news of the seizure through a letter from Commander Williams (mentioned above), wrote to Lord Lyons, the British minister at Washington, reciting the circumstances and saying in part:

"Her Majesty's Government, therefore, trust that when this matter shall have been brought under the consideration of the Government of the United States, that Government will, of its own accord, offer to the British Government such redress as alone could satisfy the British nation, namely, the liberation of the four gentlemen and their delivery to your lordship, in order that they may again be placed under British protection, and a suitable apology for the aggression which has been committed."

On the 3d of December, the French Government also made an informal protest, through its minister at Washington, M. Mercier.

On the 26th of December, Mr. Seward wrote at length to Lord Lyons, reviewing the case, and saying that the commissioners would be "cheerfully liberated." In the course of the letter Mr. Seward said:

"If I decide this case in favor of my own Government, I must disavow its most cherished principles, and reverse and forever abandon its essential policy. The country cannot afford the sacrifice. If I maintain those principles, and adhere to that policy, I must surrender the case itself. It will be seen, therefore, that this Government could not deny the justice of the claim presented to us in this respect upon its merits. We are asked to do the British nation just what we have always insisted all nations ought to do to us."

Accordingly, on the 1st of January, 1862, the commissioners and their secretaries were placed on board the English vessel *Rinaldo*, at Provincetown, Mass., which had been designated by Lord Lyons to receive them. After a voyage of unusual rigor, during which they were compelled by storms to alter the first plan of going by way of Halifax and to run to Bermuda, the commissioners arrived at Southampton, England, on the 29th of January.— EDITORS.

# EARLY OPERATIONS ON THE POTOMAC RIVER.

## BY PROFESSOR J. RUSSELL SOLEY, U. S. N.

THE first active naval operations of the war were those on the Potomac River, in May and June, 1861. At this time the larger vessels of the navy were engaged in setting on foot the blockade of the coast, in pursuance of the President's proclamations of April 19th and 27th. The *Niagara*, *Minnesota*, *Roanoke*, and *Susquehanna* on the Atlantic coast, under Flag-Officer Silas H. Stringham, and the *Colorado*, *Mississippi*, *Powhatan*, and *Brooklyn* in the Gulf, under Flag-Officer William Mervine, took the initial steps to render the blockade effective. Smaller vessels were sent to the blockading stations as rapidly as they could be prepared.

The Potomac River, although officially within the limits of the Atlantic Squadron, became early in the war a nearly independent command, owing to its distance from the flag-ship, and its nearness to Washington. In May the Potomac flotilla was organized, under Commander James H. Ward. It was originally composed of the small side-wheel steamer *Thomas Freeborn*, purchased, May 7th, at New York, and the tugs *Anacostia* and *Resolute*, but was considerably enlarged in the course of the year. Its organization was closely connected with the service of the Washington Navy Yard, and other vessels attached to the yard occasionally coöperated with it. Its movements were under the direct supervision of the department.

In the early part of May, 1861, the Navy of the State of Virginia began the erection of batteries on the Potomac, in order to close the navigation of the river to Federal vessels proceeding to and from Washington. Works were thrown up under the direction of Captain William F. Lynch, Commander Frederick Chatard, and other officers at Aquia Creek, the terminus of the Richmond and Fredericksburg Railroad, at Mathias Point, and later at Quantico. A small steamer, the *George Page*, coöperated with the forces on shore. The batteries were manned chiefly by infantry acting as artillerists. The first duty of the Potomac flotilla was to clear the Virginia banks of these obstructions to navigation and open the river. With this object in view, the *Freeborn*, under Commander Ward, on the 31st of May, attacked the works at Aquia Creek. The attack, which may be called the first naval engagement of the war, was ineffectual, the light guns of the *Freeborn* producing little impression. On the other hand, the necessity of economizing ammunition led the Confederates to reserve their fire. On the next day, June 1st, the attack was repeated by the *Freeborn*, which had meantime been joined by the *Pawnee*, under Commander S. C. Rowan. The bombardment was continued for five hours, but no casualties occurred on either side. The railroad pier and its buildings were set on fire and blown up by the Confederate forces, and both the batteries and the vessels received several shot, but no material injury was inflicted.

On the 27th of June, the *Freeborn* made an attack upon Mathias Point, where a considerable force of Confederates was posted, although no batteries had as yet been erected. In this attack Commander Ward was assisted by two boats from the *Pawnee*, under Lieutenant Chaplin. A landing was effected by the party, led by Commander Ward in person, and after some skirmishing the Confederate pickets were driven in; but upon the approach of the main body of the enemy a retreat was ordered to the boats. Commander Ward returned to the *Freeborn*, and directed her fire at the advancing force, enabling Chaplin to make a second landing. Breastworks were rapidly thrown up, but they were no sooner completed than the landing party was ordered to return, Commander Ward having received a fatal gunshot wound while sighting his bow-gun. Late in the afternoon, Lieutenant Chaplin, with great skill and coolness, embarked his men under a galling musketry fire. The only casualties in this somewhat rash undertaking were one killed and four wounded. Immediately after, the Confederates erected formidable works at the Point.

Two days after Ward's death, on the 29th of June, the steamer *St. Nicholas*, a passenger vessel still making regular trips between Baltimore and Georgetown, was captured by a stratagem of the Confederates. A party of armed men, more or less disguised, under Colonel Thomas, went on board as passengers at Baltimore, and were joined by Captain George N. Hollins and others at Point Lookout. As the *St. Nicholas* was on her way up the Potomac, the Confederates threw off their disguise, and, overpowering the crew and passengers, took possession of the vessel. She subsequently made several prizes, and was burnt at Fredericksburg in 1862.

Commander Thomas T. Craven succeeded Commander Ward in the command of the Potomac flotilla. The force was increased by the addition of eight or ten vessels, but it was unable to dislodge the Confederates from their positions, and although the navigation of the river was not actually closed to armed vessels, a virtual blockade of Washington, as far as the Potomac was concerned, was maintained until March, 1862, when the Confederate forces retired to the line of the Rappahannock River. The guns were then removed from the batteries, and the *George Page* was burnt.

During the remainder of the war, the Potomac flotilla, commanded successively by Commodore A. A. Harwood and Commanders R. H. Wyman and Foxhall A. Parker, was chiefly occupied in patrolling the river and the adjacent waters to insure the safety of water communication from Washington, and to prevent contraband trade between the frontiers. It seconded the operations of the army at various points, and occasionally its vessels had smart brushes with the enemy, but its principal occupation was that of a water-police, and its efforts were mainly directed against illicit trade and guerrilla warfare.

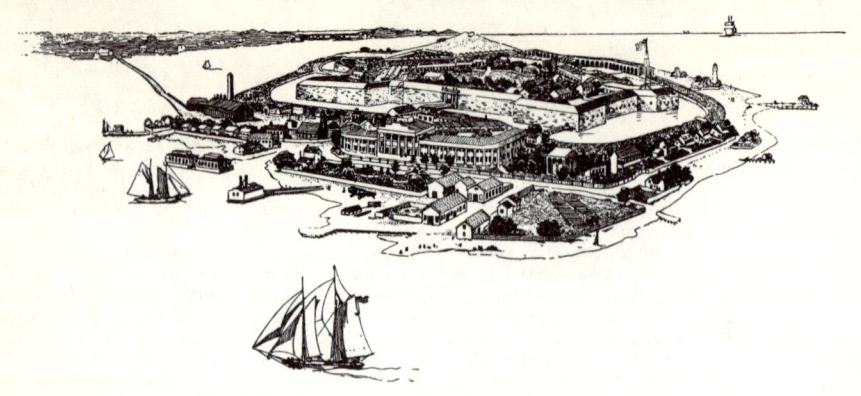

FORT MONROE — AND THE OLD HYGEIA HOTEL, SINCE TORN DOWN. FROM A LITHOGRAPH.

## OPERATIONS OF 1861 ABOUT FORT MONROE.

### BY JOSEPH B. CARR, BREVET MAJOR-GENERAL, U. S. V.

ON the 24th of May, 1861, I arrived at Fort Monroe, with my regiment, the 2d New York Volunteers. Two days before Major-General B. F. Butler had arrived and assumed command of the department. Previous to our arrival the fort contained, besides the regular garrison of four companies of artillery, the 4th Massachusetts Volunteers, a regiment of "three-months" men. We went into camp just over the border of Mill Creek, a stream dividing the fort from Virginia, and pitched our tents on a plowed field near a mansion known as the Segar House. This camp was first called Camp Troy, and, later, Camp Hamilton. Pickets were placed immediately on our arrival, and at once began operations by the capture of nine Confederate officers — one of them a surgeon. The prisoners were brought before General Butler, confessed to being in arms under the Confederacy, and stated that, when captured, they were on their way to join their regiments after a day spent in looking after their homes, located in our neighborhood. General Butler saw fit to release them unconditionally.

Within a few days of our arrival in camp we were ordered to proceed to Hampton Village, where we expected to encounter Confederates and acquire our first knowledge of warfare. In this we were disappointed; the Confederates had departed, having burned the bridge at Hampton. Save for the evident approach of war, that portion of the peninsula occupied by Union troops in 1861 seemed a paradise. Great fields of corn and wheat grew on the sunny plain, and the neighboring farms teemed with stock of all kinds. But the villas and mansions of the inhabitants were deserted and uncared for; families were scattered, industries stopped, and sources of income abandoned or destroyed. The lower portion of the peninsula, to within a few miles of the Bethels, was occupied by General Butler's troops. Within the limits of his command General Butler sought to maintain strict discipline, and to that end issued various orders relating to the rights and duties of his command, but particularly the rights of property-owners in our vicinity. Foraging and depredations of all kinds were forbidden, and as a rule the orders were obeyed, yet cases of disobedience constantly came to light, for it was only by stern experience that officers and men were taught the peculiar duties of a soldier. Food was at times irregularly issued to the men, and again was unwholesome and repellent, thus rendering the soldier doubly liable to fall under the temptations of generous foraging.

Some of the clothing issued to the men during the early days of the civil war was made of the vilest "shoddy" and literally fell from their bodies. In Fort Monroe men in the 2d New York Volunteers appeared on parade with blankets wrapped about them to conceal a lack of proper garments, and sometimes stood sentinel with naked feet and almost naked bodies. The only reason for this hardship was the dishonesty of contractors, and the lack of experience and celerity in the subordinates of the Quartermaster-General's department at Washington.

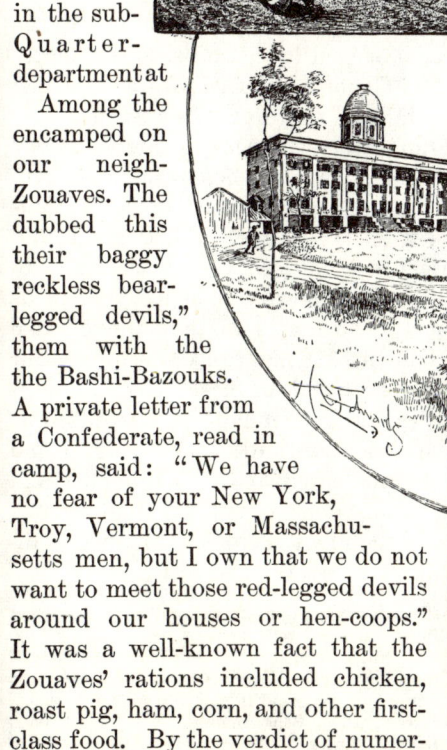

Among the liveliest soldiers encamped on any field were our neighbors, Duryee's Zouaves. The Confederates had dubbed this regiment, from their baggy red trousers and reckless bearing, "the redlegged devils," and had invested them with the characteristics of the Bashi-Bazouks. A private letter from a Confederate, read in camp, said: "We have no fear of your New York, Troy, Vermont, or Massachusetts men, but I own that we do not want to meet those red-legged devils around our houses or hen-coops." It was a well-known fact that the Zouaves' rations included chicken, roast pig, ham, corn, and other first-class food. By the verdict of numerous squads in all the regiments, many articles of food near at hand were declared "contraband of war,"

1.—LIGHT-HOUSE, FORT MONROE. 2.—CHESAPEAKE HOSPITAL, HAMPTON, VA. 3.—SALLY-PORT, FORT MONROE. FROM WAR-TIME PHOTOGRAPHS.

ARRIVAL OF THE ORIGINAL "CONTRABAND." FROM A WAR-TIME SKETCH.

on the ground that if left on farms or in gardens "aid and comfort" to the enemy might ensue. There were few cases of real lawlessness, consequently the "Beauty and Booty" proclamation ☆ of General Beauregard was uncalled for, and even in the vague and uncertain light of that day was absurd.

The negroes in Virginia, learning of our presence, began to arrive at our camp in large numbers. While other commanders were hesitating and quibbling over the question, General Butler promptly declared slaves of Confederates "contraband of war," inasmuch as they gave, or had given, aid and comfort to the enemy. Contrabands at this date were not anxious to serve as soldiers, and no commander had the temerity to employ them as such. Commanding officers were seriously in error as to the value of men in the early days of the war. In my regiment, 118 men were discharged for disability, who enlisted later in other regiments, making first-class soldiers.

During the time in which General Butler was in command at Fort Monroe, he developed remarkable ability in civil organization, and showed courage and determination in any project in which he was interested. While just and even generous in dealing with the men in his department his manner was decidedly autocratic. He rarely tolerated conduct savoring of insubordination, and yet under peculiar circumstances he overlooked it. ∫

---

☆ This proclamation by General Beauregard was dated "Department of Alexandria, Camp Pickens, June 5th, 1861," and was addressed "To the Good People of the Counties of Loudoun, Fairfax, and Prince William," in which, referring to the Union forces, he says: "All rules of civilized warfare are abandoned, and they proclaim by their acts, if not on their banners, that their war-cry is 'Beauty and Booty.'"— EDITORS.

∫ On one occasion, when residents were complaining of acts of vandalism, Butler was informed that a certain regiment was guilty. Lieutenant Butler, the general's nephew, then quite young, was sent to summon the colonel of the regiment. Entering the colonel's tent, he said, "Colonel, Uncle Ben wants you, and is going to give you hell!" "Who is Uncle Ben?" inquired the colonel. "Why, General Butler!" "Very well, I will attend, but not to 'get hell,' young man, I did not come here for that purpose." "That's right," said the lieutenant, "I like to see men who are not afraid of Uncle Ben."—J. B. C.

Among other prominent soldiers at Fort Monroe, at this time, was General J. W. Phelps, then colonel of a Vermont regiment. Brave, cool, and capable, he was thoroughly liked by his men and by his superior officers. He spoke with a long, drawling "Yankee" accent, and his piquant sayings were very entertaining. Hating display and egotism, he invariably showed his displeasure when in the presence of men who were guilty of either. A dapper young lieutenant attached to one of the regiments at Newport News had shown great fondness for his dress uniform, supplemented by a scarlet-lined cloak, and dislike for ranking his personality below the chief-officer. Strutting into General Phelps's tent on one occasion, he said, without salute or preface, "I am going down to the fort, sir." "Are you?" said General Phelps, as he took in at a glance the gorgeous uniform scarlet-lined cloak and superabundant self-esteem of the young man. "Are you? Neow, I guess not, young man. Go to your colonel, get his permission, and then, if you can get *mine*, you may go down to the fort. Not otherwise. Go, now." On another occasion when the camp was all commotion and excitement owing to firing in the direction of our pickets, General Phelps, not excited in the least degree, walked into the writer's tent, and said, "Carr, that's not picket shooting. It is your men shooting p-e-e-g-s." His surmise proved correct.

Entering General Butler's quarters the colonel saluted, and said, "You sent for me, General?" "Sit down, sir," roared the exasperated chief; then, wheeling in his chair, the general recited the crimes charged, and, concluding, said, "I'll send your whole regiment to the Rip-Raps; what have you to say, sir, in your defense?" The colonel, now as angry as his chief, rose, and said, "I have this to say: Any man who says that my men are guilty of the crimes you enumerate, lies, sir!"

"Do you dare tell *me* that I lie?" roared the general. "I tell you or any man uttering the charges, that he lies," was the reply. General Butler stared at the colonel for a few seconds, then, taking a cigar from his pocket, tendered it to the colonel, saying, "Smoke, Colonel, we will talk of this matter later." General Butler showed no further resentment, but thereafter favored the colonel. Events proved that the regiment was innocent of the crimes charged.—J. B. C.

CAMP OF DURYÉE'S ZOUAVES, NEAR FORT MONROE. FROM A SKETCH MADE IN JULY, 1861.

On the 10th of June, 1861, occurred the disastrous fight at Big Bethel,—battle we scarce may term it. Up to this time but few soldiers had been under fire, and the confidence which must exist between men and officers to make an army effective was lacking. To the want of that experience and confidence a great measure of the failure at Big Bethel may be attributed.

At noon of Sunday, the 9th of June, General Ebenezer W. Peirce received an order to go at once to headquarters at Fort Monroe. Arriving at General Butler's quarters, he was shown a plan of attack on both Little and Big Bethel. Minute directions for conducting the attack were given, and Peirce was assigned to command the expedition. The march was begun about midnight, June 9th. Peirce was to lead one column from Camp Hamilton to a point near Little Bethel, where the column advancing from Newport News was to meet him, and together they were to surprise and attack both Bethels. The troops taking part in the action on the following day were 5 New York regiments, the 1st, 2d, 3d, 5th, and 7th, detachments from the 4th Massachusetts and 1st Vermont, and a detachment of United States Regular Artillery (11 men), with 2 field-pieces, under command of Lieutenant Greble. Reports credit us with 2500 men engaged; I believe we had not less than 3500 men. General Butler had taken precautions against errors when our men should meet, having given the watchword "Boston" to be shouted when unrecognized troops should approach. Colonel Bendix, of the 7th New York regiment, did not receive information on this point. The several detachments were approaching the point designated as a place for meeting, and some troops had already departed for the rear of Little Bethel, when Townsend's (3d New York) and Bendix's troops approached each other, a dense wood having intervened for part of the march. Bendix, seeing troops in gray uniforms approaching,— the uniform of early regiments were in many cases gray in color,— and supposing them to be the enemy, opened fire on them with musketry and one piece of artillery. The watchword was shouted, but Bendix, being ignorant of its significance, continued firing. Townsend retreated a short distance, and the error was then discovered. Duryée (5th New York) and Washburn (1st Vermont), who were in advance, hearing the firing, concluded that the Confederates had reached their rear, and immediately retraced their march. The possibility of surprising the enemy was now past. The shots of Bendix's and Townsend's men had aroused the Confederates, and preparation for defense was made by

UNIFORM OF DURYEE'S ZOUAVES.

THE OPPOSING FORCES AT BIG BETHEL, VA.— JUNE 10TH, 1861.

*Union Forces:* Brigadier-General Ebenezer W. Peirce. 4th Mass. (5 co's), Maj. Horace O. Whittemore; 1st N. Y., Col. William H. Allen; 2d N. Y., Col. Joseph B. Carr; 3d N. Y., Col. Frederick Townsend; 5th N. Y., Col. Abram Duryée; 7th N. Y., Col. John E. Bendix; 1st Vt. (5 co's), Lieut.-Col. Peter T. Washburn; Regular artillery (4 guns), Lieut. John T. Greble (k).

Total Union loss: 18 killed, 53 wounded, and 5 missing = 76.

*Confederate Forces:* Col. J. Bankhead Magruder. 1st N. C., Col. Daniel H. Hill; 3d Va. (detachment), Lieut.-Col. William D. Stuart; Va. Cavalry Battalion, Maj. E. B. Montague; Va. Howitzer Battalion, Maj. Geo. W. Randolph. Total Confederate loss: 1 killed and 7 wounded = 8.

them. About this time Peirce sent for reënforcements, and the 1st and 2d New York regiments, under Colonels Allen and Carr, were hurried forward. The latter was ordered to wait orders at New Market Bridge. Advancing through Little Bethel, which they found evacuated, to a position near Big Bethel, the troops under General Peirce found the Confederates occupying a strong position, well intrenched, with earth-works covering the bridge, which crossed a stream running in front of the Confederate position. Colonel J. B. Magruder, formerly an officer in the United States Army, was in command, having, it was said, about 1800 men under him, but having actually only 300 or 400 men and about 5 guns.

Duryea's Zouaves moved up the road on the left of the woods, and the fight opened by the discharge of a Parrott gun in the Confederate works. Greble, with his battery, consisting of 2 6-pounder guns, took position on the road with Bendix's regiment and 3 companies of Massachusetts troops. Duryea went through the orchard and cornfield, Townsend on his right and rear. The Confederate firing was inaccurate for a time, but soon the range was found, and our troops were soon seeking the shelter of the woods, after a vain attempt to drive the enemy from his works. A short time after the troops had gone to the shelter of the woods, or about 11 o'clock, A. M., I arrived on the ground with my regiment. Orders to go forward had been received at 7 o'clock, and we marched as rapidly as possible; yet the delay incident to dragging a gun, by hand, for ten miles, and the time used in getting the gun over the burned bridge at Hampton, with the hot and wearying roads, made an earlier arrival impossible. On approaching, we were surprised and puzzled at the condition of the troops. For at least one mile from the scene of action the men and officers were scattered singly and in groups, without form or

THE 4TH MASSACHUSETTS REGIMENT FORTIFYING CAMP BUTLER AT NEWPORT NEWS.
FROM A SKETCH MADE IN 1861.

CONFEDERATE EARTH-WORKS AT BIG BETHEL. FROM A SKETCH MADE APRIL 4, 1862.

organization, looking far more like men enjoying a huge picnic than soldiers awaiting battle. I reported my regiment to General Peirce, who consented to give me support for a charge on the Confederate works. Colonel Townsend promptly volunteered to support me with his regiment, and departed to make the necessary preparations. Having placed the 2d New York on the right and left of the road, I was preparing for the charge, when a message reached me from General Peirce, stating that, after consultation with the colonel, he found that troops could not be formed to make the charge effective, and that during the consultation an order had been received from General Butler ordering a retreat; therefore, I was commanded to cover the retreat about to commence. The pursuit made by the Confederates was easily checked by the 2d New York, and the men reached their camps without further mishap. The only firing occurring after 12 o'clock on that day was from the gun brought up by my regiment, and in command of Lieutenant Greble. About one dozen shots had been fired when Greble was killed. The gun was abandoned on the field and Greble's body was left beside it. I called for volunteers to rescue the gun, and Captain Wilson, with his company of the 2d New York, responded, and in the face of the enemy gallantly rescued the gun, bringing it in with Greble's body lying on it. Major Winthrop's death during the early part of this engagement was a notable event. Although unattached to any regiment, he had volunteered for the expedition, and was killed

J. B. Moore, of Richmond, writes as follows:

"Major Winthrop headed a force, intending to turn our left flank. On our left was a slight earth-work. About 75 yards in front of this was a rail fence. Our attention was called by cheering to his advance. Looking up, we saw the major and two privates on the fence. His sword was drawn, and he was calling on his troops to follow him. Our first volley killed these three; those following, being protected by the peculiar formation of the ground, were not injured, but upon the fall of their leader they beat a precipitate retreat. I was among the first to reach these men. All were dead, having been instantly killed. Major Winthrop was shot in the breast, and the others in the head. About ten days afterward, a flag of truce came up asking for Major Winthrop's body. Having assisted in burying him, I was sent with the party to find the body, which was given to his friends. Among the incidents of this skirmish, none is more indelibly impressed on my mind than the gallant bearing of this unfortunate young man, when I first saw him, calling his men to follow, and confident that he had accomplished his object."

EDITORS.

while far in advance of the troops, and within one hundred yards of the enemy's works. General Butler arrived at Hampton Creek in time to meet the men coming in, but saw no part of the engagement. Among the first officers met by Butler were a major and lieutenant-colonel from one of the regiments engaged. Both were seated in a carriage driving leisurely home. Butler noticed the odd style of retreat, and also that there was crockery in the bottom of the carriage. The effects of this battle have been variously stated. Save as an encouragement to the Confederates, it had no important result.

After the battle of Big Bethel and up to the arrival of General McClellan the events of the war in and around Fort Monroe were, with few exceptions, of minor importance. On July 1st, 1861, Brigadier-General Peirce, under orders from General Butler, occupied Hampton, and at once proceeded to intrench. In this work the volunteers were assisted by former slaves. When General Magruder sent some cavalry to Hampton with orders to burn the village, a stampede of the Union soldiers occurred. Our forces on the east side of the bridge were greatly surprised when the disorganized troops and the contrabands came dashing over. The Confederate cavalrymen sent to burn the beautiful village remained, and at night we saw flames issuing from several buildings. We could readily discern the incendiaries going about the streets setting fire to the houses. In August, 1861, General John E. Wool was appointed to succeed General Butler in command at Fort Monroe.

MAJOR THEODORE WINTHROP. FROM A PORTRAIT.

Early in the fall of 1861 I was ordered, with my regiment, the 2d New York, to report to General Stone for duty in operations about Ball's Bluff, but Colonel E. D. Baker, with his regiment, was sent in my place. It appeared, later, that Colonel Baker had desired that he should be substituted, and when objections were made he succeeded in overruling them [see p. 123].

After the battle between the *Monitor* and *Merrimac* [see Vol. I., p. 692], General Wool, seeing the advantage of opening the blockade of the James River, prepared for an attempt to recapture Norfolk.

President Lincoln, with Secretaries Stanton and Chase, came to Fort Monroe, and on May 8th, 1862, the order was given and a movement made. Rear-Admiral Goldsborough, who had been ordered to assist, attacked the Confederate batteries at Sewell's Point, but, the *Merrimac* coming out, he retired, and for the hour, at least, the expedition was abandoned. News came to headquarters later in the day that General Huger was preparing to retire, and General Wool, after a trip to Willoughby's Point, decided to land his troops at Ocean View, thus taking in reverse the Confederate works. The landing of our troops was easily effected, and had more energy been displayed it is doubtful whether the enemy would have had time and opportunity to commit to the flames so much valuable material of war. While the movement was progressing, a delay

RUINS OF HAMPTON, VA. FROM A SKETCH MADE IN APRIL, 1862.

was caused by a dispute between two general officers as to rank. Our troops finally entered the intrenchments of the enemy unopposed. The mayor of Norfolk met General Wool and formally surrendered the city. While our troops were absent on this expedition, General Mansfield and myself were summoned to Fort Monroe by President Lincoln. Arriving there, Lincoln said: "Colonel Carr, where is your command?" "At Camp Hamilton, sir." (My command was the 2d, 7th, and 10th New York, and 29th Massachusetts.) "Why are you not on the other side at Norfolk?" "I am awaiting orders." Turning to Mansfield, Lincoln said, "Why are you here? Why not on the other side?" "I am ordered to the fort by General Wool," replied Mansfield. President Lincoln with vehement action threw his tall hat on the floor, and, uttering strongly his disapproval and disappointment, he said finally: "Send me some one who can write." Colonel LeGrand B. Cannon, of Wool's staff, responded, and Lincoln dictated an order to General Wool requiring that troops at Camp Hamilton be at once ordered to Norfolk, and that the troops already there be pushed rapidly forward. The order was issued, and I reported to General Viele at Norfolk and was assigned to the command of the exterior lines of defense at Portsmouth. The delays occurring in forwarding and pushing the troops allowed the Confederates time to burn the Navy Yard at Portsmouth, and to destroy the shipping. These troops remained at Norfolk until about June 1st, when we received orders to report to McClellan at Fair Oaks. General Wool was relieved of his command soon after the affair at Norfolk, and General John A. Dix was appointed in his stead.

INSPECTION. FROM A WAR-TIME SKETCH.

## CAMPAIGNING TO NO PURPOSE.

### RECOLLECTIONS OF A PRIVATE.—II. BY WARREN LEE GOSS.

WHILE we were in camp at Washington in February, 1862, we were drilled to an extent which to the raw "thinking soldier" seemed unnecessary. Our colonel was a strict disciplinarian. His efforts to drill out of us the methods of action and thought common to citizens, and to substitute in place thereof blind, unquestioning obedience to military rules, were not always appreciated at their true value. In my company there was an old drill-sergeant (let us call him Sergeant Hackett) who was in sympathetic accord with the colonel. He had occasion to reprove me often, and, finally, to inflict a blast of profanity at which my self-respect rebelled. Knowing that swearing was a breach of discipline, I waited confidently upon the colonel, with the manner of one gentleman calling upon another. After the usual salute, I opened complaint by saying: "Colonel, Mr. Hackett has——" The colonel interrupted me angrily, and, with fire in his eye, exclaimed: "*Mister?* There *are* no misters in the army." "I thought, sir——" I began apologetically. "Think? think?" he cried. "What right have *you* to think? *I* do the thinking for this regiment! Go to your quarters!"

I did not tarry. There seemed to be no common ground on which he and I could argue questions of personal etiquette. But I should do injustice to his character as a commander if I failed to illustrate another manner of reproof which he sometimes applied.

One day, noticing a corporal in soiled gloves, he said: "Corporal, you set a bad example to the men with your soiled gloves. Why do you?"

"I've had no pay, sir, since entering the service, and can't afford to hire washing."

The colonel drew from his pocket a pair of gloves spotlessly white, and, handing them to the corporal, said: "Put on those; I washed them myself!"

This was an unforgotten lesson to the whole regiment that it was a soldier's duty to attend himself to his personal neatness.

IN a camp of soldiers, rumor, with her thousand tongues, is always speaking. The rank and file and under-officers of the line are not taken into the confidence of their superiors. Hence the private soldier is usually in ignorance as to his destination. What he lacks in information is usually made up in surmise and conjecture; every hint is caught at and worked out in possible and impossible combinations. He plans and fights imaginary battles. He manœuvres for position, with pencil and chalk, on fanciful fields, at the same time knowing no more of the part he is actually performing in some great or little plan than the knapsack he bears. He makes some shrewd guesses (the Yankee's birthright), but he knows absolutely nothing. It is this which makes the good-will and confidence of the rank and file in the commander so important a factor in the *morale* of an army.

How we received the report or whence it came I know not, but it was rumored one morning that we were about to move. The order in reality came at last, to the distress and dismay of the sutlers and the little German woman who kept the grocery round the corner. We left her disconsolate over the cakes, pies, and goodies which had been liberally purchased, but which were yet unpaid for when we fell into two ranks, were counted off, and marched to conquer the prejudices of other sutlers.

We took the cars on February 25th and were hurried through a number of little sleepy-looking villages of Maryland [see map, p. 124]. The next morning found us at Sandy Hook, about half a mile from Harper's Ferry; thence, after about three hours' delay, we marched to a place opposite the promon-

A SUTLER'S TENT. BASED UPON A WAR-TIME PHOTOGRAPH.

HARPER'S FERRY IN 1862, FROM THE NORTH. BASED UPON A WAR-TIME PHOTOGRAPH.

tory on and around which is situated the picturesque village of Harper's Ferry, at the confluence of the Potomac and Shenandoah rivers. It was cold at our camping-place, between the canal and the river. There were no rations awaiting our arrival, and we were suffering from the hunger so common to soldiers. Who ever saw one off duty who was not in pursuit of something to eat? We couldn't get anything for love or money. We had at last reached a place where the people showed some of the distress incident to war, and a strong disinclination to feed or believe in us. We were grieved, but it couldn't be helped.

The bridge from the Maryland to the Virginia or Harper's Ferry shore had been destroyed by fire, leaving only the granite abutments (which were afterward built upon again), and we were soon set at work conveying some flat-bottomed scows from Sandy Hook to Harper's Ferry. As early as 9 o'clock about one hundred men came down opposite the ferry, just above the old bridge, and broke into little groups, in military precision. Four or five with spades and other implements improvised a wooden abutment on the shore; another party rowed against the stream, moored a scow, and let it drift down until it was opposite the wooden abutment; then a party of ten advanced, each two men carrying a claw-balk, or timbers fitted with a claw, one of which held the gunwale of the boat, the other the shore abutment. Twenty men now came down on the left with planks, one inch thick, six inches wide, and fifteen feet long, narrowed at each end; these they laid across the five joists or balks, and returned on the right. Another party meanwhile moored another boat, which dropped down-stream opposite the one already bridged; five joists, each twenty feet long, were laid upon the gunwale by five men; these were fastened by those in the boat, by means of ropes, to cleats or hooks pro-

CONFEDERATE PRISONERS. BASED UPON A WAR-TIME PHOTOGRAPH.

vided for the purpose on the side of the scows, which were shoved off from the shore until the shore end of the balk rested upon the shore boat. These were covered with planks in the same manner as before; side-rails of joists were lashed down with ropes to secure the whole. So one after another of the boats was dropped into position until a bridge several hundred feet long reached from the Maryland to the Virginia shore, for the passage of artillery and every description of munitions for an army. Owing to the force of the current, a large rope-cable was stretched from shore to shore fifty feet above the bridge, and the upper end of each boat was stayed to the cable by a smaller rope. The rushing bent the bridge into a half-moon curve. The clock-like precision with which these men worked showed them to be the drilled engineers and pontoniers of the regular army. After the bridge was built, a slight, short man, with sandy hair, in military dress, came out upon it and congratulated the engineers on their success. This unassuming man was George B. McClellan, commander of the Army of the Potomac.

It was on this boat-bridge that the army of General Banks crossed to the Virginia shore in 1862. Officers were not allowed to trot their horses; troops in crossing were given the order, "Route step," as the oscillation of the cadence step or trotting horse is dangerous to the stability of a bridge of any kind.

I crossed the bridge soon after it was laid, visited Jefferson Rock, the ruins of the burned armory, and the town in general. The occasional crack of a musket among the hills on the other side of the Shenandoah told that the enemy's scouts were still there. Colonel Geary's men were engaged in driving them from the hills, preparatory to the advance of General Banks. During the day fifteen or twenty were captured and marched through the town, presenting a generally shabby and unmilitary appearance. They did not impress me, as they did afterward when charging on our lines, with their unmusical yell and dauntless front.

The ruins of the burned armory of the United States were noticeable from the Maryland shore; also the masses of men moving in ceaseless tramp over the long and almost crescent-like bridge. The murmur of many voices, the mellow, abrupt call of the negro drivers to their mules, the glistening arms of the infantry reflected in the sunlight, the dull rumble of artillery wheels and baggage-wagons, live in memory to-day as one of the pictures of "war's wrinkled front," framed in the routine of more ordinary scenes.

The next day we were sent by rail back to Washington, and into camp upon our old grounds. A few mornings afterward an inspection was ordered. It came with the usual hurry and parade. Knapsacks and equipments were in shining order; every musket, bayonet, and button, boot and belt, as bright as rubbing and fear of censure or police duty could make them. Inspection over, the last jingle of ramrod in resounding musket was heard, and we were dismissed, with an intimation that on the morrow we were to go on a march.

The sun rose through the mists of the morning,—one of those quiet mornings when every sound is heard with distinctness. The waters of the Potomac were like a sheet of glass as we took up our line of march across the Long Bridge, making the old structure shake with our cadence step. Our moods varied: some laughed and joked; some, in suppressed tones, talked with their comrades as to their destination. Not much was said about fighting, but I, for one, did a great deal of thinking on that tender subject.

After we passed

A CAMP OVEN. FROM A WAR-TIME SKETCH.

the fort, which commanded the bridge on the Virginia side, we encountered one of the most powerful allies of the enemy, particularly during the winter and spring campaigns in Virginia,—MUD. No country equals a Virginia road for mud. We struck it thick, and sometimes knee-deep. It was verily "heavy marching." The foot sank insidiously into the mud, and came out again reluctantly; it had to be coaxed, and while you were persuading your left, the willing right was sinking as deep. The noise of walking was like that of a suction-pump when the water is exhausted.

The order was given, "Route step"; we climbed the banks of the road in search of firm earth, but it couldn't be found, so we went on pumping away, making about one foot in depth to two in advance. Our feet seemingly weighed twenty pounds each. We carried a number six into the unknown depths of mud, but it came out a number twelve, elongated, yellow, and nasty. Occasionally a boot or shoe would be left in the mud, and it would take an exploring expedition to find it. Wad Rider declared that though Virginia was once in the Union, she was now in the mud. The boys called their shoes "pontons," "mud-hooks," "soil-excavators," and other names not quite so polite.

The mud was in constant league with the enemy; an efficient ally in defensive warfare; equivalent to reënforcements of twenty thousand infantry. To realize the situation, spread tar a foot deep all over your back-yard, and then try to walk through it; particularly is this experiment recommended to those citizens who were constantly crying, "Why doesn't the army move?"

Mud took the military valor all out of a man. Any one would think, from reading the Northern newspapers, that we soldiers had macadamized roads over which to charge at the enemy. It would have pleased us much to have seen those "On to Richmond" people put over a 5-mile course in the Virginia mud, loaded with a 40-pound knapsack, 60 rounds of cartridges, and haversacks filled with 4 days' rations.

Without exaggeration, the mud has never had full credit for the immense help it afforded the enemy, as it prevented us from advancing upon them. The ever-present foe, winter and spring, in Old Virginia, was Mud. Summer and fall it was Dust, which was preferable; though marching without water, and with dust filling one's nostrils and throat, was not pleasant.

That first night out we went into camp near a small brook, where we washed off enough of the mud to recognize our feet. We had hard-tack and coffee for supper. And didn't it "go good!" What sauce ever equaled that of hunger? Truly the feast is in the palate. How we slept! Feet wet, boots for a pillow, the mud oozing up around our rubber blankets, but making a soft bed withal, and we sleeping the dreamless sleep of tired men. I would be willing, occasionally, to make another such march, through the same mud, for such a sleep.

At early daylight we fell in for rations of hot coffee and hard-tack. Immediately after, we took up our line of march, or, as Wad Rider expressed it, "began to pull mud." With intervals of rest, we "pulled mud" until about 4 o'clock in the afternoon, when we halted near Manassas Junction. Who has not heard of the "Quaker guns" at Manassas? We met the logs mounted on wheels, around the fortifications of Manassas, and can assure you they were not so formidable as the mud.

After thoroughly inspecting our enemies,—the logs,—we re-formed our ranks and took the back track for Washington. The rain soon began to fall, coming down literally in sheets; it ran down our backs in rivulets, and we should have run had we met the enemy about that time—that is, if the mud had permitted; for there is nothing which will so take the courage out of a soldier as to wet the seat of his trousers. On we went pumping and churning up and down in the mud, till about 10 o'clock, when we pitched camp near the roadside, as wet and bedraggled a set of men as ever panted for military glory, or pursued the bubble reputation at the wooden cannon's mouth. We arrived at our old camp near Washington the following evening.

Virginia mud has never been fully comprehended. To fully understand it you must march in it, sleep in it, be encompassed round about by it. Great is mud — Virginia mud.

In the early spring of 1862, when the Army of the Potomac was getting ready to move from Washington, the constant drill and discipline, the brightening of arms and polishing of buttons, and the exasperating fussiness on the part of company and regimental officers during inspections, conveyed to us a hint, as one of our comrades expressed it, that "some one higher in command was punching them to punch us." There was unusual activity upon the Potomac in front of our camp. Numerous steam-tugs were pulling huge sailing vessels here and there, and large transports, loaded with soldiers, horses, bales of hay, and munitions for an army, swept majestically down the broad river. Every description of water conveyance, from a canal-boat to a huge three-decked steamboat, seemed to have been pressed into the service. At last, when drills and inspections had made us almost frantic with neatness and cleanliness, our marching orders came. We formed in two ranks and boarded a little steamer lying at the wharf near by. All heavy baggage was left behind. I had clung to the contents of my knapsack with dogged tenacity; but, notwithstanding my most earnest protest, I was required to leave about one-half of them, including a pair of heavy boots and a choice brick from the Harper's Ferry engine-house. To my mind I was now entirely destitute of comforts.

The general opinion among us was that at last we were on our way to make an end of the Confederacy. We gathered in little knots on the deck: here and there a party were playing "penny ante"; others slept or dozed, but the majority smoked and discussed the probabilities of our destination, about which we really knew nothing, except that we were sailing down the Potomac.

TRANSPORTS ON THE POTOMAC. BASED UPON A WAR-TIME PHOTOGRAPH.

FORT MONROE — PARADE OF THE 3D PENNSYLVANIA ARTILLERY. FROM A PHOTOGRAPH.

## THE PENINSULAR CAMPAIGN.

BY GEORGE B. McCLELLAN, MAJOR-GENERAL, U. S. A.

IN the following pages I purpose to give a brief sketch of the Peninsular campaign of 1862. As it is impossible, within the limits available, to describe even the most important battles, I shall confine myself to strategical considerations. But even this requires a rapid review of the circumstances under which, from a small assemblage of unorganized citizens, utterly ignorant of war and almost of the use of arms, was evolved that mighty Army of the Potomac, which, unshaken alike in victory and defeat, during a long series of arduous campaigns against an army most ably commanded and the equal in heroism of any that ever met the shock of battle, proved itself worthy to bear on its bayonets the honor and fate of the nation.

In July, 1861, after having secured solidly for the Union that part of western Virginia north of the Kanawha and west of the mountains, I was suddenly called to Washington on the day succeeding the first battle of Bull Run. Reaching the capital on the 26th, I found myself assigned to the command of that city and of the troops gathered around it.

All was chaos and despondency; the city was filled with intoxicated stragglers, and an attack was expected. The troops numbered less than fifty thousand, many of whom were so demoralized and undisciplined that they could not be relied upon even for defensive purposes. Moreover, the term of service of a large part had already expired, or was on the point of doing so. On the Maryland side of the Potomac no troops were posted on the roads leading into the city, nor were there any intrenchments. On the Virginia side the condition of affairs was better in these respects, but far from satisfactory. Sufficient and fit material of war did not exist. The situation was difficult and fraught with danger.

MAJOR-GENERAL JOHN E. WOOL [SEE P. 168]. FROM A PHOTOGRAPH.

The first and most pressing demand was the immediate safety of the capital and the Government. This was secured by enforcing the most rigid discipline, by organizing permanent brigades under regular officers, and by placing the troops in good defensive positions, far enough to the front to afford room for manœuvring and to enable the brigades to support each other.

The contingency of the enemy's crossing the Potomac above the city was foreseen and promptly provided for. Had he attempted this "about three months after the battle of Manassas," he would, upon reaching "the rear of Washington," have found it covered by respectable works, amply garrisoned, with a sufficient disposable force to move upon his rear and force him to "a decisive engagement."⸗ It would have been the greatest possible good fortune for us if he had made this movement at the time in question, or even some weeks earlier. It was only for a very few days after the battle of Bull Run that the movement was practicable, and every day added to its difficulty.

Two things were at once clear: first, that a large and thoroughly organized army was necessary to bring the war to a successful conclusion; second, that Washington must be so strongly fortified as to set at rest any reasonable apprehensions of its being carried by a sudden attack, in order that the active army might be free to move with the maximum strength and on any line of operations without regard to the safety of the capital.

These two herculean tasks were entered upon without delay or hesitation. They were carried to a successful conclusion, without regard to that impatient and unceasing clamor — inevitable among a people unaccustomed to war — which finally forced the hand of the general charged with their execution. He regarded their completion as essential to the salvation of his country, and determined to accomplish them, even if sacrificed in the endeavor. Nor has he, even at this distant day, and after much bitter experience, any regret that he persisted in his determination. Washington was surrounded by a line of strong detached works, armed with garrison artillery, and secure against assault. Intermediate points were occupied by smaller works, battery epaulements, infantry intrenchments, etc. The result was a line of defenses which could easily be held by a comparatively small garrison against any assault, and could be reduced only by the slow operations of a regular siege, requiring much time and material, and affording full opportunity to bring all the resources of the country to its relief. At no time during the war was the enemy able to undertake the siege of Washington, nor, if respectably garrisoned, could it ever have been in danger from an assault. The maximum garrison necessary to hold the place against a siege from any and every quarter was 34,000 troops, with 40 field-guns; this included the requisite reserves.

With regard to the formation of the Army of the Potomac, it must suffice to say that everything was to be created from the very foundation. Raw men and officers were to be disciplined and instructed. The regular army was too small to furnish more than a portion of the general officers, and a very small portion of the staff, so that the staff-departments and staff-officers were to be fashioned mainly out of the intelligent and enthusiastic, but per-

⸗ The words quoted are General Beauregard's. (See Vol. I., p. 221).— EDITORS.

162                THE PENINSULAR CAMPAIGN.

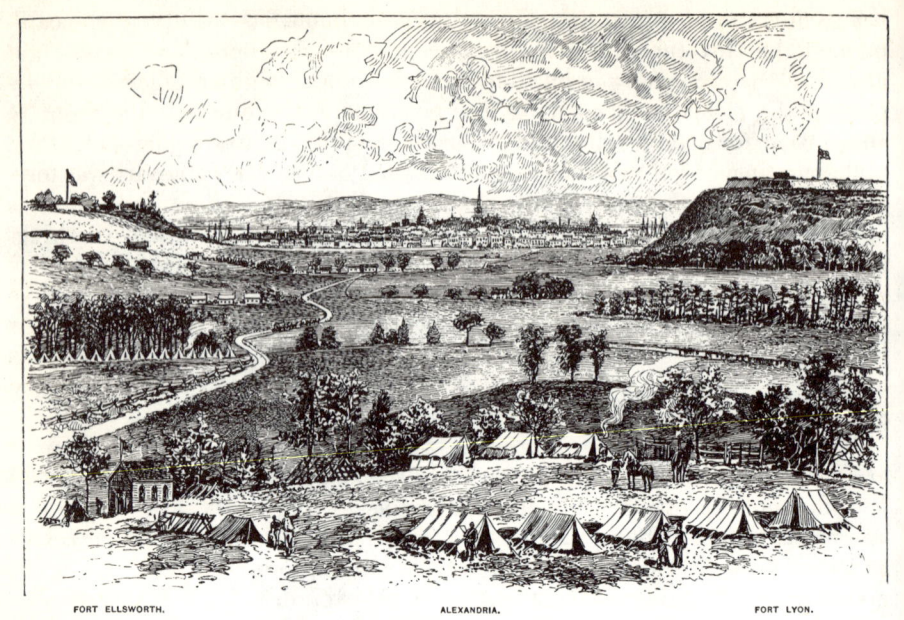

FORT ELLSWORTH.   ALEXANDRIA.   FORT LYON.
VIEW OF ALEXANDRIA FROM THE CAMP OF THE 40TH NEW YORK VOLUNTEERS.
FROM A SKETCH MADE IN NOVEMBER, 1861.

fectly raw, material furnished. Artillery, small-arms, and ammunition were to be fabricated, or purchased from abroad; wagons, ambulances, bridge trains, camp equipage, hospital stores, and all the vast *impedimenta* and material indispensable for an army in the field, were to be manufactured. So great was the difficulty of procuring small-arms that the armament of the infantry was not satisfactorily completed until the winter, and a large part of the field-batteries were not ready for service until the spring of 1862. As soon as possible divisions were organized, the formation being essentially completed in November.

On the 1st of November, upon the retirement of General Winfield Scott, I succeeded to the command of all the armies, except the Department of Virginia, which comprised the country within sixty miles of Fort Monroe. Upon assuming the general command, I found that the West was far behind the East in its state of preparation, and much of my time and large quantities of material were consumed in pushing the organization of the Western armies. Meanwhile the various coast expeditions were employed in seizing important points of the enemy's sea-board, to facilitate the prevention of blockade-running, and to cut or threaten the lines of communication near the coast, with reference to subsequent operations.

The plan of campaign which I adopted for the spring of 1862 was to push forward the armies of Generals Halleck and Buell to occupy Memphis, Nashville, and Knoxville, and the line of the Memphis and Danville Railroad, so as to deprive the enemy of that important line, and force him to adopt the circuitous routes by Augusta, Branchville, and Charleston. It was also intended to seize Washington, North Carolina, at the earliest practicable moment, and to open the Mississippi by effecting a junction between Generals Halleck and Butler. This movement of the Western armies was to be followed by that of the Army of the Potomac from Urbana, on the lower Rappahannock [see map, next page], to West Point and Richmond, intending, if we failed to gain Richmond by a rapid march, to cross the James and attack the city in rear, with the James as a line of supply.

So long as Mr. Cameron was Secretary of War I received the cordial support of that department; but when he resigned, the whole state of affairs changed. I had never met Mr. Stanton. before reaching Washington, in 1861. He at once sought me and professed the utmost personal affection, the expression of which was exceeded only by the bitterness of his denunciation of the Government and its policy. I was unaware of his appointment as Secretary of War until after it had been made, whereupon he called to ascertain whether I desired him to accept, saying that to do so would involve a total sacrifice of his personal interests, and that the only inducement would be the desire to assist me in my work. Having no reason to doubt his sincerity, I desired him to accept, whereupon he consented, and with great effusion exclaimed: "Now we two will save the country."

On the next day the President came to my house to explain why he had appointed Mr. Stanton without consulting me; his reason being that he supposed Stanton to be a great friend of mine, and that the appointment would naturally be satisfactory, and that he feared that if I had known it beforehand it would be said that I had dragooned him into it.

The more serious difficulties of my position began with Mr. Stanton's accession to the War Office. It at once became very difficult to approach

HEADQUARTERS OF BRIGADIER-GENERAL JOHN SEDGWICK, ON THE LEESBURG TURNPIKE, NEAR WASHINGTON.
FROM A SKETCH MADE IN JANUARY, 1862.

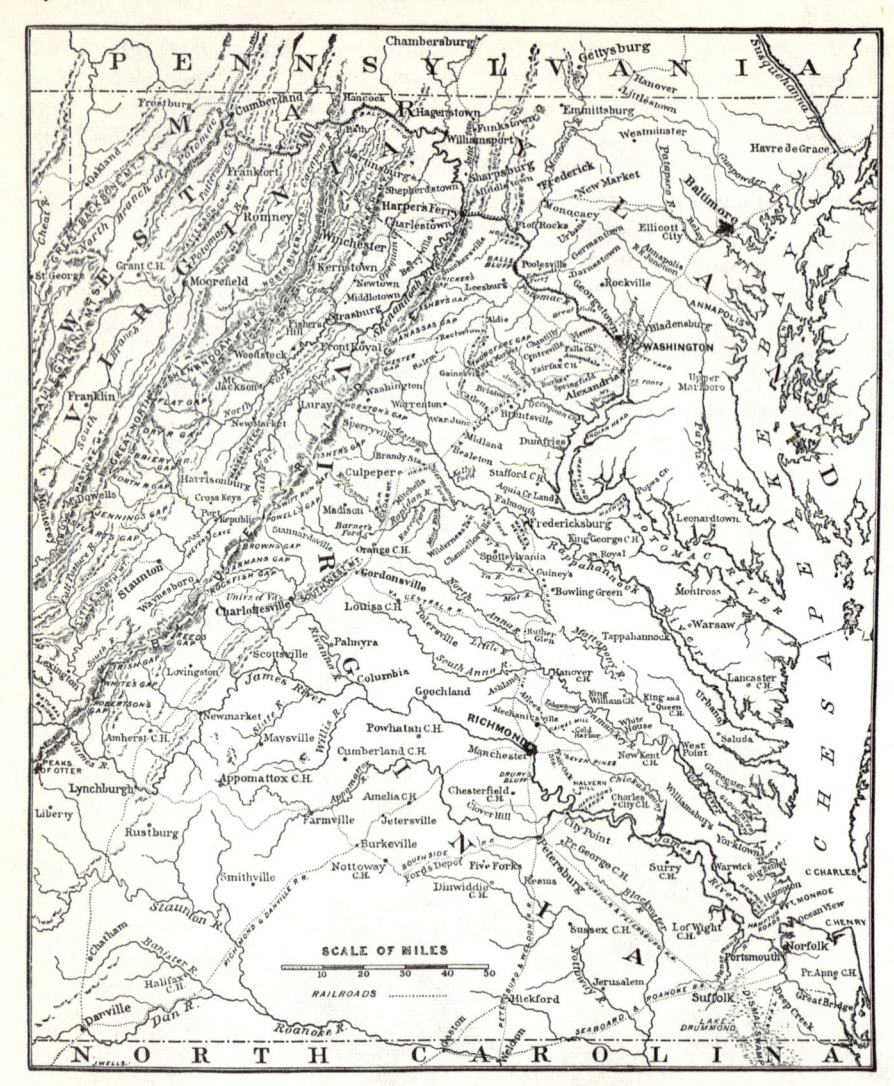

MAP OF THE VIRGINIA CAMPAIGNS.

him, even for the transaction of ordinary current business, and our personal relations at once ceased. The impatience of the Executive immediately became extreme, and I can attribute it only to the influence of the new Secretary, who did many things to break up the free and confidential intercourse that had heretofore existed between the President and myself. The Government soon manifested great impatience in regard to the opening of the Baltimore and Ohio Railroad and the destruction of the Confederate batteries on the Potomac. The first object could be permanently attained only by occupying the Shenandoah Valley with a force strong enough to resist any attack by the Confederate army then at Manassas; the second only by

QUARTERMASTER'S DOCK, FORT MONROE. FROM A SKETCH MADE IN 1862.

a general advance of the Army of the Potomac, driving the enemy back of the Rapidan. My own view was that the movement of the Army of the Potomac from Urbana would accomplish both of these objects, by forcing the enemy to abandon all his positions and fall back on Richmond. I was therefore unwilling to interfere with this plan by a premature advance, the effect of which must be either to commit us to the overland route, or to minimize the advantages of the Urbana movement. I wished to hold the enemy at Manassas to the last moment — if possible until the advance from Urbana had actually commenced, for neither the reopening of the railroad nor the destruction of the batteries was worth the danger involved.

The positive order of the President, probably issued under the pressure of the Secretary of War, forced me to undertake the opening of the railway. For this purpose I went to Harper's Ferry in February, intending to throw over a force sufficient to occupy Winchester. To do this it was necessary to have a reliable bridge across the Potomac — to insure supplies and prompt reënforcements. The pontoon-bridge, thrown as a preliminary, could not be absolutely trusted on a river so liable to heavy freshets; therefore it was determined to construct a canal-boat bridge. It was discovered, however, when the attempt was made, that the lift-lock from the canal to the river was too narrow for the boats by some four or five inches, and I therefore decided to rebuild the railroad bridge, and content myself with occupying Charlestown until its completion, postponing to the same time the advance to Winchester. I had fully explained my intentions to the President and Secretary before leaving Washington, providing for precisely such a contingency. While at Harper's Ferry I learned that the President was dissatisfied with my action, and on reaching Washington I laid a full explanation before the Secretary, with which he expressed himself entirely satisfied, and told me that the President was already so, and that it was unnecessary for me to communicate with him on the subject. I then proceeded with the preparations necessary to force the evacuation of the Potomac batteries. On the very day appointed for the division commanders to come to headquarters to receive their final orders, the President sent for me. I then learned that he had received no explanation of the Harper's Ferry affair, and that the Secretary was not authorized to make the statement already referred to; but after my repetition of it the President became fully satisfied with my course. He then, however, said that there was another "very ugly matter" which he desired to talk about, and that was the movement by the lower Chesapeake. He said that it had been suggested that I proposed this movement with the "traitorous" purpose of leaving Washington uncovered and exposed to attack. I very promptly objected to the coupling of any such adjective with my purposes, whereon he disclaimed any intention of conveying the idea that he expressed his own opinion, as he merely repeated the suggestions of others. I then explained the purpose and effect of fortifying Washington, and, as I thought, removed his apprehensions, but informed him that the division commanders were to be at headquarters that morning, and suggested that my plans should be laid before them that they might give their opinion as to whether the capital would be endangered; I also said that in order to leave them perfectly untrammeled I would not attend the meeting. Accordingly they met on the 8th of March and approved my plans.

On the same day was issued, without my knowledge, the order forming army corps and assigning the senior general officers to their command. ‡ My own views were that, as the command of army corps involved great responsibility and demanded ability of a high order, it was safer to postpone their formation until trial in the field had shown which general officers could best perform those vital functions. An incompetent division commander could not often jeopardize the safety of an army; while an unfit corps commander could easily lose a battle and frustrate the best-conceived plan of campaign. Of the four corps commanders, one only had commanded so much as a regiment in the field prior to the Bull Run campaign. On the next day intelligence arrived that the enemy was abandoning his positions. I crossed to the Virginia side to receive information more promptly and decide upon what should be done. During the night I determined to advance the whole army, to take advantage of any opportunity to strike the enemy, to break up the permanent camps, give the troops a little experience on the march and in bivouac, get rid of extra baggage, and test the working of the staff-departments. If this were done at all, it must be done promptly, and by moving the troops by divisions, without waiting to form the army corps. Accordingly, I telegraphed to the Secretary, explaining the state of the case and asking authority to postpone the army corps formation until the completion of the movement. The reply was an abrupt and unreasonable refusal. I again telegraphed, explaining the situation and throwing the responsibility upon the Secretary, whereupon he gave way.

Meanwhile, as far back as the 27th of February, orders had been given for collecting the transportation necessary to carry out the Urbana movement.

‡ First Corps, McDowell — Divisions: Franklin, McCall, and King; Second Corps, Sumner — Divisions: Richardson, Blenker, and Sedgwick; Third Corps, Heintzelman — Divisions: Porter, Hooker, and Hamilton; Fourth Corps, Keyes — Divisions: Couch, Smith, and Casey. The reserve artillery (Henry J. Hunt), the regular infantry (George Sykes), and regular cavalry (Philip St. George Cooke) and engineer troops were attached to headquarters.— EDITORS.

## THE PENINSULAR CAMPAIGN. 167

This conclusion had been reached after full discussion. On the 27th of January had been issued the President's General War Order No. 1, directing a general movement of the land and naval forces against the enemy on the 22d of February. On the 31st of January was issued the President's Special War Order No. 1, directing the Army of the Potomac to advance to the attack of Manassas on the 22d of February. The President, however, permitted me to state my objections to this order, which I did, at length, in a letter of February 3d, to the Secretary of War. As the President's order was not insisted upon, although never formally revoked, it is to be assumed that my letter produced, for a time at least, the desired effect. When Manassas had been abandoned by the enemy and he had withdrawn behind the Rapidan, the Urbana movement lost much of its promise, as the enemy was now in position to reach Richmond before we could do so. The alternative remained of making Fort Monroe and its vicinity the base of operations.

MAP OF THE PENINSULAR CAMPAIGN.

The plan first adopted was to commence the movement with the First Corps as a unit, to land north of Gloucester and move thence on West Point; or, should circumstances render it advisable, to land a little below Yorktown to turn the defenses between that place and Fort Monroe. The Navy Department were confident that we could rely upon their vessels to neutralize the *Merrimac* and aid materially in reducing the batteries on the York River, either by joining in the attack or by running by them and gaining their rear. As transports arrived very slowly, especially those for horses, and the great impatience of the Government grew apace, it became necessary to embark divisions as fast as vessels arrived, and I decided to land them at Fort Monroe, holding the First Corps to the last, still intending to move it in mass to turn Gloucester. On the 17th of March the leading division embarked at Alexandria. The campaign was undertaken with the intention of taking some 145,000 troops, to be increased by a division of 10,000 drawn from the troops in the vicinity of Fort Monroe, giving a total of 155,000. Strenuous efforts were made to induce the President to take away Blenker's German division of 10,000 men. Of his own volition he at first declined, but the day before I left Washington he yielded to the non-military pressure and reluctantly gave the order, thus reducing the expected force to 145,000.

While at Fairfax Court House, on the 12th of March, I learned that there had appeared in the daily papers the order relieving me from the general command of all the armies and confining my authority to the Department of the Potomac. I had received no previous intimation of the intention of the Government in this respect. Thus, when I embarked for Fort Monroe on the 1st of April, my command extended from Philadelphia to Richmond, from the Alleghanies, including the Shenandoah, to the Atlantic; for an order had been issued a few days previous placing Fort Monroe and the Department of Virginia under my command, and authorizing me to withdraw from the troops therein ten thousand, to form a division to be added to the First Corps.

The fortifications of Washington were at this time completed and armed. I had already given instructions for the refortification of Manassas, the reopening of the Manassas Gap Railroad, the protection of its bridges by blockhouses, the intrenchment of a position for a brigade at or near the railroad crossing of the Shenandoah, and an intrenched post at Chester Gap. I left about 42,000 troops for the immediate defense of Washington, and more than 35,000 for the Shenandoah Valley — an abundance to insure the safety of Washington and to check any attempt to recover the lower Shenandoah and threaten Maryland. Beyond this force, the reserves of the Northern States were all available.

On my arrival at Fort Monroe on the 2d of April, I found five divisions of infantry, Sykes's brigade of regulars, two regiments of cavalry, and a portion of the reserve artillery disembarked. Another cavalry regiment and a part of a fourth had arrived, but were still on shipboard; comparatively few wagons had come. On the same day came a telegram stating that the Department of Virginia was withdrawn from my control, and forbidding me to form the division of ten thousand men without General Wool's sanction. I was thus deprived of the command of the base of operations, and the ultimate strength of the army was reduced to 135,000 — another serious departure from the plan of campaign. Of the troops disembarked, only four divisions, the regulars, the majority of the reserve artillery, and a part of the cavalry, could be moved, in consequence of the lack of transportation. Casey's division was

HEADQUARTERS OF GENERAL HEINTZELMAN, COMMANDING THE THIRD ARMY CORPS AT HOWE'S SAW-MILL, BEFORE YORKTOWN [SEE MAP, P. 188]. FROM A SKETCH MADE AT THE TIME.

unable to leave Newport News until the 16th, from the impossibility of supplying it with wagons.

The best information obtainable represented the Confederate troops around Yorktown as numbering at least fifteen thousand, with about an equal force at Norfolk; and it was clear that the army lately at Manassas, now mostly near Gordonsville, was in position to be thrown promptly to the Peninsula. It was represented that Yorktown was surrounded by strong earth-works, and that the Warwick River, instead of stretching across the Peninsula to Yorktown,— as proved to be the case,— came down to Lee's Mills from the North, running parallel with and not crossing the road from Newport News to Williamsburg. It was also known that there were intrenched positions of more or less strength at Young's Mills, on the Newport News road, and at Big Bethel, Howard's Bridge, and Ship's Point, on or near the Hampton and Yorktown road, and at Williamsburg [see map, p. 188].

On my arrival at Fort Monroe, I learned, in an interview with Flag-Officer Goldsborough, that he could not protect the James as a line of supply, and that he could furnish no vessels to take an active part in the reduction of the batteries at York and Gloucester or to run by and gain their rear. He could only aid in the final attack after our land batteries had essentially silenced their fire.

I thus found myself with 53,000 men in condition to move, faced by the conditions of the problem just stated. Information was received that Yorktown was already being reënforced from Norfolk, and it was apprehended that the main Confederate army would promptly follow the same course. I therefore determined to move at once with the force in hand, and endeavor to seize a point — near the Halfway House — between Yorktown and Williamsburg, where the Peninsula is reduced to a narrow neck, and thus cut off the retreat of the Yorktown garrison and prevent the arrival of reënforcements. The advance commenced on the morning of the 4th of April, and was arranged to turn successively the intrenchments on the two roads; the result being that, on the afternoon of the 5th, the Third Corps was engaged with the enemy's outposts in front of Yorktown and under the artillery fire of the place. The Fourth Corps came upon Lee's Mills and found it covered by the unfordable line of the Warwick, and reported the position so strong as to render it impossible to execute its orders to assault [see map, p. 188]. Thus, all things were brought to a stand-still, and the intended movement on the Halfway House could not be carried out. Just at this moment came a telegram, dated the 4th, informing me that the First Corps was withdrawn from my command. Thus, when too deeply committed to recede, I found that another reduction of about 43,000, including several cavalry regiments withheld from me, diminished my paper force to 92,000, instead of the 155,000 on which the plans of the campaign had been founded, and with which it was intended to operate. The number of men left behind, sick and from other causes incident to such a movement, reduced the total for duty to some 85,000, from which must be deducted all camp, depot, and train guards, escorts, and non-combatants, such as cooks, servants, orderlies, and extra-duty men in the various staff-departments, which reduced the numbers actually available for battle to some 67,000 or 68,000.

The order withdrawing the First Corps also broke up the Department of the Potomac, forming out of it the Department of the Shenandoah, under General Banks, and the Department of the Rappahannock, under General McDowell, the latter including Washington. I thus lost all control of the depots at Washington, as I had already been deprived of the control of the base at Fort Monroe and of the ground subsequently occupied by the depot at White House. The only territory remaining under my command was the paltry triangle between the departments of the Rappahannock and Virginia; even that was yet to be won from the enemy. I was thus relieved from the duty of providing for the safety of Washington, and deprived of all control over the troops in that vicinity. Instead of one directing head controlling operations which should have been inseparable, the region from the Alleghanies to the sea was parceled out among four independent commanders.

On the 3d of April, at the very moment of all others when it was most necessary to push recruiting most vigorously, to make good the inevitable losses in battle and by disease, an order was issued from the War Department discontinuing all recruiting for the volunteers and breaking up all their recruiting stations. Instead of a regular and permanent system of recruiting, whether by voluntary enlistment or by draft, a spasmodic system of large drafts was thereafter resorted to, and, to a great extent, the system of forming new regiments. The results were wasteful and pernicious. There were enough or nearly enough, organizations in the field, and these should have been constantly maintained at the full strength by a regular and constant influx of recruits, who, by association with their veteran comrades, would soon

VIEW FROM UNION MORTAR BATTERY NO. 4, LOOKING TOWARD YORKTOWN.—GLOUCESTER POINT ON THE RIGHT. FROM A SKETCH MADE APRIL 16, 1862.

have become efficient. The new regiments required much time to become useful, and endured very heavy and unnecessary losses from disease and in battle owing to the inexperience of the officers and men. A course more in accordance with the best-established military principles and the uniform experience of war would have saved the country millions of treasure and thousands of valuable lives.

Then, on the 5th of April, I found myself with 53,000 men in hand, giving less than 42,000 for battle, after deducting extra-duty men and other non-combatants. In our front was an intrenched line, apparently too strong for assault, and which I had now no means of turning, either by land or water. I now learned that 85,000 would be the maximum force at my disposal, giving only some 67,000 for battle. Of the three divisions yet to join, Casey's reached the front only on the 17th, Richardson's on the 16th, and Hooker's commenced arriving at Ship Point on the 10th. Whatever may have been said afterward, no one at the time — so far as my knowledge extended — thought an assault practicable without certain preliminary siege operations. At all events, my personal experience in this kind of work was greater than that of any officer under my command; and after personal reconnoissances more appropriate to a lieutenant of engineers than to the commanding general, I could neither discover nor hear of any point where an assault promised any chance of success. We were thus obliged to resort to siege operations in order to silence the enemy's artillery fire, and open the way to an assault. All the batteries would have been ready to open fire on the 5th, or, at latest, on the morning of the 6th of May, and it was determined to assault at various points the moment the heavy batteries had performed their allotted task; the navy was prepared to participate in the attack as soon as the main batteries were silenced; the *Galena*, under that most gallant and able officer, John Rodgers, was to take part in the attack, and would undoubtedly have run the batteries at the earliest possible moment; but during the night of the 3d and 4th of May the enemy evacuated his positions, regarding them as untenable under the impending storm of heavy projectiles.

Meanwhile, on the 22d of April, Franklin's division of McDowell's corps had joined me by water, in consequence of my urgent calls for reënforcements.

The moment the evacuation of Yorktown was known, the order was given for the advance of all the disposable cavalry and horse batteries, supported by infantry divisions, and every possible effort was made to expedite the movement of a column by water upon West Point, to force the evacuation of the lines at Williamsburg, and, if possible, cut off a portion of the enemy's force and trains.

The heavy storms which had prevailed recommenced on the afternoon of the 4th, and not only impeded the advance of troops by land, but delayed the movement by water so much that it was not until the morning of the 7th that the leading division — Franklin's — disembarked near West Point and took up a suitable position to hold its own and cover the landing of reënforcements. This division was attacked not long after it landed, but easily repulsed the enemy.

Meanwhile the enemy's rear-guard held the Williamsburg lines against our advance, except where Hancock broke through, until the night of the 5th, when they retired [see map, p. 188].

The army was now divided: a part at the mouth of the Pamunkey, a part at Williamsburg, and a part at Yorktown prepared to ascend the York River. The problem was to reunite them without giving the enemy the opportunity of striking either fraction with his whole force. This was accomplished on the 10th, when all the divisions were in communication, and the movement of concentration continued as rapidly as circumstances permitted, so that on the 15th the headquarters and the divisions of Franklin, Porter, Sykes, and Smith reached Cumberland Landing; Couch and Casey being near New Kent Court

CLARK'S HOUSE, NEAR HOWE'S SAW-MILL, YORKTOWN, GENERAL HOSPITAL OF THE THIRD CORPS. FROM A SKETCH MADE APRIL 11, 1862.

WHARF, YORK RIVER.   McCLELLAN'S HEADQUARTERS.   NELSON HOUSE.
VIEW OF MAIN STREET, YORKTOWN, THE UNION TROOPS MARCHING IN. FROM A SKETCH MADE MAY 4, 1862.

House, Hooker and Kearny near Roper's Church, and Richardson and Sedgwick near Eltham. On the 15th and 16th, in the face of dreadful weather and terrible roads, the divisions of Franklin, Porter, and Smith were advanced to White House, and a depot established. On the 18th the Fifth and Sixth Corps were formed, so that the organization of the Army of the Potomac was now as follows: Second Corps, Sumner — Divisions, Sedgwick and Richardson; Third Corps, Heintzelman — Divisions, Kearny and Hooker; Fourth Corps, Keyes — Divisions, Couch and Casey; Fifth Corps, F. J. Porter — Divisions, Morell and Sykes and the Reserve Artillery; Sixth Corps, Franklin — Divisions, Smith and Slocum.

The cavalry organization remained unchanged, and we were sadly deficient in that important arm, as many of the regiments belonging to the Army of the Potomac were among those which had been retained near Washington.

The question now arose as to the line of operations to be followed: that of the James on the one hand, and, on the other, the line from White House as a base, crossing the upper Chickahominy.

The army was admirably placed for adopting either, and my decision was to take that of the James, operating on either bank as might prove advisable, but always preferring the southern. I had urgently asked for reënforcements to come by water, as they would thus be equally available for either line of operations. The destruction of the *Merrimac* on the 11th of May had opened the James River to us, and it was only after that date that it became available. My plan, however, was changed by orders from Washington. A telegram of the 18th from the Secretary of War informed me that McDowell would advance from Fredericksburg, and directed me to extend the right of the Army of the Potomac to the north of Richmond, in order to establish communication with him. The same order required me to supply his troops from our depots at White House. Herein lay the failure of the campaign, as it necessitated the division of the army by the Chickahominy, and caused great delay in constructing practicable bridges across that stream; while if I had been able to cross to the James, reënforcements would have reached me by water rapidly and safely, the army would have been united and in no danger of having its flank turned, or its line of supply interrupted, and the attack could have been much more rapidly pushed.

I now proceeded to do all in my power to insure success on the new line of operations thus imposed upon me. On the 20th of May our light troops reached the Chickahominy at Bottom's Bridge, which they found destroyed. I at once ordered Casey's division to ford the stream and occupy

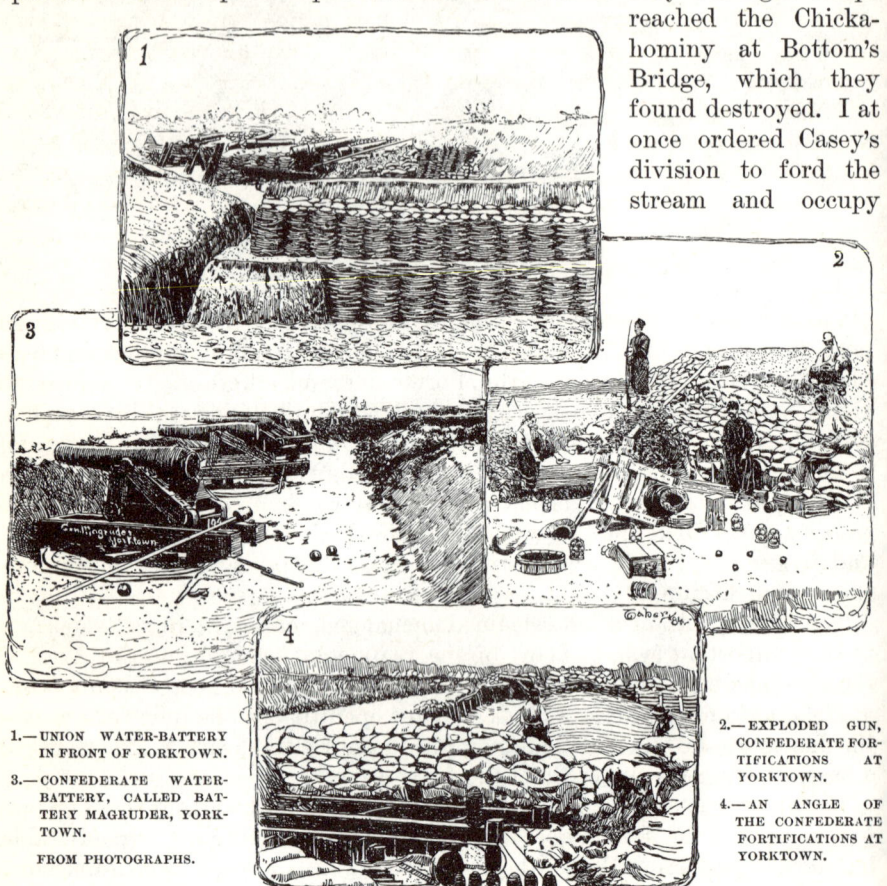

1.—UNION WATER-BATTERY IN FRONT OF YORKTOWN.
3.—CONFEDERATE WATER-BATTERY, CALLED BATTERY MAGRUDER, YORKTOWN.
FROM PHOTOGRAPHS.

2.—EXPLODED GUN, CONFEDERATE FORTIFICATIONS AT YORKTOWN.
4.—AN ANGLE OF THE CONFEDERATE FORTIFICATIONS AT YORKTOWN.

the heights beyond, thus securing a lodgment on the right bank. Heintzelman was moved up in support of Keyes. By the 24th, Mechanicsville was carried, so that the enemy was now all together on the other side of the river. Sumner was near the railroad, on the left bank of the stream; Porter and Franklin were on the same bank near Mechanicsville.

It is now time to give a brief description of the Chickahominy. This river rises some fifteen miles north-westward of Richmond, and unites with the James about forty miles below that city. Our operations were on the part between Meadow and Bottom's bridges, covering the approaches to Richmond from the east. Here the river at its ordinary stage is some forty feet wide, fringed with a dense growth of heavy forest-trees, and bordered by low marshy lands, varying from half a mile to a mile in width. Within the limits above mentioned the firm ground, above high-water mark, seldom approaches the river on either bank, and in no place did the high ground come near the stream on both banks. It was subject to frequent, sudden, and great variations in the volume of water, and a single violent storm of brief duration sufficed to cause an overflow of the bottom-lands for many days, rendering the river absolutely impassable without long and strong bridges. When we reached the river it was found that all the bridges, except that at Mechanicsville, had been destroyed. The right bank, opposite New, Mechanicsville, and Meadow bridges, was bordered by high bluffs, affording the enemy commanding positions for his batteries, enfilading the approaches, and preventing the rebuilding of important bridges. We were thus obliged to select other less exposed points for our crossings. Should McDowell effect the promised junction, we could turn the head-waters of the Chickahominy, and attack Richmond from the north and north-west, still preserving our line of supply from White House. But with the force actually available such an attempt would expose the army to the loss of its communications and to destruction in detail; for we had an able and savage antagonist, prompt to take advantage of any error on our part. The country furnished no supplies, so that we could not afford a separation from our depots. All the information obtained showed that Richmond was intrenched, that the enemy occupied in force all the approaches from the east, that he intended to dispute every step of our advance, and that his army was numerically superior. Early on the 24th of May I received a telegram from the President, informing me that McDowell would certainly march on the 26th, suggesting that I should detach a force to the right to cut off the retreat of the Confederate force in front of Fredericksburg, and desiring me to march cautiously and safely. On the same day another dispatch came, informing me that, in consequence of Stonewall Jackson's advance down the Shenandoah, the movement of McDowell was suspended. Next day the President again telegraphed that the movement against General Banks seemed so general and connected as to show that the enemy could not intend a very desperate defense of Richmond; that he thought the time was near when I "must either attack Richmond or give up the job, and come back to the defense of Washington." I replied that all my information agreed that the mass of the enemy was still in the immediate vicinity of Richmond, ready to defend it, and that the object of Jackson's movement was probably to prevent reënforcements being sent to me. On the 26th General Stoneman, with my advanced guard, cut the Virginia Central Railroad in three places. On the same day I learned that a very considerable force of the enemy was in the vicinity of Hanover Court House, to our right and rear, threatening our communications, and in position to reënforce Jackson or oppose McDowell, whose advance was then eight miles south of Fredericksburg. I ordered General F. J. Porter to move next morning to dislodge them. He took with him his own old division, Warren's provisional brigade and Emory's cavalry brigade. His operations in the vicinity of Hanover Court House were entirely successful, and resulted in completely clearing our flank, cutting the railroads in several places, destroying bridges, inflicting a severe loss upon the enemy, and fully opening the way for the advance of McDowell's corps. As there was no indication of its immediate approach, and the position at Hanover Court House was too much exposed to be permanently held, General Porter's command was withdrawn on the evening of the 29th, and returned to its old position with the main army. The campaign had taken its present position in consequence of the assurance that I should be joined by McDowell's corps. As it was now clear that I could not count with certainty upon that force, I had to do the best I could with the means at hand.

The first necessity was to establish secure communications between the two parts of the army, necessarily separated

NEW KENT COURT HOUSE. FROM A SKETCH MADE MAY 19, 1862.

by the Chickahominy. Richmond could be attacked only by troops on the right bank. As the expectation of the advance of McDowell was still held out, and that only by the land route, I could not yet transfer the base to the James, but was obliged to retain it on the Pamunkey, and therefore to keep on the left bank a force sufficient to protect our communications and cover the junction of McDowell. It was still permissible to believe that sufficient attention would be paid to the simplest principle of war to push McDowell rapidly on Jackson's heels, when he made his inevitable return march to join the main Confederate army and attack our right flank. The failure of McDowell to reach me at or before the critical moment was due to the orders he received from Washington. The bridges over the Chickahominy first built were swept away by the floods, and it became necessary to construct others

SECTION OF THE ENCAMPMENT OF THE ARMY OF THE POTOMAC NEAR WHITE HOUSE, VA. PROCESS REPRODUCTION OF A PHOTOGRAPH.

"We were now [middle of May] encamped on the old Custis place, at present owned by General Fitzhugh Lee [Gen. W. H. F. Lee] of the Rebel cavalry service. On every side of us were immense fields of wheat, which, but for the presence of armies, promised an abundant harvest. . . . It was marvelous that such quiet could exist where a hundred thousand men were crowded together, yet almost absolute stillness reigned throughout the vast camp during the whole of this pleasant Sabbath."—From George T. Stevens's "Three Years in the Sixth Corps." The picture represents the space occupied by about one brigade.—EDITORS.

more solid and with long log approaches, a slow and difficult task, generally carried on by men working in the water and under fire. The work was pushed as rapidly as possible, and on the 30th of May the corps of Heintzelman and Keyes were on the right bank of the Chickahominy, the most advanced positions being somewhat strengthened by intrenchments; Sumner's corps was on the left bank, some six miles above Bottom's Bridge; Porter's and Franklin's corps were on the left bank opposite the enemy's left. During the day and night of the 30th torrents of rain fell, inundating the whole country and threatening the destruction of our bridges.

Well aware of our difficulties, our active enemy, on the 31st of May, made a violent attack upon Casey's division, followed by an equally formidable one on Couch, thus commencing the battle of Fair Oaks or Seven Pines. Heintzelman came up in support, and during the afternoon Sumner crossed the river with great difficulty, and rendered such efficient service that the enemy was checked. In the morning his renewed attacks were easily repulsed, and the ground occupied at the beginning of the battle was more than recovered; he had failed in the purpose of the attack. The ground was now so thoroughly soaked by the rain, and the bridges were so much injured, that it was impracticable to pursue the enemy or to move either Porter or Franklin to the support of the other corps on the south bank. Our efforts were at once concentrated upon the restoration of the old and the building of new bridges.

On the 1st of June the Department of Virginia, including Fort Monroe, was placed under my command. On the 2d the Secretary telegraphed that as soon as Jackson was disposed of in the Shenandoah, another large body of troops would be at my service; on the 5th, that he intended sending a part of General McDowell's force as soon as it could return from Front Royal (in the Shenandoah Valley, near Manassas Gap, and about one hundred and fifteen miles north-west of Richmond), probably as many as I wanted; on the 11th, that McCall's force had embarked to join me on the day preceding, and that it was intended to send the residue of General McDowell's force to join me as speedily as possible, and that it was clear that a strong force was operating with Jackson for the purpose of preventing the forces there from joining me.

On the 26th the Secretary telegraphed that the forces of McDowell, Banks, and Frémont would be consolidated as the Army of Virginia, and would operate promptly in my aid by land.

Fortunately for the Army of the Potomac, however, I entertained serious doubts of the aid promised by the land route, so that, on the 18th, I ordered a number of transports, with supplies of all kinds, to be sent up the James, under convoy of the gun-boats, so that I might be free to cut loose from the Pamunkey and move over to the James, should circumstances enable me or render it desirable to do so.

The battle of Fair Oaks was followed by storms of great severity, continuing until the 20th of June, and adding vastly to the difficulties of our position, greatly retarding the construction of the bridges and of the defensive works regarded as necessary to cover us in the event of a repulse, and making the ground too difficult for the free movements of troops.

WHITE HOUSE, THE HOME OF GENERAL W. H.
F. LEE, McCLELLAN'S BASE OF SUPPLIES
ON THE PAMUNKEY.
FROM SKETCHES MADE AT THE TIME.

RUINS OF THE WHITE HOUSE, WHICH WAS BURNED JUNE
28, DURING THE "CHANGE OF BASE."

On the 19th Franklin's corps was transferred to the south side of the Chickahominy, Porter's corps, reënforced by McCall's division (which, with a few additional regiments, had arrived on the 12th and 13th), being left alone on the north side.

This dangerous distribution was necessary in order to concentrate sufficient force on the south side to attack Richmond with any hope of success; and, as I was still told that McDowell would arrive by the overland route, I could not yet change the base to the James.

It was not until the 25th that the condition of the ground and the completion of the bridges and intrenchments left me free to attack. On that day the first step was taken, in throwing forward the left of our picket-line, in face of a strong opposition, to gain ground enough to enable Sumner and Heintzelman to support the attack to be made next day by Franklin on the rear of Old Tavern. The successful issue of this attack would, it was supposed, drive the enemy from his positions on the heights overlooking Mechanicsville, and probably enable us to force him back into his main line of works. We would then be in position to reconnoiter the lines carefully, determine the points of attack, and take up a new base and line of supply if expedient.

During the night of the 24th information arrived confirming the anticipation that Jackson was moving to attack our right and rear, but I persisted in the operation intended for the 25th, partly to develop the strength of the enemy opposite our left and center, and with the design of attacking Old Tavern on the 26th, if Jackson's advance was so much delayed that Porter's corps would not be endangered.

Late in the afternoon of the 25th, Jackson's advance was confirmed, and it was rendered probable that he would attack next day. All hope of the advance of McDowell's corps in season to be of any service had disappeared; the dangerous position of the army had been faithfully held to the last moment. After deducting the garrisons in rear, the railroad guards, non-combatants, and extra-duty men, there were not more than 75,000 men for battle. The enemy, with a force larger than this, the strong defenses of Richmond close at hand in his rear, was free to strike on either flank. I decided then to carry into effect the long-considered plan of abandoning the Pamunkey and taking up the line of the James.

The necessary orders were given for the defense of the depots at the White House to the last moment and its final destruction and abandonment; it was also ordered that all possible stores should be pushed to the front while communications were open.

The ground to the James had already been reconnoitered with reference to this movement.

During the night of the 26th Porter's siege-guns and wagon-trains were brought over to the south side of the Chickahominy. During the afternoon of that day his corps had been attacked in its position on Beaver Dam Creek, near Mechanicsville, and the enemy repulsed with heavy losses on their part. It was now clear that Jackson's corps had taken little or no part in this attack, and that his blow would fall farther to the rear. I therefore ordered the Fifth Corps to fall back and take position nearer the bridges, where the flanks would be more secure. This was skillfully effected early on the 27th, and it was decided that this corps should hold its position until night. All the corps commanders on the south side were on the 26th directed to be prepared to send as many troops as they could spare in support of Porter on the next day. All of them thought the enemy so strong in their respective fronts as to require all their force to hold their positions. ☆

---

☆ Soon after the appearance of General McClellan's article the following letter was received from the daughter of General Heintzelman:

"In 'The Century' for May, 1885, General McClellan has an article, 'The Peninsular Campaign,' in which there are one or two misstatements in regards to the Third Corps, commanded by General Heintzelman. Fortunately my father's papers, which are in my possession, contain replies to both allegations,— one in the handwriting of General Heintzelman's adjutant-general, and the other the rough draft of a letter addressed to General Lorenzo Thomas, then Adjutant-General of the army. General McClellan says [see above]:

"'All the corps commanders on the south side were on the 26th directed to be prepared to send as many troops as they could spare in support of Porter on the next day. All of them thought the enemy so strong in their respective fronts as to require all their force to hold their positions.'

"Upon the demand for troops General Heintzelman replied as follows:

"'HEADQUARTERS THIRD CORPS, 4 P. M., June 26, 1862. GENERAL MARCY, Chief of Staff: I think I can hold the intrenchments with four brigades for twenty-four hours; that would leave two (2) brigades available for service on the other side of the river, but the men are so tired and worn out that I fear they would not be in a condition to fight after making a march of any distance. . . . S. P. HEINTZELMAN, Brigadier-General.'

"This is far from being a statement that all his forces were required to hold his own lines.

"General McClellan says [see p. 183]:

"'Meanwhile, through a misunderstanding of his orders, and being convinced that the troops of Sumner and Franklin at Savage's Station were ample for the purpose in view, Heintzelman withdrew his troops during the afternoon, crossed the swamp at Brackett's Ford, and reached the Charles City road with the rear of his column at 10 P. M.'

"When the same statement was first made in

Shortly after noon on the 27th the attack commenced upon Porter's corps, in its new position near Gaines's Mill, and the contest continued all day with great vigor.

The movements of the enemy were so threatening at many points on our center and left as to indicate the presence of large numbers of troops, and for a long time created great uncertainty as to the real point of his main attack. General Porter's first call for reënforcement and a supply of axes failed to reach me; but, upon receiving a second call, I ordered Slocum's division to cross to his support. The head of the division reached the field at 3:30 and immediately went into action. At about 5 P. M. General Porter reported his position as critical, and the brigades of French and Meagher — of Richardson's division — were ordered to reënforce him, although the fearless commander of the Second Corps, General Sumner, thought it hazardous to remove them from his own threatened front. I then ordered the reserve of Heintzelman to move in support of Sumner, and a brigade of Keyes's corps to headquarters for such use as might be required. Smith's division, left alone when Slocum crossed to the aid of Porter, was so seriously threatened that I called on Sumner's corps to send a brigade to its support.

French and Meagher reached the field before dusk, just after Porter's corps

---

1863, General Heintzelman wrote the following letter:

"'HEADQUARTERS DEFENSES OF WASHINGTON, April 11th, 1863. GENERAL L. THOMAS, ADJUTANT-GENERAL, U. S. A., WASHINGTON. GENERAL: I find in the "New York Tribune" of the 8th of April a "Preliminary Report of the Operations of the Army of the Potomac, since June 25th, 1862," made by General G. B. McClellan. . . .

"'In a paragraph commencing "On the 28th Porter's corps was also moved across the White Oak Swamp," etc., is the following:

"They were ordered to hold this position until dark, then to fall back across the swamp and rejoin the rest of the army. This order was not fully carried out, nor was the exact position I designated occupied by the different divisions concerned."

"'I was furnished with a map marked in red with the positions we should occupy.

"'As I had the fortified lines thrown up some time before by the troops in my command, I had no difficulty in knowing where to go, and I did occupy these lines. General Sumner's were more indefinite, and he occupied a position in advance of the one designated. This left a space of half a mile unoccupied, between his right and Franklin's left. In the morning I was informed that some rebels were already at or near Dr. Trent's house, where General McClellan's headquarters had been; I sent and found this to be the case. General Franklin had also called at my headquarters and told me that the enemy were repairing the bridges of the Chickahominy, and would soon cross in force. About 1 P. M. I saw some of our troops filing into the fields between Dr. Trent's house and Savage's Station, and a few moments later Generals Franklin and W. F. Smith came to me and reported the enemy approaching, and urged me to ride to General Sumner and get him to fall back and close this gap. I rode briskly to the front, and on the Williamsburg road, where it passed between my two divisions, met General Sumner's troops falling back. He wished me to turn back with him to arrange for ulterior operations, but as my right flank was entirely uncovered by these movements, I declined until after I had seen my division commanders and given them orders how to fall back, On my return there was some difficulty in finding General Sumner, and when found he informed me he had made his arrangements. I returned to my command, and on the way found the ground filled with troops, more than could be used to any advantage, and if the enemy planted a few batteries of artillery on the opposite side of the railroad, they would have been cut in pieces.

"'An aide to General McClellan having reported to me the day before to point out to me a road across the White Oak Swamp, opening from the left flank of my position of the fortified lines, I did not hesitate to retreat by that road, and left at 3 P. M. General Smith, of Franklin's corps, having sent to the rear all his batteries earlier in the day, I, at his request, let him have two of mine (Osborn's and Bramhall's), and they did good service that afternoon in checking and defeating the rebel attack.

"'My remaining would have been no aid to General Sumner, as he already had more troops than he could defile through the narrow road in his rear, and the road I took covered his left flank.

"'Before dark the advance of my corps was across the swamp, and by 10 P. M. the rear was over, with but little molestation from the enemy. I immediately sought General McClellan, and reported to him what I had done, and this is the first intimation I have had that my conduct was not entirely satisfactory.

"'To hold my position till dark, by which time I was to receive orders, would have been impossible. After Generals Franklin and Sumner had fallen back, my right flank and rear were uncovered, and by a road which passed entirely in my rear; and beyond my right flank my only line of retreat would have been cut off, and I would have lost my entire corps. I did not know where General McClellan was, and it was, therefore, impossible to report to him for orders.

"'When General Birney reached Fisher's Ford, the enemy were there, but not in force; they soon arrived in force, and he had to take another road more to our left. Had we been a little later they would have been in possession, and our retreat by this road cut off.

S. P. HEINTZELMAN.'

"I trust that you will be able to find space for these letters.— MARY L. HEINTZELMAN."

EDITORS.

had been forced by superior numbers to fall back to an interior position nearer the bridges, and, by their steady attitude, checked all further progress of the enemy and completed the attainment of the purpose in view, which was to hold the left bank of the river until dark, so that the movement to the James might be safely commenced. The siege-guns, material, and trains on the left bank were all safe, and the right wing was in close connection with the rest of the army. The losses were heavy, but the object justified them, or rather made them necessary. At about 6 o'clock next morning the rear-guard of regulars crossed to the south side and the bridges were destroyed.

I now bent all my energies to the transfer of the army to the James, fully realizing the very delicate nature of a flank march, with heavy trains, by a single road, in face of an active enemy, but confident that I had the army well in hand and that it would not fail me in the emergency. I thought that the enemy would not anticipate that movement, but would assume that all my efforts would be directed to cover and regain the old depots; and the event proved the correctness of this supposition. It seemed certain that I could gain one or two days for the movement of the trains, while he remained uncertain as to my intentions; and that was all I required with such troops as those of the Army of the Potomac.

During the night of the 27th I assembled the corps commanders at headquarters, informed them of my intentions, and gave them their orders. Keyes's corps was ordered to move at once, with its trains, across White Oak Swamp, and occupy positions on the farther side, to cover the passage of the remainder of the army. By noon of the 28th this first step was accomplished. During the 28th Sumner, Heintzelman, and Franklin held essentially their old positions; the trains converged steadily to the White Oak Swamp and crossed as rapidly as possible, and during this day and the succeeding night Porter followed the movement of Keyes's corps and took position to support it.

Early on the 28th, when Franklin's corps was drawing in its right to take a more concentrated position, the enemy opened a sharp artillery fire and made at one point a spirited attack with two Georgia regiments, which were repulsed by the two regiments on picket.

Sumner's and Heintzelman's corps and Smith's division of Franklin's were now ordered to abandon their intrenchments, so as to occupy, on the morning of the 29th, a new position in rear, shorter than the old and covering the crossing of the swamp. This new line could easily be held during the day, and these troops were ordered to remain there until dark, to cover the withdrawal of the rest of the trains, and then cross the swamp and occupy the positions about to be abandoned by Keyes's and Porter's corps. Meanwhile Slocum's division had been ordered to Savage's Station in reserve, and, during the morning, was ordered across the swamp to relieve Keyes's corps. This was a critical day; for the crossing of the swamp by the trains must be accomplished before its close, and their protection against attack from Richmond must be assured, as well as communication with the gun-boats.

A sharp cavalry skirmish on the Quaker road indicated that the enemy was alive to our movement, and might at any moment strike in force to intercept the march to the James. The difficulty was not at all with the movement of the troops, but with the immense trains that were to be moved virtually by a single road, and required the whole army for their protection. With the exception of the cavalry affair on the Quaker road, we were not troubled during this day south of the swamp, but there was severe fighting north of it. Sumner's corps evacuated their works at daylight and fell back to Allen's farm, nearly two miles west of Savage's Station, Heintzelman being on their left. Here Sumner was furiously attacked three times, but each time drove the enemy back with much loss.

Soon afterward Franklin, having only one division with him, ascertained that the enemy had repaired some of the Chickahominy bridges and was advancing on Savage's Station, whereupon he posted his division at that point and informed Sumner, who moved his corps to the same place, arriving a little after noon. About 4 P. M. Sumner and Franklin — three divisions in all — were sharply attacked, mainly by the Williamsburg road; the fighting continued until between 8 and 9 P. M., the enemy being at all times thoroughly repulsed, and finally driven from the field.

Meanwhile, through a misunderstanding of his orders, and being convinced that the troops of Sumner and Franklin at Savage's Station were ample for the purpose in view, Heintzelman withdrew his troops during the afternoon, crossed the swamp at Brackett's Ford, and reached the Charles City road with the rear of his column at 10 P. M.

Slocum reached the position of Keyes's corps early in the afternoon, and, as soon as the latter was thus relieved, it was ordered forward to the James, near Malvern Hill, which it reached, with all its artillery and trains, early on the 30th. Porter was ordered to follow this movement and prolong the line of Keyes's corps to our right. The trains were pushed on in rear of these corps and massed under cover of the gun-boats as fast as they reached the James, at Haxall's plantation. As soon as the fighting ceased with the final repulse of the enemy, Sumner and Franklin were ordered to cross the swamp; this was effected during the night, the rear-guard crossing and destroying the bridge at 5 A. M. on the 30th. All the troops and trains were now between the swamp and the James, and the first critical episode of the movement was successfully accomplished.

The various corps were next pushed forward to establish connection with Keyes and Porter, and hold the different roads by which the enemy could advance from Richmond and strike our line of march. I determined to hold the positions now taken until the trains had all reached a place of safety, and then concentrate the army near the James, where it could enjoy a brief rest after the fatiguing battles and marches through which it was passing, and then renew the advance on Richmond.

General Franklin, with Smith's division of his own corps, Richardson's of the Second, and Naglee's brigade were charged with the defense of the White Oak Swamp crossing. Slocum held the ground thence to the Charles City road; Kearny from that road to the Long Bridge road; McCall on his left; Hooker thence to the Quaker road; Sedgwick at Nelson's farm, in rear

CAPTAIN LE CLERC.   DUC DE CHARTRES.   COMTE DE PARIS.   PRINCE DE JOINVILLE.   CAPTAIN MOHAIN.

THE ORLÉANS PRINCES AND SUITE AT DINNER. FROM A PHOTOGRAPH.

of McCall and Kearny. The Fifth Corps was at Malvern Hill, the Fourth at Turkey Bridge. The trains moved on during this day, and at 4 P. M. the last reached Malvern Hill and kept on to Haxall's, so that the most difficult part

General McClellan contributed an article to "The Century" magazine for February, 1884, on "The Princes of the House of Orléans," in which he spoke as follows of the services of the Comte de Paris and his brother, the Duc de Chartres:

"In August, 1861, the two brothers, accompanied by the Prince de Joinville, sailed for New York. Toward the close of September they arrived in Washington, and the young Princes at once received authority from the President to enter the army as aides-de-camp, being permitted to serve without taking the oath of allegiance, and without pay; it was also understood that they should be permitted to leave the service should family or political exigencies require it. They were borne on the army register as Louis Philippe d'Orléans and Robert d'Orléans, additional aides-de-camp in the regular army, with the rank of captain, and were assigned to the staff of the major-general commanding the Army of the Potomac. The Prince de Joinville accepted no rank, and simply accompanied headquarters, on the invitation of the general commanding, as an amateur and friend. The position held by these "young gentlemen"— as the Prince de Joinville always designated them— was not free from difficulties. Princes who might at any time be called upon to assume their places in the government of a great nation, yet serving in the army of a republic whose cause was not regarded with very friendly eyes by the existing government of their own country, they had many contradictions to reconcile, many embarrassments to overcome. Connected by family ties with so of the task was accomplished, and it only remained for the troops to hold their ground until nightfall, and then continue the march to the positions selected near Malvern Hill.

The fighting on this day (June 30th) was very severe, and extended along the whole line. It first broke out between 12 and 1, on General Franklin's command, in the shape of a fierce artillery fire, which was kept up through the day and inflicted serious losses. The enemy's infantry made several attempts to cross near the old bridge and below, but was in every case thrown back. Franklin held his position until after dark, and during the night fell back to Malvern. At half-past 2 Slocum's left was attacked in vain on the Charles City road. At about 3 McCall was attacked, and, after 5 o'clock, under the pressure of heavy masses, he was forced back; but Hooker came up from the left, and Sedgwick from the rear, and the two together not only stopped the enemy, but drove him off the field.

At about 4 P. M. heavy attacks commenced on Kearny's left, and three ineffectual assaults were made. The firing continued until after dark. About midnight Sumner's and Heintzelman's corps and McCall's division withdrew from the positions they had so gallantly held, and commenced their march to Malvern, which they reached unmolested soon after daybreak. Just after the rear of the trains reached Malvern, about 4 P. M., the enemy attacked Porter's corps, but were promptly shaken off.

Thus, on the morning of July 1st, the army was concentrated at Malvern, with the trains at Haxall's, in rear. The supplies which had been sent from White House on the 18th were at hand in the James.

After consultation with Commodore Rodgers, I decided that Harrison's Landing was a better position for the resting-place of the army, because the channel passed so close to City Point as to enable the enemy to prevent the passage of transports if we remained at Malvern. It was, however, necessary to accept battle where we were, in order to give ample time for the trains to reach Harrison's, as well as to give the enemy a blow that would check his farther pursuit.

---

many of the royal families of Europe, always received by them as of royal rank, the elder regarded by so many in France as the rightful heir to the throne, they could never lose sight of the dignity of their position, while it was at the same time necessary for them to perform their duties in a subordinate grade, and to win the confidence and friendship of their new comrades, who were sure to weigh men by their personal qualities and abilities, not by their social position across the Atlantic. Their task was accomplished with complete success, for they gained the full confidence, respect, and regard of their commander and their comrades. From the moment they entered the service, they were called upon to perform precisely the same duties and in precisely the same manner as their companions on the personal staff of their commander. . . .

"Their conduct was characterized by an innate love for a soldier's life, by an intense desire to perfect themselves in the profession of arms by actual experience of war on a large scale, and by unswerving devotion to duty. Not only this, their heads and hearts were with us in our hour of trial, and I believe that, next to their own France, they most loved this country, for which they so freely and so often exposed their lives on the field of battle.

"Soon after the beginning of the peninsular campaign, the Princes were strongly urged by their friends at home to return at once to England, partly to receive the large numbers of their adherents expected to attend the Exhibition of 1862, and partly because the French expedition to Mexico had greatly strained the relations between this country and France. They persisted in remaining with the army until the close of the Seven Days, and left only when assured that the immediate resumption of the attack on Richmond was improbable. Had the prompt receipt of reinforcements rendered a new advance practicable, it is certain that no considerations would have withdrawn them from the field until the completion of the operations against Richmond. Although warmly attached to them and very unwilling to lose their services, their commander fully recognized the imperative nature of the reasons for their departure, and entirely acquiesced in the propriety of their prompt return to Europe."

Soon after the termination of the war, the Comte de Paris began his extensive "History of the Civil War in America," the first volume of the American edition being issued in 1875.— EDITORS.

Accordingly, the army was carefully posted on the admirable position of Malvern Hill, with the right thrown back below Haxall's. The left was the natural point of attack, and there the troops were massed and the reserve artillery placed, while full preparations were made to frustrate any attempt to turn our right. Early in the forenoon the army was concentrated and ready for battle, in a position of unusual strength — one which, with such troops as held it, could justly be regarded as impregnable. It was, then, with perfect confidence that I awaited the impending battle.

The enemy began feeling the position between 9 and 10 A. M., and at 3 P. M. made a sharp attack upon Couch's division, which remained lying on the ground until the enemy were within close range, when they rose and delivered a volley which shattered and drove back their assailants in disorder. At 4 P. M. the firing ceased for a while, and the lull was availed of to rectify the position and make every preparation for the approaching renewal of the attack. It came at 6 P. M., opened by the fire of all their artillery and followed by desperate charges of infantry advancing at a run. They were always repulsed with the infliction of fearful loss, and in several instances our infantry awaited their approach within a few yards, poured in a single volley, and then dashed forward with the bayonet. At 7 P. M. the enemy was accumulating fresh troops, and the brigades of Meagher and Sickles were sent from Sumner's and Heintzelman's corps to reënforce Porter and Couch; fresh batteries were moved forward from the reserve artillery and the ammunition was replenished.

The enemy then repeated his attacks in the most desperate style until dark, but the battle ended with his complete repulse, with very heavy losses, and without his even for one moment gaining a foothold in our position. His frightful losses were in vain. I doubt whether, in the annals of war, there was ever a more persistent and gallant attack, or a more cool and effective resistance.

Although the result of this bloody battle was a complete victory on our part, it was necessary, for the reasons already given, to continue the movement to Harrison's, whither the trains had been pushed during the night of the 30th of June and the day of the 1st of July. Immediately after the final repulse the orders were given for the withdrawal of the army. The movement was covered by Keyes's corps. So complete was the enemy's discomfiture, and so excellent the conduct of the rear-guard, that the last of the trains reached Harrison's after dark on the 3d, without loss and unmolested by the enemy.

This movement was now successfully accomplished, and the Army of the Potomac was at last in a position on its true line of operations, with its trains intact, no guns lost save those taken in battle, when the artillerists had proved their heroism and devotion by standing to their guns until the enemy's infantry were in the midst of them.

During the "Seven Days" the Army of the Potomac consisted of 143 regiments of infantry, 55 batteries, and less than 8 regiments of cavalry, all told. The opposing Confederate army consisted of 187 regiments of infantry, 79 batteries, and 14 regiments of cavalry. The losses of the two armies from June 25th to July 2d were: ☆

|  | Killed. | Wounded. | Missing. | Total. |
|---|---|---|---|---|
| Confederate Army | 2,823 | 13,703 | 3,223 | 19,749 |
| Army of the Potomac | 1,734 | 8,062 | 6,053 | 15,849 |

The Confederate losses in killed and wounded alone were greater than the total losses of the Army of the Potomac in killed, wounded, and missing.

No praise can be too great for the officers and men who passed through these seven days of battle, enduring fatigue without a murmur, successfully meeting and repelling every attack made upon them, always in the right place at the right time, and emerging from the fiery ordeal a compact army of veterans, equal to any task that brave and disciplined men can be called upon to undertake. They needed now only a few days of well-earned repose, a renewal of ammunition and supplies, and reënforcements to fill the gaps made in their ranks by so many desperate encounters, to be prepared to advance again, with entire confidence, to meet their worthy antagonists in other battles. It was, however, decided by the authorities at Washington, against my earnest remonstrances, to abandon the position on the James, and the campaign. The Army of the Potomac was accordingly withdrawn, and it was not until two years later that it again found itself under its last commander at substantially the same point on the bank of the James. It was as evident in 1862 as in 1865 that there was the true defense of Washington, and that it was on the banks of the James that the fate of the Union was to be decided.

☆ Tables (to follow) of the "Opposing Forces" of the "Seven Days," made from the fullest revised data of the War Records office, will show that the Army of the Potomac consisted of 150 regiments of infantry; 2 regiments and 1 battalion of engineers; 1 regiment of heavy or siege artillery; 58 batteries; and 10 regiments of cavalry. The Confederate forces consisted of 173 regiments and 12 battalions of infantry; 71 batteries; and 12 regiments of cavalry. General McClellan correctly estimates the Union loss, but the Confederate loss, according to the revised returns, was: killed, 3286; wounded, 15,909; missing, 940. Total, 20,135.—EDITORS.

CONFEDERATE BATTERY AT MATHIAS POINT, OR BUDD'S FERRY, ON THE POTOMAC [SEE ARTICLE, P. 143, AND MAP, P. 164]. FROM A SKETCH MADE IN FEBRUARY, 1862.

188

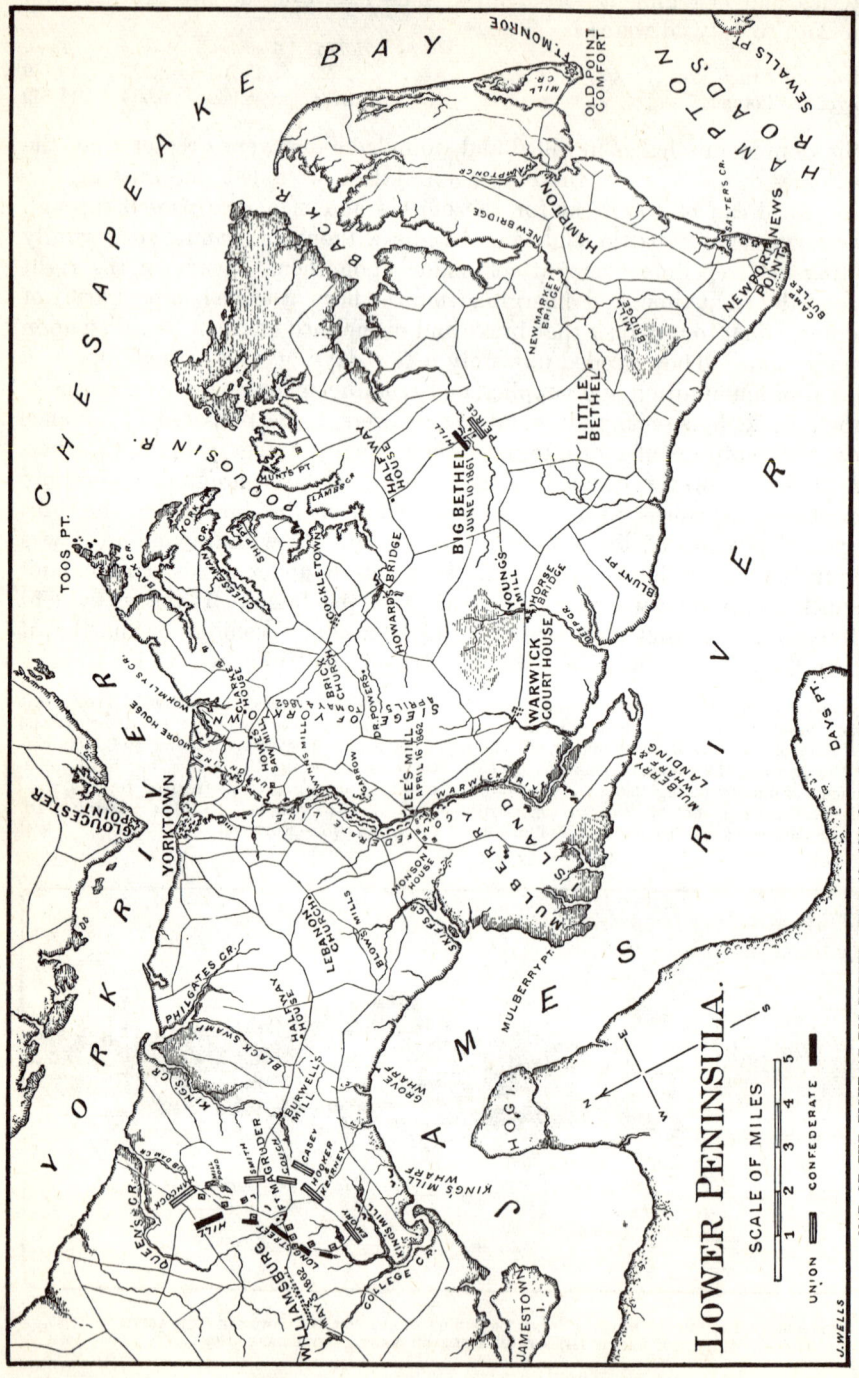

# YORKTOWN AND WILLIAMSBURG.

RECOLLECTIONS OF A PRIVATE.—III. BY WARREN LEE GOSS.

IT was with open-eyed wonder that, as part of McClellan's army, we arrived at Old Point Comfort and gazed upon Fort Monroe, huge and frowning. Negroes were everywhere, and went about their work with an air of importance born of their new-found freedom. These were the "contrabands" for whom General Butler had recently invented that sobriquet. We pitched our tents amid the charred and blackened ruins of what had been the beautiful and aristocratic village of Hampton. The first thing I noticed about the ruins, unaccustomed as I was to Southern architecture, was the absence of cellars. The only building left standing of all the village was the massive old Episcopal church. Here Washington had worshiped, and its broad aisles had echoed to the footsteps of armed men during the Revolution. In the church-yard the tombs had been broken open. Many tombstones were broken and overthrown, and at the corner of the church a big hole showed that some one with a greater desire for possessing curiosities than reverence for ancient landmarks had been digging for the corner-stone and its buried mementos.

Along the shore which looks toward Fort Monroe were landed artillery, baggage-wagons, pontoon trains and boats, and the level land back of this was crowded with the tents of the soldiers. Here and there were groups frying hard-tack and bacon. Near at hand was the irrepressible army mule, hitched to and eating out of pontoon boats; those who had eaten their ration of grain and hay were trying their teeth, with promise of success, in eating the boats. An army mule was hungrier than a soldier, and would eat anything, especially a pontoon boat or rubber blanket. The scene was a busy one. The red cap, white leggins, and baggy trousers of the Zouaves mingled with the blue uniforms and dark trimmings of the regular infantry-men, the short jackets and yellow trimmings of the cavalry, the red stripes of the artillery, and the dark blue with orange trimmings of the engineers; together with the ragged, many-colored costumes of the black laborers and teamsters, all busy at something.

One morning we broke camp and went marching up the Peninsula. The roads were very poor and muddy with recent rains, and were crowded with the indescribable material of the vast army which was slowly creeping through the mud over the flat, wooded country. It was a bright day in April — a perfect Virginia day; the grass was green beneath our feet, the buds of the trees were just unrolling into leaves under the warming sun of spring, and in the woods the birds were singing. The march was at first orderly, but

MRS. T——'S EXODUS.

under the unaccustomed burden of heavy equipments and knapsacks, and the warmth of the weather, the men straggled along the roads, mingling with the baggage-wagons, ambulances, and pontoon trains, in seeming confusion.

During our second day's march it rained, and the muddy roads, cut up and kneaded, as it were, by the teams preceding us, left them in a state of semi-liquid filth hardly possible to describe or imagine. When we arrived at Big Bethel the rain was coming down in sheets. A dozen houses of very ordinary character, scattered over an area of a third of a mile, constituted what was called the village. Just outside and west of the town was an insignificant building from which the place takes its name. It did not seem large enough or of sufficient consequence to give name to a hamlet as small as Big Bethel. Before our arrival it had evidently been occupied as officers' barracks for the enemy, and looked very little like a church.

I visited one of the dwelling-houses just outside the fortifications (if the insignificant rifle-pits could be called such) for the purpose of obtaining something more palatable than hard-tack, salt beef, or pork, which, with coffee, comprised the marching rations. The woman of the house was communicative, and expressed her surprise at the great number of Yanks who had "come down to invade our soil." She said she had a son in the Confederate army, or, as she expressed it, "in our army," and then tearfully said she should tremble for her boy every time she heard of a battle. I expressed the opinion that we should go into Richmond without much fighting. "No!" said she, with the emphasis of conviction, "you all will drink hot blood before you all get thar!"

While wandering about, I came to the house of a Mrs. T——, whose husband was said to be a captain in the Confederate service and a "fire-eating" secessionist. Here some of our men were put on guard for a short time, until relieved by guards from other parts of the army as they came up, whereupon we went on. A large, good-looking woman, about forty years old, who, I learned, was Mrs. T——, was crying profusely, and I could not induce her to tell me why. One of the soldiers said her grief was caused by the fact that some of our men had helped themselves to the contents of cupboard and cellar. She was superintending the loading of an old farm-wagon, into which she was putting a large family of colored people, with numerous bundles. The only white person on the load as it started away was the mistress, who sat amid her dark chattels in desolation and tears. Returning to the house, after this exodus, I found letters, papers, and odds and ends of various kinds littering the floor; whether overturned in the haste of the mistress or by the visiting soldiers, I could only guess. No other building at Big Bethel was so devastated, and I did not see another building so treated on our whole route. The men detailed to guard it declined to protect the property of one who was in arms fighting against us.

After leaving Big Bethel we began to feel the weight of our knapsacks. Castaway overcoats, blankets, parade-coats, and shoes were scattered along the route in reckless profusion, being dropped by the overloaded soldiers, as if after plowing the roads with heavy teams they were sowing them for a harvest. I lightened my knapsack without much regret, for I could not see the wisdom of carrying a blanket or overcoat when I could pick one up almost anywhere along the march. Very likely the same philosophy actuated those who preceded me or came after. The colored people along our route occupied themselves in picking up this scattered property. They had on their faces a distrustful look, as if uncertain of the tenure of their harvest. The march up the peninsula seemed very slow, yet it was impossible to increase our speed, owing to the bad condition of the roads. I learned in time that marching on paper and the actual march made two very different impressions. I can easily understand and excuse our fireside heroes, who fought their or our battles at home over comfortable breakfast-tables, without impediments of any kind to circumscribe their fancied operations; it is so much easier to manœuvre and fight large armies around the corner grocery, than to fight, march, and manœuvre in mud and rain, in the face of a brave and vigilant enemy.

CONFEDERATE BATTERY ON THE TERRACED MAGAZINE COMMANDING THE LAND APPROACH TO THE GOSPORT NAVY-YARD. [SEE PAGE 152.] FROM A WAR-TIME SKETCH.

The baggage-trains were a notable spectacle. To each baggage-wagon were attached four or six mules, driven usually by a colored man, with only one rein, or line, and that line attached to the bit of the near leading mule, while the driver rode in a saddle upon the near wheel mule. Each train was accompanied by a guard, and while the guard urged the drivers the drivers urged the mules. The drivers were usually expert, and understood well the wayward, sportive natures of the creatures over whose destinies they presided. On our way to Yorktown our pontoon and baggage trains were sometimes blocked for miles, and the heaviest trains were often unloaded by the guard to facilitate their removal from the mud. It did seem at times as if there were needless delays with the trains, partly due, no doubt, to fear of danger ahead. While I was guarding our pontoon train, after leaving Big Bethel, the teams stopped all along the line. Hurrying to the front, I found one of the leading teams badly mired, but not enough to justify the stopping of the whole train. The lazy colored driver was comfortably asleep in the saddle. "Get that team out of the mud!" I yelled, bringing him to his senses. He flourished his long whip, shouted his mule lingo at the team, and the mules pulled frantically, but not together. "Can't you make your mules pull together?" I inquired. "Dem mules pull right smart!" said the driver. Cocking and capping my unloaded musket, I brought it to the shoulder and again commanded the driver, "Get that team out of the mud!" The negro rolled his eyes wildly and woke up all over. He first patted his saddle mule, spoke to each one, and then, flourishing his long whip with a crack like a pistol, shouted, "Go 'long dar! what I feed yo' fo'!" and the mule team left the slough in a very expeditious manner.

When procuring luxuries of eggs or milk, we paid the people at first in silver, and they gave us local scrip in change; but we found on attempting to pay it out again that they were rather reluctant to receive it, even at that early stage in Confederate finance, and much preferred Yankee silver or notes.

On the afternoon of April 5th, 1862, the advance of our column was brought

"GET THAT TEAM OUT OF THE MUD!"

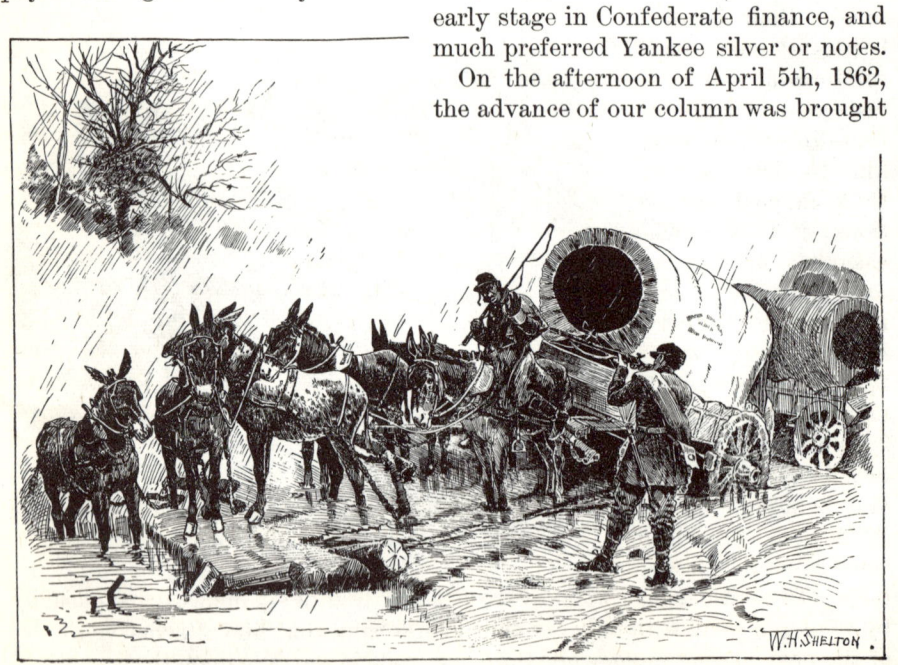

## YORKTOWN AND WILLIAMSBURG.

SKIRMISH AT LEE'S MILLS BEFORE YORKTOWN, APRIL 16, 1862. [SEE MAP, P. 188.] FROM A SKETCH MADE AT THE TIME.

to a standstill, with the right in front of Yorktown, and the left by the enemy's works at Lee's mills [see p. 188]. We pitched our camp on Wormley Creek, near the Moore house, on the York River, in sight of the enemy's water-battery and their defensive works at Gloucester Point. One of the impediments to an immediate attack on Yorktown was the difficulty of using light artillery in the muddy fields in our front, and at that time the topography of the country ahead was but little understood, and had to be learned by reconnoissance in force. We had settled down to the siege of Yorktown; began bridging the streams between us and the enemy, constructing and improving the roads for the rapid transit of supplies, and for the advance. The first parallel was opened about a mile from the enemy's fortifications, extending along the entire front of their works, which reached from the York River on the left to Warwick Creek on the right, along a line about four miles in length. Fourteen batteries and three redoubts were planted, heavily armed with ordnance.

We were near Battery No. 1, not far from the York River. On it were mounted several 200-pounder guns, which commanded the enemy's water-batteries. One day I was in a redoubt on the left, and saw General McClellan with the Prince de Joinville, examining the enemy's works through their field-glasses. They very soon drew the fire of the observant enemy, who opened with one of their heavy guns on the group, sending the first shot howling and hissing over and very close to their heads; another, quickly following it, struck in the parapet of the redoubt. The French prince, seemingly quite startled, jumped and glanced nervously around, while McClellan quietly knocked the ashes from his cigar.

Several of our war-vessels made their appearance in the York River, and occasionally threw a shot at the enemy's works; but most of them were kept busy at Hampton Roads, watching for the iron-clad *Merrimac*, which was still afloat. The firing from the enemy's lines was of little consequence, not amounting to over ten or twelve shots each day, a number of these being directed at the huge balloon which went up daily on a tour of inspection, from near General Fitz John Porter's headquarters. One day the balloon broke from its mooring of ropes and sailed majestically over the enemy's works; but fortunately for its occupants it soon met a counter-current of air which returned it safe to our lines. The month of April was a dreary one, much of the time rainy and uncomfortable. It was a common expectation among us that we were about to end the rebellion. One of my comrades wrote home to his father that we should probably finish up the war in season for him to be at home to teach the village school the following winter; in fact, I believe he partly engaged to teach it. Another wrote to his mother: "We have got them hemmed in on every side, and the only reason they don't run is because they can't." We had at last corduroyed every road and bridged every creek; our guns and mortars were in position; Battery No. 1 had actually opened on the enemy's works, Saturday, May 3d, 1862, and it was expected that our whole line would open on them in the morning. About 2 o'clock of Saturday night, or rather of Sunday morning, while on guard duty, I observed a bright illumination, as if a fire had broken out within the enemy's lines. Several guns were fired from their works during the early morning hours, but soon after daylight of May 4th it was reported that they had abandoned their works in our front, and we very quickly found the report to be true. As soon as I was relieved from guard duty, I went over on "French leave" to view our enemy's fortifications. They were prodigiously strong. A few tumble-down tents and houses and seventy pieces of heavy ordnance had been abandoned as the price of the enemy's safe retreat.

UNION MORTAR-BATTERY BEFORE YORKTOWN. FROM A PHOTOGRAPH.

As soon as it was known that the Confederates had abandoned the works at Yorktown, the commanding general sent the cavalry and horse artillery under Stoneman in pursuit to harass the retreating column. The infantry divisions of Smith (Fourth Corps) and Hooker (Third Corps) were sent forward by two roads to support the light column. General Sumner (the officer second in rank in the Army of the Potomac) was directed to proceed to the front and assume command until McClellan's arrival. Stoneman overtook Johnston's rear-guard about noon, six miles from Williamsburg, and skirmished with the cavalry of Stuart, following sharply until 4 o'clock, when he was confronted by a line of redoubts before Williamsburg. The works consisted of a large fort (Magruder) at the junction of two roads running from Yorktown to Williamsburg, and small redoubts on each side of this, making an irregular chain of fortifications extending, with the creeks upon which they rested on either flank, across the peninsula. The Confederate brigades of

THE 61ST NEW YORK REGIMENT IN CAMP AT SHIP POINT, BELOW YORKTOWN.
[SEE MAP, P. 188.] FROM A WAR-TIME SKETCH.

Kershaw and Semmes, of Magruder's command, occupied the works when Stoneman came in front of them, and, on finding his advance stubbornly opposed, Stoneman sent his cavalry upon reconnoissances over the field, and waited for the infantry under Hooker and Smith to come to his support. These divisions marched from Yorktown on parallel roads until Smith's column was halted by a burning bridge, and compelled to turn into the road by which Hooker was advancing. Sumner accompanied Smith's column, and, immediately on the arrival before Williamsburg, formed the brigades of Hancock and Brooks for an advance through a piece of woods which screened the Confederate rifle-pits. The result is given in Sumner's official report as follows:

"After entering the woods I found the underbrush much thicker than I expected, and the lines became entangled, and shortly afterward it became so dark it was impossible to advance, and I ordered the troops to halt and lie on their arms."

General Hooker was delayed on the road so long that he did not reach the field until early on the morning of May 5th, when he found himself on the left of Smith's division, and in front of Fort Magruder. The position of the Union troops then was: Smith on the right, and Hooker on the left, confronting the enemy's works, the latter having the heaviest obstacle before him, and the divisions of Kearny, Casey, and Couch struggling on toward the front, over crowded, muddy roads. General Sumner says in his report:

"I had a careful reconnoissance made on the left of the enemy's works, on the morning of the 5th, and found two of their forts unoccupied. I immediately ordered General Hancock to advance with a brigade and ten pieces of artillery, and hold those works, it being my intention to force their left."

This was about 11 A. M. Meantime, at 7:30 A. M., General Hooker, on his own responsibility, had advanced his lines. In his official report he says:

"Being in pursuit of a retreating army, I deemed it my duty to lose no time in making the disposition to attack, regardless of their number and position, except to accomplish the result with the least possible sacrifice of life."

Hooker sent forward Grover's brigade, and Bramhall's and Webber's batteries, and very soon all opposition on his front was silenced for a time.

Longstreet, however, ordered up reënforcements, and soon had a section of Pelham's battery, and the three fresh brigades of Wilcox, Pickett, and A. P. Hill on the ground, driving Hooker back, with the loss of all his cannon, and heavy casualties. During his desperate engagement, Hooker reported his situation to Sumner, and Kearny was promptly ordered up with his division, while Heintzelman, the proper commander of the Third Corps, was sent to the spot to take charge. [See "Opposing Forces," p. 200.]

A comrade in Hooker's division gave me an account of his experiences about as follows: "Marching over the muddy road late in the afternoon, we found our farther advance prevented by a force which had preceded us, and we halted in the mud by the roadside just as it began to rain. About 5 o'clock we resumed our march by crossing over to the Hampton road, and did not halt till 11 in the evening, when we lay down in our blankets, bedraggled, wet, and tired, chewing hard-tack and the cud of reflection, the tenor of which was, 'Why did we come for a soldier?' Before daylight we were on the march, plodding in the rain through the mire. By daybreak we came out on the edge of the dense woods in front of Fort Magruder. The main fort was a strong earth-work with a bastioned front and a wide ditch. In front of this muddy-looking heap of dirt was a level plain, sprinkled plentifully with smaller earth-works; while between us and the level plain the dense forest, for a distance of a quarter of a mile, had been felled, thus forming a labyrinth of tangled abatis difficult to penetrate. A mile away lay the village of Williamsburg.

A TEMPTING BREASTWORK.

"We were soon sent out as skirmishers, with orders to advance as near the enemy's rifle-pits as possible. They immediately opened fire upon us with heavy guns from the fort, while from their rifle-pits came a hum of bullets and crackle of musketry. Their heavy shot came crashing among the tangled abatis of fallen timber, and plowed up the dirt in our front, rebounding and tearing through the branches of the woods in our rear. The constant hissing of the bullets, with their sharp *ping* or *bizz* whispering around and sometimes into us, gave me a sickening feeling and a cold perspiration. I felt weak around my knees — a sort of faintness and lack of strength in the joints of my legs, as if they would sink from under me. These symptoms did not decrease when several of my comrades were hit. The little rifle-pits in our front fairly blazed with musketry, and the continuous *snap, snap, crack, crack* was murderous. Seeing I was not killed at once, in spite of all the noise, my knees recovered from their unpleasant limpness, and my mind gradually regained its balance and composure. I never afterward felt these disturbing influences to the same degree.

"We slowly retired from stump to stump and from log to log, finally regaining the edge of the wood, and took our position near Webber's and Bramhall's batteries, which had just got into position on the right of the road, not over seven hundred yards from the hostile fort. While getting into position several of the battery men were killed, as they immediately drew the artillery fire of the enemy, which opened with a noise and violence that astonished me. Our two batteries were admirably handled, throwing a number of shot and shell into the enemy's works, speedily silencing them, and by 9 o'clock the field in our front, including the rifle-pits, was completely 'cleaned out' of artillery and infantry. Shortly afterward we advanced along the edge of the wood to the left of Fort Magruder, and about 11 o'clock we saw emerging from the little ravine to the left of the fort a swarm of Confederates, who opened on us with a terrible and deadly fire. Then they charged upon us with their peculiar yell. We took all the advantage possible of the stumps and trees as we were pushed back, until we reached the edge of the wood again, where we halted and fired upon the enemy from behind all the cover the situation afforded. We were none of us too proud, not even those who had the dignity of shoulder-straps to support, to dodge behind a tree or stump. I called out to a comrade, 'Why don't you get behind a tree?' 'Confound it,' said he, 'there ain't enough for the officers.' I don't mean to accuse officers of cowardice, but we had suddenly found out that they showed the same general inclination not to get shot as privates did, and were anxious to avail themselves of the privilege of their rank by getting in our rear. I have always thought that pride was a good substitute for courage, if well backed by a conscientious sense of duty; and most of our men, officers as well as privates, were too proud to show the fear which I have no doubt they felt in common with myself. Occasionally a soldier would show symptoms which pride could not overcome. One of our men, Spinney, ran into the woods and was not seen until after the engagement. Some time afterward, when he had proved a good soldier, I asked him why he ran, and he replied that every bullet which went by his head said 'Spinney,' and he thought they were calling for him. In all the pictures of battles I had seen before I ever saw a battle, the officers were at the front on prancing steeds, or with uplifted swords were leading their followers to the charge. Of course, I was surprised to find that in a real battle the officer gets in the rear of his men, as is his right and duty,—that is, if his ideas of duty do not carry him so far to the rear as to make his sword useless.

"The 'rebs' forced us back by their charge, and our central lines were almost broken. The forces withdrawn from our right had taken the infantry support from our batteries, one of which, consisting of four guns, was captured. We were tired, wet, and exhausted when supports came up, and we were allowed to fall back from under the enemy's fire, but still in easy reach of the battle. I asked one of my comrades how he felt, and his reply was characteristic of the prevailing sentiment: 'I should feel like a hero if I wasn't so blank wet.' The bullets had cut queer antics among our men. A private, who had a canteen of whisky when he went into the engagement, on endeavoring to take a drink found the canteen quite empty, a bullet having tapped it for him. Another had a part of his thumb-nail taken off. Another had a bullet pass into the toe of his boot, down between two toes, and out along the sole of his foot, without much injury. Another had a scalp-wound from a bullet, which took off a strip of hair about three inches in length from the top of his head. Two of my regiment were killed outright and fourteen badly wounded, besides quite a number slightly injured. Thus I have chronicled my first day's fight, and I don't believe any of my regiment were ambitious to 'chase the enemy' any farther just at present. Refreshed with hot coffee and hardtack, we rested from the fight, well satisfied that we had done our duty."

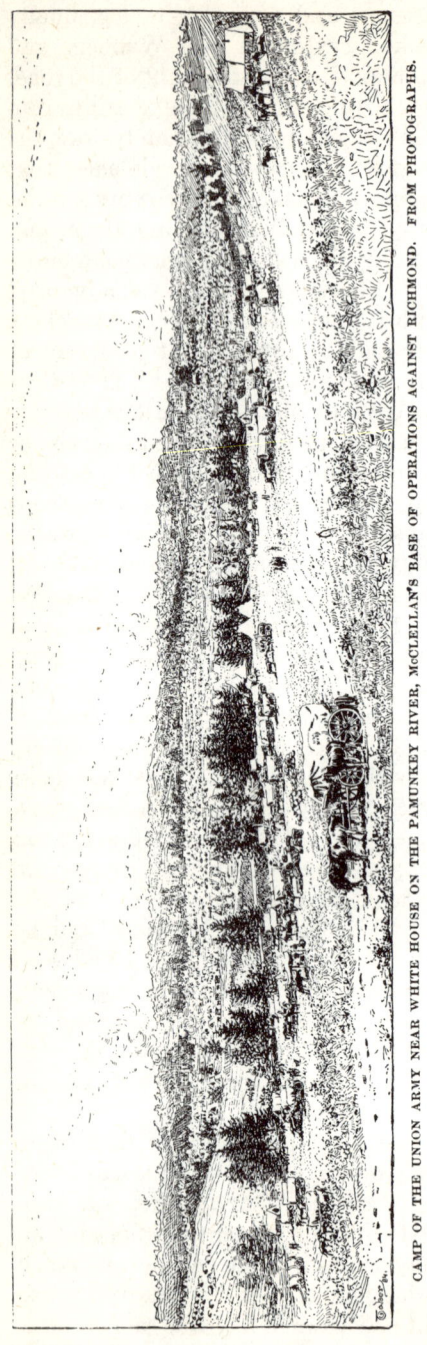

On the Confederate side, according to Longstreet's account, the march of the rear column northward in retreat from the town was being delayed all day on the 5th by impassable roads, and he ordered fresh troops from time to time to countermarch to the field at Williamsburg, relieving those whose ammunition was exhausted in this unexpected engagement. After Hooker had been forced back from Fort Magruder, the threatening position of Hancock on the Confederate left was noted by the enemy, and D. H. Hill went forward with Early's brigade, Early and Hill in person leading, toward the crest where Hancock's infantry was posted.

The Confederates were met by a severe musketry fire, and at length by a counter charge, led by Hancock, in which the bayonet was used in open field. Generals Sumner, Keyes, and Smith all mentioned Hancock's victory, which was brilliant and decisive. General Smith said in his report, "The brilliancy of the plan of battle, the

CAMP OF THE UNION ARMY NEAR WHITE HOUSE ON THE PAMUNKEY RIVER, McCLELLAN'S BASE OF OPERATIONS AGAINST RICHMOND. FROM PHOTOGRAPHS.

coolness of its execution, the seizing of the proper instant for changing from the defensive to the offensive, the steadiness of the troops engaged, and the completeness of the victory, are subjects to which I earnestly call the attention of the General-in-Chief for just praise." General Keyes wrote, "If Hancock had failed, the enemy would not have retreated."‡

The division of Kearny, that was coming to Hooker's aid, was delayed by crowded roads, and reached the field by brigades between 2:30 and 4 o'clock, and, taking position on Hooker's field, became engaged in a somewhat irregular fight to the extent of five regiments of the brigades of Berry and Birney. Berry's brigade made a desperate charge, recovering some of the ground yielded by Hooker earlier in the day. The heavy losses at Williamsburg fell upon Hooker and Kearny, the division of the former sustaining nearly three-fourths of the total Union loss.

After the engagement I went over the field in front of the enemy's fort. Advancing through the tangled mass of logs and stumps, I saw one of our men aiming over the branch of a fallen tree, which lay among the tangled abatis. I called to him, but he did not turn or move. Advancing nearer, I put my hand on his shoulder, looked in his face, and started back. He was dead!—shot through the brain; and so suddenly had the end come that his rigid hand grasped his musket, and he still preserved the attitude of watchfulness, literally occupying his post after death. At another place we came upon one of our men who had evidently died from wounds. Near one of his hands was a Testament, and on his breast lay an ambrotype picture of a group of children and another of a young woman.

The 6th of May was a beautiful morning, with birds singing among the thickets in which lay the dead. The next morning we marched through quaint, old-fashioned Williamsburg. The most substantial buildings of the town were those of William and Mary College, which were of brick. We kindled fires from that almost inexhaustible source of supply, the Virginia fences, cooked our coffee, sang, and smoked, thoughtless of the morrow.

‡ It was of this action that McClellan telegraphed to his wife, "Hancock was superb."—EDITORS.

UNION CAMP AT CUMBERLAND LANDING BELOW WHITE HOUSE. [SEE MAP, P. 167.]

# THE OPPOSING FORCES AT WILLIAMSBURG, VA.

The composition, losses, and strength of each army as here stated give the gist of all the data obtainable in the Official Records. K stands for killed; w for wounded; m w for mortally wounded; m for captured or missing; c for captured.

## THE UNION FORCES.

Major-General George B. McClellan. Brigadier-General Edwin V. Sumner, second in command.

THIRD ARMY CORPS, Brigadier-General Samuel P. Heintzelman.

SECOND DIVISION, Brig.-Gen. Joseph Hooker.
*First Brigade*, Brig.-Gen. Cuvier Grover: 1st Mass., Col. Robert Cowdin; 11th Mass., Col. William Blaisdell; 2d N. H., Col. Gilman Marston; 26th Pa., Col. William F. Small (w), Major Casper M. Berry. Brigade loss: k, 33; w, 186; m, 34 = 253. *Second Brigade*, Col. Nelson Taylor: 70th N. Y., Col. William Dwight, Jr. (w c), Major Thomas Holt; 72d N. Y., Lieut.-Col. Israel Moses; 73d N. Y.,Col. William R. Brewster; 74th N. Y., Lieut.-Col. Charles H. Burtis. Brigade loss: k, 191; w, 349; m, 232 = 772. *Third Brigade*, Brig.-Gen. Francis E. Patterson: 5th N. J., Col. Samuel H. Starr; 6th N. J., Lieut.-Col. John P. Van Leer (k), Maj. George C. Burling; 7th N. J., Lieut.-Col. Ezra A. Carman (w), Maj. Francis Price, Jr.; 8th N. J., Col. Adolphus J. Johnson (w), Maj. Peter H. Ryerson (k). Brigade loss: k, 109; w, 353; m, 64 = 526. *Artillery*, Maj. Charles S. Wainwright: D, 1st N. Y., Capt. Thomas W. Osborn; 4th N. Y., Capt. James E. Smith; 6th N. Y., Capt. Walter M. Bramhall; H, 1st U. S., Capt. Charles H. Webber. Artillery loss: k, 4; w, 20 = 24.

THIRD DIVISION, Brig.-Gen. Philip Kearny. Staff loss: k, 2.
*First Brigade*, Brig.-Gen. Charles D. Jameson: 87th N. Y., Col. Stephen A. Dodge; 57th Pa., Col. Charles T. Campbell; 63d Pa., Col. Alexander Hays; 105th Pa., Col. Amor A. McKnight. *Second Brigade*, Brig.-Gen. David B. Birney: 3d Me., Col. Henry G. Staples; 4th Me., Col. Elijah Walker; 38th N. Y., Col. J. H. Hobart Ward; 40th N. Y., Col. Edward J. Riley. Brigade loss: k, 16; w, 92; m, 10 = 118. *Third Brigade*, Brig.-Gen. Hiram G. Berry: 2d Mich., Col. Orlando M. Poe; 3d Mich., Col. Stephen G. Champlin; 5th Mich., Col. Henry D. Terry; 37th N. Y., Col. Samuel B. Hayman. Brigade loss: k, 69; w, 223; m, 7 = 299. *Artillery*, Capt. James Thompson: B, 1st N. J., Capt. John E. Beam; E, 1st R. I., Capt. George E. Randolph; G, 2d U. S., Capt. James Thompson.

FOURTH ARMY CORPS, Brigadier-General Erasmus D. Keyes.
*Cavalry*: 5th U. S., Major Joseph H. Whittlesey.
FIRST DIVISION, Brig.-Gen. Darius N. Couch.
*First Brigade*, Col. Julius W. Adams: 65th N. Y. (1st U. S. Chasseurs), Lieut.-Col. Alexander Shaler; 67th N. Y. (1st Long Island), Lieut.-Col. Nelson Cross; 23d Pa., Col. Thomas H. Neill; 31st Pa., Col. David H. Williams; 61st Pa., Col. Oliver H. Rippey. *Second Brigade*, Brig.-Gen. John J. Peck: 55th N. Y., Col. P. Regis de Trobriand; 62d N. Y., Col. John L. Riker; 93d Pa., Col. James M. McCarter; 98th Pa., Col. John F. Ballier; 102d Pa., Col. Thomas A. Rowley. Brigade loss: k, 18; w, 82; m, 24 = 124. *Third Brigade*, Brig.-Gen. Charles Devens, Jr.: 7th Mass., Col. David A. Russell; 10th Mass., Col. Henry

S. Briggs; 2d R. I., Col. Frank Wheaton. Brigade loss (7th Mass.): k, 1; w, 2 = 3. *Artillery*, Maj. Robert M. West: C, 1st Pa., Capt. Jeremiah McCarthy; D, 1st Pa., Capt. Edward H. Flood: E, 1st Pa., Capt. Theodore Miller; H, 1st Pa., Capt. James Brady.

SECOND DIVISION, Brig.-Gen.William F. Smith.
*First Brigade*, Brig.-Gen. Winfield S. Hancock (also in temporary command of Davidson's Third Brigade): 6th Me., Col. Hiram Burnham; 43d N. Y., Col. Francis L. Vinton; 49th Pa., Col. William H. Irwin; 5th Wis., Col. Amasa Cobb. Brigade loss: k, 8; w, 76; m, 1 = 85. *Second Brigade*, Brig.-Gen. W. T. H. Brooks: 2d Vt., Col. Henry Whiting; 3d Vt., Col. Breed N. Hyde; 4th Vt., Col. Edwin H. Stoughton; 5th Vt., Lieut.-Col. Lewis A. Grant; 6th Vt., Col. Nathan Lord. Brigade loss: w, 2. *Third Brigade* (temporarily under Hancock's command): 7th Me., Col. Edwin C. Mason; 33d N. Y., Col. Robert F. Taylor; 49th N. Y., Col. Daniel D. Bidwell; 76th N. Y., Col. James B. McKean. Brigade loss (33d N. Y.): w, 10. *Artillery*, Capt. Romeyn B. Ayres: 1st N. Y., Lieut. Andrew Cowan; 3d N. Y., Capt. Thaddeus P Mott; E, 1st N. Y., Capt. Charles C. Wheeler; F, 5th U. S., Capt. Romeyn B. Ayres.

THIRD DIVISION, Brig.-Gen. Silas Casey.
*First Brigade*, Brig.-Gen. Henry M. Naglee: 11th Me., Col. John F. Caldwell; 56th N. Y., Col. Charles H. Van Wyck; 100th N. Y., Col. James M. Brown; 52d Pa., Col. John C. Dodge, Jr.; 104th Pa., Col. W. W. H. Davis. *Second Brigade*, Brig.-Gen. William H. Keim: 96th N. Y., Lieut.-Col. Charles O. Gray; 85th Pa., Col. Joshua B. Howell; 101st Pa., Col. Joseph H. Wilson; 103d Pa., Maj. Audley W. Gazzam. Brigade loss (103d Pa.): w, 2. *Third Brigade*, Brig.-Gen. Innis N. Palmer: 81st N. Y., Lieut.-Col. Jacob J. De Forest; 85th N. Y., Col. Jonathan S. Belknap; 92d N. Y., Lieut.-Col. Hiram Anderson, Jr.; 93d N. Y., Lieut.-Col. Benjamin C. Butler; 98th N. Y., Col. William Dutton. *Artillery*, Col. Guilford D. Bailey: 7th N. Y., Capt. Peter C. Regan; 8th N. Y., Capt. Butler Fitch; A, 1st N. Y., Capt. Thomas H. Bates; H, 1st N. Y., Capt. Joseph Spratt.

ADVANCE-GUARD, Brig.-Gen. George Stoneman. Brig.-Gen. P. St. George Cooke and William H. Emory, brigade commanders.
*Cavalry*: 8th Ill., Col. John F. Farnsworth; McClellan (Ill.) Dragoons, Maj. Charles W. Barker; 3d Pa., Col. William W. Averell; 1st U. S., Lieut.-Col. William N. Grier; 6th U. S., Maj. Lawrence Williams. *Artillery*, Lieut.-Col. William Hays: B and L, 2d U. S., Capt. James M. Robertson; M, 2d U. S., Capt. Henry Benson; C, 3d U. S., Capt. Horatio G. Gibson; K, 3d U. S., Capt. John C. Tidball. Advance-guard loss (mostly on May 4th): k, 15; w, 33; m, 1 = 49.

The total loss of the Union army (May 4th and 5th) was = 468 killed, 1442 wounded, and 373 captured or missing = 2283.

## THE CONFEDERATE FORCES.

General Joseph E. Johnston. Major-General James Longstreet in immediate command on the field.

SECOND DIVISION (Longstreet's).
*First Brigade*, Brig.-Gen. Ambrose P. Hill: 1st Va., Col. Louis B. Williams (w), Maj. William H. Palmer (w); 7th Va., Col. James L. Kemper; 11th Va., Col. Samuel Garland (w); 17th Va., Col. M. D. Corse. Brigade loss: k, 67; w, 245; m, 14 = 326. *Second Brigade*, Brig.-Gen. Richard H. Anderson (in command on the right), Col. Micah Jenkins: 4th S. C. (Battalion), Maj. C. S. Mattison; 5th S. C., Col. John R. R. Giles; 6th S. C., Col. John Bratton; Palmetto (S. C.) Sharp-shooters, Col. Micah Jenkins, Lieut.-Col. Joseph Walker; La. Foot Rifles,

Capt. McG. Goodwyn; Fauquier (Va.) Artillery, Capt. Robert M. Stribling; Williamsburg (Va.) Artillery, (2 guns), Capt. William R. Garrett; Richmond (Va.) Howitzers (2 guns), Capt. Edward S. McCarthy. Brigade loss: k, 10 ; w, 75; m, 6 = 91. *Third Brigade*, Brig.-Gen. George E. Pickett: 8th Va., Lieut.-Col. Norbourne Berkeley; 18th Va., Lieut.-Col. Henry A. Carrington; 19th Va., Col. John B. Strange; 28th Va., Col. Robert C. Allen; Va. Battery, Capt. James Dearing. Brigade loss: k, 26; w, 138; m, 26 = 190. *Fourth Brigade*, Brig.-Gen. Cadmus M. Wilcox: 9th Ala., Col. Samuel

200

## CONFEDERATE USE OF SUBTERRANEAN SHELLS.

Henry; 10th Ala., Col. John J. Woodward; 19th Miss., Col. Christopher H. Mott (k), Lieut.-Col. L. Q. C. Lamar. Brigade loss: k and w, 231. *Fifth Brigade*, Brig.-Gen. Roger A. Pryor: 8th Ala., Lieut.-Col. Thomas E. Irby (k); 14th Ala., Maj. O. K. McLemore; 14th La., Col. R. W. Jones; 32d Va. (detachment); Richmond (Va.) Fayette Artillery, Lieut. W. I. Clopton. Brigade loss: k, w, and m, 214. *Colston's Brigade*, Brig.-Gen. R. E. Colston: 13th N. C., Col. Alfred M. Scales; 14th N. C., Col. P. W. Roberts; 3d Va., Col. Joseph Mayo. Brigade loss not separately reported. Donaldsonville (La.) Battery (3 guns), Lieut. Lestang Fortier.
FOURTH DIVISION, Major-Gen. Daniel H. Hill (in command on the left).
*Early's Brigade*, Brig.-Gen. Jubal A. Early (w), Col. D. K. McRae: 5th N. C., Col. D. K. McRae; 23d N. C., Col. John F. Hoke, Maj. Daniel H. Christie; 24th Va., Col. William R. Terry (w), Major Richard L. Maury; 38th Va., Lieut.-Col. Powhatan B. Whittle. Brigade loss (except 5th N. C., not reported): k; 30; w, 106; m, 70 = 206. *Rodes's Brigade*, Brig.-Gen. R. E. Rodes: 5th Ala., Col. C. C. Pegues; 6th Ala., Col. John B. Gordon; 12th Ala., Col. R. T. Jones; 12th Miss., Col. W. H. Taylor. *Rains's Brigade*, Brig.-Gen. G. J. Rains: 13th Ala., Col. B. D. Fry; 26th Ala., Col. E. A. O'Neal; 6th Ga., Col. A. H. Colquitt; 23d Ga., Col. Thos. Hutcherson. *Featherston's Brigade*, Brig.-Gen. W. S. Featherston: 27th Ga., Col. Levi B. Smith; 28th Ga., Col. T. J. Warthen; 4th N. C., Col. George B. Anderson; 49th Va., Col. William Smith. *Unattached*: 2d Fla., Col. George T. Ward (k); 2d Miss. Battalion, Lieut.-Col. John G. Taylor. Unattached loss: k, 9; w, 61; m, 11 = 81.
CAVALRY BRIGADE, Brig.-Gen. J. E. B. Stuart: 3d Va., Col. Thomas F. Goode; 4th Va., Maj. William H. Payne (w), Capt. R. E. Utterback; Jeff Davis Legion, Lieut.-Col. William T. Martin; Wise Legion, Col. J. Lucius Davis; Stuart Horse Artillery, Captain John Pelham. Brigade loss: k, 1; w, 3 = 4.
The total loss of the Confederate Army was 288 killed, 975 wounded, and 297 captured or missing = 1560.

## CONFEDERATE USE OF SUBTERRANEAN SHELLS ON THE PENINSULA.

SEVERAL Union officers have written to the editors, stating that they witnessed the explosion of concealed shells or torpedoes at Yorktown — among them Fred T. Locke, assistant adjutant-general to Fitz John Porter, director of the siege, and Colonel Edward C. James, of the engineer corps. General Locke wrote in May, 1885:

"On the morning of May 4th, 1862, our pickets sent in a prisoner who said he was a Union man, had been impressed with the rebel service, and was one of a party detailed to bury some shells in the road and fields near the works. . . . A cavalry detachment passing along the road leading to Yorktown had some of its men and horses killed and wounded by these shells. Our telegraph operator was sent into Yorktown soon after our troops had got possession of the place. He trod upon one of the buried shells, which burst and terribly mangled both of his legs, from which he died soon after in great agony. . . . In the casemates and covered ways about the fortifications I saw a number of large shells, placed so that they could easily be fired by persons unaware of their presence."

The "Official Records" show that General Fitz John Porter referred to the buried shells in his report of the siege, and General William F. Barry, Inspector of Artillery, made a statement in detail, in a communication to army headquarters, August 25th, 1863. Porter's statement is that when the advance detachments entered Yorktown the command

"on the left was fired upon from the Red Fort. Those on the right experienced some losses from shells planted in the ground, which exploded when trod upon. Many of these shells were concealed in the streets and houses of the town, and arranged to explode by treading on the caps or pulling a wire attached to the doors."

General W. F. Barry wrote that buried shells were encountered when they were about to enter the abandoned Confederate lines:

"Before reaching the glacis of the main work, and at the distance of more than one hundred yards from it, several of our men were injured by the explosion of what was ascertained to be loaded shells buried in the ground. These shells were the ordinary eight or ten inch mortar or Columbiad shells, filled with powder, buried a few inches below the surface of the ground, and so arranged with some fulminate, or with the ordinary artillery friction primer, that they exploded by being trod upon or otherwise disturbed. . . . These shells were not thus placed on the glacis at the bottom of the ditch, etc., which, in view of an anticipated assault, might possibly be considered a legitimate use of them, but they were planted by an enemy who was secretly abandoning his post, on common roads, at springs of water, in the shade of trees, at the foot of telegraph poles, and, lastly, quite within the defenses of the place — in the very streets."

On the march from Williamsburg toward Richmond General Longstreet wrote to General G. J. Rains, whose brigade was on duty as rear-guard:

"It is the desire of the major-general commanding [Longstreet] that you put no shells or torpedoes behind you, as he does not recognize it as a proper or effective method of war."

In an indorsement on the above, General Rains advocated the use of buried shells in retreat and for the defense of works. He forwarded Longstreet's letter and his own comments to General D. H. Hill. The latter approvingly indorsed Rains's suggestion. This correspondence went to the Secretary of War, G. W. Randolph, whose decision, favorable to Longstreet's views, was as follows:

"It is not admissible in civilized warfare to take life with no other object than the destruction of life. . . . It is admissible to plant shells in a parapet to repel an assault, or in a wood to check pursuit, because the object is to save the work in one case and the army in the other"

A copy of the "New York Herald," containing General McClellan's report on buried torpedoes at Yorktown, reached General Johnston, who, in a letter dated May 12th, requested General D. H. Hill to ascertain if there was any truth in it. General Hill referred the matter to Rains, who on May 14th reported in part as follows:

"I commanded at Yorktown for the last seven months, and when General McClellan approached with his army of 100,000 men and opened his cannons upon us, I had but 2500 in garrison, and our whole Army of the Peninsula, under Major-General Magruder, amounted to but 9300 effective men; then at a salient angle, an accessible point of our works, as part of the defenses thereof, I had the land mined with the weapons alluded to, to destroy assailants and prevent *escalade*. Subsequently, with a similar view, they were placed at spots I never saw. . . . And again when, at Williamsburg, we were ordered to turn upon our assailants and combat them, . . . some 6 or 7 miles this side of Williamsburg, my command forming the rear-guard of the army, . . . some 4 small shells, found abandoned by our artillery, were hastily prepared by my efforts, and put in the road near a tree felled across, mainly to have a moral effect in checking the advance of the enemy (for they were too small to do more). . . ." [Compare p. 205.] EDITORS.

# MANASSAS TO SEVEN PINES.

BY JOSEPH E. JOHNSTON, GENERAL, C. S. A.

ALREADY in this work [Vol. I., p. 240] I have discussed Mr. Davis's statements in his "Rise and Fall of the Confederate Government," so far as they bore upon the responsibilities of the First Bull Run. I will now consider his remarks upon the operations following the withdrawal from Manassas and including the battle of Seven Pines.

As to the question of the forces on the Peninsula Mr. Davis says: "Early in April General McClellan had landed about 100,000 men at or near Fortress Monroe" ["Rise and Fall," II., 84]. According to John Tucker, Assistant Secretary of War, 121,000 Federal troops landed before the 5th of April. Mr. Davis further says: "At this time General Magruder occupied the lower Peninsula with his force of seven or eight thousand men" [II., 84]. General Magruder reported that he had eleven thousand men. Mr. Davis also says:

CONFEDERATE SHARP-SHOOTER.

"After the first advance of the enemy, General Magruder was reënforced by some troops from the south side of James River, and General Wilcox's brigade, which had been previously detached from the army under General Johnston."

These reënforcements, together, made about five thousand men [II , p. 85]. He says, on the same page:

"On the 9th of April, General Magruder's command, thus reënforced, amounted to about 12,000. On that day General Early joined with his division from the Army of Northern Virginia. . . . . This division had about 8000 officers and men for duty. General Magruder's force was thus increased to about 20,000."

The same order detached Early's, D. R. Jones's, and D. H. Hill's divisions from the Army of Northern Virginia, and they were transported as fast as the railroad trains could carry them. The two latter divisions had together about 10,000 men, so that Magruder's army was raised to about 33,000 men, instead of 20,000, as Mr. Davis said.

Coming to the plan of withdrawal Mr. Davis says:

"As soon as it was definitely ascertained that General McClellan, with his main army, was on the Peninsula, General J. E. Johnston was assigned ↓ to the command of the Department of the Peninsula and Norfolk, and directed to proceed thither to examine the condition of affairs there.

↓ That assignment was made after the conference at Richmond mentioned on page 203.— EDITORS.

After spending a day on General Magruder's defensive line, he returned to Richmond and recommended the abandonment of the Peninsula, and that we should take up a defensive position nearer to Richmond " [II., 86].

The President has forgotten my recommendation, or misunderstood it at the time. I represented to him that General McClellan's design was, almost certainly, to demolish our batteries with his greatly superior artillery, and turn us by the river, either landing in our rear or moving directly to Richmond; so that our attempting to hold Yorktown could only delay the enemy two or three weeks. Instead of that, I proposed that all our available forces should be united near Richmond, Magruder's troops to be among the last to arrive; the great army thus formed about Richmond not to be in a defensive position, as Mr. Davis supposes, but to fall with its whole force upon McClellan when the Federal army was expecting to besiege only the troops it had followed from Yorktown. If the Federal army should be defeated a hundred miles away from its place of refuge, Fort Monroe, it could not escape destruction. This was undoubtedly our best hope [see maps, pp. 167 and 188].

In the conference that followed the President took no part. But the Secretary of War, G. W. Randolph, once a naval officer, opposed the abandonment of the valuable property in the Norfolk Navy Yard; and General Lee opposed the plan proposed, because it would expose Charleston and Savannah to capture. I maintained that if those places should be captured, the defeat of the principal Federal army would enable us to recover them; and that, unless that army should be defeated, we should lose those sea-ports in spite of their garrisons. Mr. Davis says:

"After hearing fully the views of the several officers named, I decided to resist the enemy on the Peninsula. . . . Though General J. E. Johnston did not agree with this decision, he did not ask to be relieved. . . ." [II., 87].

Not being in command, I could not be relieved. My assignment was included in the order to oppose McClellan at Yorktown; that order added to my then command the departments of Norfolk and the Peninsula. It is not easy to reconcile this increase of my command by the President, with his very numerous disparaging notices of me.

General Keyes, before the Committee on the Conduct of the War, confirmed my opinion in saying that "Gloucester must have fallen upon our [McClellan's] getting possession of Yorktown, and the York River would then have been open."

Mr. Davis expresses the opinion that "General McClellan certainly might have sent a detachment from his army, which, after crossing York River, could have turned the position at Gloucester Point" [II., 90]. That would have been needless; the driving us from Yorktown would have compelled us to abandon Gloucester Point. Then [Vol. II., p. 91] he says:

"Whether General McClellan . . . would have made an early assault . . . or have waited to batter our earth-works in breach . . . is questionable" [II., 91].

We did not apprehend "battering in breach," but believed that the heavy sea-coast rifles to be mounted in the batteries, about completed, would demolish our water-batteries, drive us from the intrenchments at Yorktown, and enable the enemy to turn us by the river. Mr. Davis quotes from one of his dispatches to me:

"Your announcement to-day [May 1st] that you would withdraw to-morrow night takes us by surprise, and must involve enormous losses, including unfinished gun-boats. Will the safety of your army allow more time ?" [II., 92].

My own announcement was made April 27th, not May 1st, and reached Richmond in ten hours; so the President had abundant time to prevent the withdrawal. The appearance of the enemy's works indicated that fire from them might open upon us the next morning. The withdrawal just then was to avoid waste of life. With regard to the property abandoned he says:

"The loss of public property, as was anticipated, was great, the steamboats expected for its transportation not having arrived before the evacuation was made. From a narrative by General Early I make the following extract: 'A very valuable part of the property so lost . . . consisted of a very large number of picks and spades. . . . All of our heavy guns, including some recently arrived and not mounted, together with a good deal of ammunition piled upon the wharf, had to be left behind'" [II., 94].

The steamboats he mentions were controlled in Richmond. As to the loss of very valuable picks and spades, Colonel Henry T. Douglas, chief engineer at Yorktown, wrote to me, May 12th, 1883:

"I was at Yorktown the evening before the evacuation commenced. I did not see any quantity of picks and shovels there, and cannot understand how they could have accumulated there when they were needed so much from Redoubt Number Five to Lee's Mills— that is, on the extreme right of our line."

General D. H. Hill, who commanded in and near Yorktown, said, in his official report: "We lost very little by the retreat, save some medical stores which Surgeon Coffin deserted in his flight, May 1st. The heavy guns were all of the old navy pattern." We had very little ammunition on hand at the time. The heavy guns could have been saved only by holding the place, which was impossible.

Mr. Davis says that General Magruder's "absence at this moment was the more to be regretted, as it appears that the positions of the redoubts he had constructed [before Williamsburg] were not all known to the commanding general"

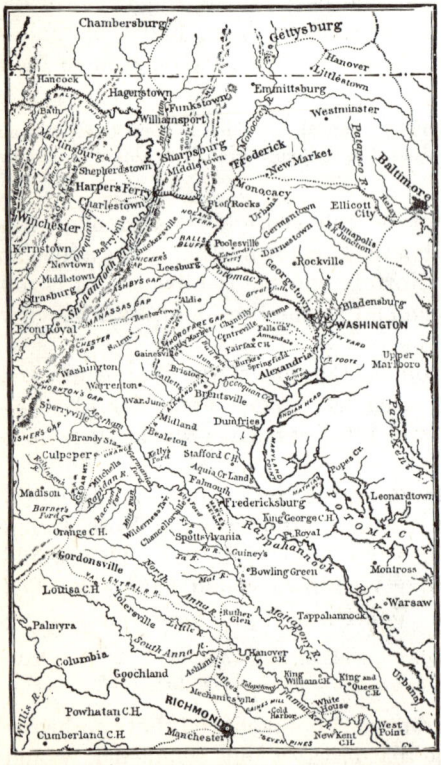

REGION BETWEEN WASHINGTON AND RICHMOND.

[II., 94]. The positions of the redoubts were "all known." But to a body of troops serving merely as a rear-guard, it was necessary to occupy only those nearest the road. A rear-guard distributed in all the redoubts intended for an army could have held none of them. The event showed that the proper redoubts were occupied. It is singular that Mr. Davis's only notice of the conflict at Williamsburg, in which our troops behaved admirably, relates to a detached affair, unimportant, because it had, and could have, no influence upon the real event. Mr. Davis says of General Early's account of his attack upon Hancock at Williamsburg:

"He [Early] confidently expresses the opinion that had his attack been supported promptly and vigorously, the enemy's force there engaged must have been captured" [II., 96].

General Early sent an officer to report that there was a battery in front of him which he could take, and asked authority to do so. The message was delivered to General Longstreet, who referred the messenger to me, we being together. I authorized the attempt, but desired the general to look carefully first. Under the circumstances he could not have expected support, for he moved out of reach of it.

Mr. Davis speaks of the employment of sub-terra shells to check a marching column, and quotes from General Rains as follows:

"Fortunately we found in a mud-hole a broken ammunition wagon containing five loaded shells. Four of these, armed with a sensitive fuse-primer, were planted in our rear, near some trees cut down as obstructions to the road. A body of the enemy's cavalry came upon these sub-terra shells, and they exploded with terrific effect" [II., 97].

This event was not mentioned in General D. H. Hill's report, although General Rains belonged to his division, nor was it mentioned by our cavalry which followed Hill's division. Such an occurrence would have been known to the whole army, but it was not; so it must have been a dream of the writer. [But see p. 201.—EDITORS.]

Mr. Davis says: "The next morning after the battle of the 5th, at Williamsburg, Longstreet's and D. H. Hill's divisions being those there engaged" [II., 98]. But one regiment of Hill's division was engaged.

In the Federal reports of this action, it is treated as a battle in which the whole Confederate army was engaged. It was an affair with our rear-guard, the object of which was to secure our baggage trains. For that it was necessary to detain the Federal army a day, which was accomplished by the rear-guard. In those Federal reports a victory is claimed.‡ The proofs

‡ General McClellan's statement was as follows:

"Notwithstanding the report I received from General Heintzelman during the night [of the 5th], that General Hooker's division had suffered so much that it could not be relied upon next day, and that Kearny's could not do more than hold its own without reënforcements, being satisfied that the result of Hancock's engagement was to give us possession of the decisive point of the battle-field, during the night I countermanded the order for the advance of the divisions of Sedgwick and Richardson and directed them to return to Yorktown. . . . On the next morning we found the enemy's position abandoned, and occupied Fort Magruder and the town of Williamsburg, which was filled with the enemy's wounded. . . . Colonel Averell was sent forward at once with a strong cavalry force to endeavor to overtake the enemy's rear-guard. He found several guns abandoned and picked up a large number of stragglers, but the condition of the roads and the state of his supplies forced him to return after advancing a few miles. . . . The supply trains had been forced out of the roads on the 4th and 5th to allow troops and artillery to pass to the front, and the roads were now in such a state, after thirty-six hours' continuous rain, that it was almost impossible to pass even empty wagons over them. General Hooker's division had suffered so severely that it was in no condition to follow the enemy, even if the roads had been good. Under these circumstances an immediate pursuit was impossible." EDITORS.

are: (1) That what deserves to be called fighting ceased at least two hours before dark, yet the Confederates held the ground until the next morning, having slept on the field, and then resumed their march; (2) that they fought only to protect their trains, and accomplished the object; (3) that although they marched but twelve miles the day after the affair, they saw no indications of pursuit, unless the seeing a scouting party once can so be called; (4) that they inflicted a loss much greater than that they suffered; (5) and that in the ten days following the fight they marched but thirty-seven miles. They left four hundred wounded in Williamsburg, because they had no means of transporting them. But they captured five cannon and destroyed the carriages of five more, and took four hundred prisoners and several colors.

Mr. Davis says:

"In the meantime, Franklin's division had gone up the York River and landed a short distance below West Point, on the south side of York River, and moved into a thick wood in the direction of the New Kent road, thus threatening the flank of our line of march. [McClellan wrote that the divisions of Franklin, Sedgwick, Porter, and Richardson were sent from Yorktown by water to the right bank of the Pamunkey, near West Point.— J. E. J.] Two brigades of General G. W. Smith's division, Hampton's and Hood's, were detached under the command of General Whiting to dislodge the enemy, which they did after a short conflict, driving him through the wood to the protection of his gun-boats in York River" [II., 98].

The Federal force engaged was very much less than a division.

Mr. Davis says, lower down: "The loss of the enemy [in the battle of Williamsburg] greatly exceeded our own, which was about 1200." He means exclusive of General Early's loss. According to General McClellan's report his loss was 2228. General Hooker stated under oath that his was 1700.↓ But Kearny's, Couch's, and two-thirds of Smith's division, and Peck's brigade were engaged also; a loss of 528 is very small among so many. ♭

Mr. Davis says:

" Soon after General Johnston took position on the north of the Chickahominy, accompanied by General Lee, I rode out to his headquarters. . . . A long conversation followed, which was so inconclusive that it lasted until late in the night, so late that we remained until the next morning. As we rode back to Richmond, . . . General Lee confessed himself, as I was unable to draw from it any more definite purpose than that the policy was to . . . improve his [Johnston's] position as far as practicable, and wait for the enemy to leave his gun-boats, so that an opportunity might be offered to meet him on land" [II., 101].

I explained that I had fallen back that far to clear my left flank of the navigable water, and so avoid having it turned; that as we were too weak to assume the offensive, and as the position I then held was an excellent one, I intended to await the Federal attack there. These explanations covered the whole ground, so that the President had no cause to complain, especially as he suggested nothing better. And he was satisfied then; for, three days later, he wrote to me by Colonel G. W. C. Lee: " . . . If the enemy proceed as heretofore indicated, your position and policy, as you stated it in

↓ The total Union loss was 2283, and Hooker's loss, 1575. See tables, p. 200.— EDITORS.

♭ Peck's brigade (five regiments) belonged to Couch's division and was the only brigade of that division which took part in the battle. Five regiments of Kearny's division (2 of Birney's brigade and 3 of Berry's) and 6 of Smith's division (4 of Hancock's and 2 of Davidson's) were engaged, so the loss (exclusive of Hooker's) of 528 belonged, in fact, to only 16 regiments.— EDITORS.

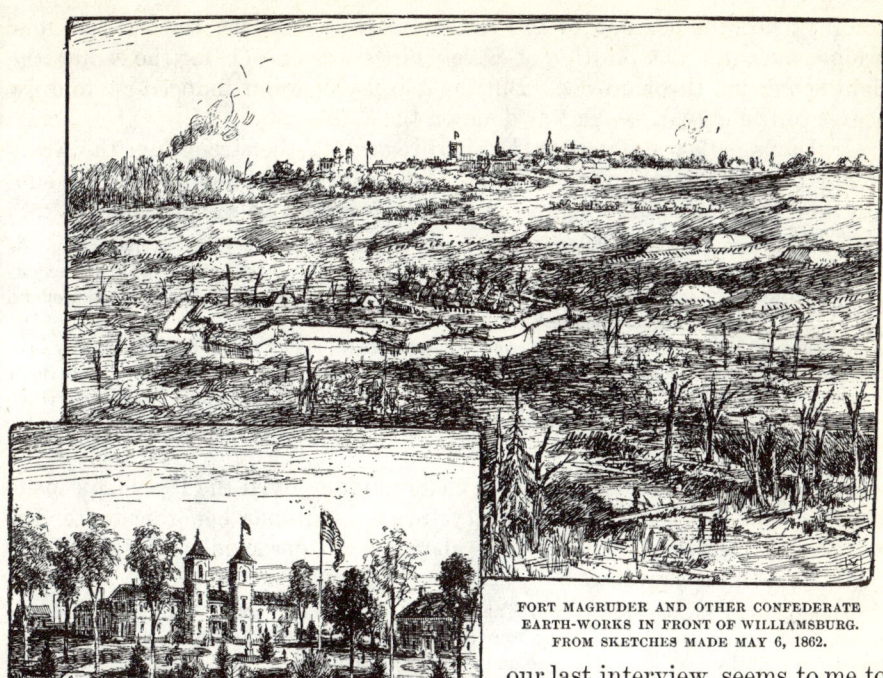

FORT MAGRUDER AND OTHER CONFEDERATE
EARTH-WORKS IN FRONT OF WILLIAMSBURG.
FROM SKETCHES MADE MAY 6, 1862.

WILLIAM AND MARY COLLEGE, WILLIAMSBURG, USED
AS A UNION HOSPITAL.

our last interview, seems to me to require no modification." This is the interview called "inconclusive." Mr. Davis says:

"After the repulse of the enemy's gun-boats at Drewry's Bluff [May 15th, 1862], I wrote to General Johnston a letter to be handed to him by my aide, Colonel G. W. C. Lee. . . . I soon thereafter rode out to visit General Johnston at his headquarters, and was surprised, in the suburbs of Richmond, . . . to meet a portion of the light artillery, and to learn that the whole army had crossed the Chickahominy" [II., 103].

The army crossed the Chickahominy immediately after the affair of Drewry's Bluff. So that if Colonel Lee delivered a letter to me then, he of course reported to the President that I had crossed the river. And as the army's nearest approach to Richmond was on the 17th, his meeting with the light artillery must have occurred that day. So one cannot understand his surprise.

He says on the same page:

"General Johnston's explanation of this (to me) unexpected movement was, that he thought the water of the Chickahominy unhealthy. . . . He also adverted to the advantage of having the river in front rather than in the rear of him."

The army crossed the Chickahominy because the possession of James River by the enemy suggested the probability of a change of base to that river. And it was necessary that we should be so placed as to be able to meet the United States army approaching either from York River or along the James. Water was not considered, for we did not use that of the Chickahominy; nor the position of the little stream behind us, for we had four bridges over it. The position of Seven Pines was chosen for the center, the right somewhat thrown back. But the scarcity of water induced me to draw nearer to Richmond, which was done on the 17th.

Mr. Davis makes statements [II., 106] regarding the strength of the Army of Northern Virginia, on the 21st and 31st of May; but as he treats the subject more minutely farther on, we will examine what he says [p. 153]:

"In the Archives Offices of the War Department in Washington, there are on file some of the field and monthly returns of the Army of Northern Virginia. . . . The following statements have been taken from those papers by Major Walter H. Taylor, of the staff of General Lee. . . .

"A statement of the strength of the troops under General Johnston shows that on May 21st, 1862, he had present for duty, as follows: Smith's division, . . . 10,592; Longstreet's division, . . . 13,816; Magruder's division, . . . 15,680 [240 too little.— J. E. J.]; D. H. Hill's division, . . . 11,151; cavalry brigade, 1289; reserve artillery, 1160;⸲ total effective men, 53,688."

The above is from Major Taylor's memorandum given the President, made from estimates of brigades, not from returns. Without being accurate, it is not far from the truth; corrected as above, Magruder should be given 15,920 men. Mr. Davis continues:

"Major Taylor in his work ('Four Years with General Lee') states: 'In addition to the troops above enumerated, . . . there were two brigades subject to his orders, then stationed in the vicinity of Hanover Junction, one under the command of General J. R. Anderson, and the other under the command of General Branch. They were subsequently incorporated into the division of General A. P. Hill.' [Mr. Davis continues]: . . . He estimates the strength of the two at 4000 effective.

" . . . Previous to the battle of Seven Pines, General Johnston was reënforced by General Huger's division of three brigades. The total strength of these three brigades, according to the 'Reports of the Operations of the Army of Northern Virginia,' was 5008 effectives. Taylor says: 'If the strength of these five be added to the return of May 21st, we shall have 62,696 as the effective strength of the army under General Johnston on May 31st, 1862.'"

But according to General Huger's report to me, there were 7000 men (instead of 5008) in his three brigades, which does not exceed the ordinary strength of brigades then (that is to say, three average brigades would have had not less than 7000 men); and what Mr. Davis calls two brigades of "4000 effective" were, in fact, Anderson's division sent to observe McDowell's corps at Fredericksburg, and so large that General Lee called it the army of the North, and estimated it as 10,000 men;☆ and the second, Branch's brigade, greatly strengthened to protect the railroad at Gordonsville, and estimated by General Lee as 5000 men.⌋ When these troops were united on the Chickahominy, General Anderson's estimate of their numbers was, of the first, 9000, and of the other, 4000; 20,000 then, and not 9008, is the number to be added

---

⸲ According to General Johnston's memorandum of May 21st, 1862, "Official Records," Vol. XI., Part III., p. 531, the reserve artillery numbered 920.— EDITORS.

☆ " I advised you, April 23d, of certain troops ordered to report to General Field, viz.: two regiments from Richmond, two light batteries, a brigade from South Carolina, and one from North Carolina (Anderson's), in all 8000, in addition to those [2500.— J. E. J.] previously there."— General Lee's letter, May 8th.—"Official Records," Vol. XI., Part III., pp 500-1.—J. E. J.

⌋ " Two brigades, one from North Carolina (Branch's) and one from Norfolk, have been ordered to Gordonsville to reënforce that line."— General Lee's letter, as above.— J. E. J.

to the return of May 21st, 1862, to show the effective strength of that army May 31st, viz., 73,928, including the correction of the number in Magruder's division.

Referring to our withdrawal from the north side of the Chickahominy to the vicinity of Richmond, Mr. Davis says:

"Remembering a remark of General Johnston's that the Spaniards were the only people who now undertook to hold fortified towns, I had written to him that he knew the defense of Richmond must be made at a distance from it" [II., 120].

Mr. Davis is mistaken. No such letter was sent to me then. We communicated with each other only orally, excepting a note he sent me to point out that I had been absent from a skirmish the day before. He knew that the fact that the enemy was then able to approach Richmond either from York River or by the James compelled me to prepare for either event, by placing the army near the city. A short time before, he wrote: "To you it is needless to say that the defense must be made outside of the city." His next sentence, approving the course I was pursuing, has been quoted in connection with what the President said of an "inconclusive" conversation with me.

Mr. Davis continues, a little farther down [II., 120]:

"It had not occurred to me that he [Johnston] meditated a retreat which would uncover the capital, nor was it ever suspected, until, in reading General Hood's book, published in 1880, the evidence was found that General Johnston, when retreating from Yorktown, told his volunteer aide, Mr. McFarland, that 'he [Johnston] expected or intended to give up Richmond.'"

MAJOR-GENERAL JOHN B. MAGRUDER, C. S. A.
FROM A PHOTOGRAPH.

This story of Mr. McFarland is incredible. He, a very rich, fat old man, could not have been an aide-de-camp. As I did not know him at all until four years later, and then barely, he could not have been my aide-de-camp. And lastly, I had no volunteer aide. Besides, the Confederate President had abundant evidence that I had no such expectation, in the fact that, so far from giving up Richmond, I stood between it and the Federal army for three weeks, until I was disabled by desperate wounds received in its defense. Under such circumstances his accusation is, to say the least, very discreditable. E. J. Harvie, late Colonel and Assistant Inspector-General, C. S. A., now in the "War Records" Office, Washington, in answer to my question, "Had I ever a volunteer aide-de-camp named McFarland, or any volunteer aide-de-camp after leaving Manassas, while serving in Virginia?" wrote me, under date of January 28th, 1885, as follows: "To my knowledge, you certainly had not.

My position as your staff-officer justifies me in saying that Mr. McFarland was not with you in any capacity."

Surgeon A. M. Fauntleroy, in answer to my question, "Had I a volunteer aide-de-camp in May, 1862, especially when the army was moving from Yorktown toward Richmond; or did you ever in that time see an old gentleman of Richmond, named McFarland, about my headquarters?" writes:

"I never did. I cannot well see how such a person could have escaped my observation, if he was there at any time."

And J. B. Washington, president of the Baltimore and Philadelphia Railway, writes me as follows:

"You had not on your staff after leaving Manassas a volunteer aide-de-camp, especially during May, 1862, when the army was between Yorktown and Richmond. I was personally acquainted with Mr. McFarland of Richmond, but never saw him at our headquarters, nor heard of his ever having been there. Having served as aide-de-camp on your staff from May, 1861, to February, 1864, I was in the position to know of the circumstances of which I have written."

Mr. Davis says:

"Seeing no preparation to keep the enemy at a distance . . . I sent for General Lee . . . and told him why and how I was dissatisfied with the condition of affairs. He asked me what I thought it was proper to do. . . . I answered that McClellan should be attacked on the other side of the Chickahominy, before he matured his preparations for a siege of Richmond. To this he promptly assented. . . . He then said: 'General Johnston should, of course, advise you of what he expects or proposes to do. Let me go and see him.' . . . When General Lee came back, he told me that General Johnston proposed, on the next Thursday, to move against the enemy, as follows: 'General A. P. Hill was to move down on the right flank and rear of the enemy. General G. W. Smith, as soon as Hill's guns opened, was to cross the Chickahominy at the Meadow Bridge, attack the enemy in flank, and, by the conjunction of the two, it was expected to double him up. Then Longstreet was to cross on the Mechanicsville bridge and attack him in front. From this plan the best results were hoped by both of us" [II., 120].

It is certain that General Lee could have had no such hopes from this plan, nor have been a party to it; for it would not only have sent our army where there was no enemy, but left open the way to Richmond. For the Meadow Bridge is 2½ miles from Mechanicsville, and that place about 6 miles above the Federal right. So, after two-thirds of our troops had crossed the Chickahominy, the Federal army could have marched straight to Richmond, opposed by not more than one-fifth of its number in Magruder's and D. H. Hill's divisions. This plan is probably the wildest on record.

As to what is described [II., 121], G. W. Smith's division was never in the place indicated, and General Longstreet's was never on the Mechanicsville road near the bridge, before General Lee crossed the Chickahominy to fight at Gaines's Mills.

A glance at the map will show how singularly incorrect is Mr. Davis's description [II., 122–3] of the vicinity of Seven Pines and of the disposition of the Federal troops.

On the 23d of May, Keyes's Federal corps crossed to the south side of the Chickahominy, and a detachment attacked Hatton's Confederate brigade, which was in observation near Savage's Station. The detachment was driven back, and Hatton's object having been accomplished (to learn whether the enemy had crossed the stream), he was recalled. I was advised to hold that position with the army, but preferred to let the enemy advance, which would increase the interval between his left and the right, which was beyond the Chickahominy. McDowell's corps of 40,000 men‡, was then at Fredericksburg, observed by a division under Brigadier-General J. R. Anderson; and a large Confederate brigade, under Brigadier-General Branch, was at Gordonsville.

On the 24th our cavalry was driven across the Chickahominy, principally at Mechanicsville. This extension of the right wing of the enemy to the west made me apprehend that the two detachments (Anderson and Branch) above mentioned might be cut off. They were therefore ordered to fall back to the Chickahominy. Near Hanover Court House the brigade was attacked by Porter's corps and driven off, escaping with a loss of 66 killed, and 177 wounded, as General Branch reported.↓ A division was formed of Anderson's and Branch's troops, to the command of which Major-General A. P. Hill was assigned.

That evening General Anderson sent word that his scouts left near Fredericksburg reported that McDowell's troops were marching southward. As the object of this march was evidently the junction of this corps with the main army, I determined to attack McClellan before McDowell could join him; and the major-generals were desired to hold their troops ready to move. But at night, when those officers were with me to receive instructions for the expected battle, General J. E. B. Stuart, who also had a detachment of cavalry observing McDowell's corps, reported that it had returned to Fredericksburg. As my object was to bring on the inevitable battle before McClellan should receive an addition of 40,000 men to his forces, this intelligence made me return to my first design — that of attacking McClellan's left wing on the Williamsburg road as soon as, by advancing, it had sufficiently increased its distance from his right, north of the Chickahominy.

The morning of the 30th, armed reconnoissances were made under General D. H. Hill's direction — on the Charles City road by Brigadier-General Rodes, and on the Williamsburg road by Brigadier-General Garland. The latter found Federal outposts five miles from Richmond — or two miles west of Seven Pines — in such strength as indicated that a corps was near. On receiving this information from General Hill, I informed him that he would lead an attack on the enemy next morning. Orders were given for the concentration of twenty-two of our twenty-eight brigades against McClellan's left wing, about two-fifths of his army. Our six other brigades were guarding the river from New Bridge to Meadow Bridge, on our extreme left. Longstreet and Huger were directed to conduct their divisions to D. H. Hill's position on the Williamsburg road, and G. W. Smith to march with his to the junction

---

‡ McDowell says, May 22d, 1862, "Official Records," Vol. XII., Part III., p. 214, that he would require subsistence for 38,000 men. This included both effectives and non-effectives. A fair deduction would leave McDowell about 35,000 combatants, to compute by the basis on which the Confederate generals always estimated their strength. — EDITORS.

↓ Exclusive of the loss of the 28th North Carolina, of Lane's command, which as far as reported was 7 killed and 15 wounded. — EDITORS.

MAJOR-GENERAL BENJAMIN HUGER, C. S. A.
FROM A PHOTOGRAPH.

of the Nine-mile road with the New Bridge road, where Magruder was with four brigades.

Longstreet, as ranking officer of the troops on the Williamsburg road, was instructed verbally to form D. H. Hill's division as first line, and his own as second, across the road at right angles, and to advance in that order to attack the enemy; while Huger's division should march by the right flank along the Charles City road, to fall upon the enemy's flank when our troops were engaged with him in front. Federal earth-works and abatis that might be found were to be turned. G. W. Smith was to protect the troops under Longstreet from attack by those of the Federal right wing across the Chickahominy; and, if such transfer should not be threatened, he was to fall upon the enemy on the Williamsburg road. Those troops were formed in four lines, each being a division. Casey's was a mile west of Seven Pines, with a line of skirmishers a half mile in advance; Couch's was at Seven Pines and Fair Oaks — the two forming Keyes's corps. Kearny's division was near Savage's Station, and Hooker's two miles west of Bottom's Bridge — the two forming Heintzelman's corps.

Longstreet's command of the right was to end when the troops approached Seven Pines and I should be present to direct the movements, after which each major-general would command his own division. The rain began to fall violently in the afternoon of the 30th, and continued all night. In the morning the little streams near our camps were so much swollen as to make it probable that the Chickahominy was overflowing its banks and cutting the communication between the wings of the Federal army. Being confident that Longstreet and D. H. Hill, with their forces united, would be successful in the earlier part of the action against adversaries formed in several lines, with wide intervals between them, I left the immediate control on the Williamsburg road to them, under general instructions, and placed myself on the left, where I could soonest learn of the approach of Federal reënforcements from their right. For this scouts were sent forward to discover all movements that might be made by the enemy.]

The condition of the ground and little streams delayed the troops in marching; yet those of Smith, Longstreet, and Hill were in position quite early enough. But the soldiers from Norfolk, who had seen garrison service only,

---

] The map of Seven Pines, printed with this paper in "The Century Magazine" for May, 1885, was prepared by the editors, and has been canceled because of incorrectness as to the positions of the opposing forces on the night of May 31st, as well as on the morning of June 1st.— EDITORS.

were unnecessarily stopped in their march by a swollen rivulet. This unexpected delay led to interchange of messages for several hours between General Longstreet and myself, I urging Longstreet to begin the fight, he replying. But, near 2 o'clock, that officer was requested to go forward to the attack; the hands of my watch marked 3 o'clock at the report of the first field-piece.\ The Federal advanced line — a long line of skirmishers, supported by several regiments — was encountered at 3 o'clock. The greatly superior numbers of the Confederates soon drove them back to the main position of Casey's division. It occupied a line of rifle-pits, strengthened by a redoubt and abatis. Here the resistance was very obstinate; for the Federals, commanded by an officer of skill and tried courage, fought as soldiers generally do under good leaders; and time and vigorous efforts of superior numbers were required to drive them from their ground. But the resolution of Garland's and G. B. Anderson's brigades, that pressed forward on our left through an open field, under a destructive fire, the admirable service of Carter's and Bondurant's batteries, and a skillfully combined attack upon the Federal left, under General Hill's direction, by Rodes's brigade in front and that of Rains in flank, were at last successful, and the enemy abandoned their intrenchments. Just then reënforcements from Couch's division came up, and an effort was made to recover the position. But it was to no purpose; for two regiments of R. H. Anderson's brigade reënforced Hill's troops, and the Federals were driven back to Seven Pines.

Keyes's corps (Casey's and Couch's divisions) was united at Seven Pines and reënforced by Kearny's division, coming from Savage's Station. But the three divisions were so vigorously attacked by Hill that they were broken and driven from their intrenchments, the greater part along the Williamsburg road to the intrenched line west of Savage's Station. Two brigades of their left, however, fled to White Oak Swamp.

General Hill pursued the enemy a mile; then, night being near, he re-formed his troops, facing toward the Federals. Longstreet's and Huger's divisions, coming up, were formed between Hill's line and Fair Oaks.

For some cause the disposition on the Charles City road was modified. Two of General Huger's brigades were ordered to advance along that road, with three of Longstreet's under Brigadier-General Wilcox. After following that road some miles, General Wilcox received orders to conduct his troops to the Williamsburg road. On entering it, he was ordered to the front, and two of his regiments joined Hill's troops near and approaching Seven Pines.

When the action just described began, the musketry was not heard at my position on the Nine-mile road, from the unfavorable condition of the air; and I supposed for some time that we were hearing only an artillery duel. But a staff-officer was sent to ascertain the facts. He returned at 4 o'clock with intelligence that our infantry as well as artillery had been engaged an hour, and all were pressing on vigorously. As no approach of troops from beyond the Chickahominy had been discovered, I hoped that the enemy's

---

\ General D. H. Hill, who directed the onset, says in his report: "At 1 o'clock the signal guns were fired, and my division moved off in fine style." In their reports, the Union commanders name 12:30 and 1 o'clock as the time of the Confederate attack.— EDITORS.

bridges were impassible, and therefore desired General Smith to move toward Seven Pines, to be ready to coöperate with our right. He moved promptly along the Nine-mile road, and his leading regiment soon became engaged with the Federal skirmishers and their reserves, and in a few minutes drove them off.

On my way to Longstreet's left, to combine the action of the two bodies of troops, I passed the head of General Smith's column near Fair Oaks, and saw the camps of about a brigade in the angle between the Nine-mile road and the York River Railroad, and the rear of a column of infantry moving in quick time from that point toward the Chickahominy by the road to the Grapevine ford. A few minutes after this, a battery near the point where this infantry had disappeared commenced firing upon the head of the Confederate column. A regiment sent against it was received with a volley of musketry, as well as canister, and recoiled. The leading brigade, commanded by Colonel Law, then advanced, and so much strength was developed by the enemy that General Smith brought his other brigades into action on the left of Law's. An obstinate contest began, and was maintained on equal terms, although we engaged superior numbers on ground of their own choosing.

LIEUTENANT-GENERAL DANIEL H. HILL, C. S. A. FROM A PHOTOGRAPH.

I had passed the railroad a few hundred yards with Hood's brigade when the firing commenced, and stopped to see it terminated. But being confident that the enemy opposing us were those whose camp I had just seen, and therefore only a brigade, I did not doubt that General Smith was more than strong enough to cope with them. Therefore, General Hood was directed to go on in such a direction as to connect his right with Longstreet's left and take his antagonists in flank. The direction of that firing was then nearly south-west from Fair Oaks. It was then about 5 o'clock.

In that position my intercourse with Longstreet was maintained through staff-officers, who were assisted by General Stuart of the cavalry, which was then unemployed; their reports were all of steady progress.

At Fair Oaks, however, no advantage was gained on either side, and the contest was continued with unflagging courage. It was near half-past 6 o'clock before I admitted to myself that Smith was engaged, not with a brigade, as I had obstinately thought, but with more than a division; but I thought that it would be injudicious to engage Magruder's division, our only reserve, so late in the day.

The firing was then violent at Seven Pines, and within a half hour the three Federal divisions were broken and driven from their position in confusion. It was then evident, however, from the obstinacy of our adversaries at Fair Oaks, that the battle would not be decided that day. I said so to the staff-officers near me, and told them that each regiment must sleep where it might be standing when the firing ceased for the night, to be ready to renew it at dawn next morning.

About half-past 7 o'clock I received a musket-shot in the shoulder, and was unhorsed soon after by a heavy fragment of shell which struck my breast. I was borne from the field — first to a house on the roadside, thence to Richmond. The firing ceased before I had been carried a mile from it. The conflict at Fair Oaks was terminated by darkness only.

Mr. Davis's account of what he saw and did at Fair Oaks (II., 123) indicates singular ignorance of the topography of the vicinity, as well as of what was occurring. He says that the enemy's line was on the bank of the river. It was at right angles to and some three miles from it. He says that soon after his arrival I was brought from the right wounded. This proves that his "arrival" was near sunset. He also describes the moving of reënforcements from the left to the right. This was not being done. The right was abundantly strong. He says that he made a reconnoissance — then sent three couriers one after the other, with an order to Magruder "to send a force" by the wooded path under the bluff, to attack the enemy in flank and reverse. If the first courier had been dispatched before the reconnoissance, and delivered the order to Magruder promptly, his "force," marching little more than a mile by the straight Nine-mile road, could scarcely have come up before dark. The route described would have been (if found) five or six miles long.

The only thing he ought to have done, or had time to do, was postponed almost twenty hours — the putting General Lee, who was near, in command of the army.

The operations of the Confederate troops in this battle were very much retarded by the broad ponds of rain-water, — in many places more than knee-deep, — by the deep mud, and by the dense woods and thickets that covered the ground.

Brigadier-General Hatton was among the killed, and Brigadier-Generals Pettigrew and Hampton were severely wounded. The latter kept his saddle, and served to the end of the action. Among the killed on the Williamsburg road were Colonels Moore, of Alabama, Jones, and Lomax. In the two days' battle, the Confederate loss, so far as the reports indicate, was 6134 (including the loss in G. W. Smith's division, which was 1283); and the Federal loss, according to the revised returns, was 5031.

Prisoners to the number of 350, 10 pieces of artillery, 6700 muskets and rifles in excellent condition, a garrison flag and 4 regimental colors, medical, commissary, quartermaster and ordnance stores, tents and sutler's property, were captured and secured.

The troops on the ground at nightfall were: on the Confederate side, 22 brigades, more than half of which had not been in action; and on the Federal side 6 divisions in 3 corps, two-thirds of which had fought, and half of which

BURYING THE DEAD, AND BURNING HORSES, AT THE TWIN HOUSES NEAR CASEY'S REDOUBT, AFTER THE SECOND DAY'S FIGHT. FROM A SKETCH MADE AT THE TIME.

had been totally defeated. Two Federal divisions were at Fair Oaks, and three and a half at Savage's, three miles off, and half a one two miles nearer Bottom's Bridge. The Southern troops were united, and in a position to overwhelm either fraction of the Northern army, while holding the other in check.

Officers of the Federal army have claimed a victory at Seven Pines. The Confederates had such evidences of victory as cannon, captured intrenchments, and not only sleeping on the field, but passing the following day there, so little disturbed by the Federal troops as to gather, in woods, thickets, mud, and water, 6700 muskets and rifles. ☆ Besides, the Federal army had been advancing steadily until the day of this battle; after it they made not another step forward, but employed themselves industriously in intrenching.

MAJOR-GENERAL GUSTAVUS W. SMITH, C. S. A. FROM A PHOTOGRAPH.

In a publication of mine ["Johnston's Narrative"] made in 1874, I attempted to show that General Lee did not attack the enemy until June 26th, because he was engaged from June 1st until then in forming a great army, bringing to that which I had commanded 15,000 men from North Carolina under General Holmes, 22,000 from South Carolina and Georgia, and above 16,000 in the divisions of Jackson and Ewell. My authority for the 15,000 was General Holmes's statement, May 31st, that he had that number waiting the President's order to join me. When their arrival was announced, I supposed the number was as stated.

General Ripley, their best-informed and senior officer, was my authority for the 22,000 from South Carolina and Georgia. I thought, as a matter of course, that all of these troops had been brought up for the great crisis. Mr. Davis is eager to prove that but 2 of the 4 bodies of them came to Richmond in time. One who, like me, had opportunity to observe that Mr. Davis was almost invariably too late in reënforcing threatened from unthreatened points, has no apology for the assumption that this was an exception. General Ripley reported officially that he brought 5000 from Charleston, and explained in writing that, arriving before them, he was assigned to the command of

---

☆ The Union position at Fair Oaks was, in general, maintained on both days of the battle. Part of the field east of Seven Pines (but not Casey's camp, which was west) was regained on the second day by General Heintzelman, who reported that "our troops pushed as far forward as the battle-field of the previous day, where they found many of our wounded and those of the enemy." General Daniel E. Sickles, who advanced to Casey's camp on June 2d, the Confederates having withdrawn in the night, states in his report that "the fields were strewn with Enfield rifles, marked 'Tower, 1862,' and muskets, marked 'Virginia,' thrown away by the enemy in his hurried retreat. In the camp occupied by General Casey and General Couch on Saturday before the battle of Seven Pines, we found rebel caissons filled with ammunition, a large number of small-arms and several baggage wagons."— EDITORS.

the brigade of 2366, his 5000 being distributed as they arrived in detachments. General Lawton stated in writing that he brought about 6000 men from Georgia to the Valley; but as they had never marched before, they were incapable of moving at Jackson's rate, and he estimated that 2500 had been unable to keep their places when they arrived at Gaines's Mill, where, as he states, he had 3500. But the laggards rejoined him in two or three days.

I estimated Jackson's and Ewell's forces at 16,000, because Ewell told me that his was 8000, and Jackson's had been usually about twenty-five per cent. larger. Mr. Davis puts the joint force at 8000. His authority has stated it also at 12,000 (see "Personal Reminiscences of General Lee," p. 6), and this is far below the fact. My object in this is to show that I consulted respectable authorities. Mr. Davis proves that his forces were not well employed.

## OPPOSING FORCES AT SEVEN PINES, MAY 31–JUNE 1, 1862.

The composition, losses, and strength of each army as here stated give the gist of all the data obtainable in the Official Records. K stands for killed; w for wounded; m w for mortally wounded; m for captured or missing; c for captured.

### THE UNION ARMY.
Major-General George B. McClellan.

SECOND ARMY CORPS, Brig.-Gen. Edwin V. Sumner.
FIRST DIVISION, Brig.-Gen. Israel B. Richardson.
*First Brigade*, Brig.-Gen. Oliver O. Howard (w), Col. Thomas J. Parker: 5th N. H., Col. E. E. Cross (w), Lieut.-Col. Samuel G. Langley; 61st N. Y., Col. Francis C. Barlow; 64th N. Y., Col. T. J. Parker, Capt. Rufus Washburn; 81st Pa., Col. James Miller (k), Lieut.-Col. Charles F. Johnson. Brigade loss: k, 95; w, 398; m, 64 = 557. *Second Brigade*, Brig.-Gen. Thomas F. Meagher: 63d N. Y., Col. John Burke; 69th N. Y., Col. Robert Nugent; 88th N. Y., Lieut.-Col. Patrick Kelly. Brigade loss: k, 7; w, 31; m, 1 = 39. *Third Brigade*, Brig.-Gen. William H. French: 52d N. Y., Col. Paul Frank; 57th N. Y., Col. Samuel K. Zook; 66th N. Y., Col. Joseph C. Pinckney; 53d Pa., Col. John R. Brooke. Brigade loss: k, 32; w, 188; m, 22 = 242. *Artillery*, Capt. G. W. Hazzard: B, 1st N. Y., Capt. Rufus D. Pettit; G, 1st N. Y., Capt. John D. Frank; A and C, 4th U. S., Capt. G. W. Hazzard.
SECOND DIVISION, Brig.-Gen. John Sedgwick.
*First Brigade*, Brig.-Gen. Willis A. Gorman: 15th Mass., Lieut.-Col. John W. Kimball; 1st Minn., Col. Alfred Sully; 34th N. Y., Col. James A. Suiter; 82d N. Y., (2d Militia), Lieut.-Col. Henry W. Hudson; 1st Co. Mass. Sharp-shooters, Capt. John Saunders; 2d Co. Minn. Sharp-shooters, Capt. William F. Russell. Brigade loss: k, 40; w, 153; m, 3 = 106. *Second Brigade*, Brig.-Gen. William W. Burns: 69th Pa., Col. Joshua T. Owen; 71st Pa., Maj. Charles W. Smith; 72d Pa., Col. De Witt C. Baxter; 106th Pa., Col. Turner G. Morehead. Brigade loss: k, 5; w, 30 = 35. *Third Brigade*, Brig.-Gen. N. J. T. Dana: 19th Mass., Col. Edward W. Hinks; 20th Mass., Col. W. Raymond Lee; 7th Mich., Col. Ira R. Grosvenor, Maj. John H. Richardson; 42d N. Y., Col. E. C. Charles. Brigade loss: k, 16; w, 95 = 111. *Artillery*, Col. Charles H. Tompkins: A, 1st R. I., Capt. John A. Tompkins; B, 1st R. I., Capt. Walter O. Bartlett; G, 1st R. I., Capt. Charles D. Owen; I, 1st U. S., Lieut. Edmund Kirby. Artillery loss: k, 1; w, 4 = 5. *Cavalry:* K, 6th N. Y., Capt. Riley Johnson.
THIRD ARMY CORPS, Brig.-Gen. S. P. Heintzelman (commanded the Third and Fourth Corps, combined).
SECOND DIVISION, Brig.-Gen. Jos. Hooker. Staff loss: w, 1.
*Second Brigade*, Brig.-Gen. Daniel E. Sickles: 70th N. Y. (1st Excelsior), Maj. Thomas Holt; 71st N. Y. (2d Excelsior), Col. George B. Hall; 72d N. Y. (3d Excelsior), Col. Nelson Taylor; 73d N. Y. (4th Excelsior), Maj. John D. Moriarty, Capt. Charles B. Elliott; 74th N. Y. (5th Excelsior), Col. Charles K. Graham. Brigade loss: k, 7; w, 61; m, 6 = 74. *Third Brigade*, Brig.-Gen. Francis E. Patterson, Col. Samuel H. Starr: 5th N. J., Col.

Samuel H. Starr; Maj. John Ramsey; 6th N. J., Col. Gershom Mott. Brigade loss: k, 9; w, 67; m, 3 = 79. *Artillery*, Maj. Charles S. Wainwright: D, 1st N. Y., Capt. Thos. W. Osborn; 6th N. Y., Capt. Walter M. Bramhall.
THIRD DIVISION, Brig.-Gen. Phil. Kearny. Staff loss: w, 1.
*First Brigade*, Brig.-Gen. Charles D. Jameson: 87th N. Y., Col. Stephen A. Dodge (w), Lieut.-Col. Richard A. Bachia; 57th Pa., Col. Charles T. Campbell (w), Lieut.-Col. E. W. Woods; 63d Pa., Col. Alexander Hays; 105th Pa., Col. Amor A. McKnight (w). Brigade loss: k, 86; w, 297; m, 36 = 419. *Second Brigade*, Brig.-Gen. David B. Birney, Col. J. H. Ward: 3d Me., Col. Henry G. Staples; 4th Me., Col. Elijah Walker; 38th N. Y., Col. J. H. H. Ward, Maj. William H. Baird; 40th N. Y., Lieut.-Col. Thomas W. Egan. Brigade loss: k, 23; w, 174; m, 10 = 207. *Third Brigade*, Brig.-Gen. Hiram G. Berry: 2d Mich., Col. Orlando M. Poe; 3d Mich., Col. S. G. Champlin (w), Lieut.-Col. A. A. Stevens; 5th Mich., Col. Henry D. Terry; 37th N. Y., Lieut.-Col. Gilbert Riordan (temporarily), Col. Samuel B. Hayman. Brigade loss: k, 84; w, 344; m, 36 = 464.
FOURTH ARMY CORPS, Brig.-Gen. E. D. Keyes.
*Cavalry*, 8th Pa., Col. D. McM. Gregg. Loss: w, 2; m, 2 = 4.
FIRST DIVISION, Brig.-Gen. D. N. Couch. Staff loss: w, 1.
*First Brigade*, Brig.-Gen. John J. Peck: 55th N. Y., Lieut.-Col. Louis Thourot; 62d N. Y., Col. J. Lafayette Riker (k), Lieut.-Col. David J. Nevin; 93d N. Y., Col. J. M. McCarter (w), Capt. John E. Arthur; 102d Pa., Col. Thomas A. Rowley (w), Lieut.-Col. J. M. Kinkead. Brigade loss: k, 47; w, 236; m, 64 = 347. *Second Brigade*, Brig.-Gen. John J. Abercrombie: 65th N. Y. (1st U. S. Chasseurs), Col. John Cochrane; 67th N. Y. (1st Long Island), Col. Julius W. Adams; 23d Pa., Col. Thomas H. Neill; 31st Pa., Col. David H. Williams; 61st Pa., Col. Oliver H. Rippey (k), Capt. Robert L. Orr. Brigade loss: k, 124; w, 433; m, 67 = 624.
*Third Brigade*, Brig.-Gen. Charles Devens, Jr. (w), Col. Charles H. Innes: 7th Mass., Col. David A. Russell; 10th Mass., Col. Henry S. Briggs (w), Capt. Ozro Miller; 36th N. Y., Col. Charles H. Innes, Lieut.-Col. D. E. Hungerford. Brigade loss: k, 34; w, 136; m, 8 = 178. *Artillery*, Maj. Robert M. West: C, 1st Pa., Capt. Jeremiah McCarthy; D, 1st Pa., Capt. Edward H. Flood; E, 1st Pa., Capt. Theodore Miller; H, 1st Pa., Capt. James Brady. Artillery loss: k, 2; w, 12 = 14.
SECOND DIVISION, Brig.-Gen. Silas Casey.
*Provost Guard:* w, 1; m, 2 = 3.
*First Brigade*, Brig.-Gen. Henry M. Naglee: 11th Me., Col. Harris M. Plaisted; 56th N. Y., Lieut.-Col. James

## OPPOSING FORCES AT SEVEN PINES. 219

Jourdan; 100th N. Y., Col. James M. Brown (k); 52d Pa., Col. John C. Dodge, Jr.; 104th Pa., Col. W. W. H. Davis (w), Capt. Edward L. Rogers. Brigade loss: k, 89; w, 383; m, 167 = 639. *Second Brigade*, Brig.-Gen. Henry W. Wessells: 96th N. Y., Col. James Fairman; 85th Pa., Col. Joshua B. Howell; 101st Pa., Lieut.-Col. David B. Morris (w), Capt. Charles W. May; 103d Pa., Maj. A. W. Gazzam. Brigade loss: k, 35; w, 264; m, 59 = 358. *Third Brigade*, Brig.-Gen. Innis N. Palmer: 81st N. Y., Lieut.-Col. Jacob J. De Forest (w), Capt. W. C. Raulston; 85th N. Y., Col. J. S. Belknap; 92d N. Y., Col. Lewis C. Hunt (w), Lieut.-Col. Hiram Anderson, Jr.; 98th N. Y., Lieut.-Col. Charles Durkee. Brigade loss: k, 46; w, 251; m, 95 = 392.* *Artillery*, Col. Guilford D. Bailey (k), Maj. D. H. Van Valkenburgh (k), Capt. Peter C. Regan: A, 1st N. Y., Lieut. George P. Hart; H, 1st N. Y., Capt. Joseph Spratt (w), Lieut. Charles E. Mink; 7th N. Y., Capt. Peter C. Regan; 8th N. Y., Capt. Butler Fitch. Artillery loss: k, 7; w, 28; m. 2 = 37. *Unattached*: E, 1st U. S. Artillery, Lieut. Alanson M. Randol. Loss : k, 1; w, 3 = 4.

— The total Union loss (Revised Official Returns) was 790 killed, 3594 wounded, and 647 captured or missing = 5031.

### THE CONFEDERATE ARMY.

General Joseph E. Johnston (w); Major-General Gustavus W. Smith; General Robert E. Lee.

RIGHT WING, Major-General James Longstreet.
LONGSTREET'S DIVISION, Brig.-Gen. Richard H. Anderson (temporarily).
*Kemper's Brigade*, Col. James L. Kemper: 1st Va.; 7th Va.; 11th Va.; 17th Va., Col. M. D. Corse. *Anderson's (R. H.) Brigade*, Col. Micah Jenkins: 5th S. C., Col. J. R. R. Giles (k), Lieut.-Col. A. Jackson; 6th S. C., Col. John Bratton (w and c), Lieut.-Col. J. M. Steedman; Palmetto (S. C.) Sharp-shooters, Maj. William Anderson; Va. Battery, Capt. Robert M. Stribling. *Pickett's Brigade*, Brig.-Gen. George E. Pickett: 8th Va., Lieut.-Col. N. Berkeley; 18th Va., Col. R. E. Withers; 19th Va., Col. John B. Strange; 28th Va., Col. William Watts; Va. Battery, Capt. James Dearing. Brigade loss: k and w, 350. *Wilcox's Brigade*, Brig.-Gen. Cadmus M. Wilcox: 9th Ala., Lieut.-Col. Stephen F. Hale; 10th Ala., Maj. J. J. Woodward; 11th Ala., Col. Sydenham Moore (m w); 19th Miss., Maj. John Mullins. Brigade loss: k and w, 101. *Colston's Brigade*, Brig.-Gen. R. E. Colston: 13th N. C.; 14th N. C.; 3d Va. *Pryor's Brigade*, Brig.-Gen. Roger A. Pryor: 8th Ala.; 14th Ala.; 14th La.
HILL'S DIVISION, Maj.-Gen. Daniel H. Hill.
*Garland's Brigade*, Brig.-Gen. Samuel Garland, Jr.: 2d Fla., Col. E. A. Perry; 2d Miss. Battalion, Lieut.-Col. John G. Taylor; 5th N. C., Col. D. K. McRae, Maj. P. J. Sinclair; 23d N. C., Col. Daniel H. Christie, Lieut.-Col. R. D. Johnston (w); 24th Va., Maj. Richard L. Maury (w); 38th Va., Col. E. C. Edmonds; Ala. Battery, Capt. J. W. Bondurant. Brigade loss: k, 98; w, 600; m, 42 = 740. *Rodes's Brigade*, Brig.-Gen. R. E. Rodes (w), Col. John B. Gordon: 5th Ala., Col. C. Pegues; 6th Ala., Col. John B. Gordon; 12th Ala., Col. R. T. Jones (k), Lieut.-Col. B. B. Gayle; 12th Miss., Col. W. H. Taylor; 4th Va. Battalion, Capt. C. C. Otey (k), Capt. John R. Bagby; Va. Battery, Capt. Thomas H. Carter. Brigade loss: k, 241; w, 853; m, 5 = 1099. *Rains's Brigade*, Brig.-Gen. Gabriel J. Rains: 13th Ala., Col. D. B. Fry (w); 26th Ala., Col. E. A. O'Neal (w); 6th Ga.; 23d Ga. *Featherston's Brigade*, Col. George B. Anderson: 27th Ga., Col. Levi B. Smith (w), Lieut.-Col. Charles T. Zachry; 28th Ga.,

Capt. John N. Wilcox; 4th N. C., Maj. Bryan Grimes; 49th Va., Col. William Smith (w). Brigade loss: k, 149; w, 680; m. 37 = 866.
HUGER'S DIVISION, Brig. Gen. Benjamin Huger.
*Armistead's Brigade*, Brig.-Gen. Lewis A. Armistead: 5th Va. Battalion; 9th Va., Col. D. J. Godwin (w); 14th Va.; 53d Va., Col. H. B. Tomlin. *Mahone's Brigade*, Brig.-Gen. William Mahone: 3d Ala., Col. Tennent Lomax (k); 12th Va.; 41st Va. *Blanchard's Brigade*, Brig.-Gen. A. G. Blanchard: 3d Ga.; 4th Ga.; 22d Ga.; 1st La, ARTILLERY (not previously mentioned): La. Battery, Capt. Victor Maurin; Va. Battery, Capt. David Watson. Total loss of the Right Wing, as reported by Gen. Longstreet: 816 killed, 3739 wounded, and 296 missing = 4851.
LEFT WING, Major-General Gustavus W. Smith.
*Couriers*: Capt. R. W. Carter's Co. 1st Va. Cav.
SMITH'S DIVISION, Brig.-Gen. W. H. C. Whiting (temporarily).
*Whiting's Brigade*, Col. E. McIver Law: 4th Ala.; 2d Miss.; 11th Miss.; 6th N. C. Brigade loss: k, 28; w, 286; m, 42 = 346. *Hood's Brigade*, Brig.-Gen. John B. Hood: 18th Ga., Col. W. T. Wofford, or Lieut.-Col. S. Z. Ruff; 1st Tex., Col. A. T. Rainey; 4th Tex., Col. John Marshall; 5th Tex., Col. James J. Archer. Brigade loss: w, 13. *Hampton's Brigade*, Brig.-Gen. Wade Hampton, (w): 14th Ga.; 19th Ga.; 16th N. C.; Hampton (S. C.) Legion, Lieut.-Col. M. W. Gary. Brigade loss: k, 45; w, 284 = 329. *Hatton's Brigade*, Brig.-Gen. Robert Hatton (k): 1st Tenn.; 7th Tenn.; 14th Tenn. Brigade loss: k, 44; w, 187; m, 13 = 244. *Pettigrew's Brigade*, Brig.-Gen. J. J. Pettigrew (w and c): Arkansas Battalion; 35th Ga.; 22d N. C.; 47th Va. Brigade loss: k, 47; w, 240; m, 54 = 341.
The "Official Records" indicate that Semmes's and Griffith's brigades were in position for action, but were not actually engaged. The total loss of the Left Wing, as reported by General Smith, was 164 killed, 1010 wounded, and 109 missing = 1283. The aggregate Confederate loss on May 31st and June 1st was 980 killed, 4749 wounded, and 405 missing = 6134.

### RELATIVE STRENGTH OF THE OPPOSING FORCES.

The following synopsis, from the "Records" and other data, is by General Gustavus W. Smith:

The Union Army numbered 98,008, of which about 5000 were on detached service: "Present for duty," Sumner's Corps, 17,412; Heintzelman's Corps, 10,999; Keyes's Corps, 17,132; Porter's Corps, 17,546; Franklin's Corps, 19,580; Engineers, Cavalry and Provost Guard, 4767. Each corps was composed of two divisions of nearly equal strength.
The aggregate present for duty in the three Union Corps that were engaged was 51,543. The number " in close action " on the Williamsburg road, May 31st, was about 11,853, with full complement of artillery; these included 4253 in Casey's division, about 4000 in Couch's division, and about 3600 in Kearny's division. Near Fair Oaks, there were engaged about 9000, with 10 pieces of artillery: these included Sedgwick's division, about 7000, and 4 regiments of Couch's division, about 2000.
The Union troops engaged, June 1st, numbered about 14,000: Richardson's division, about 7000, with 4 batteries; 1 brigade of Kearny's division, about 1500; and 1 brigade and 2 regiments of Hooker's division, about 3500; there was no artillery with Kearny and Hooker.
General Johnston estimates the strength of his army at 73,928. Other authorities place it at 62,696. The "Official Records" show that, on the 21st of May, Johnston's army was 53,688: Smith's division, 10,592; Longstreet's division, 13,816; Magruder's division (including D. R. Jones's division), 15,920; D. H. Hill's division, 11,151; cavalry and reserve artillery, 2209. Before May 31st, this force was increased by the arrival of A. P. Hill's division (estimated), 4000, and Huger's division (estimated), 5008. One of the five brigades of D. H. Hill's division was detached before May 31st.
The aggregate of the 4 Confederate divisions engaged was about 39,000. The number " in close action " on the Williamsburg road, May 31st, was about 9520, with 2 batteries—including Pettigrew's 7580 in D. H. Hill's division, and 1950 of Longstreet's division. Near Fair Oaks, 4 brigades of G. W. Smith's division (under Whiting), 8670; no artillery.
The number of Confederates engaged, June 1, was about 8300: in Huger's division about 3300; in Longstreet's division, about 5000. No artillery was advanced into action.

# TWO DAYS OF BATTLE AT SEVEN PINES (FAIR OAKS).

### BY GUSTAVUS W. SMITH, MAJOR-GENERAL, C. S. A.

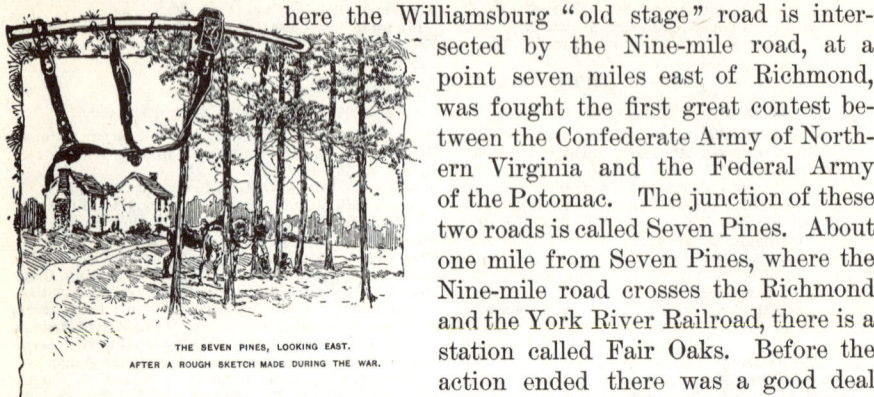

THE SEVEN PINES, LOOKING EAST.
AFTER A ROUGH SKETCH MADE DURING THE WAR.

Where the Williamsburg "old stage" road is intersected by the Nine-mile road, at a point seven miles east of Richmond, was fought the first great contest between the Confederate Army of Northern Virginia and the Federal Army of the Potomac. The junction of these two roads is called Seven Pines. About one mile from Seven Pines, where the Nine-mile road crosses the Richmond and the York River Railroad, there is a station called Fair Oaks. Before the action ended there was a good deal of fighting near the latter place. The Federals called the action of May 31st and June 1st the battle of Fair Oaks.

Before describing this contest, a sketch will be given of the movements of the two armies from the time the Confederates withdrew from Williamsburg. It is well, however, to say here that, in preparing an account of the battle, I have felt constrained to refer to some important matters in more detail than would have been considered essential, if there was not such direct conflict of "high authorities" in regard to them. For instance, nearly all the descriptions of this action heretofore published give as the intention of the Confederate commander that Longstreet's division was to move to the Williamsburg road and support D. H. Hill's division on that road. In "asserting" that this is an error, I have felt that, under the circumstances, it is incumbent on me to prove what I say on that subject.

It is broadly stated by many authorities that General Johnston intended Huger's division should attack the Federal left flank and rear, Huger's attack to be followed by D. H. Hill's division falling on the Federal front; and it is claimed by many that the slowness of Huger's division caused the failure of complete Confederate success the first day. In refutation of these statements and claims, I have felt constrained to give proofs, and not leave these questions to be decided by mere "assertion."

The position of the Confederate troops at dark, May 31st, has been erroneously stated by General Johnston, and in such particularity of detail as at the time to satisfy me that, in the main, he was correct. But the "Official Records," recently published, show beyond question that General Johnston is in error on this point. It has, therefore, been considered necessary in this article to give definite proof in regard to the position of the Confederate

---

In the Confederate attack, in the irregular and desperate fighting, and in the duration and changing success of this first great battle in the East, there are striking resemblances to (as well as wide divergences from) the two days' battle at Shiloh, the first great clash of arms in the West.— EDITORS.

forces when the command of the army devolved upon me, by reason of General Johnston's being wounded. His statement of the reasons for my not having ordered the attack to be renewed the next morning (June 1st) calls for specific proof that I did order the attack to be renewed, and for a detailed exhibit of General Longstreet's battle-field notes to me on that day.

Without specifying further, at this time, in regard to the "misunderstanding," misapprehension, and other causes that have led to erroneous published accounts of important events in this battle,— to some extent on the Federal, but more on the Confederate, side,— it may be added that the recent publication of the "Official Records," when carefully studied, throws a great deal of light upon these events, the accounts of which have heretofore been nearly as dark and confusing as were the dense, tangled wood and swamps in which most of the close and desperate fighting took place. The Federal accounts, as now officially published, are full; they embrace the reports of nearly every regimental, brigade, division, and corps commander engaged; but many of the Confederate reports are missing, those in D. H. Hill's division being the only ones that are complete in regard even to brigade commanders. There are, however, enough others, when taken in connection with the full Federal reports, to give quite a clear understanding of the main facts on both sides.

THE affair at Williamsburg, May 5th, was an incident in the withdrawal of the Confederate army from its fortified lines, near Yorktown, to the open country between the Pamunkey and the Chickahominy rivers, where General Johnston intended to halt, near the Richmond and York River Railroad, and contest the farther advance of General McClellan's army. From Williamsburg, Longstreet's and Hill's divisions, both under General Longstreet, moved on the Charles City road, which crosses the Chickahominy at Long Bridge; the division of G. W. Smith and Magruder's forces — commanded by him before Johnston's army arrived at the Yorktown lines — moved on the road that passes through Barhamsville and New Kent Court House and crosses the Chickahominy at Bottom's Bridge. All the Confederate troops on the latter road were under my command, and they were followed by the Federal army. Excepting occasional collisions between our rear-guard and the Federal advance-guard, nothing of special interest occurred after we left Barhamsville, near which place, below West Point, the Federals landed quite a large force, and seemed disposed to move out against us. General Johnston ordered nearly the whole of his army to Barhamsville, and came there in person. The next day, May 7th, the Federal skirmishers advanced, but their main force gave us no opportunity to cut them off from their gun-boats. At this point there was a good deal of sharp fighting for several hours.‡ From this time

‡ Reference is had here to the York River expedition, under General W. B. Franklin, which McClellan dispatched from Yorktown on the 5th with instructions to seize and hold a landing near West Point, situated at the confluence of the York and Pamunkey rivers, and the terminus of the Richmond and York River Railroad. This movement on West Point, if successful, would secure the so-called Urbana route of communications, the advantages of which are explained in McClellan's letter to the War Department of March 19th, 1862.

Franklin moved up the York River on the 6th, his troops in transports and under convoy of a the Confederates were more worried by the deep mud through which they were patiently trudging than they were by any movements of the Federals. In a letter to me from Palo Alto, on the Charles City road, dated Headquarters, Second Corps, May 8th, General Longstreet says:

"If your road can beat this for mud, I don't want to see it." "If you see the General [Johnston], say to him that we are as happy as larks over here, till we get 126 wagons [the total number] up to the hub at one time." "I don't fear McClellan or any one in Yankeedom."

When my command had passed the Baltimore Cross-roads, four and a half miles west of New Kent Court House, and had reached position about halfway between the Pamunkey and Chickahominy rivers, on good ground, they were halted. Longstreet's corps was again within easy supporting distance of mine, and General Johnston intended in that vicinity to contest the further advance of McClellan's army. We remained there about five days. The troops, having rested from the tiresome service in the trenches near Yorktown, and the fatiguing march, were now furnished with abundant supplies from Richmond, and were elated at the prospect of meeting the enemy on an open field of battle.

General Johnston then supposed that something effective had been done by the Government for the local defense of Richmond, during the month that had elapsed since his army moved from there to the peninsula. On the 14th of May he learned, through his chief engineer, that little or nothing — either in the way of fortifications or of troops — had been provided; and that the enemy, on the James River, were above City Point, and threatening Drewry's Bluff, as well as the obstruction in the Appomattox, four and a half miles below Petersburg. This report closed with the remark: "The danger is on the south side of James River."

On the same day General Johnston received intelligence of the destruction of the Confederate iron-clad *Virginia* — called by the Federals the *Merrimac*.

MAJOR-GENERAL SAMUEL P. HEINTZELMAN.
FROM A PHOTOGRAPH.

number of gun-boats, and made a landing the same day. General Franklin, in a letter on this subject, dated November 25th, 1881, says:

"My instructions were to await orders after landing, and not to advance. . . . We were attacked on the 7th, the object of the enemy being to drive us into the river. We had not made any attempt to advance, as such an attempt would have been in conflict with my orders."

General John Newton, commander of the Federal brigade most heavily engaged, states:

"The enemy was not only repelled in his attempt upon our position, but at the end of the day we occupied with our troops a position in advance of that held at the commencement of the action."

General Gustavus W. Smith, who commanded the Confederate troops engaged, says:

"On the morning of the 7th, after becoming satisfied that the enemy did not intend to advance in force from under the protection of their gun-boats, I directed General Whiting to drive their skirmishers from the dense woods, and endeavor to get position in the open ground between the woods and the river, from which he could reach their place of landing and their transports with his artillery fire."

In this action the Union losses were 48 killed, 110 wounded, 28 missing; total, 186. The Confederate losses were 8 killed and 40 wounded; total, 48.— EDITORS.

The next day news was received of the attack on Drewry's Bluff [see p. 271], and of the confusion and fright in Richmond. In this state of affairs, General Johnston decided that it was expedient to cross the Chickahominy and take position nearer the city, rather than continue to wait, north of that stream, for the advance of McClellan from the Pamunkey. Accordingly, orders were issued that night for Longstreet's "corps" to cross the Chickahominy at Long Bridge, and for my command to cross at Bottom's Bridge. A regiment of riflemen was sent direct to aid in the defense of Drewry's Bluff. On the 17th, Longstreet's division was about five miles from Richmond, in the direction of the James River defenses; D. H. Hill's division, on Longstreet's left, guarded the Charles City road, and was about three miles from Richmond; G. W. Smith's division was on the Williamsburg road, and north of it, two or three miles from the city, with one brigade in observation at Bottom's Bridge; whilst Magruder's troops extended from Old Tavern, on the Nine-mile road, to New Bridge, thence along the crest of the Chickahominy Bluffs to the Mechanicsville road.

McClellan's army approached the Chickahominy slowly. On the 23d Keyes's corps crossed at Bottom's Bridge; on the 25th he reached the position known later as the "third line of defense," at which point, as well as at Bottom's Bridge, strong earth-works were constructed; on the 27th the leading division of Keyes's corps occupied and commenced to fortify a position across the Williamsburg road at Seven Pines. In the meantime Heintzelman's corps had crossed at Bottom's Bridge; one division remained near that place, and the other division was posted at White Oak Bridge. Three corps of McClellan's army were still on the north side of the Chickahominy, their left near the railroad, their right, thrown back in a naturally strong position, on the left bank of Beaver Dam Creek, with an intrenched outpost at Mechanicsville. All the bridges and fords along the Chickahominy in their front were in possession of the Federals; and they were rapidly constructing new bridges.

In the meantime there had been no material change in the position of the Confederate forces. General Johnston was closely watching the movements of the Federals approaching on the Williamsburg road; but, in his opinion, the proper time to strike McClellan's left wing had not come. On the morning of the 27th our pickets were closely pressed just east of Old Tavern. This was some indication that the enemy were probably coming nearer in large force, and would soon be within our effective reach, on the Williamsburg or Nine-mile road, or on both. Our attention was, however, almost immediately diverted to McClellan's right flank, on the opposite side of the Chickahominy.

At 1 P. M. that day I received a note from General Johnston, stating he had just been informed that McDowell was advancing from Fredericksburg in force. This put a new phase on Confederate affairs around Richmond. It was well understood by us that McDowell had an army of about 40,000 men; ‡ McClellan's forces were known to be about 100,000, and we could not afford to wait until McDowell reached him.

‡ About 35,000 effectives. McDowell asked for subsistence for 38,000 men, including, of course, the non-effectives.— EDITORS.

General Johnston determined to attack the Federal right before McDowell could come up. I was ordered to move my division to the vicinity of Meadow Bridge, bring up A. P. Hill's division from the vicinity of Ashland, and make preparations, as soon as possible, to attack at Mechanicsville and Beaver Dam Creek. Longstreet's division was ordered to take position north and east of Richmond, and D. H. Hill's division was ordered to the ground vacated by mine on the Williamsburg road. Magruder's troops were not moved; but, at my request, I was relieved from longer commanding General Magruder, and he was ordered to report, in future, direct to General Johnston. At the same time D. R. Jones's division, two brigades, of Magruder's proper command, posted on our extreme left, remained temporarily under my control, for service in the proposed attack. Brigadier-General Whiting was regularly assigned, temporarily, to the command of my division.

About sunset, May 28th, I reported to General Johnston that A. P. Hill's division would be close in front of Mechanicsville, on the north side of the Chickahominy, before midnight, with orders to attack that place at dawn on the 29th. As soon as A. P. Hill's attack commenced, my division and D. R. Jones's division would cross the Meadow and Mechanicsville bridges, and the three divisions, constituting the new left wing of Johnston's army under my command, would make a prompt and combined attack on the right of the Federals, strongly posted at Beaver Dam Creek. I was satisfied that the three divisions could carry the works at that place by open assault, but it would be a bloody business—called for, however, by the necessity for prompt action before McDowell could join McClellan. I did not know, in any detail, what General Johnston intended to do with the rest of his forces during the contest I was ordered to initiate, but I was perfectly satisfied that he would use the whole strength of his army against McClellan, and, if possible, defeat him before McDowell could arrive.

On receiving my report General Johnston stated that his latest information showed McDowell's army had returned to Fredericksburg; and it was believed he was moving north from that place. In this state of affairs, there was no longer any necessity for crossing the Chickahominy, attacking the three Federal corps on the north side of that stream, and moving against the very strong position at Beaver Dam Creek; while there were but two Federal corps on our side, gradually coming within striking distance where the natural features of the ground were not against us. General Johnston ordered the contemplated attack on the Federal right to be suspended, and directed me to withdraw A. P. Hill's division, bring it to the south side of the Chickahominy, and place it on our extreme left.

General Longstreet, who was present, then proposed that an attack be made early next morning, the 29th, in the direction of Seven Pines. General Johnston said that it was not quite certain that McDowell had moved north; the disposition made of our troops whilst it was supposed McDowell was coming was too strong on the left to admit of immediate and advantageous attack being made in the direction of Seven Pines; that Huger's division from Norfolk was expected to join us very soon; and that the enemy, east of us, had not yet approached near enough, in force worth crushing, to justify the engagement of the mass of our army in the swamps around Seven Pines, whilst the Federals were threatening the city on the north side. No orders were given to attack on the 29th, but it was distinctly understood that, in case McDowell did not promptly come on, General Johnston would revert to his former intention, and endeavor to strike a sudden and, if possible, crushing blow, in full force, against the Federals in the vicinity of Seven Pines, and destroy them before they could be reënforced either from the troops in their rear, now on our side of the Chickahominy, or by forces sent across from the opposite side. When I was assigned to the command of the left wing of the army, General Longstreet became the ranking officer on the right and was anxious to attack in that direction on the 29th. These matters are mentioned in General Johnston's letter of that date to General Whiting.

On the 30th my division, under Whiting, was drawn back to ground about midway between Meadow Bridge and Richmond; and A. P. Hill's division was brought nearer the bridges. The other commands were still in the positions to which they were assigned when it was first heard that McDowell was moving to join McClellan. In the meantime Huger's division had arrived and was encamped east of the city, north of the Williamsburg road, on Gilliss Creek.

MAJOR-GENERAL ERASMUS D. KEYES. FROM A PHOTOGRAPH.

About noon on the 30th General D. H. Hill reported to General Johnston that reconnoissances satisfied him that the enemy was not in force on the Charles City road, but was on the Williamsburg road and fortified about Seven Pines. General Johnston promptly determined to attack. His intention was that General Longstreet's division should move by the Nine-mile road, that of General D. H. Hill by the Williamsburg stage road, and General Huger's by the Charles City road. In his order for my division to move, a copy of which was sent by him direct to Whiting, General Johnston says:

"Please be ready to move by the Nine-mile road, coming as early as possible to the point at which the road to New Bridge turns off [at Old Tavern]. Should there be cause of haste, General McLaws, on your approach, will be ordered to leave his ground for you, that he may reënforce General Longstreet."

In written instructions, May 30th, to Huger, General Johnston says:

"I wish to concentrate the troops of your division on the Charles City road. . . . Be ready, if an action should be begun on your left, to fall upon the enemy's left flank."

On May 31st General Johnston wrote to General Huger:

"I fear that in my note of last evening, of which there is no copy, I was too positive on the subject of your attacking the enemy's left flank. . . . It will be necessary for your progress to the front to conform at first to that of General Hill. If you find no strong body in your front, it will be well to aid General Hill; but then a strong reserve should be retained to cover our right."

There seem to have been no written instructions given either to General Longstreet or to General D. H. Hill; but, in his official report, General Johnston says the divisions of G. W. Smith, Longstreet, D. H. Hill, and Huger were ordered to move at daybreak. At sunrise General Johnston confidently expected that Keyes's corps would be crushed, or routed, before 8 A. M. At that season daybreak was at about 4 A. M. Magruder's command and A. P. Hill's division were not moved.

In order to form a proper conception of Johnston's plan it will be well to glance at the position of the Federal forces on the morning of May 31st. One division of Keyes's corps was across the Williamsburg road, a little more than half a mile west of Seven Pines; the other division was across that road at Seven Pines. Both lines were strengthened by rifle-pits extending a short distance on each side of the road, with abatis or felled timber in front. In the first line there was a small, unfinished pentangular redoubt; and the abatis of the second line extended in a curve to the rear, across the Nine-mile road. The left of the position was protected by the almost impracticable White Oak Swamp. But the ground on the right offered no strong features for defense, and was not fortified. About one thousand yards in front of the first line of rifle-pits, and nearly at right angles to the Williamsburg road, a skirmish-line extended from the White Oak Swamp to the Chickahominy River. Two regiments were detached to support the skirmish-line,— one near the railroad, the other farther to the right, on the Nine-mile road; whilst two regiments and a battery were detached and posted near Fair Oaks Station, to guard the depot of supplies at that place, where there were no artificial defenses. Keyes's lines were provided with ample artillery. On the morning of the 31st the two divisions were in camp just in rear of their earth-works; whilst strong working parties were engaged upon the unfinished trenches and other artificial defenses.

The "third line of defense," across the Williamsburg road, two miles in rear of the first line, was unoccupied. Heintzelman's corps was five miles in rear of Seven Pines; and Sumner's corps was three or four miles from Keyes, with the Chickahominy between them. The two other Federal corps on the north side of that stream were still farther off. In this part of its course the Chickahominy, at ordinary stages of water, is a sluggish stream, from thirty to sixty feet in width, from three to four feet deep, with low, muddy banks. It is bordered by flat bottom-lands for some distance, to the foot of rather abrupt bluffs about one hundred feet high. In times of freshet it rises rapidly, extends over the bottom-lands in depth of two or three feet to the bluffs; and at this stage the stream becomes a very serious military obstacle.

The ground upon which Keyes's corps fought that day is level, or very slightly undulating, and most of it, except the small open spaces at the earth-

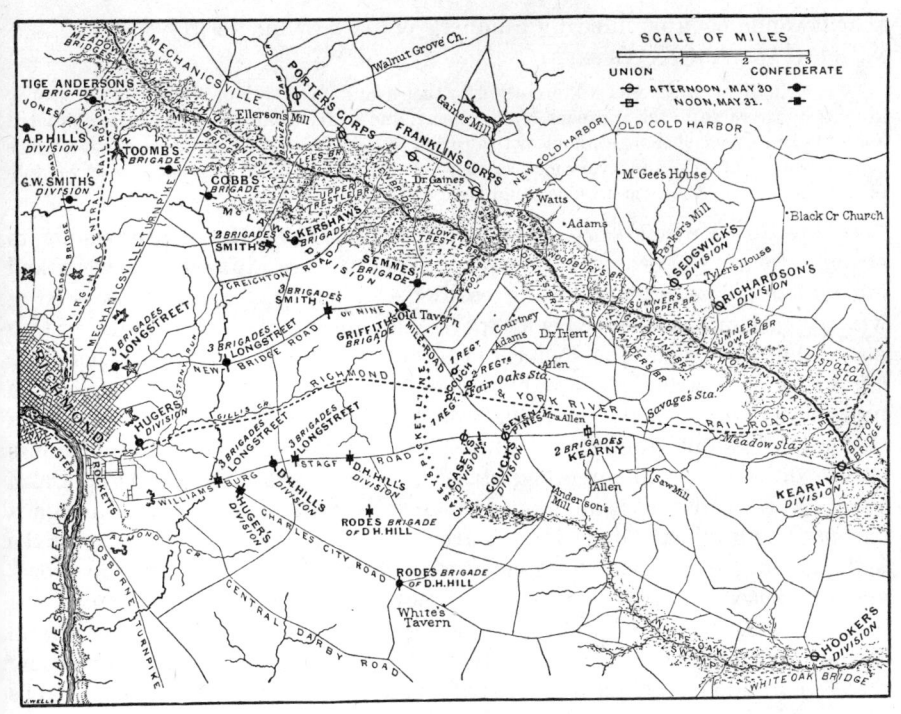

MAP SHOWING POSITIONS PRELIMINARY TO THE BATTLE OF SEVEN PINES.

works, was densely wooded and swampy. The soil in all that region, when wet, is very soft and spongy, making passage over it difficult even for infantry. In the dense woods the thick undergrowth is matted with tangled vines, and the luxuriant foliage, in the full bloom of spring, rendered it in many places impossible to distinguish objects ten paces distant. A violent rain-storm set in about 5 P. M. on the 30th, a few hours after General Johnston had determined to attack next morning. The heavy rain continued all night, and the face of the country was literally flooded. At daylight on the 31st the Chickahominy was booming, passable only at the bridges, and continued to rise during the day, although it had ceased to rain.

General Keyes gives a still closer view of his condition at that time. On the morning of the 31st he reported to General McClellan's chief-of-staff:

"Everything on the part of the Confederates indicates an attack on my position, which is only tolerably strong, and my forces are too weak to defend it properly. Brigadier-General Sumner told me yesterday he should probably cross the Chickahominy last night. If he did so, and takes post nigh Old Tavern and this side, I should feel more secure than I do now."

Sumner did not cross at the time referred to, and there is no other indication that he had orders or authority to do so. But General Keyes's report, made that morning, develops the fact that there was a dangerous gap between these two corps, and shows that there was a strong probability that it would soon be filled by Sumner's corps. In his "Fifty Years' Observations," General Keyes says:

"The left of my lines was all protected by the White Oak Swamp, but the right was on ground so favorable to the approach of the enemy, and so far from the Chickahominy, that if Johnston had attacked there an hour or two earlier than he did, I could have made but a feeble defense comparatively, and every man of us would have been killed, captured, or driven into the swamp or river before assistance could have reached us."

Isolated as Keyes's corps was, every effort should have been made to strongly fortify the ground it occupied. The defenses in front were weak and incomplete. The vulnerable and easily accessible right flank—the point at which attack ought to have been expected, because Confederate success at that place would have cut the Federal army in two, and would have exposed its left wing to destruction—ought to have been strongly fortified instead of being left entirely open. All this would have been practically illustrated if General Johnston's intentions had been carried into effect—that is, if Longstreet's division in full force had struck Keyes's right flank near Fair Oaks, when D. H. Hill's division moved against Keyes's front. But, through a "misunderstanding," General Longstreet transferred his own division to the Williamsburg road, instead of moving to the attack by the Nine-mile road, and he caused that division to take precedence of Huger's division at the crossing of Gilliss Creek, which at daylight was a raging torrent. General Huger, in a report, says: "Longstreet's division got the road at the crossing first"; and adds that his own troops "had to wait until they [Longstreet's division] had passed. The delay after that was the time necessary to cross." ☆

Captain B. Sloan, of Huger's staff, says in a letter dated August 17th, 1885:

"Longstreet's brigades as they successively reached the plain above the creek halted and remained for an hour or two resting on their arms. This plain (in front of General Huger's headquarters) was perhaps between three and four miles in rear of the battle-field. Here, at a farm-house, Huger met Longstreet and Hill, and a discussion was had as to the movements of the divisions, and as to the relative rank of the division commanders. Longstreet claimed (by instructions from General Johnston) to be in command of that portion of the army. After protest Huger acquiesced."

It was "then possibly 10 A. M. or 11 A. M." After that time "Huger's movements were directed by Longstreet."

Governor William E. Cameron, who was then adjutant of the 12th Virginia,

---

☆ On the 20th of September, 1862, General Huger wrote to General Johnston:

"I beg to refer you to my letter of the 20th ultimo. I have waited one month, and no reply has been received from General Longstreet. As you have indorsed his erroneous statements, to my injury, I must hold you responsible, and desire to know from you if you have any reason to believe an answer will be made by General Longstreet. You must perceive that by postponing an answer your published report is allowed to go down to history as true. I cannot conceive that you desire to perpetrate such an injustice, for, though it may ruin me, it cannot redound to your credit. . . . I send you herewith an abstract of such parts of your report as refer to my division, with my remarks annexed, to which I invite your attention."

In Huger's abstract of Johnston's report we find:

"Major-General Longstreet, unwilling to make a partial attack, . . . waited from hour to hour for General Huger's division. . . . Had Major-General Huger's division been in position and ready for action when those of Smith, Longstreet, and Hill moved, I am satisfied that Keyes's corps would have been destroyed instead of merely defeated. . . . Had it gone into action at 4 o'clock, the victory would have been much more complete."

In his remarks on these abstracts, Huger says:

"When General Longstreet's troops moved to support General Hill's attack, General Huger's division moved down the Charles City road at the same time with three brigades of Longstreet's division . . . to the last paragraph I have only to say that if it [Huger's division] did not go into action by 4 o'clock, it was because General Longstreet did not require it, as it was in position and awaiting his orders."  G. W. S.

of Mahone's brigade, Huger's division, says:

"Longstreet [three brigades] moved that morning from Fairfield racecourse, and arrived at the crossing of the [Gilliss] creek in front of the command. We waited till Longstreet cleared the way — crossed the creek about 10:30 A. M.— moved as far as the Tudor House — rested there until 1 P. M." [Mahone's brigade then moved out on the Charles City road]; "the men were fresh, eager, and in light marching-trim. The roads were bad, but there was no physical obstruction of any moment, and we met no enemy."

The following is from a letter by General R. E. Colston, commander of one of the three brigades of Longstreet's division that moved at 6:30 A. M., from a point three and a half miles out on the Nine-mile road:

"A little brook [Gilliss Creek] near Richmond was greatly swollen, and a long time was wasted crossing it on an improvised bridge made of planks, a wagon mid-stream serving as a trestle. Over this the division passed in single file, you may imagine with what delay. If the division commander had given orders for the men to sling their cartridge-boxes, haversacks, etc., on their muskets and wade without breaking formation, they could have crossed by fours at least, with water up to their waists, . . . and hours would have been saved. . . . When we got across we received orders to halt on the roadside until Huger's division passed us. There we waited for five or six hours."

MAJOR-GENERAL W. H. C. WHITING. FROM A PHOTOGRAPH.

These movements of Longstreet's division are in very marked contrast with General Johnston's intention that this division should start at daylight, move on the Nine-mile road, and attack the enemy on D. H. Hill's left, as early as possible that morning.

At 6:30 A. M. General D. H. Hill wrote to General Rodes: "I am ordered to attack the enemy this morning. . . . Have your men ready to start at a moment's notice." Rodes's brigade was in observation, three and a half miles out, on the Charles City road, and had to cross an almost impracticable swamp in order to reach the position on the Williamsburg road from which Hill's division was to advance to the attack. General Rodes says that the order to move reached him between 10 and 11 A. M., and adds:

"The progress of the brigade was considerably delayed by the washing away of a bridge near the head of White Oak Swamp. . . . At this point the character of the crossing was such that it was absolutely necessary to proceed with great caution, to prevent the loss of both ammunition and life."

When the signal for attack was given, only two regiments of Rodes's brigade had reached Hill's position on the Williamsburg road, about one thousand yards in front of the Federal picket-line. But the other regiments of this brigade came up soon after. At 1 o'clock the signal-guns were fired, and Hill's division at once moved forward.

The foregoing details in reference to the movements of these three divisions could not well be omitted, because General Johnston "asserts" that the divisions of Hill and Longstreet were in position early enough "to be ready to commence operations by 8 A. M.," and that General Longstreet "waited from hour to hour for General Huger's division." Having thus seen D. H. Hill's division start out alone at 1 P. M. to attack the Federals, it will be well to glance at the preparations made to receive him.

Whilst Hill's troops were coming into position, their movements had been reported to General Silas Casey, who commanded the Federal first line of defense. He at once ordered one regiment to go forward about eight hundred yards on the Williamsburg road, and support the picket-line; the working parties were called in, batteries harnessed up, and the troops formed, ready to take their assigned places. In a short time the Confederate signal-guns were heard, and the division was ordered into position to resist attack. The camps of these troops were immediately in rear of the earth-works. Palmer's brigade on the left, Wessells's in the center, and Naglee's on the right. Two regiments of Naglee's brigade were detached, supporting the picket-line, as already stated. About one-half of this division was placed in the rifle-pits on the right and left of the redoubt; the others were put in front, with orders to contest the advance of the Confederates against the first abatis, and Spratt's battery was placed four hundred yards in advance of the earth-works, on the north side of the road, closely supported by three regiments of Naglee's brigade and one of Palmer's.

In moving to attack, Rodes's brigade was on the south side of the road, supported by Rains; Garland's brigade, on the north side of the road, was supported by G. B. Anderson. All were in the dense and marshy woods, wading through water occasionally from two to three feet deep, the whole way obstructed by undergrowth, which often prevented commanders from seeing more than one company of their men at a time. General Hill had taken the precaution to order every man to wear in action a white strip of cloth around his hat as a battle-badge. Garland moved a few minutes before Rodes was ready. His skirmishers soon struck the Federal picket-line, and the shock of Garland's brigade fell upon the small regiment of raw troops that had been ordered into the woods to support the Federal pickets. That regiment fell back to the abatis just in time to prevent being enveloped and destroyed. And it was soon driven through the abatis in great disorder. It had lost about one-fourth its numbers in a few minutes, and was broken to pieces in crossing the abatis under close and deadly fire. This regiment could not again be rallied. General Keyes says that it "retreated, joined by a great many sick. The numbers, as they passed down the road as stragglers, conveyed an exaggerated idea of surprise and defeat."

The field-hospitals of the division were in the camps at the front; there was a large number of sick; some men of the working parties did not resume their arms and join their regiments; these, with the teamsters and army followers, suddenly finding themselves under the fire of a large Confederate force rapidly emerging from the dark woods, fled in wild disorder.

But Garland, who encountered Spratt's battery and its supports at the first abatis, says:

"We had now reached the edge of the wood where the abatis impeded our farther advance, and the troops were under heavy fire. . . . The regimental commanders, who had received my orders to move by the left flank, were unable to effect the movement in good order under the galling fire. The alternative was adopted — to push the regiments forward through the abatis."

General Garland soon found that his brigade unaided could not accomplish the work in hand. His losses were very heavy. But he adds: "G. B. Anderson's brigade arrived upon the field just at the proper time."

The latter officer, having put in three regiments to aid Garland, moved to the left with the 27th Georgia and endeavored to turn the right of the Federals. He encountered one of Naglee's detached regiments and drove it back; but the other detached regiment of Naglee's brigade came on the ground, and one regiment sent by General Keyes came up. G. B. Anderson then withdrew from the advanced position he had gained, but continued the fighting on the ground where it had been commenced on this part of the field.

In the meantime the contest around the battery at the abatis was close and desperate. Rodes's brigade was hotly engaged on the south side of the road, and General Hill had ordered Carter's battery to the front. The Federals stubbornly held their ground, and Hill now detached General Rains to make a wide flank movement through the woods to the right in order to turn the left of Casey's earth-works. From the edge of the wood, south of the Williamsburg road, Rains's brigade commenced firing on the flank and rear of the troops posted in Casey's rifle-pits. General Hill says:

"I now noticed commotion in the camps and redoubt and indications of evacuating the position. Rodes took skillful advantage of this commotion, and moved up his brigade in beautiful order and took possession of the redoubt and rifle-pits."

Pending this contest for Casey's earth-works, General Keyes had sent two regiments from the second line direct to Casey's assistance, and a short time before those works were carried he sent General Couch, with two regiments, to attack the Confederate left, and thus relieve the pressure on Casey's front. Before Couch could get into position Casey's line was carried, and General Keyes made immediate preparations for the defense of the line at Seven Pines, held by Couch's division. Peck's brigade was on the left, Devens in the center, and the regiments of Abercrombie's brigade, that had not been detached, were on the right. Casey's troops, in falling back from their earth-works, endeavored to make a stand at the abatis in front of Couch's line, and General Keyes sent forward one regiment of Devens's brigade to assist in checking the advance of the Confederates. Casey's men were driven through the abatis, and the regiment of Devens's brigade was hurled back in disorder, and could not be rallied until they had retreated beyond the earth-works from which they had advanced. A large proportion of the men of

Palmer's and Wessells's brigades having been thrown into great disorder whilst retiring through the second abatis, and finding the earth-works of the second line already crowded, continued to retreat; but some of them, with nearly the whole of Naglee's brigade, remained upon the field. The Confederates in the immediate front of Seven Pines were now pressing into the second abatis, and there seemed to be strong probability that they would soon break through it and carry the earth-works of Keyes's second line. Thus, after more than two hours' close and bloody fighting, Hill's division unaided had cap-

THE TWIN FARM-HOUSES BEHIND CASEY'S REDOUBT (SEEN INDISTINCTLY ON THE LEFT). FROM A PHOTOGRAPH.

The upper picture looks toward Richmond; the grove stands between the Williamsburg stage road and the houses which front squarely on the road, perhaps 300 feet away. Four hundred dead of the battle of Seven Pines were buried in the foreground (behind the houses), where also stood a part of Casey's camp.

The foreground of lower picture shows either a corner of Casey's redoubt or the works between it and the Williamsburg road.

On the Official Map of the Campaign of 1864 the twin houses are named "Kuhn." In 1886 only one of them remained. A persimmon tree stood at that time on the site of Casey's redoubt, and there were slight traces of the old earth-works that for the most part were erected after the battle of Seven Pines.

tured the Federal first line of defense, and was closely pressing upon their second line.

THE TWIN FARM-HOUSES AS SEEN FROM CASEY'S REDOUBT. FROM A PHOTOGRAPH.

Hill then sent to Longstreet for another brigade. In a few minutes "the magnificent brigade of R. H. Anderson" came to Hill's support. The latter says:

"A portion of this force, under Colonel Jenkins, consisting of the Palmetto Sharp-shooters and the 6th South Carolina, was sent on the extreme left to scour along the railroad and Nine-mile road, and thus get in rear of the enemy."

These two regiments were conducted by General (then Colonel) G. B. Anderson to the position in which he had left the 27th Georgia. The three regiments soon became engaged with the two regiments under General Couch, previously referred to. The latter says:

"I advanced with Neill's and Rippey's regiments through a close wood, moving by the flank . . . . We at once came upon a large column of the enemy in reserve, but apparently moving toward Fair Oaks. . . . Immediately engaged. . . . Here Colonel Rippey and all his field-officers fell, and in twenty minutes the enemy had passed over the [Nine-mile] road leading to my center, cutting off the advance at Fair Oaks."

In reference to this affair General Keyes says:

"Both regiments were badly cut up. . . . Casualties in Rippey's amount to 263, and are heavier than in any other regiment in Couch's division."

He adds that, after Couch was thrown back, Neill's regiment "took part in the hard fighting which closed the day near the Seven Pines," but Rippey's regiment "withdrew in detachments, some of which came again into action near my headquarters."

So far, the fighting done by the Federal troops for the safety of their second line of defense was not so effective as the resistance made by Casey's division at the first line. After the three Confederate regiments had fought their way across the Nine-mile road, not far south of Fair Oaks Station, they changed direction and moved toward Seven Pines. Leaving them for the present, attention will be called to the state of affairs in the vicinity of the redoubt in Casey's captured line.

When General Hill ordered the two South Carolina regiments to join the 27th Georgia and "scour along the railroad and Nine-mile road, and thus get in rear of the enemy," he directed General R. H. Anderson, with the other portion of his brigade, to attack the Federals in a wood north, and within cannon-range of the redoubt. This wood was then occupied by two regiments and some companies of Naglee's brigade that had been, previous to the commencement of the action, supporting the picket-line. In reference to the fighting at this point, General Naglee says in his official report:

MAJOR-GENERAL SILAS CASEY.
FROM A PHOTOGRAPH.

"The Confederates opened a most destructive cross-fire upon them from the pieces near the redoubt that had not been spiked, and this, with the [musketry] fire from their immediate front, was no longer to be endured, and they [his men] were withdrawn and marched down the Nine-mile road and placed in position in rear of this road, about three hundred yards from the Seven Pines."

Whilst these operations were in progress on Hill's left, the state of affairs at the second abatis, just in front of Seven Pines, and in the woods south and east of the redoubt had materially changed against the Confederates, who were first checked at the second abatis, and on the right were forced back to the redoubt. Previous to this the brigades of Rodes, Garland, and G. B. Anderson were engaged at the second abatis, and General Hill, having "resolved to drive" the Federals out of the woods on the south of the road, where they now appeared in strong force, ordered General Rains, who was near them, "to move farther to the right," and adds:

"I regret that that gallant and meritorious officer did not advance farther in that direction. He would have taken the Yankees in flank, and the direct attack of Rodes in front would have been less bloody. The magnificent brigade of Rodes moved over the open ground to assault the Yankees, strongly posted in the woods. He met a most galling fire, and his advance was checked. A portion of his command met with a disastrous repulse. Kemper's brigade was now sent me by General Longstreet, and directed by me to move directly to the support of Rodes. This brigade, however, did not engage the Yankees, and Rodes's men were badly cut up."

General Rodes was severely wounded, but did not turn over the command of his brigade to the senior colonel, John B. Gordon, until the firing had ceased. The latter says:

"Notified that I was placed in command, I reported to Major-General Hill for orders. Under his direction I moved the brigade about half a mile to the rear, and ordered them to encamp on either side of the Williamsburg road."

General G. B. Anderson says: "After night we were ordered by the major-general commanding the division to take position in the woods, in rear of the clearing"— that is, in the edge of the wood on the Richmond side of Casey's line. General Garland says that his brigade bivouacked that night with G. B. Anderson's. General Rains says that his brigade "ultimately passed the night in line of battle, without fire or light, in another part of the woods, ready to receive and check the enemy, should he advance." He makes no mention of any fighting done by his brigade after Casey's camp was captured.

Attention will now be called to the Federal movements that caused the right of D. H. Hill's division to fall back from the second abatis.

At 12 M. Berry's brigade of Kearny's division, from Bottom's Bridge, arrived at the third line of defense; and about the same time Birney's brigade, of the same division, reached the same line, but was near the railroad. At 3 P. M. the latter brigade was ordered to move along the railroad and support Keyes's right; but, owing to subsequent conflicting orders, it did not go into action that day. About 3:30 P. M. Berry's brigade, now at the third line of defense, was ordered to Seven Pines to support Keyes; and, at the same time, General Kearny "sent written orders for Jameson's brigade, camped at the *tête-de-pont*, near Bottom's Bridge (three miles in rear), to come up without delay." It was about 4 P. M. when the advance of Berry's brigade reached Seven Pines. At that time one regiment of Devens's brigade had just been routed in the second abatis. General Kearny says: "On arriving at the field of battle, we found certain zigzag rifle-pits sheltering crowds of men, and the enemy firing from abatis and timber in their front." Berry's brigade was moved forward in the woods on the south side of the Williamsburg road. That officer says: "We steadily drove the enemy so far that I had serious fears of being flanked by the enemy, as they were driving our troops down the [Nine-mile] road." He evidently refers to the effect being produced by the advance of the three regiments under Colonel Jenkins. General Berry adds:

"We were at this time in the woods extending from the edge of the slashings up the woods and on the left [south] of the camping-ground of General Casey's division, completely commanding his old camp and the earth-works with our rifles."

In the meantime the head of Jameson's brigade had reached the field. Two regiments were sent in advance of Seven Pines, in the abatis and woods on the south side of the road, supporting Berry's brigade; one regiment was posted in the earth-works of the second line, and the other regiment of Jameson's brigade had not yet come up.

General Kearny says:

"It was perhaps near 6 o'clock, when our center and right [the forces in the earth-works at Seven Pines, and those that had been sent to resist the Confederates advancing in rear of the Nine-mile road], defended by troops of the other divisions, with all their willingness, could no longer resist the enemy's right central flank attacks, pushed on with determined discipline and with the impulsion of numerous concentrated masses. Once broken, our troops fled incontinently, and a dense body of the enemy, pursuing rapidly, yet in order, occupied the Williamsburg road, . . . and, penetrating deep into the woods on either side, soon interposed between my division and my line of retreat." He says that he "checked the enemy in his intent of cutting us off against the White Oak Swamp. This enabled the advanced regiments . . . to retire by a remaining wood path, known to our scouts (the Saw-mill road), until they once more arrived at and remanned the impregnable position [the third line of defense]."

BRIGADIER-GENERAL HENRY M. NAGLEE. FROM A PHOTOGRAPH.

Besides Kearny's troops on the south side of the Williamsburg road, a large portion of those in the earth-works at Seven Pines retreated by the Saw-mill road; but some of the regiments from the earth-works, and others that had been contesting Colonel Jenkins's advance along the Nine-mile road, fell back on the Williamsburg road. The latter were re-formed, and again contested Colonel Jenkins's advance. It does not appear that any of D. H. Hill's division, except the regiment that was with Colonel Jenkins, succeeded in getting beyond the second abatis; but it is very certain that the effective fire, across that abatis, from Hill's musketry and artillery, materially aided Colonel Jenkins in "bursting across the Williamsburg road."

Having given the Federal account of the manner in which the two South Carolina regiments and the 27th Georgia forced their way to and crossed the Nine-mile road a little south of Fair Oaks, it is now proposed to give extracts from Colonel Jenkins's report, showing the advance of these three regiments to and across the Williamsburg road, and then along the latter road to a point within about one mile of the Federal third line of defense. Colonel Jenkins says:

"I advanced my regiment through the abatis under a very heavy fire. . . . I instructed Colonel Bratton [6th South Carolina] to keep his left touching my right; and the enemy's line, after a stubborn resistance, having given way to our attack, . . . I executed, under fire from the right front, a change of front obliquely forward. . . . We drove the enemy to the front and right, passing over their second camp. . . . The enemy, heavily reënforced, made a desperate stand, and our fighting was within seventy-five yards. . . . Our advance continued, . . . the enemy steadily giving back, . . . I halted the lines, dressed them, and then changed front obliquely forward. . . . Our steady advance was not to be resisted. . . . The enemy gave back to our left and right across the Williamsburg road, about a mile or more from General Casey's headquarters. Following the latter and heavier body, they were again reënforced and took position in a wood parallel [to] and about three hundred yards on the right [south] of the Williamsburg road."

In describing his progress thus far, Colonel Jenkins speaks repeatedly of the obstinate resistance he met with, the terrible slaughter of the enemy, and his own severe losses. Bearing in mind the movement of Kearny's troops in the meanwhile against D. H. Hill's right, and the effect of Kearny's fire on Rodes's brigade, the Federals have good cause to regret the conflicting orders that prevented Birney's brigade, on the railroad, from closely supporting Keyes's right. It should be also borne in mind that, whilst Colonel Jenkins was fighting his way to the Williamsburg road, there were four Federal regiments and a battery at Fair Oaks that had not been in action that day. Two of these regiments were the regular guards of the depot of supplies, and the other two had been ordered from Seven Pines to support Couch, but, missing their way, reached Fair Oaks just before the two regiments under Couch were cut up. It was very fortunate for the Confederates that Birney's brigade and the force at Fair Oaks Station were not thrown against the rear of Colonel Jenkins's three regiments, that were so gallantly fighting, and were so determinedly resisted in their brilliant movement to the Williamsburg road, in rear of the Federal second line of defense, and far in rear of Kearny's successful advance.

Resuming Colonel Jenkins's account, it appears that five companies of his regiment pushed after that portion of the Federals which fell back along the Williamsburg road. With the rest of his force Colonel Jenkins was preparing to move against the enemy in the woods south of that road, when it was reported to him that a heavy column of Federals was advancing upon the five companies. Learning just then that the 5th South Carolina was not far to the rear, Colonel Jenkins sent for it to come up as soon as possible ordered the commander of the five companies to advance upon the approaching Federal column, and determined to break the enemy south of the road before the column advancing on the road could reach him. He says:

"Having to pass across an open field on this advance, I lost heavily, but succeeded in routing and dispersing the enemy in my front, driving them at least a quarter of a mile; then, gathering my men promptly, . . . I moved by the flank . . . and took up line of battle oblique to the [Williamsburg] road and to the left, so as to present front at once to the enemy's advance by the road and to any rallied party that might recover from my last attack. . . . We have evidence of the near approach of the enemy by hearing their words of command and their cheers. . . . I advanced my line toward them. . . . The enemy poured in a heavy fire . . . The supporting regiment [27th Georgia], under a terrible fire, gave back. . . The enemy, encouraged, redoubled his fire . . . and advanced, and I determined to meet him In prompt obedience, the two regiments . . . resumed their old, steady advance, firing ful in the face of the foe. The two lines neared each other to 30 or 40 yards. ... Losing heavily I pressed on, and the enemy sullenly and slowly gave way. ... We had advanced some 200 or 300 yards. ... By this time ... the 5th South Carolina ... came up at a double-quick. ... The 27th Georgia ... rallied and came forward. ... Jackson [5th South Carolina] came up on their right, sweeping before him the rallied fragments, who had collected and resumed fire from the woods to the right, and thus, at 7:40 P. M., we closed our busy day."

Out of thirteen brigades composing the right wing of the Confederate army, but five were put in close action that day. General Pickett says:

"On the afternoon of May 31st, and just as the battle of Seven Pines was being opened by General Longstreet, I was directed by that officer to move with my brigade to the York River Railroad, cover the same, [and] repel any advance of the enemy up that road."

General Longstreet held Pickett's brigade back in that position until daybreak, June 1st. From this it would seem that Longstreet was not in need of help on that side from troops not under his command. Attention will now be called to the five brigades under Longstreet's control on the Charles City road.

General Wilcox, in his official report, says that the three brigades under his command were in camp near the "Mechanicsville" road. He tells me, however, that he had no map of the country, knew very little about the names of the roads, but distinctly remembers that the road his troops were on passed close to General Johnston's headquarters near the north-east suburb of Richmond and led to New Bridge,— that is, the Nine-mile road. Whatever may have been the name of the road on which his troops were in camp, he says they were three and a half miles from the city, and moved, at 6:30 A. M., "by by-paths across to the junction of the Charles City and Williamsburg roads, and remained at this point till 3:30 P. M. I was then ordered to move with three brigades — my own, Colston's, and Pryor's — on the Charles City road, in rear of a part of Huger's division (Blanchard's and Armistead's brigades), as a support to these troops."

MAJOR-GENERAL DAVID B. BIRNEY.
FROM A PHOTOGRAPH.

The Charles City road is south of the White Oak Swamp; it bears rapidly away from the point where the battle had been raging for more than two hours; and there was no enemy on that road. General Wilcox adds:

"This order was soon modified, and my three brigades ordered to precede Huger's two. Having passed Huger's brigades, the march was continued but for a short time, when orders were again received, and this time to countermarch to the Williamsburg road and follow on in rear of the troops then advancing. The brigades had retraced their steps near one mile, and orders were again given to face about and march down the Charles City road. . . . Again orders were received in writing to move across to the Williamsburg road, following country roads and paths through woods and fields . . . in many places covered with water, and at one point waist-deep. . . . It was about 5 P. M. when the head of the column reached the Williamsburg road."

The plain words of General Wilcox, written at the time and addressed to his immediate commander, are more significant of the real truth than any skillfully formed sentences, framed now, could possibly be. With Wilcox's report before him, General Longstreet says:

"I was obliged to send three of my small brigades on the Charles City road to support the one of Major-General Huger's which had been ordered to protect my right flank."

Three brigades of Huger's division were then on that road.

In order to form a proper conception of the folly exhibited by the marching and countermarching of five Confederate brigades up and down the Charles City road between 3 and 5 P. M., it is necessary to glance at the movements then being made by the Federals from the north side of the Chickahominy. At 1 P. M., when the firing of Hill's attack was first heard, General McClellan ordered General Sumner to form the two divisions of his corps, and be ready to move across the Chickahominy, at a moment's notice, to aid Keyes. Sumner at once put his two divisions under arms, marched them to their respective bridges, and, with the heads of the columns on the bridges, awaited further orders. General Sumner says: "At 2:30 o'clock P. M. I received the order to cross the river." And he adds: "The columns immediately moved over the river and marched rapidly to the field of battle by two roads." It is not proposed, just now, to describe the earnest haste with which Sumner's troops pressed forward, through the deep mud, to the assistance of their friends. The head of Sumner's leading column reached the immediate vicinity of Fair Oaks before the head of the column of five brigades of Longstreet's command, from the Charles City road, reached the Williamsburg road, far in rear of the fighting.

The leading brigade of Wilcox's command arrived at Casey's captured redoubt a little before the firing of Kearny's rear-guard in the wood, south of the Williamsburg road, ceased. Three companies of the leading regiment of Wilcox's troops were sent to dislodge a party of the enemy — Kearny's detached rear-guard — whose fire was still annoying the Confederates in the open between Casey's earth-works and the second abatis. In this contest these three companies lost 66 men in a few minutes. The five brigades with Wilcox went into bivouac between the first and the second abatis. Hill's division ☆ was afterward withdrawn and bivouacked in the woods west of Casey's redoubt and rifle-pits.

☆ On the Confederate side the losses, May 31st, in D. H. Hill's division were 2915, being more than one-third of his effective strength. The losses in R. H. Anderson's brigade (of Longstreet's division) are not reported; but it is known that the 6th South Carolina Regiment lost 269 out of 521 in action. The losses in this brigade may fairly be estimated to have been more than 600, and the total losses in Longstreet's division that day may be placed at 700. These figures, whilst showing that the losses in the six brigades of Longstreet's division were not one-fourth as great as the losses

In his "Narrative," p. 132, General Johnston says:

"An hour or two later [than noon, May 30th] orders were given for the concentration of 23 of our 27 brigades against McClellan's left wing."

The result of that alleged "concentration" has been described. McClellan's left wing was attacked by five brigades; and General Johnston, who was wounded on another part of the field about sunset that day, says, in his official report:

"The skill, vigor, and decision with which these operations were conducted by General Longstreet are worthy of the highest praise."

Without discussing here General Johnston's opinion in regard to the manner in which General Longstreet conducted the operations of the three

ALLEN'S FARM-HOUSE NEAR THE WILLIAMSBURG ROAD, NOT FAR FROM THE "THIRD LINE OF DEFENSE." DESERTED IN 1885 WHEN THIS SKETCH WAS MADE.

divisions on the right, reference will now be made to the movements of the division on the Nine-mile road, directed by General Johnston in person.

In addition to the action already described, there was a sharp contest north of Fair Oaks Station late in the afternoon, May 31st, between reënforcements, under General Sumner, sent from the north side of the Chickahominy to aid Keyes at Seven Pines, and my division, under General Whiting. It will be borne in mind that when three Confederate regiments, under Colonel Jenkins, crossed the Nine-mile road just south of Fair Oaks, a little after 4 P. M., four regiments and a battery of Couch's division were cut off from the Federals in the four brigades of D. H. Hill's division, indicate clearly enough that Hill's division did the greater part of the fighting; but all honor is due the brilliant, successful, and bloody work done that day by the two South Carolina regiments of Longstreet's division under Colonel Jenkins.

On the Federal side the losses in the operations described were: Kearny's division, less 1 brigade, 873; Couch's division, less 4 regiments, 1049; Casey's division, 1426. It is not amiss to give here the following from General Casey's official report. After stating that 8 of the 13 regiments that composed his division were raw troops, and had suffered from the inclemency of the weather, at times without tents or blankets, and poorly supplied with rations and medical stores, he adds: "Notwithstanding all these drawbacks, and the fact that there were not five thousand men in line of battle, they withstood for three hours the attack of an overwhelming force of the enemy. . . . It is true that the division, after being nearly surrounded by the enemy and losing one-third of the number actually engaged, retreated to the second line. They would all have been prisoners of war had they delayed their retreat a few minutes longer."— G. W. S.

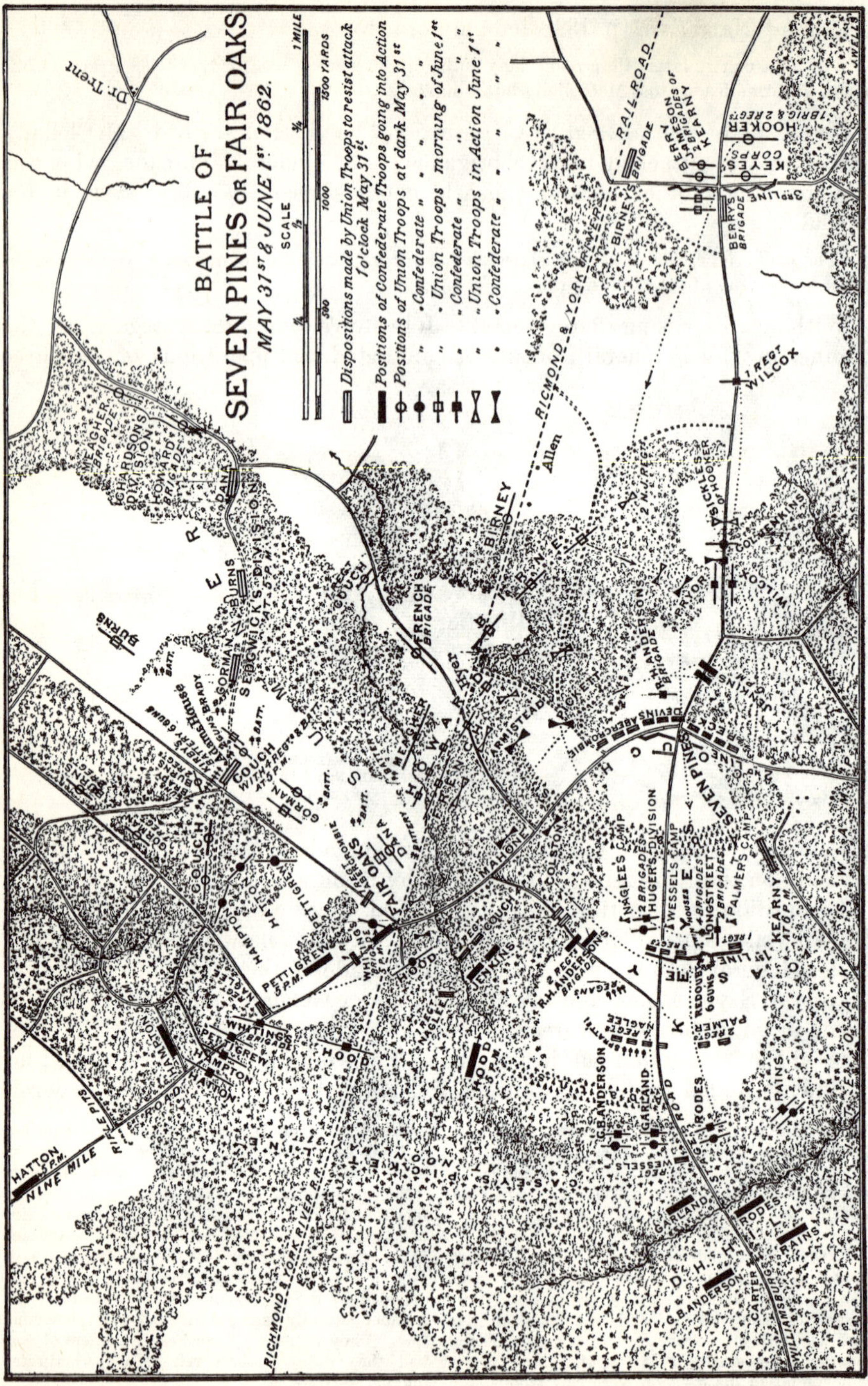
BATTLE OF
SEVEN PINES OR FAIR OAKS
MAY 31ST & JUNE 1ST 1862.
SCALE
1 MILE
1300 YARDS
Dispositions made by Union Troops to resist attack 1 o'clock May 31st
Positions of Confederate Troops going into Action
Positions of Union Troops at dark May 31st
" Confederate " " " "
" Union Troops morning of June 1st
" Confederate " " "
" Union Troops in Action June 1st
" Confederate " " "

opposed to D. H. Hill. Immediately after being thus cut off, General Couch communicated with Birney's brigade on the railroad, a mile or more east of Fair Oaks, and endeavored to make arrangements by which the cut off forces could rejoin Keyes. Just then it was reported to General Couch that a large Confederate force on the Nine-mile road was rapidly advancing on Fair Oaks, and the four regiments and battery retreated in the direction of Sumner's bridges. On reaching a point about one thousand yards north of Fair Oaks, General Couch was informed that the leading troops of Sumner's corps were closely approaching. Couch halted his forces, formed line of battle, facing nearly south, placed two guns on each side of the road, and prepared to defend the position until Sumner's troops could come up.

It is now proposed to give in some detail an account of the movements that day of my division under Whiting which prevented Sumner's forces from reaching Keyes at Seven Pines, and incidentally deprived Keyes and Heintzelman of the services of two brigades and a battery of their own troops.

LINE OF BATTLE OF GENERAL DEVENS'S BRIGADE, BETWEEN THE WILLIAMSBURG AND NINE-MILE ROADS — GENERAL DEVENS WOUNDED. FROM A SKETCH MADE AT THE TIME.

In my official report (as originally submitted to General Johnston), it is stated that

"on arriving at the headquarters of General Johnston about sunrise [May 31st], I learned from him that his intention was that General Longstreet's division should move by the Nine-mile road, that of General D. H. Hill by the Williamsburg road, and General Huger's by the Charles City road. The enemy, it was understood, had already upon this side of the Chickahominy a force variously estimated at from 20,000 to 40,000 men. The recent rains had materially increased the difficulty of crossing that stream, and, notwithstanding the very bad condition of the roads over which we had to pass, and the boggy, swampy condition of the fields and woods through which our troops would have to operate, it was believed that an energetic attack early in the morning, properly supported and followed up, would result in defeat to that portion of the enemy already upon this side before the other portion of their army could cross the swollen river — either to reënforce their troops or to attack the city in our rear. . . . General Johnston's intentions, as then explained to me, were, that whilst General D. H. Hill's division was attacking the enemy's advanced position on the Williamsburg stage road in front, . . . General Longstreet's division would engage the enemy on Hill's left."

About 6 A. M. the head of the division under Whiting reached the vicinity of General Johnston's headquarters. There its way, to a point on the Nine-mile road near the suburb, was blocked by troops of Longstreet's division. General Whiting wrote to General Johnston asking that the route should be cleared. In reply, a staff-officer wrote: "General Johnston directs me to say, in answer to yours of this date, that Longstreet will precede you." This quieted Whiting for a time, but, as the delay continued, he became impatient, and having heard that I was at General Johnston's headquarters, he came there to see if I could not have his line of march cleared of Longstreet's troops. About 8 A. M. I sent my aide-de-camp, Captain Beckham, to see General Longstreet in regard to this matter. Captain Beckham asked me where General Longstreet was to be found. I referred him to General Johnston who, with several others, was present. General Johnston said General Longstreet's division was on the Nine-mile road and he was probably with it; but, if not, he might be found on the Williamsburg road with that part of his command.

I now quote again from the suppressed portion of my official report:

"In about an hour I learned by note from Captain Beckham that neither General Longstreet nor any portion of his command was on the Nine-mile road. This note was immediately shown to General Johnston, who dispatched his aide-de-camp, Lieutenant Washington, to General Longstreet with directions to turn his division into the Nine-mile road, provided it could be done without material loss of time. This message did not reach General Longstreet."

It was about 9 A. M. when I handed Captain Beckham's note to General Johnston, who was amazed at the information and for a time strongly inclined to discredit it, thinking that my aide had not gone far enough on the Nine-mile road to come up with Longstreet's troops. Johnston then sent one of his own aides, Lieutenant J. B. Washington, to Longstreet, with orders for the latter "to send three brigades by the Nine-mile road." Washington rode at full speed along the Nine-mile road, and soon found himself within the Federal picket-line—captured. ♭ As I first wrote in my report:

"An hour later Captain Beckham reported that he had found Longstreet's division on the Williamsburg road, halted, for the purpose of allowing General D. H. Hill's troops to file by."

In a letter to me dated February 7th, 1863, Captain Peckham says it was about 10 A. M. when he reached General Longstreet. He adds:

"Kemper's brigade, which formed a part of General Longstreet's division, was at a halt when I got to General Longstreet's headquarters, and, what surprised me most, was accompanied by wagons loaded with baggage and camp-equipage."

During these delays the firing of cannon across the Chickahominy, and reports from our troops guarding the river between New Bridge and Mechanicsville, indicated threatening movements of the Federals on that side. About 11 A. M. General Johnston directed me to take Hampton's and Hatton's brigades, proceed to the Chickahominy bluffs, and assume command of all the forces on that side, in case the Federals made any attempt to cross the river. At the same time, the other three brigades, after about five hours' delay near the suburbs of the city, accompanied by General Johnston, proceeded on the Nine-mile road, and halted near the point at which the road to New Bridge turns off. Finding nothing that required my presence on the banks of the river, I placed Hampton's and Hatton's brigades in position from which they could promptly resist the passage of the river at New Bridge or above, and could support the other three brigades when needed, and then joined Generals Johnston and Whiting, near Old Tavern. About 2:30 P. M., nothing having been heard from General Longstreet since my aide returned from the Williamsburg road, the chief of my staff, Major Whiting, requested to be

♭ General Casey says this incident helped to put him on his guard.— EDITORS.

allowed to go over to that road and find out the state of affairs there. I tendered his services in this matter to General Johnston.

In my official report it is stated:

"Between 4 and 5 o'clock a note was received [by General Johnston] from General Longstreet, stating that he had attacked and beaten the enemy after several hours' severe fighting; that he had been disappointed in not receiving assistance upon his left; and, although it was now nearly too late, that an attack, by the Nine-mile road, upon the right flank and rear of the enemy would probably enable him to drive them into the Chickahominy before night."

All of the foregoing quotations from my report were omitted from the copy that was put on file, in compliance with General Johnston's request, contained in his letter to me, June 28th, 1862, in which he said:

"I inclose herewith the three first sheets of your report, to ask a modification — or omission, rather. They contain two subjects which I never intended to make generally known, and which I have mentioned to no one but yourself, and mentioned to you as I have been in the habit of doing everything of interest in the military way. I refer to the mention of the misunderstanding between Longstreet and myself in regard to the direction of his division, and that of his note to me, received about 4 o'clock, complaining of my slowness, which note I showed you. As it seems to me that both of these matters concern Longstreet and myself alone, I have no hesitation in asking you to strike them out of your report, as they in no manner concern your operations. I received information of L.'s misunderstanding (which may be my fault, as I told you at the time) while his troops were moving to the Williamsburg road, and sent to L. to send three brigades by the Nine-miles road, if they had not marched so far as to make the change involve a serious loss of time; this, after telling you of the misunderstanding. Your march from General Semmes's headquarters [he means the advance made by the division under Whiting, from the point where it was halted, near Old Tavern.— G. W. S.] was not in consequence of the letter from L. Whiting [Major] had gone at my request, with your permission, to ascertain the state of things with Longstreet. Just before 4 o'clock we heard musketry for the first time, and Whiting [General] was ordered to advance. Just then Major W. rode up and reported from L., and a moment after the note was brought me — which, after reading it, I showed to you."

MAJOR-GENERAL DARIUS N. COUCH.
FROM A PHOTOGRAPH.

In his official report General Johnston says that General Longstreet received verbal instructions, and that the division of General Longstreet was to support the attack made by D. H. Hill's division. General Longstreet, in his official report, makes no mention of the preliminary movements of his own division, except that he was obliged to send three of his small brigades on the Charles City road to support the brigade of Huger's division, which had been ordered to protect his (Longstreet's) right flank. Indefinite as these reports are in reference to the direction in which Longstreet's division was to move, it may, on the preceding evidence, be now considered established that General Johnston intended Longstreet's division should move into action on the Nine-mile road, and support Hill by attacking Keyes's right flank. It is noticeable that General Johnston, in his official report, makes no mention of the information he received in regard to the transfer of Longstreet's division to the Williamsburg road, or of the attempt made to have at least three brigades sent back to the Nine-mile road. No allusion is made, in either of their official reports, to the note from Longstreet, received by Johnston about 4 P. M.

The anxiety felt by those near Old Tavern was extreme in the hours of suspense previous to 4 P. M., during which all were expecting to hear that the fighting on the Williamsburg road had commenced. In my official report it is stated that "as the day wore on and nothing decisive was heard from General Longstreet's attack, except occasional firing of cannon, and, for some two or three hours, but little musketry, it seemed that no real attack was likely to be made that day." Previous to 4 P. M. it was believed by all on the Nine-mile road that no attack had yet been made; the division on that road could not be advanced beyond McLaws's picket-line without bringing on the battle which General Johnston intended should be initiated by the divisions of Hill and Longstreet. The division under Whiting was there for the purpose of holding in check reënforcements from the north side of the river that would surely be sent to Keyes as soon as he was attacked in force; and Whiting was only to reënforce Longstreet "should there be cause of haste." The information finally received not only warned General Johnston that the battle had been raging for several hours, but the character of Longstreet's note conveyed the distinct impression that the delay from 8 A. M. to the afternoon had enabled the Federals to reënforce Keyes to such an extent that Longstreet had met with more opposition than the whole of his command could well overcome. In this state of affairs General Johnston ordered the division under Whiting to move forward as rapidly as possible, and himself urged and led the division against "the right flank of Longstreet's adversaries" without further regard to reënforcements from the north side of the Chickahominy. This advance was so rapid that no artillery was carried forward, on account of the almost impracticable condition of the ground. Very soon after this movement commenced, General Johnston directed Hood's brigade to bear strongly to the right, and go direct to the assistance of Longstreet, who was supposed to be in front of the enemy, near Seven Pines. But it has already been seen that Colonel Jenkins's command had then burst across the Nine-mile road a little south of Fair Oaks, and was "scouring" the rear of that road; and that 8 of the 13 brigades under Longstreet's control had not been put in action. Nothing of this, however, was then known to General Johnston. When the head of the column on the Nine-mile road, in the hurried movement to aid Longstreet, reached the vicinity of Fair Oaks Station, General Johnston censured General Whiting for hesitating to cross the railroad before disposing of a Federal force, north of that station, in position to threaten the left flank and rear of Whiting's command in case he moved farther. I was not present, but the following extracts from a letter to me, written in 1868 by Colonel B. W. Frobel, of the Confederate States Engineer Corps, gives an account of what occurred on that occasion. Colonel Frobel was then a major on General Whiting's staff. He says:

"Generals Johnston and Whiting were following immediately after Whiting's brigade. As Whiting's brigade reached the road near the railroad crossing, I was sent to halt it. On returning after doing this, I joined Generals Whiting and Johnston, who were riding toward the crossing. General Whiting was expostulating with General Johnston about taking the division across the railroad — insisting that the enemy were in force on our left flank and rear. General Johnston replied: 'Oh! General Whiting, you are too cautious.' At this time we reached the crossing, and nearly at the same moment the enemy opened an artillery fire from the direction pointed out by General Whiting. We moved back up the road near the small white house. Whiting's brigade [a portion of it] was gone; it had been ordered forward to charge the batteries [two separated sections of one battery] which were firing on us. The brigade was repulsed, and in a few minutes came streaming back through the little skirt of woods to the left of the Nine-mile road near the crossing. There was only a part of the brigade in this charge. Pender [commanding regiment] soon rallied and re-formed those on the edge of the woods. General Whiting sent an order to him to reconnoiter the batteries, and if he thought they could be taken, to try it again. Before he could do so some one galloped up, shouting, 'Charge that battery!' The men moved forward at a double-quick, but were repulsed as before, and driven back to the woods."

Of the Federal resistance to this attack, General E. V. Sumner, in his official report, says:

"On arriving on the field, I found General Couch with four regiments and two companies of infantry and Brady's battery. These troops were drawn up in line near Adams's house, and there was a pause in the battle."

General Sedgwick, commander of Sumner's leading division, says: "Upon debouching into the open field near Adams's house, we found Abercrombie's brigade of Couch's division sustaining a severe attack and hard pushed by the enemy."

Kirby's six Napoleon guns were promptly placed in position facing south. The infantry of Sedgwick's division was put on the right and left, in Couch's defensive line. The Federal accounts show that repeated attempts were made by the Confederates to carry the position, but without success; that the contest continued until dark, at which time Kirby's battery faced west, without having otherwise changed position, and the infantry on the left of the battery was also facing west, with its left very near the railroad, a little east of Fair Oaks Station. On the immediate right of Kirby's battery the line of infantry still faced nearly south. There was no change in this part of the Federal lines; but on the extreme right the line was facing almost west, and had not been closely engaged.

In the meantime, before the action north of Fair Oaks commenced, when the head of Pettigrew's brigade reached the point in the large wood about three-fourths of a mile from the railroad crossing, I halted for the purpose of giving instructions to General Wade Hampton, whose brigade had reached the rear of Pettigrew's. Generals Johnston and Whiting had gone on with the two leading brigades, and I did not again see either of them until after dark. I directed General Hampton to lead his brigade to the left, on the wood road, a little more than a brigade length, and then resume his march in a direction

SUMNER'S CORPS CROSSING THE OVERFLOWED "GRAPEVINE" BRIDGE TO REËNFORCE COUCH AT FAIR OAKS. [SEE MAP, P. 226.] FROM A SKETCH MADE AT THE TIME.

parallel to the Nine-mile road, which would bring Hampton into line of battle on Pettigrew's left, in the attack General Johnston proposed to make. I remained at that point until Hampton's brigade had filed out of the Nine-mile road; then gave directions to Hatton's brigade to continue moving on the Nine-mile road, which would bring it into position as a reserve, to the line of battle formed by the brigades of Whiting, Pettigrew, and Hampton. In the meantime the action had commenced near Fair Oaks. On reaching the eastern edge of the wood I saw the leading troops moving north from Fair Oaks in direction almost exactly opposite to that in which I had given General Hampton to understand that General Johnston's movement would be made. In a short time I saw our leading troops retiring. This was the second repulse spoken of by Colonel Frobel. I notified General Whiting of Hampton's position, and soon learned from him that the previous attacks had been conducted without proper knowledge of the enemy's position; but that a reconnoissance had been made, and a combined attack by the three brigades would capture the battery in a few minutes. Before this attack was arranged, Kirby's battery of six pieces and the first brigade of Sedgwick's division reached Couch's line and the attack was repulsed. By this time Hatton's brigade had come up and was in the open field, close to the north side of the Nine-mile road. One regiment of Pettigrew's brigade, in reserve, was in the same field about two hundred yards north of the road. Soon after the repulse of the three brigades, the firing on the Federal side greatly increased. General Johnston, who was at the small grove north of Fair Oaks, sent word to me to have all the available troops brought up quickly. The only troops within reach, not already up, were a brigade and a half of Magruder's command stationed along the New Bridge road. I sent General Johnston's order direct to these brigade commanders; and seeing that Whiting's brigade was pressed back on the right, and learning that Hampton and Pettigrew were suffering great losses in the small wood, 600 or 800 yards north of Fair Oaks, it seemed to me that the Federal reënforcements from the north side of the river were likely to break through the division and reach Longstreet's left flank and rear. I therefore ordered Hatton's brigade and Pettigrew's reserve regiment to move into the woods and aid the troops closely engaged there. Believing that Whiting had, on the right, as much as he could well attend to, I went with Hatton's brigade to the extreme front line of Hampton and Pettigrew in the woods, and soon learned that General Pettigrew had been wounded, it was supposed mortally, and was a prisoner. General Hatton was killed at my side just as his brigade reached the front line of battle; and in a very few minutes General Hampton was severely wounded. In this state of affairs, I sent word to General Whiting that I would take executive control in that wood, which would relieve him, for the time, of care for the left of the division, and enable him to give his undivided attention to the right.

In the wood the opposing lines were close to each other, in some places not more than twenty-five or thirty yards apart. The contest continued until dark without material variation in the position of either line on that part of the field after I reached the extreme front, until the firing had ceased at dark, when I ordered the line to fall back to the edge of the field and re-form. In the meantime Whiting's brigade and the right of Pettigrew's had been forced back to the clump of trees just north of Fair Oaks Station, where the contest was kept up until night. ⸗

On reaching the open field in rear of the line where Hampton's and Hatton's brigades had been engaged, I heard for the first time that General Johnston had been very seriously wounded and taken from the field an hour or more before. I was second in rank in his army, therefore the command, for the time being, devolved upon me.

In further illustration of views held at that time on the Confederate side in regard to the events of the first day at Seven Pines, the following extracts from a letter dated June 7th, 1862, from Longstreet to Johnston, are not irrelevant, however erroneous the opinions he expresses may be. He says:

"The failure of complete success on Saturday [May 31st] I attribute to the slow movements of General Huger's command. This threw perhaps the hardest part of the battle upon my own poor division. . . . Our ammunition was nearly exhausted when Whiting moved, and I could not, therefore, move on with the rush that we could had his movement been earlier. . . . I can't but help think that a display of his forces on the left flank of the enemy by General Huger would have completed the affair and given Whiting as easy and pretty a game as was ever had upon a battle-field."

It is not deemed necessary to make any comments on this letter. The facts already stated and proved are sufficient.

⸗ In the action north of Fair Oaks the four Confederate brigades engaged lost 1061 killed and wounded.— G. W. S.

General Johnston says [see p. 214]:

"It was near half-past 6 o'clock before I admitted to myself that Smith was engaged, not with a brigade, as I had obstinately thought, but with more than a division."

It may not be amiss to mention here that Colonel Frobel, in the letter to me above referred to, says:

"General W. H. C. Whiting was at that time commanding your division, you being in command of the left wing of the army. . . . Whiting was directly under General Johnston, who was with the division the whole day until he was wounded, late in the afternoon."

Without dwelling now upon the persistency with which General Johnston insists that I was then in command of the division which bore my name, it may be stated here that General Whiting was clearly of opinion then and ever after, that but for General Johnston's determination to press on across the railroad to Longstreet's assistance, Couch would have been beaten and his battery captured before Sumner's leading troops reached the field.

Before describing what occurred on the second day, allusion will be made to some of the erroneous views which have been widely promulgated in regard to these operations. General Johnston, in his official report, says: "Major-General G. W. Smith succeeded to the command. He was prevented from renewing his attack on the enemy's position next morning by the discovery of strong intrenchments not seen on the previous evening." On page 141 of his published "Narrative," he says: "Sumner's corps at Fair Oaks [June 1st] was six miles from those of Heintzelman and Keyes, which were near Bottom's Bridge." In reference to the position of the Confederates at that time, he places D. H. Hill's division in line of battle across the Williamsburg road, at right angles to it, more than a mile east of Seven Pines, the left of Hill's line, near the railroad, facing north; Longstreet's and Huger's divisions on Hill's left, parallel to the railroad and extending a short distance west of Fair Oaks Station, uniting there with the division under Whiting; and says, "Magruder's division in reserve" "was under arms near." ☆ On the map in his book he represents Sumner's corps in one line facing west, its left on the railroad a little west of Fair Oaks, with Longstreet's and Huger's divisions close on Sumner's left flank and rear. Having thus placed the contending forces, he adds: "Such advantage of position and superiority of numbers would have enabled the Confederates to defeat Sumner's corps, had the engagement been renewed Sunday morning [June 1st] before any aid could have come from Heintzelman, after which his troops could not have made

MAJOR-GENERAL EDWIN V. SUMNER.
FROM A PHOTOGRAPH.

☆ "Narrative of Military Operations," by Joseph E. Johnston, pp. 137, 119.— G. W. S.

SUMNER'S MARCH TO REËNFORCE COUCH AT FAIR OAKS STATION.

Lieutenant Edmund Kirby, Battery I, First U. S. Artillery, says in his official report: "The roads were almost impassable for artillery, and I experienced great difficulty in getting my guns along. I was obliged at times to unlimber and use the prolonge, the cannoneers being up to their waists in water. About 4:30 P. M. I was within three-quarters of a mile of Fair Oaks Station, with three pieces [twelve-pounder Napoleons] and one caisson, the remainder of the battery being in the rear, and coming up as fast as circumstances would permit."

effectual resistance." He claims that the battle was "unfinished in consequence of the disabling of their commander [Johnston]," and states that after he was disabled, the *only thing* President Davis " ought to have done, or had time to do, was postponed almost twenty hours — the putting General Lee, who was near, in command of the army."

General Johnston also states that three Federal corps on the Richmond side "were completely separated from the two corps of their right beyond the Chickahominy by the swollen stream, which had swept away their bridges." This, if true, was not known or believed on our side. Anxiety on account of Federal reënforcements from the north side of the Chickahominy was felt, on the 1st of June as well as on the 31st of May, by the Confederate commander. But General Longstreet seems to have ignored all consideration of that subject on both days.

In the official report of the chief engineer of McClellan's army it is stated:

" At 8:15 A. M. (June 1st) the pontoon-bridge at the site of New Bridge was complete and passable to infantry, cavalry, and artillery. About noon the upper trestle-bridge was practicable for infantry. It was not till night that a practicable bridge for infantry was obtained at the lower trestle-bridge."

The railroad-bridge had been made practicable for all arms, and was not affected by the freshet.

The specific details given by General Johnston in regard to the positions occupied by the divisions of D. H. Hill, Longstreet, and Huger on the morning of June 1st, accorded, in the main, with General Longstreet's report to me at the time; and I never questioned the accuracy of General Johnston's statement in regard to the general positions occupied by these three divisions until I saw the recently published "Official Records." But I knew there was a gap between Whiting's right and Longstreet's left, and I knew, too, that Magruder's troops were not concentrated at Old Tavern.

Only one of the many remarkable statements made by General Longstreet in regard to the operations of the second day will be mentioned here. In a letter written in 1874 to General George W. Mindil, Federal, for the avowed purpose of throwing light upon the Confederate side, General Longstreet says:

"I do not remember to have heard of any fighting on the second day, except a sharp skirmish reported by General Pickett as he was retiring, under the orders of General Lee, to resume our former position."

Without dwelling upon what might have happened if General Johnston had not been disabled, or discussing what President Davis "ought to have done, or had time to do," it is proposed to show that General Johnston is greatly in error in reference to the positions of the contending forces on the morning of June 1st, and to present evidence that will refresh General Longstreet's memory in regard to the fighting he "heard of" that day.

In reference to the positions occupied by the three divisions under General Longstreet, it has already been stated and proved that D. H. Hill's division was in bivouac in the woods west of Casey's earth-works; and that large portions of the divisions of Longstreet and Huger were around Casey's redoubt, in the open field west of the second abatis. Before midnight, May 31st, Colonel Jenkins's command was withdrawn to Seven Pines, and the brigades of Wilcox and Pryor moved forward from the redoubt and bivouacked on the sides of the Williamsburg road, in advance of Seven Pines, the head of their column being on the ground where Colonel Jenkins ceased fighting. Pickett's brigade was still far back on the railroad, where it was posted by Longstreet's order when the attack was commenced, May 31st, and Mahone's brigade was three and a half miles out on the Charles City road.

Two brigades of the division under Whiting were in line of battle, facing nearly east, the right being on the railroad about five hundred yards west of Fair Oaks, the left in the woods on the north of the Nine-mile road, and the other three brigades within close supporting distance. There were six brigades in Magruder's command. Two of them were guarding the Mechanicsville and Meadow Bridge roads. The positions of the other four brigades are given in a note, dated 11 P. M., May 31st, addressed to me by their immediate commander, General McLaws. He says:

"General Cobb, five regiments, [posted] from the Mechanicsville road to General Harvey's place; General Kershaw from General Harvey's to Baker's; Generals Griffith and Semmes from General Kershaw's right to New Bridge, and on the line down New Bridge road."

Magruder's six brigades were the only forces guarding the crossings of the Chickahominy from New Bridge to Meadow Bridge.

On the Federal side Keyes's corps, with abundant artillery, occupied that part of the Federal third line of defense which was on the south side of the

# TWO DAYS OF BATTLE AT SEVEN PINES. 251

Williamsburg road, one and three-eighths miles east of Seven Pines. One brigade and two regiments of Hooker's division were close in rear of Keyes, and two brigades of Kearny's division were in the trenches of the third line of defense, on the north side of the Williamsburg road; whilst Birney's brigade of that division was about half a mile in advance, with three regiments in line of battle, facing nearly south-west, their right resting on the railroad, and in close connection with Sumner's corps. In fact, the lines of Sumner and Heintzelman overlapped here at the time the Confederate attack was made. Sumner's corps (instead of being drawn up in one line, facing nearly west, as represented by General Johnston) was in two lines, nearly at right angles to each other. Sedgwick's division, with Couch's cut-off forces and five batteries, were in line, facing nearly west, the left being a little north of the railroad, a short distance east of Fair Oaks. Richardson's division was on Sedgwick's left, in three lines, nearly parallel to the railroad, with four batteries. In front of Richardson's position was a dense and tangled wood; on his right, and in front of Sedgwick, the ground was open for several hundred yards.

HOUSES ON THE BATTLE-FIELD, USED AS UNION HOSPITALS. FROM PHOTOGRAPHS TAKEN SOON AFTER THE BATTLE.

I find no reasonable cause to doubt the substantial accuracy of the Federal official reports in regard to the position of their forces, or in reference to their accounts of the actual fighting, a synopsis of which will presently be given. I am far from agreeing with General Johnston in the rose-colored view he takes of the situation, at the time he was wounded, when there were, practically, three Federal corps upon the field. But I gave orders for the renewal of the attack, with no expectation, however, of the easy, complete, and certain success he pictures for that day.

When I assumed command of the army, I could learn nothing from those around me in reference to what had occurred on the Williamsburg road later than the information contained in the note received from General Longstreet, at 4 P. M. Hood's brigade had been recalled before it reached D. H. Hill's lines, and returned after the action north of Fair Oaks was ended. I sent staff-officers with several different parties to communicate with General Longstreet and request him to meet me as soon as possible at the headquarters on the Nine-mile road, near Old Tavern. A few minutes later General J. E. B.

MAJOR-GENERAL OLIVER O. HOWARD. FAC-SIMILE REPRODUCTION OF A PHOTOGRAPH TAKEN BEFORE THE BATTLE OF SEVEN PINES, ON THE SECOND DAY OF WHICH GENERAL HOWARD LOST HIS RIGHT ARM.

Stuart reported to me that the enemy had made no advance during the day on the Charles City road, and that our troops had captured the Federal works at Seven Pines some time before sunset and had advanced beyond that point—he did not know how far. He had good guides with him, and offered to go in person to General Longstreet and have him piloted to headquarters. A little after 11 P. M. I received a note from General Stuart, stating that at 10:30 he had failed to find General Longstreet.

In the meantime General McLaws, who was at New Bridge, reported large forces opposite that point, and that they were building a pontoon-bridge. He added: "If this position is forced, your command will be in great danger, as you are aware."

Guided by one of my staff, who had succeeded in finding him about midnight, General Longstreet reached headquarters after 1 A. M. He reported that D. H. Hill's division and a portion of his own, after prolonged fighting and heavy losses, had succeeded in driving the enemy from Seven Pines late in the afternoon, and had pursued them more than a mile, until dark. On learning from him that a portion of his own division had not been in action, and that Huger's division, recalled from the Charles City road, though now at the front, had not been engaged at all, I directed General Longstreet to send a brigade of Huger's division to the Nine-mile road. That brigade was to support McLaws at New Bridge, or Whiting at Fair Oaks, as might be required. General Longstreet was ordered to renew the attack with the rest of his command as soon after daybreak as practicable, and to fight north rather than attempt to force his way any farther toward Bottom's Bridge. He left me a little after 2 A. M., and returned to the Williamsburg road. I wrote to General Lee, who was stationed in Richmond, in general charge of military operations, informing him of the orders I had given. In reply, dated 5 A. M., June 1st, General Lee says: "Your movements are judicious, and determination to strike the enemy right." In my official report it is stated:

" General Longstreet was directed to push his successes of the previous day as far as practicable, pivoting his movement upon the position of General Whiting, on his left. The latter was directed to make a diversion in favor of General Longstreet's real attack."

Soon after daylight there was sharp firing for a few minutes between Hood's skirmishers, near the railroad, and the extreme right of Richardson's position. These skirmishers were promptly recalled, and Whiting was ordered to make no advance until the attack by the right wing was well developed, in full force. In this affair Hood lost thirteen wounded. No part of the division under Whiting was again engaged during the day; because, although there was a good deal of heavy firing in the right wing that morning, nothing was observed from the Nine-mile road that indicated to me a real and determined attack, in full force by the right wing, such as I intended Whiting should support.

At 6:30 A. M. firing in the wood commenced, a little south of the railroad, about half a mile or more east of Fair Oaks, and was sufficiently heavy to indicate that the movement Longstreet had been ordered to make had begun. This heavy firing continued for an hour or more, nearly at the same place, but did not develop into an attack in full force. It lulled for a while, and was presently renewed, but now at a point several hundred yards south of the railroad. Longstreet's troops were evidently losing ground without his having made an attack with more than a very small portion of the Right Wing.

In the meantime my chief of staff, who was on the Chickahominy bluffs, had, from time to time, reported movements of troops, pontoons, etc., on the north side of the river, showing preparations for sending over additional Federal reënforcements. The first information received from General Longstreet was contained in a note from him, dated 8 A. M., saying: "I have ordered a brigade of General Huger's, as agreed upon. Please send a guide for it." About 10:30 A. M. the following was received from General Longstreet: "The brigade cannot be spared. Every man except a brigade is in action." In a few minutes this came from him: "The entire army seems to be opposed to me. I trust that some diversion may be made in my favor during these successive attacks, else my troops cannot stand it. The ammunition gives out too readily." And directly after, a note, dated 10 A. M., was received, saying: "Can you reënforce me? The entire army seems to be opposed to me. . . . If I can't get help, I fear I must fall back."

His leading troops had fallen back some time before; this was evident from observations made on the Nine-mile road. In Longstreet's dire extremity, as shown in the three notes received almost at one time, there were two ways in which I could then, possibly, help him,— one was by ordering Whiting forward over the open ground, and in deep mud, against the strong lines and numerous batteries of Sedgwick and Richardson; the other was to strip the Chickahominy of its defenders above New Bridge, and send reënforcements direct to Longstreet on the Williamsburg road. I adopted the latter course, and requested General McLaws to go to General Longstreet, inform him that about five thousand men had been ordered to reënforce him, assure him that the whole Federal army was not in his front, tell him that he must not fall back any farther, but drive the enemy, and, if possible, regain the ground he had lost.

About 1 P. M. I received a note from General McLaws, stating: "Longstreet says he can hold his position with five thousand more men. He has now the same ground the enemy held yesterday." A little after 2 P. M. I received a letter from General Longstreet, dated 1:30 P. M., in which he says:

"The next attack will be from Sumner's division. I think that if we can whip it we shall be comparatively safe. . . . I sincerely hope that we may succeed against them in their next effort. Oh, that I had ten thousand men more!"

When I received that note from Longstreet there had been little or no firing for several hours, and there was none of any consequence after that time. On reading in the "Official Records" the detailed reports of subordinate fighting commanders on both sides, I asked General D. H. Hill what orders he received from General Longstreet that day. His reply, dated June 26th, 1885, authorizes me to state: "General Hill says

FARM-HOUSE NEAR FAIR OAKS, USED AS A UNION HOSPITAL. FROM SKETCHES MADE AT THE TIME.

that he got no orders from General Longstreet on Sunday [June 1st] whatever." This information was to me like lightning from a clear sky, and it cleared the murky atmosphere which had surrounded some of the

HYER'S HOUSE, NEAR FAIR OAKS, USED AS A UNION HOSPITAL. BURNED JUNE 29, 1862.

recently published official reports on the Confederate side, and enabled me to comprehend things that appeared to be inexplicable before I knew that Longstreet had made no attempt to obey my order.

The Federal reports of regimental, brigade, and division commanders of troops closely engaged the second day are given in such detail in the "Official Records," that, by comparing them with the limited number of Confederate reports found there, a clear idea may be formed of what actually occurred. This comparison eliminates nearly all of those exaggerated elements in the accounts which relate to the wondrous results claimed to have been achieved by so-called "bayonet-charges" on the one side, and the bloody repulse of "ten times" their own numbers on the other.

It has already been shown that on May 31st the Confederates struck Keyes's corps, isolated at Seven Pines, with four brigades, and increased the attacking force to five brigades after Keyes had been reënforced by Heintzelman. June 1st, the Confederate attack was made against the left wing of French's brigade, which, with one regiment of Howard's brigade on its left, formed the front line of .Richardson's division. On the left of that division was Birney's brigade of Kearny's division. In his official report, Richardson says:

"Near our left two roads crossed the railroad, and up these the enemy moved his columns of attack. At 6:30 A. M. . . . the enemy opened a heavy rolling fire of musketry within fifty yards. . . . It soon became the heaviest musketry-firing that I had ever experienced during an hour and a half. . . . I now ordered in General Howard to reënforce the first line with his brigade. . . . Soon after this the whole line of the enemy fell back for the first time, unable to stand our fire, and for half an hour the firing ceased on both sides."

In this attack the regiment of Howard's brigade on the extreme left of Richardson's front line was broken, fell back behind the second line, and was not again in action. The regiment next to it on the right was forced back a short distance. The left of Richardson's front line was so rudely shaken that all available means were used to strengthen it; a battery and Meagher's brigade were put in to cover the gap, and Burns's brigade, previously detached to cover the communications with the bridges, was recalled and hurriedly sent by General Sumner to Richardson's assistance.

It will be seen later that this staggering blow against the left of Richardson's line was from three regiments of Armistead's brigade and three regiments of Mahone's brigade, both of Huger's division. It will be seen, too, that these six regiments were the only Confederate forces that attacked the Federals during the second day.

It was about 8 A. M. when General Howard, with two regiments of his brigade, relieved the left wing of French's brigade and took up the fighting. Just at that time the three regiments of Birney's brigade south of the railroad, whose strong advanced guards had been slowly driven back, were rapidly thrown forward. The regiment next the railroad struck the flank of the Confederates just at the time Howard was advancing against their front; and under these two attacks the Confederates gave way in great disorder. The center regiment, of Birney's three, met with but little resistance until it struck a Confederate force in strong position on a wood road parallel to and three hundred to four hundred yards south of the railroad, in front of the left wing of French's brigade. The two regiments of Howard's brigade, in their forward movement, soon struck the same Confederates in the densely tangled wood. These three Federal regiments, after repeated efforts to dislodge the Confederates,— Pickett's brigade,— were repulsed with severe losses, and resumed position in the lines from which they had advanced.

General Howard was wounded just as his two regiments were coming to close quarters with Pickett's brigade. The command of Howard's brigade then devolved upon Colonel Cross, of the 5th New Hampshire, who says:

"Finding that the three other regiments of the brigade had been some time in action and severely handled, I directed that they should move out of the woods and re-form in the rear of

Meagher's brigade, while I advanced my regiment to occupy the ground. We moved forward in line of battle through a thick wood, and about three hundred yards from the railroad track encountered the rebel line of battle. . . . The fire was now very close and deadly, the opposing lines being several times not over thirty yards apart. When about ordering another [the third] charge I was struck by a rifle-ball. . . . Lieutenant-Colonel Langley then took command of the regiment, and, the rebels endeavoring to flank us, he brought off the regiment in excellent order, carrying most of our wounded."

It was now about 11 A. M., perhaps earlier. The fighting was practically ended when the 5th New Hampshire withdrew from in front of the position defended by Pickett's brigade. In the meantime, however, there had been some sharp firing, and for a short time a little close fighting, on the Williamsburg road, between the two Confederate brigades under General Wilcox and seven regiments of Hooker's division and the left regiment of Birney's three. The two regiments of the right wing of French's brigade also advanced into the wood a short time before the action was ended. [For losses, see p. 218.]

On the Confederate side, General D. H. Hill, in his official report, says that at daylight, June 1st, he "learned that heavy reënforcements had come up to the support of Keyes," and "that General G. W. Smith had been checked upon the Nine-mile road, and that no help could be expected in that direction." He adds: "I therefore resolved to concentrate my troops around the captured works." This resolution was formed in the absence of any instructions "whatever" from his chief, General Longstreet, and he certainly received none from me. It now appears that after Longstreet, about 10 A. M., May 31st, assumed control of Huger and Huger's division, all the brigades, when sent to the front, were ordered to report to General D. H. Hill. I did not know that General Longstreet had, for the time being, virtually given up to General Hill the command of the three divisions on the Williamsburg road; much less did I know, or even suspect, that General Longstreet made no attempt, June 1st, to carry into effect the order I gave him to renew the attack. The official reports show that D. H. Hill commanded the thirteen brigades in the right wing that day. It is now proposed to tell what he did with them. It will be seen that he ordered the brigades of Pickett and Mahone to attack, and, by inference, that Armistead's brigade was ordered to attack; that the brigades of Wilcox and Pryor were ordered to retire, and that the brigades of Mahone and Colston, just as the fighting ended, were ordered to assist Pickett in the defensive position he had taken up after Armistead's three regiments were repulsed.

General Pickett, in his official report, says that his brigade marched at daylight from its position back on the railroad, and, in compliance with General Longstreet's orders given the evening before, reported to General D. H. Hill at Casey's redoubt. He adds:

"My brigade had marched on some four hundred yards in advance of this point when it was there halted. General Hill directed me to ride over to the railroad and communicate with Brigadier-General Hood, whose right was resting on that road. I asked General Hill of the whereabouts of the enemy. He said they were some distance in advance — in fact, I had no definite idea where."

It is very clear that to the Confederates on the Williamsburg road the expression "in advance" meant toward the east. But Pickett's instructions from Hill required him in person to go north in search of Hood. On his route, Pickett soon met a small "plundering party" of Confederates rushing past him. He says:

" One fellow riding a mule with a halter I seized on and detained for explanation. He said the enemy was within a few yards of us, and entreated me to let him save himself. I immediately rode back with him at a gallop, and as briefly as possible informed General Hill of the circumstances. He ordered me to attack, and I supposed [the] same order was given to other brigade commanders."

HOUSE NEAR FAIR OAKS, USED AFTER THE BATTLE AS QUARTERS FOR THE OFFICERS OF THE 1ST MINNESOTA. FROM A SKETCH MADE AT THE TIME.

It is well to call attention here to the fact that the three regiments of Birney's brigade [Federal] had strong outposts well to their front, stationed in the woods several hundred yards south of the railroad, for the purpose of holding any advance of the Confederates in check long enough to enable Kearny, with the rest of his division, to reach and support Birney if closely pressed. The Federal accounts show that these outposts did seriously delay the Confederates advancing east on the south side of the railroad.

General Pickett says that his brigade was "in line of battle nearly perpendicular to the railroad," and that Armistead was on his left. It will be noticed that, advancing in the line he describes, Pickett's brigade moved nearly parallel to the railroad, and that Armistead's brigade was between Pickett and the railroad. Pickett encountered the strong outposts of Birney's brigade. Continuing his account, he says his brigade

"struck the enemy within a short distance (who opened heavily upon us), drove him through an abatis over a cross-road leading to [the] railroad, and was advancing over a second abatis, when I had discovered Armistead's brigade had broken and were leaving the field pell-mell. At this moment I was on foot and half-way across the abatis, the men moving on beautifully and carrying everything before them."

He had certainly not yet struck Richardson's line, and never did reach it. He called on General Hill for reënforcements, and he says that he threw back the left of his brigade so as to oppose a front to the Federals on the side where Armistead's men had given way, and adds:

"As a matter of course, from having been the attacking party, I now had to act on the defensive. Fortunately the enemy seemed determined on attacking and carrying my front, and driving me out of the abatis, which our men succeeded in preventing, though with considerable loss."

The "Official Records" contain no report from any commander in that portion of Armistead's or of Mahone's brigades engaged in the attack on Richardson's line. But General Mahone, in a letter to Captain Benj. Huger, October 13th, 1862, says that his brigade moved early on the morning of June 1st from its position on the Charles City road, and reported to General Hill, at the redoubt, "at the same time that General Pickett's brigade reported upon the field," and that his own "brigade was in a few moments thereafter *thrown* into action, a report of which General Huger has." That report cannot be found; but General Mahone now says, in letters to me, December, 1885, and January, 1886:

"At the moment I was reporting to General Hill, some person rode up and excitedly stated to him that the enemy were in the wood on the north side of the [Williamsburg] road. . . . General Hill said: 'General Mahone, take your brigade in there,' referring to the wood in which the enemy were supposed to be." "I am quite certain that Armistead's brigade was on my immediate right, and I suppose it went into the fight about the time my brigade went in. There was no fighting which would indicate an attack by either side before my leading regiments went in, . . . and none on my left during the engagement that followed. Armistead's brigade and mine must have struck the enemy about the same time." "The impetus of the charge of the 3d Alabama, a splendid regiment, I am satisfied must have severely shocked and disordered Richardson's line, and if there had been any intelligent understanding of the position of the enemy, and instructions as to what we were to do, it can be seen *now* how easy a destructive blow might have been given."

From different but authentic sources, I learn that the losses in Mahone's brigade were 339, of which 175 were in the 3d Alabama, 112 in the 41st Virginia, and 52 in the 12th Virginia. The other two regiments were detached.

I have not succeeded in getting specific information from any one engaged in either of the regiments of Armistead's brigade that attacked the extreme left of Richardson's line. The effect produced by that attack shows it was of a very determined character, and from the nature of the Federal counter-attack on Armistead, the losses of the latter must have been very heavy. That Armistead's three regiments did not, then, retire from the wood is shown by the published official report of Colonel H. B. Tomlin, of the 53d Virginia, which had been kept back during the night, May 31st, at General Longstreet's headquarters, and did not get to the front before the other three regiments had been repulsed. On reaching the redoubt, this regiment was ordered to join the other three in the woods. In the tangled undergrowth it became engaged by mistake with one of Mahone's regiments; and, whilst they were firing into each other, one of the regiments of French's Federal brigade came up, and Armistead's regiment, in confusion, fell back to the redoubt, "apprehending more danger from friends than the enemy." In this fiasco that regiment lost one killed and eighteen wounded, and the regiment of French's brigade lost one killed and five wounded. These incidents have been referred to because of the exaggerated importance attached by the Federals to the "bayonet-charge" made by the right of French's brigade.

General Wilcox, commanding his own brigade and Pryor's, says that on the morning of June 1st, having no orders, he formed his brigade in line of battle across and at right angles to the Williamsburg road about half a mile east of Seven Pines, and Pryor's brigade on the left, but facing nearly north. The Federals moved against Wilcox about 8 A. M. In his official report he says that after the firing had continued for some time, the engagement became serious on his entire front, and the contest "was going on as well as could be desired," when "an order was sent to me to withdraw my command, which was instantly done." General Wilcox adds:

"The order given me to retire my command on the second morning was given in writing by D. H. Hill, and for the reason, as he stated in his note, that Mahone's men had acted badly."

After the withdrawal of these two brigades they were placed in position near the redoubt. In this affair the losses in Wilcox's brigade were 44; those in Pryor's brigade are not stated. The Federal accounts of operations on this part of the field show great misapprehension of the real state of affairs on the Confederate side. General Hooker says:

"Our advance on the rebels . . . was slow, . . . the fire brisk and unerring. After an interchange of musketry of this character for more than an hour, directions were given to advance with the bayonet, when the enemy were thrown into wild confusion, throwing away their arms, hats, and coats, and broke through the forest in the direction of Richmond."

A good deal of this "magnificence" vanishes before the plain statements made by General Wilcox; but, in fairness, it should be stated that "extravagances" are also found in the Confederate reports. General Hill says: "Pickett held his ground against the odds of ten to one for several hours."

Pickett's frantic appeals to Hill for help gave color of probability to General Hill's opinion; but the Federal reports, now published, show that Pickett's strong defensive position was attacked by four regiments only. Hill finally sent two brigades to Pickett's assistance, and on their appearance the 5th New Hampshire withdrew from Pickett's front; or, as he expresses it, "the enemy retreated to their bushy cover, and their fire immediately slackened." He adds: "No other attempt was made by them to advance, and about 1 P. M., I judge, by General Hill's order, I withdrew the whole of our front line." He evidently means his own brigade and the two brigades that had been sent to aid him. The losses in the 4 regiments of Pickett's brigade were 350.

General Hill had now succeeded in concentrating the right wing of the army "around the captured works." He says:

"The [remainder of the] day was spent in removing 6700 muskets and rifles in fine condition, ordnance, commissary and medical stores. Ten captured guns had been removed the night before. . . . General Longstreet sent me an order after dark to withdraw my whole command. The thirteen brigades were not got together until near midnight."

General Pickett says:

"General Hill sent for me about 1 o'clock at night, or, rather, morning of June 2d, and I went to the redoubt in search of him. . . . General Hill gave me orders to cover [the] withdrawal of the troops with my brigade. . . . The whole of our force filed past by half an hour after sunrise. I then leisurely moved off, not a Yankee in sight or even a puff of smoke."

The Federals resumed the positions they held that morning, with the exception of Sickles's brigade of Hooker's division, which occupied the ground where Colonel Jenkins's command ceased fighting the previous day. Some time after

SECOND LINE OF UNION WORKS AT THE "TWIN HOUSES" ON THE WILLIAMSBURG ROAD, LOOKING WEST. FROM A SKETCH MADE AT THE TIME.

After the battle of Seven Pines this position was greatly strengthened, as may be seen by comparing the above picture with the sketches of the same position on page 216.

sunrise, June 2d, the Federal pickets discovered that the Confederates had retired from Casey's captured works. At 5 P. M. that day General Hooker reported the result of an armed reconnoissance from which he had just returned. He says that a short distance in front of Casey's camp "the enemy appeared to have a regiment of cavalry and three of infantry, but as the latter were most concealed in the forest, it was not prudent to determine their number." At 3 A. M. that day the chief of staff of McClellan's army wrote to General Sumner: "The general commanding says, in reply to your dispatch, that you must do the best you can to hold your own if attacked. General Heintzelman will support you." At 11:50 P. M., June 3d, General Sumner wrote to General Kearny:

"From information I have received, I have reason to expect a formidable attack to-morrow morning. Please advance with your division at 2 A. M. in order to attack the flank of the enemy if he assails me in large force. Everything may depend upon this movement of yours."

The *theory* that the "Confederates attacked in full force," were repulsed, retreated in "disorganization and dismay," "which sent them to Richmond in a panic on the night of June 1st," is not in accordance with the facts already established, nor with any that are likely to be brought to light hereafter.

The divisions of Longstreet and Hill leisurely returned to the positions they occupied when the order to attack was given; but Huger's division remained well out on the Williamsburg road in advance of D. H. Hill's position. The latter fact is made clear by the following written statement of General Longstreet, dated June 3d, 1862. He says:

"The entire division of General Huger was left in advance upon retiring with the forces from the late battle-field. He was absent yesterday, but not coming to report after being sent for, I ordered General Stuart to take command of the division."

This in itself shows, beyond doubt, that General Longstreet was exercising control over Huger and Huger's division during these operations.

On the Nine-mile road the division under Whiting remained, for some days after the battle was ended, closely confronting Sumner's corps near Fair Oaks. In the letter already referred to, Colonel Frobel says:

"We remained in the position indicated until the afternoon, when the brigades were withdrawn a short distance to the shelter of heavy woods in our rear. I do not think after this that we changed our position for several days."

In his official report of what occurred the day after he was disabled and left the field, General Johnston says: "In the evening [June 1st] our troops quietly returned to their own camps."

The camps of the division under Whiting were on the Meadow Bridge road; this division remained on the Nine-mile road, a mile or more in advance of Magruder's line at Old Tavern. The camps of Huger's division were on the banks of Gilliss Creek, close to the suburbs of Richmond; this division remained on the Williamsburg road, more than a mile in advance of Hill's camps. The two divisions that did return to their camps left the field on the morning of June 2d — not "in the evening" of June 1st.

To complete this sketch of the battle of Seven Pines, it is essential to mention that, when I received General Longstreet's note, dated 1:30 P. M., June 1st, which ended with the exclamation, "Oh, that I had ten thousand men more," General Lee had just taken command of the army. He seemed very much impressed by the state of affairs on the Williamsburg road as depicted in General Longstreet's note. I assured him, however, that Longstreet was mistaken in supposing that the whole Federal army was opposed to him; that I had several hours before nearly stripped the Chickahominy, between New Bridge and Mechanicsville, in order to send him reënforcements; and that the danger to Richmond, if any, was not then on the Williamsburg road, if it ever had been.

General Lee gave me no orders that day. The fact that Longstreet's and D. H. Hill's divisions were sent back to their former camps induces me to believe that this was in compliance with orders given by General Lee to General Longstreet — perhaps for the reason that on May 31st we had not fully succeeded in crushing one Federal corps isolated at Seven Pines, and on June 1st had lost all the ground beyond Seven Pines that we had gained the day previous.

I was completely prostrated on the 2d of June by an attack of paralysis, no symptom of which was manifested within eighteen hours after Lee relieved me of the command of the army. But, for that misfortune, I would certainly

AFTER THE BATTLE OF SEVEN PINES — PETTIT'S BATTERY IN FORT RICHARDSON, IN FRONT OF FAIR OAKS STATION, BETWEEN THE NINE-MILE ROAD AND THE RAILROAD. FROM A PHOTOGRAPH.

have required all subordinates to report to me events that took place on the field in their respective commands whilst I was in control of the army.

The detailed reports of regimental and brigade commanders on both sides in this battle show many instances of close, persistent, and bloody fighting, such as have been seldom equaled by any troops on any field. Cases of temporary confusion and disorder occurred, but fair examination shows there was good reason for this. In reference to the general management, however, it may well be said that General McClellan committed a grave error in allowing Keyes's corps to remain isolated for several days within easy striking distance of General Johnston's army. The intention of the latter to throw Longstreet's division against Keyes's exposed and weak right flank was the best plan that could have been adopted. The first great blunder consisted in Longstreet's taking his division from the Nine-mile road to the Williamsburg road, and the next in placing six brigades on the Charles City road, where there was no enemy. Five of these brigades were marching and countermarching on the latter road, and struggling through the White Oak Swamp, in mud and water waist-deep, to reach the Williamsburg road miles in rear of the fighting, where General Longstreet then was, whilst Colonel Jenkins's three regiments were scouring the rear of the Nine-mile road from Fair Oaks to Seven Pines; thus not only saving the right of Hill's division from being driven out of Casey's captured works by Federal reënforcements under Kearny, but forcing Keyes and Heintzelman to their third line of defense. No one can fairly doubt what would have been the result, if at 3 P. M., when Hill's division alone had carried Casey's works, the five brigades that had been sent to the Charles City road had been within supporting distance of Hill, and had been promptly put in close action, and Pickett's brigade had

AFTER THE BATTLE OF SEVEN PINES — PUTTING THE WOUNDED ON CARS. FROM A SKETCH MADE AT THE TIME.

been thrown forward instead of being held far back on the railroad by Longstreet's order "to repel any advance of the enemy up that road." Instead of putting his own troops into the fight, even late in the afternoon, Longstreet called on General Johnston for help, and complained of the latter's "slowness."

It is not proposed to speculate here upon what might have happened on the second day, if General Longstreet had made any attempt to carry out the orders he received to renew the attack. But it may be well to emphasize the fact that if Longstreet's division had promptly moved, on the Nine-mile road, at daybreak, May 31st, and been put in close action on that side, whilst D. H. Hill's division attacked in front,— as Johnston certainly intended,— there would have been no occasion to make excuses for the failure of complete Confederate success in wiping out Keyes's corps, early in the morning of May 31st, before it could have been reënforced by either Heintzelman or Sumner.‡

‡ On the 15th of May, the Union gun-boats opened fire on the forts at Drewry's Bluff, twelve miles below Richmond, and soon after Johnston's army retired, opening the way for McClellan's advance to within seven miles of Richmond, whose citizens believed at this time that the Confederate authorities would be compelled to evacuate the city. The archives were shipped to Columbia, S. C., the public treasure was kept on cars ready for transportation to a place of safety. Confidence was restored before the battle of Seven Pines. On May 25th and 26th, Lieutenant F. C. Davis, of the 3d Pennsylvania Cavalry, with eleven men rode from Bottom's Bridge, by way of White Oak Bridge and Charles City Court House, to the James River and communicated with the gun-boat fleet. After the battle of Seven Pines, General Lee determined to defend Richmond on the line then held by his army. This fact, in connection with the success of General Jackson in freeing the Shenandoah Valley of Union forces, restored the confidence of the people at Richmond. A large draft of soldiers from the ranks furnished a laboring force to build intrenchments, and slaves in the counties around Richmond were impressed for the work.

On the 18th of June, Brigadier-General Cuvier Grover's brigade, of Hooker's division, made a reconnoissance between the Williamsburg road and the railroad, and found the Confederates in force behind earth-works. The divisions of Hooker and Kearny advanced on the 25th to a point called Oak Grove, about four miles from Richmond, in front of Seven Pines. This was the nearest approach to Richmond during the investment by McClellan.— EDITORS.

ON THE GUN-DECK OF THE CONFEDERATE IRON-CLAD, "MERRIMAC."

## THE NAVY IN THE PENINSULAR CAMPAIGN.

### BY PROFESSOR JAMES RUSSELL SOLEY, U. S. N.

AT the opening of the Peninsular campaign, April 1st, 1862, the North Atlantic Squadron, with its headquarters at Hampton Roads, was commanded by Flag-Officer Louis M. Goldsborough. The command included not only the operations in the Chesapeake and its tributary waters, but an entirely distinct series of operations in the sounds of North Carolina, and a third distinct and also very important service,— that of the Wilmington blockade. This concentration of command at a distance from the various fields of action was not without injurious results. The attention of the flag-officer could not be successfully directed at the same instant of time to such varied and complicated movements as were simultaneously in progress in the York River, the James River, Hampton Roads, Albemarle Sound, and the entrance to Wilmington.

Of the various plans for a direct movement upon Richmond considered by the civil and military authorities in the winter of 1861–62, that by way of Urbana on the Rappahannock River was finally adopted, but the withdrawal of General Johnston from Centreville led to a change of plan at the last moment; and on the 13th of March it was decided to advance from Fort Monroe as a base. The detailed plan of General McClellan comprehended an attack by the navy upon the batteries at Yorktown and Gloucester, on opposite sides of the York River. It was upon the navy that he chiefly relied to reduce these obstacles to his progress and to clear the way to his proposed base, the White House on the Pamunkey River. This fact was made known to the War Department, but apparently the Navy Department was not fully apprised of it. The question was asked of the Navy Department whether the *Merrimac*, at that time lying in the Elizabeth River, could be held in check, and Assistant Secretary Fox replied that the *Monitor* would be sufficient for that purpose. Captain Fox said:

"It was determined that the army should go by way of Fort Monroe. The Navy Department never was consulted at all, to my knowledge, in regard to anything connected with the matter. No statement was ever made to us why they were going there beyond this."⸸

General McClellan arrived at Old Point on the 2d of April, and immediately communicated with Flag-Officer Goldsborough. The advance of the army was to begin at once. Notwithstanding that he had previously considered it an essential part of his plan that Yorktown should be reduced by the navy, McClellan does not appear even at this time to have strenuously urged it, for Goldsborough afterward stated to the Committee on the Conduct of the War that he performed every service in connection with army operations which was requested of him by General McClellan. It may be that the naval attack on Yorktown and Gloucester was not pressed because McClellan learned in this interview that it was impracticable. On this point Fox said:

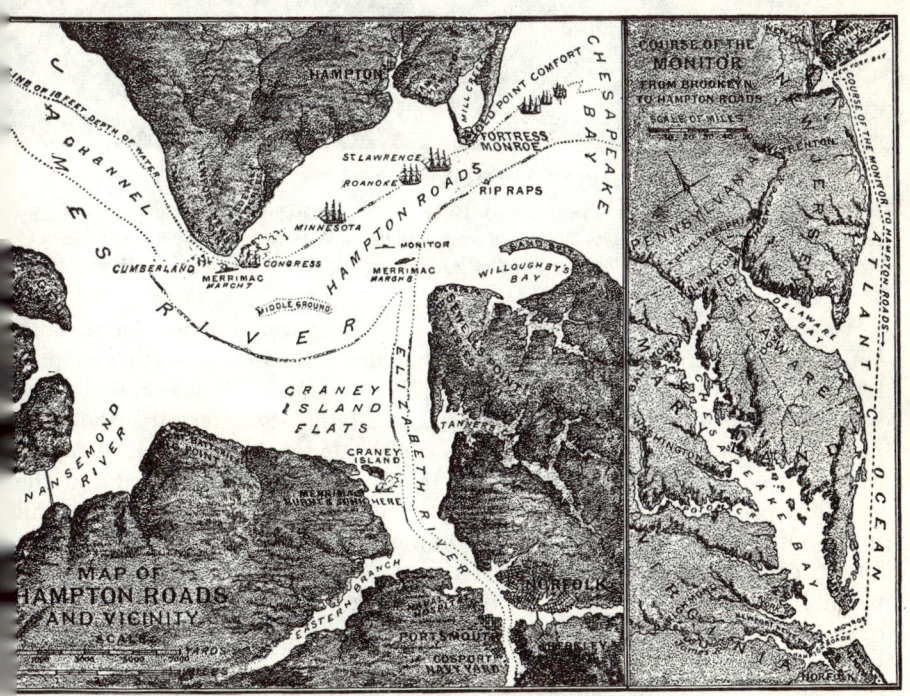

MAPS OF THE "MONITOR" AND "MERRIMAC" FIGHT [SEE ALSO VOL. I., P. 692], AND OF OPERATIONS IN THE YORK AND JAMES RIVERS.

⸸ On the 14th of March, Secretary Welles wrote to Secretary Stanton regarding McClellan's call for naval assistance:

"If a movement is to be made upon Norfolk, always a favorite measure of this Department, instant measures will be taken to advise and strengthen Flag-Officer Goldsborough; but unless such be the case, I should be extremely reluctant to take any measure that would even temporarily weaken the efficiency of the blockade."

On the 17th Gen. McDowell wrote to McClellan: "In connection with General Barnard I have had a long conference with Assistant Secretary Fox, as to naval coöperation. He promises all the power of the Department shall be at our disposal." EDITORS.

IN THE TURRET OF THE "MONITOR."

"Wooden vessels could not have attacked the batteries at Yorktown and Gloucester with any degree of success. The forts at Yorktown were situated too high, were beyond the reach of naval guns, and *I understand that General McClellan never expected any attack to be made on them by the navy.*"

At McClellan's request Goldsborough sent 7 gun-boats under Commander William Smith into the York River, the *Marblehead* on the 4th of April, followed the next day by the *Wachusett*, *Penobscot*, and *Currituck*, and later by the *Sebago*, *Corwin*, and *Chocura*. The *Maratanza* afterward took the place of the *Penobscot*. The rest of the fleet, including the *Monitor*, remained to watch the *Merrimac*. On the 1st of May, during an attack made on the left flank of the army, the fleet shelled the enemy's artillery, posted on a hill to the left, and forced it to retire. On the 5th, the day following the evacuation of Yorktown, the fleet moved up to a position off the town, and a reconnoissance made by the *Chocura* and *Corwin* showed that the river was open as far as West Point. On the 6th, Commander Smith moved the gun-boats up to that place, escorting the transports carrying General Franklin's division. On the 7th, before the landing of the troops was completed, a sharp attack was made by the enemy and repulsed, the gun-boats rendering efficient assistance. On the 17th, the *Sebago* and *Currituck* passed up the Pamunkey, which resulted in the destruction of the enemy's store-vessels. When the *Wachusett* was withdrawn to the James, five boats remained to protect McClellan's base, under the command of Lieutenant Alexander Murray.

During the siege of Yorktown the presence of the *Merrimac* had, of course, paralyzed the efforts of the navy in the waters adjoining Hampton Roads. It was necessary that she should be neutralized at all hazards, or her appearance either in the York or James River would become a serious obstacle to the success of the campaign. But for the negligence of the Navy Department in postponing the building of iron-clads until six months after the war had begun, and that of the War Department in omitting, during the six following months, when it had 150,000 men lying inactive around Washington, to send 50,000 of them to capture Norfolk, the *Merrimac* would never have become a serious factor in the situation. As, however, General McClellan had been satisfied to leave Norfolk to be turned by his advance on the Peninsula, and as the Navy Department had thus far succeeded in getting afloat only one iron-clad, the efforts of the force at Hampton Roads were necessarily concentrated on holding the enemy in check. This was the first consideration of the flag-officer from March 9th, when the engagement took place between the *Monitor* and *Merrimac* [see Vol. I., p. 692], until May 11th, when the latter was destroyed. During most of this time — that is, from April 5th to May 4th — the Army of the Potomac was conducting the siege of Yorktown.

After the battle of the 9th of March, Tattnall had taken command of the *Merrimac*, and on the 4th of April she came out of the dock thoroughly repaired, and, except for her engines, in good condition. On the morning of the 11th she steamed down Elizabeth River and came out into the Roads, advancing to a position between Sewell's Point and Newport News. Goldsborough, with the *Minnesota*, the *Monitor*, and other vessels of his squadron, was lying near Fort Monroe. The

FORT DARLING. [SEE MAP, P. 272.] FROM A PHOTOGRAPH.

transports and store-ships at this time in the neighborhood had been warned of the danger of lying near Hampton, and most of them had withdrawn under the protection of the fort. Three vessels of the quartermaster's department still remained near Newport News. They had been run on shore. The Confederate gun-boats *Jamestown* and *Raleigh*, under Captain Barney and Captain Alexander, were sent to tow them off. This was handsomely done, in full view of the Union vessels, which offered no opposition, notwithstanding the challenge offered by the captors in hoisting the flags of their prizes Union down. This event, rendered all the more humiliating by the presence of a foreign ship-of-war, was suffered by Goldsborough because, in accordance with the wishes of the Department, it was his duty to hold in check the *Merrimac*; and he feared that a collision between the gun-boats might bring on a general engagement.

During April the squadron was gradually increased by the addition of new vessels, including the new iron-clad *Galena*, and several fast steamers, the *Arago, Vanderbilt, Illinois*, and *Ericsson*, as rams. When it was apparent that the Confederates would shortly be compelled to abandon Norfolk, a squadron, consisting of the *Galena*, the gun-boat *Aroostook*, and the double-ender *Port Royal*, was sent up the James River on the 8th of May, by direction of the President. On the same day a demonstration made by the fleet against the battery at Sewell's Point led the *Merrimac* to come out again from the river. The *Monitor* had orders to fall back into fair channel-way, and only engage the *Merrimac* seriously in such a position as to enable the *Minnesota* and the other vessels to run her down if an opportunity offered. According to Flag-Officer Goldsborough, "the *Merrimac* came out, but was even more cautious than ever. The *Monitor* was kept well in advance, and so that the *Merrimac* could have engaged her without difficulty had she been so disposed; but she declined to do it, and soon returned and anchored under Sewell's Point." Commodore Tattnall said:

REAR-ADMIRAL JOHN RODGERS. FROM A PHOTOGRAPH.

"We passed the battery and stood directly for the enemy for the purpose of engaging him and I thought an action certain, particularly as the *Minnesota* and *Vanderbilt*, which were anchored below Fortress Monroe, got under way and stood up to that point, apparently with the intention of joining their squadron in the Roads. Before, however, we got within gunshot the enemy ceased firing and retired with all speed under the protection of the guns of the fortress, followed by the *Virginia*, until the shells from the Rip-Raps passed over her. The *Virginia* was then placed at her moorings near Sewell's Point."

This was the last exploit of the *Merrimac*. On the 10th, Norfolk was abandoned, and was immediately occupied by the Union forces under General Wool. Early the next morning Commodore Tattnall, being unable to carry out his plan of taking the *Merrimac* up the James River, destroyed her near Craney Island. Meantime, the *Galena* and her consorts under Commander John Rodgers had been working their way up the James River. On the first day two batteries were encountered. The first, at Rock Wharf, was silenced. The resistance of the second, at Hardin's Bluff, was more obstinate, but Rodgers, in the *Galena*, lay abreast of the enemy's guns and kept up a steady fire disconcerting their aim while the wooden boats went by. During the next week Rodgers continued on his course up the James, meeting with no serious impediment until he arrived at Drewry's Bluff, eight miles below Richmond.

At this time, May 15th, the flotilla had been increased by the addition of

FORT DARLING, LOOKING DOWN THE JAMES. FROM A PHOTOGRAPH.

SUNKEN STEAMBOATS AND OTHER OBSTRUCTIONS IN THE JAMES RIVER, NEAR FORT DARLING, ON DREWRY'S BLUFF. FROM A PHOTOGRAPH.

the *Monitor* and the *Naugatuck*. Fort Darling (Commander E. Farrand, C. S. N.), at Drewry's Bluff, was a strong position, two hundred feet above the river, and mounting a number of heavy guns. At the foot of the bluff an obstruction had been placed in the river formed of sunken vessels secured by chains. The light armor of the *Galena* had not as yet been seriously tested, and Rodgers had no great confidence in her ability to stand a severe fire; nevertheless, he decided to make the test. In a private letter written shortly after, he said: "I was convinced as soon as I came on board that she would be riddled under fire, but the public thought differently, and I resolved to give the matter a fair trial." Accordingly, he ran the *Galena* up to a point opposite the battery, where the width of the stream was not more than double the ship's length. According to an officer in the fort, the *Galena* "steamed up to within seven or eight hundred yards of the bluff, let go her starboard anchor, ran out the chains, put her head inshore, backed astern, let go her stream-anchor from the starboard quarter, hove ahead, and made ready for action before firing a gun." Nothing could have been more beautiful than the neatness and precision of movement with which Rodgers placed the *Galena*, as if at target-practice, directly under the enemy's fire. In the words of the officer already quoted, "It was one of the most masterly pieces of seamanship of the whole war."

In this position the *Galena* remained for three hours and twenty minutes until she had expended all her ammunition. She came out of the action badly shattered, having been struck 28 times and perforated in 18 places. The *Monitor* passed for a short time above the *Galena*, but being unable to elevate her guns sufficiently to reach the bluff, she again dropped below. The wooden vessels coöperated as far as possible, but of course could not accomplish much. The attack made it clear that the obstructions could not be passed without first reducing the fort, and that the fort could not be reduced without the coöperation of the army. Notwithstanding the vital importance of such a movement, seeing that Fort Darling was the only obstacle to the direct passage up the river to Richmond, and that a small force would have sufficed to accomplish the work, nothing was done by General McClellan. According to Goldsborough's testimony, he went in person to the White House to see McClellan, and, showing him Rodgers's report of the fight, offered the coöperation of the squadron, if McClellan would make the attack with a land force. "General McClellan," he adds, "replied to me that he would prefer to defer his answer until he got his army on the other side of the Chickahominy." On the 17th of May, Flag-Officer Goldsborough, in the *Susquehanna*, with the *Wachusett*, *Dacotah*, and *Maratanza*, had destroyed the two abandoned batteries of the enemy at Rock Wharf and Hardin's Bluff. All this time, and during the campaign, James River was open to Fort Darling.

On the 18th of May, Commander William Smith arrived at City Point in the *Wachusett*, and relieved Rodgers of the command, being the senior officer. The force was gradually increased, and in June comprised, in addition to the vessels already mentioned, the *Mahaska*, *Jacob Bell*, *Southfield*, *Maratanza*, *Stepping Stones*, and *Delaware*. Commander Gillis shortly after relieved Smith. Occasional attacks were made upon passing gun-boats by field-batteries of the Confederates stationed along the river-banks. The difficulties of the channel and the unprotected character of the vessels rendered them liable to serious injury from such attacks, and the *Jacob Bell*, under Lieutenant McCrea, narrowly escaped severe loss at Watkin's Bluff on the 21st of June. On the 27th, a demonstration was made up the Appomattox, but nothing was accomplished, the channel proving to be too shoal for successful operations.

On the 29th, McClellan's retreating army opened communication with Rodgers, who now commanded the vessels in the James River. Little change had taken place in the composition of the force since the 1st of June, the *Wachusett* only having left the squadron, and the *Satellite* having joined it. The gun-boats rendered efficient assistance to the army, especially in the battle at Malvern Hill on the 1st of July. By the 4th of July, McClellan's position was comparatively secure.

On July 6th, the James River flotilla was organized as a separate command under Captain Charles Wilkes, and so remained, until disbanded, on August 31st, the withdrawal of the army rendering its presence no longer necessary.

## STUART'S RIDE AROUND McCLELLAN.

### BY W. T. ROBINS, COLONEL, C. S. A.

TROOPER OF THE VIRGINIA CAVALRY, 1861.

THE battle of "Seven Pines," or "Fair Oaks," had been fought with no result. The temporary success of the Confederates early in the engagement had been more than counterbalanced by the reverses they sustained on the second day, and the two armies lay passively watching each other in front of Richmond. At this time the cavalry of Lee's army was commanded by General J. E. B. Stuart, and this restless officer conceived the idea of flanking the right wing of the Federal army near Ashland, and moving around to the rear, to cross the Chickahominy River at a place called Sycamore Ford, in New Kent County, march over to the James River, and return to the Confederate lines near Deep Bottom, in Henrico County. In carrying out this plan, Stuart would completely encircle the army of General McClellan. At the time of this movement the writer was adjutant of the 9th Virginia cavalry. When the orders were issued from headquarters directing the several commands destined to form the expedition to prepare three days' rations, and the ordnance officers to issue sixty rounds of ammunition to each man, I remember the surmises and conjectures as to our destination. The officers and men were in high spirits in anticipation of a fight, and when the bugles rang out "Boots and Saddles," every man was ready. The men left behind in camp were bewailing their luck, and those forming the detail for the expedition were elated at the prospect of some excitement. "Good-bye, boys; we are going to help old Jack drive the Yanks into the Potomac,"☆ I heard one of them shout to those left behind.

On the afternoon of June 12th we went out to the Brooke turnpike, preparatory to the march. The cavalry column was the 9th Virginia, commanded by Colonel W. H. F. Lee, the 1st Virginia, led by Colonel Fitz Lee, and the Jeff Davis Legion, under Colonel Martin. A section of the Stuart Horse Artillery, commanded by Captain Pelham, accompanied the expedition. The whole numbered twelve hundred men. The first night was passed in bivouac in the vicinity of Ashland, and orders were issued enforcing strict silence and forbidding the use of fires, as the success of the expedition would depend upon secrecy and celerity. On the following morning, at the break of dawn, the troopers were mounted and the march was begun without a bugle blast, and the column headed direct for Hanover Court House, distant about two hours' ride. Here we had the first sight of the enemy. A scouting party of the 5th U. S. Cavalry was in the village, but speedily decamped when our troops were ascertained to be Confederates. One prisoner was taken after a hot chase across country. We now moved rapidly to Hawes's Shop, where a Federal picket was surprised and captured without firing a shot. Hardly had the prisoners been disarmed and turned over to the provost guard when the Confederate advance was driven in upon the main body by a squadron of Federal cavalry, sent out from Old Church to ascertain by reconnoissance whether the report of a Confederate advance was true or false. General Stuart at once ordered Colonel W. H. F. Lee, commanding the regiment leading the column, to throw forward a squadron to meet the enemy. Colonel Lee directed Captain Swann, chief of the leading squadron of his regiment, to charge with the saber. Swann moved off at a trot, and, turning a corner of the road, saw the enemy's squadron about two hundred yards in front of him. The order to charge was given, and the men dashed forward in fine style. The onset was so sudden that the Federal cavalry broke and scattered in confusion. The latter had a start of barely two hundred yards, but the Confederate yell that broke upon the air lent them wings, and only a few fell into our hands. The rest made their escape after a chase of a mile and a half. Now the road became very narrow, and the brush on either side was a place so favorable for an ambuscade that Captain Swann deemed it prudent to draw rein and sound the bugle to recall his men. Stuart, who had been marching steadily onward with the main body of the Confederate column, soon arrived at the front, and the advance-guard, which I had all along commanded, was directed to move forward again. I at once dismounted the men, and pushed forward up a hill

---

☆ Stuart's raiders left camp ostensibly to go to Northern Virginia.—EDITORS.

271

in my front. Just beyond the hill, I ran into a force of Federal cavalry drawn up in column of fours, ready to charge. Just as my advance-guard was about to run into him, I heard their commanding officer give the order to charge. I fell back and immediately notified General Stuart of the presence of the enemy. Captain Latané, commanding a squadron of the 9th Virginia, was directed to move forward and clear the road. He moved up the hill at a trot, and when in sight of the enemy in the road gave the command to charge, and with a yell the men rushed forward. At the top of the hill, simultaneously with Latané's order to charge, a company of Federal cavalry, deployed as skirmishers in the woods on the right of the road, were stampeded, and rushed back into the woods to make good their retreat to their friends. The head of Latané's squadron, then just fairly up the hill, was in the line of their retreat and was separated from the rest of the squadron, cut off by the rush of the Federals, and borne along with them up the road toward the enemy. I was riding at the side of Latané, and just at the time when the Federal company rushed back into the road Captain Latané fell from his horse, shot dead. The rush of the Federals separated myself and six of the leading files of the squadron from our friends, and we were borne along by the flying Federals. Although the Federal cavalry both in front and rear were in full retreat, our situation was perilous in the extreme. Soon we were pushed by foes in our rear into the ranks of those in our front, and a series of hand-to-hand combats ensued. To shoot or to cut us down was the aim of every Federal as he neared us, but we did what we could to defend ourselves. Every one of my comrades was shot or cut down, and I alone escaped unhurt. After having been borne along by the retreating enemy for perhaps a quarter of a mile, I leaped my horse over the fence into the field and so got away.

Now came the rush of the Confederate column, sweeping the road clear, and capturing many prisoners. At this point my regiment was relieved by the 1st Virginia, and Colonel Lee continued the pursuit. The Federals did not attempt to make a stand until they reached Old Church. Here their officers called a halt, and made an attempt to rally to defend their camp. Fitz Lee soon swept them out, and burned their camp. They made no other attempt to stand, and we heard no more of them as an organized body, but many prisoners were taken as we passed along. We had surprised them, taken them in detail, and far outnumbered them at all points. The Federal forces, as we afterward learned, were commanded by General Philip St. George Cooke, father-in-law to General Stuart, to whom the latter sent a polite message. The casualties in this skirmish were slight—one man killed on each side, and about fifteen or twenty wounded on the Confederate side, mostly saber-cuts.

We halted for a short time at Old Church, and the people of the neighborhood, hearing of our arrival, came flocking out to greet us and wish us God-speed. They did not come empty-handed, but brought whatever they could snatch up on the spur of the moment, rightly supposing that anything to allay hunger or thirst would be acceptable to us. Some of the ladies brought bouquets, and presented them to the officers as they marched along. One of these was given to General Stuart, who, always gallant, vowed to preserve it and take it into Richmond. He kept his promise.

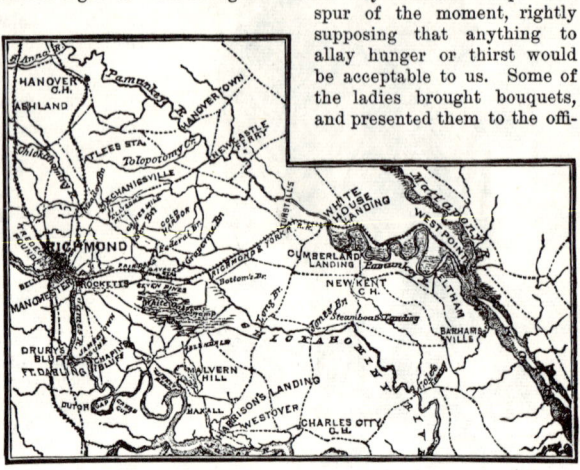

MAP OF STUART'S RIDE AROUND McCLELLAN.

We were soon far in rear of McClellan's army, which lay directly between us and Richmond. It was thought probable that the Federal cavalry was concentrating in *our* rear to cut off our retreat. We kept straight on, by Smith's store, through New Kent County to Tunstall's station, on the York River Railroad. I had been in charge of the Confederate advance-guard up to the time when Colonel Fitz Lee came to the front with the 1st Virginia, relieving the 9th of that duty. When well down in New Kent County, General Stuart sent for me again to the front. Hurrying on, I soon reached the head of the column, where I found the general, and was directed by him to take thirty men as an advance-guard, and to precede the column by about half a mile. Further, I was directed to halt at the road running from the mills to the White House long enough to cut the telegraph wire on that road; thence to proceed to Tunstall's station on the York River Railroad, at which place, the prisoners had informed the general, a company of Federal infantry was posted. At Tunstall's station I was directed to charge the infantry, disperse or capture them, cut the telegraph, and obstruct the railroad. Here was our point of danger. Once across the railroad, we were comparatively safe. But in possession of the railroad, with its rolling-stock the enemy could easily throw troops along its line to any given point. However, no timely information had been furnished to the Federal general. We moved with such celerity that we carried with us the first news of our arrival. Pushing forward at a trot, and picking up straggling prisoners every few hundred yards, the advance-guard at length reached the telegraph road. At this point we overtook an ordnance wagon, heavily loaded with canteens and Colt's revolvers. The horses had stalled in a mud-hole, and the driver, cutting them out from the wagon, made his escape. The sergeant in charge stood his ground and was captured. Here was a prize indeed, as in those days we were poorly armed. In order to save time, a man furnished with an ax was sent to cut the telegraph wire, while the rest of the party was engaged in rifling the wagon. While these operations were in progress a body of Federal cavalry, suddenly turning a bend in the road, made their appearance. As soon as the Federal officer in command saw us he called a halt, and, standing still in the road, seemed at a loss to know what to do. His men drew their sabers, as if about to charge, but they did not come on. By this time the telegraph had been cut and the wagon disposed of. Our men were hastily mounted and formed into column of fours, with drawn sabers, ready for any emergency. There we stood, eying each other, about two hundred yards apart, until the head of the main Confederate column came in sight, when the Federals retreated down the road leading to the White House. One man of the Federal party was sent back along the road to Tunstall's station, now only about half a mile off. I supposed, of course, that this messenger was sent to warn the Federal troops at Tunstall's of our approach. I was, however, afterward informed that he galloped through Tunstall's but never stopped, and when some one called to him, "What's to pay?" he dashed along, calling out, at the top of his voice, "Hell's to pay!"

The road now being clear, we marched on briskly, and arriving near the station charged down upon it with a yell. We could see the enemy scattered about the building and lounging around before we charged them. The greater part scattered for cover, and were pursued by our people. I pushed straight for the station-house, where I found the captain of the company of infantry, with thirteen of his men, standing in front of the building, but with no arms in their hands. Only one of them seemed disposed to show fight. He ran to the platform where the muskets were stacked, and, seizing one of them, began to load. Before he could ram his cartridge home, a sweep of the saber, in close proximity to his head, made him throw down his gun, and, jumping into a ditch, he dodged under the bridge over the railroad and made his escape. I had no time to pursue him; but, turning to look after the others, met the captain, who, sword in hand, advanced and surrendered himself and his company as prisoners of war. I then proceeded to obstruct the railroad. To do this effectually, I caused a tree to be cut down which was standing on the side of the road. It fell across the railroad. In addition to this, I placed across the tracks an oak-sill about a foot square and fourteen feet long. I had barely time to do this before a train from the direction of Richmond came thundering down. At this time General Stuart, with the main body, arrived at the station. The engine driver of the coming train, probably seeing the obstructions on the track and a large force of cavalry there, suspected danger, and, being a plucky fellow, put on all steam, and came rushing down. The engine, striking the obstructions, knocked them out of the way and passed on without accident. General Stuart had dismounted a number of his men, and posted them on a high bank overlooking a cut in the road, just below the station, through which the train was about to pass. They threw in a close and effective fire upon the passing train, loaded with troops. Many of these were killed and wounded.

It was now the second night since leaving camp, and the well-filled haversacks with which we started from camp had long since been empty. The march had been so rapid that there was little opportunity of foraging for man or beast. Except a little bread and meat, brought out to the column by the country people as we passed along, we had had nothing since daybreak. The men were weary and hungry, and the horses almost exhausted by the long fast and severe exercise. As soon as a proper disposition had been made of the prisoners and of the captured horses and mules, the column moved on. Down through New Kent County, to a place called New Baltimore, we marched as rapidly as our condition would permit. I was still in the command of the advance-guard, marching some distance ahead of the column, and had orders to halt at this point, and await the coming up of the main body. Fortunately, an enterprising Yankee had established a store here, to catch the trade of all persons passing from McClellan's army to his base of supplies at the White House. He had crackers, cheese, canned fruits, sardines, and many other dainties dear to the cavalryman; and in the brief hour spent with him we of the advance were made new men. I fear little was left to cheer and to invigorate those in the rear. The main body arriving, "forward" was the order — straight down through New Kent to Sycamore Ford on the Chickahominy.

A beautiful full moon lighted our way and cast weird shadows across our path. Expecting each moment to meet the enemy, every bush in the distance looked like a sentinel, and every jagged tree bending over the road like a vidette. Marching all night, we arrived at the ford between daybreak and sunrise; and here our real troubles began. To our chagrin, we found the stream swollen by recent rains almost out of its banks, and running like a torrent. No man or horse could get over without swimming, and it happened that the entrance to the ford on our side was below the point at which we had to come out on the other side. Therefore, we had to swim against the current. Owing to the mud and mire, it was not practicable for any number of horses to approach the river at any point except by the road

DUEL BETWEEN A UNION CAVALRYMAN AND A CONFEDERATE TROOPER.

leading to the ford. We therefore tried it there for two long hours. The 9th Cavalry made the trial. After repeated efforts to swim the horses over we gave up, for we had crossed over only seventy-five men and horses in two hours. While we were trying to reach the opposite bank Stuart came up, and, finding crossing at this point impracticable, rode off to find another farther down the river.‡ At a point about one mile below, known as Forge Bridge, he succeeded in throwing across one branch of the river a bridge strong enough to bear the artillery, and upon which the men, having been dismounted, could walk. Here the approach on our side was higher up stream than the point at which we would come out on the other side. So the horses were formed into a column of fours, pushed into the water, and, swimming down stream, they easily landed on the other side. After a few horses had been crossed in this manner we found no difficulty, the others following on quite readily. The column was now upon an island formed by the two branches of the Chickahominy, and to reach the mainland it was necessary to cross the other branch of that river.

This was, however, accomplished, but with some difficulty. The ford at this crossing was at that time very deep, and the river out of its banks and overflowing the flats to the depth of about two feet for at least a half-mile. At this place the limber to a caisson stuck fast in the mud, and we left it.

On leaving the river, General Stuart directed me to take charge of the rear-guard, and, when all had crossed, to burn the bridge. In accordance with these orders, I directed the men to collect piles of fence rails, heap them on the bridge, and set them afire. By my orders the horses had been led some distance back from the river into the brush, where they were concealed from view. The men were lounging about on the ground when the bridge fell in. I was seated under a tree on the bank of the river, and at the moment that the hissing of the burning timbers of the bridge let me know that it had fallen into the water, a rifle-shot rang out from the other side, and the whistling bullet cut off a small limb over my head, which fell into my lap. The shot was probably fired by some scout who had been following us,

‡ General Stuart says in his report: "The progress in crossing was very slow at the point chosen, just above Forge Bridge, and learning that at the bridge proper enough of the débris of the old bridge remained to facilitate the construction of another, material for which was afforded by a large warehouse adjacent, I moved to that point at once. . . . In three hours it was ready to bear artillery and cavalry. . . ."— EDITORS.

but who was afraid to fire until the bridge was gone. With a thankful heart for his bad aim, I at once withdrew the men, and pushed on after the column. When I came to the ford, I found it necessary to swim the horses a short distance, it having been deepened by the crossing of such a large body of horse. Soon the column was in sight, and the march across Charles City County to the James River was made as vigorously as the jaded horses were able to stand. The men, though weary and hungry, were in fine spirits, and jubilant over the successful crossing of the Chickahominy. About sunset we neared the James, at the plantation of Colonel Wilcox. Here we rested for about two hours, having marched into a field of clover, where the horses ate their fill. In the twilight, fires were lighted to cook the rations just brought in by our foragers.

We were now twenty-five miles from Richmond, on the "James River Road." Had the enemy been aware of our position, it would have been easy for him to throw a force between us and Richmond, and so cut us off. But the Federal general was not well served by his scouts, nor did his cavalry furnish him with accurate information of our movements. Relying upon the mistakes of the enemy, Stuart resolved to march straight on into Richmond by the River road on which we now lay. To accomplish this with the greater safety, it was necessary for him to march at once. Accordingly, I was ordered to take the advance guard and move out. As soon as the cravings of hunger were appeased, sleep took possession of us. Although in the saddle and in motion, and aware that the safety of the expedition depended on great vigilance in case the enemy should be encountered, it was hard to keep awake. I was constantly falling asleep, and awaking with a start when almost off my horse. This was the condition of every man in the column. Not one had closed his eyes in sleep for forty-eight hours.

The full moon lighted us on our way as we passed along the River road, and frequently the windings of the road brought us near to and in sight of the James River, where lay the enemy's fleet. In the gray twilight of the dawn of Sunday, we passed the "Double Gates," "Strawberry Plains," and "Tighlman's gate" in succession. At "Tighlman's" we could see the masts of the fleet, not far off. Happily for us, the banks were high, and I imagine they had no lookout in the rigging, and we passed by unobserved. The sight of the enemy's fleet had aroused us somewhat, when "Who goes there?" rang out on the stillness of the early morning. The challenger proved to be a vidette of the 10th Virginia Cavalry, commanded by Colonel J. Lucius Davis, who was picketing that road. Soon I was shaking hands with Colonel Davis and receiving his congratulations. Then we crossed the stream by the jug factory, up toward "New Market" heights, by the drill-house, and about a mile beyond we called halt for a little rest and food. From this point the several regiments were dismissed to their respective camps.

We lost one man killed and a few wounded, and no prisoners.☆ The most important result was the confidence the men had gained in themselves and in their leaders. The country rang out with praises of the men who had raided entirely around General McClellan's powerful army, bringing prisoners and plunder from under his very nose. The Southern papers were filled with accounts of the expedition, none accurate, and most of them marvelous.

## ANECDOTES OF THE PENINSULAR CAMPAIGN.

### I.— GENERAL JOHNSTON TO THE RESCUE. BY F. Y. DABNEY.

IT was the morning of the day on which the battle of Williamsburg was fought that the following incident occurred. Late in the afternoon of the preceding day, general orders had been issued by General Joseph E. Johnston, informing us of the intended retrograde movement on the next morning. Among the instructions was one to the effect that any gun caisson, quartermaster, or commissary wagon which might become set in the mud so as to impede the line of march must be destroyed at once. In other words, the road must be kept clear. At that time the writer was a lieutenant in Snowden Andrews's battery of light artillery, and, as such, commanded one section of 2 guns, which, with their caissons, required 4 teams of 6 horses each. Of these 4 teams, 3 were in fair condition for service, but the fourth was notoriously weak. When the general's order was read, I became very anxious about this team, especially as nothing is considered more humiliating to a battery than to have to part with a portion of its equipment, no matter what the cause may be; so that when the retreat was commenced the next morning I endeavored to keep all the men of my section well in hand, and ready to assist at a moment's notice. For six miles north of Williamsburg the entire army was falling back over a single road, and as there had been frequent rains, this road was badly cut up, and the mud in many places was up to the axles of the guns. Finally my weak team balked with the gun — a 12-pounder Napoleon — in a deep hole. Every effort was made by the drivers to dislodge the gun, but without avail; and I found when I got to the wheels, with as many men as could be utilized, that the horses could not be made to work in concert. The whole line to the rear was at a dead stand-still, when I observed a party of mounted officers coming down the road from the front, and in a few moments more I recognized General Johnston

---

☆ General Stuart reported the capture of 165 prisoners, including teamsters and other non-combatants, 260 horses and mules, with more or less harness, and some small-arms.— EDITORS.

at their head. We all were covered with mud and straining every muscle to extricate the gun, when the general, resplendent in uniform, white gauntlets, and polished cavalry boots, rode up and halted by our side. I gave the military salute and stood like a criminal awaiting sentence. To my surprise he remarked in a very kindly tone: "Well, Lieutenant, you seem to be in trouble." "Yes, sir," I replied; "and I am afraid we shall have to abandon this gun." "Oh, no; I reckon not! Let me see what I can do." Whereupon he leaped from his horse, waded out in the mire, seized one of the wheel-spokes, covered as it was with mud, and called out, "Now, boys, altogether!" The effect was magical, and the next moment the gun jumped clear of the mud-hole. After that our battery used to swear by "Old Joe."

SANTA ROSA, CAL., August 10th, 1886.

### II.—HOOD "FEELING THE ENEMY." BY J. H. L.

IMMEDIATELY after the battle of Williamsburg, as the Confederates under Johnston were moving back toward Richmond, neither by land nor water, but by a half-and-half mixture of both, General Johnston ordered me to go at once to General Hood. "Tell him," he said, "that a force of the enemy, estimated at from three to five thousand, have landed on York River, and are ravaging the country. His brigade must immediately check the advance of this force. He is to feel the enemy gently and fall back, avoiding an engagement and drawing them from under the protection of their gun-boats, as an ample force will be sent in their rear, and if he can draw them a few miles from the river, their capture is certain."

The order was given. General Hood repeated it to the colonel of his brigade; and the Texas boys, who were "sp'iling for a fight," charged upon the enemy, who outnumbered them greatly, drove them back to the shelter of their gun-boats, killing and capturing several hundred. Returning to headquarters, I had to report a result not at all in accordance with the orders or expectations of the general in command. General Johnston seemed greatly annoyed, and sternly ordered me to repeat the exact verbal orders given Hood. Just as I did so, General Hood rode up. He was asked by General Johnston to repeat the orders received from me. When he did so, "Old Joe," with the soldierly and game-cock air which characterized him, said: "General Hood, have you given an illustration of the Texas idea of feeling an enemy gently and falling back? What would your Texans have done, sir, if I had ordered them to charge and drive back the enemy?" Hood replied: "I suppose, General, they would have driven them into the river, and tried to swim out and capture the gun-boats." With a smile, General Johnston replied: "Teach your Texans that the first duty of a soldier is literally to obey orders."

### III.— CHARACTERISTICS OF GENERAL WISE. BY J. H. L.

GOVERNOR HENRY A. WISE was one of the most gifted men it has been my fortune to know. His eloquence produced a greater effect upon a popular assembly than that of any one I ever heard; he would dazzle, surprise, and shock with electric touches of sentiment, wit, and pathos. Though brave, vigilant, and fertile in resource, his military career was by no means a success. Floyd and himself quarreled in West Virginia, and his relations had not been pleasant with any commanding officer. When General Wise was in command of the James River defenses opposite Drewry's Bluff, I visited him on official business. He received me most cordially, walked with me all the morning round his lines, explaining his views most eloquently, quoting from the great masters in the art of war,—with whom he seemed to be perfectly familiar,— interspersing these learned and scientific disquisitions with the most scathing criticisms on men and measures, denouncing the Confederate Executive and Congress and the narrow curriculum of West Point, but winding up always with a stream of fiery invective against the Yankees. General Wise was camped on the plantation of one of the richest and most influential citizens of Richmond. He annoyed Wise greatly with complaints of depredations committed by the Wise Legion on his property. Wise was greatly enraged when he presumed to charge some of his men with stealing, and after a fierce altercation ordered him out of his tent. As the gentleman was mounting his horse Wise came out, and, calling him by name, said: "Sir, before you leave, I think it due both to you and myself to make you an apology." "I'm glad, General Wise, that you show some sense of what is becoming to us both." "My apology," replied General Wise, "is that, having on my slippers, I could not possibly do you justice: I ought to have kicked you out of my tent, and will do so now if you will wait till I pull on my boots!" Then he poured a broadside upon his retreating enemy.

A few days after this Wise said: "General Lee came down to see me; fortunately, my wife and several other ladies were spending the day at my headquarters. We had a good dinner and a charming time. You know 'Marse Bob' was always very fond of ladies' society, and when he asked me to take a walk with him, I suspected what was coming. After telling me of the complaints made of my treatment of the Richmond man, and hearing my account of the affair, not omitting the apology and broadside, he laid his hand upon my arm, and, with that grace and cordiality which at such times tempered his usual stately dignity, said: ' Wise, you know, as well as I do, what the army regulations say about profanity; but, as an old friend, let me ask you if that dreadful habit cannot be broken — and remind you that we have both already passed the meridian of life,' etc. Seeing he was in for a sermon, and one that I could not answer, I replied: 'General Lee, you certainly play Washington to perfection, and your whole life is a constant reproach to me. Now I am perfectly willing that Jackson and yourself shall do the praying for the whole army of Northern Virginia; but, in Heaven's name, let me do the *cussin'* for one small brigade.'

Lee laughed and said, 'Wise, you are incorrigible,' and then rejoined the ladies."

Apropos of this a friend told me that, stopping at a farmer's in Appomattox after the surrender, he found the old man deriving comfort from but one thing, of which he frequently spoke: "Anyhow, Gineral Wise *cussed* the Yankees to the last."

## IV.—ORIGIN OF THE LEE TOMATOES—BY W. ROY MASON, MAJOR, C. S. A.

ONE day in June, 1862, General Lee rode over to General Charles W. Field's headquarters at Meadow Bridge and asked for me. I would say here that on leaving home to enter the army I carried a family letter of introduction to General Lee; and on account of that, and also my relationship to Colonel Charles Marshall, an aide on his staff, my visits at army headquarters were exceptionally pleasant. When General Lee approached me on this occasion, he said: "Captain, can General Field spare you a little while?" I replied, "Certainly, General; what can I do for you?" "I have some property," he answered, "in the hands of the enemy, and General McClellan has informed me that he would deliver it to me at any time I asked for it." Then, putting aside his jesting manner, he told me that his wife and Miss Mary Lee, his daughter, had been caught within the Federal lines at the White House, the residence of General W. H. F. Lee, his son, and he desired me to take a courier and proceed with a flag of truce to Meadow Bridge and carry a sealed dispatch to General McClellan. At the Federal headquarters I would meet the ladies, and escort them to Mrs. Gooch's farm, inside our lines. I passed beyond the pickets to the second bridge, where I waved my flag of truce, and was asked by the Union officer of the guard to enter. When I reached the picket, the officer said he had been ordered not to permit any flag of truce to pass through his lines until he had communicated with the headquarters of General McClellan. I waited on the bridge, and when the courier returned he had orders to bring me before the general. The officer insisted on blindfolding me, and positively forbade my courier accompanying me. I was then led through the camps, where I could hear the voices of thousands laughing, talking, or hallooing. After riding an hour, a distance, as I supposed, of three or four miles, I reached headquarters and was relieved of my bandage. The general came out and gave me a hearty welcome; and when he heard that I had been blindfolded, he was so indignant that he placed the officer, my guide, under arrest. I had never seen him so excited. He asked me into the house, produced his liquors, and gave me a dinner of the best, after which we discussed the situation at length. He asked me no questions which it would compromise our cause to answer, but we calmly reviewed the position of things from our separate points of view, and he inquired anxiously after all his old friends. (General McClellan and my brother-in-law, General Dabney H. Maury, C. S. A., formerly captain, U. S. A., had been classmates and devoted friends, and the general had visited my father's house and my own at Fredericksburg.)

About 3 o'clock in the afternoon, looking down the road, we saw a carriage approaching. The curtains were cut off, and it was drawn by a mule and a dilapidated old horse, driven by a negro of about ten or twelve years, and followed by a cavalry escort. General McClellan, jumping up hastily, said: "There are Mrs. Lee and Miss Mary, now." As the carriage stopped before the door, General McClellan, greeting the ladies with marked cordiality, at once introduced me, and remarked to Mrs. Lee that the general (her husband) had chosen me as her escort through the lines, and that by a strange coincidence, he (McClellan) had found in me a personal friend. He offered to accompany us in person to the river, but this was declined by Mrs. Lee as entirely unnecessary.

When we reached Mrs. Gooch's farm and our own pickets, cheer after cheer went down the long line of soldiers. Near the house we were met by General Lee and a large number of officers assembled to honor the wife and daughter of their chief.

Before leaving for Richmond, Mrs. Lee handed me from a basket, under the carriage-seat, two fine tomatoes, the finest I had ever seen, remarking that she supposed such things were scarce in the Confederacy. The seeds of these tomatoes I preserved, and, some years after the war, General Lee ate some tomatoes at my table, and praised them; whereupon we told him, to his astonishment, that those were the Lee tomatoes, and that they had been distributed all over the State under that name, from the seed of those given me by his wife.

# WEST VIRGINIA OPERATIONS UNDER FRÉMONT.[†]

BY JACOB D. COX, MAJOR-GENERAL, U. S. V.

THE campaign of the spring of 1862 was an interesting one in its details, but as it became subordinate to that against Jackson in the Shenandoah and was never completed as Frémont had planned, a very brief sketch of it must suffice. On the 29th of March Frémont assumed command of the "Mountain Department," including West Virginia, eastern Kentucky, and East Tennessee as far as Knoxville. There was a little too much sentiment and too little practical war in the construction of a department out of five hundred miles of mountain ranges, and the appointment of the "path-finder" to command it was consistent with the romantic character of the whole. The mountains formed an admirable barrier at which comparatively small bodies of troops could cover and protect the Ohio Valley behind them, but extensive military operations across and beyond the Alleghanies from west or east were impracticable, because a wilderness a hundred miles wide, crossed by few and most difficult roads, rendered it impossible to supply troops from depots on either side. The country was so wild that not even forage for mules could be found in it, and the teams could hardly haul their own provender for the double trip. Quick "raids" were therefore all that ever proved feasible.

Frémont had formed a plan of campaign which consisted in starting with Blenker's division (which had been taken from the Army of the Potomac and given to him) from Romney in the valley of the south branch of the Potomac, ascending this valley toward the south, picking up Schenck's and Milroy's brigades in turn, the latter joining the column at Monterey, on the great watershed, by way of the Cheat Mountain Pass. From Monterey Frémont intended to move upon Staunton and thence, following the south-western trend of the valleys, to the New River near Christiansburg. Here he would come into communication with me, whose task it would have been to advance from Gauley Bridge on two lines, the principal one by Fayette and Raleigh Court House over Flat-top Mountain to Princeton and the Narrows of New River, and a subordinate one on the turnpike to Lewisburg. The plan looked to continuing the march to the south-west with the whole column till Knoxville should be reached, the last additions to the force to be from the troops in the Big Sandy Valley of eastern Kentucky.

The plan would probably have failed, first, from the impossibility of supplying the army on the route, as it would have been without any reliable or safe base; and second, because the railroads east of the mountains ran on routes specially well adapted to enable the enemy quickly to concentrate any needed force at Staunton, at Lynchburg, at Christiansburg, or at Wytheville to overpower the column. The Union army would be committed to a whole season of marching in the mountains, while the Confederates could concentrate the needed force and quickly return it to Richmond when its work was done, making but a brief episode in a larger campaign. But the plan was not

[†] A continuation of "McClellan in West Virginia." See Vol. I., p. 126.—EDITORS.

destined to be thoroughly tried. Stonewall Jackson, after his defeat by Kimball at Kernstown, March 23d, had retired to the Upper Shenandoah Valley with his division, numbering about 10,000 men; Ewell was waiting to coöperate with him, with his division, at the gaps of the Blue Ridge on the east, and General Edward Johnson was near Staunton with a similar force facing Milroy. In April General Banks, commanding the National forces in the Shenandoah Valley, had ascended it as far as Harrisonburg, and Jackson observed him from Swift Run Gap in the Blue Ridge, on the road from Harrisonburg to Gordonsville. Milroy also pushed eastward from Cheat Mountain summit, in which high regions winter still lingered, and had made his way through snows and rains to McDowell, ten miles east of Monterey, at the crossing of Bull Pasture River, where he threatened Staunton. But Banks was thought to be in too exposed a position, and was directed by the War Department to fall back to Strasburg, and on the 5th of May had gone as far as New Market. Blenker's division had not yet reached Frémont, who was waiting for it at Petersburg. Jackson saw his opportunity and determined to join General Johnson by a rapid march to Staunton, to overwhelm Milroy first and then return to his own operations in the Shenandoah. ⚑ Moving with great celerity, he attacked Milroy at McDowell

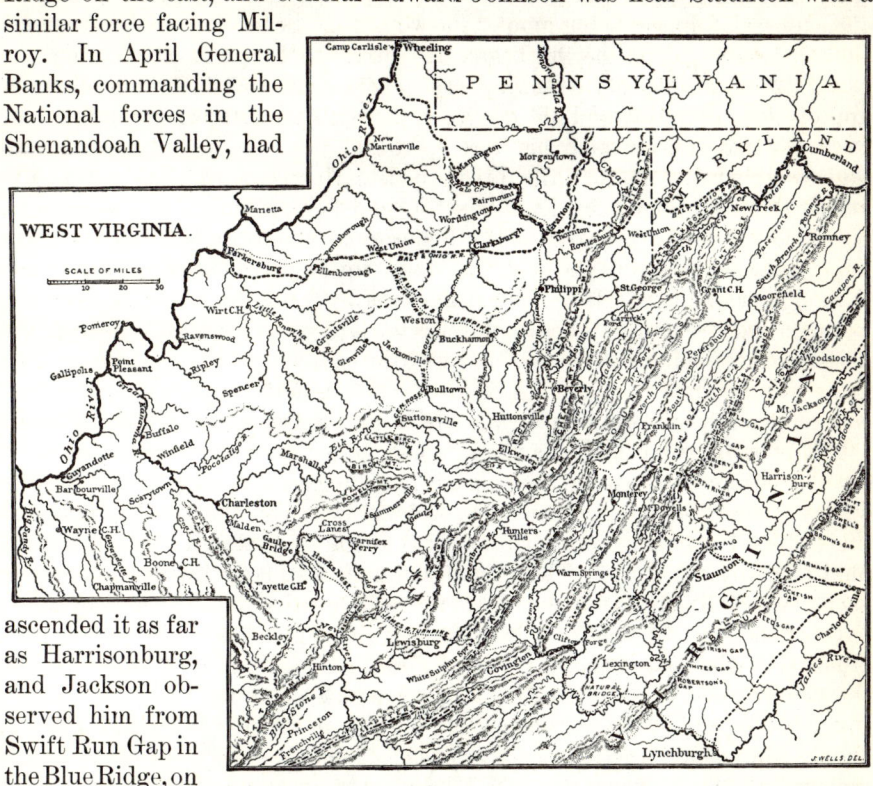

⚑ The object of Jackson in this movement is stated in his report of this campaign:

"At this time, Brigadier-General Edward Johnson, with his troops, was near Buffalo Gap, west of Staunton, so that, if the enemy was allowed to effect a junction, it would probably be followed not only by the seizure of a point so important as Staunton, but must compel General Johnson to abandon his position, and he might succeed in getting between us. To avoid these results, I determined, if practicable, after strengthening my own division by a union with Johnson's, first to strike at Milroy and then to concentrate the forces of Ewell and Johnson with my own against Banks." EDITORS.

on the 8th, and the latter calling upon Frémont for help, Schenck was sent forward to support him, who reached McDowell, having marched 34 miles in 24 hours. Jackson had not fully concentrated his forces, and the Union generals held their ground and delivered a sharp combat,[‡] in which their casualties of all kinds numbered 256, while the Confederate loss was 498, General Johnson being among the wounded. Schenck as senior assumed the command, and on the 9th began his retreat to Franklin, abandoning the Cheat Mountain road. Franklin was reached on the 11th, but Jackson approached cautiously and did not reach there till the 12th, when, finding that Frémont had concentrated his forces, he did not attack, but returned to McDowell, whence he took the direct road to Harrisonburg, and marched to attack Banks at Strasburg, Ewell meeting and joining him in this movement.

Frémont resumed preparations for his original campaign, but Banks's defeat deranged all plans, and those of the Mountain Department were abandoned. A month passed in efforts to destroy Jackson by concentration of McDowell's, Banks's, and Frémont's troops; but it was too late to remedy the ill effects of the division of commands at the beginning of the campaign. On the 26th of June Pope was assigned to command all the troops in northern Virginia, Frémont was relieved by his own request, and the Mountain Department ceased to exist.

The operations on the Kanawha line had kept pace with those in the north during the month of April. Leaving a brigade to garrison the Lower Kanawha Valley, I sent forward another under Colonel Crook on the Lewisburg Turnpike, whilst I moved in person with the two remaining (Scammon's and Moor's) on the Princeton route. The brigades numbered about two thousand men each. Wagons were so few that tents were discarded, and the men bivouacked without shelter. On the 7th of May my advanced guard occupied Giles Court House (Parisburg) and the Narrows of New River, and on the 16th the rest of the two brigades on this line were at the East River, Crook's brigade occupying Lewisburg. We were thus prepared to join Frémont's column when it should approach Christiansburg. Instead of this we got news of Jackson's movements and of Schenck's and Milroy's retreat, and Frémont was obliged to telegraph that his plans were suspended, and that I must look out for myself.

The enemy had made strong efforts to concentrate a sufficient force to protect the railway, and the brigades of Generals Humphrey Marshall, Heth, and Williams were assigned to this duty, under the command of Marshall as senior. My own orders required me to converge toward Crook's line of movement as I advanced, and from Flat-top Mountain my line of supplies was exposed to a hostile movement on the right flank. On the 16th of May Marshall, leaving Heth to hold the passes of New River, marched by the Wytheville road on

---

[‡] General Schenck in his report says:

"A little observation served to show at once that McDowell, as a defensive position, was entirely untenable, and especially against the largely outnumbering force that was ascertained to be advancing; and if it had been otherwise, there was no choice left on account of an entire destitution of forage. I determined, therefore, to obey, with as little delay as possible, your orders to fall back with the force of our two brigades to this place [Franklin]. Such a movement, however, could not with any safety or propriety be commenced before night, nor did it seem advisable to undertake it without first ascertaining or feeling the actual strength of the rebel force before us, and also, perhaps, taking some step that would serve to check or disable him from his full power or disposition to pursue. This was effectually done by our attack of his position on the mountain in the afternoon, and in the night following I was enabled to withdraw our whole little army along the road through the narrow gorge, which afforded the only egress from the valley in which McDowell is situated, in the direction of Franklin."—EDITORS.

Princeton, driving out my small detachment there after a stubborn resistance. In the night I marched Moor's brigade back from East River and drove Marshall out in turn. I recalled Scammon's brigade also on the 17th, and offered battle in front of the town. Marshall took strong position on the hills south of the place, but did not attack, nor did Heth, who followed Scammon part of the way from the Narrows. Princeton could easily have been turned by roads on the west, and I determined while awaiting the resumption of the general plan of campaign to retire to Flat-top Mountain, a very strong position, directing Crook on the other side of New River to halt at Lewisburg, where we could support each other. On May 23d Heth with his brigade tried to dislodge Crook, but was beaten, with the loss of 38 killed and many wounded, of whom 66 fell into our hands. Crook also captured 4 cannon and 300 stand of small-arms. Crook's loss was 13 killed, 53 wounded, and 7 missing.

When General Pope assumed command he directed a defensive policy to be pursued in West Virginia, and made arrangements to transfer part of my command to his army in the field. About the middle of August I took two brigades by way of the Kanawha and Ohio Rivers to Parkersburg, and thence by rail to Washington. Gauley Bridge was made the advanced post in the Kanawha Valley, and no important movement was again made on that line.

It is an interesting fact, that, so confident was General Halleck that Pope would be joined by McClellan's army in time to keep Lee in the neighborhood of Richmond, my original orders were to march through the mountains by way of Staunton, and join Pope at Charlottesville. I had several detachments out pursuing guerrillas and scattered bands of Confederate troops operating in my rear toward the Kentucky line, and this necessarily caused a few days' delay in beginning the directed movement. I took advantage of the interval to lay before General Pope, by telegraph, the proof that the march ordered meant fifteen days of uninterrupted mountain travel, most of it through a wilderness destitute of supplies, and with the enemy upon the flank. Besides this, there was the very serious question whether the Army of Virginia would be at Charlottesville when I should approach that place. On the other hand, my calculation was that we could reach Washington in ten days or less by the way we came. On this evidence Pope, with Halleck's assent, gave permission to move as suggested. The march from Flat-top Mountain to the head of navigation on the Kanawha, ninety miles, was made in three days, and the Kanawha Division reached Washington within the time appointed. One train-load of two regiments joined Pope at Warrenton Junction when the railroad was cut at Manassas Junction by Stonewall Jackson. Two other regiments got as far as Bull Run bridge and had a lively affair with the enemy. Afterward I was ordered into the forts on Upton's and Munson's hills to cover the front of Washington toward Centreville. Here, with McClellan in person, we listened to the cannonade of the Second Bull Run, and through our lines Pope and McDowell retired within the defenses of Washington. It has often been a subject of interested speculation to inquire what would have been the fate of the Kanawha Division, had it been approaching Charlottesville at this time, in accordance with Halleck's original order.

# STONEWALL JACKSON IN THE SHENANDOAH.

### BY JOHN D. IMBODEN, BRIGADIER-GENERAL, C. S. A.

SOON after the battle of Bull Run Stonewall Jackson was promoted to major-general, and the Confederate Government having on the 21st of October, 1861, organized the Department of Northern Virginia, under command of General Joseph E. Johnston, it was divided into the Valley District, the Potomac District, and Aquia District, to be commanded respectively by Major-Generals Jackson, Beauregard, and Holmes. On October 28th General Johnston ordered Jackson to Winchester to assume command of his district, and on the 6th of November the War Department ordered his old "Stonewall" brigade and six thousand troops under command of Brigadier-General W. W. Loring to report to him. These, together with Turner Ashby's cavalry, gave him a force of about ten thousand men all told.

His only movement of note in the winter of 1861–62 was an expedition at the end of December to Bath and Romney, to destroy the Baltimore and Ohio railroad and a dam or two near Hancock on the Chesapeake and Ohio canal.↓ The weather set in to be very inclement about New Year's, with snow, rain, sleet, high winds, and intense cold. Many in Jackson's command were opposed to the expedition, and as it resulted in nothing of much military importance, but was attended with great suffering on the part of his troops, nothing but the confidence he had won by his previous services saved him from personal ruin. He and his second in command, General Loring, had a serious disagreement. He ordered Loring to take up his quarters, in January, in the exposed and cheerless village of Romney, on the south branch of the upper Potomac. Loring objected to this, but Jackson was inexorable. Loring and his principal officers united in a petition to Mr. Benjamin, Secretary of War, to order them to Winchester, or at least away from Romney. This document was sent direct to the War Office, and the Secretary, in utter disregard

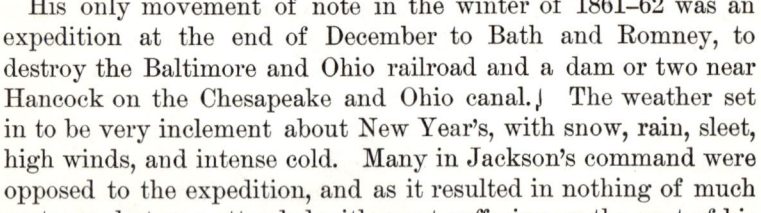

---

↓ When Jackson took command in the Valley in November, 1861, the Union forces held Romney and occupied the north side of the Potomac in strong force. The Confederates had only a weak body of militia at Jackson's disposal, until reënforcements came from the east. After receiving the four brigades of R. B. Garnett, Wm. B. Taliaferro, William Gilham, and S. R. Anderson, Jackson moved against the Union communications along the Potomac, aiming to destroy the Chesapeake and Ohio canal. Under cover of demonstrations made against various places along the Potomac east of the objective point, a Confederate force was concentrated near Dam No. 5, December 17th, and after four days' labor a breach was made in the dam. On the 1st of January another force moved from Winchester, northward, the two columns uniting, and on the 4th instant the town of Bath was occupied, after being abandoned by a body of Union troops composed of cavalry, infantry, and artillery. Jackson followed the retreating Union troops to the river and promptly bombarded Hancock, Md., without, however, securing a surrender, and on the 7th he withdrew from the Potomac region toward Romney. On his approach the Union troops at that post evacuated without a struggle, yielding the town on January 10th. The Confederates now went into winter quarters along the south branch of the Potomac, at Romney and vicinity. — EDITORS.

of "good order and discipline," granted the request without consulting Jackson. As soon as information reached Jackson of what had been done, he indignantly resigned his commission. Governor Letcher was astounded, and at once wrote Jackson a sympathetic letter, and then expostulated with Mr. Davis and his Secretary with such vigor that an apology was sent to Jackson for their obnoxious course. The orders were revoked and modified, and Jackson was induced to retain his command. This little episode gave the Confederate civil authorities an inkling of what manner of man "Stonewall" Jackson was.

In that terrible winter's march and exposure, Jackson endured all that any private was exposed to. One morning, near Bath, some of his men, having crawled out from under their snow-laden blankets, half-frozen, were cursing him as the cause of their sufferings. He lay close by under a tree, also snowed under, and heard all this; and, without noticing it, presently crawled out, too, and, shaking the snow off, made some jocular remark to the nearest men, who had no idea he had ridden up in the night and lain down amongst them. The incident ran through the little army in a few hours, and reconciled his followers to all the hardships of the expedition, and fully reëstablished his popularity.

In March Johnston withdrew from Manassas, and General McClellan collected his army of more than one hundred thousand men on the Peninsula. Johnston moved south to confront him. McClellan had planned and organized a masterly movement to capture, hold, and occupy the Valley and the Piedmont region; and if his subordinates had been equal to the task, and there had been no interference from Washington, it is probable the Confederate army would have been driven out of Virginia and Richmond captured by midsummer, 1862.

BRIGADIER-GENERAL JOHN D. IMBODEN, C. S. A. FROM A PHOTOGRAPH.

Jackson's little army in the Valley had been greatly reduced during the winter from various causes, so that at the beginning of March he did not have over 5000 men of all arms available for the defense of his district, which began to swarm with enemies all around its borders, aggregating more than ten times his own strength. Having retired up the Valley, he learned that the enemy had begun to withdraw and send troops to the east of the mountains to coöperate with McClellan. This he resolved to stop by an aggressive demonstration against Winchester, occupied by General Shields, of the Federal army, with a division of 8000 to 10,000 men.

A little after the middle of March, Jackson concentrated what troops he could, and on the 23d he occupied a ridge at the hamlet of Kernstown, four

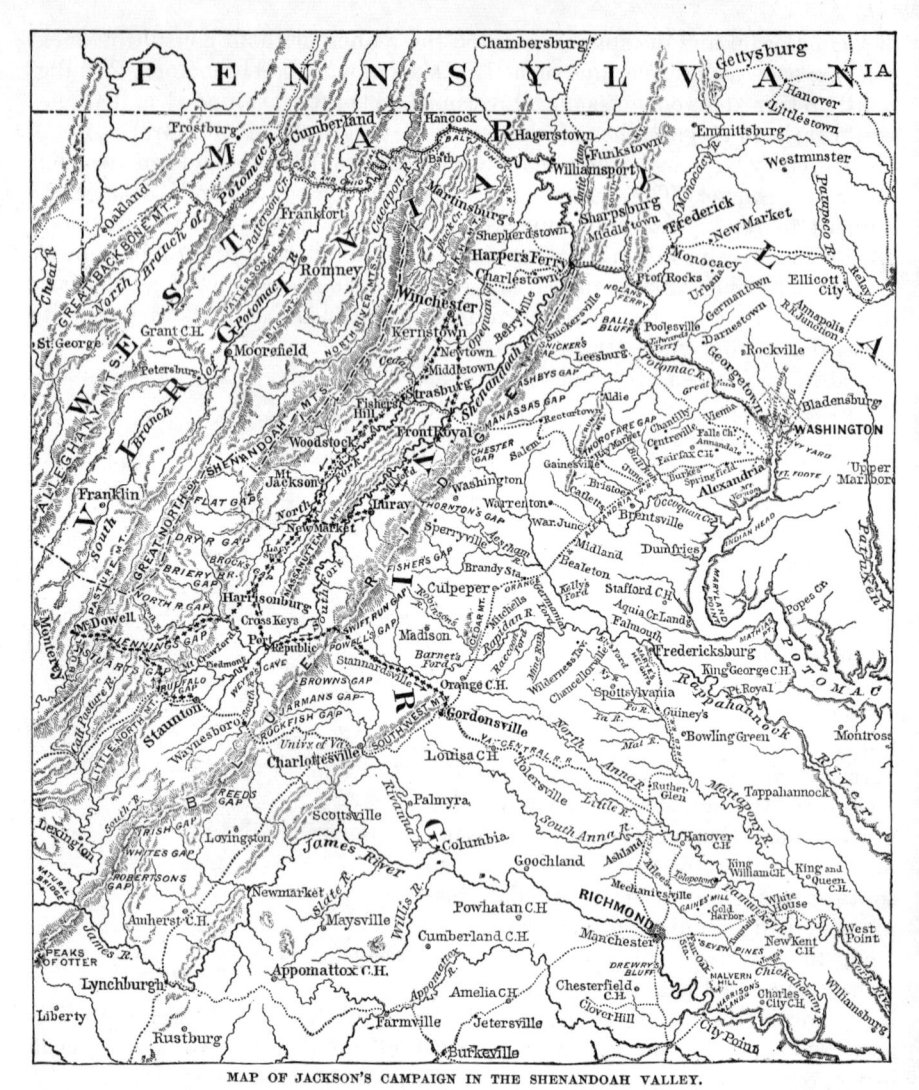

MAP OF JACKSON'S CAMPAIGN IN THE SHENANDOAH VALLEY.

The crossed line and arrows indicate Jackson's movements in the Valley. On May 6th he was at Staunton; he fought Milroy and Schenck near McDowell on May 8th; Banks at Front Royal, Newtown, and Winchester on May 23d, 24th, and 25th; Frémont at Cross Keys on June 8th; Tyler at Port Republic on June 9th.— EDITORS.

miles south of Winchester. Shields promptly attacked him, and a severe engagement of several hours ensued, ending in Jackson's repulse about dark, followed by an orderly retreat up the Valley to near Swift Run Gap in Rockingham county. The pursuit was not vigorous nor persistent.✠ Although

✠ General Jackson's first announcement of the battle to General Johnston, dated March 24th, contained the following:

"As the enemy had been sending off troops from the district, and from what I could learn were still doing so, and knowing your great desire to prevent it, and having a prospect of success, I engaged him yesterday about 3 P. M., near Winchester, and fought until dusk, but his forces were so superior to mine that he repulsed me with the loss of valuable officers and men killed and wounded; but from the obstinacy with which our troops fought and from their advantageous position I am of the opinion that his loss was greater than mine in troops, but I lost one piece of artillery and three caissons."

See also p. 302.  EDITORS.

Jackson retired before superior numbers, he had given a taste of his fighting qualities that stopped the withdrawal of the enemy's troops from the Valley.

The result was so pleasing to the Richmond government and General Johnston that it was decided to reënforce Jackson by sending General Ewell's division to him at Swift Run Gap, which reached him about the 1st of May, thus giving Jackson an aggregate force of from 13,000 to 15,000 men to open his campaign with. At the beginning of May the situation was broadly about as follows: Milroy, with about 4087 men, was on the Staunton and Parkersburg road at McDowell, less than forty miles from Staunton, with Schenck's brigade of about 2500 near Franklin. The rest of Frémont's army in the mountain department was then about 30,000 men, of whom 20,000 were concentrating at Franklin, fifty miles north-west of Staunton, and within supporting distance of Milroy. Banks, who had fortified Strasburg, seventy miles north-east of Staunton by the great Valley turnpike, to fall back upon in an emergency, had pushed forward a force of 20,000 men to Harrisonburg, including Shields's division, 10,000 strong. General McDowell, with 34,000 men, exclusive of Shields's division, was at points east of the Blue Ridge, so as to be able to move either to Fredericksburg or to the Luray Valley and thence to Staunton. Not counting Colonel Miles's, later Saxton's, command, at Harper's Ferry, which was rapidly increased to 7000 men, sent from Washington and other points north of the Potomac, before the end of May, Jackson had about 80,000 men to take into account (including all Union forces north of the Rappahannock and east of the Ohio) and to keep from a junction with McClellan in front of Richmond. Not less than 65,000↓ of these enemies were in some part of the Valley under their various commanders in May and June [see p. 299].

Besides Ewell's division already mentioned, General Johnston could give no further assistance to Jackson, for McClellan was right in his front with superior numbers, and menacing the capital of the Confederacy with almost immediate and certain capture. Its only salvation depended upon Jackson's ability to hold back Frémont, Banks, and McDowell long enough to let Johnston try doubtful conclusions with McClellan. If he failed in this, these three commanders of an aggregate force then reputed to be, and I believe in fact, over one hundred thousand ♭ would converge and move down upon Richmond from the west as McClellan advanced from the east, and the city and its defenders would fall an easy prey to nearly, if not quite, a quarter of a million of the best-armed and best-equipped men ever put into the field by any government.

Early in May, Jackson was near Port Republic contemplating his surroundings and maturing his plans. What these latter were no one but himself knew.

Suddenly the appalling news spread through the Valley that he had fled to

---

↓ This seems to us an overestimate of the Union forces actually in the Valley during the operations of May and June. April 30th, Banks had 9178 "present for duty"; May 31st, Frémont had 14,672 (Cox and Kelley not in the Valley); McDowell's force that reached the Valley (including Shield's division, which on May 31st numbered 10,203), aggregated about 21,000. Total, 44,840. Saxton had about 7000 at Harper's Ferry, which were not engaged.— EDITORS.

♭ We estimate that there were not above 80,000 Union troops in the three departments that could have been moved toward Richmond.— EDITORS.

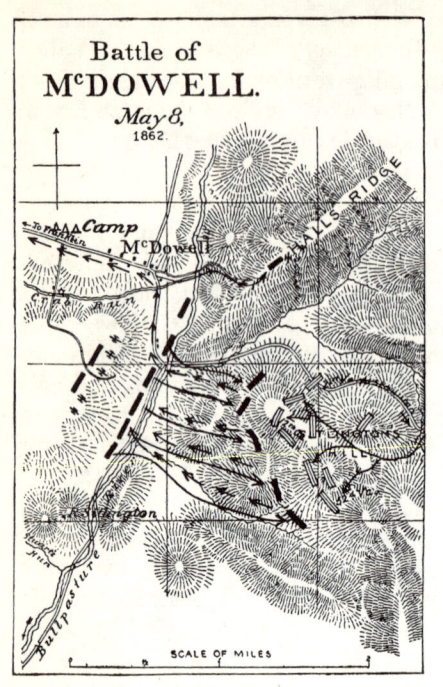

MAP OF THE BATTLE OF McDOWELL. [SEE P. 298.]

By Major Jed. Hotchkiss, Topographical Engineer Valley District Army of Northern Virginia.

The Confederate commands (indicated by white bars) of Generals Edward Johnson and W. B. Taliaferro were posted on Setlington's Hill in the following order, beginning on the left: 52d, 10th, 58th, 31st, and 23d Virginia; 12th Georgia; 37th Virginia.

General Milroy's troops (indicated by black bars) moved from the valley of the Bull Pasture River against the Confederate position, and were engaged from right to left, as follows: 25th, 75th, 32d, and 82d Ohio, and 3d W. Virginia, with Johnson's 12th Ohio battery on Hall's Ridge, the extreme left.

The attack opened on the Union right and ended with a flank movement by the regiments on the left.

the east side of the Blue Ridge through Brown's and Swift Run Gaps. Only Ashby remained behind with about one thousand cavalry, scattered and moving day and night in the vicinity of McDowell, Franklin, Strasburg, Front Royal, and Luray, and reporting to Jackson every movement of the enemy. Despair was fast settling upon the minds of the people of the Valley. Jackson made no concealment of his flight, the news of which soon reached his enemies. Milroy advanced two regiments to the top of the Shenandoah Mountain, only twenty-two miles from Staunton, and was preparing to move his entire force to Staunton, to be followed by Frémont.

Jackson had collected, from Charlottesville and other stations on the Virginia Central Railroad, enough railway trains to transport all of his little army. That it was to be taken to Richmond when the troops were all embarked no one doubted. It was Sunday, and many of his sturdy soldiers were Valley men. With sad and gloomy hearts they boarded the trains at Mechum's River Station. When all were on, lo! they took a westward course, and a little after noon the first train rolled into Staunton.

News of Jackson's arrival spread like wild-fire, and crowds flocked to the station to see the soldiers and learn what it all meant. No one knew.

As soon as the troops could be put in motion they took the road leading toward McDowell, the general having sent forward cavalry to Buffalo Gap and beyond to arrest all persons going that way. General Edward Johnson, with one of Jackson's Valley brigades, was already at Buffalo Gap. The next morning, by a circuitous mountain-path, he tried to send a brigade of infantry to the rear of Milroy's two regiments on Shenandoah Mountain, but they were improperly guided and failed to reach the position in time, so that when attacked in front both regiments escaped. Jackson followed as rapidly as possible, and the following day, May 8th, on top of the Bull Pasture Mountain, three miles east of McDowell, encountered Milroy reënforced by Schenck, who commanded by virtue of seniority of commission. The conflict lasted four

UNION CAMP AT FRONT ROYAL. FROM A WAR-TIME SKETCH.

hours, and was severe and bloody. It was fought mainly with small-arms, the ground forbidding much use of artillery. Schenck and Milroy fled precipitately toward Franklin, to unite with Frémont. The route lay along a narrow valley hedged up by high mountains, perfectly protecting the flanks of the retreating army from Ashby's pursuing cavalry, led by Captain Sheetz. Jackson ordered him to pursue as vigorously as possible, and to guard completely all avenues of approach from the direction of McDowell or Staunton till relieved of this duty. Jackson buried the dead and rested his army, and then fell back to the Valley on the Warm Springs and Harrisonburg road.↘

The morning after the battle of McDowell I called very early on Jackson at the residence of Colonel George W. Hull of that village, where he had his headquarters, to ask if I could be of any service to him, as I had to go to Staunton, forty miles distant, to look after some companies that were to join my command. He asked me to wait a few moments, as he wished to prepare a telegram to be sent to President Davis from Staunton, the nearest office to McDowell. He took a seat at a table and wrote nearly half a page of foolscap; he rose and stood before the fireplace pondering it some minutes; then he tore it in pieces and wrote again, but much less, and again destroyed what he had written, and paced the room several times. He suddenly stopped, seated himself, and dashed off two or three lines, folded the paper, and said, "Send that off as soon as you reach Staunton." As I bade him "good-bye," he remarked: "I may have other telegrams to-day or to-morrow, and will send them to you for transmission. I wish you to have two or three well-mounted couriers ready to bring me the replies promptly."

↘ See note by General Schenck, p. 298, and also p. 280.— EDITORS.

I read the message he had given me. It was dated "McDowell," and read about thus: "Providence blessed our arms with victory at McDowell yesterday." That was all. A few days after I got to Staunton a courier arrived with a message to be telegraphed to the Secretary of War. I read it, sent it off, and ordered a courier to be ready with his horse, while I waited at the telegraph office for the reply. The message was to this effect: "I think I ought to attack Banks, but under my orders I do not feel at liberty to do so." In less than an hour a reply came, but not from the Secretary of War. It was from General Joseph E. Johnston, to whom I supposed the Secretary had referred General Jackson's message. I have a distinct recollection of its substance, as follows: "If you think you can beat Banks, attack him. I only intended by my orders to caution you against attacking fortifications." Banks was understood to have fortified himself strongly at Strasburg and Cedar Creek, and he had fallen back there. I started the courier with this reply, as I supposed, to McDowell, but, lo! it met Jackson only twelve miles from Staunton, to which point on the Harrisonburg and Warm Springs turnpike he had marched his little army, except part of Ashby's cavalry, which, under an intrepid leader, Captain Sheetz, he had sent from McDowell to menace Frémont, who was concentrating at Franklin in Pendleton County, where he remained in blissful ignorance that Jackson had left McDowell, till he learned by telegraph some days later that Jackson had fallen upon Banks at Front Royal and driven him through Winchester and across the Potomac.

BREVET MAJOR-GENERAL JOHN R. KENLY. FROM A PHOTOGRAPH.

Two hours after receiving this telegram from General Johnston, Jackson was *en route* for Harrisonburg, where he came upon the great Valley turnpike. By forced marches he reached New Market in two days. Detachments of cavalry guarded every road beyond him, so that Banks remained in total ignorance of his approach. This Federal commander had the larger part of his force well fortified at and near Strasburg, but he kept a strong detachment at Front Royal, about eight miles distant and facing the Luray or Page Valley. ☆

From New Market Jackson disappeared so suddenly that the people of the Valley were again mystified. He crossed the Massanutten Mountain, and,

☆ Banks's total force now numbered 9178 present for duty as against 16,000 to 17,000 of Jackson.— EDITORS.

VIEW FROM BANKS'S FORT, NEAR STRASBURG, ACROSS TO FISHER'S HILL.
FROM A PHOTOGRAPH TAKEN IN 1885.

passing Luray, hurried toward Front Royal. He sometimes made thirty miles in twenty-four hours with his entire army, thus gaining for his infantry the sobriquet of "Jackson's foot cavalry." Very early in the afternoon of May 23d he struck Front Royal. The surprise was complete and disastrous to the enemy, who were commanded by Colonel John R. Kenly. After a fruitless resistance they fled toward Winchester, twenty miles distant, with Jackson at their heels.∫ A large number were captured within four miles by a splendid cavalry dash of Colonel Flournoy and Lieutenant-Colonel Watts.

News of this disaster reached Banks at Strasburg, by which he learned that Jackson was rapidly gaining his rear toward Newtown. The works Banks had constructed had not been made for defense in that direction, so he abandoned them and set out with all haste for Winchester; but, *en route*, near Newtown (May 24th), Jackson struck his flank, inflicting heavy loss, and making large captures of property, consisting of wagons, teams, camp-equipage, provisions, ammunition, and over nine thousand stand of arms, all new and in perfect order, besides a large number of prisoners.⚓

Jackson now chased Banks's fleeing army to Winchester, where the latter made a stand, but after a sharp engagement with Ewell's division on the 25th he fled again, not halting till he had crossed the Potomac, congratulating himself and his Government in a dispatch that his army was at last safe in Maryland. General Saxton, with some 7000 men, held Harper's Ferry, 32

---

∫ Colonel Kenly, in his report, says that he was attacked about 2 P. M., and that he maintained his position in front of his camp until nearly 5 o'clock, when he found that he was flanked. Retiring, he made a stand at the river in his rear, and again at the cross-road leading to Middletown. At the last point his men were run down by overwhelming numbers and captured in detachments.— EDITORS.

⚓ Banks reports on April 30th, as present for duty, 9178; and on June 16th, 7113,— being a reduction of 2065. Jackson reports the capture in all of 3050 of Banks's men.— EDITORS.

ARRIVAL OF FRÉMONT'S VANGUARD ABOVE STRASBURG, IN VIEW OF JACKSON'S TRAINS MOVING TOWARD FISHER'S HILL. FROM A SKETCH MADE AT THE TIME.

miles from Winchester. Jackson paid his respects to this fortified post, by marching a large part of his forces close to it, threatening an assault, long enough to allow all the captured property at Winchester to be sent away toward Staunton, and then returned to Winchester. His problem now was to escape the clutches of Frémont, knowing that that officer would be promptly advised by wire of what had befallen Banks. He could go back the way he came, by the Luray Valley, but that would expose Staunton (the most important depot in the valley) to capture by Frémont, and he had made his plans to save it.

I had been left at Staunton organizing my recruits. On his way to attack Banks, Jackson sent me an order from New Market to throw as many men as I could arm, and as quickly as possible, into Brock's Gap, west of Harrisonburg, and into any other mountain-pass through which Frémont could reach the valley at or south of Harrisonburg. I knew that within four miles of Franklin, on the main road leading to Harrisonburg, there was a narrow defile hemmed in on both sides by nearly perpendicular cliffs, over five hundred feet high. I sent about fifty men, well armed with long-range guns, to occupy these cliffs, and defend the passage to the last extremity.

On the 25th of May, as soon as Frémont learned of Banks's defeat and retreat to the Potomac, he put his army of about 14,000 in motion from Franklin to cut off Jackson's retreat up the valley. Ashby's men were still in his front toward McDowell, with an unknown force; so Frémont did not attempt that route, but sent his cavalry to feel the way toward Brock's Gap, on the direct road to Harrisonburg. The men I had sent to the cliffs let the head of the column get well into the defile or gorge, when, from a position of perfect safety to themselves, they poured a deadly volley into the close column. The attack being unexpected, and coming from a foe of unknown strength, the Federal column halted and hesitated to advance. Another volley and the "rebel yell" from the cliffs turned them back, never to appear again. Frémont took the road to Moorefield, and thence to Strasburg, though he had been peremptorily ordered on May 24th by President Lincoln to proceed direct to Harrisonburg. It shows how close had been Jackson's calculation of chances, to state that as his rear-guard marched up Fisher's Hill, two miles from Strasburg, Frémont's advance came in sight on the mountain-side on the road from Moorefield, and a sharp skirmish took place. Jackson continued to Harrisonburg, hotly pursued by Frémont, but avoiding a conflict.

The news of Banks's defeat created consternation at Washington, and Shields was ordered to return from east of the Blue Ridge to the Luray Valley in all haste to coöperate with Frémont. Jackson was advised of Shields's approach, and his aim was to prevent a junction of their forces till he reached a point where he could strike them in quick succession. He therefore sent cavalry detachments along the Shenandoah to burn the bridges as far as Port Republic, the river being at that time too full for fording. At Harrisonburg he took the road leading to Port Republic, and ordered me from Staunton, with a mixed battery and battalion of cavalry, to the bridge over North River near Mount Crawford, to prevent a cavalry force passing to his rear.

At Cross Keys, about six miles from Harrisonburg, he delivered battle to Frémont, on June 8th, and, after a long and bloody conflict, as night closed in he was master of the field. Leaving one division — Ewell's — on the ground, to resist Frémont if he should return next day, he that night marched the rest of his army to Port Republic, which lies in the forks of the river, and made his arrangements to attack the troops of Shields's command next morning on the Lewis farm, just below the town.

On the day of the conflict at Cross Keys I held the bridge across North River at Mount Crawford with a battalion of cavalry, four howitzers, and a Parrott gun, to prevent a cavalry flank movement on Jackson's trains at Port Republic. About 10 o'clock at night I received a note from Jackson, written in pencil on the blank margin of a newspaper, directing me to report with my command at Port Republic before daybreak. On the same slip, and as a postscript, he wrote, "Poor Ashby is dead. He fell gloriously."

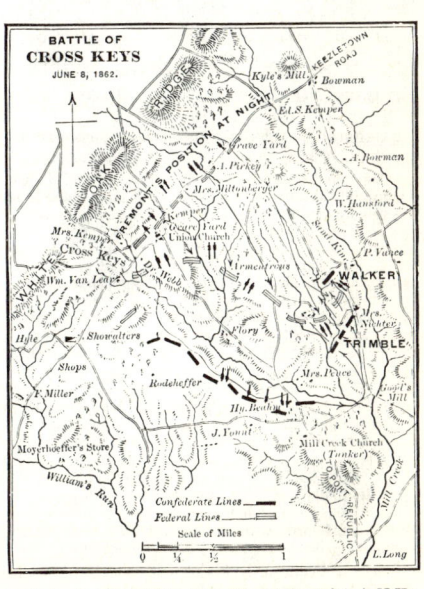

BATTLE OF CROSS KEYS, JUNE 8, 1862.

By Major Jed. Hotchkiss, Top. Eng. Valley Dist. A. N. Va.

VIEW OF THE BATTLE OF CROSS KEYS, FROM THE UNION POSITION, LOOKING EAST.
FROM A SKETCH MADE AT THE TIME.

... I know you will join with me in mourning the loss of our friend, one of the noblest men and soldiers in the Confederate army." I carried that slip of paper till it was literally worn to tatters.

It was early, Sunday, June 8th, when Jackson and his staff reached the bridge at Port Republic. General E. B. Tyler, who, with two brigades of Shields's division, was near by on the east side of the river, had sent two

↓ General Ewell, the Confederate commander on the field, in his report says of the Union advance:

"The general features of the ground were a valley and a rivulet in my front, woods on both flanks, and a field of some hundreds of acres where the road crossed the center of my line, my side of the valley being more defined and commanding the other. . . . About 10 o'clock the enemy felt along my front with skirmishers, and shortly after posted his artillery, chiefly opposite mine. He advanced under cover on General Trimble, with a force, according to his own statement, of two brigades, which were repulsed with such signal loss that they did not make another determined effort. General Trimble had been reënforced by the 13th and 25th Virginia Regiments, Colonel J. A. Walker and Lieutenant-Colonel P. B. Duffy, of General Elzey's brigade. These regiments assisted in the repulse of the enemy. General Trimble in turn advanced and drove the enemy more than a mile, and remained on his flank ready to make the final attack. . . . The enemy's attack was decided by 4 P. M., it being principally directed against General Trimble, and, though from their own statement they outnumbered us on that flank two to one, it had signally failed. General Trimble's . . . brigade captured one of their colors."

General Frémont in his report describes the desperate fighting as follows:

"Urging vigorously forward his brigade, General Stahel encountered in the first belt of woods a strong line of skirmishers, which with hard fighting was driven out of the timber and pushed by the 8th and 45th New York over the open ground beyond the edge of the woods, where these regiments suddenly came upon the right of the enemy's main line. . . . Two of General Stahel's best regiments, the 27th Pennsylvania and the 41st New York, had been diverted to the right in the timber, and the shock of the entire force here was sustained by the 8th and 45th New York; and principally by the 8th, which was attacked in front and flank by four regiments. . . . The enemy now brought up additional artillery into the open ground on my extreme left, and General Taylor's reserve brigade [Confederate] entering the woods, the fighting continued with great severity continuously along the timber in front of our position. A Mississippi regiment, charging with yells upon Buell's battery, was gallantly met with a bayonet charge by the 27th Pennsylvania, under cover of which the battery was withdrawn. A Louisiana regiment of Taylor's brigade, undertaking a charge upon Dilger's battery, was received with a fire of canister and grape, delivered with such precision and rapidity as nearly destroyed it. Every attempt of the enemy to emerge from the cover of the woods was repulsed by artillery and counter-attacks of infantry." . .

EDITORS.

guns and a few men under a green and inefficient officer to the bridge. They arrived about the same time as Jackson, but, his troops soon coming up, the Federal officer and his supports made great haste back to the Lewis farm, losing a gun at the bridge.

I reached Port Republic an hour before daybreak of June 9th, and sought the house occupied by Jackson; but not wishing to disturb him so early, I asked the sentinel what room was occupied by "Sandy" Pendleton, Jackson's adjutant-general. "Upstairs, first room on the right," he replied.

Supposing he meant our right as we faced the house, I went up, softly opened the door, and discovered General Jackson lying on his face across the bed, fully dressed, with sword, sash, and boots all on. The low-burnt tallow candle on the table shed a dim light, yet enough by which to recognize him. I endeavored to withdraw without waking him. He turned over, sat up on the bed, and called out, "Who is that?"

He checked my apology with "That is all right. It's time to be up. I am glad to see you. Were the men all up as you came through camp?"

"Yes, General, and cooking."

"That's right. We move at daybreak. Sit down. I want to talk to you."

I had learned never to ask him questions about his plans, for he would never answer such to any one. I therefore waited for him to speak first. He referred very feelingly to Ashby's death, and spoke of it as an irreparable loss. When he paused I said, "General, you made a glorious winding-up of your four weeks' work yesterday."

He replied, "Yes, God blessed our army again yesterday, and I hope with his protection and blessing we shall do still better to-day."

Then seating himself, for the first time in all my intercourse with him, he outlined the day's proposed operations. I remember perfectly his conversation. He said: "Charley Winder [Brigadier-General commanding his old 'Stonewall' brigade] will cross the river at daybreak and attack Shields on the Lewis farm [two miles below]. I shall support him with all the other troops as fast as they can be put in line. General 'Dick' Taylor will move through the woods on the side of the mountain with his Louisiana brigade, and rush upon their left flank by the time the action becomes general. By 10 o'clock we shall get them on the run, and I'll now tell you what I want with you. Send the big new rifle-gun you have [a 12-pounder Parrott] to Poague [commander of the Rockbridge artillery] and let your mounted men report to the cavalry. I want you in person to

BATTLE OF PORT REPUBLIC
JUNE 9, 1862.
By Major Jed. Hotchkiss,
Top. Eng. Valley Dist. A. N. Va.

PENNSYLVANIA "BUCKTAILS."

COLONEL JOHNSON, MOUNTED.

THE FIRST MARYLAND (CONFEDERATE) REGIMENT AT HARRISONBURG, JUNE 6, 1862, AND THE DEATH OF ASHBY.

In the affair of the rear-guard at Harrisonburg on the 6th of June, 1862, the 1st Maryland Regiment, Colonel (afterward General) Bradley T. Johnson, was ordered by General Ewell to charge through the woods to the left in support of the 58th Virginia, then closely engaged with the Pennsylvania 13th ("Bucktails"). They charged with a cheer, but soon began to suffer from a fire in the flank and rear. Colonel Johnson gave the command, "By the right flank, file right, march!" As soon as the colors came into line—"By the left flank, *charge!*" The right companies charged at double-quick, the left companies coming up on a run — thus changing front to the right under fire. At the same instant a volley from the enemy swept down the front files of the color company and color guard, killed the horses of General Turner Ashby and Colonel Johnson, and in a second after killed Ashby. Johnson, disentangling himself from his horse, led his regiment on, and, according to Ewell, "drove the enemy off with heavy loss," wounding and capturing their commanding officer, Lieutenant-Colonel Thomas L. Kane. General Frémont wrote that "a battalion of Colonel Kane's (Pennsylvania) regiment entered the woods under the direction of Brigadier-General [George D.] Bayard, and maintained for half an hour a vigorous attack, in which both sides suffered severely, driving the enemy." Ashby was directing when he fell not thirty yards from the enemy. Three Confederate color-sergeants were shot at one flag. As the regiment was moving into the battle of Cross Keys, June 8th, General Ewell directed Colonel Johnson to carry one of the bucktails captured from the enemy affixed to his colors as a trophy.— EDITORS.

take your mountain howitzers to the field, in some safe position in rear of the line, keeping everything packed on the mules, ready at any moment to take to the mountain-side. Three miles below Lewis's there is a defile on the Luray road. Shields may rally and make a stand there. If he does, I can't reach him with the field-batteries on account of the woods. You can carry your 12-pounder howitzers on the mules up the mountain-side, and at some good place unpack and shell the enemy out of the defile, and the cavalry will do the rest."

This plan of battle was carried out to the letter. I took position in a ravine about two hundred yards in rear of Poague's battery in the center of the line. General Tyler, who had two brigades of Shields's division, made a very stubborn fight, and by 9 o'clock matters began to look very serious for us. Dick Taylor had not yet come down out of the woods on Tyler's left flank.

Meanwhile I was having a remarkable time with our mules in the ravine. Some of the shot aimed at Poague came bounding over our heads, and occasionally a shell would burst there. The mules became frantic. They kicked, plunged, and squealed. It was impossible to quiet them, and it took three or four men to hold one mule from breaking away. Each mule had about three hundred pounds weight on him, so securely fastened that the load could not be dislodged by any of his capers. Several of them lay down and tried to wallow their loads off. The men held these down, and that suggested the idea of throwing them all on the ground and holding them there. The ravine sheltered us so that we were in no danger from the shot or shell which passed over us.

Just about the time our mule "circus" was at its height, news came up the line from the left that Winder's brigade near the river was giving way. Jackson rode down in that direction to see what it meant. As he passed on the brink of our ravine, his eye caught the scene, and, reining up a moment, he accosted me with, "Colonel, you seem to have trouble down there." I made some reply which drew forth a hearty laugh, and he said, "Get your mules to the mountain as soon as you can, and be ready to move."

Then he dashed on. He found his old brigade had yielded slightly to overwhelming pressure. ▷ Galloping up, he was received with a cheer; and, calling

BRIGADIER-GENERAL TURNER ASHBY, C. S. A. FROM A PHOTOGRAPH.

---

▷ The first Confederate assault was made by Winder's (Stonewall) brigade, and was repulsed by the troops of Carroll's brigade. An incident of the counter-charge is thus described by Colonel Henry B. Kelly, C. S. A.:

"While victoriously driving back the line of the Confederate left, the advancing Federal infantry were themselves suddenly assailed in flank, on their left, by a charge of two regiments of Virginia infantry, the 44th and 58th, led by Colonel Scott."

The attack on the other flank by troops brought up from Cross Keys, by General Ewell, determined the result. Colonel Kelly says:

"At the word of command, the line moved forward,

out at the top of his voice, "The 'Stonewall' brigade never retreats; follow me!" led them back to their original line. Taylor soon made his appearance, and the flank attack settled the work of the day. A wild retreat began. The pursuit was vigorous. No stand was made in the defile. We pursued them eight miles. I rode back with Jackson, and at sunset we were on the battle-field at the Lewis mansion.

Jackson accosted a medical officer, and said, "Have you brought off all the wounded?" "Yes, all of ours, but not all of the enemy's." "Why not?" "Because we were shelled from across the river." "Had you your hospital flag on the field?" "Yes." "And they shelled that?" "Yes." "Well, take your men to their quarters; I would rather let them all die than have one of my men shot intentionally under the yellow flag when trying to save their wounded." ⸱

Frémont, hearing the noise of the battle, had hurried out from near Harrisonburg to help Tyler; but Jackson had burnt the bridge at Port Republic, after Ewell had held Frémont in check some time on the west side of the river and escaped, so that when Frémont came in sight of Tyler's battle-field, the latter's troops had been routed and the river could not be crossed.

The next day I returned to Staunton, and found General W. H. C. Whiting, my old commander after the fall of General Bee at Bull Run, arriving with a division of troops to reënforce Jackson. Taking him and his staff to my house as guests, General Whiting left soon after breakfast with a guide to call on Jackson at Swift Run Gap, near Port Republic, where he was resting his troops. The distance from Staunton was about twenty miles, but Whiting returned after midnight. He was in a towering passion, and declared that Jackson had treated him outrageously. I asked, "How is that possible, General, for he is very polite to every one?"

"Oh! hang him, he was polite enough. But he didn't say one word about his plans. I finally asked him for orders, telling him what troops I had He simply told me to go back to Staunton, and he would send me orders

soon coming into plain view of the batteries and of the infantry of the enemy beyond the ravine, which at once opened fire on the advancing brigade. With one volley in reply, and a Confederate yell heard far over the field, the Louisianians rushed down the rough declivity and across the ravine, and carried the batteries like a flash. . . . By the impetus of the charge over the rough ground all formation was lost, and officers and men were all thrown into one unorganized mass around the captured guns. While this exultant crowd were rejoicing and shouting over their victory, suddenly a scathing fire of canister was poured into them by a section of Clark's battery which had been rapidly brought over from the Federal right to within two hundred yards of the position of the captured guns. . . .

"At the outset of the attempt of the Federals to retake their batteries, Lieutenant-Colonel Peck, of the 9th Louisiana, called out to the men about the captured guns to shoot the horses, which was done. When, therefore, the Federals retook and held for a time, as they did, the ground where the guns were, they were unable, when again driven off, to take more than one gun with them for want of battery horses." EDITORS.

⸱ The official references to this incident are comprised in the following.

General Jackson says in his report:

"While the forces of Shields were in full retreat, and our troops in pursuit, Frémont appeared on the opposite bank of the south fork of the Shenandoah with his army, and opened his artillery upon our ambulances and parties engaged in the humane labors of attending to our dead and wounded, and the dead and wounded of the enemy."

Frémont says in his report of his action at Port Republic:

"Parties (Confederate) gathering the dead and wounded, together with a line of prisoners, awaiting the movements of the rebel force near by, was all, in respect to troops on either side, now to be seen. A parting salvo of carefully aimed rifle-guns, duly charged with shell, hastened the departure of the rebels with the unlucky, though most gallant convoy, and the whole were speedily out of sight."

It is hardly necessary to state that intentional shelling of an ambulance and relief parties is denied by Union officers. EDITORS.

to-morrow. I haven't the slightest idea what they will be. I believe he hasn't any more sense than my horse."

Seeing his frame of mind, and he being a guest in my house, I said little. Just after breakfast, next morning, a courier arrived with a terse order to embark his troops on the railroad trains and move to Gordonsville at once, where he would receive further orders. This brought on a new explosion of wrath. "Didn't I tell you he was a fool, and doesn't this prove it? Why, I just came through Gordonsville day before yesterday."

However, he obeyed the order; and when he reached Gordonsville he found Jackson there, and his little Valley army coming after him; a few days later McClellan was astounded to learn that Jackson was on his right flank on the Chickahominy. Shortly after the seven days' battle around Richmond, I met Whiting again, and he then said: "I didn't know Jackson when I was at your house. I have found out now what his plans were, and they were worthy of a Napoleon. But I still think he ought to have told me his plans; for if he had died McClellan would have captured Richmond. I wouldn't have known what he was driving at, and might have made a mess of it. But I take back all I said about his being a fool."

From the date of Jackson's arrival at Staunton till the battle of Port Republic was thirty-five days. He marched from Staunton to McDowell, 40 miles, from McDowell to Front Royal, about 110, from Front Royal to Winchester, 20 miles, Winchester to Port Republic, 75 miles, a total of 245 miles, fighting in the meantime 4 desperate battles, and winning them all.

On the 17th of June, leaving only his cavalry, under Brigadier-General B. H. Robertson, and Chew's battery, and the little force I was enlisting in the valley (which was now no longer threatened by the enemy), Jackson moved all his troops south-east, and on the 25th arrived at Ashland, seventeen miles from Richmond. This withdrawal from the valley was so skillfully managed that his absence from the scene of his late triumphs was unsuspected at Washington. On the contrary, something like a panic prevailed there, and the Government was afraid to permit McDowell to unite his forces with McClellan's lest it should uncover and expose the capital to Jackson's supposed movement on it.

Jackson's military operations were always unexpected and mysterious. In my personal intercourse with him in the early part of the war, before he had become famous, he often said there were two things never to be lost sight of by a military commander: "Always mystify, mislead, and surprise the enemy, if possible; and when you strike and overcome him, never let up in the pursuit so long as your men have strength to follow; for an army routed, if hotly pursued, becomes panic-stricken, and can then be destroyed by half their number. The other rule is, never fight against heavy odds, if by any possible manœuvring you can hurl your own force on only a part, and that the weakest part, of your enemy and crush it. Such tactics will win every time, and a small army may thus destroy a large one in detail, and repeated victory will make it invincible."

His celerity of movement was a simple matter. He never broke down his men by too-long-continued marching. He rested the whole column very often, but only for a few minutes at a time. I remember that he liked to see the men lie down flat on the ground to rest, and would say, "A man rests all over when he lies down."

## NOTES ON THE BATTLE OF McDOWELL.

### I.—BY ROBERT C. SCHENCK, MAJOR-GENERAL U. S. V.

ON the 7th of May I left Franklin with about 2000 men to join and support General Milroy, menaced with attack by Stonewall Jackson, near McDowell, about forty miles distant. During this forced march my troops made the remarkable time of 34 miles in 23 hours. When I arrived, on the morning of the 8th, I found Milroy, with his small force in the village at the foot of the mountain, defending himself against the enemy occupying the heights above, shut in, in fact, in a sort of amphitheater. The only easy escape from the position was down the narrow valley and small stream back by the road by which I had arrived. I, of course, assumed the command by right of seniority. The only question was how best to extricate ourselves from this disadvantageous position in the presence of a force of the enemy largely superior in numbers. My whole force, after my arrival at McDowell and junction with Milroy, was but about 4000 men.

General Milroy, always moved by undaunted and impetuous, though rather uncalculating, bravery, would have remained to challenge and await attack. But, after conference, it was agreed that the better plan would be to send, that evening, whatever portion of our united force was available for the attack up the side of the mountain to assault the enemy and deliver a blow, if we could, and then retire from his front before he had recovered from the surprise of such a movement. I gave the order accordingly. No officer could have carried it out more effectively than did General Milroy.

The movement was executed successfully. The attacking force was composed of a good part of Milroy's men and of those of my immediate command who were least fatigued. The whole number engaged was 2600; of these we had just ten per cent. killed and wounded. We remained at McDowell, at the foot of the mountain, the point from which our troops moved to the attack through that night, buried our dead, sent off the wounded and all stores, and withdrew in good order toward Franklin in the early morning. Our march back to Franklin, which occupied three days, was orderly and was not seriously molested by Ashby's cavalry or any force of the rebels in pursuit.

At Franklin we kept Jackson with his whole force at bay with our still much inferior numbers, until General Frémont arrived there on the 13th of May. With the troops I had left behind at Franklin, when I marched to the relief of Milroy, I had at no time before Frémont arrived to take command more than 6500 men. On the 8th of May, Frémont was at Petersburg on his march from Lost Creek to Franklin, and certainly nowhere within less than 50 or 60 miles of McDowell. That was poor "supporting distance."

### II.—EXTRACTS FROM THE REPORT OF GENERAL R. H. MILROY.

"MAY 7th I was first advised by my scouts and spies that a junction had been effected between the armies of Generals [Stonewall] Jackson and [Edward] Johnson, and that they were advancing to attack me at McDowell. Having the day previous sent out a large portion of the 3d West Virginia and 32d and 75th Ohio Regiments to Shaw's Ridge and upon Shenandoah Mountain for the purpose of protecting my foraging and reconnoitering parties, I immediately ordered my whole command to concentrate at McDowell, and, expecting reënforcements, prepared for defense there. . . . Upon the next morning (the 8th instant) the enemy was seen upon the Bull Pasture Mountain, about one and three-fourths miles distant from McDowell, on my right and front. I commenced shelling them and sent out parties of skirmishers to endeavor to ascertain their numbers. At about 10 A. M. your brigade arrived. Desultory firing of a section of Hyman's battery and occasional skirmishing engaged the attention of the enemy during the morning. . . . In the afternoon, at about 3 o'clock, being informed by Captain George R. Latham, of the 2d West Virginia Volunteer Infantry, who, with his company, was engaged in skirmishing, that the rebels were endeavoring to plant a battery upon the mountain, which would command our whole encampment, with your permission I made a reconnoissance for the purpose of obtaining accurate information of their strength and position. . . . Under my order the 25th Ohio and 75th Ohio Regiments (the former under the command of Lieutenant-Colonel W. P. Richardson, and the latter under the command of Colonel N. C. McLean and Major Robert Reily) advanced in the most gallant manner up the face of the hill and attacked the enemy in their front. Numbering less than one thousand men, unprotected by any natural or artificial shelter, they advanced up a precipitous mountain-side upon an adversary protected by intrenchments and the natural formation of the mountain, and unsupported drove them (being at least twice their numerical strength) over the crest of the mountain, and for one and a half hours maintained unaided, while exposed to a deadly fire, the position from which they had so bravely driven the foe."

# THE OPPOSING FORCES IN THE VALLEY CAMPAIGNS.
## March 23d–June 10th, 1862.

The composition, losses, and strength of each army as here stated give the gist of all the data obtainable in the Official Records. K stands for killed; w for wounded; m w for mortally wounded; m for captured or missing; c for captured.

## THE UNION ARMY.

### FORCES AT KERNSTOWN, MARCH 23D, 1862.

Brigadier-General James Shields (w), Colonel Nathan Kimball. Staff loss: w, 1.

*First Brigade*, Col. Nathan Kimball (also commanded the division on the field of battle): 14th Ind., Lieut.-Col. William Harrow; 8th Ohio, Col. Samuel S. Carroll; 67th Ohio, Lieut.-Col. Alvin C. Voris; 84th Pa., Col. William G. Murray (k). Brigade loss: k, 45; w, 200; m, 1 = 246. *Second Brigade*, Col. Jeremiah C. Sullivan: 39th Ill., Col. Thomas O. Osborn; 13th Ind., Lieut.-Col. Robert S. Foster; 5th Ohio, Lieut.-Col. John H. Patrick; 62d Ohio, Col. Francis B. Pond. Brigade loss: k, 23; w, 69 = 92. *Third Brigade*, Col. Erastus B. Tyler: 7th Ind., Lieut.-Col. John F. Cheek; 7th Ohio, Lieut.-Col. William R. Creighton; 29th Ohio, Col. Lewis P. Buckley; 110th Pa., Col. William D. Lewis, Jr.; 1st W. Va., Col. Joseph Thoburn. Brigade loss: k, 43; w, 171; m, 21 = 235. *Cavalry*, Col. Thornton F. Brodhead: 1st Squadron Pa., Capt. John Keys; Indpt. Co's, Md., Captains Henry A. Cole, William Firey, and John Horner; 1st W. Va. (Battalion), Maj. B. F. Chamberlain; 1st Ohio (Co's A and C), Capt. Nathan D. Menken; 1st Mich. (Battalion), Lieut.-Col. Joseph T. Copeland. Cavalry loss: k, 3; w, 6 = 9. *Artillery*, Lieut.-Col. Philip Daum: A, W. Va., Capt. John Jenks; B, W. Va.; H, 1st Ohio, Capt. James F. Huntington; L, 1st Ohio, Capt. Lucius N. Robinson; E, 4th U. S., Capt. Joseph C. Clark, Jr. Artillery loss: k, 4; w, 2 = 6. Total loss (March 22d and 23d): killed, 118; wounded, 450; missing, 22 = 590.

General Shields reports ("Official Records," XII., Pt. I., p. 342): "Our force in infantry, cavalry, and artillery did not exceed 7000.... We had 6000 infantry, a cavalry force of 750, and 24 pieces of artillery."

### FORCES AT McDOWELL, VA., MAY 8TH, 1862.

Brigadier-General Robert C. Schenck.

*Milroy's Brigade*, Brig.-Gen. Robert H. Milroy: 25th Ohio, Lieut.-Col. W. P. Richardson; 32d Ohio, Lieut.-Col. Ebenezer H. Swinney; 73d Ohio, Col. Orland Smith; 75th Ohio, Col. Nathaniel C. McLean; 2d W. Va., Col. John W. Moss; 3d W. Va., Lieut.-Col. Francis W. Thompson; I, 1st Ohio Art'y, Capt. Henry F. Hyman; 12th Ohio Batt'y, Capt. Aaron C. Johnson; 1st W. Va. Cav. (3 co's), Maj. John S. Krepps. Brigade loss: k, 20; w, 177; m, 2 = 199. *Schenck's Brigade*, Brig.-Gen. R. C. Schenck: 55th Ohio, Col. John C. Lee; 82d Ohio, Col. James Cantwell; 5th W. Va., Col. John L. Zeigler; 1st Battalion Conn. Cav., Maj. Judson M. Lyon; K, 1st Ohio Art'y, Capt. William L. De Beck. Brigade loss (82d Ohio): k, 6; w, 50; m, 1 = 57.

Total loss: killed, 26; wounded, 227; missing, 3 = 256. General Schenck says ("Official Records," XII., Pt. I., pp. 462, 463), that he "brought into the field an aggregate of only 1300 infantry, besides De Beck's battery ... and about 250 of the 1st Battalion Connecticut Cavalry." ... "Adding to the 1768 of Milroy's brigade about 500 of the 82d Ohio, which was the number in action, the entire force we had engaged was 2268."

### BANKS'S COMMAND, MAY 23D–25TH, 1862.

Major-General Nathaniel P. Banks.

FIRST DIVISION, Brig.-Gen. Alpheus S. Williams.

*First Brigade*, Col. Dudley Donnelly: 5th Conn., Lieut.-Col. George D. Chapman; 28th N. Y., Lieut.-Col. Edwin F. Brown; 46th Pa., Col. Joseph F. Knipe; 1st Md., Col. John R. Kenly (w and c). Brigade loss: k, 17; w, 98; m, 735 = 850. *Third Brigade*, Col. George H. Gordon: 2d Mass., Lieut.-Col. George L. Andrews; 29th Pa., Col. John K. Murphy (c), Capt. Samuel M. Zulich; 27th Ind., Col. Silas Colgrove; 3d Wis., Col. Thomas H. Ruger. Brigade loss: k, 22; w, 80; m, 507 = 609. *Cavalry*: 1st Mich. (5 co's), Col. Thornton F. Brodhead, Maj. Angelo Paldi. Loss: k, 10; w, 9; m, 35 = 54. *Artillery*, Capt. Robert B. Hampton: M, 1st N. Y., Lieut. James H. Peabody; F, Pa., Lieut J. Presley Fleming; F, 4th U. S., Lieut. Franklin B. Crosby. Artillery loss: k, 2; w, 14; m, 12 = 28.

CAVALRY BRIGADE, Brig.-Gen. John P. Hatch: 1st Me. (5 co's), Lieut.-Col. Calvin S. Douty; 1st Vt., Col. Charles H. Tompkins; 5th N. Y., Col. Othneil De Forest; 1st Md. (5 co's), Lieut.-Col. Charles Wetschky. Brigade loss: k, 5; w, 25; m, 294 = 324. UNATTACHED: 10th Me., Col. Geo. L. Beal; 8th N. Y. Cav. (5 co's, dismounted), Lieut.-Col. Charles R. Babbitt; Pa. Zouaves d'Afrique, Capt. Charles H. T. Collis; E, Pa. Art'y (section), Lieut. Charles A. Atwell. Unattached loss: k, 6; w, 17: m, 131 = 154.

The total loss of Banks's troops at Front Royal, Middletown, Newtown, Winchester, etc., from May 23d to 25th, is reported as 62 killed, 243 wounded, and 1714 captured or missing = 2019. But Jackson claims ("Official Records," Vol. XII., Pt. I., p. 708) that the whole number of prisoners captured by his command was about 3050, including about 750 sick and wounded in the hospitals at Winchester and Strasburg. The effective strength of Banks's command was reported, April 30th, at 9178, and June 16th (after the battle) at 7113.

### FORCES AT HARPER'S FERRY, MAY 26TH–30TH, 1862.

Brigadier-General Rufus Saxton.

*Brigade Commanders:* Brig.-Gens. James Cooper and John P. Slough, and Col. Dixon S. Miles. *Troops*: Cole's Md. Cav., Capt. Henry A. Cole; 1st Md. Cav. (6 co's), Maj. James M. Deems; 5th N. Y. Cav. (4 co's), Maj. George H. Gardner; 8th N. Y. Cav. (4 co's, dismounted), Maj. William L. Markell; K, 1st N. Y. Art'y, Capt. Lorenzo Crounse; L, 1st N. Y. Art'y, Capt. John A. Reynolds; 60th N. Y., Col. William B. Goodrich; 78th N. Y., Col. Daniel Ullmann; 102d N. Y., Lieut.-Col. William B. Haywood; 109th Pa., Col. Henry J. Stainrook; 111th Pa., Col. Matthew Schlaudecker; 3d Del., Col. William O. Redden; 1st Md., P. H. B., Col. William P. Maulsby; Purnell Legion, Md., Col. William J. Leonard; 3d Md., Col. David P. De Witt; 1st D. C., Col. James A. Tait; 8th and 12th U. S. (battalion), Capt. Thomas G. Pitcher; Naval Battery, Lieut. C. H. Daniels.

The loss in Saxton's command was 1 killed, 6 wounded, and 8 captured or missing = 15. The forces consisted "of not more than 7000 effective men." (See "Official Records," Vol. XII., Pt. I., p. 641.)

## FRÉMONT'S COMMAND, JUNE 1ST–9TH, 1862.

Major-General John C. Frémont. Staff loss: k, 1.

BLENKER'S DIVISION, Brig.-Gen. L. Blenker. Staff loss: w, 2.

*First Brigade*, Brig.-Gen. Julius Stahel: 8th N. Y., Col. Francis Wutschel (w); 39th N. Y.; 41st N. Y., Col. Leopold von Gilsa (w), Maj. Detleo von Einsiedel; 45th N. Y., Col. George von Amsberg; 27th Pa., Col. Adolphus Buschbeck; 2d N. Y. Battery, Capt. Louis Schirmer, Lieut. Hermann Jahn; C, W. Va. Art'y, Capt. Frank Buell. Brigade loss: k, 68; w, 240; m, 90 = 398. *Second Brigade*, Col. John A. Koltes: 29th N. Y., Lieut.-Col. Clemens Soest; 68th N. Y.; 73d Pa., Lieut.-Col. Gust. A. Muhleck; 13th N. Y. Battery, Capt. Julius Dieckmann. Brigade loss: w, 1; m, 8 = 9. *Third Brigade*, Brig.-Gen. Henry Bohlen: 54th N. Y., Col. Eugene A. Kozlay; 58th N. Y., Col. Wladimir Krzyzanowski; 74th Pa., Lieut.-Col. John Hamm; 75th Pa., Lieut.-Col. Francis Mahler; I, 1st N. Y. Art'y, Capt. Michael Wiedrich. Brigade loss: k, 13; w, 52; m, 8 = 73. *Cavalry:* 4th N. Y., Col. Christian F. Dickel.

UNATTACHED CAVALRY: 6th Ohio, Col. William R. Lloyd; 3d W. Va. (detachment), Capt. Everton J. Conger.

ADVANCE BRIGADE, Col. Gustave P. Cluseret: 60th Ohio, Col. William H. Trimble; 8th W. Va., Lieut.-Col. Lucien Loeser. Brigade loss: k, 4; w. 12; m, 3 = 19.

MILROY'S BRIGADE, Brig.-Gen. Robert H. Milroy: 2d W. Va., Maj. James D. Owens; 3d W. Va., Lieut.-Col. Francis W. Thompson; 5th W. Va., Col. John L. Zeigler; 25th Ohio, Lieut.-Col. William P. Richardson; 1st W. Va. Cav. (detachment), Maj. John S. Krepps; G, W. Va. Art'y, Captain Chatham T. Ewing; I, 1st Ohio Art'y, Capt. Henry F. Hyman; 12th Ohio Battery, Capt. Aaron C. Johnson. Brigade loss: k, 23; w, 122; m, 14 = 159.

SCHENCK'S BRIGADE, Brig.-Gen. Robert C. Schenck: 32d Ohio, Lieut.-Col. Ebenezer H. Swinney; 55th Ohio, Col. John C. Lee; 73d Ohio, Col. Orland Smith; 75th Ohio, Col. Nathaniel C. McLean; 82d Ohio, Col. James Cantwell; 1st Battalion Conn. Cav., Capt. Louis N. Middlebrook; K, 1st Ohio Art'y, Capt. William L. De Beck; Ind. Battery, Capt. Silas F. Rigby. Brigade loss: k, 4; w, 7; m, 4 = 15.

BAYARD'S BRIGADE (detached from McDowell's command), Brig.-Gen. George D. Bayard: 1st N. J. Cav., Col. Percy Wyndham (c), Lieut.-Col. Joseph Kargé; 1st Pa. Cav., Col. Owen Jones; 13th Pa. Reserves or 1st Rifles (battalion), Lieut.-Col. Thomas L. Kane (w and c), Capt. Hugh McDonald; 2d Me. Battery, Capt. James A. Hall. Brigade loss: k, 1; w, 7 = 8.

The total loss of Frémont's forces at Cross Keys (as above given in detail) was 114 killed, 443 wounded, and 127 captured or missing = 684. In the affairs at Mount Carmel, Strasburg, Woodstock, Mount Jackson, and Harrisonburg, etc., June 1st–7th, the loss aggregated 11 killed, 52 wounded, and 39 captured or missing = 102.

General Frémont reports ("Official Records," Vol. XII., Pt. I., p. 19) that "10,500 men is a liberal estimate of force in hand and for duty" with his command, June 8th.

### SHIELDS'S DIVISION, JUNE 8TH–9TH, 1862.

Brigadier-General James Shields. Staff loss: w, 1.

*First Brigade*, Brig.-Gen. Nathan Kimball: 14th Ind., Col. William Harrow; 4th Ohio, Col. John S. Mason; 8th Ohio, Lieut.-Col. Franklin Sawyer; 7th W. Va., Col. James Evans. *Second Brigade*, Brig.-Gen. Orris S. Ferry: 39th Ill., Col. Thomas O. Osborn; 13th Ind., Lieut.-Col. Robert S. Foster; 62d Ohio, Col. Francis B. Pond; 67th Ohio, Lieut.-Col. Alvin C. Voris. *Third Brigade*, Brig.-Gen. Erastus B. Tyler: 5th Ohio, Col. Samuel H. Dunning; 7th Ohio, Lieut.-Col. William R. Creighton; 29th Ohio, Col. Lewis P. Buckley; 66th Ohio, Col. Charles Candy. Brigade loss: k, 51; w, 234; m, 431 = 716. *Fourth Brigade*, Col. Samuel S. Carroll: 7th Ind., Col. James Gavin; 84th Pa., Maj. Walter Barrett; 110th Pa., Col. William D. Lewis; 1st W. Va., Col. Joseph Thoburn. Brigade loss: k, 12; w, 145; m, 113 = 270. *Artillery*, Col. Philip Daum: H, 1st Ohio, Capt. James F. Huntington; L, 1st Ohio, Capt. Lucius N. Robinson; A, 1st W. Va., Capt. John Jenks; B, 1st Va., Lieut. John V. Keeper; E, 4th U. S., Capt. Joseph C. Clark. Artillery loss: K, 4; w, 13; m, 14 = 31. *Cavalry:* 1st Ohio (detachment), Capt. John H. Robinson; 1st R. I. (battalion), Maj. David B. Nelson; 1st W. Va. (detachment), Maj. Benjamin F. Chamberlain.

The loss of the Third and Fourth Brigades, three batteries of artillery, and a detachment of cavalry, which were the only troops of this division engaged at and near Port Republic, June 8th and 9th, aggregated 67 killed, 393 wounded, and 558 captured or missing = 1018. The Union loss during the entire campaign approximated 264 killed, 1146 wounded, and 3199 captured or missing = 4609. In his official report ("Official Records," Vol. XII., Pt. I., p. 684) General Shields gives his effective force in the engagement of June 9th as not exceeding 2500 men. General Tyler, who had immediate command of the troops in action, says ("Official Records," Vol. XII., Pt. I., p. 697) his force could not have exceeded 3000 men. The strength of Shields's entire division, on May 30th, is reported at 10,900 men ("Official Records," Vol. XII., Pt. III., p. 290). According to the same authority Ord's division, of McDowell's command, which remained at Front Royal during Shields's advance up the Luray Valley, numbered 9000.

## THE CONFEDERATE ARMY.

### FORCES AT KERNSTOWN, MARCH 23D, 1862.

Major-General Thomas J. Jackson.

*Garnett's Brigade*, Brig.-Gen. R. B. Garnett: 2d Va., Col. J. W. Allen; 4th Va., Lieut.-Col. Charles A. Ronald, Maj. A. G. Pendleton; 5th Va., Col. William H. Harman; 27th Va., Col. John Echols (w), Lieut.-Col. A. J. Grigsby; 33d Va., Col. Arthur C. Cummings; Va. Battery (Rockbridge Art'y), Capt. William McLaughlin; Va. Battery (West Augusta Art'y), Capt. James H. Waters; Va. Battery, Capt. Joseph Carpenter. Brigade loss: k, 40; w, 168; m, 153 = 361. *Burks's Brigade*, Col. Jesse S. Burks: 21st Va., Lieut.-Col. John M. Patton, Jr.; 42d Va., Lieut.-Col. D. A. Langhorne; 1st Va. (Irish) Battalion, Capt. D. B. Bridgford; Va. Battery, Lieut. James Pleasants. Brigade loss: k, 24; w, 114; m, 39 = 167. *Fulkerson's Brigade*, Col. Samuel V. Fulkerson: 23d Va., Lieut.-Col. Alex. G. Taliaferro; 37th Va., Lieut.-Col. R. P. Carson; Va. Battery (Danville Art'y), Lieut. A. C. Lanier. Brigade loss: k, 15; w, 76; m, 71 = 162. *Cavalry*, 7th Va., Col. Turner Ashby; Va. Battery, Capt. R. P. Chew Cavalry loss: k, 1; w, 17 = 18.

Total loss (March 22d and 23d): killed, 80; wounded, 375; missing, 263 = 718.

General Jackson, in his report ("Official Records," XII., Pt. I., p. 383), says: "Our number present on the evening of the battle was, of infantry, 3087, of which 2742 were engaged; 27 pieces of artillery, of which 18 were engaged. Owing to recent heavy cavalry duty and the extent of country to be protected, only 290 of this arm were present to take part in the engagement."

# THE OPPOSING FORCES IN THE VALLEY CAMPAIGNS.

## FORCES AT McDOWELL, VA., MAY 8TH, 1862.
### Major-General Thomas J. Jackson.

ARMY OF THE VALLEY: *Second Brigade*, Col. John A. Campbell: 21st Va., Lieut.-Col. R. H. Cunningham; 42d Va., Maj. Henry Lane; 48th Va., Maj. James C. Campbell (w), Lieut. Samuel Hale; 1st Va. (Irish) Battalion, Capt. B. W. Leigh. Brigade loss: w, 9. *Third Brigade*, Brig.-Gen. William B. Taliaferro: 10th Va., Col. S. B. Gibbons (k), Lieut.-Col. E. T. H. Warren; 23d Va., Col. A. G. Taliaferro; 37th Va., Col. Samuel V. Fulkerson. Brigade loss: k, 12; w, 89 = 101.

ARMY OF THE NORTH-WEST, Brig.-Gen. Edward Johnson (w), in command on the field. Staff loss: w, 1.

*First Brigade*, Col. Z. T. Conner: 12th Ga., Maj. Willis A. Hawkins; 25th Va., Col. George H. Smith (w); 31st Va., Lieut.-Col. Alfred H. Jackson, Col. John S. Hoffman. Brigade loss: k, 43; w, 223 = 266. *Second Brigade*, Col. W. C. Scott: 44th Va., Maj. Norvell Cobb; 52d Va., Col. Michael G. Harman; 58th Va., Lieut.-Col. F. H. Board. Brigade loss: k, 20; w, 102 = 122.

Total loss: killed, 75; wounded, 424 = 499.

The strength of the Confederate forces is not officially stated. Colonel Allan ("Campaign in the Valley of Virginia, 1861-62," p. 78) estimates it at about 6000.

## FORCES IN THE OPERATIONS OF MAY 20TH–JUNE 10TH, 1862.
### Major-General Thomas J. Jackson.

JACKSON'S DIVISION. *First Brigade*, Brig.-Gen. Charles S. Winder: 2d Va., Col. J. W. Allen; 4th Va., Col. Charles A. Ronald; 5th Va., Col. W. S. H. Baylor, Lieut.-Col. J. H. S. Funk; 27th Va., Col. A. J. Grigsby; 33d Va., Col. John F. Neff. Brigade loss: Winchester, k, 10; w, 27 = 37. Port Republic, k, 13; w, 154; m, 32 = 199. *Second Brigade*, Col. J. A. Campbell (w), Lieut.-Col. John M. Patton: 21st Va., Col. John M. Patton, Lieut.-Col. R. H. Cunningham; 42d Va., Maj. Henry Lane (w), Capt. John E. Penn, Lieut.-Col. William Martin; 48th Va., Captain Samuel Hale (w), Maj. J. B. Moseley, Lieut.-Col. Thomas S. Garnett; 1st Va. (Irish) Battalion, Capt. B. W. Leigh, Maj. John Seddon. Brigade loss: Winchester, k, 2; w, 14 = 16. Cross Keys and Port Republic, k, 4; w, 16 = 20. *Third Brigade*, Col. Samuel V. Fulkerson, Brig.-Gen. William B. Taliaferro: 10th Va., Col. E. T. H. Warren; 23d Va., Col. A. G. Taliaferro, Lieut.-Col. George W. Curtis; 37th Va., Maj. T. V. Williams, Col. Samuel V. Fulkerson. Brigade loss: Winchester, k, 2; w, 34 = 36. Port Republic, k, 9; m, 1 = 10. *Artillery*, Col. S. Crutchfield (chief of artillery of Jackson's entire command): Va. Battery, Capt. Joseph Carpenter; Va. Battery, Capt. William H. Caskie; Va. Battery (joined at Port Republic), Capt. James McD. Carrington; Va. Battery, Capt. W. E. Cutshaw (w), Lieut. John C. Carpenter; Va. Battery, Capt. William T. Poague; Va. Battery, Capt. George W. Wooding. Artillery loss: Winchester, k, 3; w, 21 = 24. Port Republic, w, 9; m, 1 = 10.

EWELL'S DIVISION, Major-General Richard S. Ewell. *Second Brigade*, Col. W. C. Scott, Brig.-Gen. George H. Steuart (w), Col. W. C. Scott: 1st Md. (assigned to brigade June 6th), Col. Bradley T. Johnson; 44th Va., Col. W. C. Scott; 52d Va., Lieut.-Col. James H. Skinner; 58th Va., Col. Samuel H. Letcher. Brigade loss: Cross Keys, k, 7; w, 65 = 72. Port Republic, k, 30; w, 169 = 199. *Fourth Brigade*, Brig.-Gen. Arnold Elzey (w), Col. J. A. Walker: 13th Va., Col. J. A. Walker; 31st Va., Col. John S. Hoffman; 25th Va., Lieut.-Col. Patrick B. Duffy; 12th Ga., Col. Z. T. Conner. Brigade loss: Cross Keys, k, 5; w, 62 = 67. Port Republic, k, 15; w, 80; m, 4 = 99. *Seventh Brigade*, Brig.-Gen. Isaac R. Trimble: 21st N. C., Col. W. W. Kirkland (w); 21st Ga., Col. J. T. Mercer; 15th Ala., Col. James Cantey; 16th Miss., Col. Carnot Posey (w). Brigade loss: Winchester, k, 22; w, 75 = 97. Cross Keys, k, 23; w, 109; m, 6 = 138. *Eighth Brigade*, Brig.-Gen. Richard Taylor: 6th La., Col. Isaac G. Seymour; 7th La., Col. H. T. Hays (w), Maj. David B. Penn; 8th La., Col. H. B. Kelly; 9th La., Col. Leroy A. Stafford; La. Battalion, Maj. C. R. Wheat. Brigade loss: Front Royal and Winchester, k, 21; w, 109; m, 3 = 133. Cross Keys, k, 1; w, 8 = 9. Port Republic, k, 33; w, 256; m, 9 = 298. *Maryland Line* (attached to Second Brigade June 6th), Brig.-Gen. George H. Steuart (assigned to command of the cavalry May 24th): 1st Infantry, Col. Bradley T. Johnson; Co. A, Cav., Capt. Ridgely Brown; Baltimore Battery, Capt. J. B. Brockenbrough. *Artillery:* Va. Battery, Lieut. J. W. Latimer; Captain A. R. Courtney; Va. Battery, Capt. John A. M. Lusk; Va. Battery, Capt. Charles I. Raine; Va. Battery. Capt. William H. Rice. Artillery loss: Cross Keys, k, 8; w, 20; m, 8 = 36.

CAVALRY, Col. Thomas S. Flournoy, Brig.-Gen. George H. Steuart, Brig.-Gen. Turner Ashby (k), Col. Thomas T. Munford: 2d Va., Lieut.-Col. James W. Watts; Col. Thomas T. Munford; 6th Va., Col. Thomas S. Flournoy; 7th Va., Col. Turner Ashby (promoted Brig.-Gen. May 23d); Va. Battery, Capt. R. P. Chew. Cavalry loss: Front Royal and Winchester (partial report), k, 11; w, 15 = 26. (Other casualties in the cavalry during the campaign are not specifically stated.)

General Jackson reported his losses at Front Royal, Winchester, etc., from May 23d to 31st, as 68 killed, 329 wounded, and 3 missing = 400. At Cross Keys and Port Republic the casualties were 139 killed, 951 wounded, and 60 missing = 1150. As nearly as can be ascertained from the "Official Records," the loss in the campaign was 230 killed, 1373 wounded, and 232 captured or missing = 1878. The strength of Jackson's command is nowhere authoritatively stated. Colonel William Allan says in his "Jackson's Valley Campaign," p. 146: "Jackson had moved against Banks, on May 19th, with a total effective force of 16,000 or 17,000 men. . . . His effective force [at Cross Keys] could not have exceeded 13,000, even if it reached that amount."

# FIGHTING JACKSON AT KERNSTOWN.

## BY NATHAN KIMBALL, BREVET MAJOR-GENERAL, U. S. V.

EARLY in 1862 the division of the Union army afterward commanded by General James Shields was reorganized by General Frederick W. Lander, under whose lead it had taken part in the hardships of a winter campaign through the mountains and in the valleys of the upper Potomac. On the 1st of March orders were received directing General Lander to move his division from West Virginia into the valley of the Shenandoah, to unite with the divisions under General Banks in the operations already begun against "Stonewall" Jackson.[J] But the brave Lander was not again to lead us. When the order came, it found him overcome by exposures and hardships, and on the 2d of March he died, at the camp of the division, on the Great Cacapon River. The division began the movement under this order on the 5th, and on the 7th, while we were on the way, General Shields arrived from Washington and assumed command.

General Banks had already crossed the Potomac with his divisions, and with but little opposition had occupied Harper's Ferry, Charlestown, and Martinsburg, the enemy retiring toward Winchester.[‡] When our division arrived at Martinsburg on the 10th, General C. S. Hamilton's had moved forward, and was then advancing near Winchester. Expecting that the enemy would resist his farther advance, General Hamilton requested General Shields to push forward to his support. General Shields, complying, sent forward, on the evening of the 11th, his First Brigade (my own), which, after a night's hard march, united, early on the morning of the 12th, with Hamilton's division, and advanced with it, and at 2 P. M. General Hamilton's troops occupied the city and its defenses without serious opposition. Jackson, having abandoned the place, retreated up the valley toward Strasburg. On the 13th, General Shields arrived with his Second and Third Brigades (Sullivan's and Tyler's), having left detachments to garrison Martinsburg, while other forces of General Banks's command remained at Harper's Ferry and Charlestown. General Hamilton, commanding the First Division, having received orders assigning him to duty elsewhere, General Banks assigned General Alpheus S. Williams to the command of that division.

Early on the morning of March 17th, Shields, under orders from General Banks to make a reconnoissance, moved out from Winchester, following the route taken by Jackson along the turnpike up the valley toward Staunton, with flanking parties of cavalry upon the Front Royal and other parallel roads.

---

[J] For an account of Jackson's early operations in the valley, see Vol. I., p. 111.

[‡] The object of this movement under Banks was the protection of the reopening of the Baltimore and Ohio Railroad west of Harper's Ferry. The region of the upper Potomac and the Shenandoah Valley was at this time included in the department under General McClellan's immediate control, comprising the field of operations of the Army of the Potomac, that is, northern Virginia. Banks's command was the Fifth Corps, Army of the Potomac, and consisted of two divisions, that of Hamilton, afterward Williams's, and Lander's, afterward Shields's. During the Peninsular campaign, Banks was given a separate command, the "Department of the Shenandoah."— EDITORS.

In the afternoon of the 17th, a force of the enemy with cavalry and artillery was met at Fisher's Hill, near Strasburg, where brisk skirmishing was commenced and continued until toward the close of the day, when Shields ordered the advance of the Second Brigade, the enemy retreated, and Shields's division encamped for the night in possession of the positions which had been held by the enemy. .

On the morning of the 18th, General Shields pushed forward — meeting with but little resistance — as far as Woodstock; then, halting with his infantry, he sent his cavalry forward, following the enemy to Mount Jackson, where, having crossed the Shenandoah, he had disappeared. General Shields here discontinued the pursuit, and, returning, encamped again on the night of the 18th at Fisher's Hill and Strasburg. On the morning of the 19th, waiting until the arrival of his cavalry,— at 10 o'clock,— he marched for Winchester, where the command arrived late in the evening without loss, and without being followed by the enemy.

General Shields reported to General Banks that Jackson had fled with his army from the valley, leaving only a small force under Ashby for observation, and that he had driven this force beyond the Shenandoah at Mount Jackson.

General Banks, now satisfied that Jackson had abandoned the valley, or that his force was too small and he too cautious to return to attack, and in compliance with orders previously received, removed all of his forces from Winchester (excepting Shields's division) east of the Blue Ridge.

BRIGADIER-GENERAL FREDERICK W. LANDER.
FROM A PHOTOGRAPH.

On the morning of the 22d, the last of his troops having moved, General Banks departed for Washington, leaving the division of Shields, the only force at and around Winchester, as the guardians of the valley. The enemy meantime had not been idle, having been kept well informed, daily and hourly,— by his friends and emissaries,— of every movement made by our forces, and also of the number and positions of the troops remaining under General Shields. Stonewall Jackson now returned, intent upon victory, the recapture of Winchester, and the possession of the beautiful valley.

At 4 P. M., March 22d, Jackson announced his appearance in our front by the guns of Ashby's artillery. Ashby, advancing from the direction of Strasburg, forced our outposts back upon their reserves, and attacked them with his cavalry. At the sound of the first gun, General Shields hurried to the front with reënforcements, returned the fire of the enemy with artillery and musketry, and, advancing his line, compelled the enemy to retire. Upon starting to the front General Shields had sent an officer of his staff to me with orders directing me "to move the residue of my brigade with one battery to a point on the Strasburg turnpike, two miles south of the city, with the least practicable delay." Complying at once my command was moved rapidly forward, and within an hour reached the point indicated. Here I met the general, who was being conveyed to his quarters in the city, having been severely wounded in the recent engagement. After giving me information as to the fight and the position of the forces, he directed me to take command. Our line of infantry and artillery was advanced in front of the toll-gate and in position to the right and left of the turnpike, with cavalry upon the diverging roads and flanks. No further movement on the part of the enemy took place, and night closing in, too dark for an advance, my troops bivouacked in line to await the developments of the coming Sabbath. During the night General Shields sent me instructions directing me to move forward at the earliest light with my brigade and battery, with one squadron of cavalry, along the turnpike, and drive or capture the enemy, as the force in my front was nothing more than an observation force of Ashby's cavalry.

At daylight, on the 23d, my command was moving; so was the enemy's. Advancing with infantry from the hills in my front, he opened upon my line a heavy fire of musketry and artillery, which was promptly returned, and soon our forces were engaged in severe conflict. The enemy halting, I ordered my line forward, giving and receiving heavy volleys, the dash of our men compelling the enemy to give way. With loud cheers my soldiers pushed forward, and before 8 A. M. we had the pleasure of taking possession of the positions which the enemy had held on the high ridge overlooking the village below, his forces now retreating to their supports in the woods beyond. This engagement, though of short duration, was the beginning of the battle at Kernstown.

Seeing that the force I had thus far opposed to me had been greatly reënforced, I halted for rest, observation, and further developments on the part of the enemy. Having informed the commanding general of the result of the morning's work, I awaited further orders, which were soon received through Major Armstrong with directions to move forward at once. Colonel Sullivan, with his brigade, was within supporting distance, and the force in my front, the general thought, was not strong enough to resist me. But the enemy had by this time become active and was forming his lines, his force greatly increased by infantry. Calling Major Armstrong's attention to the movements, strength, and position already presented to view, I requested him to return to the general and request him to send me reënforcements. I was satisfied that not only was the force of Ashby present, but the entire army of Stonewall Jackson, with that general in command, in person. The position I held was good for defense, and I determined to hold it. Sullivan coming forward with his brigade and one battery, I placed them in position on a continuation of the ridge on the left of the turnpike and of my brigade, thus extending our line in that direction.

The enemy had been active, and now relieved me from the execution of the movement directed by the general, by undertaking a like movement against me. Moving forward with infantry and artillery against Sullivan on the left and my own brigade on the right, he forced my skirmish line to retire until under cover of our main line and batteries, and still advanced until my fire compelled him to halt; then Carroll, Sawyer, and Voris were ordered forward from my lines, and their well-directed fire, with the storm of grape and canister poured from the well-managed guns of Clark's, Jenks's, and Robinson's batteries, forced the enemy to retreat to his former position. At 10 A. M., while I awaited his further movements, General Shields sent the following:

"COLONEL KIMBALL: Major Armstrong informs me that the enemy at present occupies a position on an eminence on the right flank, also another on the left flank, leaving the center unsupported, which I take to be the Strasburg turnpike. If this be the state of the case, I would recommend to push a column of cavalry, four pieces of artillery, and a body of infantry along the turnpike to advance far enough to take them in the rear when they commence to retreat. This body, however, must be preceded by active skirmishing to avoid falling into a trap. When this column advances far enough, a simultaneous charge may be made upon both batteries while the center column cuts off retreat. I leave the management of this to your own discretion, not being able to be on the ground in person. I cannot accurately describe what ought to be done. If the force before you be what I suppose it is, the only way to do is to close around them by some such move as this, or some other equally decisive move as you may deem practicable. My own opinion is that there is no force before you but that we encountered the other day."

BRIGADIER-GENERAL JAMES SHIELDS.
FROM A PHOTOGRAPH.

Convinced that the general did not comprehend the situation, the strength of the enemy, nor the positions held by the respective forces, and satisfied that from his bed in the city five miles to the rear he could not properly conduct the movements which might be required by the exigencies of the situation, I determined to remain on the defensive and in the position now held by my line, from which I had an unobstructed view across the little valley and the enemy's lines to the front; the danger was, our force being less than his, that he might turn one or the other of our flanks. Responding to my request, General Shields sent me the desired support, with the following:

"COLONEL KIMBALL: — I have ordered the 13th Indiana, and 39th Illinois Infantry, and a battery, and will follow them with cavalry and other infantry. I hope you will keep me advised of the motions of the enemy by intelligent orderlies who can explain themselves when they come. Tyler's brigade has been ordered within supporting distance and will communicate with you. Our whole force is now in your hands. If there is a greater force of the enemy against you than I supposed, increase the strength of the center column and take them in flank."

Near 2 P. M. Jackson again moved forward to the attack with artillery and infantry, while his cavalry threatened my left flank. His advancing column came boldly forward, seemingly intent upon driving us from our position and moving directly forward to Winchester. My gallant line of skirmishers opened their fire upon the deploying column, but were forced back under cover of our main line, which once more poured its destructive fire from rifles and batteries into the ranks of the gallant enemy, and *again* compelled him to fall back to the point from which he had advanced. While making this second attempt by direct attack, Jackson was moving troops to his left, with the aim of passing beyond my right. Colonel Tyler coming to the front in person just after this last repulse of the enemy, I pointed out the unprotected condition of my right and the open and unoccupied position beyond it, and the movement of the enemy's forces in that direction, and directed him to move his brigade as quickly as possible to secure the position. I also ordered what cavalry I had to move to the right of Tyler's brigade and in support of it. When repulsed in the last attack, the enemy's troops retreated from the front of my right toward the point in the woods where Jackson had massed his forces for an attack against my extreme right, and to move around that flank. Satisfied by this and other movements from the enemy's right of his intentions, I prepared to meet him and end the contest. At 3:30 P. M. the enemy commenced his movement, announcing it by solid shot upon my line from the hills behind which his forces were moving, and advanced across the open field toward the point to which I had ordered Tyler's brigade. The enemy's skirmishers, advancing, met Tyler's just as they were emerging from the wood and checked their advance. Tyler soon deployed and, advancing, forced this line back to their main line now under protection of a stone-wall, when the enemy poured such fire from his muskets and batteries as to check Tyler's farther advance.

The enemy made frequent attempts to advance, but they were held by Tyler's gallant men to their cover, and the battle now raged in all its fury, neither line giving way. Jackson had withdrawn his brigades from his right, leaving only a small force to guard that flank. To meet his masses, now moving to force Tyler back, regiments and batteries were drawn from our left to strengthen our center. The time having come for the decisive movement, my First Brigade, with the supports from the left, and Sullivan's, were made ready. Directing Colonel Sullivan to follow the movements of forces on our right, I ordered the line forward. With a quick move at right-half-wheel, the gallant fellows, under Harrow, Patrick, Foster, Murray, and Voris, with loud cheers, dashed forward through the terrific storm of shot and shell from the enemy's stone-wall and batteries; nor did they halt or falter until the enemy was driven from his protection, and his advancing lines were checked. Our line now had the wall so long held by Jackson. But soon the sturdy foe, reënforced, advanced again to retake the position; they were met by men as gallant and as determined as themselves, and in answer to their wild "rebel yell" loud cheers were given from our line as it dashed forward. With Tyler's gallant brigade and our fearless little band of cavalry rounding his flank, the enemy was forced back across the field to the woods, where he once more attempted to check our advancing lines. With cheers from right to left, our gallant soldiers pushed forward, and as the sun went down, the stubbornly yielding foe, who had thrice advanced to the attack, gave way, and Jackson's army was badly beaten — his shattered brigades in full retreat from the field over which they had so gallantly fought.‡ Night closing in too dark for pursuit, our weary soldiers bivouacked in positions from which they had driven the enemy. Our troops had fought without food since the evening of the 22d, and it was after midnight before this want was supplied.♭ At earliest light on the morning of the 24th our troops were again on the march, in pursuit of the enemy, whose rear-guard was overtaken near Middletown. The enemy retreated across Cedar Creek to his main force, under fire from our batteries. While here skirmishing with the enemy, I had made such disposition of our

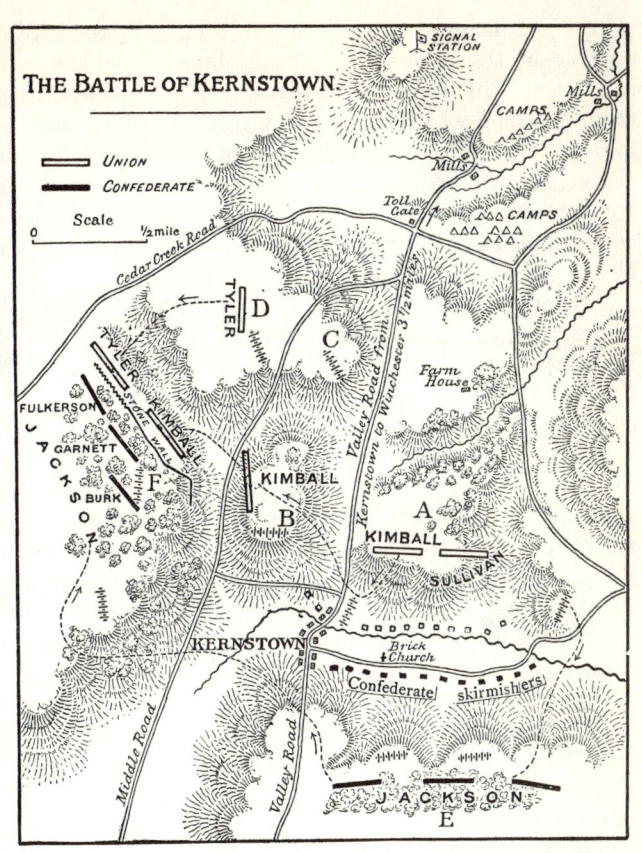

MAP OF THE BATTLE OF KERNSTOWN, VA., MARCH 23, 1862.

Based upon the maps in the "Official Records," Vol. XII., Part I., pp. 362-365. A represents the first position of Kimball's and Sullivan's brigades on the morning of March 23d. Sullivan remained to hold the Union left, while Kimball moved to the position at B, and finally to the main battle-field, F (evening of March 23d), where he joined Tyler, who had previously been in position first at C, and then at D, whence he advanced to oppose Stonewall Jackson in his flanking position at F, to which Jackson had marched by wood roads from his first position at E.— EDITORS.

‡ Colonel E. H. C. Cavins, of the 14th Indiana, writing under date of July 9th, 1887, says of this charge:

"The Confederates fell back in great disorder, and we advanced in disorder just as great, over stone-walls and over fences, through blackberry-bushes and undergrowth. Over logs, through woods, over hills and fields, the brigades, regiments, and companies advanced, in one promiscuous, mixed, and uncontrollable mass. Officers shouted themselves hoarse in trying to bring order out of confusion, but all their efforts were unavailing along the front line, or rather what ought to have been the front line. Yet many of the brave Virginians who had so often followed their standards to victory, lingered in the rear of their retreating comrades, loading as they slowly retired, and rallying in squads in every ravine and behind every hill — or hiding singly among the trees. They continued to make it very hot for our men in the advance."

♭ The losses at Kernstown were: Union, 118 killed, 450 wounded, 22 missing = 590 ; Confederate, 80 killed, 375 wounded, 263 missing = 718.

troops as I believed would result in their rout and capture of their trains, by moving up the creek with a strong flanking detachment to the back or dirt road from Winchester to Strasburg, while my other troops followed along the turnpike upon which the enemy's trains were moving. I hoped thus to head him off before he could reach Fisher's Hill beyond Strasburg. Major-General Banks, arriving as this movement was being commenced, assumed command. He deemed it prudent to await reënforcements, and our army remained in camp at Middletown and Cedar Creek that night, while the enemy escaped to Fisher's Hill.

Having been reënforced by the return of Williams's division, the army under General Banks moved forward on the morning of the 25th, and after light skirmishing occupied Strasburg and Fisher's Hill, the enemy continuing his retreat toward Woodstock and Mount Jackson. Our army remained in camp at Strasburg and Fisher's Hill, awaiting supplies, until April 1st.

On the morning of April 1st our forces moved forward, with three days' rations, but without tents or baggage, to Woodstock, the enemy having continued his retreat to Mount Jackson. Receiving additional supplies, we moved forward from Woodstock on the 8th, meeting and skirmishing with the enemy daily. On the 15th our army arrived near Mount Jackson, finding the enemy in force, and after a brisk engagement compelling him to fall back and his main force to cross the Shenandoah at Mount Jackson, beyond which he took position at Rude's Hill, covering the village and the crossings of the river.

General Banks, on the morning of the 17th, directed a forward movement to force a passage across the river. The river was much swollen by rains, rendering it impossible to ford. There being but one bridge, it became the center of contest, the enemy having failed to destroy it, although he had set fire to it. A splendid dash by a detachment of our cavalry through the bridge drove the enemy away and extinguished the flames. This gallant charge was made by two companies of the 1st Ohio, under Captains Menken and Robinson, and one company of the 1st Michigan, led by a little corporal. Dismounting, they put out the fire, carrying water from the river in their old slouched hats for the purpose. (The name of this dashing corporal was George R. Maxwell, who afterward, by his gallantry and daring achievements, rose to the command of his regiment and brigade under the heroic Sheridan.) The bridge secured, our army moved forward under a heavy fire from the enemy's line and batteries. By 11 A. M. the crossing was completed, and the enemy, forced from his position, retreated beyond New Market toward Harrisonburg and Port Republic, and our forces encamped in positions in advance of New Market.

In this engagement our forces captured one company of cavalry, and inflicted other heavy losses upon the enemy, our loss being light. For his success General Banks received that night the thanks of the President.

On the 19th and 20th our forces, under General Williams, advanced and occupied Harrisonburg, while Shields's division held the roads to Luray, the crossings of the Shenandoah, and New Market. General Banks, in "General Orders, No. 20," dated New Market, Virginia, April 21st, 1862, congratulated

BATTLE-FIELD OF KERNSTOWN, VA. FROM A PHOTOGRAPH TAKEN IN 1885.
On this side of the stone-wall Jackson formed his line of battle, March 23, 1862.—See F on map, p. 307.

"the troops under his command upon the success of their achievement, and the permanent expulsion of the rebel army from the valley of Virginia."

General Shields, who had remained out of the field on account of wounds received in the engagement of the 22d of March with Ashby's cavalry in front of Winchester, now arrived, and in "General Orders, No. 28," dated New Market, April 30th, 1862, relieving me from command of the division, said:

" The general commanding the division, having so far recovered from his wounds as to be able to serve in the field with his brave troops, desires to make it known to them that he places himself again at their head. Brigadier-General Kimball will rejoin the First Brigade, and again resume command of it. And, thus directing, the general cannot suffer the occasion to pass without expressing to that gallant officer and his staff his grateful acknowledgments for the efficient manner in which they managed the division and directed its affairs while he was compelled by his condition to be absent from the field. His special thanks are due to General Kimball for his devotion to the interests and honor of the command and the signal service he has rendered it in this emergency."

With a commission, now as brigadier-general (for my victory over Stonewall Jackson at Kernstown), I resumed command of my gallant old brigade, rejoiced to be freed from the greater responsibilities, gratified with the success attending me while in command of the division, and grateful to the Government for the recognition of my services.

Stonewall Jackson, although out of the valley, was still immediately in our front. He was daily increasing in strength by reënforcements, and was active in demonstrations. On the 1st of May, Jackson's army made movements threatening our right at Harrisonburg, and our left near the crossing of the Shenandoah toward Luray. Under cover of these a part of the force under Edward Johnson moved, on the 7th, to prevent the capture of Staunton by

Milroy.  Meeting General Milroy at McDowell and checking Milroy's advance, Jackson again returned to our front. Both sides claimed success in the affair at McDowell on the 8th of May [see p. 286].

The operations against "Stonewall Jackson" were successful, with the valley of Virginia in our possession, and Jackson's army held in check beyond the Shenandoah by Banks and Shields. General McDowell, with his army, held Fredericksburg and the line of the Rappahannock, General Frémont moving toward Staunton from the west, and General McClellan, with the Army of the Potomac, was advancing up the peninsula, confronting the Confederate army under Johnston. Thus was Washington protected, and the ruin of the Confederacy imminent, when a blunder in the management of our armies in Virginia was made. The order directing Shields's division to join General McDowell's army at Fredericksburg was most unfortunate. The divisions were indignant in contemplation of the results, knowing the situation as they did. On receipt of the order General Banks said:

"Results are not for us to consider, and orders are received to be obeyed. I regret it because I feel that the policy of which this order is a part is to end in allowing the grand army of the rebels to escape unharmed from Virginia, and add another year to the war. It is impossible to anticipate what work lies before us; I feel the imperative necessity of making preparations for the worst."

And by this order the worst came, and the opportunity was given to Stonewall Jackson for the display of his peculiar strategic ability.

On the 12th of May General Shields moved from New Market for Falmouth, and General Banks moved down the valley to Strasburg, thus opening the way for Jackson [see map, p. 284]. With Shields's division far away at Fredericksburg,↑ and Frémont beyond the Shenandoah mountains, Jackson, on the 23d, with his army of about 1500, dashed down upon Banks's 9000, mostly stationed in detachments at Strasburg and Front Royal, nearly 20 miles apart, by the route Banks was forced to take.

But not until after three days of hard fighting did he force the heroic soldiers of Banks's division from the valley. ☆ With the information of this

↑ Colonel Franklin Sawyer, in his history of the 8th Ohio, of Kimball's brigade, records the following incident, which took place at Falmouth, opposite Fredericksburg:

"Kimball's brigade was ordered into a newly fenced field for its camp, and no sooner were the men dismissed from ranks than the entire fence disappeared. General King, who was in command at this place, seeing this *movement* from his quarters at the Phillips Mansion, sent down an aide-de-camp to arrest all of our officers, and compel the men to rebuild the fence. Officers laughed and the men jeered at him. The rails were soon on fire, and our dinners cooking. King called up his adjutant, Major Barstow, who had been General Lander's adjutant when he commanded us, and ordered him to detail sufficient troops to arrest our whole division, exclaiming: 'Who are these vandals?' 'Why,' said Barstow, 'they are Lander's old troops from Western Virginia; you had better keep your guards here at headquarters, for you'll be devilish lucky if they don't steal your house-roof before morning!' King was dumfounded, but his fence was never rebuilt." EDITORS.

☆ Jackson made his attack at Front Royal on the 23d, and, after a stubborn resistance, captured the command of Colonel John R. Kenly, composed of the 1st Maryland, 2 companies of the 29th Pennsylvania, and a section of Knaps's Pennsylvania Battery, acting as guard to Banks's communications. The latter says in his report:

"The extraordinary force of the enemy could no longer be doubted. It was apparent also that they had a more extended purpose than the capture of the brave little band at Front Royal. This purpose could be nothing less than the defeat of my own command or its possible capture by occupying Winchester, and by this movement intercepting supplies or reënforcements, and cutting off all possibility of retreat. . . . It was determined, therefore, to enter the lists with the enemy in a race or a battle, as he should choose, for the possession of Winchester, the key of the valley, and for us the position of safety."

Jackson pushed his advance rapidly from Front Royal to Middletown, and on the 24th intercepted Banks's column, meeting, however, with repulse. At Newtown another Confederate force was met and driven off by Banks; his rear-guard also repulsed an attack near Kernstown.

reverse came the order directing Shields's division to move back to the Shenandoah, while Frémont crossed the mountains to strike the army of Jackson before it could retreat from the valley. On the 25th Shields's division commenced its return, and, without halting, reached Rectortown on the evening of the 28th, where we stopped for rest and to await supplies. At 4 P. M. of the 29th the following order was received: "COLONEL KIMBALL, commanding First Brigade: You will march immediately; leave your teams and wagons, take only ambulances, ammunition-wagons, and provisions, as much as on hand in haversacks. SHIELDS, Brigadier-General commanding."

At 6 P. M. my command was moving for Front Royal. Marching all night (save 2½ hours for rest and refreshment at Manassas Gap), we arrived and took position at 11:30 A. M., May 30th, upon the ridge east of and overlooking the village, before our presence was known to the enemy. Having only one company (30 men) of cavalry, my infantry was sent to surround the Confederates, but before this could be accomplished the attempt was discovered. The enemy, setting fire to the depots, warehouses, and railroad freight trains, made away in retreat under rapid firing from our battery.* My cavalry pushed forward fearlessly after the enemy, closely followed by a portion of my infantry, to the junction of the Strasburg and Middletown roads, beyond the branches of the river; here, being completely exhausted, my troops halted, the enemy having gone from view in the direction of Strasburg and Winchester. That portion of our command left in the village had saved the loaded freight trains, but the warehouses and depots were completely destroyed, with most of their contents. General Shields came up at 5 P. M. with the other brigades of the division, and the town and the captures were left to his direction.∫ With the regiments of my brigade and the 4th, Colonel Carroll's, I returned to the front and encamped in line for the night.

On the 31st the enemy appeared in considerable force in our front. I directed Carroll to move out with his command and attack them, which was promptly done, and after a sharp conflict the enemy was forced back, Carroll taking several prisoners and one piece (11-pounder) of artillery. The enemy having retreated and night having set in, Carroll returned to his position.

Our command was aroused from its slumbers early on the morning of the 1st of June by the roar of cannon away to our left toward Strasburg. Frémont had passed over the mountains and attacked Jackson's forces at Fisher's Hill. General Shields, at Front Royal, was informed of the fight going on at Strasburg and came to the front, but declined to send our forces to join in the fight, and directed us to remain in our position to await the arrival of General Irvin McDowell and Ord's (Ricketts's) division.

General McDowell arrived on the evening of June 1st. Ord's division

---

* At Winchester, another stand was made on the 25th. General Banks says: "I determined to test the substance and strength of the enemy by actual collision, and measures were promptly taken to prepare our troops to meet them." The Confederates were held in check several hours, and that night Banks's retreat was continued toward Martinsburg. See p. 288.— EDITORS.

∫ The captures at Front Royal were: 1 piece of artillery, 3 heavily laden trains with stores, and 8 wagons, with teams, retreating with commissary stores, and 160 prisoners, including Miss Belle Boyd, a famous spy in the service of the Confederates. We also recaptured many comrades of Banks's division, captured during the fight of a few days before.— N. K.

relieved ours in front, and Bayard's cavalry was sent to aid Frémont. Our division returned to Front Royal and encamped two miles south on the road to Luray.

By the wisdom (?) of Generals McDowell and Shields, our division was sent up the Luray valley, east of the south branch of the Shenandoah and Massanutten mountain, while Jackson's army, pursued by Frémont, was moving up the valley, along the Staunton turnpike. Jackson had destroyed all bridges and other means of crossing the Shenandoah, from Front Royal to Port Republic, rendering it impossible for Shields's division either to strike Jackson or communicate with Frémont. Shields's division reached Luray June 4th, after having marched 1150 miles in forty-three days, fighting one severe battle and many lesser engagements. Forty per cent. of the command were now without shoes, two per cent. without trousers, and other clothing was deficient. And now, without any supplies, officers and men were well-nigh worn out.

On the 5th, Carroll's brigade, now partially supplied, moved with only 1200 men and 1 battery, by order of General Shields, for Port Republic, to secure and hold the bridge at that crossing, if it should not already be destroyed. On the 6th, Tyler's brigade of 2000 men and 1 battery followed to support Carroll. Ferry's brigade was at Columbia crossing, 8 miles south, and mine was 6 miles north of Luray. Frémont's and Jackson's guns were distinctly heard beyond the river and mountain, but we were powerless to render assistance to our friends because of the impassable river. On the 7th, Frémont forced the enemy from Mount Jackson, and pursued him to New Market and Harrisonburg, but failed to bring him to battle.

BREVET MAJOR-GENERAL NATHAN KIMBALL.
FROM A PHOTOGRAPH.

On the 8th, Carroll reached the bridge at Port Republic with Tyler yet fifteen miles in rear. My brigade, under orders for Stanardsville, passed Luray and encamped with Ferry's, and on the 9th moved forward, leaving Ferry in his position.

On the 8th, Frémont brought Jackson to bay, and engaged him in battle at Cross Keys.‡ Jackson, being hard pressed, prepared to save his army by retreat. Sending one brigade, with artillery, to secure a crossing for his army at Port Republic, he met Carroll, and, forcing him back, secured the bridge. That night, Jackson's entire force fled from Frémont, crossed the bridge, burned it, and was free from the destruction that had threatened him.

Jackson, on the morning of the 9th, with his army, attacked the now united detachments of Tyler and Carroll, and with his overwhelming force com-

‡ See pp. 291-293 for details of the engagements at Port Republic and Cross Keys.

pelled the retreat of our small but gallant command. Jackson's own old Stonewall Brigade was first repulsed by Carroll's, and Jackson himself was compelled to rally and lead them back to the contest; then, with "Dick" Taylor's and other brigades and batteries, he forced our men from the field.↓

On the 9th, at sundown, Shields, now with me, received by the gallant Myles W. Keogh↑ news from Tyler of his disaster. My brigade was ordered at once to move forward, to be followed by Ferry's, then ten miles in my rear. At 10 o'clock on the morning of the 10th, after a terrible night's march, we reached Conrad's store, some six miles below the field of action, where I met our worn and defeated comrades of Tyler's and Carroll's commands; and here I formed a new line, and in position awaited the expected attack from Jackson, and the arrival of Ferry's brigade.

Ferry came with our supports, but Jackson, having been severely handled by a small detachment, although he had defeated it, was satisfied, now that he was free from Frémont, not to try conclusions with the division, united, that had defeated him at Kernstown.

In the afternoon General Frémont succeeded in communicating with General Shields, and arranging for the crossing of his army. It was the intention, thus united, to follow Jackson, now retreating toward Gordonsville to join Lee's army near Richmond, but before the morning of the 11th Shields received peremptory orders, directing him to return with his command to Front Royal, where we arrived on the 16th of June.

↓ See pp. 291–293 for details of the engagements at Port Republic and Cross Keys.
↑ As captain in the 7th United States Cavalry, Keogh was killed in the massacre, by the Sioux, of Custer's command, June 25th, 1876, on a branch of the Little Big Horn River, Montana.— EDITORS.

## THE OPPOSING FORCES IN THE SEVEN DAYS' BATTLES.
### June 25th – July 1st, 1862.

The composition, losses, and strength of each army as here stated give the gist of all the data obtainable in the Official Records. K stands for killed; w for wounded; m w for mortally wounded; m for captured or missing; c for captured.

### THE UNION FORCES.
Army of the Potomac, Major-General George B. McClellan.

GENERAL HEADQUARTERS: *Provost Marshal's and Hdq'rs Guard*, Brig.-Gen. Andrew Porter: 2d U. S. Cavalry (7 co's), and McClellan (Ill.) Dragoons (2 co's), Maj. Alfred Pleasonton; 93d N. Y. (4 co's), and Sturges (Ill.) Rifles, Maj. Granville O. Haller; 8th U. S. Inf. (2 co's), Capt. Royal T. Frank and Lieut. Eugene Carter. *Escort*: 4th U. S. Cav. (2 co's), and Oneida (N. Y.) Cavalry, Capt. James B. McIntyre. *Volunteer Engineer Brigade*, Brig.-Gen. Daniel P. Woodbury: 15th N. Y., Col. J. McLeod Murphy; 50th N. Y., Col. Charles B. Stuart. Brigade loss: m, 12. *Battalion U. S. Engineers*, Capt. James C. Duane. Loss: w, 2; m, 9 = 11. *Casey's Command* (at White House), Brig.-Gen. Silas Casey: 4th Pa. Cav. (squadron), Capt. William Shorts; 11th Pa. Cav. (5 co's), Col. Josiah Harlan; F, 1st N. Y. Arty., Capt. Wm. R. Wilson; 93d N. Y. (6 co's), Col. Thos. F. Morris.

SECOND CORPS, Brig.-Gen. E. V. Sumner. Staff loss: w, 1.
*Cavalry*: D, F, H, and K, 6th N. Y., Lieut.-Col. Duncan McVicar.

FIRST DIVISION, Brig.-Gen. Israel B. Richardson.
*First Brigade*, Brig.-Gen. John C. Caldwell: 5th N. H., Lieut.-Col. Samuel G. Langley, Capt. Edward E. Sturtevant; 7th N. Y., Col. George W. von Schack; 61st N. Y., Col. Francis C. Barlow; 81st Pa., Col. Charles F. Johnson (w), Lieut.-Col. Eli T. Conner (k), Maj. H. Boyd McKeen. Brigade loss: k, 61; w, 356; m, 137 = 554. *Second Brigade*, Brig.-Gen. Thomas F. Meagher, Col. Robert Nugent, Brig.-Gen. Thomas F. Meagher: 29th Mass., Col. Ebenezer W. Peirce (w), Lieut.-Col. Joseph H. Barnes; 63d N. Y., Col. John Burke (w), Lieut.-Col. Henry Fowler, Capt. Joseph O'Neill; 69th N. Y., Col. Robert Nugent; 88th N. Y., Col. Henry M. Baker, Maj. James Quinlan. Brigade loss: k, 34; w, 227, m, 232 = 493. *Third Brigade*, Brig.-Gen. William H. French: 2d Del., Lieut.-Col. William P. Baily, Capt. D. L. Stricker; 52d N. Y., Col. Paul Frank; 57th N. Y., Col. Samuel K. Zook; 64th N. Y., Col. Thomas J. Parker; 66th N. Y., Col. Joseph C. Pinckney; 53d Pa., Col. John R. Brooke. Brigade loss: k, 3; w, 43; m, 162 = 208. *Artillery*, Capt.

## 314   THE OPPOSING FORCES IN THE SEVEN DAYS' BATTLES.

George W. Hazzard (m w): B, 1st N. Y., Capt. Rufus D. Pettit; A and C, 4th U. S., Capt. George W. Hazzard, Lieut. Rufus King, Jr. Artillery loss: w, 19; m, 10 = 29.
SECOND DIVISION, Brig.-Gen. John Sedgwick.
*First Brigade*, Col. Alfred Sully: 15th Mass., Lieut.-Col. John W. Kimball; 1st Minn., Lieut.-Col. Stephen Miller; 1st Co. Mass. Sharp-shooters, Capt. John Saunders; 34th N. Y., Col. James A. Suiter; 82d N. Y., Col. Henry W. Hudson; 2d Co. Minn. Sharp-shooters, Capt. William F. Russell. Brigade loss: k, 12; w, 82; m, 152 = 246. *Second Brigade*, Brig.-Gen. William W. Burns (w.: 69th Pa., Col. Joshua T. Owen; 71st Pa., Lieut.-Col. William G. Jones; 72d Pa., Col. De Witt C. Baxter; 106th Pa., Col. Turner G. Morehead. Brigade loss: k, 40; w, 193; m, 172 = 405. *Third Brigade*, Brig.-Gen. N. J. T. Dana: 19th Mass., Col. Edward W. Hinks (w), Capt. Edmund Rice, Lieut.-Col. Arthur F. Devereux; 20th Mass., Col. William R. Lee; 7th Mich., Col. Ira R. Grosvenor; 42d N. Y., Col. Edmund C. Charles (w and c), Lieut.-Col. James J. Mooney. Brigade loss: k, 51; w, 262; m, 153 = 466. *Artillery*, Col. Charles H. Tompkins: A, 1st R. I., Capt. John A. Tompkins; I, 1st U. S., Lieut. Edmund Kirby. Artillery loss: w, 12; m, 4 = 16.
RESERVE ARTILLERY: G, 1st N. Y., Capt. John D. Frank; B, 1st R. I., Capt. Walter O. Bartlett; G, 1st R. I., Capt. Charles D. Owen. Reserve artillery loss: w, 6; m, 2 = 8.
THIRD CORPS, Brig.-Gen. S. P. Heintzelman. *Cavalry*: 3d Pa., Col. William W. Averell. Loss: k, 6; w, 2; m, 3 = 11.
SECOND DIVISION, Brig.-Gen. Joseph Hooker.
*First Brigade*, Brig.-Gen. Cuvier Grover: 1st Mass., Col. Robert Cowdin; 11th Mass., Col. William Blaisdell; 16th Mass., Col. Powell T. Wyman (k), Lieut.-Col. George A. Meacham (w), Maj. Daniel S. Lamson; 2d N. H., Col. Gilman Marston; 26th Pa., Lieut.-Col. George D. Wells. Brigade loss: k, 25; w, 214; m, 116 = 355. *Second Brigade*, Brig.-Gen. Daniel E. Sickles: 70th N. Y., Maj. Thomas Holt; 71st N. Y., Col. George B. Hall; 72d N. Y., Col. Nelson Taylor; 73d N. Y., Capt. Alfred A. Donalds; 74th N. Y., Col. Charles K. Graham. Brigade loss: k, 26; w, 173; m, 109 = 308. *Third Brigade*, Col. Joseph B. Carr: 5th N. J., Maj. John Ramsey; 6th N. J., Col. Gershom Mott; 7th N. J., Col. Joseph W. Revere, Capt. Henry C. Bartlett; 8th N. J., Maj. William A. Henry; 2d N. Y., Lieut.-Col. William A. Olmsted. Brigade loss: k, 4; w, 24; m, 31 = 59. *Artillery*: D, 1st N. Y., Capt. Thomas W. Osborn; 4th N. Y., Lieut. Joseph E. Nairn; H, 1st U. S., Capt. Charles H. Webber. Artillery loss: w, 1; m, 7 = 8.
THIRD DIVISION, Brig.-Gen. Philip Kearny.
*First Brigade*, Brig.-Gen. John C. Robinson: 20th Ind., Col. William L. Brown; 87th N. Y., Lieut.-Col. Richard A. Bachia; 57th Pa., Lieut.-Col. Elhanon W. Woods; 63d Pa., Col. Alexander Hays; 105th Pa., Col. Amor A. McKnight, Lieut.-Col. William W. Corbet, Capt. Calvin A. Craig. Brigade loss: k, 56; w, 310; m, 161 = 527. *Second Brigade*, Brig.-Gen. David B. Birney: 3d Me., Lieut.-Col. C. A. L. Sampson, Maj. Edwin Burt; 4th Me., Col. Elijah Walker; 38th N. Y., Col. J. H. H. Ward; 40th N. Y., Col. Thomas W. Egan; 101st N. Y., Col. Enrico Fardella. Brigade loss: k, 10; w, 53; m, 185 = 248. *Third Brigade*, Brig.-Gen. Hiram G. Berry: 2d Mich., Maj. Louis Dillman, Capt. William Humphrey; 3d Mich., Col. Ambrose A. Stevens; Maj. Byron R. Pierce; 5th Mich., Maj. John D. Fairbanks (m w), Capt. Judson S. Farrer; 1st N. Y., Col. Garrett Dyckman; 37th N. Y., Col. Samuel B. Hayman. Brigade loss: k, 28; w, 225, m, 176 = 429. *Artillery*: E, 1st R. I., Capt. George E. Randolph; G, 2d U. S., Capt. James Thompson. Artillery loss: k, 2; w, 16; m, 5 = 23.
RESERVE ARTILLERY, Capt. Gustavus A. De Russy: 6th N. Y., Capt. Walter M. Bramhall; 2d N. J., Capt. John E. Beam (k), Lieut. John B. Monroe; K, 4th U. S., Lieut. Francis W. Seeley. Loss: k, 1; w, 3; m, 1 = 5.
FOURTH CORPS, Brig.-Gen. Erasmus D. Keyes.
*Cavalry*: 8th Pa., Col. David McM. Gregg.
FIRST DIVISION, Brig.-Gen. Darius N. Couch.
*First Brigade*, Brig.-Gen. Albion P. Howe: 55th N. Y., Lieut.-Col. Louis Thourot; 62d N. Y., Col. David J. Nevin; 93d Pa., Capt. John S. Long; 98th Pa., Col. John

F. Ballier; 102d Pa., Col. Thomas A. Rowley. Brigade loss: k, 27; w, 148; m, 33 = 208. *Second Brigade*, Brig.-Gen. John J. Abercrombie: 65th N. Y. (1st U. S. Chasseurs), Lieut.-Col. Alexander Shaler; 67th N. Y. (1st Long Island), Lieut.-Col. Nelson Cross; 23d Pa., Col. Thomas H. Neill; 31st Pa., Col. David H. Williams; 61st Pa., Lieut.-Col. Frank Vallee. Brigade loss: k, 19; w, 168; m, 16 = 203. *Third Brigade*, Brig.-Gen. Innis N. Palmer: 7th Mass., Col. David A. Russell; 10th Mass., Maj. Ozro Miller (m w), Capt. Frederick Barton; 36th N. Y., Maj. James A. Raney; 2d R. I., Col. Frank Wheaton. Brigade loss: k, 23; w, 194; m, 48 = 265. *Artillery*: C, 1st Pa., Capt. Jeremiah McCarthy; D, 1st Pa., Capt. Edward H. Flood.
SECOND DIVISION, Brig.-Gen. John J. Peck.
*First Brigade*, Brig.-Gen. Henry M. Naglee: 11th Me., Col. Harris M. Plaisted; 56th N. Y., Col. Charles H. Van Wyck; 100th N. Y., Lieut.-Col. Phineas Staunton; 52d Pa., Lieut.-Col. Henry M. Hoyt; 104th Pa., Lieut.-Col. John W. Nields. *Second Brigade*, Brig.-Gen. Henry W. Wessells: 81st N. Y., Col. Edwin Rose; 85th N. Y., Col. Jonathan S. Belknap; 92d N. Y., Lieut.-Col. Hiram Anderson, Jr.; 96th N. Y., Col. James Fairman; 98th N. Y., Lieut.-Col. Charles Durkee; 85th Pa., Col. Joshua B. Howell; 101st Pa., Capt. Charles W. May; 103d Pa., Col. Theodore F. Lehmann. Brigade loss: k, 1; w, 2; m, 121 = 124. *Artillery*: H, 1st N. Y., Lieut. Charles E. Mink; 7th N. Y., Capt. Peter C. Regan.
RESERVE ARTILLERY, Maj. Robert M. West: 8th N. Y., Capt. Butler Fitch; E, 1st Pa., Capt. Theodore Miller; H, 1st Pa., Capt. James Brady; M, 5th U. S., Capt. James McKnight.
FIFTH CORPS, Brig.-Gen. Fitz John Porter. Staff loss: m, 1.
*Cavalry*: 8th Ill., Col. John F. Farnsworth. Loss: k, 3; w, 9; m, 3 = 15.
FIRST DIVISION, Brig.-Gen. George W. Morell.
*First Brigade*, Brig.-Gen. John H. Martindale: 2d Me., Col. Charles W. Roberts; 18th Mass. (detached with Stoneman's command), Col. James Barnes; 22d Mass., Col. Jesse A. Gove (k), Maj. William S. Tilton (w and c), Capt. Walter S. Sampson, Capt. D. K. Wardwell; 1st Mich., Col. Horace S. Roberts; 13th N. Y., Col. Elisha G. Marshall, Maj. Francis A. Schoeffel; 25th N. Y., Maj. Edwin S. Gilbert (c), Captain Shepard Gleason; 2d Co. Mass. Sharp-shooters, Lieut. Charles D. Stiles. Brigade loss: k, 114; w, 443; m, 329 = 886. *Second Brigade*, Brig.-Gen. Charles Griffin: 9th Mass., Col. Thomas Cass (w), Lieut.-Col. Patrick R. Guiney; 4th Mich., Col. Dwight A. Woodbury (k), Lieut.-Col. Jonathan W. Childs (w), Capt. John M. Randolph; 14th N. Y., Col. James McQuade; 62d Pa., Col. Samuel W. Black (k), Lieut.-Col. Jacob B. Sweitzer (w and c), Capt. James C. Hull. Brigade loss: k, 182; w, 772; m, 199 = 1153. *Third Brigade*, Brig.-Gen. Daniel Butterfield: 12th N. Y., Lieut.-Col. Robert M. Richardson, 17th N. Y. (detached with Stoneman's command), Col. Henry S. Lansing; 44th N. Y., Lieut.-Col. James C. Rice; 16th Mich., Col. T. B. W. Stockton (c), Lieut.-Col. John V. Ruehle; 83d Pa., Col. John W. McLane (k), Capt. Hugh S. Campbell (w); Brady's Co. Mich. Sharp-shooters, Capt. Kin S. Dygert. Brigade loss: k, 166; w, 546; m, 269 = 981. *Artillery*, Capt. William B. Weedcn: 3d Mass., Capt. Augustus P. Martin; 5th Mass., Lieut. John B. Hyde; C, 1st R. I., Lieut. Richard Waterman; D, 5th U. S., Lieut. Henry W. Kingsbury. Artillery loss: k, 9; w, 38; m, 9 = 56. *Sharp-shooters*: 1st U. S., Col. Hiram Berdan. Loss: k, 8; w, 35; m, 13 = 56.
SECOND DIVISION, Brig.-Gen. George Sykes.
*First Brigade*, Col. Robert C. Buchanan: 3d U. S., Maj. Nathan B. Rossell (k), Capt. Thomas W. Walker, Capt. John D. Wilkins; 4th U. S., Maj. Delozier Davidson (c), Capt. Joseph B. Collins; 12th U. S., Maj. Henry B. Clitz (w and c), Capt. John G. Read, Capt. Matthew M. Blunt; 14th U. S., Captain John D. O'Connell. Brigade loss: k, 89; w, 297; m, 181 = 567. *Second Brigade*, Lieut.-Col. William Chapman, Maj. Charles S. Lovell: 2d U. S., Capt. Adolphus F. Bond, Lieut. John S. Poland; 6th U. S., Capt. Thomas Hendrickson; 10th U. S., Maj. Charles S. Lovell, Maj. George L. Andrews; 11th U. S., Maj. De

## THE OPPOSING FORCES IN THE SEVEN DAYS' BATTLES. 315

Lancey Floyd-Jones; 17th U. S., Maj. George L. Andrews. Brigade loss: k, 38; w, 228; m, 93 = 359. *Third Brigade*, Col. Gouverneur K. Warren: 5th N. Y., Lieut.-Col. Hiram Duryée; 10th N. Y., Col. John E. Bendix. Brigade loss: k, 47; w, 154; m, 85 = 286. *Artillery*, Capt. Stephen H. Weed: L and M, 3d U. S., Capt. John Edwards; I, 5th U. S., Capt. S. H. Weed. Artillery loss: k, 4; w, 24; m, 4 = 32. THIRD DIVISION, Brig.-Gen. George A. McCall (c), Brig.-Gen. Truman Seymour. Staff loss: k, 1; w, 1; m, 1 = 3. *First Brigade*, Brig.-Gen. John F. Reynolds (c), Col. Seneca G. Simmons (k), Col. R. Biddle Roberts: 1st Pa. Res., Col. R. Biddle Roberts, Maj. Lemuel Todd; 2d Pa. Res., Lieut.-Col. William McCandless; 5th Pa. Res., Col. Seneca G. Simmons, Lieut.-Col. Joseph W. Fisher; 8th Pa. Res., Col. George S. Hays; 13th Pa. Res. (1st Rifles — 6 co's), Maj. Roy Stone. Brigade loss: k, 109; w, 497; m, 403 = 1009. *Second Brigade*, Brig.-Gen. George G. Meade (w), Col. Albert L. Magilton: 3d Pa. Res., Col. Horatio G. Sickel; 4th Pa. Res., Col. Albert L. Magilton; 7th Pa. Res., Col. Elisha B. Harvey; 11th Pa. Res., Col. Thomas F. Gallagher (c), Capt. Daniel S. Porter. Brigade loss: k, 107; w, 284; m, 1009 = 1400. (The wounded of the 11th Reserves at Gaines's Mill are counted among the captured or missing.) *Third Brigade*, Brig.-Gen. Truman Seymour, Col. C. Feger Jackson: 6th Pa. Res. (detached with Casey's command), Col. William Sinclair; 9th Pa. Res., Col. C. Feger Jackson, Capt. John Cuthbertson (w); 10th Pa. Res., Col. James T. Kirk; 12th Pa. Res., Col. John H. Taggart. Brigade loss: k, 78; w, 339; m, 142 = 559. *Artillery*: A, 1st Pa., Capt. Hezekiah Easton (k), Lieut. Jacob L. Detrich, Lieut. John G. Simpson; B, 1st Pa., Capt. James H. Cooper; G, 1st Pa., Capt. Mark Kerns (w), Lieut. Frank P. Amsden; C, 5th U. S., Capt. Henry V. De Hart (m w), Lieut. Eben G. Scott. Artillery loss: k, 21; w, 42; m, 11 = 74. *Cavalry*: 4th Pa., Col. James H. Childs. Cavalry loss: k, 2; w, 13; m, 7 = 22. ARTILLERY RESERVE, Col. Henry J. Hunt. *First Brigade* (Horse Artillery), Lieut.-Col. William Hays: A, 2d U. S., Capt. John C. Tidball; B and L, 2d U. S., Capt. James M. Robertson; M, 2d U. S., Capt. Henry Benson; C and G, 3d U. S. (detached with Casey's command), Capt. Horatio G. Gibson. Brigade loss: w, 6; m, 2 = 8. *Second Brigade*, Lieut.-Col. George W. Getty: E and G, 1st U. S., Lieut. Alanson M. Randol; K, 1st U. S., Lieut. Samuel S. Elder; G, 4th U. S., Lieut. Charles H. Morgan; A, 5th U. S., Lieut. Adelbert Ames; K, 5th U. S., Capt. John R. Smead. Brigade loss: k, 7; w, 29; m, 6 = 42. *Third Brigade*, Maj. Albert Arndt: A, 1st Battalion N. Y., Capt. Otto Diederichs; B, 1st Battalion N. Y., Capt. Adolph Voegelee; C, 1st Battalion N. Y., Capt. John Knieriem; D, 1st Battalion N. Y., Capt. Edward Grimm. Brigade loss: k, 4; w, 11; m, 4 = 19. *Fourth Brigade*, Maj. Edward R. Petherbridge: A. Md., Capt. John W. Wolcott; B, Md., Capt. Alonzo Snow. Brigade loss: k, 2; w, 22; m, 1 = 25. *Fifth Brigade*, Capt. J. Howard Carlisle: 5th N. Y. (dismounted and officers and men attached elsewhere), Capt. Elijah D. Taft; E, 2d U. S., Capt. J. Howard Carlisle; F and K, 3d U. S., Capt. La Rhett L. Livingston. Brigade loss: k, 2; w, 5 = 7. SIEGE TRAIN: 1st Conn. Heavy Artillery, Col. Robert O. Tyler. Loss: k, 2; w, 4; m, 29 = 35.

SIXTH CORPS, Brig.-Gen. William B. Franklin. *Cavalry*: 1st N. Y., Col. Andrew T. McReynolds. FIRST DIVISION, Brig.-Gen. Henry W. Slocum. *First Brigade*, Brig.-Gen. George W. Taylor: 1st N. J., Lieut.-Col. Robert McAllister, Col. A. T. A. Torbert; 2d N. J., Col. Isaac M. Tucker (k), Maj. Henry O. Ryerson (w), Lieut.-Col. Samuel L. Buck; 3d N. J., Col. Henry W. Brown; 4th N. J., Col. James H. Simpson (c). Brigade loss: k, 116; w, 380; m, 582 = 1078. *Second Brigade*, Col. Joseph J. Bartlett: 5th Me., Col. Nathaniel J. Jackson (w), Lieut.-Col. William S. Heath (k), Capt. Clark S. Edwards; 16th N. Y., Col. Joseph Howland (w), Maj. Joel J. Seaver; 27th N. Y., Lieut.-Col. Alexander D. Adams; 96th Pa., Col. Henry L. Cake. Brigade loss: k, 69; w, 400; m, 68 = 546. *Third Brigade*, Brig.-Gen. John Newton: 18th N. Y., Lieut.-Col. George R. Myers, Maj. John C. Meginnis; 31st N. Y., Col. Calvin E. Pratt (w), Maj. Alexander Raszewski; 32d N. Y., Col. Roderick Matheson; 95th Pa., Col. John M. Gosline (m w), Lieut.-Col. Gustavus W. Town. Brigade loss: k, 40; w, 279; m, 114 = 433. *Artillery*, Capt. Edward R. Platt: 1st Mass., Capt. Josiah Porter; 1st N. J., Capt. William Hexamer; D, 2d U. S., Lieut. Emory Upton. Artillery loss: k, 1; w, 13; m, 4 = 18. SECOND DIVISION, Brig.-Gen. William F. Smith. *First Brigade*, Brig.-Gen. Winfield S. Hancock: 6th Me., Col. Hiram Burnham; 43d N. Y., Col. Francis L. Vinton; 49th Pa., Col. William H. Irwin; 5th Wis., Col. Amasa Cobb. Brigade loss: k, 9; w, 93; m, 98 = 200. *Second Brigade*, Brig.-Gen. W. T. H. Brooks (w): 2d Vt., Col. Henry Whiting; 3d Vt., Lieut.-Col. Wheelock G. Veazey; 4th Vt., Col. Edwin H. Stoughton; 5th Vt., Lieut.-Col. Lewis A. Grant; 6th Vt., Col. Nathan Lord, Jr. Brigade loss: k, 45; w, 271; m, 139 = 455. *Third Brigade*, Brig.-Gen. John W. Davidson; 7th Me., Col. Edwin C. Mason; 20th N. Y., Col. Francis Weiss; 33d N. Y., Col. Robert F. Taylor; 49th N. Y., Col. Daniel D. Bidwell; 77th N. Y., Col. James B. McKean. Brigade loss: k, 12; w, 23; m, 87 = 122. *Artillery*, Capt. Romeyn B. Ayres: E, 1st N. Y., Capt. Charles C. Wheeler; 1st N. Y., Capt. Andrew Cowan; 3d N. Y., Capt. Thaddeus P. Mott; F, 5th U. S., Capt. Romeyn B. Ayres. Artillery loss: k, 3; w, 4; m, 15 = 22. *Cavalry*: I and K, 5th Pa., Capt. John O'Farrell. Loss: k, 1. CAVALRY RESERVE, Brig.-Gen. P. St. George Cooke. *First Brigade*: 6th Pa., Col. Richard H. Rush; 5th U. S. (5 co's), Capt. Charles J. Whiting (c), Capt. Joseph H. McArthur. *Second Brigade*, Col. George A. H. Blake: 1st U. S. (4 co's), Lieut.-Col. William N. Grier; 6th U. S. (with Stoneman's command), Capt. August V. Kautz. Cavalry Reserve loss: k, 14; w, 55; m, 85 = 154. [Brig.-Gen's George Stoneman and William H. Emory operated on the right flank of the army with a mixed command of infantry, cavalry, and artillery.] Total loss of the Army of the Potomac: 1734 killed, 8062 wounded, and 6053 captured or missing = 15,849. The "present for duty equipped," or effective force of this army (exclusive of Dix's command at and about Fort Monroe), on June 20th, 1862, was 1511 engineers, 6513 cavalry, 6446 artillery, and 90,975 infantry, in all 105,445. See "Official Records," XI., Pt. III., p. 238.

## THE CONFEDERATE FORCES.

Army of Northern Virginia, General Robert E. Lee.

JACKSON'S COMMAND, Maj.-Gen. T. J. Jackson. *Cavalry*: 2d Va., Col. Thomas T. Munford. WHITING'S DIVISION, Brig.-Gen. William H. C. Whiting. Staff loss: k, 1; w, 1 = 2. *First Brigade*, Brig.-Gen. John B. Hood: 18th Ga., Lieut.-Col. S. Z. Ruff; 1st Tex., Col. A. T. Rainey (w); 4th Tex., Col. John Marshall (k), Capt. W. P. Townsend; 5th Tex., Col. J. B. Robertson; Hampton (S. C.) Legion, Lieut.-Col. M. W. Gary. Brigade loss: k, 92; w, 526; m, 5 = 623. *Third Brigade*, Col. E. McIver Law: 4th Ala., Lieut.-Col. O. K. McLemore (w), Capt. L. H. Scruggs; 2d Miss., Col. J. M. Stone; 11th Miss., Col. P. F. Liddell; 6th N. C., Lieut.-Col. I. E. Avery (w), Maj. R. F. Webb. Brigade loss: k, 66; w, 482; m, 5 = 553. *Artillery*: Va. Battery (Staunton Arty.), Capt. W. L. Balthis (w); N. C. Battery (Rowan Arty.), Capt. James Reilly. Artillery loss: w, 16. JACKSON'S DIVISION. *First Brigade*, Brig.-Gen. Charles S. Winder: 2d Va., Col. J. W. Allen (k), Lieut.-Col. Lawson Botts; 4th Va., Col. Charles A. Ronald; 5th Va., Col. William S. H. Baylor; 27th Va., Col. A. J. Grigsby (w), Capt. G. C. Smith;

33d Va., Col. John F. Neff; Va. Battery (Alleghany Arty.), Lieut. John C. Carpenter; Va. Battery (Rockbridge Arty.), Capt. William T. Poague. Brigade loss: k, 30; w, 149 = 179. *Second Brigade*, Lieut.-Col. R. H. Cunningham, Jr., Brig.-Gen. J. R. Jones (w), Lieut.-Col. R. H. Cunningham, Jr.: 21st Va., Maj. John B. Moseley, Lieut.-Col. R. H. Cunningham, Jr., Maj. John B. Moseley; 42d Va., Lieut.-Col. William Martin; 48th Va., Capt. John M. Vermillion; 1st Va. (Irish) Battalion, Capt. B. W. Leigh; Va. Batty. (Hampden Arty.), Capt. William H. Caskie. Brigade loss: k, 1; w, 15 = 16. *Third Brigade*, Col. S. V. Fulkerson (m w), Col. E. T. H. Warren, Brig.-Gen. Wade Hampton: 10th Va., Col. E. T. H. Warren; 23d Va., Capt. A. V. Scott; 37th Va., Maj. T. V. Williams; Va. Battery (Danville Arty.), Capt. George W. Wooding. Brigade loss: k, 2; w, 15; m, 1 = 18. *Fourth Brigade*, Brig.-Gen. Alexander R. Lawton: 13th Ga., Col. Marcellus Douglass; 26th Ga., Col. E. N. Atkinson; 31st Ga., Col. C. A. Evans (w); 38th Ga., Lieut.-Col. L. J. Parr (w), Capt. William H. Battey; 60th Ga., Lieut.-Col. W. H. Stiles; 61st Ga., Col. John H. Lamar. Brigade loss: k, 115; w, 452 = 567.
EWELL'S DIVISION, Maj.-Gen. Richard S. Ewell. *Fourth Brigade*, Brig.-Gen. Arnold Elzey (w), Col. James A. Walker, Brig.-Gen. Jubal A. Early: 12th Va., Capt. James G. Rodgers; 13th Va., Col. James A. Walker; 25th Va., Lieut.-Col. John C. Higginbotham; 31st Va., Col. John S. Hoffman; 44th Va., Lieut.-Col. Norvell Cobb; 52d Va., Lieut.-Col. J. H. Skinner; 58th Va., Col. F. H. Board. Brigade loss: k, 52; w, 229; m, 3 = 284. *Seventh Brigade*, Brig.-Gen. Isaac R. Trimble: 15th Ala., Col. James Cantey; 21st Ga., Maj. T. W. Hooper (w); 16th Miss., Col. Carnot Posey; 21st N. C., Lieut.-Col. W. W. Kirkland; 1st N. C. Battalion Sharp-shooters, Maj. Rufus W. Wharton; Va. Battery, Capt. A. R. Courtney. Brigade loss: k, 71; w, 280; m, 49 = 400. *Eighth Brigade*, Brig.-Gen. Richard Taylor, Col. I. G. Seymour (k), Col. Leroy A. Stafford: 6th La., Col. I. G. Seymour; 7th La., Lieut.-Col. David B. Penn; 8th La., Col. Henry B. Kelly; 9th La., Col. Leroy A. Stafford; 1st La. Special Battalion, Maj. C. R. Wheat (k); Va. Battery (Charlottesville Arty.), Capt. J. McD. Carrington. Brigade loss: k, 56; w, 236 = 292. *Maryland Line*: 1st Inf., Col. Bradley T. Johnson; A, Cav., Capt. Ridgely Brown; Balto. Battery, Capt. J. B. Brockenbrough. Maryland line loss: k, 3; w, 8 = 11.
HILL'S DIVISION, Maj.-Gen. Daniel H. Hill. *First Brigade*, Brig.-Gen. Robert E. Rodes, Col. John B. Gordon: 3d Ala., Lieut.-Col. Charles Forsyth, Maj. Robert M. Sands; 5th Ala., Col. C. C. Pegues (m w), Maj. E. L. Hobson; 6th Ala., Col. John B. Gordon, Maj. B. G. Baldwin; 12th Ala., Col. B. B. Gayle; 26th Ala., Col. E. A. O'Neal; Va. Battery (King William Arty.), Capt. Thomas H. Carter. Brigade loss: k, 112; w, 458 = 570. *Second Brigade*, Brig.-Gen. George B. Anderson (w), Col. C. C. Tew: 2d N. C., Col. C. C. Tew; 4th N. C., Col. E. A. Osborne; 14th N. C., Lieut.-Col. William A. Johnston; 30th N. C., Col. Francis M. Parker; Ala. Battery, Capt. R. A. Hardaway. Brigade loss: k, 159; w, 704 = 863. *Third Brigade*, Brig.-Gen. Samuel Garland, Jr.: 5th N. C., Col. D. K. McRae; 12th N. C., Col. Benjamin O. Wade; 13th N. C., Col. Alfred M. Scales; 20th N. C., Col. Alfred Iverson (w), Lieut.-Col. Franklin J. Faison (k), Maj. William H. Toon: 23d N. C., Col. Daniel H. Christie (w), Lieut. I. J. Young (w); Ala. Battery (Jeff Davis Arty.), Capt. J. W. Bondurant. Brigade loss: k, 192; w, 637; m, 15 = 844. *Fourth Brigade*, Col. Alfred H. Colquitt: 13th Ala., Col. Birkett D. Fry; 6th Ga., Lieut.-Col. J. M. Newton; 23d Ga., Col. Emory F. Best; 27th Ga., Col. Levi B. Smith; 28th Ga., Col. T. J. Warthen. Brigade loss: k, 75; w, 474; m, 5 = 554. *Fifth Brigade*, Brig.-Gen. Roswell S. Ripley: 44th Ga., Col. Robert A. Smith (m w), Capt. John W. Beck; 48th Ga., Col. William Gibson; 1st N. C., Col. M. S. Stokes (k), Capt. H. A. Brown, Lieut.-Col. William P. Bynum; 3d N. C., Col. Gaston Meares (k), Lieut.-Col. William L. De Rosset. Brigade loss: k, 171; w, 707; m, 30 = 908. *Artillery*: Va. Battery (Hanover Arty.), Capt. G. W. Nelson. (See, also, Jones's Battalion in Reserve Artillery, temporarily attached to this division.)

MAGRUDER'S COMMAND, Maj.-Gen. J. B. Magruder. JONES'S DIVISION, Brig.-Gen. David R. Jones. Staff loss: w, 1. *First Brigade*, Brig.-Gen. Robert Toombs: 2d Ga., Col. Edgar M. Butt (w), Lieut.-Col. William R. Holmes; 15th Ga., Col. William M. McIntosh (m w), Lieut.-Col. William T. Millican, Maj. T. J. Smith, Capt. S. Z. Hearnsberger; 17th Ga., Col. Henry L. Benning; 20th Ga., Col. J. B. Cumming. Brigade loss: k, 44; w, 380; m, 6 = 430. *Third Brigade*, Col. George T. Anderson: 1st Ga. (regulars), Col. William J. Magill; 7th Ga., Lieut.-Col. W. W. White (w), Maj. E. W. Hoyle (w), Capt. George H. Carmical; 8th Ga., Col. L. M. Lamar (w and c), Capt. George O. Dawson; 9th Ga., Col. R. A. Turnipseed; 11th Ga., Lieut.-Col. William Luffman. Brigade loss: k, 64; w, 327; m, 46 = 437. *Artillery*, Maj. John J. Garnett: Va. Battery (Wise Arty.), Capt. James S. Brown; S. C. Battery (Washington Arty.), Capt. James F. Hart; La. Battery (Madison Arty.), Capt. George V. Moody; Va. Battery, Capt. W. J. Dabney. Artillery loss: k, 3; w, 11 = 14.
MCLAWS'S DIVISION, Maj.-Gen. Lafayette McLaws. *First Brigade*, Brig.-Gen. Paul J. Semmes: 10th Ga., Col. Alfred Cumming (w), Capt. W. C. Holt; 53d Ga., Col. L. T. Doyal; 5th La., Col. T. G. Hunt; 10th La., Lieut.-Col. Eugene Waggaman (w and c); 15th Va., Col. T. P. August (w); 32d Va., Lieut.-Col. William R. Willis; N. C. Battery, Capt. Basil C. Manly. Brigade loss: k, 31; w, 121; m, 63 = 215. *Fourth Brigade*, Brig.-Gen. Joseph B. Kershaw: 2d S. C., Col. John D. Kennedy, Maj. F. Gaillard; 3d S. C., Colonel James D. Nance; 7th S. C., Col. D. Wyatt Aiken; 8th S. C., Col. John W. Henagan; Va. Battery (Alexandria Arty.), Capt. Del Kemper. Brigade loss: k, 70; w, 349; m, 38 = 457.
MAGRUDER'S DIVISION. *Second Brigade*, Brig.-Gen. Howell Cobb: 16th Ga., Col. Goode Bryan; 24th Ga., Col. Robert McMillan; Ga. Legion (Cobb's) ——: 2d La., Col. J. T. Norwood (m w); 15th N. C., Col. Henry A. Dowd (w); Ga. Battery (Troup Arty.), Capt. Henry H. Carlton. Brigade loss: k, 66; w, 347; m, 2 = 415. *Third Brigade*, Brig.-Gen. Richard Griffith (m w), Col. William Barksdale: 13th Miss., Col. William Barksdale, Lieut.-Col. J. W. Carter (w), Maj. Kennon McElroy; 17th Miss., Col. W. D. Holder (w), Lieut.-Col. John C. Fiser; 18th Miss., Col. Thomas M. Griffin (w), Lieut.-Col. William H. Luse; 21st Miss., Col. Benjamin G. Humphreys, Lieut.-Col. W. L. Brandon (w), Capt. William C. F. Brooks; Va. Battery (1st Richmond Howitzers), Capt. E. S. McCarthy. Brigade loss: k, 91; w, 434 = 525.
ARTILLERY, Lieut.-Col. Stephen D. Lee: Ga. Battery (Pulaski Arty.), Capt. J. P. W. Read; Va. Battery (James City Arty.), Capt. L. W. Richardson; Va. Battery (Magruder Arty.), Capt. T. Jeff. Page, Jr.
LONGSTREET'S DIVISION, Maj.-Gen. James Longstreet (also in command of A. P. Hill's division), Brig.-Gen. Richard H. Anderson. *First Brigade*, Brig.-Gen. James L. Kemper: 1st Va., Capt. G. F. Norton; 7th Va., Col. W. T. Patton; 11th Va., Capt. K. Otey; 17th Va., Col. M. D. Corse; 24th Va., Lieut.-Col. Peter Hairston; Va. Battery (Loudoun Arty.), Capt. Arthur L. Rogers. Brigade loss: k, 44; w, 205; m, 165 = 414. *Second Brigade*, Brig.-Gen. Richard H. Anderson, Col. Micah Jenkins: 2d S. C. (Rifles), Col. J. V. Moore; 4th S. C. (Battalion), Maj. C. S. Mattison; 5th S. C., Lieut.-Col. A. Jackson; 6th S. C., Col. John Bratton; Palmetto (S. C.) Sharp-shooters, Col. Micah Jenkins, Lieut.-Col. Joseph Walker. Brigade loss: k, 136; w, 638; m, 13 = 787. *Third Brigade*, Brig.-Gen. George E. Pickett (w), Col. John B. Strange, Col. Eppa Hunton, Col. John B. Strange: 8th Va., Col. Eppa Hunton; 18th Va., Col. R. E. Withers (w); 19th Va., Col. John B. Strange; 28th Va., Col. Robert C. Allen; 56th Va., Col. W. D. Stuart. Brigade loss: k, 72; w, 563; m, 19 = 654. *Fourth Brigade*, Brig.-Gen. Cadmus M. Wilcox: 8th Ala., Lieut.-Col. Y. L. Royston (w); 9th Ala., Maj. J. H. J. Williams, Capt. J. H. King (w); 10th Ala., Col. J. J. Woodward (k), Maj. J. H. Caldwell (w); 11th Ala., Lieut.-Col. S. F. Hale (w), Capt. George Field (w); Va. Battery (Thomas Arty.), Captain Edwin J. Anderson. Brigade loss: k, 229; w, 806; m, 20 = 1055. *Fifth Brigade*, Brig.-

# THE OPPOSING FORCES IN THE SEVEN DAYS' BATTLES.

Gen. Roger A. Pryor: 14th Ala., Lieut.-Col. D. W. Baine (k); 2d Fla., Col. E. A. Perry; 14th La., Col. Z. York; 1st La. Battalion, Lieut.-Col. G. Coppens, 3d Va., Lieut.-Col. J. V. Scott (w); La. Battery (Donaldsonville Arty.), Capt. Victor Maurin. Brigade loss: k, 170; w, 681; m, 11 = 862. *Sixth Brigade*, Brig.-Gen. Winfield S. Featherston (w); 12th Miss., Maj. W. H. Lilly (w), Capt. S. B. Thomas; 19th Miss., Maj. John Mullins (w); 2d Miss. Battalion, Lieut.-Col. John G. Taylor (k); Va. Battery (3d Richmond Howitzers), Capt. Benjamin H. Smith, Jr. Brigade loss: k, 115; w, 543; m, 9 = 667. *Artillery:* La. Battalion (Washington Arty.), Col. J. B. Walton; Va. Battery (Lynchburg Arty.), Capt. James Dearing; Va. Bat'y (Dixie Arty.), Capt. W. H. Chapman.

HUGER'S DIVISION, Maj.-Gen. Benjamin Huger.

*Second Brigade*, Brig.-Gen. William Mahone: 6th Va., Col. G. T. Rogers; 12th Va., Col. D. A. Weisiger; 16th Va., Lieut.-Col. Joseph H. Ham; 41st Va., Lieut.-Col. William A. Parham (w); 49th Va., Col. William Smith; Va. Battery (Portsmouth Artillery), Capt. Carey F. Grimes; Va. Battery, Capt. M. N. Moorman. Brigade loss: k, 66; w, 274; m, 124 = 464. *Third Brigade*, Brig.-Gen. Ambrose R. Wright: 44th Ala., Col. James Kent; 3d Ga., Maj. J. R. Sturges (k), Capt. R. B. Nisbet; 4th Ga., Col. George Doles; 22d Ga., Col. R. H. Jones, Maj. Joseph Wasden; 1st La., Lieut.-Col. W. R. Shivers (w), Capt. M. Nolan; Va. Battery, Capt. Frank Huger. Brigade loss: k, 93; w, 483; m, 90 = 666. *Fourth Brigade*, Brig.-Gen. Lewis A. Armistead: 9th Va., Lieut.-Col. James S. Gilliam; 14th Va., Col. James G. Hodges; 38th Va., Col. E. C. Edmonds; 53d Va., Capt. William R. Aylett, Maj. George M. Waddill, Capt. R. W. Martin, Col. H. B. Tomlin; 57th Va., Lieut.-Col. Waddy T. James; 5th Va. Battalion, Capt. William E. Alley; Va. Battery (Fauquier Arty.), Capt. Robert M. Stribling; Va. Battery, Capt. William H. Turner. Brigade loss: k, 51; w, 281; m, 69 = 401.

HILL'S (LIGHT) DIVISION (attached to Longstreet's command June 29th–July 1st), Maj.-Gen. Ambrose P. Hill.

*First Brigade*, Brig.-Gen. Charles W. Field: 40th Va., Col. J. M. Brockenbrough; 47th Va., Col. Robert M. Mayo; 55th Va., Col. Francis Mallory; 60th Va., Col. William E. Starke (w), Lieut.-Col. B. H. Jones, Col. William E. Starke, Maj. J. C. Summers. Brigade loss: k, 78; w, 500; m, 2 = 580. *Second Brigade*, Brig.-Gen. Maxcy Gregg: 1st S. C., Col. D. H. Hamilton; 1st S. C. (Rifles), Col. J. Foster Marshall; 12th S. C., Col. Dixon Barnes (w); 13th S. C., Col. O. E. Edwards; 14th S. C., Col. Samuel McGowan. Brigade loss: k, 152; w, 773; m, 4 = 929. *Third Brigade*, Brig.-Gen. Joseph R. Anderson (w), Col. Edward L. Thomas: 14th Ga., Lieut.-Col. Robert W. Folsom (w); 35th Ga., Col. Edward L. Thomas (w); 45th Ga., Col. Thomas Hardeman (w); 49th Ga., Col. A. J. Lane (w); 3d La. Battalion, Lieut.-Col. Edmund Pendleton. Brigade loss: k, 62; w, 300; m, 2 = 364 (estimated). *Fourth Brigade*, Brig.-Gen. L. O'B. Branch: 7th N. C., Col. Reuben P. Campbell (k), Lieut.-Col. E. Graham Haywood (w), Maj. J. L. Hill; 18th N. C., Col. Robert H. Cowan; 28th N. C., Col. James H. Lane; 33d N. C., Lieut.-Col. Robert F. Hoke; 37th N. C., Col. Charles C. Lee (w), Lieut.-Col. William M. Barbour. Brigade loss: k, 105; w, 706; m, 28 = 839. *Fifth Brigade*, Brig.-Gen. James J. Archer: 5th Ala. Battalion, Capt. A. S. Van de Graaf (w); 19th Ga., Lieut.-Col. Thomas C. Johnson (k); 1st Tenn., Lieut.-Col. J. C. Shackelford (k); 7th Tenn., Col. John F. Goodner (w); 14th Tenn., Col. W. A. Forbes. Brigade loss: k, 92; w, 443 = 535. *Sixth Brigade*, Brig.-Gen. William D. Pender: 2d Ark. Battalion, Maj. W. N. Bronaugh (k); 16th N. C., Lieut.-Col. John S. McElroy; 22d N. C., Col. James Conner (w), Lieut.-Col. R. H. Gray; 34th N. C., Col. Richard H. Riddick (w); 38th N. C., Col. William J. Hoke (w); 22d Va. Battalion, Capt. J. C. Johnson. Brigade loss: k, 130; w, 692 = 822 (approximate). *Artillery*, Lieut.-Col. Lewis M. Coleman: Md. Battery, Capt. R. Snowden Andrews; S. C. Battery (German Arty.), Capt. William K. Bachman; Va. Battery (Fredericksburg Arty.), Capt. Carter M. Braxton; Va. Battery, Capt. William G. Crenshaw; Va. Battery (Letcher Arty.), Capt. Greenlee Davidson; Va. Battery, Capt. Marmaduke Johnson; Masters's Battery, Capt. L. Masters; S. C. Battery (Pee Dee Arty.), Capt. D. G. McIntosh; Va. Battery (Purcell Arty.), Capt. W. J. Pegram. Artillery loss: k, 12; w, 96 = 108.

HOLMES'S DIVISION, Maj.-Gen. Theophilus H. Holmes.

*Second Brigade* (temporarily attached to Huger's division), Brig.-Gen. Robert Ransom, Jr.: 24th N. C., Col. William J. Clarke; 25th N. C., Col. Henry M. Rutledge; 26th N. C., Col. Z. B. Vance; 35th N. C., Col. M. W. Ranson (w), Lieut.-Col. O. C. Petway (k); 48th N. C., Col. Robert C. Hill; 49th N. C., Col. S. D. Ramseur (w). Brigade loss: k, 95; w, 453; m, 76 = 624. *Third Brigade*, Brig.-Gen. Junius Daniel: 43d N. C., Col. T. S. Kenan; 45th N. C., Lieut-Col. J. H. Morehead; 50th N. C., Col. M. D. Craton; Va. Cavalry Battalion, Maj. Edgar Burroughs. Brigade loss: k, 2; w, 22 = 24. *Fourth Brigade*, Brig.-Gen. John G. Walker, Col. Van H. Manning: 3d Ark., Col. Van H. Manning; 2d Ga. Battalion, Maj. George W. Ross; 27th N. C., Col. John R. Cooke; 46th N. C., Col. E. D. Hall; 30th Va., Col. A. T. Harrison; Va. Cavalry Company, Capt. Edward A. Goodwyn. Brigade loss: w, 12. *Artillery*, Col. James Deshler: Va. Battery, Capt. James R. Branch; N. C. Battery, Capt. T. H. Brem; Va. Battery, Capt. David A. French; Va. Battery, Capt. Edward Graham. Artillery loss: w, 17.

WISE'S COMMAND (temporarily attached to Holmes's Division), Brig.-Gen. Henry A. Wise: 26th Va., Col. P. R. Page; 46th Va., Col. R. T. W. Duke; Va. Battery, Capt. W. G. Andrews; Va. Battery, Capt. J. H. Rives.

RESERVE ARTILLERY, Brig.-Gen. William N. Pendleton.

*First Va. Artillery*, Col. J. Thompson Brown: Williamsburg Artillery, Capt. John A. Coke; Richmond Fayette Arty., Lieut.William I. Clopton; Watson's Battery, Capt. David Watson. Loss: w, 1.

JONES'S BATTALION (temporarily attached to D. H. Hill's Division), Maj. Hilary P. Jones: Va. Battery, Capt. P. H. Clark; Va. Battery (Orange Arty.), Lieut. C. W. Fry; S. C. Bat'y, Capt. A. Burnet Rhett. Loss: k, 5; w, 24 = 29.

*First Battalion (Sumter), Artillery*, Lieut.-Col. A. S. Cutts: Ga. Battery, Capt. James Ap Blackshear; Ga. Battery, Capt. John Lane; Ga. Battery, Capt. John V. Price; Ga. Battery, Capt. H. M. Ross; Ga. Battery (Regulars), Capt. S. P. Hamilton. Loss: k, 3; w, 6 = 9. *Second Battalion*, Maj. Charles Richardson: Va. Battery (Fluvanna Arty.), Capt. John J. Ancell; Ga. Battery, Capt. John Milledge, Jr.; Va. Battery (Ashland Arty.), Lieut. James Woolfolk. Loss: k, 1; w, 4 = 5. *Third Battalion*, Maj. William Nelson: Va. Battery (Fluvanna Arty.), Capt. Charles T. Huckstep; Va. Battery (Amherst Arty.), Capt. Thomas J. Kirkpatrick; Va. Battery (Morris Arty.), Capt. R. C. M. Page. Loss: k, 1; w, 1 = 2.

CAVALRY, Brig.-Gen. James E. B. Stuart: 1st N. C., Lieut.-Col. James B. Gordon, Col. Lawrence S. Baker; 1st Va., Col. Fitzhugh Lee; 3d Va., Col. Thomas F. Goode; 4th Va., Capt. F. W. Chamberlayne; 5th Va., Col. Thomas L. Rosser; 9th Va., Col. W. H. F. Lee, 10th Va., Col. J. Lucius Davis; Ga. Legion, Col. Thomas R. R. Cobb; 15th Va. Battalion, Maj. J. Critcher; Hampton (S. C.) Legion (squadron), Capt. Thomas E. Screven; Jeff Davis (Miss.) Legion, Lieut.-Col. W. T. Martin; Stuart Horse Artillery, Capt. John Pelham. Cavalry loss (incomplete): k, 5; w, 26; m, 40 = 71.

Total Confederate loss (approximate): 3286 killed, 15,909 wounded, and 940 captured or missing = 20,135.

The strength of the Confederates is not officially stated, but it probably ranged from 80,000 to 90,000 effectives.

RUSH'S LANCERS — THE 6TH PENNSYLVANIA CAVALRY. FROM A SKETCH MADE IN 1862.

## HANOVER COURT HOUSE AND GAINES'S MILL.

BY FITZ JOHN PORTER, MAJOR-GENERAL, U. S. V.

UNDER the direction of General McClellan certain measures for the protection of the right flank of the army in its advance upon Richmond were put in my hands, beginning simultaneously with the march of the army from the Pamunkey.↲ Among these were the clearing of the enemy from the upper Peninsula as far as Hanover Court House or beyond, and, in case General McDowell's large forces, then at Fredericksburg, were not to join us, the destruction of railroad and other bridges over the South and Pamunkey rivers, in order to prevent the enemy in large force from getting into our rear from that direction, and in order, further, to cut the Virginia Central Railroad, the one great line of the enemy's communications between Richmond and Northern Virginia.

A portion of this duty had been accomplished along the Pamunkey as far as was deemed prudent by Colonel G. K. Warren's forces, posted at Old Church, when on the 26th of May, preparatory to an immediate advance upon Richmond, General McClellan directed me to complete the duty above specified, so that the enemy in Northern Virginia, then occupying the attention of McDowell, Banks, and Frémont, could not be suddenly thrown upon our flank and rear nor otherwise strengthen the enemy in Richmond. I was allowed to adopt my own plans, and to select such additional forces as I deemed necessary.

↲ The army left its camp at White House Landing, on the Pamunkey, May 17th to 20th. The 6th Corps, under Franklin, advanced along the north bank of the Chickahominy, and on the 23d and 24th Davidson's brigade of Smith's division occupied Mechanicsville after a brief encounter with a Confederate column of Magruder's command, under General Paul J. Semmes.— EDITORS.

At 4 A. M. on the 27th General G. W. Morell, commanding the division consisting of J. H. Martindale's, Daniel Butterfield's, and James McQuade's brigades, marched from New Bridge preceded by an advance-guard of two regiments of cavalry and a battery of artillery under command of General W. H. Emory. At the same hour Colonel Warren with his brigade moved from Old Church. Cavalry under General George Stoneman and regular infantry under General George Sykes followed at a later hour, to protect our left flank and rear. The first two commands were to fall upon the enemy, who I had reason to believe were camped in strong force near Hanover Court House. The first command, under my immediate direction, was to take the enemy in front, while Colonel Warren, taking the road along the Pamunkey, was to fall upon him in flank and rear. In a pelting storm of rain, through deep mud and water for about 14 miles, the command struggled and pushed its way to Peake's Station on the Virginia

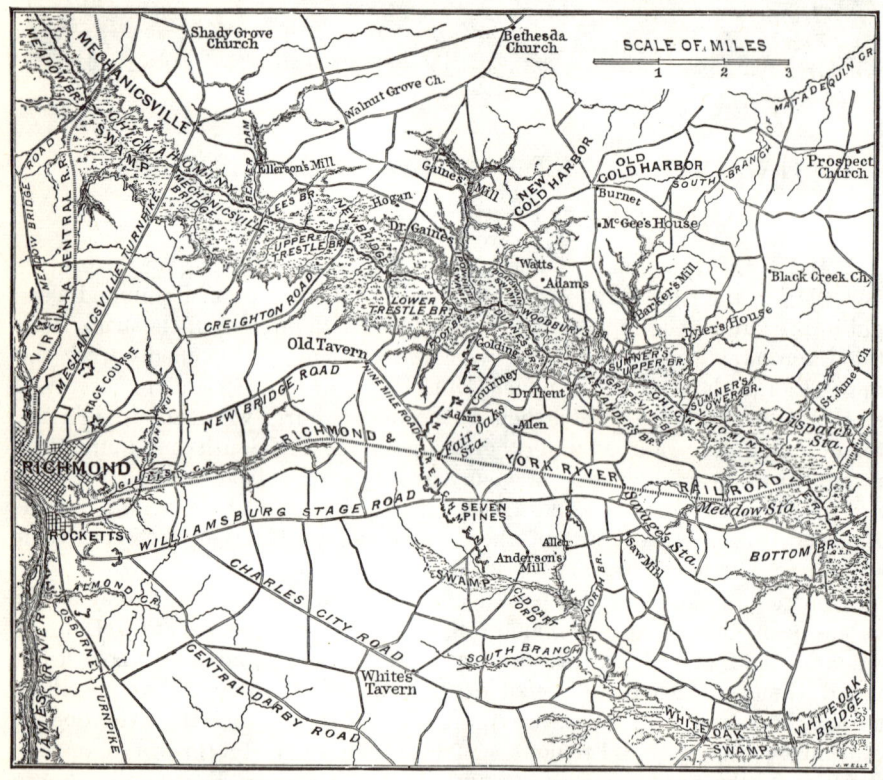

MAP OF THE UPPER CHICKAHOMINY AND NEIGHBORING COUNTRY. [FOR HANOVER COURT HOUSE, SEE MAP, P. 272.]

During the battles of Mechanicsville and Gaines's Mill, the Union army, except Porter's corps and the cavalry engaged in protecting McClellan's right flank and communications, was posted on the south side of the Chickahominy behind the line of intrenchments here shown. The divisions of Longstreet and the two Hills who had confronted McClellan were withdrawn, in order to unite with Jackson's three divisions (coming from the Shenandoah) in the attack in force upon Porter's corps at Gaines's Mill. Magruder's and Huger's divisions were left to engage the attention of Sumner, Keyes, Heintzelman, and Franklin. The attack of Lee's six divisions fell upon Porter's corps, which was reënforced during the battle by Slocum's three brigades of Franklin.

Central Railroad, 2 miles from Hanover Court House, where we came in presence of the enemy.

At once a force of infantry (Colonel C. A. Johnson's 25th New York Volunteers and Berdan's Sharp-shooters), protected by artillery, was sent forward to hold the enemy in check, pending the arrival of Morell, who was slowly pushing along the swampy roads. Cavalry and artillery were sent to the left along the Ashland road, to guard

PROFESSOR T. S. C. LOWE OBSERVING THE BATTLE OF SEVEN PINES FROM HIS BALLOON "INTREPID," ON THE NORTH SIDE OF THE CHICKAHOMINY.

our flank and destroy the railroad and telegraph at the crossing. On Martindale's arrival he was sent in support of this force, and with it soon became engaged with very persistent opponents. Butterfield was sent to the front, where, deploying in line, he moved rapidly upon the enemy, put them to flight, and captured many prisoners and one cannon and caisson.

REPLENISHING THE GAS OF PROFESSOR LOWE'S MILITARY BALLOON "INTREPID." FROM PHOTOGRAPHS. ☆

As the enemy gave way, the troops were pushed on toward Hanover Court House in pursuit of the fleeing foe and to strike their camp, which I had been informed was near by, but which was found abandoned. Suddenly the signal officers notified me of a large force attacking our flank and rear, and especially the troops under Martindale. At once the infantry were faced about, and at double-quick step hastened to the aid of their imperiled comrades. McQuade's brigade, on arriving opposite the contending forces, moved in line to the attack. Butterfield, now in rear as faced

☆ Colonel Auchmuty, of New York City, who made many ascensions by this balloon from the camp near Doctor Gaines's before the battle, says that the Confederates had a Whitworth gun at Mrs. Price's, on the south side of the Chickahominy, with which they would fire at the balloon. The usual height of observation was 1000 feet; and when lower than 300 feet high the balloon was within range of this gun. General Porter made no fewer than a hundred such ascensions.— EDITORS.

CONFEDERATE RETREAT THROUGH MECHANICSVILLE BEFORE THE ADVANCE OF McCLELLAN'S ARTILLERY, MAY 24TH. FROM A WAR-TIME SKETCH.

The view is from the east, and the retreat is in the direction of the Mechanicsville Bridge.

about, pushed his brigade through the woods and fell with vigor upon the enemy's flank. The united attack quickly routed the enemy, inflicting heavy losses in killed and wounded and prisoners.‡

Warren, greatly delayed by muddy roads, swollen streams, and the work of building bridges, arrived about 3 P. M., at the close of the first battle, and was sent northward in pursuit of the enemy, and to destroy bridges and boats on the Pamunkey. He, with Rush of the 6th Pennsylvania Cavalry, captured a company of North Carolina infantry just before reaching the wagon road bridge, which they destroyed. Night put an end to the contest.

The succeeding day was occupied in gathering in the results of our victory and in pushing the troops to Ashland, destroying two of the enemy's railroad trains, abandoned camps, and railroad and other bridges over the Pamunkey and South Anna, and injuring the railroad tracks — it having been decided at Washington that McDowell was not to join us, and that a large portion of his command had been ordered to Northern Virginia in pursuit of Jackson, then on a raid into the Shenandoah Valley. Our movement had caused the rapid retreat to Richmond of General Joseph R. Anderson's command, thereby releasing McDowell's command for active operations in Northern Virginia, as well as opening the way for him to join us. The destruction of the railroad bridges was accomplished by Major Lawrence Williams, 6th U. S. Cavalry, who, while on the South Anna, fell in with some of McDowell's scouts, who were hourly looking for the advance of their corps.

McClellan joined me on the battle-field, and was well pleased with the results of our labors. Besides the destruction of the bridges, trains, etc., we were in possession of a large number of arms and one cannon, of some 730 prisoners,

‡ The affair at Hanover Court House was with the brigade of General L. O'B. Branch, who says in his report that he contended against odds in the hope that Confederate troops would come to his assistance. His loss was 73 killed and 192 wounded.— EDITORS.

and had buried some 200 killed. By General McClellan's directions we returned to our camp on the 29th of May.

This was the first occasion that the corps had had to show its good qualities, all being in action at once. The behavior of the officers and men showed the benefit of the good training before Washington, during the fall and winter of 1861, given by their brigade and regimental commanders. The regiments, without exception, behaved most gallantly.

On our return to camp all rejoiced at the success of our mission in securing for a reasonable time our flank from injury and preparing the whole army for a rapid advance on Richmond, and also by rendering McDowell's presence unnecessary for the defense of Washington, giving the War Department the opportunity of sending his corps by water to join us. If that had been done, none of the enemy could have been detached from Richmond to threaten Washington, and his forces in Northern Virginia would have been called to defend Richmond. But a mightier power interfered, and through years of trial and sufferings delayed the happy victory we then hoped was in our hands.‡

After the battle of Fair Oaks, during the greater part of the month of June, 1862, the Army of the Potomac, under General McClellan, and the Army of Northern Virginia, under General Lee, confronted each other, east of Richmond. The two armies were of nearly equal strength. [See foot-note, p. 187.] McClellan's forces, divided by the Chickahominy, were extended south of that

‡ The Union loss at Hanover Court House was 62 killed; 223 wounded; 70 missing = 355. — EDITORS.

UNION ARTILLERY AT MECHANICSVILLE SHELLING THE CONFEDERATE WORKS SOUTH OF THE CHICKAHOMINY.

This sketch was made several days before the beginning of the Seven Days' Battles. The road to Richmond crosses the stream by the Mechanicsville Bridge, the half-dozen houses composing the town being to the left of the ground occupied by the battery. It was by this road that the troops of D. H. Hill's and Longstreet's division crossed to join Jackson and A. P. Hill in the attack upon the right of McClellan's army.

stream, from New Bridge to White Oak Swamp, leaving north of the river only the Fifth Army Corps. The Confederate troops faced the Federal army throughout its length, from White Oak Swamp to New Bridge, and thence up the right bank of the Chickahominy, covering the important crossings at Mechanicsville and Meadow Bridge, north of the city.

South of the Chickahominy each army was secured against surprise in flank or successful attack in front by that swollen stream; by marshy lands and muddy roads; by redoubts studded with artillery and rifle-pits well manned, all flanked or covered by swamps, tangled thickets, and slashed timber. Notwithstanding the apparent quiet, both armies were actively engaged in the erection of those defensive works which permit large forces to be detached, at opportune moments, for aggressive action, or for the defense of menaced positions. These preparations for offensive and defensive action, known to both commanders, plainly impressed on each the necessity of guarding against any errors in position, and the importance of preparing promptly to take advantage of any opening in his opponent's line which promised results commensurate with the risks involved.

It was apparent to both generals that Richmond could only be taken in one of two ways: by regular approaches, or by assault. An assault would require superior forces, supported by ample reserves. It was equally apparent that an attack could readily be made from Richmond, because that city's well armed and manned intrenchments would permit its defense by a small number of men, while large forces could be concentrated and detached for offensive operations.

The faulty location of the Union army, divided as it was by the Chickahominy, was from the first realized by General McClellan, and became daily an increasing cause of care and anxiety to him; not the least disturbing element of which was the impossibility of quickly reënforcing his right wing or promptly drawing it to the south bank. That this dilemma was known to so intelligent and vigilant a commander as General Lee could not be doubted; and that it was certainly demonstrated to him by General J. E. B. Stuart's dashing cavalry raid around the Union army, on June 14th, was shown in many ways. [See page 271.] One evidence of it was his immediate erection of field-works on his left, and his increasing resistance to the efforts of Union scouts to penetrate into the roads leading to Richmond from the north. This indicated that Lee was preparing to guard against the reënforcement of McClellan's right, and also against information reaching us of Confederate reënforcements from the north.

McClellan had been forced into this faulty position on the Chickahominy and held there by the oft-repeated assurances that McDowell's corps of 40,000 men, then at Fredericksburg, would be advanced to Richmond and formed on his immediate right, which would make that wing safe. ▶ On the 27th of May, under promise that McDowell would join him at once, McClellan cleared his front of all opposition to his rapid march, by operations at Hanover Court

---

▶ See Stanton's letter of May 18th: "You are instructed to coöperate so as to establish this communication as soon as possible, by extending your right wing to the north of Richmond."—F. J. P.

House. If McDowell had joined McClellan then, it would have resulted in the capture of Richmond. That junction could also easily have been brought about immediately after the battle of Fair Oaks, and even then Richmond could have been taken. But the Confederate authorities so skillfully used Jackson, in the Valley of Virginia, as to draw off McDowell; while the fears of the Administration, then aroused for the safety of Washington, together with a changed policy, caused him to be held back from the Army of the Potomac; and, although orders were several times issued requiring McDowell to unite with McClellan, and assurances were given as late as June 26th that he would so unite, yet he never arrived, and the right wing of McClellan's army, then left exposed, became the object of attack. McClellan saw the coming storm, and guarded against it as best he could. Realizing the faultiness of his position, resulting from McDowell's withdrawal to the north, he desired to correct the error by changing his base from York River to the James, where he could be easily reënforced, and from which point his communications would be safe. This change could not be made so long as McDowell's advance was to be expected, nor in any event could it be effected without great risk to the safety of his own army in the face of a vigilant and active foe, and without seriously jeopardizing the success of the cause to which he was devoting all his energies. He, however, secured by careful examination full information of the roads and the character of the country over which he would be obliged to move, if circumstances or policy should require a change of base, and as early as June 18th sent vessels loaded with supplies to the James River.

In the middle of June General McClellan intrusted to me the management of affairs on the north bank of the Chickahominy, and confided to me his plans as well as his hopes and apprehensions. His plans embraced defensive arrangements against an attack from Richmond upon our weak right flank. We did not fear the results of such an attack if made by the forces from Richmond alone; but if, in addition, we were to be attacked by Jackson's forces, suspicions of whose approach were already aroused, we felt that we should be in peril. But as Jackson had thus far prevented McDowell from joining us, we trusted that McDowell, Banks, and Frémont, who had been directed to watch Jackson, would be able to prevent him from joining Lee, or, at least, would give timely warning of his escape from their front and follow close upon his heels.

With McClellan's approval, my command was distributed as follows:

General Geo. G. Meade's brigade of General Geo. A. McCall's division of Pennsylvania Reserves was posted at Gaines's house, protecting a siege-battery controlling New Bridge; Generals John F. Reynolds's and Truman Seymour's brigades held the rifle-pits skirting the east bank of Beaver Dam Creek and the field-works covering the only crossings near Mechanicsville and Ellerson's Mill. These field-works, well armed with artillery, and the rifle-pits, well manned, controlled the roads and open fields on the west bank of that creek, and were concealed by timber and brush from an approaching foe. The infantry outposts from the same division, and their supports, west of Mechanicsville to Meadow Bridge, were instructed, if attacked or threatened by superior forces, to fall back by side approaches to the rear of Reynolds, at the upper crossing, thus leaving the main approaches open to the fire of their artillery and infantry defenders.

North from Meadow Bridge to the Pamunkey Federal cavalry pickets kept vigilant watch, and protected detachments who were felling timber in order to obstruct the roads against the rapid march of any force upon the flank or rear of the right wing.

Cooke's cavalry, near Cold Harbor, guarded the right rear and scouted toward Hanover Court House, while Morell's and Sykes's divisions were conveniently camped so as to cover the bridge-crossings and to move quickly to any threatened point.

Such was the situation on the 24th of June, when, at midnight, General McClellan telegraphed me that a pretended deserter, whom I had that day sent him, had informed him that Jackson was in the immediate vicinity, ready to unite with Lee in an attack upon my command. Though we had reason to suspect Jackson's approach, this was the first intimation we had of his arrival; and we could obtain from Washington at that time no further confirmation of our suspicions, nor any information of the fact that he had left the front of those directed to watch him in Northern Virginia.

Reynolds, who had special charge of the defenses of Beaver Dam Creek and of the forces at and above Mechanicsville, was at once informed of the situation. He prepared to give our anticipated visitors a warm welcome. The infantry division and cavalry commanders were directed to break camp at the first sound of battle, pack their wagons and send them to the rear, and, with their brigades, to take specified positions in support of troops already posted, or to protect the right flank.

On the 25th the pickets of the left of the main army south of the Chickahominy were pushed forward under strong opposition, and, after sharp fighting, gained considerable ground, so as to enable the Second and Third Corps (Sumner's and Heintzelman's) to support the attack on Old Tavern which it was intended to make next day with the Sixth Corps (Franklin's). The result of the fighting was to convince the corps commanders engaged that there had been no reduction of forces in their front to take part in any movement upon our right flank.

Early on the 26th I was informed of a large increase of forces opposite Reynolds, and before noon the Confederates gave evidence of their intention to cross the river at Meadow Bridge and Mechanicsville, while from our cavalry scouts along the Virginia Central Railroad came reports of the approach from the north of large masses of troops.

Thus the attitude of the two armies toward each other was changed. Yesterday, McClellan was rejoicing over the success of his advance toward Richmond, and he was confident of reënforcement by McDowell. To-day, all the united available forces in Virginia were to be thrown against his right flank, which was not in a convenient position to be supported. The prizes now to be contended for were: on the part of McClellan, the safety of his right wing,

THE UNION DEFENSES AT ELLERSON'S MILL. FROM A SKETCH MADE AT THE TIME.

protection behind his intrenchments with the possibility of being able to remain there, and the gain of sufficient time to enable him to effect a change of base to the James; on the part of Lee, the destruction of McClellan's right wing, and, by drawing him from his intrenchments and attacking him in front, the raising of the siege of Richmond.

The morning of Thursday, June 26th, dawned clear and bright, giving promise that the day would be a brilliant one. The formation of the ground south of the Chickahominy opposite Mechanicsville, and west to Meadow Bridge, largely concealed from view the forces gathered to execute an evidently well-planned and well-prepared attack upon my command. For some hours, on our side of the river, all was quiet, except at Mechanicsville and at the two bridge-crossings. At these points our small outposts were conspicuously displayed for the purpose of creating an impression of numbers and of an intention to maintain an obstinate resistance. We aimed to invite a heavy attack, and then, by rapid withdrawal, to incite such confidence in the enemy as to induce incautious pursuit.

In the northern and western horizon vast clouds of dust arose, indicating the movements of Jackson's advancing forces. They were far distant, and we had reason to believe that the obstacles to their rapid advance, placed in their way by detachments sent for that purpose, would prevent them from making an attack that day. As before stated, we did not fear Lee alone; we did fear his attack, combined with one by Jackson on our flank; but our fears were allayed for a day.

General McClellan's desire to make the earliest and quickest movements at that time possible, and his plans for the accomplishment of that desire, as expressed to me, were substantially conveyed in the following dispatch of June 23d from his chief-of-staff:

> "Your dispositions of your troops are approved by the commanding general. . . . If you are attacked, be careful to state as promptly as possible the number, composition, and position of the enemy. The troops on this side will be held ready either to support you directly or to attack the enemy in their front. If the force attacking you is large, the general would prefer the latter course, counting upon your skill and the admirable troops under your command to hold their own against superior numbers long enough for him to make the decisive movement which will determine the fate of Richmond."

The position selected on Beaver Dam Creek for our line of defense was naturally very strong. The banks of the valley were steep, and forces advancing on the adjacent plains presented their flanks, as well as their front, to the fire of both infantry and artillery, safely posted behind intrenchments. The stream was over waist-deep and bordered by swamps. Its passage was difficult for infantry at all points, and impracticable for artillery, except at the bridge-crossing at Ellerson's Mill, and at the one above, near Mechanicsville.

Quite early in the day I visited General Reynolds, near the head of the creek, and had the best reasons not only to be contented, but thoroughly gratified, with the admirable arrangements of this accomplished officer, and to be encouraged by the cheerful confidence of himself and his able and gallant assistants, Seymour on his left, at Ellerson's Mill, and Colonel Seneca G. Simmons and Major Roy Stone in his front. Each of these officers commanded a portion of the Pennsylvania Reserves — all under the command of the brave and able veteran, McCall. These troops were about to engage in their first battle, and bore themselves then, as they did on trying occasions immediately following, with the cheerful spirit of the volunteer and the firmness of the

PLAN OF THE BATTLE OF BEAVER DAM CREEK, JUNE 26.

*a, a, a*, Approach of D. H. Hill and Longstreet from Richmond; *b, b, b*, Approach of A. P. Hill; *c, c, c*, Route of D. H. Hill to Old Cold Harbor, the day after the battle, to join Jackson's attack on Union right; *d, d, d*, Route of A. P. Hill to New Cold Harbor, to attack Union center; *e, e, e*, Route of Longstreet to Dr. Gaines's, to attack Union left. Of the five Confederate brigades engaged in this battle, one (Ripley's) was attached to the division of D. H. Hill and came up as a reënforcement to Pender, who, with Field, Archer, and Anderson, were part of the division of A. P. Hill, his other two divisions, Gregg and Branch, being held in reserve. The losses in their hopeless attack fell chiefly upon Archer, who made the first advance about 5 P. M., and later upon Pender and Ripley. Pegram's battery was badly cut up, losing forty-seven men and many horses. On the Union side, Martindale, Griffin, and Meade came up after the battle had begun, reënforcing Reynolds and Seymour. When firing ceased, about 9 P. M., Porter's troops held their position; but Jackson's approach on their right flank compelled its evacuation early in the morning.— EDITORS.

veteran soldier — examples inspiring emulation in these trying "seven days' battles."

Part of the general details previously adopted was then ordered to be followed, and subsequently was enforced as near as practicable in all the battles in which my corps engaged: that under no circumstances should the men expose themselves by leaving their intrenchments, or other cover, merely to pursue a repulsed foe; nor, except in uneven ground which would permit the fire of artillery to pass well over their heads, was infantry or cavalry to be posted in front of a battery, or moved so as to interfere with its fire. Bullet, shot, and shell were to be relied upon for both repulse and pursuit.

Sitting for hours near the telegraph operator at my quarters, prior to the attack, I listened to the constant and rapid "ticking" of his instrument, and was kept informed, by the various intercommunicating messages at the head-quarters of the army, of the condition of affairs in front of the three corps farthest to the left. Reports often came from them that the enemy's camps seemed to be largely deserted, confirming the information that the enemy had gathered in front of Franklin and myself. Yet, the following day, when I called for aid to resist the forces of Lee and Jackson at Gaines's Mill, known to be immensely superior to mine, the commanders of these three corps expressed the belief that they were about to be attacked by bodies larger than their own, and objected to detaching any part of their troops. [See foot-note, p. 180.]

From the cavalry scouts of Colonel John F. Farnsworth, Stoneman, and General P. St. George Cooke, whose forces stretched, in the order named, from Meadow Bridge north to the Pamunkey, reports came that Jackson was advancing slowly upon my flank.‡ I was also informed that the departure of Jackson from Northern Virginia was suspected, but not positively known, at Washington; but that at this critical moment no assistance whatever could be expected from that vicinity.

Perhaps at this time the Administration had been crippled by its own acts, and could not respond to General McClellan's calls for aid. About April 1st, when our army began active operations in the field and recruiting should have been encouraged, the enrollment of troops was ordered to be stopped. The War Governor of Pennsylvania [Andrew G. Curtin] notably disregarded this order. His foresight was afterward recognized at Antietam, where he was able to render valuable assistance. In the month of June, however, the policy had begun to change, and the troops in Northern Virginia were being placed in charge of an officer [General John Pope] called to Washington "to take command of Banks and Frémont, perhaps McDowell, take the field against Jackson, and eventually supersede McClellan." At the day the order

---

‡ The outposts at Meadow Bridge, the extreme western front of Porter's line, were attacked by Confederates advancing from Richmond under A. P. Hill, about noon on the 26th, and during the afternoon the columns under Jackson encountered the cavalry pickets on the Hanover Court House road, six miles north of Mechanicsville, and at Hundley's Corner, at the crossing of Totopotomoy Creek. The cavalry under General Cooke and Colonel Farnsworth moved with the main army, and the force under Stoneman, consisting of cavalry and infantry, retired down the Pamunkey to White House Landing, and joined the force there under General Casey.— EDITORS.

of assignment was issued, June 27th, however, there was no enemy confronting that officer — Jackson having disappeared from Northern Virginia, and being in my front at Gaines's Mill.

About 2 o'clock P. M., on the 26th, the boom of a single cannon in the direction of Mechanicsville resounded through our camps. This was the signal which had been agreed upon, to announce the fact that the enemy were crossing the Chickahominy. The curtain rose; the stage was prepared for the first scene of the tragedy. At once tents were struck, wagons packed and sent to the rear to cross to the right bank of the Chickahominy. The several divisions were promptly formed, and took the positions to which they had previously been assigned. General McCall assumed command at Beaver Dam Creek; Meade joined him, taking position behind Seymour; Martindale and General Charles Griffin, of Morell's division, went, respectively, to the right and rear of Reynolds; Butterfield was directed to support General Cooke's, and subsequently Martindale's right, while Sykes was held ready to move wherever needed. Reynolds and Seymour prepared for action and concealed their men.

About 3 o'clock the enemy, under Longstreet, D. H. and A. P. Hill, in large bodies commenced rapidly to cross the Chickahominy almost simultaneously at Mechanicsville, Meadow Bridge, and above, and pushed down the left bank, along the roads leading to Beaver Dam Creek. In accordance with directions previously given, the outposts watching the access to the crossings fell back after slight resistance to their already designated position on the east bank of Beaver Dam Creek, destroying the bridges as they retired.

After passing Mechanicsville the attacking forces were divided, a portion taking the road to the right to Ellerson's Mill, while the larger body directed their march to the left into the valley of Beaver Dam Creek, upon the road covered by Reynolds. Apparently unaware, or regardless, of the great danger in their front, this force moved on with animation and confidence, as if going to parade, or engaging in a sham battle. Suddenly, when half-way down the bank of the valley, our men opened upon it rapid volleys of artillery and infantry, which strewed the road and hill-side with hundreds of dead and wounded, and drove the main body of the survivors back in rapid flight to and beyond Mechanicsville. So rapid was the fire upon the enemy's huddled masses clambering back up the hill, that some of Reynolds's ammunition was exhausted, and two regiments were relieved by the 4th Michigan and 14th New York of Griffin's brigade. On the extreme right a small force of the enemy secured a foothold on the east bank, but it did no harm, and retired under cover of darkness.

The forces which were directed against Seymour at Ellerson's Mill made little progress. Seymour's direct and Reynolds's flank fire soon arrested them and drove them to shelter, suffering even more disastrously than those who had attacked Reynolds. Late in the afternoon, greatly strengthened, they renewed the attack with spirit and energy, some reaching the borders of the stream, but only to be repulsed with terrible slaughter, which warned them not to attempt a renewal of the fight. Little depressions in the ground shielded many from our fire, until, when night came on, they all fell back beyond the range of our guns. Night put an end to the contest.

The Confederates suffered severely. All night the moans of the dying and the shrieks of the wounded reached our ears. Our loss was only about 250 of the 5000 engaged, while that of the Confederates was nearly 2000 out of some 10,000 attacking.↓

General McClellan had joined me on the battle-field at an early hour in the afternoon. While we discussed plans for the immediate future, influenced in our deliberations by the gratifying results of the day, numerous and unvarying accounts from our outposts and scouts toward the Pamunkey warned us of the danger impending on the arrival of Jackson, and necessitated a decision as to which side of the Chickahominy should be held in force. He left me late at night, about 1 A. M. (June 27th), with the expectation of receiving information on his arrival at his own headquarters from the tenor of which he would be enabled to decide whether I should hold my present position or withdraw to a well-selected and more advantageous one east of Gaines's Mill, where I could protect the bridges across the Chickahominy, over which I must retire if compelled to leave the left bank. He left General Barnard, of the Engineers, with me, to point out the new line of battle in case he should decide to withdraw me from Beaver Dam Creek. The orders to withdraw reached me about 3 o'clock A. M., and were executed as rapidly as possible.

The position selected for the new stand was east of Powhite Creek, about six miles from Beaver Dam Creek. The line of battle was semicircular, the extremities being in the valley of the Chickahominy, while the intermediate portion occupied the high grounds along the bank of a creek and curved around past McGehee's to Elder Swamp. Part of the front was covered by the ravine of the creek. The east bank was lined with trees and underbrush, which afforded concealment and protection to our troops and artillery.

From the point where the line of the creek turns suddenly to the east, the front was a series of boggy swamps covered extensively with tangled brush. Near McGehee's and beyond, the ground, elevated and drier, was filled with ravines swept by our artillery and infantry, who were covered by depressions in the ground. The high land embraced within the semicircle was cleared ground, but undulating, and often, with the aid of fences and ditches, giving concealment and cover, breast-high, to both infantry and artillery.

Before sunrise of the 27th the troops were withdrawn from Beaver Dam Creek and sent to their new position east of Powhite Creek, destroying the bridges across it after them.

Some batteries and infantry skirmishers, left as a ruse at Beaver Dam Creek, by their fire so fully absorbed the attention of the foe that our purpose

↓ Union forces engaged, 11 regiments, 6 batteries. Confederate forces engaged, 21 regiments, 8 batteries.— F. J. P.

According to the official returns the total Union loss at Mechanicsville was 361, but little more than that of the 44th Georgia alone (335). The Confederate loss, exclusive of Field's and Anderson's brigades and of the batteries, is reported at 1589. General Longstreet is quoted by William Swinton as authority for putting the aggregate at "between three and four thousand." ("Campaigns of the Army of the Potomac," p. 145.)— EDITORS.

THE BATTLE OF GAINES'S MILL. FROM A PHOTOGRAPH OF THE PAINTING BY THE PRINCE DE JOINVILLE, 1862, MADE FROM PERSONAL OBSERVATION. Persons represented: 1. Gen. F. J. Porter; 2. Gen. G. W. Morell; 3. Gen. George G. Meade (on horseback in the distance), and the following aides-de-camp: 4, Comte de Paris; 5. Colonel Radowitz; 6. Major Hammerstein; 7. Duc de Chartres; 8. Captain Mason.

The view is from the left of the Federal position, looking in a north-westerly direction up the Chickahominy, shown at the left. The out-buildings (on the right) belonged to the Watts house, which, during the thick of the fight, was the headquarters of General Fitz John Porter. The wooded ravine in the middle of the picture was the point of contact of this part of the opposing lines. The horsemen in the swampy bottom-lands are intended to represent Cooke's Union cavalry. General Longstreet's extreme right did not extend out of the woods; his left reached to a point about two-thirds across the picture, where it joined A. P. Hill's and, later, Whiting's division.

suddenly and rapidly to abandon the intrenchments seemed unsuspected. But when they discovered our withdrawal, their infantry pressed forward in small detachments, the main body and the artillery being delayed to rebuild the bridges. Seymour's brigade, the last to start, under its skillful commander, with Captain John C. Tidball's and Captain James M. Robertson's well-managed horse batteries on its flanks. kept the enemy at a respectful distance and enabled all, horse, foot, and artillery, wagons and wounded, to reach, with little loss, their designated posts in the new position; my brave and efficient aide, Lieutenant S. M. Weld, however, was taken prisoner.

The siege guns were safely removed by hand from the works overlooking New Bridge and taken to the south bank of the Chickahominy, where, protected by Franklin's corps, they were posted and used with damaging effect upon the enemy as they advanced that afternoon to attack the left of our line.

Our new line of battle was well selected and strong, though long and requiring either more troops to man it than I had, or too great a thinning of my line by the use of the reserves. The east bank of the creek, from the valley of the Chickahominy to its swampy sources, was elevated, sloping, and timbered. The bed of the stream was nearly dry, and its west bank gave excellent protection to the first line of infantry posted under it to receive the enemy descending the cleared field sloping to it. The swampy grounds along the sources of the creek were open to our view in front for hundreds of yards, and were swept by the fire of infantry and artillery. The roads from Gaines's Mill and Old Cold Harbor, along which the enemy were compelled to advance, were swept by artillery posted on commanding ground.

Along the ground thus formed and close to its border were posted the divisions of Morell and Sykes,— the latter on the right; Captain A. P. Martin's Massachusetts battery between,— each brigade having in reserve, immediately in its rear, two of its regiments. Sections or full batteries of the division artillery were posted to sweep the avenues of approach, and the fields on which these avenues opened. Wherever possible and useful, guns were placed between brigades and on higher ground, in front or rear, as judgment dictated. The unemployed guns were in reserve with their divisions. Batteries of Hunt's Artillery Reserve were in rear of the left, covered by timber from view of the enemy, but ready to move at a moment's call, or from their stand to pour their irresistible fire into the enemy's face in case they broke our line.

MAJOR-GENERAL FITZ JOHN PORTER.
FROM A PHOTOGRAPH.

McCall's division formed a second line, near the artillery in reserve, in rear of Morell, and immediately behind the woods on the left. Reynolds, the first to leave Beaver Dam Creek, had gone to Barker's Mill to cover the approaches from Cold Harbor and Dispatch Station to Grapevine Bridge; but, hearing the battle raging on our left, and having no enemy in his front, while Emory, of Cooke's cavalry, with artillery, was near at hand to do the duty assigned to him, he hastened to join McCall, arriving opportunely in rear of Griffin's left.

General Cooke was instructed to take position, with cavalry, under the hills in the valley of the Chickahominy — there, with the aid of artillery, to guard our left flank. He was especially enjoined to intercept, gather, and hold all stragglers, and under no circumstances to leave the valley for the purpose of

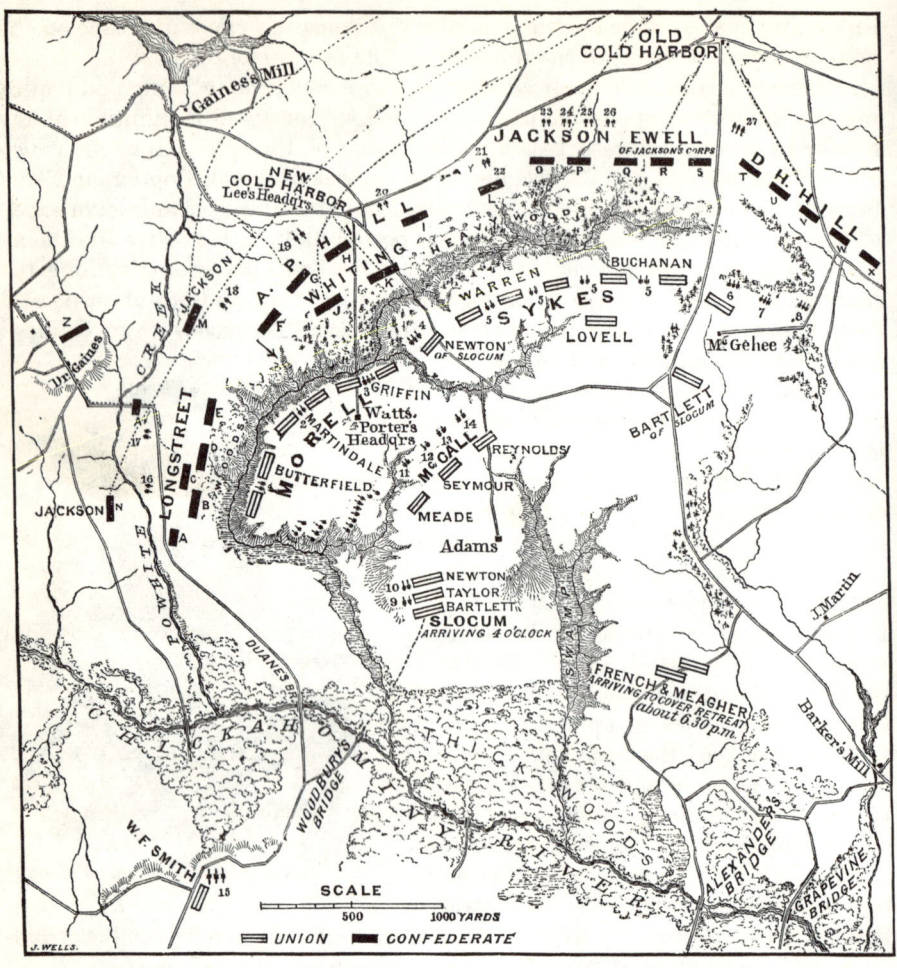

MAP OF THE BATTLE-FIELD OF GAINES'S MILL, SHOWING APPROXIMATELY THE POSITIONS OF INFANTRY AND ARTILLERY ENGAGED. (THE TOPOGRAPHY FROM THE OFFICIAL MAP.)

Confederate brigades: A, A, Anderson (R. H.); B, Wilcox; C, Featherston; D, Pryor; E, Pickett; Z, Kemper; F, G, H, J, L, Y, line of A. P. Hill's six brigades at the opening of the battle, as follows: Archer, Field, Anderson (J. R.), Branch, Gregg, Pender; I, K, Hood and Law (Whiting's division of Jackson's corps), replacing Archer, Field, Anderson; M, N, O, P, Jackson's old division, as follows: Fulkerson (3d Va.), Cunningham (2d Va.), Lawton, and Winder; Q, R, S, Seymour, Trimble, and Elzey; T, U, V, W, X, line at first: Ripley, Colquitt, Rodes, Anderson (G. B.), Garland. General directions of approach are indicated by dotted lines.

Union batteries: 1, Allen; 2, 3, Weeden; 4, Martin; 5, 5, 5, Edwards; 6, Weed; 7, Tidball; 8, Kingsbury; 9, Hexamer; 10, Upton; 11, 12, 13, 14, Kerns, Easton, De-Hart, Cooper; 15, Diederichs, Knieriem, and Tyler; also Voegelee, Smead, Porter, and Robertson. Total, 124 guns.

Confederate batteries: 16, 17, 18, Longstreet's artillery; 19, Braxton; 20, Pegram; 21, Johnson; 22, Crenshaw; 23, Pelham; 24, Brockenbrough; 25, Carrington; 26, Courtney; 27, Boudurant; also other guns not here indicated.

At 2 o'clock P. M., after a sharp engagement between Gaines's Mill and New Cold Harbor, A. P. Hill made the first severe attack on the Union center and left, and after two hours' fighting was repulsed in such disorder that Longstreet was ordered up to relieve the pressure by a feint on the right, which he converted into an attack in force. Thus, up to 4 o'clock, the Confederate assault was mainly on the Union left center and left. About this hour D. H. Hill's division got fully into action, and Jackson's corps (consisting of Ewell's, Whiting's, and Jackson's divisions) was thrown in where needed from the direction of Old Cold Harbor. Major Dabney, Jackson's chief-of-staff, in a letter to General Hill, thus describes the movements of Jackson's corps: "The column," he says, "came on the eastern extension of Gaines's Mill road at Old Cold Harbor, and, passing the old tavern a little way, soon ran afoul of McClellan's right wing, with infantry and artillery in position. Your division had taken the lead, and became, therefore, the left of our whole line of battle. Jackson put Ewell in position on your right. He seemed to think that A. P. Hill was to drive the enemy into his corps. But in a coming upon the hill held by our infantry, or pass in front of our line on the left. Stoneman's detachment of cavalry and infantry, miles to the north, was no longer available. Fearing it might be cut off by Jackson, I sent Stoneman word to make his way as best he could to White House, and in proper time to rejoin the army—wherever it might be.

Believing my forces too small to defend successfully this long line, I asked General Barnard, when he left me, to represent to General McClellan the necessity of reënforcements to thicken and to fill vacant spaces in my front line. He himself promised me axes. This was my first request for aid, but none came in response. The axes did not arrive till near dark, and were useless; but with the few obtained early in the day from the artillery, and in the little time at command, trees were felled along a small portion of our front, and barriers were erected, which were filled in with rails and knapsacks.

While withdrawing from Beaver Dam, I had seen, to my delight, General H. W. Slocum's division of Franklin's corps crossing the river to my assistance. McClellan had promised to send it, and I needed it; it was one of the best divisions of the army. Its able, experienced, and gallant commander and his brave and gifted subordinates had the confidence of their well-trained soldiers. They were all worthy comrades of my well-tried and fully trusted officers, and of many others on that field, subsequently honored by their countrymen. But to our disappointment, through some misunderstanding, the division was almost immediately recalled to Franklin. In response, however, to a later call, it returned at a time when it was greatly needed, and rendered invaluable services.

I fixed my headquarters at first at the Adams house; but early in the battle that locality became a hospital, and I advanced to the Watts house, on more elevated ground, whence I could see the greater part of the field and communicate readily with all parts of it.

Thus far, it will be seen, all plans were defensive; I had reason to believe that the enemy largely outnumbered me—three to one. Evidently it was their plan and their policy to crush me, if possible. Their boldness and

---

little while the state of the firing convinced him that Porter 'didn't drive worth a cent,' and he bestirred himself to let out his full strength. Then it was that, after ordering Ewell's advance, he wheeled on me and began to give instructions about putting in his six other brigades, which were then standing idle in the road by which we had come. I sent them in from left to right *en échelon*, each brigade to support its left-hand neighbor, and to move to the sound of the firing. The strangest divergencies, however, took place in consequence of the coppices and woods and lack of guides. Law and Hood kept the proper relation to Ewell's right, and thus helped A. P. Hill's beaten division, attacked the enemy's center or left center, and about 6 P. M. drove it in. But Lawton, bearing too much by his own left, unwittingly crossed Hood's line of march and reënforced Ewell—a most timely providence, for Ewell's line was about done for. The 2d Virginia brigade seems to have borne as much too far to the right and, at last, near sunset, found themselves behind Longstreet's extreme right,— the brigade of R. H. Anderson, whom they assisted in driving the enemy. The 3d Virginia brigade brought up behind Longstreet's left, passing near Gaines's Mill, and near sunset participated in the victory. The Stonewall brigade, under Winder, bore too much to the left and entered the fight on your right. Pickett's brigade, headed by the 'Old Ironsides' (18th Virginia), broke Porter's line just west of the Watts house." With regard to this break, General Law, in a letter to the Editors, says: "Whiting's division covered the ground on which J. R. Anderson's, Archer's, and Field's brigades had previously attacked. We passed over some of these men as we advanced to the assault. We carried the Federal line in our front, and Longstreet on our right, bringing up his reserves, again attacked and carried his front." At the last and successful advance the line from left to right was: Longstreet (Anderson, Pickett), Whiting (Hood and Law), Jackson (Winder and Lawton), Ewell (one or two brigades), and D. H. Hill (Rodes, Anderson, and Garland). General Porter thinks the first break in his line was made by Hood from the direction indicated on the map by an arrow. Of the Union reserves, McCall's division was put in on the line of Morell,— except a part of Reynolds's brigade, which went to the assistance of Warren; Slocum's division also went to the left,— except Bartlett's brigade, which was sent to the right of Sykes around the McGehee house.

NOTE.—The map is incorrect in one regard: Longstreet's right did not extend so far south as Morell's left.

EDITORS.

confidence, I might add incaution, if not imprudence and rashness in exposure and attack, confirmed my belief that at first they deemed the task an easy one.

I, however, determined to hold my position at least long enough to make the army secure. Though in a desperate situation, I was not without strong hope of some timely assistance from the main body of the army, with which I might repulse the attack and so cripple our opponents as to make the capture of Richmond by the main body of the army, under McClellan, the result of any sacrifice or suffering on the part of my troops or of myself. I felt that the life or death of the army depended upon our conduct in the contest of that day, and that on the issue of that contest depended an early peace or a prolonged, devastating war — for the Union cause could never be yielded. Our brave and intelligent men of all grades and ranks fully realized this, and thousands of them freely offered up their lives that day to maintain the sacred cause which they had voluntarily taken up arms to defend to the last extremity.

UNIFORM OF THE 83D PENNSYLVANIA OF BUTTERFIELD'S BRIGADE, MORELL'S DIVISION, FIFTH CORPS.

The Confederates, under Longstreet and A. P. Hill, following us from Mechanicsville, moved cautiously by the roads leading by Dr. Gaines's house to New Cold Harbor, and by 2 P. M. had formed lines of battle behind the crest of the hills east of Powhite Creek. These lines were parallel to ours, and extended from the valley of the Chickahominy through New Cold Harbor around Morell's front, so as nearly to reach Warren's brigade — the left of Sykes's division. At Gaines's Mill, Colonel Thomas Cass's gallant 9th Massachusetts Volunteers of Griffin's brigade obstinately resisted A. P. Hill's crossing, and were so successful in delaying his advance, after crossing, as to compel him to employ large bodies to force the regiment back to the main line. This brought on a contest which extended to Morell's center and over Martin's front — on his right — and lasted from 12:30 to near 2 o'clock — Cass and his immediate supports falling back south of the swamps. This persistent and prolonged resistance gave to this battle one of its well-known names. ☦

Another column of the enemy, D. H. Hill's, from Beaver Dam Creek, and Jackson's column, from Northern Virginia, with which it had united, came opposite my right front from the direction of Old Cold Harbor and deployed, connecting with A. P. Hill's on the left and extending to our right beyond McGehee's. The advance column of these troops came a little earlier than those under Longstreet and A. P. Hill, but were more cautious and for some hours not so aggressive. Believing that they were passing on down the river to intercept our communications, and thinking that I might strike them to good advantage while in motion, I asked permission to follow,

☦ All the severe battles in this campaign began after noon: Seven Pines, 1 o'clock; Beaver Dam Creek, 3 to 4; Gaines's Mill at 12:30; Savage's Station at 4; White Oak Swamp, 12 to 1; Frayser's Farm, 3 to 4; Malvern Hill after 1.— EDITORS.

intending to attack with Sykes's division and Emory of Cooke's cavalry, leaving Morell and McCall to hold the other lines in check. Information, however, soon poured in, convincing me that this force was larger than any I could use against them, and that still larger forces were forming to attack our left and center. This compelled me to keep my troops united and under cover, and also again to ask aid from the south bank of the Chickahominy. My first message to General McClellan was not delivered, as already stated; my second one was responded to by the speedy arrival of Slocum.↓

Soon after 2 P. M., A. P. Hill's force, between us and New Cold Harbor, again began to show an aggressive disposition, independent of its own troops on its flanks, by advancing from under cover of the woods, in lines well formed and extending, as the contest progressed, from in front of Martin's battery to Morell's left. Dashing across the intervening plains, floundering in the swamps, and struggling against the tangled brushwood, brigade after brigade seemed almost to melt away before the concentrated fire of our artillery and infantry; yet others pressed on, followed by supports as dashing and as brave as their predecessors, despite their heavy losses and the disheartening effect of having to clamber over many of their disabled and dead, and to meet their surviving comrades rushing back in great disorder from the deadly contest. For nearly two hours the battle raged, extending more or less along the whole line to our extreme right. The fierce firing of artillery and infantry, the crash of the shot, the bursting of shells, and the whizzing of bullets, heard above the roar of artillery and the volleys of musketry, all combined was something fearful.

Regiments quickly replenished their exhausted ammunition by borrowing from their more bountifully supplied and generous companions. Some withdrew, temporarily, for ammunition, and fresh regiments took their places ready to repulse, sometimes to pursue, their desperate enemy, for the purpose of retaking ground from which we had been pressed and which it was necessary to occupy in order to hold our position.

The enemy were repulsed in every direction. An ominous silence reigned. It caused the inference that their troops were being gathered and massed for a desperate and overwhelming attack. To meet it, our front line was concentrated, reënforced, and arranged to breast the avalanche, should it come. I again asked for additional reënforcements. French's and Meagher's brigades, of Sumner's corps, were sent forward by the commanding general, but did not arrive till near dark.

At 2 P. M., when I took my station beyond the Watts house, my anxieties and responsibilities had been substantially relieved, at least so far as related to the establishment of a line of battle, in which all engaged felt their power to resist attack. At that time the practicability of our defensive position, in charge of troops having implicit confidence in each other, had been demonstrated by the successful resistance for nearly two hours against the strong

↓ The forces in this battle were: Union, 50 regiments, 20 batteries (several not engaged), in all about 30,000 fighting men; Confederate, 129 regiments, 19 batteries, in all about 65,000 men.— F. J. P.

CAPTURE OF ABANDONED UNION GUNS AT THE BATTLE OF GAINES'S MILL.
FROM A SKETCH MADE AT THE TIME.

and persistent attacks upon our center and right. The troops were well shielded, with their reserves within immediate call. Commanders of divisions, of brigades, and of batteries were in the midst of their men, all confident and determined to hold their posts to the utmost, to resist and drive back the enemy, prepared to call up their reserves, replenish ammunition, and communicate to me such needs as they could not fill, and furnish all necessary information for my action. They had been left to their own judgment and energy, to determine in what manner they could accomplish the best results with the means at their command and with the least exposure.

From my post in advance of the Watts house, the field in front of Sykes was visible, and it was easily understood, by the sound of battle in the woods and by the fire of the enemy in his advance and repulse, that the center and left still remained solid and undisturbed. All available means were used by which I could be kept informed so that I could provide, in the best possible manner, for the many rapid changes and wants suddenly springing up. The Prince de Joinville and his two nephews — the Comte de Paris and Duc de Chartres — and Colonels Gantt, Radowitz, and Hammerstein, from the commanding general's staff, joined me as volunteer aides. Each of these, with my own staff, Locke, Kirkland, Mason, Monteith, and McQuade, exposed themselves to danger, not only quickly and cheerfully carrying every message, but often voluntarily throwing themselves where needed, to direct, to lead, to encourage, and to rally.

During the greater part of the afternoon, D. H. Hill's troops, in detachments, were more or less aggressive on the right. The silence which followed the repulse, already referred to, lasted but a short time. The renewed attacks raged with great fierceness and fury, with slight intermission, along the most of our front, till after five o'clock. Large and numerous bodies of infantry from the direction of Old Cold Harbor, under cover of artillery, directed their attacks upon Sykes's division and Martin's battery; others, from the west side of Powhite Creek, were hurled in rapid succession against Martindale and Butterfield. These furious attacks were successfully repelled, but were immediately renewed by fresh troops. McCall's Pennsylvania Reserves, as needed, were pushed as rapidly as possible into the woods, in support of Martindale and Griffin, whose brigades for a long time bore the brunt of the attacks and whose regiments were relieved as soon as their ammunition was expended. All our positions were held against enormous odds, and the enemy was driven back by our fresh troops, successively thrown into action. At each repulse they advanced new troops upon our diminishing forces, and in such numbers and so rapidly that it appeared as though their reserves were inexhaustible. The action extended along our entire line. At 4 o'clock, when Slocum arrived, all our reserves were exhausted. His brigades were necessarily separated and sent where most needed. Newton's brigade, being in advance, was led to the right of Griffin, there to drive back the enemy and retake ground only held by the enemy for an instant. Taylor's brigade filled vacant spaces in Morell's division, and Bartlett's was sent to Sykes, just in time to render invaluable service, both in resisting and attacking.

On the right, near McGehee's, the enemy captured one of our batteries, which had been doing them great damage by enfilading their lines and preventing their advance. They gained thereby a temporary foothold by advancing some infantry; but, prompt to act, Sykes directed its recapture, and the 16th New York,♭ with arms shifted to the right shoulder, and moving at a double-quick, was soon in possession of the prize, which again renewed its fire.

At times, the enemy on the right would gain an advantage, but in such a case our infantry, supported by the fire of artillery, would move immediately at a rapid gait and regain the lost ground. This occurred frequently in Sykes's command and in the brigades serving near it, all of which were, more or less, in exposed ground. Not less deserving of praise were the divisions of McCall, Morell, and Slocum in their stubborn resistance to the oft-repeated and determined onslaughts of their assailants, who vastly outnumbered them.

About 6:30, preceded by a silence of half an hour, the attack was renewed all along the line with the same apparent determination to sweep us by the force of numbers from the field, if not from existence. The result was evidently a matter of life or death to our opponent's cause. This attack, like its predecessors, was successfully repulsed throughout its length. The sun had sunk below the horizon, and the result seemed so favorable that I began to cherish the hope that the worst that could happen to us would be a withdrawal after dark, without further injury — a withdrawal which would be forced upon us by the exhausted condition of our troops, greatly reduced by casualties, without food and with little ammunition.

♭ The men of this regiment wore on this field, for the first time in battle, the white straw hats which made them so conspicuous during the "Seven Days." These hats were presented by Mrs. Joseph Howland, wife of the colonel. As the hats drew upon them the particular attention of the enemy, they were discarded after the retreat to the James River.— EDITORS.

As if for a final effort, as the shades of evening were coming upon us, and the woods were filled with smoke, limiting the view therein to a few yards, the enemy again massed his fresher and re-formed regiments, and threw them in rapid succession against our thinned and wearied battalions, now almost without ammunition, and with guns so foul that they could not be loaded rapidly. In preparation for defeat, should it come, I had posted artillery in large force just in rear of our center and left, ready for any emergency — and especially to be used against a successful foe, even if his destruction involved firing upon some of our own retreating troops, as might have been necessary. The attacks, though coming like a series of apparently irresistible avalanches, had thus far made no inroads upon our firm and disciplined ranks. Even in this last attack we successfully resisted, driving back our assailants with immense loss, or holding them beyond our lines, except in one instance, near the center of Morell's line, where by force of numbers and under cover of the smoke of battle our line was penetrated and broken; this at a point where I least expected it. This was naturally the weakest point of our line, owing to the closer proximity of the woods held by the enemy. Under his cover they could form, and with less exposure in time and ground than elsewhere, and launch their battalions in quick succession upon our men. I believed I had guarded against the danger by strongly and often reënforcing the troops holding this part of the line. Here the greater part of McCall's and Slocum's forces were used. Just preceding this break, to my great surprise, I saw cavalry, Rush's Lancers, which I recognized as ours, rushing in numbers through our lines on the left, and carrying off with sudden fright the limbers of our artillery, then prepared to pour their irresistible fire into a pursuing foe. With no infantry to support, and with apparent disaster before them, such of the remainder of these guns as could be moved were carried from the field; some deliberately, others in haste, but not in confusion.

In no other place was our line penetrated or shaken. The right, seeing our disaster, fell back united and in order, but were compelled to leave behind two guns, the horses of which had been killed. The troops on the left and center retired, some hastily, but not in confusion, often turning back to repulse and pursue the advancing enemy.\ All soon rallied in rear of the Adams house behind Sykes and the brigades of French and Meagher sent to our aid, and who now, with hearty cheers, greeted our battalions as they retired and re-formed. We lost in all twenty-two cannon; some of these broke down while we were withdrawing, and some ran off the bridges at night while we were crossing to the south bank of the Chickahominy. The loss of the guns was due to the fact that some of Cooke's cavalry which had been directed

---

\ We are informed by Colonel Auchmuty, then assistant adjutant-general of Morell's division, that there was no running or panic when the line broke. The men fell back in small groups, turning and firing as they went, and carrying many of the wounded with them. On the crest of the hill in the rear of the line of battle a stand was made, and from that point regimental organizations were preserved. Near the close of the war General Griffin said to Colonel Auchmuty that he regarded Gaines's Mill as the hardest-fought battle in his experience.

The same officer informs us that after the line of battle had been formed in the morning, and while the attack was momentarily expected, the mail arrived from the North, and the newsboys went along the line crying the New York and Philadelphia papers. — EDITORS.

RUINS OF GAINES'S MILL, LOOKING EAST. FROM A PHOTOGRAPH MADE IN THE SPRING OF 1885.

At the time of the battle, this building was of five stories, and was, it is said, one of the finest grist-mills in Virginia. The wooden structure, dovetailed into the ruins, now covers but one pair of burrs. The mill was not injured in the fight, but was burned by Sheridan's cavalry in May, 1864, the fire extending to a dwelling-house which stood just beyond the mill. The main conflict was a mile farther to the south-east, but the ridge shown in the picture was the scene of a most gallant resistance to the Confederate advance by the 9th Massachusetts regiment, acting as a rear-guard to Porter's corps. The road to New Cold Harbor and the battle-ground runs to the right. The mill-stream runs into Powhite Swamp, and thence into the Chickahominy.

to be kept, under all circumstances, in the valley of the Chickahominy, had been sent to resist an attack of the enemy upon our left. The charge, executed in the face of a withering fire of infantry and in the midst of our heavy cannonading, as well as that of the enemy, resulted, as should have been expected, in confusion. The bewildered and uncontrollable horses wheeled about, and, dashing through the batteries, satisfied the gunners that they were charged by the enemy. To this alone I always attributed the failure on our part longer to hold the battle-field and to bring off all our guns, with few exceptions, in an orderly retreat. Most unaccountably this cavalry was not used to cover our retreat or gather the stragglers, but was peremptorily ordered to cross to the south bank of the river.☆ I never again saw their commander.

At night I was called to General McClellan's headquarters, where the chiefs of corps, or their representatives, were gathered. The commanding general, after hearing full reports, was of the opinion that the final result would be disastrous if we undertook longer to hold the north bank of the

☆ See "Official Records," Vol. XI., Part II., pp. 43, 223, 273, 282.— F. J. P.

river with my command in the condition in which it was left by a hard fight and the loss of rest for two nights. In this opinion all concurred; and I was then instructed to withdraw to the south bank and destroy the bridges after me. The plans to move to the James River were then explained, together with the necessity for the movement, and the orders were given for their execution.∫

My command was safely withdrawn to the south bank of the river, and the bridges were destroyed soon after sunrise on the 28th.✧

The Prince de Joinville and his two nephews, the Comte de Paris and the Duc de Chartres, were on the field as volunteer aides-de-camp, actively engaged in encouraging the men, carrying messages, and performing other duties of aides. Each of these officers was in the midst of flying musket-balls, and was liable to be struck at any moment [see p. 184]. At one time the Comte de Paris, regardless of himself, begged me to send his uncle to General McClellan with a message which would at once and permanently remove him from the dangers of the battle, since the family interests at stake were too important to permit him to be so exposed. I had shortly before asked Colonel Thomas L. Gantt, another of McClellan's aides, to hasten to that general and hurry up reënforcements, as our lines would soon be broken. The danger was now imminent, and I asked the Prince to carry the same message, telling him that he was selected because of the speed of his horse. He turned as if to go, and I went to attend to the field. Soon the Count returned, with tears in his eyes, and with choking utterance, expressive of his care and affection, begged me again to send away his uncle. This also I did. Scarcely had the Prince left the second time when our cavalry fell back on us as I have related, our line was broken, and our artillery rendered unserviceable. The Prince and Colonel Gantt afterward told me that they did not leave, as I had directed, because all seemed favorable to us, and they

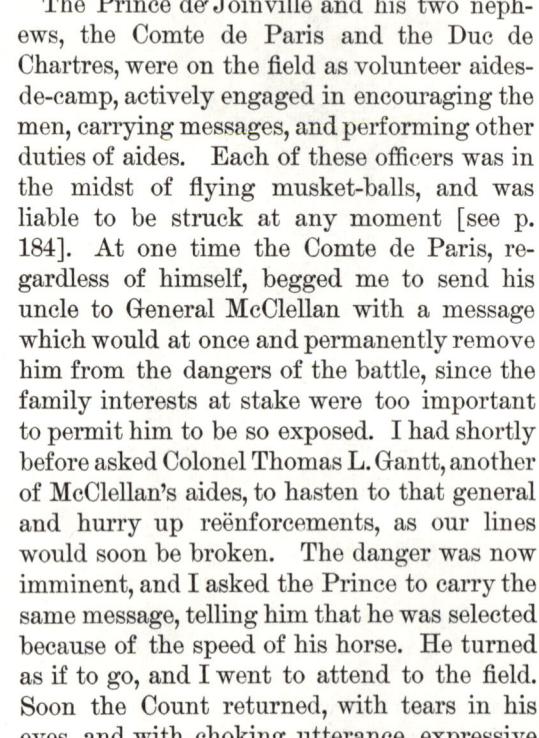

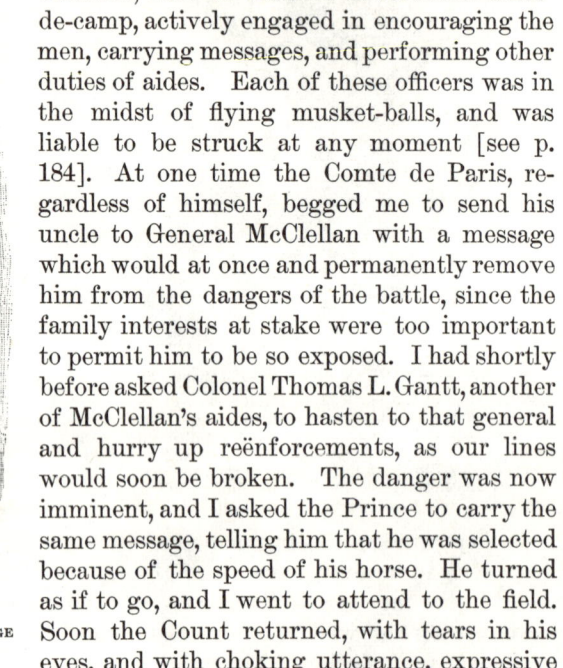

BREVET MAJOR-GENERAL PHILIP ST. GEORGE COOKE. FROM A PHOTOGRAPH.

∫ At Gaines's Mill the Union loss was: Killed, 894; wounded, 3107; missing, 2836,—total, 6837. On the Confederate side the losses of Jackson, Ewell, Whiting, and D. H. Hill were: Killed, 589; wounded, 2671; missing, 24,— total, 3284. Of these, Whiting (*i. e.*, Hood's and Law's brigades) lost 1017. The losses of A. P. Hill and Longstreet for this battle are not reported separately, but a safe estimate from their losses in the campaign would probably bring the total considerably beyond the Union loss, that of the killed and wounded certainly much higher. Almost the whole of two Union regiments, the 11th Pennsylvania Reserves and the 4th New Jersey, were captured.— EDITORS.

✧ The landing at White House and the railroad south from Tunstall's station were abandoned, the infantry and artillery embarking for Fort Monroe, and the cavalry marching to Yorktown.— EDITORS.

thought I could not be in earnest or that I had greatly misjudged the situation. This shows how suddenly the tide may turn in battle and on what little incidents success may depend.

The forces arrayed against us, and especially those which had thus far been launched upon my command, were the chosen of Southern manhood from Maryland to Texas. No braver or more spirited body of men was to be found among the Confederates, or any who more strongly believed in their own invincibility.‡ Their general officers, from the chief down, had been selected for earnest devotion to their cause, and well-earned reputation for intelligent and energetic performance of duty in other fields. With few exceptions they had been my personal friends, and many of them my intimate associates. In the varied relations to them as subaltern, as instructor, as academical and regimental comrade, in social life, as competitor for honor in war and in garrison life, and engaged in watching those performing trying duty in Kansas, Utah, and elsewhere, I learned to know them well and to respect their decision under conviction of duty, when, to my regret, they left the cause of the Union. Notwithstanding my friendship, my personal regard for these old friends and former comrades, which never varied, it was my duty to oppose them, when arrayed against the Union, to the utmost. At the earliest moment, when separation was attempted, and afterward, my efforts were continuously directed against the success of their cause. One of the results of those efforts was manifested on this battle-field. I was enabled, after great labor and care, to meet these friends and comrades in command of men, than whom there could be none more intelligent, better disciplined, braver, more confiding in each other, and more determined on success. They embraced soldiers from Maine, Michigan, Illinois, Pennsylvania, New York, and all New England — together with all the regular army, then at the East, from all parts of the country. Their commanders were not excelled by those in any other corps in ability or experience; they had the highest confidence in each other, in the army, and in their own men, and were fully competent to oppose their able adversaries.

I have said we did not fear Lee alone at Beaver Dam Creek. Nor, though anxious, did we fear the combined attack of Lee and Jackson at Gaines's Mill. Defeat to us was necessarily great damage to them. Our flanks were secure and could not be turned; though fewer in numbers, the advantages of our position, combined with the firm discipline of our own brave men, overcame the odds. Our adversaries were forced to meet us face to face. All day they struggled desperately for success, and near night, after fearful destruction, broke our line at one point, just at a time when a most unforeseen mismanagement on our part aided to crown their labors with possession of the field. Still, our confidence was not broken; and, as we shall see in a succeeding paper, under like circumstances victory crowned our arms with success against the same opponents, strongly reënforced, at Malvern Hill.

‡ The known presence of President Davis and General Lee, to oversee, direct, encourage, and urge, was another influential power in favor of the Confederates in this movement.— F. J. P.

## THE CHARGE OF COOKE'S CAVALRY AT GAINES'S MILL.

### BY PHILIP ST. GEORGE COOKE, BREVET MAJOR-GENERAL, U. S. A.

IN "The Century" for June, 1885, there is an article on the battle of Gaines's Mill, signed by Fitz John Porter, in which appear singular errors of statement regarding the action of the "Cavalry Reserve," affecting also the conduct and reputation of its commander. He says [see p. 340 of the present volume]:

"We lost in all twenty-two cannon; some of these broke down while we were withdrawing, and some ran off the bridges at night while we were crossing to the south bank of the Chickahominy. The loss of the guns was due to the fact that some of Cooke's cavalry, which had been directed to be kept, under all circumstances, in the valley of the Chickahominy, had been sent to resist an attack of the enemy upon our left. The charge, executed in the face of a withering fire of infantry and in the midst of our heavy cannonading as well as that of the enemy, resulted, as should have been expected, in confusion. The bewildered and uncontrollable horses wheeled about, and, dashing through the batteries, satisfied the gunners that they were charged by the enemy. To this alone I always attributed the failure on our part longer to hold the battle-field, and to bring off all our guns [with few exceptions,] in an orderly retreat. Most unaccountably this cavalry was not used to cover our retreat or gather the stragglers, but was peremptorily ordered to cross to the south bank of the river." [Footnote: "See 'Official Records,' Vol. XI., Part II., pp. 43, 223, 273, 282.— F. J. P."]

To silence forever the injurious statements and insinuation of the last sentence, I give here evidence of two witnesses who were present, and whose high character is known to all. Major-General Wesley Merritt, colonel Fifth Cavalry, superintendent United States Military Academy, writes me, April 8th, 1885:

"The cavalry remained, with you in immediate command, on that portion of the field, until after midnight on the 27th of June, 1862. It provided litter-bearers and lantern-bearers for our surgeons who went over the field of battle, succoring and attending the wounded. . . . The cavalry was the last force to leave the field and to cross the Chickahominy,✠ and the bridge on which it crossed, between 12 midnight on the 27th and 2 A. M. on the 28th of June, was, I think, rendered impassable by your order."

Brevet Lieutenant-Colonel J. P. Martin, assistant adjutant-general United States Army, wrote me from Fort Leavenworth, April 30th, 1885:

"The artillery did not drive the enemy from his front; the enemy was not driven from his front, but the charge of your cavalry did *stop the advance* of the enemy, and

this enabled Porter's troops to get off the field. I am by no means alone in the belief that the charge of the cavalry at Gaines's Mill, on June 27th, 1862, *saved Fitz John Porter's corps from destruction*. . . . You *did not* direct your command at once to cross the river. There were no frightened men in your vicinity. All the frightened men were far to your right; you could not have reached the retiring crowd; and if *you* could have stopped them, you could have done more than Porter himself did do, and he was amidst them, for I saw him. Your command, at least a part of it, was the very last to cross the river."

It should be observed that in the short extract from "The Century," above, General Porter repeats the assertion that the cavalry caused the loss of the (22) guns,— emphasizes, makes plainer, the meaning of the opening sentence: to the charge "*alone* I always attributed the failure on our part to longer hold the battle-field and to bring off *all* our guns in an orderly retreat."

Captain W. B. Weeden, commanding Battery C, 1st Rhode Island Artillery, reports, Vol. XI., Pt. II., p. 282, "Official Records," the loss of a section by stress of the enemy's attacks; the two other sections "held in support in rear of Griffin's brigade" opened fire; "The smoke had filled the whole field to the woods, and it was impossible to direct the fire. The batteries were limbering to the *rear* in good order" when, he says, the cavalry fugitives ran through them, but he only lost one more piece "mired in the woods." But General Griffin reports that the artillery "opened fire upon the enemy advancing upon our left; but it was too late; our infantry had already begun to fall back, and nothing being left to give confidence to the artillerymen, it was impossible to make them stand to their work." And that was just when the cavalry did go in and give confidence to the three batteries on the left, and the saving work was done.

I have examined the "Official Records" and found reports of about twenty batteries engaged in the battle, and the above is the only mention of the cavalry fugitives to be found in them; their losses are attributed to other causes. Here I will give the account of the loss of whole batteries:

General Truman Seymour reports, p. 402, of Captain Easton, "This gallant gentleman fell and his battery was lost with him."

---

⸸ Insertion by General Porter in the revision of his article for the present work.— EDITORS.

✠ Major William H. Powell, of the 4th Regular Infantry, wrote to the Editors on September 8th, 1885: "Probably not much credit attaches to the particular organized force which was the last to cross the Chickahominy River after the battle of Gaines's Mill; but in order to settle the question I desire to state that the cavalry was not the last to cross the river — even if they did leave at the time General Merritt states. The 4th United States Infantry was the last organization which crossed, and that regiment passed over about *two hours after daylight* on the morning of the 28th, and a bridge had to be partly relaid to enable it to do so. This regiment was posted on the extreme right flank of the army at the battle of Gaines's Mill, and was ordered to support Weed's battery. Weed was afterward reënforced by Tidball's battery, and the 4th Infantry held its position from the commencement of the engagement (about 11 A. M.) until twilight of the 27th, without receiving an order or stirring from its position until Weed reported that he had no more ammunition, and retired from the field by way of the Cold Harbor road, covered by the 4th Infantry. Night came upon the regiment as it was retiring on this road. It went into bivouac in line of battle, in the Chickahominy Valley, on the road by which it retired from the field. When daylight came we expected orders to renew the engagement, and took up our march to return to the battle-field, about a mile and a half distant. It was then that some wounded were met, who informed us that all the army had crossed during the night. We then marched from Grapevine Bridge to Alexander's Bridge, in sight of the enemy's pickets, and when we arrived on the south side we were astonished to find that it was thought we had been captured. We learned afterward that orders had been sent to the 4th Infantry during the action, but the officer who started with them was killed; another who took them was wounded before they could be delivered, and an orderly who was subsequently dispatched with them did not arrive at his destination, and was never heard of afterward."

Captain Mark Kerns was wounded, but "loaded and fired the last shots himself, and brought *four* of the guns off the field." Of another battery he reports, "No efforts could now repel the rush of a successful foe, under whose fire rider and horse went down, and guns lay immovable on the field." Captain J. H. Cooper, Battery B, 1st Pennsylvania Artillery, reports, p. 410:

"The remaining infantry falling back, we were compelled to retire from our guns. The charge being too sudden and overpowering, it was impossible to remove them, many of the horses being killed by the enemy's fire."

Was General Porter prevented from bringing off *all these* guns by the cavalry charge? General Porter says, p. 322:

"Just *preceding* this break" (in Morell's line) " I saw cavalry, which I recognized as ours, rushing in numbers through our lines on the left."

All the evidence goes to disprove this very deliberate statement, and that all the infantry on the left had broken and was fast disappearing before the first advance of the cavalry. Again he says:

"General Cooke was instructed to take position, with cavalry, under the hills in the valley of the Chickahominy — there with the aid of artillery to guard our left flank. He was especially enjoined to intercept, gather, and hold all stragglers, and under no circumstances to leave the valley for the purpose of coming upon the hill held by our infantry, or pass in front of our line on the left."

What strange folly of self-contradiction is betrayed between this order "to guard our left flank" and the violent condemnation in the first extract, which we have been considering, of the march "to resist an attack of the enemy on our left, . . ." in a "charge executed in the face of a withering fire of infantry, and in the midst of our heavy cannonading as well as that of the enemy." Could a poet laureate say more?

" Cannon to right of them,
Cannon to left of them
Volley'd and thundered —
. . . . . . .
Then they rode back —

Ay, there's the rub.

When I reported to General Porter before the battle, I remember that he proposed that I should take post in the narrow open meadow on the extreme left. I urged that the flank of the army was virtually covered by the Chickahominy; that, moreover, it was covered by three reserve batteries and 3 29-pounder batteries on the opposite side of the river; while the position I had taken on the hill-slope was within view, and also within cavalry striking distance. If I had gone there, I should not have been able, when the time came, to *face*, and, with artillery aid, to stop the enemy in the flush of his success. To some such objections which I made General Porter evidently yielded, instead of "enjoining" me; for the cavalry *remained* quite near his first station, Adams's house; and I was there with him repeatedly. An order "under no circumstances to leave the valley for the purpose of coming on the hill" would have been to a general officer not only unprecedented, but insulting.

How strange, to military ears, would sound an order "to intercept, gather, and hold all stragglers" on the extreme front and flank! — and the warning not to " pass in *front* of our line on the left!" Such extravagance of action — marching, with no earthly object, between two lines of fire — is seldom thus forestalled! Seriously, this passes the bounds of sanity. But it is emphasized by his map, which represents my cavalry as actually making a flank march between the lines of battle, — Morell's and Longstreet's.

It seems necessary to add the statements of eye-witnesses, from different points of view, — men of well-known high character, — to corroborate my assertions and my corrections of the misrepresentations of the part played by the cavalry and myself in the battle, as found in " The Century " article.

Next morning, at Savage's Station, the Prince de Joinville approached me with both hands extended, saying with *empressement*, " I saw you make your *charge* yesterday"; and next day he wrote to the Duc d'Aumale [see " New York Times," August 13th, 1862]:

. . . "Those fresh troops rush in good order upon our left, which falters, flies, and passing through the artillery draws on in disorder the troops of our center. The enemy advances rapidly. The fusillade and cannonade are so violent that the projectiles striking the ground raise a permanent cloud of dust. At that moment General Cooke charged at the head of his calvary; but that movement does not succeed, and his horsemen on their return only increase the disorder. He makes every effort, aided by all who felt a little courage, to stop the panic, but in vain."

The Comte de Paris wrote to me, February 2d, 1877:

. . . "I was with De Hart's battery on the crest of the hill when you advanced on our left. . . . The sacrifice of some of the bravest of the cavalry certainly saved a part of our artillery; as did, on a larger scale, the Austrian cavalry on the evening of Sadowa. . . . The main fact is, that with your cavalry you did all that cavalry could do to stop the rout."

General W. Merritt wrote me, February 2d, 1877:

"I thought at the time, and subsequent experience has convinced me, that your cavalry and the audacity of its conduct at that time, together with the rapid firing of canister at short range by the battery mentioned, did much, if not everything, toward preventing the entire destruction of the Union army at Gaines's Mill. The circumstances were these:

"The enemy had emerged from a wood, where his ranks were more or less disorganized, into an open field. Instead of finding the way clear before him he was met by a determined charge of cavalry and a heavy artillery fire. In his mind a new line of fresh troops were before him. It was but natural, at that stage of our military experience, that he should hesitate and halt, to prepare for a new emergency. He did so; and that night the cavalry bivouacked as near the scene of these events as the enemy did."

Brevet Lieut.-Colonel J. P. Martin wrote to me, March 24th, 1870:

"It is my opinion that but for the charge of the 5th Cavalry on that day, the loss in the command of General Fitz John Porter would have been immensely greater than it was; indeed, I believe that the charge, more than any other thing, was instrumental in saving that part of the army on the north bank of the Chickahominy."

"You were the last general officer of General Porter's command on the field on the left, General Porter himself leaving before you did; you had, therefore, an excellent opportunity of seeing what was going on."

Colonel G. A. H. Blake, United States Army, wrote me, June 16th, 1879:

"About sundown you advanced the brigade under a warm fire and I deployed the 5th and 1st Cavalry in two lines, and a little to the rear of (the interval of) reserve batteries of artillery, which had opened a rapid fire. The infantry of the left wing had then disappeared from the top of the hill. You then rode off to a battery further to the left, where Rush's Lancers had been ordered. The 5th Cavalry soon charged, and I saw no more of them. You had ordered me to support them; there was a warm fire, and the smoke and dust made everything obscure. I saw none of the 5th, after it was broken, pass through the battery, which was very near. It was soon forced to retire, and was followed by the 1st in its rear."

Finally, General William N. Grier, United States Army, wrote me, July 19th, 1879:

"The reserve was stationed on the hill, . . . in full view of the slopes of the hill, down to the timber through which the enemy debouched in large numbers. The United States batteries were on the slope of the hill, a little to our right front. You ordered the 5th to make a charge, directing me to make a second charge after the 5th would rally. I never saw that regiment again on that day, after it was enveloped in a cloud of dust, making the charge — but soon after saw a battery or two emerge from the dust, . . . withdrawing from the contest. I then wheeled my squadrons into column of fours, at a trot along the top of the hill, until getting in rear of the batteries — receiving the enemy's fire at a loss of an officer and many men and horses — and, as I then supposed, saving the batteries from further loss."

The orders actually given were to support the batteries to the last moment, and then charge, if necessary, to save them.

DETROIT, June, 1885.

## RECOLLECTIONS OF A PARTICIPANT IN THE CHARGE.
### BY THE REV. W. H. HITCHCOCK.

REMEMBERING clearly the incidents connected with the cavalry charge, I wish to clear up a point in regard to that charge, so far as the regiment (the 5th Regular Cavalry) with which I had the honor of being connected was concerned.

The battle did not begin till noon. We were stationed on the left of our position. As the hours passed, the battle became more and more furious. About 5 P. M. we were moved up near to the crest of the hill on our left, and within some 20 rods of the 5 or 6 batteries planted on the crest of the hill.

It was something marvelous to watch those brave men handle their guns; never a man flinched or was dismayed, though a most withering fire of musketry and artillery was poured upon them.

Just before dark, when we could tell, by the sound of the musketry fire and by the constantly advancing yells of the charging foe, that he was getting near the guns in our front, General Philip St. George Cooke, commanding the cavalry, rode to our front. I was on the right of the front line of the first squadron, and I heard his order to Captain Whiting, commanding the five companies of our regiment that were present on the field. He said, "Captain, as soon as you see the advancing line of the enemy rising the crest of the hill, charge at once, without any further orders, to enable the artillery to bring off their guns." General Cooke then rode back around the right of our squadron.

Captain Whiting turned to us and said, "Cavalry! Attention! Draw saber!" then added something to the effect, "Boys, we must charge in five minutes." Almost immediately, the bayonets of the advancing foe were seen, just beyond our cannon, probably not fifty rods from us. Captain Whiting at once gave the order, "Trot! March!" and as soon as we were fully under way he shouted, "Charge!"

We dashed forward with a wild cheer, in solid column of squadron front; but our formation was almost instantly broken by the necessity of opening to right and left to pass our guns. So furiously were our brave gunners fighting that I noticed this incident: The gun directly in my front had just been loaded; every man had fallen before it could be fired. As I bore to the right to pass this gun, I saw the man at the breech, who was evidently shot through the body, drawing himself up by the spokes of the wheel, and reaching for the lanyard, and I said, "He will fire that gun," and so kept to the right, and almost immediately felt the shock of the explosion. Then I closed in to re-form the line, but could find no one at my left, so completely had our line been shattered by the musketry fire in front and the artillery fire in our rear. I rushed on, and almost instantly my horse reared upright in front of a line of bayonets, held by a few men upon whom I had dashed. My horse came down in front of the line, and ran away partly to our rear, perfectly uncontrollable. I dropped my saber, which hung to my wrist by the saber-knot, and so fiercely tugged at my horse's bit as to cause the blood to flow from her mouth, yet could not check her. The gun I had passed, now limbered up, was being hauled off at a gallop. I could direct my horse a little to right or left, and so directed her toward the gun. As she did not attempt to leap the gun, I gained control of her, and at once turned about and started back upon my charge. After riding a short distance I paused. The firing of artillery and infantry behind and of infantry in front was terrific. None but the dead and wounded were around me. It hardly seemed that I could drive Lee's battle-scarred veterans alone, and so I rode slowly off the field. The regiment had only about 250 men in action. Our commissioned officer was the only one not wounded, except some who were captured. Only about 100 returned from that bloody field for duty the next day. Some were captured, but a large number fell in that terrible charge, and sleep with the many heroes who on that day gave their lives for the Union. So far as those of the 5th Regular Cavalry present in this charge were concerned, we certainly did our whole duty, just as we were ordered. We saved *some* guns, and tried to save all.

FAIRVIEW, ILL., June 13th, 1885.

# LEE'S ATTACKS NORTH OF THE CHICKAHOMINY.

### BY DANIEL H. HILL, LIEUTENANT-GENERAL, C. S. A.

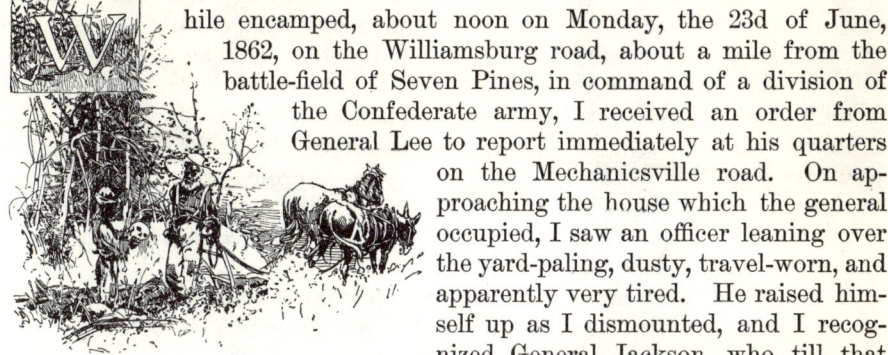

"W'AT WAR DEY FIGHTIN' 'BOUT!"

While encamped, about noon on Monday, the 23d of June, 1862, on the Williamsburg road, about a mile from the battle-field of Seven Pines, in command of a division of the Confederate army, I received an order from General Lee to report immediately at his quarters on the Mechanicsville road. On approaching the house which the general occupied, I saw an officer leaning over the yard-paling, dusty, travel-worn, and apparently very tired. He raised himself up as I dismounted, and I recognized General Jackson, who till that moment I had supposed was confronting Banks and Frémont far down the Valley of Virginia. He said that he had ridden fifty-two miles since 1 o'clock that morning, having taken relays of horses on the road. We went together into General Lee's office. General Jackson declined refreshments, courteously tendered by General Lee, but drank a glass of milk. Soon after, Generals Longstreet and A. P. Hill came in, and General Lee, closing the door, told us that he had determined to attack the Federal right wing, and had selected our four commands to execute the movement. He told us that he had sent Whiting's division to reënforce Jackson, and that at his instance the Richmond papers had reported that large reënforcements had been sent to Jackson "with a view to clearing out the Valley of Virginia and exposing Washington." He believed that General McClellan received the Richmond papers regularly, and he (Lee) knew of the nervous apprehension concerning Washington.∫ He then said that he would retire to another room to attend to some office work, and would leave us to arrange the details among ourselves. The main point in his mind seemed to be that the crossings of the Chickahominy should be uncovered by Jackson's advance down the left bank, so that the other three divisions might not suffer in making a forced passage.

During the absence of General Lee, Longstreet said to Jackson: "As you have the longest march to make, and are likely to meet opposition, you had better fix the time for the attack to begin." Jackson replied: "Daylight of the 26th." Longstreet then said: "You will encounter Federal cavalry and roads blocked by felled timber, if nothing more formidable: ought you not to give yourself more time?" When General Lee returned, he ordered

∫ I do not know how far the Federals were deceived by the announcement of reënforcements sent to Jackson, but during the Seven Days' battles I read in a Northern paper a letter from Strasburg, Va., of the 25th of June, stating that they were expecting Stonewall Jackson there, and were so well fortified that they would give him a warm reception. Jackson's corps was then at Ashland, within twelve miles of Richmond. He certainly had slipped off without observation.— D. H. H.

A. P. Hill to cross at Meadow Bridge, Longstreet at the Mechanicsville Bridge, and me to follow Longstreet. The conference broke up about nightfall.

It may be of interest to the student of history to know how Jackson managed to slip off so often and so easily. His plan was to press his infantry as near as possible to the enemy, without bringing on a general engagement; then to occupy these advanced points with dismounted cavalry pickets, and to start his "foot cavalry" in the other direction with all possible speed. His stealthy marches to the rear were made without consulting his highest officers, and even without their knowing his destination.‡

It was characteristic of Jackson to select for his chief-of-staff, not a military man, but a Presbyterian minister, a professor in a theological seminary, and to clothe him with the power of carrying out his mysterious orders when he was temporarily absent. Jackson's confidence was well bestowed, and he found in the Rev. R. L. Dabney, D. D., a faithful, zealous, and efficient staff-officer. To him, now a professor in the State University of Texas, I am indebted for the following account of the unexpected appearance of Jackson on the Federal right wing before Richmond:

"General Jackson's forced march from Mount Meridian, in the neighborhood of the Port Republic battle-field, began in earnest on Wednesday, June 18th, the general and a few of the troops having left the evening before. About midday on Thursday, the 19th, we were at Mechum's River Station, about ten miles west of Charlottesville, with the head of the column. The general called me into a room in the hotel, locked the door, and told me that he was about to go in advance of his corps by rail to Richmond to see the commander-in-chief; that the corps was going to Richmond to join in a general attack upon McClellan, but that he would return to his command before we got there; that I was to march the corps toward Richmond, following the line of railroad, as near as the country roads would permit, by Charlottesville and Gordonsville, General Ewell's division to form the head of the column with which I was personally to proceed; that strict precautions of secrecy were to be observed — which he then dictated to me. He then got on an express train and left us. I dined that day with General Ewell, and I remember that he complained to me with some bitterness of General Jackson's reserve, saying, 'Here, now, the general has gone off on the railroad without intrusting to me, his senior major-general, any order, or any hint whither we are going; but [Major J. A.] Harman, his quartermaster, enjoys his full confidence, I suppose, for I hear that he is telling the troops that we are going to Richmond to fight McClellan.'

"'You may be certain, General Ewell,' I replied, 'that you stand higher in

---

‡ This was a source of annoyance to Loring in '61, and later on to Ewell. When Jackson's corps was so strangely left at Winchester after the battle of Sharpsburg, or Antietam, and General Lee had gone to the Rappahannock (we were making a feint every day of holding the gaps in the Blue Ridge, with strict orders not to bring on an engagement), I said to Jackson one day: "I am the next in rank, and should you be killed or captured in your many scouts around, I would not know what the corps was left for, or what it was expected to do." He then told me that he had suggested to General Lee, who had to move back to protect Richmond, that he could remain and remove our wounded and stores, and that his presence on McClellan's flank and rear would keep him from attacking Lee. In case of any casualty to himself, the removal was to go on till completed.—D. H. H.

**CONFEDERATE SKIRMISH-LINE DRIVEN IN BY THE UNION ADVANCE.**
The original sketch for this picture was made from personal observation. It describes an incident of McClellan's advance up the Peninsula.

General Jackson's confidence than any one else, as your rank and services entitle you. As for Major Harman, he has not heard a word more than others. If he thinks that we are going to Richmond, it is only his surmise, which I suppose every intelligent private is now making.'

"The column reached Gordonsville, Saturday, June 21st, about noon. To my surprise, on riding into town, I got an order to go to the general — at a private house, where he was lodging. On reaching Gordonsville, Thursday afternoon, he had been met by news which alarmed the outpost there: that a heavy Federal force was on the Rapidan, about sixteen miles away. He therefore had postponed going to Richmond until he could effectually clear up this rumor. The chief mode adopted was characteristic: it was to send out by night an intelligent private citizen, thoroughly acquainted with the Rapidan people and country, as his scout. This gentleman came back, after thorough inquiry, with the news that the rumor was unfounded. About half an hour before sunset on Saturday, the general got into an express car with no one but me and the conductor, and came to Frederick's Hall Station in the county of Louisa, arriving about dawn on Sunday, the 22d. We spent the Sabbath there at the house of Mr. N. Harris, attending camp-preaching in the afternoon. At this house were General W. H. C. Whiting and General Hood, then commanding a Texas brigade. At 1 o'clock that night General Jackson arose, took an orderly whom I had selected for him as trustworthy and well acquainted with the road, and started for Richmond with impressed horses.

He had me wake up General Whiting and make *him* sign a pass and an impressment order (which no one under the rank of major-general had a right to do). He had about fifty-two miles to ride to Richmond; to the Nine-mile bridge, near which General Lee was in person, I suppose the distance was as great, so that the ride occupied him, with the time lost in impressing relays of horses, about ten hours. He must have reached his rendezvous with General Lee and his three major-generals about noon on the 23d. If he rode into the city first, the meeting would have been a few hours later. He rejoined his corps at Beaver Dam Station on Tuesday (24th), and assembled the whole of it around Ashland Wednesday night, the 25th. About two hours by sun on the 26th we came into collision with McClellan's outposts. We were much mystified at first to know why the general should put a battery in position and cannonade the bushes furiously for ten minutes only to drive away a picket. We found out afterward this was his signal to you [General D. H. Hill], and in a little while the distant sound of your guns at Ellerson's mill told us that the ball had opened."

It will be seen from the narrative of Major Dabney that General Jackson, who fought some of his most desperate battles on Sunday, would not start to Richmond till Sunday had passed. He had the pass and impressment order from General Whiting that he might not be known on the road; he wore no insignia of rank, and as he would have been known in Richmond he did not go to that city. It was 3 P. M. on the 23d when I saw him at General Lee's headquarters. Major Dabney is mistaken in saying that the signal-guns were intended for me. A. P. Hill was farther up the Chickahominy, and he was to cross first, and, being nearer to Jackson, could hear his guns better

EXTERIOR LINE OF DEFENSES OF RICHMOND ON THE MECHANICSVILLE ROAD (LOOKING SOUTH-EAST).
FROM A SKETCH MADE AT THE TIME OF McCLELLAN'S ADVANCE.

MECHANICSVILLE FROM THE NORTH-WEST — SCENE OF THE OPENING OF THE SEVEN DAYS' BATTLES. FROM A PHOTOGRAPH TAKEN IN THE SPRING OF 1885.

The cross-roads (Mechanicsville proper) are indicated by the two houses at the extreme right. The woods in the left distance show the line of Beaver Dam Creek at the crossing of the upper road from the town. A. P. Hill advanced from Meadow Bridge and along the road in the foreground, his troops deploying at this point on both sides of the road about 4 P. M. The house at the left center (Horn's) marks the location of the Union battery which opened upon Hill's troops as they came along this road, from which the Confederate artillery (McIntosh's and Pegram's) replied as they advanced. Anderson's brigade was sent to the left to flank the Union guns, which, together with the single regiment left in the town by General Porter, withdrew before the enemy to the strong position beyond the creek.— EDITORS.

than those of us lower down the stream. On the 25th there was a brisk fight about King's school-house on the Williamsburg road, between Hooker's division and parts of the divisions of Generals T. H. Holmes and Benjamin Huger. That night my division marched across to the neighborhood of Mechanicsville Bridge. To conceal the movement our camp-fires were freshly lighted up by a detachment after the troops had left, and a company was sent some miles down the Charles City road to send up rockets, as though signaling an advance in that direction. General Lee's order, issued on the 24th of June, says:

"At 3 o'clock Thursday morning, the 26th instant, General Jackson will advance on the road leading to Pole Green Church, communicating his march to General Branch [seven miles above Meadow Bridge], who will immediately cross the Chickahominy and take the road leading to Mechanicsville. As soon as the movements of these columns are discovered, General A. P. Hill, with the rest of his division, will cross the Chickahominy near Meadow Bridge. . . . The enemy being driven from Mechanicsville, and the passage across the bridge opened, General Longstreet, with his division and that of General D. H. Hill, will cross the Chickahominy at or near that point — General D. H. Hill moving to the support of General Jackson, and General Longstreet supporting General A. P. Hill — the four divisions keeping in communication with each other, and moving *en échelon* on separate roads, if practicable; the left division in advance, with skirmishers and sharp-shooters extending their front, will sweep down the Chickahominy, and endeavor to drive the enemy from his position above New Bridge, General Jackson bearing well to his left, turning Beaver Dam Creek, and taking the direction toward Cold Harbor, etc."

General Jackson was unable to reach the point expected on the morning of the 26th. General A. P. Hill says: "Three o'clock P. M. having arrived, and no intelligence from Jackson or Branch, I determined to cross at once, rather than hazard the failure of the whole plan by longer deferring it."

Heavy firing was heard at 3 P. M. at Meadow Bridge, and the Federal outposts were seen fleeing toward Mechanicsville, pursued by A. P. Hill. We could see a line of battle drawn up at that village ready to receive Hill. My division being nearest the bridge, Longstreet ordered me to cross first. Some delay was made in repairing the bridge, and A. P. Hill became hotly engaged before we could get to his relief. At this time President Davis and staff hurried past us, going "to the sound of the firing." Ripley's brigade was pushed forward to the support of three batteries of artillery of Major H. P. Jones's battalion, and the two under Captains R. A. Hardaway and J. W. Bondurant. The five batteries soon silenced the Federal artillery, and the whole plateau about Mechanicsville was abandoned to the Confederates, the Federals retiring across Beaver Dam Creek, which was strongly fortified. Our engineers seem to have had little knowledge of the country, and none of the fortifications on the creek. The maps furnished the division commanders were worthless. At a request from General W. D. Pender, who had been roughly handled in attacking works on the creek, Brigadier-General Ripley, of my division, was directed to coöperate with him, and the attack was made about dark. The enemy had intrenchments of great strength and development on the other side of the creek, and had lined the banks with his magnificent artillery. The approach was over an open plain exposed to a murderous fire of all arms, and across an almost impassable stream. The result was, as might have been foreseen, a bloody and disastrous repulse. Nearly every field-officer in the brigade was killed or wounded. It was unfortunate for the Confederates that the crossing was begun before Jackson got in rear of Mechanicsville. The loss of that position would have necessitated the abandonment of the line of Beaver Dam Creek, as in fact it did, the next day. We were lavish of blood in those days, and it was thought to be a great thing to charge a battery of artillery or an earth-work lined with infantry. "It is magnificent, but it is not war," was the sarcastic remark of the French general as he looked on at the British cavalry charge at Balaklava. The attacks on the Beaver Dam intrenchments, on the heights of Malvern Hill, at Gettysburg, etc., were all grand, but of exactly the kind of grandeur which the South could not afford.

A brisk cannonade was kept up on the morning of the 27th for an hour or more from the Federal artillery along the line of Beaver Dam, which was held by a thin line of skirmishers, the main force having retreated to Gaines's

CHARGE OF CONFEDERATES UNDER RIPLEY AND PENDER AT BEAVER DAM CREEK, JUST ABOVE ELLERSON'S MILL.

Mill and New Cold Harbor. A. P. Hill's division was ordered to pursue on to the mill, and my division to take the Bethesda Church road to join Jackson. The works on that road were turned by my division, and some sixty or seventy prisoners holding them were captured. Major Dabney says:

"General Jackson continued his march on the morning of the 27th. When I overtook him he was dismounted in the turnpike road with his cap off before a gentleman sitting on a cedar-stump, who was speaking to him in a suppressed voice. An old acquaintance whom I met told me that this gentleman was General Lee. The conference soon ended, and the march was resumed — deflecting strongly to the east."

General Lee's object in pressing down the Chickahominy was to unmask New Bridge, and thus to establish close communication between the forces defending Richmond and the six divisions attacking the Federal right. A. P. Hill, who marched close to the Chickahominy, succeeded in driving off the Federal troops defending the creek at Gaines's Mill, and advanced until he developed their full line of battle at New Cold Harbor, half a mile beyond. After waiting till 2:30 P. M. to hear from Longstreet, ☆ he advanced his division without support to the attack of the intrenched position of the Federals. He kept up a struggle for two hours, was repulsed and driven back, and in turn repulsed his pursuers. His report says:

"From having been the attacking I now became the attacked; but stubbornly and gallantly was the ground held. My division was thus engaged full two hours before assistance was received. We failed to carry the enemy's lines, but we paved the way for the successful attacks afterward, in which attacks it was necessary to employ the whole of our army on that side of the Chickahominy."

☆ General Lee in his official report says: "The arrival of Jackson on our left was momentarily expected, and it was supposed that his approach would cause the extension of the enemy's line in that direction. Under this impression, Longstreet was held back until this movement should commence."— EDITORS.

OLD COLD HARBOR TAVERN. FROM A PHOTOGRAPH MADE IN 1885.

This view is from the south, from the road by which the Confederate left under Stonewall Jackson and D. H. Hill advanced to attack Porter's right. Five roads meet at this point. Old Cold Harbor consists of one or two houses and a smithy. During the battle of Gaines's Mill the tavern was within the Confederate lines. Two years later, during the bloody engagement of General Grant's campaign, it was within the Union lines. The name is sometimes written Cool Harbor, Coal Harbor, or Cool Arbor; but Mr. Burnet, the present owner of the tavern, says that family tradition admits only Cold Harbor.— EDITORS.

Longstreet came into action after 4 o'clock. He thus describes the difficulties before him:

"In front of me the enemy occupied the wooded slope of Turkey Hill, the crest of which is fifty or sixty feet higher than the plain over which my troops must pass to make an attack. The plain is about a quarter of a mile wide; the farther side was occupied by sharp-shooters. Above these, and on the slope of the hill, was a line of infantry behind trees, felled so as to form a good breastwork. The crest of the hill, some forty feet above the last line, was strengthened by rifle-trenches and occupied by infantry and artillery. In addition to this the plain was enfiladed by batteries on the other side of the Chickahominy. I was, in fact, in the very position from which the enemy wished us to attack him."

All was done that mortals could do by the two gallant divisions struggling against such disadvantages, but nothing decisive could be effected until the full Confederate forces could be brought into action. In the meanwhile, Jackson moved forward on what we afterward found to be the Grapevine Bridge road, my division in advance. A few squads of Federal stragglers were picked up, and some wagons and ambulances were captured. One sutler, in his desperate desire to save his fancy stock, tried to dash his wagon through J. R. Anderson's brigade. He paid no attention to the orders to halt, or to the presented bayonets. Fortunately for him, his horses did not have so much at stake as he had in canned fruits and vegetables, and were quite willing to surrender. Some poor ragged graybacks got toothsome delicacies then, from which they had been long debarred, and of which before nightfall they had no need forever.

About 2 P. M. we reached the neighborhood of McGehee's house, an elevated knoll, which was the Federal right, and from which a dense and tangled swamp extended westward in an irregular curve to Gaines's Mill. Bondurant's battery was brought up to feel the position. Jackson remained with it for a time after the firing began. The battery was badly crippled, and was withdrawn by my order when I perceived the superiority of the enemy's artillery— always the most effective arm of his service. So little was known of the condition of the battle and of the roads, that Jackson posted my division in the woods to the left of the road, and facing toward the firing at Gaines's Mill, in order to intercept the forces that Longstreet and A. P. Hill might drive in that direction! Jackson's report says:

"Hoping that Generals A. P. Hill and Longstreet would soon drive the Federals toward me, I directed General D. H. Hill to move his division to the left of the road, so as to leave between him and the wood on the right of the road an open space, across which I hoped that the enemy would be driven. . . . But it soon becoming apparent from the direction and sound of the firing that General A. P. Hill was hard pressed, I ordered a general advance of my entire corps, which began with General D. H. Hill on the left and extending to the right, through Ewell's, Jackson's, and Whiting's divisions . . . in the order named."

The swamp was to be gotten through, filled with sharp-shooters, and obstructed with felled timber and choked with brushwood. The report continues:

"In advancing to the attack, General D. H. Hill had to cross this swamp densely covered with tangled undergrowth and young timber. This caused some confusion and a separation of regiments. On the farther edge of the swamp he encountered the enemy. The conflict was fierce and bloody. The Federals fell back from the wood under the protection of a fence, ditch, and hill. Separated now from them by an open field, some four hundred yards wide, he promptly determined to press forward. Before doing so, however, it was necessary to capture a battery on his left which could enfilade his line upon its advance. . . ↓ Again pressing forward, the Federals again fell back, but only to select a position for a more obstinate defense, when at dark, under the pressure of our batteries,— which had then begun to play with marked effect upon the left,— of the other concurring events of the field, and of the bold and dashing charge of General Hill's infantry, in which the troops of Brigadier-General C. S. Winder joined, the enemy yielded the field and fled in disorder."

I have always believed that this was the first break in the Federal line; it disposed of Sykes's division of regulars who had been so stubborn and so troublesome all day. The Comte de Paris says of their retreat: "Fearfully reduced as they are, they care less for the losses they have sustained than for the mortification of yielding to volunteers." The general advance of our whole line and their intrepid onset everywhere made the defeat of the regulars possible, but credit should be given to the troops that did it. We discovered that our line

---

↓ The words of Jackson's report, omitted in the quotation, are as follows:

"The battery was captured with severe loss and held for a short time — sufficiently long, however, to enable the division to move on free from its terrific fire, when it was again retaken by the enemy."

This refers to the battle around the McGehee house, the right of Porter's line under command of General George Sykes. The latter gives an account of the contest with Hill differing from that of the Confederate generals. He says:

"It was now 5:30 P. M. The enemy still continued to pour in fresh troops against 4500 men who had baffled him at every point since 11 o'clock in the morning. The excess of strength compelled the 12th and 14th [Regulars] to occupy the crest of a secondary ridge somewhat in rear of the position they had previously won. . . . Previous to this a brigade of volunteers, under Colonel J. J. Bartlett, consisting of the 16th and 27th New York, 5th Maine, and 96th Pennsylvania volunteers, and Kingsbury's battery Regular Artillery, joined my command. Under my direction, Colonel Bartlett posted the regiments of his brigade with great daring in front of and around the McGehee house, and firmly maintained himself until the center of Porter's army was pierced, the troops in his front driven in, his left flank exposed, and his position no longer tenable."

General Bartlett states in his report that he maintained his ground at the McGehee farm until after dark. See also pp. 339, 340. EDITORS.

overlapped that of the Federal forces, and saw two brigades (afterward ascertained to be under Lawton and Winder) advancing to make a front attack upon the regulars. Brigadier-Generals Samuel Garland and G. B. Anderson, commanding North Carolina brigades in my division, asked permission to move forward and attack the right flank and rear of the division of regulars. The only difficulty in the way was a Federal battery with its infantry supports, which could enfilade them in their advance. Two regiments of Elzey's brigade, which had got separated in going across the swamp, were sent by me, by way of my left flank, to the rear of the battery to attack the infantry supports, while Colonel Alfred Iverson, of the 20th North Carolina, charged it in front. The battery was captured and held long enough for the two brigades to advance across the open plain. "The effect of our appearance," says Garland's official report, "at this opportune juncture [upon the enemy's flank], cheering and charging, decided the fate of the day. The enemy broke and retreated, made a second brief stand, which induced my immediate command to halt under good cover of the bank on the roadside and return their fire, when, charging forward again, they broke and scattered in every direction." Their retreat was to the woods between the field and the river. Swinton gives credit

THE BATTLE-FIELD OF BEAVER DAM CREEK AT ELLERSON'S MILL. AFTER A PHOTOGRAPH TAKEN IN 1885.

This view is taken from the left of the Union position on the east slope, looking up-stream, the ruins of Ellerson's Mill being shown in the middle-ground. The house at the left is Dr. Catlin's. The road past the mill, bending at the bridge over the creek, follows the bed of an old mill-dam (not in use at the time of the fight) for a quarter of a mile, and turns again to the left to Mechanicsville, which is three-quarters of a mile farther, and, from the observer's point of view, directly beyond the Catlin house. The Confederate advance from Mechanicsville was by this road, and by another which strikes the creek nearly a mile farther up. The Union position at this point was held by General Seymour, of McCall's division, with artillery intrenchments, rifle-pits, and abatis. The Confederates came across the open hills and down the slope and along the road (offering their flank to the Union artillery) to the line of the creek (shown by the trees below the bridge), but did not cross it. Their loss in this engagement was frightful. Dr. Catlin's son says that the slope of the hill was fairly covered with dead and wounded. The Catlin farm was occupied chiefly by Ripley's brigade of D. H. Hill's division, and by Pender's brigade of A. P. Hill's. The 44th Georgia alone lost 335 killed and wounded, and its efforts to reform in the rear without officers are described as pathetic. "Good heavens!" said the spectators, "is this all of the 44th Georgia?"

to Hood and Law for making the first break in the Federal line, and quotes from Jackson's report: "Dashing on with unfaltering step in the face of those murderous discharges of canister and musketry, General Hood and Colonel E. M. Law at the head of their respective brigades rushed to the charge with a yell. Moving down a precipitous ravine, leaping ditch and stream, clambering up a difficult ascent, and exposed to an incessant and deadly fire from the intrenchments, these brave and determined men pressed forward, driving the enemy from his well-selected and fortified position. In this charge, in which upward of a thousand men fell killed and wounded before the fire of the enemy, and in which fourteen pieces of artillery and nearly a regiment were captured, the 4th Texas, under the lead of General Hood, was the first to pierce these strongholds and seize the guns." It is evident that Jackson means to compliment Hood for being the first to pierce the intrenchments on the Federal left. But the word "first" has been misleading as to the point where the break was first made in the Federal line.

General Lawton in his official report stated that after the forces were broken in front of him on our left, a staff-officer rode up and called for assistance to charge a battery on the left, and that after marching two or three hundred yards by the *right* flank, "the shouts of victory from our friends announced that the last battery had been taken and the rout complete." In a letter to me just received, General Lawton says: "I do believe that the first break was on the right of the Federal line, and I moved against that line in front. My knowledge of the position of the battery to be charged was derived solely from the lips of a staff-officer, who rode up to me at full speed on the field, and returned immediately to his chief. My recollection is, that very promptly after I heard the shouts of victory from our friends, the same messenger came again to request me to halt. . . . I cannot feel that my memory fails me when I say that you struck the enemy in flank, while Winder's command and mine moved directly on his front. The effect of these several attacks was promptly felt, and soon became conspicuous."

It was now quite dark, and I took the responsibility of halting all the troops on our left. General Winder thought that we ought to pursue into the woods, on the right of the Grapevine Bridge road; but, not knowing the position of our friends, nor what Federal reserves might be awaiting us in the woods, I thought it advisable not to move on. General Lawton concurred with me. I had no artillery to shell the woods in advance, as mine had not got through the swamp. No Confederate officer on the field knew that the Federals had but one bridge over which to retreat, else all the artillery that could have been collected would have opened fire upon the Federal masses crowded into a narrow space in the woods, and there would have been a general advance of our line under cover of this fire. Winder was right; even a show of pressure must have been attended with great results. I made my headquarters at McGehee's house, and ordered my artillery and infantry to occupy the hill around it. The artillery, however, did not get into position until sunrise next morning. Before the infantry was in place, we heard huzzaing on the bridge road, and understood by that that reënforcements had come to cover up the Federal

CHARGE OF A SUTLER UPON J. R. ANDERSON'S BRIGADE AT GAINES'S MILL.

retreat. They took up their position across the road and showed a determined front, but might have been broken by an artillery fire from our elevated plateau; unfortunately for us, there was no artillery to do this work.

Between 9 and 10 o'clock General Lawton and myself walked out alone to examine the line of battle across the road, afterward discovered to be Meagher's Irish brigade. We got within thirty yards of the Federals, and must have been seen, but we were not fired upon, probably because we were mistaken for a party of their own men sent up to get water at McGehee's well. We met the party going back, and saw them go into their own lines. Not a word was spoken by them or by us. At such times "Silence is golden."

After this paper appeared in "The Century" magazine, I received a letter from William H. Osborne, of East Bridgewater, Mass., of which the following is a part:

"I read your article on the battle of Gaines's Mill, Va. I was especially interested in the circumstances related by you concerning the water party sent out from the Irish Brigade to McGehee's well, and the adventure of yourself and General Lawton. I remember the incident with great vividness, as I was one of the party. I was a member of Company "C," 29th Regiment, Massachusetts Volunteers, which was a part of the brigade referred to, but I have always supposed, till I read your article, that

In his attack upon General McClellan's right wing General Lee had 50,000 men. General Fitz John Porter, who commanded the Federals at Cold Harbor, handled his 40,000 men with an ability unsurpassed on any field during the war. He had greatly the advantage in position, and he had improved this superiority with intrenchments, log breastworks, rifle-pits, and abatis. He had an immense preponderance in artillery, and that of the most superb character. Many of our field-batteries did not get across the swamp at all, and those which did get over were inferior in range and power to General Porter's. Artillery seems to have been a favorite arm with General McClellan, and he had brought it to the highest point of efficiency.

I do not know how much of our infantry straggled in the swamp. Ripley got lost, and his fine brigade was not in action at all. Of Colquitt's brigade, the 6th and 27th Georgia regiments were engaged; the other three regiments in coming out of the swamp found themselves behind Jackson's corps and were not engaged. Rodes, Garland, and Anderson kept their brigades well in hand and did brilliant service. (These three splendid officers were all killed, subsequently, in battle.) I do not know how many men the other five divisions lost by the difficulties of the swamp.

Riding in advance of his skirmish-line through the swamp attended by a few staff-officers, General Jackson found himself in the presence of fifteen or twenty Federal soldiers on outpost duty. He judged it the part of prudence to assume the offensive and charge upon them before they fired upon him. I am indebted to Major T. O. Chestney, then assistant adjutant-general of Elzey's brigade, for the following account:

"As Elzey's brigade was pressing forward to the line held by the Confederates at the bloody battle of Gaines's Mill, a squad of fifteen or twenty soldiers were encountered on their way to the rear. A tall fellow at the head of the little party drew special attention to himself by singing out to us at the top of his voice with an oath, 'Gentlemen, we had the honor of being captured by Stonewall Jackson himself,'— a statement which he repeated with evident pride all along the line, as our men tramped past. We subsequently learned that his story was true. General Jackson, having ridden some distance in advance, had come suddenly upon the bluecoats, and with his characteristic impetuosity had charged among them and ordered them to surrender, which they made haste to do."

One of the saddest things connected with the miserable fratricidal war was the breaking up of ties of friendship and of blood. The troops opposing mine on that murderous field that day were the regulars of General George Sykes, a Southerner by birth, and my room-mate at West Point,— a man admired by all for his honor, courage, and frankness, and peculiarly endeared to me by his social qualities. During the negotiations of the cartel for the exchange of prisoners, intrusted to General Dix and myself, I sent word to General Sykes, through Colonel N. B. Sweitzer, of General McClellan's staff, that

it was later in the night when we started. I have also always supposed that in going for water we went inside the Confederate lines. I remember that several times during the night we approached very near your lines, on one occasion actually seeing your men gathered about a smoldering camp-fire in the woods. I suppose you will not blame me for saying that we should all have esteemed it a great honor if we had made your acquaintance that night."
— D. H. H.

Dabney, in his "Life of Jackson," puts the Confederate force at 40,000. Swinton estimates Porter's forces at 30,000 and Lee's at 70,000 — an under and an over estimate respectively, I think.— D. H. H.

General Porter (see foot-note, p. 337) estimates his fighting strength at 30,000, and that of the Confederates at 65,000.— EDITORS.

"CAPTURED BY STONEWALL JACKSON HIMSELF." (SEE P. 359.)

"had I known that he was in front of me at Cold Harbor, I would have sent some of my North Carolina boys up to take him out of the *cold*." He replied through the same source: "I appreciate the sarcasm, but our time will be next and the tables will be turned." Alas! it was a true prophecy. About 9 P. M. on the 27th, Major H. B. Clitz was brought into my room at the McGehee house, headquarters for the night, wounded in the leg, and a prisoner. He was very young and boyish-looking when he entered West Point, and was a very great favorite with us of maturer years. It flashed upon my mind how, in the Mexican war, as his regiment filed past, I had almost a fatherly fear lest he should be struck; and now he was here, wounded by one of my own men! He was tenderly cared for by my medical director, Doctor Mott, and I was delighted to learn that he would not lose his leg. The next morning General John F. Reynolds was brought in as a prisoner. He had been my messmate in the old army for more than a year, and for half that time my tent-mate. Not an unkind word had ever passed between us. General Reynolds seemed confused and mortified at his position. He sat down and covered his face with his hands, and at length said: "Hill, we ought not to be enemies." I told him that there was no bad feeling on my part, and that he ought not to fret at the fortunes of war, which were notoriously fickle. He was placed in my ambulance and sent over to Richmond, declining a loan of Confederate money. General Reynolds had gone to sleep in the woods between the battle-ground and the Chickahominy, and when he awoke, his troops were gone and the bridge was broken down.

Winder, Anderson, and Garland, probably the most promising of all our young brigadiers, fell fighting for the cause they loved. Reynolds, one of the noblest of mankind, fell doing his duty on his side at Gettysburg. Sykes, as the friend of McClellan, never received the recognition which his knightly qualities demanded. Worst of all, Porter, who commanded on the field the most creditable to the Federal arms, received that condemnation so much worse than death from the country he had served ably and loyally.

In these battles, the great want with the Confederates, strange as it may seem, was accurate knowledge of the country in their front. The map furnished me (and I suppose the six other major-generals had no better) was very full in regard to everything within our own lines; but a red line on the east side of the Chickahominy and nearly parallel to it, without any points marked on it, was our only guide to the route on which our march was to be made.[†] None of us knew of the formidable character of the works on Beaver Dam. The blood shed by the Southern troops there was wasted in vain, and worse than in vain; for the fight had a most dispiriting effect on our troops. They could have been halted at Mechanicsville until Jackson had turned the works on the creek, and all that waste of blood could have been avoided. Ripley's brigade was sent to the assistance of Pender, by the direct order, through me, of both Mr. Davis and General Lee. They both felt pressing upon them the vast importance of keeping near Richmond, and of opening up communications with it as soon as possible. The crossing of the river by General A. P. Hill before hearing from Jackson precipitated the fight on the first day; and it having begun, it was deemed necessary to keep it up, without waiting for Jackson. The same necessity compelled Lee on the second day to attack his antagonist on his own strong and well-chosen position. Lee knew that McClellan depended upon the York River Railroad for his supplies, and by moving upon that road he could have compelled the battle upon his own selected ground, with all the advantages thereof. The lack of transportation, and the fear of the capture of Richmond while he was making this détour to the Federal rear, constrained him to surrender the advantage of position wisely chosen by the Federals and skillfully arranged for defense.

During Lee's absence Richmond was at the mercy of McClellan; but

---

[†] General E. M. Law, writing on this point in the "Southern Bivouac," says:

"The real trouble was that the Confederate officers, even those in high command, knew little or nothing of the topography of the country in which they were operating. An accurate map in the hands of each division commander would have saved many valuable lives at Gaines's mill as well as at Ellerson's, and time enough would have been gained to have brought the whole Confederate force upon the field at the former place several hours before it actually reached there. If Porter's lines had been broken at 4 o'clock instead of at half-past 6, he would not have had the cover of night to withdraw his routed troops, and his whole command could have been captured or destroyed in attempting the passage of the Chickahominy. There was no reason why this was not done, except the one given. The Federals, on the other hand, knew the country thoroughly; they had occupied it for several weeks, and during that time their engineer officers had inspected it carefully. . . . There was no earthly reason why the Confederate authorities should not have been possessed of the same information. The Federal Government had been all the previous winter preparing for the advance upon Richmond. McClellan was a long time getting from Yorktown to his position on the Chickahominy, and all his movements indicated the probable position he would take up in front of Richmond. There was no lack of time, therefore, to map the locality accurately, and no lack of warning that it would be of the most vital importance. To undertake the defense of a city, without attempting to learn the topography of the country around it, was a new principle in modern warfare." EDITORS.

Magruder was there to keep up a "clatter," as Swinton expresses it. No one ever lived who could play off the Grand Seignior with a more lordly air than could "Prince John," as Magruder was called.‡ During the absence of Lee he kept up such a clatter that each of McClellan's corps commanders was expecting a special visit from the much-plumed cap and the once-gaudy attire of the master of ruses and strategy. He put on naturally all those grand and imposing devices which deceive the military opponent.

The fortifications around Richmond at that time were very slight. McClellan could have captured the city with very little loss of life. The want of supplies would have forced Lee to attack him as soon as possible, with all the disadvantages of a precipitated movement. But McClellan seems to have contemplated nothing of the kind; and as he placed the continuance of the siege upon the hazard of Cold Harbor, he was bound to put every available man into that fight.

Just before we crossed the Chickahominy, I asked General Garland if he remembered what Napoleon said at Austerlitz when one of his marshals had begged permission to attack a column of the Austro-Russian army which was making a flank movement. Garland replied: "I, too, was just thinking that McClellan was saying to his officers, as Napoleon did, 'When your enemy is making a false movement, do not strike him till he has completed it'; and it may be that he will gobble up Richmond while we are away."

While we were lying all day idle on the 28th, unable to cross the Chickahominy, the clouds of smoke from the burning plunder in the Federal camps and the frequent explosions of magazines indicated a retreat; but Whiting kept insisting upon it that all this was but a *ruse de guerre* of McClellan preparatory to a march upon Richmond. I made to him some such reply as that once made to General Longstreet, when a cadet at West Point, by Professor Kendrick. The Professor asked Longstreet, who never looked at his chemistry, how the carbonic acid of commerce was made. Longstreet replied: "By burning diamonds in oxygen gas." "Yes," said Professor Kendrick, "that will do it; but don't you think it would be a *leetle* expensive?"↓ "Don't you think," I said to Whiting, "that this *ruse* of McClellan is a leetle expensive?" The old West Point yarn had a very quieting effect upon his apprehensions.

---

‡ In ante-bellum days (so the old army story used to run) Magruder was a lieutenant of artillery at Rouse's Point. There his mess entertained some British officers, two of whom were scions of nobility. The visit having been expected, the mess had borrowed or rented gold plate and silver plate, cut-glass ware, rich furniture, and stylish equipages for conveying the noble guests. Prince John assured them that these were but the débris of the former splendor of the regimental mess. "Only the débris, my lord; the schooner bringing most of the mess plate from Florida was wrecked." On the second day of the festival one of the dazzled noblemen said to Prince John: "We do not wish to be inquisitive, but we have been so much impressed with this magnificence that we are constrained to believe that American officers must be paid enormously. What is your monthly pay?" Assuming an indifferent air, Prince John said: "Damned if I know"; then, turning to his servant, "Jim, what is my monthly pay?" The servant was discreetly silent, it may be from a wink, or it may be that to remember $65 was too heavy a tax upon his memory also.— D. H. H.

↓ The professor would never contradict any one. The following is a specimen of his style of questioning. X. Y. Z. (whose name is now a household word) was on examination: Professor K. "What is its color?" X. Y. Z. "White, sir." Professor K. "Yes, you mean a kind of grayish white. In fact, you might call it coal-black, might you not?" X. Y. Z. "Yes, sir, that's it."— D. H. H.

## ON THE CONFEDERATE RIGHT AT GAINES'S MILL.[†]

### BY E. M. LAW, MAJOR-GENERAL, C. S. A.

BY 5 o'clock on the 27th of June the battle of Gaines's Mill was in full progress all along the line. Longstreet's and A. P. Hill's men were attacking in the most determined manner, but were met with a courage as obstinate as their own by the Federals who held the works. After each bloody repulse the Confederates only waited long enough to re-form their shattered lines or to bring up their supports, when they would again return to the assault. Besides the terrific fire in front, a battery of heavy guns on the south side of the Chickahominy was in full play upon their right flank. There was no opportunity for manœuvring or flank attacks, as was the case with D. H. Hill on our extreme left. The enemy was directly in front, and he could only be reached in that direction. If he could not be driven out before night it would be equivalent to a Confederate disaster, and would involve the failure of General Lee's whole plan for the relief of Richmond. . . . It was a critical moment for the Confederates, as victory, which involved the relief or the loss of their capital, hung wavering in the balance. Night seemed about to close the account against them, as the sun was now setting upon their gallant, but so far fruitless efforts.

While matters were in this condition Whiting's division, after crossing with much difficulty the wooded and marshy ground below Gaines's Mill, arrived in rear of that portion of the line held by the remnants of A. P. Hill's division. When Whiting advanced to the attack a thin and irregular line of General Hill's troops was keeping up the fight, but, already badly cut up, could effect nothing, and were gradually wasting away under the heavy fire from the Federal lines. From the center of the division to the Chickahominy swamp on the right the ground was open; on the left were thick woods. The right brigade (Law's) advanced in the open ground, the left (Hood's) through the woods.

As we moved forward to the firing we could see the straggling Confederate line lying behind a gentle ridge that ran across the field parallel to the Federal position. We passed one Confederate battery in the edge of the field badly cut to pieces and silent. Indeed, there was no Confederate artillery then in action on that part of the field. The Federal batteries in front were in full play. The fringe of woods along the Federal line was shrouded in smoke, and seemed fairly to vomit forth a leaden and iron hail. General Whiting rode along his line and ordered that there should be no halt when we reached the slight crest occupied by the few Confederate troops in our front, but that the charge should begin at that point in double-quick time, with trailed arms and without firing. Had these orders not been strictly obeyed the assault would have been a failure. No troops could have stood long under the withering storm of lead and iron that beat into their faces as they became fully exposed to view from the Federal lines. As it was, in the very few moments it took them to pass over the slope and down the hill to the ravine, a thousand men were killed or wounded.

Law's brigade advanced to the attack in two lines, the 11th Mississippi regiment (Colonel Liddell) and the 4th Alabama (Lieutenant-Colonel McLemore) forming the first line, and the 2d Mississippi (Colonel Stone) and the 6th North Carolina (Colonel Avery) the second. Hood had a similar formation on our left, but just as we came under fire, and before reaching the slope where the charge began, General Hood passed rapidly across my rear at the head of the 4th Texas regiment, closely followed by the 18th Georgia, both of his brigade. They came up on my right, extending our line in that direction. The 1st and 5th Texas regiments and the Hampton Legion of the same brigade remained on the left in the woods. Passing over the scattering line of Confederates on the ridge in front, the whole division "broke into a trot" down the slope toward the Federal works. Men fell like leaves in an autumn wind, the Federal artillery tore gaps in the ranks at every step, the ground in rear of the advancing column was strewn thickly with the dead and wounded; not a gun was fired in reply; there was no confusion, and not a step faltered as the two gray lines swept silently and swiftly on; the pace became more rapid every moment; when the men were within thirty yards of the ravine, and could see the desperate nature of the work in hand, a wild yell answered the roar of Federal musketry, and they rushed for the works. The Confederates were within ten paces of them when the Federals in the front line broke cover, and, leaving their log breastworks, swarmed up the hill in their rear, carrying away their second line with them in their rout. Then we had our "innings." As the blue mass surged up the hill in our front, the Confederate fire was poured into it with terrible effect. The target was a large one, the range short, and scarcely a shot fired into that living mass could fail of its errand. The debt of blood contracted but a few moments before was paid, and with interest.

Firing as they advanced, the Confederates leaped into the ravine, climbed out on the other side, and over the lines of breastworks, reaching the crest of the hill beyond with such rapidity as to capture all of the Federal artillery (fourteen pieces) at that point. We had now reached the high plateau in rear of the center of General Porter's position, his line having been completely cut in two, and thus rendered no longer tenable. From the flanks of the great gap where Whiting's division had torn through, the Federal lines gave way in both directions. R. H. Anderson's brigade, till then

---

[†] This description of the fighting in front of Morell's line is from an extended paper on "The Fight for Richmond in 1862," which appeared in "The Southern Bivouac" for April, 1887.— EDITORS.

in reserve, passed through on the right, and led the way for Longstreet's division, while on the left the roll of musketry receded toward the Chickahominy, and the cheering of the victorious Confederates announced that Jackson, Ewell, and D. H. Hill were sweeping that part of the field.

The battle was won; the Federal infantry was in full flight toward the swamps of the Chickahominy and the bridges in their rear, leaving a large portion of their artillery in the hands of the Confederates. But the fighting was not all over. Several Federal batteries, posted in reserve on the further side of the plateau which the Confederates had gained, opened a rapid but rather ineffective fire, with the view of covering the retreat of their infantry. The 4th Texas and 18th Georgia regiments of Hood's, and the 11th Mississippi and 4th Alabama of Law's brigade, continued their advance across the plateau directly upon these batteries. And here occurred an incident of the battle which has been a subject of much acrimonious dispute among Federal officers, especially Generals Porter and Philip St. George Cooke, the latter commanding the cavalry on Porter's extreme left next to the Chickahominy. In order to protect the guns upon which Law and Hood were advancing, General Cooke withdrew a portion of his command from the low grounds near the river and ordered a charge by a battalion of the 5th United States Cavalry upon the advancing Confederates. Our line was ragged and irregular, as every soldier knows will be the case after such fighting as it had passed through, and the opportunity seemed favorable to check its farther advance and save the batteries from capture. The charge was directed upon the center of the Confederate line, which was halted and partly re-formed to receive it. Though delivered in most gallant style, it was repulsed with heavy loss, including all but *one* of the officers who entered it. This episode consumed scarcely more time than it takes to write it. In the meantime, those of the cavalry who escaped retreated through the artillery they were attempting to save, and in the confusion of the retreat most of the guns were captured.

General Porter represents this charge as having been made on his extreme left (Longstreet's right), and beyond the stream along which his infantry line was originally formed, and severely censures General Cooke, charging him with throwing the artillery into confusion by retreating through it and preventing it from checking the Confederate advance. His statement as to the locality of the cavalry attack and his charges against General Cooke cannot be reconciled; for, had Cooke's cavalry attacked where General Porter says it did, it would have been utterly impossible for its line of retreat to have passed anywhere near the position of the batteries, and its flight after the repulse could have had no effect whatever upon the loss of the guns. Hood's and Law's line of advance was directly across the plateau from the left center of Porter's original line, where they had broken in, passing south of and near the Watts house on the plateau; and as the cavalry charge was made upon *them*, and *they* captured the guns, it follows that the charge could only have been made *there*, and *not* half a mile nearer the Chickahominy, where it would have been objectless, and indeed ridiculous. I speak positively on this point, as I was an eye-witness of the whole affair, commanded the troops who received the charge, and was engaged in the capture of the guns. Whatever may be said to the contrary, it is certain that the batteries, having no infantry supports, did not check our advance for a moment. The diversion by the cavalry, on the other hand, did delay their capture for the short period it took to repulse it, and gave time for the artillerists to save some of their guns.

While these events were taking place on the plateau, heavy firing was going on immediately upon the left of the gap in the Federal line through which we had passed, now some distance in our rear. As the front was clear, my brigade was halted and re-formed. This had scarcely been done when a Confederate cheer rose from the woods in the direction of the firing, and a large body of Federals rushed out upon the plateau on our left and rear, retreating rapidly and in great confusion. Part of them passed to our left, while the greater portion were running across our rear in the attempt to escape to the Chickahominy swamp in that direction. My rear rank was faced about, and they were called on to surrender. No attention was paid to the first summons, and a few shots were fired into our ranks. A volley from our rear rank, which now faced them, induced them to listen to reason, and they at once threw down their arms in token of surrender.☆ The 1st and 5th Texas regiments and the Hampton Legion (Hood's brigade), which it will be remembered were on the left of Law's brigade in the original line of

---

☆ These troops were the 11th Pennsylvania Reserves, of McCall's division, and the 4th New Jersey, Slocum's division. The 11th lost 50 killed, and 634, including wounded, were made prisoners.

Colonel J. H. Simpson, of the 4th New Jersey, explains the circumstances of the capture in a letter written from the military prison, Richmond, Va., July 8th, 1862, in which he says:

"To relieve my friends of all apprehension about my safety, I write to say that I am now here a prisoner of war, with a large portion of my regiment, and in good health and spirits. My regiment was posted in the wood to sustain the center in the battle near Gaines's Mill, on Friday, June 27th, and nobly did it hold its ground till about an hour after the right and left wings of the army had fallen back. Mine (4th New Jersey) and Colonel Gallagher's 11th Pennsylvania Reserve were the last to leave the front, and only did so when we found that the rest of the army had given way, and we were literally surrounded by the infantry and batteries of the Confederate forces.

"Being in the woods, and trusting to our superior officers to inform us when to retreat, and not being able to see on account of the woods what was going on toward our right and left, we continued fighting probably an hour after every other regiment had left the ground. The consequence was inevitable. We were surrounded by ten times our number, and though we could have fought till every man of us was slain, yet humanity, and, as I think, wisdom, dictated that we should at last yield. . . . Our casualties, so far as known, were: killed, 38; wounded, 111,—total 149,— besides 75 missing, of whom a number probably was killed and wounded. Considering the great jeopardy in which we were, I look upon it as a great mercy we all were not shot down." EDITORS.

attack, had not driven the Federal line in their front at the same time with the rest of the division; but they had now forced it, and were closely following the fugitives. The prisoners, about 800 in number, were turned over to the 5th Texas regiment, which was close on their heels.

## THE CAUSE OF A SILENT BATTLE.

BY PROFESSOR JOHN B. DE MOTTE, DE PAUW UNIVERSITY, IND.

REFERENCE has been made to the supposed effect of the wind in preventing, as in the case of the heavy cannonading between the *Merrimac* and *Congress*, the transference of sound-waves a distance of not over three and one-half miles over water; and at another time, during the bombardments of the Confederate works at Port Royal, a distance of not more than two miles. "The day was pleasant," says the writer, "and *the wind did not appear unusually strong.*" Yet "people living in St. Augustine, Florida, told me afterward that the Port Royal cannonade was heard at that place, 150 miles from the fight."

It occurs to me that the effect of the wind is greatly exaggerated in these instances. How an ordinary breeze could " carry all sounds of the conflict away from people standing within plain sight of it " and yet carry the same sound 150 miles in the opposite direction, is rather too strongly opposed to scientific fact to remain on record undisputed.

In all of these cases, is it not probable that the varying density of the air had much more to do with this strange acoustic opacity than the wind? These instances call to mind the prevalent belief that fog, snow, hail, and rain, indeed, any conditions of the atmosphere that render it optically opaque, render it also acoustically opaque; which, up to the time of Mr. Tyndall's experiments in the English Channel, off Dover, had scarcely been questioned. His tests made in 1873–74 proved conclusively, as is now well known, that on clear days the air may be composed of differently heated masses, saturated in different degrees with aqueous vapors, which produce exactly the deadening effects described above.

I submit as a case in point a similar effect, and its explanation as furnished by Mr. R. G. H. Kean to Professor Tyndall, and considered by the latter of sufficient value to find a place in his published works:

"On the afternoon of June 27th, 1862, I rode, in company with General G. W. Randolph, then Secretary of War of the Confederate States, to Price's house, about nine miles from Richmond. The evening before General Lee had begun his attack on McClellan's army, by crossing the Chickahominy about four miles above Price's, and driving in McClellan's right wing.

"The battle of Gaines's Mill was fought the afternoon to which I refer. The valley of the Chickahominy is about one and a half miles wide from hill-top to hill-top. Price's is on one hill-top, that nearest to Richmond; Gaines's farm, just opposite, is on the other, reaching back in a plateau to Cold Harbor.

"Looking across the valley, I saw a good deal of the battle, Lee's right resting in the valley, the Federal left wing the same. My line of vision was nearly in the line of the lines of battle. I saw the advance of the Confederates, their repulse two or three times, and in the gray of the evening the final retreat of the Federal forces. I distinctly saw the musket-fire of both lines, the smoke, individual discharges, the flash of the guns. I saw batteries of artillery on both sides come into action and fire rapidly. Several field-batteries on each side were plainly in sight. Many more were hid by the timber which bounded the range of vision.

"Yet looking for nearly two hours, from about 5 to 7 P. M. on a midsummer afternoon, at a battle in which at least 50,000 men were actually engaged, and doubtless at least 100 pieces of field-artillery, through an atmosphere optically as limpid as possible, *not a single sound of the battle* was audible to General Randolph and myself. I remarked it to him at the time as astonishing.

"Between me and the battle was the deep, broad valley of the Chickahominy, partly a swamp shaded from the declining sun by the hills and forest in the west (my side). Part of the valley on each side of the swamp was cleared: some in cultivation, some not. Here were conditions capable of providing several belts of air, varying in the amount of watery vapor (and probably in temperature), arranged like laminæ at right angles to the acoustic waves as they came from the battle-field to me."

---

For references to the phenomena of irregular transmission of sound at the battles on the Chickahominy, see the articles of Generals Joseph E. Johnston, Gustavus W. Smith, and Wm. B. Franklin, pp. 213, 244, and 368, respectively. In Vol. I., p. 713, General R. E. Colston, mentions the interesting fact about the engagement between the *Congress* and *Merrimac*, at the mouth of the James River, March 8th, 1862.

The Port Royal incident was related in a communication to "The Century" magazine by Mr. S. H. Prescott, of Concord, N. H., in part as follows: "At the bombardment of the Confederate works at Port Royal, South Carolina, in November, 1861, the transport my regiment was on lay near enough inshore to give us a fine view of the whole battle; but only in some temporary lull of the wind could we hear the faintest sound of firing. The day was a pleasant one, and the wind did not appear to be unusually strong; but I noticed then and afterward that a breeze on the coast down that way was very different from the erratic gusts and flaws I had been used to in the New England States, the whole atmosphere seeming to move in a body, giving sound no chance to travel against it, but carrying it immense distances to the leeward. People living at St. Augustine, Florida, told me afterward that the Port Royal cannonade was heard at that place, 150 miles from where the fight took place. A portion of the siege-batteries at Morris Island, South Carolina, were not more than two miles from our camp, but at times the firing from them and the enemy's replies could only be heard very faintly even at that short distance, while at others, when the wind blew from the opposite direction, the sounds were as sharp and distinct as if the battle were taking place within a few rods of us."

General E. M. Law, of Lee's army, in the "Southern Bivouac" for May, 1887, speaks as follows of the "silent battle" of Gaines's Mill: "To the troops stationed near the river, on the Richmond side, the action at Gaines's Mill was plainly visible, that part of it, at least, which took place in the open ground. I have been told by an eye-witness that from Price's house, on the opposite side, he could distinctly see the Confederate lines advancing to the attack through the open ground beyond the Chickahominy swamp, and could distinguish the direction of the lines of battle by the volume of smoke arising from the woods farther to the Confederate center and left. But it was all like a pantomime; not a sound could be heard, neither the tremendous roar of the musketry nor even the reports of the artillery. As they saw our assaulting lines recoil from the onset, as they were several times compelled to do early in the fight, the anxiety of our friends 'over the river' to help was intense; but the enemy was in their front also, and their time for action would soon come." EDITORS.

# REAR-GUARD FIGHTING DURING THE CHANGE OF BASE.

### BY WILLIAM B. FRANKLIN, MAJOR-GENERAL, U. S. V.

THE positions of the troops holding the Union line on the south side of the Chickahominy on the 26th of June, 1862 (the day before the battle of Gaines's Mill), were the following: General W. F. Smith's division of my corps, the Sixth, held the right of the line, its right resting on the hill overlooking the Chickahominy [two miles north of Fair Oaks station], and my other division, General Slocum's, was next on the left. Going toward the left, General Sumner's corps came next, then General Heintzelman's, and then, on the extreme left reaching to White Oak Swamp, General Keyes's corps.↓ On the 26th an epaulement was thrown up by the troops of the Sixth Corps in a wheat-field in front of our lines on Golding's farm, which was ready for guns on the morning of the 27th. During the night of the 26th five batteries of the Artillery Reserve, under the command of Colonel (now General) G. W. Getty, were collected in rear of the epaulement, ready to take position in it and commence a heavy artillery fire on the enemy's line opposite. [See map, p. 384.] Golding's is near the Chickahominy on the extreme right of the Union intrenched line. Five days' rations, cold tea in the canteens, etc., etc., had been issued, so that everything was ready to follow up the projected bombardment, which it was presumed would commence on the morning of the 27th. But on the evening of the 26th the fight at Beaver Dam Creek occurred, and General McClellan called at my headquarters on his way to confer with General Porter as to his operations of the next day. I was then absent at General Slocum's headquarters, conferring with him in regard to the attack we were expecting to make, and therefore missed General McClellan, so that I received no word from him until the next morning.

About daylight on the 27th I received orders to send General Slocum's division across the Chickahominy to report to General Porter. This order was countermanded a short time after the division had started by way of Woodbury's Bridge, and it returned to its station. About 10:30 o'clock in the morning the enemy opened on our artillery with theirs, doubtless unaware of

UNIFORM OF THE 72D PENNSYLVANIA, BAXTER'S FIRE ZOUAVES.

---

↓ General Heintzelman's corps, the 3d, advanced to the positions held by its outposts on the 26th, after a sharp engagement along the whole line on the 25th, known as Oak Grove, or King's School House. Oak Grove was the first of the Seven Days' battles. The Union loss was 67 killed, 504 wounded, 55 missing. The Confederate reports show a total loss of 441. (For the strategy of this movement see General McClellan's article, page 179.) The ground secured by this action varied in front of the different brigades, and was from a quarter of a mile to one mile in advance of the line that had been held by the Third Corps since the battle of Seven Pines.— EDITORS.

UNION TROOPS BUILDING THE CORDUROY APPROACHES TO GRAPEVINE BRIDGE. FROM A WAR-TIME PHOTOGRAPH.
It was mainly by this bridge that the Union troops were withdrawn the night after the battle of Gaines's Mill.

the five batteries of reserve artillery mentioned above. The fire was kept up for an hour, and as theirs slackened, so did ours, until both sides ceased firing. Two hours before the bombardment began I received orders not to do anything to bring on a general engagement, and after the cessation of the artillery fire everything was quiet in our front for several hours. At 2 o'clock I was ordered again to send General Slocum's division to report to General Porter. The division went, became engaged at once in the battle of Gaines's Mill, where it lost very heavily, and did not return to its station until after nightfall.

During the afternoon several of the heavy guns with us were used with effect on columns of the enemy on the north side of the Chickahominy moving against General Porter, causing them to fall back and seek some other route of attack. The range was about two and one-half miles. About sundown General Hancock's brigade, which held the extreme right of General Smith's line, was attacked furiously by the enemy. It was nearly dark when the fight began, and the combatants were not fifty yards apart; but General Hancock was, as usual, equal to the occasion, and the enemy was driven back. This fight was preceded by a severe artillery fire from the enemy, which, however, was soon silenced. This day's operations of Smith's division were known as "The Action at Golding's [or Garnett's] Farm."

The position held by General Smith's division was about one and one-half miles from the Gaines's Mill field; and, possibly because the interval was

THE RETREAT FROM THE CHICKAHOMINY. FROM A SKETCH MADE ON THE FIELD AT THE TIME.

The scene is near McClellan's headquarters at Dr. Trent's farm, before daylight on Sunday, June 29th; the Sixth Corps (Franklin's) is falling back; the fires are from the burning of commissary stores and forage; the artillery in position underneath the guns. The regiment in the middle-ground is the 16th New York, who wore straw hats in this campaign, and were, partly in consequence, such conspicuous targets for the enemy that in the Seven Days' fighting they lost 228 men.— EDITORS.

filled with dense timber, not a gun of the Gaines's Mill battle was heard by the troops in our vicinity.

The next morning, the 28th of June, General Smith's division was moved to the rear and left of the clearing of Golding's farm; General Slocum's division remaining to the rear and right of Smith, where it had taken position the night before. During this retrograde movement the enemy kept up a lively cannonade from the left, front, and right, but did remarkably little harm. A sharp infantry attack, however, was made upon the 49th Pennsylvania regiment, Colonel Irwin, and the 33d New York regiment, Colonel Taylor, who were the last to evacuate the position. The time of the attack was about the middle of the afternoon, and the attacking force was the 7th and 8th Georgia regiments. It was handsomely repulsed, and Colonels Lamar and Towers of the Georgia regiments with 50 officers and men were taken prisoners, and more than 100 were killed and wounded. [This action of the 28th, as also that of the 27th,— see p. 367,— is known as Golding's and Garnett's Farms.]‡ That evening the corps commanders were assembled at General McClellan's headquarters at the Trent house.

DR. TRENT'S FARM-HOUSE, McCLELLAN'S HEADQUARTERS.
FROM A PHOTOGRAPH TAKEN IN 1885.

General McClellan's tents were under the two trees at the right. The Chickahominy lies to the left behind the house, and is a little more than half a mile distant.

The commanding general announced to us his purpose to begin a movement to the James River on the next day, and each corps commander was furnished with a map on which were laid down the positions that the respective corps were to hold until the next evening, when all the troops remaining near their present positions were to move across the White Oak Swamp *en route* for the James. The assembly broke up about 2 o'clock in the morning, each corps commander having received all the information necessary to determine his action for the 29th, should nothing unforeseen occur.

The relative position of the Sixth Corps was not changed. Smith's division was still to have its right on the Chickahominy, extending down the river, where it was to touch the left of McCall's division (that crossed the Chickahominy during the night of the 27th), which, however, played no part in holding the line on June 29th, as it crossed White Oak Swamp early in the day.

‡ Also on the 28th a detachment of Cobb's Georgia Legion (cavalry) had a skirmish at Dispatch Station with the pickets of the 8th Illinois Cavalry.—EDITORS.

THE BATTLE OF SAVAGE'S STATION. FROM A SKETCH MADE AT THE TIME.

The 2500 sick and wounded in the field-hospitals, and their attendants, were left behind when the army fell back from Savage's Station, during the night following the engagement. The explosion on the railway is of a Union ordnance train. Other ordnance trains were set on fire and were run back to Bottom's bridge, where they plunged into the Chickahominy, as shown in the picture on the next page.

General Slocum's division was to be at Savage's Station, in reserve. Then came Sumner's corps and Heintzelman's. Keyes's corps was to cross the White Oak Swamp at once. Porter's corps had already crossed the swamp, and was under orders to press forward to a position on the James River.

This new line was about two miles nearer the White Oak Bridge than the intrenched line in front of Fair Oaks and Golding's farm (described above), and was nearly parallel. It was much shorter than the old line, its left reaching nearly to the swamp, and its right to the brink of the Chickahominy hills. This second line was about three-quarters of a mile in front of Savage's Station on the York River Railroad, which had been the depot for unloading and storing supplies for the troops that held the old line, and where had been gathered in tents 2500 sick and wounded, most of the latter from Gaines's Mill.

General Slocum's and General Smith's divisions both moved to their new positions before daylight of Sunday, the 29th of June — the day of the fighting at Savage's Station. As General Slocum's division had suffered so severely in the battle of Gaines's Mill, and had not yet recovered from its exhaustion, General McClellan ordered it to cross White Oak Swamp at once, and it accordingly left its position. Through some inadvertence I was not informed of this change of plan; so when I joined General Smith early in the morning, I found him in his proper position, but with an interval of more than a mile between him and the troops on the left. It was soon learned, by sending out cavalry, that General Sumner had not moved from the position that he held the day before, and was, at the very time we learned this fact, engaged with the enemy at Allen's farm.↓ It was also apparent that straggling parties of the enemy were in front of the interval already mentioned. These circumstances showed an alarming state of things, and General Smith and I rode over to Savage's Station to learn something of the positions of other troops. We found no troops in the vicinity except General Meagher's brigade and the 15th Massachusetts Infantry, which had been sent to the station to destroy the stores that had to be abandoned. I at once wrote General Sumner, describing the situation, and informing him that I should move General Smith's division to Savage's Station, the vicinity of which offered a good fighting position, and advising him to bring his corps to that place. He answered the note at once, telling me that he was then engaged with the enemy, and that as soon as things were quiet he would join me with his corps. Soon after I had sent to General Sumner General Heintzelman rode up, and I told him what I had done. He approved, and said that he would also join us at the station with his corps. He afterward changed his mind, however, and instead of halting in the wood in front of the station, as we naturally supposed he would, he marched off toward White Oak Bridge, hidden from us by the woods, and crossed the swamp, so that we saw him no more that day, supposing, nevertheless, until we were attacked by the enemy, that his troops were in position on a part of our front.♭ General Smith's division arrived at the station about noon or shortly after, and took position on the left in a wood. General Sumner's corps, consisting of General John Sedgwick's and General Israel B. Richardson's divisions, arrived about 2 P. M.

RUNNING AMMUNITION TRAINS INTO THE CHICKAHOMINY.

There was a cleared field of several acres on the north side of the railroad, filled with hospital tents laid out in rows, each tent containing fifteen or

---

↓ Sumner's corps, retiring, left the works at Fair Oaks at daylight and halted for bivouac on Allen's farm, between the Williamsburg road and the railroad. The Confederates of Magruder's command opened on the troops at 9 A. M. with musketry and artillery, and a spirited fight was kept up until 11 o'clock. This engagement is known also as the Peach Orchard.— EDITORS.

♭ General Heintzelman in his report says: "The whole open space near Savage's was crowded with troops — more than I supposed could be brought into action judiciously." He then states that an aide of the commanding general was with him to point out the road for his crossing. "I ordered the whole of my corps to take this road, with the exception of Osborn's and Bramhall's batteries." These were turned over to General Smith's division.— W. B. F.

VIEW OF SAVAGE'S STATION FROM THE NORTH SIDE OF THE RAILROAD. FROM A SKETCH MADE BEFORE THE BATTLE.

The railroad passes close to the south side of Savage's house. In the foreground are shown burial trenches, and in the peach orchard the graves of officers. The negro cabins on the left were used by the Sanitary Commission; the barn, on the right, was a hospital, but most of the wounded were sheltered in the tents.

twenty men on comfortable, clean beds, with the necessary surgeons and attendants. South of the railroad, and between it and the Williamsburg road, was another clearing, east of which was a ravine running obliquely across the railroad, its edges skirted by trees, and the ravine itself filled with undergrowth. This clearing was nearly square, and was about one-third or one-half mile in length and breadth. In front of the ravine were some small hills which made good shelter for the troops; and west of the clearing was timber, where we supposed General Heintzelman's troops to be; on the left of the Williamsburg road was timber also, and General Smith's division was in position therein. Sumner's corps took position in the clearing between the Williamsburg road and the railroad. Burns's brigade of Sedgwick's division was in front, Sedgwick's other two brigades being just behind. The three brigades of Richardson's division, Meagher having joined him, were farther to the rear, but more to the right. Three batteries of field-artillery, Hazzard's, Pettit's, and Osborn's, were posted toward the left, near the front of the ravine.

The day was hot and sultry and wore away slowly as we waited either to be attacked or at nightfall to start for White Oak Bridge. Large quantities of all kinds of quartermasters' and other stores, partly in cars, were burning at the station, and at intervals shells would burst as the fire reached them, jarring the nerves of the tired and expectant men.

Shortly before 4 o'clock General Sedgwick and I rode over to the hospital to visit some of our wounded friends, whose condition was found to be as comfortable as could be expected under the circumstances. From the hospital we started to make a call upon General Heintzelman, whose supposed position has already been described. As we rode over the open field we saw a group of men come out of a wood on the north of the railroad, but some distance from the place where we expected to find Heintzelman. I thought they were our men, but General Sedgwick looked at them more closely, stopped, and exclaimed: "Why, those men are rebels!" We then turned back in as dignified a manner as the circumstances would permit. But we had hardly started when they opened on us with a field-piece, keeping up a lively and uncomfortable fire. A second piece soon joined the first, and they kept up the fire until they were silenced by our batteries. This ludicrous incident prevented what might have been a disastrous surprise for our whole force. A few minutes afterward, before we had reached our troops, the signal-officers reported the approach of a force of infantry and a railroad car upon which was a rifled cannon, from the direction of Richmond. This artillery car halted in a cut of the railroad a little distance in front of the station, and at once began to shell the troops in the open field, and so about 5 o'clock the fight was begun. I immediately sought General Sumner, to inform him of the situation and get instructions. He had been fighting at the head of his corps during the morning [at the peach orchard], and, being much exhausted, was asleep when I reached his headquarters. I awoke him, and in a short time he had ordered two regiments of General Burns's brigade to attack at a point in the timber in front near the Williamsburg road, where the enemy's infantry had by this time appeared. These regiments entered the wood, and before they became engaged were joined by the 1st Minnesota Regiment. General Burns extended his line to the vicinity of the railroad, so that its center was necessarily weak. During this movement the enemy's artillery played with effect upon our troops, but was answered and finally silenced by the three batteries on our side already mentioned.

The enemy made the infantry attack with great fury, and pierced the center of General Burns's line. General Burns was wounded, but remained on the field. At this time General Sumner placed himself in front of two regiments and waved his hat. With a cheer they moved forward at double time to the endangered place in General Burns's line, enabling him to rectify it and drive the enemy from his front. Several other regiments joined General Burns's line at about the same time, but the fight was over not long after the charge, and the enemy was driven from the wood. A Confederate battery placed near the Williamsburg road was compelled to withdraw in haste. On the left General Brooks's brigade of General Smith's division, Sixth Corps, moved forward, with its right on the Williamsburg road, against a force of the enemy that was moving south of that road in the wood skirting the open field. It steadily drove back the enemy, meeting with heavy loss, particularly in the 5th Vermont Regiment. Darkness ended the fight. General Brooks was wounded in the leg, but did not leave the field. Hancock's and Davidson's brigades [Smith's division] were posted some distance to the rear to repel an anticipated attack from the right and rear, but were not engaged. When the fight

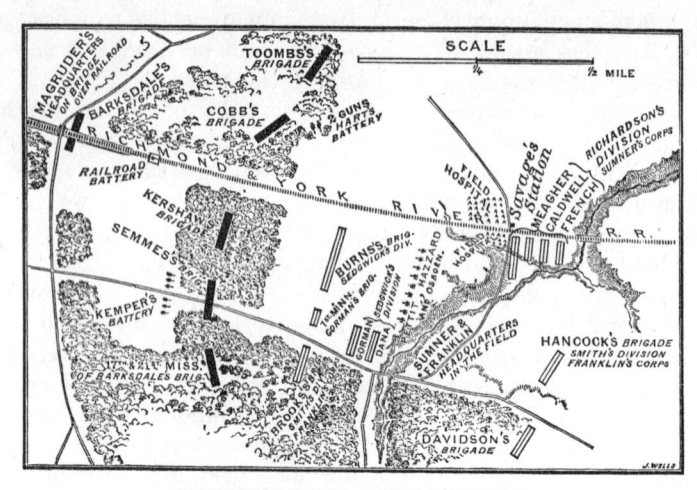

PLAN OF THE BATTLE AT SAVAGE'S STATION.

The order in which the Union troops entered the fight is thus described by General William W. Burns, in a letter dated Governor's Island, May 10th, 1885:

"The enemy appearing in the woods west of Savage's Station, General Sumner sent me forward to occupy the space between the Williamsburg road and the railroad. Thinking that two regiments of my brigade would suffice, I led them forward to the fences, at the edge of the woods on the west side of the clearing, about five hundred yards distant from the ravine on the east side of the clearing. General Sumner had his headquarters east of this wooded ravine and could not observe what was occurring on the west side of the open field.

"When I reached the fences I sent skirmishers through the belt of trees, and found the enemy advancing on the Williamsburg road and on the railroad, where General Lee's famous railroad monitor was slowly approaching. I had to throw back the right company of the right regiment, the 72d Pennsylvania, to rake the monitor. Then I found my two regiments not enough to extend across between the Williamsburg road and the railroad. I sent an aide in haste after my other two regiments, informing General Sumner of the situation. The 1st Minnesota, of Gorman's brigade, being most handy, was first sent, my two reserve regiments following. While placing the 1st Minnesota on the left to extend across the Williamsburg road, the battle began. My right flank swept the railroad monitor, which had advanced to the edge of the woods, and it ran back. The battle moved to my left, and I discovered that our works east of Seven Pines had been evacuated by Heintzelman. I threw back the left flank of the 1st Minnesota across the Williamsburg road and sent the 69th Pennsylvania of my brigade to prolong the left, to prevent the turning movement of the enemy; at the same time informing General Sumner of the conditions in front. He would not believe that Heintzelman had withdrawn until I sent my last mounted man, urging and demanding reënforcements. The 71st Pennsylvania (also called the 1st California), of my brigade, arriving, I placed it behind the center of my line where a gap had been made by extending the 1st Minnesota to the left. General Franklin sent General Brooks's brigade to the left of my line to check the turning movement of the enemy, and Sumner, when he realized that Heintzelman had withdrawn, sent Gorman's and Dana's brigades to my support in front.

"General Sumner formed the 88th New York, of Meagher's brigade, and the 5th New Hampshire, of Caldwell's brigade, for a charge. A mass of men came up in my rear in full yell. I halted the crowd and asked for their commander. 'I am Captain McCartan of the 88th New York, sir,' exclaimed an officer. I got them into line (about 250 men), facing up the Williamsburg road, which was raked by the grape and canister of the enemy's batteries. I gave the command, double quick — charge! They went in with a hurrah, and the enemy's battery fell back. General McClellan mistakenly gave the credit of that gallant charge to the 69th New York. It seems that the 5th New Hampshire halted before the charge which General Sumner had put in motion reached me.

"I was shot in the face with a minie-ball at the time the enemy broke through the gap in the center. There we had a hand-to-hand encounter, which determined the day in our favor. At nightfall I relieved the first line, its ammunition being exhausted, with the 71st Pennsylvania, the 15th and 20th Massachusetts, and the 82d New York. My report of the Seven Days' fighting was made at Harrison's Bar in hot July. I was prostrated with my wound, malaria, and twenty-eight days of constant strain, and was unable to write or to collect my thoughts. The battle at Glendale on the 30th of June, the next day after that of Savage's Station, was saved by my brigade, which kept the enemy from piercing the center of the Army of the Potomac; but, like the instance above, history has given the credit to 'General Misunderstanding,' who, in history, fights most battles."

Parts of Hazzard's, Pettit's, and Osborn's batteries were engaged on the Union side.

The Confederate infantry north of the railroad (Cobb's, Toombs's, and Anderson's brigades) did not take an active part in the battle. Anderson's brigade is not shown, its position being outside the northern bounds of the map.

The Confederate artillery engaged comprised Kemper's battery, two guns of Hart's battery, and Lieutenant Barry's "32-pounder rifled gun mounted on a rail-car, and protected from cannon-shot by a sloping roof, in front, covered with plates of iron, through which a port-hole had been pierced," — EDITORS.

was over, our troops held the contested ground. Their behavior throughout the fight had been admirable.

The Confederate force engaged in this fight was commanded by General J. B. Magruder, and consisted of Semmes's and Kershaw's brigades, Kemper's battery, and two regiments of Barksdale's brigade opposite our left. Cobb's division and two guns of Hart's battery were north of the railroad to the right of our line. Cobb's infantry was not engaged.

About a half-hour after the fight was ended, I suggested to General Sumner that if he had no objection I would carry out the commanding general's orders, so far as I was concerned, and cross the White Oak Swamp with General Smith's division. We were then on the field. His answer was, "No, General, you shall not go, nor will I go—I never leave a victorious field. Why! if I had twenty thousand more men, I would crush this rebellion." I then told him that I would show him a dispatch from General McClellan directing that all of the troops should cross during that night. With some difficulty a candle was found and lighted, and the general read the dispatch. After reading it he exclaimed, with some excitement, "General McClellan did not know the circumstances when he wrote that note. He did not know that we would fight a battle and gain a victory." I was at my wit's end. I knew that General McClellan's arrangements did anticipate a fight exactly like that just over, and that unless the whole force was on the other side of the swamp by the next morning, his movement might be seriously delayed. Moreover, I believed that if we staid where we were, the enemy would be upon us in force enough to defeat us utterly on the next morning, endangering the remainder of the army. Yet by all military usage I was under General Sumner's orders. At this juncture General Smith asked me to introduce Lieutenant Mathew Berry, his aide-de-camp, to General Sumner. After the introduction, Lieutenant Berry told General Sumner that he had seen General McClellan only a short time before, that he knew there had been a fight, and fully expected that all of the troops would cross the swamp that night. General Sumner was convinced by this statement, and with great reluctance permitted me to continue the movement toward the swamp, he following immediately after.

General Smith's division crossed the White Oak Bridge about 3 o'clock on the morning of June 30th, and went into position on the left of the road leading from the bridge toward the James River. The batteries of the division were already there in position. It faced about so that its left rested upon the road, the division bearing southward from the road. At the same time I reported to McClellan at his headquarters.

The rear of Sumner's corps, Richardson's division, crossed the bridge at 10 o'clock in the morning, destroyed it, and took position some distance on Smith's left, nearly in line with him. Both divisions guarded the crossing.

After the fight at Savage's Station was over, Hazzard's battery of Richard-

---

General E. M. Law says in the "Southern Bivouac" for May, 1887: "The battle of Savage's Station, although a 'drawn fight' as far as the possession of the field was concerned, was practically a victory for the Federals. Though their loss was three times as great as that of the Confederates, they accomplished the main purpose of the battle, which was to gain time for the passage of trains, artillery, and troops across White Oak Swamp."

son's division was unhitched, its captain not supposing there was to be any further movement that night, and the men and horses went to sleep, as usual when there was opportunity, which was not often in those days. The division, as has been told, moved off, and by accident no notice of the movement was sent to Captain Hazzard. On the next morning he heard reveille sounded by drums and trumpets from positions that he knew our troops did not hold the evening before. Everything in his vicinity was quiet. He took in the situation at once. He had been left behind, and the enemy might be upon him at any moment. He had the battery quietly hitched up, sent the caissons off in advance, and, bringing up the rear with two guns ready to open on a pursuing force, started off at a walk. When he was clear of the field he ordered the battery to trot. He arrived without harm at the White Oak Bridge at that pace just as General Richardson was on the point of destroying it. He found on the road many stragglers who were coolly wandering along with no suspicion that they were behind everybody, and by his warning was the means of saving many soldiers from a Richmond prison. The pluck and coolness shown in this exploit of Captain Hazzard were admirable. He was killed the next day while doing excellent work with his battery.

As the result of the dispositions made by the commanding general of the troops (a part of whose operations has just been described) a whole day was gained in getting a large part of the army to the James River without serious opposition, and into a proper defensive position; the enormous trains and heavy artillery had been given a start of twenty-four hours, insuring their safe arrival at the river. The rear of the army also had crossed White Oak Swamp, leaving the way clear to the James River, while at the same time a strong force was ready to protect the movement during its completion.

On the enemy's side, the slowness of Jackson in getting his force to the south side of the Chickahominy (he only arrived at Savage's Station at 3 o'clock on the morning of June 30th) had prevented us from being defeated in the fight of June 29th. The 28th and 29th had been occupied by Jackson in disposing of the dead and wounded at Gaines's Mill and in repairing Grapevine Bridge.

On the north (the enemy's) side of White Oak Swamp, the road for more than a quarter of a mile approaches the White Oak Bridge through low ground, open to artillery fire from the south side. [See map, p. 384.] On the right of the enemy, looking to the rear, there were hills covered with thick woods approaching the road, forming good cover for artillery, and making it possible for a large force to gather in the wood unseen from our side. The same range of hills continues up the stream, and approaches quite near it at Brackett's Ford, about one mile above White Oak Bridge. Both of these crossings were passable for artillery, but the bridges had been destroyed by our troops in the morning, after everything had crossed and before the appearance of the enemy.

On our side of the swamp, the ground rises from the bridge, and the road passes along the right, or east, of a ravine and joins the Long Bridge road about one and a quarter miles from the swamp. On the left of the ravine was a cleared space about a half-mile long in the direction of the swamp and running back about the same distance. At the swamp the clearing was fringed with trees and underbrush, and about half-way up the clearing to the left of the ravine were a small farm-house and some slight out-buildings. On the right of the ravine was a similar clearing, extending from the swamp about a furlong back. All other ground in the vicinity was covered with timber and underbrush. (The troops were disposed as shown on the map, p. 470.)

The cleared space at this time had in it many wagons of the train, and Colonel R. O. Tyler's 1st Connecticut Heavy Artillery, which I ordered to the rear at once. Glad enough would I have been to keep this accomplished officer, with his gallant regiment and heavy guns, but we both knew that he was needed at the James River. At about 10:30 in the morning, as near as I can now recollect, I accompanied General McClellan to the intersection of the Charles City and Quaker roads, about two miles from the White Oak Bridge. I found General Slocum's division posted somewhat in rear of the intersection of those roads, and in front of the road leading from Brackett's Ford. A small portion of his infantry and one gun

MAJOR-GENERAL WILLIAM B. FRANKLIN.
From a photograph taken in August, 1862, when General Franklin was temporarily at home on sick leave.

were posted near Brackett's Ford. His division formed the right of the force which later in the day fought the battle of Glendale or Frayser's farm. The small force at Brackett's Ford defeated an attack at that point, some time during the day.

At the junction of the Charles City and Quaker roads General McClellan had a conference with the corps commanders (Sumner, Heintzelman, and Franklin), and when it was ended he went toward the James River. A short time afterward I received an order directing me to take charge of the force guarding the White Oak Bridge, and I immediately started back. I had gone but a short distance when a bombardment commenced in the direction of the bridge, the severity of which I had never heard equaled in the field. The wood through which I was riding seemed torn to pieces with round shot and exploding shells. But the danger was really greater from falling branches than from the shot, which did small damage.

It appears that Jackson, having left Savage's Station early in the morning, arrived at the vicinity of White Oak Bridge about noon, without exciting suspicion of his presence on our part, the whole movement being hidden by the woods. Here, masked by the trees, he massed about thirty guns, which opened simultaneously on the troops in the clearings, and on the rear part of the wagon train, which had not yet started from the clearing where it had passed the night. The troops immediately got under cover of the wood, except Caldwell's brigade [Richardson's division], which was guarding the batteries. It remained in the open ground, and lost many men, but the effect of the firing was otherwise small, except on the wagon train, which was thrown into some confusion, many of the wagons not being hitched up. These were at first abandoned by the drivers, but nearly all got away during the day. One field-piece was dismounted. The batteries were, however, soon in position to return the enemy's fire, which they did with such effect that many of his guns were silenced. It was here that Captain Hazzard, already mentioned, was mortally wounded, ending a brilliant career with a glorious death. Captain (afterward General) Romeyn B. Ayres, who commanded the artillery of Smith's division, used his guns with excellent effect. One of the enemy's batteries came into view near the bridge, but was forced to retire almost immediately. The bombardment lasted with great severity for about a half-hour, when it slackened and gradually fell off, opening again at intervals during the day, but never with its original vigor. A cavalry force which was sent over by the enemy just after the bombardment had reached its height was forced to retire much faster than it advanced.

The development of our defense of the crossing convinced General Jackson that it would be impossible for him to force it. At any rate, he made no attempt during the day to cross his infantry, unless sending sharp-shooters across to pick off our pickets may be so considered. The fight at White Oak Bridge was entirely with artillery, there being little musketry firing.

About 4 o'clock the enemy made a movement to our left, threatening Brackett's Ford, where I knew we were very weak. This was met by Dana's and Colonel Alfred Sully's brigades of Sedgwick's division, which were sent by General Sumner upon information of the danger. There was no further movement in that direction after these troops appeared, and they were returned to General Sumner about 5 o'clock, in time to do good service at Glendale. Toward sundown, at the request of General Sumner, Caldwell's and Meagher's brigades of Richardson's division were also sent to reënforce him.

No other movement was made by General Jackson's force during the day. Our artillery fired at whatever could be seen on the other side, and was answered by theirs in what seemed a reluctant manner. When the bombardment began, the mules belonging to an engineer ponton-train were being watered at the swamp. The noise stampeded them, and they rushed to the rear, going through one of the regiments of Meagher's brigade, and disabling more men than were hurt in the brigade during the remainder of the day. The mules were seen no more, and the ponton-train was deserted. Captain (afterward General) M. T. McMahon, of my staff, volunteered to burn the train about 5 o'clock. It was a plucky thing to do, for the train was under the guns of the enemy, who knew its value as well as we did, and the presumption was that he would open his guns on it. But Captain McMahon got ten volunteers, and the train was soon in flames. He found four mules already harnessed, and brought off in triumph the most valuable wagon with this team.

In the house which has been described as about the middle of the left clearing lived an old man with a young wife and a child about two years old. He came to me about 10 o'clock and asked if I thought there would be a fight there that day. I told him that there certainly would be. He then asked when I thought it would begin. I thought in about half an hour. "Then," said he, "I will have time to take my wife and child to my brother, who lives about half a mile down the swamp, and get back before it begins."

"Yes," said I, "but why come back at all?"

"Why," said he, "if I don't your men will take all my chickens and ducks."

So he departed with his wife and child and in a little while returned. General Smith's headquarters were near this house, so it was a fair target for the enemy. Several shots went through it, and one of them took off the leg of the poor old man, who bled to death in a few minutes. He had sacrificed himself for his poultry.

One of the brigadier-generals of the command during a lull in the firing came to my headquarters, leaving his brigade to take care of itself. Finding his stay too long, I had him sent back to his post, and a short time afterward I was informed that he had been carried off the field on a stretcher, wounded. I thought it my duty to go to the brigade and find how things were going with it, and asked General Smith to accompany me. We started out, and almost at once the enemy opened on us with great vigor. I looked back, and found to my horror that all my own and General Smith's staff were following us, and that a large cavalry escort belonging to headquarters was also in the procession. The enemy had evidently taken us for a cavalry regiment. Getting rid of them all, we finally arrived at the right of the brigade, unharmed. Making inquiry of a staff-officer about the general, he replied, "Oh, no, sir, he is not wounded, he felt unwell and has gone to the wood to lie down and will soon be back." I turned off in great disgust to return, when another officer, looking as neat and clean as if he had just joined the army, stepped up with the air of a private secretary of some grand official, and, touching his hat, said, "Who shall I say called, sir?" General Smith and I did not hear the last of that expedition for a long time.

During the day a staff-officer of General Smith had explored a road toward James River about two miles in rear of that which the troops at Glendale were to take, and found it practicable. About 10 in the evening, assuming that my instructions to hold the crossing until nightfall had been obeyed, I sent word to General Heintzelman and General Sumner that I should move

THE REAR-GUARD AT WHITE OAK SWAMP—SHOWING GENERAL W. F. SMITH'S DIVISION. DRAWN BY JULIAN SCOTT AFTER HIS PAINTING OWNED BY THE UNION LEAGUE CLUB, NEW YORK.

to the James River by that road. General Richardson, with French's brigade, was instructed to remain, to deceive the enemy as to our movements by firing field-pieces in the direction of the bridge, and then, after an hour, to march. General Henry M. Naglee was to follow Smith's division. These instructions were carried out, and the command arrived at the James about daylight. The discovery of this road made the concentration of the troops at Malvern Hill a completed manœuvre by noon of the 1st of July, and was due to the fertile brain of General Smith, who ordered the exploration.

The military results of the defense of White Oak Bridge and the battle of Glendale were: (1) The enemy was repulsed at all points, except in the single case of McCall's division at Glendale, which was overpowered by numbers, after it had captured three of the enemy's colors; (2) The trains and heavy artillery arrived in safety at the James River (except those wagons which were destroyed by the bombardment at White Oak Bridge, not exceeding fifty out of more than four thousand), the road along which they passed not having been molested by the enemy; (3) The troops arrived in good time at the river, so that they were all in the positions desired by the commanding general, to await the attack at Malvern Hill, long before that attack was made.

General Jackson in his report intimates that his whole command, consisting of three divisions and D. H. Hill's division of five brigades, were all at White Oak Bridge on the 30th of June. He says: "It was soon seen that the enemy occupied such a position beyond a thick intervening wood on the right of the road as enabled him to command the crossing. Captain Wooding's battery was consequently recalled." General Lee says: "Jackson having been unable to force the passage of White Oak Swamp, Longstreet and A. P. Hill were without the expected support" at the battle of Glendale. It must be evident to any military reader that Jackson ought to have known of the existence of Brackett's Ford, only one mile above White Oak Bridge, and ought to have discovered the weakness of our defense at that point. He had troops enough to have attacked the ford and the bridge with forces at both points exceeding ours at the bridge, and the two attacks, to say the least, would have embarrassed us exceedingly. Had he made two attacks simultaneously, the result of the day at Glendale and White Oak Bridge might have been different. There may be reasons for his inaction in this matter that I do not understand, but, as the record now shows, he seems to have been ignorant of what General Lee expected of him, and badly informed about Brackett's Ford. When he found how strenuous was our defense at the bridge, he should have turned his attention to Brackett's Ford also. A force could have been as quietly gathered there as at the bridge; a strong infantry movement at the ford would have easily overrun our small force there, placing our right at Glendale, held by Slocum's division, in great jeopardy, and turning our force at the bridge by getting between it and Glendale. In fact, it is likely that we should have been defeated on that day had General Jackson done what his great reputation seems to make it imperative that he should have done.

A short time after I separated from General McClellan (as mentioned above) at the junction of the Charles City and Quaker roads, I bade farewell to the

Prince de Joinville, who told me that he and his nephews were about to leave us and return to Europe. He had always been very friendly, and now expressed many good wishes for my future. Holding my hand in his, he said, with great earnestness, "General, advise General McClellan to concentrate his army at this point, and fight a battle to-day; if he does, he will be in Richmond to-morrow." I was much impressed by his manner and by what he said, and from the purely military point of view the advice may have been good; but it was impracticable for me to adopt the suggestion. General McClellan was then well on his way to the James River, and I had no right to leave my command. It was impossible to concentrate the army there that day early enough to give battle, and had it been possible to risk a general engagement there, it would have been contrary to General McClellan's views as to his responsibility connected with the safety of the army, views which were actuating him in the very movement then taking place. It is likely from what we know now, that had it been possible to follow the prince's advice, his military forecast might have proved correct. But no one at that hour could have predicted the paralysis of Jackson's large force in our rear for the whole of that day, nor General Lee's ignorance of McClellan's intentions. Had a general engagement taken place, and had we been defeated, the army would have reached the James River, it is true, but instead of getting there as it did, with its *morale* unharmed, and with slight damage to its men and material, it would have been a disorganized mob, and as an army would have perished miserably. General McClellan believed that the destruction of the Army of the Potomac at that time would have been ruin to our cause, and his actions, for which he alone is responsible, were guided by that belief and by the conviction that at any sacrifice the preservation of that army, *at that time*, was paramount to every other consideration.

I cannot finish without a word as to the conduct of the men. My experience during the period generally known as "the Seven Days" was with the Sixth and Second Corps. During the whole time between June 26th and July 2d, there was not a night in which the men did not march almost continually, nor a day on which there was not a fight. I never saw a skulker during the whole time, nor heard one insubordinate word. Some men fell by the wayside, exhausted, and were captured; but their misfortune was due to physical inability to go on. They had no food but that which was carried in their haversacks, and the hot weather soon rendered that uneatable. Sleep was out of the question, and the only rest obtained was while lying down awaiting an attack, or sheltering themselves from shot and shell. No murmur was heard; everything was accepted as the work for which they had enlisted. They had been soldiers less than a year, yet their conduct could not have been more soldierly had they seen ten years of service. No such material for soldiers was ever in the field before, and their behavior in this movement foreshadowed their success as veterans at Appomattox.

WOODBURY'S BRIDGE ACROSS THE CHICKAHOMINY [SEE NEXT PAGE].  FROM A WAR-TIME PHOTOGRAPH.

## McCLELLAN'S CHANGE OF BASE AND MALVERN HILL.

### BY DANIEL H. HILL, LIEUTENANT-GENERAL, C. S. A.

FIVE of the six Confederate divisions north of the Chickahominy at the close of the battle of Gaines's Mill remained in bivouac all the next day (June 28th), it being deemed too hazardous to force the passage of the river. Ewell was sent with his division to Dispatch Station on the York River Railroad. He found the station and the railroad-bridge burnt. J. E. B. Stuart, who followed the retreating Federal cavalry to White House on the Pamunkey, found ruins of stations and stores all along the line. These things proved that General McClellan did not intend to retreat by the short line of the York River Railroad; but it was possible he might take the Williamsburg road. General Lee, therefore, kept his troops on the north side of the river, that he might be ready to move on the Federal flank, should that route be attempted. New Bridge was repaired on Saturday (the 28th), and our troops were then ready to move in either direction. The burnings and explosions in the Federal camp Saturday afternoon and night showed that General McClellan had determined to abandon his strong fortifications around Richmond. Ewell, who was watching him at Bottom's Bridge, and the cavalry, holding the crossings lower down, both reported that there was no attempt at the Williamsburg route. Longstreet and A. P. Hill were sent across the river at New Bridge early on Sunday morning to move down the Darbytown road to the Long Bridge road to intercept the retreat to the James River. This movement began before it was known that General

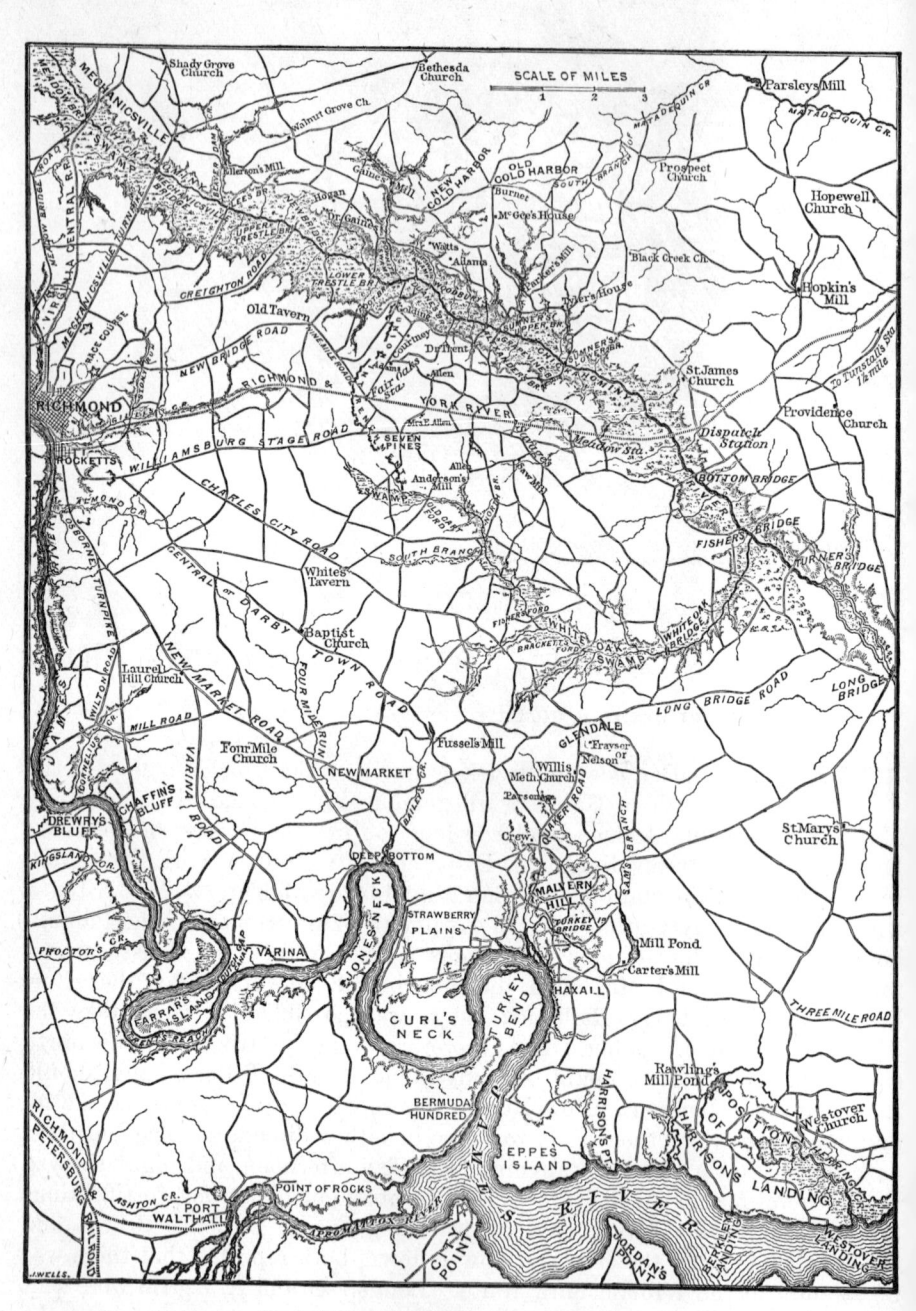

REGION OF THE SEVEN DAYS' FIGHTING.

A SAMPLE OF THE CHICKAHOMINY SWAMP. FROM A PHOTOGRAPH OF 1862.

McClellan had evacuated his stronghold. Lee gave here the first illustration of a quality for which he became noted — the remarkable discernment of his adversary's plans through the study of his character. McClellan could have retreated to Yorktown with as little loss as Johnston sustained on his retreat from it. The roads from Richmond to Yorktown lead through a wooded and swampy country, on which strong rear-guards could have afforded perfect protection to a retreating column without bringing on a general engagement. General Johnston, on his retreat from Yorktown, did fight at Williamsburg, but it was a battle of his own choosing, and not forced upon him by the vigor of pursuit. Lee had but little idea that McClellan would return to Yorktown, judging rightly that the military pride of his distinguished opponent would not permit him to march back a defeated column to the point from which he had started, a few months before, for the capture of the Confederate capital, with his splendid army and magnificent outfit.] It is a proof of Lee's sagacity that he predicated his orders for an advance upon the belief that General McClellan was too proud a man to fall back by the same route by which the triumphal advance had been made. A great commander must study the mental and moral characteristics of the opposing leader, and Lee was specially endowed with an aptitude in that direction. At the battle of Salzbach, Montecuculi, the Austrian commander, noticed the French troops making a movement so different from the cautious style of his famous rival that he exclaimed, "Either Turenne is dead or mortally wounded." So it proved to be; the French marshal had been killed by a cannon-ball before the movement began.

In pursuance of General Lee's plan, Huger was directed (on the 29th) to take the Charles City road to strike the retreating column below White Oak Swamp. Holmes was to take possession of Malvern Hill, and Magruder to follow the line of retreat, as soon as the works were abandoned. The abandonment became known about sunrise on Sunday morning, but Grapevine Bridge was not completed till sunset. Jackson then crossed his corps at that point, my division leading. We bivouacked that night near Savage's Station, where McLaws's division had had a severe fight a few hours before. Just at dawn on Monday, the 30th, we were in motion, when I discovered what appeared to be a line of battle drawn up at the station, but which proved to be a line of sick and of hospital attendants, 2500 in number. About half a mile from the station we saw what seemed to be an entire regiment of Federals cold in death, and learned that a Vermont regiment [the 5th] had been in the desperate charge upon the division of McLaws, and had suffered great loss [killed, 31; wounded, 143]. From the time of crossing the river, we had evidence everywhere of the precipitate nature of the Federal retreat.‡ Dabney, in his life of Jackson, says:

"The whole country was full of deserted plunder, army wagons, and pontoon-trains partially burned or crippled; mounds of grain and rice and hillocks of mess beef smoldering; tens of thousands of axes, picks, and shovels; camp kettles gashed with hatchets; medicine chests with their drugs stirred into a foul medley, and all the apparatus of a vast and lavish host; while the mire under foot was mixed with blankets lately new, and with overcoats torn from the waist up. For weeks afterward agents of our army were busy in gathering in the spoils. Great stores of fixed ammunition were saved, while more were destroyed."

In our march from Savage's Station my division picked up a thousand prisoners, stragglers from the retreating army, and gathered a large number of abandoned rifles. I detached two regiments (the Fourth and Fifth North

] The capture of Petersburg would have been almost as disastrous to the South as the capture of Richmond, and for many days Petersburg was at the mercy of the Federal army. There were no troops and no fortifications there when McClellan reached the James. Some two weeks after the battle of Malvern Hill the first earth-works were begun at Petersburg, by my order.— D. H. H.

‡ The Union reports do not indicate precipitancy. The greater part of McClellan's army was within three miles of the original lines at the close of the second day after the battle of Gaines's Mill, that is, on the evening of June 29th. The third day after that battle, the Army of the Potomac fought on three separate fields (White Oak Bridge, Charles City road, and Glendale), at distances of from 7 to 10 miles from the old positions in front of Richmond. General Wm. B. Franklin was with the rear columns of the army during the movement to the James River. [See p. 366.]—EDITORS.

UNION FIELD-HOSPITAL AT SAVAGE'S STATION, AFTER THE BATTLE OF GAINES'S MILL.
FROM A PHOTOGRAPH TAKEN BEFORE THE ARMY WITHDREW, EARLY ON THE MORNING OF JUNE 30TH.

Carolina) to take the prisoners and arms to Richmond. We reached White Oak Swamp about noon, and there found another hospital camp, with about five hundred sick in it. Truly, the Chickahominy swamps were fatal to the Federal forces. A high bluff was on our side of the little stream called White Oak, and a large uncultivated field on the other side. In this field could be seen a battery of artillery, supported by a brigade of infantry — artillerists and infantry lying down and apparently asleep. Under cover of Thomas T. Munford's 2d Virginia cavalry, thirty-one field-pieces were placed upon the bluff, and were ordered to open fire as soon as the cavalry mask was removed. The battery fired its loaded guns in reply, and then galloped off, followed by its infantry supports and the long lines of infantry farther back in the field. Munford crossed his regiment over the ford, and Jackson and myself went with him to see what had become of the enemy. We soon found out. The battery had taken up a position behind a point of woods, where it was perfectly sheltered from our guns, but could play upon the broken bridge and ford, and upon every part of the uncultivated field. It opened with grape and canister upon us, and we retired rapidly. Fast riding in the wrong direction is not military, but it is sometimes healthy. We had taken one prisoner, a drunken Irishman, but he declined the honor of going back with us, and made fight with his naked fists. A soldier asked me näively whether he should shoot the Irishman or let him go. I am glad that I told him to let the man go, to be a comfort to his family. That Irishman must have had a charmed life. He was under the shelter of his gum-cloth coat hung on a stick, near the ford, when a citizen fired at him four times, from a distance of about fifty paces; and the only recognition that I could see the man make was to raise his hand as if to brush off a fly.‡ One of the shells set the farm-house on fire. We learned from the owner that Franklin's corps was in front of us.

Our cavalry returned by the lower ford, and pronounced it perfectly practicable for infantry. But Jackson did not advance. Why was this? It was the critical day for both commanders, but especially for McClellan. With consummate skill he had crossed his vast train of five thousand wagons and his immense parks of artillery safely over White Oak Swamp, but he was more exposed now than at any time in his flank march. Three columns of attack were converging upon him, and a strong corps was pressing upon his rear. Escape seemed impossible for him, but he *did* escape, at the same time inflicting heavy damage upon his pursuers. General Lee, through no fault in his plans, was to see his splendid prize slip through his hands. Longstreet and A. P. Hill struck the enemy at Frayser's farm (or Glendale) at 3 P. M. on the 30th, and, both being always ready for a fight, immediately attacked. Magruder, who followed them down the Darbytown road, was ordered to the assistance of General Holmes on the New Market road, who was not then engaged, and their two divisions took no part in the action. Huger, on the Charles City road, came upon Franklin's left flank, but made no attack. I sent my engineer officer, Captain W. F. Lee, to him through the swamp, to ask him whether he could not engage Franklin. He replied that the road was obstructed by fallen timber. So there were five divisions within sound of the firing, and within supporting distance, but not one of them moved. Longstreet and A. P. Hill made a desperate fight, contending against Sumner's corps, and the divisions of McCall, Kearny, and Hooker; but they failed to gain possession of the Quaker road, upon which McClellan was retreating. That night Franklin glided silently by them. He had to pass within easy range of the artillery of Longstreet and Hill, but they did not know he was there. It had been a gallant fight on their part. General Lee reported: "Many prisoners, including a general of division, McCall, were captured, and several batteries, with some thousands of small-arms, were taken." But as an obstruction to the Federal retreat, the fight amounted to nothing.

‡ After the appearance of this article in "The Century" magazine, E. McLaughlin, of East Saginaw, Michigan, wrote me that he was a member of Co. C of the 7th Maine Volunteers, General W. F. Smith's division, and said: "The statement in regard to the drunken Irishman is true. That man belonged to my company and told us, when he came to the company at Malvern Hill, that he had been inside your lines and had been repeatedly shot at. He further said that if he had had one more canteen of whisky he could have held the position all day."— D. H. H.

**THE ARTILLERY ENGAGEMENT AT WHITE OAK BRIDGE. FROM A SKETCH MADE AT THE TIME.**

The view is from Franklin's position south of the bridge, Jackson's and D. H. Hill's troops being seen in the distance.

Major Dabney, in his life of Jackson, thus comments on the inaction of that officer: "On this occasion it would appear, if the vast interests dependent upon General Jackson's coöperation with the proposed attack upon the center were considered, that he came short of the efficiency in action for which he was everywhere else noted." After showing how the crossing of White Oak might have been effected, Dabney adds: "The list of casualties would have been larger than that presented on the 30th, of one cannoneer wounded; but how much shorter would have been the bloody list filled up the next day at Malvern Hill? This temporary eclipse of Jackson's genius was probably to be explained by physical causes. The labor of the previous days, the sleeplessness, the wear of gigantic cares, with the drenching of the comfortless night, had sunk the elasticity of his will and the quickness of his invention for the nonce below their wonted tension. And which of the sons of man is so great as never to experience this?"

I think that an important factor in this inaction was Jackson's pity for his own corps, worn out by long and exhausting marches, and reduced in numbers by its numerous sanguinary battles. He thought that the garrison of Richmond ought now to bear the brunt of the fighting. None of us knew that the veterans of Longstreet and A. P. Hill were unsupported; nor did we even know that the firing that we heard was theirs. Had all our troops been at Frayser's farm, there would have been no Malvern Hill.

Jackson's genius never shone when he was under the command of another. It seemed then to be shrouded or paralyzed. Compare his inertness on this occasion with the wonderful vigor shown a few weeks later at Slaughter's [Cedar] Mountain in the stealthy march to Pope's rear, and later still in the capture of Harper's Ferry. MacGregor on his native heath was not more different from MacGregor in prison than was Jackson his own master from Jackson in a subordinate position. He wrote once to Richmond requesting that he might have "fewer orders and more men." That was the keynote to his whole character. The hooded falcon cannot strike the quarry.

The gentleman who tried his "splendid rifle" on the drunken Irishman was the Rev. L. W. Allen. Mr. Allen had been raised in that neighborhood, and knew Malvern Hill well. He spoke of its commanding height, the difficulties of approach to it, its amphitheatrical form and ample area, which would enable McClellan to arrange his 350 field-guns tier above tier and sweep the plain in every direction. I became satisfied that an attack upon the concentrated Federal army so splendidly posted, and with such vast superiority in artillery, could only be fatal to us. The anxious thought then was, Have Holmes and Magruder been able to keep McClellan from Malvern Hill? General Holmes arrived at Malvern at 10:30 A. M. on the 30th, with 5170 infantry, 4 batteries of artillery, and 130 improvised or irregular cavalry. He did not attempt to occupy the hill, although only 1500 Federals had yet reached it. Our cavalry had passed over it on the afternoon of the 29th, and had had a sharp skirmish with the Federal cavalry on the Quaker road.

As General Holmes marched down the river, his troops became visible to the gun-boats, which opened fire upon them, throwing those awe-inspiring shells familiarly called by our men "lamp-posts," on account of their size and appearance. Their explosion was very much like that of a small volcano, and had a very demoralizing effect upon new troops, one of whom expressed the general sentiment by saying: "The Yankees throwed them lamp-posts about too careless like." The roaring, howling gun-boat shells were usually harmless to flesh, blood, and bones, but they had a wonderful effect upon the nervous system. General Junius Daniel, a most gallant and accomplished officer, who had a brigade under General Holmes, gave me an incident connected with the affair on the 30th, known as the "Battle of Malvern Cliff." General Holmes, who was very deaf, had gone into a little house concealed from the boats by some intervening woods, and was engaged in some business when the bellowing of the "lamp-posts" began. The irregular cavalry stampeded and made a brilliant charge to the rear. The artillerists of two guns of Graham's Petersburg battery were also panic-struck, and cutting their horses loose mounted them, and, with dangling traces, tried to catch up with the fleet-footed cavaliers. The infantry troops were inexperienced in the wicked ways of war, having never been under fire before. The fright of the fleeing cavalry would have pervaded their ranks also with the same mischievous result but for the strenuous efforts of their officers, part of whom were veterans. Some of the raw levies crouched behind little saplings to get protection from the shrieking, blustering shells. At this juncture General Holmes, who from his deafness, was totally unaware of the rumpus, came out of the hut, put his hand behind his right ear, and said: " I thought I heard firing." Some of the pale-faced infantry thought that they also had heard firing.

Part of Wise's brigade joined Holmes on the 30th, with two batteries of artillery and two regiments of cavalry. His entire force then consisted of 5820 infantry, 6 batteries of artillery, and 2 regiments of cavalry. He remained inactive until 4 P. M., when he was told that the Federal army was passing over Malvern Hill in a demoralized condition. He then opened upon the supposed fugitives with six rifled guns, and was speedily undeceived in regard to the disorganization in the Army of the Potomac by a reply from thirty guns, which in a brief time silenced his own. The audacity of the Federals and the large number of their guns (which had gone in advance of the main body of Porter's corps) made General Holmes believe that he was about to be attacked, and he called for assistance, and, by Longstreet's order, Magruder was sent to him. After a weary march, Magruder was recalled to aid Longstreet; but the day was spent in fruitless marching and countermarching, so that his fine body of troops took no part in what might have been a decisive battle at Frayser's farm. General Holmes was a veteran soldier of well-known personal courage, but he was deceived as to the strength and intentions of the enemy. General Porter says that the force opposed to General Holmes consisted of Warren's brigade and the Eleventh U. S. Infantry; in all, 1500 infantry and 30 pieces of artillery. Here was afforded an example of the proneness to overestimate the number of troops opposed to us. The Federals reported Holmes to have 25,000 men, and he thought himself confronted by a large part of McClellan's army. That night he fell back to a stronger position,☆ thinking apparently that there would be an "on to Richmond" movement by the River road. He lost 2 killed, 49 wounded, 2 pieces of artillery, and 6 caissons. The guns and caissons, General Porter states, were afterward abandoned by the Federals. General Holmes occupied the extreme Confederate right the next day, July 1st, but he took no part in the attack upon Malvern Hill, believing, as he says in his official report, "that it was out of the question to attack the strong position of Malvern Hill from that side with my inadequate force."

Mahone's brigade had some skirmishing with Slocum's Federal division on the 30th, but nothing else was done on that day by Huger's division. Thus it happened that Longstreet and A. P. Hill, with the fragments of their divisions which had been engaged at Gaines's Mill, were struggling alone, while Jackson's whole corps and the divisions of Huger, Magruder, Holmes, McLaws, and my own were near by.

Jackson moved over the swamp early on the first of July, Whiting's division leading. Our march was much delayed by the crossing of troops and trains. At Willis's Church I met General Lee. He bore grandly his terrible disappointment of the day before, and made no allusion to it. I gave him Mr. Allen's description of Malvern Hill, and presumed to say, "If General McClellan is there in force, we had better let him alone." Longstreet laughed and said, "Don't get scared, now that we have got him whipped." It was this belief in the demoralization of the Federal army that made our leader risk the attack. It was near noon when Jackson reached the immediate neighbor-

☆ Half a mile below the upper gate at Curl's Neck. (See "Official Records," Vol. XI., Part II., p. 908.)—D. H. H.

SKETCH MAP OF THE VICINITY OF MALVERN HILL (JULY 1, 1862).

The Union troops reached the field by the so-called Quaker road (more properly the Church road); the Confederates chiefly by this and the Long Bridge road. The general lines were approximately as indicated above. The Confederates on the River road are the troops of General Holmes, who had been repulsed at Turkey Island Bridge the day before by Warren's brigade, with the aid of the gun-boats. The main fighting was in the space between the words "Confederate" and "Union," together with one or two assaults upon the west side of the Crew Hill from the meadow. Morell's and Couch's divisions formed the first Union line, and General Porter's batteries extended from the Crew house to the West house.

hood of Malvern Hill. Some time was spent in reconnoitering, and in making tentative efforts with our few batteries to ascertain the strength and position of the enemy. I saw Jackson helping with his own hands to push Reilly's North Carolina battery farther forward. It was soon disabled, the woods around us being filled with shrieking and exploding shells. I noticed an artilleryman seated comfortably behind a very large tree, and apparently feeling very secure. A moment later a shell passed through the huge tree and took off the man's head. This gives an idea of the great power of the Federal rifled artillery. Whiting's division was ordered to the left of the Quaker road, and mine to the right; Ewell's was in reserve. Jackson's own division had been halted at Willis's Church. The divisions of Magruder, Huger, and McLaws were still farther over to my right. Those of Longstreet and A. P. Hill were in reserve on the right and were not engaged.

At length we were ordered to advance. The brigade of General George B. Anderson first encountered the enemy, and its commander was wounded and borne from the field. His troops, however, crossed the creek and took position in the woods, commanded by Colonel C. C. Tew, a skillful and gallant man. Rodes being sick, his brigade was commanded by that peerless soldier, Colonel J. B. Gordon. Ripley, Garland, and Colquitt also got over without serious loss. My five brigade commanders and myself now made an examination of the enemy's position. He was found to be strongly posted on a commanding hill, all the approaches to which could be swept by his artillery and were guarded by swarms of infantry, securely sheltered by fences, ditches, and ravines. Armistead was immediately on my right. We remained a long while awaiting orders, when I received the following:

"July 1st, 1862.

"GENERAL D. H. HILL: Batteries have been established to act upon the enemy's line. If it is broken, as is probable, Armistead, who can witness the effect of the fire, has been ordered to charge with a yell. Do the same. R. H. CHILTON, A. A. G."

A similar order was sent to each division commander. However, only one battery of our artillery came up at a time, and each successive one, as it took position, had fifty pieces turned upon it, and was crushed in a minute. Not knowing what to do under the circumstances, I wrote to General Jackson that the condition upon which the order was predicated was not fulfilled, and that I wanted instructions. He replied to advance when I heard the shouting. We did advance at the signal, and after an unassisted struggle for an hour and a half, and after meeting with some success, we were compelled to fall back under cover of the woods. Magruder advanced at the same signal, having portions of the divisions of Huger and McLaws, comprising the brigades of Mahone, Wright, Barksdale, Ransom, Cobb, Semmes, Kershaw, Armistead, and G. T. Anderson; but he met with some delay, and did not get in motion till he received a second order from General Lee, and we were then beaten.

The Comte de Paris, who was on McClellan's staff, gives this account of the charge of my gallant division:

"Hill advanced alone against the Federal positions. . . . He had therefore before him Morell's right, Couch's division, reënforced by Caldwell's brigade, . . . and finally the left of Kearny. The woods skirting the foot of Malvern Hill had hitherto protected the Confederates, but as soon as they passed beyond the edge of the forest, they were received by a fire from all the batteries at once, some posted on the hill, others ranged midway, close to the Federal infantry. The latter joined its musketry fire to the cannonade when Hill's first line had come within range, and threw it back in disorder on the reserves. While it was re-forming, new [Confederate] battalions marched up to the assault in their turn. The remembrance of Cold Harbor doubles the energy of Hill's soldiers. They try to pierce the line, sometimes at one point, sometimes at another, charging Kearny's left first, and Couch's right, . . . and afterward throwing themselves upon the left of Couch's division. But, here also, after nearly reaching the Federal positions, they are repulsed. The conflict is carried on with great fierceness on both sides, and, for a moment, it seems as if the Confederates are at last about to penetrate the very center of their adversaries and of the formidable artillery, which but now was dealing destruction in their ranks. But Sumner, who commands on the right, detaches Sickles's and Meagher's brigades successively to Couch's assistance. During this time, Whiting on the left, and Huger on the right, suffer Hill's soldiers to become exhausted without supporting them. Neither Lee nor Jackson has sent the slightest order, and the din of the battle which is going on in their immediate vicinity has not sufficed to make them march against the enemy. . . . At seven o'clock Hill reorganized the débris of his troops in the woods; . . . his tenacity and the courage of his soldiers have only had the effect of causing him to sustain heavy losses." (Pp. 141, 142, Vol. II.)

WILLIS'S CHURCH, ON THE QUAKER ROAD, NEAR GLENDALE. USED AS A CONFEDERATE HOSPITAL AFTER THE BATTLE OF MALVERN HILL.

Truly, the courage of the soldiers was sublime! Battery after battery was in their hands for a few moments, only to be wrested away by fresh troops of the enemy. If one division could effect this much, what might have been done had the other nine coöperated with it! General Lee says:

"D. H. Hill pressed forward across the open field and engaged the enemy gallantly, breaking and driving back his first line; but a simultaneous advance of the other troops not taking place, he found himself unable to maintain the ground he had gained against the overwhelming numbers and the numerous batteries of the enemy. Jackson sent to his support his own division, and that part of Ewell's which was in reserve; but owing to the increasing darkness, and the intricacy of the forest and swamp, they did not arrive in time to render the desired assistance. Hill was therefore compelled to abandon part of the ground that he had gained, after suffering severe loss and inflicting heavy damage upon the enemy."

I never saw anything more grandly heroic than the advance after sunset of the nine brigades under Magruder's orders.✠ Unfortunately, they did not move together, and were beaten in detail. As each brigade emerged from the woods, from fifty to one hundred guns opened upon it, tearing great gaps in its ranks; but the heroes reeled on and were shot down by the reserves at the guns, which a few squads reached. Most of them had an open field half a mile wide to cross, under the fire of field-artillery in front, and the fire of the heavy ordnance of the gun-boats in their rear. It was not war—it was murder.

Our loss was double that of the Federals at Malvern Hill. Not only did the fourteen brigades which were engaged suffer, but also the inactive troops and those brought up as reserves too late to be of any use met many casualties from the fearful artillery fire which reached all parts of the woods. Hence, more than half the casualties were from field-pieces—an unprecedented thing in warfare. The artillery practice was kept up till nine o'clock at night, and the darkness added to the glory of the pyrotechnics. It was quite late when I had posted for the night the last of the reënforcements that had come up when the battle was over. A half-hour before, an incident occurred which is thus related by General Trimble:

"I proposed to General D. H. Hill to ride forward and reconnoiter the enemy's position. We approached within one hundred steps of the enemy's batteries, and could hear plainly the ordinary tone of conversation. The guns were then firing on the woods to our left, where the last attack had been made, at right angles to that part of the field we were then in. I suggested to General Hill the advantage of making an attack on this battery, and that it must be successful, as the enemy would not expect one from our position, and under cover of the darkness we could approach them undiscovered. General Hill did not seem inclined to make the movement."

The chivalrous Trimble proposed to make the attack with his own brigade, but there were many troops now in the woods, and I thought that the attack would but expose them to a more intense artillery fire. We saw men going about with lanterns, looking up and carrying off the dead and wounded. There were no pickets out, and the rumbling of wheels in the distance seemed to indicate that the retreat had begun. The morning revealed the bare plateau stripped of its terrible batteries. The battle of Malvern Hill was a disaster to the Confederates, and the fourteen brigades that had been so badly repulsed were much demoralized. But there were six divisons intact, and they could have made a formidable fight on the 2d.

✠ Toombs's brigade belonged to Magruder, but had moved to my assistance by my order when we were hard pressed. It was not, therefore, in the final attack made by Magruder.—D. H. H.

Possibly owing to the belief that Longstreet and A. P. Hill were making a march between Malvern and Harrison's Landing, the retreat was the most disorderly that took place. Wagons and ambulances were abandoned; knapsacks, cartridge-boxes, clothing, and rifles by the thousand were thrown away by the Federals. Colonel James D. Nance, of the 3d South Carolina regiment, gathered 925 rifles in fine condition that had been thrown away in the wheat-field at Shirley, a farm between Malvern and Haxall's. The fruits of the Seven Days' Fighting were the relief of Richmond, the capture of 9000 prisoners [including 3000 in hospitals], 52 pieces of artillery, and 35,000 stand of arms, and the destruction or capture of many military stores.

I crossed the Chickahominy with 10,000 effective men. Of these 3907 were killed or wounded and 48 were reported missing, either captives or fugitives from the field. With the infantry and artillery detached, and the losses before Malvern Hill, I estimate that my division in that battle was 6500 strong, and that the loss was 2000. Magruder puts his force at between 26,000 and 28,000 (I think a high estimate), and states his loss as 2900.

Throughout this campaign we attacked just when and where the enemy wished us to attack. This was owing to our ignorance of the country and lack of reconnoissance of the successive battle-fields. Porter's weak point at Gaines's Mill was his right flank. A thorough examination of the ground would have disclosed that; and had Jackson's command gone in on the left of the road running by the McGehee house, Porter's whole position would have been turned and the line of retreat cut off. An armed reconnoissance at Malvern would have shown the immense preponderance of the Federal artillery, and that a contest with it must be hopeless. The battle, with all its melancholy results, proved, however, that the Confederate infantry and Federal artillery, side by side on the same field, need fear no foe on earth.

Both commanders had shown great ability. McClellan, if not always great in the advance, was masterly in retreat, and was unquestionably the greatest of Americans as an organizer of an army. Lee's plans were perfect; and had not his dispositions for a decisive battle at Frayser's farm miscarried, through no fault of his own, he would have won a most complete victory. It was not the least part of his greatness that he did not complain of his disappointment, and that he at no time sought a scape-goat upon which to lay a failure. As reunited Americans, we have reason to be proud of both commanders.

GEORGE W. RANDOLPH, SECRETARY OF WAR OF THE CONFEDERACY FROM MARCH 17, 1862, UNTIL NOVEMBER 17, 1862. FROM A PHOTOGRAPH.

# "THE SEVEN DAYS," INCLUDING FRAYSER'S FARM.[†]

BY JAMES LONGSTREET, LIEUTENANT-GENERAL, C. S. A.

WHEN General Joseph E. Johnston was wounded at the battle of Seven Pines, and General Lee assumed his new duties as commander of the Army of Northern Virginia, General Stonewall Jackson was in the Shenandoah Valley, and the rest of the Confederate troops were east and north of Richmond in front of General George B. McClellan's army, then encamped about the Chickahominy River, 100,000 strong, and preparing for a regular siege of the Confederate capital. The situation required prompt and successful action by General Lee. Very early in June he called about him, on the noted Nine-mile road near Richmond, all his commanders, and asked each in turn his opinion of the military situation. I had my own views, but did not express them, believing that if they should be unfolded privately to the commanding general. The next day I called on General Lee, and suggested my plan for driving the Federal forces away from the Chickahominy. McClellan had a small force at Mechanicsville, and farther back, at Beaver Dam Creek, a considerable portion of his army in a stronghold that was simply unassailable from the front. The banks of Beaver Dam Creek were so steep as to be impassable except on bridges. I proposed an echelon movement, and suggested that Jackson be called down from the Valley, and passed to the rear of the Federal right, in order to turn the position behind Beaver Dam, while the rest of the Confederate forces who were to engage in the attack could cross the Chickahominy at points suitable for the succession in the move, and be ready to attack the Federals as soon as they were thrown from their position. After hearing me, General Lee sent General J. E. B. Stuart on his famous ride around McClellan. The dashing horseman, with a strong reconnoitering force of cavalry, made a forced reconnoissance, passing above and around the Federal forces, recrossing the Chickahominy below them, and returning safe to Confederate headquarters. He made a favorable report of the situation and the practicability of the proposed plan. On the 23d of June General Jackson was summoned to General Lee's headquarters, and was there met by General A. P. Hill, General D. H. Hill, and myself. A conference resulted in the selection of the 26th as the day on which we should move against the Federal position at Beaver Dam. General Jackson was ordered down from the Valley. General A. P. Hill was to pass the Chickahominy with part of his division, and hold the rest in readiness to cross at Meadow Bridge, following

"GIN'L LONGSTREET'S BODY-SARVANT, SAH, ENDU'IN' DE WAH!"

---

[†] The usual spelling is Frazier or Frazer. The authority for the form here adopted is Captain R. E. Frayser, of Richmond.— EDITORS.

Jackson's swoop along the dividing ridge betewen the Pamunkey and the Chickahominy. D. H. Hill and I were ordered to be in position on the Mechanicsville pike early on the 26th, ready to cross the river at Mechanicsville Bridge as soon as it was cleared by the advance of Jackson and A. P. Hill.

Thus matters stood when the morning of the 26th arrived. The weather was clear, and the roads were in fine condition. Everything seemed favorable to the move. But the morning passed and we received no tidings from Jackson. As noon approached, General Hill, who was to move behind Jackson, grew impatient at the delay and begged permission to hurry him up by a fusillade. General Lee consented, and General Hill opened his batteries on Mechanicsville, driving the Federals off. When D. H. Hill and I crossed at the Mechanicsville Bridge we found A. P. Hill severely engaged, trying to drive the Federals from their strong position behind Beaver Dam Creek. Without Jackson to turn the Federal right, the battle could not be ours. Although the contest lasted until some time after night, the Confederates made no progress. The next day the fight was renewed, and the position was hotly contested by the Federals until 7 o'clock in the morning, when the advance of Jackson speedily caused the Federals to abandon their position, thus ending the battle. ☙

☙ According to General Fitz John Porter, it was not Jackson's approach, but information of that event, that caused the withdrawal of the Union troops, who, with the exception of "some batteries and infantry skirmishers," were withdrawn before sunrise on the 27th.
— EDITORS.

MAP OF THE BATTLE OF FRAYSER'S FARM (CHARLES CITY CROSS-ROADS OR GLENDALE), JUNE 30, 1862, SHOWING APPROXIMATE POSITIONS OF UNION AND CONFEDERATE TROOPS. ALSO DISPOSITION OF TROOPS DURING THE ARTILLERY ENGAGEMENT AT WHITE OAK BRIDGE.

Union brigades: 1, Sickles; 2, Carr; 3, Grover; 4, Seymour; 5, Reynolds (Simmons); 6, Meade (this brigade should be represented as north of the road); 7, Robinson; 8, Birney; 9, Berry; 10, Newton; 11, Bartlett; 12, 12, Taylor; 13, Burns; 14, 14, Dana; 15, 15, Sully; 16, 16, Caldwell; 17, French; 18, Meagher; 19, Naglee (of Keyes's corps); 20, Davidson; 21, Brooks; 22, Hancock. Randol's battery was on the right of the road, Kerns's and Cooper's on the left, and Diederichs's and Knieriem's yet farther to the left. Thompson's battery of Kearny's division was with General Robinson's brigade (7).

Confederate brigades: a, Kemper; b, Pickett (Hunton); c, R. H. Anderson (Jenkins); d, Wilcox; e, Featherston; f, Pryor; g, Branch; h, Archer; i, Field; j, J. R. Anderson; k, Pender; l, Gregg; m, n, o, p, Armistead, Wright, Mahone, and Ransom. Of the Confederate batteries, Rogers's, Dearing's, the Thomas artillery, Pegram's, Davidson's, and others were engaged.

The action at White Oak Bridge, about 11 A. M., and that between Huger and Slocum to the left, beginning about 3 P. M., were of artillery only, and were successful from the Union point of view, in that they prevented the Confederate forces at these points from reënforcing Longstreet, while they enabled four Union brigades (12, 14, 15, and 16) to reënforce his opponents. The battle of Frayser's farm, beginning about 4 P. M., resulted in the accomplishment of General McClellan's object, the protection of his trains from rear and flank attack as they were passing down the Long Bridge and Quaker roads to the James River. General Kearny's report characterized this battle as "one of the most desperate of the war, the one the most fatal if lost." The fighting began in force on the left of Seymour's brigade (4), and the brunt of the attack fell upon McCall and the left of Kearny. "Of the four divisions that day engaged," says General McCall's report, "each manœuvred and fought independently." McCall's division, being flanked on the left by Longstreet's right, was driven from its position after a stubborn resistance; its place was taken by Burns's brigade, reënforced by Dana's and Sully's, and these troops recovered part of the ground lost by McCall. The fury of the battle now shifted to the front of Kearny, who was reënforced by Taylor's and Caldwell's brigades. The Confederates gained some ground, but no substantial advantage, and the Union troops withdrew during the night to Malvern Hill.— EDITORS.

FRAYSER'S FARM-HOUSE, FROM THE QUAKER OR CHURCH ROAD, LOOKING SOUTH. FROM A PHOTOGRAPH TAKEN IN 1885.

This house was used as General Sumner's headquarters and as a hospital during the battle. The fighting took place from half to three-quarters of a mile to the right, or westward. The National Cemetery is shown in the middle distance.

It is easy to see that the battle of the previous day would have been a quick and bloodless Confederate victory if Jackson could have reached his position at the time appointed. In my judgment the evacuation of Beaver Dam Creek was very unwise on the part of the Federal commanders. We had attacked at Beaver Dam, and had failed to make an impression at that point, losing several thousand men and officers. This demonstrated that the position was safe. If the Federal commanders knew of Jackson's approach on the 26th, they had ample time to reënforce Porter's right before Friday morning (27th) with men and field defenses, to such extent as to make the remainder of the line to the right secure against assault. So that the Federals in withdrawing not only abandoned a strong position, but gave up the *morale* of their success, and transferred it to our somewhat disheartened forces; for, next to Malvern Hill, the sacrifice at Beaver Dam was unequaled in demoralization during the entire summer.

From Beaver Dam we followed the Federals closely, encountering them again under Porter beyond Powhite Creek, where the battle of Gaines's Mill occurred. General A. P. Hill, being in advance, deployed his men and opened the attack without consulting me. A very severe battle followed. I came up with my reserve forces and was preparing to support Hill, who was suffering very severely, when I received an order from General Lee to make a demonstration against the Federal left, as the battle was not progressing to suit him. I threw in three brigades opposite the Federal left and engaged them in a severe skirmish with infantry and artillery. The battle then raged with great fierceness. General Jackson was again missing, and General Lee grew fearful of the result. Soon I received another message from General Lee, saying that unless I could do something the day seemed to be lost. I then determined to make the heaviest attack I could. The position in front of me was very strong. An open field led down to a difficult ravine a short distance beyond the Powhite Creek. From there the ground made a steep ascent, and was covered with trees and slashed timber and hastily made rifle-trenches. General Whiting came to me with two brigades of Jackson's men and asked me to put him in. I told him I was just organizing an attack and would give him position. My column of attack then was R. H. Anderson's and Pickett's brigades, with Law's and Hood's of Whiting's division. We attacked and defeated the Federals on their left, capturing many thousand stand of arms, fifty-two pieces of artillery, a large quantity of supplies, and many prisoners,— among them General Reynolds, who afterward fell at Gettysburg. The Federals made some effort to reënforce and recover their lost ground, but failed, and during the afternoon and night withdrew their entire forces from that side of the Chickahominy, going in the direction of James River. On the 29th General Lee ascertained that McClellan was marching toward the James. He determined to make a vigorous move and strike the enemy a severe blow. He decided to intercept them in the neighborhood of Charles City cross-roads, and with that end in view planned a pursuit as follows: I was to march to a point below Frayser's farm with General A. P. Hill. General Holmes was to take up position below me on the New Market or River road, to be in readiness to coöperate with me and to attack such Federals as would come within his reach. Jackson was to pursue closely the Federal rear, crossing at the Grapevine Bridge, and coming in on the north of the cross-roads. Huger was to attend to the Federal right flank, and take position on the Charles City road west of the cross-roads. Thus we were to envelop the Federal rear and make the destruction of that part of McClellan's army sure. To reach my position south of the cross-roads, I had about sixteen miles to march. I marched 14 miles on the 29th, crossing over into the Darbytown road and moving down to its intersection, with the New Market road, where I camped for the night, about 3 miles south-west of Frayser's farm. On the morning of the 30th I moved two miles nearer up and made preparation to intercept the Federals as they retreated toward James River. General McCall, with a division of ten thousand Federals, was at the cross-roads and about Frayser's farm. My division, being in advance, was deployed in front of the enemy. I placed such of my batteries as I could find position for, and kept Hill's troops in my rear. As I had twice as far to march as the other commanders, I considered it certain that Jackson and

UNIFORM OF A NON-COMMISSIONED OFFICER OF THE 1ST. NEW YORK, BERRY'S BRIGADE, KEARNY'S DIVISION, 3D CORPS.

OPENING OF THE BATTLE OF FRAYSER'S FARM: SLOCUM'S ARTILLERY ENGAGED WITH THAT OF HUGER, AT BRACKETT'S, ON THE CHARLES CITY ROAD. FROM A SKETCH MADE AT THE TIME.

Huger would be in position when I was ready. After getting my troops in position I called upon General A. P. Hill to throw one of his brigades to cover my right and to hold the rest of his troops in readiness to give pursuit when the enemy had been dislodged. My line extended from near the Quaker road across the New Market road to the Federal right. The ground upon which I approached was much lower than that occupied by General McCall, and was greatly cut up by ravines and covered with heavy timber and tangled undergrowth. On account of these obstructions we were not disturbed while getting into position, except by the firing of a few shots that did no damage. Holmes got into position below me on the New Market road, and was afterward joined by Magruder, who had previously made an unsuccessful attack on the Federal rear-guard at Savage's Station.

By 11 o'clock our troops were in position, and we waited for the signal from Jackson and Huger. Everything was quiet on my part of the line, except occasional firing between my pickets and McCall's. I was in momentary expectation of the signal. About half-past 2 o'clock artillery firing was heard on my left, evidently at the point near White Oak Swamp where Huger was to attack. I very naturally supposed this firing to be the expected signal, and ordered some of my batteries to reply, as a signal that I was ready to coöperate. While the order to open was going around to the batteries, President Davis and General Lee, with their staff and followers, were with me in a little open field near the rear of my right. We were in pleasant conversation, anticipating fruitful results from the fight, when our batteries opened. Instantly the Federal batteries responded most spitefully. It was impossible for the enemy to see us as we sat on our horses in the little field, surrounded by tall, heavy timber and thick undergrowth; yet a battery by chance had our range and exact distance, and poured upon us a terrific fire. The second or third shell burst in the midst of us, killing two or three horses and wounding one or two men. Our little party speedily retired to safer quarters. The Federals doubtless had no idea that the Confederate President, commanding general, and division commanders were receiving point-blank shot from their batteries. Colonel Micah Jenkins was in front of us, and I sent him an order to silence the Federal battery, supposing that he could do so with his long-range rifles. He became engaged, and finally determined to charge the battery. That brought on a general fight between my division and the troops in front of us. Kemper on my right advanced his brigade over difficult ground and captured a battery. Jenkins moved his brigade forward and made a bold fight. He was followed by the other four brigades successively.

The enemy's line was broken, and he was partly dislodged from his position. The batteries were taken, but our line was very much broken up by the rough ground we had to move over, and we were not in sufficiently solid form to maintain a proper battle. The battle was continued, however, until we encountered succor from the corps of Generals Sumner and Heintzelman, when we were obliged to halt and hold the position the enemy had left. This line was held throughout the day, though at times, when vigorous combinations were made against me, McCall regained points along his line. Our counter-movements, however, finally pushed him back again, and more formidable efforts from our adversary were required. Other advances were made, and reënforcements came to the support of the Federals, who contested the line with varying fortune, sometimes recovering batteries we had taken, and again losing them. Finally McCall's division was driven off, and fresh troops seemed to come in to their relief. Ten thousand men of A. P. Hill's division had been held in reserve, in the hope that Jackson and Huger would come up on our left, enabling us to dislodge the Federals, after which Hill's troops could be put in fresh to give pursuit, and follow them down to Harrison's Landing. Jackson found Grapevine Bridge destroyed and could not reach his position; while for some unaccountable reason Huger failed to take part, though near enough to do so.↓ As neither Jackson nor Huger came up, and as night drew on, I put Hill in to relieve my troops. When he came into the fight the Federal line had been broken at every point except one. He formed his line and followed up in the position occupied by my troops. By night we succeeded in getting the entire field, though all of it was not actually occupied until we advanced in pursuit next day. As the enemy moved off they continued the fire of their artillery upon us from various points, and it was after 9 o'clock when the shells ceased to fall. Just before dark General McCall, while looking up a fragment of his division, found us where he supposed his troops were, and was taken prisoner. At the time he was brought in General Lee happened to be with us. As I had known General McCall pleasantly in our

---

↓ General Huger says, in his official report, that the road was very effectively obstructed.— EDITORS.

**CHARGE OF CONFEDERATES UPON RANDOL'S BATTERY AT FRAYSER'S FARM.**

The contest for this battery was one of the most severe encounters of the day. The Confederates (the 55th and 60th Virginia Regiments) advanced out of formation, in wedge shape, and with trailing arms, and began a hand-to-hand conflict over the guns, which were finally yielded to them [see p. 413].

service together in the 4th Infantry, I moved to offer my hand as he dismounted. At the first motion, however, I saw he did not regard the occasion as one for renewing the old friendship, and I merely offered him some of my staff as an escort to Richmond.♭ But for the succoring forces, which should have been engaged by Jackson, Huger, Holmes, and Magruder, McCall would have been entirely dislodged by the first attack. All of our other forces were within a radius of 3 miles, and in easy hearing of the battle, yet of the 50,000 none came in to coöperate. (Jackson should have done more for me than he did. When he wanted me at the Second Manassas, I marched two columns by night to clear the way at Thoroughfare Gap, and joined

---

♭ Major W. Roy Mason, who served on the staff of General C. W. Field, C. S. A., gives this account of the capture of General McCall at Glendale, on the evening of June 30th:

"We occupied as headquarters [at the close of the battle] the center of an old road that ran through a dense pine-wood which the enemy had occupied only two hours before, and the dead and wounded were lying about us. General Field asked me to remain with the other members of the staff, and volunteered to go down to a watercourse, where he had seen water trickling, to fill the canteens and make some coffee for me, for I was much exhausted, having been thrown violently by a wounded horse during the battle. While General Field was absent we saw, in the shadows, three or four men riding toward us, one of them being in advance and having a cloak thrown around him. I recognized the figure at once as that of a Federal officer. 'What command is this?' he asked. 'General Field's, sir,' was my answer. 'General Field! I don't know him.' 'Perhaps not, as you are evidently in the wrong place.'

"He at once turned to retreat, spurring his horse, and I gave the alarm. A soldier of the 47th Virginia (S. Brooke Rollins) now came forward and seized the bridle of the horse, saying to the rider, 'Not so fast.' The captured officer proved to be General McCall, of the Pennsylvania Reserves."

The staff-officers were fired upon while attempting to ride back, and Captain H. J. Biddle, McCall's adjutant-general, was instantly killed. Owing to the darkness the others escaped.— EDITORS.

him in due season.) Hooker claimed at Glendale to have rolled me up and hurriedly thrown me over on Kearny,— tennis-like, I suppose; but McCall showed in his supplementary report that Hooker could as well claim, with a little tension of the hyperbole, that he had thrown me over the moon. On leaving Frayser's farm the Federals withdrew to Malvern Hill, and Lee concentrated his forces and followed them.

On the morning of July 1st, the day after the battle at Frayser's farm, we encountered the enemy at Malvern Hill, and General Lee asked me to make a reconnoissance and see if I could find a good position for the artillery. I found position offering good play for batteries across the Federal left over to the right, and suggested that sixty pieces should be put in while Jackson engaged the Federal front. I suggested that a heavy play of this cross-fire on the Federals would so discomfit them as to warrant an assault by infantry. General Lee issued his orders accordingly, and designated the advance of Armistead's brigade as the signal for the grand assault. Later it was found that the ground over which our batteries were to pass into position on our right was so rough and obstructed that of the artillery ordered for use there only one or two batteries could go in at a time. As our guns in front did not engage, the result was the enemy concentrated the fire of fifty or sixty guns upon our isolated batteries, and tore them into fragments in a few minutes after they opened, piling horses upon each other and guns upon horses. Before night, the fire from our batteries failing of execution, General Lee seemed to abandon the idea of an attack. He proposed to me to move around to the left with my own and A. P. Hill's division, turning the Federal right. I issued my orders accordingly for the two divisions to go around and turn the Federal right, when in some way unknown to me the battle was drawn on. We were repulsed at all points with fearful slaughter, losing six thousand men and accomplishing nothing.

The Federals withdrew after the battle, and the next day I moved on around by the route which it was proposed we should take the day before. I followed the enemy to Harrison's Landing, and Jackson went down by another route in advance of Lee. As soon as we reached the front of the Federal position we put out our skirmish-lines, and I ordered an advance, intending to make another attack, but revoked it on Jackson urging me to wait until the arrival of General Lee. Very soon General Lee came, and, after carefully considering the position of the enemy and of their gun-boats on the James, decided that it would be better to forego any further operations. Our skirmish-lines were withdrawn, we ordered our troops back to their old lines around Richmond, and a month later McClellan's army was withdrawn to the North.

The Seven Days' Fighting, although a decided Confederate victory, was a succession of mishaps. If Jackson had arrived on the 26th,— the day of his own selection,— the Federals would have been driven back from Mechanicsville without a battle. His delay there, caused by obstructions placed in his road by the enemy, was the first mishap. He was too late in entering the fight at Gaines's Mill, and the destruction of Grapevine Bridge kept him from

GENERAL GEORGE A. McCALL. FROM A PHOTOGRAPH.

reaching Frayser's farm until the day after that battle. If he had been there, we might have destroyed or captured McClellan's army. Huger was in position for the battle of Frayser's farm, and after his batteries had misled me into opening the fight he subsided. Holmes and Magruder, who were on the New Market road to attack the Federals as they passed that way, failed to do so.

General McClellan's retreat was successfully managed; therefore we must give it credit for being well managed. He had 100,000 men, and insisted to the authorities at Washington that Lee had 200,000. In fact, Lee had only 90,000. General McClellan's plan to take Richmond by a siege was wise enough, and it would have been a success if the Confederates had consented to such a programme. In spite of McClellan's excellent plans, General Lee, with a force inferior in numbers, completely routed him, and while suffering less than McClellan, captured over six thousand of his men.\ General Lee's

\ In this estimate General Longstreet follows General Lee's unspecific report. The Union returns state the "Captured or missing" of McClellan's army at 6053, and the total loss at 15,849. The Confederate loss was 20,135.— EDITORS.

plans in the Seven Days' Fight were excellent, but were poorly executed. General McClellan was a very accomplished soldier and a very able engineer, but hardly equal to the position of field-marshal as a military chieftain. He organized the Army of the Potomac cleverly, but did not handle it skillfully when in actual battle. Still I doubt if his retreat could have been better handled, though the rear of his army should have been more positively either in his own hands or in the hands of Sumner. Heintzelman crossed the White Oak Swamp prematurely and left the rear of McClellan's army exposed, which would have been fatal had Jackson come up and taken part in Magruder's affair of the 29th near Savage's Station.

I cannot close this sketch without referring to the Confederate commander when he came upon the scene for the first time. General Lee was an unusually handsome man, even in his advanced life. He seemed fresh from West Point, so trim was his figure and so elastic his step. Out of battle he was as gentle as a woman, but when the clash of arms came he loved fight, and urged his battle with wonderful determination. As a usual thing he was remarkably well-balanced — always so, except on one or two occasions of severe trial when he failed to maintain his exact equipoise. Lee's orders were always well considered and well chosen. He depended almost too much on his officers for their execution. Jackson was a very skillful man against such men as Shields, Banks, and Frémont, but when pitted against the best of the Federal commanders he did not appear so well. Without doubt the greatest man of rebellion times, the one matchless among forty millions for the peculiar difficulties of the period, was Abraham Lincoln.

GENERAL HEINTZELMAN'S HEADQUARTERS AT NELSON'S HOUSE, JUNE 30, DURING THE BATTLE OF GLENDALE, FROM A SKETCH MADE AT THE TIME.

# THE BATTLE OF MALVERN HILL.

BY FITZ JOHN PORTER, MAJOR-GENERAL, U. S. V.

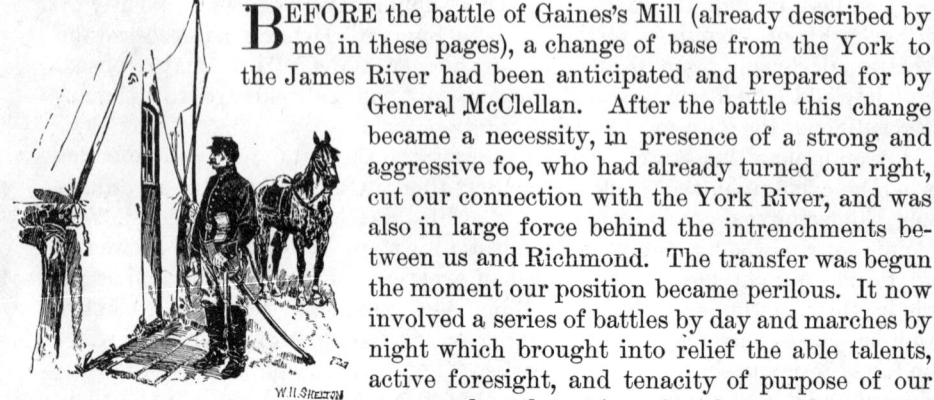

BEFORE the battle of Gaines's Mill (already described by me in these pages), a change of base from the York to the James River had been anticipated and prepared for by General McClellan. After the battle this change became a necessity, in presence of a strong and aggressive foe, who had already turned our right, cut our connection with the York River, and was also in large force behind the intrenchments between us and Richmond. The transfer was begun the moment our position became perilous. It now involved a series of battles by day and marches by night which brought into relief the able talents, active foresight, and tenacity of purpose of our commander, the unity of action on the part of his subordinates, and the great bravery, firmness, and confidence in their superiors on the part of the rank and file.

AN ORDERLY AT HEADQUARTERS.

These conflicts from the beginning of the Seven Days' fighting were the engagement at Oak Grove, the battles of Beaver Dam Creek and Gaines's Mill, the engagements at Golding's and Garnett's farms, and at Allen's farm or Peach Orchard; the battle of Savage's Station; the artillery duel at White Oak Swamp; the battle of Glendale (or Charles City cross-roads); the action of Turkey Creek, and the battle of Malvern Hill. Each was a success to our army, the engagement of Malvern Hill being the most decisive. The result of the movement was that on the 2d of July our army was safely established at Harrison's Landing, on the James, in accordance with General McClellan's design. The present narrative will be confined to events coming under my own observation, and connected with my command, the Fifth Army Corps.

Saturday, June 28th, 1862, the day after the battle of Gaines's Mill, my corps spent in bivouac at the Trent farm on the south bank of the Chickahominy. Artillery and infantry detachments guarded the crossings at the sites of the destroyed bridges. Our antagonists of the 27th were still north of the river, but did not molest us. We rested and recuperated as best we could, amid the noise of battle close by, at Garnett's and Golding's farms, in which part of Franklin's corps was engaged, refilling the empty cartridge-boxes and haversacks, so as to be in readiness for immediate duty.

Our antagonists on the north bank of the river were apparently almost inactive. They seemed puzzled as to our intentions, or paralyzed by the effect of their own labors and losses, and, like ourselves, were recuperating for a renewal of the contest in the early future; though to them, as well as to us, it was difficult to conjecture where that renewal would be made. The only evidence of activity on their part was the dust rising on the road down the river, which we attributed, with the utmost unconcern, to the movements of troops seeking to interrupt our already abandoned communications with York River. The absence of any indication of our intention to maintain those communications, together with the rumble of our artillery, which that night was moving southward, opened the eyes of our opponents to the fact that we had accomplished the desired and perhaps necessary object of withdrawing to the south bank of the Chickahominy, and for the first time had aroused their suspicion that we were either intending to attack Richmond or temporarily abandon the siege, during a change of base to the James River. But the active spurts on the 27th and 28th of June made by the defenders of that city against our left created the false impression that they designed to attack the Second, Third, and Fourth Corps, and thereby succeeded in preventing an attack upon them. So, in order to thwart our plans, whatever they might be, promptly on the 29th our opponents renewed their activity by advancing from Richmond, and by recrossing to the south bank of the river all their forces lately employed at Gaines's Mill. But at that time the main body of our army was beyond their immediate reach, taking positions to cover the passage of our trains to the new base and to be ready again to welcome our eager and earnest antagonists.

Between 2 and 9 P. M. on the 28th, my corps was in motion and marched by the way of Savage Station to the south side of White Oak Swamp; and at the junction of the roads from Richmond (Glendale) to be prepared to repel attacks from the direction of that city. General Morell, leading the advance, aided General Woodbury, of the engineer corps, to build the causeways and bridges necessary for the easy passage of the trains and troops over the swamps and streams. Sykes and McCall followed at 5 and 9 o'clock, respectively, McCall being accompanied by Hunt's Artillery Reserve. We expected to reach our destination, which was only ten miles distant, early on the 29th; but, in consequence of the dark night and of the narrow and muddy roads, cut up and blocked by numerous trains and herds of cattle, the head of the column did not arrive till 10 A. M., the rear not until midnight. McCall arrived latest, and all were greatly fatigued.

The enemy not having appeared at Glendale on the afternoon of the 29th, and other troops arriving to take the place of mine, General McClellan ordered me to move that night by the direct road to the elevated and cleared lands (Malvern Hill) on the north bank of Turkey Creek, there to select and hold a position behind which the army and all its trains could be withdrawn with safety. General Keyes was to move by a different road and form to my right and rear.

Again the dangers and difficulties of night marches attended us, followed by the consequent delay, which, though fortunately it was counterbalanced by the slowness of our opponents in moving to the same point, endangered the safety of our whole army. Although we started before dark, and were led by an intelligent cavalry officer who had passed over the route and professed to know it, my command did not reach Turkey Creek, which was only five miles distant, until 9 A. M. on the 30th. In fact, we were misled up the

THE PARSONAGE, NEAR MALVERN HILL.

This house was in the rear of the Confederate line, which was formed in the woods shown in the background. It was used as a Confederate hospital after the fight. The road is the Church road (known also as the Quaker road), and the view is from near C. W. Smith's, which was for a short time the headquarters of General Lee. The trees of this neighborhood were riddled with bullets and torn with shell, and in 1885, when this view was photographed, the corn was growing out of many a soldier's grave.— EDITORS.

Long Bridge road toward Richmond until we came in contact with the enemy's pickets. Then we returned and started anew. Fortunately I was at the head of the column to give the necessary orders, so that no delay occurred in retracing our steps.

Our new field of battle embraced Malvern Hill, just north of Turkey Creek and Crew's Hill, about one mile farther north. Both hills have given name to the interesting and eventful battle which took place on July 1st, and which I shall now attempt to describe.

The forces which on this occasion came under my control, and were engaged in or held ready to enter the contest, were my own corps, consisting of Morell's, Sykes's and McCall's divisions, Colonel H. J. Hunt's Artillery Reserve of one hundred pieces, including Colonel R. O. Tyler's Connecticut siege artillery, Couch's division of Keyes's corps, the brigades of John C. Caldwell and Thomas F. Meagher of Sumner's corps, and the brigade of D. E. Sickles of Heintzelman's corps. Though Couch was placed under my command, he was left uncontrolled by me, as will be seen hereafter. The other brigades were sent to me by their respective division commanders, in anticipation of my needs or at my request.

This new position, with its elements of great strength, was better adapted for a defensive battle than any with which we had been favored. It was elevated, and was more or less protected on each flank by small streams or by swamps, while the woods in front through which the enemy had to pass to attack us were in places marshy, and the timber so thick that artillery could not be brought up, and even troops were moved in it with difficulty. Slightly in rear of our line of battle on Crew's Hill the reserve artillery and infantry were held for immediate service. The hill concealed them from the view of the enemy and sheltered them to some extent from his fire. These hills, both to the east and west, were connected with the adjacent valleys by gradually sloping plains except at the Crew house, where for a little distance the slope was quite abrupt, and was easily protected by a small force. With the exception of the River road, all the roads from Richmond, along which the enemy would be obliged to approach, meet in front of Crew's Hill. This hill was flanked with ravines, enfiladed by our fire. The ground in front was sloping, and over it our artillery and infantry, themselves protected by the crest and ridges, had clear sweep for their fire. In all directions, for several hundred yards, the land over which an attacking force must advance was almost entirely cleared of forest and was generally cultivated.

MAJOR-GENERAL GEORGE W. MORELL.
FROM A PHOTOGRAPH.

I reached Malvern Hill some two hours before my command on Monday, June 30th; each division, as it came upon the field, was assigned to a position covering the approaches from Richmond along the River road and the debouches from the New Market, Charles City, and Williamsburg roads. Warren, with his brigade of about six hundred men, took position on the lowlands to the left, to guard against the approach of the enemy along the River road, or over the low, extensive, and cultivated plateau beyond and extending north along Crew's Hill. Warren's men were greatly in need of rest. The brigade had suffered greatly at Gaines's Mill, and was not expected to perform much more than picket duty, and it was large enough for the purpose designed, as it was not probable that any large force would be so reckless as to advance on that road. Warren was supported by the 11th U. S. Infantry, under Major Floyd-Jones, and late in the afternoon was strengthened by Martin's battery of 12-pounders and a detachment of the 3d Pennsylvania cavalry under Lieutenant Frank W. Hess.

On the west side of Malvern Hill, overlooking Warren, were some thirty-six guns, some of long range, having full sweep up the valley and over the cleared lands north of the River road. These batteries comprised Captain S. H. Weed's Battery I, 5th U. S. Artillery, Captain John Edwards's Batteries L and M, 3d U. S. Artillery, J. H. Carlisle's Battery E, 2d U. S. Artillery, John R. Smead's Battery K, 5th U. S. Artillery, and Adolph Voegelee's, Battery B, 1st N. Y. Artillery Battalion, with others in reserve. To these, later in the day, were added the siege-guns of the 1st Connecticut Artillery, under Colonel Robert O. Tyler, which were placed on elevated

THE CREW HOUSE. THE UPPER PICTURE SHOWS THE OLD HOUSE, AND IS FROM A COLOR-SKETCH TAKEN SOON AFTER THE WAR; THE NEW HOUSE SHOWN IN THE LOWER PICTURE IS FROM A PHOTOGRAPH TAKEN EARLY IN 1885.

The old building, sometimes called Dr. Mellert's, was the headquarters of General Morell; during the battle members of the Signal Corps were at work on the roof. It was burned after the war and rebuilt on the old foundations. The view in each case is from the east.

The lane, in the lower picture, leads to the Quaker road and was the line of Griffin's guns. McQuade's repulse of the attack on the hill took place behind the cabin on the left of the picture. The Crew farm is said to be one of the most fertile on the Peninsula.— EDITORS.

ground immediately to the left of the Malvern house, so as to fire over our front line at any attacking force, and to sweep the low meadow on the left.

To General (then Colonel) Hunt, the accomplished and energetic chief of artillery, was due the excellent posting of these batteries on June 30th, and the rearrangement of all the artillery along the whole line on Tuesday (July 1st), together with the management of the reserve artillery on that day.

Major Charles S. Lovell, commanding Colonel William Chapman's brigade of Sykes's division, supported some of these batteries, and, with the brigade of Buchanan on his right, in a clump of pines, extended the line northward, near the Crew (sometimes called the Mellert) house.

Morell, prolonging Sykes's line on Crew's Hill, with headquarters at Crew's house, occupied the right of the line extending to the Quaker road. To his left front, facing west, was the 14th New York Volunteers, under Colonel

## THE BATTLE OF MALVERN HILL.    411

McQuade, with a section of Captain W. B. Weeden's Battery C, 1st Rhode Island Artillery, both watching the Richmond road and the valley and protecting our left. On their right, under cover of a narrow strip of woods, skirting the Quaker road, were the brigades of Martindale and Butterfield, while in front of these, facing north, was Griffin's brigade. All were supporting batteries of Morell's division, commanded by Captain Weeden and others, under the general supervision of Griffin, a brave and skilled artillery officer.↓

About 3 o'clock on Monday the enemy was seen approaching along the River road, and Warren and Hunt made all necessary dispositions to receive them. About 4 o'clock the enemy advanced and opened fire from their artillery upon Warren and Sykes and on the extreme left of Morell, causing a few casualties in Morell's division. In return for this intrusion the concentrated rapid fire of the artillery was opened upon them, soon smashing one battery to pieces, silencing another, and driving back their infantry and cavalry in rapid retreat, much to the satisfaction of thousands of men watching the result. The enemy left behind in possession of Warren a few prisoners, two guns and six caissons, the horses of which had been killed. The battery which had disturbed Morell was also silenced by this fire of our artillery. On this occasion the gun-boats in the James [see p. 268] made apparent their welcome presence and gave good support by bringing their heavy guns to bear upon the enemy. Though their fire caused a few casualties among our men, and inflicted but little, if any, injury upon the enemy, their large shells, bursting amid the enemy's troops far beyond the attacking force, carried great moral influence with them, and naturally tended, in addition to the effect of our artillery, to prevent any renewed attempt to cross the open valley on our left. This attacking force formed a small part of Wise's brigade of Holmes's division. They were all raw troops, which accounts for their apparently demoralized retreat. This affair is known as the action of Turkey Bridge or Malvern Cliff. ⚓

Our forces lay on their arms during the night, in substantially the positions I have described, patiently awaiting the attack expected on the following day.

↓ These batteries as located on Tuesday, the day of the battle, were those of Edwards, Livingston, Kingsbury, Ames, part of Weeden's under Waterman, part of Allen's under Hyde, and Bramhall's. Other batteries as they arrived were posted in reserve south of Crew's Hill, and were used to replace batteries whose ammunition was exhausted, or were thrown forward into action to strengthen the line.

The different commands as soon as they were posted prepared to pass the night [June 30th] in securing the rest greatly needed both by man and beast. Later on June 30th Couch's division of Keyes's corps came up and took its place, extending Morell's line to the right of the Quaker road. The greater part of the supply trains of the army and of the reserve artillery passed safely beyond Turkey Creek through the commands thus posted, the movement only ceasing about 4 o'clock in the afternoon.—F. J. P.

⚓ Some idea may be formed from the following incident of how indifferent to noises or unconscious of sudden alarms one may become when asleep, under the sense of perfect security or from the effect of fatigue. For several days I had been able to secure but little sleep, other than such as I could catch on horseback, or while resting for a few minutes. During this heavy artillery firing I was asleep in the Malvern house. Although the guns were within one hundred yards of me, and the windows and doors were wide open, I was greatly surprised some two hours afterward to learn that the engagement had taken place. For weeks I had slept with senses awake to the sound of distant cannon, and even of a musket-shot, and would be instantly aroused by either. But on this occasion I had gone to sleep free from care, feeling confident that however strong an attack might be made, the result would be the repulse of the enemy without much damage to us. My staff, as much in need of rest as myself, sympathized with me and let me sleep.—F. J. P.

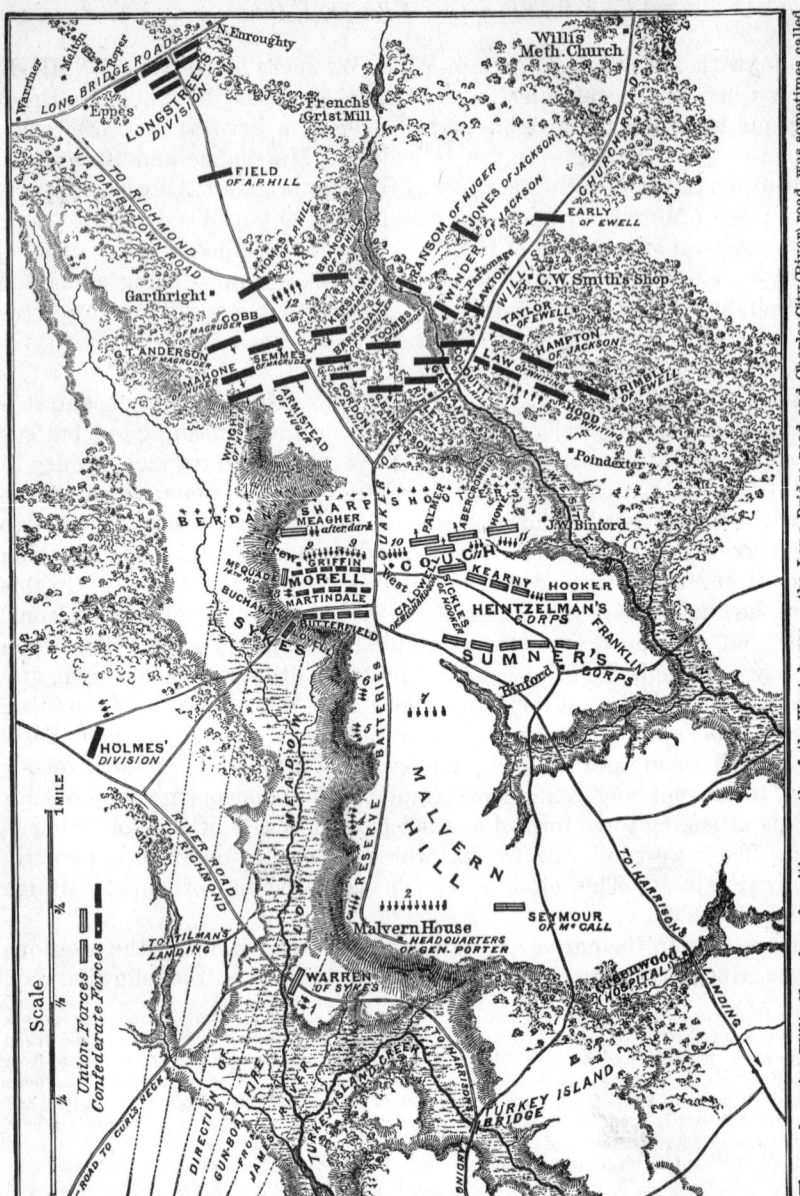

MAP OF THE BATTLE OF MALVERN HILL, SHOWING, APPROXIMATELY, POSITIONS OF BRIGADES AND BATTERIES.

The Union batteries, as indicated on the map, were: 1, Martin's; 2, Tyler's; 3, 4, 5, 6, batteries in reserve; 7, Hunt's reserve artillery; 8 and 11, first and second positions of Waterman's (Weeden's); 9—9, Edwards's, Livingston's, Ames's, Kingsbury's, and Hyde's; 10, Snow's, Frank's, and Hyde's; 11, Kingsbury's and Seeley's.

On the Union side the chief variations from these positions were the advance of a part of Butterfield's brigade, between Griffin and Couch, and the transfer of batteries from Morell to Couch. During the afternoon Sickles's brigade took the place of Caldwell's, which had come up to Couch's aid and had suffered severely. Meagher advanced about 5 o'clock, accompanied by 32-pounders under Colonel H. J. Hunt, which did terrible execution.

The Confederate brigades are placed in the order of their attack; those marked with an arrow were in the charges or in the front line after dark. It is difficult to fix the positions of the Confederate artillery. In general, 12 indicates Moorman's, Grimes's, and Pegram's; and 13 denotes the position of Balthis's, Poague's, and Carpenter's. In other positions, the batteries of Wooding (one section under Lieutenant Jones), Carrington, Hardaway, Bondurant, Hart, McCarthy, and the Baltimore Light Artillery were engaged to some extent.— EDITORS.

412

McCall's division of Pennsylvania Reserves, now under General Truman Seymour, arrived during the night and was posted just in front of the Malvern house, and was held in reserve, to be called upon for service only in case of absolute necessity.↓

Early on Tuesday our lines were re-formed and slightly advanced to take full advantage of the formation of the ground, the artillery of the front line being reposted in commanding positions, and placed under General Griffin's command, but under Captain Weeden's care, just behind the crest of the hill. The infantry was arranged between the artillery to protect and be protected by its neighbors, and prepared to be thrown forward, if at any time advisable, so as not to interfere with the artillery fire.

BERDAN'S SHARP-SHOOTERS (OF MORELL'S DIVISION) SKIRMISHING IN THE MEADOW WHEAT-FIELD.

↓ This division had reached me at New Market cross-roads, at midnight of the 29th, greatly in need of rest. This fact, and the necessity that a reliable force should hold that point until the whole army had crossed the White Oak Swamp and the trains had passed to the rear, compelled the assignment of McCall to the performance of that duty. During the afternoon of the 30th he was attacked by large forces of the enemy, which he several times repulsed; but he failed to enjoy the advantages of his success through the recklessness and irrepressible impetuosity of his men or the forgetfulness of orders by infantry subordinates. They were strictly cautioned, unless unusual fortune favored them, not to pass through a battery for the purpose of pursuing a repulsed enemy, and under no circumstances to return in face of one, so as to check its fire. In the excitement of presumed success at repulsing a heavy attack, a brigade pushed after a rapidly fleeing foe, and was impulsively joined by its neighbors, who wished not to be excelled in dash or were perhaps encouraged by injudicious orders. Passing through their own batteries as they advanced, they lost the benefit of their fire, as they did also when returning after being repulsed and pursued by the enemy's reserves. Disregard of these principles at this time caused heavy losses of men, and led to the demoralization at a critical moment of one good volunteer battery and the capture, through no fault of its commander, of one of the best batteries of the regular army [see p. 402]. This battery was commanded by Lieutenant A. M. Randol, a brave and accomplished artillery officer of the regular army. This division had otherwise suffered heavily. At Gaines's Mill it had lost, by capture, one of the ablest generals, John F. Reynolds, with other gallant and efficient officers and men, captured, killed, or wounded. Its misfortunes culminated in the capture at New Market cross-roads of McCall, the wounding of General George G. Meade, his able assistant, and the loss of many excellent subordinates. Fortunately the brave and experienced soldier, General Seymour, with his worthy officers, escaped to lead the survivors of the division to our camp, where they were welcomed by their sympathizing comrades.—F. J. P.

THE WEST HOUSE, LOOKING TOWARD THE CREW HOUSE. FROM A PHOTOGRAPH TAKEN EARLY IN 1885.

This house was the dividing point between Couch's division and Morell's line, the artillery fronting the fence and being nearly on the line indicated by it. The West house was occupied as headquarters by General Couch.—EDITORS.

The corps of Heintzelman and Sumner had arrived during the night and taken position in the order named to the right and rear of Couch's division, protecting that flank effectively toward Western Run. They did not expect to be seriously engaged, but were ready to resist attack and to give assistance to the center and left, if circumstances should require it. At an early hour in the day Sumner kindly sent me Caldwell's brigade, as he thought I might need help. This brigade I placed near Butterfield, who was directed to send it forward wherever it should be needed or called for. He sent it to Couch at an opportune moment early in the day.

General McClellan, accompanied by his staff, visited our lines at an early hour, and approved my measures and those of General Couch, or changed them where it was deemed advisable. Though he left me in charge of that part of the field occupied by Couch, I at no time undertook to control that general, or even indicated a desire to do so, but with full confidence in his ability, which was justified by the result of his action, left him free to act in accordance with his own judgment. I coöperated with him fully, however, having Morell's batteries, under Weeden, posted so as to protect his front and sending him help when I saw he needed it. The division of Couch, though

Franklin's corps, and French's brigade of Sumner's corps, arrived at Malvern Hill on the morning of July 1st. During the day Franklin's columns were in line of battle on the right of Sumner.—EDITORS.

it suffered severely in the battle of Fair Oaks, had seen less service and met with fewer losses in these "Seven Days' battles" than any one of my three, and was prepared with full ranks to receive an attack, seeming impatient and eager for the fight. Its conduct soon confirmed this impression. Batteries of Hunt's Artillery Reserve were sent to him when needed — and also Caldwell's brigade, voluntarily sent to me early in the day by Sumner, and Sickles's brigade, borrowed of Heintzelman for the purpose.

About 10 A. M. the enemy's skirmishers and artillery began feeling for us along our line; they kept up a desultory fire until about 12 o'clock, with no severe injury to our infantry, who were well masked, and who revealed but little of our strength or position by retaliatory firing or exposure.

Up to this time and until nearly 1 o'clock our infantry were resting upon their arms and waiting the moment, certain to come, when the column of the enemy rashly advancing would render it necessary to expose themselves. Our desire was to hold the enemy where our artillery would be most destructive, and to reserve our infantry ammunition for close quarters to repel the more determined assaults of our obstinate and untiring foe. Attacks by brigade were made upon Morell, both on his left front and on his right, and also upon Couch; but our artillery, admirably handled, without exception, was generally sufficient to repel all such efforts and to drive back the assailants in confusion, and with great loss.

VIEW FROM THE MEADOW WEST OF THE CREW HOUSE. FROM A PHOTOGRAPH TAKEN EARLY IN 1885.

The Crew house is in the extreme right of the picture. The hill to the left is the high ground shown on p. 419. The ravine between the two is the ravine shown in the right of the picture on p. 418. At the time of the battle the low ground was in wheat, partly shocked, affording protection for the Union sharp-shooters under Berdan. Farther to the left, up this valley, and in the rear of the hill, was the right of the Confederate line, which late in the evening made several assaults upon the Crew Hill, by way of the ravine and meadow.— EDITORS.

SCENE OF THE CONFEDERATE ATTACK ON THE WEST SIDE OF CREW'S HILL, LOOKING FROM THE CREW HOUSE SOUTH-WEST TOWARD THE JAMES RIVER. FROM A PHOTOGRAPH TAKEN EARLY IN 1885.

The Confederates came down the valley or meadow from the right, and advanced up this slope toward the two guns of Weeden, which were supported by the Fourteenth New York Volunteers. The road across the meadow leads to Holmes's position on the River road.— EDITORS.

While the enemy's artillery was firing upon us General Sumner withdrew part of his corps to the slope of Malvern Hill, to the right of the Malvern house, which descended into the valley of Western Run. Then, deeming it advisable to withdraw all our troops to that line, he ordered me to fall back to the Malvern house; but I protested that such a movement would be disastrous, and declined to obey the order until I could confer with General McClellan, who had approved of the disposition of our troops. Fortunately Sumner did not insist upon my complying with the order, and, as we were soon vigorously attacked, he advanced his troops to a point where he was but little disturbed by the enemy, but from which he could quickly render aid in response to calls for help or where need for help was apparent.※

The spasmodic, though sometimes formidable attacks of our antagonists, at different points along our whole front, up to about 4 o'clock, were presumably demonstrations or feelers, to ascertain our strength, preparatory to their engaging in more serious work. An ominous silence, similar to that which had preceded the attack in force along our whole line at Gaines's Mill, now intervened, until, at about 5:30 o'clock, the enemy opened upon both Morel

※ On one occasion, when I sent an urgent request for two brigades, Sumner read my note aloud, and, fearing he could not stand another draft on his forces, was hesitating to respond, when Heintzelman, ever prompt and generous, sprang to his feet and exclaimed : "By Jove! if Porter asks for help, I know he needs it and I will send it." The immediate result was the sending of Meagher by Sumner and Sickles by Heintzelman. This was the second time that Sumner had selected and sent me Meagher's gallant Irish brigade, and each time i rendered invaluable service. I had served under General Heintzelman up to the capture of Yorktown, and I ever appreciated his act as the prompting of a thoughtful, generous, and chivalrou nature.— F. J. P.

and Couch with artillery from nearly the whole of his front, and soon afterward pressed forward his columns of infantry, first on one and then on the other, or on both. As if moved by a reckless disregard of life, equal to that displayed at Gaines's Mill, with a determination to capture our army, or destroy it by driving us into the river, regiment after regiment, and brigade after brigade, rushed at our batteries; but the artillery of both Morell and Couch mowed them down with shrapnel, grape, and canister; while our infantry, withholding their fire until the enemy were within short range, scattered the remnants of their columns, sometimes following them up and capturing prisoners and colors. ☆

As column after column advanced, only to meet the same disastrous repulse, the sight became one of the most interesting imaginable. The havoc made by the rapidly bursting shells from guns arranged so as to sweep any position

REPULSE OF THE CONFEDERATES ON THE SLOPE OF CREW'S HILL [SEE P. 416].

☆ Captain William B. Weeden, in a letter dated May 24th, 1885, says of the battle :

"It was a fine afternoon, hot but tempered by a cooling breeze. The soldiers waited; patience, not courage, kept them steady. The ranks were full now; each knew that in himself he might be a possible victor or a possible victim at nightfall. Crew's deserted house, more hospitable than its owner, had furnished a luxury seldom enjoyed on the field. Water, not warm in the canteen, but iced in a delf pitcher, with glasses, was literally 'handed round.' Pickets and skirmishers had kept us informed of the opposing formations and of batteries going into position. The sharp-shooters' bullets began to thicken. Action might begin at any moment, and between 2 and 3 o'clock it did begin. Out of the woods, puffs of smoke from guns and nearer light wreaths from their shells lent new colors to the green of woods and fields and the deep blue sky. The musketry cracked before it loudened into a roar, and whizzing bullets mingled with ragged exploding shells. The woods swarmed with butternut coats and gray. These colors were worn by a lively race of men and they stepped forward briskly, firing as they moved. The regimental formations were plainly visible, with the colors flying. It was the onset of battle with the good order of a review. In this first heavy skirmish — the prelude of the main action — Magruder's right made a determined attack by way of the meadow to pierce Griffin's line to turn Ames's Battery and to break the solid advantages of position held by the Union forces.

"The brunt of the blow fell upon Colonel McQuade's 14th New York. This was a gallant regiment which had suffered much in the rough work at Gaines's Mill. The Confederate charge was sudden and heavy. The New Yorkers began to give ground, and it looked for a moment as if the disasters of Gaines's Mill might be repeated. But only for a moment. The men stiffened up to the color line, charged forward with a cheer, and drove back the enemy. Weeden's Rhode Island Battery of three-inch rifled ordnance guns had lost three pieces at Gaines's Mill. The remaining guns, under command of Lieutenant Waterman, were stationed south and west of Crew's, fronting left and rearward. It was the angle of our position, and so far west that Tyler's heavy guns mistook it for the enemy and fired 4½-inch shells into it. One caused severe casualties. The battery was withdrawn from this dangerous range, and later in the afternoon, when the main action was raging, Waterman's three guns, with two of the same type under Lieutenant Phillips of Massachusetts, relieved Kingsbury and Hazlitt's regular batteries of Parrotts on Couch's right. The service here was admirable. Waterman with only half a battery had a whole company of experienced gunners. When the ammunition gave out they were in turn relieved by a fresh battery."   EDITORS.

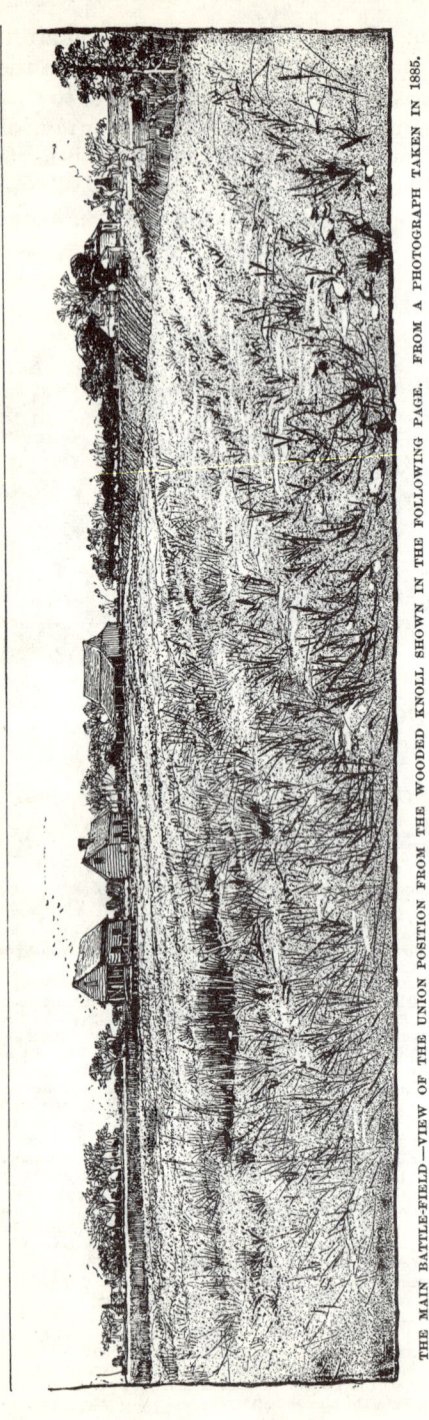

THE MAIN BATTLE-FIELD.—VIEW OF THE UNION POSITION FROM THE WOODED KNOLL SHOWN IN THE FOLLOWING PAGE. FROM A PHOTOGRAPH TAKEN IN 1885.

Morell's line extended from the Crew house on the right to the West house in the extreme left of the picture. Couch extended the line a third of a mile to the left of the West house. The ravine, to the right of the barn and buildings in the middle-ground, descends to the meadow; it was by this ravine and the shelter of the out-buildings that the Confederates effected a lodgment on the hill, at dusk, compelling Griffin to shift his guns to avoid capture.

General A. R. Wright, who commanded a brigade in Huger's division, in his official report describes as follows the aspect of the Federal position, as seen from the wooded knoll shown on the following page: "I suggested to General Armistead that we go forward to the edge of the field, and, under protection of a strong force of skirmishers, ascend a high knoll or hill which abruptly sprang from the meadow below and on our right, from the summit of which we would be able to observe the enemy's movements. Having reached this position, we were enabled to get a very complete view of McClellan's army. Immediately in our front, and extending one mile, stretched a field, at the farther extremity of which was situated the dwelling and farm-buildings of Mr. Crew (formerly Dr. Mellert). In front and to our left the land rose gently from the edge of the woods up to the farm-yard, when it became high and rolling, and valleys, which ran out at right angles to a line drawn from our position to that of the enemy, and all of which terminated upon our extreme right in a precipitous bluff, which dropped suddenly down upon a low, flat meadow, covered with wheat and intersected with a number of ditches, which ran from the bluff across the meadow to a swamp or dense woods about five hundred yards farther to our right. This low, flat meadow stretched up to, and swinging around, Crew's house, extended as far as Turkey Bend, on James River. The enemy had drawn up his artillery (as well as could be ascertained about fifty pieces) in a crescent-shaped line, the convex line being next to our position, with its right (on our left) resting upon a road which passed three hundred yards to the left of Crew's house on to Malvern Hill, the left of their advanced line of batteries resting upon the high bluff which overlooked the meadow to the right (our right) and rear of Crew's house. Their infantry, a little in the rear of the artillery, and protected by the crest of the ridge upon which the batteries were placed, extended from the woods on our left along the crest of the hill and through a lane in the meadow on our right to the dense woods there. In rear of this and beyond a narrow ravine, the sides of which were covered with timber, and which ran parallel to their line of battle and but a few rods in the rear of Crew's house, was another line of infantry, its right resting upon a heavy, dense woods, which covered the Malvern Hill farm on the east. The left of this line rested upon the precipitous bluff which overhung the low meadow on the west of the farm. At this point the high bluff stretched out to the west for two hundred yards in a long ridge or ledge (nearly separating the meadow from the lowlands of the river), upon the extreme western terminus of which was planted a battery of heavy guns. This latter battery commanded the whole meadow in front of it, and by a direct fire was able to dispute the manœuvring of troops over any portion of the meadow. Just behind the ravine which ran in rear of Crew's house, and under cover of the timber, was planted a heavy battery in a small redoubt, whose fire swept across the meadow. These two batteries completely controlled the meadow from one extremity of it to the other, and effectually prevented the movement of troops in large masses upon it. The whole number of guns in these several batteries could not have fallen far short of one hundred. The infantry force of the enemy I estimated at least 25,000 or 30,000 from what I saw. Large numbers, as I ascertained afterward, were posted in the woods on our extreme right and left, and the line of ditches across the meadow were lined with sharp-shooters."— EDITORS.

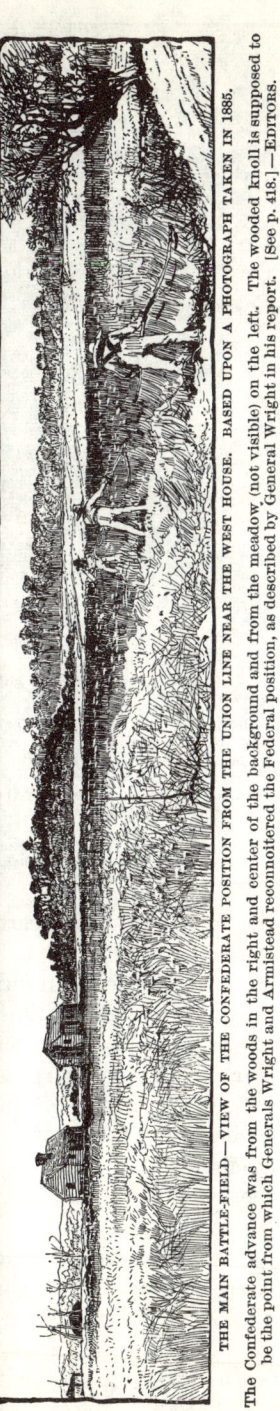

far and near, and in any direction, was fearful to behold. Pressed to the extreme as they were, the courage of our men was fully tried. The safety of our army — the life of the Union — was felt to be at stake. In one case the brigades of Howe, Abercrombie, and Palmer, of Couch's division, under impulse, gallantly pushed after the retreating foe, captured colors, and advantageously advanced the right of the line, but at considerable loss and great risk. The brigades of Morell, cool, well-disciplined, and easily controlled, let the enemy return after each repulse, but permitted few to escape their fire. Colonel McQuade, on Morell's left, with the 14th New York, against orders and at the risk of defeat and disaster, yielding to impulse, gallantly dashed forward and repulsed an attacking party. Assisted by Buchanan of Sykes's division, Colonel Rice, with the 44th New York Volunteers, likewise drove a portion of the enemy from the field, taking a flag bearing the inscription "Seven Pines." Colonel Hunt, directing the artillery, was twice dismounted by having his horse shot under him, but though constantly exposed continued his labors until after dark. General Couch, who was also dismounted in like manner, took advantage of every opportunity to make his opponents feel his blows.

It is not to be supposed that our men, though concealed by the irregularities of the ground, were not sufferers from the enemy's fire. The fact is that before they exposed themselves by pursuing the enemy, the ground was literally covered with the killed and wounded from dropping bullets and bursting shells and their contents; but they bravely bore the severe trial of having to remain inactive under a damaging fire.

As Morell's front ranks became thinned out and the ammunition was exhausted, other regiments eagerly advanced; all were stimulated by the hope of a brilliant and permanent success, and nerved by the approving shouts of their comrades and the cry of "Revenge, boys!" "Remember McLane!" "Remember Black!" "Remember Gove!" or "Remember Cass!" Black and McLane and Gove had been killed at Gaines's Mill;

MALVERN HILL, FROM THE DIRECTION OF TURKEY ISLAND BRIDGE. FROM A SKETCH MADE SOON AFTER THE WAR.

VIEW FROM MALVERN HILL, LOOKING TOWARD THE JAMES. FROM A PHOTOGRAPH TAKEN IN 1885.

This view is taken from near the position of Tyler's siege-guns (see map). The engagement of Malvern Cliff, or Turkey Island bridge, on the 30th of June, between Generals Warren and Holmes, took place on the road at the foot of the hill which passes near the house in the middle-ground. The bridge is to the left on this road. The winding stream is Turkey Creek. In the middle distance is the position of the three gun-boats which shelled the woods at the right both on the 30th of June and the 1st of July.— EDITORS.

Woodbury and Cass were then lying before them.‍‍‍‍‍‍‍‍‍‍‍‍‍ ‍‍‍‍‍‍‍‍‍‍ Colonel McQuade was the only regimental commander of Griffin's brigade who escaped death during the Seven Days, and he was constantly exposed.

During that ominous silence of which I have spoken, I determined that our opponents should reap no advantage, even if our lines yielded to attack, and therefore posted batteries, as at Gaines's Mill, to secure against the disaster of a break in our lines, should such a misfortune be ours. For this purpose I sent Weed, Carlisle, and Smead, with their batteries, to the gorge of the roads on Crew's Hill, from which the enemy must emerge in pursuit if he should break our lines; instructing them to join in the fight if necessary, but not to permit the advance of the foe, even if it must be arrested at the risk of firing upon friends. To these Colonel Hunt added three batteries of horse artillery. Though they were all thus posted and their guns loaded with double canister, "they were," as Captain Smead reported, "very happy to find their services not needed on that occasion."

‍‍‍‍‍‍‍‍‍ Colonel Samuel W. Black, of the 62d Pennsylvania, Colonel John W. McLane, of the 83d Pennsylvania, Colonel Jesse A. Gove, of the 22d Massachusetts, Colonel Dwight A. Woodbury, of the 4th Michigan, and Colonel Thomas Cass, of the 9th Massachusetts.— EDITORS.

It was at this time, in answer to my call for aid, that Sumner sent me Meagher, and Heintzelman sent Sickles, both of whom reached me in the height of battle, when, if ever, fresh troops would renew our confidence and insure our success. While riding rapidly forward to meet Meagher, who was approaching at a "double-quick" step, my horse fell, throwing me over his head, much to my discomfort both of body and mind. On rising and remounting I was greeted with hearty cheers, which alleviated my chagrin. This incident gave rise to the report, spread through the country, that I was wounded. Fearing that I might fall into the hands of the enemy, and if so that my diary and dispatch-book of the campaign, then on my person, would meet with the same fate and reveal information to the injury of our cause, I tore it up, scattering the pieces to the winds, as I rode rapidly forward, leading Meagher into action. I have always regretted my act as destroying interesting and valuable memoranda of our campaign.

Advancing with Meagher's brigade, accompanied by my staff, I soon found that our forces had successfully driven back their assailants. Determined, if possible, satisfactorily to finish the contest, regardless of the risk of being fired upon by our artillery in case of defeat, I pushed on beyond our lines into the woods held by the enemy. About fifty yards in front of us, a large force of the enemy suddenly rose and opened with fearful volleys upon our advancing line. I turned to the brigade, which thus far had kept pace with my horse, and found it standing "like a stone-wall," and returning a fire more destructive than it received and from which the enemy fled. The brigade was planted. My presence was no longer needed, and I sought General Sickles, whom I found giving aid to Couch. I had the satisfaction of learning that night that a Confederate detachment, undertaking to turn Meagher's left, was met by a portion of the 69th New York Regiment, which, advancing, repelled the attack and captured many prisoners.

BREVET BRIGADIER-GENERAL JAMES McQUADE. (DIED 1885.) AT MALVERN HILL COLONEL OF THE 14TH NEW YORK. FROM A PHOTOGRAPH.

After seeing that General Sickles was in a proper position, I returned to my own corps, where I was joined by Colonel Hunt with some 32-pounder howitzers. Taking those howitzers, we rode forward beyond our lines, and, in parting salutation to our opponents, Colonel Hunt sent a few shells, as a warning of what would be ready to welcome them on the morrow if they undertook to disturb us.

THE MALVERN HOUSE. FROM A PHOTOGRAPH TAKEN IN 1885.

During the engagement at Turkey bridge and the battle of Malvern Hill, this house was the headquarters of General Porter, and was a signal-station in communication with the gun-boats in the James River, toward which it fronts. It was built of imported English brick, of a dark but vivid red. The main battle-field is in the direction of the trees on the right, and Tyler's siege-guns were near the small trees in the left distance.— EDITORS.

Almost at the crisis of the battle — just before the advance of Meagher and Sickles — the gun-boats on the James River opened their fire with the good intent of aiding us, but either mistook our batteries at the Malvern house for those of the enemy, or were unable to throw their projectiles beyond us. If the former was the case, their range was well estimated, for all their shot landed in or close by Tyler's battery, killing and wounding a few of his men. Fortunately members of our excellent signal-service corps were present as usual on such occasions, and the message signaled to the boats, "For God's sake, stop firing," promptly relieved us from further damage and the demoralization of a "fire in the rear." Reference is occasionally seen in Confederate accounts of this battle to the fearful sounds of the projectiles from those gun-boats. But that afternoon not one of their projectiles passed beyond my headquarters; and I have always believed and said, as has General Hunt, that the enemy mistook the explosions of shells from Tyler's siege-guns and Kusserow's 32-pounder howitzers, which Hunt had carried forward, for shells from the gun-boats.

While Colonel Hunt and I were returning from the front, about 9 o'clock we were joined by Colonel A. V. Colburn, of McClellan's staff. We all rejoiced over the day's success. By these officers I sent messages to the commanding general, expressing the hope that our withdrawal had ended and that we should hold the ground we now occupied, even if we did not assume the offensive. From my standpoint I thought we could maintain our position, and perhaps in a few days could improve it by advancing. But I knew only the circumstances before me, and these were limited by controlling influences. It was now after 9 o'clock at night. Within an hour of the time that Colonels Hunt and Colburn left me, and before they could have reached the commanding general, I received orders from him to withdraw, and to direct Generals Sumner and Heintzelman to move at specified hours to Harrison's Landing and General Couch to rejoin his corps, which was then under way to the same point.‡

These orders were immediately sent to the proper officers, and by daybreak, July 2d, our troops, preceded by their trains, were well on their way to their destination, which they reached that day, greatly wearied after a hard march over muddy roads, in the midst of a heavy rain. That night, freed from care and oblivious of danger, all slept a long sleep; and they awoke the next morning with the clear sun, a happier, brighter, and stronger body of men than that which all the day before, depressed and fatigued, had shivered in the rain.

The conduct of the rear-guard was intrusted to Colonel Averell, commander of the 3d Pennsylvania Cavalry, sustained by Colonel Buchanan, with his brigade of regulars, and the 67th New York Regiment. No trying trust was ever better bestowed or more satisfactorily fulfilled. At daybreak Colonel Averell found himself accidentally without artillery to protect his command in its difficult task of preventing an attack before our rear was well out of range. He at once arranged his cavalry in bodies to represent horse-batteries, and, manœuvring them to create the impression that they were artillery ready for action, he secured himself from attack until the rest of the army and trains had passed sufficiently to the rear to permit him to retire rapidly without molestation. His stratagem was successful, and without loss he rejoined the main body of the army that night. Thus ended the memorable "Seven Days' battles," which, for severity and for stubborn resistance and endurance of hardships by the contestants, were not surpassed during the war. Each antagonist accomplished the result for which he aimed: one insuring the temporary relief of Richmond; the other gaining security on the north bank of the James, where the Union army, if our civil and military authorities were disposed, could be promptly reënforced, and from whence only, as subsequent events proved, it could renew the contest successfully. Preparations were commenced and dispositions were at once made under

---

‡ The order referred to read as follows:
"HEADQUARTERS ARMY OF THE POTOMAC, 9 P. M., JULY 1ST, 1862; BRIGADIER-GENERAL F. J. PORTER, COMMANDING FIFTH PROVISIONAL CORPS.— GENERAL: The General Commanding desires you to move your command at once, the artillery reserve moving first to Harrison's Bar. In case you should find it impossible to move your heavy artillery, you are to spike the guns and destroy the carriages. Couch's command will move under your orders. Communicate these instructions to him at once. The corps of Heintzelman and Sumner will move next. Please communicate to General Heintzelman the time of your moving. Additional gun-boats, supplies, and reënforcements will be met at Harrison's Bar. Stimulate your men by informing them that reënforcements, etc., have arrived at our new base. By command of MAJOR-GENERAL MCCLELLAN, JAMES A. HARDIE, LIEUTENANT-COLONEL, A. D. C., A. A. A. G."

424                THE BATTLE OF MALVERN HILL.

I.—HEADQUARTERS OF GENERAL HEINTZELMAN ON THE RIVER SIDE OF MALVERN HILL.
II.—TURKEY BRIDGE, UNDER MALVERN HILL. FROM WAR-TIME SKETCHES.

every prospect, if not direct promise, of large reënforcements for a renewal of the struggle on the south side of the James, and in the same manner as subsequently brought a successful termination of the war.

In the Fifth Corps, however, mourning was mingled with rejoicing. Greatly injured by the mishap of a cavalry blunder at Gaines's Mill, it had at Malvern, with the brave and gallant help of Couch and the generous and chivalric assistance of Heintzelman and Sumner, successfully repulsed the foe in every quarter, and was ready to renew the contest at an opportune moment. Our killed and wounded were numbered by thousands; the loss of the Confederates may be imagined. ↓

While taking Meagher's brigade to the front, I crossed a portion of the ground over which a large column had advanced to attack us, and had a fair opportunity of judging of the effect of our fire upon the ranks of the enemy.

↓ It is impossible to estimate the casualties of each of these battles, so quickly did one follow another. Our total loss in these battles is recorded as 15,849, while that of the Confederates sums up to 20,135. The loss in the Fifth Corps was 7601. This does not include the losses of Slocum's division and Cooke's cavalry engaged with us at Gaines's Mill, nor of Couch's division and the brigades of Caldwell, Meagher, and Sickles serving with it at Malvern. [See pp. 314–318.]—F. J. P.

GENERAL FITZ JOHN PORTER'S HEADQUARTERS IN THE WESTOVER MANSION, CAMP AT HARRISON'S LANDING, JULY, 1862. FROM A WAR-TIME SKETCH.

It was something fearful and sad to contemplate; few steps could be taken without trampling upon the body of a dead or wounded soldier, or without hearing a piteous cry, begging our party to be careful. In some places the bodies were in continuous lines and in heaps. In Mexico I had seen fields of battle on which our armies had been victorious, and had listened to pitiful appeals; but the pleaders were not of my countrymen then, and did not, as now, cause me to deplore the effects of a fratricidal war.

Sadder still were the trying scenes I met in and around the Malvern house, which at an early hour that day had been given up to the wounded, and was soon filled with our unfortunate men, suffering from all kinds of wounds. At night, after issuing orders for the withdrawal of our troops, I passed through the building and the adjoining hospitals with my senior medical officer, Colonel George H. Lyman. Our object was to inspect the actual condition of the men, to arrange for their care and comfort, and to cheer them as best we could. Here, as usual, were found men mortally wounded, by necessity left unattended by the surgeons, so that prompt and proper care might be given to those in whom there was hope of recovery.

While passing through this improvised hospital I heard of many sad cases. One was that of the major of the 12th New York Volunteers, a brave and gallant officer, highly esteemed, who was believed to be mortally wounded. While breathing his last, as was supposed, a friend asked him if he had any message to leave. He replied, "Tell my wife that in my last thoughts were blended herself, my boy, and my flag." Then he asked how the battle had gone, and when told that we had been successful he said, "God bless the old fla——" and fell back apparently dead. For a long time he was mourned as dead, and it was believed that he had expired with the prayer left unfinished on his closing lips. Though still an invalid, suffering from the wound then received, that officer recovered to renew his career in the war.♭

On the occasion of this visit we frequently witnessed scenes which would melt the stoutest heart: bearded men piteously begging to be sent home; others requesting that a widowed mother or orphan sisters might be cared for; more sending messages to wife or children, or to others near and dear to them. We saw the amputated limbs and the bodies of the dead hurried out of the room for burial. On every side we heard the appeals of the unattended, the moans of the dying, and the shrieks of those under the knife of the surgeon. We gave what cheer we could, and left with heavy hearts.

At noon on the 4th of July the usual national salute was fired, and the different corps were reviewed. General McClellan, as opportunity offered, made a few remarks full of hope and encouragement, thanking the men in most feeling terms for their uniform bravery, fortitude, and good conduct, but intimating that this was not the last of the campaign.

Contrary, however, to his expectations, the Peninsular campaign of the Army of the Potomac for 1862 virtually ended on the 4th of July. From that date to August 14th, when the army at sundown took up its march for Fort Monroe, its commander was engaged in the struggle to retain it on the James, as against the determination of the Secretary of War to withdraw it to the line of the Rappahannock, there to act in conjunction with the Army of Virginia.

Although General McClellan was assured, in writing, that he was to have command of both armies after their junction, he preferred, as a speedy and the only practicable mode of taking Richmond, to remain on the James, and

♭ Afterward Brevet Major-General Henry A. Barnum.— EDITORS.

SUPPLYING THE HUNGRY ARMY AT HARRISON'S LANDING. FROM A WAR-TIME SKETCH.

**BERKELEY, HARRISON'S LANDING, AS SEEN FROM McCLELLAN'S HEADQUARTERS TENTS. FROM A WAR-TIME SKETCH.**

This house was the birthplace of General (afterward President) William Henry Harrison. During the month of July, 1862, it was used as a hospital and signal station.

renew the contest from the south bank, for which he had commenced operations. During this period he omitted nothing which would insure the removal of the army without loss of men and material. The withdrawal of the army changed the issue from the capture of Richmond to the security of Washington, transferred to the Federals the anxiety of the Confederates for their capital, and sounded an alarm throughout the Northern States.

It was publicly announced that Halleck would assume command and take the field. Pope had reason to believe that "he would eventually supersede McClellan," and McDowell had been so satisfied of his future supremacy that he confided to a friend that "he would be at the highest round of the ladder."— F. J. P.

## THE ARMY OF THE POTOMAC AT HARRISON'S LANDING.

### BY GEORGE L. KILMER, CO. D, 27TH NEW YORK VOLUNTEERS.

THE withdrawal of General McClellan's army from Malvern Hill, a position that seemed to be impregnable, was a surprise to the men in the ranks, and for the first time in the campaign they became discouraged. During July 2d rain fell copiously, and when the columns arrived at Harrison's Landing the fields were soaked and the soil was quickly reduced to paste by the men and trains. The infantry and the division wagons and batteries were drawn up in an immense field of standing wheat near the Harrison mansion, also called Berkeley. The grain was trampled into the soil, or laid down so as to serve under the tents as protection from the wet ground. Neither wood nor boards were to be had, and the army was exceedingly uncomfortable. Transports in the James landed rations, which proved a great blessing, since many of the men had not had food in forty-eight hours. The rain continued all night, and the flimsy wheat floors were soon floating in pools of water; besides, the soil would not hold the tent-pins, and in the morning the tents were nearly all down, exposing men whose beds were sinking deeper and deeper into the mud to the pelting rain. About 8 o'clock, while some of the men were yet asleep and others were attempting to get breakfast, the camp was startled by a sudden outburst of artillery fire, and shells came whistling over the plain. The shots were scattering, and seemed to be directed principally at the shipping. The troops were summoned to arms, but, as very little damage was done by the shells, the affair was soon turned to account as a joke. General J. E. B. Stuart for some days had been operating in the center of the Peninsula, and learning of the exposed position of McClellan's army on the James had hastened there and stationed his battery near Westover Church, across Herring Creek, north of the landing. A few shells from our gun-boats caused his guns to speedily shift their position, and General Nathan Kimball, of Shields's division (just arrived from the Shenandoah), advanced and cleared the field after some lively skirmishing.

The army immediately took position on the high ground about Harrison's Landing, and went into camp on an intrenched line several miles in extent. The air was filled with rumors about future operations. To the soldiers McClellan was less a hero now, perhaps, than before, but he was more a martial leader than ever. The unusual strain imposed upon the men, the malarial character of the region around Richmond, the lack of proper nourishment, the want of rest, combined with the excitement of the change of base, and the midsummer heat prostrated great numbers. In my notes written at the time, it is stated that 50 of the regiment, about 15 per cent. of the duty men, were sick in the camp hospital July 24th. This was in addition to the casualties of 162 sustained in the "Seven Days." According to the report of Surgeon Jonathan Letterman, Medical Director (Vol. XI., Part I., "Official Records," pp. 210-220), about 6000 sick were sent away soon after the army reached Harrison's Landing, over 12,000 remaining in camp. On July 30th, the report says, there were 12,000 sick with the army, and of these only 2000 were able to take the field. Fortunately the Sanitary Commission hastened to our relief with tents, food, medical supplies, and competent nurses.

⚓ A Confederate force under General S. G. French had been sent out from the command of D. H. Hill, at Petersburg. General W. N. Pendleton reported that

After the departure of Stuart from Westover, July 4th, the army did not see or hear the enemy, with a slight exception, until search was made for him toward Richmond early in August. The exception was on the night of Thursday, July 31st. About midnight the whole army was startled by a lively cannonade and by shells flying over the lines, some bursting within them. The troops turned out under arms, and it was soon discovered that a mild fusillade from across the James was being directed on the shipping and on the supply depots near the camps. ⚓ Comparatively little damage was done. The next day a Union force was thrown across the river to seize Coggins's Point, where the elevated ground favored that style of attack on our camps. The army soon became restless for want of work, and there was great rejoicing at the prospect of a forward movement. On the 2d of August, Hooker marched a portion of his division to Malvern Hill, and on the 4th extended his advance to Charles City Cross-roads, near Glendale. But orders came to withdraw from the Peninsula, so we marched to Williamsburg, Yorktown, Newport News, and Fort Monroe. The Fifth and Third Corps embarked, on August 20th and 21st, for Aquia Creek and Alexandria; also for Alexandria the Sixth (Aug. 23d and 24th), the Second (Aug. 26th), and the Fourth (except Peck's division, which remained at Yorktown), Aug. 29th.

1000 rounds were fired. The casualties in the Union camps, as reported by General McClellan, were 10 killed and 15 wounded.—G. L. K.

DUMMIES AND QUAKER GUNS LEFT IN THE WORKS AT HARRISON'S LANDING ON THE EVACUATION BY THE ARMY OF THE POTOMAC. FROM A SKETCH MADE AT THE TIME.

# WITH THE CAVALRY ON THE PENINSULA.

## BY WILLIAM W. AVERELL, BREVET MAJOR-GENERAL, U. S. A.

A PART OF THE FORTIFIED CAMP AT HARRISON'S LANDING. AFTER A SKETCH MADE AT THE TIME.

IN the Peninsular campaign of 1862 there were employed fourteen regiments of cavalry, entire or in parts, and two independent squadrons [see p. 314]. Considerably over half this force was composed of volunteers, and had been in existence about six months. In the regular cavalry three years had been regarded as necessary to transform a recruit into a good cavalryman. The amount of patient and persistent hard work required to convert 1200 untrained citizens, unaccustomed to the care of a horse or to his use under the saddle, and wholly inexperienced in the use of arms, into the semblance of a cavalry regiment in six months is known only to those who have done it.

The topography and soil of the peninsula presented a most difficult field for cavalry operations. From Fort Monroe to Hanover Court House there was hardly a field with sufficient scope for the manœuvres of a single regiment of cavalry. After a rain the deep alluvium became, under the tread of horses, a bed of mortar knee-deep. The forests between the York and the James rivers were filled with tangled thickets and unapproachable morasses. The tributaries of the rivers, mostly deep, crooked, and sluggish, became more tortuous as they approach their confluence, and the expanse of floods is converted by evaporation into stagnant swamps. A heavy rain in a few hours rendered these streams formidable obstacles. Above this dismal landscape the fierce rays of the sun were interrupted only at night, or by deluges of rains, so that men and animals were alternately scorched and drenched. These conditions made cavalry operations in this region affairs of squadrons.

The cavalry had been organized into a division under General George Stoneman, chief of cavalry, and distributed by assignment to the corps of the army, excepting the cavalry reserve under General P. St. George Cooke and that portion which was attached to general headquarters. During the month of the siege of Yorktown not an hour was lost which could be applied to cavalry instruction. Alertness and steadiness soon characterized our cavalrymen. No incident was fruitless. When grindstones were procured and the sabers of my regiment were sharpened at Hampton, it produced a similar effect upon the men.

Few but cavalry names reached the ears of the army on the day of the evacuation and pursuit. Stoneman and Cooke, on the right, with the 1st and 6th Regulars, struck cavalry, infantry, batteries, redoubts, and ravines, and pushed their attack with audacity. Cavalrymen galloped around field-works. We soon heard of the gallantry of Colonel Grier, Major Lawrence Williams, Captains Sanders, Davis, Baker, and others in cavalry charges, and that the French Princes were among the first in the advance. Lieutenant-Colonel Grier, commanding the 1st ("Old Billy Grier, the *bueno commandante*"), had led a charge and engaged two of the enemy in personal combat, wounding one and himself receiving a wound. Then came tidings of the dash of Chambliss and McLean leading Hancock's column and crowding the left-center of the enemy's line, and soon the 3d Pennsylvania cavalry met the enemy in the woods and drove him out with skirmishers and canister, and cleared our left toward the James of the enemy's cavalry under Stuart. During the following day, the cavalry were spectators of the battle at Williamsburg (except the 3d Pennsylvania actively engaged on our left) and were only occupied with the rather serious business of procuring food for the horses.

Although pursuit was again undertaken on the morning of the 6th by squadrons of the 3d Pennsylvania and 8th Illinois Cavalry and was continued for four miles, and five pieces of artillery were recovered and some prisoners were captured, it came to a dead halt from necessity. During the succeeding twenty days the cavalry swept the country in advance of our marching army by day and hovered around its bivouacs by night.

When the army was in line about seven miles from Richmond, on the 25th of May, I was directed to communicate with the gun-boats on the James River at City Point. Lieutenant Davis, of the 3d Pennsylvania, with ten men, was selected for the duty, and he made his way along various roads infested with the pickets and patrols of the enemy to the bank of the James, where, taking a skiff, with two negroes, he went on board the *Galena* and communicated to Captain Rodgers the position of the army, and received from the captain a statement of the position of the gun-boats.

On the 27th, not satisfied with the picnic appearance of our front on our left, south of the Chickahominy, I reported its perilous condition to McClellan, who at once sent Colonel N. B. Sweitzer, of his staff, to me, and together we rode to the front. As a result, orders were given at once for slashing the forest, and positions for batteries and outposts were determined,— precautions which, three days later, disclosed their value in the battle of Fair Oaks.

On the same day (27th) we were scratching the ground away up to our right at Hanover Court House, in invitation to McDowell to come down from Fredericksburg. Almost within his sight, and quite within his hearing, the principal northern gate to Richmond was set ajar, the Virginia Central and the Richmond and Fredericksburg railroads were destroyed. In the resultant mêlée about Hanover Court House, the cavalry, under Emory, Royall, Lawrence Williams, Chambliss, Whiting, Harrison, and Arnold, and Rush's 6th Pennsylvania, aggressively attacked infantry, captured whole companies with arms, swept right, left, and rear, and generally filled the ideal of cavalry activities in such a battle.

General Lee assumed command June 1st. On the 13th he announced himself, through his cavalry, in Stuart's raid around our army. This expedition was appointed with excellent judgment, and was conducted with superb address. Stuart pursued the line of least resistance, which was the unexpected. His subordinate commanders were Colonels Fitz Lee, W. H. F. Lee, and W. T. Martin, all intrepid cavalrymen. It was an easy thing to do, but being his first raid, Stuart was nervous, and, imagining perils which did not exist, neglected one great opportunity—the destruction of our base of supplies at the White House. Had he, at Garlick's, exchanged purposes with his detachment, sending it on the road home while he with the main body bent all his energies to the destruction of our base of supplies, we might have had something to lament even had we captured his command. On our side were developed many things to remember with pride, and one thing to regret with mortification. The memories are glorious that not a single vedette or picket was surprised, and that never was outpost duty more honorably and correctly performed than by Captain W. B. Royall and Lieutenant McLean of the 5th United States Cavalry. They met the enemy repeatedly, and the lieutenant gave his life and the captain was prostrated with saber wounds in resisting Stuart's column. The killing of the dashing Confederate Captain Latané and several men with the saber, and the checking of the invading forces for an hour attest the courage and devotion of Royall and his picket. We had to regret that there was no reserve to the outpost within supporting distance, and that when the reserve was alarmed in its camp precious time was lost by indirections. This raid of Stuart's added a new feature to cavalry history. A similar expedition, however, had been projected previously. Just before the Army of the Potomac advanced on Manassas, in March, '62, in a conference with General McClellan, it was suggested that I should take my brigade, consisting of the 3d and 8th Pennsylvania Cavalry, the first brigade of cavalry formed in the war, and go around the enemy, then at Manassas, destroying the bridge at Rappahannock Station, and that at Fredericksburg; but the immediate movement of the enemy from Manassas prevented its being carried out.

Our general's plans were not disturbed by Stuart's raid, and two days after it was over the 3d Pennsylvania Cavalry crossed the Pamunkey River on our right and rear, ascended to King William Court House and Ellett's Mills, burned the bridge and ferry-boat, and a schooner and other boats, and a storehouse containing 30,000 bushels of grain. Scouts were pushed out many miles in quest of news of Jackson's coming. This was the last extension of our hands toward McDowell, for Jackson came sooner than he was expected, on the 26th, the day upon which a general advance had been determined and the battle of Gaines's Mill was opened.

McClellan met and mastered the occasion. Alert, radiant, and cheerful, he stood out in front of his tent in his shirt-sleeves nearly all day of the 26th listening to his army. To the north, across the Chickahominy, his clipped right wing, environed with our cavalry, was sullenly retracting its lines to the position at Gaines's Mill. Stoneman, with infirmities that would have kept a man of less fortitude in hospital, was in the saddle confronting Stuart's cavalry and covering the White House Landing.

The ensuing night was without rest for the cavalry. The strain of the following day to help the Fifth Corps to hold its ground until dark will never be forgotten, and it was not devoid of heroic cavalry effort. Fragments of the reserve under General Cooke massed in the valley of the Chickahominy, on its left bank. About 5 P. M., when it was evident that we were being pressed on the right and left of our line by all the force the enemy could bring into action against Porter, and that we were not likely to be able to resist his attack, the cavalry was moved from its masked position to the edge of the hill and placed in a formation to charge, should a charge seem likely to do good. It was there exposed to the enemy's fire, and must either retire, advance, or be destroyed. In a few minutes the order to charge was given to the 5th Regulars, not 300 strong. Chambliss, leading, rode as straight as man ever rode, into the face of Longstreet's corps, and the 5th Cavalry was destroyed and dispersed. Six out of the seven officers present and fifty men were struck down. Chambliss, hit by seven balls, lost consciousness, and when he recovered found himself in the midst of the enemy. The charge at Balaklava had not this desperation and was not better ridden. Chambliss lay on the field ten days, and was finally taken to Richmond, where he was rescued from death by the kind care of Generals Hood and Field. In this battle there were two and a half squadrons of the 5th and two squadrons of the 1st U. S. Cavalry, three squadrons Rush's Lancers (6th Pennsylvania Cavalry), and one squadron 4th Pennsylvania (Col. Childs).

Two or three weeks before this several officers of the 3d Pennsylvania Cavalry, Newhall, Treichel, W. E. Miller, and others, penetrated the region between the Chickahominy and the James, taking bearings and making notes. Their fragmentary sketches, when put together, made a map which exhibited all the roadways, fields, forests, bridges, the streams, and houses, so that our commander knew the country to be traversed through the seven days far better than any Confederate commander.

On the evening of June 27th, my pickets from Tunstall's Station and other points were called in, and at 6:30 A. M., on the 28th, the regiment crossed White Oak Swamp, leading Keyes's corps, and advanced to the Charles City road. Lieutenant Davis was again sent to communicate with the gun-boats on the James.

At daylight, on the 29th, Captain White's squadron, with 200 infantry and 2 guns, was sent to picket and hold Jones's Bridge on the Chickahominy. About 9 A. M. my scouts reported a regiment of the enemy's cavalry advancing in column about a mile away. Some woodland intervened. Between this and my position was an open field a quarter of a mile across. A picket was quickly posted at the hither edge of the wood, with orders to fire upon the enemy when he should come within range and then turn and run away, thus inviting pursuit. On my position two guns were already placed to enfilade the road, and a few squadrons held in readiness to charge. The enemy came, was fired upon, and the picket fled, followed by the enemy in hot pursuit. Upon arriving within two hundred yards of our position, the picket quitted the road through the gaps in the fences made for that purpose, thus unmasking the enemy's column; the two guns of Major West fired two rounds, and two squadrons, led by Captains Walsh and Russell, of the 3d Pennsylvania, were let loose upon the enemy, and over 60 of his officers and men were left on the ground, whilst the survivors fled in great disorder toward Richmond. The command was the 1st North Carolina and 3d Virginia Cavalry, led by Colonel Lawrence Baker, a comrade of mine in the old army. The 3d Pennsylvania lost 1 man killed and 5 wounded.

After this affair I galloped back to see General McClellan, and found him near a house south of White Oak Swamp Bridge. Near him were groups of a hundred officers eagerly but quietly discussing our progress and situation. So soon as McClellan descried me, he came with the Prince de Joinville to the fence, where I dismounted. After telling him all I knew and had learned from prisoners and scouts, I ventured to suggest that the roads were tolerably clear toward Richmond, and that we might go there. The Prince seemed to exhibit a favorable interest in my suggestion, but the general, recognizing its weakness, said promptly: "The roads will be full enough to-morrow"; and then earnestly, "Averell, if any army can save this country, it will be the Army of the Potomac, and it must be saved for that purpose." The general rode to the front with me, and reconnoitered the ground in all directions. In the afternoon, with Hays's regiment of infantry and Benson's battery, I established our outposts and pickets within one mile of New Market, where we were first touched with some of the enemy's infantry during the night. On the 30th, there were battles on our center and right, and having joined the Fifth Corps, I proceeded to Malvern Hill in the evening and rode over the field with Captain Colburn, my classmate and the favorite aide of McClellan, and made a topographical sketch of the position, which was of some use afterward in posting the infantry and artillery as they arrived.

During the night of the 30th, the general commanding asked me for two officers for hazardous service. Lieutenants Newhall and Treichel, because of their intimate knowledge of the country, were sent to communicate with our right and center, and a second time that night made their way for a mile and a half through the enemy's camps.

During the battle of July 1st (Malvern Hill), my cavalry was deployed as a close line of skirmishers with drawn sabers in rear of our lines, with orders to permit no one to pass to the rear who could not show blood. The line of battle was ready and reserves of infantry and artillery in position some time before the enemy came in force and developed his attack. There were some preliminary bursts of artillery, but the great crash of all arms did not begin before 6 P. M. It lasted about two hours. The commanding general, with his mounted staff, was standing on the plateau in front of the farm-house at the rear verge of the hill, a conspicuous group, when a round shot from the enemy struck the ground a few yards directly in front of him and threw dirt and gravel over the little group around him. General Porter, with whom I was riding, had just started toward the front when he turned and said to McClellan: "General, everything is all right here and you are not needed; if you will look after our center and right that would help us here more than you can by remaining." Then we separated from them and rode toward our left, at Crew's house. The wounded were already coming away from the lines.

When the battle was over and the field had become quiet, the cavalry bivouacked half a mile in rear of the line of battle. Men and horses were too tired to do aught but sleep for hours. At midnight I found myself in the saddle with a cup of hot coffee held to my lips, a portion of its contents having scalded its way down my throat. When awakened I was informed by the Duc de Chartres that General McClellan desired to see me. We found him near by, in a little orchard by a camp-fire, giving orders rapidly to his generals and staff-officers. When my turn came, McClellan said: "Averell, I want you to take command of the rear-guard at daylight in the morning, and hold this position until our trains are out of the way. What force do you want?" I asked for just enough to cover the front with a strong skirmish line. The orders were given for Buchanan's brigade of Sykes's division, Fifth Corps, to report to me at daylight, and also a battery.

At daylight the cavalry advanced toward the front. There was a fog so dense that we could not see a man at fifty paces distance. Colonel

Buchanan was met with his staff returning from the front on foot, their horses being led. He informed me that the enemy was threatening his pickets, and advancing on both flanks. I asked him to halt his command until further orders, and galloped to the front, where our line of battle had been the night before. I could see nothing, but could hear shrieks, and groans, and the murmur of a multitude, but no sounds of wheels nor trampling horses. I ordered the line reëstablished, with skirmishers and a squadron of cavalry on either flank. Colonel Hall, with the 2d Regiment Excelsior Brigade, also reported for duty, and took position in the line. The battery not having reported, some cavalry was organized into squads, resembling sections of artillery, at proper intervals behind the crest. By this time the level rays of the morning sun from our right were just penetrating the fog, and slowly lifting its clinging shreds and yellow masses. Our ears had been filled with agonizing cries from thousands before the fog was lifted, but now our eyes saw an appalling spectacle upon the slopes down to the woodlands half a mile away. Over five thousand dead and wounded men were on the ground, in every attitude of distress. A third of them were dead or dying, but enough were alive and moving to give to the field a singular crawling effect. The different stages of the ebbing tide are often marked by the lines of flotsam and jetsam left along the sea-shore. So here could be seen three distinct lines of dead and wounded marking the last front of three Confederate charges of the night before. Groups of men, some mounted, were groping about the field.

As soon as the woodland beyond, which masked the enemy, could be clearly seen, I offered battle by directing the infantry lines to show on the crest, the sham sections of artillery to execute the movements of going "into battery, action front," and the flank squadrons to move toward the enemy until fired upon. All these details were executed simultaneously at the sound of the trumpet. The squadrons had not proceeded three hundred yards when they were fired upon and halted. At the same time, a horseman from among those on the field approached our line with a white flag. An aide was sent to meet and halt him. The Confederate horseman, who was an officer, requested a truce of two hours in which to succor their wounded. I was about to send a demand that his request be put in writing, when I reflected that it would be embarrassing for me to reply in writing, so word was sent to him to dismount and wait until his request had been submitted to the commanding general. In the meantime the scattered parties of the enemy withdrew hastily from the field to the woods, and there was some threatening desultory firing on my flanks, killing one man and wounding another. After waiting thirty minutes, word was sent to the officer with the flag that the truce was granted, and that their men could come out without arms, and succor their wounded. I had no idea that the flag was properly authorized, else there would have been no firing on my flanks, but time was the precious thing I wished to gain for our trains which crowded the bottom-lands below Malvern. My squadrons were withdrawn to the line, the infantry lay down, while officers took position in front of the line to prevent conversation with the enemy. In a few minutes thousands of men swarmed from the woods and scattered over the field. I kept myself informed by couriers of the movements of our army and trains, and had already sent officers to reassure our rear of its security, and also to bring me back a battery of artillery. Captain Frank with his battery responded. I sent a request to General Wessells, commanding Keyes's rear brigade, to select a good position about two miles in my rear in case I should need a checking force when the time for withdrawal should come. That excellent soldier had already chosen such a position and established his brigade in line of battle.

When the quasi-truce had expired, at the sound of the trumpet, the line resumed its attitude of attack, and the officer with the flag again appeared with a request that the truce be extended two hours. After a reasonable wait, answer was returned that the time was extended but that no further extension would be granted. I had come on the line at 4 A. M., and these manœuvres and truces had consumed the time until after 9 o'clock. The Army of the Potomac was then at its new base on the James, and all its trains were safely on the way there, with Keyes's corps some miles below in my rear awaiting the enemy. So when the extended truce had expired, my command, with the exception of the cavalry, had left the field. Our dead and wounded, about 2500 in number, had been cared for during the night. Not above a dozen bodies could be found on our field during the truce, and these were buried. Twelve stalled and abandoned wagons were destroyed, and two captured guns which could not be removed were spiked and their carriages were broken. The 3d Pennsylvania Cavalry, which had led the Army of the Potomac across White Oak Swamp, now saw its last serviceable man safe beyond Malvern Hill, before it left that glorious field, about 10 A. M., July 2d. A heavy rainstorm was prevailing. When everything movable was across Turkey Bridge it was destroyed by my rear squadron. My command passed through Wessells's lines about noon, and the lines of General Naglee a little later. Everything was now quiet and in good order, and the 3d Pennsylvania proceeded to camp at Westover after dark.

The 8th Pennsylvania Cavalry, under Colonel D. McM. Gregg, had scoured the left bank of the Chickahominy, on the 28th, and had swum the river to the right bank, rafting its arms across at Long Bridge. He subsequently picketed the front of our center and right on the 30th, and on July 1st and 2d — an extremely important service. The 4th Pennsylvania Cavalry, after its efficient service, at and about Gaines's Mill, during the day and night of the 27th of June, performed similar duties with General McCall at Charles City road on the 30th. The 11th Pennsylvania, Colonel Harlan, which, on the 13th, had covered the White House Landing during Stuart's raid, on the 28th, joined Stoneman on similar duty, and retired with him.

Colonel Farnsworth, 8th Illinois, after his active

participation in covering our right wing on the 26th, and guiding trains and maintaining steadiness of lines on the 27th, guided Keyes's corps to the James River below Malvern, on the 29th, and assisted the 8th Pennsylvania in covering that corps on the 30th and 1st of July. The 2d U. S. Cavalry and McClellan Dragoons, under Major Pleasonton, escorted Colonel B. S. Alexander, of the Corps of Engineers, on the 29th, to Carter's Landing, on the James. Captains Norris and Green, of the 2d, performed scouting service in the direction of the Chickahominy and Charles City Court House, after the arrival of the regiment on the James. And so ended the first lesson of the cavalry service of the Army of the Potomac.☆

Near the White House, on the morning of the 29th of June (at the very time that the 3d Pennsylvania Cavalry was repelling the 1st North Carolina and 3d Virginia Cavalry at Willis Church, south of the Chickahominy), Stuart received a note from General Lee asking for his impressions in regard to the designs of the Union Army. He replied that there was no evidence of a retreat down the Williamsburg road, and that he had no doubt that it was endeavoring to reach the James. On the 30th, while we were establishing our advance on Malvern Hill, Stuart, north of the Chickahominy, was directing his cavalry columns toward the bridges of that river behind us. Had the disposition of his forces been reversed at the outset, and had he, with his main body, gone to Charles City road and obstructed and defended the crossings of White Oak Swamp, he could have annoyed and perhaps embarrassed our movements. Finally, had his cavalry ascertained on July 1st, any time before 3 P. M., that the center and right of our lines were more vulnerable and favorable to attack than the left, the enemy need not have delivered the unsuccessful and disastrous assault on Malvern Hill, but, while maintaining a strong demonstration at that point, might have thrown two or three corps upon our center below Malvern with hopes of dividing the Union Army. Undoubtedly Gregg and Farnsworth, with the 8th Pennsylvania and 8th Illinois cavalry, would have successfully prevented the reconnoissance of our center and right, but that it was not attempted was a discredit to Stuart's cavalry.

At Harrison's Landing, General Stoneman having taken sick-leave and General Cooke having been relieved, on the 5th of July I was appointed acting Brigadier-General and placed in command of all the cavalry of the Army of the Potomac, and at once issued orders organizing it into a cavalry corps, and the history of cavalry brigades was begun. Stoneman, returning the same day, resumed command, and I took the First Brigade, composed of the 5th United States, the 3d and 4th Pennsylvania, and the 1st New York Cavalry.

Active scouting followed in the direction of Richmond and up the Chickahominy. On the 3d of August I crossed the James, with the 5th United States and 3d Pennsylvania Cavalry, to explore the ways to Petersburg, encountering the 13th Virginia Cavalry in a charge led by Lieutenant McIntosh, of the 5th United States, supported by Captain Miller, of the 3d Pennsylvania. The enemy was driven over seven miles, and his camp and supplies destroyed.

All the successes and sacrifices of the army were now to be worse than lost — they were to be thrown away by the withdrawal of the army from the Peninsula, instead of reënforcing it.

☆ The total losses of our cavalry reported in the Seven Days' battles was 234; that of the Confederates 71, of which number 61 were credited to the 3d Pennsylvania Cavalry, at Willis Church, on the 29th of June.—W. W. A.

ROLL-BOOK OF CO. D, 27TH NEW YORK REGIMENT. FROM THE "HISTORY OF THE 27TH NEW YORK VOLUNTEERS."

The scars show where a bullet passed through the roll-book and entered the heart of Lieutenant (formerly Orderly-Sergeant) John L. Bailey, who carried the roll-book in his breast-pocket. Lieutenant Bailey was shot by a Confederate picket named W. Hartley, of the 4th Alabama, the night of May 6th, 1862, at West Point on the York River. Hartley was shot and instantly killed by Corporal H. M. Crocker, whose name, the eighth in the list of corporals, was obliterated by the tear and the blood-stains.— EDITORS.

# THE REAR-GUARD AT MALVERN HILL.

## I.— BY HENRY E. SMITH, BREVET MAJOR, U. S. A.

REFERRING to the retreat from Malvern Hill, July 2d, General McClellan gives Keyes's corps the credit of furnishing the entire rear-guard. According to the report of Colonel Averell, of the 3d Pennsylvania Cavalry, the rear-guard was made his command and consisted of his regiment of Heintzelman's corps, First Brigade of Regular Infantry, consisting of the 3d, 4th, 12th, and 14th Infantry, of Porter's corps, and the New York Chasseurs, of Keyes's corps. The "Official Records," Vol. XI., Part II., p. 235, confirm this statement. In the same volume, p. 193, will be found Keyes's official report, but no mention of Averell. In fact, Averell was the rear-guard to Turkey Bridge and a mile beyond that point, where he found General Wessells of Keyes's corps. The official reports of Fitz John Porter, Sykes, and Buchanan all speak of Averell as having covered this retreat. The writer was a first lieutenant in the 12th Infantry, and in command of Company D, First Battalion, at Malvern Hill, and remembers distinctly that the First Brigade of Regulars slept on the field on the night of July 1st in line of battle. We were surprised the next morning to find that the entire army had retreated during the night, leaving Averell with his small command as a rear-guard to cover the retreat, which was done in the masterly manner stated by General McClellan, but by Averell, and not by Keyes.

UNITED SERVICE CLUB, PHILADELPHIA, May 25th, 1885.

## II.— BY ERASMUS D. KEYES, MAJOR-GENERAL, U. S. V.

A FEW days ago, in Switzerland, my attention was called to a communication in the August [1885] number of "The Century," p. 642, which falsifies history. It is under the heading, "The Rear-Guard after Malvern Hill," and is signed Henry E. Smith. Mr. Smith asserts that it was General Averell who commanded the rear-guard, and that to Averell, and not to Keyes, belongs the credit which General McClellan gives the latter in his article. Mr. Smith cites authorities for his statements, and refers to the "Official Records of the Rebellion," Vol. XI., Part II., p. 235, and to my report, p. 193, same volume, in which he says there is "no mention of Averell." It is not unreasonable to suppose that Mr. Smith had read General McClellan's and my reports, since he refers to them, but it is certain that he discredits both, and that he rejects my claim to approval unceremoniously [see p. 435]. General McClellan says, in his book, "Report . . . of the Army of the Potomac," etc., p. 273:

"The greater portion of the transportation of the army having been started for Harrison's Landing during the night of the 30th of June and the 1st of July, the order for the movement of the troops was at once issued upon the final repulse of the enemy at Malvern Hill. The order prescribed a movement by the left and rear, General Keyes's corps to cover the manœuvre. It was not carried out in detail as regards the divisions on the left, the roads being somewhat blocked by the rear of our trains. Porter and Couch were not able to move out as early as had been anticipated, and Porter found it necessary to place a rear-guard between his command and the enemy. Colonel Averell, of the 3d Pennsylvania Cavalry, was intrusted with this delicate duty. He had under his command his own regiment and Lieutenant-Colonel Buchanan's brigade of regular infantry and one battery. By a judicious use of the resources at his command, he deceived the enemy so as to cover the withdrawal of the left wing without being attacked, remaining himself on the previous day's battle-field until about 7 o'clock of the 2d of July. Meantime General Keyes, having received his orders, commenced vigorous preparations for covering the movement of the entire army, and protecting the trains. It being evident that the immense number of wagons and artillery pertaining to the army could not move with celerity along a single road, General Keyes took advantage of every accident of the ground to open new avenues, and to facilitate the movement. He made preparations for obstructing the roads after the army had passed, so as to prevent any rapid pursuit, destroying effectually Turkey Bridge, on the main road, and rendering other roads and approaches temporarily impassable, by felling trees across them. He kept the trains well closed up, and directed the march so that the troops could move on each side of the road, not obstructing the passage, but being in good position to repel an attack from any quarter. His dispositions were so successful that, to use his own words, 'I do not think that more vehicles or more public property were abandoned on the march from Turkey Bridge than would have been left, in the same state of the roads, if the army had been moving toward the enemy, instead of away from him'— and when it is understood that the carriages and teams belonging to this army, stretched out in one line, would extend not far from forty miles, the energy and caution necessary for their safe withdrawal from the presence of an enemy vastly superior in numbers, will be appreciated. . . . Great credit must be awarded to General Keyes for the skill and energy which characterized his performance of the important and delicate duties intrusted to his charge."

The above extract defines General Averell's duties on the field of Malvern, and gives him credit, and it is equally distinct in reference to me, but General McClellan's article is vague in its expressions regarding the same subjects. As Mr. Smith's article is historically erroneous, I trust you will consider it just to give place to this explanation, and to the following short account of "The Rear-Guard after Malvern Hill."

After the battle of Malvern Hill, which was fought on the 1st of July, 1862, the army retired to Harrison's Landing. Late in the evening of that day I received orders from Adjutant-General Seth Williams to command the rear-guard. I spent nearly the whole night making preparatory arrangements; dispatched a party to destroy Turkey Bridge; selected twenty-five expert axe-men under Captain Clarke, 8th Illinois Cavalry, with orders to chop nearly through all the large trees that lined the road below the bridge. All my orders were well executed, and within fifteen minutes after the tail of the column passed, the bridge was destroyed without blowing up, and the road blocked beyond the possibility of passage by wheels and cavalry, and made difficult for infantry for several hours.

The force composing the rear-guard consisted of Peck's division of infantry and four batteries of artillery of my own corps, Gregg's 8th Pennsylvania Cavalry and Farnsworth's 8th Illinois Cavalry. Averell's regiment of cavalry was also designated in a dispatch sent me by Adjutant-General Williams, and he may have taken part below the bridge, but I do not remember to have seen him during the day.

The danger to the trains arose from the fact that the narrow country roads were insufficient in number, and their composition was mostly clay, which was soon converted into mud by the torrents of rain which fell nearly the whole day, and from the liability to attack on the flank. The main road was skirted with woods on the left the entire distance, which is about seven miles from Turkey Bridge to Harrison's Landing. The opposite side of the main road was open, and the columns of troops could move parallel with the wagons. When General W. F. Smith came along at the head of his division, I was opposite an opening in the woods at the highest point of the road. Smith exclaimed to me: "Here's a good place for a battle!" "Would you like to have a fight?" said I. "Yes; just here, and now!" While the columns of troops were moving alongside the trains I felt no apprehension, but after they had all passed there still remained in rear not less than five hundred wagons struggling in the mud, and it was not above ten minutes after the last vehicle had entered the large field bordering the intended camp when the enemy appeared and commenced a cannonade upon us. Fortunately I had in position Miller's and McCarthy's batteries, and they replied with such effect that the attack was discontinued.

The anxiety at headquarters was such that I was authorized, in case of necessity, to cut the traces and drive the animals forward without their loads. Nothing of that kind was done, and we saved all the wagons except a small number that broke down and were as necessarily abandoned as a vessel in a convoy would be after it had sunk in the ocean.

About the middle of the day I received a note from headquarters at Harrison's Landing, of which the following is a copy:

"GENERAL: I have ordered back to your assistance all the cavalry that can be raised here. It is of the utmost importance that we should save all our artillery, and as many of our wagons as possible; and the commanding general feels the utmost confidence that you will do all that can be done to accomplish this. Permit me to say that if you bring in everything you will accomplish a most signal and meritorious exploit, which the commanding general will not fail to represent in its proper light to the Department. Very respectfully,
R. B. MARCY,
July 2d. *Chief of Staff.*
"BRIGADIER-GENERAL KEYES."

General McClellan came out half a mile and met me. I was engaged sending forward sheaves of wheat to fill the ruts in the road near camp, which were so deep that in spite of all efforts to fill them, about 1200 wagons were parked for the night under guard outside. The general appeared well satisfied with what had been done by the rear-guard, and after all the proofs cited above, it is scarcely probable that he made a mistake in the name of its commander.

BLANGY, SEINE-INFÉRIEURE, FRANCE, August 20, 1885.

## THE ADMINISTRATION IN THE PENINSULAR CAMPAIGN.

BY RICHARD B. IRWIN, LIEUTENANT-COLONEL AND ASSISTANT ADJUTANT-GENERAL, U. S. V.

THE views entertained by General McClellan as to the manner and extent to which his plans and operations on the Peninsula were interfered with or supported by the Government having been fully set forth by him in these pages, it is now proper to show, as far as this can be done from the official reports, how the case must have presented itself to the President and the Secretary of War.

Appointed on the 25th of July, 1861, immediately after Bull Run, to the command of the shattered and reduced forces then gathered about Washington, at one time not exceeding 42,000 all told, General McClellan was rapidly reënforced, until on the 15th of March, 1862, he had under his command within the division or department of the Potomac 203,213 men present for duty. The field-artillery was increased from 30 guns to 520; to these had been added a siege train of nearly 100 heavy guns. From these materials he organized the Army of the Potomac.

In the last days of October General McClellan presented to the Secretary of War a written statement of his views as to the conduct of operations, in which, after representing the Confederate forces in his front at not less than 150,000, his own movable force as 76,285, with 228 guns, and the force required for active operations as 150,000 men, with 400 guns, he recommended that all operations in other quarters be confined to the defensive, and that all surplus troops be sent to reënforce the Army of the Potomac.

"A vigorous employment of these means [he proceeds] will, in my opinion, enable the Army of the Potomac to assume successfully this season the offensive operations which, ever since entering upon the command, it has been my anxious desire and diligent effort to prepare for and prosecute. The advance should not be postponed beyond the 25th of November, if possible to avoid it.

"Unity in councils, the utmost vigor and energy in action are indispensable. The entire military field should be grasped as a whole, and not in detached parts. One plan should be agreed upon and pursued; a single will should direct and carry out these plans. The great object to be accomplished, the crushing defeat of the rebel army (now) at Manassas, should never for one instant be lost sight of, but all the intellect and means and men of the Government poured upon that point."

On the 1st of November, 1861, the President, "with the concurrence of the entire Cabinet," designated General McClellan "to command the whole army" of the United States. No trust approaching this in magnitude had ever before been confided to any officer of the United States.

Everywhere the armies remained inactive. For seven months the Army of the Potomac was held within the defenses of Washington. Its only important movement had resulted in the disheartening disaster of Ball's Bluff. The Confederates, with headquarters at Manassas, confronted them with an army, represented by General McClellan, on the faith of his secret-service department, as numbering at least 115,500, probably 150,000, but now known to have at no time exceeded 63,000. ⸸ The Potomac was closed to navigation by Confederate batteries established on its banks within twenty-three miles of the capital. Norfolk, with its navy-yard, was left untouched and unmenaced. The loyal States had furnished three-quarters of a million of soldiers, and the country had rolled up a daily increasing war debt of $600,000,000. There is no indication that General McClellan appreciated, or even perceived, the consequences that must inevitably follow the loss of confidence on the part of the people, as month after month passed without action and without success in any quarter, or the position in which, under these circumstances, he placed the President, with respect to the continued support of the people and and their representatives, by withholding full information of his plans. In his "Own Story" he tells how he refused to give this information when called upon by the President in the presence of his Cabinet.

The President having, on the 31st of January, ordered the movement of all the disposable force of the Army of the Potomac, for the purpose of seizing a point on the railroad beyond Manassas Junction, General McClellan on the same day submitted his own plan for moving on Richmond by way of Urbana, on the lower Rappahannock. On the 8th of March, yielding to General McClellan's views, supported by the majority of his division commanders, the President approved the Urbana movement, with certain conditions; but on the 9th the Confederates evacuated Manassas, and thus rendered the whole plan inoperative. On the 13th, upon General McClellan's recommendation, supported by the commanders of all four of the newly constituted army corps, the President authorized the movement by Fort Monroe, as it was finally made.

McClellan expected to take with him to the Peninsula 146,000 men of all arms, to be increased to 156,000 by a division to be drawn from Fort Monroe. On the 31st of March, the President informed him that he had been obliged to order Blenker's division of about 10,000 men, ⸸ with 18 guns, to Frémont. "I did this with great pain," he says, "knowing that you would wish it otherwise. If you could know the full pressure of the case, I am confident you would approve."

The council of corps commanders had annexed to their approval, among other conditions, the following: "Fourth, that the force to be left to cover Washington shall be such as to give an entire feeling of security for its safety from menace. . . . NOTE.—That with the forts on the right bank of the Potomac fully garrisoned and those on the left bank occupied, a covering force in front of the Virginia line of 25,000 men would suffice (Keyes, Heintzelman, and McDowell). A total of 40,000 men for the defense of the city would suffice. (Sumner.)" Upon this point the President's orders were: "1st. Leave such a force at Manassas Junction as shall make it entirely certain that the enemy shall not repossess himself of that position and line of communication. 2d. Leave Washington secure."

On the 1st of April, as he was on the point of sailing, General McClellan reported from his headquarters on board the steamer *Commodore*, the arrangements he had made to carry out these provisions, and at once set out for Fort Monroe without knowing whether they were satisfactory to the Government or not. They were not. General McClellan had arranged to leave 7780 men at Warrenton, 10,859 at Manassas, 1350 on the Lower Potomac, and 18,000 men for the garrisons and the front of Washington, to be augmented by about 4,000 new troops from New York. The President, deeming this provision wholly insufficient for the defense of the capital, ordered McDowell with his corps of 33,510 men and 68 guns to remain, and charged him with the duty of covering and defending Washington.

This led to a telegraphic correspondence, thus characterized in the President's letter to General McClellan, dated April 9th: "Your dispatches complaining that you are not properly sustained, while they do not offend me, pain me very much." Then, after again explaining the detachment of Blenker and the retention of McDowell, Mr. Lincoln concludes with these noteworthy admonitions: "I suppose the whole force which has gone forward to you is with you by this time; and if so, I think it is the precise time for you to strike a blow. By delay, the enemy will steadily gain on you — that is, he will gain faster by fortifications and reënforcements than you can by reënforcements alone.

"And once more, let me tell you, it is indispensable to *you* ↓ that you strike a blow! I am powerless to help this. You will do me the justice to remember I always insisted that going down the bay in search of a field instead of fighting at or near Manassas, was only shifting and not surmounting a difficulty; that we would find the same enemy and the same or equal intrenchments at either place. The country will not fail to note — is noting now — that the present hesitation to move upon an intrenched enemy is but the story of Manassas repeated.

"I beg to assure you that I have never written or spoken to you in greater kindness of feeling than now, nor with a fuller purpose to sustain you, so far as in my most anxious judgment I consistently can. *But you must act.*" ↓

On the 11th of April, Franklin's division was

---

⸸ Of which only 44,563 were at Manassas. ↓ Original italicized.
⸸ General McClellan's figures. The latest return, Feb. 28th, showed 8396 for duty.— R. B. I.

ordered to the Peninsula, in response to General McClellan's earnest renewal of his request.

General McClellan estimates his force before Franklin's arrival at 85,000, apparently meaning fighting men, since the returns show 105,235 present for duty on the 13th of April. On the 30th, including Franklin, this number was increased to 112,392. General McClellan also estimated the Confederate forces at "probably not less than 100,000 men, and possibly more,"[) "probably greater a good deal than my own."{ We now know that their total effective strength on the 30th of April was 55,633 of all arms. When the Army of the Potomac halted before the lines of the Warwick, Magruder's whole force was but 11,000. General McClellan estimated it at only 15,000, and his own, confronting it, at the same period, at 53,000.

The plan of a rapid movement up the Peninsula having resolved itself into an endeavor to take Yorktown by regular approaches in front, leaving its rear necessarily open, General McClellan thus describes the result:

"Our batteries would have been ready to open on the morning of the 6th of May at latest; but on the morning of the 4th it was discovered that the enemy had already been compelled to evacuate his position during the night."

The effect of these delays on Mr. Lincoln's mind is curiously indicated by his telegram of May 1st:

"Your call for Parrott guns from Washington alarms me, chiefly because it argues indefinite procrastination. Is anything to be done?"

Then followed the confused and unduly discouraging battle of Williamsburg; the attempt to cut off the Confederate retreat by a landing at West Point came to nothing; and on the 20th of May, the Army of the Potomac, having moved forward 52 miles in 16 days, reached the banks of the Chickahominy. There it lay, astride of that sluggish stream, imbedded in its pestilential swamps, for thirty-nine days.

On the 31st of May, at Fair Oaks, Johnston failed, though narrowly missing success, in a well-meant attempt to crush McClellan's forces on the right bank of the swollen stream before they could be reënforced. On the 1st of June the Confederate forces were driven back in disorder upon the defenses of Richmond, but the damage suffered by the Union forces on the first day being over-estimated, and their success on the second day insufficiently appreciated, or inadequately represented, and no apparent advantage being taken of them, the general effect was to add to the discouragement already prevailing.

Reënforcements continuing to be urgently called for, Fort Monroe, with its dependencies, reporting 9277 for duty, was placed under General McClellan's orders; McCall's division, with 22 guns, was detached from McDowell, and arrived by water 9514 strong on the 12th and 13th of June; while McDowell, with the rest of his command, was ordered to march to join McClellan by land: this movement was, however, promptly brought to

) Telegram to Stanton, April 7th, 1862.

naught by Jackson's sudden incursion against Banks in the Shenandoah.

Meanwhile, the flow of telegrams indicated an ever-increasing tension, the Executive urging to action, the General promising to act soon, not acting, yet criticising and objecting to the President's orders to him and to others. On the 25th of May the President said: "I think the time is near when you must either attack Richmond or give up the job and come to the defense of Washington." McClellan replied: "The time is very near when I shall attack Richmond." Then, June 10th, he says: "I shall be in perfect readiness to move forward to take Richmond the moment that McCall reaches here and the ground will admit the passage of artillery." June 14th: "If I cannot control all his (McDowell's) troops I want none of them, but would prefer to fight the battle with what I have, and let others be responsible for the results." On the 18th: "After to-morrow we shall fight the rebel army as soon as Providence will permit. We shall await only a favorable condition of the earth and sky and the completion of some necessary preliminaries." While appealing to the President when some of his telegrams to the Secretary remained for a time unanswered, General McClellan allowed Mr. Stanton's cordial assurances of friendship and support to pass unnoticed.

At last, on the 25th, General McClellan advanced his picket lines on the left to within four miles of Richmond, and was apparently preparing for a further movement, though none was ordered, and the next day, as at Manassas and Yorktown and Fair Oaks, his adversary once more took the initiative out of his hands. Jackson had come from the Valley.

As soon as this was known, on the evening of the 25th, General McClellan reported it to Mr. Stanton, added that he thought Jackson would attack his right and rear, that the Confederate force was stated at 200,000, that he regretted his great inferiority in numbers, but was in no way responsible for it, and concluded:

"I will do all that a general can do with the splendid army I have the honor to command, and if it is destroyed by overwhelming numbers can at least die with it and share its fate. But if the result of the action, which will probably occur to-morrow, or within a short time, is a disaster, the responsibility cannot be thrown on my shoulders; it must rest where it belongs."

The battle of Gaines's Mill followed, where, on the 27th, one-fifth of the Union forces contended against the whole Confederate army, save Magruder's corps and Huger's division; then the retreat, or "change of base," to the James, crowned by the splendid yet unfruitful victory of Malvern; then a month of inaction and discussion at Harrison's Landing.

At 12:20 A. M., on the 28th of June, General McClellan sent a long telegram, of which these sentences strike the key-note:

"Our men [at Gaines's Mill] did all that men could do . . . but they were overwhelmed by vastly superior numbers, even after I brought my last reserves into action. . . . I have lost this battle because my force is too small. . . . The Government must not and can-

{ Telegram to Stanton, May 5th, 1862.

not hold me responsible for the result. I feel too earnestly to-night. I have seen too many dead and wounded comrades to feel otherwise than that the Government has not sustained this army. . . . If I save this army now, I tell you plainly that I owe no thanks to you *or to any other persons in Washington. You have done your best to sacrifice this army.* ☆

On reaching the James River, General McClellan reported that he had saved his army, but it was completely exhausted and would require reënforcements to the extent of 50,000 men. On the 3d of July, he wrote more fully from Harrison's Landing, then saying that "reënforcements should be sent to me rather much over, than much less, than 100,000 men." He referred to his memorandum of the 20th of August, 1861. That memorandum called for 273,000 men. General Marcy, his chief-of-staff, who bore this dispatch to Washington, telegraphed back:

"I have seen the President and Secretary of War. 10,000 men from Hunter, 10,000 from Burnside, and 11,000 from here have been ordered to reënforce you as soon as possible. Halleck [who had been originally called on for 25,000 men which he had reported he could not spare] has been urged by the President to send you at once 10,000 men from Corinth. The President and Secretary speak very kindly of you and find no fault."

The dispatches of the President and Secretary breathe the same spirit.

"Allow me to reason with you a moment [wrote Mr. Lincoln on the 2d of July, adding that he had not fifty thousand men who could be sent promptly]. If, in your frequent mention of responsibility, you have the impression that I blame you for not doing more than you can, please be relieved of such impression. I only beg that in like manner you will not ask impossibilities of me. If you think you are not strong enough to take Richmond just now, I do not ask you to try just now. Save the army, material and personal, and I will strengthen it for the offensive again as fast as I can. The governors of 18 States offer me a new levy of 300,000, which I accept."

On the 5th, Mr. Stanton wrote that he had nominated all the corps commanders for promotion.

"The gallantry of every officer and man in your noble army shall be suitably acknowledged. General Marcy will take you cheering news. Be assured that you shall have the support of this Department and the Government as cordially and faithfully as ever was rendered by man to man, and if we should ever live to see each other face to face, you will be satisfied that you have never had from me anything but the most confiding integrity."

The next day Mr. Stanton followed this by a personal letter, couched in still warmer terms.

"No man [he wrote] had ever a truer friend than I have been to you, and shall continue to be. You are seldom absent from my thoughts, and I am ready to make any sacrifice to aid you. Time allows me to say no more than that I pray Almighty God to deliver you and your army from all perils and lead you on to victory."

General McClellan's reply was long, cold, and formal. He reviewed their past relations, and alluded to the Secretary's official conduct toward him as "marked by repeated acts done in such manner as to be deeply offensive to my feelings, and calculated to affect me injuriously in public estimation."

"After commencing the present campaign [he continued], your concurrence in the withholding of a large portion of my force, so essential to the success of my plans, led me to believe that your mind was warped by a bitter personal prejudice against me. Your letter compels me to believe that I have been mistaken in regard to your real feelings and opinions, and that your conduct, so unaccountable to my own fallible judgment, must have proceeded from views and motives which I did not understand."

The campaign had failed. The President visited Harrison's Landing to see for himself what was to be done next. Then General McClellan handed him his well-known letter "upon a civil and military policy covering the whole ground of our national trouble." He called Mr. Stanton's attention to this letter, in the reply we have just cited, and told him that for no other policy would our armies continue to fight. This must have been the last straw. ∫ On one point, however, he was in accord with the President. He wound up by recommending the appointment of a commander-in-chief of the army who should possess the President's confidence. On the 11th General Halleck was appointed.

On the 26th General Halleck arrived at General McClellan's camp. He reports that McClellan "expressed the opinion that with 30,000 reënforcements he could attack Richmond, with 'a good chance of success.' I replied that I was authorized by the President to promise only 20,000, and that if he could not take Richmond with that number we must devise some plan for withdrawing his troops from their present position to some point where they could unite with those of General Pope without exposing Washington. . . . He . . . the next morning informed me he would attack Richmond with the reënforcements promised. He would not say that he thought the probabilities of success were in his favor, but that there was 'a chance,' and he was 'willing to try it.'

"With regard to the force of the enemy he expressed the opinion that it was not less than 200,000."

The orders for the removal followed. "There was, to my mind," General Halleck says, "no alternative." "I have taken the responsibility of doing so and am to risk my reputation on it."

Upon whatever side, if upon either, of these many-sided controversies, history shall at last adjudge the right to be, upon whatever shoulders and in whatever degree the burden of blame shall finally rest, certain it is that no fair account of these operations can ever be written without taking note of these delays, whereby the initiative was transferred to the adversary; of these disasters, these unproductive victories, this ceaseless flow of telegrams, surcharged with the varying words of controversy, criticism, objection, reproach; and of the inevitable effect of all these causes combined, in weakening the confidence of the President and in undermining his authority and influence, which, however, to the last were exerted to uphold the general of his first choice at the head of his greatest army.

☆ Original not italicized. These words are omitted in the dispatch as printed in the report of the Committee on the Conduct of the War.— R. B. I. ∫ Confirmed by Chase and Welles.— R. B. I.

## RICHMOND SCENES IN '62.

### BY CONSTANCE CARY HARRISON.

THE first winter of the war was spent by our family in Richmond, where we found lodgings in a dismal rookery familiarly dubbed by its new occupants "The Castle of Otranto." It was the old-time Clifton Hotel, honeycombed by subterranean passages, and crowded to its limits with refugees like ourselves from country homes within or near the enemy's lines—or "'fugees," as we were all called. For want of any common sitting-room, we took possession of what had been a doctor's office, a few steps distant down the hilly street, fitting it up to the best of our ability; and there we received our friends, passing many merry hours. In rainy weather we reached it by an underground passage-way from the hotel, an alley through the catacombs; and many a dignitary of camp or state will recall those "Clifton" evenings. Already the pinch of war was felt in the commissariat; and we had recourse occasionally to a contribution supper, or "Dutch treat," when the guests brought brandied peaches, boxes of sardines, French prunes, and bags of biscuit, while the hosts contributed only a roast turkey or a ham, with knives and forks. Democratic feasts those were, where major-generals and "high privates" met on an equal footing. The hospitable old town was crowded with the families of officers and members of the Government. One house was made to do the work of several, many of the wealthy citizens generously giving up their superfluous space to receive the new-comers. The only public event of note was the inauguration of Mr. Davis as President of the "Permanent Government" of the Confederate States, which we viewed by the courtesy of Mr. John R. Thompson, the State Librarian, from one of the windows of the Capitol, where, while waiting for the exercises to begin, we read "Harper's Weekly" and other Northern papers, the latest per underground express. That 22d of February was a day of pouring rain, and the concourse of umbrellas in the square beneath us had the effect of an immense mushroom-bed. As the bishop and

THE OLD CLIFTON HOTEL.

FRONT AND REAR VIEWS OF THE VIRGINIA ARMORY, RICHMOND.

The armory, which was completed in 1805, was garrisoned during the war by a company known as the State Guard. The building was destroyed in the fire that followed the evacuation in April, 1865.

the president-elect came upon the stand, there was an almost painful hush in the crowd. All seemed to feel the gravity of the trust our chosen leader was assuming. When he kissed the book a shout went up; but there was no elation visible as the people slowly dispersed. And it was thought ominous afterward, when the story was repeated, that, as Mrs. Davis, who had a Virginia negro for coachman, was driven to the inauguration, she observed the carriage went at a snail's pace and was escorted by four negro men in black clothes, wearing white cotton gloves and walking solemnly, two on either side of the equipage; she asked the coachman what such a spectacle could mean, and was answered, "Well, ma'am, you tole me to arrange everything as it should be; and this is the way we do in Richmon' at funerals and sich-like." Mrs. Davis promptly ordered the outwalkers away, and with them departed all the pomp and circumstance the occasion admitted of. In the mind of a negro, everything of dignified ceremonial is always associated with a funeral.

About March 1st martial law was proclaimed in Richmond, and a fresh influx of refugees from Norfolk claimed shelter there. When the spring opened, as the spring does open in Richmond, with a sudden glory of green leaves, magnolia blooms, and flowers among the grass, our spirits rose after the depression of the latter months. If only to shake off the atmosphere of doubts and fears engendered by the long winter of disaster and uncertainty, the coming activity of arms was welcome! Personally speaking, there was vast improvement in our situation, since we had been fortunate enough to find a real home in a pleasant brown-walled house on Franklin street, divided from the pavement by a garden full of bounteous greenery, where it was easy to forget the discomforts of our previous mode of life. I shall not attempt to describe the rapidity with which thrilling excitements succeeded each other in our experiences in this house. The gathering of many troops around the town filled the streets with a continually moving panorama of war, and we spent our time in greeting, cheering, choking with sudden emotion, and quivering in anticipation of what was yet to follow. We had now finished other battle-flags [see "Virginia Scenes in '61," Vol. I., p. 160], and one of them was bestowed upon the "Washington Artillery" of New Orleans, a body of admirable soldiers who had wakened to enthusiasm the daughters of Virginia in proportion, I dare say, to the woe they had created among the daughters of Louisiana in bidding them good-bye. One morning an orderly arrived to request that the ladies would be out upon the veranda at a given hour; and, punctual to the time fixed, the travel-stained battalion filed past our house. These were no holiday soldiers. Their gold was tarnished and their scarlet faded by sun and wind and gallant service — they were veterans now on their way to the front, where the call of duty never failed to find the flower of Louisiana. As they came in line with us, the officers saluted with their swords, the band struck up "My Maryland," the tired soldiers sitting upon the caissons that dragged heavily through the muddy street set up a rousing cheer. And there in the midst of them, taking the April wind with daring color, was our flag, dipping low until it passed us! One must grow old and cold indeed before such things are forgotten.

A few days later, on coming out of church — it is a curious fact that most of our exciting news spread over Richmond on Sunday, and just at that hour — we heard of the crushing blow of the fall of New Orleans and the destruction of our iron-clads. My brother had just reported aboard one of those splendid ships, as yet unfinished. As the news came directly from our kinsman, General Randolph, the Secretary of War, there was no doubting it; and while the rest of us broke into lamentation, Mr. Jules de St. Martin, the brother-in-law of Mr. Judah P. Benjamin, merely shrugged his shoulders, with a thoroughly characteristic gesture, making no remark.

"This must affect your interests," some one said to him inquiringly.

"I am ruined, *voilà tout!*" was the rejoinder — and this was soon confirmed. This debonair little gentleman was one of the greatest favorites of our war society in Richmond. His cheerfulness, his wit, his exquisite courtesy, made him friends everywhere; and although his nicety of dress, after the pattern of the *boulevardier fini* of Paris, was the subject of much wonderment to the populace when he first appeared upon the streets, it did not prevent him from joining the volunteers before Richmond when occasion called, and roughing it in the trenches like a veteran. His cheerful endurance of hardship during a freezing winter of camp life became a proverb in the army later in the siege.

For a time nothing was talked of but the capture of New Orleans. Of the midshipman, my brother, we heard that on the day previous to the taking of the forts, after several days' bombardment by the United States fleet under

RICHMOND FROM THE MANCHESTER SIDE OF THE JAMES.

Flag-Officer Farragut, he had been sent in charge of ordnance and deserters to a Confederate vessel in the river; that Lieutenant R——, a friend of his, on the way to report at Fort Jackson during the hot shelling, had invited the lad to accompany him by way of a pleasure trip; that while they were crossing the moat around Fort Jackson, in a canoe, and under heavy fire, a thirteen-inch mortar-shell had struck the water near, half filling their craft; and that, after watching the fire from this point for an hour, C—— had pulled back again alone, against the Mississippi current, under fire for a mile and a half of the way—passing an astonished alligator who had been hit on the head by a piece of shell and was dying under protest. Thus ended a trip alluded to by C—— twenty years later as an example of juvenile foolhardiness.

Aboard the steamship *Star of the West*,☆ next day, he and other midshipmen in charge of gold and silver coin from the mint and banks of New Orleans, and millions more of paper money, over which they were ordered to keep guard with drawn swords, hurried away from the doomed city, where the enemy's arrival was momentarily expected, and where the burning ships and steamers and bales of cotton along the levee made a huge crescent of fire. Keeping just ahead of the enemy's fleet, they reached Vicksburg, and thence went overland to Mobile, where their charge was given up in safety.

And now we come to the 31st of May, 1862, when the eyes of the whole continent turned to Richmond. On that day Johnston assaulted the Federals who had been advanced to Seven Pines [see pp. 203, 220]. In face of recent reverses, we in Richmond had begun to feel like the prisoner of the Inquisition in Poe's story, cast into a dungeon of slowly contracting walls. With the sound of guns, therefore, in the direction of Seven Pines, every heart leaped as if deliverance were at hand. And yet there was no joy in the wild pulsation, since those to whom we looked for succor were our own flesh and blood, barring the way to a foe of superior numbers, abundantly provided, as we

☆ The same vessel that drew the opening shots of the war at Charleston; seized at Indianola, Tex., in April, 1861; later, sunk by the Confederates in the Yazoo, near Fort Pemberton.—EDITORS.

were not, with all the equipments of modern warfare, and backed by a mighty nation as determined as ourselves to win. Hardly a family in the town whose father, son, or brother was not part and parcel of the defending army.

When on the afternoon of the 31st it became known that the engagement had begun, the women of Richmond were still going about their daily vocations quietly, giving no sign of the inward anguish of apprehension. There was enough to do now in preparation for the wounded; yet, as events proved, all that was done was not enough by half. Night brought a lull in the cannonading. People lay down dressed upon beds, but not to sleep, while the weary soldiers slept upon their arms. Early next morning the whole town was on the street. Ambulances, litters, carts, every vehicle that the city could produce, went and came with a ghastly burden; those who could walk limped painfully home, in some cases so black with gunpowder they passed unrecognized. Women with pallid faces flitted bareheaded through the streets searching for their dead or wounded. The churches were thrown open, many people visiting them for a sad communion-service or brief time of prayer; the lecture-rooms of various places of worship were crowded with ladies volunteering to sew, as fast as fingers could fly, the rough beds called for by the surgeons.

FOOD FOR THE CONFEDERATE WOUNDED.

Men too old or infirm to fight went on horseback or afoot to meet the returning ambulances, and in some cases served as escort to their own dying sons. By afternoon of the day following the battle, the streets were one vast hospital. To find shelter for the sufferers a number of unused buildings were thrown open. I remember, especially, the St. Charles Hotel, a gloomy place, where two young girls went to look for a member of their family, reported wounded. We had tramped in vain over pavements burning with the intensity of the sun, from one scene of horror to another, until our feet and brains alike seemed about to serve us no further. The cool of those vast dreary rooms of the St. Charles was refreshing; but such a spectacle! Men in every stage of mutilation lying on the bare boards, with perhaps a haversack or an army blanket beneath their

IN THE STREETS OF RICHMOND — WOUNDED FROM THE BATTLE OF SEVEN PINES.

heads,— some dying, all suffering keenly, while waiting their turn to be attended to. To be there empty-handed and impotent nearly broke our hearts. We passed from one to the other, making such slight additions to their comfort as were possible, while looking in every upturned face in dread to find the object of our search. This sorrow, I may add, was spared, the youth arriving at home later with a slight flesh-wound. The condition of things at this and other improvised hospitals was improved next day by the offerings from many churches of pew-cushions, which, sewn together, served as comfortable beds; and for the remainder of the war their owners thanked God upon bare benches for every "misery missed" that was "mercy gained." To supply food for the hospitals the contents of larders all over town were emptied into baskets; while cellars long sealed and cobwebbed, belonging to the old Virginia gentry who knew good Port and Madeira, were opened by the Ithuriel's spear of universal sympathy. There was not much going to bed that night, either; and I remember spending the greater part of it leaning from my window to seek the cool night air, while wondering as to the fate of those near to me. There was a summons to my mother about midnight. Two soldiers came to tell her of the wounding of one close of kin; but she was already on duty elsewhere, tireless and watchful as ever. Up to that time the younger girls had been regarded as superfluities in hospital service; but on Monday two of us found a couple of rooms where fifteen wounded men lay upon pallets around the floor, and, on offering our services to the surgeons in charge, were proud to have them accepted and to be installed as responsible nurses, under direction of an older and more experienced woman. The constant activity our work entailed was a relief from the strained excitement of life after the battle of Seven Pines. When the first flurry of distress was over, the residents of those pretty houses standing back in gardens full of roses set their cooks to work, or, better still, went themselves into the kitchen, to compound delicious messes for the wounded, after the appetizing old Virginia recipes. Flitting about the streets in the direction of the hospitals were smiling, white-jacketed negroes, carrying silver trays with dishes of fine porcelain under napkins of thick white damask, containing soups, creams, jellies, thin biscuit, eggs *à la crême*, boiled chicken, etc., surmounted by clusters of freshly gathered flowers. A year later we had cause to pine after these culinary glories when it came to measuring out, with sinking hearts, the meager portions of milk and food we could afford to give our charges.

As an instance, however, that quality in food was not always appreciated by the patients, my mother urged upon one of her sufferers (a gaunt and soft-voiced Carolinian from the "piney woods district") a delicately served trifle from some neighboring kitchen.

"Jes ez you say, old miss," was the weary answer; "I ain't a-contradictin' you. It mout be good for me, but my stomick's kinder sot agin it. There ain't but one thing I'm sorter yarnin' arter, an' that's a dish o' greens en bacon fat, with a few molarses poured onto it."

VIEW OF WASHINGTON MONUMENT, IN CAPITOL SQUARE, RICHMOND.

From our patients, when they could syllable the tale, we had accounts of the fury of the fight, which were made none the less horrible by such assistance as imagination could give to the facts. I remember they told us of shot thrown from the enemy's batteries, that plowed their way through lines of flesh and blood before exploding in showers of musket-balls to do still further havoc. Before these awful missiles, it was said, our men had fallen in swaths, the living closing over them to press forward in the charge.

It was at the end of one of these narrations that a piping voice came from a pallet in the corner: "They fit right smart, them Yanks did, I tell *you!*" and not to laugh was as much of an effort as it had just been not to cry.

From one scene of death and suffering to another we passed during those days of June. Under a withering heat that made the hours preceding dawn the only ones of the twenty-four endurable in point of temperature, and a shower-bath the only form of diversion we had time or thought to indulge in, to go out-of-doors was sometimes worse than remaining in our wards. But one night after several of us had been walking about town in a state of panting exhaustion, palm-leaf fans in hand, a friend persuaded us to ascend to the small platform on the summit of the Capitol, in search of fresher air. To reach it was like going through a vapor-bath, but an hour amid the cool breezes above the tree-tops of the square was a thing of joy unspeakable.

Day by day we were called to our windows by the wailing dirge of a military band preceding a soldier's funeral. One could not number those sad pageants: the coffin crowned with cap and sword and gloves, the riderless horse following with empty boots fixed in the stirrups of an army saddle; such soldiers as could be spared from the front marching after with arms reversed and crape-enfolded banners; the passers-by standing with bare, bent heads. Funerals less honored outwardly were continually occurring. Then and thereafter the green hillsides of lovely Hollywood were frequently upturned to find resting-places for the heroic dead. So much taxed for time and for attendants were those who officiated that it was not unusual to perform the last rites for the departed at night. A solemn scene was that in the July moonlight, when, in the presence of the few who valued him most, we laid to rest one of my own nearest kinsmen, of whom in the old service of the United States, as in that of the Confederacy, it was said, "He was a spotless knight."

Spite of its melancholy uses, there was no more favorite walk in Richmond than Hollywood, a picturesquely beautiful spot, where high hills sink into velvet undulations, profusely shaded with holly, pine, and cedar, as well as by trees of deciduous foliage. In spring the banks of the stream that runs through the valley were enameled with wild flowers, and the thickets were full of May-blossom and dogwood. Mounting to the summit of the bluff, one may sit under the shade of some ample oak, to view the spires and roofs of the town, with the white colonnade of the distant Capitol. Richmond, thus seen beneath her verdant foliage "upon hills, girdled by hills," confirms what an old writer felt called to exclaim about it, "Verily, this city hath a pleasant seat." On the right, below this point, flows the rushing yellow river, making ceaseless turmoil around islets of rock whose rifts are full of birch and willow, or leaping impetuously over the bowlders of granite that strew its bed. Old-time Richmond folk used to say that the sound of their favorite James (or, to be exact, "Jeems") went with them into foreign countries, during no matter how many years of absence, haunting them like a strain of sweetest music; nor would they permit a suggestion of superiority in the flavor of any other fluid to that of a draught of its amber waters. So blent with my own memories of war is the voice of that tireless river, that I seem to hear it yet, over the tramp of rusty battalions, the short imperious stroke of the alarm-bell, the clash of passing bands, the gallop of eager horsemen, the roar of battle, the moan of hospitals, the stifled note of sorrow!

During all this time President Davis was a familiar and picturesque figure on the streets, walking through the Capitol square from his residence to the executive office in the morning, not to return until late in the afternoon, or riding just before nightfall to visit one or another of the encampments near the city. He was tall, erect, slender, and of a dignified and soldierly bearing, with clear-cut and high-bred features, and of a demeanor of stately courtesy to all. He was clad always in Confederate gray cloth, and wore a soft felt hat with wide brim. Afoot, his step was brisk and firm; in the saddle he rode admirably and with a martial aspect. His early life had been spent in the Military Academy at West Point and upon the then north-western frontier in the Black Hawk War, and he afterward greatly distinguished himself at Monterey and Buena Vista in Mexico; at the time when we knew him, everything in his appearance and manner was suggestive of such a training. He was reported to feel quite out of place in the office of President, with executive and administrative duties, in the midst of such a war; General Lee always spoke of him as the best of military advisers; his own inclination was to be with the army, and at the first tidings of sound of a gun, anywhere within reach of Richmond, he was in the saddle and off for the spot — to the dismay of his staff-officers, who were expected to act as an escort on such occasions, and who never knew at what hour of the night or of the next day they should get back to bed or to a meal. The stories we were told of his adventures on such excursions were many, and sometimes amusing. For instance, when General Lee had crossed the Chickahominy, President Davis, with several staff-officers, overtook the column, and, with the Secretary of War and a few other non-combatants, forded the river just as the battle at Mechanicsville began. General Lee, surrounded by members of his own staff and other officers, was found a few hundred yards north of the bridge, in the middle of the broad road, mounted and busily engaged in directing the attack then about to be made by a brigade sweeping in line over the fields to the east of the road and toward Ellerson's Mill, where in a few minutes a hot engagement commenced. Shot, from the enemy's guns out of sight, went whizzing overhead in quick succession, striking every moment nearer the group of horsemen in the road as the gunners improved their range. General Lee observed the President's approach, and was evidently annoyed at what he considered a foolhardy expedition of needless exposure of the head of the Government, whose duties were elsewhere. He turned his back for a moment, until Colonel Chilton had been dispatched at a gallop with the last direction to the commander of the attacking brigade; then, facing the cavalcade and looking like the god of war indignant, he exchanged with the President a salute, with the most frigid reserve of anything like welcome or cordiality. In an instant, and without allowance of opportunity for a word from the President, the general, looking not at him but at the assemblage at large, asked in a tone of irritation:

"Who are all this army of people, and what are they doing here?"

No one moved or spoke, but all eyes were upon the President; everybody perfectly understood that this was only an order for him to retire to a place of safety, and the roar of the guns, the rattling fire of musketry, and the bustle of a battle in progress, with troops continually arriving across the bridge to go into action, went on. The President twisted in his saddle, quite taken aback at such a greeting—the general regarding him now with glances of growing severity. After a painful pause the President said, deprecatingly: "It is not my army, General." "It certainly is not *my* army, Mr. President," was the prompt reply, "and this is no place for it"—in an accent of command. Such a rebuff was a stunner to Mr. Davis, who, however, soon regained his serenity and answered:

"Well, General, if I withdraw, perhaps they will follow," and, raising his hat in another cold salute, he turned his horse's head to ride slowly toward the bridge—seeing, as he turned, a man killed immediately before him by a shot from a gun which at that moment got the range of the road. The President's own staff-officers followed him, as did various others; but he presently drew rein in a stream, where the high bank and the bushes concealed him from General Lee's repelling observation, and there remained while the battle raged. The Secretary of War had also made a show of withdrawing, but improved the opportunity afforded by rather a deep ditch on the roadside to attempt to conceal himself and his horse there for a time from General Lee, who at that moment was more to be dreaded than the enemy's guns.

When on the 27th of June the Seven Days' strife began, there was none of the excitement that had attended the battle of Seven Pines. People had shaken themselves down, as it were, to the grim reality of a fight that must be fought. "Let the war bleed, and let the mighty fall," was the spirit of their cry.

It is not my purpose to deal with the history of those awful Seven Days. Mine only to speak of the other side of that canvas in which heroes of two armies were passing and repassing, as on some huge Homeric frieze, in the manœuvres of a strife that hung our land in mourning. The scars of war are healed when this is written, and the vast "pity of it" fills the heart that wakes the retrospect.

What I have said of Richmond before these battles will suffice for a picture of the summer's experience. When the tide of battle receded, what wrecked hopes it left to tell the tale of the Battle Summer! Victory was ours, but in how many homes was heard the voice of lamentation to drown the shouts of triumph! Many families, rich and poor alike, were bereaved of their dearest; and for many of the dead there was mourning by all the town. No incident of the war, for instance, made a deeper impression than the fall in battle of Colonel Munford's beautiful and brave young son, Ellis, whose body, laid across his own caisson, was carried that summer to his father's house at nightfall, where the family, unconscious of their loss, were sitting in cheerful talk around the portal. Another son of Richmond, whose death was keenly felt by everybody, received his mortal wound at the front of the first charge to break the enemy's line at Gaines's Mill. This was Lieutenant-Colonel Bradfute Warwick, a young hero who had won his spurs in service with Garibaldi. Losses like these are irreparable in any community; and so, with lamentations in nearly every household, while the spirit along the lines continued unabated, it was a chastened "Thank God" that went up among us when we knew the siege of Richmond was over.

# THE SECOND BATTLE OF BULL RUN.[¶]

## BY JOHN POPE, MAJOR-GENERAL, U. S. A.

PICKETING THE RAPIDAN.

EARLY in June, 1862, I was in command of the army corps known as the "Army of the Mississippi," which formed the left wing of the army engaged in operations against Corinth, Miss., commanded by General Halleck. A few days after Corinth was evacuated I went to St. Louis on a short leave of absence from my command, and while there I received a telegram from Mr. Stanton, Secretary of War, requesting me to come to Washington immediately. I at once communicated the fact to General Halleck by telegraph, and received a reply from him strongly objecting to my leaving the army which was under his command. I quite concurred with him both as to his objections to my going to Washington for public reasons and as to the unadvisability of such a step on personal considerations. I was obliged, however, to go, and I went accordingly, but with great reluctance and against the urgent protests of my friends in St. Louis, and subsequently of many friends in the Army of the West.

When I reached Washington the President was absent at West Point, but I reported in person to Secretary Stanton. I had never seen him before, and his peculiar appearance and manners made a vivid impression on me. He was short and stout. His long beard, which hung over his breast, was slightly tinged with gray even at that time, and he had the appearance of a man who had lost much sleep and was tired both in body and mind. Certainly, with his large eye-glasses and rather disheveled appearance, his presence was not imposing. Although he was very kind and civil to me, his manner was abrupt and his speech short and rather dictatorial. He entered at once on the business in hand, seemingly without the least idea that any one should object to, or be reluctant to agree to, his views and purposes. He was surprised, and, it seemed to me, not well pleased, that I did not assent to his plans with effusion; but went on to unfold them in the seeming certainty that they must be submitted to. He informed me that the purpose was to unite the armies under McDowell, Frémont, and Banks, all three of whom were my seniors in rank, and to place me in general command. These armies were scattered over the northern part of Virginia, with little or no communication or concert of action with one another; Frémont and Banks being at Middletown, in the Shenandoah Valley, and McDowell's corps widely separated, King's division at Fredericksburg, and Ricketts's at and beyond Manassas Junction.

The general purpose at that time was to demonstrate with the army toward Gordonsville and Charlottesville and draw off as much as possible of the force

[¶] Accompanying General Beauregard's paper on the First Battle of Bull Run (Vol. I., pp. 196–227) are maps and many pictures of interest with reference to the second battle.— EDITORS.

in front of General McClellan, who then occupied the line of the Chickahominy, and to distract the attention of the enemy in his front so as to reduce as far as practicable the resistance opposed to his advance on Richmond.

It became apparent to me at once that the duty to be assigned to me was in the nature of a forlorn-hope, and my position was still further embarrassed by the fact that I was called from another army and a different field of duty to command an army of which the corps commanders were all my seniors in rank. I therefore strongly urged that I be not placed in such a position, but be permitted to return to my command in the West, to which I was greatly attached and with which I had been closely identified in several successful operations on the Mississippi. It was not difficult to forecast the delicate and embarrassing position in which I should be placed, nor the almost certainly disagreeable, if not unfortunate, issue of such organization for such a purpose.

It would be tedious to relate the conversations between the President, the Secretary of War, and myself on this subject. Sufficient to say that I was finally informed that the public interests required my assignment to this command, and that it was my duty to submit cheerfully. An order from the War Department was accordingly issued organizing the Army of Virginia, to consist of the army corps of McDowell, Banks, and Frémont, and placing me in command.

One result of this order was the very natural protest of General Frémont against being placed under the command of his junior in rank, and his request to be relieved from the command of his corps.⚓

⚓ This request was complied with, and on the 29th of June, 1862, General Franz Sigel assumed command of the First Corps.—EDITORS.

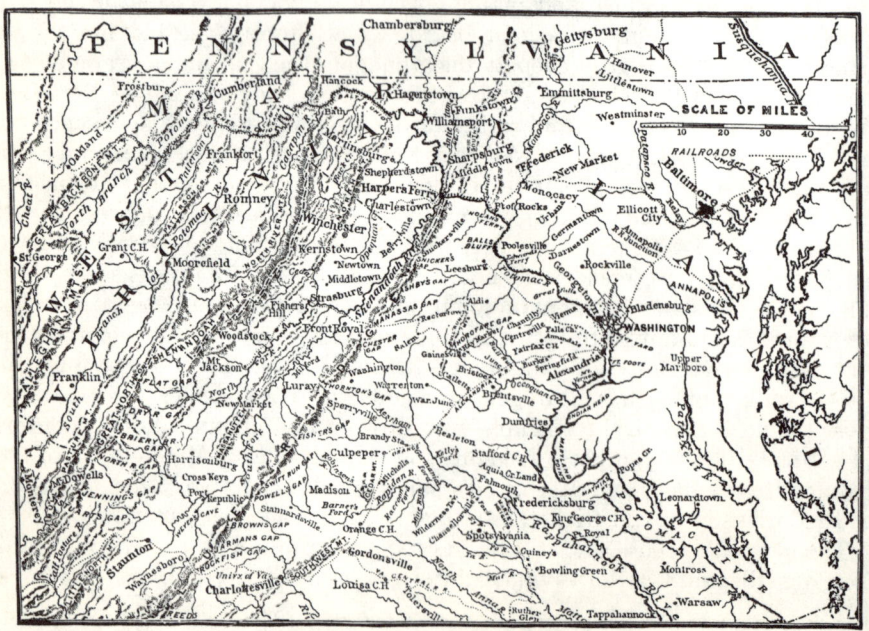

OUTLINE MAP OF THE CAMPAIGN.

It was equally natural that the subordinate officers and the enlisted men of those corps should have been ill-pleased at the seeming affront to their own officers, involved in calling an officer strange to them and to the country in which they were operating, and to the character of the service in which they were engaged, to supersede well-known and trusted officers who had been with them from the beginning, and whose reputation was so closely identified with their own. How far this feeling prevailed among them, and how it influenced their actions, if it did so at all, I am not able to tell; but it is only proper for me to say (and it is a pleasure as well as a duty to say it) that Generals McDowell and Banks never exhibited to me the slightest feeling on the subject either in their conversation or acts. Indeed, I think it would be hard to find officers more faithful to their duty or more deeply interested in the success of the army. To General McDowell especially is due my gratitude for his zeal and fidelity in what was and ought to have been considered a common cause, the success of the Union Army.

VIEW IN CULPEPER DURING THE OCCUPATION BY POPE. FROM A PHOTOGRAPH.
The building with the ball and vane is the Court House, in which Confederate prisoners were confined.

Knowing very well the difficulties and embarrassments certain to arise from all these sources, and the almost hopeless character of the service demanded of me, I, nevertheless, felt obliged, in deference to the wish of the President and Secretary of War, to submit; but I entered on this command with great reluctance and serious forebodings.

On the 27th of June, accordingly, I assumed command of the Army of Virginia, which consisted of the three corps above named, which numbered as follows: Frémont's corps, 11,500; Banks's corps, 8000, and McDowell's corps, 18,500,—in all, 38,000 men.‡ The cavalry numbered about 5000, but most of it was badly organized and armed, and in poor condition for service. These forces were scattered over a wide district of country, not within supporting

‡ On the 27th of June, according to the "Official Records," the strength of the Army of Virginia appears to have been about as follows: Headquarters, 200; Sigel's corps (Frémont's), 13,200; Banks's, 12,100; McDowell's, 19,300; cavalry, 5800. Total of the three army corps, 44,600, or 6600 more than General Pope's estimate: Aggregate, 50,600, or 7600 more than General Pope's estimate. On the 31st of July the consolidated report showed 46,858 "effectives." An error in the report of Banks's corps reduced this aggregate to 40,358. After the battle of Cedar Mountain, and when he had been reënforced by Reno (7000), Pope estimated his force at barely 40,000. With this force were 25 field-batteries numbering about 150 guns.—EDITORS.

distance of one another, and some of the brigades and divisions were badly organized and in a more or less demoralized condition. This was especially the case in the army corps of General Frémont, as shown in the report of General Sigel which was sent me when he had assumed command of it.

My first object was, therefore, to bring the three corps of the army together, or near enough together to be within supporting distance of one another, and to put them in as efficient a condition for active service as was possible with the time and means at my disposal. When I assumed this command, the troops under General Stonewall Jackson had retired from the valley of the Shenandoah to Richmond, so there was not at that time any force of the enemy of any consequence within several days' march of my command. I accordingly sent orders to General Sigel to move forward, cross the Shenandoah at Front Royal, and, pursuing the west side of the Blue Ridge to Luray, and then crossing it at Thornton's Gap, take post at Sperryville. At the same time I directed General Banks to cross the Shenandoah at Front Royal and proceed by way of Chester Gap to Little Washington. Ricketts's division of McDowell's corps, then at and beyond Manassas Junction, was ordered to move forward to Waterloo Bridge, where the turnpike from Warrenton to Sperryville crosses the Rappahannock, there known as Hedgman's River. In deference to the wishes of the Government, and much against my opinion, King's division of the same corps was kept at Fredericksburg. The wide separation of this division from the main body of the army not only deprived me of its use when, as became plain afterward, it was much needed, but left us exposed to the constant danger that the enemy might interpose between us.

The partial concentration of the corps so near to the Blue Ridge and with open communications with the Shenandoah Valley seemed to me best to fulfill the object of covering that valley from any movements from the direction of Richmond with any force less than the army under my command. The position was one also which gave most favorable facilities for the intended operations toward Gordonsville and Charlottesville.

At the date of my orders for this concentration of the army under my command,‡ the Army of the Potomac under General McClellan occupied both banks of the Chickahominy, and it was hoped that his advance against Richmond, so long delayed, might be facilitated by vigorous use of the Army of Virginia.

During the preparation for the march of the corps of Banks and Sigel toward Sperryville and Little Washington, began the series of battles which preceded and attended the retreat of General McClellan from the Chickahominy toward Harrison's Landing.

When first General McClellan began to intimate by his dispatches that he designed making this retreat toward the James River, I suggested to the President the impolicy of such a movement, and the serious consequences

---

‡ The President's order constituting the Army of Virginia is dated June 26th. On that day the second of the Seven Days' battles referred to in the next paragraph began with Lee's attack on McClellan's right near Mechanicsville. General Pope took command on the 27th; on that day was fought the battle of Gaines's Mill, and the march to the James began that night.—EDITORS.

FROM A PHOTOGRAPH TAKEN SINCE THE WAR.

*Jno. Pope*

that would be likely to result from it; I urged upon him that he send orders to General McClellan, if he were unable to maintain his position on the Chickahominy, and were pushed by superior forces of the enemy, to mass his whole force on the north side of that stream, even at the risk of losing some of his material of war, and endeavor to retire in the direction of Hanover Court House, but in no event to retreat farther south than the White House on the Pamunkey River. I told the President that by the movement to the James River the whole army of the enemy would be interposed between General McClellan and myself, and that they would then be able to strike in either direction as might seem most advantageous to them; that this movement would leave entirely unprotected, except so far as the small force under my command could protect it, the whole region in front of Washington, and that it would therefore be impossible to send him any of my troops without putting it in the power of the enemy to exchange Richmond for Washington; that to them the loss of Richmond would be comparatively a small loss, while to us the loss of Washington would be almost a fatal blow. I was so impressed with these opinions that I several times urged them upon the attention of the President and the Secretary of War.

The soundness of these views can be easily tested by subsequent facts. The enemy actually did choose between the danger of losing Richmond and the chance of capturing Washington.♭ Stonewall Jackson's corps was detached from Lee's army confronting McClellan at Harrison's Landing early in July, and on the 19th of that month was concentrated at Gordonsville in my front; while Stuart's cavalry division, detached from Lee's army about the same time, was at or near Fredericksburg watching our movements from that direction. On the 13th of August Longstreet's whole corps was dispatched to join Jackson at Gordonsville, to which place he had fallen back from Cedar Mountain, and the head of Longstreet's corps had joined Jackson at that place on August 15th. These forces were commanded by Lee in person, who was at Gordonsville on that day. The first troops of the Army of the Potomac which left Harrison's Landing moved out from that place on August 14th,↑ at which date there was nothing of Lee's army, except D. H. Hill's corps, left in front

♭ General Lee says in his report dated April 18th, 1863:

"To meet the advance of the latter [Pope] . . . General Jackson, with his own and Ewell's divisions, was ordered to proceed toward Gordonsville on July 13th. Upon reaching that vicinity he ascertained that the force under General Pope was superior to his own, but the uncertainty that then surrounded the designs of McClellan rendered it inexpedient to reënforce him from the army at Richmond. . . . Assistance was promised should the progress of General Pope put it in our power to strike an effectual blow without withdrawing the troops too long from the defense of the capital. The army at Westover [Harrison's Landing], continuing to manifest no intention of resuming active operations, and General Pope's advance having reached the Rapidan, General A. P. Hill, with his division, was ordered on July 27th to join General Jackson. At the same time, in order to keep McClellan stationary, or, if possible, to cause him to withdraw, General D. H. Hill, commanding south of James River, was directed to threaten his communications."

And in his report, dated June 8th, 1863:

"The victory at Cedar Run [August 9th] effectually checked the progress of the enemy for the time, but it soon became apparent that his army was being largely increased. The corps of Major-General Burnside from North Carolina, which had reached Fredericksburg [August 4th and 5th], was reported to have moved up the Rappahannock a few days after the battle, to unite with General Pope, and a part of General McClellan's army was believed to have left Westover for the same purpose. It therefore seemed that active operations on the James were no longer contemplated, and that the most effectual way to relieve Richmond from any danger of attack from that quarter would be to reënforce General Jackson and advance upon General Pope." EDITORS.

↑ On the 30th of July General Halleck ordered General McClellan to send away his sick as rapidly as possible. On the 3d of August General Halleck telegraphed: "It is determined to withdraw your army from the Peninsula to Aquia Creek. You will take immediate measures to effect this. . . . Your material and transportation should be removed first." General McClellan protested against the movement, as did Generals Dix, Burnside, and Sumner. General Halleck replied to General McClellan that he saw no alternative. "There is no change of plans." "I . . . have taken the responsibility . . . and am to risk my reputation on it."

The movement of the sick began at once. Between the 1st of August, when the order was received, and the 16th, when the evacuation of Harrison's Landing was completed, 14,159 were sent away, many of them necessarily to the North. The first troops arrived at Aquia within seven days, and the last of the infantry within 26 days, after the receipt of the order.

(The original movement of the Army of the Potomac, from Alexandria to Fort Monroe, had taken 37 days, and Mr. Tucker, who had superintended its transport, said of it: "I confidently submit that for economy and celerity this expedition is without a parallel on record.")

In the terms of General Halleck's order of August 3d, there were to be transported first the 14,159 sick; next all the material of the army, and the transportation, embracing 3100 wagons, 350 ambulances, 13,000 horses and mules; then 89,407 officers and men, 360 guns, and 13,000 artillery and cavalry horses, together with the baggage and stores in use; but in order to hasten the movement this routine was not rigidly observed, and the movement of Peck's division (ordered to move last) of 7581 men and 10 guns was countermanded by General Halleck.—EDITORS.

of McClellan or near to him. Hill's corps could have opposed but little effective resistance to the advance of the Army of the Potomac upon Richmond.

It seems clear, then, that the views expressed to the President and Secretary of War, as heretofore set forth, were sound, and that the enemy had left McClellan to work his will on Richmond, while they pushed forward against the small army under my command and to the capture of Washington. This movement of Lee was, in my opinion, in accordance with true military principle, and was the natural result of McClellan's retreat to Harrison's Landing, which completely separated the Army of the Potomac from the Army of Virginia and left the entire force of the enemy interposed between them.

RETREAT OF THE UNION TROOPS ACROSS THE RAPPAHANNOCK AT RAPPAHANNOCK STATION. AFTER A SKETCH MADE AT THE TIME.

The retreat of General McClellan to Harrison's Landing was, however, continued to the end. During these six days of anxiety and apprehension Mr. Lincoln spent much of his time in the office of the Secretary of War, most of that time reclining on a sofa or lounge. The Secretary of War was always with him, and from time to time his Cabinet officers came in. Mr. Lincoln himself appeared much depressed and wearied, though occasionally, while waiting for telegrams, he would break into some humorous remark, which seemed rather a protest against his despondent manner than any genuine expression of enjoyment. He spoke no unkind word of any one, and appeared to be anxious himself to bear all the burden of the situation; and when the final result was reported he rose with a sorrowful face and left the War Department.

A day or two after General McClellan reached the James River I was called before the President and his Cabinet to consult upon means and movements to relieve him. I do not know that it would be proper even at this day for me to state what occurred or what was said during this consultation, except so far as I was myself directly concerned. General McClellan was calling for reënforcements, and stating that "much over rather than under one hundred thousand men" were necessary before he could resume operations against Richmond. I had not under my command one-half that force.

I stated to the President and Cabinet that I stood ready to undertake any movement, however hazardous, to relieve the Army of the Potomac. Some suggestions which seemed to me impracticable were made, and much was said which under the circumstances will not bear repetition.

I stated that only on one condition would I be willing to involve the army

THE BATTLE OF CEDAR MOUNTAIN — VIEW FROM THE UNION LINES. FROM A SKETCH MADE AT THE TIME.
The picture shows the artillery duel and deployment of troops before the main attack toward the right, in the middle distance.

under my command in direct operations against the enemy to relieve the Army of the Potomac. That condition was, that such peremptory orders be given to General McClellan, and in addition such measures taken in advance as would render it certain that he would make a vigorous attack on the enemy with his whole force the moment he heard that I was engaged.

In face of the extraordinary difficulties which existed and the terrible responsibility about to be thrown on me, I considered it my duty to state plainly to the President that I could not risk the destruction of my army in such a movement as was suggested if it were left to the discretion of General McClellan or any one else to withhold the vigorous use of his whole force when my attack was made.

The whole plan of campaign for the army under my command was necessarily changed by the movement of the Army of the Potomac to Harrison's Landing. A day or two after General McClellan had reached his position on James River I addressed him a letter stating to him my position, the disposition of the troops under my command, and what was required of them, and requesting him in all good faith and earnestness to write me freely and fully his views, and to suggest to me any measures which he thought desirable to enable me to coöperate with him, and offering to render any assistance in my power to the operations of the army under his command. I stated to him that I was very anxious to assist him in his operations, and that I would undertake any labor or run any risk for that purpose. I therefore requested him to feel no hesitation in communicating freely with me, as he might rest assured that any suggestions he made would meet all respect and consideration from me, and that, so far as was within my power, I would carry out his wishes with all energy and all the means at my command. In reply to this communication I received a letter from General McClellan very general in its terms and proposing nothing toward the accomplishment of the purpose I suggested to him.

It became very apparent, therefore, considering the situation in which the Army of the Potomac and the Army of Virginia were placed in relation to each other and the absolute necessity of harmonious and prompt coöperation between them, that some military superior both of General McClellan and myself should be placed in general command of all the operations in Virginia, with power to enforce joint action between the two armies within that field of operations. General Halleck was accordingly called to Washington and assigned to the command-in-chief of the army,☆ though Mr. Stanton was opposed to it and used some pretty strong language to me concerning General Halleck and my action in the matter. They, however, established friendly relations soon after General Halleck assumed command.

The reasons which induced me, in the first instance, to ask to be relieved from the command of the Army of Virginia, as heretofore set forth, were greatly intensified by the retreat of General McClellan to James River and the bitter feelings and controversies which it occasioned, and I again requested the President to relieve me from the command and permit me to return to the West. The utter impossibility of sending General McClellan anything like the reënforcements he asked for, the extreme danger to Washington involved in sending him even a fraction of the small force under my command, and the glaring necessity of concentrating these two armies in some judicious manner and as rapidly as possible, resulted in a determination to withdraw the Army of the Potomac from the James River and unite it with the Army of Virginia. The question of the command of these armies when united was never discussed in my presence, if at all, and I left Washington with the natural impression that when this junction was accomplished General Halleck would himself assume the command in the field. Under the changed condition of things brought about by General McClellan's retreat to James River, and

BRIGADIER-GENERAL CHARLES S. WINDER, C. S. A., KILLED AT CEDAR MOUNTAIN. FROM A PHOTOGRAPH.

---

☆ The first step toward calling General Halleck to Washington appears in the President's telegram of July 2d asking if he could not come "for a flying visit." On the 6th Governor Sprague was sent to him at Corinth, on a confidential mission, arriving there on the 10th. Meanwhile the President had visited General McClellan and received from his hands the Harrison's Bar letter. On the 11th, General Halleck was appointed General-in-chief. Mr. Chase says in his diary (see "Life and Public Services of S. P. Chase," by J. W. Schuckers, p. 447) that he and Mr. Stanton "proposed to the President to send Pope to the James and give [Ormsby M.] Mitchel the command of the front of Washington. . . . The President was not prepared for anything so decisive, and sent for Halleck and made him Commander-in-chief." Secretary Welles says ("Lincoln and Seward," p. 191): "Pope also . . . uniting with Stanton and General Scott in advising that McClellan should be superseded and Halleck placed in charge of military affairs at Washington."— EDITORS.

the purpose to withdraw his army and unite it with that under my command, the campaign of the Army of Virginia was limited to the following objects:

1. To cover the approaches to Washington from any enemy advancing from the direction of Richmond, and to oppose and delay its advance to the last extremity, so as to give all the time possible for the withdrawal of the Army of the Potomac from the James River.

2. If no heavy forces of the enemy moved north, to operate on their lines of communication with Gordonsville and Charlottesville, so as to force Lee to make heavy detachments from his force at Richmond and facilitate to that extent the withdrawal of the Army of the Potomac.

Halleck was of the opinion that the junction of the two armies could be made on the line of the Rappahannock, and my orders to hold fast to my communications with Fredericksburg, through which place McClellan's army was to make its junction with the Army of Virginia, were repeated positively.

The decision of the enemy to move north with the bulk of his army was promptly made and vigorously carried out, so that it became apparent, even before General McClellan began to embark his army, that the line of the Rappahannock was too far to the front. That fact, however, was not realized by Halleck until too late for any change which could be effectively executed.

Such was the organization of the Army of Virginia, and such its objects and the difficulties with which it was embarrassed from the very beginning. This rather long preface appears to me to be essential to any sufficient understanding of the second battle of Bull Run, and why and how it was fought.

HOUSE ON THE BATTLE-FIELD OF CEDAR MOUNTAIN WHERE GENERAL C. S. WINDER DIED. FROM A PHOTOGRAPH.

General Winder, who was in command of Stonewall Jackson's old division, was struck by a shell while directing the movements of the batteries of his division.— EDITORS.

It is also necessary as a reply to a statement industriously circulated at the time and repeated again and again for obvious purposes, until no doubt it is generally believed, that I had set out to capture Richmond with a force sufficient for the purpose, and that the falling back from the Rapidan was unexpected by the Government, and a great disappointment to it. The whole campaign was, and perhaps

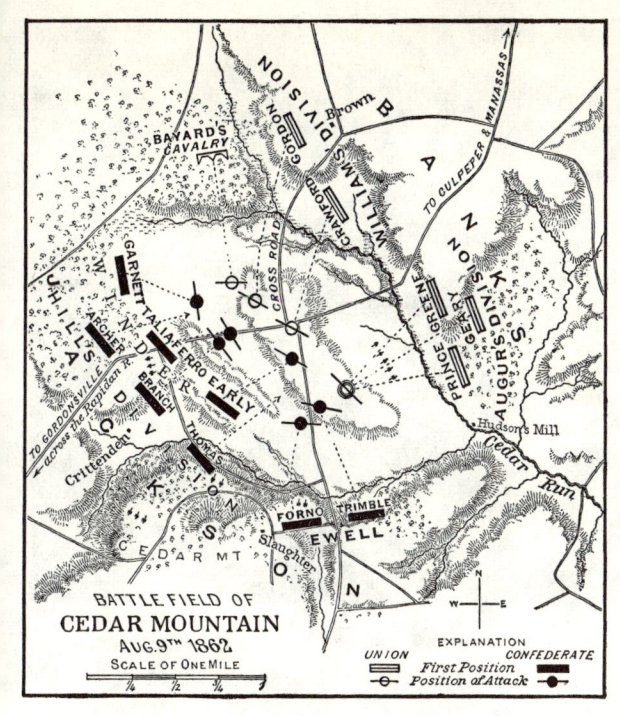

Banks's line was formed in the valley of Cedar Run, and overlapped the Confederate left. Geary and Prince, advancing, encountered Early and Taliaferro on the broad cultivated plateau south of the Culpeper road, while Crawford closed in from the north on the enemy's left. The advantage was with Banks. At 6 o'clock the battle was at its height; Garnett struck the flank of Crawford, and the fresh brigades of Hill's division were led against Prince and Geary. The extreme right of Banks's line, the brigade of General G. H. Gordon (Williams's division), now charged up to the point where Crawford had gone in, and General G. S. Greene's brigade (Augur's division) moved to the aid of Prince and Geary. Meanwhile, Banks's artillery having been forced back by the guns on the mountain-sides, Ewell threw forward his brigades on the right, Thomas (Hill's division) came forward into the gap between Early and Forno, and the battle was decided by the repulse everywhere of Banks's troops. The last charge was made by Bayard's cavalry on the extreme Union right. The advance of Branch brought fresh muskets against Bayard, and the successes of Jackson all along the line closed the day. After dark Banks withdrew to his first position north of Cedar Creek and was there met by Ricketts's division and by General Pope in person.

NOTE ON THE BATTLE OF CEDAR MOUNTAIN: On the 13th of July, the regular command of Jackson, consisting of the divisions of Ewell and Winder, marched from Mechanicsville, on the Chickahominy, under orders to dispute the advance of Pope's army south of the Rapidan. The column reached Gordonsville on the 19th, and Jackson, on learning that Pope's forces outnumbered his own, remained inactive until reënforced early in August by the division of A. P. Hill. Pope was now on the Upper Rappahannock, with the corps of Banks and Sigel, the former at Culpeper, the latter at Sperryville. The outposts of infantry and cavalry under Generals S. W. Crawford and George D. Bayard were along the Rapidan, covering the approaches to Culpeper and Sperryville [see map, p. 450]. On the 8th Bayard's pickets discovered the enemy crossing at Barnett's Ford in large force, and retired along the Orange Court House road toward Culpeper.

Jackson's object was to strike Banks at Culpeper before the latter could be reënforced. On Jackson's approach, Pope ordered Banks's corps forward to Cedar Mountain, about eight miles beyond Culpeper, where it arrived in detachments, being in hand by noon of the 9th, in two divisions, numbering about 8000 men, under Generals C. C. Augur and A. S. Williams. General J. B. Ricketts's division, of McDowell's corps, was coming up as support. The Confederate divisions of Generals C. S. Winder and R. S. Ewell were now disposed along the northern base of the mountain, the brigades of General I. R. Trimble, Colonel H. Forno, and General J. A. Early, of Ewell's division, on the right, with those of General W. B. Taliaferro and Lieutenant-Colonel T. S. Garnett, of Winder's division, on the left, and Winder's "Stonewall" brigade, under Colonel C. A. Ronald, in reserve. The brigades of Generals L. O'B. Branch, J. J. Archer, and E. L Thomas, of A. P. Hill's division, were within call, the entire command under Jackson on the field, numbering at least 20,000. The Confederates opened the battle, sending forward Early and Taliaferro at 3 o'clock, but moving with caution. [See p. 496.]

The journal of General L. O'B. Branch, written August 13th, contains the following description of the battle: "General Jackson came to me and told me his left was beaten and broken, and the enemy was turning him and he wished me to advance. I was already in line of battle and instantly gave the order, 'Forward, march.' I had not gone 100 yards through the woods before we met the celebrated Stonewall Brigade, utterly routed and fleeing as fast as they could run. After proceeding a short distance farther we met the enemy pursuing. My brigade opened upon them and quickly drove the enemy back from the woods into a large field. Following up to the edge of the field, I came in view of large bodies of the enemy, and having a very fine position, I opened upon them with great effect. The enemy's cavalry attempted to charge us in two columns, but the fire soon broke them and sent them fleeing across the field in every direction. The infantry then retreated also. Advancing into the field, I halted near the middle of it, in doubt which direction to take. Just at that moment General Jackson came riding up from my rear alone. I reported my brigade as being solid, and asked for orders. My men recognized him and raised a terrific shout as he rode along the line with his hat off. He evidently knew how to appreciate a brigade that had gone through a hot battle and was then following the retreating enemy without having broken its line of battle, and remained with me . . . until the pursuit ceased."

General S. W. Crawford gives this account of the flank movement attempted by his brigade: "Onward these regiments charged, driving the enemy's infantry back through the wood beyond. . . . But the reserves of the enemy were at once brought up and thrown upon the broken ranks. The field-officers had all been killed, wounded, or taken prisoners; the support I looked for did not arrive, and my gallant men, broken, decimated by that fearful fire, that unequal contest, fell back again across the space, leaving most of their number upon the field." Crawford's brigade lost 494 killed or wounded, and 373 missing, out of a total of 1767 engaged.—EDITORS.

CHARGE OF UNION CAVALRY UPON THE CONFEDERATE ADVANCE NEAR BRANDY STATION, AUGUST 20, 1862. FROM A SKETCH MADE AT THE TIME.

is yet, misunderstood because of the false impressions created by this statement.

Under the orders heretofore referred to, the concentration of the three corps of the Army of Virginia (except King's division of McDowell's corps) was completed, Sigel's corps being at Sperryville, Banks's at Little Washington, and Ricketts's division of McDowell's corps at Waterloo Bridge. I assumed the command in person July 29th, 1862.

As this paper is mainly concerned with the second battle of Bull Run, I shall not recount any of the military operations beyond the Rappahannock, nor give any account of the battle of Cedar Mountain [see p. 459] and the skirmishes which followed.

It is only necessary to say that the course of these operations made it plain enough that the Rappahannock was too far to the front, and that the movements of Lee were too rapid and those of McClellan too slow to make it possible, with the small force I had, to hold that line, or to keep open communication with Fredericksburg without being turned on my right flank by Lee's whole army and cut off altogether from Washington.

On the 21st of August, being then at Rappahannock Station, my little army confronted by nearly the whole force under General Lee, which had compelled the retreat of McClellan to Harrison's Landing, I was positively assured that two days more would see me largely enough reënforced by the Army of the Potomac to be not only secure, but to assume the offensive against Lee, and I was instructed to hold on "and fight like the devil."

I accordingly held on till the 26th of August, when, finding myself to be outflanked on my right by the main body of Lee's army, while Jackson's corps having passed Salem and Rectortown the day before were in rapid march in the direction of Gainesville and Manassas Junction, and seeing that none of the reënforcements promised me were likely to arrive, I determined to abandon the line of the Rappahannock and communications with Fredericksburg, and concentrate my whole force in the direction of Warrenton and Gainesville, to cover the Warrenton pike, and still to confront the enemy rapidly marching to my right.

Stonewall Jackson's movement on Manassas Junction was plainly seen and promptly reported, and I notified General Halleck of it. He informed me on the 23d of August that heavy reënforcements would begin to arrive at Warrenton Junction on the next day (24th), and as my orders still held me to the Rappahannock I naturally supposed that these troops would be hurried forward to me with all speed. Franklin's corps especially, I asked, should be sent rapidly to Gainesville. I also telegraphed Colonel Herman Haupt, chief of railway transportation, to direct one of the strongest divisions coming forward, and to be at Warrenton Junction on the 24th, to be put in the works at Manassas Junction. A cavalry force had been sent forward to observe the Thoroughfare Gap early on the morning of the 26th, but nothing was heard from it.

On the night of August 26th Jackson's advance, having passed Thoroughfare Gap, struck the Orange and Alexandria railroad at Manassas Junction, and made it plain to me that all of the reënforcements and movements of the troops promised me had altogether failed. Had Franklin been even at Centreville, or had Cox's and Sturgis's divisions been as far west as Bull Run on that day, the movement of Jackson on Manassas Junction would not have been practicable.

As Jackson's movement on Manassas Junction marks the beginning of the second battle of Bull Run, it is essential to a clear understanding of subsequent operations to give the positions of the army under my command on the night of August 26th, as also the movements and operations of the enemy as far as we knew them.

Reynolds's division of Porter's corps, having arrived at Aquia on August 13th and 20th, joined General Pope on the 22d, and was assigned to McDowell's corps. General Porter reported to General Burnside (who had arrived at Aquia on August 5th with about 12,000 men from North Carolina) for orders on the 21st. Being pushed out toward the Upper Rappahannock to connect with Reno, his advance under Morell, on the 24th, found Reno and Reynolds gone; no troops of General Pope's were to be seen or heard of (except one company of cavalry, afterward discovered, which had been left to guard Kelly's ford), nor were any orders from General Pope or any information as to his whereabouts received by General Porter or General Burnside until the 26th. So far as appears, no information of this movement was communicated to General Halleck. On the 24th, in reply to General McClellan's inquiry from Falmouth, 9:40 P. M., "Please inform me exactly where General Pope's troops are. . . .

Up to what point is the Orange and Alexandria railroad now available? Where are the enemy in force?" General Halleck telegraphed: "You ask me for information which I cannot give. I do not know either where General Pope is or where the enemy in force is. These are matters which I have all day been most anxious to ascertain."—EDITORS.

General Pope's orders of the 25th disposed his troops on the line of the Rappahannock, from Waterloo to Kelly's Ford, as for an advance toward the Rapidan. Reno was ordered back to Kelly's Ford to resume communication with the forces under Burnside at Falmouth.— EDITORS.

The first information appears to have been received in a communication between the telegraph operators at Pope's headquarters and at Manassas Junction, dated 8:20 P. M., on August 26th. From this time until the 30th all direct communication between General Pope and Washington remained cut off, and nothing was heard of him except *via* Falmouth.— EDITORS.

From the 18th until the night of the 26th of August the troops had been marching and fighting almost continuously. As was to be expected under such circumstances, the effective force had been greatly diminished by death, by wounds, by sickness, and by fatigue.↓

Heintzelman's corps, which had come up from Alexandria, was at Warrenton Junction, and numbered, as he reported to me, less than eight thousand men,↓ but it was without wagons, without artillery, without horses even for the field-officers, and with only forty rounds of ammunition to the man. The corps of General F. J. Porter consisted of about ten thousand men, and was by far the freshest if not the best in the army. He had made very short and deliberate marches from Fredericksburg, and his advance division, mainly troops of the regular army under Sykes, had arrived at Warrenton Junction by eleven o'clock on the morning of the 27th, Morell's division of the same corps arriving later in the same day.

I saw General F. J. Porter at Warrenton Junction about 11 o'clock on the morning of the 27th. Sykes's division of his corps was encamped near; Morell's was expected in a few hours. I had seen General Porter at West Point while we were both cadets, but I think I never had an acquaintance with him there,

BREVET MAJOR-GENERAL JOHN W. GEARY.
FROM A PHOTOGRAPH MADE IN 1866.

nor do I think I ever met him afterward in the service except for about five minutes in Philadelphia in 1861, when I called at his office for a pass, which was then required to go to Washington *via* Annapolis. This, I think, was the first and only time I ever met him previous to the meeting at Warrenton Junction. He had so high a reputation in the army and for services since the outbreak of the war, that I was not only curious to see him, but was exceedingly glad that he had joined the army under my command with a corps which I knew to be one of the most effective in the service. This feeling was so strong that I expressed it warmly and on several occasions. He appeared to me a most gentlemanlike man, of a soldierly and striking appearance. I had but little

↓ August 18th, skirmishes at Rapidan Station and on Clark's Mountain, near Orange Court House; 20th, skirmishes at Raccoon Ford, Stevensburg, Brandy Station, Rappahannock Station, and near Kelly's Ford; 21st, skirmishes along the Rappahannock, at Kelly's, Beverly (or Cunningham's), and Freeman's Fords; 22d, actions at Freeman's Ford and Hazel River, and skirmishes along the Rappahannock; 23d, engagement at Rappahannock Station, action at Beverly Ford, and skirmish at Fant's Ford; 23d and 24th, actions at Sulphur (or Warrenton) Springs; 24th and 25th, actions at Waterloo Bridge; 25th, skirmish at Sulphur Springs; 26th, skirmishes at Bristoe Station, Bull Run Bridge, Gainesville, Haymarket, Manassas Junction, and Sulphur Springs.— EDITORS.

↓ Heintzelman's infantry (effectives) numbered 15,011 on the 10th of August, and the full corps, replenished by six new regiments, reported 16,000 for duty September 10th. There are no intermediate reports.— EDITORS.

conversation with him, as I was engaged, as he was, in writing telegrams. He seemed to me to exhibit a listlessness and indifference not quite natural under the circumstances, which, however, it is not unusual for men to assume in the midst of dangers and difficulties, merely to impress one with their superior coolness.

The troops were disposed as follows: McDowell's corps and Sigel's corps were at Warrenton under general command of General McDowell, with Banks's corps at Fayetteville as a reserve. Reno's corps was directed upon the Warrenton turnpike to take post three miles east of Warrenton. Porter's corps was near Bealeton Station moving slowly toward Warrenton Junction; Heintzelman at Warrenton Junction, with very small means to move in any direction.

Up to this time I had been placed by the positive orders of General Halleck much in the position of a man tied by one leg and fighting with a person much his physical superior and free to move in any direction. The following telegrams will explain exactly the situation as heretofore indicated:

"August 25th, 1862.

"MAJOR-GENERAL HALLECK: Your dispatch just received. Of course I shall be ready to recross the Rappahannock at a moment's notice. You will see from the positions taken that each army corps is on the best roads across the river. You wished forty-eight hours to assemble the forces from the Peninsula behind the Rappahannock, and four days have passed without the enemy yet being permitted to cross. I don't think he is yet ready to do so. In ordinarily dry weather the Rappahannock can be crossed almost anywhere, and these crossing-places are best protected by concentrating at central positions to strike at any force which attempts to cross. I had clearly understood that you wished to unite our whole forces before a forward movement was begun, and that I must take care to keep united with Burnside on my left, so that no movement to separate us could be made. This withdrew me lower down the Rappahannock than I wished to come. I am not acquainted with your views, as you seem to suppose, and would be glad to know them so far as my own position and operations are concerned. I understood you clearly that, at all hazards, I was to prevent the enemy from passing the Rappahannock. This I have done, and shall do. I don't like to be on the defensive if I can help it, but must be so as long as I am tied to Burnside's forces, not yet wholly arrived at Fredericksburg. Please let me know, if it can be done, what is to be my own command, and if I am to act independently against the enemy. I certainly understood that, as soon as the whole of our forces were concentrated, you designed to take command in person, and that, when everything was ready, we were to move forward in concert. I judge from the tone of your dispatch that you are dissatisfied with something. Unless I know what it is, of course I can't correct it. The troops arriving here come in fragments. Am I to assign them to brigades and corps? I would suppose not, as several of the new regiments coming have been assigned to army corps directly from your office. In case I commence offensive operations I must know what forces I am to take and what you wish left, and what connection must be kept up with Burnside. It has been my purpose to conform my operations to your plans, yet I was not informed when McClellan evacuated Harrison's Landing, so that I might know what to expect in that direction; and when I say these things in no complaining spirit I think that you know well that I am anxious to do everything to advance your plans of campaign. I understood that this army was to maintain the line of the Rappahannock until all the forces from the Peninsula had united behind that river. I have done so. I understood distinctly that I was not to hazard anything except for this purpose, as delay was what was wanted.

"The enemy this morning has pushed a considerable infantry force up opposite Waterloo Bridge, and is planting batteries, and long lines of his infantry are moving up from Jeffersonville toward Sulphur Springs. His whole force, as far as can be ascertained, is massed in front of me, from railroad crossing of Rappahannock around to Waterloo Bridge, their main body being opposite Sulphur Springs. "JOHN POPE, Major-General."

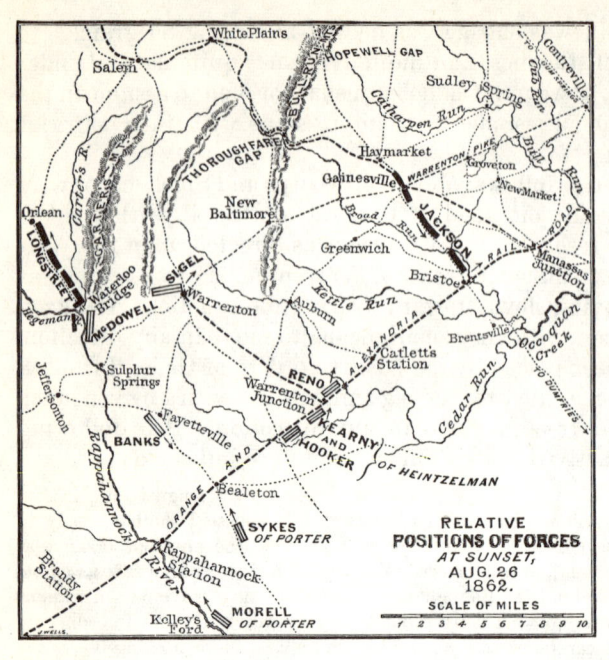

"U. S. MILITARY TELEGRAPH. (Received Aug. 26th, 1862, from War Dep't, 11 : 45 A. M.)

"MAJOR-GENERAL POPE:— Not the slightest dissatisfaction has been felt in regard to your operations on the Rappahannock. The main object has been accomplished in getting up troops from the Peninsula, although they have been greatly delayed by storms. Moreover, the telegraph has been interrupted, leaving us for a time ignorant of the progress of the evacuation. . . . If possible to attack the enemy in flank, do so, but the main object now is to ascertain his position. Make cavalry excursions for that purpose, especially toward Front Royal. If possible to get in his rear, pursue with vigor. H. W. HALLECK, "General-in-Chief."

The movements of the enemy toward my right forced me either to abandon the line of the Rappahannock and the communications with Fredericksburg, or to risk the loss of my army and the almost certain loss of Washington. Of course between these two alternatives I could not hesitate in a choice. I considered it my duty, at whatever sacrifice to my army and myself, to retard, as far as I could, the movement of the enemy toward Washington, until I was certain that the Army of the Potomac had reached Alexandria.

The movement of Jackson presented the only opportunity which had offered to gain any success over the superior forces of the enemy. I determined, therefore, on the morning of the 27th of August to abandon the line of the Rappahannock and throw my whole force in the direction of Gainesville and Manassas Junction, to crush any force of the enemy that had passed through Thoroughfare Gap, and to interpose between Lee's army and Bull Run. Having the interior line of operations, and the enemy at Manassas being inferior in force, it appeared to me, and still so appears, that with even ordinary promptness and energy we might feel sure of success.

In the meantime heavy forces of the enemy still confronted us at Waterloo Bridge,↘ while his main body continued its march toward our right, following the course of Hedgman's River (the Upper Rappahannock). I accordingly sent orders, early on the 27th of August, to General McDowell to move rapidly on Gainesville by the Warrenton pike with his own corps, reënforced by Reynolds's division and Sigel's corps. I directed Reno, followed by Kearny's division of Heintzelman's corps, to move on Greenwich, so as to reach there

↘ On the afternoon of August 26th, Longstreet's corps moved to Hinson's Mill Ford, six miles above, leaving R. H. Anderson's division (about 6000 effectives) at Waterloo Bridge.— EDITORS.

THE SECOND BATTLE OF BULL RUN. 465

THE REAR OF THE COLUMN. FROM A WAR-TIME SKETCH.

that night, to report thence at once to General McDowell, and to support him in operations against the enemy which were expected near Gainesville. With Hooker's division of Heintzelman's corps I moved along the railroad toward Manassas Junction, to reopen our communications and to be in position to coöperate with the forces along the Warrenton pike.

On the afternoon of that day a severe engagement took place between Hooker's division and Ewell's division of Jackson's corps, near Bristoe Station, on the railroad. Ewell was driven back along the railroad, but at dark still confronted Hooker along the banks of Broad Run. The loss in this action was about three hundred killed and wounded on each side. Ewell left his dead, many of his wounded, and some of his baggage on the field.⚓

I had not seen Hooker for many years, and I remembered him as a very handsome young man, with florid complexion and fair hair, and with a figure agile and graceful. As I saw him that afternoon on his white horse riding in rear of his line of battle, and close up to it, with the excitement of battle in his eyes, and that gallant and chivalric appearance which he always presented under fire, I was struck with admiration. As a corps commander, with his whole force operating under his own eye, it is much to be doubted whether Hooker had a superior in the army.

The railroad had been torn up and the bridges burned in several places just west of Bristoe Station. I therefore directed General Banks, who had reached Warrenton Junction, to cover the railroad trains at that place until General Porter marched, and then to run back the trains toward Manassas as

⚓ This engagement is known as Kettle Run (see map, p. 467). The Confederate force consisted of Early's brigade, with two regiments of Forno's, two of Lawton's, and Brown's and Johnson's batteries. After disputing Hooker's advance for some hours, Ewell withdrew under fire.—EDITORS.

far as he could and rebuild the railroad bridges. Captain Merrill of the Engineers was also directed to repair the railroad track and bridges toward Bristoe. This work was done by that accomplished officer as far east as Kettle Run on the 27th, and the trains were run back to that point next morning.

At dark on the 27th Hooker informed me that his ammunition was nearly exhausted, only five rounds to the man being on hand. Before this time it had become apparent that Jackson, with his whole force, was south of the Warrenton pike and in the immediate neighborhood of Manassas Junction.

McDowell reached his position at Gainesville during the night of the 27th, and Kearny and Reno theirs at Greenwich. It was clear on that night that we had completely interposed between Jackson and the enemy's main body, which was still west of the Bull Run range, and in the vicinity of White Plains.

In consequence of Hooker's report, and the weakness of the small division which he commanded, and to strengthen my right wing moving in the direction of Manassas, I sent orders to Porter at dark, which reached him at 9 P. M., to move forward from Warrenton Junction at 1 A. M. night, and to report to me at Bristoe Station by daylight next morning (August 28th).

There were but two courses left to Jackson by this sudden movement of the army. He could not retrace his steps through Gainesville, as that place was occupied by McDowell with a force equal if not superior to his own. To retreat through Centreville would carry him still farther away from the main body of Lee's army. It was possible, however, to mass his whole force at Manassas Junction and assail our right (Hooker's division), which had fought a severe battle that afternoon, and was almost out of ammunition. Jackson, with A. P. Hill's division, retired through Centreville. Thinking it altogether within the probabilities that he might adopt the other alternative, I sent the orders above mentioned to General Porter. He neither obeyed them nor attempted to obey them,☆ but afterward gave as a reason for not doing so that his men were tired, the night was too dark to march, and that there was a wagon train on the road toward Bristoe. The distance was nine miles along the railroad track, with a wagon road on each side of it most of the way; but his corps did not reach Bristoe Station until 10:30 o'clock next morning, six hours after daylight; and the moment he found that the enemy had left our front he asked to halt and rest his corps. Of his first reason for not complying with my orders, it is only necessary to say that Sykes's division had reached Warrenton Junction at 11 o'clock on the morning of the 27th, and had been in camp all day. Morell's division arrived later in the day at Warrenton Junction, and would have been in camp for at least eight hours before the time it was ordered to march. The marches of these two divisions from Fredericksburg had been extremely deliberate, and involved but little more exercise than is needed for good health. The diaries of these marches make

---

☆ Porter marched about 3 A. M., instead of at 1, as ordered. The leading brigade lit candles to look for the road. On the Confederate side Colonel Henry Forno, 5th Louisiana, reports: "After 12 o'clock at night of the 27th, the brigade was put in motion with orders to follow General Early, but owing to the darkness I was unable to find him." Two orders addressed by Pope at Bristoe to McDowell at Gainesville fell into the hands of A. P. Hill, at Centreville. Some of the Confederates (Jackson, Trimble, and Stuart) mention the darkness of the night of the 26th; and General McDowell lost his way from this cause on the night of the 28th.— EDITORS.

Porter's claim of fatigue ridiculous. To compare the condition of this corps and its marches with those of any of the troops of the Army of Virginia is a sufficient answer to such a pretext. The impossibility of marching on account of the darkness of that night finds its best answer in the fact that nearly every other division of the army, and the whole of Jackson's corps, marched during the greater part of the night in the immediate vicinity of Porter's corps, and from nearly every point of the compass. The plea of darkness and of the obstruction of a wagon train along the road will strike our armies with some surprise in the light of their subsequent experience of night marches. The railroad track itself was clear and entirely practicable for the march of infantry.

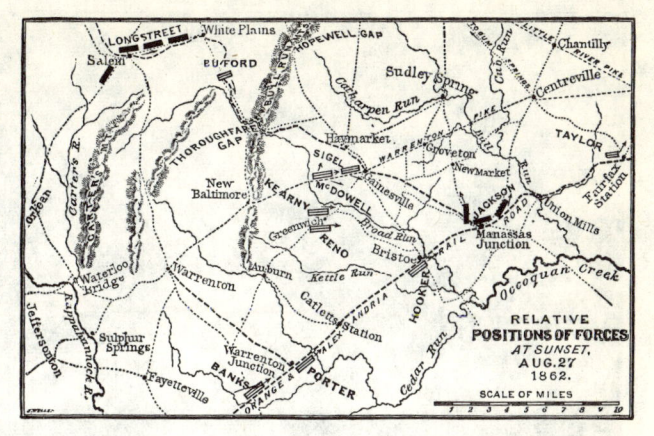

According to the testimony of Colonel Myers, quartermaster in charge of the train, the train was drawn off the roads and parked after dark that night; and even if this had not been the case, it is not necessary to tell any officer who served in the war that the infantry advance could easily have pushed the wagons off the road to make way for the artillery. Colonel Myers also testified that he could have gone on with his train that night, and that he drew off the road and parked his train for rest and because of the action of Hooker's division in his front, and not because he was prevented from continuing his march by darkness or other obstacles.

At 9 o'clock on the night of the 27th, satisfied of Jackson's position, I sent orders to General McDowell at Gainesville to push forward at the earliest dawn of day upon Manassas Junction, resting his right on the Manassas Gap Railroad and extending his left to the east. I directed General Reno at the same time to march from Greenwich, also direct on Manassas Junction, and Kearny to move from the same place upon Bristoe Station. This move of Kearny was to strengthen my right at Bristoe and unite the two divisions of Heintzelman's corps.↓

Jackson began to evacuate Manassas Junction during the night (the 27th) and marched toward Centreville and other points of the Warrenton pike west of that place, and by 11 o'clock next morning was at and beyond Centreville and north of the Warrenton pike.‡ I arrived at Manassas Junction shortly after the last of Jackson's force had moved off, and immediately pushed for-

---

↓ General Pope's orders of the 27th for the movements of the 28th directed his whole army upon Manassas. Full information of these dispositions reached General A. P. Hill early the next morning, through the captured orders.— EDITORS.

‡ At this time Jackson's command was concen-

COLLISION ON THURSDAY, AUGUST 28, BETWEEN REYNOLDS'S DIVISION AND JACKSON'S RIGHT WING.

The view is from the north side of the turnpike (from a war-time sketch), east of Gainesville, and looking toward Groveton. The smoke along the woods indicates the position of the Confederates, who fell back toward Groveton, while Reynolds turned off to the right toward Manassas. During the battles of Friday and Saturday (the 29th and 30th), the lines were nearly reversed. Jackson was then to the left, looking south toward Manassas, and Longstreet's lines, facing like Reynolds's in the above picture, but extending farther to the right, and confronting McDowell and Porter (see maps, pp. 473 and 482).— EDITORS.

ward Hooker, Kearny, and Reno upon Centreville,↓ and sent orders to Porter to come forward to Manassas Junction. I also wrote McDowell the situation and directed him to call back to Gainesville any part of his force which had moved in the direction of Manassas Junction, and march upon Centreville along the Warrenton pike with the whole force under his command to intercept the retreat of Jackson toward Thoroughfare Gap. With King's division in advance, McDowell, marching toward Centreville, encountered late in the afternoon the advance of Jackson's corps retreating toward Thoroughfare Gap.♭ Late in the afternoon, also, Kearny drove the rear-guard of Jackson trated near Groveton. General Pope says in his report: "I reached Manassas Junction . . . about 12 o'clock . . . less than an hour after Jackson, in person, had retired." Jackson was, however, on the old "battle-field of Manassas" at 8 A. M., as appears from the order of that date to A. P. Hill, and about noon when he sent orders to Taliaferro to attack the Federal troops (evidently Reynolds), supposed to be marching on Centreville, but actually moving from Gainesville to Manassas under Pope's first orders. Jackson says: "My command had hardly concentrated north of the turnpike before the enemy's advance reached the vicinity of Groveton from the direction of Warrenton." In the above sketch, Meade's brigade and Cooper's battery are seen deploying for action.— EDITORS.

↓ At 1:20 or 2 P. M. Pope repeated his orders sent "a few minutes ago" to McDowell to march toward Gum Springs, distant 20 miles in the direction of Aldie Gap. The note sent "a few minutes ago," reached McDowell at 3:15 P. M. The orders to march on Centreville were dated 4:15 P. M., and McDowell appears to have received the second while preparing to execute the first.— EDITORS.

♭ Jackson says: "Dispositions were promptly made to attack the enemy, based upon the idea that he would continue to press forward upon the turnpike toward Alexandria; but as he did not appear to advance in force, and there was reason to believe that his main body was leaving the road and inclining toward Manassas Junction, my command was advanced through the woods, leaving Groveton on the left, until it reached a commanding position near Brawner's house. By this time it was sunset; but as his column appeared to be moving by, with its flank exposed, I determined to attack at once, which was vigorously done by the divisions of Taliaferro and Ewell."— EDITORS.

out of Centreville and occupied that place with his advance beyond it toward Gainesville. A very severe engagement occurred between King's division and Jackson's forces near the village of Groveton on the Warrenton pike, which was terminated by the darkness, both parties maintaining their ground.\ The conduct of this division in this severe engagement was admirable, and reflects the utmost credit both upon its commanders and the men under their command. That this division was not reënforced by Reynolds☆ and Sigel⫮ seems unaccountable. The reason given, though it is not satisfactory, was the fact that General McDowell had left the command just before it encountered the enemy, and had gone toward Manassas Junction, where he supposed me to be, in order to give me some information about the immediate country in which we were operating, and with which, of course, he was much more familiar from former experience than I could be. ⚓ I had

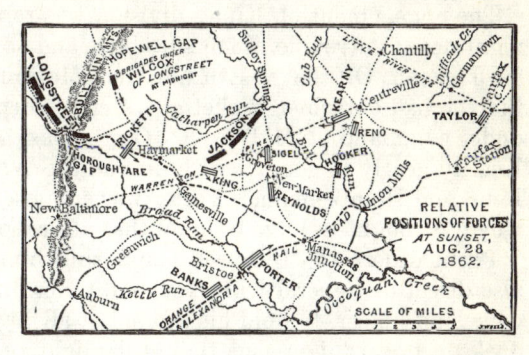

\ King's division (which had not been at Gainesville on the night of the 27th, but near Buckland Mills, and was consequently near the Warrenton pike instead of at Manassas, when, by General Pope's 4:15 P. M. order, the army was directed upon Centreville instead of upon Manassas, encountered Jackson's forces in position as stated in the preceding note about 5:30 P. M. Gibbon's brigade, with two regiments of Doubleday's (the 56th Pennsylvania and 76th New York), contended against Taliaferro's division and two brigades (Lawton's and Trimble's) of Ewell's division. General Jackson says:

"The batteries of Wooding, Poague, and Carpenter were placed in position in front of Starke's brigade, and above the village of Groveton, and, firing over the heads of our skirmishers, poured a heavy fire of shot and shell upon the enemy. This was responded to by a very heavy fire from the enemy, forcing our batteries to select another position. By this time Taliaferro's command, with Lawton's and Trimble's brigades on his left, was advanced from the woods to the open field, and was now moving in gallant style until it reached an orchard on the right of our line and was less than 100 yards from a large force of the enemy. The conflict here was fierce and sanguinary. Although largely reënforced, the Federals did not attempt to advance, but maintained their ground with obstinate determination. Both lines stood exposed to the discharges of musketry and artillery until about 9 o'clock, when the enemy slowly fell back, yielding the field to our troops. The loss on both sides was heavy, and among our wounded were Major-General Ewell and Brigadier-General Taliaferro."

Gibbon's brigade lost 133 killed, 539 wounded, 79 missing, total, 751, "or considerably over one-third of the command." King held his ground until 1 A. M. on the 29th, when, being without support, without communication with either of the generals in command over him, and without orders since those of 4:15 P. M., he marched to Manassas Junction.—EDITORS.

☆Reynolds, ordered to march *en échelon* on King's right, was moving toward Manassas (see note to picture, p. 468), when, at 5 P. M., he received McDowell's order, based on Pope's of 4:15, to march on Centreville. He turned off at Bethlehem Church and took the Sudley Springs road toward the Warrenton pike. General Reynolds says:

"About this time heavy cannonading was heard both to our front and left, the former supposed to be from Sigel's corps, and the latter from King's division, which had taken the Warrenton pike from Gainesville. I sent word to the column to hasten its march, and proceeded to the left at once myself in the direction of the firing, arriving on the field just before dark, and found that Gibbon's brigade, of King's division, was engaged with the enemy, with Doubleday's and Patrick's brigades in the vicinity. After the firing ceased I saw General King, who, determining to maintain his position, I left about 9 o'clock P. M. to return to my division, promising to bring it up early in the morning to his support. Before leaving, however, I heard the division moving off, and I learned from General Hatch that it was moving by Gainesville toward Manassas. I then returned to my own division, which I reached at daylight."
EDITORS.

⫮ Sigel was ordered to move at 2:45 A. M. and to march *en échelon* on Reynolds's right. His advance appears to have reached Manassas about noon. He states that during the afternoon he was ordered by General Pope to march by New Market on Centreville, and arrived on the field of the First Bull Run, near the Henry house (see p. 473), too late to take part in King's engagement.—EDITORS.

⚓ According to General McDowell, this was "after putting these divisions in motion (under the 4:15 P. M. order) and going with Reynolds's left Manassas Junction, however, for Centreville. Hearing the sound of the guns indicating King's engagement with the enemy, McDowell set off to rejoin his command, but lost his way, and I first heard of him next morning at Manassas Junction. As his troops did not know of his absence, there was no one to give orders to Sigel and Reynolds.

The engagement of King's division was reported to me about 10 o'clock at night near Centreville. I felt sure then, and so stated, that there was no escape for Jackson. On the west of him were McDowell's corps (I did not then know that he had detached Ricketts ↘), Sigel's corps, and Reynolds's division, all under command of McDowell. On the east of him, and with the advance of Kearny nearly in contact with him on the Warrenton pike, were the corps of Reno and Heintzelman. Porter was supposed to be at Manassas Junction, where he ought to have been on that afternoon.

I sent orders to McDowell (supposing him to be with his command), and also direct to General King,↓ several times during that night and once by his own staff-officer, to hold his ground at all hazards, to prevent the retreat of Jackson toward Lee, and that at daylight our whole force from Centreville and Manassas would assail him from the east, and he would be crushed between us. I sent orders also to General Kearny at Centreville to move forward cautiously that night along the Warrenton pike; to drive in the pickets of the enemy, and to keep as closely as possible in contact with him during the night, resting his left on the Warrenton pike and throwing his right to the north, if practicable, as far as the Little River pike, and at daylight next morning to assault vigorously with his right advance, and that Hooker and Reno would certainly be with him shortly after daylight. I sent orders to General Porter, who I supposed was at Manassas Junction, to move upon Centreville at dawn, stating to him the position of our forces, and that a severe battle would be fought that morning (the 29th).

With Jackson at and near Groveton, with McDowell on the west, and the rest of the army on the east of him, while Lee, with the mass of his army, was still west of Thoroughfare Gap, the situation for us was certainly as favorable as the most sanguine person could desire, and the prospect of crushing Jackson, sandwiched between such forces, were certainly excellent. There is no doubt, had General McDowell been with his command when King's division of his corps became engaged with the enemy, he would have brought forward to its support both Sigel and Reynolds, and the result would have been to hold the ground west of Jackson at least until morning brought against him also the forces moving from the direction of Centreville.

division to near Manassas"; and in compliance with General Pope's request of 1:20 or 2 P. M., viz., "Give me your views fully; you know the country much better than I do." General McDowell found Reynolds at daybreak on the 29th.— EDITORS.

↘ In the exercise of his discretion McDowell, then commanding two corps, sent Ricketts to Thoroughfare Gap on the morning of the 28th, to delay Longstreet's advance, notwithstanding General Pope's orders to move on Manassas with his whole command. But for this, the movement on Manassas as ordered in the morning, as well as the movement on Centreville as ordered in the afternoon, would have left no troops except Buford's broken down cavalry between Longstreet and Jackson, or between Longstreet and Pope's left.— EDITORS.

† But see Captain Charles King's denial on page 495.— EDITORS.

## THE SECOND BATTLE OF BULL RUN. 471

To my great disappointment and surprise, however, I learned toward daylight the next morning (the 29th) that King's division had fallen back toward Manassas Junction, and that neither Sigel nor Reynolds had been engaged or had gone to the support of King. The route toward Thoroughfare Gap had thus been left open by the wholly unexpected retreat of King's division, due to the fact that he was not supported by Sigel and Reynolds, and an immediate change was necessary in the disposition of the troops under my command. Sigel and Reynolds were near Groveton, almost in contact with Jackson; Ricketts had fallen back toward Bristoe from Thoroughfare Gap, after offering (as might have been expected) ineffectual resistance to the passage of the Bull Run range by very superior forces; King had fallen back to Manassas Junction; Porter was at Manassas Junction or near there; Reno♮ and Hooker near Centreville; Kearny at Centreville and beyond toward Groveton; Jackson near Groveton with his whole corps; Lee with the main army of the enemy, except three brigades of Longstreet which had passed Hopewell Gap, north of Thoroughfare Gap.

The field of battle was practically limited to the space between the old railroad grade from Sudley to Gainesville if prolonged across the Warrenton pike and the Sudley Springs road east of it. The railroad grade indicates almost exactly the line occupied by Jackson's force, our own line confronting it from left to right.

The ridge which bounded the valley of Dawkins's Branch on the west, and on which were the Hampton Cole and Monroe houses, offered from the Monroe house a full view of the field of battle from right to left, and the Monroe house being on the crest of the ridge overlooked and completely commanded the approach to Jackson's right by the Warrenton turnpike. To the result of the battle this ridge was of the last importance, and, if seized and held by noon, would absolutely have prevented any reënforcement of Jackson's right from the direction of Gainesville. The northern slope of this ridge was held by our troops near the Douglass house, near which, also, the right of Jackson's line rested. The advance of Porter's corps at Dawkins's Branch was less than a mile and a half from the Monroe house, and the road in his front was one of several which converged on that point.

The whole field was free from obstacles to movement of troops and nearly so to manœuvres, with only a few eminences, and these of a nature to have been seized and easily held by our troops even against very superior numbers. The ground was gently undulating and the water-courses insignificant, while the intersecting system of roads and lanes afforded easy communication with all parts of the field. It would be difficult to find anywhere in Virginia a more perfect field of battle than that on which the second battle of Bull Run was fought.

About daylight, therefore, on the 29th of August, almost immediately after I received information of the withdrawal of King's division toward Manassas Junction, I sent orders to General Sigel, in the vicinity of Groveton, to attack

♮ Reno appears not to have been at Centreville at this time, since General Pope's headquarters "near Bull Run" were between him and Centreville at 3 A. M. on the 30th.—EDITORS.

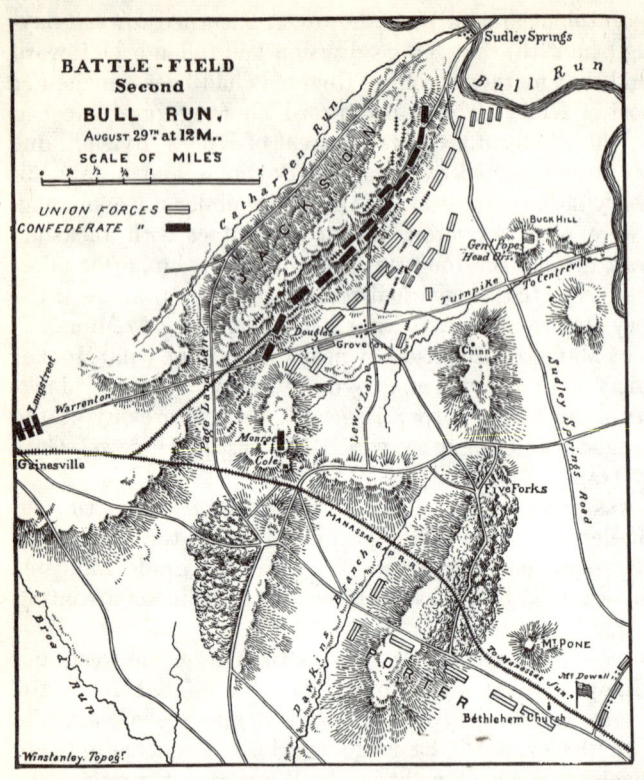

RELATIVE POSITIONS AT NOON, FRIDAY, AUGUST 29TH.

This map represents General Pope's view of the situation at noon, August 29th, with Longstreet placed at Gainesville; but, according to General Longstreet (see p. 510) and others (see p. 525), Longstreet was at that hour on Jackson's right and capable of resisting an advance on the part of Porter.— EDITORS.

the enemy vigorously at daylight and bring him to a stand if possible. ☆ He was to be supported by Reynolds's division. I instructed Heintzelman ǀ to push forward from Centreville toward Gainesville on the Warrenton pike at the earliest dawn with the divisions of Kearny and Hooker, and gave orders also to Reno with his corps to follow closely in their rear. They were directed to use all speed, and as soon as they came up with the enemy to establish communication with Sigel, and to attack vigorously and promptly. I also sent orders to General Porter ☩ at Manassas Junction to move forward rapidly with his own corps and King's division of McDowell's corps, which was there also, upon Gainesville by the direct route from Manassas Junction to that place. I urged him to make all possible speed, with the purpose that he should come up with the enemy or connect himself with the left of our line near where the Warrenton pike is crossed by the road from Manassas Junction to Gainesville.

Shortly after sending this order I received a note from General McDowell, whom I had not been able to find during the night of the 28th, dated Manassas

---

☆ These orders to Sigel are not found in the "Official Records," but they correspond with the orders given to Kearny and Heintzelman at 9:50 and 10 P. M., on the 28th. General Sigel says he received them during the night, made his preparations at night, and "formed in order of battle at daybreak." Such of the subordinate reports as mention the time, as well as the reports of Generals McDowell and Reynolds, tend to confirm General Sigel's statement.— EDITORS.

ǀ These orders to Heintzelman are dated 10 P. M.,

August 28th; similar orders to Kearny direct are dated 9:50 P. M.— EDITORS.

☩ At 3 A. M. on the 29th, General Pope ordered Porter, then at Bristoe, to "move upon Centreville at the first dawn of day." In the order of the 29th to Porter, "Push forward with your corps and King's division, which you will take with you upon Gainesville," the hour is not noted, but General Pope testified on the Porter court-martial that he sent it between 8 and 9 A. M. Porter appears to have received it about 9:30.— EDITORS.

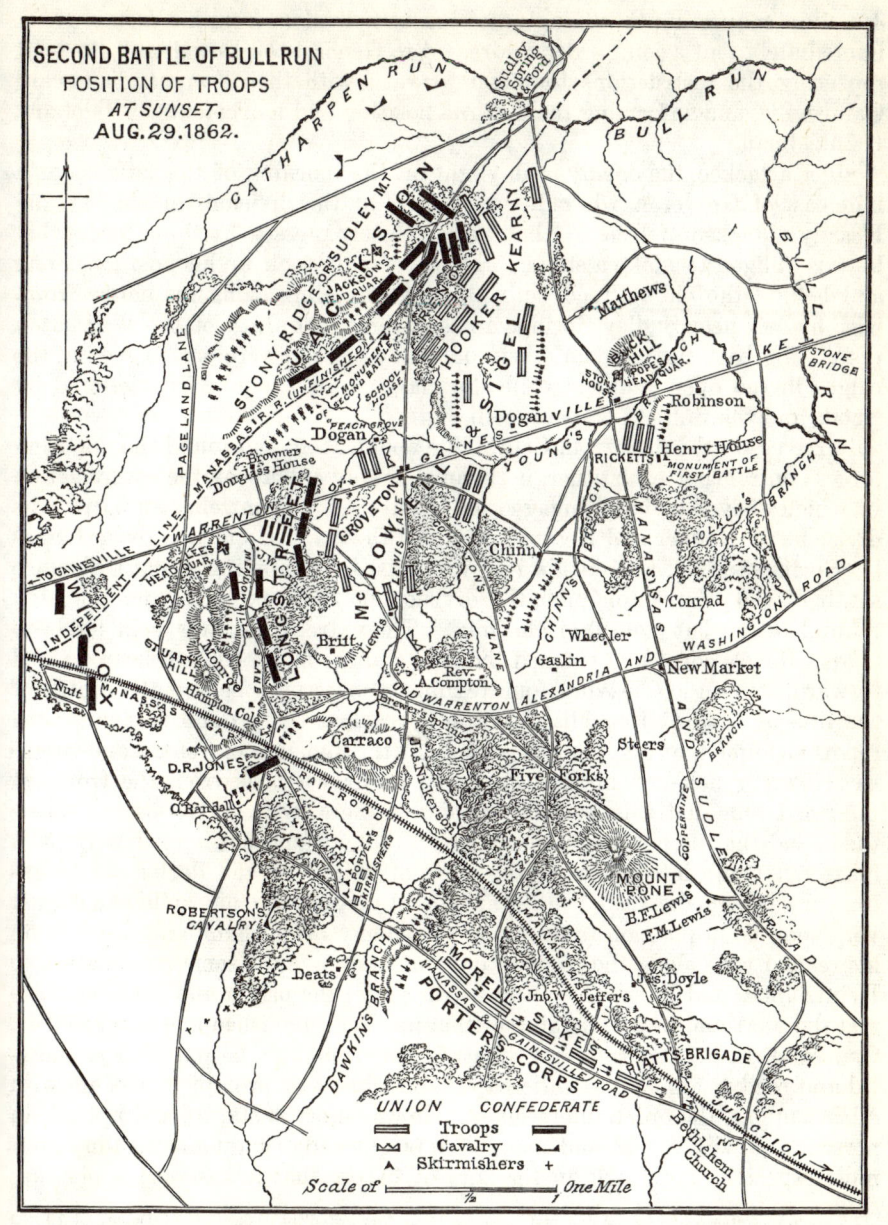

RELATIVE POSITIONS AT SUNSET, FRIDAY, AUGUST 29TH.

At noon of that day Porter's corps was in much the same position as at sunset. According to General Pope, at noon Porter, with very little resistance to overcome, might have occupied the hill of the Monroe and Hampton Cole houses, a position of great importance. But, according to other authorities (see p. 527), Longstreet was in position between Jackson and Porter by noon. At that hour the right of the Union army was arrayed in continuous line in front of Jackson from a point on the turnpike three-quarters of a mile west of Groveton to the point where the Sudley Springs road crosses the unfinished railroad which was Jackson's stronghold. The map above illustrates the situation at the time of the greatest success on the right, when Jackson's left had been turned upon itself by Kearny's, Reno's, and Hooker's divisions.— EDITORS.

Junction, requesting that King's division be not taken from his command. I immediately sent a joint order, addressed to Generals McDowell and Porter,↓ repeating the instructions to move forward with their commands toward Gainesville, and informing them of the position and movements of Sigel and Heintzelman.

Sigel attacked the enemy at daylight on the morning of the 29th about a mile east of Groveton, where he was joined by the divisions of Hooker and Kearny. Jackson fell back,♭ but was so closely pressed by these forces that he was obliged to make a stand. He accordingly took up his position along and behind the old railroad embankment extending along his entire front, with his left near Sudley Springs and his right just south of the Warrenton pike. His batteries, some of them of heavy caliber, were posted behind the ridges in the open ground, while the mass of his troops were sheltered by woods and the railroad embankment.

I arrived on the field from Centreville about noon, and found the opposing forces confronting each other, both considerably cut up by the severe action in which they had been engaged since daylight. Heintzelman's corps (the divisions of Hooker and Kearny) occupied the right of our line toward Sudley Springs. Sigel was on his left, with his line extending a short distance south of the Warrenton pike, the division of Schenck occupying the high ground to the left (south) of the pike. The extreme left was held by Reynolds. Reno's corps had reached the field and the most of it had been pushed forward into action, leaving four regiments in reserve behind the center of the line of battle. Immediately after I reached the ground, General Sigel reported to me that his line was weak, that the divisions of Schurz and Steinwehr were much cut up and ought to be drawn back from the front. I informed him that this was impossible, as there were no troops to replace them, and that he must hold his ground; that I would not immediately push his troops again into action, as the corps of McDowell and Porter were moving forward on the road from Manassas Junction to Gainesville, and must very soon be in position to fall upon the enemy's right flank and possibly on his rear. I rode along the front of our line and gave the same information to Heintzelman and Reno. I shall not soon forget the bright and confident face and the alert and hearty manner of that most accomplished and loyal soldier, General J. L. Reno. From first to last in this campaign he was always cheerful and ready; anxious to anticipate if possible, and prompt to execute with all his might, the orders he received. He was short in stature and upright in person, and with a face and manner so bright and engaging at all times, but most especially noticeable in the fury of battle, that it was both a pleasure

↓ This joint order refers to the one just cited as having been sent "an hour and a half ago," under which Porter was marching toward Gainesville when McDowell joined him near Manassas Junction. After receiving the joint order, General McDowell again joined Porter, at the front, and showed him a dispatch just received from Buford, dated 9:30 A. M., and addressed to Ricketts. It appears to have escaped notice that this dispatch was forwarded by Ricketts to McDowell at 11:30 A. M., which fixes the time of the meeting between Generals McDowell and Porter at the front as *after* 11:30.—EDITORS.

♭ Not mentioned by Jackson or any of the subordinate commanders of either army. Jackson appears to have received the attack in position as stated by General Pope in the next sentence.— EDITORS.

and a comfort to see him. In his death, two weeks afterward, during the battle of South Mountain, when he led his troops with his usual gallantry and daring, the Government lost one of its best and most promising officers. Had he lived to see the end of the war, he would undoubtedly have attained one of the highest, if not the very highest position in the army. His superior abilities were unquestioned, and if he lacked one single element that goes to make a perfect soldier, certainly it was not discovered before his death.

The troops were permitted to rest for a time, and to resupply themselves with ammunition. From 1:30 to 4 o'clock P. M. very severe conflicts occurred repeatedly all along the line, and there was a continuous roar of artillery and small-arms, with scarcely an intermission. About two o'clock in the afternoon three discharges of artillery were heard on the extreme left of our line or right of the enemy's, and I for the moment, and naturally, believed that Porter and McDowell had reached their positions and were engaged with the enemy. I heard only three shots, and as nothing followed I was at a loss to know what had become of these corps, or what was delaying them, as before this hour they should have been, even with ordinary marching, well up on our left. Shortly afterward I received information that McDowell's corps was advancing to join the left of our line by the Sudley Springs road, and would probably be up within two hours [about 4 P. M.—EDITORS]. At 4:30 o'clock I sent a peremptory order to General Porter, who was at or near Dawkins's Branch, about four or five miles distant from my headquarters, to push forward at once into action on the enemy's right, and if possible on his rear, stating to him generally the condition of things on the field in front of me. At 5:30 o'clock, when General Porter should have been going into action in compliance with this order, I directed Heintzelman and Reno to attack the enemy's left. The attack was made promptly and with vigor and persistence, and the left of the enemy was doubled back toward his center. After a severe and bloody action of an hour Kearny forced the position on the left of the enemy and occupied the field of battle there.

By this time General McDowell had arrived on the field, and I pushed his corps, supported by Reynolds, forward at once into action along the Warrenton pike toward the enemy's right, then said to be falling back. This attack along the pike was made by King's division near sunset; but, as Porter made no movement whatever toward the field, Longstreet, who was pushing to the front, was able to extend his lines beyond King's left with impunity, and King's attack did not accomplish what was expected, in view of the anticipated attack which Porter was ordered to make, and should have been making at the same time.

From 5 o'clock in the day until some time after dark the fighting all along our lines was severe and bloody, and our losses were very heavy. To show clearly the character of the battle on the 29th, I embody extracts from the official reports of General Lee, of General T. J. Jackson, and of Longstreet and Hill, who commanded the enemy's forces on that day. I choose the reports of the officers commanding against us for several reasons, but especially to show Longstreet's movements and operations on the afternoon of the 29th of August, when, it is alleged, he was held in check by Porter. General Lee says:

THE BATTLE OF GROVETON, AUGUST 29TH, AS SEEN FROM CENTREVILLE. FROM A SKETCH MADE AT THE TIME.

... "Generals Jones and Wilcox bivouacked that night [28th] east of the mountain; and on the morning of the 29th the whole command resumed the march, the sound of cannon at Manassas announcing that Jackson was already engaged. Longstreet entered the turnpike near Gainesville, and, moving down toward Groveton, the head of his column came upon the field in rear of the enemy's left, which had already opened with artillery upon Jackson's right, as previously described. He immediately placed some of his batteries in position, but before he could complete his dispositions to attack, the enemy withdrew; not, however, without loss from our artillery. Longstreet took position on the right of Jackson, Hood's two brigades, supported by Evans, being deployed across the turnpike, at right angles to it. These troops were supported on the left by three brigades under General Wilcox, and by a light force on the right under General Kemper. D. R. Jones's division formed the extreme right of the line, resting on the Manassas Gap railroad. The cavalry guarded our right and left flanks; that on the right being under General Stuart in person. After the arrival of Longstreet the enemy changed his position and began to concentrate opposite Jackson's left, opening a brisk artillery fire, which was responded to with effect by some of General A. P. Hill's batteries. Colonel Walton placed a part of his artillery upon a commanding position between the lines of Generals Jackson and Longstreet, by order of the latter, and engaged the enemy vigorously for several hours. Soon afterward General Stuart reported the approach of a large force from the direction of Bristoe Station, threatening Longstreet's right. The brigades under General Wilcox were sent to reënforce General Jones, but no serious attack was made, and after firing a few shots the enemy withdrew. While this demonstration was being made on our right, a large force advanced to assail the left of Jackson's position, occupied by the division of General A. P. Hill. The attack was received by his troops with their accustomed steadiness, and the battle raged with great fury. The enemy was repeatedly repulsed, but again pressed on to the attack with fresh troops Once he succeeded in penetrating an interval between General Gregg's brigade, on the extreme left, and that of General Thomas, but was quickly driven back with great slaughter by the 14th South Carolina regiment, then in reserve, and the 49th Georgia, of Thomas's brigade. The contest was close and obstinate: the combatants sometimes delivering their fire at ten paces General Gregg, who was most exposed, was reënforced by Hays's brigade under Colonel Forno and successfully and gallantly resisted the attacks of the enemy, until, the ammunition of hi brigade being exhausted, and all his field-officers but two killed or wounded, it was relieved, afte several hours of severe fighting, by Early's brigade and the 8th Louisiana regiment. General Early drove the enemy back, with heavy loss, and pursued about two hundred yards beyond the line of battle, when he was recalled to the position of the railroad where Thomas, Pender, and Archer had firmly held their ground against every attack. While the battle was raging on Jackson's left, General Longstreet ordered Hood and Evans to advance, but before the order could be obeyed Hood was himself attacked, and his command at once became warmly engaged. General Wilcox was recalled from the right and ordered to advance on Hood's left, and one of Kemper's brigades, under Colonel Hunton, moved forward on his right. The enemy was repulsed by Hood after a severe contest, and fell back, closely followed by our troops. The battle continued until 9 P. M., the enemy retreating until he reached a strong position, which he held with a large force. The darkness of the night put a stop to the engagement, and our troops remained in their advanced position until early next morning, when they were withdrawn to their first line. One piece of artillery, several stands of colors, and a number of prisoners were captured. Our loss was severe in this engagement; Brigadier-Generals Field and Trimble, and Colonel Forno, commanding Hays's brigade, were severely wounded, and several other valuable officers killed or disabled whose names are mentioned in the accompanying reports."

General Jackson in his report, dated April 27th, 1863, says:

... "My troops on this day were distributed along and in the vicinity of the cut of an unfinished railroad (intended as a part of the track to connect the Manassas road directly with Alexandria), stretching from the Warrenton turnpike in the direction of Sudley's Mill. It was mainly along the excavation of this unfinished road that my line of battle was formed on the 29th: Jackson's division, under Brigadier-General Starke, on the right; Ewell's division, under Brigadier-General Lawton, in the center; and Hill's division on the left. In the morning, about 10 o'clock, the Federal artillery opened with spirit and animation upon our right, which was soon replied to by the batteries of Poague, Carpenter, Dement, Brockenbrough, and Latimer, under Major [L. M.] Shumaker. This lasted for some time, when the enemy moved around more to our left, to another point of attack. His next effort was directed against our left. This was vigorously

BREVET MAJOR-GENERAL CUVIER GROVER.
FROM A PHOTOGRAPH.

⁊ Both on Friday and Saturday afternoons there was desperate fighting about the railroad cut and embankment opposite, and to the right of the site of the battle monument (see map, p. 473). On Friday afternoon Grover's brigade, of Hooker's division, here charged Jackson's center before Kearny's successful and bloody charge on Jackson's left. Grover led 5 regiments, altogether about 1500 men, and in 20 minutes lost 486, or nearly one-third of his command. In his report, General Grover says:

"I rode over the field in front as far as the position of the enemy would admit. After rising the hill under which my command lay, an open field was entered, and from one edge of it gradually fell off in a slope to a valley, through which ran a railroad embankment. Beyond this embankment the forest continued, and the corresponding heights beyond were held by the enemy in force, supported by artillery. At 3 P. M. I received an order to advance in line of battle over this ground, pass the embankment, enter the edge of the woods beyond, and hold it. Dispositions for carrying out such orders were immediately made. Pieces were loaded, bayonets fixed, and instructions given for the line to move slowly upon the enemy until it felt his fire, then close upon him rapidly, fire one well-directed volley, and rely upon the bayonet to secure the position on the other side. We rapidly and firmly pressed upon the embankment, and here occurred a short, sharp, and obstinate hand-to-hand conflict with bayonets and clubbed muskets. Many of the enemy were bayoneted in their tracks, others struck down with the butts of pieces, and onward pressed our line. In a few yards more it met a terrible fire from a second line, which, in its turn, broke. The enemy's third line now bore down upon our thinned ranks in close order, and swept back the right center and a portion of our left. With the gallant 16th Massachusetts on our left I tried to turn his flank, but the breaking of our right and center and the weight of the enemy's lines caused the necessity of falling back, first to the embankment, and then to our first position, behind which we rallied to our colors."

EDITORS.

THE HALT ON THE LINE OF BATTLE. FROM A WAR-TIME SKETCH.

repulsed by the batteries of Braxton, Crenshaw, and Pegram. About 2 o'clock P. M. the Federal infantry, in large force, advanced to the attack of our left, occupied by the division of General Hill. It pressed forward in defiance of our fatal and destructive fire with great determination, a portion of it crossing a deep cut in the railroad track, and penetrating in heavy force an interval of nearly 175 yards, which separated the right of Gregg's from the left of Thomas's brigade. For a short time Gregg's brigade, on the extreme left, was isolated from the main body of the command. But the 14th South Carolina regiment, then in reserve, with the 49th Georgia, left of Colonel Thomas, attacked the exultant enemy with vigor and drove them back across the railroad track with great slaughter." . . .

General Longstreet says in his report, dated October 10th, 1862:

. . . "Early on the 29th [August] the columns [that had passed Thoroughfare and Hopewell Gaps] were united, and the advance to join General Jackson was resumed. The noise of battle was heard before we reached Gainesville. The march was quickened to the extent of our capacity. The excitement of battle seemed to give new life and strength to our jaded men, and the head of my column soon reached a position in rear of the enemy's left flank, and within easy cannon-shot.

"On approaching the field some of Brigadier-General Hood's batteries were ordered into position, and his division was deployed on the right and left of the turnpike, at right angles with it, and supported by Brigadier-General Evans's brigade. Before these batteries could open, the enemy discovered our movements and withdrew his left. Another battery (Captain Stribling's) was placed upon a commanding position to my right, which played upon the rear of the enemy's left and drove him entirely from that part of the field. He changed his front rapidly, so as to meet the advance of Hood and Evans.

"Three brigades, under General Wilcox, were thrown forward to the support of the left; and three others, under General Kemper, to the support of the right of these commands. General D. R. Jones's division was placed upon the Manassas Gap railroad to the right, and en échelon with regard to the last three brigades. Colonel Walton placed his batteries in a commanding position between my line and that of General Jackson, and engaged the enemy for several hours in a severe and successful artillery duel. At a late hour in the day Major-General Stuart reported the approach of the enemy in heavy columns against my extreme right. I withdrew General

Wilcox, with his three brigades, from the left, and placed his command in position to support Jones in case of an attack against my right. After some few shots the enemy withdrew his forces, moving them around toward his front, and about 4 o'clock in the afternoon began to press forward against General Jackson's position. Wilcox's brigades were moved back to their former position, and Hood's two brigades, supported by Evans, were quickly pressed forward to the attack. At the same time Wilcox's three brigades made a like advance, as also Hunton's brigade, of Kemper's command.

"These movements were executed with commendable zeal and ability. Hood, supported by Evans, made a gallant attack, driving the enemy back till 9 o'clock at night. One piece of artillery, several regimental standards, and a number of prisoners were taken. The enemy's entire force was found to be massed directly in my front, and in so strong a position that it was not deemed advisable to move on against his immediate front; so the troops were quietly withdrawn at 1 o'clock the following morning. The wheels of the captured piece were cut down, and it was left on the ground. The enemy seized that opportunity to claim a victory, and the Federal commander was so imprudent as to dispatch his Government, by telegraph, tidings to that effect. After withdrawing from the attack, my troops were placed in the line first occupied, and in the original order."

General A. P. Hill says in his report, dated February 25th, 1863:

. . . "Friday morning, in accordance with orders from General Jackson, I occupied the line of the unfinished railroad, my extreme left resting near Sudley Ford, my right near the point where the road strikes the open field, Gregg, Field, and Thomas in the front line; Gregg on the left and Field on the right; with Branch, Pender, and Archer as supports. . . .

"The evident intention of the enemy this day was to turn our left and overwhelm Jackson's corps before Longstreet came up, and to accomplish this the most persistent and furious onsets were made, by column after column of infantry, accompanied by numerous batteries of artillery. Soon my reserves were all in, and up to 6 o'clock my division, assisted by the Louisiana brigade of General Hays, commanded by Colonel Forno, with a heroic courage and obstinacy almost beyond parallel, had met and repulsed six distinct and separate assaults, a portion of the time the majority of the men being without a cartridge. . . .

"The enemy prepared for a last and determined attempt. Their serried masses, overwhelming superiority of numbers, and bold bearing made the chances of victory to tremble in the balance; my own division exhausted by seven hours' unremitted fighting, hardly one round per man remaining, and weakened in all things save its unconquerable spirit. Casting about for help, fortunately it was here reported to me that the brigades of Generals Lawton and Early were near by, and, sending to them, they promptly moved to my front at the most opportune moment, and this last charge met the same disastrous fate that had befallen those preceding. Having received an order from General Jackson to endeavor to avoid a general engagement, my commanders of brigades contented themselves with repulsing the enemy and following them up but a few hundred yards."

General J. E. B. Stuart says in his report, dated February 28th, 1863:

. . . "I met with the head of General Longstreet's column between Hay Market and Gainesville, and there communicated to the commanding general General Jackson's position and the enemy's. I then passed the cavalry through the column so as to place it on Longstreet's right flank, and advanced directly toward Manassas, while the column kept directly down the pike to join General Jackson's right. I selected a fine position for a battery on the right, and one having been sent to me, I fired a few shots at the enemy's supposed position, which induced him to shift his position. General Robertson, who, with his command, was sent to reconnoiter farther down the road toward Manassas, reported the enemy in his front. Upon repairing to that front, I found that Rosser's regiment was engaged with the enemy to the left of the road, and Robertson's vedettes had found the enemy approaching from the direction of Bristoe Station toward Sudley. The prolongation of his line of march would have passed through my position, which was a very fine one for artillery as well as observation, and struck Longstreet in flank. I waited his approach long enough to ascertain that there was at least an army corps, at the same

COLLECTING THE WOUNDED.

In his "Recollections of a Private" [see "The Century" magazine for January, 1886] Warren Lee Goss says: "At the end of the first day's battle, August 29th, so soon as the fighting ceased, many sought without orders to rescue comrades lying wounded between the opposing lines. There seemed to be an understanding between the men of both armies that such parties were not to be disturbed in their mission of mercy. After the failure of the attempt of Grover and Kearny to carry the railroad embankment, the Confederates followed their troops back and formed a line in the edge of the woods. When the fire had died away along the darkling woods, little groups of men from the Union lines went stealthily about, bringing in the wounded from the exposed positions. Blankets attached to poles or muskets often served as stretchers to bear the wounded to the ambulances and surgeons. There was a great lack here of organized effort to care for our wounded. Vehicles of various kinds were pressed into service. The removal went on during the entire night, and tired soldiers were roused from their slumbers by the plaintive cries of comrades passing in the comfortless vehicles. In one instance a Confederate and a Union soldier were found cheering each other on the field. They were put into the same Virginia farm-cart and sent to the rear, talking and groaning in fraternal sympathy."

time keeping detachments of cavalry dragging brush down the road from the direction of Gainesville, so as to deceive the enemy,— a ruse which Porter's report shows was successful,— and notified the commanding general, then opposite me on the turnpike, that Longstreet's flank and rear were seriously threatened, and of the importance to us of the ridge I then held. Immediately upon the receipt of that intelligence, Jenkins's, Kemper's, and D. R. Jones's brigades, and several pieces of artillery were ordered to me by General Longstreet, and, being placed in position fronting Bristoe, awaited the enemy's advance. After exchanging a few shots with rifle-pieces this corps withdrew toward Manassas, leaving artillery and supports to hold the position until night. Brigadier-General Fitz Lee returned to the vicinity of Sudley, after a very successful expedition, of which his official report has not been received, and was instructed to coöperate with Jackson's left. Late in the afternoon the artillery on this commanding ridge was, to an important degree, auxiliary to the attack upon the enemy, and Jenkins's brigade repulsed the enemy in handsome style at one volley, as they advanced across a corn-field. Thus the day ended, our lines having considerably advanced."

What would have been the effect of the application on the enemy's right at, or any time after, 4 o'clock that afternoon of ten or twelve thousand effective men who had not been in battle at all, I do not myself consider doubtful.

In this battle the Fifth Corps, under General F. J. Porter, took no part whatever, but remained all day in column, without even deploying into line of battle or making any effort in force to find out what was in their front. ☆ That General Porter knew of the progress of the battle on his right, and that he believed the Union army was being defeated, is shown by his own dispatches to McDowell, several times repeated during the day. That subjoined will be sufficient:

"GENERALS McDOWELL AND KING : — I found it impossible to communicate by crossing the woods to Groveton. The enemy are in great force on this road, and as they appear to have driven our forces back, the fire of the enemy having advanced and ours retired, I have determined to withdraw to Manassas. I have attempted to communicate with McDowell and Sigel, but my messengers have run into the enemy. They have gathered artillery and cavalry and infantry, and the advancing masses of dust show the enemy coming in force. I am now going to the head of the column to see what is passing and how affairs are going, and I will communicate with you. Had you not better send your train back?
"F. J. PORTER, Major-General."

Not the artillery only, but the volleys of musketry in this battle were also plainly heard on their right and front by the advance of Porter's troops much of the day. In consequence of his belief that the army on his right was being defeated, as stated in more than one of these dispatches, he informed General McDowell that he intended to retire to Manassas, and advised McDowell to send back his trains in the same direction.

For this action, or non-action, he has been on the one hand likened to Benedict Arnold, and on the other favorably compared with George Washington. I presume he would not accept the first position, and probably would hardly lay claim to the second. Certainly I have not the inclination, even had I the power, to assign him to either or to any position between the two; and if he were alone concerned in the question, I should make no comment at all on the subject at this day. Many others than himself and the result of a battle, however, are involved in it, and they do not permit silence when the second battle of Bull Run is discussed. Without going into the merits of the case, which has been obscured and confused by so many and such varied controversies, I shall confine myself to a bare statement of the facts as they are known to me personally, or communicated officially by officers of rank and standing, and by the official reports of both armies engaged in the battle. General Porter was tried by court-martial a few months after the battle and was cashiered. The reasons given by him at the time for his failure to go into action, or take any part in the battle, were: first, that he considered himself under General McDowell's orders, who told him that they were too far to

☆ For another account of Porter's action see "The Fitz John Porter Case," to follow.— EDITORS.

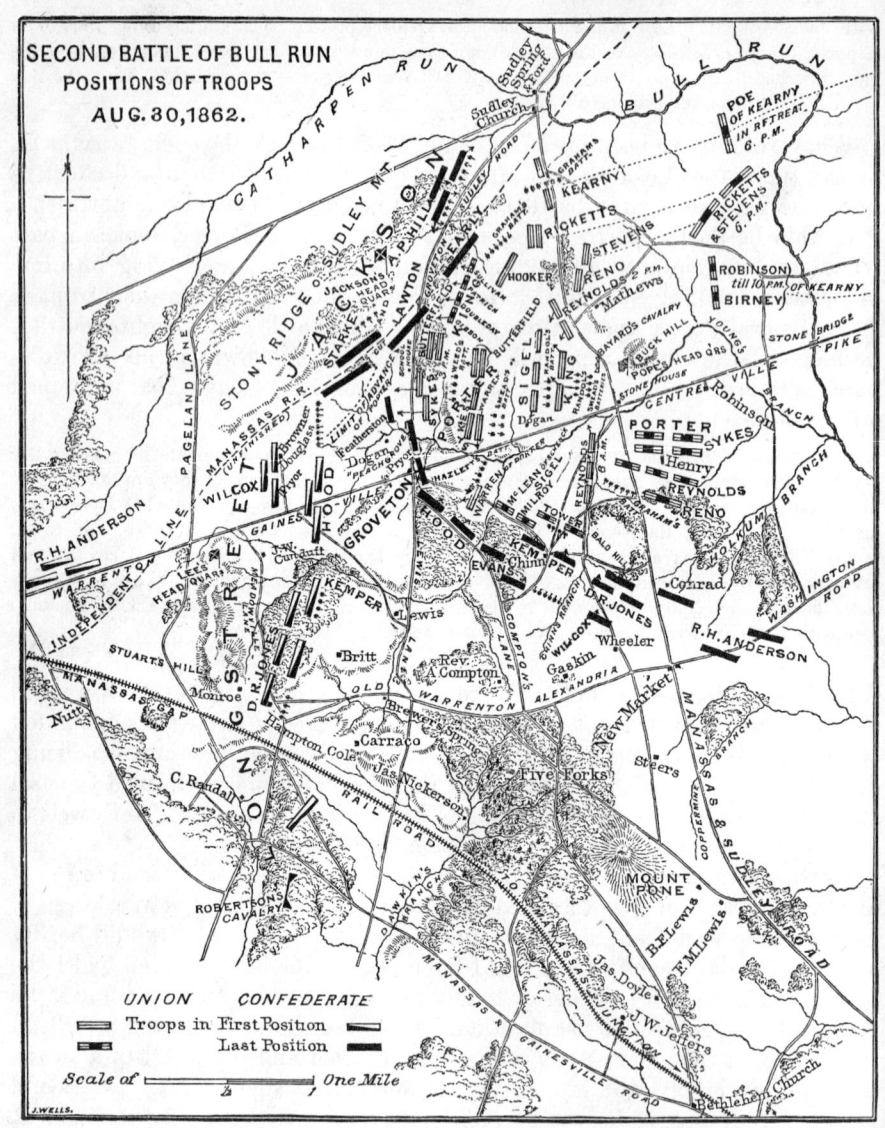

**FIRST AND LAST POSITIONS IN THE FIGHTING OF AUGUST 30TH.**

During the assault by Porter's corps and King's division, Jackson's forces were behind the unfinished railway. When that assault failed, the Unionists north of the turnpike were attacked by the brigades of Featherston and Pryor (of Wilcox), which were acting with some of Jackson's troops and with one brigade of Hood. Wilcox, with his own proper brigade, passed far to the right and fought his way to an advanced position, after Evans and D. R. Jones had compelled Sigel and McDowell to loosen their hold on and west of Bald Hill. [NOTE.— Tower, Milroy, and McLean, on the map, should be placed more to the east on and near Bald Hill.] At dark the Confederates were somewhat in advance of the positions indicated on the map.— EDITORS.

the front for a battle; and, second, that the enemy was in such heavy force in his front that he would have been defeated had he attacked. General McDowell stated before the court-martial that, so far from saying that they were too far to the front for battle, he directed General Porter before leaving him to put his corps into the action where he was, and that he (McDowell) would move farther to the right and go into the battle there. Upon Porter remarking that he could not go in there without getting into a fight, McDowell replied, "I thought that was what we came here for."

General J. E. B. Stuart, who commanded the cavalry in Lee's army, tells in his official report above quoted precisely what was in General Porter's front, and what means he took to produce upon General Porter the impression that there were heavy forces in front of him and advancing toward him. General Porter certainly made no reconnoissance in force to ascertain whether or not there was a heavy force in his front; and Stuart's report makes it quite certain that, at the time referred to by him, Porter could easily have moved forward from Dawkins's Branch and seized the ridge on which are the Hampton Cole and Monroe houses, from which he would have had a complete view of the field from right to left. Not only this, but his occupation of that ridge would have connected him closely with our left and absolutely prevented Longstreet from forming on Jackson's right until he had dislodged Porter, which would have occupied him too long to have permitted the effective use of his troops for any other purpose, and certainly for the advance which he subsequently made against our left. Longstreet now asserts that he was in front of Porter with part of his corps at some indefinite hour of the day, variously fixed, but according to him by 11 o'clock in the morning, about the time that Porter's corps reached Dawkins's Branch. He further asserts, somewhat extravagantly, that if Porter had attacked he (Longstreet) would have annihilated him. He seems to have thought it a simple matter to annihilate an army corps of ten or twelve thousand men, much of which was composed of regular troops, but perhaps his statement to that effect would hardly be accepted by military men. If such an assertion made by a corps commander of one army is sufficient reason for a corps commander of the opposing army not to attack, even under orders to do so, it is hard to see how any general commanding an army could direct a battle at all; and certainly if such assertions as Longstreet's are considered reliable, there would have been no battle fought in our civil war, since they could easily have been had from either side in advance of any battle that was fought.

MAJOR-GENERAL GEORGE SYKES. FROM A PHOTOGRAPH.

It seems pertinent to ask why General Longstreet did not annihilate Porter's corps during the day if it were so easily in his power to do so. It is also proper to suggest that it would have required a long time and all of his force to do this annihilating business on such a corps as Porter's; and in that case, what would have become of Jackson's right deprived of Longstreet's active support, which barely enabled Jackson to hold the ground that afternoon, Longstreet himself falling back at least a mile from our front at 1 o'clock that night after several hours of severe fighting?

I shall not discuss the various statements concerning the time of Longstreet's arrival on the field. That he may have been there in person at the hour he mentions is of course possible; but that his corps was with him, that it was in line of battle at any such hour, or was in any such condition to fight as Porter was, can neither be truthfully asserted nor successfully maintained. Whatever Porter supposed to be Longstreet's position, however, in no respect touches his obligation to move forward under the circumstances and force Longstreet to develop what he really had, which he (Porter) certainly did not know and had taken no measures to know. The severe fighting on his right, which he heard and interpreted into a defeat for the Union army, did not permit him to rest idle on the field with his troops in column and with no sufficient effort even to find out anything of the field in front of him.

If a mere impression that the enemy is in heavy force and that an attack or further advance might be hazardous is a sufficient reason for a corps commander to keep out of a battle, raging in his hearing, especially when he thinks that his friends are being defeated, it is extremely difficult to see how any army commander would venture to engage in battle at all, unless he could ascertain in advance and keep himself acquainted during the day with the impressions of his corps commanders about the propriety of going into the battle. Certainly Porter did not know at that time that Longstreet was in his front, and his non-action was based on fancy, and not on any fact that he knew.

But wherever Longstreet was in the morning, it is certain that at 4 o'clock that day, or about 4 o'clock, according to his own official report, he withdrew the larger part of his force and advanced to Jackson's right flank to resist the last attack of the Union army on Jackson's line, and that for several hours he was engaged in a severe battle on our left, utterly ignoring Porter and presenting his right flank to Porter's attack during that whole time. He seems also to have entirely forgotten that he was "held in check," as he was good-natured enough to say he was years afterward. During these long hours General Porter still remained idle with his corps in column, and many of them lying on the ground, for ease of position probably, as they were not under fire.

Taking the enemy's own account of the battle that afternoon, which lasted several hours, and its result, it is not unreasonable to say that, if General Porter had attacked Longstreet's right with ten or twelve thousand men while the latter was thus engaged, the effect would have been conclusive. Porter's case is the first I have ever known, or that I find recorded in military history, in which the theory has been seriously put forth that the hero of a battle is the man who keeps out of it. With this theory in successful operation, war will be stripped of most of its terrors, and a pitched battle need not be much more dangerous to human life than a militia muster.

# THE SECOND BATTLE OF BULL RUN. 485

When the battle ceased on the 29th of August, we were in possession of the field on our right, and occupied on our left the position held early in the day, and had every right to claim a decided success. What that success might have been, if a corps of twelve thousand men who had not been in battle that day had been thrown against Longstreet's right while engaged in the severe fight that afternoon, I need not indicate. To say that General Porter's non-action during that whole day was wholly unexpected and disappointing, and that it provoked severe comment on all hands, is to state the facts mildly.

Every indication during the night of the 29th and up to 10 o'clock on the morning of the 30th pointed to the retreat of the enemy from our front. Paroled prisoners of our own army, taken on the evening of the 29th, who came into our lines on the morning of the 30th, reported the enemy retreating during the whole night in the direction of and along the Warrenton pike (a fact since confirmed by Longstreet's report).☆ Generals McDowell and Heintzelman, who reconnoitered the position held by the enemy's left on the evening of the 29th, also confirmed this statement. They reported to me the evacuation of these positions by the enemy, and that there was every indication of their retreat in the direction of Gainesville. On the morning of the 30th, as may be easily believed, our troops, who had been marching and fighting almost continuously for many days, were greatly exhausted. They had had

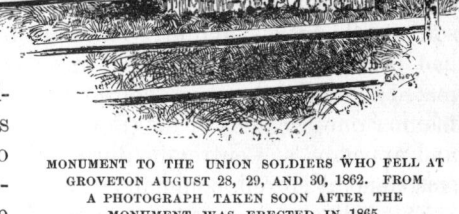

MONUMENT TO THE UNION SOLDIERS WHO FELL AT GROVETON AUGUST 28, 29, AND 30, 1862. FROM A PHOTOGRAPH TAKEN SOON AFTER THE MONUMENT WAS ERECTED IN 1865.

This view is taken from the edge of the railway cut, looking toward the Union lines. The shaft is of brown sandstone, and in design and material is like the monument erected on the Henry hill at the same time. The shot and shell that were fixed with mortar to the base and to the top of the shaft, and every vestige of the inclosing fence, have been carried off by relic-hunters. In May, 1884, the monument was partly hidden by the four evergreens which were planted at the corners. The field behind the railway cut and behind the embankment, east of the cut, was even then strewn with the tins of cartridge-boxes, rusty camp utensils, and bits of broken accouterments.— EDITORS.

little to eat for two days, and artillery and cavalry horses had been in harness and under the saddle for ten days, and had been almost out of forage for the last two days. It may be readily imagined how little these troops, after such severe labors and hardships, were in condition for further active marching and fighting. On the 28th I had telegraphed General Halleck our condition, and had begged of him to have rations and forage sent forward to us from Alexandria with all speed; but about daylight on the 30th I received a note from

---

☆ According to General Longstreet's and other Confederate reports, their troops withdrew at night to their line of battle of the day, occupying the same positions and in the same order. General Pope's orders for the 30th directed that the corps of McDowell, Heintzelman, and Porter, with the necessary cavalry, should move "forward in pursuit of the enemy," and "press him vigorously all day." The command of the pursuit was assigned to General McDowell.— EDITORS.

General Franklin, written by direction of General McClellan, informing me that rations and forage would be loaded into the available wagons and cars at Alexandria as soon as I should send back a cavalry escort to guard the trains. Such a letter, when we were fighting the enemy and when Alexandria was full of troops, needs no comment. Our cavalry was well-nigh broken down completely, and certainly we were in no condition to spare troops from the front, nor could they have gone to Alexandria and returned within the time by which we must have had provisions and forage or have fallen back toward supplies; nor am I able to understand of what use cavalry could be to guard railroad trains. It was not until I received this letter that I began to be hopeless of any successful issue to our operations; but I felt it to be my duty, notwithstanding the broken-down condition of the forces under my command, to hold my position. I had received no sort of information of any troops coming forward to reënforce me since the 24th, and did not expect on the morning of the 30th that any assistance would reach me from the direction of Washington, but I determined again to give battle to the enemy and delay as long as possible his farther advance toward Washington. I accordingly prepared to renew the engagement.

General Porter, with whose non-action of the day before I was naturally dissatisfied, had been peremptorily ordered that night to report to me in person with his corps, and arrived on the field early in the morning. His corps had been reënforced by Piatt's brigade of Sturgis's division, and was estimated to be about twelve thousand strong; but in some hitherto unexplained manner one brigade ⸸ of his (Porter's) corps had straggled off from the corps and appeared at Centreville during the day. With this straggling brigade was General Morell, commander of the division to which it belonged.

This brigade remained at Centreville all day, in sight and sound of the battle in which the corps to which it belonged was engaged, but made no move to join it or to approach the field of battle. On the contrary, the brigade commander made requisition for ten thousand pairs of shoes on one of my aides-de-camp who was at Centreville in charge of the headquarters train. The troops under General Sturgis and General A. Sanders Piatt had followed this brigade by a misunderstanding of the situation; but the moment they found themselves away from the battle these two officers, with true soldierly spirit, passed Morell and brought their commands to the field and into the battle, where they rendered gallant and distinguished services.

Between 12 and 2 o'clock during the day I advanced Porter's corps, supported by King's division of McDowell's corps, and supported also on their left by Sigel's corps and Reynolds's division, to attack the enemy along the Warrenton pike. At the same time the corps of Heintzelman and Reno on our right were directed to push forward to the left and front toward the pike and attack the enemy's left flank. For a time Ricketts's division of McDowell's corps was placed in support of this movement. I was obliged to assume the

---

⸸ Griffin's brigade. Griffin testified that he was ordered by General Morell to follow Sykes, who was supposed to have gone to Centreville. Griffin moved thence toward the battle-field about 5 P. M. He found the road blocked, and the bridge over Cub Run broken.—EDITORS.

aggressive or to fall back, as from want of provisions I was not able to await an attack from the enemy or the result of any other movement he might make.

Every moment of delay increased the odds against us, and I therefore pushed forward the attack as rapidly as possible. Soon after Porter advanced to attack along the Warrenton pike and the assault was made by Heintzelman and Reno on the right, it became apparent that the enemy was massing his forces as fast as they arrived on the right of Jackson, and was moving forward to force our left. General McDowell was therefore directed to recall Ricketts's division from our right, and put it so as to strengthen our left thus threatened.

Porter's corps was repulsed after some severe fighting, and began to retire, and the enemy advancing to the assault, our whole line was soon furiously engaged. The main attack of the enemy was made against our left, but was met with stubborn resistance by the divisions of Schenck and Reynolds, and the brigade of Milroy, who were soon reënforced on the left by Ricketts's division. The action was severe for several hours, the enemy bringing up heavy reserves and pouring mass after mass of his troops on our left. He was able also to present at least an equal force all along our line of battle. Porter's corps was halted and re-formed, and as soon as it was in condition it was pushed forward to the support of our left, where it rendered distinguished service, especially the brigade of regulars under Colonel (then Lieutenant-Colonel) Buchanan.

McLean's brigade of Schenck's division, which was posted in observation on our left flank, and in support of Reynolds, became exposed to the attack of the enemy on our left when Reynolds's division was drawn back to form line to support Porter's corps, then retiring from their attack, and it was fiercely assailed by Hood and Evans, in greatly superior force. This brigade was commanded in person by General Schenck, the division commander, and fought with supreme gallantry and tenacity. The enemy's attack was repulsed several times with severe loss, but he returned again and again to the assault.

It is needless for me to describe the appearance of a man so well known to the country as General R. C. Schenck. I have only to say that a more gallant and devoted soldier never lived, and to his presence and the fearless exposure of his person during these attacks is largely due the protracted resistance made by this brigade. He fell, badly wounded, in the front of his command, and his loss was deeply felt and had a marked effect on the final result in that part of the field.

Tower's brigade of Ricketts's division was pushed forward to his support, and the brigade was led by General Tower in person with conspicuous gallantry. The conduct of these two brigades and their commanders in plain view of our whole left was especially distinguished, and called forth hearty and enthusiastic cheers. Their example was of great service, and seemed to infuse new spirit into the troops that witnessed their intrepid conduct.

I have always considered it a misfortune to the country that in this action General Tower received a severe wound which disabled him from active

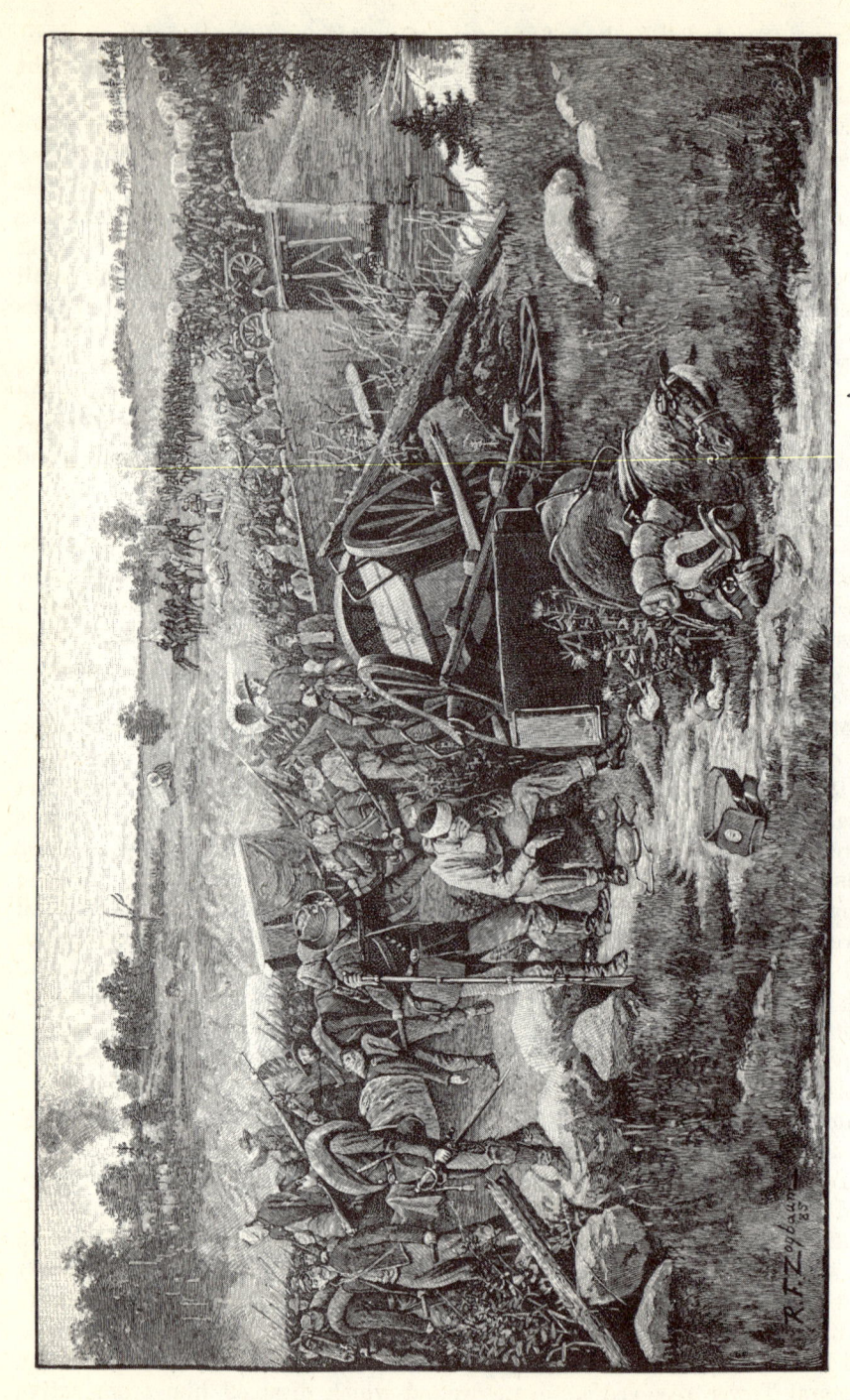

THE RETREAT OVER THE STONE BRIDGE, SATURDAY EVENING, AUGUST 30TH.

service. He is a man of very superior abilities, zealous, and full of spirit and *élan*, and might easily have expected to serve his country in a much higher position than the one that he held on that field.

Reno's corps was withdrawn from our right center late in the afternoon and thrown into action on our left, where the assaults of the enemy were persistent and unintermitting. Notwithstanding the disadvantages under which we labored, our troops held their ground with the utmost firmness and obstinacy. The loss on both sides was heavy. By dark our left had been forced back half or three-fourths of a mile, but still remained firm and unbroken and still held the Warrenton pike on our rear, while our right was also driven back equally far, but in good order and without confusion. At dark the enemy took possession of the Sudley Springs road, and was in position to threaten our line of communication *via* stone bridge. After 6 o'clock in the evening I learned, accidentally, that Franklin's corps had arrived at a point about 4 miles east of Centreville, or 12 miles in our rear, and that it was only about 8000 strong. [But see General Franklin's statement, p. 539.]

The result of the battle of the 30th convinced me that we were no longer able to hold our position so far to the front, and so far away from the absolute necessaries of life, suffering, as were men and horses, from fatigue and hunger, and weakened by the heavy losses in battle. About 8 o'clock in the evening, therefore, I sent written orders to the corps commanders to withdraw leisurely to Centreville, and stated to them what route each should pursue and where they should take position at and near Centreville. General Reno, with his corps, was ordered to take post to cover this movement. The withdrawal was made slowly, quietly, and in good order, no attempt whatever being made by the enemy to obstruct our movement. A division of infantry, with its batteries, was posted to cover the crossing of Cub Run.

☆ Captain William H. Powell, of the 4th Regular Infantry, in a letter to "The Century," dated Fort Omaha, Nebraska, March 12th, 1885, thus describes the retreat upon Washington and McClellan's reception by his old army:

"The last volley had been fired, and as night fell upon us the division of regulars of Porter's corps was ordered to retire to Centreville. It had fought hard on the extreme left to preserve the line of retreat by the turnpike and the stone bridge. We were gloomy, despondent, and about 'tired out'; we had not had a change of clothing from the 14th to the 31st of August, and had been living, in the words of the men, on 'salt horse,' 'hard-tack,' and 'chicory juice.' As we filed from the battle-field into the turnpike leading over the stone bridge, we came upon a group of mounted officers, one of whom wore a peculiar style of hat which had been seen on the field that day, and which had been the occasion of a great deal of comment in the ranks. As we passed these officers, the one with the peculiar hat called out in a loud voice:

"'What troops are these?'

"'The regulars,' answered somebody.

"'Second Division, Fifth Corps,' replied another.

"'God bless them! they saved the army,' added the officer, solemnly. We learned that he was General Irvin McDowell.

"As we neared the bridge we came upon confusion. Men singly and in detachments were mingled with sutlers' wagons, artillery, caissons, supply wagons, and ambulances, each striving to get ahead of the other. Vehicles rushed through organized bodies, and broke the columns into fragments. Little detachments gathered by the roadside, after crossing the bridge, crying out the numbers of their regiments as a guide to scattered comrades.

"And what a night it was! Dark, gloomy, and beclouded by the volumes of smoke which had risen from the battle-field. To our disgust with the situation was added the discomfort of a steady rain setting in after nightfall. With many threats to reckless drivers, and through the untiring efforts of our officers,— not knowing how, when, or where we should meet the enemy again,— we managed to preserve our organization intact, keeping out of the road as much as possible, in order to avoid mingling with others. In this way we arrived at Centreville some time before midnight, and on the morning of the 31st of August we were placed in the old Confederate earth-works surrounding that village to await developments.

"It was Sunday. The morning was cold and rainy; everything bore a look of sadness in unison with our feelings. All about were the *disjecta membra* of a shattered army; here were stragglers plodding through the mud, inquiring for their regiments; little squads, just issuing from their shelterless bivouac on the wet ground; wagons wrecked and forlorn; half-formed regiments, part of the men with guns and part without; wanderers driven in by the patrols; while every one you met had an unwashed, sleepy, downcast aspect, and looked as if he would like to hide his head somewhere from all the world.

"During the afternoon of Sept. 1st, a council of war was held in the bivouac of the regular division, at which

The exact losses in this battle I am unable to give, as the reports from corps commanders only indicated the aggregate losses since August 22d, but they were very heavy. [See " Opposing Forces," p. 497.—EDITORS.]

Before leaving the field I sent orders to General Banks, at Bristoe Station, where the railroad was broken, to destroy the cars and such of the stores as he could not take off in the wagon trains, and join me at Centreville. I had previously sent him instructions to bring off from Warrenton Junction and Bristoe Station all of the ammunition and all of the sick and wounded who could bear transportation, throwing personal baggage and property out of the regimental trains, if necessary, for the purpose.

At no time during the 29th, 30th, or 31st of August was the road between Bristoe and Centreville interrupted by the enemy. The orders will show conclusively that every arrangement was made in the minutest detail for the security of our wagon train and supplies; and General Banks's subsequent report to me is positive that none of the wagons or mules were lost. I mention this matter merely to answer the wholly unfounded statements made at the time, and repeated often since, of our loss of wagons, mules, and supplies.

I arrived personally at Centreville about 9 or 10 o'clock that night [the 30th]. The next morning the various corps were posted in the old intrenchments in and around Centreville, and ammunition trains and some supplies were brought up during the day and distributed. We spent that whole day resting the men and resupplying them with ammunition and provisions as far as our means permitted.

Franklin's corps arrived at Centreville late on the afternoon of the 30th; Sumner's the next day. What was then thought by the Government of our operations up to this time is shown in the subjoined dispatch:

I noticed all the prominent generals of that army. It was a long one, and apparently not over-pleasant, if one might judge of it by the expressions on the faces of the officers when they separated. The information it developed, however, was that the enemy was between the Army of the Potomac and Washington; that Kearny was then engaged with him at Chantilly, and that we must fall back toward the defenses of the city. Dejection disappeared, activity took the place of immobility, and we were ready again to renew the contest. But who was to be our leader? and where were we to fight? Those were the questions that sprang to our lips. We had been ordered to keep our camp-fires burning brightly until 'tattoo'; and then, after the rolls had been called, we stole away — out into a gloomy night, made more desolate by the glare of dying embers. Nothing occurred to disturb our march; we arrived at Fairfax Court House early on the morning of the 2d of September. At this point we were turned off on the road to Washington, and went into bivouac. Here all sorts of rumors reached us; but, tired out from the weary night march, our blankets were soon spread on the ground, and we enjoyed an afternoon and night of comparative repose.

"About 4 o'clock on the next afternoon, from a prominent point, we descried in the distance the dome of the Capitol. We would be there at least in time to defend it! Darkness came upon us and still we marched. As the night wore on, we found at each halt that it was more and more difficult to arouse the men from the sleep into which they would fall apparently as soon as they touched the ground. During one of these halts, while Colonel Buchanan, the brigade commander, was resting a little off the road, some distance in advance of the head of the column, it being starlight, two horsemen came down the road toward us. I thought I observed a familiar form, and, turning to Colonel Buchanan, said:

"'Colonel, if I did not know that General McClellan had been relieved of all command, I should say that he was one of that party,' adding immediately, 'I do really believe it is he!'

"'Nonsense,' said the colonel; 'what would General McClellan be doing out in this lonely place, at this time of night, without an escort?'

"The two horsemen passed on to where the men of the column were lying, standing, or sitting, and were soon lost in the shadowy gloom. But a few moments had elapsed, however, when Captain John D. Wilkins, of the 3d Infantry (now colonel of the 5th) came running toward Colonel Buchanan, crying out:

"'Colonel! Colonel! General McClellan is here!'

"The enlisted men caught the sound! Whoever was awake aroused his neighbor. Eyes were rubbed, and those tired fellows, as the news passed down the column, jumped to their feet, and sent up such a hurrah as the Army of the Potomac had never heard before. Shout upon shout went out into the stillness of the night; and as it was taken up along the road and repeated by regiment, brigade, division, and corps, we could hear the roar dying away in the distance. The effect of this man's presence upon the Army of the Potomac — in sunshine or rain, in darkness or in daylight, in victory or defeat — was electrical, and too wonderful to make it worth while attempting to give a reason for it. Just two weeks from this time this defeated army, under the leadership of McClellan, won the battles of South Mountain and Antietam, having marched ten days out of the two weeks in order to do it."

WASHINGTON, August 31st, 1862. 11 A. M.

MY DEAR GENERAL: You have done nobly. Don't yield another inch if you can avoid it. All reserves are being sent forward. . . . I am doing all I can for you and your noble army. God bless you and it. . . . H. W. HALLECK, General-in-chief.

The enemy's cavalry appeared in front of Cub Run that morning, but made no attempt to attack. Our cavalry, under Buford and Bayard, was completely broken down, and both of these officers reported to me that not five horses to the company could be forced into a trot. No horses whatever had reached us for remounts since the beginning of operations. It was impracticable, therefore, to use the cavalry as cavalry to cover our front with pickets or to make reconnoissances of the enemy's front.

This paper would be incomplete indeed did it fail to contain some short, if entirely insufficient, tribute to that most gallant and loyal soldier, John Buford. I remember very well how surprised I was when I was first placed in command of the Army of Virginia that General Buford, then only a major in the inspector-general's department, reported to me for duty as inspector.

MAJOR-GENERAL ROBERT C. SCHENCK.
FROM A PHOTOGRAPH.

I asked him how he could possibly remain in such a position while a great war was going on, and what objections he could have (if he had any) to being placed in a command in the field. He seemed hurt to think I could have even a doubt of his wish to take the field, and told me that he had tried to get a command, but was without influence enough to accomplish it. I went at once to the Secretary of War and begged him to have Major Buford appointed a brigadier-general of volunteers and ordered to report to me for service. The President was good enough to make the appointment, and certainly a better one was never made. Buford's coolness, his fine judgment, and his splendid courage were known of all men who had to do with him; but besides, and in addition to these high qualities, he acquired in a few months, through his presence and manner, an influence over men as remarkable as it was useful. His quiet dignity, covering a fiery spirit and a military sagacity as far-reaching as it was accurate, made him in the short period of his active service one of the most respected and trusted officers in the service. His death, brought about by disease contracted during the months of active service and constant exposure, was widely lamented in the army.

On the morning of the 1st of September I directed General Sumner to push forward a reconnoissance toward Little River pike, which enters the

Warrenton pike at Fairfax, with two brigades, to ascertain if the enemy was making any movement toward our right by that road. The enemy was found moving again slowly toward the right, heavy columns moving along the Little River pike in the direction of Fairfax. This movement had become so developed by the afternoon of that day, and was so evidently directed to turn our right, that I made the necessary disposition of troops to fight a battle between the Little River pike and the road from Fairfax to Centreville. General Hooker was sent early in the afternoon to Fairfax Court House, and directed to concentrate all the troops in that vicinity and to push forward to Germantown with his advance. I instructed McDowell to move along the road from Centreville toward Fairfax Court House, as far as Difficult Creek, and to connect on his right with Hooker. Reno was directed to push forward north of the road to Centreville, and in the direction of Chantilly, toward the flank of the enemy's advance; Heintzelman's corps to support Reno. Just before sunset the enemy attacked us toward our right, but was met by Hooker, McDowell, and Reno, and by Kearny's division of Heintzelman's corps. A very severe action was fought in the midst of a terrific thunder-storm, and was only ended by the darkness. The enemy was driven back entirely from our front, and did not again renew his attack upon us.

MAJOR-GENERAL PHILIP KEARNY. FROM A PHOTOGRAPH.

In this short but severe action the army lost two officers of the highest capacity and distinction, whose death caused general lamentation in the army and country. The first was Major-General Philip Kearny, killed in advance of his division and while commanding it. There have been few such officers as Kearny in our own or any other army. In war he was an enthusiast, and he never seemed so much at home and so cheerful and confident as in battle. Tall and lithe in figure, with a most expressive and mobile countenance, and a manner which inspired confidence and zeal in all under his command, no one could fail to admire his chivalric bearing and his supreme courage. He seemed to think that it was his mission to make up the shortcomings of others, and in proportion as these shortcomings were made plain, his exertions and exposure were multiplied. He was a great and most accomplished soldier, and died as he would himself have wished to die, and as became his heroic character, at the head of his troops and in the front of the battle.

General Isaac I. Stevens, who was killed at the same time and nearly on the same ground, was an officer in many respects contrasted to Kearny. He was short and rather stout, with a swarthy complexion and very bright dark eyes. He was a man of very superior abilities and of marked skill and courage. His extreme political opinions before the war, ardently asserted, as was his habit in all matters which interested him, made it somewhat difficult for him to secure such a position in the army as one of his capacity might well have expected. The prejudice against him on this account was soon shown to be utterly groundless, for a more zealous and faithful officer never lived. His conduct in the battle in which he lost his life, and in every other operation of the campaign, was marked by high intelligence and the coolest courage, and his death in the front of battle ended too soon a career which would have placed him among the foremost officers of the war. As an officer of engineers before the war, and as Governor of, and delegate to Congress from Washington Territory, he was always a man of note, and possessed the abilities and the force to have commanded in time any position to which he might have aspired. The loss of these two officers was a heavy blow to the army, not so much perhaps because of their soldierly capacity as because of their well-known and unshakable fidelity to duty, and their entire loyalty to their comrades in arms.

On the morning of the 2d of September the army was posted behind Difficult Creek from Flint Hill to the Alexandria pike. The enemy disappeared from our front, moving toward the Upper Potomac with no attempt to force our position. And here the second battle of Bull Run may be said to terminate. On that day I received orders from General Halleck to take position in the intrenchments in front of Washington, with a view to reorganizing the army and eliminating such of the discordant elements in it as had largely caused the misfortunes of the latter part of that campaign.

The transactions at Alexandria and Washington City during these eventful days, as also at Centreville during part of them, are as closely connected with these battles, and had nearly as much to do with their results, as any part of the operations in the field; but they demand more space than is accorded to this article. The materials to write a complete account of these matters are at hand, and it is quite probable that the course of events may yet make their publication necessary.

There are other matters which, although not important, seem not out of place in this paper. A good deal of cheap wit has been expended upon a fanciful story that I published an order or wrote a letter or made a remark that my "headquarters would be in the saddle." It is an expression harmless and innocent enough, but it is even stated that it furnished General Lee with

MAJOR-GENERAL ISAAC I. STEVENS.
FROM A PHOTOGRAPH.

the basis for the only joke of his life. I think it due to army tradition, and to the comfort of those who have so often repeated this ancient joke in the days long before the civil war, that these later wits should not be allowed with impunity to poach on this well-tilled manor. This venerable joke I first heard when a cadet at West Point, and it was then told of that gallant soldier and gentleman, General W. J. Worth, and I presume it could be easily traced back to the Crusades and beyond. Certainly I never used this expression or wrote or dictated it, nor does any such expression occur in any order of mine; and as it has perhaps served its time and effected its purpose, it ought to be retired.

I thus conclude for the present this account of the second battle of Bull Run. The battle treated of, as well as the campaign which preceded it, have been, and no doubt still are, greatly misunderstood. Probably they will remain during this generation a matter of controversy, into which personal feeling and prejudice so largely enter that dispassionate judgment cannot now be looked for.

I submit this article to the public judgment with all confidence that it will be fairly considered, and as just a judgment passed upon it as is possible at this time. I well understood, as does every military man, how difficult and how thankless was the task imposed on me, and I do not hesitate to say that I would gladly have avoided it if I could have done so consistent with duty.

To confront with a small army greatly superior forces, to fight battles without the hope of victory, but only to gain time by delaying the forward movement of the enemy, is a duty the most hazardous and the most difficult that can be imposed upon any general or any army. While such operations require the highest courage and endurance on the part of the troops, they are unlikely to be understood or appreciated, and the results, however successful in view of the object aimed at, have little in them to attract public commendation or applause.

At no time could I have hoped to fight a successful battle with the superior forces of the enemy which confronted me, and which were able at any time to outflank and bear my small army to the dust. It was only by constant movement, incessant watchfulness, and hazardous skirmishes and battles, that the forces under my command were saved from destruction, and that the enemy was embarrassed and delayed in his advance until the army of General McClellan was at length assembled for the defense of Washington.

I did hope that in the course of these operations the enemy might commit some imprudence, or leave some opening of which I could take such advantage as to gain at least a partial success. This opportunity was presented by the advance of Jackson on Manassas Junction; but although the best dispositions possible in my view were made, the object was frustrated by causes which could not have been foreseen, and which perhaps are not yet completely known to the country.

## IN VINDICATION OF GENERAL RUFUS KING.

### BY CHARLES KING, CAPTAIN, U. S. A.

IN writing for "The Century" magazine his recollections of "The Second Battle of Bull Run," General Pope has, perhaps inadvertently, used the exact language which, in 1863, and long after, so bitterly hurt one of his most loyal subordinates. In the course of his article appear these words [see p. 470]:

"I sent orders to McDowell (supposing him to be with his command), and also direct to General King, several times during that night and once by his own staff-officer, to hold his ground at all hazards."

Now the casual reader, ignoring the commas before and after the words "and also direct to General King," would say that orders were sent to King several times that night and once by his own staff-officer. Indeed, these words have been used as authority in the army, in histories, even in Congressional debate, for the statement that General King received repeated orders to hold his ground on the evening of August 28th, 1862, and abandoned it in spite of them.

*No order or message of any kind, sort, or description reached General King that night from General Pope or any other superior officer; no staff-officer of General King saw or heard of General Pope that night;* and, in point of fact, no matter how many he may have sent to McDowell, Pope has since admitted that he sent none to King.

Early in 1863, when those words first met General King's eyes, he wrote at once to his late commander to have the error rectified. General Pope claimed that the construction of the sentence proved that McDowell was meant as the one to whom the repeated orders were sent, but at that time he thought he *had* sent *one* message to King by a staff-officer. I quote from his letter now in my possession, the italics being mine:

"It was far from my intention to imply even that any blame attached to you in the matter. . . . The officer came into my camp about 10 o'clock looking for McDowell, to report the result of your action. I told him I had no idea where McDowell was, but to return at once to you with the message to hold your ground. He got something to eat, I think with Ruggles, and went off. . . . Whether he was on your staff or not I really do not know, though I thought he was your staff-officer. "Several officers of McDowell's staff came to me during the night looking for him, and to more than one of them I gave the same message *for McDowell*. If McDowell had been with his command, as I supposed he was, Sigel and Reynolds could have been brought to your support. I was disappointed, of course, but did not for a moment attach any sort of blame to you. *I never knew whether the aide-de-camp reached you that night or not*, but I felt always perfectly satisfied that whether he did or not you had done the very best you could have done under the circumstances."

Now the aide-de-camp in question was Major D. C. Houston, Chief of Engineers, of General McDowell's staff. He had witnessed the severe engagement of King's division, west of Groveton, and some time after dark had ridden off through the woods in search of his general, who had not been seen by King or his officers since 2 o'clock in the afternoon. McDowell, in hunting for Pope, got lost in the woods, and Houston, hunting for McDowell, stumbled in on Pope's camp late at night, told there of King's battle, got refreshment, he says, of Ruggles, and went off; but he remembered no message from Pope to King, and if there was one, which he doubts, he did not deliver it, for he never attempted to return to King, but went on in search of McDowell until he found him late the following day. No other officer from King got within range of Pope that night, so far as rigid investigation has ever disclosed, and that none at all came from Pope to King is beyond peradventure. Indeed, in 1878 General Pope declared it was to McDowell that all the orders were sent. ☆

As to King's falling back to Manassas Junction, that was the result of the conference between him and his four brigade commanders, and was vehemently urged upon him as the only practicable way to save what was left of the command after the fierce conflict that raged at sunset. King's orders were to march to Centreville, which was objected to strenuously by Stonewall Jackson's corps, and they were in the majority. The brigade commanders voted for a deflection to the right toward Manassas, General John Gibbon being most urgent, and the following extract from a letter from him to King, dated Baltimore, March 7th, 1863, gives his views:

"I deem it not out of place to say that that retreat was suggested and urged by myself as a necessary military measure . . . I do not hesitate to say, and it is susceptible of proof, that of the two courses which I considered open to you, of obeying your orders to march to Centreville or retreat on Manassas on your own responsibility, the one you adopted was the proper one. "Having first suggested the movement and urged it on military grounds, I am perfectly willing to bear my full share of the responsibility, and you are at liberty to make any use of this communication you may deem proper. I am, General, very respectfully, your obedient servant, JOHN GIBBON, Brig.-Gen. Vols."

☆ General Pope also repeated this statement in a conversation with me in July, 1887, and expressed his regret that this phraseology had not been corrected in his article which appeared in "The Century" magazine for January, 1886.— C. K.

## THE OPPOSING FORCES AT CEDAR MOUNTAIN, VA.

### August 9th, 1862.

The composition, losses, and strength of each army as here stated give the gist of all the data obtainable in the Official Records. K stands for killed; w for wounded; m w for mortally wounded; m for captured or missing; c for captured.

### THE UNION ARMY.

ARMY OF VIRGINIA. — Major-General John Pope.

*Escort:* A and C, 1st Ohio Cavalry, Capt. Nathan B. Menken. Loss: m, 2.

SECOND ARMY CORPS, Maj.-Gen. N. P. Banks.
*Escort:* L, 1st Mich. Cav., Capt. Melvin Brewer; M, 5th N. Y. Cav., Lieut. Eugene Dimmick; H, 1st W. Va. Cav., Capt. Isaac P. Kerr. Escort loss: k, 5; w, 5; m, 6 = 16.

FIRST DIVISION, Brig.-Gen. A. S. Williams. Staff loss: m, 1.
*Escort:* M, 1st Mich. Cav., Capt. R. C. Dennison.
*First Brigade,* Brig.-Gen. Samuel W. Crawford: 5th Conn., Col. George B. Chapman (w and c); 10th Me.,

Col. George L. Beal; 28th N. Y., Col. Dudley Donnelly (m w), Lieut.-Col. Edwin F. Brown (w); 46th Pa., Col. Joseph F. Knipe (w), Lieut.-Col. James L. Selfridge. Brigade loss: k, 97; w, 397; m, 373 = 867. *Third Brigade*, Brig.-Gen. George H. Gordon: 27th Ind., Col. Silas Colgrove; 2d Mass., Col. George L. Andrews; Pa. Zouaves d'Afrique, Lieut. S. A. Barthoulot; 3d Wis., Col. Thomas H. Ruger. Brigade loss: k, 74; w, 191; m, 79 = 344.
SECOND DIVISION, Brig.-Gen. Christopher C. Augur (w), Brig.-Gen. Henry Prince (c), Brig.-Gen. George S. Greene. Staff loss: w, 1; m, 2 = 3.
*First Brigade*, Brig.-Gen. John W. Geary (w), Col. Charles Candy: 5th Ohio, Lieut.-Col. John H. Patrick; 7th Ohio, Col. William R. Creighton; 29th Ohio, Capt. Wilbur F. Stevens; 66th Ohio, Col. Charles Candy; 28th Pa. (on a reconnoissance and not in the action), Lieut.-Col. Hector Tyndale. Brigade loss: k, 61; w, 385; m, 19 = 465. *Second Brigade*, Brig.-Gen. Henry Prince, Col. David P. De Witt: 3d Md., Col. David P. De Witt; 102d N. Y., Maj. Joseph C. Lane; 109th Pa., Col. Henry J. Stainrook; 111th Pa., Maj. Thomas M. Walker; 8th and 12th U. S. (Battalion), Capt. Thomas G. Pitcher (w), Capt. Thomas M. Anderson. Brigade loss: k, 58; w, 311; m, 83 = 452. *Third Brigade*, Brig.-Gen. George S. Greene: 1st D. C., Col. James A. Tait; 78th N. Y., Lieut.-Col. Jonathan Austin. Brigade loss: w, 3; m, 23 = 26. *Artillery*, Capt. Clermont L. Best: 4th Me., Capt. O'Neil W. Robinson; 6th Me., Capt. Freeman McGilvery; K, 1st N. Y., Capt. Lorenzo Crounse; L, 1st N. Y., Capt. John A. Reynolds; M, 1st N. Y., Capt. George W. Cothran; I, 2d N. Y., Capt. Jacob Roemer; 10th N. Y., Capt. John T. Bruen; E, Pa., Capt. Joseph M. Knap; F, 4th U. S., Lieut. E. D. Muhlenberg. Artillery loss: k, 7; w, 27; m, 6 = 40.

THIRD ARMY CORPS, Maj.-Gen. Irvin McDowell.
SECOND DIVISION, Brig.-Gen. James B. Ricketts.
*First Brigade*, Brig.-Gen. Abram Duryée: 97th N. Y., Lieut.-Col. John P. Spofford; 104th N. Y., Maj. Lewis C. Skinner; 105th N. Y., Col. James M. Fuller; 107th Pa., Lieut.-Col. Robert W. McAllen. Brigade loss: w, 12; m, 1 = 13. *Second Brigade*, Brig.-Gen. Zealous B. Tower: 26th N. Y., Col. William H. Christian; 94th N. Y., Col. Adrian R. Root; 88th Pa., Col. George P. McLean; 90th Pa., Col. Peter Lyle. Brigade loss: w, 1. *Third Brigade*, Brig.-Gen. George L. Hartsuff: 12th Mass., Col. Fletcher Webster; 13th Mass., Col. Samuel H. Leonard; 83d N. Y. (9th Militia), Col. John W. Stiles; 11th Pa., Col. Richard Coulter. Brigade loss: k, 2; w, 11; m, 4 = 17. *Fourth Brigade*, Col. Samuel S. Carroll: 7th Ind., Lieut.-Col. John F. Cheek; 84th Pa., Col. Samuel M. Bowman; 110th Pa., Col. William D. Lewis, Jr.; 1st W. Va., Col. Joseph Thoburn. Brigade loss: w, 54; m, 15 = 69. *Artillery*, Maj. Davis Tillson: 2d Me., Capt. James A. Hall; 5th Me., Capt. George F. Leppien; F, 1st Pa., Capt. Ezra W. Matthews; C, Pa., Capt. James Thompson. Artillery loss: w, 2. *Unattached:* 16th Ind. Battery, Capt. Charles A. Naylor; 13th Pa. Reserve or 1st Rifles (Battalion), Capt. Hugh McDonald.
CAVALRY, Brig.-Gen. George D. Bayard: 1st Me., Col. Samuel H. Allen; 1st N. J., Lieut.-Col. Joseph Kargé; 1st Pa., Col. Owen Jones; 1st R. I., Col. Alfred N. Duffié. Cavalry loss: k, 10; w, 45; m, 6 = 61.
Total Union loss: killed, 314; wounded, 1445; captured or missing, 622 = 2381.
The number engaged on the Union side is not specifically stated, but it is estimated that Pope's effective force in Banks's and McDowell's commands and the cavalry, on the field from first to last, aggregated about 17,900.

## THE CONFEDERATE ARMY.

Major-General Thomas J. Jackson.

FIRST DIVISION, Brig.-Gen. Charles S. Winder (k), Brig.-Gen. W. B. Taliaferro. Staff loss: k, 1; w, 1 = 2.
*First Brigade*, Col. Charles A. Ronald: 2d Va., Lieut.-Col. Lawson Botts; 4th Va., Lieut.-Col. R. D. Gardner; 5th Va., Maj. H. J. Williams; 27th Va., Capt. Charles L. Haynes; 33d Va., Lieut.-Col. Edwin G. Lee. Brigade loss: k, 10; w, 48 = 58. *Second Brigade*, Lieut.-Col. Thomas S. Garnett: 21st Va., Lieut.-Col. R. H. Cunningham (k), Capt. W. A. Witcher; 42d Va., Maj. Henry Lane (m w), Capt. Abner Dobyns; 48th Va., Capt. William Y. C. Hannum; 1st Va. (Irish) Battalion, Maj. John Seddon. Brigade loss: k, 91; w, 210 = 301. *Third Brigade*, Brig.-Gen. William B. Taliaferro, Col. Alexander G. Taliaferro: 10th Va., Maj. Joshua Stover; 23d Va., Col. Alexander G. Taliaferro, Lieut.-Col. George W. Curtis (m w), Maj. Simon T. Walton; 37th Va., Col. T. V. Williams (w), Maj. H. C. Wood; 47th Ala., Lieut.-Col. James W. Jackson; 48th Ala., Col. James L. Sheffield (w), Lieut.-Col. Abner A. Hughes. Brigade loss: k, 51; w, 271 = 322. *Fourth Brigade*, Col. Leroy A. Stafford; 2d La., ——; ⟩ 9th La., ——; 10th La., ——; 15th La., ——. Brigade loss: k, 4; w, 20 = 24. *Cavalry*, Brig.-Gen. Beverly H. Robertson: 7th Va., Col. William E. Jones; 17th Va. Battalion, Maj. W. Patrick. Cavalry loss: k, 1; w, 18 = 19. *Artillery*, Maj. R. Snowden Andrews: Va. Battery (Alleghany Art'y), Capt. Joseph Carpenter (w), Lieut. John C. Carpenter; Va. Battery (Rockbridge Art'y), Capt. William T. Poague; Va. Battery (Hampden Art'y), Capt. William H. Caskie. Artillery loss: w, 6.
LIGHT DIVISION, Maj.-Gen. A. P. Hill. Staff loss: w, 2.
*Branch's Brigade*, Brig.-Gen. L. O'B. Branch: 7th N. C., Col. Edward G. Haywood; 18th N. C., Lieut.-Col. T. J. Purdie; 28th N. C., Col. James H. Lane; 33d N. C., Col. Robert F. Hoke; 37th N. C.,——. Brigade loss: k, 2; w, 88 = 100. *Archer's Brigade*, Brig.-Gen. James J. Archer: 5th Ala. Battalion, ——; 19th Ga., ——; 1st Tenn. (Prov. Army), Col. Peter Turney: 7th Tenn.,——;

14th Tenn., Col. W. A. Forbes. Brigade loss: k, 19; w, 116 = 135. *Thomas's Brigade*, Col. Edward L. Thomas: 14th Ga., Col. R. W. Folsom; 35th Ga., ——; 45th Ga., ——; 49th Ga., ——. Brigade loss: k, 24; w, 133 = 157. *Field's Brigade*, Brig.-Gen. Charles W. Field: 22d Va. Battalion, ——; 40th Va., ——; 55th Va., ——. Brigade loss: k, 7; w, 6 = 13. *Pender's Brigade*, Brig.-Gen. William D. Pender: 16th N. C.,——; 22d N. C., Lieut.-Col. Robert H. Gray; 34th N. C., Col. Richard H. Riddick; 38th N. C., Capt. John Ashford. Brigade loss: k, 2; w, 11; m, 2 = 15. *Artillery*, Lieut.-Col. R. L. Walker; Va. Battery (Purcell Art'y), Capt. W. J. Pegram; Va. Battery (Middlesex Art'y), Lieut. W. B. Hardy; Va. Battery (Fredericksburg Art'y), Capt. Carter M. Braxton; N. C. Battery (Branch Art'y), Capt. A. C. Latham. Artillery loss: k, 2; w, 12 = 14.
THIRD DIVISION, Maj.-Gen. Richard S. Ewell.
*Fourth Brigade*, Brig.-Gen. Jubal A. Early: 12th Ga., Capt. William F. Brown; 13th Va., Col. James A. Walker; 25th Va., Maj. John C. Higginbotham; 31st Va., Lieut.-Col. Alfred H. Jackson (w); 44th Va.,——; 52d Va., Lieut.-Col. James H. Skinner; 58th Va., Maj. John G. Kasey. Brigade loss: k, 16; w, 145; m, 2 = 163. *Seventh Brigade*, Brig.-Gen. Isaac R. Trimble: 15th Ala., Maj. A. A. Lowther; 21st Ga., ——; 21st N. C., ——. Brigade loss: k, 1; w, 17 = 18. *Eighth Brigade*, Col. Henry Forno: 5th La., ——; 6th La., ——; 7th La., ——; 8th La., ——; 14th La., ——. Brigade loss: w, 8. *Artillery*, Maj. A. R. Courtney: 1st Md., Battery, Capt. William F. Dement; 4th Md. Battery (Chesapeake Art'y), Capt. William D. Brown; La. Battery, Capt. Louis E. D'Aquin; Va. Battery (Courtney Art'y), Capt. J. W. Latimer; Va. Battery (Bedford Art'y), Lieut. Nathaniel Terry. Artillery loss: w, 8.
Total Confederate loss: killed, 241; wounded, 1120; missing, 4 = 1365. Estimated strength on the field at least 20,000.

⟩ NOTE.—In these tables the dash indicates that the name of the commanding officer has not been found in the "Official Records."— EDITORS.

# THE OPPOSING FORCES AT THE SECOND BULL RUN.

August 16th–September 2d, 1862.

The composition, losses, and strength of each army as here stated give the gist of all the data obtainable in the Official Records. K stands for killed; w for wounded; m w for mortally wounded; m for captured or missing; c for captured.

## THE UNION FORCES.

ARMY OF VIRGINIA.—Major-General John Pope. Staff loss: m, 2.

*Escort:* A and C, 1st Ohio Cav., Capt. Nathan D. Menken. Loss: w, 1; m, 20=21.

FIRST ARMY CORPS, Maj.-Gen. Franz Sigel. *Escort:* 1st Ind. Cav. (2 co's), Capt. Abram Sharra. Loss: w, 1; m, 1=2.

FIRST DIVISION, Brig.-Gen. Robert C. Schenck (w), Brig.-Gen. Julius Stahel. Staff loss: w, 1.

*First Brigade,* Brig.-Gen. Julius Stahel, Col. Adolphus Buschbeck: 8th N. Y., Lieut.-Col. Carl B. Hedterich; 41st N. Y., Lieut.-Col. Ernest W. Holmstedt; 45th N. Y., Lieut.-Col. Edward C. Wratislaw; 27th Pa., Col. Adolphus Buschbeck, Lieut.-Col. Lorenz Cantador; 2d N. Y. Battery, Capt. Louis Schirmer, Lieut. F. J. T. Blume. Brigade loss (incomplete): k, 40; w, 96; m, 33=169. *Second Brigade,* Col. Nathaniel C. McLean: 25th Ohio, Col. William P. Richardson; 55th Ohio, Col. John C. Lee; 73d Ohio, Col. Orland Smith; 75th Ohio, Maj. Robert Reily; K, 1st Ohio Art'y, Lieut. George B. Haskin. Brigade loss: k, 57; w, 272; m, 105=434.

SECOND DIVISION, Brig.-Gen. Adolph von Steinwehr. *First Brigade,* Col. John A. Koltes (k), Lieut.-Col. Gust. A. Muhleck: 29th N. Y., Col. Clemens Soest (w), Maj. Louis Hartmann; 68th N. Y., Lieut.-Col. John H. Kleefisch (m w); 73 Pa., Lieut.-Col. Gust. A. Muhleck. Brigade loss: k, 47; w, 294; m, 60=401.

THIRD DIVISION, Brig.-Gen. Carl Schurz. *First Brigade,* Brig.-Gen. Henry Bohlen (k), Col. Alexander Schimmelfennig: 61st Ohio, Col. Newton Schleich, Lieut.-Col. Stephen J. McGroarty; 74th Pa., Maj. Franz Blessing; 8th W. Va., Capt. Hedgman Slack; F, Penn. Art'y, Capt. Robert B. Hampton. Brigade loss: k, 26; w, 96; m, 36=158. *Second Brigade,* Col. Wladimir Krzyzanowski: 54th N. Y., Lieut.-Col. Charles Ashby; 58th N. Y., Maj. William Henkel (w), Capt. Frederick Braun; 75th Pa., Lieut.-Col. Francis Mahler (w); L, 2d N. Y., Art'y, Capt. Jacob Roemer. Brigade loss: k, 48; w, 274; m, 50=372. *Unattached:* C, 3d W. Va. Cav., Capt. Jonathan Stahl; I, 1st Ohio Art'y, Capt. Hubert Dilger. Unattached loss: w, 4.

INDEPENDENT BRIGADE, Brig.-Gen. Robert H. Milroy. 2d W. Va., Col. George R. Latham; 3d W. Va., Col. David T. Hewes; 5th W. Va., Col. John L. Zeigler; 82d Ohio; Col. James Cantwell (k); C, E, and L, 1st W. Va. Cav., Maj. John S. Krepps; 12th Ohio Bat'y, Capt. Aaron C. Johnson. Brigade loss: k, 70; w, 286; m, 81=437.

CAVALRY BRIGADE, Col. John Beardsley. 1st Conn. (Bat'l'n), Capt. L. N. Middlebrook; 1st Md., Lieut.-Col. C. Wetschky; 4th N. Y., Lieut.-Col. Ferries Nazer; 9th N. Y., Maj. Charles McL. Knox; 6th Ohio, Col. William R. Lloyd. Brigade loss: k, 3; w, 15; m, 65=83.

RESERVE ARTILLERY, Capt. Frank Buell (k), Capt. Louis Schirmer. I, 1st N. Y., Capt. Michael Wiedrich; 13th N. Y., Capt. Julius Dieckmann; C, W. Va., Lieut. Wallace Hill. Artillery Reserve loss: k, 4; w, 22=26.

SECOND ARMY CORPS, Maj.-Gen. Nathaniel P. Banks. (This corps, excepting its cavalry, was not engaged in any of the principal battles.)

FIRST DIVISION, Brig.-Gen. Alpheus S. Williams. *First Brigade,* Brig.-Gen. Samuel W. Crawford: 5th Conn., Capt. James A. Betts; 10th Me., Col. George L. Beal; 28th N. Y., Capt. William H. H. Mapes; 46th Pa., Lieut.-Col. James L. Selfridge. Brigade loss: m, 15. *Third Brigade,* Brig.-Gen. George H. Gordon: 2d Mass., Col. George L. Andrews; 27th Ind., Col. Silas Colgrove; 3d Wis., Col. Thomas H. Ruger.

SECOND DIVISION, Brig.-Gen. George S. Greene. *First Brigade,* Col. Charles Candy, Col. John H. Patrick: 5th Ohio, Col. John H. Patrick, Maj. John Collins; 7th Ohio, Col. William R. Creighton, Capt. Frederick A. Seymour, Capt. Orrin J. Crane; 29th Ohio, Capt. Wilbur F. Stevens, Capt. Jonas Schoonover, Lieut. Theron E. Winship; 66th Ohio, Lieut.-Col. Eugene Powell; 28th Pa., Col. Gabriel De Korponay. *Second Brigade,* Col. Matthew Schlaudecker, Col. Thomas B. Van Buren: 3d Md., Col. David P. De Witt; 102d N. Y., Col. Thomas B. Van Buren; 109th Pa., Col. Henry J. Stainrook; 111th Pa., Maj. Thomas M. Walker. Brigade loss: k, 2; w, 25; m, 3 = 30. *Third Brigade,* Col. James A. Tait: 3d Del., Col. William O. Redden, Lieut.-Col. Samuel H. Jenkins; 1st D. C., Lieut.-Col. Lemuel Towers, Capt. Marvin P. Fisher; 60th N. Y., Col. William B. Goodrich; 78th N. Y., Lieut.-Col. Jonathan Austin; Purnell Legion, Md., Col. William J. Leonard (c), Lieut.-Col. Benjamin L. Simpson. Brigade loss: k, 2; w, 11; m, 65=78. *Artillery,* Capt. Clermont L. Best: 4th Me., Capt. O'Neil W. Robinson, Jr.; M, 1st N. Y., Capt. George W. Cothran; 10th N. Y., Capt. John T. Bruen; E, Pa., Capt. Joseph M. Knap; F, 4th U. S., Lieut. Edward D. Muhlenberg.

CAVALRY BRIGADE, Brig.-Gen. John Buford. 1st Mich., Col. Thornton F. Brodhead (m w), Maj. Charles H. Town; 5th N. Y., Col. Othniel De Forest; 1st Vt., Col. Charles H. Tompkins; 1st W. Va., Lieut.-Col. Nathaniel P. Richmond. Brigade loss: k, 15; w, 35; m, 150=200.

THIRD ARMY CORPS, Maj.-Gen. Irvin McDowell. FIRST DIVISION, Brig.-Gen. Rufus King, Brig.-Gen. John P. Hatch (w), Brig.-Gen. Abner Doubleday. Staff loss: w, 1.

*First Brigade,* Brig.-Gen. John P. Hatch, Col. Timothy Sullivan: 22d N. Y., Col. Walter Phelps, Jr.; 24th N. Y., Col. Timothy Sullivan; 30th N. Y., Col. Edward Frisby (k); 84th N. Y. (14th Militia), Lieut.-Col. Edward B. Fowler (w), Maj. William H. de Bevoise; 2d U. S. Sharp-shooters, Col. Henry A. V. Post. Brigade loss: k, 95; w, 382; m, 295=772. *Second Brigade,* Brig.-Gen. Abner Doubleday, Col. William P. Wainwright: 56th Pa., Col. Sullivan A. Meredith (w), Lieut.-Col. J. William Hofmann; 76th N. Y., Col. William P. Wainwright; 95th N. Y., Lieut.-Col. James B. Post. Brigade loss: k, 18; w, 192; m, 237=447. *Third Brigade,* Brig.-Gen. Marsena R. Patrick: 21st N. Y., Col. William F. Rogers; 23d N. Y., Lieut.-Col. Nirom M. Crane; 35th N. Y., Col. Newton B. Lord; 80th N. Y. (20th Militia), Col. George W. Pratt (m w), Lieut.-Col. Theodore B. Gates. Brigade loss: k, 56; w, 334; m, 178=568. *Fourth Brigade,* Brig.-Gen. John Gibbon: 2d Wis., Col. Edgar O'Connor (k), Lieut.-Col. Lucius Fairchild; 6th Wis., Col. Lysander Cutler (w), Lieut.-Col. Edward S. Bragg; 7th Wis., Col. William W. Robinson (w), Lieut.-Col. Charles A. Hamilton (w), Lieut.-Col. Lucius Fairchild; 19th Ind., Col. Solomon Meredith. Brigade loss: k, 148; w, 626; m, 120=894. *Artillery,* 1st N. H., Capt. George A. Gerrish (c), Lieut. Frederick M. Edgell; D, 1st R. I., Capt. J. Albert Monroe; L, 1st N. Y., Capt. John A. Reynolds; B, 4th U. S., Capt. Joseph B. Campbell. Artillery loss: k, 7; w, 25; m, 14=46.

SECOND DIVISION, Brig.-Gen. James B. Ricketts. *First Brigade,* Brig.-Gen. Abram Duryea: 97th N. Y., Lieut.-Col. John P. Spofford; 104th N. Y., Maj. Lewis C. Skinner; 105th N. Y., Col. Howard Carroll; 107th Pa., Col. Thomas F. McCoy. Brigade loss: k, 29; w, 138; m, 224=391. *Second Brigade,* Brig.-Gen. Zealous B. Tower (w), Col. William H. Christian: 26th N. Y., Col. William H. Christian, Lieut.-Col. Richard H. Richardson; 94th N.Y., Col. Adrian R. Root (w); 88th Pa., Lieut.-Col. Joseph A. McLean (k), Maj. George W. Gile; 90th Pa., Col. Peter Lyle. Brigade loss: k, 66; w, 338; m, 292=696. *Third*

# THE OPPOSING FORCES AT THE SECOND BULL RUN.

*Brigade*, Brig.-Gen. George L. Hartsuff, Col. John W. Stiles: 12th Mass., Col. Fletcher Webster (k), Lieut.-Col. Timothy M. Bryan, Jr.; 13th Mass., Col. Samuel H. Leonard; 83d N. Y. (9th Militia), Col. John W. Stiles, Lieut.-Col. William Atterbury; 11th Pa., Col. Richard Coulter, Brigade loss: k, 87; w, 305; m, 265 = 657. *Fourth Brigade*, Col. Joseph Thoburn (w); 7th Ind., Lieut.-Col. John F. Cheek; 84th Pa., Col. Samuel M. Bowman; 110th Pa., Col. William D. Lewis, Jr.; 1st W. Va., Lieut.-Col. Henry B. Hubbard. Brigade loss (incomplete): k, 5; w, 34; m, 75 = 114. *Artillery:* 2d Me., Capt. James A. Hall; 5th Me., Capt. G. F. Leppien; F, 1st Pa., Capt. Ezra W. Matthews; C, Pa., Capt. James Thompson. Artillery loss: k, 5; w, 30; m, 19 = 54.
CAVALRY BRIGADE, Brig.-Gen. George D. Bayard.
1st Me., Col. Samuel H. Allen; 2d N. Y., Col. J. Mansfield Davies; 1st N. J., Lieut.-Col. Joseph Kargé (w), Maj. Ivins D. Jones; 1st Pa., Col. Owen Jones; 1st R. I., Col. A. N. Duffié. Brigade loss: k, 13; w, 44; m, 70 = 127.
REYNOLDS'S DIVISION (temporarily attached), Brig.-Gen. John F. Reynolds.
*First Brigade*, Brig.-Gen. George G. Meade: 3d Pa. Reserves, Col. Horatio G. Sickel; 4th Pa. Reserves, Col. Albert L. Magilton; 7th Pa. Reserves, Lieut.-Col. Robert M. Henderson (w), Col. Henry C. Bolinger; 8th Pa. Reserves, Capt. William Lemon; 13th Pa. Reserves or 1st Rifles (6 co's), Col. Hugh W. McNeil. Brigade loss: k, 12; w, 96; m, 77 = 186. *Second Brigade*, Brig.-Gen. Truman Seymour: 1st Pa. Reserves, Col. R. Biddle Roberts; 2d Pa. Reserves, Col. William McCandless (w); 5th Pa. Reserves, Col. Joseph W. Fisher, Lieut.-Col. George Dare; 6th Pa. Reserves, Col. William Sinclair. Brigade loss: k, 13; w, 83; m, 42 = 138. *Third Brigade*, Brig.-Gen. Conrad F. Jackson, Col. Martin D. Hardin (w), Col. James T. Kirk (w), Lieut.-Col. Robert Anderson: 9th Pa. Reserves, Lieut.-Col. Robert Anderson, Maj. J. McK. Snodgrass; 10th Pa. Reserves, Col. James T. Kirk; 11th Pa. Reserves, Lieut.-Col. Samuel M. Jackson; 12th Pa. Reserves, Col. Martin D. Hardin, Capt. Richard Gustin. Brigade loss: k, 33; w, 172; m, 82 = 287. *Artillery*, Capt. Dunbar R. Ransom: A, 1st Pa., Capt. John G. Simpson; B, 1st Pa., Capt. James H. Cooper; G, 1st Pa., Capt. Mark Kerns (m w); Lieut. Frank P. Amsden; C, 5th U. S., Capt. Dunbar R. Ransom. Artillery loss: k, 8; w, 48; m, 10 = 66.
UNATTACHED: 3d Me. Battery (Pontonniers), Capt. James G. Swett; 16th Ind. Battery, Capt. Charles A. Naylor; E, 4th U. S. Art'y, Capt. Joseph C. Clark, Jr., 3d Ind. Cav. (detachment) ——; C, G, H, and I, 13th Pa. Reserves (1st Rifles), Lieut.-Col. Thomas L. Kane. Unattached loss: w, 5; m, 21 = 26.
RESERVE CORPS, Brig.-Gen. Samuel D. Sturgis.
*Piatt's Brigade* (temporarily attached to Fifth Army Corps August 27th-31st), Brig.-Gen. A. Sanders Piatt: 63d Ind. (4 co's), Lieut.-Col. John S. Williams; 86th N. Y., Col. Benajah P. Bailey. Brigade loss: k, 16; w, 84; m, 45 = 145. *Unattached:* 2d N. Y. H'y Art'y, Col. Gustav Waagner; 11th N. Y. Battery, Capt. Albert A. von Puttkammer; C, 1st N. Y. Art'y (detachment), Lieut. Samuel R. James. Unattached loss: w, 10; m, 67 = 77.

## ARMY OF THE POTOMAC.

THIRD ARMY CORPS, Maj.-Gen. S. P. Heintzelman.
FIRST DIVISION, Maj.-Gen. Philip Kearny (k), Brig.-Gen. David B. Birney. Staff loss: k, 1; m, 1 = 2.
*First Brigade*, Brig.-Gen. John C. Robinson: 20th Ind., Col. William L. Brown (k), Maj. John Wheeler; 63d Pa., Col. Alexander Hays (w), Capt. James F. Ryan; 105th Pa., Lieut.-Col. Calvin A. Craig (w), Maj. Jacob W. Greenawalt. Brigade loss: k, 26; w, 166; m, 25 = 217. *Second Brigade*, Brig.-Gen. David B. Birney, Col. J. H. Hobart Ward: 3d Me., Capt. Moses B. Lakeman, Maj. Edwin Burt; 4th Me., Col. Elijah Walker; 1st N. Y., Maj. Edwin Burt, Capt. Joseph Yeamans; 38th N. Y., Col. J. H. Hobart Ward; 40th N. Y., Col. Thomas W. Egan; 101st N. Y., Lieut.-Col. Nelson A. Gesner; 57th Pa., Maj. William Birney. Brigade loss: k, 56; w, 459; m, 114 = 629. *Third Brigade*, Col. Orlando M. Poe: 3'th N. Y., Col. Samuel B. Hayman; 99th Pa., Col. Asher S. Leidy; 2d Mich., Lieut.-Col. Louis Diillman; 3d Mich., Col. Stephen G. Champlin, Maj. Byron R. Pierce; 5th Mich., Capt. William Wakenshaw. Brigade loss: k, 25; w, 115; m, 38 = 178. *Artillery:* E, 1st R. I., Capt. George E. Randolph; K, 1st U. S., Capt. William M. Graham. Artillery loss: k, 2; w, 1 = 3.
SECOND DIVISION, Maj.-Gen. Joseph Hooker, Brig.-Gen. Cuvier Grover.
*First Brigade*, Brig.-Gen. Cuvier Grover, Col. Robert Cowdin: 2d N. H., Col. Gilman Marston; 1st Mass., Col. Robert Cowdin, Capt. Clark B. Baldwin; 11th Mass., Col. William Blaisdell; 16th Mass., Maj. Gardner Banks; 26th Pa., Maj. Robert L. Bodine. Brigade loss: k, 55; w, 329; m, 103 = 487. *Second Brigade*, Col. Nelson Taylor: 70th N. Y., Capt. Charles L. Young; 71st N. Y., Lieut.-Col. Henry L. Potter (w), Capt. Owen Murphy; 72d N. Y., Capt. Harman J. Bliss; 73d N. Y., Capt. Alfred A. Donalds (m w), Capt. M. William Burns; 74th N. Y., Maj. Edward L. Price. Brigade loss: k, 47; w, 217; m, 65 = 329. *Third Brigade*, Col. Joseph B. Carr: 2d N. Y., Capt. Sidney W. Park; 5th N. J., Lieut.-Col. William J. Sewell; 6th N. J., Col. Gershom Mott (w), Lieut.-Col. George C. Burling; 7th N. J., Col. Joseph W. Revere; 8th N. J., Lieut.-Col. William Ward (w), Capt. John Tuite (k), Capt. George Hoffman, Capt. Oliver S. Johnson, Capt. Daniel Blauvelt, Jr.; 115th Pa., Lieut.-Col. Robert Thompson. Brigade loss: k, 48; w, 238; m, 107 = 393. *Unattached:* 6th Me. Battery, Capt. Freeman McGilvery. Loss: k, 4; w, 9; m, 5 = 18.
FIFTH ARMY CORPS, Maj.-Gen. Fitz-John Porter.
FIRST DIVISION, Maj.-Gen. George W. Morell.
*First Brigade*, Col. Charles W. Roberts: 2d Me., Maj. Daniel F. Sargent; 18th Mass., Capt. Stephen Thomas, Maj. Joseph Hayes; 22d Mass. (not in action), Capt. Mason W. Burt; 13th N. Y., Col. Elisha G. Marshall; 25th N. Y., Col. Charles A. Johnson; 1st Mich., Col. Horace S. Roberts (k), Capt. Emery W. Belton. Brigade loss: k, 103; w, 374; m, 99 = 576. *Second Brigade* (not in action), Brig.-Gen. Charles Griffin: 9th Mass., Col. Patrick R. Guiney; 32d Mass., Col. Francis J. Parker; 14th N. Y., Col. James McQuade; 62d Pa., Col. Jacob B. Sweitzer; 4th Mich., Col. Jonathan W. Childs. *Third Brigade*, Brig.-Gen. Daniel Butterfield (commanded First and Third Brigades in battle of August 30th), Col. Henry S. Lansing, Col. Henry A. Weeks (w), Col. James C. Rice: 12th N. Y., Col. Henry A. Weeks, Capt. Augustus I. Root (w), Capt. William Huson, Capt. Ira Wood; 17th N. Y., Col. Henry S. Lansing, Maj. W. T. C. Grower (w), Capt. John Vickers; 44th N. Y., Col. James C. Rice, Maj. Freeman Conner; 83d Pa., Lieut.-Col. Hugh S. Campbell (w), Maj. William H. Lamont (w), Capt. John Graham (w), Capt. Orpheus S. Woodward; 16th Mich., Capt. Thomas J. Barry (w), Capt. Henry H. Sibley. Brigade loss: k, 70; w, 357; m, 163 = 590. *Sharp-shooters:* 1st U. S., Col. Hiram Berdan. Loss: k, 5; w, 45; m, 15 = 61. *Artillery:* 3d Mass. (not in action), Capt. Augustus P. Martin; C, 1st R. I., Capt. Richard Waterman; D, 5th U. S., Lieut. Charles E. Hazlett. Artillery loss: w, 5; m, 1 = 6.
SECOND DIVISION, Brig.-Gen. George Sykes.
*First Brigade*, Lieut.-Col. Robert C. Buchanan: 3d U. S., Capt. John D. Wilkins; 4th U. S., Capt. Joseph B. Collins (w), Capt. Hiram Dryer; 12th U. S. (1st Battalion), Capt. Matthew M. Blunt; 14th U. S., (1st Battalion), Capt. John D. O'Connell (w), Capt. W. Harvey Brown; 14th U. S. (2d Battalion), Capt. David B. McKibbin. Brigade loss: k, 31; w, 189; m, 65 = 285. *Second Brigade*, Lieut.-Col. William Chapman: G, 1st U. S., Capt. Matthew R. Marston; 2d U. S., Maj. Charles S. Lovell; 6th U. S., Capt. Levi C. Bootes; 10th U. S., Maj. Charles S. Lovell; 11th U. S., Maj. De Lancey Floyd-Jones; 17th U. S., Maj. George L. Andrews. Brigade loss: k, 19; w, 159; m, 40 = 218. *Third Brigade*, Col. Gouverneur K. Warren: 5th N. Y., Capt. Cleveland Winslow; 10th N. Y., Col. John E. Bendix. Brigade loss: k, 102; w, 235; m, 75 = 412. *Artillery*, Capt. Stephen H. Weed: E and G, 1st U. S., Lieut. Alanson M. Randol; I, 5th U. S., Capt. Stephen H. Weed; K, 5th U. S., Capt. John R. Smead (k), Lieut. William E. Van Reed. Artillery loss: k, 1; w, 2 = 3.

## THE OPPOSING FORCES AT THE SECOND BULL RUN.

FIRST BRIGADE, FIRST DIVISION, SIXTH ARMY CORPS (engaged only at Bull Run Bridge, August 27th), Brig.-Gen. George W. Taylor (m w), Col. Henry W. Brown.
1st N. J., Maj. William Henry, Jr.; 2d N. J., Col. Samuel L. Buck; 3d N. J., Col. Henry W. Brown; 4th N. J., Capt. Napoleon B. Aaronson, Capt. Thomas M. Fetters. Brigade loss: k, 9; w, 126; m, 204=339.
NINTH ARMY CORPS, Maj.-Gen. Jesse L. Reno.
FIRST DIVISION, Maj.-Gen. Isaac I. Stevens (k), Col. Benjamin C. Christ. Staff loss: k, 1.
*First Brigade*, Col. Benjamin C. Christ, Lieut.-Col. Frank Graves: 50th Pa., Lieut.-Col. Thomas S. Brenholtz (w), Maj. Edward Overton, Jr., 8th Mich., Lieut.-Col. Frank Graves, Capt. Ralph Ely. Brigade loss: k, 29; w, 175; m, 27=231. *Second Brigade*, Col. Daniel Leasure (w), Lieut.-Col. David A. Leckey: 46th N. Y. (5 co's), Col. Rudolph Rosa (w), Maj. Julius Parcus; 100th Pa., Lieut.-Col. David A. Leckey, Capt. James E. Cornelius (w), Capt. Hillery W. Squier. Brigade loss: k, 20; w, 133; m, 10=163. *Third Brigade*, Col. Addison Farnsworth (w), Lieut.-Col. David Morrison: 28th Mass., Maj. George W. Cartwright (w), Capt. Andrew P. Caraher; 79th N. Y., Maj. William St. George Elliot (w), Lieut.-Col. David Morrison. Brigade loss: k, 42; w, 267; m, 30=339. *Artillery:* 8th Mass., Capt. Asa M. Cook; E, 2d U. S., Lieut. Samuel N. Benjamin. Artillery loss: k, 3; w, 10=13.
SECOND DIVISION, Maj.-Gen. Jesse L. Reno.
*First Brigade*, Col. James Nagle: 6th N. H., Col. Simon G. Griffin; 48th Pa., Lieut.-Col. Joshua K. Sigfried; 2d Md., Lieut.-Col. J. Eugene Duryea. Brigade loss: k, 76; w, 259; m, 183=518. *Second Brigade*, Col. Edward Ferrero: 21st Mass., Col. William S. Clark; 51st N. Y., Lieut.-Col. Robert B. Potter; 51st Pa., Col. John F. Hartranft. Brigade loss: k, 33; w, 156; m, 69=258.
KANAWHA DIVISION—(En route to Pope from W. Va.)
*First Provisional Brigade* (engaged only at Bull Run Bridge, August 27th), Col. E. Parker Scammon: 11th Ohio, Maj. Lyman J. Jackson, Lieut.-Col. Augustus H. Coleman; 12th Ohio, Col. Carr B. White. Brigade loss: k, 14; w, 50; m, 42=106. *Unattached*, 30th Ohio, Lieut.-Col. Theodore Jones; 36th Ohio, Col. George Crook.

The loss of the Union army in the battles of August 29th and 30th is not separately reported. In all the combats of the campaign from the Rappahannock to the Potomac, the casualties amounted (approximately) to 1747 killed, 8452 wounded, and 4263 captured or missing = 14,462.

## THE CONFEDERATE FORCES.

### ARMY OF NORTHERN VIRGINIA—General Robert E. Lee.

RIGHT WING, OR LONGSTREET'S CORPS, Maj.-Gen. James Longstreet.
ANDERSON'S DIVISION, Maj.-Gen. Richard H. Anderson.
*Armistead's Brigade*, Brig.-Gen. Lewis A. Armistead: 9th Va., ——; 14th Va., ——; 38th Va., ——; 53d Va., ——; 57th Va., ——; 5th Va. Battalion, ——. Brigade loss: k, 2; w, 18=20. *Mahone's Brigade*, Brig.-Gen. William Mahone: 6th Va., ——; 12th Va., ——; 16th Va., ——; 41st Va., ——. Brigade loss: k, 38; w, 196=234. *Wright's Brigade*, Brig.-Gen. Ambrose R. Wright: 44th Ala., ——; 3d Ga., ——; 22d Ga., ——; 48th Ga., ——. Brigade loss: k, 32; w, 150; m, 8=190.
JONES'S DIVISION, Brig.-Gen. David R. Jones. Staff loss: m, 1.
*Toombs's Brigade*, Col. Henry L. Benning, Brig.-Gen. Robert Toombs: 2d Ga., Lieut.-Col. William R. Holmes; 15th Ga., Col. William T. Millican; 17th Ga., Maj. John H. Pickett (w), Capt. A. C. Jones (k), Capt. Hiram L. French; 20th Ga., Maj. J. D. Waddell. Brigade loss: k, 40; w, 327=367. *Drayton's Brigade*, Brig.-Gen. Thomas F. Drayton: 50th Ga., ——; 51st Ga., ——; 15th S. C., ——; Phillips's (Ga.) Legion, ——. Brigade loss: k, 13; w, 80=93. *Jones's Brigade*, Col. George T. Anderson: 1st Ga. (regulars), Maj. John D. Walker; 7th Ga., Col. W. T. Wilson (m w), 8th Ga., Lieut.-Col. John R. Towers; 9th Ga., Col. Benjamin Beck; 11th Ga., Lieut.-Col. William Luffman. Brigade loss: k, 103; w, 701; m, 5=809.
WILCOX'S DIVISION, Brig.-Gen. Cadmus M. Wilcox.
*Wilcox's Brigade*, Brig.-Gen. Cadmus M. Wilcox: 8th Ala., Maj. H. A. Herbert; 9th Ala., Maj. J. H. J. Williams; 10th Ala., Maj. John H. Caldwell; 11th Ala., Capt. J. C. C. Sanders; Va. Battery (Thomas Art'y), Capt. Edwin J. Anderson. Brigade loss: k, 9; w, 61=70. *Pryor's Brigade*, Brig.-Gen. Roger A. Pryor: 14th Ala., ——; 5th Fla., ——; 8th Fla., ——; 3d Va., ——. Brigade loss: k, 15; w, 76; m, 4=95. *Featherston's Brigade*, Brig.-Gen. Winfield S. Featherston, Col. Carnot Posey: 12th Miss., ——; 16th Miss., Col. Carnot Posey; 19th Miss., ——; 2d Miss. Battalion, ——; Va. Battery (Dixie Art'y), Capt. W. H. Chapman. Brigade loss: k, 26; w, 142=168.
HOOD'S DIVISION, Brig.-Gen. John B. Hood.
*Hood's Brigade*, Brig.-Gen. John B. Hood: 18th Ga., Col. William T. Wofford; Hampton (S. C.) Legion, Lieut.-Col. M. W. Gary; 1st Tex., Lieut.-Col. P. A. Work; 4th Tex., Lieut.-Col. B. F. Carter; 5th Tex., Col. J. B. Robertson (w), Capt. K. Bryan (w), Capt. I. N. M. Turner. Brigade loss: k, 75; w, 550; m, 13=638. *Whiting's Brigade*, Col. E. M. Law: 4th Ala., Lieut.-Col. O. K. McLemore; 2d Miss., Col. J. M. Stone; 11th Miss., Col. P. F. Liddell; 6th N. C., Maj. Robert F. Webb. Brigade loss: k, 56; w, 268=324. *Artillery*, Maj. B. W. Frobel: S. C. Battery (German Art'y), Capt. W. K. Bachman; S. C. Battery (Palmetto Art'y), Capt. Hugh R. Garden; N. C. Battery (Rowan Art'y), Capt. James Reilly. Artillery loss: k, 1; w, 9=10.
KEMPER'S DIVISION, Brig.-Gen. James L. Kemper.
*Kemper's Brigade*, Col. Montgomery D. Corse (w), Col. William R. Terry: 1st Va., Lieut.-Col. F. G. Skinner; 7th Va., Col. W. T. Patton (w); 11th Va., Maj. Adam Clement; 17th Va., Lieut.-Col. Morton Marye (w), Maj. Arthur Herbert; 24th Va., Col. William R. Terry. Brigade loss: k, 33; w, 240; m, 1=274. *Jenkins's Brigade*, Brig.-Gen. Micah Jenkins (w), Col. Joseph Walker: 1st S. C., Col. Thomas J. Glover (k); 2d S. C. (Rifles) ——; 5th S. C., ——; 6th S. C., ——; 4th S. C. Battalion, ——; Palmetto (S. C.) Sharp-shooters, Col. Joseph Walker. Brigade loss: k, 59; w, 408; m, 2=469. *Pickett's Brigade*, Col. Eppa Hunton: 8th Va., ——; 18th Va., ——; 19th Va., ——; 28th Va., ——; 56th Va.,——. Brigade loss: k, 21; w, 209; m, 4=234. *Evans's Independent Brigade*, Brig.-Gen. Nathan G. Evans (on Aug. 30th also in command of Hood's division), Col. P. F. Stevens: 17th S. C., Col. John H. Means (m w), Lieut.-Col. F. W. McMaster; 18th S. C., Col. J. M. Gadberry (k), Lieut.-Col. W. H. Wallace; 22d S. C., Col. S. D. Goodlett (w); 23d S. C., Col. H. L. Benbow (w), Capt. M. V. Bancroft; Holcombe (S. C.) Legion, Col. P. F. Stevens, Lieut.-Col. F. G. Palmer (w), Maj. W. J. Crawley; S. C. Battery (Macbeth Art'y), Capt. R. Boyce. Brigade loss: k, 133; w, 593; m, 8=734.
ARTILLERY: *Washington (La.) Artillery*, Col. John B. Walton: 1st Company, Capt. C. W. Squires; 2d Company, Capt. J. B. Richardson; 3d Company, Capt. M. B. Miller; 4th Company, Capt. B. F. Eshleman. Loss: k, 9; w, 23=32. *Lee's Battalion*, Col. Stephen D. Lee: Va. Battery, Capt. J. L. Eubank; Va. Battery (Grimes's), Lieut. Thomas J. Oakham; Va. Battery (Bedford Art'y), Capt. T. C. Jordan; Va., Battery, Capt. W. W. Parker; S. C. Battery (Rhett's) Lieut. William Elliott; Va. Battery, Capt. J. S. Taylor. Loss: w, 6. *Miscellaneous:* Va. Battery (Huger's), ——; Va. Battery (Leake's), ——; La. Battery (Donaldsonville Art'y), ——; Va. Battery (Moorman's) ——; Va. Battery (Loudoun Art'y), Capt. A. L. Rogers; Va. Battery (Fauquier Art'y), Capt. R. M. Stribling.

LEFT WING, OR JACKSON'S CORPS, Maj.-Gen. Thomas J. Jackson. Staff loss: w, 1.
FIRST (JACKSON'S) DIVISION, Brig.-Gen. William B. Taliaferro (w), Brig.-Gen. William E. Starke.
*First Brigade*, Col. W. S. H. Baylor (k), Col. A. J. Grigsby (w): 2d Va., Lieut.-Col. Lawson Botts (m w), Capt. J. W. Rowan, Capt. Rawley T. Colston; 4th Va., Lieut.-Col. R. D. Gardner; 5th Va., Maj. H. J. Williams; 27th Va., Col. A. J. Grigsby; 33d Va., Col. John F. Neff (k). Brigade loss: k, 65; w, 346 = 411. *Second Brigade*, Maj. John Seddon, Col. Bradley T. Johnson: 21st Va., Capt. William A. Witcher; 42d Va., Capt. John E. Penn; 48th Va., Lieut. Virginius Dabney (w), Capt. W. W. Goldsborough (w); 1st Va. (Irish) Battalion, Maj. John Seddon, Capt. O. C. Henderson. Brigade loss: k, 18; w, 102 = 120. *Third Brigade*, Col. Alexander G. Taliaferro: 47th Ala., Col. James W. Jackson; 48th Ala., Col. J. L. Sheffield; 10th Va., Lieut.-Col. S. T. Walker (w); 23d Va., ——; 37th Va., ——. Brigade loss: k, 22; w, 147 = 169. *Fourth Brigade*, Brig.-Gen. William E. Starke, Col. Leroy A. Stafford: 1st La., ——; 2d La., Col. J. M. Williams; 9th La., Col. Leroy A. Stafford; 10th La., ——; 15th La., Col. Edmund Pendleton; Coppens's (La.) Battalion, Maj. G. Coppens. Brigade loss: k, 110; w, 269; m, 6 = 385. *Artillery*, Maj. L. M. Shumaker: Md. Battery (Baltimore Art'y), Capt. J. B. Brockenbrough; Va. Battery, Capt. Joseph Carpenter; Va. Battery, (Hampden Art'y), Capt. William H. Caskie; Va. Battery, Capt. W. E. Cutshaw; Va. Battery (Rockbridge Art'y), Capt. William T. Poague; Va. Battery (Lee Art'y), Capt. Charles I. Raine; Va. Battery, Capt. W. H. Rice; Va. Battery (Danville Art'y), Capt. George W. Wooding. Artillery loss: k, 8; w, 13 = 21.

SECOND, OR LIGHT DIVISION, Major-General A. P. Hill.
*Branch's Brigade*, Brig.-Gen. L. O'B. Branch: 7th N. C., Capt. R. B. MacRae; 18th N. C., Lieut.-Col. T. J. Purdie; 28th N. C., Col. James H. Lane; 33d N. C., Col. Robert F. Hoke; 37th N. C., ——. Brigade loss: k, 44; w, 280; m, 3 = 327. *Pender's Brigade*, Brig.-Gen. William D. Pender: 16th N. C., Capt. L. W. Stowe (w); 22d N. C., Maj. C. C. Cole; 34th N. C., Col. Richard H. Riddick (m w); 38th N. C., Capt. John Ashford (w). Brigade loss: k, 26; w, 197 = 223. *Thomas's Brigade*, Col. Edward L. Thomas: 14th Ga., Col. R. W. Folsom; 35th Ga., ——; 45th Ga., Maj. W. L. Grice; 49th Ga., Lieut.-Col. S. M. Manning. Brigade loss: k, 33; w, 199 = 232. *Artillery*, Lieut.-Col. R. L. Walker: Va. Battery (Fredericksburg Art'y), Capt. Carter M. Braxton; Va. Battery, Capt. W. G. Crenshaw; Va. Battery (Letcher Art'y), Capt. Greenlee Davidson; Va. Battery (Middlesex Art'y), Lieut. W. B. Hardy; N. C. Battery (Branch Art'y), Lieut. John R. Potts; S. C. Battery (Pee Dee Artillery), Capt. D. G. McIntosh; Va. Battery (Purcell Art'y), Capt. W. J. Pegram. Artillery loss: k, 4; w, 8 = 12. *Gregg's Brigade*, Brig.-Gen. Maxcy Gregg: 1st S. C., Maj. Edward McCrady, Jr. (w), Capt. C. W. McCreary; 1st S. C. (Orr's Rifles), Col. J. Foster Marshall (k), Capt. Joseph J. Norton, Capt. G. McD. Miller, Capt. Joseph J. Norton; 12th S. C., Col. Dixon Barnes; 13th S. C., Col. O. E. Edwards (w), Capt. —— Duncan; 14th S. C., Col. Samuel McGowan (w), Lieut.-Col. W. D. Simpson. Brigade loss: k, 116; w, 606 = 722. *Archer's Brigade*, Brig.-Gen. James J. Archer: 5th Ala. Battalion, Capt. Thomas Bush (k), Lieut. Charles M. Hooper; 19th Ga., Capt. F. M. Johnston; 1st Tenn. (Provisional Army), Col. Peter Turney; 7th Tenn., Maj. S. G. Shepard; 14th Tenn., Col. W. A. Forbes (m w), Maj. James W. Lockert. Brigade loss: k, 21; w, 213 = 234. *Field's Brigade*, Brig.-Gen. Charles W. Field (w), Col. J. M. Brockenbrough: 40th Va., Col. J. M. Brockenbrough; 47th Va. [Col. Robert M. Mayo (w)]; 55th Va. [Col. Frank Mallory]; 22d Va. Battalion, ——. Brigade loss: k, 15; w, 80 = 95.

THIRD DIVISION, Maj.-Gen. Richard S. Ewell (w), Brig.-Gen. A. R. Lawton. Staff loss: w, 1.
*Lawton's Brigade*, Brig.-Gen. A. R. Lawton, Col. M. Douglass: 13th Ga., Col. M. Douglass; 26th Ga., ——; 31st Ga., ——; 38th Ga., ——; 60th Ga., Maj. T. J. Berry; 61st Ga., ——. Brigade loss: k, 139; w, 368; m, 5 = 512. *Trimble's Brigade*, Brig.-Gen. Isaac R. Trimble (w), Capt. W. F. Brown (k): 15th Ala., Maj. A. A. Lowther; 12th Ga., Capt. W. F. Brown; 21st Ga., Capt. Thomas C. Glover; 21st N. C., Lieut.-Col. Saunders Fulton (k); 1st N. C. Battalion, ——. Brigade loss: k, 109; w, 331; m, 7 = 447. *Early's Brigade*, Brig.-Gen. Jubal A. Early: 13th Va., Col. James A. Walker; 25th Va., Col. George H. Smith (w); 31st Va., Col. John S. Hoffman; 44th Va., ——; 49th Va., Col. William Smith; 52d Va., ——; 58th Va., ——. Brigade loss: k, 29; w, 187; m, 4 = 220. *Hays's Brigade*, Col. Henry Forno (w), Col. H. B. Strong: 5th La., Maj. B. Menger; 6th La., Col. H. B. Strong; 7th La., ——; 8th La., Maj. T. D. Lewis; 14th La., ——. Brigade loss: k, 87; w, 263; m, 11 = 361. *Artillery*: Va. Battery (Staunton Art'y), Lieut. A. W. Garber; Md. Battery (Chesapeake Art'y), Capt. William D. Brown; La. Battery (La. Guard Art'y), Capt. L. E. D'Aquin; Md. Battery, Capt. W. F. Dement; Va. Battery, Capt. John R. Johnson; Va. Battery (Courtney Art'y), Capt. J. W. Latimer. Artillery loss: k, 6; w, 20; m, 1 = 27.
CAVALRY DIVISION, Maj.-Gen. James E. B. Stuart.
*Robertson's Brigade*, Brig.-Gen. Beverly H. Robertson: 2d Va., Col. Thomas T. Munford (w); 6th Va., Col. Thomas S. Flournoy; 7th Va., Col. William E. Jones, Capt. Samuel B. Myers; 12th Va., Col. A. W. Harman; 17th Va. Battalion, Maj. W. Patrick (m w). Brigade loss: k, 18; w, 78; m, 18 = 114. *Lee's Brigade*, Brig.-Gen. Fitzhugh Lee: 1st Va., Col. L. T. Brien; 3d Va., ——; 4th Va., Col. W. C. Wickham; 5th Va., Col. Thomas L. Rosser; 9th Va., Col. W. H. F. Lee. Brigade loss (not reported). *Artillery*: Va. Battery (Stuart Horse Art'y), Capt. John Pelham. Loss: k, 1; w, 5 = 6. The losses sustained by Longstreet's corps are reported ("Official Records," Vol. XII., Pt. II., p. 568) as 663 killed, 4016 wounded, and 46 missing, in all 4725. Jackson reported his losses at 805 killed, 3547 wounded, and 35 missing, or a total of 4387 ("Official Records," Vol. XII., Pt. II., p. 648), but the reports of his subordinate commanders aggregate 871 killed, 3713 wounded, and 45 missing = 4629. Adopting these latter figures as Jackson's loss, we have, after including the loss of 120 in Stuart's cavalry (less Fitzhugh Lee's brigade, not reported), a grand total of 1553 killed, 7812 wounded, and 109 missing = 9474.

Unquestionably the casualties given in these tables for both armies are too small, but they are the nearest approximation attainable from the records.

It is impossible to compute with precision the number of men actually present on the field of battle at Groveton and Bull Run. The official returns and reports are not only imperfect, but often contradictory. However, a careful study of the subject, based upon the best information obtainable, justifies the conclusion that the effective strength of the army under Pope's command was at least 63,000, and that of the Confederate army about 54,000,— of all arms. The computation of Pope's forces includes his own proper command (exclusive of Banks's corps, which did not reach the scene of action), Reno's corps, and the reënforcements received from the Army of the Potomac. The Confederate force has been estimated by some writers as low as 47,000. Others concede the number given above. Colonel William Allan, late chief-of-ordnance, Second Corps, Army of Northern Virginia, in a paper upon the subject, contributed to the Military Historical Society of Massachusetts, concludes that on the 28th of August, Pope had 70,000 men (including Banks's corps), and Lee about 49,000.

RAID UPON A UNION BAGGAGE TRAIN BY STUART'S CAVALRY. FROM A WAR-TIME SKETCH.

## JACKSON'S RAID AROUND POPE.

BY W. B. TALIAFERRO, MAJOR-GENERAL, C. S. A.

ON the morning of the 25th of August, 1862, Stonewall Jackson, with Ewell's and A. P. Hill's divisions and his own old division under my command, marched northward from Jeffersonton, Virginia, to cut Pope's communications and destroy his supplies. Quartermasters and commissaries, with their forage and subsistence stores, were left behind, their white tilted wagons parked conspicuously. The *impedimenta* which usually embarrass and delay a marching column had been reduced to a few ambulances and a limited ordnance train; three days' meager rations had been cooked and stowed away in haversacks and pockets; and tin cans and an occasional frying-pan constituted the entire camp-equipage. The men had rested and dried off, and as they marched out they exulted with the inspiration of the balmy summer atmosphere and the refreshing breezes which swept down from the Blue Mountains.

No man save one in that corps, whatever may have been his rank, knew our destination. The men said of Jackson that his piety expressed itself in obeying the injunction, "Let not thy left hand know what thy right hand doeth." No intelligence of intended Confederate movements ever reached the enemy by any slip of his. The orders to his division chiefs were like this: "March to a cross-road; a staff-officer there will inform you which fork to take; and so to the next fork, where you will find a courier with a sealed direction pointing out the road."

This extreme reticence was very uncomfortable and annoying to his subordinate commanders, and was sometimes carried too far; but it was the real secret of the reputation for ubiquity which he acquired, and which was so well expressed by General McClellan in one of his dispatches: "I am afraid of Jackson; he will turn up where least expected."

Naturally his destination was supposed to be Waterloo Bridge, there to force the passage of the river; but the road leading to Waterloo was passed and the northward march continued. The Rappahannock (locally the Hedgeman) is here confined in narrow limits by bold hills and rocky cliffs, and some miles above the bridge there is a road through these crossing the river at Hinson's Mill. The picturesque surroundings of the ford at this place and the cool bath into which the men plunged were not the less enjoyed because of the unexpected absence of opposition by the enemy; and after the inevitable delay which accompanies any crossing of a watercourse by an army, Jackson's corps stood on the same side of the river with the entire Federal army.

After crossing, Colonel Thomas T. Munford's 2d Virginia Cavalry picketed the roads leading in the direction of the enemy, whose whole force, now confronting Longstreet alone, was massed within lines drawn from Warrenton and Waterloo on the north to the Orange and Alexandria Railroad (now called the Midland) on the south. But Jackson's course was not directed toward the enemy. We were marching toward the lower Valley of Virginia, with our destination shrouded in mystery.

From the crossing at Hinson's Mills, Jackson's course still took the same direction—through the little village of Orlean, along the base of a small mountain which crops up in Fauquier County, and on to the little town of Salem, where his "foot cavalry," after a march of over twenty-six miles on a midsummer's day, rested for the night. At dawn on the 26th the route was resumed—this day at right angles with the direction of that of the preceding, and now, with faces set to the sunrise, the troops advanced toward the Bull Run Mountains, which loomed up across the pathway.

Thoroughfare Gap, of this range, is the outlet by which the Manassas Gap Railroad, passing from the Shenandoah Valley, penetrates the last mountain obstruction on its way to tide-water. Marching along the graded bed of this road, between the spurs and cliffs which rise on either side, and refreshed by the cooler atmosphere of the mountain elevation, the Confederate troops poured through the narrow pathway and streamed down into the plain below. Used to scanty diet, they had early learned the art of supplementing their slender commissariat, and the tempting corn-fields along which they passed were made to pay tribute.

At Gainesville, on the Warrenton and Alexandria turnpike, we were overtaken by Stuart, who, with Fitz Lee's and Robertson's brigades, had crossed the Rappahannock that morning and pursued nearly the same route with Jackson; and our subsequent movements were greatly aided and influenced by the admirable manner in which the cavalry was employed and managed by Stuart and his accomplished officers.

Late in the afternoon Ewell's division, preceded by Munford's cavalry, reached the Orange and Alexandria Railroad at Bristoe Station, the other two divisions being halted for the night a little short of that point. Munford, with his cavalry, dashed upon the station, dispersed a party of the same arm, and had a sharp skirmish with a company of infantry who took shelter in the houses; but he failed to stop a train which sped recklessly past, throwing aside the obstructions he had placed upon the track and effecting its escape. General Henry Forno's (Hays's) brigade, of General Ewell's division, however, quickly reënforcing him, two other trains and several prisoners were captured.

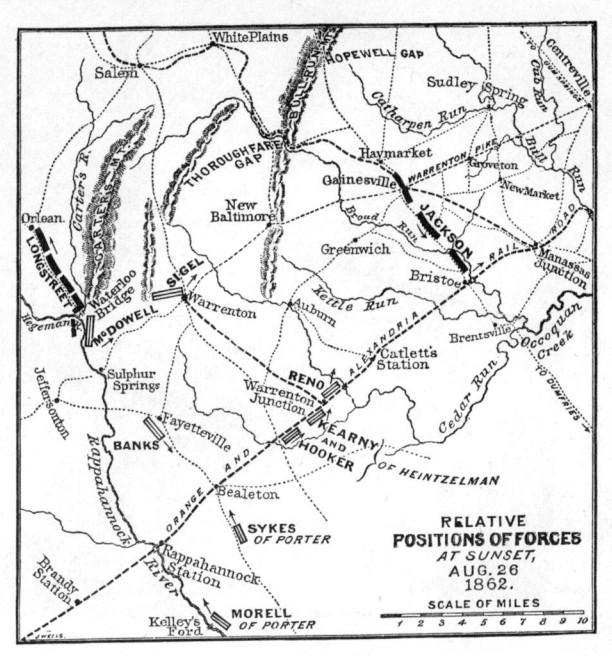

Wearied, as they were, with a march of over thirty miles, Jackson determined, nevertheless, to tax still further the powers of endurance of his men. At Manassas Junction was established a vast depot of quartermaster's, commissary, and ordnance stores; and it was also a "city of refuge" for many runaway negroes of all ages and of both sexes. The extent of the defenses, and of the force detailed for its protection, could not be known; but as it was far in the rear of the Federal army, not very distant from Alexandria, and directly on the line of communication and reënforcement, it was not probable that any large force had been detached for its protection. General Stonewall Jackson's habit in the valley had been to make enforced requisitions upon the Federal commissaries for his subsistence supplies; and the tempting opportunity of continuing this policy and rationing his hungry command, as well as inflicting almost irreparable loss upon the enemy, was not to be neglected. General Trimble volunteered to execute the enterprise with five hundred men, and his offer was readily accepted; but "to increase the prospect of success," Stuart, with a portion of his cavalry, was ordered to coöperate with him. The enemy were not taken by surprise, and opened with their artillery upon the first intimation of attack, but their force was too small; their cannon were taken at the point of the bayonet, and without the loss of a man killed, and with but fifteen wounded, the immense stores, eight guns, and three hundred prisoners fell into our

SUPPER AFTER A HARD MARCH.

hands.] Early next morning A. P. Hill's division and mine were moved to the Junction, Ewell's remaining at Bristoe.

Our troops at Manassas had barely been placed in position before a gallant effort was made by General Taylor, with a New Jersey brigade, to drive off the supposed raiding party and recapture the stores; but, rushing upon overwhelming numbers, he lost his own life, two hundred prisoners, and the train that had transported them from Alexandria. The railroad bridge over Bull Run was destroyed, severing communication with Alexandria, the roads were picketed, and Fitz Lee's cavalry pushed forward as far as Fairfax Court House on the turnpike and Burke's Station on the railroad. The long march of over fifty-six miles in two days entitled Jackson's men to a holiday, and the day of rest at Manassas Junction was fully enjoyed. There was no

]The guns captured at Manassas Junction appear to have belonged to the 11th New York battery, Captain Albert A. von Puttkammer, who lost 6 guns; one section of Battery C, 1st New York Artillery, Lieutenant Samuel R. James, 2 guns. Part of one company of the 12th Pennsylvania Cavalry, which had been driven in from Bristoe, was captured. Captain von Puttkammer saved two of his guns and presently fell in with the advance of the 2d New York Heavy Artillery, Colonel Gustav Waagner (about 600 strong), which had been hurried forward from Washington. These forces, later in the morning, had a brief contest with Branch's brigade, moving on Union Mills at the head of A. P. Hill's division. Waagner's force was soon driven off, and in his retreat was harried by Fitzhugh Lee's cavalry from Centreville to Fairfax, where they met the 14th Massachusetts regiment (1st Massachusetts Heavy Artillery), Col. W. B. Greene, which had also been ordered forward. Colonel L. B. Pierce, 12th Pennsylvania Cavalry, was ill and in the hospital at Manassas; the rest of his regiment had been sent toward White Plains, and a portion of it seems to have encountered the advance of Stuart's cavalry at Hay Market and Gainesville; "the remains" of this regiment, as General McClellan describes them, were reunited near Alexandria.

Shortly after driving off Waagner's force, A. P. Hill's advance met and overpowered Taylor's New Jersey brigade of Slocum's division supported by part of Scammon's brigade of the Kanawha division. Taylor and Scammon were hurrying forward from Washington.—EDITORS.

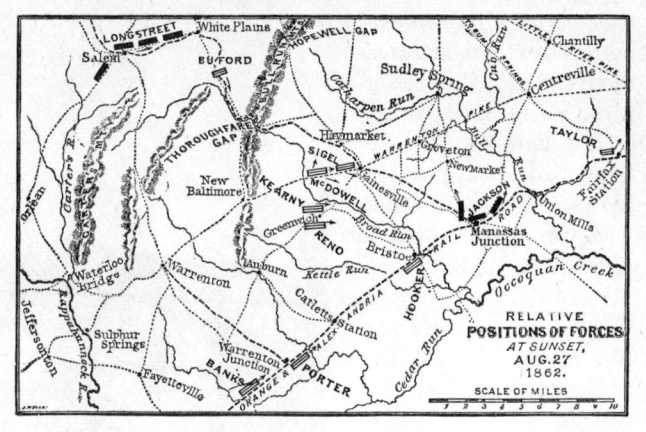

lack or stint of good cheer, in the way of edibles, from canned meats to caramels.

Stonewall Jackson had now severed the communications of the enemy, broken down the bridges behind them, and destroyed their enormous reserve supplies. But this, which might have been accomplished by a raiding party, was by no means the only object of his enterprise; the object was beyond that—to deliver a stunning blow upon his adversary, if possible without hazard to himself. His plans, no doubt conditionally discussed with General Lee before he started on the expedition, were determined without hesitation at Manassas. He could throw himself north of Bull Run and await the coming of Pope,— who he believed would retreat along the line of the railroad and turnpike,—thus taking the chances of holding him in check until Longstreet came in to crush him from behind. The conditions of the problem were these: he must place himself on the enemy's flank, so as to avoid the full shock of his whole force if Longstreet should be delayed, and at the same time where he could himself strike effectively; he must remain within reach of Longstreet, in order to insure a more speedy concentration; and he must seek some point from which, in the event that Longstreet's advance should be barred, he might aid in removing the obstacle, or, in case of necessity, withdraw his corps and reunite it with the rest of the army behind the Bull Run Mountains.

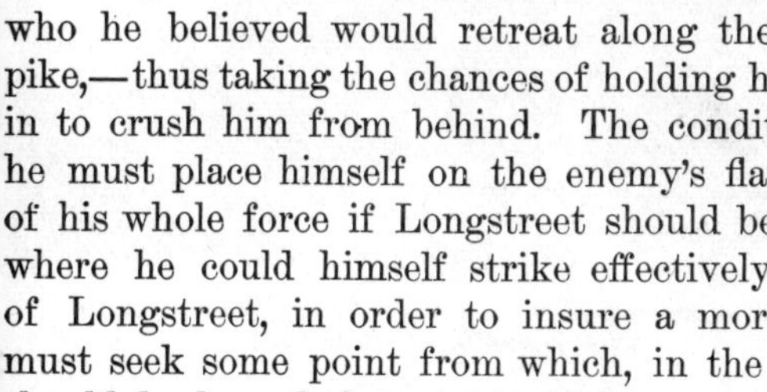

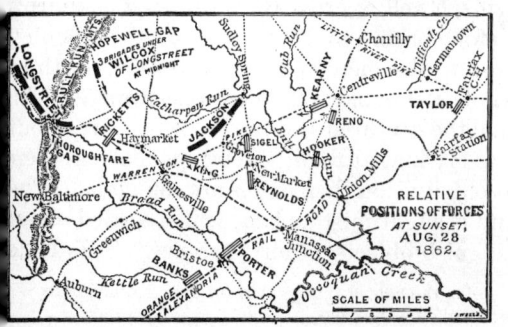

The point that satisfied these requirements was west of Bull Run and north of the Warrenton turnpike, and within striking distance of Aldie Gap as the line of retreat. That position Jackson determined to occupy, and there was nothing to prevent or disconcert his plans. A glance at the map will show that Jackson was really master of the situation—that neither General Lee nor himself had forced his command into a trap, but, on the contrary, he was at that time not even menaced; and if he had been, the gateways of retreat were wide open. His march had been made with such celerity, his flanks guarded with such consummate skill, that he was in no hurry to execute those tactical movements which he recognized as essential to his safety and to the delivery of his heaviest blows. On one flank, Fitz Lee was as near to Alexandria as to Manassas Junction; and, on the other, Munford and Rosser were in advance of Bristoe. Jackson was resting — as a man full of life and vigor, ready to start into action at the first touch — but he rested in the consciousness of security. The Federal commander, around whose flank and rear fourteen brigades of infantry, two of cavalry, and eighteen light batteries had passed, was also resting — but in profound ignorance. On the 26th he ordered Heintzelman "to send a regiment" from Warrenton to Manassas, "to repair the wires and protect the railroad." Aroused, however, on the evening of the 27th, to some appreciation of the condition of affairs, he sent one division (Hooker's) of Heintzelman's corps to Bristoe, which attacked the brigades of Lawton, Early, and Forno (Hays's) of Ewell's division, who successively retired, as they had been directed to do, with little loss, upon the main body at Manassas Junction.

THE STONE BRIDGE, BULL RUN, FROM THE NORTH BANK. FROM A SKETCH MADE IN 1884.

At his leisure, Jackson now proceeded to execute his projected movements. A. P. Hill was ordered to Centreville, Ewell to cross Bull Run at Blackburn's Ford and follow the stream to the stone bridge, and my division by the Sudley road, to the left of the other routes, to the vicinity of Sudley Mills, north of the Warrenton pike, where the whole command was to be concentrated. The immense accumulation of stores and the captured trains were set on fire about midnight and destroyed ⚓ [see p. 511]; and at night the troops took up their march, Jackson accompanying his old division then under my command. The night was starlit but moonless, and a slight mist or haze which settled about the earth made it difficult to distinguish objects at any distance. Still, little

⚓ None of the Federal reports mention seeing the light of this great fire or that at Union Mills on the same night.— EDITORS.

encumbered by baggage, and with roads free from the blockade of trains, the march was made without serious impediment or difficulty. The enemy was again deceived. A. P. Hill's march to Centreville was mistaken for that of the whole command; Jackson was supposed to be between Bull Run and Washington; and now, instead of a regiment, the whole Federal army was ordered to concentrate on Manassas for the pursuit.

Early on the morning of the 28th, Colonel Bradley T. Johnson, commanding a brigade of my division, was ordered down the Warrenton road toward Gainesville, with directions to picket the roads converging upon the turnpike near that place. Stuart had already placed a small cavalry force on this road and north of it, at Hay Market. Johnson, holding Groveton as his reserve, picketed the road as directed, pushed Captain George R. Gaither's troop of cavalry, which he found on picket, still farther on in the direction of Warrenton, and made dispositions to prevent surprise, and to check, if necessary, any advance of the enemy.

THE UNION MONUMENT NEAR THE "DEEP CUT." FROM A SKETCH MADE IN 1884. (SEE MAPS, PP. 473, 509.)

Ewell's division having now come up and united with the troops of my command, Jackson determined to rest and await further developments.

Captain Gaither had the good fortune to capture a courier conveying a dispatch from General McDowell to Generals Sigel and Reynolds, which revealed General Pope's intention of concentrating on Manassas Junction, Sigel being ordered to march on that point from Gainesville, with his right resting on the Manassas Gap Railroad; Reynolds, also from Gainesville, to keep his left on the Warrenton road; and King's division to move *en échelon* in support of the other two.

In the execution of this order, Reynolds's column struck Johnson's command; but after a short conflict, which was well sustained on both sides, the Federal commander, mistaking Johnson's force for a reconnoitering party, turned off to the right, on the road to Manassas. Johnson then, by order of General Stuart, took position, which he held for the rest of the day, north and west of the turnpike.

Johnson's messenger, bearing the captured order, found the Confederate headquarters established on the shady side of an old-fashioned worm fence, in the corners of which General Jackson and his two division commanders were profoundly sleeping after the fatigues of the preceding night, notwithstanding the intense heat of that August day. There was not so much as an ambulance at those headquarters. The headquarters' train was back beyond the Rappahannock (at Jeffersonton), with servants, camp-equipage, and all the arrangements for cooking and serving food. All the property of the gen-

THE "DEEP CUT." FROM A SKETCH MADE IN 1884.

If this picture were extended a little to the left it would include the Union monument. General Bradley T. Johnson, commanding a brigade in Jackson's old division, in his official report describes Porter's assault at this point on Saturday, August 30th, as follows:

"About 4 P.M. the movements of the enemy were suddenly developed in a decided manner. They stormed my position, deploying in the woods in brigade front and then charging in a run, line after line, brigade after brigade, up the hill on the thicket held by the 48th, and the railroad cut occupied by the 42d. . . . Before the railroad cut the fight was most obstinate. I saw a Federal flag hold its position for half an hour within ten yards of a flag of one of the regiments in the cut, and go down 6 or 8 times; and after the fight 100 dead men were lying 20 yards from the cut, some of them within two feet of it. The men fought until their ammunition was exhausted and then threw stones. Lieutenant —— —— of the battalion killed one with a stone, and I saw him after the fight with his skull fractured. Dr. Richard P. Johnson, on my volunteer staff, having no arms of any kind, was obliged to have recourse to this means of offense from the beginning. As line after line surged up the hill time after time, led up by their officers, they were dashed back on one another until the whole field was covered with a confused mass of struggling, running, routed Yankees." [See note to picture, p. 485.]
— EDITORS.

eral, the staff, and of the headquarters' bureau, was strapped to the pommels and cantles of the saddles, and these formed the pillows of their weary owners.

The captured dispatch aroused Jackson like an electric shock. He was essentially a man of action; he rarely, if ever, hesitated; he never asked advice; he did not seem to reflect, or reason out a purpose; but he leaped by instinct and not by the slower process of ordinary ratiocination to a conclusion, and then as rapidly undertook its execution. He called no council to discuss the situation disclosed by this communication, although his ranking officers were almost at his side; he asked no conference, no expression of opinion; he made no suggestion, but simply, without a word except to repeat the language of the dispatch, turned to me and said, "Move your division and attack the enemy"; and to Ewell, "Support the attack." The slumbering soldiers sprang from the earth with the first summons. There was nothing for them to do but to form, and take their pieces. They were sleeping almost in ranks and by the time the horses of their officers were saddled, the long lines of infantry were moving to the anticipated battle-field.

The two divisions, after marching some distance to the north of the turnpike, finding no enemy, were halted and rested, and the prospect of an engagement on that afternoon [the 28th] seemed to disappear with the lengthening shadows. The enemy did not come — he could not be found — the Warrenton pike, along which it was supposed he would march, was in view — but it was as free from Federal soldiery as it had been two days before, when Jackson's men had streamed along its highway.

Ewell's division was in rear of mine, both lines fronting the turnpike. Beyond this road a pleasant farm-house, with shaded lawn and conspicuous dairy, invited the heated soldiers to its cool retreat and suggested tempting visions of milk and butter. Application was made by some of the men for permission to test the hospitality of the residents and the quality of their dairy products. They went and returned just as General Ewell happened to ride to the front. He heard their favorable report, and, laughingly suggesting that a canteen of buttermilk was a delicacy not to be despised on such an evening by the commander-in-chief himself, requested another party to procure for him the coveted luxury. As these men reached the farmhouse a straggling party of the enemy, doubtless attracted by the same object, came in sight and made straight for what they supposed to be their comrades. A closer approach revealed the distinctive uniforms of enemies and brought about a brief but lively skirmish, from which both parties soon retired upon their respective friends — the Confederates, however, bearing off the *spolia opima*. General Ewell reaped the fruits of the contest, for he obtained and enjoyed his canteen of buttermilk.

Shortly after this, then late in the afternoon, the Federal columns were discovered passing, and the Con-

JACKSON'S LINE ON THE AFTERNOON OF THE LAST DAY, AUGUST 30TH.

The topography is after General Beauregard's map, made from survey after the first battle of Bull Run. The deep cut and the embankment as far as the "Dump" were the scene of the fighting with stones, illustrated on p. 534. Here the unfinished railroad embankment is made of earth and blasted rock taken from the cut. The "Dump" was a break in the embankment, or rather a space which was never filled in; several hundred Union soldiers were buried near it. — EDITORS.

SUDLEY CHURCH, FROM THE SUDLEY SPRINGS ROAD. A HOSPITAL IN BOTH BULL RUN BATTLES. FROM A PHOTOGRAPH TAKEN SHORTLY BEFORE THE SECOND BATTLE.

federate line, formed parallel to the turnpike, moved rapidly forward to the attack. There was no disposition on the part of the Federals to avoid the onset, but, on the contrary, they met us half-way.

It was a sanguinary field; none was better contested during the war. The Federal artillery was admirably served, and at one time the annihilation of our batteries seemed inevitable, so destructive was the fire; but the Confederate guns, although forced to retire and seek new positions, responded with a determination and pluck unshaken by the fiery tempest they had encountered.

A farm-house, an orchard, a few stacks of hay, and a rotten "worm" fence were the only cover afforded to the opposing lines of infantry; it was a stand-up combat, dogged and unflinching, in a field almost bare. There were no wounds from spent balls; the confronting lines looked into each other's faces at deadly range, less than one hundred yards apart, and they stood as immovable as the painted heroes in a battle-piece. There was cover of woods not very far in rear of the lines on both sides, and brave men — with that instinct of self-preservation which is exhibited in the veteran soldier, who seizes every advantage of ground or obstacle — might have been justified in slowly seeking this shelter from the iron hail that smote them; but out in the sunlight, in the dying daylight, and under the stars, they stood, and although they could not advance, they would not retire. There was some discipline in this, but there was much more of true valor.

In this fight there was no manœuvring, and very little tactics — it was a question of endurance, and both endured.

The loss was unusually heavy on both sides. On ours, both division commanders, Ewell and myself, were seriously wounded, and several field-officers were killed or wounded. Federal reports state that "more than one-third of their commanders were left dead or wounded on the field," while Confederate accounts claim that the enemy slowly fell back about 9 o'clock at night but the other side assert that they did not retire until 1 o'clock. It was dark and the Confederates did not advance, and it may be called a drawn battle as a tribute due by either side to the gallantry of the other.

Five of Jackson's brigades took part in the conflict, Lawton's and Trimble's of Ewell's, and Starke's, Taliaferro's, and Baylor's, of Jackson's old division. Early's, Forno's, and Johnson's brigades were not engaged, nor were any of the brigades of General A. P. Hill's division. The Federal troops encountered were those of King's division, and consisted of the brigade of Gibbon and two regiments of Doubleday's brigade.↧

During our engagement at Groveton the white puffs in the air, seen away off to the Confederate right, and the sounds of sharp but distant explosions coming to our ears, foretold the passage of Thoroughfare Gap; and the next day, before noon, Longstreet's advance, under Hood, mingled their hurrahs with those of our men.♭ The march and the manœuvres of Jackson had been a success;⹋ the army was reunited, and ready, under its great head, to strike with both of its strong arms the blows he should direct.

↧ In this battle the right of the Confederate line was held by Taliaferro's brigade of Virginia and Alabama troops, commanded by Colonel Alexander G. Taliaferro, 23d Virginia; next on the left was Jackson's old brigade, all Virginians (lately commanded by General C. S. Winder, killed at Slaughter's [Cedar] Mountain),— officially designated as the "Stonewall," in honor of the steadiness and gallantry which it displayed on the same field [the First Bull Run] twelve months before, and which gained for their commander his well-known sobriquet,— now commanded by Colonel Baylor, 5th Virginia. Next came the Louisiana brigade, lately commanded by Colonel Stafford, and now by General William E. Starke, who took command about August 19th, and who was killed three weeks afterward at Antietam; then the Georgia brigade, commanded by General Alexander R. Lawton; and upon the extreme left General I. R. Trimble's brigade of Georgia, Mississippi, North Carolina, and Alabama troops. The batteries engaged were those of Wooding, Poague, and Carpenter, much outnumbered by the Federal guns, but, toward the close of the contest, ably supplemented by two pieces brought to their support by the "boy-major" Pelham, of Stuart's Horse Artillery, already famous for his skill and gallantry. Jackson ordered up twenty additional guns, but before they could be brought night and fatigue had closed the contest.— W. B. T.

♭ Jackson's force in this raid consisted of three divisions, as follows: Ewell's division, composed of the brigades of Lawton, Early, Hays (Forno commanding), and Trimble, with the batteries of Brown, Dement, Latimer, Balthis, and D'Aquin; Hill's division, of the brigades of Branch, Gregg, Field, Pender, Archer, and Thomas, with the batteries of Braxton, Latham, Crenshaw, McIntosh, Davidson, and Pegram; and Jackson's old division consisted of the brigades of Starke, Taliaferro (Col. A. G. Taliaferro commanding), Winder (Col. Baylor commanding), and Campbell (Major John Seddon commanding), with the batteries of Brockenbrough, Poague, Wooding, Carpenter, Caskie, and Raine. After the 26th, Colonel Bradley T. Johnson commanded Campbell's brigade. General Stuart, with the brigades of Fitz Lee and Robertson, coöperated with Jackson.— W. B. T.

⹋ The results of Jackson's raid on Manassas Junction were reported by General R. E. Lee to be — "eight pieces of artillery, with their horses and equipments, were taken. More than 300 prisoners, 175 horses, besides those belonging to the artillery, 200 new tents, and immense quantities of quartermaster's and commissary stores fell into our hands. . . . 50,000 pounds of bacon, 1000 barrels of corned beef, 2000 barrels of salt pork, and 2000 barrels of flour, besides other property of great value, were burned."— EDITORS.

RUINS OF THE HENRY HOUSE, BURNED DURING THE FIRST BATTLE OF BULL RUN. FROM A PHOTOGRAPH PROBABLY TAKEN IN MARCH, 1862.

## Our March Against Pope

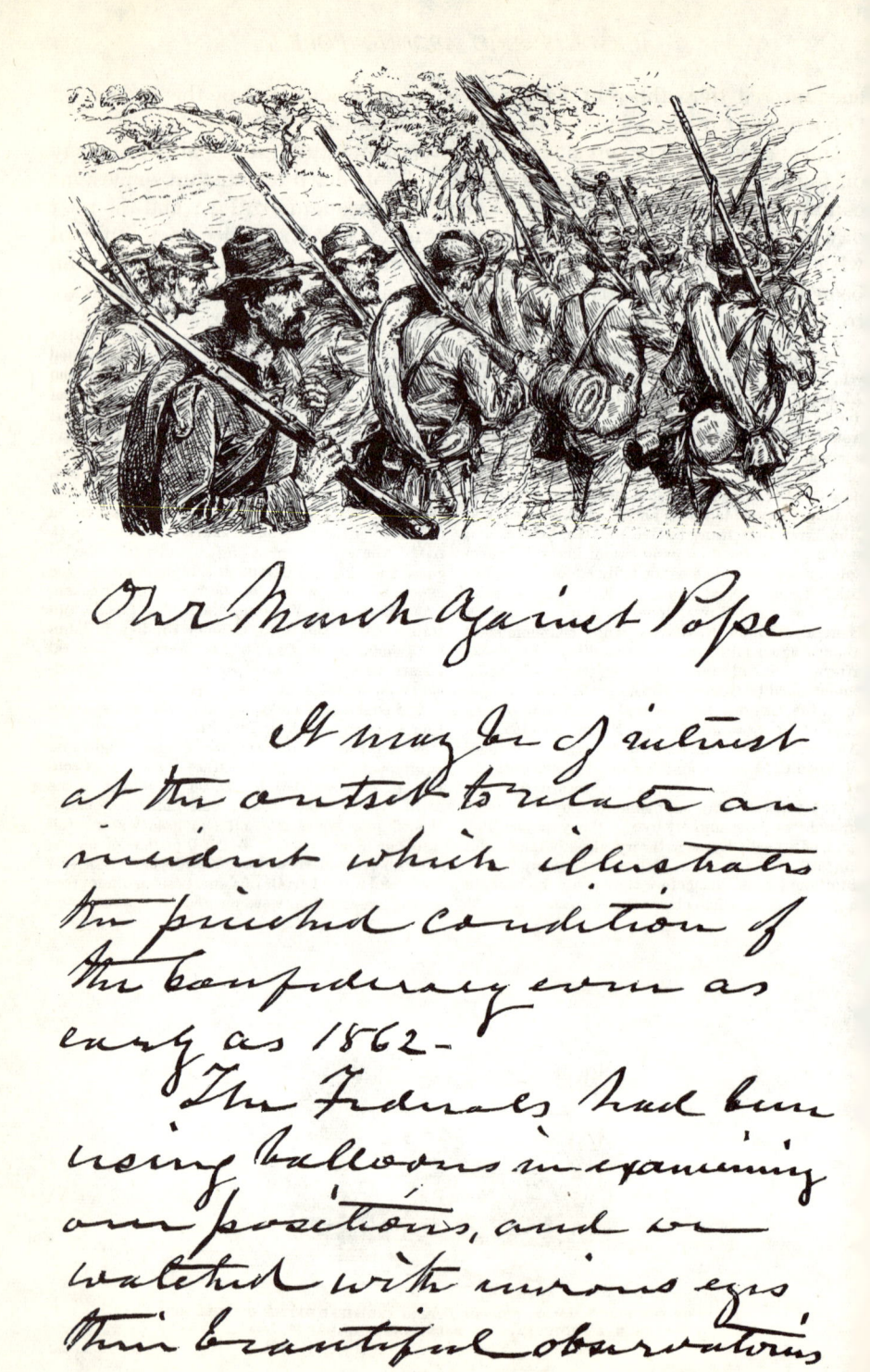

It may be of interest at the outset to relate an incident which illustrates the pinched condition of the Confederacy even as early as 1862.

The Federals had been using balloons in examining our positions, and we watched with envious eyes their beautiful observatories as they floated high up in the air, well out of the range of our guns. While we were longing for the balloons that poverty denied us, a genius arose for the occasion and suggested that we send out and gather together all the silk dresses in the Confederacy and make a balloon. It was done, and soon we had a great patchwork ship of many and varied hues which was ready for use in the Seven Days' campaign. We had no gas except in Richmond, and it was the custom to inflate the balloon there, tie it securely to an engine, and run it down the York River Railroad to any point at which we desired to send it up. One day it was on a steamer down the James when the tide went out and left vessel and balloon high and dry on a bar. The Federals gathered it in, and with it the last silk dress in the Confederacy. This capture was the meanest trick of the war and one I have never yet forgiven.

By the Seven Days' fighting around Richmond General Lee frustrated McClellan's plans for a siege. At the end of that campaign Lee retired to Richmond and McClellan withdrew his forces to Westover Landing, where intrenchments and gun-boats made him secure from attack. As his new position, thus guarded and protected by the navy, was not assailable, General Lee, resuming the defensive at Richmond, resolved to strike out by his left in the direction of Washington, with the idea that the Army of the Potomac might be forced to abandon the James River, in defense of its own capital, threatened by this move.

Contemporaneously with our operations on the Chickahominy, the Washington authorities had been organizing the Army of Virginia of three efficient corps d'armée; and, continuing the search for a young Napoleon, had assigned General Pope, fresh from the West, with his new laurels, to command this select organization. This army, under its dashing leader, was at the same time moving toward Richmond by the Orange and Alexandria Railway, so that our move by the left had also in view the Army of Virginia, as the first obstacle in the way of relief to Richmond — an obstacle to be removed, if possible, before it could be greatly reënforced from other commands.

The assignment of General John Pope to command was announced in Richmond three days after the orders were issued in Washington, and the flourish of trumpets over the manner in which the campaign was to be conducted soon followed. He was reported to have adopted a favorite expression of General Worth's, "Headquarters in the saddle, sir!" and to be riding with as much confidence as that old chieftain when searching the everglades of Florida for the Seminole Indians.⌡ Lee had not known Pope intimately, but accepted the popular opinion of him as a boastful man, quite ambitious to accomplish great results, but unwilling to study closely and properly the means necessary to gratify his desires in that direction. Pope was credited with other expressions, such as that he cared not for his rear; that he hoped in Virginia to see the faces of the rebels, as in the West he had been able to see only their backs.

When General Lee heard of these strange utterances his estimate of Pope was considerably lessened. The high-sounding words seemed to come from

⌡ See General Pope's denial, p. 493; and the text of his address, p. 530.— EDITORS.

LONGSTREET'S MARCH THROUGH THOROUGHFARE GAP.

a commander inexperienced in warfare. For centuries there has been among soldiers a maxim: "Don't despise your enemy." General Pope's words would seem to indicate great contempt for his enemy. Unfortunately for him our troops, at that time, were not so well clad that they cared to show their backs. With the double purpose of drawing McClellan away from Westover, and of checking the advance of the new enemy then approaching from Washington by the Orange and Alexandria Railroad, General Lee sent Stonewall Jackson to Gordonsville, while I remained near Richmond to engage McClellan in case he should attempt an advance upon the Confederate capital. Jackson had his own division and that of General R. S. Ewell, and later A. P. Hill was sent to reënforce him. McDowell was already in coöperation with Pope, part of his command, however, being still at Fredericksburg. On the 9th of August Jackson encountered the enemy near Slaughter or Cedar Mountain. [See page 459.] There the battle of Cedar Run was fought and the Federals were repulsed. In this fight, about 5 o'clock in the afternoon, the Federals, by a well-executed move, were pressing the Confederates back, when the opportune approach of two brigades changed the scene, and a counter-attack from our side drove them back in disorder and left us masters of the field. We followed them some distance, but Jackson thought them too strongly reënforced for us to continue the pursuit and risk severe battle in a disjointed way; so, after caring for our wounded and dead, we retired to a position behind the Rapidan to await the arrival of General Lee with other forces. Thus on his first meeting with the Confederates in Virginia the new Federal commander went to the rear — a direction he was wholly unused to. At that time General Lee was feeling very certain that Richmond was in no immediate danger from an advance by McClellan's forces. He therefore began at once preparations for a vigorous campaign against Pope. Divisions under Generals R. H. Anderson, Lafayette McLaws, J. G. Walker, and D. H. Hill were left to watch McClellan, with instructions to follow the main body of the army as soon as the Federals were drawn away from Westover.

On the 13th of August my command was ordered to Gordonsville, and General Lee accompanied me there. Jackson's troops were stationed on the left of the Orange and Alexandria Railroad, and I went into camp on the right of Gordonsville. Northward was the Rapidan River, several miles distant

Farther on, at Culpeper Court House, was the army of Pope, and farther still was the Rappahannock River. A little in advance of my position was Clark's Mountain, rising several hundred feet above the surrounding hills. With General Lee I proceeded to the mountain, and, climbing to its summit, we raised our glasses and turned them to the north. There, between the two rivers, clustering around Culpeper Court House, and perhaps fifteen miles away, we saw the flags of Pope's army floating placidly above the tops of the trees. From the summit of the mountain we beheld the enemy occupying ground so weak as to invite attack. Realizing the situation, General Lee determined on speedy work, and gave orders that his army should cross the Rapidan on the 18th and make battle. He was exceedingly anxious to move at once, before Pope could get reënforcements. For some reason not fully explained, our movements were delayed and we did not cross the Rapidan until the 20th. In the meantime a dispatch to General Stuart was captured by Pope, which gave information of our presence and contemplated advance. This, with information Pope already had, caused him to withdraw to a very strong position behind the Rappahannock River, and there, instead of at Culpeper Court House, where the attack was first meant to be made, General Lee found him. I approached the Rappahannock at Kelly's Ford, and Jackson approached higher up at Beverly Ford, near the Orange and Alexandria Railroad bridge.

A STRAGGLER ON THE LINE OF MARCH.

We reached the river on the morning of the 21st, without serious opposition, and found Pope in an almost unassailable position, with heavy reënforcements summoned to his aid. General Lee's intention was to force a passage and make the attack before Pope could concentrate. We hoped to be able to interpose, and to strike Pope before McClellan's reënforcements could reach him. We knew at that time that McClellan was withdrawing from Westover. I was preparing to force a passage at Kelly's Ford, when I received an order from General Lee to proceed to Beverly Ford and mask the movements of Jackson, who was to be sent up the river to cross by a left flank movement. On the 22d Jackson withdrew carefully and went on the proposed move. He sought an opportunity to cross farther up the stream, and succeeded in putting part of his command across at Warrenton Springs Ford and in occupying a position there. The flooding rains interrupted his operations, making the river past fording and crippling all attempts at forcing a passage. Jackson therefore withdrew his forces at night by a temporary bridge. As the lower fords become impassable by reason of the floods, the Federals seemed to concentrate against Jackson's efforts.

On the 23d I had quite a spirited artillery combat at Beverly Ford with a force of the enemy that had crossed at the railroad bridge near where I was stationed. The superior position and metal of the Federals gave them an advantage, which they improved by skillful practice. We had more guns, however, and by practice equally clever at length gained the advantage. A little before night the Federals withdrew from the combat.

Pending our movements south-west of the Rappahannock, General Stuart had been making an effort to go around Pope's army, but, fearing to remain on the Washington side of the river in the face of such floods as had come, recrossed with some important dispatches he had captured by a charge upon Pope's headquarters train [see p. 528]. This correspondence confirmed the information we already had, that the Federal army on the James under McClellan and the Federal troops in the Kanawha Valley under Cox had been ordered to reënforce Pope [see p. 278]. Upon receipt of that information, General Lee was more anxious than ever to cross at once. Pope, however, was on the alert, and Lee found he could not attack him to advantage in his stronghold behind the Rappahannock. Lee therefore decided to change his whole plan, and was gratified, on looking at the map, to find a very comfortable way of turning Pope out of his position. It was by moving Jackson off to our left, and far to the rear of the Federal army, while I remained in front with thirty thousand men to engage him in case he should offer to fight.

On the 25th Jackson crossed the Rappahannock at Hinson's Mill, four miles above Waterloo Bridge, and that night encamped at Salem. The next day he passed through Thoroughfare Gap and moved on by Gainesville, and when sunset came he was many miles in the rear of Pope's army, and between it and Washington. This daring move must have staggered the Federal commander. From the Rappahannock, Jackson had gone without serious opposition to within a stone's-throw of the field where the first battle of Manassas was fought. When he arrived at Bristoe Station, just before night, the greater part of the Federal guard at that point fled, and two trains of cars coming from the direction of Warrenton were captured. Jackson sent a force forward seven miles and captured Manassas Junction, taking eight pieces of artillery, a lot of prisoners, and great quantities of commissary and quartermaster's stores. He left a force at Bristoe Station and proceeded to the Junction, arriving there himself on the morning of the 27th.

During the afternoon the enemy attacked our troops at Bristoe Station, coming from the direction of Warrenton Junction in such force that it was evident Pope had discovered the situation and was moving with his entire army upon Jackson. The Confederates at the station withdrew, after a sharp engagement, and the Federals halted there. Jackson appropriated such of the supplies captured at Manassas as he could use, and burned the rest. He then moved over to a position north of the turnpike leading from Warrenton to Alexandria. There, on the old battle-field, Jackson waited for the Federals. On the evening of the 28th King's division came moving eastward down the turnpike and Jackson met them. A bloody fight ensued, lasting until 9 o'clock at night. The enemy withdrew, leaving the Confederates in possession of the field.

That same evening I arrived at Thoroughfare Gap. But I should say that during Jackson's march I had been engaging Pope at different points along the Rappahannock, to impress him with the idea that I was attempting to force a passage in his front. On the afternoon of the 26th, Pope's army broke away from its strong position to meet Jackson's daring and unexpected move. General Lee decided that I should follow at once, and asked whether I would prefer to force a passage of the river, now rapidly falling, or take the route by which Jackson had gone. From the crossing along the route to Warrenton were numerous strongly defensive positions where a small force could have detained me an uncertain length of time. I therefore decided to take Jackson's route, and on the 26th I started. On the 28th, just before night, I arrived at Thoroughfare Gap. As we approached, a report was made to me that the pass was unoccupied, and we went into bivouac on the west side of the mountain, sending a brigade under Anderson down to occupy the pass. As the Confederates neared the gap from one side, Ricketts's division of Federals approached from the other and took possession of the east side. Thoroughfare Gap is a rough pass in the Bull Run Mountains, at some points not more than a hundred yards wide. A turbid stream rushes over its rugged bottom, on both sides of which the mountain rises several hundred feet. On the north the face of the gap is almost perpendicular. The south face is less precipitous, but is covered with tangled mountain ivy and projecting bowlders, forming a position unassailable when occupied by a small infantry and artillery force. Up to this moment we had received reports from General Jackson, at regular intervals, assuring us of his successful operations, and of confidence in his ability to baffle all efforts of the enemy till we should reach him. This sudden interposition of a force at a mountain pass indicated a purpose on the part of the adversary to hold me in check, while overwhelming forces were being brought against Jackson. This placed us in a desperate strait; for we were within relieving distance, and must adopt prompt and vigorous measures that would burst through all opposition. Three miles north was Hopewell Gap, and it was necessary to get possession of this in advance of the Federals, in order to have that vantage-ground for a flank movement, at the same time that we forced our way by footpaths over the mountain heights at Thoroughfare Gap. During the night I sent Wilcox with three brigades through that pass, while Hood was climbing over the mountain at Thoroughfare by a trail. We had no trouble in getting over, and our apprehensions were relieved at the early dawn of the 29th by finding that Ricketts had given up the east side of the gap and was many

VIEW OF JACKSON'S POSITION AS SEEN FROM GROVETON CORNERS. FROM A RECENT PHOTOGRAPH.

The farthest ridge is the line of the unfinished railway. Jackson's center occupied the ground in the right of the picture. There, on elevated open ground, the front of a deep cut, stands the Union monument. [See map, p. 509.]

hours in advance of us, moving in the direction of Manassas Junction. His force, instead of marching around Jackson, could have been thrown against his right and rear. If Ricketts had made this move and the forces in front had coöperated with him, such an attack, well handled, might have given us serious trouble before I reached the field.

As we found the pass open at early dawn and a clean road in front, we marched leisurely to unite our forces on Manassas plains. Before reaching Gainesville we heard the artillery combat in front, and our men involuntarily quickened their steps. Our communications with Jackson were quite regular, and as he had not expressed a wish that we should hurry, our troops were allowed to take their natural swing under the inspiration of impending battle. As we approached the field the fire seemed to become more spirited, and gave additional impulse to our movements. According to the diary of the Washington Artillery we filed down the turnpike at Gainesville at 11:30 A. M.‡ The general impression was that we were there earlier; but this is the only record of time we made on the ground. We marched steadily from daylight till we reached the field, with the exception of an hour's halt to permit Stuart's cavalry to file from east to west of us. There were many of Jackson's men — several thousand — straggling at points along the road, who were taken for my men, and reported as such.

Passing through Gainesville we filed off to the left down the turnpike, and

‡ GAINESVILLE, GA., 8th January, 1886. My attention has just been called to a dispatch of the Federal General John Buford, written on August 29th, 1862, at 9:30 A. M., in which he gives information of my troops moving through Gainesville [Va.] some three-quarters of an hour before his note was written. This would place the head of my column at Gainesville about 9 A. M., and the line deployed and ready for battle at 12 M., which agrees with my recollection, and with my evidence in the F. J. Porter case. It seems that the Washington Artillery was halted some distance in rear to await my selection of the position to which it was assigned — hence the late hour (11:30) mentioned in the diary from which I have quoted above in fixing the hour of our arrival at Gainesville.— J. L. [In this connection see also the testimony of others, p. 527.]

soon came in sight of the troops held at bay by Jackson. Our line of march brought us in on the left and rear of the Federals. At sight of this favorable opportunity our artillery was ordered up, with the leading brigades for its support. Our advance was discovered, however, and the Federals withdrew from attack, retiring their left across the pike behind Groveton, and taking strong defensive ground. The battalion of Washington Artillery was thrown forward to a favorable position on Jackson's right, and from that point my line was deployed so as to extend it to the right some distance beyond the Manassas Gap Railroad. A Federal corps was reported to be at Manassas Junction that morning, and we trail-traced Ricketts's division from Thoroughfare Gap toward the same point; my line was now arranged for attack in front and also to guard against the force in the direction of the Junction. This preparation must have taken an hour—possibly more.

As soon as the troops were arranged, General Lee expressed his wish to have me attack. The change of position on the part of the Federals, however, involved sufficient delay for a reconnoissance on our part. To hasten matters I rode over in the direction of Brewer's Spring, east of the Hampton Cole House [see map, p. 482], to see the new position, and had a fair view of the Federal line, then extending some distance south of the turnpike. The position was not inviting, and I so reported to General Lee.

The two great armies were now face to face upon the memorable field of 1861; both in good defensible positions and both anxious to find a point for an entering wedge into the stronghold of the adversary. It appeared easy for us, except for the unknown quantity at Manassas Junction, to overleap the Federal left and strike a decisive blow. This force at the Junction was a thorn in our side which could not be ignored. General Lee was quite disappointed by my report against immediate attack along the turnpike, and insisted that by throwing some of the brigades beyond the Federal left their position would be broken up and a favorable field gained. While talking the matter over, General Stuart reported the advance of heavy forces from the direction of Manassas Junction against my right. It proved to be McDowell and Porter. I called over three brigades, under Wilcox, and prepared to receive the attack. Battle was not offered, and I reported to General Lee some time afterward that I did not think the force on my right was strong enough to attack us. General Lee urged me to go in, and of course I was anxious to meet his wishes. At the same time I wanted, more than anything else, to know that my troops had a chance to accomplish what they might undertake. The ground before me was greatly to the advantage of the Federals, but if the attack had come from them it would have been a favorable opportunity for me. After a short while McDowell moved toward the Federal right, leaving Porter in front of my right with nine thousand men. My estimate of his force, at the time, was ten thousand. General Lee, finding that attack was not likely, again became anxious to bring on the battle by attacking down the Groveton pike. I suggested that, the day being far spent, it might be as well to advance just before night upon a forced reconnoissance, get our troops into the most favorable positions, and have all things ready for battle at daylight the next morning. To this he reluctantly gave consent, and our plans were laid accordingly. Wilcox returned to position on the left of the turnpike. Orders were given for an advance, to be pursued under cover of night until the main position could be carefully examined. It so happened that an order to advance was issued on the other side at the same time, so that the encounter was something of a surprise on both sides. A very spirited engagement was the result, we being successful, so far at least as to carry our point, capturing a piece of artillery and making our reconnoissance before midnight. As none of the reports received of the Federal positions favored attack, I so explained to General Lee, and our forces were ordered back to their original positions. The gun which we had captured was ordered to be cut down, spiked, and left on the ground.

When Saturday the 30th broke, we were a little apprehensive that Pope was going to get away from us, and Pope was afraid that we were going to get away from him. He telegraphed to Washington that I was in full retreat and he was preparing to follow, while we, thinking he was trying to escape, were making arrangements for moving by our left across Bull Run, so as to get over on the Little River pike and move down parallel to his lines and try to interpose between him and Washington. We had about completed our arrangements, and took it for granted that Pope would move out that night by the Warrenton and Centreville pike, and that we could move parallel with him along the Little River pike. General Lee was still anxious to give Pope battle on Manassas plains, but had given up the idea of attacking him in his strong position.

COLONEL W. S. H. BAYLOR, C. S. A., COMMANDING THE "STONEWALL" BRIGADE; KILLED AUGUST 30, 1862. FROM A PHOTOGRAPH.

Shortly before nine on the 30th, Pope's artillery began to play a little, and not long afterward some of his infantry force was seen in motion. We did not understand that as an offer of battle, but merely as a display to cover his movements to the rear. Later a considerable force moved out and began to attack us on our left, extending and engaging the whole of Jackson's line. Evidently Pope supposed that I was gone, as he was ignoring me entirely. His whole army seemed to surge up against Jackson as if to crush him with an overwhelming mass. At the critical moment I happened to be riding to the front of my line to find a place where I might get in for my share of the battle. I reached a point a few rods in front of my line on the left of the pike where I could plainly see the Federals as they rushed in heavy masses against the obstinate ranks of the Confederate left. It was a grand display of well-organized attack, thoroughly concentrated and operating cleverly. So terrible was the onslaught that Jackson sent to me and begged for reënforcements. About the same time I received an order from General Lee to the same effect. To retire from my advanced position in front of the Federals and get to Jackson would have taken an hour and a half. I had discovered a prominent position that commanded a view of the great struggle, and realizing the opportunity, I quickly ordered out three batteries, making twelve guns. Lieutenant Wm. H. Chapman's Dixie Battery of four guns was the first to report and was placed in position to rake the Federal ranks that seemed determined to break through Jackson's lines. In a moment a heavy fire of shot and shell was being poured into the thick columns of the enemy, and in ten minutes their stubborn masses began to waver and give back. For a moment there was chaos; then order returned and they re-formed, apparently to renew the attack. Meanwhile my other eight pieces reported to me, and from the crest of the little hill the fire of twelve guns cut them down. As the cannon thundered the ranks broke, only to be formed again with dogged determination. A third time the batteries tore the Federals to pieces, and as they fell back under this terrible fire, I sprung everything to the charge. My troops leaped forward with exultant yells, and all along the line we pushed forward. Farther and still farther back we pressed them, until at 10 o'clock at night we had the field; Pope was across Bull Run, and the victorious Confederates lay down on the battle-ground to sleep, while all around were strewn thousands—friend and foe, sleeping the last sleep together.

The next morning the Federals were in a strong position at Centreville. I sent a brigade across Bull Run under General Pryor and occupied a point over there near Centreville. As our troops proceeded to bury their dead, it began to rain, as it had done on the day after the first battle of Manassas. As soon as General Lee could make his preparations, he ordered Jackson to cross Bull Run near Sudley's and turn the position of the Federals occupying Centreville; and the next day, September 1st, I followed him. But the enemy discovered our turning movement, abandoned Centreville, and put out toward Washington. On the evening of September 1st Jackson encountered a part of the Federal force at Ox Hill [or Chantilly; see map, p. 450], and, attacking it, had quite a sharp engagement. I came up just before night and found his men retiring in a good deal of confusion. I asked Jackson what the situation was, and added that his men seemed to be pretty well dispersed. He said, "Yes, but I hope it will prove a victory."

I moved my troops out and occupied the lines where he had been, relieving the few men who were on picket. Just as we reached there General Kearny, a Federal officer, came along looking for his line, that had disappeared. It was raining in the woods, and was so late in the day that a Federal was not easily distinguished from a Confederate. Kearny did not seem to know that he was in the Confederate line, and our troops did not notice that he was a Federal. He began to inquire about some command, and in a moment or so the men saw that he was a Federal officer. At the same moment he realized where he was. He was called upon to surrender, but instead of doing so he wheeled his

VIEW FROM THE HENRY HILL DURING THE ATTACK UPON JACKSON, ABOUT FOUR O'CLOCK, AUGUST 30TH. FROM A SKETCH MADE AT THE TIME.

In the foreground Reynolds's division is marching to the defense of the left flank, where Milroy is fighting on Bald Hill. The stone house on the turnpike is seen in the hollow.— EDITORS.

horse, lay flat on the animal's neck, clapped spurs into his sides and dashed off. Instantly a half-dozen shots rang out, and before he had gone thirty steps he fell. He had been in the army all his life, and we knew him and respected him. His body was sent over the lines under a flag of truce. [See p. 538.] The forces we had been fighting at Ox Hill proved to be the rear-guard covering the retreat of the Federals into Washington.❧ They escaped and we abandoned further pursuit.

The entire Bull Run campaign up to Ox Hill was clever and brilliant. It was conceived entirely by General Lee, who held no such consultation over it as he had done in beginning the Seven Days' campaign. The movement around Pope was not as strong as it should have been. A skillful man could have concentrated against me or Jackson, and given us severe battles in detail. I suppose Pope tried to get too many men against Jackson before attacking. If he had been satisfied with a reasonable force he might have overwhelmed him.

General Pope, sanguine by nature, was not careful enough to keep himself informed about the movements of his enemy. At half-past four on the afternoon of the 29th, he issued an order for Porter to attack Jackson's right, supposing I was at Thoroughfare Gap, when in fact I had been in position since noon, and was anxiously awaiting attack. It has been said that General Stuart, by raising a dust in front of Porter, so impressed him that he did not offer battle. I know nothing of the truth of the story, and never heard of it till after the war. If from any such cause Porter was prevented from attacking me, it was to our disadvantage and delayed our victory twenty-four hours. Porter knew I was in his front. He had captured one or two of my men, which gave him information of my position before he actually saw me. If Porter had not appeared when he did I would have attacked by our right

❧ It appears from the official reports that the Union force encountered by Jackson at Chantilly (Ox Hill) was the advance of Pope's army, which had changed front in anticipation of attack down Little River Pike. (See pp. 492, 493.) — EDITORS.

early in the afternoon. In that event Porter would have had a fine opportunity to take me on the wing and strike a fearful blow. As it was, he was a check upon my move against Pope's main position. If I had advanced upon Pope I would have been under an enfilade fire from Porter's batteries, and if I had advanced upon Porter I would have been under a fire from the batteries on Pope's front as severe as the raking fire from my batteries the next day, when Pope was massed against Jackson. Had Porter attacked me between noon and night on the 29th, I should have received his nine thousand with about double that number. I would have held my line to receive the attack, and as soon as his line developed his strength I would have thrown three brigades forward beyond his extreme left.

MAJOR-GENERAL ROBERT H. MILROY.
FROM A PHOTOGRAPH.

When my line of battle had broken up the attack, as it certainly would have done, these three brigades would have been thrown forward at the flank, and at the same time my main line would have pushed on in the pursuit. The result would have been Porter's retreat in confusion, and I might possibly have reached Pope's left and rear in time to cut him off. When his army was well concentrated on the 30th he was badly cut up and defeated. It does not seem unreasonable to conclude that attack on the 29th in his disjointed condition would have been attended with more disastrous results to him. If I had been attacked under the 4:30 order [see p. 475] the result might have been less damaging, as Porter would have had the night to cover his retreat, and the Federal army could have availed itself of the darkness to screen its move across Bull Run. But Porter's attack at night, if not followed by the back retreat of the army, would have drawn me around the Federal left and put me in a position for striking the next day.

Colonel Charles Marshall, of General Lee's staff, in his evidence before the Fitz John Porter Board, puts my forces on the 29th at 30,000. It is difficult to see how Porter with 9000 men was to march over 30,000 of the best soldiers the world ever knew. Any move that would have precipitated battle would have been to our advantage, as we were ready at all points and waiting for an opportunity to fight. The situation will be better understood when we reflect that the armies were too evenly balanced to admit mistakes on either side. I was waiting for an opportunity to get into the Federal lines close upon the heels of their own troops. The opportunity came on the 30th, but the

Federal army was then concentrated; had it come on the 29th I would have been greatly pleased.

It is proper to state that General Lee, upon hearing my guns on the 30th, sent me word that if I had anything better than reënforcing Jackson to pursue it, and soon afterward rode forward and joined me. Jackson did not respond with spirit to my move, so my men were subjected to a severe artillery fire from batteries in front of him. General Lee, seeing this, renewed his orders for Jackson to press on to the front. The fire still continued severe, however, and General Lee, who remained with me, was greatly exposed to it. As we could not persuade him to drop back behind it, I finally induced him to ride into a ravine which threw a traverse between us and the fire, which was more annoying than fire from the front.

On the 31st we were engaged in caring for our wounded and cleaning up the battle-field. General Lee was quite satisfied with the results of the campaign, though he had very little to say. He was not given to expressions of pride. Under all circumstances he was a moderate talker, and in everything was unassuming. His headquarters were exceedingly simple. He had his tents of the same kind as the other officers—perhaps a few more, to accommodate his larger staff. He made no display of position or rank. Only when he was specially engaged could a sentinel be seen at the door of his tent. On the march he usually had his headquarters near mine.

COLONEL FLETCHER WEBSTER.
FROM A PHOTOGRAPH.

Colonel Webster (son of Daniel Webster) commanded the 12th Massachusetts Volunteers (Ricketts's division) and was mortally wounded August 30th, in the defense of Bald Hill [see map, p. 482].

I was graduated with Pope at West Point. He was a handsome, dashing fellow, and a splendid cavalryman, sitting his horse beautifully. I think he stood at the head for riding. He did not apply himself to his books very closely. He studied about as much as I did, but knew his lessons better. We were graduated in 1842, but Pope saw little of active service till the opening of the Civil War. When he assumed command of the Army of Virginia he was in the prime of life, less than forty years old, and had lost little if any of the dash and grace of his youth. D. H. Hill, Lafayette McLaws, Mansfield Lovell, Gustavus W. Smith, R. H. Anderson, A. P. Stewart, and Earl Van Dorn were among the Confederate commanders who were graduated in the same class with me. Of the Federal commanders, there were of that class—besides Pope—Generals John Newton, W. S. Rosecrans, George Sykes, Abner Doubleday, and others less prominent. Stonewall Jackson came on four years after my class. General Lee had preceded us about fourteen years. General Ewell, who was hurt in this battle, was in the same class with Tecumseh Sherman and George H. Thomas. A truer soldier and nobler spirit than Ewell never drew sword.

"Jeb" Stuart was a very daring fellow and the best cavalryman America ever produced. At the Second Manassas, soon after we heard of the advance of McDowell and Porter, Stuart came up and made a report to General Lee. When he had done so General Lee said he had no orders at that moment, but he requested Stuart to wait awhile. Thereupon Stuart turned round in his tracks, lay down on the ground, put a stone under his head and instantly fell asleep. General Lee rode away and in an hour returned. Stuart was still sleeping. Lee asked for him, and Stuart sprang to his feet and said, "Here I am, General."

General Lee replied, "I want you to send a message to your troops over on the left to send a few more cavalry over to the right."

"I would better go myself," said Stuart, and with that he swung himself into the saddle and rode off at a rapid gallop, singing as loud as he could, 'Jine the cavalry.'"

General Toombs, our Georgia fire-eater, was given to criticising pretty severely all the officers of the regular army who had joined their fortunes with those of the Confederacy. He was hot-blooded and impatient, and chafed at the delays of the commanders in their preparations for battle. His general idea was that the troops went out to fight, and he thought they should be

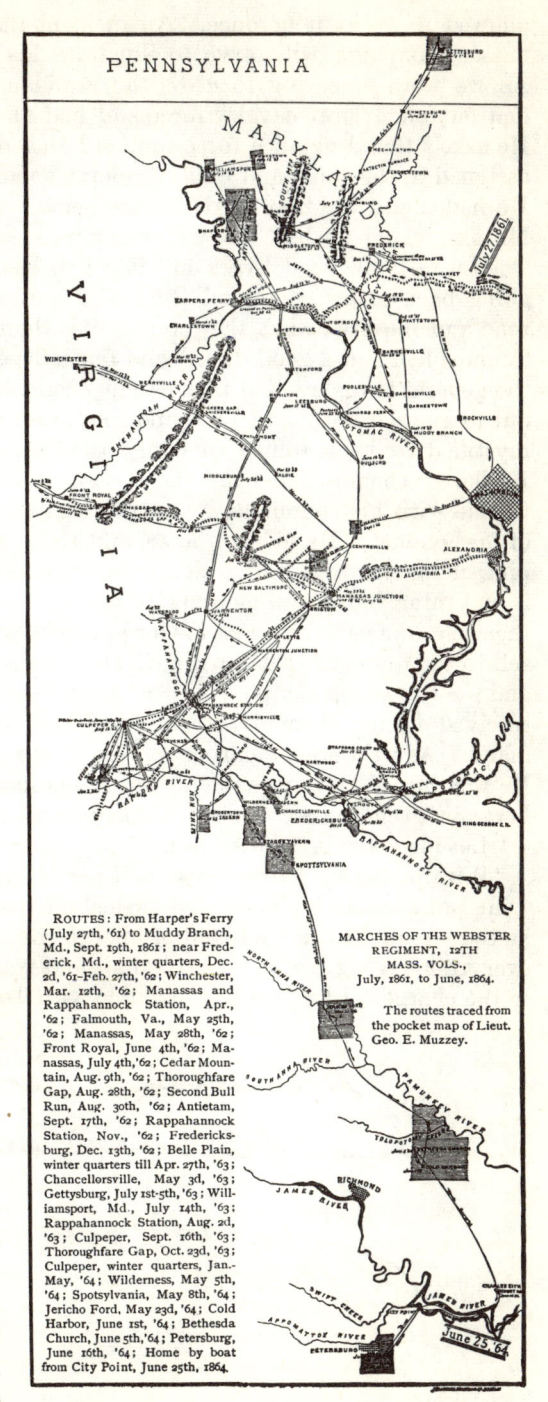

ROUTES: From Harper's Ferry (July 27th, '61) to Muddy Branch, Md., Sept. 19th, 1861; near Frederick, Md., winter quarters, Dec. 2d, '61-Feb. 27th, '62; Winchester, Mar. 12th, '62; Manassas and Rappahannock Station, Apr., '62; Falmouth, Va., May 25th, '62; Manassas, May 28th, '62; Front Royal, June 4th, '62; Manassas, July 4th,'62; Cedar Mountain, Aug. 9th, '62; Thoroughfare Gap, Aug. 28th, '62; Second Bull Run, Aug. 30th, '62; Antietam, Sept. 17th, '62; Rappahannock Station, Nov., '62; Fredericksburg, Dec. 13th, '62; Belle Plain, winter quarters till Apr. 27th, '63; Chancellorsville, May 3d, '63; Gettysburg, July 1st-5th, '63; Williamsport, Md., July 14th, '63; Rappahannock Station, Aug. 2d, '63; Culpeper, Sept. 16th, '63; Thoroughfare Gap, Oct. 23d, '63; Culpeper, winter quarters, Jan.-May, '64; Wilderness, May 5th, '64; Spotsylvania, May 8th, '64; Jericho Ford, May 23d, '64; Cold Harbor, June 1st, '64; Bethesda Church, June 5th,'64; Petersburg, June 16th, '64; Home by boat from City Point, June 25th, 1864.

MARCHES OF THE WEBSTER REGIMENT, 12TH MASS. VOLS., July, 1861, to June, 1864.

The routes traced from the pocket map of Lieut. Geo. E. Muzzey.

allowed to go at it at once. An incident that occurred in the second Manassas campaign will serve to illustrate his characteristic hot-headedness. As we were preparing to cross the Rapidan, Stuart sent me word that he had cut off a large cavalry force and had all the fords guarded except one. He asked that I detail a force to guard that point of escape. The work was assigned to the command under General Toombs, who was absent at the time. He had met a kindred spirit in the person of a wealthy Virginian named Morton, whom he had known in Congress, and was out dining with him. They were both good livers and loved to have their friends with them. In going back to his command General Toombs came upon his troops on the road and inquired what they were doing there. The explanation was made. Toombs had had a good dinner and felt independent. He said he would give the general to understand that he must consult him before sending his troops out to guard a ford, and thereupon he ordered them back to camp. As the mystified troops marched solemnly back, the matter was reported to me and I ordered Toombs under arrest. As we marched against Pope I allowed him to ride with his command, expecting that he would make some explanation of his conduct. He did not do so, and the next I heard of him he was stopping along the route and making stump-speeches to the troops and referring in anything but complimentary terms to the commander of his division. I then sent him back in arrest to Gordonsville, with instructions to confine himself to the limits of that town until further orders. He obeyed the command and went to Gordonsville. Just as I was leaving the Rappahannock, having received a long letter of apology from him, I directed him to join his command. As we were preparing for the charge at Manassas, Toombs arrived. He was riding rapidly, with his hat in his hand, and was very much excited. I was just sending a courier to his command with a dispatch.

"Let me carry it!" he exclaimed.

"With pleasure," I responded, and handed him the paper.

He put spurs to his horse and dashed off, accompanied by a courier. When he rode up and took command of his brigade there was wild enthusiasm, and, everything being ready, an exultant shout was sent up, and the men sprang to the charge. I had no more trouble with Toombs.

*We were ever afterwards warm personal friends*

*James Longstreet.*

## THE TIME OF LONGSTREET'S ARRIVAL AT GROVETON.

D. M. PERRY, sergeant in Company E, 76th New York (of Doubleday's brigade, King's division, McDowell's corps), wrote to the editors in 1886 to say that he was wounded in the attack made on the flank of King's division as it was passing Jackson's front on the evening of August 28th, was left on the field, was taken prisoner, hobbled off the next morning, and again fell into the hands of the enemy, Hood's men, of Longstreet's corps. By an ingenious device he managed to retain possession of his watch. He says:

"I awoke at 7 A. M., August 29th, by the Warrenton Pike, near Douglass's woods. A few yards away, under the trees, were several wounded comrades. . . . I made use of a broken musket as a crutch, and was well on my way to the shelter of the trees, when some one called out: 'Throw down that gun.' It was not until the order had been repeated that I was aware it was addressed to me. Looking round, I saw a company of the enemy's cavalry approaching. I dropped the gun, and they rode up and claimed us as prisoners.

"A few of the Confederates remained with us nearly two hours, and were then compelled to retire before Schenck's skirmishers, who passed through the woods, and remained west of us, possibly thirty minutes, when they in turn retired whence they came, followed by those of the enemy, with whom they exchanged a few shots. The enemy's skirmishers passed down the pike and through the field south of it, followed by the 2d Mississippi, of Hood's division, which halted a few yards east of us. The enemy now began to arrive in force, and occupied the woods. Hood's troops remained here from 11 A. M. until nearly sundown, when they went forward and engaged our troops under Hatch south-east of Groveton.

"This action between Hood and Hatch at sunset, August 29th, was fought east, rather than west of Groveton, as laid down on the map [p. 473], which would have been only a few yards from us, and within full view. The battle took place, I should think, at least a mile east of Douglass's woods. Participants in that action, who visited the field with me in October, 1883, were positive regarding the locality of the fight.

"My recollection of the time of Hood's arrival is concurred in by fellow-prisoners with whom I have recently corresponded. They say, '10 A. M., and the woods were full of the enemy's troops at 11 o'clock.'

"General Lee's headquarters during the 29th and 30th were on the elevation between Pageland lane and Meadowville lane [see p. 473], a few hundred yards west of us. When he moved on the 31st, the band stopped and played 'Dixie' for us in good old Southern style."

William R. Houghton, attorney-at-law, of Hayneville, Alabama, writes to the editors as follows:

"I belonged to Toombs's brigade of D. R. Jones's division, and we were ready to march from the eastern end of Thoroughfare Gap at daylight on the morning of the 29th of August, but other troops filing past occupied the road, so that we did not move until a little after sunrise. We moved at a quick pace, without halting, until we filed to the right of the road near Groveton. My recollection of the distance we marched is that it was eight or nine miles. At the time of our arrival some of Longstreet's troops who had preceded us were formed in two lines fronting toward Centreville, while Jones's division was deployed, facing more toward Manassas Station. I do not know the exact time of our arrival, but it could not have been later than 11 o'clock. My recollection is that it was earlier than the hour named, and that Jones's whole division, in addition to the two lines of men who had preceded us, was in position on very favorable ground before 11 o'clock in the day, and between Porter's corps and Jackson's right flank. Before Porter could have attacked Jackson's right, it would have been necessary for him to remove or disperse this force, which must have been much larger than — if not double — his own. I volunteered for skirmish duty, and we remained in this position all the remainder of that day, and until about 4 o'clock in the afternoon of the 30th of August, at which time we advanced against the enemy, whose line was then at the Chinn house. I feel perfectly assured that we — that is, D. R. Jones's division of several thousand men — were in front of Porter all the day, 29th of August, and that General Pope is utterly mistaken when he says we were not."

General E. M. Law, then colonel of the 4th Alabama Regiment, commanding Whiting's brigade of Hood's division, has written as follows in the Philadelphia "Weekly Press":

"The true story of the forcing of Thoroughfare Gap has never been fully told. Bare allusions were made in some of the official reports to the fact that Hood's division was sent over the mountain by a trail north of the pass, and I have seen it stated that Hood was guided by a wood-chopper, who was familiar with the mountain. The facts are these: My brigade was leading the division when it reached the mountain. There I met General Hood, coming from the direction of the gap. He informed me that it was held on the other side in strong force by the enemy, and that Jones's division was unable to force it. He was accompanied by a man living in the vicinity, who, he said, would guide me by a trail across the mountain, a short distance above the gap. His own brigade was to follow mine. The head of my column was at once turned to the left, and, striking a slight trail, commenced the ascent. I had not gone half-way up the side of the mountain when my guide either missed the trail or it ran out. At any rate, he seemed to know as little as I did, and told me he could guide me no farther. Letting him go, I moved on through the tangled woods and huge rocks until the crest was reached. Here we were confronted by a natural wall of rock, which seemed impassable. Men were sent out on both sides to search for some opening through which we might pass, and a crevice was soon found several feet above our level, where the men could get through one at a time, the first one being lifted up by those behind, and each man as he got up lending a helping hand to the next. As I stood on the crest and heard the fighting in the gap below and the distant thundering of Jackson's battle at Manassas, I felt that the sound of each gun was a call for help, and the progress of the men, one by one, across the rocky barrier seemed painfully slow. In fact, they got through in an almost incredibly short time. As soon as the leading regiment was over, a skirmish line was pushed down the mountain, which on this side sloped gently, and presented few obstacles except a small ravine and stream which issued from the gap itself. The Federal batteries at the mouth of the gap soon came in sight. They were firing steadily but leisurely, and seemed as if they were there to stay. My whole brigade were soon over, the skirmishers in the meantime pressing forward upon the flank of the batteries, which were less than half a mile off. As they emerged into the open ground at the foot of the mountain and engaged the Federal skirmishers on the ravine already mentioned, there was a commotion among the batteries, which limbered up and rapidly moved off.

"It was now nearly dark. My skirmishers were pressing steadily forward, followed by the main line, when I received an order from a staff-officer of General Hood directing me to return at once to the gap by the way I had come — that the enemy was retiring. This was plain enough, but of what had caused him to retire Hood was at that time entirely ignorant. I remonstrated against the order, but was told that it was peremptory. I therefore had no choice but to move back, and march

527

two miles and a half in the night to reach a point less than half a mile from where I had started. We passed through the gap and camped that night on the ground that Ricketts's troops had held in the afternoon. The second battle of Bull Run was practically decided at Thoroughfare Gap. Had McDowell's whole corps been assigned to the duty of keeping Longstreet on the west side of the Bull Run Mountains, it could, properly handled, have kept him there long enough to enable General Pope to crush Jackson with the other forces at his disposal.

"At sunrise the next morning we were on the march toward Manassas, Hood's division leading. A short delay was caused near Gainesville by the passage of a portion of Stuart's cavalry from left to right across our line of march; but before 10 o'clock the head of the column reached Jackson's battle-field, where heavy artillery firing was then going on. There have been many different statements as to the time of Longstreet's arrival at Manassas on the 29th of August. I am absolutely certain that Hood's division reached there not later than the time above stated. The distance to our camp of the previous night was under eight miles, and we marched steadily from 6 o'clock until we reached the field, with the exception of less than an hour's halt caused by the passage of the cavalry already referred to. At that time, in addition to the artillery firing, heavy skirmishing was in progress along Jackson's line, which was formed on the grading of an unfinished railroad running from Sudley Ford to a point near the Warrenton turnpike in rear (north-west) of Groveton. The line formed an acute angle with the pike, and the right wing was thrown back so as partially to face that road. Federal troops were moving on and to the south of the pike, around Jackson's right, when we arrived. Our division was thrown quickly into line across the road, one brigade on each side, and pressed these troops steadily back until Jackson's flank was cleared, when we took up a line on the ridge west of Groveton, slightly in advance of Jackson's right.

"The other troops of Longstreet's command were now rapidly coming up. Kemper, with three brigades, took position to the right of Hood, and D. R. Jones's division still farther to the right, extending the line a mile and a half south of the turnpike. Evans's brigade came up in rear of Hood, and Wilcox's three brigades were posted in rear of the interval between Longstreet's left and Jackson's right, the interval itself being occupied by Colonel Walton's battalion of Washington Artillery."

Colonel John S. Mosby, C. S. A., said, in 1887, in his lecture on " War Reminiscences":

"The reason that Jackson left Manassas was that Stuart had captured a dispatch showing that Pope was concentrating his army on that point. General Jackson says: 'General Stuart kept me advised of the movements of the enemy.' In a dispatch to Fitz John Porter, on the evening of the 27th, Pope ordered him to be at Bristoe at daylight the next morning to bag Jackson, who was then five miles off. General Pope says that Jackson made a mistake in leaving Manassas before he got there. If Jackson went there to be caught, it was. If Pope had reached the place at daylight he would have found nothing but a rear-guard of Stuart's cavalry. He has censured Porter for not getting there in time to bag Jackson. Pope himself arrived about noon. It happened that the evening before I rode off to a farmer's house to get some supper and slept under a tree in the yard. The next morning I returned to the Junction thinking our army was still there. I found the place deserted and as silent as the cities of the plain. So, if General Pope and Fitz John Porter had come at that time they might have caught me, that is, if their horses were faster than mine. . . . On the evening of the 28th, Longstreet drove Ricketts's division from Thoroughfare, and the head of his column bivouacked within about six miles of Jackson. During the fight I rode with Stuart toward Thoroughfare Gap. As Ricketts was then between him and Longstreet, Stuart sent a dispatch by a trusty messenger urging him [Longstreet] to press on to the support of Jackson."

And in a letter to the editors, referring to the above, Colonel Mosby says:

"You will also see that I make some new points in Fitz John Porter's case. I was a witness against him and was somewhat prejudiced against him by the unwise attacks his friends made on Stuart, and by being a particular friend of Colonel [T. C. H.] Smith, who preferred charges against Porter. You may remember that General Pope in his 'Century' article quotes Stuart's report to convict Porter: both sides have misunderstood it. Stuart is a conclusive witness for Porter. I took nothing in my lecture second-hand."

## MARCHING ON MANASSAS.

### BY W. ROY MASON, MAJOR, C. S. A.

ON the 23d of August, as our brigade (Field's, of Hill's division) was passing through an oak forest several miles from our starting-point in the morning, General Field and his staff riding leisurely at its head, we were hailed by General Fitzhugh Lee, who, with his staff, had alighted on one side of the road. He requested us to dismount, as he had something to show us. He then slipped behind a big oak-tree, and, in a moment or two, emerged dressed in the long blue cloak of a Federal general that reached nearly down to his feet, and wearing a Federal general's hat with its big plume. This masquerade was accompanied by a burst of jolly laughter from him that might have been heard for a hundred yards. We inquired as to what this meant, and he told us that the night before he had made a raid upon Pope's headquarters, near Catlett's Station, with orders to capture him. He had surrounded his tent, but upon going in had found only the supper-table spread there, and near it a quartermaster [Major Charles N. Goulding] and one or two minor staff-officers, whom he took greatly by surprise.

Pope's cloak and hat were in the tent, and he was told that the general had taken them off on account of the heat, and had walked down through the woods to visit the headquarters of some other general,—where, they did not know. Being pressed for time, and anxious to retreat from a position that might soon become a dilemma, General Fitz Lee requested the quartermaster to open the military chest of his chief, which was found to contain (to the best of my recollection) $350,000 in greenbacks, after which, mounting the Federal officers behind three of his men, he prepared to go.☆ He did not forget to take the supper from the table, however, or the uniform coat and hat from the chair.

☆ General Stuart reports that Fitzhugh Lee's command "charged the camp, capturing a large number of prisoners, particularly officers, and securing public property to a fabulous amount." Pope's uniform, his horses and equipments and money-chests were included in the enumeration of captures.— EDITORS.

Proceeding on our way, when we reached Manassas Plains on the morning of the 27th, a mile or a mile and a half from the Junction, our brigade in the van of Jackson's corps,—a staff-officer of General Fitz Lee's,—who had preceded us again after our late encounter,—rode back to explain the new situation.

He said that Fitz Lee had reached Manassas Junction at daybreak and made his appearance before the enemy. General George W. Taylor, of the U. S. army, commanding a brigade of Franklin's division advancing from Alexandria for the protection of the stores at Manassas Junction, supposing that Lee was making a mere cavalry reconnoissance, and not aware of the Confederate forces between General Pope and himself, had demanded Fitz Lee's unconditional surrender, adding that, as Pope was in the rear and his retreat was entirely cut off, there was no alternative. Lee returned him a facetious answer, requesting an hour to consider the question, supposing by that time that General Jackson would be up with him.

When we appeared from the woods which had concealed the infantry, General Taylor, still considering, when he saw us, that we were only a brigade of infantry that supported Lee's cavalry, advanced toward us in three lines of battle. We brought our batteries, four in number, to bear, the shot and shell from which began to plow through their ranks before we opened on them with our infantry. They closed up the gaps and marched toward us in the most perfect line of battle that I had seen during the war, and it was only when General Jackson's corps enveloped them front and flanks that they broke. General Taylor was mortally wounded, almost in the first onset, and his men were nearly all captured, or rendered *hors de combat*, as we chased them toward Washington for many miles.

That evening we took possession of the enormous commissary and quartermaster stores of the enemy.

The buildings that sheltered them were sheds reaching, as well as my memory serves me, for many hundred yards, and containing everything necessary to the equipment of an army, but, having only ambulances with us, we could carry away nothing but medical supplies, which we found in abundance. The first order that General Jackson issued was to knock out the heads of hundreds of barrels of whisky, wine, brandy, etc., intended for the army. I shall never forget the scene when this was done. Streams of spirits ran like water through the sands of Manassas, and the soldiers on hands and knees drank it greedily from the ground as it ran.

General C. W. Field and staff took possession of the Federal headquarters. When we reached them, we found spread upon the table, untouched, a breakfast of cold chicken, lamb, and biscuit, and coffee that by this time, had also grown cold. It had not been spread for us, but — "*Telle est la fortune de la guerre.*" There were also a barrel of cut sugar, a sack of Java coffee, and similar luxuries. There I found for the first time a bed with feather pillows and bolster, upon which I at once threw myself, begging to be allowed to rest, if but for ten minutes.

In a short time General A. P. Hill sent us an order to burn all the quartermaster and commissary stores with all the buildings, and requested me to superintend the execution of the order. It was with the greatest pain that I complied with this order, as there were so many things that we of the South absolutely required; but we had no wagons to transfer them. It must be remembered that we were within twenty miles of Washington, with Pope's enormous army between us and Longstreet's corps, which we had left at the Fauquier White Sulphur Springs.

Before I executed my order in burning the commissary and quartermaster stores, however, I took the bolster-case from the headquarters tent, filled it with cut sugar, and tied it at one end, and filled the pillow-case with Java coffee, and succeeded in strapping both behind my horse, for which small act of providence I was amply praised by General Field. I had hoped to get an ambulance to carry these, but was unfortunate enough to miss it.

As I before remarked, the army was far from being happy about its position, of which we knew the really critical nature, and just below us, a few miles over the plains, we could hear a terrific artillery fire. I became uneasy as it continued, and seeing General Jackson, who stood in the porch of one of the commissary depots, I proposed to General Field to let me go over and ask him if General Longstreet had passed through Thoroughfare Gap. Through this he must necessarily pass to reach us, and it was known to have been held by the enemy, and was, besides, a sort of second Pass of Thermopylæ in its difficulties. When I made this proposition to General Field, who was an old army officer, he replied promptly: "No, sir,—you cannot carry any such message from me to General Jackson."

"Well, Field, then I am going over to ask on my own account," I said.

"Then let it be distinctly understood"—was the answer—"that you don't go officially."

Walking over to where General Jackson stood, and saluting him, I remarked: "General, we are all of us desperately uneasy about Longstreet and the situation, and I have come over on my own account to ask the question: Has Longstreet passed Thoroughfare Gap successfully?" With a smile General Jackson replied: "Go back to your command, and say, 'Longstreet is through, and we are going to whip in the next battle.'"

# JACKSON'S "FOOT-CAVALRY" AT THE SECOND BULL RUN.

### BY ALLEN C. REDWOOD, 55TH VIRGINIA REGIMENT, C. S. A.

IN the operations of 1862, in Northern Virginia, the men of Jackson's corps have always claimed a peculiar proprietorship. The reorganization of the disrupted forces of Banks, Frémont, and McDowell under a new head seemed a direct challenge to the soldiers who had made the Valley Campaign, and the proclamation of General Pope betokened to the "foot-cavalry" an infringement of their specialty, demanding emphatic rebuke. Some remnant of the old *esprit de corps* yet survives, and prompts this narrative.

After the check to Pope's advance at Cedar Mountain, on the 9th of August, and while we awaited the arrival of Longstreet's troops, A. P. Hill's division rested in camp at Crenshaw's farm. Our brigade (Field's) was rather a new one in organization and experience, most of us having "smelt powder" for the first time in the Seven Days before Richmond. We reached the field at Cedar Mountain too late to be more than slightly engaged, but on the 10th and 11th covered the leisurely retreat to Orange Court House without molestation. When, about a week later, Pope began to retreat in the direction of the Rappahannock, we did some sharp marching through Stevensburg and Brandy Station, but did not come up with him until he was over the river. While our artillery was dueling with him across the stream, I passed the time with my head in the scant shade of a sassafras bush by the roadside, with a chill and fever brought from the Chickahominy lowgrounds.

For the next few days there was skirmishing at the fords, we moving up the south bank of the river, the enemy confronting us on the opposite side. The weather was very sultry, and the troops were much weakened by it,

---

↓ The following is the full text of General Pope's address to his army:

"HEADQUARTERS ARMY OF VIRGINIA, WASHINGTON, D. C., July 14th, 1862.— TO THE OFFICERS AND SOLDIERS OF THE ARMY OF VIRGINIA: By special assignment of the President of the United States, I have assumed the command of this army. I have spent two weeks in learning your whereabouts, your condition, and your wants, in preparing you for active operations, and in placing you in positions from which you can act promptly and to the purpose. These labors are nearly completed, and I am about to join you in the field.

"Let us understand each other. I have come to you from the West, where we have always seen the backs of our enemies; from an army whose business it has been to seek the adversary, and to beat him when he was found; whose policy has been attack and not defense. In but one instance has the enemy been able to place our Western armies in defensive attitude. I presume that I have been called here to pursue the same system and to lead you against the enemy. It is my purpose to do so, and that speedily. I am sure you long for an opportunity to win the distinction you are capable of achieving. That opportunity I shall endeavor to give you. Meantime I desire you to dismiss from your minds certain phrases, which I am sorry to find so much in vogue amongst you. I hear constantly of 'taking strong positions and holding them,' of 'lines of retreat,' and of 'bases of supplies.' Let us discard such ideas. The strongest position a soldier should desire to occupy is one from which he can most easily advance against the enemy. Let us study the probable lines of retreat of our opponents, and leave our own to take care of themselves. Let us look before us and not behind. Success and glory are in the advance, disaster and shame lurk in the rear. Let us act on this understanding, and it is safe to predict that your banners shall be inscribed with many a glorious deed and that your names will be dear to your countrymen forever.— JNO. POPE, Major-General, Commanding."

EDITORS.

and our rations of unsalted beef, eked out with green corn and unripe apples, formed a diet unsuited to soldiers on the march, and there was much straggling. I fell behind several times, but managed to catch up from day to day. Once some cavalry made a dash across the river at our train; I joined a party who, like myself, were separated from their commands, and we fought the enemy until Trimble's brigade, the rear-guard, came up.

We were then opposite the Warrenton Springs, and were making a great show of crossing, Early's brigade having been thrown over the river where it became smartly engaged. I have since heard that this officer remonstrated more than once at the service required of him, receiving each time in reply a peremptory order from Jackson "to hold his position." He finally retorted: "Oh! well, old Jube can *die* if *that's* what he wants, but tell General Jackson I'll be —— if this position *can* be held!"

The brigade moved off next morning, leaving me in the grip of the ague, which reported promptly for duty, and, thanks to a soaking overnight, got in its work most effectually. The fever did not let go until about sundown, when I made two feeble trips to carry my effects to the porch of a house about one hundred yards distant, where I passed the night without a blanket—mine having been stolen between the trips. I found a better one next morning thrown away in a field, and soon after came up with the command, in bivouac and breakfasting on some beef which had just been issued. Two ribs on a stump were indicated as my share, and I broiled them on the coals and made the first substantial meal I had eaten for forty-eight hours. This was interrupted by artillery fire from beyond the river,

CONFEDERATE CAMP-SERVANT ON THE MARCH.

and as I was taking my place in line, my colonel ordered me to the ambulance to recruit. Here I got a dose of Fowler's solution, "in lieu of quinine," and at the wagon-camp that day I fared better than for a long time before. Meanwhile they were having a hot time down at Waterloo Bridge, which the enemy's engineers were trying to burn, while some companies of sharpshooters under Lieutenant Robert Healy of " ours"—whose rank was no measure of his services or merit—were disputing the attempt. A concentrated fire from the Federal batteries failed to dislodge the plucky riflemen, while our guns were now brought up, and some hard pounding ensued. But at sunset the bridge still stood, and I "spread down" for the night, under the pole of a wagon, fully expecting a serious fight on the morrow.

JACKSON'S TROOPS PILLAGING THE UNION DEPOT OF SUPPLIES AT MANASSAS JUNCTION.

I was roused by a courier's horse stepping on my leg, and found this rude waking meant orders to move. With no idea whither, we pulled out at half-past two in the morning, and for some time traveled by fields and "new cuts" in the woods, following no road, but by the growing dawn evidently keeping up the river. Now Hill's "Light Division" was to earn its name and qualify itself for membership in Jackson's corps. The hot August sun rose, clouds of choking dust enveloped the hurrying column, but on and on the march was pushed without relenting. Knapsacks had been left behind in the wagons, and haversacks were empty by noon; for the unsalted beef spoiled and was thrown away, and the column subsisted itself, without process of commissariat, upon green corn and apples from the fields and orchards along the route, devoured while marching; for there were no stated meal-times, and no systematic halts for rest. I recall a sumptuous banquet of "middling" bacon and "collards" which I was fortunate enough to obtain during the delay at Hinson's Mill where we forded the river, and the still more dainty fare of tea and biscuits, the bounty of some good maiden ladies at "The Plains," where our ambulance stopped some hours to repair a broken axle—the only episodes of the march which now stand out with distinctness. It was far on in the night when the column stopped, and the weary men dropped beside their stacked muskets and were instantly asleep, without so much as unrolling a blanket. A few hours of much-needed repose, and they were shaken up again long before "crack of day," and limped on in the darkness only half-awake. There was no mood for speech, nor breath to spare if there had been — only the shuffling tramp of the marching feet, the steady rumbling of wheels, the creak and rattle and clank of harness and accouterment, with an occasional order, uttered under the breath and always the same: "Close up! close up, men!"

All this time we had the vaguest notions as to our objective: at first we had expected to strike the enemy's flank, but as the march prolonged itself, a theory obtained that we were going to the Valley. But we threaded Thoroughfare Gap, heading eastward, and in the morning of the third day (August 27th) struck a railroad running north and south — Pope's "line of communication and supply." Manassas was ours.

What a prize it was! Here were long warehouses full of stores; cars loaded with boxes of new clothing *en route* to General Pope, but destined to adorn the "backs of his enemies"; camps, sutlers' shops — "no eating up" of good things. In view of the abundance, it was not an easy matter to determine what we should eat and drink and wherewithal we should be clothed; one was limited in his choice to only so much as he could personally transport, and the one thing needful in each individual case was not always readily found. However, as the day wore on, an equitable distribution of our wealth was effected by barter, upon a crude and irregular tariff in which the rule of supply and demand was somewhat complicated by fluctuating estimates of the imminence of marching orders. A mounted man would offer large odds in shirts or blankets for a pair of spurs or a bridle; and while in anxious quest of a pair of shoes I fell heir to a case of cavalry half-boots, which I would gladly have exchanged for the object of my search. For a change of underclothing and a pot of French mustard I owe grateful thanks to the major of the 12th Pennsylvania Cavalry, with regrets that I could not use his library. Whisky was, of course, at a high premium, but a keg of "lager" — a drink less popular then than now — went begging in our company.

But our brief holiday was drawing to a close, for by this time General Pope had some inkling of the disaster which lurked in his rear. When, some time after dark, having set fire to the remnant of the stores, we took the road to Centreville, our mystification as to Jackson's plans was complete. Could he actually be moving on Washington with his small force, or was he only seeking escape to the mountains? The glare of our big bonfire lighted up the country for miles, and was just dying out when we reached Centreville. The corduroy road had been full of pitfalls and stumbling-blocks, to some one of which our cracked axle had succumbed before we crossed Bull Run, and being on ahead, I did not know of the casualty until it was too late to save my personal belongings involved in the wreck. Thus suddenly reduced from affluence to poverty, just as the gray dawn revealed the features of the forlorn little hamlet, typical of this war-harried region, I had a distinct sense of being a long way from home. The night's march had seemed to put the

STARKE'S BRIGADE FIGHTING WITH STONES NEAR THE "DEEP CUT." (SEE MAP, P. 509, AND NOTE, P. 536.)

climax to the endurance of the jaded troops. Such specters of men they were,— gaunt-cheeked and hollow-eyed, hair, beard, clothing, and accouterments covered with dust,— only their faces and hands, where mingled soil and sweat streaked and crusted the skin, showing any departure from the whitey-gray uniformity. The ranks were sadly thinned, too, by the stupendous work of the previous week. Our regiment, which had begun the campaign 1015 strong and had carried into action at Richmond 620, counted off that Thursday morning (August 28th) just 82 muskets! Such were the troops about to deliver battle on the already historic field of Manassas.

We were soon on the road again, heading west; we crossed Stone Bridge, and a short distance beyond, our ambulances halted, the brigade having entered some woods on the right of the road ahead,— going into camp, I thought. This pleasing delusion was soon dispelled by artillery firing in front, and our train was moved off through the fields to the right, out of range, and was parked near Sudley Church. Everything pointed to a battle next day; the customary hospital preparations were made, but few, if any, wounded came in that night, and I slept soundly, a thing to be grateful for. My bedfellow and I had decided to report for duty in the morning, knowing that every musket would be needed. I had picked up a good "Enfield" with the proper trappings, on the road from Centreville, to replace my own left in the abandoned ambulance; and having broken my chills, and gained strength from marching unencumbered, was fit for service—as much so as were the rest at least.

Friday morning early, we started in what we supposed to be the right direction, guided by the firing, which more and more betokened that the fight was on. Once we stopped for a few moments at a field-hospital to make inquiries, and were informed that our brigade was farther along to the right. General Ewell, who had lost his leg the evening before, was carried by on a stretcher while we were there. Very soon we heard sharp musketry over a low ridge which we had been skirting, and almost immediately we became involved with stragglers from that direction—Georgians, I think they were. It looked as if a whole line was giving way, and we hurried on to gain our own colors before it should grow too hot. The proverbial effect of bad company was soon apparent. We were halted by a Louisiana major, who was trying to rally these fragments upon his own command. My companion took the short cut out of the scrape by showing his "sick-permit," and was allowed to pass; mine, alas! had been left in my cartridge-box with my other belongings in that unlucky ambulance. The major was courteous but firm; he listened to my story with more attention than I could have expected, but attached my person all the same. "Better stay with us, my boy, and if you do your duty I'll make it right with your company officers when the fight's over. They won't find fault with you when they know you've been in with the 'Pelicans,'" he added, as he assigned me to company "F."

The command was as unlike my own as it was possible to conceive. Such a congress of nations only the cosmopolitan Crescent City could have sent forth, and the tongues of Babel seemed resurrected in its speech; English, German, French, and Spanish, all were represented, to say nothing of Doric brogue and local "gumbo." There was, moreover, a vehemence of utterance and gesture curiously at variance with the reticence of our Virginians. In point of fact, we burned little powder that day, and my promised distinction as a "Pelican" *pro tem.* was cheaply earned. The battalion did a good deal of counter-marching, and some skirmishing, but most of the time we were acting as support to a section of Cutshaw's battery. The tedium of this last service my companions relieved by games of "seven up," with a greasy, well-thumbed deck, and in smoking cigarettes, rolled with great dexterity, between the deals. Once, when a detail was ordered to go some distance under fire to fill the canteens of the company, a hand was dealt to determine who should go, and the decision was accepted by the loser without demur. Our numerous shifts of position completely confused what vague ideas I had of the situation, but we must have been near our extreme left at Sudley Church, and never very far from my own brigade, which was warmly engaged that day and the day following.┘ Toward evening we were again within sight of Sudley Church.

┘ A recent letter from Lieutenant Robert Healy, of the writer's regiment, the 55th Virginia, says: "Thursday night we slept on our arms; Friday, we charged a battery and took it, and in the evening got considerably worsted in an engagement with the enemy in a field on the left. Saturday morning we lay in reserve in the edge of the woods [see Brockenbrough's brigade on the map, p. 509]; about half-past two o'clock we received urgent orders to reënforce a portion of our line in the center, which was about to give way. We proceeded at double-quick to a point in the woods

I could see the light of fires among the trees, as if cooking for the wounded was going on, and the idea occurred to me that there I could easily learn the exact position of my proper command. Once clear of my major and his polyglot "Pelicans," the rest would be plain sailing.

My flank movement was easily effected, and I suddenly found myself the *most* private soldier on that field; there seemed to be nobody else anywhere near. I passed a farm-house, which seemed to have been used as a hospital, and where I picked up a Zouave fez. Some cavalrymen were there, one of whom advised "me not to go down there," but as he gave no special reason and did not urge his views, I paid no heed to him, but went on my way down a long barren slope, ending in a small water-course at the bottom, beyond which the ground rose abruptly and was covered by small growth. The deepening twilight and strange solitude about me, with a remembrance of what had happened a year ago on this same ground, made me feel uncomfortably lonely. By this time I was close to the stream, and while noting the lay of the land on the opposite bank with regard to choice of a crossing-place, I became aware of a man observing me from the end of the cut above. I could not distinguish the color of his uniform, but the crown of his hat tapered suspiciously, I thought, and instinctively I dropped the butt of my rifle to the ground and reached behind me for a cartridge. "Come here!" he called;—his accent was worse than his hat. "Who are you?" I responded as I executed the movement of "tear cartridge." He laughed and then invited me to "come and see." Meanwhile I was trying to draw my rammer, but this operation was arrested by the dry click of several gunlocks, and I found myself covered by half a dozen rifles, and my friend of the steeple-crown, with less urbanity in his intonation, called out to me to "drop that." In our brief intercourse he had acquired a curious influence over me. I did so.

My captors were of Kearny's division, on picket. They told me they thought I was deserting until they saw me try to load. I could not account for their being where they were, and when they informed me that they had Jackson surrounded and that he must surrender next day, though I openly scouted the notion, I must own the weight of evidence seemed to be with them. The discussion of this and kindred topics was continued until a late hour that night with the sergeant of the guard at Kearny's headquarters, where I supped in unwonted luxury on hard-tack and "genuine" coffee, the sergeant explaining that the fare was no better because of our destruction of their supplies at the Junction. Kearny's orderly gave me a blanket, and so I passed the night. We were astir early in the morning (August 30th), and I saw Kearny as he

---

behind the deep cut, where we formed line. . . . We came in sight of the enemy when we had advanced a few yards, and were saluted with cannon. We pushed on, however, to the old railroad cut, in which most of Jackson's troops lay. The troops occupying this place had expended their ammunition and were defending themselves with rocks . . . which seemed to have been picked or blasted out of the bed of the railroad, chips and slivers of stone which many were collecting and others were throwing. Of course, such a defense would have been overcome in a very short time, but our arrival seemed to be almost simultaneous with that of the enemy. We had ammunition (twenty rounds to the man) and we attacked the enemy and drove them headlong down the hill, across the valley, and over the hill into the woods, when we were recalled by General Starke."—A. C. R.

## JACKSON'S "FOOT-CAVALRY" AT THE SECOND BULL RUN. 537

DEATH OF GENERAL PHILIP KEARNY, SEPTEMBER 1, 1862.

passed with his staff to the front,— a spare, erect, military figure, looking every inch the fighter he was. He fell three days later, killed by some of my own brigade.‡

‡ Captain James H. Haynes, 55th Virginia regiment, says he was on the skirmish line at Chantilly, on the edge of a brushy place with a clearing in front. It was raining heavily and growing dark when Kearny rode suddenly upon the line, and asked what troops they were. Seeing his mistake,

Near the Stone Bridge I found about 500 other prisoners, mostly stragglers picked up along the line of our march. Here my polite provost-sergeant turned me over to other guardians, and after drawing rations, hard-tack, coffee, and sugar, we took the road to Centreville. That thoroughfare was thronged with troops, trains, and batteries, and we had to stand a good deal of chaff on the way, at our forlorn appearance. We were a motley crowd enough, certainly, and it *did* look as if our friends in blue were having their return innings. More than once that day as I thought of the thin line I had left, I wondered how the boys were doing, for disturbing rumors came to us as we lay in a field near Centreville, exchanging rude badinage across the cordon of sentries surrounding us. Other prisoners came in from time to time who brought the same unvarying story, "Jackson hard-pressed—no news of Longstreet yet." So the day wore on. Toward evening there was a noticeable stir in the camps around us, a continual riding to and fro of couriers and orderlies, and now we thought we could hear more distinctly the deep-toned, jarring growl which had interjected itself at intervals all the afternoon through the trivial buzz about us. Watchful of indications, we noted, too, that the drift of wagons and ambulances was *from* the battle-field, and soon orders came for us to take the road in the same direction. The cannonading down the pike was sensibly nearer now, and at times we could catch even the roll of musketry, and once we thought we could distinguish, far off and faint, the prolonged, murmurous sound familiar to our ears as the charging shout of the gray people—but this may have been fancy. All the same, we gave tongue to the cry, and shouts of "Longstreet! Longstreet's at 'em, boys! Hurrah for Longstreet!" went up from our ranks, while the guards trudged beside us in sulky silence.

There is not much more to tell. An all-day march on Sunday through rain and mud brought us to Alexandria, where we were locked up for the night in a cotton-factory. Monday we embarked on a transport steamer, and the next evening were off Fort Monroe, where we got news of Pope's defeat. I was paroled and back in Richmond within ten days of my capture, and then and there learned how completely Jackson had made good the name of "Stonewall" on his baptismal battle-field.

he turned and started across the open ground to escape, but was fired on and killed. His body was brought into the lines and was recognized by General A. P. Hill, who said, sorrowfully, "Poor Kearny! he deserved a better death than this."

The next day General Lee ordered that the body be carried to the Federal lines, and in a note to General Pope he said: " The body of General Philip Kearny was brought from the field last night, and he was reported dead. I send it forward under a flag of truce, thinking the possession of his remains may be a consolation to his family."— A. C. R.

According to General A. P. Hill, Kearny fell in front of Thomas's brigade, but he also states that Brockenbrough's brigade held the skirmish line, and to this Captain Haynes's and Lieutenant Healy's regiment, the 55th Virginia, belonged.—EDITORS.

# THE SIXTH CORPS AT THE SECOND BULL RUN.

## BY WILLIAM B. FRANKLIN, MAJOR-GENERAL, U. S. V.

THE Sixth Corps left Harrison's Landing on the James River on August 16th, 1862, and arrived at Newport News on August 21st. On the 22d and 23d it embarked on transports for Aquia Creek. My impression is that Burnside's corps started first, landing at Aquia Creek; Porter's disembarked at Aquia Creek; Heintzelman's followed, landing at Alexandria; and the Sixth Corps followed Heintzelman's. As soon as I saw the infantry of the corps embarked at Newport News, leaving the chiefs of the quartermaster and subsistence departments and the chief of artillery to superintend the embarkation of the property for which they were responsible, with orders to hasten their departure to the utmost, I preceded the transports, and on Sunday, August 24th, about 2 o'clock, arrived at Aquia Creek, at which point I had orders to disembark and report to General McClellan. The wharves here were so encumbered with the artillery and stores that were already landed for the corps of Burnside and Porter, that McClellan directed me to have my corps landed at Alexandria, and to report upon my arrival to General Halleck. Still preceding the corps, I reported to General Halleck at Washington, arriving there about 4 o'clock P. M. The city was as quiet as though profound peace reigned; no one was at General Halleck's office to whom I could report, and I found him at his house. He told me that he felt under no apprehension about Pope's position, and that he doubted whether it would be necessary for me to go to the front at all; that in any event I could be of no use until my artillery and horses arrived—instancing the fact that Burnside had been much crippled, and had done little good so far, on account of the absence of his artillery. He directed me to go into camp in front of Alexandria, and reorganize the corps as the artillery and transportation reached the camp. The infantry arrived on Monday and Tuesday, the 25th and 26th, but no artillery horses, except sixteen, had arrived on Wednesday night.

The two division commanders and myself were constantly at work during this time, endeavoring to get horses. But we had no success, the answer to our demands always being that the teams then present were absolutely necessary to feed the troops in the forts from day to day, and that this duty was more important under the circumstances than that of providing transportation for artillery. Without transportation the artillery could not be used.

On Wednesday, the 27th, news having arrived that the enemy was at Centreville, Taylor's brigade of Slocum's division was sent there on the cars of the Orange and Alexandria Railroad to reconnoiter. It was received at the railroad bridge over Bull Run by a force of the enemy's artillery and infantry, and lost its gallant commander and many men. The brigade was withdrawn in safety in the face of a large force, four brigades of A. P. Hill's division, Jackson's corps. The order for this movement came from General Halleck. Thursday, the 28th, was employed in organizing such batteries as had arrived, with the horses, which now began to arrive slowly, and in attempting to collect a train for carrying provisions to General Pope's army. Little was accomplished, however. On Friday, the corps was started to the front with orders to communicate with General Pope, and at the same time to guard his communications with Alexandria. On the arrival of the leading division, commanded by General W. F. Smith, at Annandale, ten miles to the front, its commander reported to me that fugitives were constantly coming in, and reported a large force of the enemy near Fairfax Court House, six miles distant. As he had with him only ten rounds of ammunition for each gun, he considered it prudent to await further orders. General McClellan, upon learning this state of things, directed me to stop at Annandale for the night, and proceed the next morning at 6.

During the night more ammunition and provision wagons were collected, numbering about one hundred, and as I was starting in the morning at the designated time I received orders to delay my start until 8:30 A. M., to protect the train so formed. When I arrived at Fairfax Court House I detached a brigade of General Slocum's division and one battery to take position to guard the point where the Little River Turnpike joins the Warrenton pike between Centreville and Alexandria. The detachment of this brigade had an important effect upon the after events of the campaign, as will appear. Proceeding onwards toward Centreville I received, at 1:30 P. M., an order from General McClellan, directing me to join General Pope at once. The corps marched forward through Centreville toward Bull Run about three miles in front of Centreville, without stopping. Going to the front I found General Slocum's division formed across the road, in front of Cub Run, stopping what seemed to be an indiscriminate mass of men, horses, guns and wagons, all going pell-mell to the rear. As General Slocum expressed it, it was as bad as the Bull Run retreat of 1861. Officers of all grades, from brigadier-general down, were in the throng, but none of them exercised any authority. We gathered about three thousand in a yard near by. Presently a force of cavalry appeared to the left and front, about one mile off, and the fugitives, imagining that they were the enemy, ran to the rear as one man;—nothing could stop them.

General W. F. Smith's division was posted in a good position on hills in the vicinity, and shortly afterward Generals Pope and McDowell appeared, and I reported to General Pope. He directed me to return to Centreville, upon which place his army was falling back. The corps remained at Centreville during the 31st of August with the bulk of the army, the enormous trains in the meantime moving toward Washington. On the morning of that day, on my own responsibility, I sent a grand guard, consisting of the 5th Wisconsin infantry under Colonel Amasa Cobb, and a section of artillery, to the Cub Run Bridge, to guard the rear of the army. Large bodies of the enemy appeared in its front, but no attack was made on it. So far as I know, this was the only rear-guard between Pope and the enemy on the 31st of August.

On September 1st, the corps marched to Fairfax Court House with General Pope, and remained there until the evening of the 2d of September, when it moved back to the vicinity of Alexandria.

Colonel (afterward General) Torbert, who commanded the detachment left at Fairfax Court House on August 30th, reports that about 8 o'clock on the night of the 31st the enemy brought three pieces of artillery about three hundred yards from his pickets, and fired upon the trains then crowding the turnpike in his rear, causing great confusion. Torbert drove off the enemy's artillery, reported to General Pope, and on the next morning was reënforced by a brigade and two batteries. It appears from General J. E. B. Stuart's report of his operations that this attack was made by him. Had Colonel Torbert's brigade not been present to defend this very vulnerable point, Stuart's cavalry would easily have been in rear of the army that night; the trains would in all probability have been utterly destroyed, and another great disaster would have occurred. The wisdom of General McClellan's order, which directed me to guard General Pope's communications with Alexandria, was thus demonstrated.

HEINTZELMAN'S HEADQUARTERS AT ALEXANDRIA. FROM A SKETCH MADE SEPTEMBER 3, 1862.

## WASHINGTON UNDER BANKS.

BY RICHARD B. IRWIN, LIEUTENANT-COLONEL AND ASSISTANT ADJUTANT-GENERAL, U. S. V.

"THE 27th and 28th" [of August], writes General F. A. Walker, in his admirable "History of the Second Army Corps," "were almost days of panic in Washington." These words mildly indicate the state into which affairs had fallen at the close of August and the opening of September, 1862, on the heels of General Pope's defeat in the Second Bull Run. Yet Washington was defended by not less than 110,000 men; for, in addition to the army which Pope was bringing back, beaten certainly, but by no means destroyed, there stood before the lines of Washington not less than 40,000 veterans who had not fired a shot in this campaign, and behind the lines 30,000 good men of the garrisons and the reserves of whom at least two-thirds were veterans in discipline, though all were untried in battle.

As General McClellan's staff rode in on the morning of the 2d of September, from their heart-rending exile on the Seminary heights, condemned there to hear in helpless idleness the awful thunder of Manassas and Chantilly, we made our way through the innumerable herd of stragglers,— mingled with an endless stream of wagons and ambulances, urged on by uncontrollable teamsters,—which presently poured into Washington, overflowed it, took possession of its streets and public places, and held high orgie. Disorder reigned unchecked and confusion was everywhere. The clerks in the departments, many of whom had been hurried toward the front to do service as nurses, were now hastily formed into companies and battalions for defense; the Government ordered the arms and ammunition at the arsenal and the money in the Treasury to be shipped to New York, and the banks followed the example; a gun-boat, with steam up, lay in the river off the White House, as if to announce to the army and the inhabitants the impending flight of the Administration. It was at this juncture that the President, on his own responsibility, once more charged General McClellan with the defense of the capital.

The next day, the 3d of September, the President further confided to General Halleck ⸸ the duty of preparing an army to take the field; but since Lee did not wait for this, McClellan could not; even before the President's order reached General Halleck the Confederate army had disappeared from the front of Washington and General McClellan was putting his troops in march to meet it.

On the afternoon of the 7th, 87,000 men were in motion, and General McClellan set out for Rockville to put himself at their head. Almost at the last moment I was directed to remain in charge of the adjutant-general's department at his headquarters in Washington, to issue orders in his name and "to prevent the tail of the army from being cut off," and Lieutenant-Colonel Sawtelle was left in charge of the Quartermaster's Department, also with plenary authority, to see that the transportation and supplies went forward. On the same day, General Banks, who was reported confined to his bed, and unable to join his corps, was assigned to the immediate command of the defenses of Washington during McClellan's absence. The next day, General Banks assumed this command, having first obtained General McClellan's consent to my assignment as Assistant Adjutant-General, at the Headquarters of the Defenses, in addition to my other duties. ☨ I thought then that this was a difficult position for a young captain of twenty-two; I think now that it would have been difficult for a field-marshal of sixty-two; certainly the arrangement could not have lasted an hour, but for the determination of all concerned to make it work, and to be deaf, blind, and dumb to everything not distinctly in front of us.

Everything was at once put in motion to carry out General McClellan's orders, of which the first point was to restore order.

The forces included the Third, Fifth, and Eleventh Army Corps, commanded respectively by Heintzelman, Fitz John Porter, and Sigel, covering the fortified line on the Virginia side and numbering about 47,000 for duty; the garrisons of the works, 15,000; Casey's provisional brigades of newly arriving regiments and the town guards, 11,000,—in all, 73,000,↓ with 120 field-pieces and about 500 heavy guns in position; in brief, nearly one half of McClellan's entire army; a force a fourth or a third larger than Lee's; indeed, to all appearance, the identical command designed for General McClellan himself, before the defense of the capital had made it necessary for him to resume operations in the field by the pursuit of Lee. The improvised staff-officers were at once sent out to establish the picket lines, so broken and disconnected that virtually there were none. The troops were rapidly inspected, and their numbers, positions, and wants ascertained. With the three corps and the organized divisions this was simple enough, since their commanders had them in hand. For a few days the discoveries of scattered detachments were numerous and surprising; some only turned up after a check had been put on the commissary issues, and about ten days later, in the ward Brevet Major-General) George W. Mindil, who had been Kearny's adjutant-general, one of the most gallant and accomplished officers of our (or any) branch of the volunteer service; Lieutenant (now Colonel) G. Norman Lieber, at present Acting Judge Advocate General, and Drake DeKay, from Pope's staff.— R. B. I.

↓ Rapidly augmented by new levies, these forces must have exceeded 80,000 before the dispatch of Porter's corps to Antietam, September 12th. The returns for October 10th shows 79,535; for November 10th 80,989. The lowest point was about 60,000 after Whipple's division left, October 17th. The actual effective strength would, as always, be a fifth or a sixth less.

MAJOR-GENERAL W. F. BARRY, CHIEF-OF-ARTILLERY OF THE DEFENSES OF WASHINGTON, SEPTEMBER 1, 1862, TO MARCH 1, 1864. FROM A PHOTOGRAPH.

⸸ General McClellan seems never to have known of this order.—R. B. I.

☨ At this time General Banks was without a staff-officer. Colonel John S. Clark, A. D. C., Lieutenant-Colonel D. H. Strother, A. D. C. (the genial "Porte Crayon"), and others of his staff joined him presently. General Halleck also sent down many officers, as they happened to report to him for orders, and thus a curious yet very useful staff was soon collected, including several officers who afterward won deserved distinction; among them I recall Captains (afterward Major-General) Wesley Merritt and A. J. Alexander (afterward Brigadier-General) of the Cavalry; Captain (after-

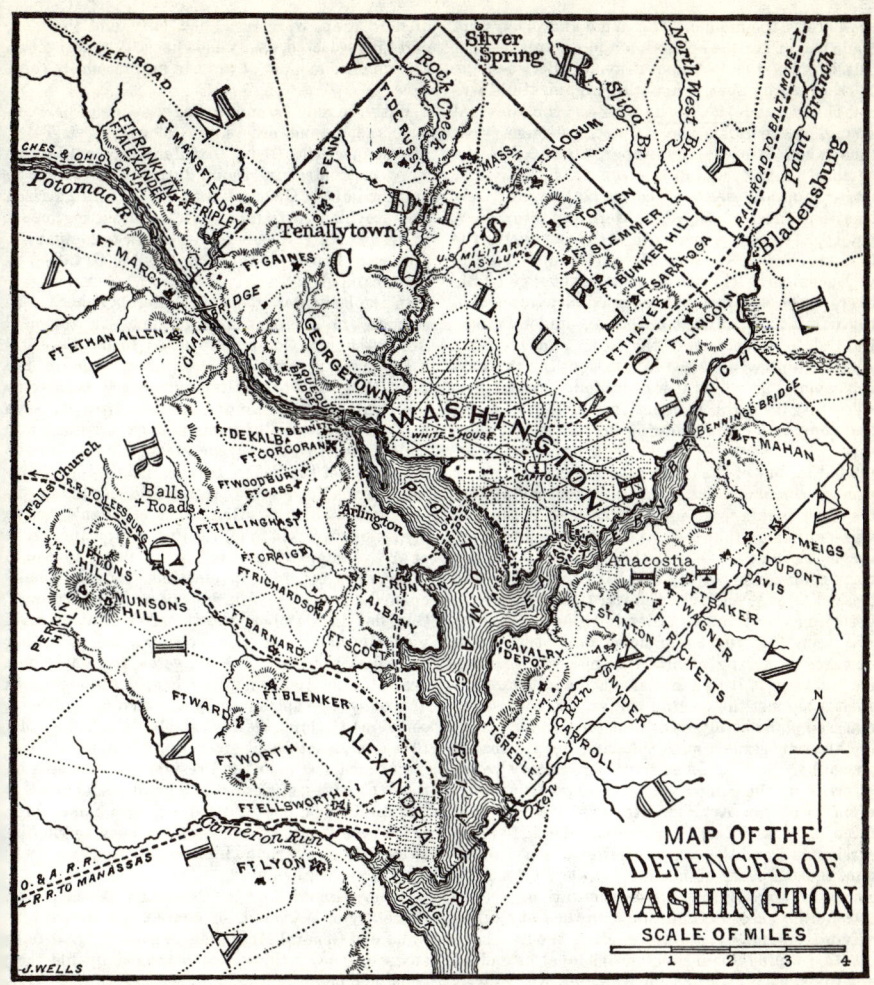

THE DEFENSES OF WASHINGTON DURING THE ANTIETAM CAMPAIGN, SEPTEMBER 1-20, 1862.

Extensive additions to the defenses of the west bank of the Potomac were made subsequently; these will be indicated hereafter on another map. Forts Alexander, Franklin, and Ripley were afterward united and called redoubts Davis, Kirby, and Cross, receiving later the name of Fort Sumner. Forts De Kalb, Massachusetts, Pennsylvania, and Blenker were afterward changed respectively to Strong, Stevens, Reno, and Reynolds.— EDITORS.

most insalubrious part of "the slashes" (now the fashionable quarter of the capital) I came upon a squadron of cavalry comfortably "waiting orders"— from anybody.

The stragglers were promptly gathered in, the hotels and bar-rooms were swept of officers of all grades "absent without leave," while heavy details of cavalry reduced to obedience even the unruly teamsters whose unbroken trains blocked the streets, and checked the reckless and senseless galloping of orderlies and other horsemen, who kept the foot-passengers in terror. Thus in two days order was restored, and it was afterward maintained.

There was quite an army of officers and men who had somehow become separated from their regiments. This happened often without any fault of their own, or with less than the frequent scoldings in general orders would have one believe. The number continued to be so enormous♭ as to be quite unmanageable by any existing method. There was already a convalescent camp near Alexandria, in charge of Colonel J. S. Belknap, of the 85th New York. Under the

♭ General McClellan estimated the number of stragglers he met on the Centreville road on the 2d at 20,000; Colonel Kelton those on the 1st at 30,000. Colonel Belknap estimates the number that passed through his hands before September 17th at 20,000.— R. B. I.

pressure of the moment, the name and place were made use of for the collection and organization of this army of the lost and strayed. Between the 17th of September, when the organization was completed, and the 30th, 17,343 convalescent stragglers, recruits, and paroled prisoners were thus taken care of; in October, 10,345; in November, 11,844, and in December, 12,238. The larger number were, of course, stragglers. At least one-third of the whole were unfit for duty, yet 16,176 were returned to the ranks during the first six weeks, 8226 in November, and 16,660 in December. The paroled and exchanged prisoners were afterward encamped separately, to the number of 3500 at one time, under Colonel Gabriel De Korponay, of the 28th Pennsylvania. As this camp was a clear innovation, the truly intolerable evils which it was intended to mitigate were forgotten the moment they ceased to press, and complaints came pouring in from every quarter. The reasonable ones were assiduously attended to, but of the other kind I recall two which came in company: one from a senator, saying that his constituents were so badly treated at the convalescent camp that they were driven to desert the service rather than remain there; the other from a corps commander, saying that his men were so well treated ("coddled" was the word) that they were deserting the colors in order to return. When it was seen that the camp must outlast the first emergency, arrangements were made to reorganize and remove it to a better place and to provide shelter against the coming winter, but these well-matured plans being set aside after General Banks left the department, such suffering ensued that in December the War Office gave peremptory orders to break up the camp; yet, as General Hunt aptly remarks of his Artillery Reserve, "such is the force of ideas" that these orders could never be carried out, and the camp remained, as it had begun, the offspring of necessity, a target for criticism, and a model for reluctant imitation.

General Casey was continued in the duty of receiving, organizing, and instructing the new regiments, forming them into "provisional brigades" and divisions; a service for which he was exactly fitted and in which he was ably assisted by Captain (afterward Lieutenant-Colonel) Robert N. Scott,⸹ as assistant adjutant-general. At this period not far from one hundred thousand men must have passed through this "dry nursery," as it was called.

General Barnard, as chief engineer of the defenses, with the full support of the Government (although Congress had, in a strange freak, forbidden it), set vigorously to work to complete and extend the fortifications, particularly on the north side and beyond the eastern branch, and to clear their front by felling the timber. Heavy details of new troops were furnished daily, and the men, carefully selected, easily and cheerfully got through an immense amount of work in an incredibly short time. ☆

With the aid of General Barry as chief of artillery, and, among others, of Colonel R. O. Tyler, 1st Connecticut Heavy Artillery, the artillerists were instructed in their duties, and with the approval of the Government a permanent garrison was provided, formed of those splendid regiments of heavy artillery, each of twelve large companies, afterward known as the "heavies" of Grant's Virginia campaigns.

In the last three weeks of September there were sent to the Army of the Potomac in the field 36,000 men, in October, 29,000; in all, 65,000. ⸹

Frequent reconnoissances to the gaps of the Blue Ridge and to the Rapidan served to disturb the Confederate communications a little, to save us from needless "alarums and excursions," and incidentally to throw some strange lights on the dark ways of the Secret Service, whose reports we thus learned to believe in if possible less than ever.

Especially during General McClellan's active operations, we used to see the President rather often of an evening, when, as in earlier days, he would "just drop in" to ask, sometimes through a half-opened doorway, "Well, how does it look now?" One day in October, shortly after Stuart's raid into Maryland and Pennsylvania, on returning on board the *Martha Washington* from a review near Alexandria, when the President seemed in unusually high spirits and was conversing freely, some one (I think DeKay) suddenly asked: "Mr. President, what about McClellan?" Without looking at his questioner the President drew a ring on the deck with a stick or umbrella and said quietly: "When I was a boy we used to play a game, three times round and out. Stuart has been round him twice; if he goes round him once more, gentlemen, McClellan will be out!"

General Banks kept the President, as well as the Secretary of War, and, of course, the General-in-Chief and General McClellan, constantly and fully advised of everything, and managed by his tact, good judgment, and experience to retain the confidence of his superiors, without which, in the remarkable state of feeling and of faction then prevailing, no one could have done anything. The President felt that the capital was safe, that the forces in its front were in hand, ready for any service at any notice; that order had quietly replaced confusion, and was maintained without fuss or excitement. In his own words, he was not bothered all day and could sleep all night if he wanted to; and this it was that toward the end of October, when it had been decided to make a change in the Department of the Gulf, led him to offer the command to General Banks.

⸹ Distinguished after the war by his invaluable public services in the organization and editing of the "Official Records of the Rebellion."—EDITORS.

☆ It was before these lines that, two years later, in his raid on Washington, Early brought up one evening; it was behind them that the dawn revealed to him the familiar Greek cross of the Sixth Army Corps, and also the four-pointed star of the Nineteenth.—R. B. I.

⸹ Porter's corps (Morell and Humphreys), 15,500; 20 new regiments in a body, 18,500; Stoneman and Whipple, 15,000; together, 49,000; add convalescents and stragglers, 16,000.—R. B. I.

# FROM THE PENINSULA TO ANTIETAM.

POSTHUMOUS NOTES BY GEORGE B. McCLELLAN, MAJOR-GENERAL, U. S. A.

IT is not proposed to give in this article a detailed account of the battles of South Mountain and Antietam, but simply a sketch of the general operations of the Maryland campaign of 1862 intended for general readers, especially for those whose memory does not extend back to those exciting days, and whose knowledge is derived from the meager accounts in so-called histories, too often intended to mislead and pander to party prejudices rather than to seek and record the truth.

THE NATIONAL CEMETERY AT SHARPSBURG— OVERLOOKING THE VALLEY OF THE ANTIETAM.

A great battle can never be regarded as "a solitaire," a jewel to be admired or condemned for itself alone, and without reference to surrounding objects and circumstances. A battle is always one link in a long chain of events; the culmination of one series of manœuvres, and the starting-point of another series — therefore it can never be fully understood without reference to preceding and subsequent events.

Restricted as this narrative is intended to be, it is nevertheless necessary to preface it by a brief story of the antecedent circumstances.

In an article already published in "The Century" [May, 1885], I have narrated the events of the Peninsular campaign up to the time when, at the

---

After General McClellan had written the article on the Peninsular Campaign (published in "The Century" magazine for May, 1885 [see p. 160]), he was requested to write an account of the battle of Antietam, which he promised to do at his leisure. He had kept the promise in mind, and as occasion served had sketched introductory portions of the proposed article. In the morning after his sudden death, these manuscript pages were found on his table, with some others freshly written, possibly on the previous day or evening. There was also an unsealed note to one of the editors (in reply to one he had received), in which he said that he would at once proceed with the article and finish it.

It was his custom in writing for the press to make a rapid but complete sketch, often abbreviating words and leaving blanks for matter to be copied from documents, and then to rewrite the entire article for publication. It would seem that in this case he had first in mind the consideration stated in the second paragraph of the article, and had given his attention to the history of the army, from the close of the Seven Days' battles to the advance from Washington toward South Mountain and Antietam. There was no manuscript relating to later

events. He had commenced what appears to be his final copy of this first portion of the article, but had completed only about three pages of foolscap, which extend in the print below to a place indicated.

It is an interesting fact that in this final copy the paragraph commencing with the words "So long as life lasts" was apparently the last written, being on a separate page and indicated by a letter A for insertion where it stands. This tribute of admiration for the army which loved him as he loved them was among the last thoughts, if it was not the very last, which his pen committed to paper.

Although this introduction to the account of Antietam is but his first sketch, and not in the final shape he would have given it for publication, it is so comprehensive and complete, and contains so much that is of historical importance, that his literary executor has considered it his duty to allow its publication in "The Century" in the form in which General McClellan left it, and thus as far as possible fulfill a promise made in the last hours of his life.

WILLIAM C. PRIME,
*Literary Executor of General McClellan.*

close of the Seven Days' battles, the Army of the Potomac was firmly established on its proper line of operations, the James River.

So long as life lasts the survivors of those glorious days will remember with quickened pulse the attitude of that army when it reached the goal for which it had striven with such transcendent heroism. Exhausted, depleted in numbers, bleeding at every pore, but still proud and defiant, and strong in the consciousness of a great feat of arms heroically accomplished, it stood ready to renew the struggle with undiminished ardor whenever its commander should give the word. It was one of those magnificent episodes which dignify a nation's history, and are fit subjects for the grandest efforts of the poet and the painter.

[Many years ago it was my good fortune, when in Europe, to make the acquaintance of a charming old Westphalian baron who was aide-de-camp to King Jerome in the days of his prosperity. In 1813 my friend was sent by his king with important dispatches to the Emperor, and, as it happened, arrived while the battle of Lutzen was in progress. He approached from the rear and for miles passed through crowds of stragglers, feeling no doubt that the battle was lost, and that he was about to witness the crushing defeat of the French. Still keeping on and on, he at last found the Emperor at the front, and to his great surprise discovered that the battle was won. Thus it very often happens in war that there are on each side two armies in the field, one of the fighting men with the colors, the other of stragglers and marauders in the rear; the relative strength of these two armies depends upon the state of discipline and the peculiar circumstances of the time.] ⚓

At the close of such a series of battles and marches the returns of the killed, wounded, and missing by no means fully measure the temporary decrease of strength; there were also many thousands unfitted for duty for some days by illness, demoralization, and fatigue. The first thing to be done was to issue supplies from the vessels already sent to the James, and to allow the men some little time to rest and recover their strength after the great fatigue and nervous tension they had undergone.

In order to permit a small number to watch over the safety of the whole army, and at the same time to prepare the way for ulterior operations so that when the army advanced again upon Richmond by either bank of the James its base of supplies might be secure with a small guard, the position was rapidly intrenched, the work being completed about the 10th of July.

Prior to the 10th of July two brigades of Shields's division, numbering about 5300 men, had joined the army, bringing its numbers for duty up to 89,549, officers and men, about the same strength as that with which it entered upon the siege of Yorktown, the reënforcements received in the shape of the divisions of Franklin and McCall, the brigades of Shields, and a few regiments from Fort Monroe having slightly more than made good the losses

⚓ The paragraph inclosed by brackets was in the first sketch of the article, but was omitted by General McClellan in the final manuscript.— W. C. P.

in battle and by disease. But among these 89,000 for duty‡ on the 10th of July were included all the extra duty men employed as teamsters, and in the various administrative services, and, with the further deductions necessary for camp guards, guards of communications, depots and trains, flank detachments, etc., reduced the numbers actually available for offensive battle to not more than [60,000?]

A few days sufficed to give the men the necessary rest, and to renew the supplies exhausted on the march across the

‡ According to General McClellan's "Tri-monthly Return," dated July 10, 1862 ("Official Records," Vol. XI., Pt. III., p. 312), he would appear to be mistaken, above, in saying that the "89,000 for duty" included "all the extra duty men," for in the return he classifies (excluding the forces under Dix) 88,435 as "present for duty, equipped," at Harrison's Landing, and in the next column he accounts for 106,466 as the "aggregate present." Obviously there is no meaning in the return if the 88,435 "present for duty, equipped," did not exclude the 18,021 (supposedly extra duty men like teamsters, etc.) which made the difference between the "present for duty, equipped," and the 106,466 "aggregate present."—EDITORS.

Peninsula; the army was once more in condition to undertake any operation justified by its numbers, and was in an excellent position to advance by either bank of the James. [End of finished draft.]

. . . . . . . . . . . . . . . . . . . . . . . . . . . . .

It was at last upon its true line of operations, which I had been unable to adopt at an earlier day in consequence of the Secretary of War's peremptory order of the 18th of May requiring the right wing to be extended to the north of Richmond in order to establish communication with General McDowell. General McDowell was then under orders to advance from Fredericksburg, but never came, because, in spite of his earnest protest, these orders were countermanded from Washington, and he was sent upon a fruitless expedition toward the Shenandoah instead of being permitted to join me, as he could have done, at the time of the affair of Hanover Court House.

I urged in vain that the Army of the Potomac should remain on the line of the James, and that it should resume the offensive as soon as reënforced to the full extent of the means in possession of the Government. Had the Army of the Potomac been permitted to remain on the line of the James, I would have crossed to the south bank of that river, and while engaging Lee's attention in front of Malvern, would have made a rapid movement in force on Petersburg, having gained which, I would have operated against Richmond and its communications from the west, having already gained those from the south.

Subsequent events proved that Lee did not move northward from Richmond with his army until assured that the Army of the Potomac was actually on its way to Fort Monroe; and they also proved that so long as the Army of the Potomac was on the James, Washington and Maryland would have been entirely safe under the protection of the fortifications and a comparatively small part of the troops then in that vicinity; so that Burnside's troops and a large part of the Union Army of Virginia might, with entire propriety, have been sent by water to join the army under my command, which—with detachments from the West—could easily have been brought up to more than 100,000 men disposable on the actual field of battle.

In spite of my most pressing and oft-repeated entreaties, the order was insisted upon for the abandonment of the Peninsula line and the return of the Army of the Potomac to Washington in order to support General Pope, who was in no danger so long as the Army of the Potomac remained on the James. With a heavy heart I relinquished the position gained at the cost of so much time and blood.

As an evidence of my good faith in opposing this movement it should be mentioned that General Halleck had assured me, verbally and in writing, that I was to command all the troops in front of Washington, including those of Generals Burnside and Pope—a promise that was not carried into effect.

As the different divisions of the Army of the Potomac reached Aquia Creek and the vicinity of Washington they were removed from my command, even to my personal escort and camp guard, so that on the 30th of August, in reply to a telegram from him, I telegraphed General Halleck from Alexandria, "I have no sharp-shooters except the guard around my camp. I have sent off every man but those, and will now send them with the train as you direct. I will also send my only remaining squadron of cavalry with General Sumner. I can do no more. You now have every man of the Army of the Potomac who is within my reach." I had already sent off even my headquarters wagons — so far as landed — with ammunition to the front.

On the same day I telegraphed to General Halleck, "I cannot express to you, etc." [The dispatch which General McClellan here indicates, as intending to insert when revising the manuscript, proceeds as follows:

"I cannot express to you the pain and mortification I have experienced to-day in listening to the distant sound of the firing of my men. As I can be of no further use here, I respectfully ask that if there is a possibility of the conflict being renewed to-morrow, I may be permitted to go to the scene of battle with my staff, merely to be with my own men, if nothing more; they will fight none the worse for my being with them. If it is not deemed best to intrust me with the command even of my own army, I simply ask to be permitted to share their fate on the field of battle. Please reply to this to-night.

"I have been engaged for the last few hours in doing what I can to make arrangements for the wounded. I have started out all the ambulances now landed. As I have sent my escort to the front, I would be glad to take some of Gregg's cavalry with me, if allowed to go.
"G. B. McCLELLAN, Major-General."

The dispatch was dated "Camp near Alexandria, Aug. 30th, 1862, 10:30 P. M." On the following day he received this answer:

"WASHINGTON, Aug. 31, 1862, 9:18 A. M.
"MAJOR-GENERAL McCLELLAN: I have just seen your telegram of 11:05 last night. The substance was stated to me when received, but I did not know that you asked for a reply immediately. I cannot answer without seeing the President, as General Pope is in command, by his orders, of the department.

"I think Couch's division should go forward as rapidly as possible, and find the battle-field.
"H. W. HALLECK, General-in-Chief."]

On the 1st of September I met General Halleck at his office in Washington, who by verbal order directed me to take charge of Washington and its defenses, but expressly prohibited me from exercising any control over the active troops under General Pope.

At this interview I informed General Halleck that from information received through one of my aides I was satisfied that affairs were not progressing favorably at the front, and urged him to go out in person to ascertain the exact state of the case. He declined doing this, but finally sent Colonel Kelton, his adjutant-general.

Next morning while at breakfast at an early hour I received a call from the President, accompanied by General Halleck.

The President informed me that Colonel Kelton had returned and represented the condition of affairs as much worse than I had stated to Halleck on the previous day; that there were thirty thousand stragglers on the roads; that the army was entirely defeated and falling back to Washington in confusion. He then said that he regarded Washington as lost, and asked me if I would, under the circumstances, consent to accept command of all the forces. Without one moment's hesitation and without making any conditions whatever, I at once said that I would accept the command and would stake my life that I would save the city. Both the President and Halleck again asserted that it was impossible to save the city, and I repeated my firm conviction that I could and would save it. They then left, the President verbally placing me in entire command of the city and of the troops falling back upon it from the front.

I at once sent for my staff-officers and dispatched them on various duties; some to the front with orders for the disposition of such corps as they met, others to see to the prompt forwarding of ammunition and supplies to meet the retreating troops. In a very short time I had made all the requisite preparations and was about to start to the front in person to assume command as far out as possible, when a message came to me from General Halleck informing me that it was the President's order that I should not assume command until the troops had reached the immediate vicinity of the fortifications. I therefore waited until the afternoon, when I rode out to Upton's Hill, the most advanced of the detached works covering the capital.

Soon after arriving there the head of Hatch's command of infantry arrived, immediately followed by Generals Pope and McDowell escorted by a regiment, or part of a regiment, of cavalry. I obtained what information I could from General Pope and dispatched the few remaining aides with me to meet the troops on the roads leading in on the left, with final orders to them, when quite a heavy distant artillery firing broke out in the direction of the Chantilly and Vienna road. Asking General Pope what that was, he replied it was probably an attack on Sumner, who commanded the rear-guard in that direction; in reply to another question he said that he thought it probably a serious affair. He and McDowell then asked if I had any objection to their proceeding to Washington. I said that they might do so, but that I was going to the firing. They then proceeded on with their escort while, with a single aide (Colonel Colburn) and three orderlies, I struck across country to intercept the column on our right by the shortest line. It was a little after dark when I reached the column.

I leave to others who were present the description of what then occurred: the frantic cheers of welcome that extended for miles along the column; the breaking of ranks and the wild appeals of the men that I should then and there take them back on the line of retreat and let them snatch victory out of defeat.‡ Let it suffice to say that before the day broke the troops were all in position to repulse attack, and that Washington was safe.

‡ In November, 1887, George Kimball of Boston wrote to the editors:

"Though a quarter of a century has passed since 'those darkest days of the war,' I still retain a vivid remembrance of the sudden and complete change which came upon the face of affairs when General McClellan was restored to command. At the time, I was serving in Company A, 12th Massachusetts Volunteers, attached to Ricketts's division of the First Army Corps. The announcement of McClellan's restoration came to us in the early evening of the 2d of September, 1862, just after reaching Hall's Hill, weary from long marching and well-nigh disheartened by recent reverses. The men were scattered about in groups, discussing the events of their ill-starred campaign, and indulging in comments that were decidedly uncomplimentary to those who had been responsible for its mismanagement. We did not know, of course, the exact significance of all that had happened, as we afterward learned it, but being mainly thinking men, we were able to form pretty shrewd guesses as to where the real difficulty lay. Suddenly, while these mournful consultations were in full blast, a mounted officer, dashing past our bivouac, reined up enough to shout, '"Little Mac" is back here on the road, boys!' The scene that followed can be more easily imagined than described. From extreme sadness we passed in a twinkling to a delirium of delight. A Deliverer had come. A real 'rainbow of promise' had appeared suddenly in the dark political sky. The feeling in our division upon the return of General McClellan had its counterpart in all the others, for the Army of the Potomac loved him as it never loved any other leader. In a few days we started upon

## FROM THE PENINSULA TO ANTIETAM. 551

On the 3d it was clear that the enemy intended an invasion of Maryland and Pennsylvania by crossing the Upper Potomac; I therefore moved the Second, Ninth, and Twelfth Corps to the Maryland side of the Potomac in position to meet any attack upon the city on that side.

As soon as this was done I reported the fact to General Halleck, who asked what general I had placed in command of those three corps; I replied that I had made no such detail, as I should take command in person if the enemy appeared in that direction. He then said that my command included only the defenses of Washington and did not extend to any active column that might be moved out beyond the line of works; that no decision had yet been made as to the commander of the active army. He repeated the same thing on more than one occasion before the final advance to South Mountain and Antietam took place.

I should here state that the only published order ever issued in regard to the extent of my command after my interview with the President on the morning of the 2d ♭ was the following:

"WAR DEPARTMENT, ADJUTANT-GENERAL'S OFFICE,
"WASHINGTON, September 2, 1862.

"Major-General McClellan will have command of the fortifications of Washington and of all the troops for the defense of the capital.

"By order of MAJOR-GENERAL HALLECK.⸸

"E. D. TOWNSEND, *Assistant Adjutant-General.*"

A few days after this and before I went to the front, Secretary Seward came to my quarters one evening and asked my opinion of the condition of affairs at Harper's Ferry, remarking that he was not at ease on the subject. Harper's Ferry was not at that time in any sense under my control, but I told Mr. Seward that I regarded the arrangements there as exceedingly dangerous; that in my opinion the proper course was to abandon the position and unite the garrison (about ten thousand men) to the main army of operations,

---

that long march into Maryland, and whenever General McClellan appeared among his troops, from the crossing of the Potomac at Washington to the grapple with Lee at Antietam, it was the signal for the most spontaneous and enthusiastic cheering I ever listened to or participated in. Men threw their caps high into the air, and danced and frolicked like school-boys, so glad were they to get their old commander back again. It is true that McClellan had always been fortunate in being able to excite enthusiasm among his troops, but demonstrations at this time took on an added and noticeable emphasis from the fact that he had been recalled to command after what the army believed to be an unwise and unjust suspension. The climax seemed to be reached, however, at Middletown, where we first caught sight of the enemy. Here, upon our arrival, we found General McClellan sitting upon his horse in the road. The enemy occupied a gap in the South Mountain, a mile or two beyond. Reno and Hatch were fighting, and the smoke of their guns could be seen half-way up the mountain. As each organization passed the general, the men became apparently forgetful of everything but their love for him. They cheered and cheered again, until they became so hoarse they could cheer no longer. It seemed as if an intermission had been declared in order that a reception might be tendered to the general-in-chief. A great crowd continually surrounded him, and the most extravagant demonstrations were indulged in. Hundreds even hugged the horse's legs and caressed his head and mane. While the troops were thus surging by, the general continually pointed with his finger to the gap in the mountain through which our path lay. It was like a great scene in a play, with the roar of the guns for an accompaniment. Another enthusiastic demonstration that I remember occurred in the afternoon of the 17th at Antietam, when the general rode along our line of battle. The cheers could not have been heartier than they were. General McClellan may have had opponents elsewhere; he had few, if any, among the soldiers whom he commanded." [See also p. 489.]

♭ On the 3d the President, by an order in his own handwriting, but signed by the Secretary of War, directed General Halleck to "organize an army for active operations . . . independent of the forces he may deem necessary for the defense of Washington, when such active army shall take the field." See "Washington under Banks," p. 542.— EDITORS.

⸸ In its original form, as it was first given to the newspapers and as it appeared in some of them, this order purported to be issued "by order of the Secretary of War."— EDITORS.

for the reason that its presence at Harper's Ferry would not hinder the enemy from crossing the Potomac; that if we were unsuccessful in the approaching battle, Harper's Ferry would be of no use to us and its garrison necessarily would be lost; that if we were successful we would immediately recover the post without any difficulty, while the addition of ten thousand men to the active army would be an important factor in securing success. I added that if it were determined to hold the position the existing arrangements were all wrong, as it would be easy for the enemy to surround and capture the garrison, and that the garrison ought, at least, to be withdrawn to the Maryland Heights, where they could resist attack until relieved.

The Secretary was much impressed by what I said, and asked me to accompany him to General Halleck and repeat my statement to him. I acquiesced, and we went together to General Halleck's quarters, where we found that he had retired for the night. But he received us in his bedroom, when, after a preliminary explanation by the Secretary as to the interview being at his request, I said to Halleck precisely what I had stated to Mr. Seward.

Halleck received my statement with ill-concealed contempt — said that everything was all right as it was; that my views were entirely erroneous, etc., and soon bowed us out, leaving matters at Harper's Ferry precisely as they were.

On the 7th of September, in addition to the three corps already mentioned (the Second, Ninth, and Twelfth), the First and Sixth Corps, Sykes's division of the Fifth Corps, and Couch's division of the Fourth Corps, were also on the Maryland side of the river; the First and Ninth Corps at Leesboro; the Second and Twelfth in front of Rockville; the Sixth Corps at Rockville; Couch's division at Offutt's Cross Roads; Sykes's division at Tenallytown.

As the time had now arrived for the army to advance, and I had received no orders to take command of it, but had been expressly told that the assignment of a commander had not been decided, I determined to solve the question for myself, and when I moved out from Washington with my staff and personal escort I left my card with *P. P. C.* written upon it, at the White House, War Office, and Secretary Seward's house, and went on my way.☆

I was afterward accused of assuming command without authority, for nefarious purposes, and in fact I fought the battles of South Mountain and Antietam with a halter around my neck, for if the Army of the Potomac had been defeated and I had survived I would, no doubt, have been tried for assuming authority without orders, and, in the state of feeling which so unjustly condemned the innocent and most meritorious General F. J. Porter, I would probably have been condemned to death. I was fully aware of the risk I ran, but the path of duty was clear and I tried to follow it. It was absolutely necessary that Lee's army should be met, and in the state of affairs I have briefly described there could be no hesitation on my part as to doing it promptly. Very few in the Army of the Potomac doubted the favorable

---

☆ General McClellan's orders from the 1st to the 8th of September, inclusive, are dated "Headquarters, Washington." On the 9th he resumed the heading, "Headquarters, Army of the Potomac," at Rockville.— EDITORS.

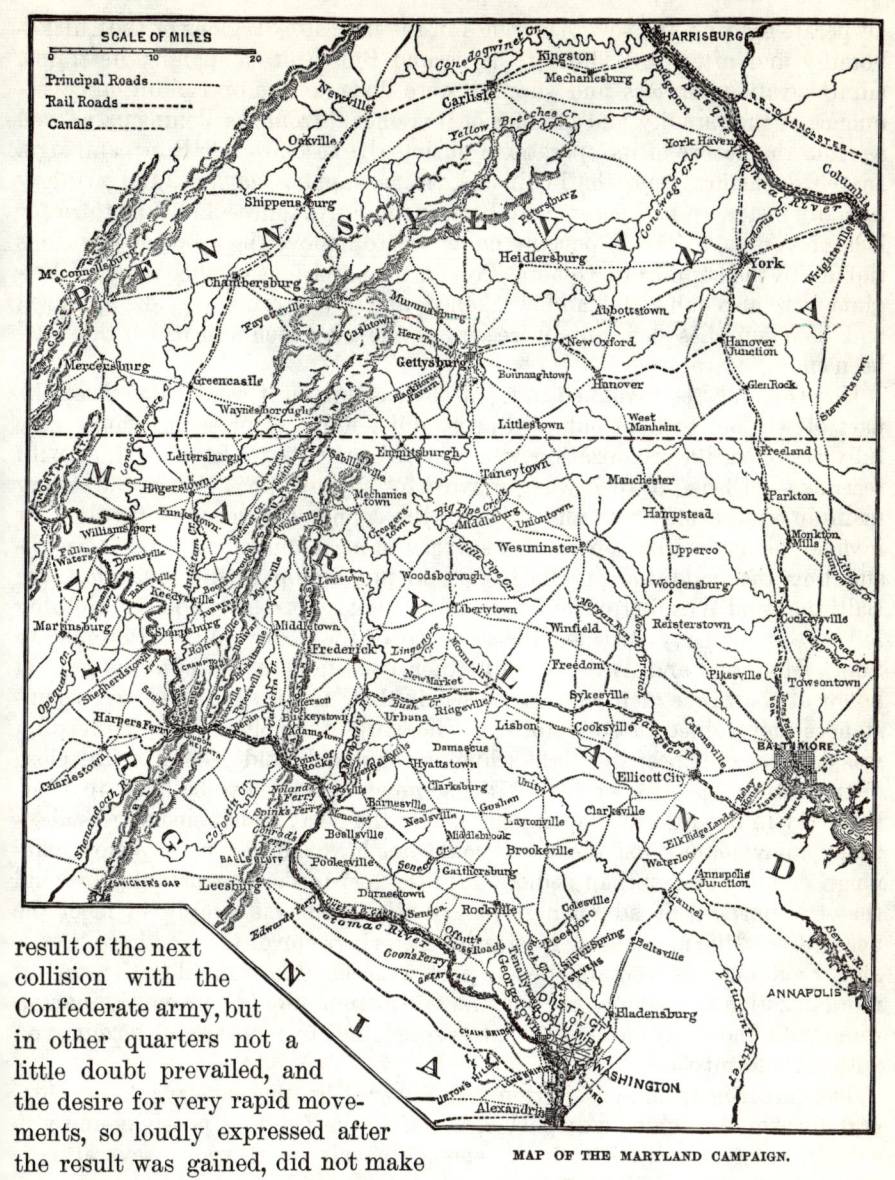

result of the next collision with the Confederate army, but in other quarters not a little doubt prevailed, and the desire for very rapid movements, so loudly expressed after the result was gained, did not make itself heard during the movements preceding the battles; quite the contrary was the case, as I was more than once cautioned that I was moving too rashly and exposing the capital to an attack from the Virginia side.

MAP OF THE MARYLAND CAMPAIGN.

As is well known, the result of General Pope's operations had not been favorable, and when I finally resumed command of the troops in and around Washington they were weary, disheartened, their organization impaired, their clothing, ammunition, and supplies in a pitiable condition.

The Army of the Potomac was thoroughly exhausted and depleted by its desperate fighting and severe marches in the unhealthy regions of the Chickahominy and afterward, during the second Bull Run campaign; its trains, administration services and supplies were disorganized or lacking in consequence of the rapidity and manner of its removal from the Peninsula as well as from the nature of its operations during the second Bull Run campaign. In the departure from the Peninsula, trains, supplies, cavalry, and artillery in many instances had necessarily been left at Fort Monroe and Yorktown for lack of vessels, as the important point was to remove the infantry divisions rapidly to the support of General Pope. The divisions of the Army of Virginia were also exhausted and weakened, and their trains were disorganized and their supplies deficient by reason of the movements in which they had been engaged.

Had General Lee remained in front of Washington it would have been the part of wisdom to hold our own army quiet until its pressing wants were fully supplied, its organization was restored, and its ranks were filled with recruits — in brief, until it was prepared for a campaign. But as the enemy maintained the offensive and crossed the Upper Potomac to threaten or invade Pennsylvania, it became necessary to meet him at any cost notwithstanding the condition of the troops, to put a stop to the invasion, save Baltimore and Washington, and throw him back across the Potomac. Nothing but sheer necessity justified the advance of the Army of the Potomac to South Mountain and Antietam in its then condition, and it is to the eternal honor of the brave men who composed it that under such adverse circumstances they gained those victories. The work of supply and reorganization was continued as best we might while on the march, and even after the close of the battles [September 14th–17th] so much remained to be done to place the army in condition for a campaign, that the delay which ensued was absolutely unavoidable, and the army could not have entered upon a new campaign one day earlier than it did. It must then be borne constantly in mind that the purpose of advancing from Washington was simply to meet the necessities of the moment by frustrating Lee's invasion of the Northern States, and, when that was accomplished, to push with the utmost rapidity the work of reorganization and supply so that a new campaign might be promptly inaugurated with the army in condition to prosecute it to a successful termination without intermission.

The advance from Washington was covered by the cavalry, under General Pleasonton, which was pushed as far to the front as possible, and was soon in constant contact with the enemy's cavalry, with whom several well-conducted and successful affairs occurred.

Partly in order to move men freely and rapidly, partly in consequence of the lack of accurate information as to the exact position and intention of Lee's army, the troops advanced by three main roads: that part near the Potomac by Offutt's Cross Roads and the mouth of the Seneca; that by Rockville to Frederick, and that by Brookville and Urbana to New Market. We were then in condition to act according to the development of the enemy's plans and to concentrate rapidly in any position. If Lee threatened our left flank by moving down the river road, or by crossing the Potomac at any of the fords from Coon's Ferry upward, there were enough troops on the river road to hold him in check until the rest of the army could move over to support them; if Lee took up a position behind the Seneca near Frederick the whole army could be rapidly concentrated in that direction to attack him in force; if he moved upon Baltimore the entire army could rapidly be thrown in his rear and his retreat would be cut off; if he moved by Gettysburg or Chambersburg upon York or Carlisle we were equally in position to throw ourselves in his rear.

The first requisite was to gain accurate information as to Lee's movements, and the second, to push the work of supply and reorganization as rapidly as possible.

General Lee and I knew each other well. In the days before the war we served together in Mexico, and we had commanded against each other in the Peninsula. I had the highest respect for his ability as a commander, and knew that he was a general not to be trifled with or carelessly afforded an opportunity of striking a fatal blow. Each of us naturally regarded his own army as the better, but each entertained the highest respect for the endurance, courage, and fighting qualities of the opposing army; and this feeling extended to the officers and men. It was perfectly natural under these circumstances that both of us should exercise a certain amount of caution,— I in my endeavors to ascertain Lee's strength, position, and intentions before I struck the fatal blow; he to abstain from any extended movements of invasion, and to hold his army well in hand until he could be satisfied as to the condition of the Army of the Potomac after its second Bull Run campaign, and as to the intentions of its commander.

. . . . . . . . . . . . . . . . . . . . . . . . . . . . . . . .

ROSTRUM IN THE NATIONAL CEMETERY AT SHARPSBURG. FROM A RECENT PHOTOGRAPH.

On Memorial Day, 1885, General McClellan addressed from this rostrum a large assembly of members of the "Grand Army of the Republic."— EDITORS.

## IN THE RANKS TO THE ANTIETAM.

### BY DAVID L. THOMPSON, CO. G, 9TH NEW YORK VOLUNTEERS.

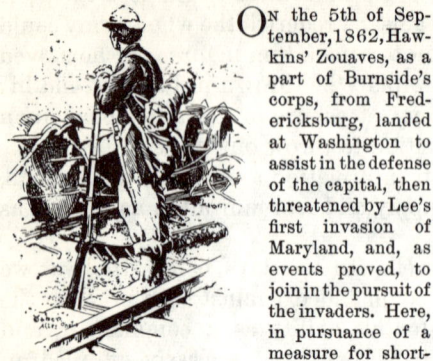

ON the 5th of September, 1862, Hawkins' Zouaves, as a part of Burnside's corps, from Fredericksburg, landed at Washington to assist in the defense of the capital, then threatened by Lee's first invasion of Maryland, and, as events proved, to join in the pursuit of the invaders. Here, in pursuance of a measure for shortening the baggage train which had lately been decided on, we were deprived of our Sibley tents — those cumbersome, conical caravansaries, in which eighteen men lie upon the ground with their feet toward the center.

Shelter tents came soon to replace the "Sibleys," and with them came marching orders — the army was moving west. At dusk we set up our new houses. A shelter or dog tent is like a bargain — it takes two to make it. Each man is provided with an oblong piece of thick, unbleached muslin about the length of a man — say six feet — and two-thirds as wide, bordered all round with buttons and button-holes alternately matching respectively the button-holes and buttons of his comrade's piece. To set it up, cut two crotched stakes, each about four feet long, point them at the uncrotched end, and drive them into the ground about six feet apart; cut a slender pole to lie horizontally from one crotch to the other, button the two pieces of muslin together and throw the resulting piece over the pole, drawing out the corners tight and pinning them down to the ground by means of little loops fastened in them. You will thus get a wedge-shaped structure — simply the two slopes of an ordinary roof — about three and a half feet high at its highest point, and open at both ends. This will accommodate two men, and in warm, pleasant weather is all that is needed. In rainy weather a third man is admitted. A piece of rope about four feet long is then tied to the top of one of the stakes and stretched out in the line of direction of the ridge pole, the free end being brought down to the ground and pinned there. The third man then buttons his piece of muslin to one slope of the roof, carries the other edge of the piece out around the tightened rope and brings it back to the edge of the other slope, to which it is buttoned. This third piece is shifted from one end of the tent to the other, according to the direction of the wind or storm. You thus get an extension to your tent in which knapsacks can be stored, leaving the rest of the space clear for sleeping purposes. This is large enough to accommodate three men lying side by side.

A DISORGANIZED PRIVATE. FROM A PHOTOGRAPH.

But will such a structure keep out rain? Certainly, just as your umbrella does — unless you touch it on the inside when it is soaked. If you do, the rain will come in, drop by drop, just where you have touched it. To keep the water from flowing in along the surface of the ground, dig a small trench about three inches deep all around the tent, close up, so that the rain shed from the roof will fall into it. Such a house is always with you potentially, for you carry the materials on your back and can snap your fingers at the baggage wagon. For three-fourths of the year it is all the shelter needed, as it keeps out rain, snow, and wind perfectly, being penetrable only by the cold.

We marched at last, and on the 12th of September entered Frederick, wondering all the way what the enemy meant. We of the ranks little suspected what sheaves he was gathering in at Harper's Ferry, behind the curtain of his main body. We guessed, however, as usual, and toward evening began to get our answer. He was right ahead, his rear-guard skirmishing with our advance. We came up at the close of the fight at Frederick, and, forming line of battle, went at double-quick through cornfields, potato patches, gardens, and backyards — the German washer-women of the 103d New York regiment going in with us on the run. It was only a measure of precaution, however, the cavalry having done what little there was to do in the way of driving out of the city a Confederate rear-guard not much inclined to stay. We pitched tents at once in the outskirts, and after a hearty supper went to explore the city.

The next morning the feeling of distrust which the night before had seemed to rule the place had disappeared, and a general holiday feeling took its place. The city was abloom with flags, houses were open everywhere, trays of food were set on the window-sills of nearly all the better class of houses, and the streets were filled with women dressed in their best, walking bareheaded, singing, and testifying in every way the general joy. September 13th in Frederick City was a bright one in memory for many a month after — a pleasant topic to discuss over many a camp-fire.

The next day our regiment went on a reconnoissance to a speck of a village, rather overweighted by its name, — Jefferson, — about eight miles from Frederick and on our left. Far up the mountain-side ahead of us we could see, in the fields confronting the edge of the woods that crowned the ridge, the scattered line of Rush's Lancers, their bright red pennons fluttering gayly from their spear heads.

We reached camp again about 10 o'clock at night, and found awaiting us marching orders for 2 o'clock the following morning. Late as it was, one of my tent-mates — an enterprising young fellow — started out on a foraging expedition, in pursuance of a vow made several days before to find something with which to vary his monotonous regimen of "hard-tack" and "salt horse." He "ran the guard"—an easy thing to do in the darkness and hubbub—and returned shortly after, struggling with a weight of miscellaneous plunder; a crock of butter, a quantity of apple-butter, some lard, a three-legged skillet weighing several pounds, and a live hen. It was a marvel how he managed to carry so much; but he was a rare gleaner always, with a comprehensive method that covered the ground. That night we had several immense flapjacks, the whole size of the pan; then, tethering the hen to one of the tent pegs, we went to sleep, to be roused an hour or so later by hearing our two-legged prize cackling and fluttering off in the darkness.

Up to the 10th the army had not marched so much as it had drifted, but from this point on our purpose seemed to grow more definite and the interest deepened steadily. There had been sporadic fighting through the day (the 13th), but it was over the hills to the west, and we heard nothing of it beyond those airy echoes that take the shape of rumor. Now, however, the ferment at the front, borne back by galloping orderlies, was swiftly leavening the mass. Occasionally, on our march we would pass a broken gun wheel or the bloated body of a slaughtered horse, and in various ways we knew that we were close upon the enemy, and that we could not now be long delayed. This would have been told us by the burden of our daily orders, always the same, to hold ourselves "in readiness to march at a moment's notice," with the stereotyped addendum, "three days' cooked rations and forty rounds." Every one lay down to sleep that night with a feeling of impending battle.

By daylight next morning we were in motion again—the whole army. The gathering of such a multitude is a swarm, its march a vast migration. It fills up every road leading in the same direction over a breadth of many miles, with long ammunition and supply trains disposed for safety along the inner roads, infantry and artillery next in order outwardly, feelers of cavalry all along its front and far out on its flanks; while behind, trailing along every road for miles (ravelings from the great square blanket which the enemy's cavalry, if active, snip off with ease), are the rabble of stragglers—laggards through sickness or exhaustion, squads of recruits, convalescents from the hospital, special duty men going up to rejoin their regiments. Each body has its route laid down for it each day, its time of starting set by watch, its place of bivouac or camp appointed, together with the hour of reaching it. If two roads come together, the corps that reaches the junction first moves on, while the other files out into the fields, stacks arms, builds fires, and boils its coffee. Stand, now, by the roadside while a corps is filing past. They march "route step," as it is called,—that is, not keeping time,—and four abreast, as a country road seldom permits a greater breadth, allowing for the aides and orderlies that gallop in either direction continually along the column. If the march has just begun, you hear the sound of voices everywhere, with roars of laughter in spots, marking the place of the company wag—generally some Irishman, the action of whose tongue bears out his calling. Later on, when the weight of knapsack and musket begins to tell, these sounds die out; a sense of weariness and labor rises from the toiling masses streaming by, voiced only by the shuffle of a multitude of feet, the rubbing and straining of innumerable straps, and the flop of full canteens. So uniformly does the mass move on that it suggests a great machine, requiring only its directing mind. Yet such a mass, without experience in battle, would go to pieces before a moderately effective fire. Catch up a handful of snow and throw it, it flies to fluff; pack it, it strikes like stone. Here is the secret of organization—the aim and crown of drill, to make the units one, that when the crisis comes, the missile may be thoroughly compacted. Too much, however, has been claimed for theoretic discipline—not enough for intelligent individual action. No remark was oftener on the lips of officers during the war than this: "Obey orders! *I* do your thinking for you." But that soldier is the best whose good sense tells him when to be merely a part of a machine and when not.

The premonitions of the night were not fulfilled next day. That day—the 14th of September— we crossed the Catoctin range of mountains, reaching the summit about noon, and descended its western slope into the beautiful valley of Middletown. Half-way up the valley's western side we halted for a rest, and turned to look back on the moving host. It was a scene to linger in the memory. The valley in which Middletown lies is four or five miles wide, as I remember it, and runs almost due north and south between the parallel ranges of Catoctin and South Mountains. From where we stood the landscape lay below us, the eye commanding the opposite slope of the valley almost at point-blank. An hour before, from the same spot, it had been merely a scene of quiet pastoral beauty. All at once, along its eastern edge the heads of the columns began to appear, and grew and grew, pouring over the ridge and descending by every road, filling them completely and scarring the surface of the gentle landscape with the angry welts of war. By the farthest northern road—the farthest we could see—moved the baggage wagons, the line stretching from the bottom of the valley back to the top of the ridge, and beyond, only the canvas covers of the wagons revealing their character. We knew that each dot was a heavily loaded army wagon, drawn by six mules and occupying forty feet of road at least. Now they looked like white beads on a string. So far away were they that no motion was perceptible. The constant swelling of the end of the line down in the valley, where the teams turned into the fields to park, gave evidence that, in this way, it was being slowly reeled along the way. The troops were marching by two roads farther south. The Confederates fighting on the western summit must have seen them plainly. Half a mile beyond us the column broke abruptly, filing off into line of battle, right and left, across the fields. From that point backward and downward, across the valley and up the farther slope, it stretched with scarcely a gap, every curve and zigzag of the way defined more sharply by its somber presence. Here, too, on all the distant portions of the line, motion was imperceptible, but could be inferred from the casual glint of sunlight on a musket barrel miles away. It was 3 o'clock when we resumed our march, turning our backs upon the beautiful, impressive picture — each column a monstrous, crawling, blue-black snake, miles long, quilled with the silver slant of muskets at a "shoulder," its sluggish tail writhing slowly up over the distant eastern ridge, its bruised head weltering in the roar and smoke upon the crest above, where was being fought the battle of South Mountain.

We were now getting nearer to the danger line, the rattle of musketry going on incessantly in the edges of the woods and behind the low stone fences that seamed the mountain-side. Then we came upon the fringes of the contest — slightly wounded men scattered along the winding road on their way to the hospital, and now and then a squad of prisoners, wounded and unwounded together, going under guard to the rear.

The brigade was ordered to the left of the road to support a regular battery posted at the top of a steep slope, with a cornfield on the left, and twenty yards or so in front, a thin wood. We formed behind the battery and a little down the slope — the 89th on the left, the 9th next, then the 103d. We had been in position but a few minutes when a stir in front advised us of something unusual afoot, and the next moment the Confederates burst out of the woods and made a dash at the battery. We had just obeyed a hastily given order to lie down, when the bullets whistled over our heads, and fell far down the slope behind us. Then the guns opened at short range, full-shotted with grape and canister. The force of the charge was easily broken, for though it was vigorously made it was not sustained — perhaps was not intended to be, as the whole day's battle had been merely an effort of the enemy to check our advance till he could concentrate for a general engagement. As the Confederates came out of the woods their line touched ours on the extreme left only, and there at an acute angle, their men nearly treading on those of the 89th, who were on their faces in the cornfield, before they discovered them. At that instant the situation just there was ideally, cruelly advantageous to us. The Confederates stood before us not twenty feet away, the full intention of destruction on their faces — but helpless, with empty muskets. The 89th simply rose up and shot them down.

It was in this charge that I first heard the "rebel yell"; not the deep-breasted Northern cheer, given in unison and after a struggle, to signify an advantage gained, but a high shrill yelp, uttered without concert, and kept up continually when the fighting was approaching a climax, as an incentive to further effort. This charge ended the contest for the day on that part of the line. Pickets were set well forward in the woods, and we remained some time in position, waiting. How a trivial thing will often thrust itself upon the attention in a supreme moment was well exemplified here. All about us grew pennyroyal, bruised by the tramping of a hundred feet, and the smell of it has always been associated in my memory with that battle.

Before the sunlight faded, I walked over the narrow field. All around lay the Confederate dead — undersized men mostly, from the coast district of North Carolina, with sallow, hatchet faces, and clad in "butternut" — a color running all the way from a deep, coffee brown up to the whitish brown of ordinary dust. As I looked down on the poor, pinched faces, worn with marching and scant fare, all enmity died out. There was no "secession" in those rigid forms, nor in those fixed eyes staring blankly at the sky. Clearly it was not "their war." Some of our men primed their muskets afresh with the finer powder from the cartridge-boxes of the dead. With this exception, each remained untouched as he had fallen. Darkness came on rapidly, and it grew very chilly. As little could be done at that hour in the way of burial, we unrolled the blankets of the dead, spread them over the bodies, and then sat down in line, munching a little on our cooked rations in lieu of supper, and listening to the firing, which was kept up on the right, persistently. By 9 o'clock this ceased entirely. Drawing our blankets over us, we went to sleep, lying upon our arms in line as we had stood, living Yankee and dead Confederate side by side, and indistinguishable. — This was Sunday, the 14th of September.

The next morning, receiving no orders to march, we set to work collecting the arms and equipments scattered about the field, and burying the dead. The weather being fine, bowers were built in the woods — generally in fence corners — for such of the wounded as could not be moved with safety; others, after stimulants had been given, were helped down the mountain to the rude hospitals. Before we left the spot, some of the country people living thereabout, who had been scared away by the firing, ventured back, making big eyes at all they saw, and asking most ridiculous questions. One was, whether we were from Mexico! Those belated echoes, it seemed, were still sounding in the woods of Maryland.

# THE BATTLE OF SOUTH MOUNTAIN, OR BOONSBORO'.

## FIGHTING FOR TIME AT TURNER'S AND FOX'S GAPS.

### BY DANIEL H. HILL, LIEUTENANT-GENERAL, C. S. A.

THE conflict of the 14th of September, 1862, is called at the North the battle of South Mountain, and at the South the battle of Boonsboro'. So many battle-fields of the Civil War bear double names that we cannot believe the duplication has been accidental. It is the unusual which impresses. The troops of the North came mainly from cities, towns, and villages, and were, therefore, impressed by some natural object near the scene of the conflict and named the battle from it. The soldiers from the South were chiefly from the country and were, therefore, impressed by some artificial object near the field of action. In one section the naming has been after the handiwork of God; in the other section it has been after the handiwork of man. Thus, the first passage of arms is called the battle of Bull Run at the North,— the name of a little stream. At the South it takes the name of Manassas, from a railroad station. The second battle on the same ground is called the Second Bull Run by the North, and the Second Manassas by the South. Stone's defeat is the battle of Ball's Bluff with the Federals, and the battle of Leesburg with the Confederates. The battle called by General Grant, Pittsburg Landing, a natural object, was named Shiloh, after a church, by his antagonist. Rosecrans called his first great fight with Bragg, the battle of Stone River, while Bragg named it after Murfreesboro', a village. So McClellan's battle of the Chickahominy,[†] a little river, was with Lee the battle of Cold Harbor, a tavern. The Federals speak of the battle of Pea Ridge, of the Ozark range of mountains, and the Confederates call it after Elk Horn, a country inn. The Union soldiers called the bloody battle three days after South Mountain from the little stream, Antietam, and the Southern troops named it after the village of Sharpsburg. Many instances might be given of this double naming by the opposing forces. According to the same law of the unusual, the war-songs of a people have generally been written by non-combatants. The bards who followed the banners of the feudal lords, sang of their exploits, and stimulated them and their retainers to deeds of high emprise, wore no armor and carried no swords. So, too, the impassioned orators, who roused our ancestors in 1776 with the thrilling cry, "Liberty or Death," never once put themselves in the way of a death by lead or steel, by musket-ball or bayonet stab. The noisy speakers of 1861, who fired the Northern heart and who fired the Southern heart, never did any other kind of *firing*.[‡]

The battle of South Mountain was one of extraordinary illusions and delusions. The Federals were under the self-imposed illusion that there was a

---

[†] Gaines's Mill.— EDITORS.
[‡] Of the political speakers of 1860 a number might be mentioned who afterward served, in some cases with distinction, in the respective armies; for example, Banks, Baker, Frank P. Blair, Jr., Logan, Garfield, Schurz, on the Union side; and Breckinridge, Toombs, Cobb, Floyd, and Pryor of the Confederates.— EDITORS.

very large force opposed to them, whereas there was only one weak division until late in the afternoon. They might have brushed it aside almost without halting, but for this illusion. It was a battle of delusions also, for, by moving about from point to point and meeting the foe wherever he presented himself, the Confederates deluded the Federals into the belief that the whole mountain was swarming with rebels. I will endeavor to explain the singular features of the battle and what caused them.

In the retirement of Lee's army from Frederick to Hagerstown and Boonsboro', my division constituted the rear-guard. It consisted of five brigades (Wise's brigade being left behind), and after the arrival at Boonsboro' was intrusted with guarding the wagon trains and parks of artillery belonging to the whole army. Longstreet's corps went to Hagerstown, thirteen miles from Boonsboro', and I was directed to distribute my five brigades so as not only to protect the wagons and guns, but also to watch all the roads leading from Harper's Ferry, in order to intercept the Federal forces that might make their escape before Jackson had completed the investment of that place. It required a considerable separation of my small command to accomplish these two objects, and my tent, which was pitched about the center of the five brigades, was not less than three miles from Turner's Gap on the National road crossing South Mountain.

During the forenoon of the 13th General Stuart, who was in an advance position at the gap in the Catoctin Mountain, east of Middletown, with our cavalry, sent a dispatch to me saying that he was followed by two brigades of Federal infantry, and asking me to send him a brigade to check the pursuit at South Mountain. I sent him the brigades of Colquitt and Garland, and the batteries of Bondurant and Lane, with four guns each. Pleasonton's Federal cavalry division came up to the mountain and pressed on till our infantry forces were displayed, when it returned without fighting. The Confederates, with more than half of Lee's army at Harper's Ferry, distant a march of two days, and with the remainder divided into two parts, thirteen miles from each other, were in good condition to be beaten in detail, scattered and captured. General Longstreet writes to me that he urged General Lee in the evening of the 13th to unite at Sharpsburg the troops which were then at Hagerstown and Boonsboro'. He said that he could effect more with one-third of his own corps, fresh and rested, than with the whole of it, when exhausted by a forced march to join their comrades. That night, finding that he could not rest, General Longstreet rose and wrote to his commander, presenting his views once more, favoring the abandonment of the defense of the mountain except by Stuart and the concentration at Sharpsburg.

I received a note about midnight of the 13th from General Lee saying that he was not satisfied with the condition of things on the turnpike or National road, and directing me to go in person to Turner's Gap the next morning and assist Stuart in its defense. In his official report General Lee says:

"Learning that Harper's Ferry had not surrendered and that the enemy was advancing more rapidly than was convenient from Fredericktown, I determined to return with Longstreet's command to the Blue Ridge to strengthen D. H. Hill's and Stuart's divisions engaged in holding the passes of the mountains, lest the enemy should fall upon McLaws's rear, drive him from the Maryland Heights, and thus relieve the garrison at Harper's Ferry."

This report and the note to me show that General Lee expected General Stuart to remain and help defend the pass on the 14th. But on reaching the Mountain House between daylight and sunrise that morning, I received a message from Stuart that he had gone to Crampton's Gap. [See map, p. 593.] He was too gallant a soldier to leave his post when a

RATIONS FROM THE STALK.

battle was imminent, and doubtless he believed that there was but a small Federal force on the National road.↓ I found Garland's brigade at the Mountain House and learned that Colquitt's was at the foot of the mountain on the east side. I found General Colquitt there without vedettes and without information of the Federals, but believing that they had retired. General Cox's Federal division was at that very time marching up the old Sharpsburg or Braddock's road, a mile to the south, seizing the heights on our right and establishing those heavy batteries which afterward commanded the pike and all the approaches to it. General Pleasonton, of the Federal cavalry, had learned the ground by the reconnoissance of the day before, and to him was intrusted the posting of the advance troops of Reno's corps on the south side of the pike. He says:

"I directed Scammon's brigade to move up the mountain on the left-hand road, gain the crest, and then move to the right, to the turnpike in the enemy's rear. At the same time I placed Gibson's battery and the heavy batteries in position to the left, covering the road on that side and obtaining a direct fire on the enemy's position in the gap."

This shows that Pleasonton knew that the Confederate forces were at the foot of the mountain. However, I brought Colquitt's brigade back to a point

↓ Generals Colquitt and Rosser have both written to me that General Stuart told them he had been followed by only a small Federal force.— D. H. H.

near the summit and placed the 23d and 28th Georgia regiments on the north side of the pike behind a stone-wall, which afforded an excellent fire upon the pike. The other three regiments, the 6th and 27th Georgia and the 13th Alabama, were posted on the south side of the pike, a little in advance of the wall and well protected by a dense wood. This brigade did not lose an inch of ground that day. The skirmishers were driven in, but the line of battle on both sides of the road was the same at 10 o'clock at night as it was at 9 o'clock in the morning. After posting Colquitt's brigade I went with Major Ratchford of my staff on a reconnoissance to our right. About three-fourths of a mile from the Mountain House we discovered, by the voices of command and the rumbling of wheels, that the old road and heights above it were occupied, and took it for granted that the occupation was by Federal troops. We did not see them, and I suppose we were not seen by them. Colonel T. L. Rosser of the cavalry had been sent that morning with his regiment and Pelham's artillery, by order of General Stuart, to seize Fox's Gap on the Braddock road. Cox had got to the heights first and confronted Rosser with a portion of his command, while the remainder of it could be plainly seen at the foot of the mountain. General Rosser writes to me that he reported the situation of things to Stuart, who was passing by on the east side of the mountain on his way south. He, Rosser, was not directed to report to me, and I did not suspect his presence. I do not know to this hour whether Ratchford and myself came near stumbling upon him or upon the enemy.

Returning through the woods we came upon a cabin, the owner of which was in the yard, surrounded by his children, and evidently expectant of something. The morning being cool, Ratchford was wearing a blue cloak which he had found at Seven Pines. In questioning the mountaineer about the roads I discovered that he thought we were Federals.

"The road on which *your* battery is," said he, "comes into the valley road near the church." This satisfied me that the enemy was on our right, and I asked him: "Are there any rebels on the pike?" "Yes; there are some about the Mountain House." I asked: "Are there many?" "Well, there are *several*; I don't know how many." "Who is in command?" "I don't know."

Just then a shell came hurtling through the woods, and a little girl began crying. Having a little one at home of about the same age, I could not forbear stopping a moment to say a few soothing words to the frightened child, before hurrying off to the work of death.

The firing had aroused that prompt and gallant soldier, General Garland, and his men were under arms when I reached the pike. I explained the situation briefly to him, directed him to sweep through the woods, reach the road, and hold it at all hazards, as the safety of Lee's large train depended upon its being held. He went off in high spirits and I never saw him again. I never knew a truer, better, braver man. Had he lived, his talents, pluck, energy, and purity of character must have put him in the front rank of his profession, whether in civil or military life.

After passing through the first belt of woods Garland found Rosser, and, conferring with him, determined to make his stand close to the junction of the roads, near the summit of the mountain (Fox's Gap). He had with him five regiments of infantry and Bondurant's battery of artillery—his infantry force being a little less than one thousand men, all North Carolinians. The 5th regiment was placed on the right of the road, with the 12th as its support; the 23d was posted behind a low stone-wall on the left of the 5th; then came the 20th and 13th. From the nature of the ground and the duty to be performed, the regiments were not in contact with each other, and the 13th was 250 yards to the left of the 20th. Fifty skirmishers of the 5th North Carolina soon encountered the 23d Ohio, deployed as skirmishers under Lieutenant-Colonel R. B. Hayes, afterward President of the United States, and the action began at 9 A. M. between Cox's division and Garland's brigade.

I will delay an account of the fight to give the strength of the forces engaged.♭ The Ninth Corps (Reno's) consisted of four divisions under Cox, Willcox, Sturgis, and Rodman; or eight brigades— Scammon and Crook (Cox); Christ and Welsh (Willcox); Nagle and Ferrero (Sturgis); and Fairchild and Harland (Rodman). It had 29 regiments of infantry, 3 companies of cavalry, and 8 batteries of artillery, 3 of them United States batteries of regulars under Benjamin, Clark, and Muhlenberg.¶

General Cox, who fought Garland, had six Ohio regiments under Brigadiers Scammon and Crook, and also the batteries of McMullin and Simmonds, and three companies of cavalry. The heavy batteries in position (20-pounder Parrotts) were of service to him also, in commanding the approaches to the scene of the conflict. The strength of the division is not given directly, but Scammon estimates his effectives at 1455. The other brigade was most likely equally strong, and I conclude that Cox's infantry, artillery, and cavalry reached three thousand.☆ Garland's brigade is estimated at "scarce a thousand."

Scammon's brigade led the attack with great spirit. The 13th North Carolina, under Lieutenant-Colonel Ruffin, and the 20th, under Colonel Alfred Iverson, were furiously assailed on the left. Both regiments were under tried and true soldiers, and they received the assault calmly. Lieutenant Crome, of McMullin's battery, ran up a section of artillery by hand, and opened with effect upon the 20th North Carolina; but the skirmishers under Captain Atwell of that regiment killed the gallant officer while he was himself serving as a gunner. The section was abandoned, but the Confederates were unable to capture it. The effort seemed to be to turn the 13th; and Colonel Ruffin in vain urged General Garland to go to the other part of his line. But with Garland the post of danger was the post of honor. Judge Ruffin, in a recent letter to me, thus speaks of the fall of the hero:

"I said to him: 'General, why do you stay here ? you are in great danger.'
"To which he replied: 'I may as well be here as yourself.'

♭ See also Table of Opposing Forces in the Maryland Campaign, p. 598.— EDITORS.

¶ According to General Cox, until the arrival of Willcox with his division, about 2 o'clock, Cox's division and a portion of Pleasonton's cavalry were the only Union troops on the field. Sturgis arrived on the field about 3 : 30.— EDITORS

☆ In effect confirmed by General Cox.—EDITORS.

BRIGADIER-GENERAL SAMUEL GARLAND, JR., C. S. A., KILLED AT SOUTH MOUNTAIN. FROM A PHOTOGRAPH.

"I said: 'No, it is my duty to be here with my regiment, but you could better superintend your brigade from a safer position.'

"Just then I was shot in the hip, and as there was no field-officer then with the regiment, other than myself, I told him of my wound, and that it might disable me, and in that case I wished a field-officer to take my place. He turned and gave some order, which I have forgotten. In a moment I heard a groan, and looked and found him mortally wounded and writhing in pain. We continued to occupy this position for some time, when I sent my adjutant to the right to see what was going on (as the furious fighting had ceased in that direction). He returned and reported that the remainder of the brigade was gone and that the ground was occupied by the enemy. I then attempted to go to the left, hoping to come in contact with some portion of your command, but was again confronted by the enemy. I next tried to retreat to the rear, but to my dismay found myself entirely surrounded. The enemy in front was pressing us, and I saw but one way out, and that was to charge those in my front, repel them, if possible, and then, before they could recover, make a dash at those in my rear and cut my way out. This plan was successfully executed. I shall never forget the feelings of relief which I experienced when I first caught sight of you. You rode up to me, and, shaking my hand, said that you had given us up for lost and did not see how it was possible for us to have escaped. You then attached us to G. B. Anderson's brigade, which had come up in the meantime. . . . I remember one remark which you made just after congratulating me upon cutting my way out that surprised me very much. You said that you were greatly gratified to find that McClellan's whole army was in your front. As I knew how small your force was, I could not understand how it could be a source of pleasure to you to find yourself assailed by twenty times your number. In a moment you made it plain to me by saying that you had feared at first that McClellan's attack upon you was but a feint, and that with his main army he would cross the mountain at some of the lower gaps and would thus cut in between Jackson's corps and the forces under Lee."

A little before this I had seen from the lookout station near the Mountain House the vast army of McClellan spread out before me. The marching columns extended back far as eye could see in the distance; but many of the troops had already arrived and were in double lines of battle, and those advancing were taking up positions as fast as they arrived. It was a grand and glorious spectacle, and it was impossible to look at it without admiration. I had never seen so tremendous an army before, and I did not see one like it afterward. For though we confronted greater forces at Yorktown, Sharpsburg, Fredericksburg, and about Richmond under Grant, these were only partly seen, at most a corps at a time. But here four corps were in full view, one of which was on the mountain and almost within rifle-range. The sight inspired more satisfaction than discomfort; for though I knew that my little force could be brushed away as readily as the strong man can brush to one side the wasp or the hornet, I felt that General McClellan had made a mistake, and I hoped to be able to delay him until General Longstreet could come up and our trains could be extricated from their perilous position.

When two distinct roars of artillery were heard south of us that morning, I thought that the nearer one indicated that McClellan was forcing his way across some gap north of Harper's Ferry with a view of cutting Lee's army in two. I suppose that Stuart believed that this would be the movement of the enemy, and for this reason abandoned Turner's Gap and hastened to what he believed to be the point of danger. McClellan was too cautious a man for so daring a venture. Had he made it, Jackson could have escaped across the Potomac, but the force under Lee in person (Longstreet's corps and my division) must have been caught. My division was very small and was embarrassed with the wagon trains and artillery of the whole army, save such as Jackson had taken with him. It must be remembered that the army now before McClellan had been constantly marching and fighting since the 25th of June. It had fought McClellan's army from Richmond to the James, and then had turned about and fought Pope's army, reënforced by parts of McClellan's, from the Rapidan to the Potomac. The order excusing barefooted men from marching into Maryland had sent thousands to the rear. Divisions had become smaller than brigades were when the fighting first began; brigades had become smaller than regiments, and regiments had become smaller than companies.‡ Dabney, a careful statistician, in his "Life of Jackson," estimates Lee's forces at Sharpsburg (Antietam) at 33,000 men, including the three arms of service. Three of Longstreet's twelve brigades had gone to Harper's Ferry with Jackson. He (Longstreet) puts the strength of his nine brigades at Hagerstown on the morning of the 14th of September at thirteen thousand men. Accepting the correctness of his estimate for the present (though I expect to prove it to be too large), I find that Lee had under his immediate command that morning but eighteen thousand men.

McClellan gives his force at Sharpsburg at 87,164. Had he made the movement which Stuart and myself thought he was making, it was hardly possible for the little force under Lee in person to have escaped, encumbered as it was with wagon trains and reserve artillery. Forming his infantry into a solid column of attack, Lee might have cut a way through the five-fold force of his antagonist, but all the trains must have been lost,— an irreparable loss to the South. Frederick the Great's campaign against the allies

---

See General Franklin's paper on the engagement at Crampton's Gap, p. 591.— EDITORS.

‡ Thus the 18th Virginia Regiment (p. 899, Vol. XIX., of the "Official Records") is put at 120 men; 56th Virginia Regiment at 80; 8th Virginia at 34; Hampton Legion (p. 931) at 77; 17th South Carolina Regiment at 59 (p. 946).— D. H. H.

According to Thomas White, Chief Clerk in the Adjutant-General's Office at Lee's headquarters, General Lee had 33,000 *infantry* at Sharpsburg, or 41,500 of all arms. Adding 2000 for the previous casualties (only partly given), the total Confederate force on the 14th would appear to be 43,500, of which 15,000 were at Harper's Ferry, on the Virginia side, and 28,500 in Maryland.— EDITORS.

shows what he would have done had he been in command of the Federal army. But the American soldier preferred to do sure work rather than brilliant work, his natural caution being increased by the carping criticisms of his enemies.

Upon the fall of Garland, Colonel McRae, of the 5th North Carolina regiment, assumed command, and ordered the two regiments on the left to close in to the right. This order either was not received or it was found to be impossible of execution. The main attack was on the 23d North Carolina behind the stone-wall. The Federals had a plunging fire upon this regiment from the crest of a hill, higher than the wall, and only about fifty yards from it. The 12th North Carolina, a badly trained regiment, on that day under the command of a young captain, deserted the field.\ The 12th Ohio, actuated by a different impulse, made a charge upon Bondurant's battery and drove it off, failing, however, to capture it. The 30th Ohio advanced directly upon the stone-wall in their front, while a regiment moved upon the 23d North Carolina on each flank. Some of the 30th Ohio forced through a break in the wall, and bayonets and clubbed muskets were used freely for a few moments. Garland's brigade, demoralized by his death and by the furious assault on its center, now broke in confusion and retreated behind the mountain, leaving some two hundred prisoners of the 5th, 23d, and 20th North Carolina in the hands of the enemy. The brigade was too roughly handled to be of any further use that day. Rosser retired in better order, not, however, without having some of his men captured, and took up a position from which he could still fire upon the old road, and which he held until 10 o'clock that night.

General Cox, having beaten the force in his front, now showed a disposition to carry out General Pleasonton's instructions, and advance to the Mountain House by the road running south from it on the summit of the mountain. There was nothing to oppose him. My other three brigades had not come up; Colquitt's could not be taken from the pike except in the last extremity. So two guns were run down from the Mountain House and opened a brisk fire on the advancing foe. A line of dismounted staff-officers, couriers, teamsters, and cooks was formed behind the guns to give the appearance of battery supports. I do not remember ever to have experienced a feeling of greater *loneliness*. It seemed as though we were deserted by "all the world and the rest of mankind." Some of the advancing Federals encountered Colquitt's skirmishers under Captain Arnold, and fell back to their former positions.

General Cox seems not to have suspected that the defeat of Garland had cleared his front of every foe. He says in his report: "The enemy withdrew

---

\ Mr. R. V. Minor, of Oxford, North Carolina, a member of the 12th North Carolina regiment, writes to the editors that on the morning of the 14th of September his regiment numbered seventy-two men, and that they advanced along the mountain crest until they were in the midst of enemies. The commander, an inexperienced captain, then gave the order to "fire and fall back." The order was obeyed, but the fire was returned so promptly, at close range, that the withdrawal was attended with confusion. However, "thirty or forty" members of the 12th regiment halted on the line of the 13th North Carolina, of their own (Garland's) brigade. Lieutenant-Colonel T. Ruffin, Jr., commander of the 13th regiment, says in his report: "I feel it to be just that I should acknowledge the fact that we were joined by a small party of the 12th North Carolina regiment early in the morning, who continued with us throughout the day and rendered us very efficient aid."

## THE BATTLE OF SOUTH MOUNTAIN, OR BOONSBORO'. 567

their battery to a new position on a ridge more to the front and right, forming their infantry in support and moving columns toward both our flanks."

It was more than half an hour after the utter rout and dispersion of Garland's brigade when G. B. Anderson arrived at the head of his small but fine body of men. ☆ He made an effort to recover the ground lost by Garland, but failed and met a serious repulse. General Cox says of this attack: "The enemy made several attempts to retake the crest, advancing with great obstinacy and boldness."

Under the strange illusion that there was a large Confederate force on the mountain, the Federals withdrew to their first position in the morning to await the arrival of the other three divisions of Reno's corps. Willcox's arrived about noon, and Sturgis's and Rodman's between 3 and 4 o'clock, but there was no advance until 5 P. M. The falling back of Cox's division is alluded to by Colonel Ewing of Scammon's brigade and by Major Lyman J. Jackson of Crook's brigade. The former says: "We fell back to the original position until the general advance at 5 P. M." Major Jackson, after speaking of fighting the enemy behind a stone-wall with the coöperation of two other regiments, adds: "We then fell back to the hillside in the open fields, where we were out of reach of their guns, and remained here *with the rest of our brigade* until an advance was made against the enemy by the Pennsylvania and Rhode Island troops on our right."

After the arrival of his whole corps General Reno arranged his line of battle as follows: Cox's division on the left, resting on the batteries already in position; Willcox's on the right, supported by the division of Sturgis. Rodman's division was divided; Fairchild's brigade was sent to the extreme left to support the batteries, and Harland's was placed on the extreme right.

In the meantime Rodes and Ripley, of my division, reported to me for orders. Rodes was sent with his brigade of twelve hundred men to a commanding knoll north of the pike or National road. Ripley was directed to attach himself to G. B. Anderson's left. Anderson, being thus strengthened, and finding there was no enemy in his immediate front, sent out the 2d and 4th North Carolina regiments of his brigade on a reconnoissance to the front, right, and rear. Captain E. A. Osborne, commanding the skirmishers of the 4th North Carolina, discovered a brigade in an old field south of Fox's Gap, facing toward the turnpike and supporting a battery with its guns turned in the same direction. Captain Osborne hastened back to Colonel Grimes, commanding the regiment, and told him that they could deliver a flank fire upon the brigade before it could change its position to meet them. But a Federal

---

☆ General Hill in his official report thus describes the posting of his forces after the defeat of Garland: "There were two mountain roads practicable for artillery on the right of the main turnpike. The defense of the farther one had cost Garland his life. It was now intrusted to Colonel Rosser of the cavalry, who had reported to me, and who had artillery and dismounted sharp-shooters. General Anderson was intrusted with the care of the nearest and best road. Bondurant's battery was sent to aid him in its defense. The brigade of Colquitt was disposed on each side of the turnpike, and that with Lane's battery was judged adequate to the task. There was, however, a solitary peak on the left, which, if gained by the Yankees, would give them control of the ridge commanding the turnpike. I had a large number of guns from Cutts's artillery placed upon the hill . . . to sweep the approaches. . . . Rodes and Ripley came up soon after Anderson."— EDITORS.

568                THE BATTLE OF SOUTH MOUNTAIN, OR BOONSBORO'.

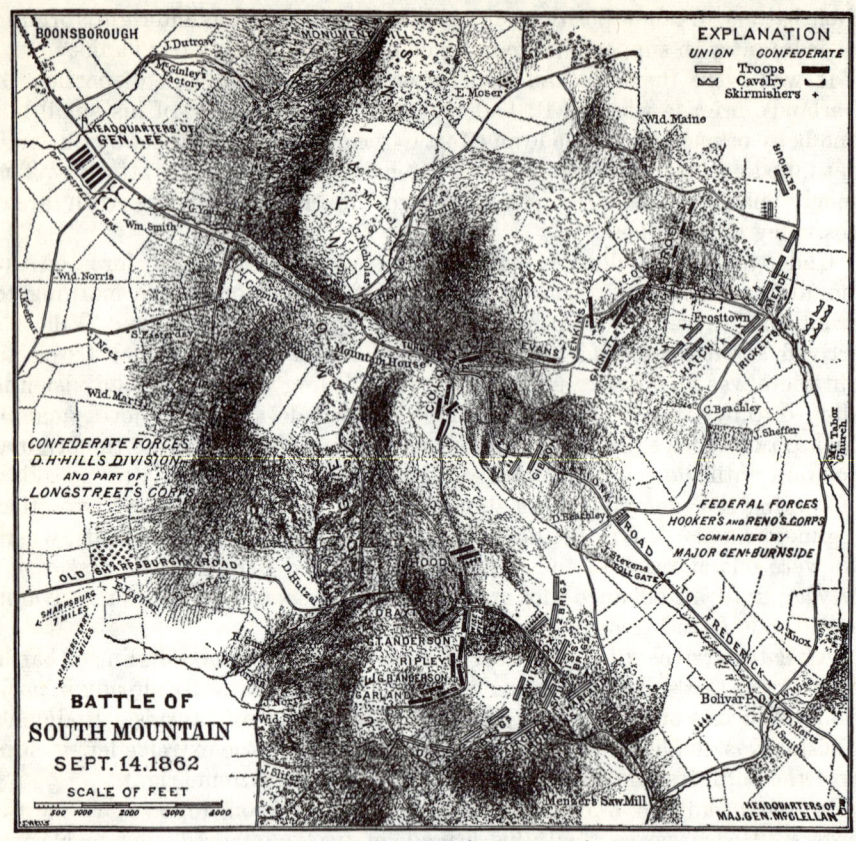

MAP OF THE POSITIONS AT FOX'S AND TURNER'S GAPS.

The fights of September 14th were so distinct as to time and place, and the positions of the troops were so often changed, that any single map would be misleading without analysis: (1) The early morning fight was mostly on the south side of Fox's Gap, between Cox's two Union brigades and Garland's brigade, the latter being assisted on its left by a part of Colquitt's brigade which was at Turner's Gap. By 10 o'clock Garland had been killed and his brigade routed. (2) Then Cox encountered G. B. Anderson's arriving brigade, repulsed it, and fell back to his position in the morning. (3) G. B. Anderson was then posted at Fox's Gap on both sides of the old Sharpsburg road. D. H. Hill's two other brigades came up toward noon, Ripley being joined to G. B. Anderson, and Rodes being sent to occupy a hill on the north side of Turner's Gap, near where Garnett is placed on the map. (4) About 2 o'clock, on the Union side, Cox's division was reënforced by the arriving divisions of Willcox, Sturgis, and Rodman; and Hooker's corps of three divisions was moving north of the National road by way of Mount Tabor Church (Hooker's headquarters) to flank the Confederate left. About the same time D. H. Hill's brigades at Fox's Gap were reënforced by Longstreet's brigades of G. T. Anderson, Drayton, Law, and Hood; and north of Turner's Gap three of Rodes's four regiments were sent still farther to the left. The defense was afterward strengthened by the posting of Longstreet's brigades of Garnett and Kemper, supported by Jenkins, on the hill first held by Rodes. Evans's brigade arrived later, and was of assistance to Rodes when the latter had been thrown back by Meade's flank movement. (5) The last severe engagements began at both gaps after 3 o'clock and lasted until after dark. Colquitt and Gibbon, in the center, joined desperately in the battle.— EDITORS.

scout had seen the captain, and the brigade was the first to open fire. The fight was, of course, brief, the regiment beating a hasty retreat. The brigade halted at the edge of the woods, probably believing that there was a concealed foe somewhere in the depths of the forest. This Federal brigade was, possibly, Benjamin C. Christ's of Willcox's division — the same which had made the successful flank movement in the previous fight. ☆

☆ This engagement is not mentioned by Cox, Willcox, or Christ. The Union brigade was more probably that of Colonel H. S. Fairchild, Rodman's division. See p. 558.— EDITORS.

## THE BATTLE OF SOUTH MOUNTAIN, OR BOONSBORO'. 569

About 3:30 P. M. the advance of Longstreet's command arrived and reported to me — one brigade under Colonel G. T. Anderson and one under General Drayton. They were attached to Ripley's left, and a forward movement was ordered. In half an hour or more I received a note from Ripley saying that he was progressing finely; so he was, to the rear of the mountain on the west side. Before he returned the fighting was over, and his brigade did not fire a shot that day. ☆ The Federal commander intrusted to General Burnside the management of the fight, but under his own eyes; Burnside ordered a general advance on both sides of the pike. The First Corps, under Hooker, was to attack on the north side of the National road, while the Ninth Corps, under Reno, was to move forward, as before, on the south side. Hooker's corps consisted of 3 divisions, 10 brigades, or 42 regiments, with 10 batteries of artillery and a battalion of cavalry. General Meade, a division commander, had under him the brigades of Seymour, Magilton, and Gallagher, containing 13 regiments with 4 batteries attached. General Hatch, division commander, had under him the brigades of Doubleday, Phelps, Patrick, and Gibbon — 17 regiments and 4 batteries. General Ricketts, division commander, had under him the brigades of Duryée, Christian, and Hartsuff — 12 regiments and 2 batteries. From the nature of the ground, none of the artillery of Hooker's corps could be used, except that which went directly up the pike with Gibbon's brigade and one battery (Cooper's) on the enemy's right.

The hour for the general advance is not specified in the reports. Some of the Federal officers, as we have seen, speak of the general advance at 5 P. M. General Sturgis says that he became engaged on the south side of the pike at 3:30 P. M. General Meade, on the north side, says that he moved toward the right at 2 P. M.,‡ while General Ricketts, who took part in the same movement, says that he did not arrive at the foot of the mountain until 5 P. M. If General Meade was not mistaken as to the time of his starting, he must have been long delayed in the thick woods through which the first part of his march was made.

Here is probably the best place to explain the extraordinary caution of the Federals, which seemed so mysterious to us on that 14th of September. An

---

☆ In "The Century" magazine for December, 1886, page 308, was printed a letter from William L. De Rosset, Colonel of the 3d North Carolina regiment, in which, after stating that General Hill disclaims any intention of reflecting on Ripley's brigade in this statement, the writer says:

"The facts are these: He [General Hill] correctly states Ripley's manœuvres at Boonsboro' until we reached a position at the foot of the mountain, — on the west side, — when General Ripley said to me that we were entirely cut off from the rest of the army, except G. B. Anderson's brigade, which was on our right, and that he assumed the command of the two brigades, directing me to take command of the three regiments Colonel Doles, with his 4th Georgia, having been detached and sent to a position on the north of the pike), and that he would remain near me, directing me at the same time to advance slowly up the mountain with a strong line of skirmishers in front. Upon reaching the summit, after toiling through the dense undergrowth of laurel, Major Thruston, in command of the skirmish line, reported troops in his front, a few minutes later confirming his first impression that they were G. B. Anderson's brigade, presenting their flank and advancing toward his left. This was promptly reported through my adjutant to General Ripley, who directed me to withdraw to my original position, which having been accomplished, I was directed to hold my then position until further orders. After nightfall I moved forward, changing front to the left, a short distance, to the support of General Drayton, remaining there 'without drawing trigger' when we took up the line of march for Sharpsburg, about 10 to 12 at night. While, therefore, we accomplished nothing tangible, we were in position to do any duty for which we might be called." — EDITORS.

‡ This is the hour at which General Meade says he received the order to move to the front, from the point where his division was halted beyond Middletown, at Catoctin creek. Meade turned off to the right, followed the old Hagerstown road to Mount Tabor Church, and then formed line at the foot of the mountain for the climb. Cooper's battery opened fire at 3:30. Hatch followed Meade, and Ricketts moved last. — EDITORS.

order of General Lee, made while at Frederick, directing Jackson to capture Harper's Ferry, and Longstreet and myself to go to Boonsboro', had fallen into the hands of the Federals, and had been carried to General McClellan. This order (known at the South as the Lost Dispatch) was addressed to me, but I proved twenty years ago that it could not have been lost through my neglect or carelessness.⁆ The Federal commander gained two facts from the order, one of which was needless and the other misleading. He learned that Jackson had gone to Harper's Ferry — a truth that he must have learned from his own scouts and spies and the roar of artillery in his own ears: the cannonading could be distinctly heard at Frederick, and it told that *some one* was beleaguering Harper's Ferry. The misleading report was that Longstreet was at Boonsboro'. ⚓ The map of the battle-field of South Mountain, prepared in 1872, ten years after the fight, by the United States Bureau of Engineers, represents ten regiments and one battalion under Longstreet at the foot of the mountain on the morning of the 14th of September, 1862. But Longstreet was then an ordinary day's march from that point. In fact, after the removal of Colquitt's brigade, about 7 A. M., there was not a Southern soldier at the foot of the mountain until 3 P. M., when Captain Park of the 12th Alabama Regiment was sent there with forty men. General McClellan in his report says: "It is believed that the force opposed to us at Turner's Gap consisted of D. H. Hill's corps (fifteen thousand) and a part if not the whole of Longstreet's, and perhaps a portion of Jackson's,— probably thirty thousand in all." ("Official Records," Volume XIX., Pt. I., p. 53.) The mistake of the Federal commander in regard to General Longstreet was natural, since he was misled by the Lost Dispatch. But it seems strange that the United States Engineers should repeat the blunder, with the light of history thrown for ten years upon all the incidents of the battle. It was incomprehensible to us of the losing side that the men who charged us so boldly and repulsed our attacks so successfully should let slip the fruits of victory and fall back as though defeated. The prisoners taken were from my division, but the victors seemed to think that Longstreet's men lay hidden somewhere in the depths of those mysterious forests. Thus it was that a thin line of men extending for miles along the crest of the mountain could afford protection for so many hours to Lee's trains and artillery and could delay the Federal advance until Longstreet's command did come up, and, joining with mine, saved the two wings of the army from being cut in two. But for the mistake about the position of our forces, McClellan could have captured Lee's trains and artillery and interposed between Jackson and Longstreet before noon on that 14th of September. The losing of the dispatch was the saving of Lee's army.

⁆ In a private letter to the editors, dated Feb. 24th, 1888, General Hill says: "I went into Maryland under Jackson's command. I was under his command when Lee's order was issued. It was proper that I should receive that order through Jackson and not through Lee. I have now before me the order received from Jackson. . . . My adjutant-general made affidavit, twenty years ago, that no order was received at our office from General Lee. But an order from Lee's office, directed to me, was lost and fell into McClellan's hands. Did the courier lose it? Did Lee's own staff-officers lose it? I do not know." See also pp. 603 and 664.— EDITORS.

⚓ "Special Orders No. 191," which was the "lost order," sent Longstreet to Boonsboro'. It was afterward modified by General Lee so as to place Longstreet at Hagerstown.— EDITORS.

About 4 P. M. I saw what appeared to be two Federal brigades emerge from the woods south of Colquitt's position and form in an open field nearly at right angles to each other — one brigade facing toward the pike, and the other facing the general direction of the mountain. This inverted V-like formation was similar to that of the 1st Mississippi Regiment at Buena Vista. If it was made anywhere else during the Civil War, I never heard of it. The V afforded a fine target from the pike, and I directed Captain Lane to open on it with his battery. His firing was wild, not a shot hitting the mark. The heavy batteries promptly replied, showing such excellent practice that Lane's guns were soon silenced. A small force in the edge of the woods on the west side of the old field opened fire upon the V. The Federals changed their formation, and, advancing in line of battle, brushed away their assailants and plunged into the woods, when heavy firing began which lasted possibly half an hour.

I suppose that the Federal force which I saw was the division of General Sturgis,↓ and that he left behind Harland's brigade of Rodman's division to guard his flank in his advance, since Harland reports that he had no casualties. General Sturgis claims that he swept everything before him. So do his comrades who fought on his left. On the other hand, General Hood, who came up a short time before this advance, with the brigades of Wofford and Law, claims that he checked and drove back the Federals. G. T. Anderson reports that only his skirmishers were engaged. The surviving officers under G. B. Anderson (who was killed at Sharpsburg, and left no report) say that the same thing was true of their brigade in the afternoon. Ripley's brigade was not engaged at all. About dusk the 2d and 13th North Carolina Regiments attacked Fairchild's brigade and the batteries protected by it on the extreme Federal left, and were repulsed disastrously. Generals Burnside and Willcox say that the fight was continued until 10 o'clock at night. Hood was mistaken, then, in thinking that he had driven back the Federal advance. The opposing lines were close together at nightfall, and the firing between the skirmishers was kept up till a late hour. Equally erroneous is the claim that any Confederates were driven except Drayton's small brigade. We held the crests of the mountain, on the National road and the old Sharpsburg road, until Lee's order for withdrawal was given. General Reno, the Federal corps commander on our right, was killed at 7 P. M., in Wise's field, where the fight began at 9 o'clock in the morning. But on our left a commanding hill was lost before night. Batteries placed upon it next morning, acting in concert with the heavy batteries placed on our right by General Pleasonton before we were aware of his presence, would have made any position untenable on the pike or the crest of the mountain. I made that statement to General Lee about 9 P. M., when he consulted with Longstreet and myself in regard to renewing the fight the next morning. Longstreet concurred in this view, remarking that I knew the ground and the situation better than he did.

General Hooker detached Gibbon's brigade, consisting of three Wisconsin

↓ Probably Willcox's division, with its right refused to avoid the enfilading fire from the batteries on the mountain.— EDITORS.

FOX'S GAP.—THE APPROACH TO WISE'S FIELD.

This sketch and the one on the next page (from photographs made in 1885) may be regarded as parts of one picture. The old Sharpsburg or Braddock road lies between the stone-wall and the rail fence. The left distance shows the Middletown valley and the Catoctin range, from which Reno approached.—EDITORS.

regiments and one Indiana regiment, from Hatch's division, and directed it to move directly up the pike with a section of artillery. Then the divisions of Meade and Hatch were formed on the north side of the pike, with the division of Ricketts in supporting distance in rear. A belt of woods had to be passed through, and then it was open field all the way to the summit, and the two detached peaks were in full view upon which the devoted little band of Rodes was posted — the 12th Alabama Regiment on one, and the 3d, 5th, 6th, and 26th Alabama regiments on the other. Under the illusion that there were ten regiments and one battalion of Longstreet's command in those woods, the progress through them was slow, but, when once cleared, the advance was steady and made almost with the precision of movement of a parade day. Captain Robert E. Park, of Macon, Georgia, who commanded the forty skirmishers in the woods, thinks that he delayed the Federal advance for a long time.▶

It is not more improbable that a few active skirmishers north of the pike should prove an obstacle to progress through the forest there, than that a

▶ Captain Park writes:

"After passing through Boonsboro', *en route* to the scene of action, we met the dead body of the gallant General Garland, when an order from General D. H. Hill, through General R. E. Rodes, to Colonel B. B. Gayle of the 12th Alabama, directed that skirmishers should be deployed in front. Colonel Gayle hurriedly ordered captains of companies to send four men each to the front to report to Lieutenant R. E. Park as sharpshooters, and I promptly reported for orders; was directed to carry my squad of forty men to the foot of South Mountain, 'and keep the enemy back as long as possible.' I hastily deployed the men, and we moved down the mountain-side. On our way down we could see the enemy, in two lines of battle, in the valley below, advancing, preceded only a few steps by their dense line of skirmishers. I concealed my men behind trees, rocks, and bushes, and cautioned them to aim well before firing. We awaited with beating hearts the sure and steady approach of the 'Pennsylvania Bucktails,' who were directly in my front, and soon near enough to fire upon. I gave the command, 'Fire,' and forty guns were almost simultaneously emptied with deadly effect, and the surviving skirmishers rushed back pell-mell to their main line, disordering it greatly. The solid, well-drilled line soon rallied, and advanced steadily forward, and my small party, as soon as they were near enough, fired again, and nearly every bullet did fatal work. At least thirty men must have been killed or wounded at the second fire, and perhaps more at the first. Though checked for some minutes, the enemy again advanced, their officers earnestly exhorting them with 'close up' and 'forward.' I directed my men to fall back slowly and to fire from everything which would screen them from observation. I had lost only four men wounded up to this time, but six or eight more became demoralized and, despite my commands, entreaties, and threats left me and hastily fled to the rear. With the brave

FOX'S GAP—WISE'S FIELD AS SEEN FROM THE PASTURE NORTH OF THE ROAD.

The stump in the middle of the field beyond the wall is near where Reno fell. Part of the struggle was for the wooded crest on the left of the field. The house is Wise's, at the crossing of the ridge and Old Sharpsburg roads. [See map, p. 568.] The Confederates here were posted behind a stone-wall. The well at Wise's house was filled with the Confederate dead.— EDITORS.

division on the south side should hesitate to penetrate a forest from which their foes had been completely driven. The success of the Federals on the north side was due to the fact that after getting through the belt of woods at the foot of the mountain, they saw exactly what was before them. The lack of complete success south of the pike was owing to the thick woods on that side, which were supposed to be full of hidden enemies. In the battle of South Mountain the imaginary foes of the Lost Dispatch were worth more to us than ten thousand men.

The advance of Hatch's division in three lines, a brigade in each, was as grand and imposing as that of Meade's division. Hatch's general and field officers were on horseback, his colors were all flying, and the alignment of his men seemed to be perfectly preserved. General Hooker, looking at the steady and precise movement from the foot of the mountain, describes it as a beautiful sight. From the top of the mountain the sight was grand and sublime, but the elements of the pretty and the picturesque did not enter into it. Doubtless the Hebrew poet whose idea of the awe-inspiring is expressed by

squad which remained, we retreated slowly, firing as rapidly as we could load, and doing fatal work with every step. The advance was very slow and cautious. It was about 3 o'clock when we had opened fire at the foot of the mountain, and now the sun was rapidly setting. Corporal Myers, of Mobile, at my request, aimed at and shot an exposed officer, receiving himself a terrible wound as he did so. I raised him tenderly, gave him water, and reluctantly was about to abandon him to his fate, when a dozen muskets were pointed at me, and I was ordered to surrender. There was a deep ravine to our left, and the 3d Alabama skirmishers having fallen back, the Federals had got in my rear, and at the same time had closed upon me in front. If I had not stopped with Myers I might have escaped capture, but I was mortified and humiliated by the necessity of yielding myself a prisoner. Certain death was the only alternative. The enemy pushed forward after my capture, and came upon Colonel Gayle and the rear support. Colonel Gayle was ordered to surrender, but, drawing his pistol and firing it in their faces, he exclaimed: 'We are flanked, boys, but let's die in our tracks,' and continued to fire until he was literally riddled by bullets.

"I was accompanied to the rear by three Federal soldiers, and could but notice, as I walked down the mountain, the great execution done by my little squad as shown by the dead and wounded lying all along the route. At the foot of the mountain ambulances were being loaded. From what I saw and gathered from my captors, my little party committed fearful havoc, and the Federals imagined that several divisions of Lee's army confronted them. . . . I was carried before some prominent officer (have heard it was General Hatch), who questioned me about my regiment, brigade, division, number of troops, etc. The information I gave could not have benefited him much."

D. H. H.

the phrase, "terrible as an army with banners," had his view of the enemy from the top of a mountain.

There was not a single Confederate soldier to oppose the advance of General Hatch. I got some guns from the reserve artillery of Colonel Cutts to fire at the three lines; but owing to the little practice of the gunners and to the large angles of depression, the cannonade was as harmless as blank-cartridge salutes in honor of a militia general. While these ineffective missiles were flying which the enemy did not honor by so much as a dodge, Longstreet came up in person with three small brigades, and assumed direction of affairs. He sent the brigade of Evans under Colonel Stevens to the aid of Rodes's men, sorely pressed and well-nigh exhausted. The brigade of Pickett (under Garnett) and that of Kemper were hurried forward to meet and check Hatch, advancing, hitherto, without opposition.

General Meade had moved the brigade of Seymour to the right to take Rodes's position in reverse, while the brigades of Magilton and Gallagher went straight to the front. Meade was one of our most dreaded foes; he was always in deadly earnest, and he eschewed all trifling. He had under him brigade commanders, officers, and soldiers worthy of his leadership. In his onward sweep the peak upon which the 12th Alabama was posted was passed the gallant Colonel Gayle was killed, and his regiment was routed and dispersed. The four other regiments of Rodes made such heroic resistance that Meade, believing his division about to be flanked, sent for and obtained Duryée's brigade of Ricketts's division. It was pitiable to see the gallant but hopeless struggle of those Alabamians against such mighty odds. Rodes claimed to have fought for three hours without support; but an over-estimate of time under such circumstances is usual and natural. He lost 61 killed, 157 wounded, and 204 missing (captured), or more than one-third of his brigade. His supports [Evans's brigade] fought gallantly and saved him from being entirely surrounded, but they got on the ground too late to effect anything else. Evans's brigade under Stevens had been wasted by two campaigns and was small when it left Hagerstown that morning, and many had fallen out on the hot and dusty forced march. Of the four regiments in the brigade, we find in Volume XIX. of the "Official Records" only the report of one, the 17th South Carolina regiment under Colonel McMaster. That says that 141 men entered the fight on South Mountain, and of these 7 are reported killed, 37 wounded, and 17 missing (captured). Colonel McMaster writes to me that his was the largest regiment in the brigade; so the brigade must have been about 550 strong. General Meade says in his report that he lost 39 men, or ten per cent. of his division. As he received the support of Duryée before or about the time that Rodes got the aid of Stevens, he fought Rodes with the advantage all the while of three to one.

When Ripley came up, as before described, the pressure was all at Fox' Gap. He was sent in there and his brigade was uselessly employed by him in marching and counter-marching. Had it been sent to strengthen Rodes the key of the position might not have been lost. But the vainest of all speculations and regrets are about "the might have been."

Meade encamped that night on the commanding eminence which he had won.

The strength of the two brigades sent to check General Hatch did not exceed eight hundred men, as I will show presently. They must have performed prodigies of valor, and their praises can best be spoken in the words of their enemies. General Patrick, commanding the leading Federal brigade, tells of a race between his men and a strong force of the enemy for the possession of a fence. Patrick won the race and delivered his fire from the fence, picking off the cannoneers at some of our guns. General Hatch was wounded at this fence, and the command devolved on General Doubleday. The latter speaks of lying down behind the fence and allowing the enemy to charge up to within fifteen paces, whereupon he opened a deadly fire. Colonel Wainwright, who succeeded Doubleday in command of his brigade, was also wounded here, and Colonel Hofmann assumed command of it. Colonel Hofmann tells us that the ammunition of the brigade was just giving out when Ricketts relieved Doubleday. Several of the reports speak of the "superior force of the enemy." General Ricketts says that "he relieved Doubleday hard-pressed and nearly out of ammunition." Before Ricketts came in person with Hartsuff's brigade, he had sent Christian's brigade to the assistance of Doubleday. The brigades of Kemper and Pickett (the latter under Garnett) must have fought valiantly, else such results could not have been achieved. General Doubleday's report contains this curious story: "I learned from a wounded prisoner that we were engaged with four to five thousand under the immediate command of General Pickett, with heavy masses in their vicinity. He stated also that Longstreet in vain tried to rally the men, calling them his pets and using every effort to induce them to renew the attack." Of course, the old rebel knew that Pickett was not there in person and that there were no heavy masses in the vicinity. The astonishing thing is that General Doubleday should believe that there were 4000 or 5000 men before him under the immediate command of Pickett. But Doubleday's belief of the story is a tribute to the efficiency of the 800 men who fought a division of 3500 men the number reported by Hatch after Gibbon had been detached), and fought it so vigorously that two brigades were sent to its assistance.

Jenkins's brigade, under Walker, came up at dusk, too late to be in the fight; but it went in on the right of Garnett and took part in the irregular firing which was kept up till a late hour. Colonel Walker's report shows a loss of 3 killed and 29 wounded, which proves that he was but slightly engaged. The tired men of both sides lay down at last to rest within a hundred yards of each other. But now Gibbon was putting in earnest work on the pike. He had a choice brigade, strong in numbers and strong in the pluck of his men, all from the North-west, where habitually good fighters are reared. He had pushed forward cautiously in the afternoon with the 7th Wisconsin regiment, followed by the 6th on the north side of the pike and the 19th Indiana, supported by the 2d Wisconsin, on the south side. The ten imaginary regiments of the Lost Dispatch retarded his progress through the woods; and at one time, believing that the 7th Wisconsin was about to be

VIEW FROM TURNER'S GAP, LOOKING SOUTH-EAST [SEE MAP, P. 568]. FROM A PHOTOGRAPH TAKEN IN 1886.

The point of view is a little to the left of the Mountain House, now the home of Mrs. Dahlgren, widow of Admiral Dahlgren. Rodes was first posted on the hill, the slope of which is seen on the left; Gibbon was farther down the road in the hollow. The white patch on the mountain to the south (on the right) is Wise's field at Fox's Gap, where Reno and Garland were killed.—EDITORS.

turned on its right flank, he sent the 6th to its assistance. There were only a few skirmishers on his right, but the Lost Dispatch made him believe otherwise. About 9 P. M. the stone-wall was reached, and several gallant efforts were made in vain to carry it. When each repulse was followed by the "rebel" yells, the young men on my staff would cry out: "Hurrah for Georgia! Georgia is having a free fight." The Western men had met in the 23d and 28th Georgia regiments men as brave as themselves and far more advantageously posted. Colonel Bragg, of the 6th Wisconsin, says in his report: "We sat down in the dark to wait another attack, but the enemy was no more seen." At midnight Gorman's brigade of Sumner's corps relieved Gibbon's.

General Gibbon reports officially 318 men killed and wounded — a loss sustained almost entirely, I think, at the stone-wall. The colonel of the 7th Wisconsin reports a loss of 147 men in killed and wounded out of 375 muskets carried into action. This shows that he had brave men and that he encountered brave men. From his report we infer that Gibbon had fifteen hundred men. On our side Colquitt had 1100 men, and lost less than 100, owing to the admirable position in which he had been placed.

And now in regard to the numbers engaged. Longstreet sent to my aid 8 brigades,—5 belonging to the division of D. R. Jones, consisting of the brigades of Drayton, Pickett, Jenkins, G. T. Anderson, and Kemper; and 3 belonging to an extemporized division of N. G. Evans, including the brigades of Evans, Hood, and Law. On page 886, Part I., Volume XIX. of the "Official Records," Jones says that after Toombs joined him from Hagerstown, his 6 brigades numbered at Sharpsburg 2430 men; *i. e.*, an average of 405 men to each brigade. Now all Longstreet's officers and men know that the ranks were fuller at Sharpsburg than at South Mountain, because there were more stragglers in the forced march from Hagerstown to the battle-field of the 14th of September than there were casualties in the battle.¶ The above average would give 810 as the number of men in the two brigades which confronted the division of Hatch aided by two brigades from Ricketts. But it is well known that the Virginia brigades were unusually small, because of the heavy draughts upon them for cavalry, artillery, and local service. Between pages 894 and 902, Volume XIX., we have the strength at South Mountain of four of the five regiments of Pickett's brigade given officially,—the 19th Regiment, 150 men; 18th Regiment, 120 men; 56th Regiment, 80 men; 8th Regiment, 34 men. The strength of the other regiment, the 28th, is not given; but, assuming that it was 96, the average of the other four regiments, we have 480 as the number of men in Pickett's brigade at South Mountain. But the report of the colonel of the 56th shows that he was turned off with his 80 muskets, and did not go in with his brigade; so that Garnett had in the battle but 400 of Pickett's men. From Kemper's brigade we have but one report giving the strength of a regiment, and that comes from Colonel Corse of the 17th Virginia. He says that at Sharpsburg he had 6 officers and 49 privates in his regiment. A calculation based upon this report would show that Kemper's brigade was smaller than Pickett's.

On page 907 we have the only report from Jenkins's brigade which gives any intimation of its strength. There the 1st South Carolina regiment is said to have 106 men at Sharpsburg. It is possible the five regiments of this brigade numbered 530 in that battle. It is true that it was considerably larger at Sharpsburg than at South Mountain, because the stragglers from the Hagerstown march much more than made up for the small loss (32) in the battle of the 14th. But with due allowance for that gain, the brigade must have been 450 strong at South Mountain. It is evident, then, that Kemper's brigade fell below 400 at South Mountain; otherwise, the brigade average in Jones's division would have exceeded 406.

Longstreet thinks that he had four thousand men at South Mountain. His estimate is too high, according to the records as I find them. Accepting

---

¶ In his official report General Hill, after stating his force on the morning of the 14th as "less than 5000 men," says: "My ranks had been diminished by some additional straggling, and the morning of the 17th [Antietam] I had but 3000 infantry." Adding to this number General Hill's losses on September 14th at Fox's and Turner's Gaps, and we have 3934 as his strength in the battle of South Mountain, without counting these additional stragglers.— EDITORS.

BRIGADIER-GENERAL GEORGE B. ANDERSON, C. S. A., KILLED AT ANTIETAM. FROM AN OIL PORTRAIT.

his numbers, I would place 2200 at Fox's Gap and 1800 north of Turner's Gap. Colquitt fought mainly and Rodes entirely with Hooker's corps. Adding the 2200 men of these two brigades to Longstreet's 1800, we have 4000 as the number opposed to Hooker. ☆

General McClellan puts the strength of the two attacking corps at thirty thousand. His figures are substantially corroborated by the reports of his subordinates, — division, brigade, and regimental commanders. They indicate, moreover, that there had been great straggling in the Federal army, as well as in our own. On p. 97, General Ingalls, chief quartermaster, reports, October 1st, 1862, means of transporation for 13,707 men in the First Corps; for 12,860 men in the Ninth Corps . . . . and for 127,818 men in the entire Army of the Potomac.│ This was after the wastage of the two

☆ According to the estimate of Mr. Thomas White, chief clerk of the adjutant-general's office at General Lee's headquarters, who had charge of the field returns during the war, the effective strength of the Confederate forces at South Mountain, or Boonsboro', was: Longstreet, 8000; D. H. Hill, 7000,— total, 15,000. According to Colonel W. H. Taylor, adjutant-general of the Army of Northern Virginia, Hill had "less than 5000"; 6 brigades of Longstreet engaged numbered 4900,— total, 9900 (with 2 of Longstreet's brigades not engaged and not included). In his official report, General D. H. Hill says "the division numbered less than 5000 men on the morning of September 14th"; of his 5 brigades, Rodes's is stated to have numbered 1200, and Garland's "scarce 1000 men." The Union returns quoted show the whole number of officers and men of all arms present for duty without deduction. If to the strength of the

First and Ninth Corps on the 20th of September we add the previous losses, these numbers will show as follows: First Corps, 15,750; Ninth Corps, 13,972. Deduct one-fifth, 5944, for non-effectives,— total available Union force, 23,778. Total available Confederate force, according to Mr. White, 15,000; according to Colonel Taylor 9900, plus the two reserve brigades of Longstreet whose strength he does not give.— EDITORS.

│ The return of the Army of the Potomac for September 30th shows a total present for duty of 98,774 officers and men, including 5714 cavalry and headquarters guard. General Ingalls's statement, partly estimated as shown on its face (he counts cavalry 7000, it being actually 4543), is obviously in error in the figures, 30,926, set down for the Fifth Corps, which the return shows to have had 17,268 for duty, and 31,688 *present and absent*.— EDITORS.

## THE BATTLE OF SOUTH MOUNTAIN, OR BOONSBORO'.

battles (14th and 17th of September), reported on page 204 as amounting to 15,203.

General Hooker was well pleased with the work of his corps. He says in his report: "When the advantages of the enemy's position are considered, and his preponderating numbers, the forcing of the passage of South Mountain will be classed among the most brilliant and satisfactory achievements of this army, and its principal glory will be awarded to the First Corps." Undoubtedly that corps had gained important positions, but it is difficult to see how 4000 men could preponderate in numbers over 13,707. Hooker's division and brigade commanders, who had been well up under musketry fire, do not speak in such glowing terms of the victory. The reports of the stubborn fighters in the Federal army on both sides of the pike are models of modest propriety. This is especially so with those who bore the heat and burden of the day,— Meade, Hatch, Cox, Willcox, Scammon, Crook, Gibbon, Ewing, Gallagher, Magilton, Phelps, White, Jackson, Callis, Bragg, and others.

In regard to the casualties of the opposing forces, the losses in killed and wounded were greater on the Federal side than on the Confederate, because the one thin line of the latter fired at the dense masses of the former, sometimes in two lines, and sometimes in three. But from their weakness the Confederates took no prisoners, while they lost over four hundred within the enveloping ranks of their enemies. The revised statement of Federal losses in Volume XIX. gives the casualties in the First Corps as 923; of the Ninth Corps as 889,— total 1812, infantry and artillery; and to this number is added one cavalryman, how killed is not explained.

I lost two brigadiers and a large number of regimental commanders within three days, so that my division reports are very meager. Of the five brigades, there is a statistical report from that of Rodes alone. By means of a very extensive correspondence I have ascertained the casualties as nearly as they can be reached at this late day:

|  | Killed and Wounded. | Missing. |
|---|---|---|
| Rodes | 218 | 204 |
| Colquitt | 92 | 7 |
| Garland | 100 | 200 |
| Anderson | 84 | 29 |
| Ripley | 0 | 0 |
|  | 494 | 440 |

Longstreet's loss must have been less than mine, as he had but four small brigades seriously engaged. Walker reports only thirty-two casualties in Jenkins's brigade; G. T. Anderson had none. Hood speaks lightly of the fight of the two brigades under him. The exact losses can, however, never be known.

In the foregoing table reference is had to prisoners taken in battle. Some of our wearied men slipped off in the woods to sleep, and were not aroused when the orders came to fall back. Colonel Parker of the 30th North Carolina regiment, a brave and efficient officer, writes to me that he could hardly keep his men awake even when the deadly missiles were flying among them. This is in confirmation of what General Hood, in charge of the rear-guard, told me when I passed him after daylight on the 15th. He said that he found it difficult to arouse and push on the tired men, who had fallen out by the wayside to get a few minutes' sleep.

If the battle of South Mountain was fought to prevent the advance of McClellan, it was a failure on the part of the Confederates. If it was fought to save Lee's trains and artillery, and to reunite his scattered forces, it was a Confederate success. The former view was taken by the President of the United States, for he telegraphed to General McClellan on the 15th of September: "God bless you and all with you. Destroy the rebel army, if possible."

But, from whatever standpoint it may be looked at, the battle of South Mountain must be of interest to the military reader as showing the effect of a hallucination in enabling 9000 men to hold 30,000 at bay for so many hours, in robbing victory of its fruits, and in inspiring the victors with such caution that a simple ruse turned them back in their triumphal career.

Every battle-field of the Civil War beheld the deadly conflict of former friends with each other. South Mountain may be taken as a specimen of this unnatural and horrible state of things. The last time I ever saw Generals McClellan and Reno was in 1848, at the table of General G. W. Smith, in the city of Mexico. Generals Meade and Scammon had both been instructors while I was at West Point. Colonel Magilton, commanding a brigade in Meade's division, had been a lieutenant in my company in the Mexican war.

MAJOR-GENERAL R. E. RODES, C. S. A. FROM A PHOTOGRAPH.

General John Gibbon (whose brigade pressed up the pike on the 14th of September) and his brother Lardner had been "best men" at my wedding. They were from North Carolina; one brother took the Northern side, while the other took the Southern.

There is another view of the picture, however. If we had to be beaten it was better to be beaten by former friends. Every true soldier loves to have "a foeman worthy of his steel." Every true man likes to attribute high qualities to those who were once friends, though now alienated for a time. The temporary estrangement cannot obliterate the recollection of noble traits of character. Some one attempted to condole with Tom Yearwood, a famous old South Carolina bully, upon the beating given him by his own son. "Hush up," said old Tom. "I am glad that no one but my own flesh and blood had a hand in my drubbing."

The sons of the South struck her many heavy blows. Farragut, of Tennessee, rose, as a reward of merit, to the highest rank in the Federal navy. A large number of his associates were from the South. In the Federal army there were of Southern blood and lineage Generals Thomas, Sykes, Reno,

Newtown, J. J. Reynolds, Canby, Ord, Brannan, William Nelson, Crittenden, Blair, R. W. Johnson, T. J. Wood, N. B. Buford, Terrill, Graham [Lawrence P.], Davidson, Cooke, Alexander, Getty, French, Frémont, Pope, Hunter. Some of these doubtless served the South better by the side they took; most of them were fine, and some superb, officers.

Moreover, the South had three hundred thousand of her sons in the Federal army in subordinate capacities.‡ Her armies surrendered when a Southern-born President and a Southern-born Vice-President were at the head of the United States Government. That the wounds of defeat and humiliation have been so soon healed has been owing largely to this balm to mortified pride. The sting of shame to Frenchmen is that their magnificent capital was captured by, and their splendid armies were surrendered to, soldiers of an alien race and religion. On the other hand, the civil wars in England have left no bitter memories behind them. Compare this forgetfulness of civil strife in England with the bitterness which Ireland still feels over her subjugation; compare it with the fact that the Roman occupation of England for five hundred years made no impression upon the language of the natives, so little intercourse was there between them and their conquerors; compare it with the fact that for four hundred years after the Norman conquest there was no fusion between the Norman and Saxon tongues. In truth, all history teaches that the humiliation of defeat by a foreign foe is felt for ages, while that of defeat by the same race is temporary and soon forgotten. The late Civil War was relieved of very much of its sectional character by the presence of so many Southerners in the Union armies. Therefore, it will be in the United States as in all the unsectional civil wars of the world's history in which race and religion were not involved,—the waves of oblivion will roll over the bitter recollections of the strife. But we trust that fragrant forever will be the memory of deeds of heroism, patience, fortitude, self-denial, and constancy to principle, whether those deeds were performed by the wearers of the blue or of the gray.

---

‡ According to a printed statement dated at the "Adjutant-General's Office, Washington, November 9th, 1880," the slave-holding States furnished troops to the Union army as follows: Delaware, 12,284; Maryland, 46,638; West Virginia, 32,068; District of Columbia, 16,534; Missouri, 109,111; Kentucky, 75,760; Tennessee, 31,092; Arkansas, 8289; North Carolina, 3156; Alabama, 2576; Florida, 1290; Louisiana, 5224; Mississippi, 545; Texas, 1965,—total, 346,532. This sum includes colored troops, but their number is not stated. The territory in actual rebellion also furnished 99,337 colored soldiers, recruited at various stations and not accredited to States. The so-called Northern, or free, States furnished to the Union army 2,419,159 men.—EDITORS.

FROM A PHOTOGRAPH.

J. E. B. Stuart
Maj'r Gen'l

CONFEDERATE DEAD AT THE CROSS-ROADS BY WISE'S HOUSE AT FOX'S GAP [SEE PP. 568 AND 573]. FROM A SKETCH MADE THE DAY AFTER THE BATTLE.

## FORCING FOX'S GAP AND TURNER'S GAP.

### BY JACOB D. COX, MAJOR-GENERAL, U. S. V.

ON the 5th of September, 1862, the Kanawha Division was ordered by McClellan to report to General Burnside, commanding the Right Wing of the Army of the Potomac. We left Upton's Hill early on the morning of the 6th, crossed the river, and marched through Washington to Leesboro, Maryland, where the First Corps (Hooker's) and the Ninth Corps (Burnside's, under Reno), constituting the right wing, were assembling. Our formal assignment to the Ninth Corps was made a day or two later. On the 8th, the division was ordered to take the advance and marched to Brookville; on the 9th to Goshen; on the 11th to Ridgeville, and on the 12th, shortly after noon, to Frederick City, being the first to enter that place, and driving out the Confederate rear-guard of cavalry under General Wade Hampton. The insignificant skirmish which occurred there had a considerable influence upon the battle of the 14th, in an indirect way. The enemy's cavalry had been driven from the banks of the Monocacy River and retired into the town. The division, consisting of two brigades (Moor's and Scammon's), had crossed at the stone bridge on the National road, and Moor's, deployed on both sides of the turnpike, advanced upon the city. Colonel Moor himself, with a troop of cavalry and a single cannon, was in the road. An impertinent criticism upon the speed of his movement, volunteered by a young staff-officer from corps head-

---

For an account of the transfer of the Kanawha Division from West Virginia to the Potomac, see p. 281. The division was not engaged in the second battle of Bull Run; but two regiments of Scammon's brigade were under fire at Bull Run Bridge, near Union Mills, August 27th.— EDITORS.

Confusion in the numbers of the First and Twelfth Corps is found in the records and correspondence. In the Army of Virginia, Sigel's corps (Eleventh) had been designated as First, Banks's (Twelfth) had been Second, and McDowell's (First) had been Third. In the Maryland campaign Hooker was assigned to McDowell's, which was sometimes called First and sometimes Third. Mansfield was assigned to Banks's. The proper designations after the consolidation of the armies were First and Twelfth. Reno had been assigned to the First, but McClellan got authority to change it, and gave that corps to Hooker, sending Reno back to the Ninth ("Official Records," XIX., Pt. II., pp. 197, 198, 279, 349).— J. D. C.

The Ninth Corps, created July 22d, 1862, was composed of the command that Burnside brought from North Carolina.— EDITORS.

quarters, stung Moor into dashing ahead at a gallop, with his escort and staff, and the gun. Just at the outskirts of the town the road turns to the left among the houses, and cannot be seen. While we were wondering at the charge by the brigade commander and his escort, he came to the turn of the road: there was a quick, sharp rattling of carbines, and Hampton's Legion was atop of the little party. There was one discharge of the cannon, and some of the brigade staff and the escort came back in disorder. I ordered up quickly the 11th Ohio, of Scammon's brigade, which was in column in the road, and they dashed into the town at a charge with fixed bayonets. The enemy's cavalry had not waited for them, but had retreated out of the place by the Hagerstown road. Moor had been ridden down, unhorsed, and captured. The artillerymen had unlimbered their gun, pointed it, and the gunner stood with the lanyard in his hand, when he was struck by a rushing horse; the gun was fired by the concussion, but at the same moment it was capsized into the ditch by the impact of the cavalry column. The enemy had no time to right the gun or carry it off, nor to stop for prisoners. They forced Moor on another horse and turned tail as the charging lines of infantry came up on right and left, together with the column in the road, for there had not been a moment's pause in the advance. Those who have a fancy for learning how Munchausen could have told this story are referred to the narrative of Major Heros Von Borcke, of J. E. B. Stuart's staff. Moor's capture, however, had consequences, as we shall see. His brigade passed to the command of Colonel George Crook, of the 36th Ohio.

Frederick was a loyal city, and as Hampton's cavalry went out at one end of the street and our infantry came in at the other, while the carbine smoke and the smell of powder still lingered, the closed window-shutters of the houses flew open, the sashes went up, the windows were filled with ladies waving their handkerchiefs and the national flag, and the men came to the column with fruits and refreshments for the marching soldiers.

We encamped just beyond the town. Pleasonton's cavalry, which had advanced by a different road (the one leading through Urbana), was sent forward next morning (September 13th) to reconnoiter the passes of Catoctin Mountain, and Rodman's division of our corps went as his support. Through some misunderstanding, Rodman did not advance on the Hagerstown road beyond Catoctin Mountain, but moved toward Franklin's line of march upon Crampton's Gap (southward). About noon of the 13th, I was ordered to march with my division to Middletown, on the National road leading to Hagerstown. McClellan himself met me as my column moved out of town, and told me of the misunderstanding in Rodman's orders, adding, that if I met him on the march I should take his division also along with me. I did not meet him, but his division returned to Frederick that night. The other two divisions of our corps crossed the Catoctin in the evening, and camped near the western base of the mountain. My own camp for the night was pitched on the western side of the village of Middletown.

The Catoctin or Middletown valley is beautifully included between Catoctin Mountain and South Mountain, two ranges of the Blue Ridge, running north-east and south-west. The valley is 6 or 8 miles wide, and the National road, as it goes north-westward, crosses South Mountain at a depression called Turner's Gap. The old Sharpsburg road leaves the turnpike a little west of Middletown, turns to the left, and crosses the mountain at Fox's Gap, about a mile from Turner's. The mountain crests are about 1300 feet above the Catoctin valley, and the "gaps" are from 200 to 300 feet lower than the summits near them.‡ These summits are like scattered and somewhat irregular hills upon the high rounded surface of the mountain-top. They are wooded, but along the south-easterly slopes, quite near the top of the mountain, are small farms with meadows and cultivated fields.

MAJOR-GENERAL JESSE L. RENO, KILLED AT FOX'S GAP. FROM A PHOTOGRAPH.

In the evening of the 13th I was ordered to support General Pleasonton in his cavalry reconnoissance to be made toward Turner's Gap in the morning. He had already been reënforced by Benjamin's and Gibson's batteries from the corps. The notion that Pleasonton was authorized to put the infantry in position for an expected battle is wholly a mistake. No battle was expected at Turner's Gap. Lee's order, of which a copy had fallen into McClellan's hands, directed the concentration of the forces under Longstreet and D. H. Hill at Boonsboro', where they were to be joined by those under Jackson as soon as Harper's Ferry should be taken. McClellan's orders and correspondence show that he expected a battle at Boonsboro', but not at South Mountain or east of it. Pleasonton had found a rear-guard at Turner's Gap, but the support of a single brigade of infantry was assumed to be enough to enable his cavalry to clear the way. Pleasonton asked for one brigade of infantry to report to him for the purpose stated, and I detailed the brigade under command of Colonel E. P. Scammon. At 6 o'clock in the morning of Sunday, September 14th, he marched out of camp at Middletown. His brigade consisted of the 12th, 23d, and 30th Ohio regiments; that of Crook, which was left in camp, was made up of the 11th, 28th, and 36th Ohio, and each brigade was nearly fifteen hundred strong. Two batteries of artillery and a squadron of cavalry also belonged to the division.

I was myself on the road when Scammon marched out, and was riding forward with him to learn how Pleasonton intended to use the troops, when, just as we crossed Catoctin Creek, I was surprised to see Colonel Moor standing

‡ These elevations are from the official map made by the U. S. Engineers.— J. D. C.

at the roadside. With astonishment, I rode to him and asked how he came there. He said he had been taken as prisoner beyond the mountain, but had been paroled the evening before, and was now finding his way back to us on foot. "But where are *you* going?" said he. I answered that Scammon's brigade was going to support Pleasonton in a reconnoissance into the gap. Moor made an involuntary start, saying, "My God! be careful"; then, checking himself, said, "But I am paroled!" and turned away.

I galloped to Scammon and told him that I should follow him in close support with Crook's brigade, and as I went back along the column I spoke to each regimental commander, warning them to be prepared for anything, big or little,— it might be a skirmish, it might be a battle. Hurrying back to the camp, I ordered Crook to turn out his brigade prepared to march at once. I then wrote a dispatch to General Reno, saying I suspected we should find the enemy in force on the mountain-top, and should go forward with both brigades instead of sending one. Starting a courier with this, I rode forward to find Pleasonton, who was about a mile in front of my camp, where the old Sharpsburg road leaves the turnpike. I found that he was convinced that the enemy's position in the gap was too strong to be carried by a direct attack, and that he had determined to let his horsemen demonstrate on the main road, supporting the batteries, one of which at least (Benjamin's) was of 20-pounder Parrott guns, while Scammon should march by the Sharpsburg road and try to reach the flank of the force on the summit. Telling him of my suspicion as to the enemy, I also informed him that I had determined to support Scammon with Crook, and if it became necessary to fight with the whole division I should do so, in which case I should assume the responsibility myself as his senior officer. To this he cordially assented.

One of my batteries contained a section of 20-pounder Parrotts, and as these were too heavy to take up the rough mountain road, I ordered them to go into action beside Benjamin's battery, near the turnpike, and to remain with it till further orders. Our artillery at this time was occupying a knoll about half a mile in front of the forks of the road, and was exchanging shots with a battery of the enemy well up toward the gap. It was about half-past 7 o'clock when Crook's column filed off on the old Sharpsburg road, Scammon having perhaps half an hour's start. We had fully two miles to go before we should reach the place where our attack was made, and, as it was a pretty steep road, the men marched slowly with frequent rests. On our way up we were overtaken by my courier who had returned from Reno with approval of my action, and the assurance that the rest of the Ninth Corps would come forward to my support. [See map, p. 568.]

At about half a mile from the summit, at Fox's Gap, the enemy had opened upon Scammon with case shot from the edge of the timber above the open fields, and the latter had judiciously turned off upon a country road leading still farther to the left and nearly parallel to the ridge above. Here I overtook him, his brigade being formed in line, under cover of the timber, facing open pasture fields, having a stone-wall along the upper side, with the forest again beyond this. Crook was brought up close in his rear. The ascent and the formation of the division had occupied more than an hour, and it was now about 9 o'clock. Bayonets were fixed, and at the word the lines charged forward with loud hurrahs. The enemy opened with musketry and shrapnel; our men fell fast, but they kept up their pace, and in a few moments they were on and over the wall, the center of Garland's North Carolina brigade breaking before them. They hung on a little longer at right and left, and for some time it was a fierce mêlée, hand to hand, but the Ohio boys were the victors. We found that there was a country road behind the wall on top of the ridge, and the cover of the forest had enabled the enemy's guns to get away toward our right. The 11th Ohio was sent from Crook's brigade beyond Scammon's left, where part of the enemy's force held a hill and summit higher than the ridge at the stone-wall. This seems to have been held by Rosser's cavalry with a battery. The 36th Ohio was, in similar manner, sent beyond Scammon's right. The whole line again sprung forward. The high knoll on the left was carried, the enemy's center was completely broken and driven down the mountain, while on the right our men pushed the routed Carolinians beyond the Sharpsburg road, through Wise's fields, and up the slope of the crest toward the Mountain House at Turner's Gap. The regiment on the enemy's extreme right had been cut off from the others and retreated south-westwardly down the mountain toward Rohrersville. Those on their left had made such resistance as they could till they were supported by Anderson's brigade, which hurried to their assistance. The cavalry also took refuge on a wooded hill west of the Mountain House. Although Garland's line had been broken in the first charge, the rallying and fighting had been stubborn for more than an hour. Our position was now diagonally across the mountain-top, the shape of the ridges making our formation a hollow curve with our right too much in the air, where it was exposed to a severe artillery fire, not only from the batteries near the Mountain House but from one on a high hill north of the turnpike. The batteries with Pleasonton did their best to assist us, and were admirably served. We had several hundred prisoners in our hands, and learned from them that D. H. Hill's division, consisting of five brigades, was opposed to us, and that Longstreet was said to be in near support. Our own losses had not been trifling, and it seemed wise to contract our lines a little, so that we might have some reserve and hold the crest we had won till the rest of the Ninth Corps should arrive. Our left and center were strongly posted, but the right was partly across Fox's Gap, at the edge of the woods beyond Wise's house, around which there had been a fierce struggle. The 30th and 36th were therefore brought back to the crest on the hither side of the gap, where we still commanded the Sharpsburg road, and making the 30th our right flank, the 36th and the 28th were put in second line. My right thus occupied the woods looking northward into Wise's fields. About noon the combat was reduced to one of artillery, and the enemy's guns had so completely the range of the sloping fields behind us that their canister shot cut long furrows in the sod, with a noise like the cutting of a melon rind.

Willcox's division reported to me at about 2 o'clock, and would have been up considerably earlier but for a mistake in the delivery of a message to him, in consequence of which he moved first toward the hill on the north of the turnpike (afterward carried by Hooker's corps), until he was recalled and given the right direction by Reno, who had arrived at Pleasonton's headquarters. As he went into position on my right, the artillery fire from the crest beyond the turnpike annoyed him, and to avoid being enfiladed by it, he formed with his right thrown back nearly at right angles to the front and facing toward the turnpike. We were not long left idle. Longstreet's divisions had been arriving on the field faster than ours, and made a most determined effort to push us back from the ridge we held. I sent two regiments of Willcox's to extend my left, which was in danger of being turned. Their strongest attack fell upon the angle of Willcox's command, and for a little while there was some confusion there, due to the raking artillery fire which came from the right; but Willcox soon reformed his lines, and after a very bloody contest, pushed across the Sharpsburg road, through Wise's fields, and into the wooded slope beyond. Along the front of the Kanawha Division the line was steadily maintained and the enemy was repulsed with severe loss. At nearly 4 o'clock, Sturgis's division arrived and relieved the left wing of Willcox's division, the latter taking ground a little more to the right and rear. Rodman was the last to arrive, and as part of Longstreet's corps again threatened to pass beyond my left flank, I sent Fairchild's brigade to extend the line in that direction, the rest of that division going to the support of Sturgis and Willcox. During all this time there was sharp fighting all along the front, the struggle being on the part of the Confederates to drive back our center and left, where we held the highest summits of the mountain, and on our part to push forward our right so as to gain the one elevation they still held on our side of the National road, at the Mountain House. On the other side of the turnpike Hooker had by this time deployed, and his corps was fighting its way up the mountain side there.

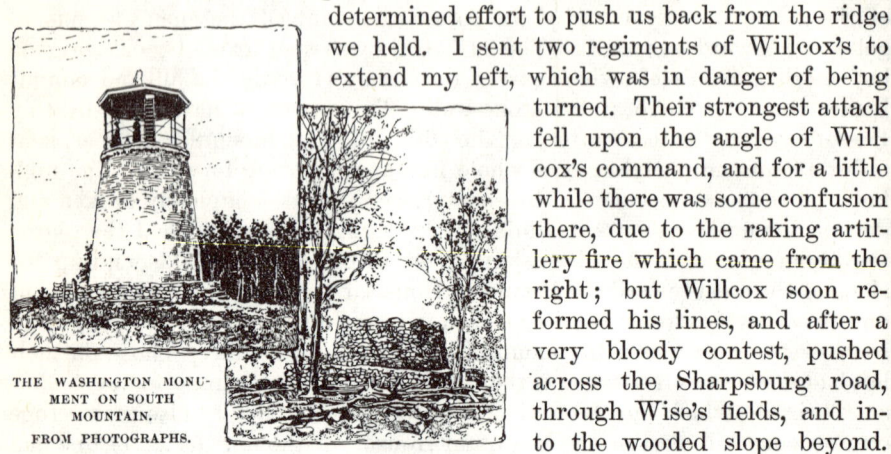

THE WASHINGTON MONUMENT ON SOUTH MOUNTAIN.
FROM PHOTOGRAPHS.

This monument, to the memory of George Washington, was first erected by the citizens of Boonsboro' and vicinity in 1827. It stands on the summit, a mile and a half north of Turner's Gap [see map, p. 568]. Originally it was twenty feet high. In its tumble-down condition, as seen on the right of the picture, it served as one of the Union signal stations during the battle of Antietam. In 1882 the monument was rebuilt, as seen on the left of the picture, by the Odd Fellows of Boonsboro'. The present height of the tower, including the observatory, is forty feet.— EDITORS.

McClellan, Burnside, and Reno had come, soon after Willcox's division, to the knoll in the valley which had been Pleasonton's position, and from that point, a central one in the midst of curving hills, had issued their orders. The Ninth Corps troops, as they came up the mountain, had reported to me for position, as I was senior on the line. Soon after the arrival of Rodman's division, the order came to advance the whole line, so as to complete the dislodgment of the enemy from the remaining summit at the Mountain House. At the center and left the advance was not difficult, for we held the ridge and pushed our opponents down the mountain. But the right had still to climb, and the ground there was rough and rocky, a fortress in itself and stoutly held. Good progress was made by both Sturgis and Willcox, but the fastness at the Mountain House had not been carried when darkness fell upon the field. A little before sunset, Reno came up in person, anxious to know why the right could not get forward quite to the summit. After a few moments' conversation with me he passed on to Sturgis; it seemed to me he was hardly gone before he was brought back upon a stretcher, dead. He had gone to the skirmish line to examine for himself the situation there, and had been shot down by the enemy posted among the rocks and trees. There was more or less firing in that part of the field till late in the evening, but when morning dawned, the Confederates had abandoned the last foothold above Turner's Gap.

On the north of the National road the First Corps under Hooker had been opposed by one of Hill's brigades and four of Longstreet's, and had gradually worked its way along the old Hagerstown road, crossing the heights in that direction after dark in the evening. Gibbon's brigade had advanced along the National road, crowding up quite close to Turner's Gap, and engaging the enemy under Colquitt in a lively combat. It has been my purpose, however, to limit any detailed account to what occurred under my own eye.

The peculiar character of the battle had been that it grew out of what was intended for a mere reconnoissance. The Kanawha Division had carried the crest at Fox's Gap early in the forenoon, while the rest of the army was miles away. General Hill has since argued that only part of his division could oppose us; but his brigades were all on the mountain summit within easy support of each other, and they had the day before them. It was five hours from the time of our first charge to the arrival of our first supports, and it was not till 3 o'clock in the afternoon that Hooker's corps reached the eastern base of the mountain and began its deployment north of the National road. Our effort was to attack the weak end of the Confederate line, and we succeeded in putting a stronger force there than that which opposed us. It is for our opponent to explain how we were permitted to do it. The two brigades of the Kanawha Division numbered less than three thousand men. Hill's division was five thousand strong, even by the Confederate method of counting their effectives, which should be increased nearly one-fifth to compare properly with our reports. In addition to these, Stuart had the principal part of the Confederate cavalry on this line, and they were not idle spectators. Part of Lee's and Hampton's brigades were certainly there, and probably the whole of Lee's. With less than half the numerical strength which was opposed to it, therefore, the Kanawha Division had carried the summit, advancing to the charge for the most part over open ground in a storm of musketry and artillery fire, and had held the crests they had gained through the livelong day, in spite of all efforts to retake them. The Ninth and the First Corps were deployed about 4 o'clock in the afternoon, and from that time till dark the proportions of the combat were enlarged to a battle which raged along two miles of mountain summits. The casualties in the Ninth Corps had been 889, of which 356 were in the Kanawha Division, which also captured some 600 of the enemy and sent them to the rear under guard. Reno on the National side and Garland on the Confederate were the officers of highest rank who were killed; but the wounded included a long list of distinguished men, among whom was Lieutenant-Colonel Rutherford B. Hayes (afterward President), who fell severely wounded in the early morning struggle on our left, where, also, Garland died, vainly trying to stay the rout of his brigade as our men covered the mountain-top.↓

On Monday morning our first duty was to bury the dead and to see that the wounded in our field-hospitals were sent back to Middletown where the general hospital had been established. During the forenoon we received orders to march toward Sharpsburg, but the road was already occupied by other troops, and when the head of my division reached it, at the place where the fight in front of Willcox's division had been most severe, we were halted for two or three hours till the corps which had the right of way should pass. Then we turned our faces toward the Antietam.

↓ General Hooker, commander of the First Corps, in his report, thus describes the action on the right of the Union Army, for the control of Turner's Gap:

"In front of us was South Mountain, the crest of the spinal ridge of which was held by the enemy in considerable force. Its slopes are precipitous, rugged, and wooded, and difficult of access to an infantry force even in absence of a foe in front. . . . Meade moved forward with great vigor and soon became engaged, driving everything before him. Every step of his advance was resisted stubbornly by a numerous enemy, and, besides, he had great natural obstacles to overcome which impeded his advance, but did not check it. . . . At this moment word was received that the enemy were attempting to turn Meade's right, when Duryée's brigade, of Ricketts's division, was dispatched to thwart it, and reached there in good time to render substantial aid in this, and also in assisting their comrades in crowning the summit with our arms. This was taken possession of in fine style between sundown and dark, and from that moment the battle was won. . . . Meantime Hatch had pressed into the forest on the left, and, after driving in their advanced pickets, encountered a heavy fire from the enemy massed in his front. The struggle became violent and protracted, his troops displaying the finest courage and determination. . . . Hatch being outnumbered, sorely pressed, and almost out of ammunition, Christian's brigade, of Ricketts's division, was ordered forward to strengthen him, and in this rendered good service. On this part of the field the resistance of the enemy was continued until after dark, and only subsided on his being driven from his position. It being very dark, our troops were directed to remain in position, and Hartsuff's brigade [of Ricketts's division] was brought up and formed a line across the valley, connecting with Meade's left and Hatch's right, and all were directed to sleep on their arms."

Brigadier-General John Gibbon reports:

". . . My brigade was detached from the division and ordered to report for duty to Major-General Burnside.

Late in the afternoon I was ordered to move up the Hagerstown turnpike [National road] with my brigade and one section of Gibbon's battery to attack the position of the enemy in the gorge. The 7th Wisconsin and the 19th Indiana were placed respectively on the right and left of the turnpike, to advance by the head of the company, preceded by two companies of skirmishers from the 6th and 2d Wisconsin, and, followed by these regiments, formed in double column at half distance, the section of the battery under Lieutenant Stewart, 4th Artillery, keeping on the pike a little in rear of the first line. The skirmishers soon became engaged and were supported by the leading regiments, while our guns moved forward on the turnpike until within range of the enemy's guns which were firing on our column from the top of the gorge, when they opened with good effect. My men steadily advanced on the enemy posted in the woods and behind stone-walls, driving him before them until he was reënforced by three additional regiments, making five in all opposed to us. Seeing we were likely to be outflanked on our right, I directed Lieutenant-Colonel Bragg, of the 6th Wisconsin, to enter the wood on his right and deploy his regiment on the right of the 7th. This was successfully accomplished, while the 19th Indiana, supported by the 2d Wisconsin, deployed, and, swinging around parallel to the turnpike, took the enemy in the flank. Thus the fight continued till long after dark, Stewart using his guns with good effect over the heads of our own men. My men, with their ammunition nearly exhausted, held all the ground they had taken. . . ."

The Confederate troops opposed to Meade appear to have been Rodes's brigade, of D. H. Hill's division, supported by Jenkins's, of D. R. Jones's division, while Hatch's advance appears to have been resisted by Kemper's and Garnett's brigades, of D. R. Jones's division, supported by Evans's independent brigade. Colquitt's brigade, of D. H. Hill's division, held the main turnpike against Gibbon.— EDITORS.

CAVALRY SKIRMISHERS.

# NOTES ON CRAMPTON'S GAP AND ANTIETAM.

### BY WM. B. FRANKLIN, MAJOR-GENERAL, U. S. V.

BETWEEN the 2d and 6th of September, the Sixth Corps remained in camp near Alexandria and collected horses and transportation for ammunition and provisions, which were gradually disembarked. On the latter date it marched to Tenallytown, beyond Georgetown, D. C., crossing the Potomac by the Long Bridge, and beginning the Maryland campaign. Its daily marches thereafter, to the date of the battle of Antietam, were regulated by orders from General McClellan, who, in turn, was in direct communication with Washington. It appears from the telegraphic correspondence which was carried on between Halleck and McClellan, that while the latter believed that General Lee's object was the invasion of Pennsylvania, the former could not divest himself of the notion that Lee was about to play the Union army some slippery trick by turning its left, getting between it and Washington and Baltimore, and then taking each city by a *coup-de-main*.

The following are extracts from some of General Halleck's dispatches:

SEPT. 9.—". . . I think we must be very cautious about stripping too much the forts on the Virginia side. It may be the enemy's object to draw off the mass of our forces, and then attempt to attack from the Virginia side of the Potomac."

SEPT. 11.—"I think the main force of the enemy is in your front; more troops can be spared from here."‡

SEPT. 13.—"I am of opinion that the enemy will send a small column toward Pennsylvania, so as to draw your forces in that direction; then suddenly move on Washington with the forces south of the Potomac, and those he may cross over."

‡ General McClellan states that he received the dispatch in this form, but as printed in the "Official Records," Vol. XIX., Pt. II., p. 253, the sentence reads: "If the main force of the enemy is in your front, more troops can be spared from here."— EDITORS.

SEPT. 14.—" Scouts report a large force still on Virginia side of the Potomac, near Leesburg. If so, I fear you are exposing your left flank, and that the enemy can cross in your rear."

SEPT. 16.—" I fear now more than ever that they [the enemy] will recross at Harper's Ferry, or below, and turn your left, thus cutting you off from Washington. . . ."

On September 12th, Mr. Lincoln telegraphed General McClellan that he believed the enemy was recrossing the Potomac, and said, "Please do not let him get off without being hurt."

These dispatches demonstrate that it was McClellan's duty as a subordinate to move slowly and cautiously in his advance, although he believed that the whole of Lee's army was in his front. And during the whole Maryland campaign his army was nearer Washington than was Lee's.

On or before September 7th, General McClellan advised that Harper's Ferry should be evacuated *via* Hagerstown, so as to hold the Cumberland Valley against an advance toward Harrisburg, and on the 10th of September he asked that the garrison at Harper's Ferry should be ordered to join him. General Halleck in answer to the last request stated, "There is no way for Colonel Miles to join you at present; his only chance is to defend his works till you can open communication with him." Yet during the night of September 14th two regiments of cavalry marched out of Harper's Ferry to Hagerstown without meeting any enemy; and the whole infantry and field-artillery force of the garrison might have escaped before the 14th had General McClellan's advice of September 7th and 10th been followed. So the Sixth Corps moved by easy marches toward the Blue Ridge, under daily orders from the commanding general, and on the 14th of September fought the battle of Crampton's Gap, gaining the completest victory gained up to that time by any part of the Army of the Potomac.

While Burnside and Hooker were forcing Turner's Gap to open the direct road to Hagerstown, I was ordered to move by Crampton's Gap, five miles farther south, and gain Rohrersville, in order to cut off McLaws and R. H. Anderson on Maryland Heights, and to relieve Harper's Ferry. About noon on the 14th of September, the head of my column, Slocum's division, came upon Munford's brigade of cavalry, comprising the 2d and 12th Virginia regiments, with Chew's battery and a section of the Portsmouth battery of naval howitzers, supported by two regiments of Mahone's brigade of R. H. Anderson's division, under Colonel William A. Parham. General McLaws had also posted the remainder of Mahone's brigade and the brigades of Semmes and Cobb of his own division within supporting distance, and ordered General Howell Cobb to take command and to hold the pass against us. With the remainder of Anderson's division and his own, General McLaws occupied Maryland Heights, distant five miles. I quote from my official report of the action which ensued:

"The enemy was strongly posted on both sides of the road, which made a steep ascent through a narrow defile, wooded on both sides and offering great advantages of cover and position. Their advance was posted near the base of the mountain, in the rear of a stone-wall, stretching to the right of the road at a point where the ascent was gradual and for the most part over open fields. Eight guns had been stationed on the road and at points on the sides and summit of the mountain to the left of the pass. It was evident that the position could be carried

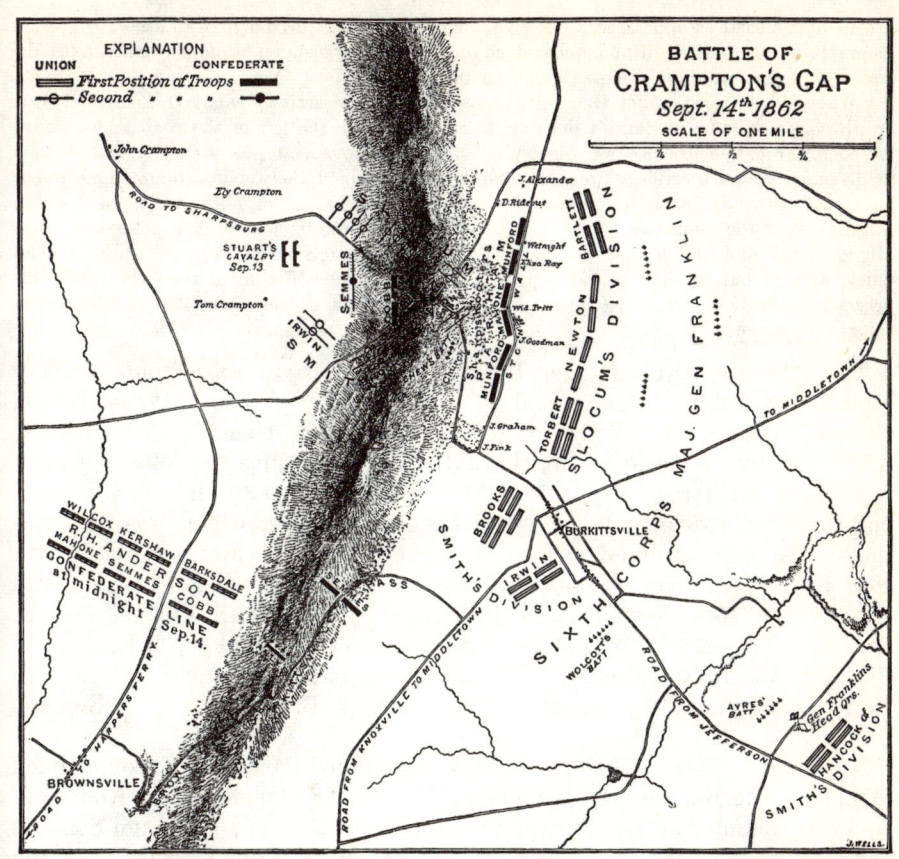

The Confederate sharp-shooters were behind their main line on higher ground, protected by trees and bowlders. After Parham's troops retired, Cobb, who had just reached the field, assumed command.—EDITORS.

only by an infantry attack. Accordingly, I directed Major-General Slocum to advance his division through the village of Burkittsville and commence the attack upon the right. Wolcott's 1st Maryland Battery was stationed on the left and to the rear of the village, and maintained a steady fire on the positions of the enemy until they were assailed and carried by our troops. Smith's division was placed in reserve on the east side of the village, and held in readiness to coöperate with General Slocum or support his attack as occasion might require. Captain Ayres's battery of this division was posted on a commanding ground to the left of the reserves, and kept up an uninterrupted fire on the principal battery of the enemy until the latter was driven from its position.

"The advance of General Slocum was made with admirable steadiness through a well-directed fire from the batteries on the mountain, the brigade of Colonel Bartlett taking the lead, and followed at proper intervals by the brigades of General Newton and Colonel Torbert. Upon fully determining the enemy's position, the skirmishers were withdrawn and Colonel Bartlett became engaged along his entire line. He maintained his ground steadily under a severe fire for some time at a manifest disadvantage, until reënforced by two regiments of General Newton's brigade upon his right, and the brigade of Colonel Torbert and the two remaining regiments of Newton's on his left. The line of battle thus formed, an immediate charge was ordered, and most gallantly executed. The men swept forward with a cheer, over the stone-wall, dislodging the enemy, and pursuing him up the mountain-side to the crest of the hill and down the opposite slope. This single charge, sustained as it was over a great distance, and on a rough ascent of unusual steepness, was decisive. The enemy was driven in the utmost confusion from a position of strength and allowed no opportunity for even an attempt to rally, until the pass was cleared and in the possession of our troops.

"When the division under General Slocum first became actively engaged, I directed General Brooks's brigade, of Smith's division, to advance upon the left of the road and dislodge the enemy from the woods upon Slocum's flank. The movement was promptly and steadily made under a severe artillery fire. General Brooks occupied the woods after a slight resistance, and then advanced, simultaneously with General Slocum, rapidly and in good order, to the crest of the mountain. The victory was complete, and its achievement followed so rapidly upon the first attack that the enemy's reserves, although pushed forward at the double-quick, arrived but in time to participate in the flight and add confusion to the rout. 400 prisoners, from 17 different organizations, 700 stand of arms, 1 piece of artillery, and 3 stand of colors were captured." . . .

The gun was a 12-pounder howitzer belonging to the Troup artillery attached to Cobb's brigade, and was captured by the 95th Pennsylvania, Colonel Gustavus W. Town, of Newton's brigade. General Cobb says it was "lost by an accident to the axle," but according to Colonel Town's report the artillerists fled before his advance, "merely disabling it temporarily by throwing off one wheel from the limber, which was left with the horses near at hand." Two of the colors were captured by the 4th New Jersey regiment, Colonel William B. Hatch, of Torbert's brigade, and one by the 16th New York, commanded by Lieutenant-Colonel Joel J. Seaver, of Bartlett's brigade. A fourth stand of colors, belonging to the 16th Virginia regiment, of Mahone's brigade, was taken by the 4th Vermont regiment, Lieutenant-Colonel Charles B. Stoughton, of Brooks's brigade.

No report appears to have been made by Colonel Parham, who commanded Mahone's brigade, nor by his division commander, General R. H. Anderson, who was wounded at Antietam, but the reports of Generals Cobb and Semmes and Colonel Munford sufficiently indicate the effect of our advance upon the forces under their command. Munford, who had eight guns, his two regiments of cavalry dismounted, and Mahone's brigade, was driven from his position behind a stone-wall at the foot of the pass. Cobb now came to his support, dividing his brigade to the right and left, but too late to change the result. One regiment, the 10th Georgia, of Semmes's brigade, also joined in Parham's defense, while the remaining three regiments, with nine guns of Manly's, Macon's, and Page's batteries, were posted for the defense of Burkittsville Gap, about a mile below toward our left, where the artillery is described, in the Confederate reports, as having done "good service." General Cobb says:

"As I was marching the last of the column, I received a message from you [McLaws] . . . that I must hold the gap if it cost the life of every man in my command. . . . Two of my regiments were sent to the right and two to the left to meet these movements of the enemy. In this we were successful, until the center gave way, pressed by fresh troops of the enemy and increased numbers. Up to this time the troops had fought well and maintained their ground against greatly superior forces. The 10th Georgia regiment, of General Semmes's brigade, had been ordered to the gap from their position at the foot of the mountain and participated in the battle with great courage and energy. After the lines were broken, all my efforts to rally the troops were unsuccessful."

A BATTERY GOING INTO ACTION.

General Semmes, who hurried forward to offer his assistance to General Cobb, thus describes the scene he witnessed on the Confederate side of the crest:

"Arriving at the base of and soon after commencing the ascent of the mountain at Crampton's Gap, I encountered fugitives from the battle-field and endeavored to turn them back. Proceeding farther up the mountain, the troops were met pouring down the road and through the wood in great disorder, where I found General Cobb and his staff, at the imminent risk of their lives, using every effort to check and rally them. I immediately joined my efforts, and those of my staff who were with me, to General Cobb's, and coöperated with him for a considerable time in the vain effort to rally the men."

General McLaws moved Wilcox's brigade of R. H. Anderson's, and later Kershaw's and Barksdale's brigades of his own division, to the support of Cobb, but not in time to take part in the engagement. The report of General McLaws shows that he accurately appreciated the effect of our success in completely shutting up his command on Maryland Heights until the surrender of Harper's Ferry opened the door for him to cross into Virginia. Accepting the estimate of Mr. Thomas White, who was chief clerk in the adjutant-general's office at General Lee's headquarters, and had charge of the returns, the whole available force under McLaws was 8000 men, and mine, on the basis of the last returns, 12,300. Couch's division (7219 men) of the Fourth Corps did not reach the field of the 14th until the fighting was over, and was detached from my command early the next morning. But these figures are at least one-fifth, if not one-fourth, beyond the actual effective strength. General Cobb estimates the Confederate forces actually engaged at 2200. Mine can hardly have exceeded 6500; heavy odds, indeed, but so are stone walls and a steep mountain pass. My losses were 533. The losses in Parham's (Mahone's) brigade, spoken of as heavy, are not reported; those in Cobb's and Semmes's brigades are given as 749.

At the end of the fight, after nightfall, the division of the corps which had borne the brunt of the fight (Slocum's), was, as it were, astride of the mountain. Of the other division (Smith's), the brigades of Brooks and Irwin were on the mountain, the reserve under Hancock being at the eastern base. Couch's division reported to me at 10 P. M.⸾ Early the next morning, Smith's division was sent into Pleasant Valley, west of the Blue Ridge, to begin the movement toward Harper's Ferry. Couch's division was sent, by order of the commanding general, to occupy Rohrersville. Slocum was to support Smith.

As I was crossing the mountain about 7 A. M., on September 15th, I had a good view of the enemy's force below, which seemed to be well posted on hills stretching across the valley, which is at this place about two miles wide. When I reached General Smith we made an examination of the position, and concluded that it would be suicidal to attack it. The whole breadth of the valley was occupied, and batteries swept the only approaches to the position. We estimated the force as quite as large as ours, and it was in a position which, properly defended, would have required a much greater force than ours to have carried. I am unable to give the numbers, but McLaws, in his report of the operations of the day, states that he formed the line across the valley with the brigades of Kershaw and Barksdale, except one regiment and two guns of the latter, and the "remnants" of the brigades of Cobb, Semmes, Mahone, and Wilcox, which he afterward states were very small.

The only force available for an attack would have been Smith's division of about 4500 men, Slocum's division being in no condition for a fight that day. Reading between the lines of General McLaws's report, he seems to have been disgusted that I did not attack him. The evidence before the court of inquiry on the surrender of Harper's Ferry shows that the white flag was shown at 7:30 A. M., on the 15th, and the firing ceased about one hour afterward. It is evident, therefore, that a fight between General McLaws's force and mine could have had no effect upon the surrender of Harper's Ferry. Success on my part would have drawn me farther away from the army and would have brought me in dangerous nearness to Jackson's force, already set free by the surrender. McLaws's supports were three and a half miles from him, while my force was seven miles from the main army.

Later on that day the enemy withdrew from Pleasant Valley and Harper's Ferry toward Sharpsburg. Couch's division joined me, and the corps remained stationary without orders from McClellan until the evening of the 16th, when I was ordered to march the next morning to join the army and to send Couch's division to occupy Maryland Heights. Accordingly the corps started at 5:30 A. M., and the advance reached the field of Antietam at 10 A. M., about twelve miles distant from the starting-point.

⸾ In October, 1862, when Mr. Lincoln visited the army, he came through Crampton's Gap; he told me that he was astonished to see and hear of what we had done there. He thanked me for it, and said that he had not understood it before. He was in all respects very kind and complimentary.— W. B. F.

General Smith's division arrived first and was immediately brought into action in the vicinity of the Dunker Church, repelling a strong attack made by the enemy at this point. The details of the part borne by the corps in the battle are graphically given in the official reports.

While awaiting the arrival of Slocum, I went to the right, held by Sumner. I found him at the head of his troops, but much depressed. He told me that his whole corps was exhausted and could do nothing more that day. It was lying in line of battle partly in a wood from which it had driven the enemy that morning. About three hundred yards in its front, across an open field, was a wood nearer the bank of the river, strongly held by the enemy. The corps had been driven back from an attack on this wood with great loss.

When General Slocum arrived I placed two brigades of his division on General Sumner's left and was awaiting the arrival of his third brigade, which was to be in reserve. With the two brigades I intended to make an attack on the wood referred to, and General Sumner was informed of my intention. The two brigades were ready to move. Just as the third brigade arrived, General Sumner rode up and directed me not to make the attack, giving as a reason for his order, that if I were defeated the right would be entirely routed, mine being the only troops left on the right that had any life in them. Major Hammerstein, of McClellan's staff, was near, and I requested him to inform General McClellan of the state of affairs, and that I thought the attack ought to be made. Shortly afterward McClellan rode up, and, after hearing the statements of Sumner and myself, decided that as the day had gone so well on the other parts of the line it would be unsafe to risk anything on the right. Of course, no advance was made by the division.

Later in the day General McClellan came again to my headquarters, and there was pointed out to him a hill on the right, commanding the wood, and it was proposed that the hill should be occupied by our artillery early the next morning, and that after shelling the wood, the attack should be made by the whole corps from the position then held by it. He assented to this, and it was understood that the attack was to be made. During the night, however, the order was countermanded. I met him about 9 o'clock on the morning of the 18th. He informed me that he countermanded the order because fifteen thousand Pennsylvania troops would soon arrive, and that upon their arrival the attack would be ordered. The troops, however, did not arrive, and the order was not renewed that day. On the 19th the corps entered the wood, expecting a fight, but the enemy had slipped off during the night.

MAJOR-GENERAL E. V. SUMNER.
FROM A PHOTOGRAPH TAKEN BEFORE THE WAR.

# THE OPPOSING FORCES IN THE MARYLAND CAMPAIGN.

The composition, losses, and strength of each army as here stated give the gist of all the data obtainable in the Official Records. K stands for killed; w for wounded; m w for mortally wounded; m for captured or missing; c for captured.

## THE UNION ARMY.

(On September 14th, the right wing of this army, consisting of the First and Ninth Corps, was commanded by Maj.-Gen. A. E. Burnside; the center, composed of the Second and Twelfth Corps, by Maj.-Gen. Edwin V. Sumner; and the left wing, comprising the Sixth Corps and Couch's division of the Fourth Corps, by Maj.-Gen. W. B. Franklin.)

ARMY OF THE POTOMAC.—Major-General George B. McClellan.

*Escort,* Capt. James B. McIntyre: Oneida (N. Y.) Cav., Capt. Daniel P. Mann; A, 4th U. S. Cav., Lieut. Thomas H. McCormick; E, 4th U. S. Cav., Capt. James B. McIntyre. *Regular Engineer Battalion,* Capt. James C. Duane. *Provost Guard,* Maj. William H. Wood: 2d U. S. Cav. (4 co's) Capt. George A. Gordon; 8th U. S. Inf. (4 co's), Capt. Royal T. Frank; G, 19th U. S. Inf., Capt. Edmund L. Smith; H, 19th U. S. Inf., Capt. Henry S. Welton. *Headquarters Guard,* Maj. Granville O. Haller: 93d N. Y., Lieut.-Col. Benjamin C. Butler. *Quartermaster's Guard:* 1st U. S. Cav. (4 co's), Capt. Marcus A. Reno.

FIRST ARMY CORPS, Maj.-Gen. Joseph Hooker (w), Brig.-Gen. George G. Meade. Staff loss: Antietam, w, 1.

*Escort:* 2d N. Y. Cav. (4 co's), Capt. John E. Naylor.

FIRST DIVISION, Brig.-Gen. Rufus King, Brig.-Gen. John P. Hatch (w), Brig.-Gen. Abner Doubleday. Staff loss: South Mountain, w, 1.

*First Brigade,* Col. Walter Phelps, Jr.: 22d N. Y., Lieut.-Col. John McKie, Jr.; 24th N. Y., Capt. John D. O'Brian (w); 30th N. Y., Col. William M. Searing; 84th N. Y. (14th Militia), Maj. William H. de Bevoise; 2d U. S. Sharp-shooters, Col. Henry A. V. Post (w). Brigade loss: South Mountain, k, 20; w, 67; m, 8=95. Antietam, k, 30; w, 120; m, 4=154. *Second Brigade,* Brig.-Gen. Abner Doubleday, Col. William P. Wainwright (w), Lieut.-Col. J. William Hofmann: 7th Ind., Maj. Ira G. Grover; 76th N. Y., Col. William P. Wainwright, Capt. John W. Young; 95th N. Y., Maj. Edward Pye; 56th Pa., Lieut.-Col. J. William Hofmann, Capt. Frederick Williams. Brigade loss: South Mountain, k, 3; w, 52; m, 4=59. Antietam, w, 10. *Third Brigade,* Brig.-Gen. Marsena R. Patrick: 21st N. Y., Col. William F. Rogers; 23d N. Y., Col. Henry C. Hoffman; 35th N. Y., Col. Newton B. Lord; 80th N. Y. (20th Militia), Lieut.-Col. Theodore B. Gates. Brigade loss: South Mountain, k, 3; w, 19; m, 1 = 23. Antietam, k, 30; w, 187; m, 17=234. *Fourth Brigade,* Brig.-Gen. John Gibbon: 19th Ind., Col. Solomon Meredith, Lieut.-Col. Alois O. Bachman (k), Capt. William W. Dudley: 2d Wis., Col. Lucius Fairchild, Lieut.-Col. Thomas S. Allen (w); 6th Wis., Lieut.-Col. Edward S. Bragg (w), Maj. Rufus R. Dawes; 7th Wis., Capt. John B. Callis. Brigade loss: South Mountain, k, 37; w, 251; m, 30=318. Antietam, k, 68; w, 275; m, 5=348. *Artillery,* Capt. J. Albert Monroe: 1st N. H., Lieut. Frederick M. Edgell; D, 1st R. I., Capt. J. Albert Monroe; L, 1st N. Y., Capt. John A. Reynolds; B, 4th U. S., Capt. Joseph B. Campbell (w), Lieut. James Stewart. Artillery loss: Antietam, k, 12; w, 46; m, 8 = 66.

SECOND DIVISION, Brig.-Gen. James B. Ricketts.

*First Brigade,* Brig.-Gen. Abram Duryée (w): 97th N. Y., Maj. Charles Northrup; 104th N. Y., Maj. Lewis C. Skinner; 105th N. Y., Col. Howard Carroll; 107th Pa., Capt. James MacThomson. Brigade loss: South Mountain, k, 5; w, 16 = 21. Antietam, k, 59; w, 233; m, 35=327. *Second Brigade,* Col. William A. Christian, Col. Peter Lyle (w): 26th N. Y., Lieut.-Col. Richard H. Richardson; 94th N. Y., Lieut.-Col. Calvin Littlefield; 88th Pa., Lieut.-Col. George W. Gile (w), Capt. Henry R. Myers; 90th Pa., Col. Peter Lyle, Lieut.-Col. William A. Leech. Brigade loss: South Mountain, k, 2; w, 6 = 8. Antietam, k, 28; w, 197; m, 29 = 254. *Third Brigade,* Brig.-Gen. George L. Hartsuff (w), Col. Richard Coulter: 12th Mass., Maj. Elisha Burbank (m w), Capt. Benjamin F. Cook; 13th Mass., Maj. J. Parker Gould; 83d N. Y. (9th Militia), Lieut.-Col. William Atterbury; 11th Pa., Col. Richard Coulter, Capt. David M. Cook. Brigade loss: South Mountain, k, 2; w, 4 = 6. Antietam, k, 82; w, 497; m, 20=599. *Artillery:* F, 1st Pa., Capt. Ezra W. Matthews; C, Pa., Capt. James Thompson. Artillery loss: Antietam, k, 3; w, 19; m, 2 = 24.

THIRD DIVISION (Pa. Reserves), Brig.-Gen. George G. Meade, Brig.-Gen. Truman Seymour.

*First Brigade,* Brig.-Gen. Truman Seymour, Col. R. Biddle Roberts: 1st Pa., Col. R. Biddle Roberts, Capt. William C. Talley; 2d Pa., Capt. James N. Byrnes; 5th Pa., Col. Joseph W. Fisher; 6th Pa., Col. William Sinclair; 13th Pa. (1st Rifles), Col. Hugh W. McNeil (k), Capt. Dennis McGee. Brigade loss: South Mountain, k, 38; w, 133=171. Antietam, k, 24; w, 131=155. *Second Brigade,* Col. Albert L. Magilton: 3d Pa., Lieut.-Col. John Clark; 4th Pa., Maj. John Nyce; 7th Pa., Col. Henry C. Bolinger (w), Maj. Chauncey A. Lyman; 8th Pa., Maj. Silas M. Baily. Brigade loss: South Mountain, k, 25; w, 63; m, 1 = 89. Antietam, k, 41; w, 181 = 222. *Third Brigade,* Col. Thomas F. Gallagher (w), Lieut.-Col. Robert Anderson: 9th Pa., Lieut.-Col. Robert Anderson, Capt. Samuel B. Dick; 10th Pa., Lieut.-Col. Adoniram J. Warner (w), Capt. Jonathan P. Smith; 11th Pa., Lieut.-Col. Samuel M. Jackson; 12th Pa., Capt. Richard Gustin. Brigade loss: South Mountain, k, 32; w, 100=132. Antietam, k, 37; w, 136; m, 2 = 175. *Artillery:* A, 1st Pa., Lieut. John G. Simpson; B, 1st Pa., Capt. James H. Cooper; C, 5th U. S., Capt. Dunbar R. Ransom. Artillery loss: Antietam, k, 3; w, 18 = 21.

SECOND ARMY CORPS, Maj.-Gen. Edwin V. Sumner. Staff loss: Antietam, w, 2.

*Escort:* D and K, 6th N. Y. Cav., Capts. Henry W. Lyon and Riley Johnson. Loss: Antietam, w, 1.

FIRST DIVISION, Maj.-Gen. Israel B. Richardson (m w), Brig.-Gen. John C. Caldwell, Brig.-Gen. Winfield S. Hancock. Staff loss: Antietam, w, 2.

*First Brigade,* Brig.-Gen. John C. Caldwell: 5th N. H., Col. Edward E. Cross; 7th N.Y., Capt. Chas. Brestel; 61st and 64th N. Y., Col. Francis C. Barlow (w), Lieut.-Col. Nelson A. Miles; 81st Pa., Maj. H. Boyd McKeen. Brigade loss: Antietam, k, 44; w, 268; m, 2 = 314. *Second Brigade,* Brig.-Gen. Thomas F. Meagher, Col. John Burke: 29th Mass., Lieut.-Col. Joseph H. Barnes; 63d N. Y., Col. John Burke, Lieut.-Col. Henry Fowler (w), Maj. Richard C. Bentley (w), Capt. Joseph O'Neill; 69th N.Y., Lieut.-Col. James Kelly (w), Maj. James Cavanagh; 88th N. Y., Lieut.-Col. Patrick Kelly. Brigade loss: Antietam, k,113; w, 422; m, 5=540. *Third Brigade,* Col. John R. Brooke: 2d Del., Capt. David L. Stricker; 52d N. Y., Col. Paul Frank; 57th N. Y., Lieut.-Col. Philip J. Parisen (k), Maj. Alford B. Chapman; 66th N. Y., Capt. Julius Wehle, Lieut.-Col. James H. Bull; 53d Pa., Lieut.-Col. Richards McMichael. Brigade loss: Antietam, k, 52; w, 244; m, 9 = 305. *Artillery:* B, 1st N. Y., Capt. Rufus D. Pettit; A and C, 4th U. S., Lieut. Evan Thomas. Artillery loss: Antietam, k, 1; w, 3 = 4.

SECOND DIVISION, Maj.-Gen. John Sedgwick (w), Brig.-Gen. Oliver O. Howard. Staff loss: Antietam, w, 2.

*First Brigade,* Brig.-Gen. Willis A. Gorman: 15th Mass., Lieut.-Col. John W. Kimball; 1st Minn., Col. Alfred Sully; 34th N. Y., Col. James A. Suiter; 82d N. Y. (2d Militia), Col. Henry W. Hudson; 1st Co. Mass. Sharp-shooters, Capt. John Saunders (k); 2d Co. Minn. Sharp-shooters, Capt. William F. Russell. Brigade loss: Antietam, k, 134; w, 539; m, 67=740. *Second Brigade,*

# THE OPPOSING FORCES IN THE MARYLAND CAMPAIGN. 599

Brig.-Gen. Oliver O. Howard, Col. Joshua T. Owen, Col. De Witt C. Baxter: 69th Pa., Col. Joshua T. Owen; 71st Pa., Col. Isaac J. Wistar (w), Lieut. Richard P. Smith, Capt. Enoch E. Lewis; 72d Pa., Col. De Witt C. Baxter; 106th Pa., Col. Turner G. Morehead. Brigade loss: Antietam, k, 93; w, 379; m, 73 = 545. *Third Brigade*, Brig.-Gen. Napoleon J. T. Dana (w), Col. Norman J. Hall: 19th Mass., Col. Edward W. Hinks (w), Lieut.-Col. Arthur F. Devereux (w); 20th Mass., Col. William R. Lee; 7th Mich., Col. Norman J. Hall, Capt. Charles J. Hunt; 42d N. Y., Lieut.-Col. George N. Bomford, Maj. James E. Mallon; 59th N. Y., Col. Wm. L. Tidball. Brigade loss: Antietam, k, 142; w, 652; m, 104 = 898. *Artillery*: A, 1st R. I., Capt. John A. Tompkins; I, 1st U. S., Lieut. George A. Woodruff. Artillery loss: Antietam, k, 4; w, 21 = 25.
THIRD DIVISION, Brig.-Gen. William H. French.
*First Brigade*, Brig.-Gen. Nathan Kimball: 14th Ind., Col. William Harrow; 8th Ohio, Lieut.-Col. Franklin Sawyer; 132d Pa., Col. Richard A. Oakford (k), Lieut.-Col. Vincent M. Wilcox; 7th W. Va., Col. Joseph Snider. Brigade loss: Antietam, k, 121; w, 510; m, 8 = 639. *Second Brigade*, Col. Dwight Morris: 14th Conn., Lieut.-Col. Sanford H. Perkins; 108th N. Y., Col. Oliver H. Palmer; 130th Pa., Col. Henry I. Zinn. Brigade loss: Antietam, k, 78; w, 356; m, 95 = 529. *Third Brigade*, Brig.-Gen. Max Weber (w), Col. John W. Andrews: 1st Del., Col. John W. Andrews, Lieut.-Col. Oliver Hopkinson (w); 5th Md., Maj. Leopold Blumenberg (w), Capt. E. F. M. Faehtz; 4th N. Y., Lieut.-Col. John D. MacGregor. Brigade loss: Antietam, k, 100; w, 449; m, 33 = 582. UNATTACHED ARTILLERY: G, 1st N. Y., Capt. John D. Frank; B, 1st R. I., Capt. John G. Hazard; G, 1st R. I., Capt. C. D. Owen. Artillery loss: Antietam, k, 1; w, 9 = 10.
FOURTH ARMY CORPS.
FIRST DIVISION (attached to Sixth Army Corps), Maj.-Gen. Darius N. Couch.
*First Brigade*, Brig.-Gen. Charles Devens, Jr.: 7th Mass., Col. David A. Russell; 10th Mass., Col. Henry L. Eustis; 36th N. Y., Col. William H. Browne; 2d R. I., Col. Frank Wheaton. *Second Brigade*, Brig.-Gen. Albion P. Howe: 62d N. Y., Col. David J. Nevin; 93d Pa., Col. James M. McCarter; 98th Pa., Col. John F. Ballier; 102d Pa., Col. Thomas A. Rowley; 139th Pa., Col. Frank H. Collier. *Third Brigade*, Brig.-Gen. John Cochrane: 65th N. Y., Col. Alexander Shaler; 67th N. Y., Col. Julius W. Adams; 122d N. Y., Col. Silas Titus; 23d Pa., Col. Thomas H. Neill; 61st Pa., Col. George C. Spear; 82d Pa., Col. David H. Williams. Brigade loss: Antietam (Sept. 18th), w, 9. *Artillery*: 3d N. Y., Capt. William Stuart; C, 1st Pa., Capt. Jeremiah McCarthy; D, 1st Pa., Capt. Michael Hall; G, 2d U. S., Lieut. J. H. Butler.
FIFTH ARMY CORPS, Maj.-Gen. Fitz John Porter.
*Escort*: Detachment 1st Me. Cav., Capt. George J. Summat.
FIRST DIVISION, Maj.-Gen. George W. Morell.
*First Brigade*, Col. James Barnes: 2d Me., Col. Charles W. Roberts; 18th Mass., Lieut.-Col. Joseph Hayes; 22d Mass., Lieut.-Col. William S. Tilton; 1st Mich., Capt. Emory W. Belton; 13th N. Y., Col. Elisha G. Marshall; 25th N. Y., Col. Charles A. Johnson; 118th Pa., Col. Charles M. Prevost; 2d Co. Mass. Sharp-shooters, Capt. Lewis E. Wentworth. Brigade loss: Shepherdstown, k, 66; w, 125; m, 130 = 321. *Second Brigade*, Brig.-Gen. Charles Griffin: 2d D. C., Col. Charles M. Alexander; 9th Mass., Col. Patrick R. Guiney; 32d Mass., Col. Francis J. Parker; 4th Mich., Col. Jonathan W. Childs; 14th N. Y., Col. James McQuade; 62d Pa., Col. Jacob B. Sweitzer. Brigade loss: Shepherdstown, k, 1; w, 10 = 11. *Third Brigade*, Col. T. B. W. Stockton: 20th Me., Col. Adelbert Ames; 16th Mich., Lieut.-Col. Norval E. Welch; 12th N. Y., Capt. William Huson; 17th N. Y., Lieut.-Col. Nelson B. Bartram; 44th N. Y., Maj. Freeman Conner; 83d Pa., Capt. Orpheus S. Woodward; Brady's Co. Mich. Sharp-shooters, Lieut. Jonas H. Titus, Jr. Brigade loss: Shepherdstown, w, 7. *Artillery*: 3d Mass., Capt. Augustus P. Martin; C, 1st R. I., Capt. Richard Waterman; D, 5th U. S., Lieut. Charles E. Hazlett. Artillery loss: Shepherdstown, m, 1. *Sharpshooters*: 1st U. S., Capt. John B. Isler. Loss: Shepherdstown, k, 2; w, 5 = 7.

SECOND DIVISION, Brig.-Gen. George Sykes.
*First Brigade*, Lieut.-Col. Robert C. Buchanan: 3d U. S., Capt. John D. Wilkins; 4th U. S., Capt. Hiram Dryer; 12th U. S. (1st Battalion), Capt. Matthew M. Blunt; 12th U. S. (2d Battalion), Capt. Thomas M. Anderson; 14th U. S. (1st Battalion), Capt. W. Harvey Brown; 14th U. S. (2d Battalion), Capt. David B. McKibbin. Brigade loss: Antietam, k, 4; w, 35 = 39. *Second Brigade*, Maj. Charles S. Lovell: 1st and 6th U. S., Capt. Levi C. Bootes; 2d and 10th U. S., Capt. John S. Poland; 11th U. S., Capt. De Lancey Floyd-Jones; 17th U. S., Maj. George L. Andrews. Brigade loss: Antietam, k, 8; w, 47; m, 1 = 56; Shepherdstown, k, 1; w, 8 = 9. *Third Brigade*, Col. Gouverneur K. Warren: 5th N. Y., Capt. Cleveland Winslow; 10th N. Y., Lieut.-Col. John W. Marshall. Brigade loss: Shepherdstown, w, 1. *Artillery*: E and G, 1st U. S., Lieut. Alanson M. Randol; I, 5th U. S., Capt. Stephen H. Weed; K, 5th U. S., Lieut. William E. Van Reed. Artillery loss: Antietam, w, 3. Shepherdstown, k, 1; w, 2 = 3.
THIRD DIVISION (reached the field of Antietam Sept. 18th), Brig.-Gen. Andrew A. Humphreys.
*First Brigade*, Brig.-Gen. Erastus B. Tyler: 91st Pa., Col. Edgar M. Gregory; 126th Pa., Col. James G. Elder; 129th Pa., Col. Jacob G. Frick; 134th Pa., Col. Matthew S. Quay. *Second Brigade*, Col. Peter H. Allabach: 123d Pa., Col. John B. Clark; 131st Pa., Lieut.-Col. William B. Shaut; 133d Pa., Col. Franklin B. Speakman; 155th Pa., Col. Edward J. Allen. *Artillery*: C, 1st N. Y., Capt. Almont Barnes; L, 1st Ohio, Capt. Lucius N. Robinson.
ARTILLERY RESERVE, Lieut.-Col. William Hays:
A, B, C, and D, 1st Battalion N. Y., Lieuts. Bernhard Wever and Alfred von Kleiser, and Capts. Robert Langner and Charles Kusserow; 5th N. Y., Capt. Elijah D. Taft; K, 1st U. S., Capt. William M. Graham; G, 4th U. S., Lieut. Marcus P. Miller. Artillery loss: Antietam, k, 5; w, 5; m, 1 = 11.

SIXTH ARMY CORPS, Maj.-Gen. William B. Franklin.
*Escort*: B and G, 6th Pa. Cav., Capt. H. P. Muirheid.
FIRST DIVISION, Maj.-Gen. Henry W. Slocum.
*First Brigade*, Col. A. T. A. Torbert: 1st N. J., Lieut.-Col. Mark W. Collet; 2d N. J., Col. Samuel L. Buck; 3d N. J., Col. Henry W. Brown; 4th N. J., Col. William B. Hatch. Brigade loss: Crampton's Pass, k, 38; w, 134 = 172. Antietam, k, 2; w, 17 = 19. *Second Brigade*, Col. Joseph J. Bartlett: 5th Me., Col. Nathaniel J. Jackson; 16th N. Y., Lieut.-Col. Joel J. Seaver; 27th N. Y., Lieut.-Col. Alexander D. Adams; 96th Pa., Col. Henry L. Cake. Brigade loss: Crampton's Pass, k, 50; w, 167 = 217. Antietam, k, 1; w, 8 = 9. *Third Brigade*, Brig.-Gen. John Newton: 18th N. Y., Lieut.-Col. George R. Myers; 31st N. Y., Lieut.-Col. Francis E. Pinto; 32d N. Y., Col. Roderick Matheson (m w), Maj. George F. Lemon (m w); 95th Pa., Col. Gustavus W. Town. Brigade loss: Crampton's Pass, k, 24; w, 98; m, 2 = 124. Antietam, k, 1; w, 20 = 21. *Artillery*, Capt. Emory Upton: A, Md., Capt. John W. Wolcott; 1st Mass., Capt. Josiah Porter; 1st N. J., Capt. William Hexamer; D, 2d U. S., Lieut. Edward B. Williston. Artillery loss: Antietam, k, 1; w, 13; m, 2 = 16.
SECOND DIVISION, Maj.-Gen. William F. Smith.
*First Brigade*, Brig.-Gen. Winfield S. Hancock, Col. Amasa Cobb: 6th Me., Col. Hiram Burnham; 43d N. Y., Maj. John Wilson; 49th Pa., Lieut.-Col. William Brisbane; 137th Pa., Col. Henry M. Bossert; 5th Wis., Col. Amasa Cobb. Brigade loss: Antietam, w, 6. *Second Brigade*, Brig.-Gen. W. T. H. Brooks: 2d Vt., Maj. James H. Walbridge; 3d Vt., Col. Breed N. Hyde; 4th Vt., Lieut.-Col. Charles B. Stoughton; 5th Vt., Col. Lewis A. Grant; 6th Vt., Maj. Oscar L. Tuttle. Brigade loss: Crampton's Pass, k, 1; w, 18 = 19. Antietam, k, 1; w, 24 = 25. *Third Brigade*, Col. William H. Irwin: 7th Me., Maj. Thomas W. Hyde; 20th N. Y., Col. Ernest von Vegesack; 33d N. Y., Lieut.-Col. Joseph W. Corning; 49th N. Y., Lieut.-Col. William C. Alberger (w), Maj. George W. Johnson; 77th N. Y., Capt. Nathan S. Babcock. Brigade loss: Antietam, k, 64; w, 247; m, 31 = 342. *Artillery*, Capt. Romeyn B. Ayres: B, Md., Lieut. Theodore J. Vanneman; 1st N. Y., Capt. Andrew Cowan; F, 5th U. S., Lieut. Leonard Martin.

NINTH ARMY CORPS, Maj.-Gen. Ambrose E. Burnside (commanded the right wing of the army at South Mountain and exercised general command on the left at Antietam), Maj.-Gen. Jesse L. Reno (k), Brig. Gen. Jacob D. Cox. Staff loss: South Mountain, k, 1.

*Escort:* G, 1st Me. Cav., Capt. Zebulon B. Blethen.

FIRST DIVISION, Brig.-Gen. Orlando B. Willcox.

*First Brigade,* Col. Benjamin C. Christ: 28th Mass., Capt. Andrew P. Caraher; 17th Mich., Col. William H. Withington; 79th N. Y., Lieut.-Col. David Morrison; 50th Pa., Maj. Edward Overton (w), Capt. William H. Diehl. Brigade loss: South Mountain, k, 26; w, 136 = 162. Antietam, k, 43; w, 198; m, 3 = 244. *Second Brigade,* Col. Thomas Welsh: 8th Mich. (transferred to First Brigade, Sept. 16th), Lieut.-Col. Frank Graves, Maj. Ralph Ely; 46th N. Y., Lieut.-Col. Joseph Gerhardt; 45th Pa., Lieut.-Col. John I. Curtin; 100th Pa., Lieut.-Col. David A. Leckey. Brigade loss: South Mountain, k, 37; w, 151 = 188. Antietam, k, 3; w, 86; m, 4 = 93. *Artillery:* 8th Mass., Capt. Asa M. Cook; E, 2d U. S., Lieut. Samuel N. Benjamin. Artillery loss: South Mountain, k, 1; w, 4 = 5. Antietam, w, 1.

SECOND DIVISION, Brig.-Gen. Samuel D. Sturgis.

*First Brigade,* Brig.-Gen. James Nagle: 2d Md., Lieut.-Col. J. Eugene Duryea; 6th N. H., Col. Simon G. Griffin; 9th N. H., Col. Enoch Q. Fellows; 48th Pa., Lieut.-Col. Joshua K. Sigfried. Brigade loss: South Mountain, w, 34; m, 7 = 41. Antietam, k, 39; w, 160; m, 5 = 204. *Second Brigade,* Brig.-Gen. Edward Ferrero: 21st Mass., Col. William S. Clark; 35th Mass., Col. Edward A. Wild (w), Lieut.-Col. Sumner Carruth (w); 51st N.Y., Col. Robert B. Potter; 51st Pa., Col. John F. Hartranft. Brigade loss: South Mountain, k, 10; w, 83; m, 23 = 116. Antietam, k, 95; w, 368; m, 6 = 469. *Artillery:* D, Pa., Capt. George W. Durell; E, 4th U. S., Capt. Joseph C. Clark, Jr. Artillery loss: Antietam, k, 2; w, 4 = 6.

THIRD DIVISION, Brig.-Gen. Isaac P. Rodman (m w). Staff loss: Antietam, w, 1.

*First Brigade,* Col. Harrison S. Fairchild: 9th N. Y., Lieut.-Col. Edgar A. Kimball; 89th N. Y., Maj. Edward Jardine; 103d N. Y., Maj. Benjamin Ringold. Brigade loss: South Mountain, k, 2; w, 18 = 20. Antietam, k, 87; w, 321; m, 47 = 455. *Second Brigade,* Col. Edward Harland: 8th Conn., Lieut.-Col. Hiram Appelman (w), Maj. John E. Ward; 11th Conn., Col. Henry W. Kingsbury (k); 16th Conn., Col. Francis Beach; 4th R. I., Col. William H. P. Steere (w), Lieut.-Col. Joseph B. Curtis. Brigade loss: Antietam, k, 133; w, 462; m, 23 = 618. *Artillery:* A, 5th U. S., Lieut. Charles P. Muhlenberg. Loss: Antietam, w, 3.

KANAWHA DIVISION, Brig.-Gen. Jacob D. Cox, Col. Eliakim P. Scammon.

*First Brigade,* Col. Eliakim P. Scammon, Col. Hugh Ewing: 12th Ohio, Col. Carr B. White; 23d Ohio, Lieut.-Col. Rutherford B. Hayes (w), Maj. James M. Comly; 30th Ohio, Col. Hugh Ewing, Lieut.-Col. Theodore Jones (c), Maj. George H. Hildt; 1st Ohio Battery, Capt. James R. McMullin; Gilmore's Co., W. Va. Cav., Lieut. James Abraham; Harrison's Co., W. Va. Cav., Lieut. Dennis Delaney. Brigade loss: South Mountain, k, 63; w, 201; m, 8 = 272. Antietam, k, 28; w, 134; m, 20 = 182. *Second Brigade,* Col. Augustus Moor (c), Col. George Crook: 11th Ohio, Lieut.-Col. Augustus H. Coleman (k), Maj. Lyman J. Jackson; 28th Ohio, Lieut.-Col. Gottfried Becker; 36th Ohio, Col. George Crook, Lieut.-Col. Melvin Clarke (k), Maj. E. B. Andrews; Chicago (Ill.) Dragoons, Capt. Frederick Schambeck; Ky. Battery, Capt. Seth J. Simmonds. Brigade loss: South Mountain, k, 17; w, 64; m, 3 = 84. Antietam, k, 8; w, 58; m, 7 = 73.

UNATTACHED TROOPS: 6th N. Y. Cav. (8 co's), Col. Thomas C. Devin; 3d Co. Ohio Cav., Lieut. Jonas Seamen; L and M, 3d U. S. Art'y, Capt. John Edwards, Jr.

TWELFTH ARMY CORPS, Maj.-Gen. Joseph K. F. Mansfield (k), Brig.-Gen. Alpheus S. Williams. Staff loss: Antietam, k, 1.

*Escort:* L, 1st Mich. Cav., Capt. Melvin Brewer.

FIRST DIVISION, Brig.-Gen. Alpheus S. Williams, Brig.-Gen. Samuel W. Crawford (w), Brig.-Gen. George H. Gordon. Staff loss: Antietam, w, 1.

*First Brigade,* Brig.-Gen. Samuel W. Crawford, Col. Joseph F. Knipe: 10th Me., Col. George L. Beal (w); 28th N. Y., Capt. William H. H. Mapes; 46th Pa., Col. Joseph F. Knipe, Lieut.-Col. James L. Selfridge; 124th Pa., Col. Joseph W. Hawley (w), Maj. Isaac L. Haldeman; 125th Pa., Col. Jacob Higgins; 128th Pa., Col. Samuel Croasdale (k), Lieut.-Col. William W. Hammersly (w), Maj. Joel B. Wanner. Brigade loss: Antietam, k, 88; w, 315; m, 27 = 430. *Third Brigade,* Brig.-Gen. George H. Gordon, Col. Thomas H. Ruger (w): 27th Ind., Col. Silas Colgrove; 2d Mass., Col. George L. Andrews; 13th N. J., Col. Ezra A. Carman; 107th N. Y., Col. R. B. Van Valkenburgh; Pa. Zouaves d'Afrique; 3d Wis., Col. Thomas H. Ruger. Brigade loss: Antietam, k, 71; w, 548; m, 27 = 646.

SECOND DIVISION, Brig.-Gen. George S. Greene.

*First Brigade,* Lieut.-Col. Hector Tyndale (w), Maj. Orrin J. Crane: 5th Ohio, Maj. John Collins; 7th Ohio, Maj. Orrin J. Crane, Capt. Frederick A. Seymour; 66th Ohio, Lieut.-Col. Eugene Powell (w); 28th Pa., Maj. Ario Pardee, Jr. Brigade loss: Antietam, k, 61; w, 308; m, 7 = 376. *Second Brigade,* Col. Henry J. Stainrook: 3d Md., Lieut.-Col. Joseph M. Sudsburg; 102d N. Y., Lieut.-Col. James C. Lane; 111th Pa., Maj. Thomas M. Walker. Brigade loss: Antietam, k, 32; w, 128; m, 16 = 176. *Third Brigade,* Col. William B. Goodrich (k), Lieut.-Col. Jonathan Austin: 3d Del., Maj. Arthur Maginnis (w), Capt. William J. McKaig; Purnell (Md.) Legion, Lieut.-Col. Benjamin L. Simpson; 60th N. Y., Lieut.-Col. Charles R. Brundage; 78th N. Y., Lieut.-Col. Jonathan Austin, Capt. Henry R. Stagg. Brigade loss: Antietam, k, 21; w, 71; m, 7 = 99. *Artillery,* Capt. Clermont L. Best: 4th Me., Capt. O'Neil W. Robinson; 6th Me., Capt. Freeman McGilvery; M, 1st N Y., Capt. George W. Cothran; 10th N.Y., Capt. John T. Bruen; E, Pa., Capt. Joseph M. Knap; F, Pa., Capt. R. B. Hampton; F, 4th U. S., Lieut. E. D. Muhlenberg. Artillery loss: Antietam, k, 1; w, 15; m, 1 = 17.

CAVALRY DIVISION, Brig.-Gen. Alfred Pleasonton.

*First Brigade,* Maj. Charles J. Whiting: 5th U. S., Capt. Joseph H. McArthur; 6th U. S., Capt. William P. Sanders. Brigade loss: Antietam, w, 1. *Second Brigade,* Col. John F. Farnsworth: 8th Ill., Maj. William H. Medill; 3d Ind., Maj. George H. Chapman; 1st Mass., Capt. Casper Crowninshield; 8th Pa., Capt. Peter Keenan. Brigade loss: Antietam, w, 6. *Third Brigade,* Col. Richard H. Rush: 4th Pa., Col. James H. Childs (k), Lieut.-Col. James K. Kerr; 6th Pa., Lieut.-Col. C. Ross Smith. Brigade loss: Antietam, k, 3; w, 10 = 13. *Fourth Brigade,* Col. Andrew T. McReynolds: 1st N. Y., Maj. Alonzo W. Adams; 12th Pa., Maj. James A. Congdon. *Fifth Brigade,* Col. Benjamin F. Davis: 8th N. Y., Col. Benjamin F. Davis; 3d Pa., Lieut.-Col. Samuel W. Owen. *Unattached,* 15th Pa. (detachment), Col. William J. Palmer. Loss: Antietam, k, 1.

The total loss of the Union Army in the three principal engagements of the campaign was as follows:

| | Killed. | Wounded. | Captured or missing. | Total. |
|---|---|---|---|---|
| South Mountain | 325 | 1403 | 85 | 1813 |
| Crampton's Pass | 113 | 418 | 2 | 533 |
| Antietam | 2108 | 9549 | 753 | 12,410 |

The casualties during the entire campaign, from September 3d to 20th (exclusive of Miles's force at Harper's Ferry, for which see page 618), aggregated 2629 killed, 11,583 wounded, and 991 captured or missing = 15,203.

## THE CONFEDERATE ARMY.

### General Robert E. Lee.

LONGSTREET'S COMMAND, Maj.-Gen. James Longstreet. Staff loss (in the campaign): w, 2.

MCLAWS'S DIVISION, Maj.-Gen. Lafayette McLaws. Staff loss (in the campaign): k, 1.

*Kershaw's Brigade,* Brig.-Gen. Joseph B. Kershaw: 2d S. C., Col. John D. Kennedy (w), Maj. Franklin Gaillard; 3d S. C., Col. James D. Nance; 7th S. C., Col. D. Wyatt Aiken (w), Capt. John S. Hard; 8th S. C., Col.

## THE OPPOSING FORCES IN THE MARYLAND CAMPAIGN. 601

John W. Henagan, Lieut.-Col. A. J. Hoole. Brigade loss (in the campaign): k, 90; w, 455; m, 6 = 551. *Cobb's Brigade*, Brig.-Gen. Howell Cobb, Lieut.-Col. C. C. Sanders, Lieut.-Col. William MacRae: 16th Ga., ——; ☆ 24th Ga., Lieut.-Col. C. C. Sanders, Maj. R. E. McMillan; Cobb's (Ga.) Legion, ——; 15th N. C., Lieut.-Col. William MacRae. Brigade loss (in the campaign): k, 76; w, 318, m, 452 = 846. *Semmes's Brigade*, Brig. Gen. Paul J. Semmes: 10th Ga., Maj. Willis C. Holt (w), Capt. P. H. Loud; 53d Ga., Lieut.-Col. Thomas Sloan (w), Capt. S. W. Marshborne; 15th Va., Capt. E. M. Morrison (w), Capt. Edward J. Willis; 32d Va., Col. E. B. Montague. Brigade loss in the campaign): k, 56; w, 274; m, 43 = 373. *Barksdale's Brigade*, Brig.-Gen. William Barksdale: 13th Miss., Lieut.-Col. Kennon McElroy (w); 17th Miss., Lieut.-Col. John C. Fiser; 18th Miss., Maj. J. C. Campbell (w), Lieut.-Col. William H. Leese; 21st Miss., Capt. John Sims, Col. Benjamin G. Humphreys. Brigade loss (in the campaign): k, 35; w, 272; m, 4 = 311. *Artillery*, Maj. S. P. Hamilton, Col. Henry C. Cabell: N. C. Battery, Capt. Basil C. Manly; Ga. Battery (Pulaski Art'y), Capt. John P. W. Read; Va. Battery (Richmond Fayette Art'y), Capt. M. C. Macon; Va. Battery (1st Co. Richmond Howitzers), Capt. E. S. McCarthy; Ga. Battery (Troup Art'y), Capt. H. H. Carlton. (Loss of the artillery included with that of the brigades to which attached.)
ANDERSON'S DIVISION, Maj.-Gen. Richard H. Anderson (w), Brig.-Gen. Roger A. Pryor. Staff loss (in the campaign): w, 1.
*Wilcox's Brigade*, Col. Alfred Cumming: 8th Ala. ——; 9th Ala., ——; 10th Ala., ——; 11th Ala., ——. Brigade loss (in the campaign): k, 34; w, 181; m, 29 = 244. *Mahone's Brigade*, Col. W. A. Parham: 6th Va., ——; 12th Va., ——; 16th Va., ——; 41st Va., ——; 61st Va., ——. Brigade loss (in the campaign): k, 8; w, 92; m, 127 = 227. *Featherston's Brigade*, Col. Carnot Posey: 12th Miss., ——; 16th Miss., Capt. A. M. Feltus; 19th Miss., ——; 2d Miss. Battalion, ——. Brigade loss (in the campaign): k, 45; w, 238; m, 36 = 319. *Armistead's Brigade*, Brig.-Gen. Lewis A. Armistead, Col. J. G. Hodges: 9th Va., ——; 14th Va., Col. J. G. Hodges; 38th Va., ——; 53d Va., ——; 57th Va., ——. Brigade loss (in the campaign): k, 5; w, 29; m, 1 = 35. *Pryor's Brigade*, Brig.-Gen. Roger A. Pryor: 14th Ala., ——; 2d Fla., ——; 8th Fla., ——; 3d Va., ——. Brigade loss (in the campaign): k, 48; w, 285; m, 49 = 382. *Wright's Brigade*, Brig.-Gen. Ambrose R. Wright: 44th Ala., ——; 3d Ga., ——; 22d Ga., ——; 48th Ga., ——. Brigade loss (in the campaign): k, 32; w, 192; m, 34 = 258. *Artillery*, Maj. J. S. Saunders: La. Battery (Donaldsville Art'y), Capt. Victor Maurin; Va. Battery (Huger's); Va. Battery, Lieut. C. R. Phelps; Va. Battery (Thompson's or Grimes's). (Loss of artillery not separately reported.)
JONES'S DIVISION, Brig.-Gen. David R. Jones.
*Toombs's Brigade*, Brig.-Gen. R. Toombs (in temporary command of a division), Col. Henry L. Benning: 2d Ga., Lieut.-Col. William R. Holmes (k), Maj. Skidmore Harris (w); 15th Ga., Col. William T. Millican (k); 17th Ga., Capt. J. A. McGregor; 20th Ga., Col. John B. Cumming. Brigade loss (in the campaign): k, 16; w, 122; m, 22 = 160. *Drayton's Brigade*, Brig.-Gen. Thomas F. Drayton: 50th Ga., Lieut.-Col. F. Kearse; 51st Ga., ——; 15th S. C., Col. W. D. De Saussure. Brigade loss (in the campaign): k, 82; w, 280; m, 179 = 541. *Pickett's Brigade*, Brig.-Gen. Richard B. Garnett: 8th Va., Col. Eppa Hunton; 18th Va., Maj. George C. Cabell; 19th Va., Col. J. B. Strange (n w), Capt. John L. Cochran, Lieut. William N. Wood; 28th Va., Capt. W. L. Wingfield; 56th Va., Col. William D. Stuart, Capt. John B. McPhail. Brigade loss (in the campaign): k, 30; w, 199; m, 32 = 261. *Kemper's Brigade*, Brig.-Gen. James L. Kemper: 1st Va., ——; 7th Va., ——; 11th Va., Maj. Adam Clement; 17th Va., Col. Montgomery D. Corse (w), Maj. Arthur Herbert; 24th Va., ——. Brigade loss (in the campaign): k, 15; w, 102; m, 27 = 144. *Jenkins's Brigade*, Col. Joseph Walker: 1st S. C., Lieut.-Col. D. Livingston (w): 2d S. C. (rifles) ——; 5th S. C., Capt. T. C. Beckham; 6th S. C., Lieut.-Col. J. M. Steedman, Capt. E. B. Cantey (w); 4th S. C. Battalion, ——; Palmetto (S. C.) Sharp-shooters, ——. Brigade loss (in the campaign): k, 27; w, 196; m, 12 = 235· *Anderson's Brigade*, Col. George T. Anderson: 1st Ga. (Regulars), Col. William J. Magill; 7th Ga., ——; 8th Ga. ——; 9th Ga., ——; 11th Ga., Maj. F. H. Little; Va. Battery (Wise Art'y), Capt. J. S. Brown (w). Brigade loss (in the campaign): k, 8; w, 80; m, 6 = 94.
WALKER'S DIVISION, Brig.-Gen. John G. Walker.
*Walker's Brigade*, Col. Van H. Manning (w), Col. E. D. Hall: 3d Ark., Capt John W. Reedy; 27th N. C., Col. John R. Cooke; 46th N. C., Col. E. D. Hall, Lieut.-Col. William A. Jenkins; 48th N. C., Col. R. C. Hill; 30th Va., ——; Va. Battery, Capt. Thomas B. French. Brigade loss (in the campaign); k, 140; w, 684; m, 93 = 917. *Ransom's Brigade*, Brig.-Gen. Robert Ransom, Jr.: 24th N. C., Lieut.-Col. John L. Harris; 25th N. C., Col. H. M. Rutledge; 35th N. C., Col. M. W. Ransom; 49th N. C., Lieut.-Col. Lee M. McAfee; Va. Battery, Capt. James R. Branch. Brigade loss (in the campaign): k, 41; w, 141; m, 4 = 186.
HOOD'S DIVISION, Brig.-Gen. John B. Hood.
*Hood's Brigade*, Col. W. T. Wofford: 18th Ga., Lieut.-Col. S. Z. Ruff; Hampton (S. C.) Legion, Lieut.-Col. M. W. Ganz; 1st Tex., Lieut.-Col. P. A. Work; 4th Tex., Lieut.-Col. B. F. Carter; 5th Tex., Capt. Ike N. M. Turner. Brigade loss (in the campaign): k, 69; w, 417; m, 62 = 548. *Law's Brigade*, Col. E. McIver Law: 4th Ala., Lieut.-Col. O. K. McLemore (m w), Capt. L. H. Scruggs (w): 2d Miss., Col. J. M. Stone (w), 11th Miss., Col. P. F. Liddell (m w), Lieut.-Col. S. F. Butler (w); 6th N. C., Maj. Robert F. Webb (w). Brigade loss (in the campaign): k, 53; w, 390; m, 25 = 468. *Artillery*, Maj. B. W. Frobel: S. C. Battery (German Art'y), Capt. W. K. Bachman; S. C. Battery (Palmetto Art'y), Capt. H. R. Garden; N. C. Battery (Rowan Art'y), Capt. James Reilly. Artillery loss (in the campaign): k, 4; w, 19 = 23.
EVANS'S BRIGADE, Brig.-Gen. Nathan G. Evans (in temporary command of a division), Col. P. F. Stevens: 17th S. C., Col. F. W. McMaster; 18th S. C., Col. W. H. Wallace; 22d S. C., Lieut.-Col. Thomas C. Watkins (k), Maj. M. Hilton; 23d S. C., Capt. S. A. Durham (w), Lieut. E. R. White; Holcombe's (S. C.) Legion, ——; S. C. Battery (Macbeth Art'y), Capt. R. Boyce. Brigade loss (in the campaign): k, 40; w, 185; m, 65 = 290.
ARTILLERY. *Washington (La.) Artillery*, Col. J. B. Walton: 1st Co., Capt. C. W. Squires; 2d Co., Capt. J. B. Richardson; 3d Co., Capt. M. B. Miller; 4th Co., Capt. B. F. Eshleman. Loss (in campaign): k, 4; w, 28; m, 2, = 34. *Lee's Battalion*, Col. S. D. Lee: Va. Battery (Ashland Art'y), Capt. Pichegru Woolfolk, Jr.; Va. Battery (Bedford Art'y), Capt. T. C. Jordan; S. C. Battery (Brooks's Art'y), Lieut. William Elliott; Va. Battery, Capt. J. L. Eubank; La. Battery (Madison Light Art'y), Capt. Geo. V. Moody; Va. Battery, Capt. W. W. Parker. Loss (in the campaign); k, 11; w, 75 = 86.
JACKSON'S COMMAND, Maj.-Gen. T. J. Jackson.
EWELL'S DIVISION, Brig.-Gen. A. R. Lawton (w), Brig.-Gen. Jubal A. Early. Staff loss: Antietam w, 2.
*Lawton's Brigade*, Col. M. Douglass (k), Maj. J. H. Lowe, Col. John H. Lamar: 13th Ga., ——; 26th Ga., ——; 31st Ga., Lieut.-Col. J. T. Crowder; 38th Ga., ——; 60th Ga., ——; 61st Ga., Col. John H. Lamar. Brigade loss: Antietam, k, 106; w, 440; m, 21 = 567. *Shepherdstown*, w, 7. *Early's Brigade*, Brig.-Gen. Jubal A. Early, Col. William Smith: 13th Va., Capt. F. V. Winston; 25th Va., ——; 31st Va., ——; 44th Va., ——; 49th Va., Col. William Smith; 52d Va., Col. M. G. Harman; 58th Va., ——. Brigade loss: Antietam, k, 18; w, 167; m, 9 = 194. *Trimble's Brigade*, Col James A. Walker (w): 15th Ala., Capt. I. B. Feagin; 12th Ga., Capt. James G. Rodgers (k); 21st Ga., Maj. Thomas C. Glover (w); 21st N. C. (1st N. C. Battalion attached), Capt. F. P. Miller (k); Va. Battery, Capt. John R. Johnson. Brigade loss: Antietam, k, 27; w, 202; m, 8 = 237. Shepherdstown, w, 1. *Hays's Brigade*, Col. H. B. Strong, Brig.-Gen. Harry T. Hays; 5th La., ——; 6th La., Col. H. B. Strong; 7th La., ——; 8th La., ——; 14th La., ——; La. Battery, Capt. Louis E. D'Aquin. Brigade loss: Antietam, k, 45;

☆ The dash indicates that the name of the commanding officer has not been found in the "Official Records". — EDITORS.

w, 289; m, 2 = 336. *Artillery*, Maj. A. R. Courtney: 1st Md. Battery, Capt. William F. Dement; Md. Battery (Chesapeake Art'y), Capt. William D. Brown; Va. Battery (Courtney Art'y), Capt. J. W. Latimer; Va. Battery (Staunton Art'y), Lieut. A. W. Garber. Artillery not engaged at Antietam.

LIGHT DIVISION, Maj.-Gen. Ambrose P. Hill.
*Branch's Brigade*, Brig.-Gen. L. O'B. Branch (k), Col. James H. Lane: 7th N. C., ———; 18th N. C., Lieut.-Col. T. J. Purdie; 28th N. C., Col. James H. Lane; 33d N. C., ———; 37th N. C., ———. Brigade loss: Harper's Ferry, w, 4. Antietam, k, 21; w, 79; m, 4 = 104. Shepherdstown, k, 3; w, 71 = 74. *Gregg's Brigade*, Brig.-Gen. Maxcy Gregg (w): 1st S. C. (Prov. Army), Col. D. H. Hamilton; 1st S. C. (Rifles), Lieut.-Col. James M. Perrin (w); 12th S. C., Col. Dixon Barnes (k), Maj. W. H. McCorkle; 13th S. C., Col. O. E. Edwards; 14th S. C., Lieut.-Col. W. D. Simpson. Brigade loss: Antietam, k, 28; w, 135; m, 2 = 165. Shepherdstown, k, 10; w, 53 = 63. *Field's Brigade*, Col. J. M. Brockenbrough: 40th Va., ———; 47th Va., ———; 55th Va., ———; 22d Va. Battalion, ———. Brigade loss not separately reported. *Archer's Brigade*, Brig.-Gen. James J. Archer, Col. Peter Turney: 5th Ala. Battalion, Capt. Charles M. Hooper; 19th Ga., Maj. James H. Neal, Capt. F. M. Johnston; 1st Tenn. (Prov. Army), Col. Peter Turney; 7th Tenn., Maj. S. G. Shepard, Lieut. G. A. Howard; 14th Tenn., Lieut.-Col. J. W. Lockert, Col. William McComb (w). Brigade loss: Harper's Ferry, k, 1; w, 22 = 23. Antietam, k, 15; w, 90 = 105. Shepherdstown, k, 6; w, 49 = 55. *Pender's Brigade*, Brig.-Gen. William D. Pender: 16th N. C., Lieut.-Col. W. A. Stowe; 28d N.C., Maj. C. C. Cole; 34th N.C., ———; 38th N.C., ———. Brigade loss: Harper's Ferry, k, 2; w, 20 = 22. Antietam, k, 2; w, 28 = 30. Shepherdstown, k, 8; w, 55 = 63. *Thomas's Brigade*, Col. Edward L. Thomas: 14th Ga., Col. R. W. Folsom; 35th Ga., ———; 45th Ga., Maj. W. L. Grice; 49th Ga., Lieut.-Col. S. M. Manning. Brigade not at Antietam; losses elsewhere not separately reported. *Artillery*, Lieut.-Col. R. L. Walker: Va. Battery, Capt. William G. Crenshaw; Va. Battery (Fredericksburg Art'y), Capt. Carter M. Braxton, Lieut. E. A. Marye; Va. Battery (Letcher Art'y), Capt. Greenlee Davidson; Va. Battery (Purcell Art'y), Capt. W. J. Pegram (w); S. C. Battery (Pee Dee Art'y), Capt. D. G. McIntosh. Artillery loss not separately reported. Division loss (in the campaign): k, 99; w, 605; m, 6 = 710.

JACKSON'S DIVISION, Brig.-Gen. John R. Jones (w), Brig.-Gen. William E. Starke (k), Col. A. J. Grigsby. Staff loss: Antietam, k, 1; m, 1 = 2.
*Winder's Brigade*, Col. A. J. Grigsby, Lieut.-Col. R. D. Gardner, Maj. H. J. Williams: 2d Va. (detached at Martinsburg), Capt. R. T. Colston; 4th Va., Lieut.-Col. R. D. Gardner; 5th Va., Maj. H. J. Williams; 27th Va., Capt. Frank C. Wilson; 33d Va., Capt. Jacob B. Golladay, Lieut. David H. Walton. Brigade loss: Antietam, k, 11; w, 77 = 88. *Taliaferro's Brigade*, Col. E. T. H. Warren, Col. James W. Jackson, Col. James L. Sheffield: 47th Ala., Col. James W. Jackson; 48th Ala., Col. James L. Sheffield; 10th Va., ———; 23d Va., ———; 37th Va., ———. Brigade loss: Antietam, k, 41; w, 132 = 173. *Jones's Brigade*, Col. Bradley T. Johnson, Capt. John E. Penn (w), Capt. A. C. Page (w), Capt. R. W. Withers: 21st Va., Capt. A. C. Page; 42d Va., Capt. R. W. Withers; 48th Va., Capt. John H. Candler; 1st Va. Battalion, Lieut. C. A. Davidson. Brigade loss not separately reported. *Starke's Brigade*, Brig.-Gen. William E. Starke, Col. Leroy A. Stafford (w), Col. Edmund Pendleton: 1st La., Lieut.-Col. M. Nolan (w); 2d La., Col. J. M. Williams (w); 9th La., Col. Leroy A. Stafford; 10th La., Capt. H. D. Monier; 15th La., Col. Edmund Pendleton; 1st La. Battalion (Zouaves), Lieut.-Col. G. Coppens. Brigade loss (partial): Antietam, k, 81; w, 189; m, 17 = 287. *Artillery*, Maj. L. M. Shumaker: Md. Battery (Baltimore Battery), Capt. J. B. Brockenbrough; Va. Battery (Alleghany Art'y), Capt. Joseph Carpenter; Va. Battery (Danville Art'y), Capt. George W. Wooding; Va. Battery (Hampden Art'y), Capt. William H. Caskie; Va. Battery, (Lee Battery), Capt. Charles I. Raine; Va. Battery (Rockbridge Art'y), Capt. W. T. Poague. Artillery loss not separately reported.

HILL'S DIVISION, Maj.-Gen. Daniel H. Hill.
*Ripley's Brigade*, Brig.-Gen. Roswell S. Ripley (w), Col. George Doles: 4th Ga., Col. George Doles; 44th Ga., Capt. John C. Key; 1st N. C., Lieut.-Col. Hamilton A. Brown; 3d N. C., Col. William L. De Rosset (w). Brigade loss: South Mountain and Antietam, k, 110; w, 506; m, 124 = 740. *Rodes's Brigade*, Brig.-Gen. R. E. Rodes (w): 3d Ala., Col. C. A. Battle; 5th Ala., Maj. E. L. Hobson: 6th Ala., Col. J. B. Gordon (w), Lieut.-Col. J. N. Lightfoot (w): 12th Ala., Col. B. B. Gayle (k); 26th Ala., Col. E. A. O'Neal (w). Brigade loss: South Mountain, k, 61; w, 157; m, 204 = 422. Antietam, k, 50; w, 132; m, 21 = 203. *Garland's Brigade*, Brig.-Gen. Samuel Garland, Jr., (k), Col. D. K. McRae (w): 5th N. C., Col. D. K. McRae, Capt. Thomas M. Garrett; 12th N. C., Capt. S. Snow; 13th N. C., Lieut.-Col. Thomas Ruffin, Jr. (w), Capt. J. H. Hyman; 20th N. C., Col. Alfred Iverson; 23d N. C., Col. Daniel H. Christie. Brigade loss: South Mountain and Antietam, k,46; w, 210; m, 187 = 443. *Anderson's Brigade*, Brig.-Gen. George B. Anderson (m w), Col. R. T. Bennett (w): 2d N. C., Col. C. C. Tew (k), Capt. G. M. Roberts; 4th N. C., Col. Bryan Grimes, Capt. W. T. Marsh (k), Capt. D. P, Latham (k); 14th N. C., Col. R. T. Bennett, Lieut.-Col. William A. Johnston (w); 30th N. C., Col. F. M. Parker (w), Maj. William W. Sillers. Brigade loss: South Mountain and Antietam, k, 64; w, 229; m, 202 = 565. *Colquitt's Brigade*, Col. A. H. Colquitt: 13th Ala., Col. B. D. Fry (w), Lieut.-Col. W. H. Betts (w); 6th Ga., Lieut.-Col. J. M. Newton (k); 23d Ga., Col. W. P. Barclay (k); 27th Ga., Col. Levi B. Smith (k); 28th Ga., Maj. Tully Graybill, Capt. N. J. Garrison (w). Brigade loss: South Mountain and Antietam, k, 129; w, 518; m, 184 = 831. *Artillery*, Maj. S. F. Pierson: Ala. Battery, Capt. R. A. Hardaway; Ala. Battery (Jeff Davis Art'y), Capt. J. W. Bondurant; Va. Battery, Capt. William B. Jones; Va. Battery (King William Art'y), Capt. Thomas H. Carter. Brigade loss: South Mountain and Antietam, k, 4; w, 30; m, 3 = 37.

RESERVE ARTILLERY, Brig.-Gen. William N. Pendleton.
*Brown's Battalion* (1st Va. Art'y), Col. J. Thompson Brown: Powhatan Art'y., Capt. Willis J. Dance; 2d Co. Richmond Howitzers, Capt. D. Watson; 3d Co. Richmond Howitzers, Capt. Benjamin H. Smith, Jr.; Salem Art'y, Capt. A. Hupp; Williamsburg Art'y, Capt. John A. Coke. *Cutts's Battalion*, Lieut.-Col. A. S. Cutts: Ga. Battery, Capt. James Ap Blackshear; Ga. Battery (Irwin Art'y), Capt. John Lane; N. C. Battery, Capt. W. P. Lloyd; Ga. Battery, Capt. G. M. Patterson; Ga. Battery, Capt. H. M. Ross. *Jones's Battalion*, Maj. H. P. Jones: Va. Battery (Morris Art'y), Capt. R. C. M. Page; Va. Battery (Orange Art'y), Capt. Jefferson Peyton; Va. Battery (Turner's); Va. Battery, Capt. A. Wimbish. *Nelson's Battalion*, Maj. William Nelson: Va. Battery (Amherst Art'y), Capt. T. J. Kirkpatrick; Va. Battery (Fluvanna Art'y), Capt. John J. Ancell; Va. Battery, Capt. Charles T. Huckstep; Va. Battery, Capt. Marmaduke Johnson; Ga. Battery (Milledge Art'y), Capt. John Milledge. *Miscellaneous* : Va. Battery, Capt. W. E. Cutshaw; Va. Battery (Dixie Art'y), Capt. W. H. Chapman; Va. Battery (Magruder Art'y), Capt. T. J. Page, Jr.; Va. Battery, Capt. W. H. Rice.

CAVALRY, Maj.-Gen. James E. B. Stuart.
*Hampton's Brigade*, Brig.-Gen. Wade Hampton: 1st N. C., Col. L. S. Baker; 2d S. C., Col. M. C. Butler: 10th Va., ———; Cobb's (Ga.) Legion, Lieut.-Col. P. M. B. Young (w), Maj. William G. Delony; Jeff. Davis (Miss.) Legion, Lieut.-Col. W. T. Martin. *Lee's Brigade*, Brig.-Gen. Fitzhugh Lee: 1st Va., Lieut.-Col. L. T. Brien; 3d Va., Lieut.-Col. John T. Thornton (m w); 4th Va., Col. W. C. Wickham; 5th Va., Col. Thomas L. Rosser; 9th Va., ———. *Robertson's Brigade*, Col. Thomas T. Munford: 2d Va., Lieut.-Col. Richard H. Burks; 7th Va., Capt. S. B. Myers; 12th Va., Col. A. W. Harman. *Horse Artillery*: Va. Battery, Capt. R. P. Chew; S. C. Battery, Capt. J. F. Hart; Va. Battery, Capt. John Pelham. Cavalry and Horse Artillery loss (in the campaign): k, 10; w, 45; m, 6 = 61.

According to the report of Lee's medical director (Dr. Guild), there was a loss of 1567 killed and 8724 wounded in the battles of South Mountain, Crampton's Pass, Harper's Ferry, Sharpsburg (or Antietam), and Shepherdstown. Dr. Guild does not give the number of missing and prisoners, and he also omits the casualties in Jones's brigade of Jackson's division, Rodes's brigade of D. H. Hill's division, and the whole of A. P. Hill's division. The corps and division commanders report 1890 killed, 9770 wounded, and 2304 captured or missing during the campaign, making a total of 13,964. Estimating four-fifths of these for the battle of Antietam, we have the following comparative result in that engagement:

|  | Killed. | Wounded. | Captured or Missing. | Total. |
|---|---|---|---|---|
| Union Army | 2108 | 9549 | 753 | 12,410 |
| Confederate Army | 1512 | 7816 | 1844 | 11,172 |

There is not the slightest reason for doubting that many of the "missing" of Lee's army were killed, and that if the number could be ascertained, it would materially increase that class of casualties. General McClellan (Vol. XIX., Pt. I., p. 67, "Official Records"), says that "about 2700 of the enemy's dead were . . . counted and buried upon the battle-field of Antietam"; also, that "a portion of their dead had been previously buried by the enemy."

### RELATIVE STRENGTH OF THE ARMIES.

According to McClellan's report the number of combatants in his command was 87,164; but the brunt of the battle was borne by not above 60,000 men. Comparing the *available* strength of the two armies, undoubtedly McClellan's doubled that of Lee's. In his official report General Lee says, "This great battle was fought by less than 40,000 men on our side."

## THE FINDING OF LEE'S LOST ORDER.

### BY SILAS COLGROVE, BREVET BRIGADIER-GENERAL, U. S. V.

IN reply to your request for the particulars of the finding of General Lee's lost dispatch, "Special Orders No. 191," and the manner in which it reached General McClellan, I beg leave to submit the following account:

The Twelfth Army Corps arrived at Frederick, Maryland, about noon on the 13th of September, 1862. The 27th Indiana Volunteers, of which I was colonel at that date, belonged to the Third Brigade, First Division, of that corps.

We stacked arms on the same ground that had been occupied by General D. H. Hill's division the evening before.

Within a very few minutes after halting, the order was brought to me by First Sergeant John M. Bloss and Private B. W. Mitchell, of Company F, 27th Indiana Volunteers, who stated that it was found by Private Mitchell near where they had stacked arms. When I received the order it was wrapped around three cigars, and Private Mitchell stated that it was in that condition when found by him. [See p. 664.]

General A. S. Williams was in command of our division. I immediately took the order to his headquarters, and delivered it to Colonel S. E. Pittman, General Williams's adjutant-general.

The order was signed by Colonel Chilton, General Lee's adjutant-general, and the signature was at once recognized by Colonel Pittman, who had served with Colonel Chilton at Detroit, Michigan, before the war, and was acquainted with his handwriting. It was at once taken to General McClellan's headquarters by Colonel Pittman. It was a general order giving directions for the movement of General Lee's entire army, designating the route and objective point of each corps. Within an hour after finding the dispatch, General McClellan's whole army was on the move, and the enemy were overtaken next day, the 14th, at South Mountain, and the battle of that name was fought. During the night of the 14th General Lee's army fell back toward the Potomac River, General McClellan following the next day. On the 16th they were overtaken again, and the battle of Antietam was fought mainly on the 17th. General D. H. Hill says in his article in the May "Century," that the battle of South Mountain was fought in order to give General Lee time to move his trains, which were then parked in the neighborhood of Boonsboro'. It is evident from General Lee's movements from the time he left Frederick City, that he intended to recross the Potomac without hazarding a battle in Maryland, and had it not been for the finding of this lost order, the battle of South Mountain, and probably that of Antietam, would not have been fought.

For confirmation of the above statements in regard to the finding of the dispatch, you are respectfully referred to Colonel Samuel E. Pittman, of Detroit, Michigan, and Captain John M. Bloss, of Muncie, Indiana.

WASHINGTON, D. C., June 2d, 1886.

NOTE.— Mr. W. A. Mitchell, the son of Private Mitchell, who, as General Silas Colgrove describes above, was the finder of Lee's order, writes to say that his father was severely wounded at Antietam. After eight months in hospital he completed his term of enlistment, three years, and three years after his discharge died at his home in Bartholomew, Indiana. As his family were then destitute, some efforts are said to have been made to procure a pension for the widow, but General Colgrove (in a letter to the editor of the "Century," dated Washington, November 15th, 1886) states that "neither the soldier nor the widow has ever filed a claim for pension, and any seeming failure of recognition is not due to neglect on the part of the Pension Office."

The following letter from General McClellan to the son is of interest:

"TRENTON, NEW JERSEY, November 18th, 1879. W. A. MITCHELL, ESQ., LA CYNGE, KANSAS.— DEAR SIR: Your letter of the 9th inst. has reached me. I cannot, at this interval of time, recall the name of the finder of the papers to which you refer— it is doubtful whether I ever knew the name. All that I can say is that on or about the 13th of September, 1862,— just before the battles of South Mountain and Antietam,— there was handed to me by a member of my staff a copy (original) of one of General Lee's orders of march, directed to General D. H. Hill, which order developed General Lee's intended operations for the next few days, and was of very great service to me in enabling me to direct the movements of my own troops accordingly. This order was stated to have been found on one of the abandoned camp-grounds of the Confederate troops by a private soldier, and, as I think, of an Indiana regiment. Whoever found the order in question and transmitted it to the headquarters showed intelligence and deserved marked reward, for he rendered an infinite service. The widow of that soldier should have her pension without a day's delay. Regretting that it is not in my power to give the name of the finder of the order, I am very truly yours, GEO. B. MCCLELLAN." EDITORS.

# JACKSON'S CAPTURE OF HARPER'S FERRY.[1]

### BY JOHN G. WALKER, MAJOR-GENERAL, C. S. A.

WHEN General Lee began his campaign against Pope I was in command of a division (of three brigades) which was not a part of either of the two corps of the Army of Northern Virginia. I was left on the James for the defense of Richmond, but after the evacuation of Harrison's Landing by McClellan's army [August 14th to 20th], the Confederate capital being no longer threatened, I was ordered by the Secretary of War to leave one of my brigades at Richmond and proceed with the other two to join General Lee in the field. Leaving Daniel's brigade on the James, I marched northward with my old brigade, the strongest and the one which had seen most service, at that time commanded by Colonel Van H. Manning, and with the brigade of General Robert Ransom.

It was our hope that we should overtake General Lee in time to take part in the fight with Pope; but when we reached the field of Bull Run we found it strewn with the still unburied dead of Pope's army, and learned that Lee was pushing for the fords of the Upper Potomac. Following him rapidly, on the night of the 6th of September my division reached the vicinity of Leesburg, and the next morning crossed the Potomac at Cheek's Ford, at the mouth of the Monocacy, and about three miles above White's Ford, where Stonewall Jackson had crossed.

At Cheek's Ford I overtook G. B. Anderson's brigade of D. H. Hill's division and crossed into Maryland with it. The next day we reached the neighborhood of Frederick. I went at once to General Lee, who was alone. After listening to my report, he said that as I had a division which would often, perhaps, be ordered on detached service, an intelligent performance of my duty might require a knowledge of the ulterior purposes and objects of the campaign.

"Here," said he, tracing with his finger on a large map, "is the line of our communications, from Rapidan Station to Manassas, thence to Frederick. It is too near the Potomac, and is liable to be cut any day by the enemy's cavalry. I have therefore given orders to move the line back into the Valley of Virginia, by way of Staunton, Harrisonburg, and Winchester, entering Maryland at Shepherdstown. [See map, p. 553.]

"I wish you to return to the mouth of the Monocacy and effectually destroy the aqueduct of the Chesapeake and Ohio canal. By the time that is accomplished you will receive orders to coöperate in the capture of Harper's Ferry, and you will not return here, but, after the capture of Harper's Ferry, will rejoin us at Hagerstown, where the army will be concentrated. My information is that there are between 10,000 and 12,000 men at Harper's Ferry, and 3000 at Martinsburg. The latter may escape toward Cumberland, but I think the chances are that they will take refuge at Harper's Ferry and be captured.

[1] For other Harper's Ferry pictures, see Vol. I., pp. 115 to 120, and Vol. II., p. 155.—EDITORS.

"Besides the men and material of war which we shall capture at Harper's Ferry, the position is necessary to us, not to garrison and hold, but because in the hands of the enemy it would be a break in our new line of communications with Richmond."

"A few days' rest at Hagerstown will be of great service to our men. Hundreds of them are barefooted, and nearly all of them are ragged. I hope to get shoes and clothing for the most needy. But the best of it will be that the short delay will enable us to get up our stragglers — not stragglers from a shirking disposition, but simply from inability to keep up with their commands.⁂ I believe there are not less than from eight to ten thousand of them between here and Rapidan Station. Besides these we shall be able to get a large number of recruits who have been accumulating at Richmond for some weeks. I have now requested that they be sent forward to join us. They ought to reach us at Hagerstown. We shall then have a very good army, and," he smilingly added, "one that I think will be able to give a good account of itself.

"In ten days from now," he continued, "if the military situation is then what I confidently expect it to be after the capture of Harper's Ferry, I shall concentrate the army at Hagerstown, effectually destroy the Baltimore and Ohio road, and march to this point," placing his finger at Harrisburg, Pennsylvania. "That is the objective point of the campaign. You remember, no doubt, the long bridge of the Pennsylvania railroad over the Susquehanna, a few miles west of Harrisburg. Well, I wish effectually to destroy that bridge, which will disable the Pennsylvania railroad for a long time. With the Baltimore and Ohio in our possession, and the Pennsylvania railroad broken up, there will remain to the enemy but one route of communication with the West, and that very circuitous, by way of the Lakes. After that I can turn my attention to Philadelphia, Baltimore, or Washington, as may seem best for our interests."

I was very much astonished at this announcement, and I suppose he observed it, for he turned to me and said:

"You doubtless regard it hazardous to leave McClellan practically on my line of communication, and to march into the heart of the enemy's country?"

I admitted that such a thought had occurred to me.

"Are you acquainted with General McClellan?" he inquired. I replied that we had served together in the Mexican war, under General Scott, but that I had seen but little of him since that time.

---

⁂ During the Maryland campaign the Federals as well as the Confederates were greatly weakened by straggling. On October 7th, twenty days after the battle of Antietam, General Halleck, in a letter to General McClellan, said:

"Straggling is the great curse of the army, and must be checked by severe measures. . . . I think, myself, that shooting them while in the act of straggling from their commands, is the only effective remedy that can be applied. If you apply the remedy you will be sustained here. . . . The country is becoming very impatient at the want of activity of your army, and we must push it on. . . . There is a decided want of legs in our troops. . . . The real difficulty is they are not sufficiently exercised in marching; they lie still in camp too long. After a hard march one day is time enough to rest. Lying still beyond that time does not rest the men. If we compare the average distances marched per month by our troops for the last year, with that of the rebels, or with European armies in the field, we will see why our troops march no better. They are not sufficiently exercised to make them good and efficient soldiers."— EDITORS.

"He is an able general but a very cautious one. His enemies among his own people think him too much so. His army is in a very demoralized and chaotic condition, and will not be prepared for offensive operations—or he will not think it so—for three or four weeks. Before that time I hope to be on the Susquehanna."

Our conversation was interrupted at this point by the arrival of Stonewall Jackson, and after a few minutes Lee and Jackson turned to the subject of the capture of Harper's Ferry. I remember Jackson seemed in high spirits, and even indulged in a little mild pleasantry about his long neglect of his friends in "the Valley," General Lee replying that Jackson had "some friends" in that region who would not, he feared, be delighted to see him.

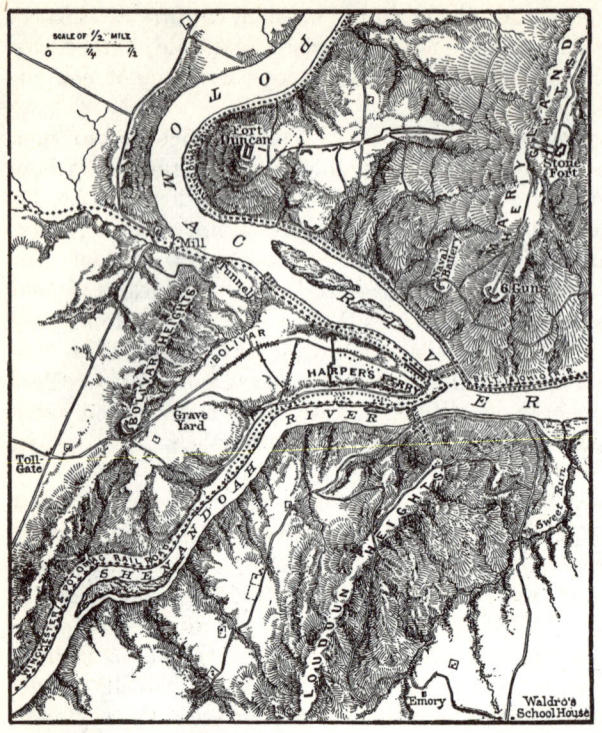

MAP OF THE DEFENSES AND APPROACHES OF HARPER'S FERRY.

The arrival of a party of ladies from Frederick and vicinity, to pay their respects to Lee and Jackson, put an end to the conversation, and soon after I took my departure.

Retracing our steps toward the Potomac, at 10 P. M. of the 9th my division arrived at the aqueduct which conveys the waters of the Chesapeake and Ohio canal across the Monocacy. The attempted work of destruction began, but so admirably was the aqueduct constructed and cemented that it was found to be virtually a solid mass of granite. Not a seam or crevice could be discovered in which to insert the point of a crow-bar, and the only resource was in blasting. But the drills furnished to my engineer were too dull and the granite too hard, and after several hours of zealous but ineffectual effort the attempt had to be abandoned. Dynamite had not then been invented, so we were foiled in our purpose, and about 3 o'clock A. M. of the 10th went into bivouac about two miles and a half west of the Monocacy.

Late in the afternoon a courier from General Lee delivered me a copy of his famous "Special Orders No. 191," directing me to coöperate with Jackson and McLaws in the capture of Harper's Ferry. That order contained the most precise and detailed information respecting the position, at its date, of every portion of the Confederate army,—where it would be during the next five or six days at least,—and inferentially revealed the ulterior designs of the Confederate commander. Possessed of the information it contained, the Federal general would be enabled to throw the weight of his whole force on that small portion of the Confederate army then with Lee, before Jackson, McLaws, and Walker could effect the capture of Harper's Ferry and go to its assistance.

General McClellan did get possession, on the 13th of September, of a copy of this order, addressed to General D. H. Hill. In what manner this happened is not positively known. General Bradley T. Johnson says that there is a tradition in Frederick that General Hill was seen to drop a paper in the streets of that town, which was supposed to be the order in question. The Comte de Paris says it was found in a house in Frederick which had been occupied by General Hill. But General Hill informed me, two years after the war, that he never received the order, and never knew of its existence until he read it in McClellan's report.‡

To whatever circumstance General McClellan owed its possession, it certainly enabled him to thwart General Lee's designs for the invasion of Pennsylvania, or a movement upon Washington. But that he obtained all the advantages he might have done will hardly be contended for by General McClellan's warmest admirer. By the exercise of greater energy he might easily have crushed Lee on the afternoon of the 15th or early on the 16th, before the arrival of Jackson from Harper's Ferry. On receiving my copy of the order I was so impressed with the disastrous consequence which might result from its loss that I pinned it securely in an inside pocket. In speaking with General Longstreet on this subject afterward, he remarked that the same thought had occurred to him, and that, as an absolutely sure precaution, he memorized the order and then "chewed it up."

Informed of the presence of a superior Federal force at Cheek's Ford, where I was ordered to pass the Potomac, and learning that the crossing at the Point of Rocks was practicable, I moved my division to that place and succeeded in landing everything safe on the Virginia shore by daylight of the 11th.

About the same time a heavy rain set in, and as the men were much exhausted by their night march, I put them into bivouac. I would here remark that the Army of Northern Virginia had long since discarded their tents, capacious trunks, carpet-bags, bowie-knives, mill-saw swords, and six-shooters, and had reduced their "kits" to the simplest elements and smallest dimensions.

Resuming our march on the morning of the 12th, we reached Hillsboro' and halted for the night. During the night I was sent for from the village inn by a woman who claimed my attendance on the ground that she was just from Washington, and had very important information to give me. Answering the call, I found seated in the hotel parlor a young woman of perhaps twenty-five, of rather prepossessing appearance, who claimed to have left

‡ See General D. H. Hill's statement, p. 570; General Colgrove's, p. 603, and the text of the order, p. 664.—EDITORS.

VIEW FROM WALKER'S POSITION ON LOUDOUN HEIGHTS OF THE UNION CAMP AND POSITION ON MARYLAND HEIGHTS. FROM A WAR-TIME SKETCH.

Washington the morning before, with important information from "our friends" in the Federal capital which she could communicate only to General Lee himself, and wished to know from me where he could be found. I saw at once that I had to do with a Federal spy; but as I did not wish to be encumbered with a woman prisoner, I professed ignorance of General Lee's whereabouts and advised her to remain quietly at the hotel, as I should, no doubt, have some information for her the next morning. Before resuming our march the next day I sent her under guard to Leesburg, directing the provost marshal at that place to hold her for three or four days and then release her.

Resuming the march at daylight on the 13th, we reached the foot of Loudoun Heights about 10 o'clock. Here I was joined by a detachment of signal men and Captain White's company of Maryland cavalry. I detached two regiments,—the 27th North Carolina and 30th Virginia,—under Colonel J. R. Cooke, directing him to ascend Loudoun Mountain and take possession of the heights, but, in case he found no enemy, not to reveal his presence to the garrison of Harper's Ferry. I sent with him the men of the Signal Corps with orders to open communication if possible with Jackson, whose force ought to be in the neighborhood, coming from the west. I then disposed of the remainder of the division around the point of the mountain, where it abuts on the Potomac.

About 2 P. M. Colonel Cooke reported that he had taken unopposed possession of Loudoun Heights, but that he had seen nothing of Jackson, yet from the movements of the Federals he thought he was close at hand. By 8 o'clock the next morning five long-range Parrott rifles were on the top of the mountain in a masked position, but ready to open fire. About half-past 10 o'clock my signal party succeeded in informing Jackson of my position and my readiness to attack.

At a reunion of the Association of the Army of Northern Virginia held at Richmond on October 23d, 1884, in an address delivered by General Bradley T. Johnson, occurs this passage:

"McLaws, having constructed a road up Maryland Heights and placed his artillery in position during the 14th, while fighting was going on at Crampton's Gap and Turner's Gap, signaled to Jackson that he was ready; whereupon Jackson signaled the order both to McLaws and Walker — 'Fire at such positions of the enemy as will be most effective.'"

I am, of course, ignorant of what Jackson may have signaled McLaws, but it is certain that I received no such order. On the contrary, as soon as he was informed that McLaws was in possession of Maryland Heights, Jackson signaled me substantially the following dispatch: "Harper's Ferry is now completely invested. I shall summon its commander to surrender. Should he refuse I shall give him twenty-four hours to remove the non-combatants, and then carry the place by assault. *Do not fire unless forced to.*"❩

Jackson at this time had, of course, no reason to suspect that McClellan was advancing in force, and doubtless supposed, as we all did, that we should have abundant leisure to rejoin General Lee at Hagerstown. But about noon I signaled to Jackson that an action seemed to be in progress at Crampton's Gap, that the enemy had made his appearance in Pleasant Valley in rear of McLaws, and that I had no doubt McClellan was advancing in force.

To this message Jackson replied that it was, he thought, no more than a cavalry affair between Stuart and Pleasonton. It was now about half-past 12 and every minute the sound of artillery in the direction of South Mountain was growing louder, which left no doubt on my mind of the advance of the whole Federal army. If this were the case, it was certain that General Lee would be in fearful peril should the capture of Harper's Ferry be much longer delayed. I thereupon asked permission to open fire, but receiving no reply, I determined to be "forced." For this purpose I placed the two North Carolina regiments under Colonel (afterward Major-General, and now U. S. Senator) M. W. Ransom, which had relieved those under Cooke, in line of battle in full view of the Federal batteries on Bolivar Heights. As I expected, they at once opened a heavy, but harmless, fire upon my regiments, which afforded me the wished-for pretext. Withdrawing the infantry to the safe side of the mountain, I directed my batteries to reply.

It is possible that some of my military readers may question the propriety of my course, and allege that it amounted virtually to disobedience of orders.

❩ See statements by General Bradley T. Johnson, p. 615, and Colonel H. Kyd Douglas, p. 617.— EDITORS.

This I freely admit, but plead the dire urgency of the case. Had Jackson compromised himself by agreeing to allow the Federal commander twenty-four hours, as he proposed, General Lee would undoubtedly have been driven into the Potomac before any portion of the Confederate force around Harper's Ferry could have reënforced him. The trouble was that Jackson could not be made to believe that McClellan's whole army was in movement.

I never knew whether or not Jackson actually made a formal demand for the surrender of the Federal garrison, but I had his own word for it that he intended to do so. Besides, such a course was in harmony with the humanity of his generous nature, and with his constant practice of doing as little harm as possible to non-combatants.

About an hour after my batteries opened fire those of A. P. Hill and Lawton followed suit, and about 3 o'clock those of McLaws. But the range from Maryland Heights being too great, the fire of McLaws's guns was ineffective, the shells bursting in mid-air without reaching the enemy. From my position on Loudoun Heights my guns had a plunging fire on the Federal batteries a thousand feet below and did great execution. By 5 o'clock our combined fire had silenced all the opposing batteries except one or two guns east of Bolivar Heights, which kept up a plucky but feeble response until night put a stop to the combat.

During the night of the 14th-15th, Major (afterward Brigadier-General) R. Lindsay Walker, chief of artillery of A. P. Hill's division, succeeded in crossing the Shenandoah with several batteries, and placing them in such a position on the slope of Loudoun Mountain, far below me, as to command the enemy's works. McLaws got his batteries into position nearer the enemy, and at daylight of the 15th the batteries of our five divisions were pouring their fire on the doomed garrison. The fire of my batteries, however, was at random, as the enemy's position was entirely concealed by a dense fog clinging to the sides of the mountain far below. But my artillerists trained their guns by the previous day's experience and delivered their fire through the fog.

The Federal batteries replied promptly, and for more than an hour maintained a spirited fire; but after that time it grew more and more feeble until about 8 o'clock, when it ceased altogether, and the garrison surrendered. Owing to the fog I was ignorant of what had taken place, but surmising it, I soon ordered my batteries to cease firing. Those of Lawton, however, continued some minutes later. This happened unfortunately, as Colonel Dixon S. Miles, the Federal commander, was at this time mortally wounded by a fragment of shell while waving a white flag in token of surrender.

It was pleasing to us, perched upon the top of the mountain, to know that more than twelve thousand "boys in blue" below us were stacking arms. Such a situation has its pathetic side too, for after the first feeling of exultation has passed there comes one of sympathy for the humiliation of the brave men, who are no longer enemies, but unfortunate fellow-soldiers.

Some hours later, accompanied by two of my staff, I rode into Harper's Ferry, and we were interested in seeing our tattered Confederates fraternizing in the most cordial manner with their well-dressed prisoners. I was introduced by General A. P. Hill to Federal Brigadier-General White. He explained to me that although of superior rank to Colonel Miles he had declined to assume command of the garrison, since he was at Harper's Ferry by accident — "an unfortunate accident too," he added.

I am of the opinion that it would have been practicable for Colonel Miles to have escaped with the infantry of his garrison during the night of the 14th–15th, as did a body of thirteen hundred cavalry under Colonel "Grimes" Davis.¶ This enterprising young officer crossed his cavalry to the Maryland side of the Potomac over the pontoon bridge, and followed the road on the berme side of the Chesapeake and Ohio canal, leading north to Sharpsburg. Mention of this very meritorious action is made in neither Federal nor Confederate accounts of the capture of Harper's Ferry that have fallen under my notice. ☆ There is a strong probability that the infantry of the garrison could have done the same. It should be stated that Davis not only escaped capture, but that he passed through Sharpsburg at daylight of the 15th,∫ and in crossing the Hagerstown and Williamsport road he destroyed the greater part of Longstreet's reserve ordnance trains. ‡ This escape of Davis from Harper's Ferry and Forrest's escape from Fort Donelson under very similar circumstances show what a bold subordinate may achieve after his superior has lost heart.

No sooner had the surrender of Harper's Ferry been assured than my division took up its line of march to join General Lee. At 2 A. M. of the 16th my advance overtook the rear of Jackson's force, and about 8 o'clock in the morning [of the day of the battle], after seeing our commands safe across the river at the ford below Shepherdstown, Jackson and myself went forward together toward Sharpsburg. As we rode along I mentioned my *ruse* in opening fire on Harper's Ferry. Knowing the strictness of Jackson's ideas in regard to military obedience, I felt a little doubtful as to what he would say. When I had finished my confession he was silent for some minutes, and then remarked: "It was just as well as it was; but I could not believe that the fire you reported indicated the advance of McClellan in force. It seemed more likely to be merely a cavalry affair." Then after an interval of silence, as if to himself, he continued: "I thought I knew McClellan" (they were classmates at West Point), "but this movement of his puzzles me."

¶ Colonel Benjamin F. Davis of the 8th New York Cavalry, familiarly known at West Point and among his old army associates as "Grimes" Davis. He was killed at Beverly Ford, June 9th, 1863. For some interesting details of his escape from Harper's Ferry and subsequent march, see page 613.— EDITORS.

☆ Mentioned by General McClellan.— EDITORS.

∫ According to a paper read by Captain William M. Luff, 12th Illinois Cavalry, before the Illinois Commandery of the Loyal Legion, the hour was 10 P. M. of the 14th.— EDITORS.

‡ Narrowly missing an encounter with the Reserve Artillery under General William N. Pendleton, which crossed Davis's track about eight miles north of Sharpsburg, about sunrise on the 15th. General Pendleton says Davis was "perhaps less than an hour ahead of us," and speaks of the large wagon train then passing, which he took immediate measures to protect.— EDITORS.

# THE CAPITULATION OF HARPER'S FERRY.

## BY JULIUS WHITE, BRIGADIER-GENERAL, U. S. V.

ON the 8th of September, 1862, being then in command of the Union forces at Martinsburg, Virginia, about 2500 of all arms, I reported to General Wool at Baltimore, commanding the Department, that the enemy was approaching from the north in a force estimated at 15,000 to 20,000, and asked for instructions. General Wool replied:

"If 20,000 men should attack you, you will of course fall back. Harper's Ferry would be the best position I could recommend." . . .

After reconnoissance, and some skirmishing with the enemy's advance [Sept. 11th], demonstrating that his force was too large to be opposed with success, especially as there were no defenses at Martinsburg, the post, in accordance with General Wool's views, was evacuated, and on the 12th Harper's Ferry was reached.

Upon my reporting to Colonel Miles, the officer in command, he showed me the following dispatch:

"WASHINGTON, D. C., Sept. 7th, 1862. COLONEL MILES, Harper's Ferry: Our army [McClellan's] is in motion; it is important that Harper's Ferry be held to the latest moment. The Government has the utmost confidence in you, and is ready to give you full credit for the defense it expects you to make. H. W. HALLECK, General-in-Chief."

In view of the foregoing dispatch, and of the fact that I had been ordered from Harper's Ferry to the command at Martinsburg a few days before by General Wool, it was manifest that the authorities intended to retain Colonel Miles in command—very properly so, as he was an officer of forty years' experience.

The defenses of Harper's Ferry, if worthy of the name, comprised a small work on the crest of Maryland Heights called Stone Fort; another well down the western slope, where a battery of heavy naval guns was established; and a line of intrenchments terminating at a work near the Potomac called Fort Duncan,—but this line was not occupied except at the upper end. [See map, p. 606.]

On Bolivar Heights a line of rifle-pits extended from near the Potomac southward to the Charlestown road, where a small work for the protection of artillery was situated.

In the rear of this line eastward, and in the upper part of the town, was an earth-work known as Camp Hill. Loudoun Heights (east of the Shenandoah) were not occupied by our troops.

The troops constituting the garrison were originally disposed by Colonel Miles as follows: on Maryland Heights, about 2000; on Bolivar Heights, from the Potomac to the Charlestown road, thence at a right angle to the Shenandoah, a distance in all of at least a mile and a half, 7000 men; in the work at Camp Hill, about 800; while the remainder, about 1000, guarded the bridges and other points on the rivers.

The distance from Maryland Heights to the nearest point on Bolivar Heights by way of the pontoon bridge was two and a quarter miles; to the intersection of the Charlestown road, three miles. Thus the principal points to be defended were not within supporting distance of each other in case of assault, nor was either of them properly fortified.

On the 13th the divisions of Generals McLaws and R. H. Anderson, by order of General Lee, reached Maryland Heights, and attacked the force stationed there, under Colonel Ford, who after some fighting abandoned the position—as he stated, by order of Colonel Miles; the latter, however, denied having given such an order. Be this as it may, it is certain that the enemy could easily have taken it with the force at his command whenever he chose.

On the same day General Walker, with a force of the enemy estimated at eight thousand, had taken possession of Loudoun Heights, and General Jackson with a much larger force had reached a position in front of Bolivar Heights—thus completing the investment of Harper's Ferry.

It has generally been considered that Colonel Miles should have tried to hold Maryland Heights (on the north side of the Potomac), even if it became necessary to mass his whole force there. The reasons given by him to the writer for not doing so were: (1) That his orders required him to hold Harper's Ferry, and this would be a violation of such orders; (2) that water would be inaccessible. Moreover, it was manifest that if the town of Harper's Ferry and the defensive line on Bolivar Heights were evacuated, the entire forces of the enemy on the Virginia side of the Potomac would recross to the north side, enveloping our small force and at the same time concentrating Lee's entire army in front of McClellan; while we should have given up the river-crossing, which, as the contending armies were then placed, constituted the only strategic value of Harper's Ferry.

Whether this view was correct or not, it is a fact that the maintenance of the line on Bolivar Heights till the morning of September 15th prevented the presence of the divisions of Generals A. P. Hill, McLaws, and Anderson with Lee, until the 17th, the day of Antietam, being four full days after General McClellan had received a copy of General Lee's orders directing the movement against Harper's Ferry, and disclosing the fact that fully one-third of his army was south of the Potomac, and much more than that, including the force under General McLaws, engaged in the movement against Harper's Ferry. Distinguished officers of the Confederate army [Generals Longstreet and Walker and Colonel Douglas, see pp. 604, 620, 663] describe the situation of that part of Lee's army north of the Potomac during the 14th, 15th, and 16th of September as one of "imminent peril," "very serious," etc., etc., virtually admitting that it might then have been defeated.

Thus it will be seen that there were two sides to the question whether Maryland Heights was the key to Harper's Ferry under the then existing circumstances, and that the detention of the Confederate forces around that place was prolonged, instead of abbreviated, by the continued occupation of Bolivar Heights by Colonel Miles.

In the afternoon of the 14th General Jackson moved forward with a view to occupy the ridge which is a prolongation of Bolivar Heights south of the Charlestown road and descends toward the Shenandoah River.

To oppose this movement troops were advanced, but after a spirited engagement it was manifest that we could not prevent his establishment in the position sought, and at night our force was withdrawn within the lines of defense.

During the evening of the 13th a consultation took place between the writer, then temporarily in command of the cavalry, Colonel B. F. Davis of the 8th New York, and Lieutenant-Colonel Hasbrouck Davis of the 12th Illinois, at which it was agreed that the mounted force could be of little use in the defense — that the horses and equipments would be of great value to the enemy if captured, and that an attempt to reach McClellan ought therefore to be made.

This proposition, made by Colonel B. F. Davis, was warmly seconded by Colonel Davis of the 12th Illinois. The question whether the whole force might not also escape was considered, but was negatived on the ground that infantry and artillery could not march fast enough to succeed. Besides, Colonel Miles considered that he had no right under his orders to evacuate the post.

After some hesitation and some sharp words between Colonels Miles and B. F. Davis, the former issued the order directing the cavalry to move out on the evening of the 14th, under the general command of the senior officer, Colonel Arno Voss, of the 12th Illinois.

Under the inspiration and immediate direction of the two Davises, who rode together at the head of the column, the escaping force accomplished the brilliant achievement of reaching the Union lines without the loss of a man, capturing on the way a Confederate ammunition train of 97 wagons and its escort of 600 men.

Graphic accounts of this daring and successful exploit have been published by Major Thomas Bell of the 8th New York, Major W. M. Luff of the 12th Illinois, and Sergeant Pettengill of the 1st Rhode Island Cavalry — all of whom were participants, and I regret that the limits of this article do not permit the recital here.

There were other incidents in the history of the events under consideration highly creditable to the troops constituting the garrison of Harper's Ferry. General Kershaw's report to General McLaws of the capture of Maryland Heights, on the 13th, states that he met with a "most obstinate resistance" from our force stationed there, "a fierce fire being kept up at a distance of one hundred yards," and it was not till he had sent General Barksdale's brigade to attack the works in rear that the heights were evacuated.

The fighting with Jackson's advance in front of Bolivar Heights, on the afternoon of the 14th and on the morning of the 15th, by the troops posted in that quarter, was deliberate, systematic, and plucky. The artillery was admirably handled, and if there had been anything like an equality of position, its effect would have been more decided. It would be invidious to specify the action of certain brigades, regiments, or batteries, but common justice to these troops requires that the foregoing statement of their service be made.

Soon after daylight on the morning of the 15th fire was opened by the enemy's artillery, comprising nearly or quite fifty pieces. Those established at the southern extremity of Bolivar Heights completely enfiladed that part of our line extending from the Charlestown road northward to the Potomac; those placed on the south-western slope of Loudoun Heights, and on the west side of the Shenandoah near by, delivered their fire at an acute angle to our line, being half enfilade; those at or near the crest of Loudoun Heights took us in reverse; and still others in the valley beyond Bolivar Heights fired directly at our front.

The fire was chiefly converged upon the batteries we had established at and near the intersection of Bolivar Heights and the Charlestown road, that being the point upon which it was manifest that General Jackson would deliver the expected assault.

The writer, being in command of the forces in this quarter, ordered the massing of the artillery there and the movements of the regiments holding Camp Hill to the front. These orders, as I afterward learned, were countermanded by Colonel Miles, who deemed it necessary to retain a force near the river-crossing; at all events the order was not executed.

The artillery fire continued until half-past 8 in the morning, when it was apparent the assault might be expected immediately. At this time Colonel Miles visited the work at the Charlestown road and said to the writer that the situation seemed hopeless, and that the place might as well be surrendered without further sacrifice of life. It was replied that such a step should only be taken upon the judgment of a council of war; whereupon Colonel Miles called the commanders of brigades together, who, after consultation, and with great reluctance on the part of some, voted unanimously for capitulation if honorable terms could be obtained, for the following reasons:

*First.* The officer commanding had lost all confidence in his ability further to defend the place, and was the first to advise surrender.

*Second.* There was no reason to hope that the attenuated line on Bolivar Heights could be maintained, even for half an hour, against the greatly superior force massed for the assault, supported if necessary by an attack on our rear by Generals Walker and McLaws.

*Third.* Great as was the disparity in numbers, the disparity in position was greater. Harper's Ferry and Bolivar Heights were dominated by Maryland and Loudoun Heights, and the other positions held by the enemy's artillery. The crest of Maryland Heights is at an elevation of 1060 feet; the southern point, nearest Harper's Ferry, 649 feet; Loudoun Heights, 954 feet. The south-western slope of the latter and the grounds near by, west of the Shenandoah, where batteries of the enemy were placed, were 300 to 600 feet high. The elevation of Bolivar Heights is about 300 feet, while Camp Hill and the town of Harper's Ferry are still lower. Thus all our movements of men or guns during the engagements of the 14th and 15th, as well as the effect of their own plunging fire, were plainly visible from the enemy's signal-station on Loudoun Heights. No effective reply could be made to the fire from these elevated positions, no suitable defenses existed from which to resist the assault, and there was no opportunity on the morning of the 15th to change our position, even if there had been a better one to occupy.

*Fourth.* To await the assault, then impending, with no hope of even a temporary successful resistance, did not seem to justify the sacrifice of life consequent upon such a course — the situation being regarded as one of the unfortunate chances of war, unavoidable under existing circumstances.

I was appointed by Colonel Miles commissioner to arrange the terms of capitulation, and at the urgent request of other officers I accepted the unwelcome duty, in the hope of obtaining honorable conditions. Immediately after the council broke up Colonel Miles was mortally wounded; he died the next day.

As commissioner I was received very courteously by the Confederate officers, and the terms of capitulation agreed upon with General A. P. Hill provided that all private property of individuals and the side-arms of officers should be retained by them. Refugees, of whom there were a considerable number, were not to be treated as prisoners, except such, if any, as were deserters from the Confederate army. There were none of this class. All the Union troops were immediately paroled, not to serve again until regularly exchanged. A number of the prominent officers of the Confederate army spoke of our situation as hopeless from the hour when the investment was completed.

Harper's Ferry is not defensible by a force inferior to that attacking it, unless the surrounding heights be well fortified, and each of them held by a force sufficient to maintain itself unsupported by the others. It was this which doubtless prompted the advice given by General McClellan to General Halleck, before the investment, that the garrison be withdrawn.

The battle of South Mountain was fought by General McClellan, on the 14th of September, against a force of the enemy not more than two-thirds as large as that encountered by him at Antietam.

After the mountain passes had been carried, if a prompt advance down Pleasant Valley had been made by his largely preponderating force, there seems good reason to believe that Harper's Ferry would have been relieved, the river-crossing at that place secured, the reunion of Lee's army, separated as it was by the Potomac, rendered difficult, if not impossible, and the capture or dispersion of a large part of it probable.

The orders issued by General McClellan to General Franklin, commanding the Sixth Corps, on the night of the 13th, announced his purpose to do these very things, and directed that Crampton's Gap — the pass nearest Harper's Ferry — be carried at whatever cost. The enemy in front of General Franklin was then to be "cut off, destroyed, or captured, and Harper's Ferry relieved." The dispatch concludes with the remark: "My general idea is to cut the enemy in two, and beat him in detail." The column to be thus interposed between the enemy and Harper's Ferry consisted of General Franklin's corps only — subsequently reënforced by General Couch's division of the Fourth Corps. The imminent peril of Harper's Ferry had been known to General McClellan from the inception of the campaign. He had advised the withdrawal of the garrison, and had predicted its loss if left there, before he left Washington.

No direct measures were taken by him, however, for the relief of the post, until after his receipt on the 13th of General Lee's order detaching a large part of his army for its capture, which force had then completed its investment. Early on the morning of the 14th General McClellan had been informed by Colonel Miles, through Major Russell of the 1st Maryland Cavalry, who, with great courage and tact, had made his way during the night through the enemy's lines, that Harper's Ferry could not be held more than forty-eight hours — from the time the courier left — viz., till the 15th.

Thus the time within which to relieve that post had been reduced to the minimum, so that success depended upon the prompt and vigorous advance of a force large enough to readily overcome such of the enemy as stood in the way. Unfortunately, General Franklin's command was not sufficient to accomplish this vitally important purpose.

After receiving the orders, he was not able to get his command into action until midday of the 14th, and met with such determined resistance that it was not until near nightfall, and after a loss of more than five hundred in killed and wounded, that he had forced the pass and found himself on the west side of the mountain in Pleasant Valley, confronted by an increased force of the enemy, with plenty of artillery advantageously posted.

The attack on Turner's Gap by the main body of the army, although successful, did not result, as General McClellan had expected, in relieving General Franklin of the enemy in his front; and the latter, as shown in his dispatches of the morning of the 15th, declined to attack unless reënforced.

But the time within which it was possible to relieve Harper's Ferry had then passed, even if the place had been held during the whole of that day.

During the afternoon of the 14th our guns at Harper's Ferry, engaged with Jackson's forces, were cheeringly responded to by those of General Franklin at Crampton's Gap; but after 4 o'clock of that day, and on the morning of the 15th, there was no sound of conflict in that direction, and the hope of relief from McClellan, which the proximity of the firing had inspired, was abandoned. Harper's Ferry was doomed, and as affecting this result, it did not matter whether the garrison occupied the town or either of the adjacent heights, nor whether the surrender took place before or after an assault, *because it was surrounded by the whole of Lee's army.*

I must not be understood as presuming to criticise the conduct of this campaign by General McClellan. The object of this article, as before stated, is only to relate the historical facts bearing upon the subject in hand; therefore, no commentary is made upon the questions whether his advice that the garrison of Harper's Ferry be withdrawn should have been adopted, whether he might have marched his army toward Harper's Ferry faster, or whether he might and should have detached a larger force for the purposes indicated in his orders to General Franklin. Manifestly it was his design to relieve that post, but the measures taken did not succeed.

It has been often asserted that Harper's Ferry might have held out a day or two longer, but of those who have claimed that it could have been longer held, no one has yet, so far as the writer is informed, stated *how* a garrison mostly of recruits under fire for the first time could have successfully defended an area of three square miles, assailed from all sides by veterans three times their number, posted, with artillery, in positions commanding the whole field. The writer, with due deference, expresses the opinion that the force under Jackson could have carried the place by assault within an hour after his arrival before it, or at any time thereafter prior to the surrender, in spite of any resistance which under the circumstances could have been made.↓

## STONEWALL JACKSON'S INTENTIONS AT HARPER'S FERRY.

### I. BY BRADLEY T. JOHNSON, BRIGADIER-GENERAL, C. S. A.

MAJOR-GENERAL J. G. WALKER, in his interesting paper in "The Century" [June, 1886], states that after he had occupied Loudoun Heights on September 14th, he received a dispatch from General Jackson, by signal, substantially as follows: "Harper's Ferry is now completely invested. I shall summon its commander to surrender. Should he refuse, I will give him twenty-four hours to remove the non-combatants, and then carry the place by assault. Do not fire unless forced to." [See p. 609.]

Referring to the statement made by me in an address before the Association of the Army of Northern Virginia, October 23d, 1884, that on the 14th of September General Jackson signaled the order to both McLaws and Walker, "Fire at such positions of the enemy as will be most effective," General Walker says: "I am, of course, ignorant of what Jackson may have signaled McLaws, but it is certain I received no such order." General Walker then goes on to show that Jackson determined to give the commanding officer of Harper's Ferry twenty-four hours before he carried the place; that he, General Walker, was satisfied that the delay of twenty-four hours would be fatal to General Lee,—as it would have been; that, therefore, against orders not to fire until he was forced to, he determined to be forced; and that he secured this end by the display of two North Carolina regiments, under Colonel M. W. Ransom, in line of battle on Loudoun Heights, in full view of the Federal batteries on Bolivar Heights. As he expected, he says, "they at once opened a heavy but harmless fire upon my regiments, which afforded me the wished-for pretext. Withdrawing the infantry to the safe side of the mountain, I directed my batteries to reply."

Thus it would appear that General Walker forced the attack on Harper's Ferry, and prevented the delay of twenty-four hours which General Jackson proposed to give; and that to this prompt attack was due the capture of Harper's Ferry, and the salvation of that part of the Army of Northern Virginia which, with Lee, Longstreet, and D. H. Hill, was waiting at Sharpsburg the reduction of the force at the former place, and the reënforcement of Lee by Jackson, McLaws, and Walker after Harper's Ferry had fallen. Twenty-four hours' delay would have postponed the fall of Harper's Ferry, and the battle of the 17th would have been fought by Longstreet and D. H. Hill alone, who would have been destroyed by McClellan before Jackson could have come up.

I prepared the address before the Association of the Army of Northern Virginia after careful study of the records and reports of both sides, and all accessible accounts of the battle of Sharpsburg, and believe every statement made by me can be substantiated by the record, or by the statements of eye-witnesses. Unless General Walker has a copy of the dispatch referred to by him, I respectfully submit that his recollection is in error; that no intention was ever entertained by Jackson of giving twenty-four hours' delay; and that General Jackson himself gave the order to Walker and McLaws to open fire, exactly as stated by me.

The reasons for believing that General Walker is mistaken in thinking that he ever received the order referred to by him, or one in any way intimating an intention of giving twenty-four hours'

---

↓ The report of the Military Commission censured Colonels Miles and Ford and Major Baird. It affirmed that there was nothing in the conduct of Colonels D'Utassy and Trimble to call for censure; and that General Julius White merited the approbation of the Commission, adding, "He appears from the evidence to have acted with decided capability and courage."—EDITORS.

delay, seem to me to be conclusive. Colonel H. Kyd Douglas was aide-de-camp to Jackson, and occupied, particularly in that campaign, peculiarly confidential relations to him. His home was near Sharpsburg and Shepherdstown, the scene of operations, and he probably knew as much of General Jackson's intentions as any man living. He tells me he never heard of any such projected delay. The "lost order" No. 191 — from General Lee to Jackson, Walker, and McLaws — specially directs Walker and McLaws to be in position on Loudoun and Maryland Heights respectively by Friday morning, September 12th, and Jackson to take possession of the Baltimore and Ohio railroad by Friday morning and "intercept such of the enemy as may attempt to escape from Harper's Ferry." Jackson's advance division reached the vicinity of Harper's Ferry during Saturday forenoon, the 13th; Walker and McLaws reached the designated points Saturday night, but were not in position for offensive action until September 14th.

Now, when the army was moving to the positions assigned by "Special Orders No. 191," it was a matter of common knowledge that McClellan's advance was in contact with our rear. Hampton had a sharp affair in the streets of Frederick late on the 12th. Fitz Lee, hanging on to the advance, located McClellan and reported his presence to Stuart, who held the mountain pass over Catoctin at Hagan's. During the 13th Stuart delayed the advance of the Federal infantry through Middletown Valley by sturdily defending the practicable points on the National road.

On the 14th, when, according to General Walker, Jackson, then a day late, proposed to give the commander of Harper's Ferry twenty-four hours' delay, and General Walker, in order to prevent that delay, drew the fire of the Federal guns on him on Loudoun Heights, Franklin's corps attacked Crampton's Gap about noon, and after a sharp defense drove Munford through the mountain pass. Now Crampton's Gap is in full sight of Loudoun Heights, not four miles off as the crow flies, and is in rear of McLaws's position on Maryland Heights. Jackson then knew that McClellan was thundering in his rear. Walker and McLaws could see the battle and hear the guns at Crampton's, and Walker could also see the fight at South Mountain.

It would have been contrary to every known characteristic of the chief of the "Foot Cavalry" for him to have given his adversary twenty-four hours' breathing-time, under any circumstances, anywhere, and utterly impossible for him to have done so under these circumstances at this time.

General Jackson did send General Walker an order by signal: "I do not desire any of the batteries to open until all are ready on both sides of the river, except you should find it necessary, of which you must judge for yourself. I will let you know when to open all the batteries."

In the War Records office may be seen the report of Captain J. L. Bartlett, signal officer of Jackson's corps. It contains the order to Walker and McLaws quoted by me in my address: "Fire at such positions of the enemy as will be most effective." This order General Walker does not recollect to have received. It certainly was sent by Captain Bartlett to Walker's signal officer, and just as certainly received by the latter. It is hardly possible that so important an order, at such a time, should not have been forwarded by the signal officer to General Walker. The following order was also sent from Captain Bartlett's signal-station to General Walker's officer on Loudoun Heights:

"*Special Orders*      HEADQUARTERS VALLEY DISTRICT,
     No. ——                         September 14, 1862.

"1. To-day Major-General McLaws will attack so as to sweep with 'his artillery the ground occupied by the enemy, take his batteries in reverse, and otherwise operate against him as circumstances may justify.

"2. Brigadier-General Walker will take in reverse the battery on the turnpike, and also sweep with his artillery the ground occupied by the enemy, and silence the battery on the island in the Shenandoah, should he find a battery there.

"3. Major-General A. P. Hill will move along the left bank of the Shenandoah, and thus turn the enemy's left flank and enter Harper's Ferry.

"4. Brigadier-General Lawton will move along the turnpike for the purpose of supporting General Hill and otherwise operating against the enemy on the left of General Hill.

"5. Brigadier-General Jones will, with one of his brigades and a battery of artillery, make a demonstration against the enemy's right; the remaining part of his division will constitute the reserve and move along the turnpike.

"By order of Major-General Jackson:
          "WILLIAM L. JACKSON,
     "Acting Assistant Adjutant-General."

Captain Bartlett, after reporting all messages and orders sent through his station, among which were the foregoing, says, "If any other dispatches or orders were sent at Harper's Ferry, it was done at other posts than mine."

Now, there was no signal officer except Captain Bartlett attached to Jackson's headquarters, communicating with Loudoun Heights, and his report thus shows all the orders sent by Jackson to Walker. The one quoted by General Walker is not among them; the one quoted by me is. Therefore, inasmuch as it appears that the investing force under Jackson was twenty-four hours behind the time fixed by General Lee for completing the investment of Harper's Ferry; and that Generals Jackson and McLaws knew that McClellan had been in Frederick on the 12th, only twenty miles off; and that McClellan was actually attacking at Crampton's, three or four miles from Harper's Ferry; and that Lee, Longstreet, and D. H. Hill were then north of the Potomac, and in imminent danger of being cut off from the rest of the army at Harper's Ferry; and that General Jackson did, in fact, send the order, cited by me, to Walker and McLaws to fire at such positions of the enemy as would be most effective, and did, in fact, as soon as his troops were in position, completing the investment, issue an order of battle for the assault on Harper's Ferry: taking all these facts into consideration, we must believe that General Walker is mistaken as to the order he thinks he received, and that General Jackson never issued such order, nor entertained the idea of delaying the attack.

## STONEWALL JACKSON'S INTENTIONS AT HARPER'S FERRY.

### II. BY HENRY KYD DOUGLAS, COLONEL, C. S. A.

IN his article in "The Century" for June, 1885, on "Harper's Ferry and Sharpsburg," General John G. Walker said, in substance, that General Jackson, after Harper's Ferry was invested, informed him that he intended to summon the Federal commander to surrender, and, should he refuse, then to give him twenty-four hours to remove the non-combatants before making an assault; but that he, General Walker, being better advised as to the movements of General McClellan, became impatient of the delay, and by a piece of mild strategy *forced* the assault, and thereby hastened the surrender of Harper's Ferry, saved Jackson from being "compromised," and Lee from being driven into the Potomac. [See pp. 604–611.]

With the help of such notes as I have, confirming my recollection, and the official reports corroborating them, I will briefly examine General Walker's statement.

I think I may safely assume that General Jackson, being in immediate communication, by signal, with General McLaws (who was in contact with the enemy), and with General Lee both by signal through McLaws and by a constant line of couriers, knew at least as much about the movements of General McClellan and the situation of the rest of our army as General Walker, on Loudoun Heights, could possibly know.

Jackson reached Harper's Ferry on Saturday, September 13th, and immediately shut up his side of the pen. McLaws and Walker were not yet in position, their delay being doubtless unavoidable. Let us see whether Jackson was in danger of compromising himself by want of activity. The next day at 7:20 A. M., in anticipation that McLaws and Walker would soon be ready, he sent to McLaws a characteristic letter of instructions. As will appear, a copy of this letter was doubtless sent to Walker, and will help to explain one of the errors into which he has fallen. That letter looks to quick work. But although Jackson was ready, there were obstacles in the way of immediate action. General Jackson says that, separated by the Potomac and Shenandoah from McLaws and Walker, he resorted to signals, "and that before the necessary orders were thus transmitted the day was far advanced." General A. P. Hill says, in effect, that it was afternoon before the signals from Maryland and Loudoun Heights notified Jackson that "all was ready," and then Jackson ordered him against the enemy. General McLaws says the morning of the 14th was occupied cutting a road for artillery, and that by 2 P. M. he had four pieces in position on Maryland Heights. General Walker says that at half-past 10 he succeeded in notifying Jackson that he was ready, and Captain Bartlett, the signal officer of Jackson, reports to the same effect. Jackson then ordered Walker to "wait" for McLaws. Every one at headquarters knew how impatient General Jackson was at the unavoidable loss of time. He had written the McLaws letter very early in the morning, and in further preparation for prompt and decisive action he dictated to Colonel Jackson his "special order" for the attack, and as soon as it was practicable issued it. It speaks for itself. He also issued his joint order to McLaws and Walker—"Fire at such positions of the enemy as will be most effective." Walker opened fire about 1 P. M.—whether shortly before or shortly after this joint order does not appear, and is of little importance. McLaws began about 2 P. M. He says Walker and Jackson were both at it before him. Hill moved promptly, and did enough of work that afternoon and night, as he says, "to seal the fate of Harper's Ferry," with the assistance of McLaws and Walker. At 3 o'clock the next morning I was sent by General Jackson to direct the movement of Jones's division at first dawn, and at daylight everybody was in action, and Harper's Ferry speedily surrendered. In energy, Jackson at Harper's Ferry simply paralleled himself; he could do no more. "Let the work be done thoroughly," he had said to McLaws; and it was.

Was General Jackson pushed to this activity by General Walker, and would he otherwise have given Colonel Miles twenty-four hours to remove non-combatants before assault, and thus have imperiled General Lee beyond hope? I will treat this question soberly, as becomes the gravity of General Walker's statement and his regard for General Jackson's reputation. But, as the matter now presents itself, I will submit the reasons for thinking General Walker is mistaken in regard to the dispatch he says he received from General Jackson respecting the twenty-four hours' delay. It is known now that Jackson never did summon the enemy to surrender, and in his report he makes no mention of such a purpose. I find in my notes this item in regard to the 14th: "It was late in the afternoon when McLaws was ready for action—too late to effect anything on that day. Preparations were made for an assault early the next morning. I am not aware that General Jackson made any demand for the surrender of the garrison." There is nothing in the reports of Hill, McLaws, Jones, or Walker, touching the matter of a contemplated demand for surrender, or any delay by reason thereof. Captain Bartlett's report as signal officer—the only one known to have sent signal dispatches between Jackson and Walker—contains no such order as the one quoted by General Walker. If such a message had been sent to Walker, it would, of course, have been sent also to Hill and McLaws, and they make no mention of it. It could not have gone to McLaws except through Bartlett, and he surely would have made a note of it. General Walker says it was after Jackson was informed that McLaws was in possession of Maryland Heights that the dispatch was sent to him. This was not earlier than 2 P. M., and before that time Walker had opened fire, and Jackson had issued the joint order, "Fire," etc., and had followed it up with his specific "special order," prepared beforehand. In fact, General Jackson knew the urgency of the situation better than General Walker, and it is simply incredible that he contemplated a delay of twenty-four hours

# 618  THE HISTORICAL BASIS OF WHITTIER'S "BARBARA FRIETCHIE."

for any purpose. General Walker must be mistaken. It does not follow, however, that he has no ground for his mistake. I have said that the substance of Jackson's early letter to McLaws must have been sent to Walker. That letter looks to an attack by Walker on an island battery in the Shenandoah, and during the morning a dispatch to Jackson from Loudoun Heights says: "Walker can't get position to bear on island,"—showing that Walker had in some way been instructed with regard to it. (It would seem that Jackson's "special order" must have been prepared in the morning and before the receipt of the dispatch from Walker, for in it he gives instructions to Walker touching that island battery.) In the McLaws letter, Jackson speaks of a flag of truce to get out non-combatants should the enemy not surrender; but the spirit of that letter is against any delay. I remember the question of a demand for surrender was vaguely talked of at headquarters by the staff. It is likely they got the idea from the McLaws letter, for I never heard the general [Jackson] say anything on the subject, and every indication was against any delay in making the assault. I merely throw out the suggestion to account for the error of memory into which I think General Walker has fallen. Whatever purpose General Jackson at first had to demand a surrender or to consider non-combatants, his ruling anxiety was for the speedy fall of Harper's Ferry. It may be that a little reflection satisfied him, after writing the McLaws letter, that the citizens of the town would be in little danger from the firing of McLaws and Walker at the enemy on Bolivar Heights, and that he dismissed that consideration from his mind. If this humane purpose ever took definite shape in his intentions, there was never any occasion to execute it, and it would now be of little consequence had not General Walker attempted to give it such strange form and significance.

## THE OPPOSING FORCES AT HARPER'S FERRY, VA.
### September 12–15, 1862.

The composition, losses, and strength of each army as here stated give the gist of all the data obtainable in the Official Records. K stands for killed; w for wounded; m w for mortally wounded; m for captured or missing; c for captured.

### THE UNION FORCES.
Col. Dixon S. Miles (m w), Brig.-Gen. Julius White.

*Brigade Commanders:* Colonels F. G. D'Utassy, William H. Trimble, Thomas H. Ford, and William G. Ward. *Troops:* 12th Ill. Cav., Col. Arno Voss; M, 2d Ill. Art'y, Capt. John C. Phillips; 65th Ill., Col. Daniel Cameron; 15th Ind. Battery, Capt. John C. H. von Sehlen; Ind. Battery, Capt. Silas F. Rigby; 1st Md. Cav. (detachment), Capt. Charles H. Russell; Battalion Md. Cav., Maj. Henry A. Cole; 1st Md., P. H. Brigade, Col. William P. Maulsby; 3d Md., P. H. Brigade, Lieut.-Col. Stephen W. Downey; 8th N. Y. Cav., Col. Benjamin F. Davis; A, 5th N. Y. H. Art'y, Capt. John H. Graham; F, 5th N. Y. H. Art'y, Capt. Eugene McGrath; 12th N. Y. (militia), Col. William G. Ward; 39th N. Y., Maj. Hugo Hildebrandt; 111th N. Y., Col. Jesse Segoine; 115th N. Y., Col. Simeon Sammon; 125th N. Y., Col. George L. Willard; 126th N. Y., Col. Eliakim Sherrill (w), Maj. William H. Baird; Ohio Battery, Capt. Benjamin F. Potts; 32d Ohio, Maj. Sylvester M. Hewitt; 60th Ohio, Lieut.-Col. Noah H. Hixon;.87th Ohio, Col. Henry B. Banning; 7th Squadron R. I. Cav., Maj. Augustus W. Corliss; 9th Vermont, Col. George J. Stannard.

The total Union loss in the actions on Maryland Heights and at Harper's Ferry and Bolivar Heights was 44 killed, 173 wounded, and 12,520 captured = 12,737. (Most of the wounded were probably counted among the captured.)

The Confederate force employed at Harper's Ferry consisted of the commands of Generals Jackson, McLaws (including R. H. Anderson's division), and Walker. For composition of these forces in detail, see pp. 600–602.

## THE HISTORICAL BASIS OF WHITTIER'S "BARBARA FRIETCHIE."
### BY GEORGE O. SEILHEIMER.[↓]

THAT Barbara Frietchie lived is not denied. That she died at the advanced age of 96 years and is buried in the burial-ground of the German Reformed Church in Frederick is also true.

There is only one account of Stonewall Jackson's entry into Frederick, and that was written by a Union army surgeon who was in charge of the hospital there at the time. "Jackson I did not get a look at to recognize him," the doctor wrote on the 21st of September, "though I must have seen him, as I witnessed the passage of all the troops through the town." Not a word about Barbara Frietchie and this incident. Dr. Oliver Wendell Holmes, too, was in Frederick soon afterward, on his way to find his son, reported mortally wounded at Antietam. Such a story, had it been true, could scarcely have failed to reach his ears, and he would undoubtedly have told it in his delightful chapter of war reminiscences, "My Hunt for the Captain," had he heard it. Barbara Frietchie had a flag, and it is now in the possession of Mrs. Handschue and her daughter, Mrs. Abbott, of Frederick. Mrs. Handschue was the niece and adopted daughter of Mrs. Frietchie, and the flag came to her as part of her inheritance, a cup out of which General Washington drank tea when he spent a night in Frederick in 1791 being among the Frietchie heirlooms. This flag which Mrs. Handschue and her daughter so religiously preserve is torn, but the banner was not rent with seam and gash from a rifle-blast; it is torn — only this and nothing more. That Mrs. Frietchie did not wave the flag at Jackson's men Mrs. Handschue positively affirms. The flag-waving act was done, however, by Mrs. Mary S. Quantrell, another Frederick woman; but Jackson took no notice of it, and

[↓] Condensed from a contribution to the "Philadelphia Times" for July 21st, 1886.—EDITORS.

as Mrs. Quantrell was not fortunate enough to find a poet to celebrate her deed she never became famous.

Colonel Henry Kyd Douglas, who was with General Jackson every minute of his stay in Frederick, declares in an article in "The Century" for June, 1886, that Jackson never saw Barbara Frietchie, and that Barbara never saw Jackson. This story is borne out by Mrs. Frietchie's relatives.

As already said, Barbara Frietchie had a flag and she waved it, not on the 6th to Jackson's men, but on the 12th to Burnside's. Here is the story as told by Mrs. Abbott, Mrs. Handschue's daughter:

"Jackson and his men had been in Frederick and had left a short time before. We were glad that the rebels had gone and that our troops came. My mother and I lived almost opposite aunt's place. She and my mother's cousin, Harriet Yoner, lived together. Mother said I should go and see aunt and tell her not to be frightened. You know that aunt was then almost ninety-six years old. When I reached aunt's place she knew as much as I did about matters, and cousin Harriet was with her. They were on the front porch, and aunt was leaning on the cane she always carried. When the troops marched along aunt waved her hand, and cheer after cheer went up from the men as they saw her. Some even ran into the yard. 'God bless you, old lady,' 'Let me take you by the hand,' 'May you live long, you dear old soul,' cried one after the other, as they rushed into the yard. Aunt being rather feeble, and in order to save her as much as we could, cousin Harriet Yoner said, 'Aunt ought to have a flag to wave.' The flag was hidden in the family Bible, and cousin Harriet got it and gave it to aunt. Then she waved the flag to the men and they cheered her as they went by. She was very patriotic and the troops all knew of her. The day before General Reno was killed he came to see aunt and had a talk with her."

The manner in which the Frietchie legend originated was very simple. A Frederick lady visited Washington some time after the invasion of 1862 and spoke of the open sympathy and valor of Barbara Frietchie. The story was told again and again, and it was never lost in the telling. Mr. Whittier received his first knowledge of it from Mrs. E. D. E. N. Southworth, the novelist, who is a resident of Washington. When Mrs. Southworth wrote to Mr. Whittier concerning Barbara, she inclosed a newspaper slip reciting the circumstances of Barbara Frietchie's action when Lee entered Frederick.

When Mr. Whittier wrote the poem ⚓ he followed as closely as possible the account sent him at the time. He has a cane made from the timber of Barbara's house,— a present from Dr. Stiener, a member of the Senate of Maryland. The flag with which Barbara Frietchie gave a hearty welcome to Burnside's troops has but thirty-four stars, is small, of silk, and attached to a staff probably a yard in length.

Barbara Frietchie was born at Lancaster, Pennsylvania. Her maiden name was Hauer. She was born December 3d, 1766, her parents being Nicholas and Catharine Hauer. She went to Frederick in early life, where she married John C. Frietchie, a glover, in 1806. She died December 18th, 1862, Mr. Frietchie having died in 1849. In 1868 the waters of Carroll Creek rose to such a height that they nearly wrecked the old home of the heroine of Whittier's poem.

⚓ Writing to the editor of "The Century" on the 10th of June, 1886, Mr. Whittier said: "The poem 'Barbara Frietchie' was written in good faith. The story was no invention of mine. It came to me from sources which I regarded as entirely reliable; it had been published in newspapers, and had gained public credence in Washington and Maryland before my poem was written. I had no reason to doubt its accuracy then, and I am still constrained to believe that it had foundation in fact. If I thought otherwise, I should not hesitate to express it. I have no pride of authorship to interfere with my allegiance to truth." Mr. Whittier, writing March 7th, 1888, informs us further that he "also received letters from several other responsible persons wholly or partially confirming the story, among whom was the late Dorothea L. Dix."— EDITORS.

UNION HOSPITAL IN A BARN NEAR ANTIETAM CREEK. AFTER A SKETCH MADE AT THE TIME.

# STONEWALL JACKSON IN MARYLAND.

BY HENRY KYD DOUGLAS, COLONEL, C. S. A.

ON the 3d of September, 1862, the Federal army under General Pope having been confounded, General Lee turned his columns toward the Potomac, with Stonewall Jackson in front. On the 5th of September Jackson crossed the Potomac at White's Ford, a few miles beyond Leesburg. The passage of the river by the troops marching in fours, well closed up, the laughing, shouting, and singing, as a brass band in front played "Maryland, my Maryland," was a memorable experience. The Marylanders in the corps imparted much of their enthusiasm to the other troops, but we were not long in finding out that if General Lee had hopes that the decimated regiments of his army would be filled by the sons of Maryland he was doomed to a speedy and unqualified disappointment. However, before we had been in Maryland many hours, one enthusiastic citizen presented Jackson with a gigantic gray mare. She was a little heavy and awkward for a war-horse, but as the general's "Little Sorrel" had a few days before been temporarily stolen, the present was a timely one, and he was not disposed to "look a gift horse in the mouth." Yet the present proved almost a Trojan horse to him, for the next morning when he mounted his new steed and touched her with his spur the loyal and undisciplined beast reared straight into the air, and, standing erect for a moment, threw herself backward, horse and rider rolling upon the ground. The general was stunned and severely bruised, and lay upon the ground for some time before he could be removed. He was then placed in an ambulance, where he rode during the day's march, having turned his command over to his brother-in-law, General D. H. Hill, the officer next in rank.

Early that day the army went into camp near Frederick, and Generals Lee, Longstreet, Jackson, and for a time "Jeb" Stuart, had their headquarters near one another in Best's grove. Hither in crowds came the good people of Frederick, especially the ladies, as to a fair. General Jackson, still suffering from his hurt, kept to his tent, busying himself with maps and official papers, and declined to see visitors. Once, however, when he had been called to General Lee's tent, two young girls waylaid him, paralyzed him with smiles and embraces and questions, and then jumped into

ROASTING GREEN CORN AT THE CAMP-FIRE.

---

‡ "We had been faring very badly since we left Manassas Junction, having had only one meal that included bread and coffee. Our diet had been green corn, with beef without salt, roasted on the end of ramrods. We heard with delight of the 'plenty' to be had in Maryland; judge of our disappointment when, about 2 o'clock at night, we were marched into a dank clover-field and the order came down the line, 'Men, go into that corn-field and get your rations — and be ready to march at 5 in the morning. Don't burn any of these fence-rails.' Of course we obeyed orders as to the corn, but, the rails suffered."— Extract from a letter written by Lieut. Robert Healy, of Jackson's corps.

JACKSON'S MEN WADING THE POTOMAC AT WHITE'S FORD.[†]

their carriage and drove off rapidly, leaving him there, cap in hand, bowing, blushing, and speechless. But once safe in his tent he was seen no more that day. The next evening, Sunday, he went into Frederick for the first time to attend church, and there being no service in the Presbyterian Church he went to the German Reformed. As usual he fell asleep, but this time more soundly than was his wont. His head sunk upon his breast, his cap dropped from his hands to the floor, the prayers of the congregation did not disturb him, and only the choir and the deep-toned organ awakened him. Afterward I learned that the minister was credited with much loyalty and courage because he had prayed for the President of the United States in the very presence of Stonewall Jackson. Well, the general didn't hear the prayer, and if he had he would doubtless have felt like replying as General Ewell did, when asked at Carlisle, Pennsylvania, if he would permit the usual prayer for President Lincoln — "Certainly; I'm sure he needs it."

General Lee believed that Harper's Ferry would be evacuated as soon as he interposed between it and Washington. But he did not know that Halleck, and not McClellan, held command of it. When he found that it was not

[†] Lieutenant Robert Healy, of the 55th Virginia, in Stonewall Jackson's command, tells the following incident of the march into Maryland: "The day before the corps waded the Potomac at White's Ford, they marched through Leesburg, where an old lady with upraised hands, and with tears in her eyes exclaimed: 'The Lord bless your dirty ragged souls!' Lieutenant Healy adds: 'Don't think we were any dirtier than the rest, but it was our luck to get the blessing.'"— EDITORS.

evacuated he knew some one had blundered, and took steps to capture the garrison and stores. On Tuesday, the 9th, he issued an order, directing General Jackson to move the next morning, cross the Potomac near Sharpsburg, and envelop Harper's Ferry on the Virginia side. In the same order he directed General McLaws to march on Harper's Ferry by way of Middletown and seize Maryland Heights, and General Walker to cross the Potomac below Harper's Ferry and take Loudoun Heights, all to be in position on the 12th, except Jackson, who was first to capture, if possible, the troops at Martinsburg.

Early on the 10th Jackson was off. In Frederick he asked for a map of Chambersburg and its vicinity, and made many irrelevant inquiries about roads and localities in the direction of Pennsylvania. To his staff, who knew what little value these inquiries had, his questions only illustrated his well-known motto, "Mystery, mystery is the secret of success." I was then assistant inspector-general on his staff, and also acting aide-de-camp. It was my turn this day to be intrusted with the knowledge of his purpose. Having finished this public inquiry, he took me aside, and after asking me about the different fords of the Potomac between Williamsport and Harper's Ferry, told me that he was ordered to capture the garrison at Harper's Ferry, and would cross either at Williamsport or Shepherdstown, as the enemy might or might not withdraw from Martinsburg. I did not then know of General Lee's order.

The troops being on the march, the general and staff rode rapidly out of town and took the head of the column. Just a few words here in regard to Mr. Whittier's touching poem, "Barbara Frietchie." An old woman, by that now immortal name, did live in Frederick in those days, but she never saw General Jackson, and General Jackson never saw "Barbara Frietchie." I was with him every minute of the time he was in that city,—he was there only twice,—and nothing like the scene so graphically described by the poet ever happened. Mr. Whittier must have been misinformed as to the incident. [See p. 619.— EDITORS.]

On the march that day, the captain of the cavalry advance, just ahead, had instructions to let no civilian go to the front, and we entered each village we passed before the inhabitants knew of our coming. In Middletown two very pretty girls, with ribbons of red, white, and blue floating from their hair, and small Union flags in their hands, rushed out of a house as we passed, came to the curbstone, and with much laughter waved their flags defiantly in the face of the general. He bowed and raised his hat, and, turning with his quiet smile to his staff, said: "We evidently have no friends in this town." And this is about the way he would have treated Barbara Frietchie!

Having crossed South Mountain, at Turner's Gap, the command encamped for the night within a mile of Boonsboro'. Here General Jackson must determine whether he would go on to Williamsport or turn toward Shepherdstown. I at once rode into the village with a cavalryman to make some inquiries, but we ran into a squadron of Federal cavalry, who without ceremony proceeded to make war upon us. We retraced our steps, and although we did not stand upon the order of our going, a squad of them escorted us out of town with great rapidity. When I tried a couple of Parthian shots at them with my revolver, they returned them with interest, and shot a hole in my new hat, which, with the beautiful plume that a lady in Frederick had placed there, rolled in the dust. This was of little moment, but at the end of the town, reaching the top of the hill, we discovered, just over it, General Jackson, walking slowly toward us, leading his horse. There was but one thing to do. Fortunately the chase had become less vigorous, and, with a cry of command to unseen troops, we turned and charged the enemy. They, suspecting trouble, turned and fled, while the general quickly galloped to the rear. I recovered my hat and plume, and as I returned to camp I picked up the gloves which the general had dropped in mounting, and took them to him. Although he had sent a regiment of infantry to the front as soon as he went back, the only allusion he made to the incident was to express the opinion that I had a very fast horse.

The next morning, having learned that the Federal troops still occupied Martinsburg, General Jackson took the direct road to Williamsport. He there forded the Potomac, the troops now singing, and the bands playing, "Carry me back to ole Virginny!" We marched on Martinsburg. General A. P. Hill took the direct turnpike, while Jackson, with the rest of his command, followed a side road, so as to approach Martinsburg from the west, and encamped four miles from the town. His object was to drive General White, who occupied Martinsburg, toward Harper's Ferry, and thus "corral" all the Federal troops in that military pen. As the Comte de Paris puts it, he "organized a kind of grand hunting match through the lower valley of Virginia, driving all the Federal detachments before him and forcing them to crowd into the blind alley of Harper's Ferry." Fatigued by the day's march, Jackson was persuaded by his host of the night to drink a whisky toddy — the only glass of spirits I ever saw him take. While mixing it leisurely, he remarked that he believed he liked the taste of whisky and brandy more than any soldier in the army; that they were more palatable to him than the most fragrant coffee, and for that reason, with others, he rarely tasted them.

The next morning the Confederates entered Martinsburg. Here the general was welcomed with great enthusiasm, and a great crowd hastened to the hotel to greet him. At first he shut himself up in a room to write dispatches, but the demonstration became so persistent that he ordered the door to be opened. The crowd, chiefly ladies, rushed in and embarrassed the general with every possible outburst of affection, to which he could only reply, "Thank you, you're very kind." He gave them his autograph in books and on scraps of paper, cut a button from his coat for a little girl, and then submitted patiently to an attack by the others, who soon stripped the coat of nearly all the remaining buttons. But when they looked beseechingly at his hair, which was thin, he drew the line there, and managed to close the interview. These blandishments did not delay his movements, however, for in the afternoon he was off again.

A GLIMPSE OF STONEWALL JACKSON.

On the 13th he invested Bolivar Heights and Harper's Ferry. On this day General McClellan came into possession, by carelessness or accident, of General Lee's order of the 9th, and he was thus notified of the division of the Confederate army and the intention to capture Harper's Ferry. From this moment General Lee's army was in peril, imminent in proportion to the promptness with which the Federal commander might use the knowledge he thus obtained. The plans of the latter were quickly and skillfully made. Had they been executed more rapidly, or had Jackson been slower and less sure, the result must have been a disastrous one to us. But military critics disposed to censure General McClellan for not being equal to his opportunities should credit him with the embarrassment of his position. He had not been in command of this army two weeks. It was a large army, but a heterogeneous one, with many old troops dispirited by recent defeat, and many new troops that had never been under fire. With such an army a general as cautious as McClellan does not take great risks, nor put the safety of his army rashly "to the touch, to win or lose it all." General McClellan was inclined by nature to magnify the forces of the enemy, and had he known General Lee's weakness he would have ventured more. Yet when we remember what Pope had done and suffered just before, and what happened to Burnside and Hooker not long after, their friends can hardly sit in judgment upon McClellan.

On the afternoon of the 13th Colonel Miles, in command at Harper's Ferry, made the fatal mistake of withdrawing his troops from Maryland Heights, and giving them up to McLaws. Napier has said, "He who wars walks in a mist through which the keenest eyes cannot always discern the right path." But it does seem that Colonel Miles might have known that to abandon these heights under the circumstances was simply suicidal.‡

Jackson met with so much delay in opening communication with McLaws and Walker, and ascertaining whether they were in position, that much of the 14th was consumed. But late in the afternoon A. P. Hill gained a foothold, with little resistance, well up on the enemy's left, and established some artillery at the base of Loudoun Heights and across the Shenandoah, so as to take the Federal line on Bolivar Heights in rear. (General Hill had been placed under arrest by General Jackson, before crossing the Potomac into Maryland, for disobedience of orders, and the command of his division devolved upon General Branch, who was killed a few days later at Antietam. Believing a battle imminent, General Hill requested General Jackson to reinstate him in command of his division until the approaching engagement was over. No one could appreciate such an appeal more keenly than General Jackson, and he at once restored General Hill to his command. The work the Light Division did at Harper's Ferry and Sharpsburg proved the wisdom of Hill's request and of Jackson's compliance with it.)

During the 14th, while Jackson was fixing his clamps on Harper's Ferry, McClellan was pushing against Lee's divided forces at Turner's Gap. Hooker and Reno, under Burnside and under the eye of General McClellan, were fighting the battle of South Mountain against D. H. Hill and Longstreet. Here Reno and Garland were killed on opposite sides, and night ended the contest before it was decided. At the same time Franklin was forcing his way through Crampton's Gap, driving out Howell Cobb commanding his own brigade and one regiment of Semmes's brigade, both of McLaws's division, Parham's brigade of R. H. Anderson's division, and two regiments of Stuart's cavalry under Colonel Munford. The military complications were losing their simplicity. Being advised of these movements, Jackson saw that his work must be done speedily. On Monday morning, at 3 o'clock, he sent me to the left to move Jones forward at first dawn, and to open on Bolivar Heights with all his artillery. This feint was executed promptly and produced confusion on the enemy's right. Troops were moved to strengthen it. Then the guns from Maryland and Loudoun Heights opened fire, and very soon, off on our right, the battle-flags of A. P. Hill rose on Bolivar Heights, and Harper's Ferry was doomed. Returning, I found General Jackson at the church in the wood on the Bolivar and Halltown turnpike, and just as I joined him a white flag was raised on Bolivar and all the firing ceased.

‡ General Julius White says in his report ("Official Records," Vol. XIX., Pt. I., p. 523): "It will be noticed that Colonel Ford claims to have been ordered by Colonel Miles to evacuate the heights. Colonel Miles, however, denied to me ever having given such an order, but said he gave orders that if it became necessary to abandon the heights the guns were to be spiked and dismounted." See also General White's statements, p. 612.—EDITORS.

LIEUTENANT-GENERAL AMBROSE P. HILL, C. S. A. FROM A PHOTOGRAPH.

Under instructions from General Jackson, I rode up the pike and into the enemy's lines to ascertain the purpose of the white flag. Near the top of the hill I met General White and staff and told him my mission. He replied that Colonel Miles had been mortally wounded, that he was in command and desired to have an interview with General Jackson. Just then General Hill came up from the direction of his line, and at his request I conducted them to General Jackson, whom I found sitting on his horse where I had left him. He was not, as the Comte de Paris says, leaning against a tree asleep, but exceedingly wide-awake. The contrast in appearances there presented was striking. General White, riding a handsome black horse, was carefully dressed and had on untarnished gloves, boots, and sword. His staff were equally comely in costume. On the other hand, General Jackson was the dingiest, worst-dressed, and worst-mounted general that a warrior who cared for good looks and style would wish to surrender to. The surrender was unconditional, and then General Jackson turned the matter over to General A. P. Hill, who allowed General White the same liberal terms that Grant afterward gave Lee at Appomattox.◊

◊ Of the expectations of Jackson's men, Lieutenant Robert Healy says, in a letter written in 1886:

"On the evening of the 14th we took position within six hundred yards of a Federal fort on Bolivar Heights. We lay that night in a deep ravine, perpendicular to the Shenandoah. The next morning by dawn I crept up the hill to see how the land lay. A few strides brought me to the edge of an abatis which extended solidly for two hundred yards, a narrow bare field being between the abatis and the foot of the fort, which was garnished with thirty guns. They were searching the abatis lazily

The fruits of the surrender were 12,520 prisoners ("Official Records"), 13,000 arms, 73 pieces of artillery, and several hundred wagons.

General Jackson, after sending a brief dispatch to General Lee announcing the capitulation, rode up to Bolivar and down into Harper's Ferry. The curiosity in the Union army to see him was so great that the soldiers lined the sides of the road. Many of them uncovered as he passed, and he invariably returned the salute. One man had an echo of response all about him when he said aloud: "Boys, he's not much for looks, but if we'd had him we wouldn't have been caught in this trap!"

General Jackson lost little time in contemplating his victory. When night came, he started for Shepherdstown with J. R. Jones and Lawton, leaving directions to McLaws and Walker to follow the next morning. He left A. P. Hill behind to finish up with Harper's Ferry. His first order had been to take position at Shepherdstown to cover Lee's crossing into Virginia, but, whether at his own suggestion or not, the order was changed, and after daylight on the 16th he crossed the Potomac there and joined Longstreet at Sharpsburg. General McClellan had, by that time, nearly all his army in position on the east bank of the Antietam, and General Lee was occupying the irregular range of high ground to the west of it, with the Potomac in his rear. Except some sparring between Hooker and Hood on our left, the 16th was allowed to pass without battle, fortunately for us. In the new dispositions of that evening, Jackson was placed on the left of Lee's army. [See map, p. 636.]

The first onset, early on the morning of the 17th, told what the day would be. The impatient Hooker, with the divisions of Meade, Doubleday, and Ricketts, struck the first blow, and Jackson's old division caught it and struck back again. Between such foes the battle soon waxed hot. Step by step and marking each step with dead, the thin Confederate line was pushed back to the wood around the Dunker Church. Here Lawton, Starke (commanding in place of Jones, already wounded), and D. H. Hill with part of his division, engaged Meade. And now in turn the Federals halted and fell back, and left their dead by Dunker Church. Next Mansfield entered the fight, and beat with resistless might on Jackson's people. The battle here grew angry and bloody. Starke was killed, Lawton wounded, and nearly all their general and field officers had fallen; the sullen Confederate line again fell back, killing Mansfield and wounding Hooker, Crawford, and Hartsuff.

And now D. H. Hill led in the rest of his division; Hood also took part, to the right and left, front and rear of Dunker Church. The Federal line was again driven back, while artillery added its din to the incessant

with grape-shot, which flew uncomfortably near at times. I thought I had never seen a more dangerous trap in my life. The order had been given that we were to charge at sunrise. I went back, and Austin Brockenbrough asked, 'How is it?' 'Well,' said I, 'we'll say our prayers and go in like men.' 'Not as bad as that?' 'Every bit; see for yourself.' He went up and came back looking very grave. Meanwhile, from the east, north-west, and north-east our cannon opened and were answered by the Federal guns from Bolivar Heights. We were down in a ravine; we could see nothing; we could only hear. Presently, along our line came the words, 'Prepare to charge!' We moved steadily up the hill; the sun had just risen; some one said: 'Colonel, what is that on the fort?' 'Halt,' cried the colonel, 'they have surrendered.' A glad shout burst from ten thousand men. We got into the place as soon as we could, but the way was so difficult it took us a half hour." EDITORS.

rattle of musketry. Then Sumner, with the fresh division of Sedgwick, re-formed the Federal line and renewed the offensive. Hood was driven back, and Hill partly; the Dunker Church wood was passed, the field south of it entered, and the Confederate left turned. Just then McLaws, hurrying from Harper's Ferry, came upon the field, and hurled his men against the victorious Sedgwick. He drove Sedgwick back into the Dunker wood and beyond it, into the open ground. Farther to our right, the pendulum of battle had been swinging to and fro, with D. H. Hill and R. H. Anderson hammering away at French and Richardson, until the sunken road became historic as "bloody lane." Richardson was mortally wounded and Hancock assumed command of his division.

For a while there was a lull in the storm. It was early in the day, but hours are fearfully long in battle. About noon Franklin, with Slocum and W. F. Smith, marched upon the field to join the unequal contest. Smith tried his luck and was repulsed. Sumner then ordered a halt. Jackson's fight was over, and a strange silence reigned around Dunker Church.

General Lee had not visited the left that day. As usual he trusted to Jackson to fight his own battle and work out salvation in his own way. How well he did it, against the ablest and fiercest of McClellan's lieutenants, history has told.

BRIGADIER-GENERAL WILLIAM E. STARKE. FROM A TINTYPE.

In the cannonade which began with dawn of the 17th, General J. R. Jones, commanding the left division of Jackson, was stunned and injured by a shell which exploded directly over his head. General Starke was directed to take command of the division, which he led against Hooker, and a half-hour later he fell pierced by three minie-balls. Of that terrible struggle Stonewall Jackson says in his report: "The carnage on both sides was terrific. At this early hour General Starke was killed. Colonel Douglass, commanding Lawton's brigade, was also killed. General Lawton, commanding division, and Colonel Walker, commanding brigade, were severely wounded. More than half of the brigades of Lawton and Hays were either killed or wounded, and more than a third of Trimble's, and all the regimental commanders in those brigades, except two, were killed or wounded."— EDITORS.

During all this time Longstreet, stripped of his troops,— sent to the help of Jackson,— held the right almost alone, with his eye on the center. He was now called into active work on his own front, for there were no unfought troops in Lee's army at Sharpsburg; every soldier on that field tasted battle.

General Burnside, with his corps of fourteen thousand men, had been lying all day beyond the bridge which now bears his name. Ordered to cross at 8 o'clock he managed to get over at 1, and by 3 was ready to advance.↧ He

↧ See General Cox's statements, p. 647.— EDITORS.

moved against the hill which D. R. Jones held with his little division of 2500 men. Longstreet was watching this advance. Jackson was at General Lee's headquarters on a knoll in rear of Sharpsburg. A. P. Hill was coming, but had not arrived, and it was apparent that Burnside must be stayed, if at all, with artillery. One of the sections, transferred to the right from Jackson at the request of General Lee, was of the Rockbridge Artillery, and as it galloped by, the youngest son of the general-in-chief, Robert E. Lee, Jr., a private at the guns, black with the grime and powder of a long day's fight, stopped a moment to salute his father and then rushed after his gun. Where else in this war was the son of a commanding general a private in the ranks?

Going to put this section in place, I saw Burnside's heavy line move up the hill, and the earth seemed to tremble beneath their tread. It was a splendid and fearful sight, but for them to beat back Jones's feeble line was scarcely war. The artillery tore, but did not stay them. They pressed forward until Sharpsburg was uncovered and Lee's line of retreat was at their mercy. But then, just then, A. P. Hill, picturesque in his red battle-shirt, with 3 of his brigades, 2500 men, who had marched that day 17 miles from Harper's Ferry and had waded the Potomac, appeared upon the scene. Tired and footsore, the men forgot their woes in that supreme moment, and with no breathing time braced themselves to meet the coming shock. They met it and stayed it. The blue line staggered and hesitated, and, hesitating, was lost. At the critical moment A. P. Hill was always at his strongest. Quickly advancing his battle-flags, his line moved forward, Jones's troops rallied on him, and in the din of musketry and artillery on either flank the Federals broke over the field. Hill did not wait for his other brigades, but held the vantage gained until Burnside was driven back to the Antietam and under the shelter of heavy guns. The day was done. Again A. P. Hill, as at Manassas, Harper's Ferry, and elsewhere, had struck with the right hand of Mars. No wonder that both Lee and Jackson, when, in the delirium of their last moments on earth, they stood again to battle, saw the form of A. P. Hill leading his columns on; but it is a wonder and a shame that the grave of this valiant Virginian in Hollywood cemetery has not a stone to mark it and keep it from oblivion.

The battle at Sharpsburg was the result of unforeseen circumstances and not of deliberate purpose. It was one of the bloodiest of the war, and a defeat for both armies. The prestige of the day was with Lee, but when on the night of the 18th he recrossed into Virginia, although, as the Comte de Paris says, he "left not a single trophy of his nocturnal retreat in the hands of the enemy," he left the prestige of the result with McClellan. And yet when it is known that General McClellan had 87,000 troops at hand, and General Lee fought the battle with less than 35,000,‡ an army depleted by battles, weakened by privations, broken down by marching, and "ruined by straggling," it was unquestionably on the Confederate side the best-fought battle of the war.

‡ See notes on pp. 565 and 603 as to the strength of the forces on each side.— EDITORS.

NORTH OF THE DUNKER CHURCH — A UNION CHARGE THROUGH THE CORN-FIELD.

# THE BATTLE OF ANTIETAM.

### BY JACOB D. COX, MAJOR-GENERAL, U. S. V.

IT was not till some time past noon of the 15th of September that, the way being clear for the Ninth Corps at South Mountain, we marched through Fox's gap to the Boonsboro' and Sharpsburg turnpike, and along this road till we came up in rear of Sumner's command. Hooker's corps, which was part of the right wing (Burnside's), had been in the advance, and had moved off from the turnpike to the right near Keedysville. I was with the Kanawha Division, assuming that my temporary command of the corps ended with the battle on the mountain. When we approached the line of hills bordering the Antietam, we received orders to turn off the road to the left, and halted our battalions closed in mass. It was now about 3 o'clock in the afternoon. McClellan, as it seemed, had just reached the field, and was surrounded by a group of his principal officers, most of whom I had never seen before. I rode up with General Burnside, dismounted, and was very cordially greeted by General McClellan. He and Burnside were evidently on terms of most intimate friendship and familiarity. He introduced me to the officers I had not known before, referring pleasantly to my service with him in Ohio and West Virginia, putting me upon an easy footing with them in a very agreeable and genial way.

We walked up the slope of the ridge before us, and looking westward from its crest the whole field of the coming battle was before us. Immediately in front the Antietam wound through the hollow, the hills rising gently on both sides. In the background on our left was the village of Sharpsburg, with fields inclosed by stone fences in front of it. At its right was a bit of wood (since known as the West Wood), with the little Dunker Church standing out white and sharp against it. Farther to the right and left the scene was closed in by wooded ridges with open farm lands between, the whole making as pleasing and prosperous a landscape as can easily be imagined. We made a large group as we stood upon the hill, and it was not long before we attracted the enemy's attention. A puff of white smoke from a knoll on the right of the Sharpsburg road was followed by the screaming of a shell over our heads. McClellan directed that all but one or two should retire behind the ridge, while he continued the reconnoissance, walking slowly to the right. I noted with satisfaction the cool and business-like air with which he made his examination under fire. The Confederate artillery was answered by a battery, and a lively cannonade ensued on both sides, though without any noticeable effect. The enemy's position was revealed, and he was evidently in force on both sides of the turnpike in front of Sharpsburg, covered by the undulations of the rolling ground which hid his infantry from our sight.

The examination of the enemy's position and the discussion of it continued till near the close of the day. Orders were then given for the Ninth Corps to move to the left, keeping off the road, which was occupied by other troops. We moved through fields and farm lands, an hour's march in the dusk of the evening, going into bivouac about a mile south of the Sharpsburg bridge, and in rear of the hills bordering the Antietam.

UNION SIGNAL STATION ON ELK MOUNTAIN, FIVE OR SIX MILES SOUTH-EAST OF SHARPSBURG. FROM A PHOTOGRAPH.

On Tuesday, September 16th, we confidently expected a battle, and I kept with my division. In the afternoon I saw General Burnside, and learned from him that McClellan had determined to let Hooker make a movement on our extreme right to turn Lee's position. Burnside's manner in speaking of this implied that he thought it was done at Hooker's solicitation and through his desire, openly evinced, to be independent in command.

I urged Burnside to assume the immediate command of the corps and allow me to lead only my own division. He objected that as he had been announced as commander of the right wing of the army composed of two corps (his own and Hooker's), he was unwilling to waive his precedence or to assume that Hooker was detached for anything more than a temporary purpose. I pointed out that Reno's staff had been granted leave of absence to

DOUBLEDAY'S DIVISION OF HOOKER'S CORPS CROSSING THE UPPER FORDS OF THE ANTIETAM. FROM A SKETCH MADE AT THE TIME.

take the body of their chief to Washington, and that my division staff was too small for corps duty; but he met this by saying that he would use his staff for this purpose and help me in every way he could, till the crisis of the campaign should be over.

The 16th passed without serious fighting, though there was desultory cannonading and picket firing. It was hard to restrain our men from showing themselves on the crest of the long ridge in front of us, and whenever they did so they drew the fire from some of the enemy's batteries, to which ours would respond. In the afternoon McClellan reconnoitered the line of the Antietam near us, Burnside being with him. As the result of this we were ordered to change our positions at nightfall, staff-officers being sent to guide each division to its new camp. Rodman's division went half a mile to the left, where a country road led to a ford in a great bend in the Antietam curving deeply into the enemy's side of the stream.∫ Sturgis's division was placed on the sides of the road leading to the stone bridge, since known as Burnside's Bridge (below the Sharpsburg bridge). Willcox's was put in reserve in rear of Sturgis. My own division was divided, Scammon's brigade going with Rodman, and Crook's going with Sturgis. Crook was ordered to take the advance in crossing the bridge, in case we should be ordered to attack.

∫ The information obtained from the neighborhood was that no fords of the Antietam were passable at that time, except one about half-way between the two upper bridges and another less than half a mile below Burnside's Bridge. We, however, found during the engagement another ford a short distance above Burnside's Bridge. The inquiry and reconnoissance for the fords was made by engineer officers of the general staff, and our orders were based on their reports.—J. D. C.

This selection was made by Burnside himself, as a compliment to the division for the vigor of its assault at South Mountain. While we were moving, we heard Hooker's guns far off on the right and front, and the cannonade continued an hour or more after it became dark.

The morning of Wednesday, the 17th, broke fresh and fair. The men were astir at dawn, getting breakfast and preparing for a day of battle. The artillery opened on both sides as soon as it was fairly light, and the positions which had been assigned us in the dusk of the evening were found to be exposed in some places to the direct fire of the Confederate guns, Rodman's division suffering more than the others. Fairchild's brigade alone reported thirty-six casualties before they could find cover. It was not till 7 o'clock that orders came to advance toward the creek as far as could be done without exposing the men to unnecessary loss. Rodman was directed to acquaint himself with the situation of the ford in front of him, and Sturgis to seek the best means of approach to the stone bridge. All were then to remain in readiness to obey further orders.

When these arrangements had been made, I rode to the position Burnside had selected for himself, which was upon a high knoll north-east of the Burnside Bridge, near a hay-stack which was a prominent landmark. Near by was Benjamin's battery of 20-pounder Parrotts, and a little farther still to the right, on the same ridge, General Sturgis had sent in Durell's battery. These were exchanging shots with the enemy's guns opposite, and had the advantage in range and weight of metal.

Whatever the reason, McClellan had adopted a plan of battle which practically reduced Sumner and Burnside to the command of one corps each, while Hooker had been sent far off on the right front, followed later by Mansfield, but without organizing the right wing as a unit so that one commander could give his whole attention to handling it with vigor. In his preliminary report, made before he was relieved from command, McClellan says:

"The design was to make the main attack upon the enemy's left — at least to create a diversion in favor of the main attack, with the hope of something more, by assailing the enemy's right — and, as soon as one or both of the flank movements were fully successful, to attack their center with any reserve I might then have in hand."

McClellan's report covering his whole career in the war, dated August 4th, 1863 (and published February, 1864, after warm controversies had arisen and he had become a political character), modifies the above statement in some important particulars. It says:

"My plan for the impending general engagement was to attack the enemy's left with the corps of Hooker and Mansfield, supported by Sumner's, and if necessary by Franklin's, and as soon as matters looked favorably there to move the corps of Burnside against the enemy's extreme right upon the ridge running to the south and rear of Sharpsburg, and having carried their position, to press along the crest toward our right, and whenever either of these flank movements should be successful, to advance our center with all the forces then disposable."

The opinion I got from Burnside as to the part the Ninth Corps was to take was fairly consistent with the design first quoted, viz., that when the attack by Sumner, Hooker, and Franklin should be progressing favorably, we were "to create a diversion in favor of the main attack, with the hope of something more." It would also appear probable that Hooker's movement was at first intended to be made by his corps alone, taken up by Sumner's two corps as soon as he was ready to attack, and shared in by Franklin if he reached the field in time, thus making a simultaneous oblique attack from our right by the whole army except Porter's corps, which was in reserve, and the Ninth Corps, which was to create the "diversion" on our left and prevent the enemy from stripping his right to reënforce his left. It is hardly disputable that this would have been a better plan than the one actually carried out. Certainly the assumption that the Ninth Corps could cross the Antietam alone at the only place on the field where the Confederates had their line immediately upon the stream which must be crossed under fire by two narrow heads of column, and could then turn to the right along the high ground occupied by the hostile army before that army had been broken or seriously shaken elsewhere, is one which would hardly be made till time had dimmed the remembrance of the actual positions of Lee's divisions upon the field.

The evidence that the plan did not originally include the wide separation of two corps to the right, to make the extended turning movement, is found in

THE SHARPSBURG BRIDGE OVER THE ANTIETAM. FROM A WAR-TIME PHOTOGRAPH.

## THE BATTLE OF ANTIETAM. 635

Hooker's incomplete report, and in the wide interval in time between the marching of his corps and that of Mansfield. Hooker was ordered to cross the Antietam at about 2 o'clock in the afternoon of the 16th by the bridge in front of Keedysville and the ford below it. He says that after his troops were over and in march, he rode back to McClellan, who told him that he might call for reënforcements and that when they came they should be under his command. Somewhat later McClellan rode forward with his staff to observe the progress making, and Hooker again urged the necessity of reënforcements. Yet Sumner did not receive orders to send Mansfield to support Hooker till evening, and the Twelfth Corps marched only half an hour before midnight, reaching its bivouac, about a mile and a half in rear of that of Hooker, at 2 A. M. of the 17th. Sumner was also ordered to be in readiness to march with the Second Corps an hour before day, but his orders to move did not reach him till nearly half-past 7 in the morning. By this time, Hooker had fought his battle, had been repulsed, and later in the morning was carried wounded from the field. Mansfield had fallen before his corps was deployed, and General Alpheus S. Williams who succeeded him was fighting a losing battle at all points but one — where Greene's division held the East Wood.

After crossing the Antietam, Hooker had shaped his course to the westward, aiming to reach the ridge upon which the Hagerstown turnpike runs, and which is the dominant feature of the landscape. This ridge is some two

GERMAN REFORMED CHURCH IN KEEDYSVILLE, USED AS A UNION HOSPITAL. FROM A PHOTOGRAPH TAKEN IN 1886.

miles distant from the Antietam, and for the first mile of the way no resistance was met. However, Hooker's progress had been observed by the enemy, and Hood's two brigades were taken from the center and passed to the left of D. H. Hill. Here they occupied an open wood (since known as the East Wood), north-east of the Dunker Church. Hooker was now trying to approach the Confederate positions, Meade's division of the Pennsylvania Reserves being in the advance. A sharp skirmishing combat ensued and artillery was also brought into action on both sides, the engagement continuing till after dark. On our side Seymour's brigade had been chiefly engaged, and had felt the enemy so vigorously that Hood supposed he had repulsed a serious effort to take the wood. Hooker was, however, aiming to pass quite beyond the flank, and kept his other divisions north of the hollow beyond the wood, and upon the ridge which reaches the turnpike near the largest reëntrant bend of the Potomac, which is here only half a mile distant. Here he bivouacked upon the northern slopes of the ridge, Doubleday's division resting with its

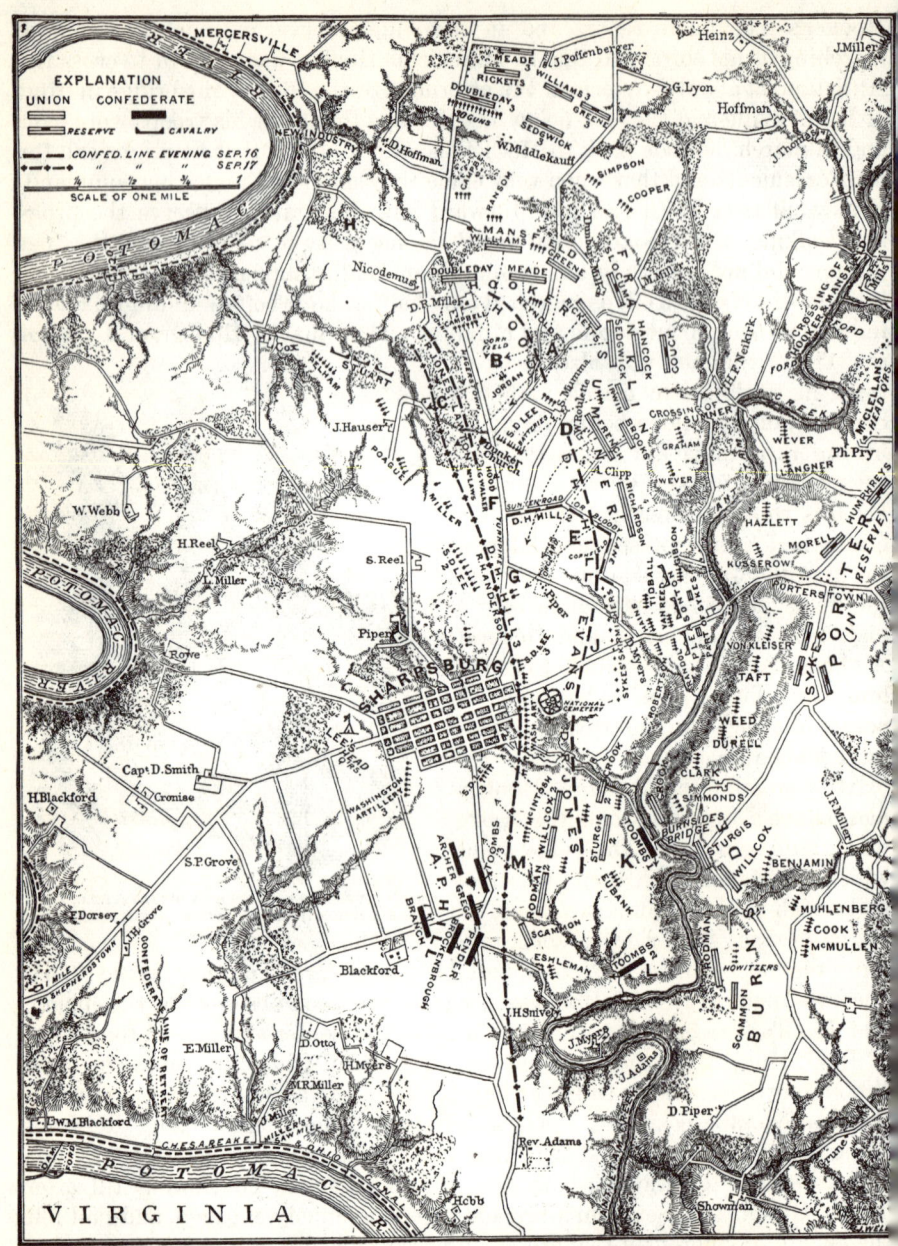

## THE FIELD OF ANTIETAM.

On the afternoon of September 16th, Hooker's corps crossed at the two fords and the bridge north of McClellan's headquarters.

A.— From near sunset till dark Hooker engaged Hood's division (of Longstreet's corps) about the "East Wood," marked A on the map. Hood was relieved by two brigades of Jackson's corps, which was in and behind the Dunker Church wood (or West Wood), C.

B.— At dawn on the 17th, Hooker and Jackson began a terrible contest which raged in and about the famous corn-field, B, and in the woods, A and C. Jackson's reserves regained the corn-field. Hartsuff's brigade, of Hooker's corps, and Mansfield's corps charged through the corn-field into the Dunker Church wood, General Mansfield being mortally wounded in front of the East Wood.

right upon the turnpike, Ricketts's division upon the left of Doubleday, and Meade covering the front of both with the skirmishers of Seymour's brigade. Between Meade's skirmishers and the ridge were the farm-house and barn of J. Poffenberger on the east of the road, where Hooker made his own quarters for the night. Half a mile farther in front was the farm of D. R. Miller, the dwelling on the east, and the barn surrounded by stacks on the west of the road.✝ Mansfield's corps, marching as it did late in the night, kept farther to the right than Hooker's, but moved on a nearly parallel course and bivouacked upon the farm of another J. Poffenberger near the road which, branching from the Hagerstown turnpike at the Dunker Church, intersects the one running from Keedysville through Smoketown to the same turnpike about a mile north of Hooker's position.

On the Confederate side, Hood's division had been so severely handled that it was replaced by Jackson's (commanded by J. R. Jones), which, with Ewell's, had been led to the field from Harper's Ferry by Jackson, reaching Sharpsburg in the afternoon of the 16th. These divisions were formed on the left of D. H. Hill and almost at right angles to his line, crossing the turnpike and facing northward. Hood's division, on being relieved, was placed in reserve near the Dunker Church, and spent part of the night in cooking rations, of which its supply had been short for a day or two. The combatants on both sides slept upon their arms, well knowing that the dawn would bring bloody work.

When day broke on Wednesday morning, the 17th, Hooker, looking south from the Poffenberger farm along the turnpike, saw a gently rolling landscape, of which the commanding point was the Dunker Church, whose white brick walls appeared on the west side of the road backed by the foliage of the West Wood, which came toward him, filling a slight hollow which ran parallel to the turnpike, with a single row of fields between. Beyond the Miller house and barns, the ground dipped into a little depression. Beyond this was seen a large corn-field between the East Wood and the turnpike, rising again

Jackson, with the aid of Hood, and a part of D. H. Hill's division, again cleared the Dunker Church wood. J. G. Walker's division, taken from the extreme right of the Confederate line, charged in support of Jackson and Hood.

C.— Sumner's corps formed line of battle in the center, Sedgwick's division facing the East Wood, through which it charged over the corn-field again, and through Dunker Church wood to the edge of the fields beyond. McLaws's division (of Longstreet's corps), just arrived from Harper's Ferry, assisted in driving out Sedgwick, who was forced to retreat northward by the Hagerstown pike.

D.— About the time that Sedgwick charged, French and Richardson, of Sumner's corps, dislodged D. H. Hill's line from Roulette's house.

E.— Hill re-formed in the sunken road, since known as the "Bloody Lane," where his position was carried by French and Richardson, the latter being mortally wounded in the corn-field, E.

F.— Irwin and Brooks, of Franklin's corps, moved to the support of French and Richardson. At the point F, Irwin's brigade was repelled.

G.— D. H. Hill, reënforced by R. H. Anderson's division of Longstreet's corps, fought for the ground about Piper's house.

H.— Stuart attempted a flank movement north of the Dunker Church wood, but was driven back by the thirty guns under Doubleday.

J.— Pleasonton, with a part of his cavalry and several batteries, crossed the Boonsboro' bridge as a flank support to Richardson, and to Burnside on the south. Several battalions of regulars from Porter's corps came to his assistance and made their way well up to the hill which is now the National Cemetery.

K.— Toombs (of Longstreet) had defended the lower bridge until Burnside moved Rodman and Scammon to the fords below.

L.— Then Toombs hurried south to protect the Confederate flank. Sturgis and Crook charged across the Burnside Bridge and gained the heights. Toombs was driven away from the fords.

M.— After 3 o'clock, Burnside's lines, being re-formed, completed the defeat of D. R. Jones's division (of Longstreet), and on the right gained the outskirts of Sharpsburg. Toombs, and the arriving brigades of A. P. Hill, of Jackson's corps, saved the village and regained a part of the lost ground.— EDITORS.

✝ Hooker's unfinished report says he slept in the barn of D. R. Miller, but he places it on the east of the road, and the spot is fully identified as Poffenberger's by General Gibbon, who commanded the right brigade, and by Major Rufus R. Dawes (afterward Brevet Brigadier-General), both of whom subsequently visited the field and determined the positions.— J. D. C.

to the higher level. There was, however, another small dip beyond, which could not be seen from Hooker's position; and on the second ridge, near the church, and extending across the turnpike eastward into the East Wood, could be seen the Confederate line of gray, partly sheltered by piles of rails taken from the fences. They seemed to Hooker to be at the farther side of the cornfield and at the top of the first rise of ground beyond Miller's. It was plain that the high ground about the little white church was the key of the enemy's position, and if that could be carried Hooker's task would be well done.

The Confederates opened the engagement by a rapid fire from a battery near the East Wood as soon as it was light, and Hooker answered the challenge by an immediate order for his line to advance. Doubleday's division was in two lines, Gibbon's and Phelps's brigades in front, supported by Patrick and Hofmann. Gibbon had the right and guided upon the turnpike. Patrick held a small wood in his rear, which is upon both sides of the road a little north of Miller's house. Some of Meade's men were supposed to be in the northernmost extension of the West Wood, and thus to cover Gibbon's right flank as he advanced. Part of Battery B, 4th United States Artillery (Gibbon's own battery), was run forward to Miller's barn and stack-yard on the right of the road, and fired over the heads of the advancing regiments. Other batteries were similarly placed more to the left. The line moved swiftly forward through Miller's orchard and kitchen garden, breaking through a stout picket fence on the near side, down into the moist ground of the hollow, and up through the corn, which was higher than their heads, and shut out every thing from view. At the southern side of the field they came to a low fence beyond which was an open field, at the farther side of which was the enemy's line. But Gibbon's right, covered by the corn, had outmarched the left which had been exposed to a terrible fire, and the direction taken had been

THE PRY HOUSE, GENERAL McCLELLAN'S HEADQUARTERS AT THE BATTLE OF ANTIETAM. FROM A PHOTOGRAPH TAKEN IN 1886.

little oblique, so that the right wing of the 6th Wisconsin, the flanking regiment, had crossed the turnpike and was suddenly assailed by a sharp fire from the West Wood on its flank. They swung back into the road, lying down along the high, stout post-and-rail fence, keeping up their fire by shooting between the rails. Leaving this little band to protect their right, the main line, which had come up on the left, leaped the fence at the south edge of the corn-field and charged across the open at the enemy in front. But the concentrated fire of artillery and musketry was more than they could bear. Men fell by scores and hundreds, and the thinned lines gave way and ran for the shelter of the corn. They were rallied in the hollow on the north side of the field. The enemy had rapidly extended his left under cover of the West Wood, and now made a dash at the right flank and at Gibbon's exposed guns. His men on the right faced by that flank and followed him bravely, though with little order, in a dash at the Confederates, who were swarming out of the wood. The gunners double-charged the cannon with canister, and under a terrible fire of both artillery and rifles the enemy broke and sought shelter.

Patrick's brigade had come up in support of Gibbon, and was sent across the turnpike into the West Wood to cover that flank. They pushed forward, the enemy retiring, until they were in advance of the principal line in the corn-field, upon which the Confederates were now advancing. Patrick faced his men to the left, parallel to the edge of the wood and to the turnpike, and poured his fire into the flank of the enemy, following it by a charge through the field and up to the fence along the road. Again the Confederates were driven back, but only to push in again by way of these woods, forcing Patrick to resume his original line of front and to retire to the cover of a ledge at right angles to the road near Gibbon's guns.

Farther to the left Phelps's and Hofmann's brigades had had similar experience, pushing forward nearly to the Confederate lines, and being driven back with great loss when they charged over open ground against the enemy. Ricketts's division entered the edge of the East Wood; but here, at the salient angle, where D. H. Hill and Lawton joined, the enemy held the position stubbornly, and the repulse of Doubleday's division made Ricketts glad to hold even the edge of the East Wood, as the right of the line was driven back.

It was now about 7 o'clock, and Mansfield's corps (the Twelfth) was approaching, for that officer had called his men to arms at the first sound of Hooker's battle and had marched to his support. The corps consisted of two divisions, Williams's and Greene's. It contained a number of new and undrilled regiments, and in hastening to the field in columns of battalions in mass, proper intervals for deployment had not been preserved, and time was necessarily lost before the troops could be put in line. General Mansfield fell mortally wounded before the deployment was complete, and the command devolved on General Williams. Williams had only time to take the most general directions from Hooker, when the latter also was wounded.‡ The Twelfth Corps attack

---

‡ Of the early morning fight in the corn-field, General Hooker says in his report:

"We had not proceeded far before I discovered that a heavy force of the enemy had taken possession of a corn-field (I have since learned about a thirty-acre field), in my immediate front, and from the sun's rays falling on their bayonets projecting above the corn could see

MAJOR-GENERAL JOSEPH K. F. MANSFIELD. ☆
FROM A PHOTOGRAPH.

seems to have been made obliquely to that of Hooker, and facing more to the westward, for General Williams speaks of the post-and-rail fences along the turnpike being a great obstruction in their front. Greene's division, on his left, moved along the ridge leading to the East Wood, taking as the guide for his extreme left the line of the burning house of Mumma, which had been set on fire by D. H. Hill's men. Doubleday, in his report, notices this change of direction of Williams's division, which had relieved him, and says Williams's brigades were swept away by a fire from their left and front, from behind rocky ledges they could not see.❧ Our officers were deceived in part as to the extent and direction of the enemy's line by the fact that the Confederate cavalry commander, Stuart, had occupied a commanding hill west of the pike and beyond our right flank, and from this position, which, in fact, was considerably detached from the Confederate line, he used his batteries with such effect as to produce the belief that a continuous line extended from this point to the Dunker Church.¶ Our true lines of attack were convergent ones, the right sweeping southward along the pike and through the narrow strip of the West Wood, while the division

that the field was filled with the enemy, with arms in their hands, standing apparently at 'support arms.' Instructions were immediately given for the assemblage of all of my spare batteries near at hand, of which I think there were five or six, to spring into battery on the right of this field, and to open with canister at once. In the time I am writing every stalk of corn in the northern and greater part of the field was cut as closely as could have been done with a knife, and the slain lay in rows precisely as they had stood in their ranks a few moments before.

"It was never my fortune to witness a more bloody, dismal battle-field. Those that escaped fled in the opposite direction from our advance, and sought refuge behind the trees, fences, and stone ledges nearly on a line with the Dunker Church, etc., as there was no resisting this torrent of death-dealing missives. . . . The whole morning had been one of unusual animation to me and fraught with the grandest events. The conduct of my troops was sublime, and the occasion almost lifted me to the skies, and its memories will ever remain near me. My command followed the fugitives closely until we had passed the corn-field a quarter of a mile or more, when I was removed from my saddle in the act of falling out of it from loss of blood, having previously been struck without my knowledge." — EDITORS.

❧ Both in the West and East Wood and on the ground south of the East Wood the Confederates were protected by outcroppings of rocks, which served as natural breastworks.—EDITORS.

¶ Stuart says he had batteries from all parts of Jackson's command, and mentions Poague's, Pegram's, and Carrington's, besides Pelham's which was attached to the cavalry. He also says he was supported part of the time by Early's brigade; afterward by one regiment of it, the 13th Virginia.—EDITORS.

☆ General Mansfield was mortally wounded early in the action. In the "History of the 1st, 10th, 29th Maine Regiments," Major John M. Gould, who was Adjutant of the 10th Maine regiment, at Antietam, in Crawford's First Brigade, of A. S. Williams's First Division, of Mansfield's Twelfth Corps, gives the following circumstantial account of this event:

"The Confederate force in our front showed no colors. They appeared to be somewhat detached from and in advance of the main rebel line, and were about where the

SUMNER'S ADVANCE.—FRENCH'S DIVISION CLOSING IN UPON ROULETTE'S BARNS AND HOUSE—RICHARDSON'S DIVISION CONTINUING THE LINE FAR TO THE LEFT. FROM A SKETCH MADE AT THE TIME.

which drove the enemy from the East Wood should move upon the commanding ground around the church. This error of direction was repeated with disastrous effect a little later, when Sumner came on the ground with Sedgwick's corps.

When Mansfield's corps came on the field, Meade, who succeeded Hooker, ↓ withdrew the First Corps to the ridge north of Poffenberger's, where it had bivouacked the night before. It had suffered severely, having lost 2470 in killed and wounded, but it was still further depleted by straggling, so that

left of General Duryée's brigade might be supposed to have retreated. To General Mansfield we appeared to be firing into Duryea's troops; therefore he beckoned to us to cease firing, and as this was the very last thing we proposed to do, the few who saw him did not understand what his motions meant, and so no attention was paid to him. He now rode down the hill from the 128th Pennsylvania, and passing quickly through H, A, K, E, I, G, and D (of the 10th Maine), ordering them to cease firing, he halted in front of C, at the earnest remonstrances of Captain Jordan and Sergeant Burnham, who asked him to see the gray coats of the enemy, and pointed out particular men of them who were then aiming their rifles at us and at him. The general was convinced, and remarked 'Yes, yes, you are right,' and was almost instantly hit. He turned and attempted to put his horse over the rails, but the animal had also been severely wounded and could not go over. Thereupon the general dismounted, and a gust of wind blowing open his coat we saw that he was wounded in the body. Sergeant Joe Merritt, Storer Knight, and I took the general to the rear, assisted for a while by a negro cook from Hooker's corps. We put the general into an ambulance in the woods in front of which we had deployed, and noticed that General Gordon was just at that moment posting the 107th New York in their front edge."

Colonel Jacob Higgins, 125th Pennsylvania regiment, commanding the brigade after Crawford was wounded, reports that some of his men carried General Mansfield "off the field on their muskets until a blanket was procured." General George H. Gordon, commanding the Third Brigade of this division, which formed on Crawford's left, reports that "General Mansfield had been mortally wounded . . . while making a bold reconnoissance of the woods through which we had just dashed."—EDITORS.

↓ The order assigning Meade to command is dated 1:25 P. M.—EDITORS.

MAJOR-GENERAL ISRAEL B. RICHARDSON. FROM A PHOTOGRAPH.

Referring in his report to the incidents accompanying General Richardson's fall, General Caldwell says: "The enemy made one more effort to break my line, and this time the attack was made in the center. Colonel Barlow [General Francis C.], hearing firing to his left, on our old front, immediately moved to the left and formed in line with the rest of the brigade. The whole brigade then moved forward in line, driving the enemy entirely out of the corn-field [see E on the map] and through the orchard beyond, the enemy firing grape and canister from two brass pieces in the orchard to our front, and shell and spherical case-shot from a battery on our right. While leading his men forward under the fire, Colonel Barlow fell dangerously wounded by a grape-shot in the groin. By command of General Richardson I halted the brigade, and, drawing back the line, re-formed it near the edge of the corn-field. It was now 1 o'clock P. M. Here we lay exposed to a heavy artillery fire, by which General Richardson was severely wounded. The fall of General Richardson (General Meagher having been previously borne from the field) left me in command of the division, which I formed in line, awaiting the enemy's attack. Not long after, I was relieved of the command by General Hancock, who had been assigned to the command of the division by General McClellan." General Richardson was carried to Pry's house, McClellan's headquarters, where he died November 3d.— EDITORS.

Meade reported less than 7000 men with the colors that evening. Its organization was preserved, however, and the story that it was utterly dispersed was a mistake.

Greene's division, on the left of the Twelfth Corps, profited by the hard fighting of those who had preceded it, and was able to drive the enemy quite out of the East Wood and across the open fields between it and the Dunker Church. Greene even succeeded, about the time of Sumner's advance, in getting a foothold about the Dunker Church itself, which he held for some time.† But the fighting of Hooker's and Mansfield's men, though lacking unity of force and of purpose, had cost the enemy dear. J. R. Jones, who commanded Jackson's division, had been wounded; Starke, who succeeded Jones, was killed; Lawton, who followed Starke, was wounded. Ewell's division, commanded by Early, had suffered hardly less. Hood was sent back into the fight to relieve Lawton, and had been reënforced by the brigades of Ripley, Colquitt, and McRae (Garland's), from D. H. Hill's division. When Greene reached the Dunker Church, therefore, the Confederates on that wing had suffered more fearfully than our own men. Nearly half their numbers were killed and wounded, and Jackson's famous "Stonewall" division was so completely disorganized that only a handful of men under Colonels Grigsby and Stafford remained and attached themselves to Early's command. Of the division under Early, his own brigade was all that retained much strength, and this, posted among the rocks in the West Wood and vigorously supported by Stuart's horse artillery on the flank, was all that covered the left of Lee's army. Could Hooker and Mansfield have attacked together,— or, still better, could Sumner's Second Corps have marched before day and united with the first onset,— Lee's left must inevitably have been crushed long before the Confederate divisions of McLaws, Walker, and A. P. Hill could have reached the field. It is this failure to carry out any intelligible plan which the historian must regard as the unpardonable military fault on the National side. To account for the hours between 4 and 8 on that morning, is the most serious responsibility of the National commander.

Sumner's Second Corps was now approaching the scene of action, or rather two divisions of it — Sedgwick's and French's — Richardson's being still delayed ‡ till his place could be filled by Porter's troops, the strange tardiness in sending orders being noticeable in regard to every part of the army. Sumner met Hooker, who was being carried from the field, and the few words he could exchange with the wounded general were enough to make him feel the need of haste, but not sufficient to give him any clear idea of the position.

Both Sedgwick and French marched their divisions by the right flank, in three columns, a brigade in each column, Sedgwick leading. They crossed the Antietam by Hooker's route, but did not march as far to the north-west as Hooker had done. When the center of the corps was opposite the Dunker Church, and nearly east of it, the change of direction was given; the troops faced to their proper front and advanced in line of battle in three lines, fully deployed, and 60 or 70 yards apart, Sumner himself being in rear of Sedgwick's first line, and near its left. When they approached the position held by Greene's division at Dunker Church, French kept on so as to form on Greene's left, while Sedgwick, under Sumner's immediate lead, diverged somewhat to the right, passing through the East Wood, crossing the turnpike on the right of Greene and of the Dunker Church, and plunged into the West Wood. At this point there were absolutely no Confederate troops in front of them. Early was

---

† Until he was driven out, about 1:30, according to Generals Williams and Greene.— EDITORS.

‡ Sumner says Richardson came about an hour later. Howard, who succeeded Sedgwick, says his division moved "about 7." French says he followed "about 7:30." Hancock, who succeeded Richardson, says that officer received his orders "about 9:30."— EDITORS.

## THE BATTLE OF ANTIETAM.

SCENE AT THE RUINS OF MUMMA'S HOUSE AND BARNS. FROM A SKETCH MADE AT THE TIME.

These buildings were fired early in the morning by D. H. Hill's men, who feared they would become a point of vantage to the Union forces. The sketch was made after the advance of French to the sunken road. Presumably, the battery firing upon the Confederate line to the right of that road is the First Rhode Island Light Artillery; for Captain John A. Tompkins, of Battery A, says, in his report, that he placed his pieces on a knoll "directly in front of some burning ruins," and opened fire upon a battery in front. "At 9:30," he continues, "the enemy appeared upon my right front with a large column, apparently designing to charge the battery. I was not aware of their approach until the head of the column gained the brow of a hill about sixty yards from the right gun of the battery. The pieces were immediately obliqued to the right and a sharp fire of canister opened upon them, causing them to retire in confusion, leaving the ground covered with their dead and wounded, and abandoning one of their battle-flags, which was secured by a regiment which came up on my right after the enemy had retreated. The enemy now opened a fire upon us from a battery in front, and also from one on the right near the white school-house [Dunker Church]. Two guns were directed to reply to the battery on the right, while the fire of the rest was directed upon the guns in front, which were silenced in about twenty minutes, and one of their caissons blown up." At noon, Tompkins was relieved by Battery G.— EDITORS.

farther to the right, opposing Williams's division of the Twelfth Corps, and now made haste under cover of the woods to pass around Sedgwick's right and to get in front of him to oppose his progress. This led to a lively skirmishing fight in which Early was making as great a demonstration as possible, but with no chance of solid success. At this very moment, however, McLaws's and Walker's divisions came upon the field, marching rapidly from Harper's Ferry. Walker charged headlong upon the left flank of Sedgwick's lines, which were soon thrown into confusion, and McLaws, passing by Walker's left, also threw his division diagonally upon the already broken and retreating lines of Sumner. Taken at such a disadvantage, these had never a chance; and in spite of the heroic bravery of Sumner and Sedgwick, with most of their officers (Sedgwick being severely wounded), the division was driven off to the north with terrible losses, carrying along in the rout part of Williams's men of the Twelfth Corps, who had been holding Early at bay. All these troops were rallied at the ridge on the Poffenberger farm, where Hooker's corps had already taken position. Here some thirty cannon of both corps were concentrated, and, supported by the organized parts of all three of the corps which had fought upon this part of the field, easily repulsed all efforts of Jackson and Stuart to resume the aggressive or to pass between them and the Potomac. Sumner himself did not accompany the routed troops to this position, but as soon as it was plain that the division could not be rallied, he galloped off to put himself in communication with French and with the headquarters of the army and try to retrieve the misfortune. From the flag-station east of the East Wood he signaled to McClellan: "Reënforcements are badly wanted. Our troops are giving way." It was between 9 and 10 o'clock when Sumner entered the West Wood, and in fifteen minutes, or a little more, the one-sided combat was over. ♭

The enemy now concentrated upon Greene at the Dunker Church, and after a stubborn resistance he too was driven back across the turnpike and the open ground to the edge of the East Wood. Here, by the aid of several batteries gallantly handled, he defeated the subsequent effort to dislodge him. French had come up on his left, and both his batteries and the numerous ones on the Poffenberger hill swept the open ground and the corn-field over which Hooker had fought, and he was able to make good his position. The enemy was content to regain the high ground near the church, and French's attack upon D. H. Hill was now attracting their attention.

The battle on the extreme right was thus ended before 10 o'clock in the morning, and there was no more serious fighting north of the Dunker Church. French advanced on Greene's left, over the open farm lands, and after a fierce combat about the Roulette and Clipp farm buildings, drove D. H. Hill's division from them. Richardson's division came up on French's left soon after, and foot by foot, field by field, from hill to hill and from fence to fence, the enemy was pressed back, till after several hours of fighting the sunken road, since known as "Bloody Lane," was in our hands, piled full of the Confederate dead who had defended it with their lives. Richardson had been mortally wounded, and Hancock had been sent from Franklin's corps to command the division. Barlow had been conspicuous in the thickest of the fight, and after a series of brilliant actions was carried off desperately wounded. On the Confederate side equal courage had been shown and a magnificent tenacity exhibited. But it is not my purpose to describe the battle in detail. I limit

♭ Sumner's principal attack was made, as I have already indicated, at right angles to that of Hooker. He had thus crossed the line of Hooker's movement both in the latter's advance and retreat. Greene's division was the only part of the Twelfth Corps troops he saw, and he led Sedgwick's men to the right of these. Ignorant, as he necessarily was, of what had occurred before, he assumed that he formed on the extreme right of the Twelfth Corps, and that he fronted in the same direction as Hooker had done. This misconception of the situation led him into another error. He had seen only a few stragglers and wounded men of Hooker's corps on the line of his own advance, and hence concluded that the First Corps was completely dispersed and its division and brigade organizations broken up. He not only gave this report to McClellan at the time, but reiterated it later in his statement before the Committee on the Conduct of the War. The truth was that he had marched westward more than half a mile south of the Poffenberger hill, where Meade was with the sadly diminished but still organized First Corps, and half that distance south of the Miller farm buildings, near which Williams's division of the Twelfth Corps held the ground along the turnpike till they were carried away in the disordered retreat of Sedgwick's men toward the right. Sedgwick had gone in, therefore, between Greene and Williams, of the Twelfth Corps, and the four divisions of the two corps alternated in their order from left to right, thus: French, Greene, Sedgwick, Williams.— J. D. C.

myself to such an outline as may make clear my interpretation of the larger features of the engagement and its essential plan.

The head of Franklin's corps (the Sixth) had arrived about 10 o'clock and taken the position near the Sharpsburg Bridge which Sumner had occupied. Before noon Smith's and Slocum's divisions were ordered to Sumner's assistance, and early in the afternoon Irwin and Brooks, of Smith's, advanced to the charge and relieved Greene's division and part of French's, holding the line from Bloody Lane by the Clipp, Roulette, and Mumma houses to the East Wood and the ridge in front. Here Smith and Slocum remained till Lee retreated, Smith's division repelling a sharp attack. French and Richardson's battle may be considered as ended at 1 or 2 o'clock.

It seems to me very clear that about 10 o'clock in the morning was the great crisis in this battle. The sudden and complete rout of Sedgwick's division was not easily accounted for, and with McClellan's theory of the enormous superiority of Lee's numbers, it looked as if the Confederate general had massed overwhelming forces on our right. Sumner's notion that Hooker's corps was utterly dispersed was naturally accepted, and McClellan limited his hopes to holding on at the East Wood and the Poffenberger hill where Sedgwick's batteries were massed and supported by the troops that had

CHARGE OF IRWIN'S BRIGADE (SMITH'S DIVISION) AT THE DUNKER CHURCH. FROM A SKETCH MADE AT THE TIME.

General Wm. F. Smith, commanding the Second Division of Franklin's corps, went to the assistance of French. On getting into position, for the most part to the right of French, General Smith, in his report, says: "Finding that the enemy were advancing, I ordered forward the Third Brigade (Colonel Irwin's), who, passing through the regular battery then commanded by Lieutenant Thomas (Fourth Artillery), charged upon the enemy and drove them gallantly until abreast the little church at the point of woods, the possession of which had been so fiercely contested. At this point a severe flank fire from the woods was received." The brigade rallied behind the crest of a slope, and remained in an advanced position until the next day.—EDITORS.

GENERAL VIEW OF THE BATTLE OF ANTIETAM. FROM A SKETCH MADE AT THE TIME.

This sketch was made on the hill behind McClellan's headquarters, which is seen in the hollow on the left. Sumner's corps is seen in line of battle in the middle-ground, and Franklin's is advancing in column to his support. The smoke in the left background is from a bursting Confederate caisson. The column of smoke is from the burning house and barn of S. Mumma, who gave the ground on which the Dunker Church stands, and after whom, in the Confederate reports, the church is frequently called "St. Mumma's." On the right is the East Wood, in which is seen the smoke of the conflict between Mansfield and Jackson.— EDITORS.

been rallied there. Franklin's corps as it came on the field was detained to support the threatened right center, and McClellan determined to help it further by a demonstration upon the extreme left by the Ninth Corps. At this time, therefore (10 A. M.), he gave his order to Burnside to try to cross the Antietam and attack the enemy, thus creating a diversion in favor of our hard-pressed right.\ Facts within my own recollection strongly sustain

\ Here, as in regard to the time at which Sumner was ordered to march to Hooker's support, is a disputed question of fact. In his official report, McClellan says he ordered Burnside to make this attack at 8 o'clock, and from the day that the latter relieved McClellan in command of the army, and especially after the battle of Fredericksburg, a hot partisan effort was made to hold Burnside responsible for the lack of complete success at Antietam as well as for the repulse upon the Rappahannock. I think I understand the limitations of Burnside's abilities as a general, but I have had, ever since the battle itself, a profound conviction that the current criticisms upon him in relation to the battle of Antietam were unjust. Burnside's official report declares that he received the order to advance at 10 o'clock. This report was dated on the 30th of September, within two weeks of the battle, and at a time when public discussion of the incomplete results of the battle was animated. It was made after he had in his hands my own report as his immediate subordinate, in which I had given about 9 o'clock as my remembrance of the time.

As I directed the details of the action at the bridge in obedience to this order, it would have been easy for him to have accepted the hour named by me, for I should have been answerable for any delay in execution after that time. But he believed he knew the time at which the order came to him upon the hill-top overlooking the field, and no officer in the whole army has a better established reputation for candor and freedom from any wish to avoid full personal responsibility for his acts. It was not till quite lately that I saw a copy of his report or learned its contents, although I enjoyed his personal friendship down to the time of his death. He was content to have stated the fact as he knew it, and did not feel the need of debating it. Several circumstances have satisfied me that his accuracy in giving the hour was greater than my own. McClellan's preliminary report (dated October 16th, 1862) explicitly states that the order to Burnside to attack was "communicated to him at 10 o'clock A. M." This exact agreement with General Burnside would ordinarily be conclusive in itself.— J. D. C.

GENERAL McCLELLAN RIDING THE LINE OF BATTLE AT ANTIETAM. FROM A SKETCH MADE AT THE TIME.

General McClellan rode his black horse, "Daniel Webster," which, on account of the difficulty of keeping pace with him, was better known to the staff as "that devil Dan."—EDITORS.

this view that the hour was 10 A. M. I have mentioned the hill above the Burnside Bridge where Burnside took his position, and to which I went after the preliminary orders for the day had been issued. There I remained until the order of attack came, anxiously watching what we could see at the right, and noting the effect of the fire of the heavy guns of Benjamin's battery.

From that point we could see nothing that occurred beyond the Dunker Church, for the East and West Woods, with farm-houses and orchards between, made an impenetrable screen. But as the morning wore on we saw lines of troops advancing from our right upon the other side of the Antietam, and engaging the enemy between us and the East Wood. The Confederate lines facing them now rose into view. From our position we looked, as it were, down between the opposing lines as if they had been the sides of a street, and as the fire opened we saw wounded men carried to the rear and stragglers making off. Our lines halted, and we were tortured with anxiety as we speculated whether our men would charge or retreat. The enemy occupied lines of fences and stone-walls, and their batteries made gaps in the National ranks. Our long-range guns were immediately turned in that direction, and we cheered every well-aimed shot. One of our shells blew up a caisson close to the Confederate line. This contest was going on, and it was yet uncertain which would succeed, when one of McClellan's staff ☆ rode up with an order to Burnside. The latter turned to me, saying we were ordered to make our

---

☆ Colonel D. B. Sackett, who says he got the order from McClellan about 9 o'clock.— EDITORS.

attack. I left the hill-top at once to give personal supervision to the movement ordered, and did not return to it, and my knowledge by actual vision of what occurred on the right ceased. The manner in which we had waited, the free discussion of what was occurring under our eyes and of our relation to it, the public receipt of the order by Burnside in the usual and business-like form, all forbid the supposition that this was any reiteration of a former order. It was immediately transmitted to me without delay or discussion, further than to inform us that things were not going altogether well on the right, and that it was hoped our attack would be of assistance to that wing. If then we can determine whose troops we saw engaged, we shall know something of the time of day; for there has been a general agreement reached as to the hours of movement during the forenoon on the right. The official map settles this. No lines of our troops were engaged in the direction of Bloody Lane and the Roulette farm-house, and between the latter and our station on the hill, till French's division made its attack. We saw them distinctly on the hither side of the farm buildings, upon the open ground, considerably nearer to us than the Dunker Church or the East Wood. In number we took them to be a corps. The place, the circumstances, all fix it beyond controversy that they were French's men, or French's and Richardson's. No others fought on that part of the field until Franklin went to their assistance at noon or later. The incident of their advance and the explosion of the caisson was illustrated by the pencil of the artist, Forbes, on the spot [see p. 647], and placed by him at the time Franklin's head of column was approaching from Rohrersville, which was about 10 o'clock. ☆

McClellan truly said, in his original report, that the task of carrying the bridge in front of Burnside was a difficult one. The depth of the valley and the shape of its curve made it impossible to reach the enemy's position at the bridge by artillery fire from the hill-tops on our side. Not so from the enemy's position, for the curve of the valley was such that it was perfectly enfiladed near the bridge by the Confederate batteries at the position now occupied by the national cemetery. [See map, p. 636.] The Confederate defense of the passage was intrusted to D. R. Jones's division of four brigades, which was the one Longstreet himself had disciplined and led till he was assigned to a larger command. Toombs's brigade was placed in advance, occupying the defenses of the bridge itself and the wooded slopes above, while the other brigades supported him, covered by the ridges which looked down upon the valley. The division batteries were supplemented by others from the reserve, and the valley, the bridge, and the ford below were under the direct and powerful fire of shot and shell from the Confederate cannon. Toombs speaks in his report in a characteristic way of his brigade

---

☆ It will not be wondered at, therefore, if to my mind the story of the 8 o'clock order is an instance of the way in which an erroneous memory is based upon the desire to make the facts accord with a theory. The actual time must have been as much later than 9 o'clock as the period during which, with absorbed attention, we had been watching the battle on the right,—a period, it is safe to say, much longer than it seemed to us. The judgment of the hour, 9 o'clock, which I gave in my report, was merely my impression from passing events, for I hastened at once to my own duties without thinking to look at my watch, while the cumulative evidence seems to prove conclusively that the time stated by Burnside, and by McClellan himself in his original report, is correct.— J. D. C.

holding back Burnside's corps; but his force, thus strongly supported, was as large as could be disposed of at the head of the bridge, and abundantly large for resistance to any that could be brought against it. Our advance upon the bridge could only be made by a narrow column, showing a front of eight men at most. But the front which Toombs deployed behind his defenses was three or four hundred yards both above and below the bridge. He himself says in his report:

"From the nature of the ground on the other side, the enemy were compelled to approach mainly by the road which led up the river for near three hundred paces parallel with my line of battle and distant therefrom from fifty to a hundred and fifty feet, thus exposing his flank to a destructive fire the most of that distance."

Under such circumstances, I do not hesitate to affirm that the Confederate position was virtually impregnable to a direct attack over the bridge, for the column approaching it was not only exposed at pistol-range to the perfectly covered infantry of the enemy and to two batteries which were assigned to the special duty of supporting Toombs, and which had the exact range of the little valley with their shrapnel, but if it should succeed in reaching the bridge its charge across it must be made under a fire plowing through its length, the head of the column melting away as it advanced, so that, as every soldier knows, it could show no front strong enough to make an impression upon the enemy's breastworks, even if it should reach the other side. As a desperate sort of diversion in favor of the right wing, it might be justifiable; but I believe that no officer or man who knew the actual situation at that bridge thinks a serious attack upon it was any part of McClellan's original plan. Yet, in his detailed official report, instead of speaking of it as the difficult task the original report had called it, he treats it as little different from a parade or march across, which might have been done in half an hour.

Burnside's view of the matter was that the front attack at the bridge was so difficult that the passage by the ford below must be an important factor in the task; for if Rodman's division should succeed in getting across there, at the bend in the Antietam, he would come up in rear of Toombs, and either the whole of D. R. Jones's division would have to advance to meet Rodman, or Toombs must abandon the bridge. In this I certainly concurred, and Rodman was ordered to push rapidly for the ford. It is important to remember, however, that Walker's Confederate division had been posted during the earlier morning to hold that part of the Antietam line, and it was

BRIGADIER-GENERAL ISAAC P. RODMAN, MORTALLY WOUNDED AT ANTIETAM. FROM A PHOTOGRAPH.

probably from him that Rodman suffered the first casualties which occurred in his ranks. But, as we have seen, Walker had been called away by Lee only an hour before, and had made the hasty march by the rear of Sharpsburg, to fall upon Sedgwick. If, therefore, Rodman had been sent to cross at 8 o'clock, it is safe to say that his column fording the stream in the face of Walker's deployed division would never have reached the farther bank,— a contingency that McClellan did not consider when arguing long afterward the favorable results that might have followed an earlier attack. As Rodman died upon the field, no full report for his division was made, and we only know that he met with some resistance from both infantry and artillery; that the winding of the stream made his march longer than he anticipated, and that, in fact, he only approached the rear of Toombs's position from that direction about the time when our last and successful charge upon the bridge was made, between noon and 1 o'clock.

The attacks at Burnside's Bridge were made under my own eye. Sturgis's division occupied the center of our line, with Crook's brigade of the Kanawha Division on his right front, and Willcox's division in reserve, as I have already stated. Crook's position was somewhat above the bridge, but it was thought that by advancing part of Sturgis's men to the brow of the hill they could cover the advance of Crook, and that the latter could make a straight dash down the hill to our end of the bridge. The orders were accordingly given, and Crook advanced, covered by the 11th Connecticut (of Rodman), under Colonel Kingsbury, deployed as skirmishers. In passing over the spurs of the hills, Crook came out on the bank of the stream above the bridge and found himself under a heavy fire. He faced the enemy and returned the fire, getting such cover for his men as he could and trying to drive off or silence his opponents. The engagement was one in which the Antietam prevented the combatants from coming to close quarters, but it was none the less vigorously continued with musketry fire. Crook reported that his hands were full, and that he could not approach closer to the bridge. But later in the contest, and about the time that the successful charge at the bridge was made, he got five companies of the 28th Ohio over by a ford above. Sturgis ordered forward an attacking column from Nagle's brigade, supported and covered by Ferrero's brigade, which took position in a field of corn on one of the lower slopes of the hill opposite the head of the bridge. The whole front was carefully covered with skirmishers, and our batteries on the heights overhead were ordered to keep down the fire of the enemy's artillery. Nagle's effort was gallantly made, but it failed, and his men were forced to seek cover behind the spur of the hill from which they had advanced. We were constantly hoping to hear something from Rodman's advance by the ford, and would gladly have waited for some more certain knowledge of his progress, but at this time McClellan's sense of the necessity of relieving the right was such that he was sending reiterated orders to push the assault. Not only were these forwarded to me, but to give added weight to my instructions Burnside sent direct to Sturgis urgent messages to carry the bridge at all hazards. I directed Sturgis to take two regiments from Ferrero's brigade, which had not

THE CHARGE ACROSS THE BURNSIDE BRIDGE. FROM A SKETCH MADE AT THE TIME.

In his report General Sturgis describes as follows the charge across the bridge:

"Orders arrived from General Burnside to carry the bridge at all hazards. I then selected the Fifty-first New York and the Fifty-first Pennsylvania from the Second Brigade, and directed them to charge with the bayonet. They started on their mission of death full of enthusiasm, and, taking a route less exposed than the regiments [Second Maryland and Sixth New Hampshire] which had made the effort before them, rushed at a double-quick over the slope leading to the bridge and over the bridge itself, with an impetuosity which the enemy could not resist; and the Stars and Stripes were planted on the opposite bank at 1 o'clock P. M., amid the most enthusiastic cheering from every part of the field from where they could be seen."

been engaged, and make a column by moving them by the flank, the one left in front and the other right in front, side by side, so that when they passed the bridge they could turn to left and right, forming line as they advanced on the run. He chose the 51st New York, Colonel Robert B. Potter, and the 51st Pennsylvania, Colonel John F. Hartranft (both names afterward greatly distinguished), and both officers and men were made to feel the necessity of success. At the same time Crook succeeded in bringing a light howitzer of Simmonds's mixed battery down from the hill-tops, and placed it where it had a point-blank fire on the farther end of the bridge. The howitzer was one we had captured in West Virginia, and had been added to the battery, which was partly made up of heavy rifled Parrott guns. When everything was ready, a heavy skirmishing fire was opened all along the bank, the howitzer threw in double charges of canister, the two regiments charged up the road in column with fixed bayonets, and in scarcely more time than it takes to tell it, the bridge was passed and Toombs's brigade fled through the woods and over the top of the hill. The charging regiments were advanced in line to the crest above the bridge as soon as they were deployed, and the rest of Sturgis's division, with Crook's brigade, were immediately brought over to strengthen the line. These were soon joined by Rodman's division with Scammon's brigade, which had crossed at the ford, and whose presence on that side of the stream had no doubt made the final struggle of Toombs's men less obstinate than it would otherwise have been, the fear of being taken in rear having always a strong moral effect upon even the best of troops. It was now about 1 o'clock, and nearly three hours had been spent in a bitter and bloody contest across the narrow stream. The successive efforts to carry the bridge had been made as closely following each other as possible. Each had been a fierce combat, in which the men, with wonderful courage, had not easily accepted defeat, and even when not able to cross the bridge had made use of the walls at the end, the fences, and every tree and stone as cover, while they strove to reach with their fire their well-protected and nearly concealed opponents. The lulls in the fighting had been short, and only to prepare new efforts. The severity of the work was attested by our losses, which, before the crossing was won, exceeded five hundred men and included some of our best officers, such as Colonel Kingsbury, of the 11th Connecticut; Lieutenant-Colonel Bell, of the 51st Pennsylvania, and Lieutenant-Colonel Coleman, of the 11th Ohio, two of them commanding regiments. The proportion of casualties to the number engaged was much greater than common, for the nature of the task required that comparatively few troops should be exposed at once, the others remaining under cover.

Our first task was to prepare to hold the height we had gained against the return assault of the enemy which we expected, and to reply to the destructive fire from the enemy's abundant artillery. The light batteries were brought over and distributed in the line. The men were made to lie down behind the crest to save them from the concentrated artillery fire which the enemy opened upon us as soon as Toombs's regiments succeeded in reaching their main line. But McClellan's anticipation of an overwhelming attack upon his right was so strong that he determined still to press our advance, and sent orders accordingly. The ammunition of Sturgis's and Crook's men had been nearly exhausted, and it was imperative that they should be freshly supplied before entering into another engagement. Sturgis also reported his men so exhausted by their efforts as to be unfit for an immediate advance. On this I sent to Burnside the request that Willcox's division be sent over, with an ammunition train, and that Sturgis's division be replaced by the fresh troops, remaining, however, on the west side of the stream as support to the others. This was done as rapidly as was practicable, where everything had to pass down the steep hill road and through so narrow a defile as the bridge. Still, it was 3 o'clock before these changes and further preparations could be made. Burnside had personally striven to hasten them, and had come over to the west bank to consult and to hurry matters, and took his share of personal peril, for he came at a time when the ammunition wagons were delivering cartridges, and the road where they were, at the end of the bridge, was in the range of the enemy's constant and accurate fire. It is proper to mention this because it has been said that he did not cross the stream. The criticisms made by McClellan as to the time occupied in these changes and movements will not seem

**BURNSIDE'S ATTACK UPON SHARPSBURG. FROM A SKETCH MADE AT THE TIME.**

In this attack Willcox's division (the right of the line) charged into the village. Colonel Fairchild, commanding a brigade in Rodman's division, on the left of the line (which included Hawkins's Zouaves, seen at the stone-wall in the picture), describes as follows in his report the advance upon Sharpsburg after the hill above the bridge had been gained: "We continued to advance to the opposite hill under a tremendous fire from the enemy's batteries, up steep embankments. Arriving near a stone fence, the enemy — a brigade composed of South Carolina and Georgia regiments — opened on us with musketry. After returning their fire I immediately ordered a charge, which the whole brigade gallantly responded to, moving with alacrity and steadiness. Arriving at the fence, behind which the enemy were awaiting us, receiving their fire, losing large numbers of our men, we charged over the fence, dislodging them and driving them from their positions down the hill toward the village, a stand of regimental colors belonging to a South Carolina regiment being taken by Private Thomas Hare, Company D, 89th New York Volunteers, who was afterward killed. We continued to pursue the enemy down the hill. Discovering that they were massing fresh troops on our left, I went back and requested General Rodman to bring up rapidly the Second Brigade to our support, which he did, they engaging the enemy, he soon afterward falling badly wounded. . . . The large force advancing on our left flank compelled us to retire from the position, which we could have held had we been properly supported."

forcible, if one will compare them with any similar movements on the field; such as Mansfield's to support Hooker, or Sumner's or Franklin's to reach the scene of action. About this, however, there is fair room for difference of opinion; what I personally know is that it would have been folly to advance again before Willcox had relieved Sturgis, and that as soon as the fresh troops reported and could be put in line, the order to advance was given. McClellan is in accord with all other witnesses in declaring that when the movement began, the conduct of the troops was gallant beyond criticism.

Willcox's division formed the right, Christ's brigade being north and Welsh's brigade south of the road leading from the bridge to Sharpsburg. Crook's brigade of the Kanawha Division supported Willcox. Rodman's division formed on the left, Harland's brigade having the position on the flank, and Fairchild's uniting with Willcox at the center. Scammon's brigade of the Kanawha Division was the reserve for Rodman on the extreme left. Sturgis's division remained and held the crest of the hill above the bridge. About half the batteries of the divisions accompanied the movement, the rest being in position on the hill-tops east of the Antietam. The advance necessarily followed the high ground toward Sharpsburg, and as the enemy made strongest resistance toward our right, the movement curved in that direction, the six brigades of D. R. Jones's Confederate division being deployed diagonally across our front, holding the stone fences and crests of the cross ridges and aided by abundant artillery, in which arm the enemy was particularly strong. The battle was a fierce one from the moment Willcox's men showed themselves on the open ground. Christ's brigade, taking advantage of all the cover the trees and inequalities of surface gave them, pushed on along the depression in which the road ran, a section of artillery keeping pace with them in the road. The direction of movement brought all the brigades of the first line in échelon, but Welsh soon fought his way up beside Christ, and they, together, drove the enemy successively from the fields and farm-yards till they reached the edge of the village. Upon the elevation on the right of the road was an orchard in which the shattered and diminished force of Jones made a final stand, but Willcox concentrated his artillery fire upon it, and his infantry was able to push forward and occupy it. They now partly occupied the town of Sharpsburg, and held the high ground commanding it on the south-east, where the national cemetery now is. The struggle had been long and bloody. It was half-past 4 in the afternoon, and ammunition had again run low, for the wagons had not been able to accompany the movement. Willcox paused for his men to take breath again, and to fetch up some cartridges; but meanwhile affairs were taking a serious turn on the left.

As Rodman's division went forward, he found the enemy before him seemingly detached from Willcox's opponents, and occupying ridges upon his left front, so that he was not able to keep his own connection with Willcox in the swinging movement to the right. Still, he made good progress in the face of stubborn resistance, though finding the enemy constantly developing more to his left, and the interval between him and Willcox widening. In fact his movement became practically by column of brigades. The view of the field to the south was now obstructed by fields of tall Indian corn, and under this cover Confederate troops approached the flank in line of battle. Scammon's officers in the reserve saw them as soon as Rodman's brigades écheloned, as these were toward the front and right. This hostile force proved to be A. P. Hill's division of six brigades, the last of Jackson's force to leave Harper's Ferry, and which had reached Sharpsburg since noon. Those first seen by Scammon's men were dressed in the National blue uniforms which they had captured at Harper's Ferry, and it was assumed that they were part of our own forces till they began to fire. Scammon quickly changed front to the left, drove back the enemy before him, and occupied a line of stone fences, which he held until he was withdrawn from it. Harland's brigade was partly moving in the corn-fields. One of his regiments was new, having been organized only three weeks, and the brigade had somewhat lost its order and connection when the sudden attack came. Rodman directed Colonel Harland to lead the right of the brigade, while he himself attempted to bring the left into position.

In performing this duty he fell mortally wounded, and the brigade broke in confusion after a brief effort of its right wing to hold on. Fairchild, also, now received the fire on his left, and was forced to fall back and change front.

Being at the center when this break occurred on the left, I saw that it would be impossible to continue the movement to the right, and sent instant orders to Willcox and Crook to retire the left of their line, and to Sturgis to come forward into the gap made in Rodman's. The troops on the right swung back in perfect order; Scammon's brigade hung on at its stone-wall with unflinching tenacity till Sturgis had formed on the curving hill in rear of them, and Rodman's had found refuge behind. Willcox's left, then united with Sturgis and Scammon, was withdrawn to a new position on the left flank of the whole line. That these manœuvres on the field were really performed in good order is demonstrated by the fact that, although the break in Rodman's line was a bad one, the enemy was not able to capture many prisoners, the whole number of missing, out of the 2340 casualties which the Ninth Corps suffered in the battle, being 115, which includes wounded men unable to leave the field. The enemy were not lacking in bold efforts to take advantage of the check we had received, but were repulsed with severe punishment, and as the day declined were content to entrench themselves along the line of the road leading from Sharpsburg to the Potomac at the mouth of the Antietam, half a mile in our front. The men of the Ninth Corps lay that night upon their arms, the line being one which rested with both flanks near the Antietam, and curved outward upon the rolling hill-tops which covered the bridge and commanded the plateau between us and the enemy. With my staff I lay upon the ground behind the troops, holding our horses by the bridles as we rested, for our orderlies were so exhausted that we could not deny them the same chance for a little broken slumber.

The conduct of the battle on the left has given rise to several criticisms, among which the most prominent has been that Porter's corps, which lay in reserve, was not put in at the same time with the Ninth Corps.❘ McClellan

---

❘ Captain Thomas M. Anderson, in 1886 Lieutenant-Colonel of the 9th Infantry, U. S. A., wrote to the editors in that year:

"At the battle of Antietam I commanded one of the battalions of Sykes's division of regulars, held in reserve on the north of Antietam creek near the stone bridge. Three of our battalions were on the south side of the creek, deployed as skirmishers in front of Sharpsburg. At the time A. P. Hill began to force Burnside back upon the left, I was talking with Colonel Buchanan, our brigade commander, when an orderly brought him a note from Captain (now Colonel) Blunt, who was the senior officer with the battalions of our brigade beyond the creek. The note, as I remember, stated in effect that Captain Dryer, commanding the 4th Infantry, had ridden into the enemy's lines, and upon returning had reported that there were but one Confederate battery and two regiments in front of Sharpsburg, connecting the wings of Lee's army.* Dryer was one of the coolest and bravest officers in our service, and on his report Blunt

asked instructions. We learned afterward that Dryer proposed that he, Blunt, and Brown, commanding the 4th, 12th, and 14th Infantries, should charge the enemy in Sharpsburg instanter. But Blunt preferred asking for orders. Colonel Buchanan sent the note to Sykes, who was at the time talking with General McClellan and Fitz John Porter, about a hundred and fifty yards from us. They were sitting on their horses between Taft's and Weed's batteries a little to our left. I saw the note passed from one to the other in the group, but could not, of course, hear what was said.

"We received no orders to advance, however, although the advance of a single brigade at the time (sunset) would have cut Lee's army in two.

"After the war, I asked General Sykes why our reserves did not advance upon receiving Dryer's report. He answered that he remembered the circumstance very well and that he thought McClellan was inclined to order in the Fifth Corps, but that when he spoke of doing so Fitz John Porter said: 'Remember, General! I command the last reserve of the last Army of the Republic.'"

* General Fitz John Porter writes to say that no such note as "Captain Dryer's report" was seen by him, and that no such discussion as to the opportunity for using the "reserve" took place between him and General McClellan. General Porter says that nearly all of his Fifth Corps (according to McClellan's report, 12,900 strong), instead of being idle at that critical hour, had been sent to reënforce the right and left wings, leaving of the Fifth Corps to defend the center a force "not then four thousand strong," according to General Porter's report.— EDITORS.

answered this by saying that he did not think it prudent to divest the center of all reserve troops.⸸ No doubt a single strong division marching beyond the left flank of the Ninth Corps would have so occupied A. P. Hill's division that our movement into Sharpsburg could not have been checked, and, assisted by the advance of Sumner and Franklin on the right, apparently would have made certain the complete rout of Lee. As troops are put in reserve, not to diminish the army, but to be used in a pinch, I am deeply convinced that McClellan's refusal to use them on the left was the result of his continued conviction through all the day after Sedgwick's defeat, that Lee was overwhelmingly superior in force, and was preparing to return a crushing blow upon our right flank. He was keeping something in hand to cover a retreat, if that wing should be driven back. Except in this way, also, I am at a loss to account for the inaction of our right during the whole of our engagement on the left. Looking at our part of the battle as only a strong diversion to prevent or delay Lee's following up his success against Hooker and the rest, it is intelligible. I certainly so understood it at the time, as my report witnesses, and McClellan's preliminary report supports this view. If he had been impatient to have our attack delivered earlier, he had reason for double impatience that Franklin's fresh troops should assail Lee's left simultaneously with ours, unless he regarded action there as hopeless, and looked upon our movement as a sort of forlorn-hope to keep Lee from following up his advantages.

PRESIDENT LINCOLN IN GENERAL MCCLELLAN'S TENT AT ANTIETAM AFTER THE BATTLE. FROM A PHOTOGRAPH.

But even these are not all the troublesome questions requiring an answer. Couch's division had been left north-east of Maryland Heights to observe Jackson's command, supposed still to be in Harper's Ferry. Why could it not have come up on our left as well as A. P. Hill's division, which was the last of

---

⸸ At this time Sykes and Griffin, of Porter's corps, had been advanced, and part of their troops were actively engaged.— EDITORS.

the Confederate troops to leave the Ferry, there being nothing to observe after it was gone? Couch's division, coming with equal pace with Hill's on the other side of the river, would have answered our needs as well as one from Porter's corps. Hill came, but Couch did not. Yet even then, a regiment of horse watching that flank and scouring the country as we swung it forward would have developed Hill's presence and enabled the commanding general either to stop our movement or to take the available means to support it; but the cavalry was put to no such use; it occupied the center of the whole line, only its artillery being engaged during the day. It would have been invaluable to Hooker in the morning as it would have been to us in the afternoon. McClellan had marched from Frederick City with the information that Lee's army was divided, Jackson being detached with a large force to take Harper's Ferry. He had put Lee's strength at 120,000 men. Assuming that there was still danger that Jackson might come upon our left with a large force, and that Lee had proven strong enough without Jackson to repulse three corps on our right and right center, McClellan might have regarded his own army as divided also for the purpose of meeting both opponents, and his cavalry would have been upon the flank of the part with which he was attacking Lee; Porter would have been in position to help either part in an extremity, or to cover a retreat, and Burnside would have been the only subordinate available to check Lee's apparent success. Will any other hypothesis intelligibly account for McClellan's dispositions and orders? The error in the above assumption would be that McClellan estimated Lee's troops at nearly double their actual numbers, and that what was taken for proof of Lee's superiority in force on the field was a series of partial reverses which resulted directly from the piecemeal and disjointed way in which McClellan's morning attacks had been made.

The same explanation is the most satisfactory one that I can give for the inaction of Thursday, the 18th of September. Could McClellan have known the desperate condition of most of Lee's brigades he would have known that his own were in much better case, badly as they had suffered. I do not doubt that most of his subordinates discouraged the resumption of the attack, for the rooted belief in Lee's preponderance of numbers had been chronic in the army during the whole year. That belief was based upon the inconceivably mistaken reports of the secret service organization, accepted at headquarters, given to the War Department at Washington as a reason for incessant demands of reënforcements, and permeating downward through the whole organization till the error was accepted as truth by officers and men, and became a factor in their morale which can hardly be over-estimated. The result was that Lee retreated unmolested on the night of the 18th, and that what might have been a real and decisive success was a drawn battle in which our chief claim to victory was the possession of the field.

The Ninth Corps occupied its position on the heights west of the Antietam without further molestation, except an irritating picket firing, till the Confederate army retreated. But the position was one in which no shelter from the weather could be had; nor could any cooking be done; and the troops were short of rations. Late in the afternoon of Thursday, Morell's division of

GENERAL McCLELLAN AND PRESIDENT LINCOLN AT ANTIETAM. FROM A PHOTOGRAPH.

The Proclamation of Emancipation was published September 22d, three days after the withdrawal of Lee to Virginia, and was communicated to the army officially on September 24th.

On October 1st President Lincoln visited the army to see for himself if it was in no condition to pursue Lee into Virginia. General McClellan says in his general report: "His Excellency the President honored the Army of the Potomac with a visit, and remained several days, during which he went through the different encampments, reviewed the troops, and went over the battle-fields of South Mountain and Antietam. I had the opportunity during this visit to describe to him the operations of the army since the time it left Washington, and gave him my reasons for not following the enemy after he crossed the Potomac." In "McClellan's Own Story" he says that the President "more than once assured me that he was fully satisfied with my whole course from the beginning; that the only fault he could possibly find was, that I was too prone to be sure that everything was ready before acting, but that my actions were all right when I started. I said to him that I thought a few experiments with those who acted before they were ready would probably convince him that in the end I consumed less time than they did."

After the President's return to Washington, October 5th, Halleck telegraphed to McClellan under date of October 6th: "The President directs that you cross the Potomac and give battle to the enemy or drive him south," etc.

On October 7th McClellan, in "General Orders No. 163," referred to the Proclamation of Emancipation. He warned the army of the danger to military discipline of heated political discussions, and reminded them that the "remedy for political errors, if any are committed, is to be found only in the action of the people at the polls." On October 5th General McClellan had said, in a letter to his wife [see "McClellan's Own Story," p. 655], "Mr. Aspinwall [W. H., of New York] is decidedly of the opinion that it is my duty to submit to the President's proclamation and quietly continue doing my duty as a soldier. I presume he is right, and am at least sure that he is honest in his opinion. I shall surely give his views full consideration."— EDITORS.

Porter's corps was ordered to report to Burnside to relieve the picket line and some of the regiments in the most exposed position. One brigade was sent over the Antietam for this purpose, ⚓ and a few of the Ninth Corps regiments were enabled to withdraw far enough to cook some rations of which they had been in need for twenty-four hours. Harland's brigade of Rodman's division had been taken to the east side of the stream on the evening of the 17th to be reorganized.

⚓ Porter in his report says that Morell took the place of the whole Ninth Corps. In this he is entirely mistaken, as the reports from Morell's division show.—J. D. C.

## WITH BURNSIDE AT ANTIETAM. ☆

BY DAVID L. THOMPSON, CO. G, 9TH N. Y. VOLS.

ON THE LINE OF A SCATTERED FENCE AT ANTIETAM. FROM A PHOTOGRAPH.

At Antietam our corps — the Ninth, under Burnside — was on the extreme left, opposite the stone bridge. Our brigade stole into position about half-past 10 o'clock on the night of the 16th. No lights were permitted, and all conversation was carried on in whispers. As the regiment was moving past the 103d New York to get to its place, there occurred, on a small scale and without serious results, one of those unaccountable panics often noticed in crowds, by which each man, however brave individually, merges his individuality for the moment, and surrenders to an utterly causeless fear. When everything was at its darkest and stealthiest one of the 103d stumbled over the regimental dog, and, in trying to avoid treading on it, staggered against a stack of muskets and knocked them over. The giving way of the two or three men upon whom they fell was communicated to others in a sort of wave movement of constantly increasing magnitude, reënforced by the ever-present apprehension of attack, till two regiments were in confusion. In a few seconds order was restored, and we went on to our place in the line — a field of thin corn sloping toward the creek, where we sat down on the plowed ground and watched for a while the dull glare on the sky of the Confederate campfires behind the hills. We were hungry, of course, but, as no fires were allowed, we could only mix our ground coffee and sugar in our hands and eat them dry. I think we were the more easily inclined to this crude disposal of our rations from a feeling that for many of us the need of drawing them would cease forever with the following day.

All through the evening the shifting and placing had gone on, the moving masses being dimly descried in the strange half lights of earth and sky. There was something weirdly impressive yet unreal in the gradual drawing together of those whispering armies under cover of the night — something of awe and dread, as always in the secret preparation for momentous deeds. By 11 o'clock the whole line, four miles or more in length, was sleeping, each corps apprised of its appointed task, each battery in place.

It is astonishing how soon, and by what slight causes, regularity of formation and movement are lost in actual battle. Disintegration begins with the first shot. To the book-soldier all order seems destroyed, months of drill apparently going for nothing in a few minutes. Next after the most powerful factor in this derangement — the enemy — come natural obstacles and the inequalities of the ground. One of the commonest is a patch of trees. An advancing line lags there inevitably, the rest of the line swinging around insensibly, with the view of keeping the alignment, and so losing direction. The struggle for the possession of such a point is sure to be persistent. Wounded men crawl to a wood for shelter, broken troops re-form behind it, a battery planted in its edge will stick there after other parts of the line have given way. Often a slight rise of ground in an open field, not noticeable a thousand yards away, becomes, in the keep of a stubborn regiment, a powerful head-land against which the waves of battle roll and break, requiring new dispositions and much time to clear it. A stronger fortress than a casual railroad embankment often proves, it would be difficult to find; and as for a sunken road, what possibilities of victory or disaster lie in that obstruction, let Waterloo and Fredericksburg bear witness.

At Antietam it was a low, rocky ledge, prefaced by a corn-field. There were woods, too, and knolls, and there were other corn-fields; but the student of that battle knows one corn-field only — *the* corn-field, now historic, lying a quarter of a mile north of Dunker Church, and east of and bordering the Hagerstown road. About it and across it, to and fro, the waves of battle swung almost from the first, till by 10 o'clock in the

☆ See p. 556.—EDITORS.

morning, when the struggle was over, hundreds of men lay dead among its peaceful blades.

While these things were happening on the right, the left was not without its excitement. A Confederate battery discovered our position in our corn-field, as soon as it was light enough to see, and began to shell us. As the range became better we were moved back and ordered to boil coffee in the protection of a hollow. The general plan of battle appears to have been to break through the Confederate left, following up the advantage with a constantly increasing force, sweep him away from the fords, and so crowd his whole army down into the narrow peninsula formed by the Potomac and Antietam Creek. Even the non-military eye, however, can see that the tendency of such a plan would be to bring the two armies upon concentric arcs, the inner and shorter of which must be held by the enemy, affording him the opportunity for reënforcement by interior lines — an immense advantage only to be counteracted by the utmost activity on our part, who must attack vigorously where attacking at all, and where not, imminently threaten. Certainly there was no imminence in the threat of our center or left — none whatever of the left, only a vague consciousness of whose existence even seems to have been in the enemy's mind, for he flouted us all the morning with hardly more than a meager skirmish line, while his coming troops, as fast as they arrived upon the ground, were sent off to the Dunker Church.

So the morning wore away, and the fighting on the right ceased entirely. That was fresh anxiety — the scales were turning perhaps, but which way? About noon the battle began afresh. This must have been Franklin's men of the Sixth Corps, for the firing was nearer, and they came up behind the center. Suddenly a stir beginning far up on the right, and running like a wave along the line, brought the regiment to its feet. A silence fell on every one at once, for each felt that the momentous "now" had come. Just as we started I saw, with a little shock, a line-officer take out his watch to note the hour, as though the affair beyond the creek were a business appointment which he was going to keep.

When we reached the brow of the hill the fringe of trees along the creek screened the fighting entirely, and we were deployed as skirmishers under their cover. We sat there two hours. All that time the rest of the corps had been moving over the stone bridge and going into position on the other side of the creek. Then we were ordered over at a ford which had been found below the bridge, where the water was waist-deep. One man was shot in mid-stream. At the foot of the slope on the opposite side the line was formed and we moved up through the thin woods. Reaching the level we lay down behind a battery which seemed to have been disabled. There, if anywhere, I should have remembered that I was soaking wet from my waist down. So great was the excitement, however, that I have never been able to recall it. Here some of the men, going to the rear for water, discovered in the ashes of some hay-ricks which had been fired by our shells the charred remains of several Confederates. After long waiting it became noised along the line that we were to take a battery that was at work several hundred yards ahead on the top of a hill. This narrowed the field and brought us to consider the work before us more attentively.

Right across our front, two hundred feet or so away, ran a country road bordered on each side by a snake fence. Beyond this road stretched a plowed field several hundred feet in length, sloping up to the battery, which was hidden in a corn-field. A stone fence, breast-high, inclosed the field on the left, and behind it lay a regiment of Confederates, who would be directly on our flank if we should attempt the slope. The prospect was far from encouraging, but the order came to get ready for the attempt.

Our knapsacks were left on the ground behind us. At the word a rush was made for the fences. The line was so disordered by the time the second fence was passed that we hurried forward to a shallow undulation a few feet ahead, and lay down among the furrows to re-form, doing so by crawling up into line. A hundred feet or so ahead was a similar undulation to which we ran for a second shelter. The battery, which at first had not seemed to notice us, now, apprised of its danger, opened fire upon us. We were getting ready now for the charge proper, but were still lying on our faces. Lieutenant-Colonel Kimball was ramping up and down the line. The discreet regiment behind the fence was silent. Now and then a bullet from them cut the air over our heads, but generally they were reserving their fire for that better shot which they knew they would get in a few minutes. The battery, however, whose shots at first went over our heads, had depressed its guns so as to shave the surface of the ground. Its fire was beginning to tell. I remember looking behind and seeing an officer riding diagonally across the field — a most inviting target — instinctively bending his head down over his horse's neck, as though he were riding through driving rain. While my eye was on him I saw, between me and him, a rolled overcoat with its straps on bound into the air and fall among the furrows. One of the enemy's grape-shot had plowed a groove in the skull of a young fellow and had cut his overcoat from his shoulders. He never stirred from his position, but lay there face downward — a dreadful spectacle. A moment after, I heard a man cursing a comrade for lying on him heavily. He was cursing a dying man. As the range grew better, the firing became more rapid, the situation desperate and exasperating to the last degree. Human nature was on the rack, and there burst forth from it the most vehement, terrible swearing I have ever heard. Certainly the joy of conflict was not ours that day. The suspense was only for a moment, however, for the order to charge came just after. Whether the regiment was thrown into disorder or not, I never knew. I only remember that as we rose and started all the fire that had been held back so long was loosed. In a second the air was full of the hiss of bullets and the hurtle of grape-shot. The mental strain was so great that I saw at that moment the singular effect mentioned, I think, in the life of Goethe on a similar occasion — the whole landscape for an instant turned slightly red. I see again, as I saw it then in a flash, a man just in front of me drop his musket and throw up his hands, stung into vigorous swearing by a bullet behind the ear. Many men fell going up the hill, but it seemed to be all over in a moment, and I found myself passing a hollow where a dozen wounded men lay —

MAJOR-GENERAL JOHN G. WALKER, C. S. A.
FROM A PHOTOGRAPH.

among them our sergeant-major, who was calling me to come down. He had caught sight of the blanket rolled across my back, and called me to unroll it and help to carry from the field one of our wounded lieutenants.

When I returned from obeying this summons the regiment (?) was not to be seen. It had gone in on the run, what there was left of it, and had disappeared in the corn-field about the battery. There was nothing to do but lie there and await developments. Nearly all the men in the hollow were wounded, one man — a recruit named Devlin, I think — frightfully so, his arm being cut short off. He lived a few minutes only. All were calling for water, of course, but none was to be had. We lay there till dusk, — perhaps an hour, when the fighting ceased. During that hour, while the bullets snipped the leaves from a young locust-tree growing at the edge of the hollow and powdered us with the fragments, we had time to speculate on many things — among others, on the impatience with which men clamor, in dull times, to be led into a fight. We heard all through the war that the army "was eager to be led against the enemy." It must have been so, for truthful correspondents said so, and editors confirmed it. But when you came to hunt for this particular itch, it was always the next regiment that had it. The truth is, when bullets are whacking against tree-trunks and solid shot are cracking skulls like egg-shells, the consuming passion in the breast of the average man is to get out of the way. Between the physical fear of going forward and the moral fear of turning back, there is a predicament of exceptional awkwardness from which a hidden hole in the ground would be a wonderfully welcome outlet.

Night fell, preventing further struggle. Of 600 men of the regiment who crossed the creek at 3 o'clock that afternoon, 45 were killed and 176 wounded. The Confederates held possession of that part of the field over which we had moved, and just after dusk they sent out detachments to collect arms and bring in prisoners. When they came to our hollow all the unwounded and slightly wounded there were marched to the rear — prisoners of the 15th Georgia. We slept on the ground that night without protection of any kind; for, with a recklessness quite common throughout the war, we had thrown away every incumbrance on going into the fight. The weather, however, was warm and pleasant, and there was little discomfort.

The next morning we were marched — about six hundred of us, fragments of a dozen different commands — to the Potomac, passing through Sharpsburg. We crossed the Potomac by the Shepherdstown ford, and bivouacked in the yard of a house near the river, remaining there all day. The next morning (the 19th) shells began to come from over the river, and we were started on the road to Richmond with a mixed guard of cavalry and infantry. When we reached Winchester we were quartered for a night in the court-house yard, where we were beset by a motley crew who were eager to exchange the produce of the region for greenbacks.

On the road between Shepherdstown and Winchester we fell in with the Maryland Battalion — a meeting I have always remembered with pleasure. They were marching to the front by companies, spaced apart about 300 or 400 feet. We were an ungainly, draggled lot, about as far removed as well could be from any claim to ceremonious courtesy; yet each company, as it passed, gave us the military salute of shouldered arms. They were noticeable, at that early stage of the war, as the only organization we saw that wore the regulation Confederate gray, all other troops having assumed a sort of revised regulation uniform of homespun butternut — a significant witness, we thought, to the efficacy of the blockade.

From Winchester we were marched to Staunton, where we were put on board cattle-cars and forwarded at night, by way of Gordonsville, to Richmond, where we entered Libby Prison. We were not treated with special severity, for Libby was not at that time the hissing it afterward became. Our time there, also, was not long. Only nine days after we entered it we were sent away, going by steamer to Camp Parole, at Annapolis. From that place I went home without ceremony, reporting my address to my company officers. Three weeks afterward they advised me that I was exchanged — which meant that I was again, legally and technically, food for powder.

# THE INVASION OF MARYLAND.

### BY JAMES LONGSTREET, LIEUTENANT-GENERAL, C. S. A.

WHEN the Second Bull Run campaign closed we had the most brilliant prospects the Confederates ever had. We then possessed an army which, had it been kept together, the Federals would never have dared attack. With such a splendid victory behind us, and such bright prospects ahead, the question arose as to whether or not we should go into Maryland. General Lee, on account of our short supplies, hesitated a little, but I reminded him of my experience in Mexico, where sometimes we were obliged to live two or three days on green corn. I told him we could not starve at that season of the year so long as the fields were loaded with "roasting ears." Finally he determined to go on, and accordingly crossed the river and went to Frederick City. On the 6th of September some of our cavalry, moving toward Harper's Ferry, became engaged with some of the Federal artillery near there. General Lee proposed that I should organize a force, and surround the garrison and capture it. I objected, and urged that our troops were worn with marching and were on short rations, and that it would be a bad idea to divide our forces while we were in the enemy's country, where he could get information, in six or eight hours, of any movement we might make. The Federal army, though beaten at the Second Manassas, was not disorganized, and it would certainly come out to look for us, and we should guard against being caught in such a condition. Our army consisted of a superior quality of soldiers, but it was in no condition to divide in the enemy's country. I urged that we should keep it well in hand, recruit our strength, and get up supplies, and then we could do anything we pleased. General Lee made no reply to this, and I supposed the Harper's Ferry scheme was abandoned. A day or two after we had reached Frederick City, I went up to General Lee's tent and found the front walls closed. I inquired for the general, and he, recognizing my voice, asked me to come in. I went in and found Jackson there. The two were discussing the move against Harper's Ferry, both heartily approving it. They had gone so far that it seemed useless for me to offer any further opposition, and I only suggested that Lee should use his entire army in the move instead of sending off a large portion of it to Hagerstown as he intended to do. General Lee so far changed the wording of his order as to require me to halt at Boonsboro' with General D. H. Hill; Jackson being ordered to Harper's Ferry *via* Bolivar Heights, on the south side; McLaws by the Maryland Heights on the north, and Walker, *via* Loudoun Heights, from the south-east. This was afterward changed, and I was sent on to Hagerstown, leaving D. H. Hill alone at South Mountain.

The movement against Harper's Ferry began on the 10th. Jackson made a wide, sweeping march around the Ferry, passing the Potomac at Williamsport, and moving from there on toward Martinsburg, and turning thence upon Harper's Ferry to make his attack by Bolivar Heights. McLaws made a hurried march to reach Maryland Heights before Jackson could get in position, and succeeded in doing so. With Maryland Heights in our possession the Federals could not hold their position there. McLaws put 200 or 300 men to each piece of his artillery and carried it up the heights, and was in position when Jackson came on the heights opposite. Simultaneously Walker appeared upon Loudoun Heights, south of the Potomac and east of the Shenandoah, thus completing the combination against the Federal garrison. The surrender of the Ferry and the twelve thousand Federal troops there was a matter of only a short time.

If the Confederates had been able to stop with that, they might have been well contented with their month's campaign. They had had a series of successes and no defeats; but the division of the army to make this attack on Harper's Ferry was a fatal error, as the subsequent events showed.

While a part of the army had gone toward Harper's Ferry I had moved up to Hagerstown. In the meantime Pope had been relieved and McClellan was in command of the army, and with ninety thousand refreshed troops was marching forth to avenge the Second Manassas. The situation was a very serious one for us. McClellan was close upon us. As we moved out of Frederick he came on and occupied that place, and there he came across a lost copy of the order assigning position to the several commands in the Harper's Ferry move.

This "lost order" has been the subject of much severe comment by Virginians who have written of the war. It was addressed to D. H. Hill, and they charged that its loss was due to him, and that the failure of the campaign was the result of the lost order. As General Hill has proved that he never received the order at his headquarters it must have been lost by some one else.↓ Ordinarily, upon getting possession of such an order, the adversary

---

↓ See General Hill's statement on p. 570, and General Colgrove's on p. 603. The following is the text of the "lost order" as quoted by General McClellan in his official report:

"SPECIAL ORDERS, } HEADQUARTERS, ARMY
NO. 191.          }    OF NORTHERN VIRGINIA,
                          September 9th, 1862.

"The army will resume its march to-morrow, taking the Hagerstown road. General Jackson's command will form the advance, and after passing Middletown, with such portions as he may select, take the route toward Sharpsburg, cross the Potomac at the most convenient point, and by Friday night take possession of the Baltimore and Ohio Railroad, capture such of the enemy as may be at Martinsburg, and intercept such as may attempt to escape from Harper's Ferry.

"General Longstreet's command will pursue the same road as far as Boonsboro', where it will halt with the reserve, supply, and baggage trains of the army.

"General McLaws, with his own division and that of General R. H. Anderson, will follow General Longstreet; on reaching Middletown he will take the route to Harper's Ferry, and by Friday morning possess himself of the Maryland Heights and endeavor to capture the enemy at Harper's Ferry and vicinity.

"General Walker, with his division after accomplishing the object in which he is now engaged, will cross the Potomac at Check's ford, ascend its right bank to Lovettsville, take possession of Loudoun Heights, if practicable, by Friday morning, Keyes's ford on his left, and the road between the end of the mountain and the Potomac on his right. He will, as far as practicable,

coöperate with General McLaws and General Jackson in intercepting the retreat of the enemy.

"General D. H. Hill's division will form the rear-guard of the army, pursuing the road taken by the main body. The reserve artillery, ordnance, and supply trains, etc., will precede General Hill.

"General Stuart will detach a squadron of cavalry to accompany the commands of Generals Longstreet, Jackson, and McLaws, and, with the main body of the cavalry, will cover the route of the army and bring up all stragglers that may have been left behind.

"The commands of Generals Jackson, McLaws, and Walker, after accomplishing the objects for which they have been detached, will join the main body of the army at Boonsboro' or Hagerstown.

"Each regiment on the march will habitually carry its axes in the regimental ordnance-wagons, for use of the men at their encampments, to procure wood, etc. By command of General R. E. Lee.

"R. H. CHILTON, Assistant Adjutant-General.
"MAJOR-GENERAL D. H. HILL, Commanding Division."

Comparison of the above with the copy of the order as printed among the Confederate Correspondence ("Official Records," Volume XIX., Part II., p. 603) shows that the latter contains two paragraphs, omitted above. In the first paragraph the officers and men of Lee's army are prohibited from visiting Fredericktown except on written permission; and in the second paragraph directions are given for the transportation of the sick and disabled to Winchester.—EDITORS.

would take it as a *ruse de guerre*, but it seems that General McClellan gave it his confidence, and made his dispositions accordingly. He planned his attack upon D. H. Hill under the impression that I was there with 12 brigades, 9 of which were really at Hagerstown, while R. H. Anderson's division was on Maryland Heights with General McLaws. Had McClellan exercised due diligence in seeking information from his own resources, he would have known better the situation at South Mountain and could have enveloped General D. H. Hill's division on the afternoon of the 13th, or early on the morning of the 14th, and then

THE OLD LUTHERAN CHURCH, SHARPSBURG. FROM A WAR-TIME PHOTOGRAPH.

The church stands at the east end of the village, on Main street, and was a Federal hospital after the battle. Burnside's skirmishers gained a hold in the first cross-street below the church, where there was considerable fighting. On the hill in the extreme distance Main street becomes the Shepherdstown road, by which the Confederates retreated.—EDITORS.

turned upon McLaws at Maryland Heights, before I could have reached either point. As it was, McClellan, after finding the order, moved with more confidence on toward South Mountain, where D. H. Hill was stationed as a Confederate rear-guard with five thousand men under his command. As I have stated, my command was at Hagerstown, thirteen miles farther on. General Lee was with me, and on the night of the 13th we received information that McClellan was at the foot of South Mountain with his great army. General Lee ordered me to march back to the mountain early the next morning. I suggested that, instead of meeting McClellan there, we withdraw Hill and unite my forces and Hill's at Sharpsburg, at the same time explaining that Sharpsburg was a strong defensive position from which we could strike the flank or rear of any force that might be sent to the relief of Harper's Ferry. I endeavored to show him that by making a forced march to Hill my troops would be in an exhausted condition and could not make a proper battle. Lee listened patiently enough, but did not change his plans, and directed that I should go back the next day and make a stand at the mountain. After lying down, my mind was still on the battle of the next day, and I was so impressed with the thought that it would be impossible for us to do anything at South Mountain with the fragments of a worn and exhausted army, that I rose and, striking a light, wrote a note to General Lee, urging him to order Hill away and concentrate at Sharpsburg. To that note I got no answer, and the next morning I marched as directed, leaving General Toombs, as ordered by General Lee, at Hagerstown to guard our trains and supplies.

We marched as hurriedly as we could over a hot and dusty road, and reached the mountain about 3 o'clock in the afternoon, with the troops much scattered and worn. In riding up the mountain to join General Hill I discovered that everything was in such disjointed condition that it would be impossible for my troops and Hill's to hold the mountain against such forces as McClellan had there, and wrote a note to General Lee, in which I stated that fact, and cautioned him to make his arrangements to retire that night. We got as many troops up as we could, and by putting in detachments here and there managed to hold McClellan in check until night, when Lee ordered the withdrawal to Sharpsburg.

On the afternoon of the 15th of September my command and Hill's crossed the Antietam Creek, and took position in front of Sharpsburg, my command filing into position on the right of the Sharpsburg and Boonsboro' turnpike, and D. H. Hill's division on the left. Soon after getting into position we found our left, at Dunker Church, the weak point, and Hood, with two brigades, was changed from my right to guard this point, leaving General D. H. Hill between the parts of my command.

That night, after we heard of the fall of Harper's Ferry, General Lee ordered Stonewall Jackson to march to Sharpsburg as rapidly as he could come. Then it was that we should have retired from Sharpsburg and gone to the Virginia side of the Potomac.

The moral effect of our move into Maryland had been lost by our discomfiture at South Mountain, and it was then evident we could not hope to concentrate

LEE'S HEADQUARTERS IN SHARPSBURG. FROM A PHOTOGRAPH.

This house, which was the residence of Jacob H. Grove, is noted in Sharpsburg as the place where Lee held a conference with Longstreet and D. H. Hill. But Lee's headquarters tents were pitched in a small grove on the right of the Shepherdstown road, just outside the town.—EDITORS.

SOUTH-EASTERN STRETCH OF THE SUNKEN ROAD, OR "BLOODY LANE." [SEE MAP, P. 636.] FROM A PHOTOGRAPH TAKEN IN 1885.

in time to do more than make a respectable retreat, whereas by retiring before the battle we could have claimed a very successful campaign.

On the forenoon of the 15th, the blue uniforms of the Federals appeared among the trees that crowned the heights on the eastern bank of the Antietam. The number increased, and larger and larger grew the field of blue until it seemed to stretch as far as the eye could see, and from the tops of the mountains down to the edges of the stream gathered the great army of McClellan. It was an awe-inspiring spectacle as this grand force settled down in sight of the Confederates, then shattered by battles and scattered by long and tiresome marches. On the 16th Jackson came and took position with part of his command on my left. Before night the Federals attacked my left and gave us a severe fight, principally against Hood's division, but we drove them back, holding well our ground. After nightfall Hood was relieved from the position on the left, ordered to replenish his ammunition, and be ready to resume his first position on my right in the morning. General Jackson's forces, who relieved Hood, were extended to our left, reaching well back toward the Potomac, where most of our cavalry was. Toombs had joined us with two of his regiments, and was placed as guard on the bridge on my right. Hooker, who had thrown his corps against my left in the afternoon, was reënforced by the corps of Sumner and Mansfield. Sykes's division was also drawn into position for the impending battle. Burnside was over against my right, threatening the passage of the Antietam at that point. On the morning of the 17th the Federals were in good position along the Antietam, stretching up and down and across it to our left for three miles. They had a good position for their guns, which were of the most approved make and metal. Our position overcrowned theirs a little, but our guns were inferior and our ammunition was very imperfect.

THE SUNKEN ROAD, OR "BLOODY LANE."
FROM A PHOTOGRAPH TAKEN SINCE THE WAR.

This view is from the second bend in the lane, looking toward the Hagerstown pike, the Dunker Church wood appearing in the background. In the foreground Richardson crossed to the left into the cornfield near Piper's house. The house in the middleground, erected since the war, marks the scene of French's hard fight after passing Roulette's house.—EDITORS.

Back of McClellan's line was a high ridge upon which was his signal station overlooking every point of our field. D. R. Jones's brigades of my command deployed on the right of the Sharpsburg pike, while Hood's brigades awaited orders. D. H. Hill was on the left extending toward the Hagerstown-Sharpsburg pike, and Jackson extended out from Hill's left toward the Potomac. The battle opened heavily with the attacks of the corps of Hooker, Mansfield, and Sumner against our left center, which consisted of Jackson's right and D. H. Hill's left. So severe and persistent were these attacks that I was obliged to send Hood to support our center. The Federals forced us back a little, however, and held this part of our position to the end of the day's work. With new troops and renewed efforts McClellan continued his attacks upon this point from time to time, while he brought his forces to bear against other points. The line swayed forward and back like a rope exposed to rushing currents. A force too heavy to be withstood would strike and drive in a weak point till we could collect a few fragments, and in turn force back the advance till our lost ground was recovered. A heroic effort was made by D. H. Hill, who collected some fragments and led a charge to drive back and recover our lost ground at the center. He soon found that his little band was too much exposed on its left flank and was obliged to abandon the attempt. Thus the battle ebbed and flowed with terrific slaughter on both sides.

The Federals fought with wonderful bravery and the Confederates clung to their ground with heroic courage as hour after hour they were mown down like grass. The fresh troops of McClellan literally tore into shreds the already ragged army of Lee, but the Confederates never gave back.

I remember at one time they were surging up against us with fearful

THE SUNKEN ROAD, LOOKING EAST FROM ROULETTE'S LANE. FROM A PHOTOGRAPH TAKEN IN 1885.

numbers. I was occupying the left over by Hood, whose ammunition gave out. He retired to get a fresh supply. Soon after the Federals moved up against us in great masses.

We were under the crest of a hill occupying a position that ought to have been held by from four to six brigades. The only troops there were Cooke's regiment of North Carolina infantry, and they were without a cartridge. As I rode along the line with my staff I saw two pieces of the Washington Artillery (Miller's battery), but there were not enough men to man them. The gunners had been either killed or wounded. This was a fearful situation for the Confederate center. I put my staff-officers to the guns while I held their horses. It was easy to see that if the Federals broke through our line there, the Confederate army would be cut in two and probably destroyed, for we were already

CONFEDERATE DEAD (OF D. H. HILL'S DIVISION) IN THE SUNKEN ROAD.
FROM A PHOTOGRAPH.

badly whipped and were only holding our ground by sheer force of desperation. Cooke sent me word that his ammunition was out. I replied that he must hold his position as long as he had a man left. He responded that he would show his colors as long as there was a man alive to hold them up. We loaded up our little guns with canister and sent a rattle of hail into the Federals as they came up over the crest of the hill.

That little battery shot harder and faster, with a sort of human energy, as though it realized that it was to hold the thousands of Federals at bay or the battle was lost. So warm was the reception we gave them that they dodged back behind the crest of the hill. We sought to make them believe we had many batteries before them. As the Federals would come up they would see the colors of the North Carolina regiment waving placidly and then would receive a shower of canister. We made it lively while it lasted. In the meantime General Chilton, General Lee's chief of staff, made his way to me and asked, "Where are the troops you are holding your line with?" I pointed to my two pieces and to Cooke's regiment, and replied, "There they are; but that regiment hasn't a cartridge."

Chilton's eyes popped as though they would come out of his head; he struck spurs to his horse and away he went to General Lee. I suppose he made some remarkable report, although I did not see General Lee again until night. After a little a shot came across the Federal front, plowing the ground in a parallel line. Another and another, each nearer and nearer their line. This enfilade fire, so distressing to soldiers, was from a battery on D. H. Hill's line, and it soon beat back the attacking column.

Meanwhile, R. H. Anderson and Hood came to our support and gave us more confidence. It was a little while only until another assault was made against D. H. Hill, and extending far over toward our left, where McLaws and Walker were supporting Jackson. In this desperate effort the lines seemed to swing back and forth for many minutes, but at last they settled down to their respective positions, the Confederates holding with a desperation which seemed to say, "We are here to die."

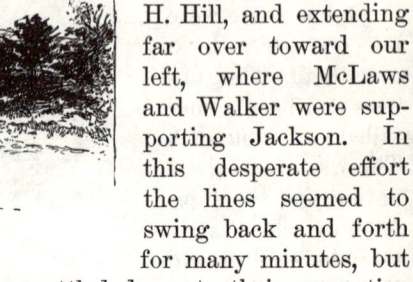

Meantime General Lee was over toward our right, where Burnside was trying to cross to the attack. Toombs, who had been assigned as guard at that point, did handsome service. His troops were footsore and worn from marching, and he had only four hundred men to meet the Ninth Corps. The little band fought bravely, but the Federals were pressing them slowly back. The delay that Toombs caused saved that part of the battle, however, for at the last moment A. P. Hill came in to reënforce him, and D. H. Hill discovered a good place for a battery and opened with it. Thus the Confederates were enabled to drive the Federals back, and when night settled down the army of Lee was still in possession of the field. But it was dearly bought, for thousands of brave soldiers were dead on the field and many gallant commands were torn as a forest in a cyclone. It was heart-rending to see how Lee's army had been slashed by the day's fighting.

ROULETTE'S FARM.

1.—View of William Roulette's farm-house. 2.— Roulette's spring-house, in which Confederate prisoners were confined during the battle. 3.— Roulette's spring, a copious fountain which refreshed many thirsty soldiers of both armies.

Nearly one-fourth of the troops who went into the battle were killed or wounded. We were so badly crushed that at the close of the day ten thousand fresh troops could have come in and taken Lee's army and everything it had. But McClellan did not know it, and [apparently] feared, when Burnside was pressed back, that Sharpsburg was a Confederate victory, and that he would have to retire. As it was, when night settled down both armies were content to stay where they were.

During the progress of the battle of Sharpsburg General Lee and I were riding along my line and D. H. Hill's, when we received a report of movements of the enemy and started up the ridge to make a reconnoissance. General Lee and I dismounted, but Hill declined to do so. I said to Hill, "If you insist on riding up there and drawing the fire, give us a little interval so that we may not be in the line of the fire when they open upon you." General Lee and I stood on the top of the crest with our glasses, looking at the movements of the Federals on the rear left. After a moment I turned my glass to the right— the Federal left. As I did so, I noticed a puff of white smoke from the mouth of a cannon. "There is a shot for you," I said to General Hill. The gunner was a mile away, and the cannon-shot came whisking through the air for three or four seconds and took off the front legs of the horse that Hill sat on and let the animal down upon his stumps. The horse's head was

AFTER THE BATTLE—POSITION OF THE CONFEDERATE BATTERIES IN FRONT OF DUNKER CHURCH. FROM A PHOTOGRAPH.

so low and his croup so high that Hill was in a most ludicrous position. With one foot in the stirrup he made several efforts to get the other leg over the croup, but failed. Finally we prevailed upon him to try the other end of the horse, and he got down. He had a third horse shot under him before the close of the battle. That shot at Hill was the second best shot I ever saw. The best was at Yorktown. There a Federal officer came out in front of our line, and sitting down to his little platting table began to make a map. One of our officers carefully sighted a gun, touched it off, and dropped a shell into the hands of the man at the little table.⁋

When the battle was over and night was gathering, I started to Lee's headquarters to make my report. In going through the town I passed a house that had been set afire and was still burning. The family was in great distress, and I stopped to do what I could for them. By that I was detained until after the other officers had reached headquarters and made their reports.

⁋ Major Alfred A. Woodhull, Surgeon, U. S. A., wrote from David's Island, N. Y., July 16th, 1886:

"General Longstreet's 'best shot' was undoubtedly the shell that shattered the plane table that First Lieutenant Orlando G. Wagner, Topographical Engineer, was using in front of Yorktown, when he was mortally wounded, precisely as described. He died April 21st, 1862.

"Early on the morning of September 17th, 1862 (about 8 or 9 o'clock), I was standing near the guns of Captain Stephen H. Weed, 5th Artillery, when a small group came in sight, directly in our front, about a mile away. There was no firing of any importance at that time on our left, and Captain Weed, who was a superb artillerist himself, aimed and fired at the single mounted man and struck the horse. I witnessed the shot, and have no doubt it was the one General Longstreet commemorates as the 'second best.' My recollection is that the horse was gray, and I had the impression that the party was somewhat to the left (south) of the turnpike. General Longstreet kindly writes me that he cannot now recall the hour, but that there was little firing at the time, and that the place 'was about twenty feet from the Boonsboro' pike, north.'"— EDITORS.

672                    THE INVASION OF MARYLAND.

My delay caused some apprehension on the part of General Lee that I had been hurt; in fact, such a report had been sent him. When I rode up and dismounted he seemed much relieved, and, coming to me very hurriedly for one of his dignified manner, threw his arms upon my shoulders and said:

"Here is my old war-horse at last."

When all the reports were in, General Lee decided that he would not be prepared the next day for offensive battle, and would prepare only for defense, as we had been doing.

The next day [the 18th] the Federals failed to advance, and both armies remained in position. During the day some of the Federals came over under a flag of truce to look after their dead and wounded. The following night we withdrew, passing the Potomac with our entire army. After we had crossed, the Federals made a show of pursuit, and a force of about fifteen hundred crossed the river and gave a considerable amount of trouble to the command under Pendleton. A. P. Hill was sent back with his division, and attacked the Federals who had crossed the river in pursuit of us. His lines extended beyond theirs, and he drove them back in great confusion. Some sprang over the bluffs of the river and were killed; some were drowned and others were shot.↓

Proceeding on our march, we went to Bunker Hill, where we remained for several days. A report was made of a Federal advance, but it turned out to be only a party of cavalry and amounted to nothing. As soon as the cavalry

FIELD-HOSPITALS OF FRENCH'S DIVISION AT ANTIETAM.
FROM A PHOTOGRAPH.

These pictures, according to a letter received by the editors from Dr. Samuel Sexton (8th Ohio), represent two field-hospitals established for the use of French's division at Antietam. The upper one was in charge of Dr. Sexton, who sent back the wounded men under his care at the front to this place during the battle, and afterward organized a hospital for all of the wounded soldiers found there,— utilizing for that purpose two or three barns, and erecting, besides, a number of shelters (shown in the cut) out of Virginia split-rails, set up on end in two parallel rows, meeting at the top, where they were secured. The sheds thus made were afterward thatched with straw, and could accommodate about 10 or 15 men each.

The lower picture shows an adjacent hospital for wounded Confederate prisoners, which was in charge of Dr. Anson Hurd of the 14th Indiana, who is seen standing on the right.

↓ Major Alfred A. Woodhull, Surgeon, U. S. A., wrote from David's Island, N. Y., July 21st, 1886, concerning this movement:

"Early Saturday, September 20th, Major Charles S. Lovell, 10th Infantry, crossed to reconnoiter with the Second Brigade (regulars), of Sykes's division, and other troops followed. On our ascent to the plateau we passed some abandoned artillery, but met with no opposition until nearly a mile from the bank, where a long infantry

BLACKFORD'S, OR BOTELER'S, FORD, FROM THE MARYLAND SIDE. FROM A RECENT PHOTOGRAPH.

This picture, taken from the tow-path of the Chesapeake and Ohio Canal, shows the ford below Shepherdstown by which Lee's army retreated after Antietam, the cliff on the Virginia side being the scene of the disaster to the 118th Pennsylvania, or Corn Exchange, regiment. When Porter's corps arrived at the Potomac in pursuit, on September 19th, Confederate artillery on the cliffs disputed the passage. A small Union force, under General Griffin, moved across the river in face of a warm fire, and, scaling the heights, captured several pieces of artillery. This attacking party was recalled during the night. Next morning, the 20th, two brigades of Sykes's division crossed and gained the heights on the left by the cement mill, while one brigade of Morell's division advanced to the right toward Shepherdstown and ascended the heights by way of the ravine. The 118th Pennsylvania formed beyond the crest and abreast of the dam. Soon the Confederates attacked with spirit. The Union forces were withdrawn without much loss, except to the 118th Pennsylvania, which was a new regiment, numbering 737 men, and had been armed, as it proved, with defective rifles. They made a stout resistance, until ordered to retreat, when most of the men fled down the precipitous face of the bluff and thence across the river, some crossing on the dam, the top of which was then dry. They were also under fire in crossing; and out of 361 in killed, wounded, and captured at this place, the 118th Pennsylvania lost 269.

retired we moved back and camped around Winchester, where we remained until some time in October. Our stragglers continued to come in until November, which shows how many we had lost by severe marches.

The great mistake of the campaign was the division of Lee's army. If General Lee had kept his forces together, he could not have suffered defeat.

line was confronted unexpectedly. Major Lovell had been informed that cavalry was to cross before us at daylight, but we were then found to be in advance, and the cavalry which was to feel the way was in our rear, and being useless was at once withdrawn. The overlapping size of the advancing force in front, its manifest effort to envelop our left flank as well, and the probability of its extension beyond our right, compelled an immediate return, which was effected with steadiness, while skirmishing. Infantry reënforcements that had crossed the river were simultaneously withdrawn, but on the right the 118th Pennsylvania, known as the "Corn Exchange" regiment, suffered severely, especially in one wing, where it was said at the time that there was a misapprehension of orders. When our men were in the stream there were dropping shots, but there was no direct infantry fire of importance. A fierce Union artillery fire was kept up to cover the retreat of our right, which indeed lost heavily. But there was no such slaughter as the Confederate reports announced (I think A. P. Hill put it at 3000, and said the Potomac was blue with the Yankee dead). Had the cavalry really been in advance, the reconnoissance could have been accomplished with comparative ease. I was a medical officer attached to the infantry, and, acting as an aide for Major Lovell, had opportunity to witness what is here stated.— EDITORS.

At Sharpsburg he had hardly 37,000 men,♭ who were in poor condition for battle, while McClellan had about 87,000, who were fresh and strong.

The next year, when on our way to Gettysburg, there was the same situation of affairs at Harper's Ferry, but we let it alone.

General Lee was not satisfied with the result of the Maryland campaign, and seemed inclined to attribute the failure to the Lost Dispatch; though I believe he was more inclined to attribute the loss of the dispatch to the fault of a courier or to other negligence than that of the officer to whom it was directed.

Our men came in so rapidly after the battle that renewed hope of gathering his army in great strength soon caused Lee to look for other and new prospects, and to lose sight of the lost campaign. But at Sharpsburg was sprung the keystone of the arch upon which the Confederate cause rested. Jackson was quite satisfied with the campaign, as the Virginia papers made him the hero of Harper's Ferry, although the greater danger was with McLaws, whose service was the severer and more important. Lee lost nearly 20,000 by straggling in this campaign,— almost twice as many as were captured at Harper's Ferry.

The battle casualties of Jackson's command from the Rappahannock to the Potomac, according to the "Official Records," were 4629, while mine, including those of R. H. Anderson's division, were 4725, making in all, 9354. That taken from the army of 55,000 at the Second Manassas left a force of 45,646 moving across the Potomac. To that number must be added the forces that joined us; namely, D. H. Hill with 5000, McLaws with 4000, and Walker with 2000. Thus Lee's army on entering Maryland was made up of nearly 57,000 men, exclusive of artillery and cavalry. As we had but 37,000 at Sharpsburg, our losses in the several engagements after we crossed the Potomac, *including stragglers*, reached nearly 20,000. Our casualties in the affairs of the Maryland campaign, including Sharpsburg, were 13,964. Estimating the casualties in the Maryland campaign preceding Sharpsburg at 2000, it will be seen that we lost at Sharpsburg 11,000 to 12,000. Only a glance at these figures is necessary to impress one with the number of those who were unable to stand the long and rapid marches, and fell by the wayside, viz., 8000 to 9000. The Virginians who have written of the war have often charged the loss of the Maryland campaign to "laggards." It is unkind to apply such a term to our soldiers, who were as patient, courageous, and chivalrous as any ever marshaled into phalanx. Many were just out of the hospitals, and many more were crippled by injuries received in battle. They were marching without sufficient food or clothing, with their muskets, ammunition, provisions, and in fact their all, packed upon their backs. They struggled along with bleeding feet, tramping rugged mountain roads through a heated season. Such soldiers should not be called "laggards" by their countrymen. Let them have their well-earned honors though the fame of others suffer thereby.

♭ This was Lee's estimate as stated to me at the time. It is much above the estimate of those who have since written of this campaign. Colonel Charles Marshall, in his evidence in the Fitz John Porter case, gives our forces at the Second Manassas on August 29th as 50,000, not including artillery or cavalry. R. H. Anderson joined me on the night of August 29th, with over 4000.— J. L.

Lee says officially that "Antietam was fought with less than 40,000 men on our side."— EDITORS.

RALLYING BEHIND THE TURNPIKE FENCE.

## SHARPSBURG.[‡]

### BY JOHN G. WALKER, MAJOR-GENERAL, C. S. A.

A LITTLE past the hour of noon on the 16th of September, 1862, General "Stonewall" Jackson and myself reached General Lee's headquarters at Sharpsburg and reported the arrival of our commands. I am thus particular in noting the hour of the arrival of my division for the reason that some writers have fallen into the error of mentioning my arrival as coincident with that of McLaws's division, which was some twenty-two hours later.

The thought of General Lee's perilous situation, with the Potomac River in his rear, confronting, with his small force, McClellan's vast army, had haunted me through the long hours of the night's march, and I expected to find General Lee anxious and careworn. Anxious enough, no doubt, he was; but there was nothing in his look or manner to indicate it. On the contrary, he was calm, dignified, and even cheerful. If he had had a well-equipped army of a hundred thousand veterans at his back, he could not have appeared more composed and confident. On shaking hands with us, he simply expressed his satisfaction with the result of our operations at Harper's Ferry, and with our timely arrival at Sharpsburg; adding that with our reënforcement he felt confident of being able to hold his ground until the arrival of the divisions of R. H. Anderson, McLaws, and A. P. Hill, which were still behind, and which did not arrive until the next day.

At four in the afternoon I received an order from General Lee to move at 3 o'clock the next morning, and take position with my division on the extreme right of his line of battle, so as to cover a ford of the Antietam, and to lend a hand, in case of necessity, to General Toombs, whose brigade was guarding the bridge over the Antietam called by Federal writers "Burnside's Bridge."

[‡] For an account of the part taken by General Walker's division in the operations leading to the surrender of Harper's Ferry, see pp. 604 to 611.— EDITORS.

BURNSIDE'S BRIDGE — I.

This picture, after a photograph taken in 1885, is a view of the Confederate position from the slope of the hill occupied by the Union batteries before a crossing was effected. At the time of the battle the buildings had not been erected, and the Confederate hill-side was covered with trees. A Confederate battery on the left enfiladed the crossing. Union sharp-shooters took advantage of the stone-wall on the right of the approach to the bridge. The continuation of the road to Sharpsburg is seen on the right across the bridge.— EDITORS.

At daybreak on the 17th I took the position assigned me, forming my line of battle on the crest of a ridge in front of the ford just mentioned. The ground, from my position to the creek, distant about five hundred yards, sloped gradually down to the crossing, just below which there was a wooded, bluff-like hill commanding the approach to the ford from the east.⚓ Here I posted a battalion of skirmishers.

While these dispositions, after a careful reconnoissance of the ground on both sides of the Antietam, were being made, the booming of artillery, at some distance on my left, warned us that the battle had begun. As the morning wore on the firing grew heavier and heavier, until Elk Mountain, to the eastward, gave back an incessant echo.

About 9 o'clock an order was brought by a staff-officer of General Lee, directing me to hurry to the left to reënforce Jackson, who was being hard pressed. Hastily recalling my skirmishers, I hurried forward, left in front, along the rear of the whole Confederate line of battle. As I passed what is now known as Cemetery Hill, I saw General Lee standing erect and calm, with a field-glass to his eye, his fine form sharply outlined against the sky, and I

⚓ The ford by which Rodman crossed after Walker's forces were withdrawn.— EDITORS.

**BURNSIDE'S BRIDGE — II.**

This picture, after a photograph taken in 1885, is a view of the Union position from the hill where Confederate artillery was planted to enfilade the bridge. From a point below, the 2d Maryland and the 6th New Hampshire charged up the road, but they were swept by such a murderous fire that only a few reached the bridge and sought shelter behind the stone-wall above. Subsequently, the bridge was carried by the 51st Pennsylvania and the 51st New York, charging from the pines on the hill-side (see p. 652).— EDITORS.

thought I had never seen a nobler figure. He seemed quite unconscious that the enemy's shells were exploding around and beyond him.

To those who have not been witnesses of a great battle like this, where more than a hundred thousand men, armed with all the appliances of modern science and skill, are engaged in the work of slaughtering each other, it is impossible by the power of words to convey an adequate idea of its terrible sublimity. The constant booming of cannon, the ceaseless rattle and roar of musketry, the glimpses of galloping horsemen and marching infantry, now seen, now lost in the smoke, adding weirdness to terror, all together make up a combination of sights and sounds wholly indescribable.

Opposite the rear of Longstreet's position I overtook General Ripley, of D. H. Hill's division, who, after having had dressed a serious wound in the neck, was returning to the command of his brigade, then hotly engaged. From him I obtained some information of the progress of the battle in the center.

Hurrying on, I was soon met by a staff-officer, who informed me that it was General Jackson's wish that I should go to the assistance of Hood, who was hard pressed and almost out of ammunition, adding that if I found the

Federals in possession of the wood on the Hagerstown road, I must drive them out, as it was the key of the battle-field.

He further explained that there was between the wood, just referred to, and the left of D. H. Hill's position, a gap of at least a third of a mile, and that I must leave a part of my command to fill it, and to support the reserve batteries under Colonel Stephen D. Lee which would also occupy the gap. For this purpose I detached the 27th North Carolina and the 3d Arkansas of Manning's brigade, and placed them under the orders of Colonel John R. Cooke, of the former regiment.↓

Moving forward, we soon reached the rear of Hood's position, and there, forming line of battle with Ransom on the left, we moved forward to Hood's relief, supported by McLaws's division, which at that moment (10:30 A. M.) arrived from Harper's Ferry. By this time the Federals [under Sedgwick] had forced Hood's men out of the wood, and were in possession of the key of the battle-field. To regain this position and restore our line was now the task before us. This we soon accomplished, but only after perhaps the severest struggle of the day.

BRIGADIER-GENERAL ROSWELL S. RIPLEY, C. S. A. FROM A PHOTOGRAPH.

The Federals contended for every foot of the ground, but, driven from rock to rock, from tree to tree, of the "West Wood," after a bloody struggle of some thirty minutes, Sedgwick's forces were pressed back into the open fields beyond, and, being there exposed to the fire of S. D. Lee's artillery, broke and fled in great disorder back to the cover of the "East Wood," beyond the Hagerstown road.

My loss in this attack was heavy, including the gallant Colonel Van H. Manning, commanding Walker's brigade, who fell severely wounded. The regiment which suffered most was the 30th Virginia. In the ardor of their pursuit of the enemy through the wood, the Virginians followed three hundred yards into the open, where they were fearfully cut up by the Federal batteries; they only saved themselves from annihilation by a timely retreat to the cover of the wood.

This ended the attempt of the Federals to drive Jackson from his position by infantry attacks. Their artillery, however, continued throughout the day to pour a heavy fire upon him, but with little effect. Our position was a most advantageous one. The space between it and the "East Wood," occupied by

---

↓ These are the troops spoken of in General D. H. Hill's report as "Walker's," who assisted in the repulse of Federal General French, later in the day. As the main body of my division was some distance to the left of the corn-fields where Cooke's regiments were posted, General Palfrey [in his volume "The Antietam and Fredericksburg," p. 94] expresses some uncertainty as to General Hill's meaning.—J. G. W.

See also General Longstreet, p. 669.—EDITORS.

the Federals, consisted of meadows and corn-fields, intersected by fences, and in passing over the ground their attacking columns were exposed to the fire of our batteries. Seventy or eighty yards in front of our position, and parallel with it, was a ridge, which, although slight, was sufficient to cover our men as they lay down among the trees and bowlders which covered the ground. The projectiles from the Federal batteries, striking this ridge, passed harmlessly over our heads, shattering the branches of the trees and tumbling them down in showers upon our men. Occasionally a shell would explode above us and send its hissing fragments in the midst of us, but our loss from this cause was surprisingly small.

The Federal infantry assaults having ceased, about half-past twelve I sought Jackson to report that from the front of my position in the wood I thought I had observed a movement of the enemy, as if to pass through the gap where I had posted Colonel Cooke's two regiments. I found Jackson in rear of Barksdale's brigade, under an apple-tree, sitting on his horse, with one leg thrown carelessly over the pommel of his saddle, plucking and eating the fruit. Without

CONFEDERATE DEAD ON THE WEST SIDE OF THE HAGERSTOWN ROAD OPPOSITE THE CORN-FIELD. FROM A PHOTOGRAPH.

making any reply to my report, he asked me abruptly: "Can you spare me a regiment and a battery?" I replied that Colonel Hill's 48th North Carolina, a very strong regiment, was in reserve, and could be spared, and that I could also give him both French's and Branch's batteries, but that they were without long-range ammunition, which had been exhausted at Harper's Ferry.

Jackson then went on to say that, owing to the nature of the ground, General Stuart's cavalry could take no part in the battle and were in the rear, but that Stuart himself had reported for such duty as he could perform.

Jackson added that he wished to make up, from the different commands on our left, a force of four or five thousand men, and give them to Stuart, with orders to turn the enemy's right, and attack him in the rear; that I must give orders to my division to advance to the front, and attack the enemy as soon as I should hear Stuart's guns—and that our whole left wing would move to the attack at the same time. Then, replacing his foot in the stirrup, he said with great emphasis: "We'll drive McClellan into the Potomac."

After giving orders for the regiment and batteries to report to Stuart, I galloped down the line where I had posted Cooke, but found that General Longstreet, having observed the danger from General French's formidable attack, had ordered Cooke forward, and that (together with D. H. Hill's division)

NORTH-WEST ANGLE OF THE "EAST WOOD" AND THE CORN-FIELD. FROM A SKETCH MADE AT THE TIME.

When the artist sketched this scene he was told that the guns in the corn-field belonged to a Maryland battery (Union), which was firing into the Dunker Church wood beyond. Most of the dead and wounded in this angle of the "East Wood" were Confederates. One of them, under the large tree at the left, had bound his shattered leg with corn-stalks and leaves to stop the flow of blood. He asked for water, of which there was none, and then begged the artist to remove his dead comrade, who was lying partly upon him, which was done. He wanted to be carried out of the woods, because he expected his friends to return and fight for them again. At the right was a tall young Georgian with a shattered ankle, sitting at the feet of one of the dead, who, he said, was his father.— EDITORS.

he was then closely engaged. Soon returning to my command, I repeated General Jackson's order to my brigade commanders and directed them to listen for the sound of Stuart's guns. We all confidently expected to hear the welcome sound by 2 o'clock, at least, and as that hour approached every ear was on the alert. Napoleon at Waterloo did not listen more intently for the sound of Grouchy's fire than did we for Stuart's. Two o'clock came, but nothing was heard of Stuart. Half-past two and then three, and still Stuart made no sign.

About half-past three a staff-officer of General Longstreet brought me an order from that general to advance and attack the enemy in my front. As the execution of this order would materially interfere with Jackson's plans, I thought it my duty before beginning the movement to communicate with General Longstreet personally. I found him in rear of the position in which I had posted Cooke in the morning, and upon informing him of Jackson's intentions, he withdrew his order.

While we were discussing this subject, Jackson himself joined us with the information of Stuart's failure to turn the Federal right, for the reason that he had found it securely *posted on the Potomac*. Upon my expressing surprise at this statement, Jackson replied that he also had been surprised, as he had supposed the Potomac much farther away; but he remarked that Stuart had an excellent eye for topography, and it must be as he represented. He added: "It is a great pity,— we should have driven McClellan into the Potomac."

By this time, with staff-officers, couriers, etc., we were a mounted group of some ten or a dozen persons, presenting so tempting a target that a Federal battery, at a distance of five hundred yards, opened fire upon us, but with no other result, strange to say, than the slaughter of the horse of one of my couriers.

The attempt of the Federals to penetrate our center, and its repulse by D. H. Hill, materially assisted by Colonel John R. Cooke's two regiments of my division,♭ ended infantry operations on our portion of the field for the day. The batteries, however, continued to pound away at each other until dark.

Late in the afternoon the direction of the firing on our extreme right was most alarming,— indicating, as it did, that the Federal left had forced a crossing of the Antietam, and that it must be perilously near our only line of retreat to the Potomac, at Shepherdstown. Could it be that A. P. Hill had come up and had been repulsed? If so, we had lost the day.

We hoped that A. P. Hill was still behind, but within striking distance. Soon the sound of musketry, which had almost ceased, roared out again with increased volume, indicating that fresh troops had been brought up, on one side or the other. For thirty minutes the sound of the firing came steadily from the same direction; then it seemed to recede eastward, and finally to die away almost entirely. We knew then that Hill *was* up; that the Federals had been driven back, and that the Confederate army had narrowly escaped defeat.

As night closed down, the firing along the whole line ceased; one of the bloodiest and most hotly contested battles of the war had been fought. The men of my division — worn out by a week's incessant marching and fighting by day and night—dropped down where they were, and could with difficulty be roused, even to take their cooked rations, brought up from our camp in the rear.

But there was little sleep for the ambulance corps; and all night long their lanterns could be seen flashing about the battle-field while they were searching for and bringing in the wounded, of friend and foe alike. In company with General Barksdale of Mississippi, whose brigade was on my left, I rode over that part of the battle-field where our own troops had been engaged, to see that none of the wounded had been overlooked. While passing along a worm fence, in the darkness, we heard a feeble voice almost under our horses' feet : " Don't let your horses t-r-e-a-d on m-e ! " We at once pulled up, and peering over the pommels of our saddles into the darkness, we could distinguish the dim outlines of a human form extended across our path. "Who are you?" we inquired. "I belong to the 20th Mas-sa-chu-setts rig-i-ment," answered the voice ; " I can't move — I think my back's broken." We sent for an ambulance and gave orders to care for the poor fellow, who was one of Sedgwick's men. This was but one of the very many instances of human suffering we encountered that night.

During the whole of the 18th the two armies rested in the positions which they had occupied at the close of the battle. There was a tacit truce, and Federal and Confederate burying-parties passed freely between the lines.

---

♭ The gallant conduct of Colonel Cooke on this occasion deservedly won for him promotion to the grade of brigadier-general. His losses in this engagement were terrible. In his own regiment, the 27th North Carolina, out of 26 commissioned officers who went into action, 18 were killed or wounded. In the 3d Arkansas the losses were equally great.—J. G. W.

We had fought an indecisive battle, and although we were, perhaps, in as good a condition to renew the struggle as the enemy were, General Lee recognized the fact that his ulterior plans had been thwarted by this premature engagement, and after a consultation with his corps commanders he determined to withdraw from Maryland. At dark on the night of the 18th the rearward movement began; and a little after sunrise of the next morning the entire Confederate army had safely recrossed the Potomac at Shepherdstown.

Detained in superintending the removal of a number of the wounded of my division, I was among the last to cross the Potomac. As I rode into the river I passed General Lee, sitting on his horse in the stream, watching the crossing of the wagons and artillery. Returning my greeting, he inquired as to what was still behind. There was nothing but the wagons containing my wounded, and a battery of artillery, all of which were near at hand, and I told him so. "Thank God!" I heard him say as I rode on.

UNION BURIAL PARTY AT ANTIETAM. FROM A PHOTOGRAPH.

## ANTIETAM SCENES.

### BY CHARLES CARLETON COFFIN.

THE cannon were thundering when at early morn, September 17th, 1862, I mounted my horse at Hagerstown, where I had arrived the preceding day, as an army correspondent, upon its evacuation by the Confederates. The people of the town, aroused by the cannonade, were at the windows of the houses or in the streets, standing in groups, listening to the reverberations rolling along the valley. The wind was south-west, the clouds hanging low and sweeping the tree-tops on South Mountain.

The cannonade, reverberating from cloud to mountain and from mountain to cloud, became a continuous roar, like the unbroken roll of a thunder-storm. The breeze, being in our direction, made the battle seem much nearer than it was. I was fully seven miles from Hooker's battle-field.

I turned down the Hagerstown and Sharpsburg turnpike at a brisk gallop, although I knew that Lee's army was in possession of the thoroughfare by the toll-gate which then stood about two miles north of Sharpsburg. A citizen who had left his home, to be beyond harm during the battle, had given me the information. The thought uppermost in my mind was to gain the left flank of the Confederate army, mingle with the citizens, and so witness the battle from the Confederate side. It would be a grand accomplishment if successful.

It would give me a splendid opportunity to see the make-up of the Confederate army. It would be like going behind the scenes of a theater. I was in citizen's dress, splashed with mud, and wore a dilapidated hat.

While wondering what would be the outcome of the venture, I came upon a group of farmers, who were listening with dazed countenances to the uproar momentarily increasing in volume. It was no longer alone the boom of the batteries, but a rattle of musketry—at first like pattering drops upon a roof; then a roll, crash, roar, and rush, like a mighty ocean billow upon the shore, chafing the pebbles, wave on wave,—with deep and heavy explosions of the batteries, like the crashing of thunderbolts. I think the currents of air must have had something to do with the effect of sound. The farmers were walking about nervously, undecided, evidently, whether to flee or to remain.

"I wouldn't go down the pike if I were you," said one, addressing me. "You will ride right into the Rebs."

"That is just where I would like to go."

"You can't pass yourself off for a Reb; they'll see, the instant they set eyes on you, that you are a Yank. They'll gobble you up and take you to Richmond," said the second.

No doubt I acted wisely in leaving the turnpike and riding to gain the right flank of the Union line. A short distance and I came upon a Confederate soldier lying beneath a tree. He doubtless supposed that I was a cavalryman, and raised his hand as if to implore me not to shoot him. His face was pale and haggard, and he had dropped from the ranks through sheer exhaustion. I left the poor fellow with the conviction that he never again would see his Southern home.

A mile farther on and I came upon the driftwood of McClellan's army. Every army has its driftwood soldiers — valiant at the mess-table, brave in the story around the bivouac fire, but faint of heart when battle begins. Some of them were old skulkers, others fresh recruits, with bright uniforms, who had volunteered under the pressure of enthusiasm. This was their first battle and was not what they had pictured a battle to be.

"Where does this road lead to?" asked one with white lips.

"To Hagerstown. But where are you going?"

"Oh, our division has been ordered to Hagerstown," was the reply as they hastened on.

Ammunition trains were winding up the hill from the road leading to Keedysville. Striking across the fields, I soon came upon the grounds on Hoffman's farm selected for the field-hospitals. Even at that hour of the morning it was an appalling sight. The wounded were lying in rows awaiting their turn at the surgeons' tables. The hospital stewards had a corps of men distributing straw over the field for their comfort.

Turning from the scenes of the hospital, I ascended the hill and came upon the men who had been the first to sweep across the Hagerstown pike, past the toll-gate, and into the Dunker Church woods, only to be hurled back by Jackson, who had established his line in a strong position behind outcropping limestone ledges.

"There are not many of us left," was the mournful remark of an officer.

I learned the story of the morning's engagement, and then rode to the line of batteries on the ridge by the house of J. Poffenberger; if my memory serves me there were thirty guns in position there pointing south-west. There was a lull in the strife. All was quiet in the woods along the turnpike, and in the corn-field beyond D. R. Miller's house,—so quiet that I thought I would ride on to the front line, not knowing that the brigade lying upon the ground near the cannon was the advanced line of the army. I rode through Poffenberger's door-yard, and noticed that a Confederate cannon-shot had ripped through the building; another had upset a hive of bees, and the angry insects had taken their revenge on the soldiers. I walked my horse down the pike past the toll-gate.

"Hold on!" It was the peremptory hail of a Union soldier crouching under the fence by the roadside. "Where are you going?"

"I thought I would go out to the front!"

"The front! you have passed it. This is the picket line. If you know what is good for yourself, you'll skedaddle mighty quick. The Rebs are in the corn right out there."

I acted upon the timely advice and retreated to a more respectful distance; and none too soon, for a moment later the uproar began again — solid shot tearing through the woods and crashing among the trees, and shells exploding in unexpected places. I recall a round shot that came ricochetting over the ground, cutting little furrows, tossing the earth into the air, as the plow of the locomotive turns its white furrow after a snow-storm. Its speed gradually diminished, and a soldier was about to catch it, as if he were at a game of base-ball, but a united yell of "Look out!" "Don't!" "Take care!" "Hold on!" caused him to desist. Had he attempted it, he would have been knocked over instantly.

Turning from the conflict on the right, I rode down the line, toward the center, forded the Antietam and ascended the hill east of it to the large square mansion of Mr. Pry, where General McClellan had established his headquarters. The general was sitting in an arm-chair in front of the house. His staff were about him; their horses, saddled and bridled, were hitched to the trees and fences. Stakes had been driven in the earth in front of the house, to which were strapped the headquarters telescopes, through which a view of the operations and movements of the two armies could be obtained.

It was a commanding situation. The panorama included fully two-thirds of the battle-field, from the woods by the Dunker Church southward to the hills below Sharpsburg.

The Fifth Corps, under Fitz John Porter, was behind the ridge extending south toward the bridge, where the artillery of the Ninth Corps was thundering. Porter, I remember, was with McClellan, watching the movements of the troops across the Antietam — French's and Richardson's divisions, which were forming in the fields east of Roulette's and Mumma's houses. What a splendid sight it was! How beautifully the lines deployed! The clouds which had hung low all the morning had lifted, and the sun was shining through the rifts, its bright beams falling on the flags and glinting from gun-barrel and bayonet. Upon the crest of the hill south of the Dunker Church, I could see Confederates on horseback, galloping, evidently with orders; for, a few moments later, there was another gleam in the sunshine from the bayonets of their troops, who were apparently getting into position to resist the threatened movement of French and Richardson.

Memory recalls the advance of the line of men in blue across the meadow east of Roulette's. They reach the spacious barn, which divides the line of men as a rock parts the current of a river, flowing around it, but uniting beyond. The orchard around the house screens the movement in part. I see the blue uniforms beneath the apple-trees. The line halts for alignment. The skirmishers are in advance. There are isolated puffs of smoke, and then the Confederate skirmishers scamper up the hill and disappear. Up the slope moves the line to the top of a knoll. Ah! what a crash! A white cloud, gleams of lightning, a yell, a hurrah, and then up in the corn-field a great commotion, men firing into each other's faces, the Confederate line breaking, the ground strewn with prostrate forms. The Confederate line in "Bloody lane" has been annihilated, the center pierced.

Just here McClellan lost a great opportunity. It was the plain dictate of common sense that then was the time when Porter's eleven thousand should have been sent across the Antietam and thrown like a thunderbolt upon the enemy. It was so plain that the rank and file saw it. "Now is the time" was the universal comment. But not a soldier stirred from his position. McClellan saw it, but issued no order. All through the day most of the Fifth Corps remained in reserve.

The battle was in the main fought by divisions — one after another. There was no concerted action, no hammering all along the line at the same time. Heavy blows were given, but they were not followed up. It has been said that McClellan's excuse for not throwing in Porter's corps at that moment was the reason given by Napoleon at Borodino when asked why he did not at a certain moment put in the Imperial Guard: "If I am defeated to-day, where is my army for to-morrow?" There was no parallel between Antietam and Borodino. The moment had come for dividing Lee's army at its center and crushing it back upon the Potomac in utter rout. A. P. Hill, on his way from Harper's Ferry to join Lee, was at that moment fording the Potomac at Shepherdstown. This General McClellan did not know, but the fact was before him that French and Richardson had pierced the Confederate center.

With the falling back of the Confederates I went up past Roulette's house to the sunken road. The hillside was dotted with prostrate forms of men in blue, but in the sunken road, what a ghastly spectacle! The Confederates had gone down as the grass falls before the scythe. Words are inadequate to portray the scene. Resolution and energy still lingered in the pallid cheeks, in the set teeth, in the gripping hand. I recall a soldier with the cartridge between his thumb and finger, the end of the cartridge bitten off, and the paper between his teeth when the bullet had pierced his heart, and the machinery of life — all the muscles and nerves — had come to a standstill. A young lieutenant had fallen while trying to rally his men; his hand was still firmly grasping his sword, and determination was visible in every line of his face. I counted fourteen bodies lying together, literally in a heap, amid the corn rows on the hillside. The broad, green leaves were sprinkled and stained with blood.

The close of the battle presented a magnificent spectacle as the artillery of both armies came into play. The arrival of A. P. Hill had a stimulating effect upon Lee's veterans, while the carrying of the bridge and the work accomplished by French's and Richardson's divisions in the center gave great encouragement to the Union army. It was plain that Lee was economical in the use of artillery ammunition. In fact, he had a short supply. The engagements at Gainesville, Groveton, Bull Run, Chantilly, Harper's Ferry, and South Mountain had depleted his ammunition-chests, and supply trains had not reached him from the west side of the Potomac.

Far up on the Union right, as well as in the center, the Union batteries were pounding. I recall a remarkable scene. The sun was going down, — its disc red and large as seen through the murky battle-cloud. One of Sumner's batteries was directly in line toward the sun, on the crest of the ridge north of the smoking ruins of Mumma's house and barn, and there was one piece of which the gunners, as they rammed home the cartridge, seemed to be standing in the sun. Beyond, hid from view by the distance and the low-hanging branches of the oaks by the Dunker Church, the Confederate guns were flashing. Immediately north of Sharpsburg, and along the hill in front, now the National Cemetery, Longstreet's cannon were in play. Half-way up the hill were Burnside's men sending out a continuous flame, with A. P. Hill's veterans confronting them. All the country was flaming and smoking; shells were bursting above the contending lines; Burnside was asking for reënforcements. How quickly Porter's eleven thousand could have rushed across Antietam bridge with no Confederates to oppose them, swept up the hillside and forced themselves like a wedge between Longstreet and A. P. Hill! — but McClellan had only Miller's battery to send him! The sun went down; the thunder died away, the musketry ceased, bivouac fires gleamed out as if a great city had lighted its lamps.

When the soldiers are seeking rest, the work of the army correspondent begins. All through the day eyes and ears have been open. The note-book is scrawled with characters intelligible to him if read at once, but wholly meaningless a few hours later. He must grope his way along the lines in the darkness, visit the hospitals, hear the narratives of all, eliminate error, get at the probable truth, keeping ever in mind that each general thinks his brigade, each colonel his regiment, every captain his company, did most of the fighting. While thus visiting the lines, I heard a song rising on the night air sweet and plaintive:

> Do they miss me at home, do they miss me?
> 'Twould be an assurance most dear
> To know that this moment some lov'd one
> Were saying, 'I wish he were here';
> To feel that the group at the fireside
> Were thinking of me, as I roam.
> Oh, yes, 'twould be joy beyond measure
> To know that they miss me at home."

Both before and after a battle, sad and solemn thoughts come to the soldier. Before the conflict they are of apprehension; after the strife there is a sense of relief; but the thinned ranks, the knowledge that the comrade who stood by your side in the morning never will stand there again, bring inexpressible sadness. The soldiers, with thoughts far away, were apprehensive that the conflict of the day was but a prelude to another struggle more fierce and bloody in the morning. They were in position and lying on their arms, ready to renew the battle at daylight; but day dawned and the cannon were silent. The troops were in line, yet there was no order to advance. I could hear now and then the isolated shots of the pickets. I could see that Lee had contracted his line between Dunker Church and Sharpsburg. His cannon were in position, his troops in line. Everybody knew that Franklin's corps was comparatively fresh; that McClellan had 29,000 men who either had as yet not fired a musket or had been only slightly engaged. Why did he not attack? No one could tell.

Riding up to the right, I found that hostilities had ceased; that the ambulance corps of both armies were gathering up the wounded in the field near the Dunker Church. ☆ Going out over the ground where the tides had ebbed and flowed, I found it thickly strewn with dead. I recall a Union soldier lying near the Dunker Church with his face turned upward, and his pocket Bible open upon his breast. I lifted the volume and read the words: "Though I walk through the valley of the shadow of death, I will fear no evil; for Thou art with me. Thy rod and Thy staff, they comfort me." Upon the fly-leaf were the words: "We hope and pray that you may be permitted by a kind Providence, after the war is over, to return."

Near by stood a wounded battery-horse and a shattered caisson belonging to one of Hood's batteries. The animal had eaten every blade of grass within reach. No human being ever looked more imploringly for help than that dumb animal, wounded beyond the possibility of moving, yet resolutely standing, as if knowing that lying down would be the end.

The assumed armistice came to an end, the pickets stood in hostile attitude once more, but the day wore away and no orders were issued for a renewal of the attack. Another morning, and Lee was beyond the Potomac. I galloped along the lines where his army had stood, and saw the wreck and ruin of battle. I recall the body of a Confederate sharp-shooter, lying in the forks of a tree by the roadside, between the Dunker Church and Sharpsburg. Shells had exploded in the streets of Sharpsburg. The horses of a Confederate battery had gone down in a heap in the public square.

Porter's corps was passing through the town. McClellan and his staff came galloping up the hill. Porter's men swung their hats and gave a cheer; but few hurrahs came from the other corps — none from Hooker's. A change had come over the army. The complacent look which I had seen upon McClellan's countenance on the 17th, as if all were going well, had disappeared. There was a troubled look instead — a manifest awakening to the fact that his great opportunity had gone by. Lee had slipped through his fingers.

☆ Surgeon Jonathan Letterman, Medical Director, Army of the Potomac, reports as follows upon the work of his department on the field: "Immediately after the retreat of the enemy from the field of Antietam, measures were taken to have all the Confederate wounded gathered in from the field, over which they lay scattered in all directions, and from the houses and barns in the rear of their lines, and placed under such circumstances as would permit of their being properly attended to, and at such points as would enable their removal to be effected to Frederick, and thence to Baltimore and Fortress Monroe to their own lines. They were removed as rapidly as their recovery would permit. . . . There were many cases both on our right and left whose wounds were so serious that their lives would be endangered by their removal; and to have every opportunity afforded them for recovery, the Antietam hospital, consisting of hospital tents and capable of comfortably accommodating nearly six hundred cases, was established at a place called Smoketown, near Keedysville, for those who were wounded on our right, and a similar hospital, but not so capacious, — the Locust Spring hospital, — was established in the rear of the Fifth Corps for those cases which occurred on our left. To one or other of these hospitals all the wounded were carried whose wounds were of such a character as to forbid their removal to Frederick or elsewhere. . . . Immediately after the battle a great many citizens came within our lines in order to remove their relatives or friends who had been injured, and in a great many instances when the life of the man depended upon his remaining at rest. It was impossible to make them understand that they were better where they were, and that a removal would probably be done only with the sacrifice of life. Their minds seemed bent on having them in a house. If that could be accomplished, all would, in their opinion, be well. No greater mistake could exist, and the results of that battle only added additional evidence of the absolute necessity of a full supply of pure air, constantly renewed — a supply which cannot be obtained in the most perfectly constructed building. Within a few yards a marked contrast could be seen between the wounded in houses and barns and in the open air. Those in houses progressed less favorably than those in the barns, those in barns less favorably than those in the open air, although all were in other respects treated alike. The capacious barns, abundantly provided with hay and straw, the delightful weather with which we were favored, and the kindness exhibited by the people afforded increased facilities to the medical department for taking care of the wounded thrown upon it by that battle. . . ."—EDITORS.

IN THE WAKE OF BATTLE.

## A WOMAN'S RECOLLECTIONS OF ANTIETAM.

BY MARY BEDINGER MITCHELL.

SEPTEMBER, 1862, was in the skies of the almanac, but August still reigned in ours; it was hot and dusty. The railroads in the Shenandoah Valley had been torn up, the bridges had been destroyed, communication had been made difficult, and Shepherdstown, cornered by the bend of the Potomac, lay as if forgotten in the bottom of somebody's pocket. We were without news or knowledge, except when some chance traveler would repeat the last wild and uncertain rumor that he had heard. We had passed an exciting summer. Winchester had changed hands more than once; we had been "in the Confederacy" and out of it again, and were now waiting, in an exasperating state of ignorance and suspense, for the next move in the great game.

It was a saying with us that Shepherdstown was just nine miles from everywhere. It was, in fact, about that distance from Martinsburg and Harper's Ferry — oft-mentioned names — and from Williamsport, where the armies so often crossed, both to and from Maryland. It was off the direct road between those places and lay, as I said, at the foot of a great sweep in the river, and five miles from the nearest station on the Baltimore and Ohio railroad. As no trains were running now, this was of little consequence; what was more important was that a turnpike road — unusually fine for that region of stiff, red clay — led in almost a straight line for thirty miles to Winchester on the south, and stretched northward, beyond the Potomac, twenty miles to Hagerstown. Two years later it was the scene of "Sheridan's ride." Before the days of steam this had been part of the old posting-road between the Valley towns and Pennsylvania, and we had boasted a very substantial bridge. This had been burned early in the war, and only the massive stone piers remained; but a mile and a half down the Potomac was the ford, and the road that led to it lay partly above and partly along the face of rocky and precipitous cliffs. It was narrow and stony, and especially in one place, around the foot of "Mount

Misery," was very steep and difficult for vehicles. It was, moreover, entirely commanded by the hills on the Maryland side, but it was the ford over which some part of the Confederate army passed every year, and in 1863 was used by the main body of infantry on the way to Gettysburg. Beyond the river were the Cumberland Canal and its willow-fringed tow-path, from which rose the soft and rounded outlines of the hills that from their farther slopes looked down upon the battle-field of Antietam. On clear days we could see the fort at Harper's Ferry without a glass, and the flag flying over it, a mere speck against the sky, and we could hear the gun that was fired every evening at sunset.

Shepherdstown's only access to the river was through a narrow gorge, the bed of a small tributary of the Potomac, that was made to do much duty as it slipped cheerily over its rocks and furnished power for several mills and factories, most of them at that time silent. Here were also three or four stone warehouses, huge empty structures, testifying mutely that the town had once had a business. The road to the bridge led through this cleft, down an indescribably steep street skirting the stream's ravine to whose sides the mills and factories clung in most extraordinary fashion; but it was always a marvel how anything heavier than a wheelbarrow could be pulled up its tedious length, or how any vehicle could be driven down without plunging into the water at the bottom.

In this odd little borough, then, we were waiting "developments," hearing first that "our men" were coming, and then that they were not coming, when suddenly, on Saturday, the 13th of September, early in the morning, we found ourselves surrounded by a hungry horde of lean and dusty tatterdemalions, who seemed to rise from the ground at our feet. I did not know where they came from, or to whose command they belonged; I have since been informed that General Jackson recrossed into Virginia at Williamsport, and hastened to Harper's Ferry by the shortest roads. These would take him some four miles south of us, and our haggard apparitions were perhaps a part of his force. They were stragglers, at all events,—professional, some of them, but some worn out by the incessant strain of that summer. When I say that they were hungry, I convey no impression of the gaunt starvation that looked from their cavernous eyes. All day they crowded to the doors of our houses, with always the same drawling complaint: "I've been a-marchin' an' a-fightin' for six weeks stiddy, and I ain't had n-a-r-thin' to eat 'cept green apples an' green cawn, an' I wish you'd please to gimme a bite to eat."

Their looks bore out their statements, and when they told us they had "clean gin out," we believed them, and went to get what we had. They could be seen afterward asleep in every fence corner, and under every tree, but after a night's rest they "pulled themselves together" somehow and disappeared as suddenly as they had come. Possibly they went back to their commands, possibly they only moved on to repeat the same tale elsewhere. I know nothing of numbers, nor what force was or was not engaged in any battle, but I saw the troops march past us every summer for four years, and I know something of the appearance of a marching army, both Union and Southern. There are always stragglers, of course, but never before or after did I see anything comparable to the demoralized state of the Confederates at this time. Never were want and exhaustion more visibly put before my eyes, and that they could march or fight at all seemed incredible.

As I remember, the next morning — it was Sunday, September 14th — we were awakened by heavy firing at two points on the mountains. We were expecting the bombardment of Harper's Ferry, and knew that Jackson was before it. Many of our friends were with him, and our interest there was so intense that we sat watching the bellowing and smoking Heights, for a long time, before we became aware that the same phenomena were to be noticed in the north. From our windows both points could be observed, and we could not tell which to watch more keenly. We knew almost nothing except that there was fighting, that it must be very heavy, and that our friends were surely in it somewhere, but whether at South Mountain or Harper's Ferry we had no means of discovering. I remember how the day wore on, how we staid at the windows until we could not endure the suspense; how we walked about and came back to them; and how finally, when night fell, it seemed cruel and preposterous to go to bed still ignorant of the result.

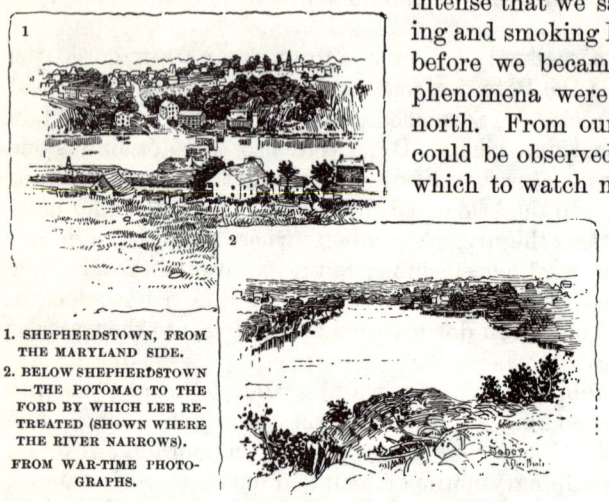

1. SHEPHERDSTOWN, FROM THE MARYLAND SIDE.
2. BELOW SHEPHERDSTOWN — THE POTOMAC TO THE FORD BY WHICH LEE RETREATED (SHOWN WHERE THE RIVER NARROWS).
FROM WAR-TIME PHOTOGRAPHS.

Monday afternoon, about 2 or 3 o'clock, when we were sitting about in disconsolate fashion, distracted by the contradictory rumors, our negro cook rushed into the room with eyes shining and face working with excitement. She had been down in "de ten-acre lot to pick a few years ob cawn," and she had seen a long train of wagons coming up from the ford, and "dey is full ob wounded men, and de blood runnin' outen dem dat deep," measuring on her outstretched arm to the shoulder. This horrible picture sent us flying to town, where we found the streets already crowded, the people all astir, and the foremost wagons, of what seemed an endless line, discharging their piteous burdens. The scene speedily became ghastly, but fortunately we could not stay to look at it. There were no preparations, no accommodations — the men could not be left in the street — what was to be done?

A Federal soldier once said to me, "I was always sorry for your wounded; they never seemed to get any care." The remark was extreme, but there was much justice in it. There was little mitigation of hardship to our unfortunate armies. We were fond of calling them Spartans, and they were but too truly called upon to endure a Spartan system of neglect and privation. They were generally ill-fed and ill-cared for. It would have been possible at this time, one would think, to send a courier back to inform the town and bespeak what comforts it could provide for the approaching wounded; but here they were, unannounced, on the brick pavements, and the first thing was to find roofs to cover them. Men ran for keys and opened the shops, long empty, and the unused rooms; other people got brooms and stirred up the dust of ages; then swarms of children began to appear with bundles of hay and straw, taken from anybody's stable. These were hastily disposed in heaps, and covered with blankets—the soldiers' own, or blankets begged or borrowed. On these improvised beds the sufferers were placed, and the next question was how properly to dress their wounds. No surgeons were to be seen. A few men, detailed as nurses, had come, but they were incompetent, of course. Our women set bravely to work and washed away the blood or stanched it as well as they could, where the jolting of the long rough ride had disarranged the hasty binding done upon the battle-field. But what did they know of wounds beyond a cut finger, or a boil? Yet they bandaged and bathed, with a devotion that went far to make up for their inexperience. Then there was the hunt for bandages. Every housekeeper ransacked her stores and brought forth things new and old. I saw one girl, in despair for a strip of cloth, look about helplessly, and then rip off the hem of her white petticoat. The doctors came up, by and by, or I suppose they did, for some amputating was done—rough surgery, you may be sure. The women helped, holding the instruments and the basins, and trying to soothe or strengthen. They stood to their work nobly; the emergency brought out all their strength to meet it.

One girl who had been working very hard helping the men on the sidewalks, and dressing wounds afterward in a close, hot room, told me that at one time the sights and smells (these last were fearful) so overcame her that she could only stagger to the staircase, where she hung, half conscious, over the banisters, saying to herself, "Oh, I hope if I faint some one will kick me into a corner and let me lie there!" She did not faint, but went back to her work in a few moments, and through the whole of what followed was one of the most indefatigable and useful. She was one of many; even children did their part.

It became a grave question how to feed so many unexpected guests. The news spread rapidly, and the people from the country neighborhoods came pouring in to help, expecting to stay with friends who had already given up every spare bed and every inch of room where beds could be put up. Virginia houses are very elastic, but ours were strained to their utmost. Fortunately some of the farmers' wives had been thoughtful enough to bring supplies of linen, and some bread and fruit, and when our wants became better known other contributions flowed in; but when all was done it was not enough.

We worked far into the night that Monday, went to bed late, and rose early next morning. Tuesday brought fresh wagon-loads of wounded, and would have brought despair, except that they were accompanied by an apology for a commissariat. Soon more reliable sources of supply were organized among our country friends. Some doctors also arrived, who—with a few honorable exceptions—might as well have staid away. The remembrance of that worthless body of officials stirs me to wrath. Two or three worked conscientiously and hard, and they did all the medical work, except what was done by our own town physicians. In strong contrast was the conduct of the common men detailed as nurses. They were as gentle as they knew how to be, and very obliging and untiring. Of course they were uncouth and often rough, but with the wounded dying about us every day, and with the necessity that we were under for the first few days, of removing those who died at once that others not yet quite dead might take their places, there was no time to be fastidious; it required all our efforts to be simply decent, and we sometimes failed in that.

We fed our men as well as we could from every available source, and often had some difficulty in feeding ourselves. The townspeople were very hospitable, and we were invited here and there, but could not always go, or hesitated, knowing every house was full. I remember once, that having breakfasted upon a single roll and having worked hard among sickening details, about 4 o'clock I turned wolfishly ravenous and ran to a friend's house down the street. When I got there I was almost too faint to speak, but my friend looked at me and disappeared in silence, coming back in a moment with a plate of hot soup. What luxury! I sat down then and there on the front doorstep and devoured the soup as if I had been without food for a week.

It was known on Tuesday that Harper's Ferry had been taken, but it was growing evident that South Mountain had not been a victory. We had heard from some of our friends, but not from all, and what we did hear was often most unsatisfactory and tantalizing. For instance, we would be told that some one whom we loved had been seen standing with his battery, had left his gun an instant to shake hands and send a message, and had then stepped back to position, while our civilian informant had come away for safety, and the smoke of conflict had hidden battery and all from view. As night drew nearer, whispers of a great battle to be fought the next day grew louder, and we shuddered at the prospect, for battles had come to mean to us, as they never had before, blood, wounds, and death.

On the 17th of September cloudy skies looked down upon the two armies facing each other on the fields of Maryland. It seems to me now that the roar of that day began with the light, and all through its long and dragging hours its thunder formed a background to our pain and terror. If we had been in doubt as to our friends' whereabouts on Sunday, there was no room for doubt now. There was no sitting at the windows now and counting discharges of guns, or watching the curling smoke. We went about our work with pale faces and trembling hands, yet trying to appear composed for the sake of our patients, who were much excited. We could hear the incessant explosions of artillery, the shrieking whistles of the shells, and the sharper, deadlier, more thrilling roll of musketry; while every now and then the echo of some charging cheer would come, borne by the wind, and as the human voice pierced that demoniacal clangor we would catch our breath and listen, and try not to sob, and turn back to the forlorn hospitals, to the suffering at our feet and before our eyes, while imagination fainted at thought of those other scenes hidden from us beyond the Potomac.

On our side of the river there were noise, confusion, dust; throngs of stragglers; horsemen galloping about; wagons blocking each other, and teamsters wrangling; and a continued din of shouting, swearing, and rumbling, in the midst of which men were dying, fresh wounded arriving, surgeons amputating limbs and dressing wounds, women going in and out with bandages, lint, medicines, food. An ever-present sense of anguish, dread, pity, and, I fear, hatred—these are my recollections of Antietam.

When night came we could still hear the sullen guns and hoarse, indefinite murmurs that succeeded the day's turmoil. That night was dark and lowering and the air heavy and dull. Across the river innumerable camp-fires were blazing, and we could but too well imagine the scenes that they were lighting. We sat in silence, looking into each other's tired faces. There were no impatient words, few tears; only silence, and a drawing close together, as if for comfort. We were almost hopeless, yet clung with desperation to the thought that we were hoping. But in our hearts we could not believe that anything human could have escaped from that appalling fire. On Thursday the two armies lay idly facing each other, but we could not be idle. The wounded continued to arrive until the town was quite unable to hold all the disabled and suffering. They filled every building and overflowed into the country round, into farm-houses, barns, corn-cribs, cabins,—wherever four walls and a roof were found together. Those able to travel were sent on to Winchester and other towns back from the river, but their departure seemed to make no appreciable difference. There were six churches, and they were all full; the Odd Fellows' Hall, the Freemasons', the little Town Council room, the barn-like place known as the Drill Room, all the private houses after their capacity, the shops and empty buildings, the school-houses,—every inch of space, and yet the cry was for room.

The unfinished Town Hall had stood in naked ugliness for many a long day. Somebody threw a few rough boards across the beams, placed piles of straw over them, laid down single planks to walk upon, and lo, it was a hospital at once. The stone warehouses down in the ravine and by the river had been passed by, because low and damp and undesirable as sanitariums, but now their doors and windows were thrown wide, and, with barely time allowed to sweep them, they were all occupied,—even the "old blue factory," an antiquated, crazy, dismal building of blue stucco that peeled off in great blotches, which had been shut up for years, and was in the last stages of dilapidation.

On Thursday night we heard more than usual sounds of disturbance and movement, and in the morning we found the Confederate army in full retreat. General Lee crossed the Potomac under cover of the darkness, and when the day broke the greater part of his force—or the more orderly portion of it—had gone on toward Kearneysville and Leetown. General McClellan followed to the river, and without crossing got a battery in position on Douglas's Hill, and began to shell the retreating army and, in consequence, the town. What before was confusion grew worse; the retreat became a stampede. The battery may not have done a very great deal of execution, but it made a fearful noise. It is curious how much louder guns sound when they are pointed at you than when turned the other way! And the shell, with its long-drawn screeching, though no doubt less terrifying than the singing minie-ball, has a way of making one's hair stand on end. Then, too, every one who has had any experience in such things, knows how infectious fear is, how it grows when yielded to, and how, when you once begin to run, it soon seems impossible to run fast enough; whereas, if you can manage to stand your ground, the alarm lessens and sometimes disappears.

Some one suggested that yellow was the hospital color, and immediately everybody who could lay hands upon a yellow rag hoisted it over the house. The whole town was a hospital; there was scarcely a building that could not with truth seek protection under that plea, and the fantastic little strips were soon flaunting their ineffectual remonstrance from every roof-tree and chimney. When this specific failed the excitement became wild and ungovernable. It would have been ludicrous had it not produced so much suffering. The danger was less than it seemed, for McClellan, after all, was not bombarding the town, but the army, and most of the shells flew over us and exploded in the fields; but aim cannot be always sure, and enough shells fell short to convince the terrified citizens that their homes were about to be battered down over their ears. The better people kept some outward coolness, with perhaps a feeling of *"noblesse oblige"*; but the poorer classes acted as if the town were already in a blaze, and rushed from their houses with their families and household goods to make their way into the country. The road was thronged, the streets blocked; men were vociferating, women crying, children screaming; wagons, ambulances, guns, caissons, horsemen, footmen, all mingled—nay, even wedged and jammed together—in one struggling, shouting mass. The negroes were the worst, and with faces of a ghastly ash-color, and staring eyes, they swarmed into the fields, carrying their babies, their clothes, their pots and kettles, fleeing from the wrath behind them. The comparison to a hornet's nest attacked by boys is not a good one, for there was no "fight" shown; but a disturbed ant-hill is altogether inadequate. They fled widely and camped out of range, nor would they venture back for days.

Had this been all, we could afford to laugh now, but there was another side to the picture that lent it an intensely painful aspect. It was the hurrying crowds of wounded. Ah me! those maimed and bleeding fugitives! When the firing commenced the hospitals began to empty. All who were able to pull one foot after another, or could bribe or beg comrades to carry them, left in haste. In vain we implored them to stay; in vain we showed them the folly, the suicide, of the attempt; in vain we argued, cajoled, threatened, ridiculed; pointed out that we were remaining and that there was less danger here than on the road. There is no sense or reason in a panic. The cannon were bellowing upon Douglas's Hill, the shells whistling and shrieking, the air full of shouts and cries; we had to scream to make ourselves heard. The men replied that the "Yankees" were crossing; that the town was to be burned; that *we* could not be made prisoners, but they could; that, anyhow, they were going as far as they could walk, or be carried. And go they did. Men with cloths about their heads went hatless in the sun, men with cloths about their feet limped shoeless on the stony road; men with arms in slings, without arms, with one leg, with bandaged sides and backs; men in ambulances, wagons, carts, wheelbarrows, men carried on stretchers or supported on the shoulder of some self-denying comrade — all who could crawl went, and went to almost certain death. They could not go far, they dropped off into the country houses, where they were received with as much kindness as it was possible to ask for; but their wounds had become inflamed, their frames were weakened by fright and over-exertion: erysipelas, mortification, gangrene set in; and long rows of nameless graves still bear witness to the results.

Our hospitals did not remain empty. It was but a portion who could get off in any manner, and their places were soon taken by others, who had remained nearer the battle-field, had attempted to follow the retreat, but, having reached Shepherdstown, could go no farther. We had plenty to do, but all that day we went about with hearts bursting with rage and shame, and breaking with pity and grief for the needless, needless waste of life. The amateur nurses all stood firm, and managed to be cheerful for the sake of keeping their men quiet, but they could not be without fear. One who had no thought of leaving her post desired to send her sister — a mere child — out of harm's way. She, therefore, told her to go to their home, about half a mile distant, and ask their mother for some yellow cloth that was in the house, thinking, of course, that the mother would never permit the girl to come back into the town. But she miscalculated. The child accepted the commission as a sacred trust, forced her way out over the crowded road, where the danger was more real than in the town itself, reached home, and made her request. The house had its own flag flying, for it was directly in range and full of wounded. Perhaps for this reason the mother was less anxious to keep her daughter with her; perhaps in the hurry and excitement she allowed herself to be persuaded that it was really necessary to get that strip of yellow flannel into Shepherdstown as soon as possible. At all events, she made no difficulty, but with streaming tears kissed the girl, and saw her set out to go alone, half a mile through a panic-stricken rabble, under the fire of a battery and into a town whose escape from conflagration was at best not assured. To come out had been comparatively easy, for she was going with the stream. The return was a different matter. The turbulent tide had now to be stemmed. Yet she managed to work her way along, now in the road, now in the field, slipping between the wagon wheels, and once, at least, crawling under a stretcher. No one had noticed her coming out, she was but one of the crowd; and now most were too busy with their own safety to pay much heed to anything else. Still, as her face seemed alone set toward the town, she attracted some attention. One or two spoke to her. Now it was, "Look-a here, little gal! don't you know you're a-goin' the wrong way?" One man looked at the yellow thing she had slung across her shoulder and said, with an approving nod:

CONFEDERATE MONUMENT AT SHEPHERDSTOWN. FROM A PHOTOGRAPH TAKEN IN 1885.

"That's right, that's right; save the wounded if ye kin." She meant to do it, and finally reached her sister, breathless but triumphant, with as proud a sense of duty done as if her futile errand had been the deliverance of a city.

I have said that there was less danger than appeared, but it must not be supposed that there was none. A friend who worked chiefly in the old blue factory had asked me to bring her a bowl of gruel that some one had promised to make for one of her patients. I had just taken it to her, and she was walking across the floor with the bowl in her hands, when a shell crashed through a corner of the wall and passed out at the opposite end of the building, shaking the rookery to its foundations, filling the room with dust and plaster, and throwing her upon her knees to the floor. The wounded screamed, and had they not been entirely unable to move, not a man would have been left in the building. But it was found that no one was hurt, and things proceeded as before. I asked her afterward if she was frightened. She said yes, when it was over, but her chief thought at the time was to save the gruel, for the man needed it, and it had been very hard to find any one composed enough to make it. I am glad to be able to say that he got his gruel in spite of bombs. That factory was struck twice. A school-house, full of wounded, and one or two other buildings were hit, but I believe no serious damage was done.

On Saturday morning there was a fight at the ford. The negroes were still encamped in the fields, though some, finding that the town was yet standing, ventured back on various errands during the day. What we feared were the stragglers and hangers-on and nondescripts that circle round an army like the great buzzards we shuddered to see wheeling silently over us. The people were still excited, anticipating the Federal crossing and dreading a repetition of the bombardment or an encounter in the streets. Some parties of Confederate cavalry rode through, and it is possible that a body of infantry remained drawn up in readiness on one of the hills during the morning, but I remember no large force of troops at any time on that day.

About noon, or a little after, we were told that General McClellan's advance had been checked, and that it was not believed he would attempt to cross the river at once—a surmise that proved to be correct. The country grew more composed. General Lee lay near Leetown, some seven miles south of us, and General McClellan rested quietly in Maryland. On Sunday we were able to have some short church services for our wounded, cut still shorter, I regret to say, by reports that the "Yankees" were crossing. Such reports continued to harass us, especially as we feared the capture of our friends, who would often ride down to see us during the day, but who seldom ventured to spend a night so near the river. We presently passed into debatable land, when we were in the Confederacy in the morning, in the Union after dinner, and on neutral ground at night. We lived through a disturbed and eventful autumn, subject to continual "alarms and excursions," but when this Saturday came to an end, the most trying and tempestuous week of the war for Shepherdstown was over.

## THE CASE OF FITZ JOHN PORTER.

BY RICHARD B. IRWIN, LIEUTENANT-COLONEL AND ASSISTANT ADJUTANT-GENERAL, U. S. V.

WITHOUT going into the intricacies of allegation, evidence, and argument on one side or the other of this many-sided controversy, some account of the proceedings and conclusions of the military tribunals appointed for its investigation seems necessary. These tribunals were four in number: First, a Court of Inquiry, ordered by the President September 5th, 1862, and which met and was finally dissolved on the 15th, without taking any action; second, the Military Commission, convened November 17th, 1862; third, the Court-martial, appointed November 25th, which sentenced General Porter to be cashiered; fourth, the Board of Officers, appointed by President Hayes April 12th, 1878, and upon whose report, reversing the findings of the court-martial, General Porter was finally reinstated in the service.

In his report of September 3d, 1862, General Pope made certain representations unfavorable to Generals Porter, Franklin, and Griffin. On the 5th, by the same order that relieved General Pope from command, the President directed that Generals Porter, Franklin, and Griffin "be relieved from their respective commands until the charges against them can be investigated by a court of inquiry." This order appears to have been suspended the next day at General McClellan's request, and was never executed, all three of the generals named remaining on duty; but on the 5th of November, by the same order that removed General McClellan from command of the Army of the Potomac, the President again directed that General Porter be relieved from command of the Fifth Corps; and this order, issued by Halleck on the 10th, was put in force on the 12th.

The Court of Inquiry, appointed on the 5th of September, was ordered to inquire into the charges preferred by General Pope against Generals Franklin, Porter, and Griffin. The detail consisted of Major-General George Cadwalader, Brigadier-Generals Silas Casey and J. K. F. Mansfield, with Colonel Joseph Holt as Judge-Advocate, and this commission met on the 6th and 8th, adjourned and was dissolved without action, General Mansfield being ordered into the field on the day last named, and Generals Franklin, Porter, and Griffin being already there.

On the 17th of November a military commission was appointed by the General-in-Chief to examine and report on charges preferred against General Porter by General Pope.

A military commission is a tribunal constituted to try civil cases when the functions of the ordinary courts of law are suspended by the state of war. Its authority rests entirely upon the supreme will of the commander. Its jurisdiction is wholly outside the articles of war by which the army itself is exclusively governed. When the soldier is arraigned before such a commission, it is for offenses for which, in time of peace, he would be tried by the civil authorities. The proceeding first contemplated would therefore, at first sight, appear to have been of a character unusual in armies and altogether different from that afterward pursued; however, the distinction was not always strictly regarded during this war, purely military cases being more than once brought before a commission, sitting really as a court of inquiry, as in the Harper's Ferry case, and in the investigation as to "the operations of the army under the command of Major-General D. C. Buell, in Kentucky and Tennessee," and punishment even inflicted, as in the former, without charges, or arraignment, and without any other trial.

No charges preferred against General Porter by General Pope have been found, save in his official reports of September 3d, 1862, and January 27th, 1863; and General Pope testified before the court-martial that he had in fact preferred none. In his letter to General Halleck of September 30th, 1862, General Pope speaks of "having laid before the Government the conduct of McClellan, Porter, and Griffin," and of being "not disposed to push the matter farther unless the silence of the Government . . . and the restoration of these officers without trial to their commands, coupled with my banishment to a distant and unimportant department, render it necessary as an act of justice to myself." In his reply, October 10th, Halleck says: "Again you complain that Porter and Griffin have not been tried on your charges against them. You know that a court was ordered for their trial and that it was suspended because all officers were required in the field. A new court has been ordered, and they are to be tried and the grounds of your charges to be fully investigated."

On November 25th, 1862, the military commission, having simply met and adjourned, was dissolved and the court-martial appointed. General Porter was now placed in arrest.

As finally constituted the court consisted of Major-Generals David Hunter and E. A. Hitchcock, and Brigadier-Generals Rufus King, B. M. Prentiss, James B. Ricketts, Silas Casey, James A. Garfield, N. B. Buford, and J. P. Slough, with Colonel Joseph Holt, Judge-Advocate-General of the Army, as Judge-Advocate.

The charges exhibited to the court were found to have been preferred by Brigadier-General Benjamin S. Roberts, Inspector-General on General Pope's staff at the time of the occurrences. The first charge, laid under the ninth article of war, alleged five instances of "disobedience of orders"; the second charge, laid under the fifty-second article of war, contained four allegations covering two acts of misbehavior in the presence of the enemy on the 29th and 30th.

The court found the accused guilty of having disobeyed three of General Pope's orders — that of August 27th, to march on Bristoe at 1 A. M.; the "joint order" on the morning of the 29th, to "move toward Gainesville"; and the order dated 4:30 that afternoon, "to push forward into action at once on the enemy's right flank"; guilty, also, of having "shamefully disobeyed" the latter order, and of having retreated without any attempt to engage the enemy; but not guilty of having permitted Griffin's and Piatt's brigades to leave the battle-field and go to Centreville. The charge of having feebly attacked the enemy on the 30th was withdrawn.

In substance the charges on which Porter was convicted were two,— that he disobeyed General Pope's order to march at 1 A. M. on the 28th, and that, in disobedience of orders, he failed to attack, but retreated, on the 29th. Upon the former we shall not dwell, since even upon the first trial it was shown that Porter delayed only two hours, on account of the darkness of the night, that he marched at 3, that nothing turned upon his delay,

that McDowell, Kearny, and Reno, with less distance to cover, under orders substantially similar, were similarly delayed. The vital point remains whether Porter did or did not disobey his orders and fail in his duty by not attacking on the 29th, and by retreating.

The sentence of the court-martial delivered on the 10th of January, 1863, was that General Porter "be cashiered and be forever disqualified from holding any office of trust or profit under the Government of the United States." On the 21st of January this sentence was approved by President Lincoln.

During the next fifteen years General Porter continually applied for a rehearing, in the light of evidence newly discovered or not available at the time of his trial.

On the 12th of April, 1878, President Hayes appointed a board of officers, consisting of Major-General John M. Schofield, Brigadier-General Alfred H. Terry, and Colonel George W. Getty, to examine the new evidence in connection with the old.

The new evidence consisted largely of the testimony and the official reports of the Confederate officers serving in the Army of Northern Virginia at the second battle of Bull Run, supplemented by new and accurate maps of the field of battle. None of this information, from the nature of the case, was, or could have been, before the court-martial. By it, if established, an entirely new light was thrown upon the circumstances as they existed in Porter's front on the 29th of August.

General Pope's orders of the 29th, which Porter was charged with disobeying, were as follows, the first, known as the "joint order," having reached him about or shortly after noon:

"GENERALS MCDOWELL AND PORTER: You will please move forward with your joint commands toward Gainesville. I sent General Porter written orders to that effect an hour and a half ago. Heintzelman, Sigel, and Reno are moving on the Warrenton turnpike, and must now be not far from Gainesville.‡ I desire that as soon as communication is established between this force and your own, the whole command shall halt. It may be necessary to fall back behind Bull Run at Centreville to-night. I presume it will be so, on account of our supplies. If any considerable advantages are to be gained by departing from this order it will not be strictly carried out. One thing must be had in view, that the troops must occupy a position from which they can reach Bull Run to-night or by morning. The indications are that the whole force of the enemy is moving in this direction at a pace that will bring them here by to-morrow night or the next day."

General McDowell almost immediately withdrew King's division, marched it round in the rear by the Sudley Springs road, did not connect or again communicate with Porter during the day, and only brought King's division into action, on the right, at 6:15 P. M.

Porter's right was not in connection or communication with Reynolds, who held the left of the main line. Between them was a very wide gap, hid-

---

‡ The orders to Generals Heintzelman, Reno, and Sigel at the same hour (not produced before the court or board) were: "If you find yourselves heavily pressed by superior numbers of the enemy, you will not push matters further. Fitz John Porter and King's division of McDowell's corps are moving on Gainesville from Manassas Junction, and will come in on your left. They have about twenty thousand men. The command must return to this place [Centreville] to-night or by morning on account of subsistence and forage."

den by a wood through which Generals McDowell and Porter were unable to pass on horseback, and in which messengers sent by Porter to communicate with McDowell and others were captured by the enemy.

The second order did not reach General Porter till 6:30 P. M., and before the dispositions immediately ordered to execute it could be completed, darkness interposed. It read:

"August 29th, 1862 — 4:30 P. M.
"MAJOR-GENERAL PORTER:
"Your line of march brings you in on the enemy's right flank. I desire you to push forward into action at once on the enemy's flank and, if possible, on his rear, keeping your right in communication with General Reynolds. The enemy is massed in the woods in front of us, but can be shelled out as soon as you engage their flank. Keep heavy reserves and use your batteries, keeping well closed to your right all the time. In case you are obliged to fall back, do so to your right and rear, so as to keep you in close communication with the right wing."

Both orders are based upon the supposition that the enemy was Jackson; that Longstreet was not there, and would not arrive till the night of the 30th or the 31st, and that Jackson was to be attacked in front and flank or rear and crushed before Longstreet joined him.

When McDowell came upon the rear of Porter's troops near Bethlehem Church he had just received Buford's dispatch of 9:30 A. M. forwarded by Ricketts at 11:30 A. M.☆ This told of Longstreet's passage through Gainesville before 9:30; it reached McDowell after 11:30. When McDowell joined Porter he found him at the head of his troops, advancing; therefore, when Porter arrived on the crest of the hills which descend to Dawkin's Branch, his advance encountered Longstreet's, already in occupation of the opposite slope.

The board of officers say in their report:

"General Porter's conduct was adjudged [by the court-martial] upon the assumption that not more than one division under Longstreet had arrived on the field, and that Porter had no considerable force in his front.

"The fact is that Longstreet, with *four* divisions of 25,000 ♩ men, was there on the field before Porter arrived with his two divisions of 9000 men; that the Confederate general-in-chief was there in person at least two or three hours before the commander of the Army of Virginia himself arrived on the field, and that Porter with his two divisions saved the Army of Virginia that day from the disaster naturally due to the enemy's earlier preparations for battle.

"If the 4:30 order had been promptly delivered a very grave responsibility would have devolved upon General Porter. The order was based upon conditions which were essentially erroneous and upon expectations which could not possibly be realized. . . .

"What General Porter actually did do . . . now seems to have been only the simple necessary action which an intelligent soldier had no choice but to take. It is not possible that any court-martial could have condemned such conduct if it had been correctly understood. On the contrary, that conduct was obedient, subordinate, faithful, and judicious. It saved the Union army from disaster on the 29th of August."

The board accordingly recommended to President Hayes to set aside the findings and sentence of the court-martial and to restore Porter to his rank in the service from the date of his dismissal.

In the absence of legislation, President Hayes considered himself as without power to act, and on the 5th of June, 1879, he submitted the proceedings and conclusions of the board for the action of Congress.

On the 4th of May, 1882, President Arthur, by letters patent, remitted so much of the sentence of the court as had not been fully executed, and thus relieved General Porter from the continuing disqualification to hold office.

On the 1st of July, 1886, President Cleveland approved an act "for the relief of Fitz John Porter" which had been passed in the House of Representatives on the 18th of February by a vote of 171 to 113, and in the Senate on the 25th of June by a vote of 30 to 17. In accordance with the provisions of this act, on the 5th of August Porter was once more commissioned as colonel of infantry in the army of the United States, to rank from May 14th, 1861, but without back pay; and on August 7th he was placed on the retired list.

☆ Ricketts's dispatch was not produced in evidence. It strongly confirms Surgeon R. O. Abbott's statement that it was "between 12 and 1 o'clock, toward 1," when he delivered one copy of the "joint order" to Porter, after delivering the other to General McDowell.— R. B. I.

♩ According to Col. Marshall of Gen. Lee's staff, 30,000.

## CANBY'S SERVICES IN THE NEW MEXICAN CAMPAIGN.

BY LATHAM ANDERSON, BREVET BRIGADIER-GENERAL, U. S. V.

THE account in this work by Captain Pettis of "The Confederate Invasion of New Mexico and Arizona,"‡ is accurate as to most details. It is open to criticism, however, in two particulars: it fails to recognize the political as well as the military importance of the campaign, and it does injustice to General Canby.

The remote and unimportant territory of New Mexico was not the real objective of this invasion. The Confederate leaders were striking at much higher game — no less than the conquest of California, Sonora, Chihuahua, New Mexico, Arizona, and Utah — and, above all, the possession of the gold supply of the Pacific coast, a source of strength considered by Mr. Lincoln to be essential to the successful prosecution of the war.

The truth of this view will be apparent when we consider what the relative positions of the two governments would have been had Sibley succeeded in his enterprise. The Confederacy would have controlled the Gulf of California and the two finest harbors on the Pacific coast with a coast-line of 1200 or 1500 miles. The conquest alone of this vast domain, in all probability, would have insured the recognition of the Confederacy by the European powers. Owing to the remoteness of this

‡ For Captain Pettis's article and accompanying maps, see Vol. II., p. 103.— EDITORS.

coast it would have been impossible for us to have effectually blockaded it. In fact the Confederates could have overpowered us in the Pacific Ocean, as all the advantages of position and materials would have been on their side. Finally, the current of gold, that, according to Mr. Lincoln, formed the life-blood of our financial credit, would have been diverted from Washington to Richmond. What then would have been the relative quotations of "Greenbacks" and "Graybacks"? Unquestionably the Confederate paper would have been worth at least as much as ours, and the oceans would have swarmed with *Alabama*s. But it may be asked, to what extent would Sibley's conquest of New Mexico have contributed to this result? If it would have rendered the conquest of California probable, then it was one of the most momentous campaigns of the war. If the reverse were true, then it was a series of insignificant skirmishes, devoid of military or political significance. The capture of Forts Craig and Union with their garrisons and supplies would have rendered highly probable the successful accomplishment of the entire plan of Sibley's campaign. Southerners and Southern sympathizers were scattered throughout the Western mountain regions. They preponderated strongly in Southern New Mexico, Arizona, and Southern California.

In the coast and river towns and cities of California, the Confederates formed a powerful faction. Had Sibley's conquest of New Mexico been complete, he would have captured 6000 or 8000 stand of arms and 25 or 30 pieces of artillery. Hardy miners and frontier desperadoes would have flocked to his standard from all parts of the Rocky Mountains. He could have enlisted California with at least twice as many men as he brought into New Mexico. As a matter of course, the entire Mormon population of Utah, Arizona, and California would have joined him joyfully, and would have furnished him most efficient aid. In the meantime the California Secessionists would not have been idle. Although General George Wright and the Unionists would have been too enterprising to enable them to effect any complete or systematic organization, a fierce guerrilla warfare would certainly have been inaugurated all over the central and southern parts of the State as soon as it was known that Sibley's victorious army was approaching. Unaided they could have accomplished nothing. The National forces had absolute control of the situation. The forts in San Francisco harbor, the arsenal at Benicia, the Mare Island navy-yard, and whatever naval force there was on the coast were all in Union hands, under the custody of a nucleus (small, it is true) of regular troops. Moreover, the Union volunteers, with whom the enemy would have had to contend, were unsurpassed as fighting material. But with an invading army of 6000 or 8000 men across the Colorado, flushed with victory and well supplied with small arms, artillery, ammunition, and transportation, the situation would have been materially changed. The Government, in order to maintain its prestige, must have continually protected many points from attack. It would thus have been compelled to divide and weaken its forces. The California desert constitutes a serious obstacle to an invading army; but, in this instance, the Confederates and their natural allies, the Mormons, preponderated so largely in that region that they could have maintained control of all the water-holes on the desert, and thus could have prevented Union scouts from observing and reporting promptly the movements of the invading army. Our forces probably could not have received notice of the route of the invading column in time to concentrate upon the Tejon Pass. Simultaneously with the arrival of the Confederate column, diversion by guerrilla attacks at various points throughout the State could, and, no doubt, would, have been made so as to compel a still further weakening of our forces at the main point of attack. Owing to all these causes it would have been impossible for the Union commander to meet Sibley with equal forces. For the Union army defeat under these circumstances in Southern California would have been defeat in an enemy's country, and it would have been very difficult for it to escape capture had it been routed. However superb the material of which the California volunteers were composed,‡ they were raw troops and would have been confronted by larger numbers of men, many of them already seasoned to war in a victorious campaign, who would, moreover, have been compelled to fight with desperation because they had the desert at their backs. It is true the fortunes of war are uncertain, and none of these things might have happened; but, in view of the above facts, the probabilities seem altogether in favor of the success of the Confederates, backed by an army which had conquered New Mexico and Arizona. Hence, in view of the situation in California and of the momentous consequences of its capture by the Confederates, the conflict in New Mexico should be regarded as one of the decisive campaigns of the war. The soundness and brilliancy of General Canby's management rendered it decisive in our favor. For the invading column the result was practically annihilation, unless the reports brought into our lines were gross exaggerations. It is to be hoped that this discussion may elicit from some of the survivors of Sibley's column a detailed account of that retreat.

Soon after Canby assumed command of the department, and before he had time to get it fairly in hand, he was confronted with the appalling disaster of San Augustine Springs. This was quickly followed by the intelligence that two expeditions were forming to attack him,— one in Northern Texas under Van Dorn, to enter by the Canadian route against Fort Union; the other at San Antonio, under Sibley, intended to reënforce Baylor at El Paso. He was therefore compelled to keep a strong force at Fort Union, another at Fort Craig, and to hold a third at an intermediate point

---

‡ A remarkable march through the hostile Indian country of Arizona to join Canby was made by eleven companies of infantry, two of cavalry, and two batteries, under Colonel J. H. Carleton, which were dispatched by General George Wright, commanding the Department of the Pacific, overland from Southern California. The column started April 13th, 1862, and arrived at Santa Fe September 20th.— EDITORS.

whence he could succor the division first attacked. This prevented him from acting aggressively against Baylor early in the campaign. After Sibley had passed Fort Craig, Canby called a meeting of his senior officers and outlined to them his plan of campaign, which was to follow the enemy closely in his march up the valley, harass him in front, flanks, and rear with the irregular troops and cavalry — burn or remove all supplies in his front, but avoid a general engagement, except where the position was strongly in our favor. The numerous adobe villages along the line gave admirable opportunities for carrying out this plan at intervals of a few miles. Canby had no confidence in the capacity of the New Mexico volunteers to face the Texans in the open field, and the results fully confirmed his judgment on that point. But the adobe villages could be quickly loop-holed and converted into admirable defenses for raw troops. By placing the New Mexicans in these improvised fortresses, and using the regulars and Colorado volunteers aggressively in the open parts of the line, the efficiency of his force would have been doubled. Should the enemy refuse to attack us in any of these strong positions until he passed Albuquerque, Canby could then form a junction with the reënforcements at Fort Union, and Sibley's fate would have been sealed. The late Major H. R. Selden, who was present at the meeting, is the writer's authority for this outline of Canby's intended plan of campaign. This plan was marred at the very outset by the impetuosity of that rash old fighter, Lieutenant-Colonel B. S. Roberts, who, at Valverde, January 21st, precipitated a decisive engagement with the enemy, where the latter had the advantage of position. It must be said in justice to Colonel Roberts, however, that had not two of his subordinates shown a lack of their commander's dash, the result of that day's battle would have been different. Mr. Pettis intimates that all went well on the field until Canby arrived. Such was not the case. Roberts had failed to dislodge the enemy from his strong position behind the sand hills. Had it not been for the fatal gap in our center, the Texan assault on McRae's battery could not have been made, as the attacking column would have been taken in flank by our center. That gap was caused by Colonel Miguel Pino's 2d New Mexican Regiment remaining under the river-bank and refusing to move forward into line. For this, of course, Canby was not responsible. His plan of pivoting on his left and doubling up the enemy's left flank so as to sweep him out of his natural intrenchment was an admirable one.

After the reverse at Valverde nothing remained for Canby but to strive for a junction with the troops at Fort Union. In this he was thwarted for a time by the fact that Colonel John P. Slough, against his instructions, brought on a decisive engagement with the enemy at Cañon Glorieta on the 28th of March. Slough's main force was driven from the field, and the defeat would have been a disastrous one had not the flanking party, under Major Chivington, of the 1st Colorado Volunteers, and Captain W. H. Lewis, 5th U. S. Infantry, succeeded in destroying the Texan train. The rumor is said to have spread among the Texans that they were being attacked in rear by Canby's column. This caused a panic among part of their force, and prevented an effective pursuit of Slough's defeated troops.

After the junction with the troops from Fort Union, and the overtaking and surprising of the enemy at Peralta, on the 15th of April, Canby had it in his power to capture the entire column. But this was impracticable, because he could not have fed his prisoners. The country was stripped of provisions of all sorts, his own troops were on short rations, and he was at Peralta, one thousand miles from his base of supplies. His only alternative was to force the Texans into their disastrous retreat.

The account of the battle of Valverde in Greeley's "American Conflict" is erroneous in two important statements. First, speaking of the fighting in the morning he says: "The day wore on with more noise than execution, until 2 P. M." As a matter of fact our losses in the morning were heavier than in the evening, when most of the casualties were confined to McRae's Battery. Also Mr. Greeley states: "Our supporting infantry, twice or thrice the Texans in number, and including more than man for man of regulars, shamefully withstood every entreaty to charge, and the Colorado volunteers vied with the regulars in this infamous flight." There were only one thousand regulars in the field altogether, and the bulk of them were on the extreme right, out of supporting distance of the battery. In the morning fight the single company of Colorado volunteers behaved admirably, showing as much steadiness as old regulars.

## CANBY AT VALVERDE.

### BY A. W. EVANS, LIEUTENANT-COLONEL, U. S. A.

COLONEL CANBY reached the field of Valverde in the afternoon, during the lull, proceeding to the position of McRae's battery. One or two shots were fired from it after his arrival without eliciting a reply. After consultation and examination of the position, he moved that battery about two hundred yards to the left and directed the placing of its supports, which had hardly — if at all — got completely into position when the Texan charge was made. It was a surprise, and the attacking force (picked men) was superior in numbers to the supports of the battery — certainly to the regulars in support. Hall's battery (its commander is now Major R. H. Hall, 22d U. S. Infantry) was an extempore one of two 24-pounders, one of which was disabled in the course of the day by the breaking of its trail, and was taken off the field. His position was on the extreme right, down the river, a mile from McRae, with a great gap between. Neither Captain Wingate's battalion nor Colonel Carson's regiment was in support of him. They were nearer McRae. Just before the charge upon the latter Major Duncan sent up for reënforcements, announcing that a charge was about to be made upon him; and Carson's regiment and Company H, 7th Infantry, Captain Ingraham, were sent, but did not reach him in time, or only got half-way. One of McRae's caissons (possibly a limber-box, but I think the former) was blown up in the fight,— it was said, by one of his sergeants firing his pistol into it to prevent its capture, but this is not authenticated. The New Mexican volunteers in support broke early, and caused much confusion. It was reported that the muzzles of the cannon had been elevated for distant firing, and that in the flurry they were not depressed, thus firing over the heads of the approaching enemy. The ammunition was, I think, only round shot and spherical case; there was no grape.

That the Union troops were successful in the morning under Colonel Roberts and were defeated in the evening under Colonel Canby was the fortune of war. It is not always correct to argue *post hoc, propter hoc.* The result would probably have been the same if the commanders had been reversed, or if Colonel Canby had remained at Fort Craig.

## SIBLEY'S NEW MEXICAN CAMPAIGN.—ITS OBJECTS AND THE CAUSES OF ITS FAILURE.

### BY T. T. TEEL, MAJOR, C. S. A.

THE object of his campaign in New Mexico was explained in detail by General H. H. Sibley to the writer in a conversation which occurred just after the former had assumed command of the army. His plans were in substance as follows: While in the United States army and stationed in Arizona, he had acquired full information as to the resources of that Territory and of New Mexico; and as to the condition of the United States forces in those Territories, the quantity of Government stores, supplies, transportation, etc. He had informed President Davis of these things, and had submitted to him the plan of campaign. President Davis had authorized him to enlist three regiments in Texas, to constitute a brigade to be mounted and mustered into the service, with such arms as could be obtained in Texas, and, upon arriving in New Mexico, the brigade was to be furnished with arms and equipments out of the supply already captured or that might be captured. His campaign was to be self-sustaining; President Davis knew that Colonel John R. Baylor, with less than five hundred troops, had captured large supplies and was in possession of all of Arizona and the lower part of New Mexico; Sibley was to utilize the results of Baylor's successes, make Mesilla the base of operations, and with the enlistment of men from New Mexico, California, Arizona, and Colorado form an army which would effect the ultimate aim of the campaign, for there were scattered all over the Western States and Territories Southern men who were anxiously awaiting an opportunity to join the Confederate army. Upon the arrival of his brigade at Mesilla, Sibley was to open negotiations with the governors of Chihuahua, Sonora, and Lower California, for supplies, etc. *The objective aim and design of the campaign was the conquest of California,* and as soon as the Confederate army should occupy the Territory of New Mexico, an army of advance would be organized, and "On to San Francisco" would be the watchword; California had to be conquered, so that there would be an outlet for slavery, the boundaries of the Confederacy, as they then existed, including none of the Territories, but with New Mexico, Arizona, California, and Utah there would be plenty of room for the extension of slavery, which would greatly strengthen the Confederate States. If the Confederates succeeded in occupying California, New Mexico, and Arizona, negotiations to secure Chihuahua, Sonora, and Lower California, either by purchase or by conquest, would be opened; the state of affairs in Mexico made it an easy thing to take those States, and the Mexican President would be glad to get rid of them and at the same time improve his exchequer. In addition to all this, General Sibley intimated that there was a secret understanding between the Mexican and the Confederate authorities, and that, as soon as our occupation of the said states was assured, a transfer of those Mexican states would be made to the Confederacy. Juarez, the President of the Republic (so called), was then in the City of Mexico with a small army under his command, hardly sufficient to keep him in his position. That date (1862) was the darkest hour in the annals of our sister republic, but it was the brightest of the Confederacy, and General Sibley thought that he would have little difficulty in consummating the ends so devoutly wished by the Confederate Government.

The direct cause of our discomfiture and the failure of our campaign was the want of supplies of all kinds for the use of our army. The territory which we occupied was no storehouse. Colonel Canby's order to destroy everything that would be of use to the Confederates had been fully enforced. Thus we were situated in the very heart of the enemy's country, with well-equipped forces in our front and rear.

General Sibley was not a good administrative officer. He did not husband his resources, and was too prone to let the morrow take care of itself. But for this the expedition never would have been undertaken, nor would he have left the enemy between him and his base of supplies, a mistake which he made at Fort Craig. The other reasons for the failure of the campaign were want of supplies, ammunition, discipline, and confidence. Under such circumstances failure was inevitable. Had Colonel John R. Baylor continued to command, the result might have been different.

# OPERATIONS IN NORTH ALABAMA.

### BY DON CARLOS BUELL, MAJOR-GENERAL, U. S. V.

THE instructions↓ which I left behind for the regulation of affairs in Tennessee, when I started from Nashville for Savannah prior to the battle of Shiloh, constituted an important part in the plan of campaign, but could not be made absolute with reference to military operations which depended so much on undetermined conditions. For East Tennessee, General George W. Morgan, the officer assigned to the command of a column operating in that direction from Kentucky, was instructed, as a first step, to take Cumberland Gap if practicable, or to hold the enemy in check on that line if his force should prove insufficient to advance. The force left in Middle Tennessee was to preserve internal order there, keep open the communications of the army, repel invasion, and occupy the Memphis and Charleston railroad when the opportunity offered. The two latter objects were chiefly intrusted to General O. M. Mitchel. Only the instructions to him,⚓ and his action under them, can here be remarked upon.

These instructions placed General Mitchel, in the beginning, mainly at Fayetteville, Tennessee, twenty-eight miles north of Huntsville, Alabama, and explained to him how his position was to be used according to circumstances; among other things to concentrate his force at Huntsville or Decatur — the occupation of the Memphis and Charleston railroad through those points having been all the time distinctly understood as a standing object, and discussed in the conversations referred to in the instructions.↓ One division, with three field-batteries (18 pieces) of artillery, a regiment of cavalry, and two companies of engineer troops, in all about 8000 effective men, constituted his command; and he was told that in case of necessity the remainder of the force in Middle Tennessee would be placed under his orders. The general dispositions included a few regiments for the immediate protection of Nashville, under the command of General Ebenezer Dumont, who besides was charged with the communications of the army, in certain respects. A regiment was also designated as a provost-guard for Nashville, with orders to answer the demands of the military governor, Andrew Johnson, for the enforcement of his authority. The fine regiment (51st Ohio) of Colonel Stanley Matthews, now a justice of the United States Supreme Court, was selected for that position, on account of the efficient and judicious character of its commander. Governor Johnson was not pleased with the limited power thus arranged for himself. He wanted a much larger force under his control, and the records exhibit earnest protests from him to the President and Secretary of War against the defenseless condition in which he considered that I had left him.

Under the instructions given to Mitchel, that officer, after hearing of the victory at Shiloh (April 7th, 1862), marched from Fayetteville at noon on the 10th of April, and reached Huntsville at 6 A. M. on the 11th, capturing, as he reports, about 200 prisoners, 15 locomotives, and other rolling-stock and

↓ See "Official Records," Vol. X., Pt. II., pp. 47, 54, 71, 75, 86.   ⚓ Page 71.   ↓ Pages 37 and 60.

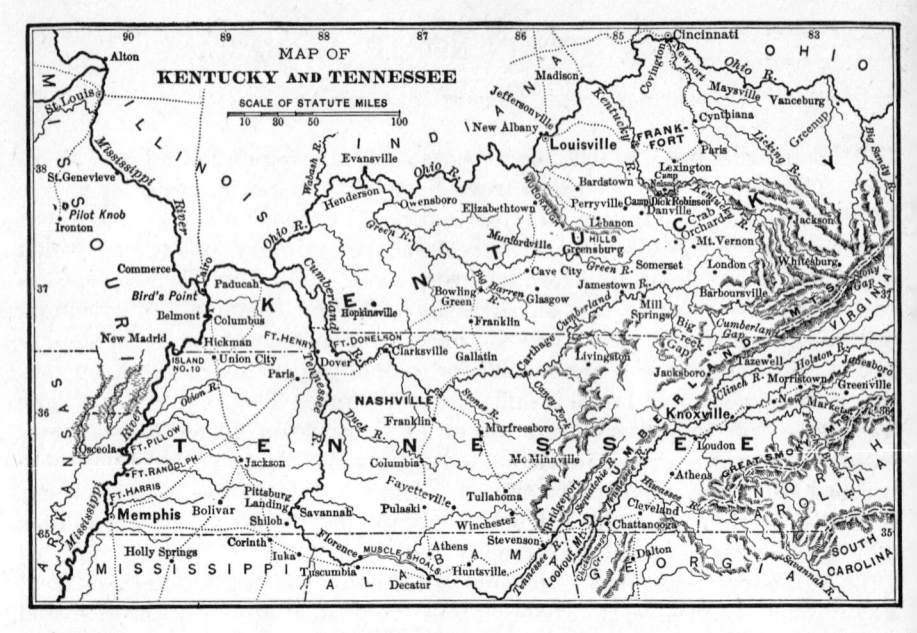

public property. On the 12th, expeditions were sent eastward to within four miles of the bridge over the Tennessee River at Bridgeport, destroying bridges in that direction and capturing five more locomotives; and westward to the Decatur bridge, twenty miles from Huntsville. Reporting these last movements on the 12th, General Mitchel says: "We have nothing more to do in this region, having fully accomplished all that was ordered."

These operations of course stopped the enemy's railroad communications through North Alabama. On the 13th a brigade under Colonel John B. Turchin was started to Tuscumbia (thirty miles west of Decatur), where it arrived about the 17th, and where I furnished it with supplies by water. It encountered no enemy, and was recalled by Mitchel on the 24th, upon a rumor that it was threatened from Corinth. As soon as it crossed again to the north side of the Tennessee the Decatur bridge was burned. As a reconnoitering measure, this expedition was well enough. The evil of it, as it turned out, was in the injury which resulted to the line of railroad — the destruction of the Decatur bridge by Mitchel himself, and other bridges by the enemy. Nothing could be more unwise than Mitchel's idea that the brigade should be reënforced from the main army so as to hold Tuscumbia, while Beauregard was at Corinth, fifty miles distant, with railroad communication, and Halleck not yet prepared to march against him from Pittsburg Landing.

On the 1st of May Mitchel reports from Huntsville to the Secretary of War, with whom he had established a correspondence: "On yesterday (properly the 29th of April), the enemy having cut our wires and attacked during the night one of our brigades, I deemed it my duty to head in person the expedition against Bridgeport," and he describes what was done. The expedition was under the command of Colonel Joshua W. Sill, a capable young officer, afterward killed at Stone's River. Mitchel represents the force of the enemy, by report, at 5000 infantry and one regiment of cavalry; and again at five regiments of infantry and 1800 cavalry. The enemy reports 450 raw infantry, 150 cavalry, and two old iron field-pieces drawn by hand. There was virtually no resistance. Sill had one man killed, and the enemy reports two men slightly wounded in retiring. The Confederates withdrew as the Federals advanced. The 50 men that remained a moment at the bridge-head retreated rapidly across at the first shot, and the whole force, after burning 450 feet at the east end of the bridge, continued the retreat, leaving behind the two iron guns. The blast which the enemy had prepared for blowing up a span at the west end failed to do its work. Mitchel reports the following incident in this affair: "A body of 40 or 50 cavalry came dashing through a wheat-field in full sight just below the bridge, supposing our troops to be theirs, and advanced to within 400 yards. Our cavalry dashed after them, while our artillery opened fire. *How many escaped I do not know.*" The enemy reports "10 or 12" of his cavalry scouts in that position, probably afraid to venture on the bridge, which was about to be destroyed. As neither the enemy nor Mitchel reports any of them killed or captured, the presumption is that *all* escaped. Mitchel at Huntsville, on May 1st, closes his report of this affair as follows: "This campaign is ended, and I can now occupy Huntsville in perfect security, while all of Alabama north of the Tennessee floats no flag but that of the Union." Thus far no resistance had been encountered, but Mitchel's movements had been well conceived and vigorous, and made a good appearance. Stanton answered his glowing dispatches naturally: "Your spirited operations afford great satisfaction to the President."

Three days after Mitchel's dispatch as quoted, he telegraphed Stanton, May 4th, in explanation of some unexpected developments of the enemy, and says:

"I shall soon have watchful guards among the slaves on the plantations from Bridgeport to Florence, and all who communicate to me valuable information I have promised the protection of my government. Should my course in this particular be disapproved, it would be impossible for me to hold my position. I must abandon the line of railway, and Northern Alabama falls back into the hands of the enemy. No reënforcements have been sent to me, and I am promised none except a regiment of cavalry and a company of scouts, neither of which have reached me. I should esteem it a great military and political misfortune to be compelled to yield up one inch of the territory we have conquered." [And again the same day, May 4th]: "I have promised protection to the slaves who have given me valuable assistance and information. If the government disapproves of what I have done, I must receive heavy reënforcements or abandon my position."

The only visible or actual ground for this sudden change from easy assurance to anxious uncertainty, was the appearance of the Confederate John Morgan on the road from Decatur to Nashville on the 2d of May with a force which Mitchel reports at 600 cavalry, including Scott's attack at Athens, and by which some careless detachments were surprised and captured. Without tarrying, Morgan continued his passage into Kentucky. He was overtaken and defeated with some loss, at Lebanon, Tennessee, by a force under General Dumont not under Mitchel's command. Morgan was promptly succeeded in Middle Tennessee by small bands of cavalry, which gave Mitchel great

MAJOR-GENERAL ORMSBY M. MITCHEL.
FROM A PHOTOGRAPH.

uneasiness and caused considerable harassment by operating on the railroads, and firing into guards and trains. It was a foretaste of what was to be experienced on a much larger scale and to a much wider extent, when the army entered North Alabama to advance into East Tennessee in July.

On the 7th of May Mitchel was authorized to employ the whole of the available force in Middle Tennessee, amounting to about 16,000 men, including what he had before. There was a considerable display of activity. A movement of two columns under General James S. Negley and Colonel William H. Lytle, about the 14th of May, interrupted the crossing of a body of Confederate cavalry, 1750 strong, under Colonel Wirt Adams from the south to the north side of the Tennessee at Lamb's ferry below Decatur. The Federals had one man killed in these operations. Adams, with 850 men, moved north of Huntsville to the Nashville and Chattanooga railroad in the vicinity of Manchester. Toward the last of May quite a large expedition was organized, to which the dispatches ascribe different objects at different times. Sometimes it is to repel a heavy force that is supposed to be invading Middle Tennessee from Chattanooga. Sometimes it is to attack Chattanooga, which it is at last reported as having attacked. It embraced, according to Mitchel's report, at least 6000 men, under the command of General Negley. A portion of it under Negley surprised Adams's cavalry at Sweeden's Cove near the railroad, compelling it to make a precipitate retreat, and capturing some camp-equipage and supplies. Negley had two men killed and seven wounded in this affair. He then advanced to the river opposite Chattanooga. A sharp fire with field-artillery was opened upon the trenches and the town, and the enemy was reported as driven out. Negley had been authorized "to take the town in case he deemed it prudent," but he had no means of crossing the river, and for the want of supplies could not have remained forty-eight hours if he had crossed, or even have held his position on the north side. His supplies were already virtually exhausted, and he was ordered back by Mitchel, June 9th, ostensibly on the ground that an imaginary force was threatening Nashville in his rear. A better reason was that he was there without any ulterior purpose, and without adequate means for advancing or remaining.

General Mitchel deprecated this withdrawal because, as he says: "If we fall back we open the door to pour in troops at the exact point they (the enemy) are already determined to use, and if we once commence to fall back it is

## OPERATIONS IN NORTH ALABAMA. 705

difficult to determine when we can halt"; and in reporting his action he says: "I am quite certain the enemy will follow." The next day he concludes that the invading force, with reference to which this formidable expedition was set on foot, did not exist. Negley had one man wounded opposite Chattanooga.

The destruction of the Bridgeport and Decatur bridges was not contrary to my orders under certain conditions. General Mitchel's position was an isolated one. It happened that the Confederate force in East Tennessee at the moment was small, but the resources of the enemy were not well understood at that early period. By the road to the east Mitchel was exposed to whatever force the enemy might be capable of sending against him, and he was not within reach of prompt succor even if the troops for that purpose could be spared from the main army on the west side of the Tennessee. Very soon, therefore, after his arrival at Huntsville, he was authorized to destroy the Bridgeport bridge. But the orders, though ample, were not imperative, as he evidently understood, for in reporting his expedition of the 29th of April, he took credit to his command for partially rescuing the bridge from destruction by the enemy. He says: "We can now hold it or destroy it as may be ordered." He did not report that upon the withdrawal of his force the bridge was totally burned by his order. That action was unnecessary, the bridge having been already sufficiently disabled by the enemy.

There was no necessity for the burning of the Decatur bridge. Mitchel had been instructed to destroy it in case he should be forced to retire from his position in North Alabama, a contingency of which he frequently expressed apprehension; but while he remained, the bridge was so completely under his control as to render its destruction unnecessary until the last moment. On April 25th Mitchel reported: "I have determined to withdraw my troops to the north side of the river, and, if necessary to our safety, to destroy the Decatur bridge." I never censured him for these acts, and do not now censure him. I only mean to make a proper account of them. Channels of communication in the field of operations of hostile armies, if not guarded, will generally be obstructed by one side or the other, and it is seldom that their importance in advance of actual use will warrant the means requisite for their preservation. These are matters of judgment at the moment, and ought not to be too narrowly criticised. A measure which proved in the end to have been superfluous, or even hurtful, may with the evidence at the time have seemed entirely advisable.

A far more serious fault was the habitual lawlessness that prevailed in a portion of General Mitchel's command. He has described it himself in a dispatch to the Secretary of War: "The most terrible outrages — robberies, rapes, arsons, and plunderings — are being committed by lawless brigands and vagabonds connected with the army"; and he asks for authority to visit the punishment of death upon the offenders. The authority was granted, but nobody was punished. Not only straggling individuals, but a whole brigade, under the open authority of its commander, could engage in these acts. Mitchel's refinement would be shocked by brutality under any circumstances, but he could not apply the means of repression when his command was the offender and the people of the country were the victims; and when a body of respectable citizens appealed to him for protection and justice in a case which was of undisputed atrocity, he answered them: "I cannot arraign before a court, civil or military, a brigade, and I most deeply regret that a portion at least of your time had not been occupied in searching for the testimony which would have fixed the charge of pillage and plunder upon some individual officer or soldier under my command!" This was to the inhabitants of a town in which he had previously reported the existence of a strong Union sentiment, and which had been given up by one of his brigade commanders to indiscriminate sack.‡ These disorders do not appear to have prevailed in the portion of the command immediately under Mitchel's eye.

The conditions which were found to exist when I arrived at Huntsville about the last of June were certainly not gratifying. The discipline of the command demanded vindication; the troops to a considerable extent were scattered, and their whereabouts unknown; the cavalry was broken down by marchings and counter-marchings that seemed not to have been well considered; a treatment partly authoritative and partly riotous, resulting from imperfect discipline and an injudicious temper on the part of the commander of the troops, had embittered even that portion of the population that would have been friendly or passive; no supplies had been provided for the army on its arrival from Corinth; substantially nothing had been done as ordered to repair the railroads to Nashville, though some steps had been taken, and the wagon train was worn down in hauling cotton for speculators. The measures that were necessary to remedy this state of affairs — the frequent calls upon General Mitchel for information, the arrest and trial of offenders whose flagrant crimes he had condoned or neglected, the breaking up of Turchin's ungoverned brigade, the orders with reference to the use of public transportation for private purposes, and other reformatory measures — seemed unavoidably to reflect upon Mitchel, and no doubt he felt them keenly, though that was in no manner their object. The records show, however, that he had been preparing the way for a transfer to the east, though I knew nothing of it at the time. I had been in Huntsville three days, when I received a letter from him tendering the resignation of his commission, and I was requested to forward it to the War Department. I sent for him in a friendly spirit to dissuade him, but I found him avowedly in a very wounded frame of mind, and apparently fixed in his purpose. I therefore said to him, "Very well; I am sorry to have you go, but if you desire I will forward your letter, and recommend that you be assigned some other duty. I cannot approve your resignation. It is not necessary that you should sacrifice your commission merely because you do not wish to serve under my command." And I forwarded his letter with an endorsement to that effect. The letter must now be on file in the War Department. The very next day orders, dated 9 : 20 A. M., were received by telegraph for him to repair to Washington, and he started immediately. The day after his departure I was surprised to

‡ See the official order promulgating the trial and dismissal of Colonel Turchin. Several other officers were tried and variously punished by the same court for similar disorders.— D. C. B.

be shown the original of a dispatch from him to the War Department, on file in the telegraph office, saying that, finding it impossible to serve his country longer under his present commander, he had forwarded his unconditional resignation, and he solicited leave of absence for twenty days. If a leave of absence was his object, he knew I could grant it as well as the Secretary of War.

Upon the whole, it is difficult to find satisfaction in an attentive study of General Mitchel's proceedings during the period referred to. The first occupation of the Memphis and Charleston railroad in April was well executed; but everywhere the pleasing impression of an apparently vigorous action is marred by exaggeration and false coloring, and inconsistency and self-seeking. The most trivial occurrence is reported with the flourish of a great battle; an old flat-boat in which he had rigged the machinery of a saw-mill, incapable of harming anything or resisting anything, is called a *gun-boat* and named the *Tennessee*, which he reports he has extemporized, and hopes will arrive in time to take part in the fight at Chattanooga, where he hopes also to receive 600 prisoners. At one moment he is appealing to be transferred to the Army of the Potomac, in order that he may have more active service; and almost in the same breath he is threatened by an overwhelming force, and is broken down by his responsibilities, and by his unceasing watchfulness night and day.

But in spite of his peculiarities, General Mitchel was a valuable officer. He was a graduate of West Point, about fifty-five years of age, a man of good bearing and pure morals, of considerable culture, and some reputation in science, having been employed as a teacher of science in a Cincinnati college, and having lectured and published entertainingly on astronomy. He was energetic in a certain way, and had some qualification from practical experience, as well as by education, in railroad construction and management, which was often useful in the war. He was not insubordinate, but was restless in ordinary service, ambitious in an ostentatious way, and by temperament unsuited to an important independent command. Until the publication of volumes X. and XVI. of the "Official Records" I knew nothing of the account which Mitchel after he went to Washington was called upon to render of his administration in North Alabama, in regard to discipline and cotton trading. He answered earnestly and no doubt satisfactorily. He had at the time reported to the War Department the use of Government transportation for getting out cotton for traders, but he did not report it to me.

Whitelaw Reid, in his sketch of him in "Ohio in the War," no doubt on Mitchel's authority, gives me a credit to which I am not entitled, as having said to Mitchel at Huntsville that I would myself resign rather than that the country should be deprived of his valuable services. General Mitchel was at last assigned to a sort of local command at Hilton Head, South Carolina, and died there from yellow fever under circumstances which inspired general sympathy, within a very few months after his departure from Huntsville.

POSTSCRIPT.—The foregoing notes were in the hands of the editors of this work when there appeared a biography of General Mitchel written by his son (Boston: Houghton, Mifflin & Co.) This biography as well as a book called "Daring and Suffering," by the Rev. William Pittenger, attach great importance to the expedition under Andrews against the Georgia railroad. [See pp. 709, 716.] There is in Pittenger's book an express assumption not adopted in the Mitchel biography, that this project was a part of a comprehensive plan of invasion devised by Mitchel, but it rests on no evidence whatever. In moving upon Huntsville Mitchel was totally unprepared for the supposed enterprise, and instead of turning his column to the east to take advantage of the occasion promptly, as he must have done if he would have availed himself of it at all, he at once spread his force to the right and left to secure both flanks — on his left destroying bridges which would have been necessary for the execution of the alleged plan; and on the right taking steps to open communication with the army before Corinth. It is not improbable, however, that he hoped that Andrews's work would give greater security to an advance upon Huntsville.

The military portion of the Mitchel biography shows on his part an unhappy misconception of his official functions, and breathes a general accent of complaint that his ability was fettered and his usefulness thwarted by the faults of his superiors. He was continually falling under hindrances and vexations which were the fruit of his vague impulses and erroneous notions of the military situation and of his relations to it. To Secretary Chase he chafes that he had hoped he "would be allowed to march on Chattanooga and Knoxville," and now fears that his line is to be abandoned; but his propositions, if they may be so called, are never submitted to his commanding officer, with information and reasons that might bring them to fruition if they deserved it. Having opened a direct correspondence with the Secretary of War, he uses the privilege to criticise the measures of his commanding officer, nominates a military governor for North Alabama, and wants authority to send rebel citizens to Northern prisons. He complains to Secretary Stanton that his "is the first instance in the history of war where a general has been deprived of the command of his own lines of supply and communication," never, apparently, realizing that in the independent sense he is not a general at all, but only the commander of a detachment for a specific subordinate duty. The demoralizing effect of his surreptitious intercourse with Washington, encouraged by Secretary Stanton, and some of it withheld from the official files but brought to light after twenty-five years in the biography, is to be seen in the whole of Mitchel's career in North Alabama, and it followed him after his departure. In a long report evidently suggested by conversations and called for by the Secretary of War, Mitchel makes the statement, July 7th, that one month before, evidently referring to Negley's expedition, he could have been "permanently established in Chattanooga." His dispatches from June 7th to the 22d explain the importance he attached to the occupation of Chattanooga and the difficulties which prevented him from seizing it. No censure is meant to be applied to General Mitchel for not seizing Chattanooga at any time, but his dispatches alluded to above and his report of July 7th show that his action was not consistent with his profession, and that his representations misled the Government and the public with reference to the responsibility of others, and the feasibility of an operation which upon his own judgment he had abandoned.

I have no recollection of ever having been at General Mitchel's quarters at Huntsville. It is not improbable, however, that on my arrival I was met by him and invited to his quarters. His son and biographer describes a scene as having occurred there on the day of my arrival: A map upon a pine-table under a tree, and on opposite sides "the two commanders," as he expresses it, one being the commander of the army and the other a subordinate officer belonging to it, consulting over a plan of campaign — "the one having the power for decision, the other being simply adviser." After many hours, during which one talked much, and the other "was, as usual, uncommunicative," no conclusion was reached. The commander of the army "rolled up his maps and withdrew." The next day, says the biographer, "the consultation was renewed at General Buell's headquarters, and the next for three successive days." "General Mitchel pleaded with General Buell for a quick occupation of the territory east." "At length," says the biographer, "Mitchel induced Buell to go to Bridgeport" to look over the ground, saying, "I will have a train ready for you to-morrow morning at 7 o'clock," "but Buell declined to go so soon." Whereupon, Mitchel gave up the struggle, and retiring to his tent telegraphed to the Secretary of War: "Finding it impossible to serve my country longer under my present commander, I have to-day forwarded through him my unconditional resignation, and respectfully solicit leave of absence for twenty days." A copy of this dispatch, the biographer adds, he sent to General Buell. The biographer then quotes "two documents," written, as he says, "within a day or two of each other," "to show how differently two men can look upon the same subject." The second in citation, though the first in date, is the report called for by Secretary Stanton and made by General Mitchel on the 7th of July, probably the next day after his arrival in Washington. It does not appear among the published war records, and I learn of its existence through the biography for the first time. It gives a so-called plan of campaign which it states that the writer, General Mitchel, had urged upon me. No plan of campaign was proposed to me by General Mitchel, and no such controversy, or discussion, or series of consultations as would be inferred from the biography, ever occurred between us.

General Mitchel failed to obtain from the War Department the recognition which he desired. The official records show in part, and a study of his son's publication will indicate more fully, by what means and with what effect his influence entered, as it nevertheless did, into the channels of public opinion and the councils of the Government. They may also explain the true cause of his many disappointments. The merely individual bearing of the inquiry, however, is now of little consequence.— D. C. BUELL.

CONFEDERATES IN PURSUIT.

## THE LOCOMOTIVE CHASE IN GEORGIA.

BY THE REV. WILLIAM PITTENGER, 2D OHIO VOLUNTEERS, ONE OF THE RAIDERS.

BEGINNING OF THE PURSUIT.

THE railroad raid in Georgia in the spring of 1862 has always been considered to rank high among the striking and novel events of the civil war. At that time General O. M. Mitchel, under whose authority it was organized [see pp. 708, 716], commanded Union forces in Middle Tennessee, consisting of a division of Buell's Army. The Confederates were concentrating at Corinth, Miss., and Grant and Buell were advancing by different routes toward that point. Mitchel's orders required him to protect Nashville and the country around, but allowed him latitude in the disposition of his division, which, with detachments and garrisons, numbered nearly seventeen thousand men. His attention had long been turned toward the liberation of East Tennessee, which he knew President Lincoln also earnestly desired, and which would, if achieved, strike a most damaging blow at the resources of the Rebellion. A Union army once in possession of East Tennessee would have the inestimable advantage, found nowhere else in the South, of operating in the midst of a friendly population, and having at hand abundant supplies of all kinds. Mitchel had no reason to believe that Corinth would detain the Union armies much longer than Fort Donelson had done, and was satisfied that as soon as it had been captured, the next movement would be eastward toward Chattanooga, thus throwing his own division in advance. He determined, therefore, to press into the heart of the enemy's country as far as possible, occupying strategical points before they were adequately defended.

On the 8th of April, 1862,— the day after the battle of Pittsburg Landing, of which, however, Mitchel had received no intelligence,— he marched swiftly southward from Shelbyville and seized Huntsville, in Alabama, on the 11th of April, and then sent a detachment westward over the Memphis and Charleston railroad to open railway communication with the Union army at Pittsburg Landing.

Another detachment, commanded by Mitchel in person, advanced on the same day 70 miles by rail directly into the enemy's territory, arriving unchecked within 30 miles of Chattanooga. In two hours' time he could have reached that point, the most important position in the West, with 2000 men. Why did he not go? The story of the railroad raid is the answer.

The night before breaking camp at Shelbyville, Mitchel sent an expedition secretly into the heart of Georgia to cut the railroad communications of Chattanooga to the south and east. The fortune of this attempt had a most important bearing upon his movements, and will now be narrated.

In the employ of General Buell was a spy, named James J. Andrews, who had rendered valuable services [see p. 716] in the first year of the war, and had secured the confidence of the Union commanders. In March, 1862, Buell had sent him secretly with eight men to burn the bridges west of Chattanooga; but the failure of expected coöperation defeated the plan, and Andrews, after visiting Atlanta, and inspecting the whole of the enemy's lines in that vicinity and northward, had returned, ambitious to make another attempt. His plans for the second raid were submitted to Mitchel, and on the eve of the movement from Shelbyville to Huntsville, the latter authorized him to take twenty-

---

↓ See "Official Records," Volume X., Part I., pp. 630–639. [For a detailed account by the present writer, see "Daring and Suffering," War Publishing Co., N. Y.]

four men, secretly enter the enemy's territory, and, by means of capturing a train, burn the bridges on the northern part of the Georgia State railroad, and also one on the East Tennessee railroad where it approaches the Georgia State line, thus completely isolating Chattanooga, which was then virtually ungarrisoned.

The soldiers for this expedition, of whom the writer was one, were selected from the three Ohio regiments belonging to General J. W. Sill's brigade, being simply told that they were wanted for secret and very dangerous service. So far as known not a man chosen declined the perilous honor. Our uniforms were exchanged for ordinary Southern dress, and all arms, except revolvers, were left in camp. On the 7th of April, by the roadside about a mile east of Shelbyville, in the late twilight, we met our leader. Taking us a little way from the road he quietly placed before us the outlines of the romantic and adventurous plan, which was: to break into small detachments of three or four, journey eastward into the mountains, and then work southward, traveling by rail after we were well within the Confederate lines, and finally meet Andrews at Marietta, Georgia, more than 200 miles away, the evening of the third day after the start. When questioned, we were to profess ourselves Kentuckians going to join the Southern army.

On the journey we were a good deal annoyed by the swollen streams and the muddy roads consequent on three days of almost ceaseless rain. Andrews was led to believe that Mitchel's column would be inevitably delayed, and as we were expected to destroy the bridges the very day that Huntsville was entered, he took the responsibility of sending word to our different groups that our attempt would be postponed one day — from Friday to Saturday, April 12th. This was a natural but a most lamentable error of judgment.

JAMES J. ANDREWS. FROM A PHOTOGRAPH.

One of the men was belated and did not join us at all. Two others were very soon captured by the enemy, and though their true character was not detected, they were forced into the Southern army, and two, who reached Marietta, failed to report at the rendezvous. Thus, when we assembled, very early in the morning, in Andrews's room at the Marietta Hotel for final consultation before the blow was struck, we were but twenty, including our leader. All preliminary difficulties had been easily overcome, and we were in good spirits. But some serious obstacles had been revealed on our ride from Chattanooga to Marietta the previous evening.‡ The railroad was found to be crowded with trains, and many soldiers were among the passengers. Then the station — Big Shanty — at which the capture was to be effected had recently been made a Confederate camp. To succeed in our enterprise it would be necessary first to capture the engine in a guarded camp, with soldiers standing around as spectators, and then to run it from 100 to 200 miles through the enemy's country, and to deceive or overpower all trains that should be met — a large contract for twenty men! Some of our party thought the chances of success so slight, under existing circumstances, that they urged the abandonment of the whole enterprise. But Andrews declared his purpose to succeed or die, offering to each man, however, the privilege of withdrawing from the attempt — an offer no one was in the least disposed to accept. Final instructions were then given, and we hurried to the ticket office in time for the northward bound mail train, and purchased tickets for different stations along the line in the direction of Chattanooga.

Our ride as passengers was but eight miles. We swept swiftly around the base of Kenesaw Mountain, and soon saw the tents of the forces camped at Big Shanty (now Kenesaw Station) gleam white in the morning mist. Here we were to stop for breakfast and attempt the seizure of the train. The morning was raw and gloomy, and a rain, which fell all day, had already begun. It was a painfully thrilling moment! We were but twenty, with an army about us and a long and difficult road before us crowded with enemies. In an instant we were to throw off the disguise which had been our only protection, and trust our leader's genius and our own efforts for safety and success. Fortunately we had no time for giving way to reflections and conjectures which could only unfit us for the stern task ahead.

When we stopped, the conductor, engineer, and many of the passengers hurried to breakfast, leaving the train unguarded. Now was the moment of action! Ascertaining that there was nothing to prevent a rapid start, Andrews, our two engineers, Brown and Knight, and the fireman hurried forward, uncoupling a section of the train consisting of three empty baggage or box cars, the locomotive and tender. The engineers and fireman sprang into the cab of the engine, while Andrews, with

‡ The different detachments reached the Georgia State railroad at Chattanooga, and traveled as ordinary passengers on trains running southward. — EDITORS.

## THE LOCOMOTIVE CHASE IN GEORGIA.

BIG SHANTY (NOW KENESAW) STATION. FROM A WAR-TIME SKETCH.

hand on the rail and foot on the step, waited to see that the remainder of the band had gained entrance into the rear box car. This seemed difficult and slow, though it really consumed but a few seconds, for the car stood on a considerable bank, and the first who came were pitched in by their comrades, while these, in turn, dragged in the others, and the door was instantly closed. A sentinel, with musket in hand, stood not a dozen feet from the engine watching the whole proceeding, but before he or any of the soldiers and guards around could make up their minds to interfere, all was done, and Andrews, with a nod to his engineer, stepped on board. The valve was pulled wide open, and for a moment the wheels of the "General" slipped around ineffectively; then, with a bound that jerked the soldiers in the box car from their feet, the little train darted away, leaving the camp and station in the wildest uproar and confusion. The first step of the enterprise was triumphantly accomplished.

According to the time-table, of which Andrews had secured a copy, there were two trains to be met. These presented no serious hindrance to our attaining high speed, for we could tell just where to expect them. There was also a local freight not down on the time-table, but which could not be far distant. Any danger of collision with it could be avoided by running according to the schedule of the captured train until it was passed; then, at the highest possible speed, we would run to the Oostenaula and Chickamauga bridges, lay them in ashes, and pass on through Chattanooga to Mitchel, at Huntsville, or wherever eastward of that point he might be found, arriving long before the close of the day. It was a brilliant prospect, and, so far as human estimates can determine, it would have been realized had the day been Friday instead of Saturday. On Friday every train had been on time, the day dry, and the road in perfect order. Now the road was in disorder, every train far behind time, and two "extras" were approaching us. But of these unfavorable conditions we knew nothing, and pressed confidently forward.

We stopped frequently, at one point tore up the track, cut telegraph wires, and loaded on crossties to be used in bridge burning. Wood and water were taken without difficulty, Andrews telling, very coolly, the story to which he adhered throughout the run, namely, that he was an agent of General Beauregard's running an impressed powder train through to that officer at Corinth. We had no good instruments for track-raising, as we had intended rather to depend upon fire; but the amount of time spent in taking up a rail was not material at this stage of our journey, as we easily kept on the time of our captured train. There was a wonderful exhilaration in passing swiftly by towns and stations through the heart of an enemy's country in this manner. It possessed just enough of the spice of danger—in this part of the run—to render it thoroughly enjoyable. The slightest accident to our engine, however, or a miscarriage in any part of our programme, would have completely changed the conditions.

At Etowah Station we found the "Yonah," an old locomotive owned by an iron company, standing with steam up; but not wishing to alarm the enemy till the local freight had been safely met, we left it unharmed. Kingston, thirty miles from the starting-point, was safely reached. A train from Rome, Ga., on a branch road, had just arrived and was waiting for the morning mail — our train. We learned that the local freight would soon come also, and, taking the side track, waited for it. When it arrived, however, Andrews saw to his surprise and chagrin that it bore a red flag, indicating another train not far behind. Stepping to the conductor, he boldly asked, "What does it mean that the road is blocked in this manner when I have orders to take this powder to Beauregard without a minute's delay?" The answer was interesting but not reassuring: "Mitchel has captured Huntsville and is said to be coming to Chattanooga, and we are getting everything out

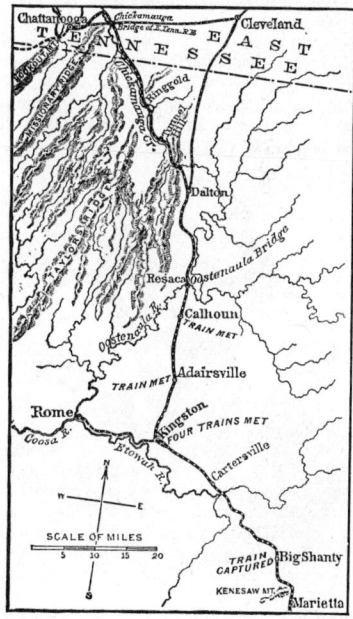

THE RAILROAD FROM MARIETTA TO CHATTANOOGA.

of there." He was asked by Andrews to pull his train a long way down the track out of the way, and promptly obeyed.

It seemed an exceedingly long time before the expected "extra" arrived; and when it did come it bore another red flag! The reason given was that the "local," being too great for one engine, had been made up in two sections, and the second section would doubtless be along in a short time. This was terribly vexatious; yet there seemed nothing to do but wait. To start out between the sections of an extra train would be to court destruction. There were already three trains around us, and their many passengers, and others, were growing very curious about the mysterious train which had arrived on the time of the morning mail, manned by strangers. *For an hour and five minutes* from the time of arrival at Kingston, we remained in this most critical position. The sixteen of us who were shut up tightly in a box car, personating Beauregard's ammunition,— hearing sounds outside, but unable to distinguish words,— had perhaps the most trying position. Andrews sent us, by one of the engineers, a cautious warning to be ready to fight in case the uneasiness of the crowd around led them to make any investigation, while he himself kept near the station to prevent the sending off of any alarming telegram. So intolerable was our suspense that the order for a deadly conflict would have been felt as a relief. But the assurance of Andrews quieted the crowd until the whistle of the expected train from the north was heard; then, as it glided up to the depot, past the end of our side track, we were off without more words.

But unexpected danger had arisen behind us. Out of the panic at Big Shanty two men emerged, determined, if possible, to foil the unknown captors of their train. There was no telegraph station, and no locomotive at hand with which to follow; but the conductor of the train, W. A. Fuller, and

PLAN OF THE BLOCKADE AT KINGSTON STATION.

Anthony Murphy, foreman of the Atlanta railway machine shops, who happened to be on board of Fuller's train, started on foot after us as hard as they could run! Finding a hand-car they mounted it and pushed forward till they neared Etowah, where they ran on the break we had made in the road and were precipitated down the embankment into the ditch. Continuing with more caution, they reached Etowah and found the "Yonah," which was at once pressed into service, loaded with soldiers who were at hand, and hurried with flying wheels toward Kingston. Fuller prepared to fight at that point, for he knew of the tangle of extra trains, and of the lateness of the regular trains, and did not think we would be able to pass. We had been gone only four minutes when he arrived and found himself stopped by three long, heavy trains of cars headed in the wrong direction. To move them out of the way so as to pass would cause a delay he was little inclined to afford — would indeed have almost certainly given us the victory. So, abandoning his engine, he, with Murphy, ran across to the Rome train, and, uncoupling the engine and one car, pushed forward with about forty armed men. As the Rome branch connected with the main road above the depot, he encountered no hindrance, and it was now a fair race. We were not many minutes ahead.

Four miles from Kingston we again stopped and cut the telegraph. While trying to take up a rail at this point, we were greatly startled. One end of the rail was loosened and eight of us were pulling at it, when distant, but distinct, we heard the whistle of a pursuing engine! With a frantic pull we broke the rail and all tumbled over the embankment with the effort. We moved on, and at Adairsville we found a mixed train (freight and passenger) waiting, but there was an express on the road that had not yet arrived. We could afford no more

CAPTAIN WM. A. FULLER, C. S. A., LEADER OF THE PURSUIT. FROM AN AMBROTYPE.

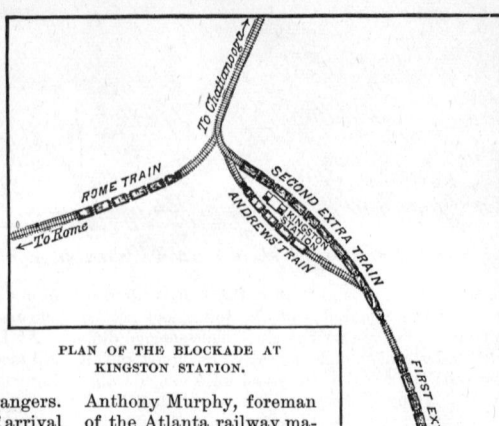

delay, and set out for the next station, Calhoun, at terrible speed, hoping to reach that point before the express, which was behind time, should arrive. The nine miles which we had to travel were left behind in less than the same number of minutes! The express was just pulling out, but, hearing our whistle, backed before us until we were able to take the side track; it stopped, however, in such a manner as completely to close up the other end of the switch. The two trains, side by side, almost touched each other, and our precipitate arrival caused natural suspicion. Many searching questions were asked which had to be answered before we could get the opportunity of proceeding. We, in the box car, could hear the altercation and were almost sure that a fight would be necessary before the conductor would consent to "pull up" in order to let us out. Here, again, our position was most critical, for the pursuers were rapidly approaching.

Fuller and Murphy saw the obstruction of the broken rail, in time to prevent wreck, by reversing their engine; but the hindrance was for the present insuperable. Leaving all their men behind, they started for a second foot-race. Before they had gone far they met the train we had passed at Adairsville and turned it back after us. At Adairsville they dropped the cars, and, with locomotive and tender loaded with armed men, they drove forward at the highest speed possible. They knew that we were not many minutes ahead, and trusted to overhaul us before the express train could be safely passed.

But Andrews had told the powder story again, with all his skill, and had added a direct request in peremptory form to have the way opened before him, which the Confederate conductor did not see fit to resist; and just before the pursuers arrived at Calhoun we were again under way. Stopping once more to cut wires and tear up the track, we felt a thrill of exhilaration to which we had long been strangers. The track was now clear before us to Chattanooga; and even west of that city we had good reason to believe that we would find no other train in the way till we had reached Mitchel's lines. If one rail could now be lifted we would be in a few minutes at Oostenaula bridge, and, that burned, the rest of the task would be little more than simple manual labor, with the enemy absolutely powerless. We worked with a will.

But in a moment the tables were turned! Not far behind we heard the scream of a locomotive bearing down upon us at lightning speed! The men on board were in plain sight and well armed! Two minutes — perhaps one — would have removed

PURSUERS OFF THE TRACK.

the rail at which we were toiling; then the game would have been in our own hands, for there was no other locomotive beyond that could be turned back after us. But the most desperate efforts were in vain. The rail was simply bent, and we hurried to our engine and darted away, while remorselessly after us thundered the enemy.

Now the contestants were in clear view, and a most exciting race followed. Wishing to gain a little time for the burning of the Oostenaula bridge we dropped one car, and shortly after, another; but they were "picked up" and pushed ahead to Resaca station. We were obliged to run over the high trestles and covered bridge at that point without a pause. This was the first failure in the work assigned us.

The Confederates could not overtake and stop us on the road, but their aim was to keep close behind so that we might not be able to damage the road or take in wood or water. In the former they succeeded, but not the latter. Both engines were put at the highest rate of speed. We were obliged to cut the wire after every station passed, in order that an alarm might not be sent ahead, and we constantly strove to throw our pursuer off the track or to obstruct the road permanently in some way so that we might be able to burn the Chickamauga bridges, still ahead. The chances seemed good that Fuller and Murphy would be wrecked. We broke out the end of our last box car and dropped cross-ties on the track as we ran, thus checking their progress and getting far enough ahead to take in wood and water at two separate stations. Several times we almost lifted a rail, but each time the coming of the Confederates, within rifle range, compelled us to desist and speed on. Our worst hindrance was the rain. The previous day (Friday) had been clear, with a high wind, and on such a day fire would have been easily and tremendously effective. But to-day a bridge could be burned only with abundance of fuel and careful nursing.

Thus we sped on, mile after mile, in this fearful chase, around curves and past stations in seemingly endless perspective. Whenever we lost sight of the enemy beyond a curve we hoped that some of our obstructions had been effective in throwing him from the track and that we would see him no more; but at each long reach backward the smoke was again seen, and the shrill whistle was like the scream of a bird of prey. The time could not have been so very long, for the terrible speed was rapidly devouring the distance, but with our nerves strained to the highest tension each minute seemed an hour. On several occasions the escape of the enemy from wreck seemed little less than miraculous. At one point a rail

THE PURSUERS PUSHING THE BURNING CAR FROM THE BRIDGE.

was placed across the track so skillfully on a curve that it was not seen till the train ran upon it at full speed. Fuller says that they were terribly jolted, and seemed to bounce altogether from the track, but lighted on the rails in safety. Some of the Confederates wished to leave a train which was driven at such a reckless rate, but their wishes were not gratified.

Before reaching Dalton we urged Andrews to turn and attack the enemy, laying an ambush so as to get into close quarters that our revolvers might be on equal terms with their guns. I have little doubt that if this had been carried out it would have succeeded. But Andrews — whether because he thought the chance of wrecking or obstructing the enemy still good, or feared that the country ahead had been alarmed by a telegram around the Confederacy by the way of Richmond — merely gave the plan his sanction without making any attempt to carry it into execution.

Dalton was passed without difficulty, and beyond we stopped again to cut wires and obstruct the track. It happened that a regiment was encamped not a hundred yards away, but they did not molest us. Fuller had written a dispatch to Chattanooga, and dropped a man with orders to have it forwarded instantly while he pushed on to save the bridges. Part of the message got through and created a wild panic in Chattanooga, although it did not materially influence our fortunes. Our supply of fuel was now very short, and without getting rid of our pursuer long enough to take in more, it was evident that we could not run as far as Chattanooga.

While cutting the wire we made an attempt to get up another rail, but the enemy, as usual, were too quick for us. We had no tool for this purpose except a wedge-pointed iron bar. Two or three bent iron claws for pulling out spikes would have given us such superiority, that, down to almost the last of our run, we would have been able to escape and to burn all the Chickamauga bridges. But it had not been our intention to rely on this mode of obstruction — an emergency only rendered necessary by our unexpected delay and the pouring rain.

We made no attempt to damage the long tunnel north of Dalton, as our enemies had greatly dreaded. The last hope of the raid was now staked upon an effort of a different kind. A few more obstructions were dropped on the track and our speed was increased so that we soon forged a considerable distance ahead. The side and end boards of the last car were torn into shreds, all available fuel was piled upon it, and blazing brands were brought back from the engine. By the time we approached a long covered bridge the fire in the car was fairly started. We uncoupled it in the middle of the bridge, and with painful suspense awaited the issue. Oh, for a few minutes till the work of conflagration was fairly begun! There was still steam-pressure enough in our boiler to carry us to the next wood-yard, where we could have replenished our fuel, by force if necessary, so as to run as near to Chattanooga as was deemed prudent. We did not know of the telegraph message which the pursuers had sent ahead. But, alas! the minutes were not given. Before the bridge was extensively fired the enemy was upon us. They pushed right into the smoke and drove the burning car before them to the next side-track.

With no car left, and no fuel, the last scrap having been thrown into the engine or upon the burning car, and with no obstruction to drop on the track, our situation was indeed desperate.

But it might still be possible to save ourselves if we left the train in a body and took a direct

END OF THE RUN — THE STOLEN ENGINE, THE "GENERAL," ABANDONED.

course toward the Union lines. Confederate pursuers with whom I have since conversed have agreed on two points — that we could have escaped in the manner here pointed out; and that an attack on the pursuing train would likely have been successful. But Andrews thought otherwise, at least in relation to the former plan, and ordered us to jump from the locomotive, and, dispersing in the woods, each endeavor to save himself.

The question is often asked, "Why did you not reverse your engine and thus wreck the one following?" Wanton injury was no part of our plan, and we could not afford to throw away our engine till the last extremity. When the raiders were jumping off, however, the engine was reversed and driven back, but by that time the steam was so nearly exhausted that the Confederate engine had no difficulty in reversing and receiving the shock without injury. Both were soon at a stand-still, and the Confederates, reënforced by a party from a train which soon arrived on the scene,— the express passenger, which had been turned back at Calhoun,— continued the chase on foot.

It is easy now to understand why Mitchel paused thirty miles west of Chattanooga. The Andrews raiders had been forced to stop eighteen miles south of the same town, and no flying train met Mitchel with tidings that all the railroad communications of Chattanooga were destroyed, and that the town was in a panic and undefended.

A few words will give the sequel to this remarkable enterprise. The hunt for the fugitive raiders was prompt, energetic, and successful. Several

were captured the same day, and all but two within a week. Even these two were overtaken and brought back, when they supposed that they were virtually out of danger. Two who had reached Marietta, but had failed to board the train (J. R. Porter,† Co. C, 21st Ohio, and Martin J. Hawkins,† Co. A, 33d Ohio), were identified and added to the band of prisoners. Now follows the saddest part of the story. Being in citizens' dress within an enemy's lines, the whole party were held as spies. A court-martial was convened, and the leader and seven out of the remaining twenty-one were condemned and executed. ☆ The others were

MEMORIAL DAY AT CHATTANOOGA, 1883. GRAVES OF ANDREWS AND HIS COMPANIONS.

☆ The participants in the raid were: James J. Andrews,* Leader; William Campbell,* a civilian who volunteered to accompany the raiders; George D. Wilson,* Co. B, 2d Ohio; Marion A. Ross,* Co. A, 2d Ohio; Perry G. Shadrack,* Co. K, 2d Ohio; Samuel Slavens,* 33d Ohio; Samuel Robinson,* Co. G, 33d Ohio; John Scott,* Co. K, 21st Ohio; Wilson W. Brown,† Co. F, 21st Ohio;

William Knight,† Co. E, 21st Ohio; Mark Wood,† Co. C, 21st Ohio; James A. Wilson,† Co. C, 21st Ohio; John Wollam,† Co. C, 33d Ohio; D. A. Dorsey,† Co. H, 33d Ohio; Jacob Parrott,‡ Co. K, 33d Ohio; Robert Buffum,‡ Co. H, 21st Ohio; William Bensinger,‡ Co. G, 21st Ohio; William Reddick,‡ Co. B, 33d Ohio; E. H. Mason,‡ Co. K, 21st Ohio; William Pittenger,‡ Co. G, 2d Ohio.— EDITORS.

\* Executed.     † Escaped.     ‡ Exchanged.

never brought to trial, probably because of the advance of Union forces and the consequent confusion into which the affairs of the Departments of East Tennessee and Georgia were thrown. Of the remaining fourteen, eight succeeded, by a bold effort,—attacking their guard in broad daylight,—in making their escape from Atlanta, Ga., and ultimately in reaching the North. The other six, who shared in this effort, but were recaptured, remained prisoners until the latter part of March, 1863, when they were exchanged through a special arrangement made by Secretary Stanton. All the survivors of this expedition received medals and promotion. The pursuers also received expressions of gratitude from their fellow Confederates, notably from the Governor and Legislature of Georgia.

## NOTES ON THE LOCOMOTIVE CHASE.

### BY JAMES B. FRY, BREVET MAJOR-GENERAL, U. S. A.

Two expeditions to burn bridges near Chattanooga were sent from the Union lines early in 1862. The first was authorized by General D. C. Buell, commanding the Army of the Ohio, who had seized Nashville in the latter part of February, and was about marching south-westward to join Grant at Savannah on the Tennessee River. Buell was not unmindful of the advantage of breaking, west of Chattanooga, the railroad which led the Confederate forces from the east and south to his flank and also directly connected them with Corinth, against which Halleck was moving. A spy by the name of Andrews, who was in Buell's service, represented early in March that with a party of six trusty men he could destroy the bridges between Chattanooga and Bridgeport, and also the important bridge over the Tennessee, at the latter place, and thus effectually prevent the enemy from using that route, either to reënforce Corinth or to return to Middle Tennessee. Buell had received but little benefit from Andrews's services ✠ and did not encourage the proposition, but in consequence mainly of the confidence and urgency of the spy, he finally directed me, his chief of staff, to confer fully with Andrews and use my discretion as to authorizing and organizing the enterprise. On the strength of Andrews's assurance that an engineer running a regular train over the road was in our interest and would use his locomotive for the purpose, I sanctioned and arranged the expedition. General Mitchel was directed to furnish six men, if volunteers for the service could be found — that is all he had to do with the original expedition. Of this operation General Buell wrote, August 5th, 1863, to the Adjutant-General of the army as follows:

"SIR: In the 'Official Gazette' of the 21st. ultimo, I see a report of Judge-Advocate General Holt, dated the 27th of March, relative to an expedition set on foot in April, 1862, under the authority and direction (as the report says) of General O. M. Mitchel, the object of which was to destroy the communication on the Georgia State railroad between Atlanta and Chattanooga. The expedition was set on foot under my authority, the plan was arranged between Mr. Andrews, whom I had had in employment from shortly after assuming command in Kentucky, and my chief of staff, Colonel James B. Fry, and General Mitchel had nothing to do either with its conception or execution, except to furnish from his command the soldiers who took part in it. He was directed to furnish 6; instead of that he sent 22. Had he conformed to the instructions given him, it would have been better, the chances of success would have been greater, and in any event several lives would have been saved. The report speaks of the plan as an emanation of genius, and of the results which it promised as absolutely sublime. It may be proper, therefore, to say that this statement is made for the sake of truth, and not to call attention to the extravagant colors in which it has been presented. Very respectfully your obedient servant,
"D. C. BUELL, Major-General."

General Buell was speaking here of the first expedition,— the one he authorized. In relation to the merits of this scheme it may be said that at the time perhaps the object was of sufficient importance to offset the probabilities of failure and the risk to the men engaged. But at best the undertaking was hardly commendable. Buell, basing no plans on the success of it, marched with the main body of his army for the field of Shiloh, without knowing the result. The effort failed, and when Andrews returned, early in April, he found Mitchel in command below Nashville, and reported to him in Buell's absence. Thereupon Mitchel, on the 7th of April, 1862, set on foot the second expedition. This expedition also failed, and with distressingly disastrous consequences to those engaged in it. The Confederates were fully aware of the importance of holding Chattanooga, and from my knowledge of the military situation at the time, the military commanders concerned, and the course of events afterward, I do not hesitate to express the opinion that if the raiders had succeeded in destroying every bridge on their proposed route it would have produced no important effect upon Mitchel's military operations, and that he would not have taken, certainly would not have held, Chattanooga. Hence it is my opinion that Mitchel's bridge-burners took desperate chances to accomplish objects of no substantial advantage.∫

---

✠ General Buell writes, March, 1888: "Andrews came into my employment in the capacity of a spy. Having traffic in quinine, etc., as an excuse for his movements, he made one trip and returned without information of any value. He started on another at a critical period, full of important facts. While the crisis was pending I expected him every day. He returned only after I entered Nashville, and then the current of events had told all he knew. . . . I had little confidence in his usefulness, apprehending that he thought more of his traffic than of the object for which he was engaged. When he proposed to attempt the destruction of bridges I did not assent. . . . He, however, interested my chief of staff, and at the request of the latter I consented to the arrangement that was completed between them."— J. B. F.

∫ General Buell writes: "The damage could only have been partial and temporary; and no condition of the contending forces then existed upon which the obstruction could have exerted any decisive influence."— J. B. F.

HALLECK'S ARMY ON THE MARCH TO CORINTH.
FROM A LITHOGRAPH.

## WITH PRICE EAST OF THE MISSISSIPPI.

### BY COLONEL THOMAS L. SNEAD.

BEAUREGARD, withdrawing his army in good order from the field of Shiloh, took position once more within the defenses of Corinth, and called for help to stay the advance of Halleck's fast-gathering forces. Of the 40,000 men who had followed Johnston out to battle, 30,000 were again in the trenches on the 9th of April, 1862. Van Dorn, after his defeat at Pea Ridge, was hastening to join them from the trans-Mississippi with the remainder of the Army of the West more than twenty thousand strong. Its advance under Price was even now embarking on the White River of Arkansas, and would be at Corinth in less than a week. Kirby Smith ⚓ sent his every available regiment from East Tennessee, and Pemberton ⚓ every man that could be spared from the coasts of Carolina and Georgia. The armies which had been assembled for the defense of New Orleans and Pensacola had already been sent to Corinth, and had fought at Shiloh. The President telegraphed on the 10th of April to the governors of South Carolina, Georgia, Alabama,

⚓ See (Vol. I., p. 262) Colonel Snead's paper on "The First Year of the War in Missouri," of which this is a continuation.— EDITORS.

⚓ Major-General E. Kirby Smith, who, as a brigadier-general, had commanded a brigade in General J. E. Johnston's Army of the Shenandoah at the battle of Bull Run (where he was wounded), and afterward a division in the Army of Northern Virginia, assumed command of the District of East Tennessee (afterward raised to a Department), with headquarters at Knoxville, on the 8th of March, 1862.— EDITORS.

⚓ Major-General John C. Pemberton at this time commanded the Confederate Department of South Carolina, with headquarters at Charleston, South Carolina.— EDITORS.

Mississippi, and Louisiana, "Beauregard must have reënforcements to meet the vast accumulation of the enemy before him. The necessity is imminent, the case of vital importance. Send forward to Corinth all the armed men that you can furnish." The Confederate Congress supported all this activity by enacting in haste on the 22d of April a stringent law for conscripting every white male between the ages of 18 and 35.

Halleck was at St. Louis, getting ready in his elaborate way to go to the Tennessee, when he was startled by learning that Grant had been attacked at Shiloh and had barely escaped a great disaster. Hastening to the front, he assumed command in person of the forces in the field on the 11th of April, and proceeded to execute deliberately his long-conceived plan of campaign.

Preëminently cautious by nature, and the more cautious now because he was sure of ultimate success, and averse always to the unnecessary shedding of human blood, Halleck, instead of advancing boldly against Beauregard as Grant would have done and risking all upon the hazard of a battle whose issue would have been uncertain, first fortified his position on the left bank of the Tennessee, and then began to strengthen his army by bringing to it all the available forces of his immense Department.

Pope was recalled from before Fort Pillow, which he was preparing to attack, and reached the Tennessee with the Army of the Mississippi on the 21st of April. He came flushed with his victories at New Madrid and at Island No. Ten — the last of which Halleck pronounced "a splendid achievement, exceeding in boldness and brilliancy all other operations of the war," and one that "would be memorable in military history and admired by future generations." Halleck did not then know how weakly the place had been defended by the officer to whom Beauregard had intrusted its defense.

Though the main body of the army with which Curtis had defeated Van Dorn at Elkhorn was still dragging itself slowly over the mountains, or floundering through the swamps of Arkansas, it, too, sent reënforcements to the Tennessee.

At length, toward the last of April, Halleck had assembled on the banks of the Tennessee an army of one hundred thousand men.

Remarkable and imposing as this great army was for its numbers and the excellence of its *personnel*, it was still more remarkable for its array of distinguished leaders. Among them were the future generals-in-chief of the armies of the United States,— Halleck himself, and after him the three most successful of all the soldiers that fought for the Union — Grant, Sherman, and Sheridan; and with them were George H. Thomas, whom Greeley believed to be the greatest soldier of them all, and Buell, and Pope, and Rosecrans, and many others that rose to high command. With it, but not of it, were also the great War Governor of Indiana, Oliver P. Morton, and the Assistant Secretary of War, Colonel Thomas A. Scott, the railway king of the future, who had come to advise and assist Halleck; while in commands more or less important were McClernand, Palmer, Oglesby, Hurlbut, John A. Logan, and Colonel Robert G. Ingersoll, Illinoisians all.

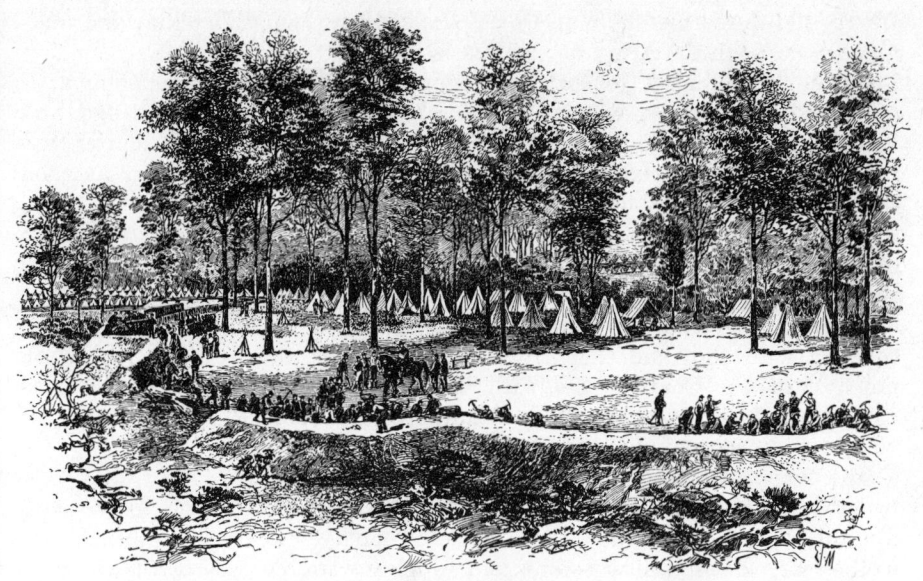

THE 31ST OHIO VOLUNTEERS BUILDING BREASTWORKS BEFORE CORINTH IN MAY, 1862.
FROM A LITHOGRAPH.

Halleck, before advancing, reorganized his army. Having little faith in Grant, he assigned him to the merely honorary position of second in command of the forces — a position analogous to and as unimportant as that of Vice-President. George H. Thomas was transferred with his division from Buell's army to Grant's — the Army of the Tennessee — and put in command of that army, which formed the right wing of the forces. Buell with the Army of the Ohio occupied the center, and Pope with the Army of the Mississippi the left.

Moving cautiously, and intrenching every time that he halted, Halleck by the middle of May approached within four miles of Corinth, some twenty miles from the Tennessee. He then seized and fortified a line extending from the Mobile and Ohio railroad on the north-west to and beyond Farmington on the south-east — some five miles or more in length — and began to mount his heavy siege guns. By the 25th of May he was almost ready to open with these upon the Confederates, some of whose intrenchments were hardly a thousand yards in his front.

Halleck's force now amounted to more than 110,000 fighting men. Beauregard's army had long ago reached its maximum, and was fast wasting away with disease. Of the 80,000 officers and men who were at Corinth, 18,000 were in the hospitals, and of the rest there were very few whose health was not affected by the pestilential air and unwholesome water of that swamp-surrounded village. Of those that were fit for duty, 5000 were on detached service and 4000 were on extra duty. There were "present for duty" 53,000 officers and men. One-third of them belonged to the Army of the West, and two-thirds to the Army of the Mississippi. The latter was commanded by

Bragg and the former by Van Dorn. Polk, Hardee, and Breckinridge commanded corps in the Army of the Mississippi.

On the 25th of May General Beauregard called his subordinate commanders together—namely, Bragg, Van Dorn, Polk, Hardee, Breckinridge, and Price‡—to discuss the propriety of evacuating Corinth. The matter was fully debated, particularly by General Hardee, who urged, with great good sense, that Corinth should be forthwith abandoned and the army withdrawn southward along the line of the Mobile and Ohio railroad. The necessity for this course had indeed become apparent to every one, and Beauregard issued the appropriate orders the same night.

It was none too soon, for Halleck would be ready within two or three days to open with shot and shell from his great guns, and to attack the weak defenses of the Confederates with an overwhelming force. He was also extending his line so as to flank Beauregard on the south and west, and to cut the railroad behind the Confederates.

The evacuation was conducted with the utmost secrecy. The troops were ordered to the front with three days' cooked rations in their haversacks, and told that they were about to attack the enemy. The sick were then sent to the rear, and all military stores and supplies were removed by the railways which were still at Beauregard's service. That the army was about to retreat was known to very few of its officers till the 29th. During that night there was a great running of cars, and the Confederates were ordered to cheer whenever a train arrived, so as to delude Halleck into believing that they were being reënforced. Before daybreak of the 30th all of Beauregard's forces except his cavalry had been withdrawn from Corinth.

Halleck had been completely deceived. Pope telegraphed him a few lines before daybreak (May 30th): "The enemy are reënforcing heavily in my front and on my left. The cars are running constantly, and the cheering is immense every time that they unload in front of me. I have no doubt that I shall be attacked in heavy force at daylight." Halleck thereupon ordered Grant to hold the reserve, and Buell the center, in readiness to reënforce Pope. It was not until 5 o'clock in the morning that any one, except some war correspondents, ♭ even suspected that the Confederates were retreating, and it was nearly 7 when the first Union troops entered the town and learned that Beauregard had certainly escaped. His army was then safe behind the Tuscumbia.

---

‡ It may be of interest to mention that General Price regarded Beauregard as the fittest of these officers for a great command.— T. L. S.

♭ General Pope's dispatch here quoted is dated May 30th, 1:20 A. M. At 6 A. M. he reported "a succession of loud explosions," adding that "everything indicates evacuation and retreat." At 5 A. M. Brigadier-General William Nelson had reported: "The prisoner who accompanies this states that the enemy have gone, and the town to me appears to be on fire." General Grant mentions, in his "Memoirs," Vol. I, p. 379, that, "probably on the 28th of May, General John A. Logan . . . said to me that the enemy had been evacuating for several days, and that, if allowed, he could go into Corinth with his brigade. Trains of cars were heard coming into and going out of Corinth constantly. Some of the men who had been engaged in various capacities on railroads before the war, claimed that they could tell by putting their ears to the rail, not only which way the trains were moving, but which trains were loaded and which were empty. They said loaded trains had been going out for several days and empty ones coming in. Subsequent events proved the correctness of their judgment."— EDITORS.

GENERAL POPE'S ENCAMPMENT BEFORE CORINTH IN MAY, 1862.

The camps, beginning at the left, are those of the 8th Wisconsin, 27th Illinois, 10th Michigan, 14th Michigan, 42d Illinois, 16th Illinois, 27th Ohio, 51st Illinois, 22d Illinois, and 39th Ohio. In the middle distance, on the right, are seen Captain Williams's siege guns. The flag marks General Pope's headquarters.

Pope's forces went in pursuit. Before night (May 30th) he reported that he had captured hundreds of barrels of beef, several hundred wagons, and seven thousand stand of arms, which Price and Van Dorn, in their haste to get away, had abandoned. Two days later (June 1st) he reported that Colonel Elliott, with a brigade of cavalry (one regiment of which was commanded by Sheridan), had, among other things done at and near Booneville on the 30th of May, destroyed 10,000 stand of small arms, 3 pieces of artillery, a great quantity of clothing and ammunition, and had paroled 2000 prisoners, who could not keep up with his cavalry; and on the 3d of June he reported "the woods for miles are full of stragglers from the enemy, who are coming in in squads. Not less than ten thousand men are thus scattered about, who will come in within a day or two."

The next day (June 4th) Halleck telegraphed to Washington:

"General Pope with 40,000 men is 30 miles south of Corinth, pushing the enemy hard. He already reports 10,000 prisoners and deserters from the enemy, and 15,000 stand of arms captured. . . . A farmer says that when Beauregard learned that Colonel Elliott had cut the railroad on his line of retreat he became frantic, and told his men to save themselves the best they could." ⸸

At that very time (June 4th) Pope himself was within 4 miles of Halleck's headquarters; Beauregard with his entire army was still within 27 miles of Corinth, and nobody was pushing him. He had already been there several days, and he remained there three or four days longer. Price and Van Dorn had *not* abandoned any wagons, nor had they abandoned any arms. Colonel Elliott had destroyed about 2000 muskets at Booneville, and had found about

⸸ General Pope afterward denied having made any such report, and complained that General Halleck's dispatch had done him injustice. See his correspondence with General Halleck, July 3d–5th, 1865, in the "Official Records," Vol. X., Pt. II., pp. 635–637. See also General Halleck's telegram to the Secretary of War, July 3d, 1862, claiming that he had "telegraphed the exact language of General Pope" ("Official Records," Vol. X., Pt. I., p. 671). No dispatch from General Pope containing this "exact language" appears in the "Official Records."—EDITORS.

2000 sick men there and several hundred stragglers. But he did not carry off a single prisoner, nor did he parole one.

Beauregard, far from being frantic with alarm and despair, assumed such a threatening attitude on the 4th that Halleck, at Pope's request, ordered Buell to the front by forced marches, with twenty thousand men to reënforce him. Reaching Booneville the next day, Buell assumed command of the combined force, amounting to about sixty thousand men, and on the 8th ordered a reconnoissance in force to be made the next morning, in order to ascertain the strength and position of the enemy.

Beauregard was already on his way to Tupelo, 25 miles farther south, and 52 miles from Corinth. Pope fired a parting shot at him by telegraphing to Halleck:

"They have lost by desertion of the Tennessee, Kentucky and Arkansas regiments near 20,000 men, since they left Corinth. All the regiments yet left from these States passed down closely guarded on both sides by Mississippi and Alabama troops."

The "Official Records" show that Beauregard lost less than 4000 on the retreat from Corinth, and many of these came in after a few days. The Army of the West, and notably Price's division, mustered more men "present for duty" the day after it reached Tupelo than when it began its retreat from Corinth.

By the series of operations which Halleck had directed since he assumed command at St. Louis in November, 1861, the Confederates had now been driven out of Missouri, north Arkansas, Kentucky, and all of western and middle Tennessee, and had lost every city and stronghold on the Mississippi except Vicksburg. No wonder that the Government was so well pleased with him that on the 8th of June, 1862, it extended his command over the whole of Kentucky and Tennessee, so that he might have abundant means to conduct the new campaign upon which he had determined, with Chattanooga as its first objective.

He began straightway to prepare for it by sending Buell's army back into middle Tennessee, and by making such disposition of his forces in western Tennessee as would assure the safety of that part of his command and of the country west of the Mississippi. In the midst of these preparations the President, whose confidence in McClellan had been greatly shaken by the latter's reverses before Richmond, appointed Halleck (July 11th) general-in-chief, and ordered him to repair forthwith to Washington. Halleck, before leaving, put Grant in command of all the troops west of the Tennessee, including those at Columbus and Cairo; ordering him, however, to send Hovey's division to Helena to reënforce Curtis, and Thomas into middle Tennessee to rejoin Buell.

As soon as Beauregard, whose health had been seriously impaired, was satisfied that Halleck did not intend to attack him at Tupelo, he turned over the command of his army temporarily to Bragg (June 17th) and went to Mobile. When the President learned this fact he relieved Beauregard, and assigned Bragg to the command of the Department.

## WITH PRICE EAST OF THE MISSISSIPPI. 723

While Halleck at Corinth and Bragg at Tupelo were engaged in the congenial business of reorganizing and disciplining their armies, a cavalry engagement took place near Booneville which, though only an affair of outposts, is worth relating, because it brought into conspicuous notice a young officer of rare merit and singular good fortune—Philip H. Sheridan. At the beginning of 1862 he was still but a captain of infantry, on duty as quartermaster and commissary of the army with which Curtis was marching against Price in Missouri. He had come to Corinth with Halleck, and was still doing duty there as quartermaster when, on the 25th of May, he was made colonel of the 2d Michigan Cavalry. Within forty-eight hours he went with Elliott on what Pope says was "the first cavalry raid of the war," and participated in the attack upon Booneville (May 30th). He was now fairly started in his new career. On the 1st of July he was in command of a brigade consisting of two cavalry regiments, and had just established his headquarters at Booneville.

Bragg, who was sending a division of infantry to Ripley, Miss., had ordered Chalmers (June 30th) to take some 1200 or 1500 cavalry, and to cover the movement of this infantry by making a feint upon Rienzi. In executing this order Chalmers encountered Sheridan (July 1st), and a stubborn engagement took place. It lasted from 8:30 in the morning till late in the afternoon, when, Sheridan having been reënforced by infantry and artillery, Chalmers retired.

Rosecrans (who, in June, upon Pope's transfer to the East, had succeeded him in the command of the Army of the Mississippi, to which Sheridan's brigade belonged) issued an order declaring that "the coolness, determination, and fearless gallantry displayed by Colonel Sheridan and the officers and men of his command in this action deserved the thanks and admiration of the army," and telegraphed Halleck: "More cavalry massed under such an officer would be of great use to us. Sheridan ought to be made a brigadier. He would not be a stampeding general." Halleck at once asked the President to promote him "for gallant conduct in battle"; and soon afterward Generals Rosecrans, J. C. Sullivan, Gordon Granger, Elliott, and Asboth telegraphed to Halleck (then in Washington): "The undersigned respectfully beg that you will obtain the promotion of Sheridan. *He is worth his weight in gold.*" He was eventually promoted to the rank of brigadier-general, his commission dating from this fight with Chalmers on July 1st.

When the army had got into camp at Tupelo, and it was apparent that hostilities would not be resumed immediately, General Price went to Richmond in order to persuade the President to send him and the Missourians back to the trans-Mississippi. Beauregard, Bragg, and Van Dorn all advised that this be done; and Van Dorn, who was still in nominal command of the country west of the Mississippi, generously urged the President to assign General Price to that command, saying, in a private letter to Mr. Davis, that as "the love of the people of Missouri was so strong for General Price, and his prestige as a commander so great there, wisdom would seem to dictate that he be put at the head of affairs in the West."

All along the route to Richmond crowds testified their great admiration for Price. At Richmond, the capital of his native State, he was fêted and honored, even in the midst of the great anxiety which was felt in the dangerous presence of McClellan's great army within sight of the capital. The General Assembly gave him a formal reception, and the people manifested for him their respect and affection.

Not so the President. He received the general courteously, but he had been strongly prejudiced against him; he had little confidence in any soldier who had not been educated at West Point, and he had been told again and again, by those who did not know the difference between a drill-sergeant and a general, that Price was not a disciplinarian, and that his army was a mere mob. I do not blame Mr. Davis for believing it, for some of the men who told these things were men of high degree,—generals, congressmen, statesmen, and many of them, I am sorry to have to add, Missourians.

President Davis asked Price to express his opinions and wishes in writing. This the general did, as he did everything, plainly, sensibly, and modestly, asking for himself nothing but permission to return with his Missourians to Arkansas, there to rally around these veterans an army with which to gain possession of their own State.

This letter was submitted to the President, who, after a few days, sent for the general. The details of this final interview, at which the Secretary of War and myself were also present, are deeply impressed upon my memory. After discussing the matter awhile, the President said that he had determined not to let the general and the Missourians return to the trans-Mississippi.

"Well, Mr. President," said General Price, with the utmost respect and courtesy of manner, "Well, Mr. President, if you will not let me serve *you*, I will nevertheless serve my *country*. You cannot prevent me from doing that. I will send you my resignation, and go back to Missouri and raise another army there without your assistance, and fight again under the flag of Missouri, and win new victories for the South in spite of the Government."

No one who ever encountered Jefferson Davis in authority, especially when he was President, can ever forget the measured articulation with which he gave force to words addressed to one who presumed to oppose his wishes or to refuse obedience to his will. And now he had been defied in the very Executive Chamber of the Confederacy by a wild Western chieftain, whom he had himself raised from insignificance as a major-general of the Missouri militia to the height of major-general in the provisional army of the Confederate States. His eye flashed with anger as he glanced to the general's flushed face, and his tone was contemptuous, as he replied with measured slowness: "Your resignation will be promptly accepted, General; and if you do go back to Missouri and raise another army, and win victories for the South, or do it any service at all, no one will be more *pleased* than myself, or," after a pause which was intended to emphasize, and did emphasize, the words that followed, "more *surprised*."

"Then I will surprise you, sir," said the general, bringing his clenched fist down upon the table with a violence which set the inkstands and everything upon it a-dancing; and out he went, indignant and furious, to return to his hotel and forward his resignation. The next day Price was informed that the President, instead of accepting his resignation, would instruct Bragg to send the Missourians to the trans-Mississippi as soon as it could safely be done.

Leaving Richmond while the Seven Days' battles were still being fought within sight of the capital, General Price arrived at Tupelo on the 2d of July. On reporting to Bragg, the latter told him that he could not spare him or the Missouri troops just then, but would give him command of the Army of the West, since Van Dorn had been sent by order of the President to relieve Lovell in the command at Vicksburg, then threatened by Farragut's fleet.

Halleck, as has been said, began to move his army toward Chattanooga immediately after occupying Corinth. One of his last acts, before laying down his Western command in order to assume the position of general-in-chief, was to order Grant to send Thomas's division eastward to Buell. This was done in obedience to the wishes of President Lincoln, who telegraphed him on the 30th of June not to do anything which would force him "to give up, or weaken, or delay the expedition against Chattanooga. To take and hold the railroad at or east of Cleveland, in east Tennessee, is, I think, fully as important as the taking and holding of Richmond."

The Confederate Government also recognized the vital importance of Chattanooga and reorganized its Western commands accordingly. The country west of the Mississippi was erected into a separate military department, and Bragg was assigned to the command of all the country lying between the Mississippi and Virginia. This was done on the 18th of July, and Bragg at once determined to transfer the bulk of his forces to Chattanooga, and, assuming the offensive before Buell was ready to oppose him, to push boldly through Tennessee into Kentucky, and call upon the people of those States to rise and help him to drive the enemy beyond the Ohio.

To this end he made his dispositions. Van Dorn was assigned to the command of the District of the Mississippi lying along the eastern bank of that river, and ordered to defend Vicksburg, to keep open communication with the trans-Mississippi, and at the same time to prevent the Union armies from occupying the north-eastern part of the State of Mississippi. Forney was left in command of the district of the Gulf. Price was placed in command of the District of the Tennessee, with orders to hold the line of the Mobile and Ohio railroad, and, above all, to watch Grant and prevent him from sending reënforcements to Buell in middle Tennessee. Kirby Smith was directed to get ready to move from Knoxville, and Humphrey Marshall out of Western Virginia into Kentucky. Polk was "Second in command of the forces"; Hardee was put in immediate command of the Army of the Mississippi, now thoroughly reorganized. On July 21st this army started for Chattanooga, the infantry being sent by rail *via* Mobile. To cover the movement, Bragg sent Wheeler with his cavalry on a raid into west Tennessee. ☆

---

☆ The Confederate cavalry brigade, at this time commanded by Colonel Joseph Wheeler, consisted at first of parts of the 1st Alabama and 1st Kentucky regiments; afterward of the 3d Georgia, 1st Kentucky, and 8th Texas regiments and 9th Tennessee battalion.— EDITORS.

Price was left with the Army of the West at Tupelo. At the time when Price assumed command of this army it consisted of two divisions of infantry, a light battery for each brigade, and a small force of cavalry. One division was commanded by Brigadier-General Henry Little, and the other by Brigadier-General Dabney H. Maury. The strength of the two was about 15,000 officers and men, but of these nearly 4000 were sick or on extra duty; there were, therefore, about 11,000 "present for duty."

As the cavalry of the Army of the West had been dismounted in Arkansas when about to be moved to Corinth, Price's mounted force consisted of only a few fractional regiments and independent companies, which, all together, could not muster one thousand men for duty. One of his first cares was to organize this force efficiently. The difficulty of the task was increased by the fact that the men were scattered in all directions on picket duty; and, moreover, they had never been accustomed to act together. With the consent of Bragg he assigned Frank C. Armstrong, who had lately been elected colonel of the 3d Louisiana infantry (one of the best regiments in the service), to the command of the cavalry, with the provisional rank of brigadier-general; and Armstrong quickly brought it to a high state of discipline and efficiency.

On leaving Tupelo, Bragg ordered other troops within the district to report to Price, whose "effective" force was thus raised to about fifteen thousand.

Hardee left Tupelo on the 29th of July, and during the next week all of the Army of the Mississippi was on its way to Chattanooga. Price at once began to get ready to move toward Corinth, in order, by threatening that place, to keep Grant from reënforcing Buell. As, however, he knew that he would have to encounter a force of at least thirty thousand men, he did not dare to make any serious advance without the coöperation of Van Dorn, to whom he therefore wrote, on the 31st of July (sending the letter by Dr. Blackburn, one of his volunteer aides, since Governor of Kentucky), that he would himself be ready within a few days to move against Grant with fifteen thousand effectives, and would gladly place himself and them under his command if he would, with his own available force, coöperate in the proposed movement.

Unfortunately Van Dorn at Vicksburg did not have any available force at that time, or for many weeks afterward. With the assistance of the gun-boat *Arkansas* he had demonstrated to Farragut the impracticability of taking Vicksburg without the coöperation of a large land force, and had caused him to return to New Orleans with his fleet, and Davis's and Ellet's to retire up the river, and on July 27th, the very day on which Farragut withdrew, he ordered Breckinridge to proceed at once to Baton Rouge with five thousand picked men and occupy that place.╯ A series of misadventures had followed that expedition, and Van Dorn, far from being able to coöperate with Price in a forward movement, was himself in great want of reënforcements for Breckinridge, and implored Price to send that officer a brigade.

Now it had so happened that when General Hardee was leaving Tupelo on the 29th of July he sent for me (I being at that time chief of staff of the District of the Tennessee), and said that he had just learned of Van Dorn's expe-

╯ For accounts of operations about Vicksburg see Vol. III. of this work.—EDITORS.

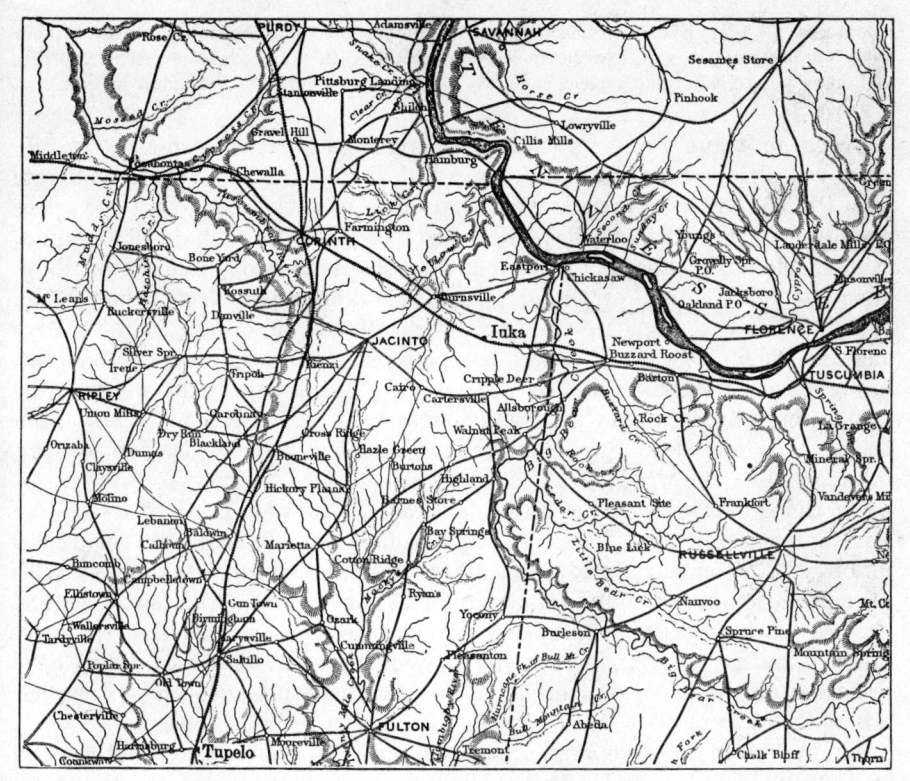

MAP OF THE CORINTH AND IUKA REGION.

dition against Baton Rouge; that he feared that it would lead Van Dorn into other adventures which would overtask his strength, and that Van Dorn would then call on General Price to help him. "Now," said he, "when this happens, as it surely will, I want you to say to General Price, for me, that the success of General Bragg's movement into Tennessee and Kentucky depends greatly upon his (Price's) ability to keep Grant from reënforcing Buell, and consequently that General Bragg would sternly disapprove the sending of any reënforcements whatever to Van Dorn. Say to General Price that I know that General Bragg expects him to keep his men well in hand, and ready to move northward at a moment's notice."

Simultaneously with Van Dorn's request for reënforcements came a telegram from Bragg (August 2d) saying that Grant had been reënforcing Buell, and that "the road was open for him (Price) into west Tennessee." Price therefore replied to Van Dorn that in view of Bragg's telegram, and considering the very important relations which the Army of the West bore to that in east Tennessee, he could not send any of his troops to Breckinridge, but must concentrate them for a forward movement.

"The enemy [said he] is still transferring his troops from Corinth and its vicinity eastward. He will, by the end of this week, have reduced the force to its minimum. We should be quick to take advantage of this, for he will soon begin to get in reënforcements under the late call for volunteers. . . . Every consideration makes it important that I shall move forward without a day's unnecessary delay. I earnestly desire your coöperation in such a movement, and will, as I have before said, gladly place my army and myself under your command in that contingency."

Bragg, to whom Price forwarded a copy of this correspondence, warmly approved Price's conduct, and ordered Van Dorn (August 11th) to coöperate with Price. Price meanwhile went vigorously to work to get ready for active operations. An efficient officer, who had been sent to Richmond for funds, came back with enough to pay off the troops and to purchase an abundance of supplies of every kind. Transportation was collected, more than enough, and the roads in our front were all put in order. Three active and intelligent officers who had been sent to Richmond for the purpose, brought back with them improved arms sufficient to supply the wants of the troops in camp, and also to arm five thousand exchanged prisoners whom Bragg had ordered to Price, but whom Van Dorn, with Mr. Davis's consent, intercepted on the way.

On the 4th of September Price telegraphed to Van Dorn: "I state for your information that I can put in the field an effective total of 13,000 infantry, 3000 cavalry, and 800 artillerymen; that they are supplied with transportation and ammunition as prescribed in General Bragg's last general orders; that subsistence has been provided to October 1st; that the commissary trains will transport seven days' provisions; and that I will have arms for all my troops, including those exchanged prisoners that Bragg has ordered sent to me."

Not only were these men well armed and equipped, well fed, well clothed, and well provided with everything that an army in the field needed, but they were thoroughly organized, drilled, and disciplined. July 24th, just before leaving Tupelo, Bragg reviewed them for the first time. When Price's old division, to the command of which Little had succeeded, had passed in review, and Little was about to resume his place at its head, Bragg turned to Little and said: "You had the reputation of having one of the finest companies in the old army. General, this is certainly as fine a division as I have ever seen." And it was. ✥ But however brave and well-disciplined his men, Price did not dare to throw them against the fortifications of Corinth, defended by twice their own number commanded by Grant and Rosecrans.

All that he could do was to send Armstrong with his cavalry into west Tennessee to harass Grant, and bring back such information as he could get.

✥ What manner of men they were that constituted it no one who has not shared their fortunes, their hardships, and their dangers in camp, on the march, and upon the field of battle, can ever know. There lie before me now two yellowing bits of coarse paper which throw some light upon their humanity. While at Richmond during the Seven Days' battles around that city, the general and those of us that were with him had seen the long files of wounded that came or were brought day by day to the crowded hospitals. Naturally, when we got back to the army we spoke of these things to the men. Within less than forty-eight hours the chaplain of Erwin's battalion was on his way to Richmond with $2350, which the officers and men of that battalion were sending to the relief of the wounded of Lee's army. A day or two afterward Colonel Gates, of the 1st Missouri Cavalry, sent a similar contribution. These men, it must be remembered, had been away from their homes for almost a year, serving much the greater part of that time without pay, and clothing themselves besides. Nor was this money depreciated currency, but it was just as good as any United States Treasury notes. Other regiments did likewise, but the record of their humanity has been lost.—T. L. S.

DWELLINGS IN IUKA. FROM PHOTOGRAPHS TAKEN IN 1884.

1. General George H. Thomas's headquarters. 2. Female seminary, used as a hospital. 3. General Price's headquarters. 4. Iuka Springs. 5. Methodist Church, used as a hospital. 6. General Rosecrans's headquarters. 7. General Grant's headquarters.

Taking 1600 men, Armstrong reached Holly Springs on the 26th of August, and having been reënforced there by 1100 men under Jackson, struck for Bolivar, Tennessee. There he encountered and defeated a force under Colonel Leggett, who, in his report of this affair, says that after fighting for seven hours with "less than 900" he "drove from the field over 6000." Armstrong then crossed the Hatchie and cut the railroad between Bolivar and Jackson. He then turned back to Tupelo. On the way he met a force under Colonel Dennis, whose brigade commander, General L. F. Ross, reported that with 800 men he met Armstrong, 6000 strong, and won "the most brilliant victory of the war"; that he himself lost only 5 men, but that "Armstrong left 179 dead upon the field." This is his *official* report; but the fact is that during the whole expedition Armstrong lost only one hundred and fifteen men killed, wounded, and missing.

Van Dorn, having brought Breckinridge and most of his men back to Jackson, Miss., announced, on the 24th of August, that he was ready to coöperate with General Price in an aggressive campaign. He proposed to move through western Tennessee into Kentucky, and thence to Paducah and "wherever circumstances might dictate." But he was not ready to move, and there was no possibility that he could get ready for two weeks to come.

On the 1st of September Bragg telegraphed Price that Buell was in full retreat upon Nashville, and that he must watch Rosecrans and prevent their junction; or, if he should escape, follow him closely. Price consequently told Van Dorn that he could wait for him no longer, but must move in three days. Van Dorn replied that he would be ready to move from Holly Springs on the 12th, but wanted men, arms, and wagons. Upon Price's refusal to give them he asked the President to order Price to do it, and also to give him command of Price and his army. After some hesitation, the President, without consulting General Bragg, or knowing the special instructions which Bragg had given to Van Dorn and Price, ordered Van Dorn by telegraph (September 11th) to assume command of both armies, and thereby unknowingly struck Bragg a heavier blow than any which he had yet received from the enemy.

Price, not knowing what had been done, was on the march to Iuka, intending to move thence into middle Tennessee, if, on reaching that place, he should find that Rosecrans had gone to Nashville, as Bragg believed. His cavalry under Armstrong entered the town on the 13th, but withdrew when the enemy appeared in force.

Moving by moonlight that night with his infantry and artillery,

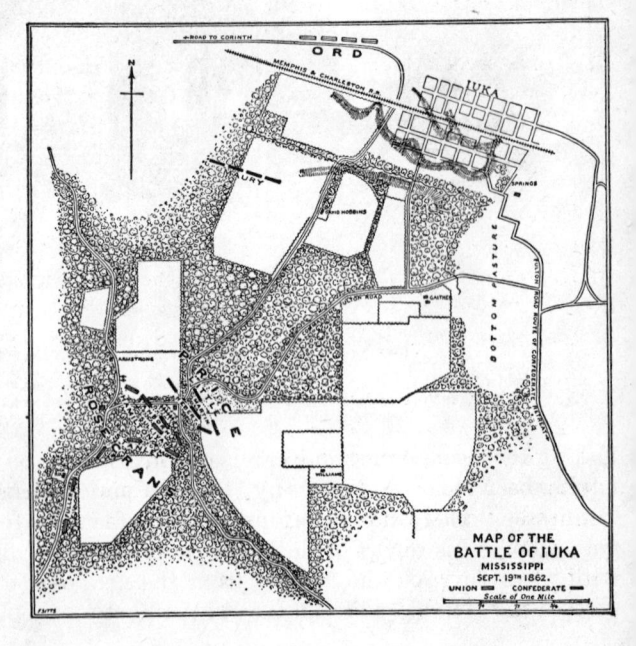

MAP OF THE BATTLE OF IUKA
MISSISSIPPI
SEPT. 19TH 1862.
UNION ■■■ CONFEDERATE ▬▬▬
Scale of One Mile

Price entered Iuka the next morning (September 14th), and quietly took possession,—the Union garrison retiring without offering any resistance, and abandoning a large amount of supplies which added greatly to the happiness of the Confederates.

Price learned as soon as he got into Iuka that though Rosecrans had sent three divisions of his army [E. A. Paine's, Jeff. C. Davis's, and Gordon Granger's] to Buell, he was himself still west of Iuka with two divisions. After some hesitation he felt that it was his duty not to go to Nashville, but to look after Rosecrans and what was left of his army; accordingly he telegraphed Van Dorn that as Rosecrans had gone to Corinth he would turn back and co-operate with Van Dorn in an attack upon that place. Hardly had he done this when Price received a telegram from Bragg urging him to hasten to Nashville. [See map, p. 702.]

This is what Price ought to have done. It is what Halleck, Grant, and Rosecrans feared that he would do. Rosecrans telegraphed Grant that he "had better watch the Old Woodpecker" (alluding to that bird's skill in deceiving its enemies), "or he would get away from them." Halleck telegraphed (September 17th): "Do everything in your power to prevent Price from crossing the Tennessee River. A junction of Price and Bragg in Tennessee would be most disastrous. They should be fought while separate." Grant replied that he "would do everything in his power to prevent such a catastrophe," and began at once to concentrate his forces against Price. Ord was pushed forward to Burnsville, where Grant established his own headquarters, and Rosecrans was ordered to concentrate his two divisions at Jacinto, and to move thence upon Iuka, in order to flank Price and cut off his retreat.

BRIGADIER-GENERAL HENRY LITTLE, C. S. A., KILLED AT IUKA. FROM A PHOTOGRAPH.

Hurlbut, who was at Bolivar, was at the same time ordered to make a strong demonstration toward Grand Junction, near which place Van Dorn had at last arrived with about 10,000 effectives. In order to deceive Van Dorn, and to keep him from helping Price by an attack upon Corinth, Hurlbut was told to make a great fuss, and to let it leak out that he was expecting heavy reënforcements from Columbus, and that as soon as they came, he, Sherman and Steele were going to make a dash for Grenada and the Yazoo country.☥

On the 18th of September, Ord with about 6500 men was advanced to within 6 miles of Iuka and directed to be ready to attack the next morning;

---

☥ On the 19th of September, 1862, General Grant telegraphed to General Halleck that before leaving Corinth he had sent instructions to General Hurlbut as indicated in the text.

Meanwhile General Grant had received General Halleck's orders of September 18th to make the very movement up the Yazoo that Hurlbut had been told to feign.—EDITORS.

but Grant, having learned that Rosecrans could not reach Iuka till the afternoon, instructed Ord not to attack till he heard Rosecrans's guns.

There was yet time for Price to obey Bragg's order and hurry to Nashville. Once across the defiles of Bear Creek, he would have been safe from pursuit, for Grant would hardly have ventured to lay open west Tennessee to the advance of Van Dorn, who was now waiting for an opportunity to enter it. Price was still undecided what to do in view of this latest order from Bragg, when, during the night of the 18th, one of Van Dorn's staff arrived, bringing the intelligence that Van Dorn had been directed by the President to take command of Price and the Army of the West. This staff-officer was also authorized to concert with General Price the movements by which the junction of the two armies should be effected. This settled the matter. Orders were issued to load the wagons and get the troops ready to move the next morning at daybreak toward Baldwyn, on the Mobile and Ohio railroad.

While preparations for this movement were being made, Price learned about 2 P. M. (September 19th) that his pickets on the Jacinto road had been driven in, and that Rosecrans was advancing on that road in force. All of Price's infantry and artillery was at that time in front of Ord, from which direction Price expected to be attacked.

Little was hastily ordered to send Hébert's brigade to the left, toward Rosecrans. It came forward on the instant, Price himself taking it to the front. Hamilton's division of Rosecrans's corps was by this time within a mile and a half of the center of the town. Seeing that he was greatly outnumbered, Price ordered Little to send up another brigade, and Martin's was quickly on the ground. The fight had already begun and was being waged with great severity. Price now ordered Little to bring up the rest of his division. After starting the men forward, Little himself galloped to the front and joined General Price in the thickest of the fight. While they were consulting, a minie-ball, crashing through Little's forehead, killed him instantly.

MAJOR-GENERAL C. S. HAMILTON.
FROM A PHOTOGRAPH.

Hamilton was already giving way. Price pushed him the more vigorously, and, capturing 9 of his guns, drove him back about 600 yards. Hamilton was now reënforced by Stanley's division. About the same time the rest of Little's division reached the field,— too late, however, to take part in the battle, for it was already dark. The Confederate division bivouacked upon the ground from which Hamilton had been driven.

General Price returned sorrowfully to town, for he had lost his most trusted lieutenant,—the very best division commander I have ever known,— Henry Little. He, nevertheless, resolved to renew the battle at daylight, and was confident of victory. Maury was ordered to move his division to the front of Rosecrans, and Armstrong and Wirt Adams were directed to occupy with the cavalry the positions in front of Ord, so as to cover the movement of our troops from that front to the front of Rosecrans, and also to hinder the advance of the Federals upon our right. General Price then went to the house of a friend, instead of to his own quarters, and told me not to let him be disturbed till an hour before day.

After burying Little by torchlight, I returned to headquarters, determined to remain awake all night. Some time after midnight Hébert, who had succeeded to the command of Little's division, came in and said that his brigade was so badly cut up and was so much disheartened by the death of Little that he was apprehensive of the morrow. While he was still there, Maury came in and said that he was convinced that Grant would attack us in overwhelming force in the morning, brush our cavalry out of his way, destroy our trains, and assail us in rear. Wirt Adams, who came in next, sustained Maury's views, and all of them insisted upon seeing General Price. I was still hesitating what to do when one of Van Dorn's staff arrived with important dispatches from Van Dorn, and asked to see the general. I hesitated no longer, but took them to his lodgings. It was nearly dawn, and he thought I had come to call him to battle. Great was his disappointment when he ascertained the true cause of our coming. He tried to convince his generals that their apprehensions were groundless, and that a victory was in their grasp, but they would not be convinced. Unwilling to give battle when all of his chief officers were so averse to it, he reluctantly directed them to carry out the orders which had been issued the preceding morning for the withdrawal of the army to Baldwyn. The trains had already been loaded and were ready to leave. They were put in motion instantly, and toward sunrise the troops followed. Every wagon, all the valuable captured stores, and all the sick and wounded that were fit to be moved, were brought away safely. Maury's division left the town about 8 A. M., and Armstrong brought up the rear with the cavalry.

Between Burnsville, where Grant was on the 19th, and the battle-field of that day, there lay a densely wooded country, much of it an impassable swamp, and it was only by making a long circuit that Rosecrans could communicate with him. The wind, too, happened during the battle to be blowing away from Burnsville. It was, therefore, not till half-past 8 o'clock the next morning that Grant knew that a battle had been fought.‡ Hastening to the front, he directed Ord to push forward. Rosecrans had meanwhile entered the town. Grant sent Hamilton's and Stanley's divisions with some cavalry in pursuit. The cavalry came up with Price's rear-guard in the afternoon, but

‡ In his "Memoirs" (Vol. I., p. 412), Grant says: "The wind was still blowing hard and in the wrong direction to transmit sound toward either Ord or me. Neither he nor I nor any one in either command heard a gun that was fired on the battle-field."—EDITORS.

having been roughly handled and driven back by McCulloch's regiment of Missouri cavalry, supported by Colonel Rogers's regiment of Texas sharpshooters and Bledsoe's battery, the pursuit was abandoned and the Confederates reached Baldwyn without further interruption.

In the battle of Iuka only two brigades of Price's army were engaged, Hébert's and Adams's brigades of Little's division. They were composed exclusively of troops from Mississippi, Alabama, Louisiana, Arkansas, and Texas, and one Missouri battery. The aggregate strength of both brigades was 3179 officers and men. Their loss was 86 killed and 408 wounded [see also p. 736]. In addition to these, about 200 of the Confederate sick were left at Iuka and on the road. Price's loss, therefore, was about 700.

Rosecrans's column, according to his own report, was 9000 strong, but the brunt of the battle fell upon two brigades of Hamilton's division. The Union loss was 141 killed, 613 wounded, and 36 missing; total, 790.

Rosecrans says that Price's loss was 1438; and Hamilton states "boldly," to use his own expression, that he, "with a force of not more than 2800 men, met and conquered a rebel force of 11,000 on a field chosen by Price." General Grant, in his report of the battle written a month afterward, discards these exaggerations of Rosecrans and Hamilton.

## THE BATTLE OF IUKA.

### BY C. S. HAMILTON, MAJOR-GENERAL, U. S. V.

IUKA is a little village on the Memphis and Charleston railway, in northern Mississippi, about thirty miles east of Corinth. In September, 1862, the Confederate authorities, to prevent reënforcements being sent by the Federal commander in Mississippi to Buell in Kentucky, sent General Sterling Price with his army corps to Iuka. A regiment of Union troops stationed at Iuka evacuated the place, leaving a considerable quantity of army stores, as also quite an amount of cotton. The latter was destroyed, the former made use of, and Price settled down, apparently at his leisure, under the nose of Grant's force, whose headquarters were at Corinth. As soon as definite information was had of this position of Price, Grant took immediate steps to beat him up. A combined attack was planned, by which Rosecrans with his two divisions (Hamilton's and Stanley's) was to move on Iuka from the south, while Ord, with a similar column, was to approach Iuka from the west. This he did, taking position within about six miles of the village, where he was to await Rosecrans's attack.

From Iuka southward ran two parallel roads, some two miles distant from each other — the most eastern known as the Fulton road, the western as the Tuscumbia. Grant's plan contemplated an approach on Iuka by way of the Fulton road, at least in part, with a view of cutting off the escape of Price by that road. Rosecrans, however, for reasons of his own, decided on taking the Tuscumbia road with his whole force, thus leaving the Fulton road open.

A rapid march from Jacinto (Hamilton's division leading, Sanborn's brigade in the advance) brought Rosecrans's column to Barnett's by noon. Hamilton, who had expected to march upon the Fulton road from that point, was furnished with a guide, and directed to continue his march on the Tuscumbia road without further instructions.

About 4 P. M. the guide gave notice that the column was within about two miles of Iuka. In fact, we were on the eve of a battle, and it is well here to note the strength and position of the opposing forces. On the Union side was Hamilton's division of 2 brigades (Sanborn's and Sullivan's) of 5 regiments and a battery each. Stanley's division was following along the same road, but as yet was some distance in the rear. It also had 2 brigades of 5 regiments each, but only 3 of these regiments reached the field in time to take any part in the conflict.

At the moment the guide gave notice of our nearness to Iuka, the whole of the leading division was halted in the road in exactly the order they had been marching. The head of the column had just finished ascending a long hill, from the top of which the ground sloped in undulations toward the front. A few hundred yards ahead, in line of battle, the enemy lay concealed in the woods. Hébert's brigade of 6 regiments lay athwart the road by which we were approaching; Martin's brigade of 4 regiments had been divided, and 2 of these regiments were thrown on the right of the Confederate line and 2 on the left, making 10 regiments in line of battle. At the commencement of the conflict, the other 2 brigades which had been ordered up had arrived on the field, making the whole strength of Little's division, 18 regiments, ready for action before a gun had been fired.

On the halting of my troops, the battalion of skirmishers was pushed rapidly forward in the direction of Iuka. An advance of four hundred yards brought them in the immediate presence of the enemy. I was immediately in rear of the skirmishers, and taking in the situation at a glance dashed back to the head of the column. If this should become enveloped by the enemy, a rout was inevitable, and our force would be doubled back on itself. I threw the leading regiment, the 5th Iowa, across the road, moving it a short distance to the right, and ordered up the nearest battery, which was placed in position on the road, and to the left of the first regiment in position. Colonel Sanborn was active in bringing up other regiments, and getting them into line. Just as the first regiment was placed, the enemy opened one of his batteries with canister. The charge passed over our heads, doing no damage beyond bringing down a shower of twigs and leaves. The Confederates were in line ready for action. Why they did not move forward and attack us at once is not understood. Their delay, which enabled us to form the nearest three regiments in line of battle before the attack began, was our salvation. An earlier attack would have enveloped the head of the column, and brought a disastrous rout.

Meantime not a moment was lost. A second regiment, and a third, with all the rapidity that men could exercise, were added to our little line; and while the Confederates were moving to the front, we had managed to get a battle line of three regiments into position. It was then the storm of battle opened. The opposing infantry lines were within close musketry shot. Our battery was handled with energy, and dealt death to the enemy. The Confederate batteries had ceased firing, their line of fire having been covered by the advance of their infantry. Our own infantry held their ground nobly against the overwhelming force moving against them, and we were enabled to add another regiment to the line of battle. At the first musketry fire of the enemy, most of the horses of our battery were killed, and the pieces could not be removed from the field. The fight became an infantry duel. I never saw a hotter or more destructive engagement. General Price says in his official report, "The fight began, and was waged with a severity I have never seen surpassed."

The regiments of Sanborn's brigade were in the front line. Sullivan's brigade was divided—a regiment thrown to the right flank, and one to the left—the remaining two being placed in rear of Sanborn's center as a reënforcement. Thus was every regiment of my command doing duty on the field. Stanley's division seemed long in coming up. The Confederate lines had moved forward, concentrating their fire on our little front, and stretching out their wings to the right and left, as though we were to be taken in at once. Our men stood their ground bravely, yielding nothing for a long time; but the pressure began to grow severe, and I feared we might be driven from our ground. Thinking General Rosecrans was in the rear, where he could hurry up the troops of Stanley's division, I dispatched an aide with the request that General Rosecrans would come forward far enough to confer with me. All the while the battle waxed hotter and more furious. The dead lay in lines along the regiments, while some of our troops gave signs of yielding. I dispatched another officer, the only one in reach, for General Rosecrans. He happened to be one of General Rosecrans's staff, and at my request he started to bear the message to his general. Our troops, as yet, had not given way. The battery under Sears was doing noble service, but had lost nearly half its men. Sanborn's brigade was held by him to their work like Roman veterans, but without help we could not much longer hold out. I dispatched my adjutant-general, Captain Sawyer, and a short time later another aide, Lieutenant Wheeler, with messages for General Rosecrans, saying that I considered it imperative he should come forward to see me, and should hurry forward fresh troops.↓

Stanley's division had now reached the vicinity of the battle-field, and General Stanley came instantly to the front, directing the division to follow as rapidly as possible. It was time, for our line had begun to give way slowly. It had been formed on the crest of the hill (up which we had come, and which sloped to our rear), and in falling back had been arrested just below the brow of the hill, where it maintained the fight. Other regiments were yielding ground slowly, but were readily stopped by the united exertions of Stanley, Sanborn, and myself. The falling back of the troops had exposed the battery, into which the Confederates had entered. A short time later, however, a desperate rally was made, and they were driven back from the battery; but returning with renewed strength, our troops were again forced below the brow of the hill. Here three of Stanley's regiments reached the field, and were pushed to the right of the line, where they made good the places of troops that had fallen to the rear. They fought bravely under Colonels Mower, Boomer, and Holman, but the fire was too deadly, and they in turn were forced back. It was growing dark. The smoke of battle added to the coming night, and it was soon too dark to distinguish the gray from the blue uniform. The storm of battle gradually lulled to entire quiet.

Our troops bivouacked on the slope of the hill. The Confederates, for several hours, were occupied with burying their dead and removing their wounded.

A consultation between General Rosecrans and his division commanders resulted in a rearrangement of the troops early in the night, and every-

---

↓ Rosecrans in his official report says: "About this time [referring to a time subsequent to the capture and recovery of Sears's battery] it was deemed prudent to order up the first brigade of Stanley's division." This shows that Stanley had reached the vicinity of the battle-field, but for some reason no one had ordered him to the front.—C. S. H.

thing was made ready for battle in the morning. The enemy, however, left the vicinity of the field during the night, leaving the battery which had been the object of such a sanguinary struggle but a short distance to the rear, and near their first line of battle.

The Fulton road being open, there was nothing to interfere with the enemy's escape. A pursuit was made the following day — but a pursuit of a defeated enemy can amount to little in a country like that of northern Mississippi, heavily wooded, and with narrow roads, when the enemy has time enough to get his artillery and trains in front of his infantry. To make an effective pursuit, it must be so close on the heels of the battle that trains, artillery, and troops can be made to blockade the roads by being mixed in an indiscriminate mass.

On the following day, September 21st, our troops were back in their old encampments at Jacinto. Just two weeks later, the same divisions and brigades were measured against each other on the field of Corinth.

## THE OPPOSING FORCES AT IUKA, MISS.
### September 19th, 1862.

The composition, losses, and strength of each army as here stated give the gist of all the data obtainable in the Official Records. K stands for killed; w for wounded; m w for mortally wounded; m for captured or missing; c for captured.

### THE UNION FORCES.
ARMY OF THE MISSISSIPPI.— Major-General William S. Rosecrans.

SECOND DIVISION, Brig.-Gen. David S. Stanley. *First Brigade*, Col. John W. Fuller: 27th Ohio, Major Zephaniah S. Spaulding; 39th Ohio, Col. Alfred W. Gilbert; 43d Ohio, Col. J. L. Kirby Smith; 63d Ohio, Col. John W. Sprague; M, 1st Mo. Art'y, Capt. Albert M. Powell; 8th Wis. Battery (section), Lieut. John D. McLean; F, 2d U. S. Art'y, Capt. Thomas D. Maurice. Brigade loss: w, 8. *Second Brigade*, Col. Joseph A. Mower: 26th Ill., Major Robert A. Gillmore; 47th Ill., Lieut.-Col. William A. Thrush; 11th Mo., Major Andrew J. Weber; 8th Wis., Lieut.-Col. George W. Robbins; 2d Iowa Battery, Capt. Nelson T. Spoor; 3d Mich. Battery, Capt. Alex. W. Dees. Brigade loss: k, 8; w, 81; m, 4 = 93. THIRD DIVISION, Brig.-Gen. C. S. Hamilton. Staff loss: w, 2. *Escort*: C, 5th Mo. Cav., Capt. Albert Borcherdt (w). Loss: k, 1; w, 2 = 3. *First Brigade*, Col. John B. Sanborn: 48th Ind., Col. Norman Eddy (w), Lieut.-Col. De Witt C. Rugg; 5th Iowa, Col. Charles L. Matthies; 16th Iowa, Col. Alexander Chambers (w), Lieut.-Col. Add. H. Sanders; 4th Minn., Capt. Ebenezer Le Gro; 26th Mo., Col. George B. Boomer (w); 11th Ohio Battery, Lieut. Cyrus Sears (w). Brigade loss: k, 127; w, 434; m, 27 = 588. *Second Brigade*, Brig.-Gen. Jeremiah C. Sullivan: 10th Iowa, Col. Nicholas Perczel; 17th Iowa, Col. John W. Rankin (injured), Capt. Samson M. Archer (w), Capt. John L. Young; 10th Mo., Col. Samuel A. Holmes; E, 24th Mo., Capt. Lafayette M. Rice; 80th Ohio, Lieut.-Col. Matthias H. Bartilson (w), Major Richard Lanning; 12th Wis. Battery, Lieut. Lorenzo D. Immell. Brigade loss: k, 5; w, 76; m, 5 = 86. CAVALRY DIVISION, Col. John K. Mizner; 2d Iowa, Col. Edward Hatch; B and E, 7th Kans., Capt. Frederick Swoyer; 3d Mich., Capt. Lyman G. Willcox. Division loss: w, 9. *Unattached*: Jenks's Co., Ill. Cav., Capt. Albert Jenks. Loss: w, 1.

Total loss of the Union Army: killed, 141; wounded, 613; captured or missing, 36 = 790.

General Rosecrans says ("Official Records," Vol. XVII., Pt. I., p. 74) that "we moved from Jacinto at 5 A. M., with 9000 men, on Price's forces at Iuka. After a march of 18 miles attacked them at 4:30 P. M. . . . with less than half our forces in action." Meanwhile the command of General E. O. C. Ord, comprising the divisions of Davies, Ross, and McArthur, numbering about 8000 men, was marching from Corinth direct on Iuka, and was within four or five miles of the battle-field on the 19th (see map, p. 730). The entire Union force near Iuka, including Ord, was about 17,000 men.

### THE CONFEDERATE FORCES.
ARMY OF THE WEST.— Major-General Sterling Price.

FIRST DIVISION, Brig.-Gen. Henry Little (k). *First Brigade*, Col. Elijah Gates: 16th Ark., ——; 2d Mo., Col. Francis M. Cockrell; 3d Mo., Col. James A. Pritchard; 5th Mo., ——; 1st Mo. (dismounted cavalry), Lieut.-Col. W. D. Maupin; Mo. Battery, Capt. William Wade. Brigade loss: w, 10. *Second Brigade*, Brig.-Gen. Louis Hébert: 14th Ark., ——; 17th Ark., Lieut.-Col. John Griffith; 3d La., Lieut.-Col. J. B. Gilmore (w); 40th Miss., Col. W. Bruce Colbert; 1st Tex. Legion (dismounted cavalry), Col. John W. Whitfield (w), Lieut.-Col. E. R. Hawkins; 3d Tex. (dismounted cavalry), Col. H. P. Mabry (w); St. Louis (Mo.) Battery, Capt. William E. Dawson; Clark (Mo.) Battery, Lieut. J. L. Faris. Brigade loss: k, 63; w, 305; m, 40 = 408. *Third Brigade*, Brig.-Gen. Martin E. Green: 7th Miss. Battalion, Lieut.-Col. J. S. Terral; 43d Miss., Col. W. H. Moore; 4th Mo., Col. A. MacFarlane; 6th Mo., Col. Eugene Erwin; 3d Mo. (dismounted cavalry), ——; Mo. Battery, Capt. Henry Guibor; Mo. Battery, Capt. John C. Landis. *Fourth Brigade*, Col. John D. Martin; 37th Ala., Col. James F. Dowdell (w); 36th Miss., Col. W. W. Witherspoon; 37th Miss., Col. Robert McLain; 38th Miss, Col. F. W. Adams. Brigade loss: k, 22; w, 95 = 117. CAVALRY, Brig.-Gen. Frank C. Armstrong: Miss. regiment, Col. Wirt Adams; 2d Ark., Col. W. F. Slemons; 2d Mo., Col. Robert McCulloch; 1st Miss. Partisan Rangers, Col. W. C. Falkner. Loss not reported.

Total Confederate loss: killed, 85; wounded, 410; captured or missing, 40 = 535.

The battle was fought on the Confederate side by Little's division, and mainly by the brigades of Hébert and Martin, numbering 3179 men. But the effective strength of Price's entire command is estimated at about 14,000, including Dabney H. Maury's division, of three brigades, which, during the 19th, was held near Iuka in readiness to confront Ord.

FILLMORE STREET, CORINTH. FROM A PHOTOGRAPH TAKEN IN 1884.

## THE BATTLE OF CORINTH.

BY WILLIAM S. ROSECRANS, MAJOR-GENERAL, U. S. V., BREVET MAJOR-GENERAL, U. S. A.

THE battle of Corinth, Miss., which is often confounded in public memory with our advance, under Halleck, from Pittsburg Landing in April and May, 1862, was fought on the 3d and 4th of October, of that year, between the combined forces of Generals Earl Van Dorn and Sterling Price of the Confederacy, and the Union divisions of Generals David S. Stanley, Charles S. Hamilton, Thomas A. Davies, and Thomas J. McKean, under myself as commander of the Third Division of the District of West Tennessee.

The Confederate evacuation of Corinth occurred on the 30th of May, General Beauregard withdrawing his army to Tupelo, where, June 27th, he was succeeded in the command by General Braxton Bragg. Halleck occupied Corinth on the day of its evacuation, and May 31st instructed General Buell, commanding the Army of the Ohio, to repair the Memphis and Charleston railway in the direction of Chattanooga — a movement to which, on June 11th, Halleck gave the objective of "Chattanooga and Cleveland and Dalton"; the ultimate purpose being to take possession of east Tennessee, in coöperation with General G. W. Morgan. To counteract these plans, General Bragg began, on June 27th, the transfer of a large portion of his army to Chattanooga by rail, via Mobile, and about the middle of August set out on the northward movement which terminated only within sight of the Ohio River. The Confederate forces in Mississippi were left under command of Generals Van Dorn and Price. About the middle of July General Halleck was called to Washington to discharge the duties of General-in-chief. He left the District of West Tennessee and the territory held in northern Mississippi under the command of General Grant. In August, by Halleck's orders, General Grant sent E. A. Paine's and Jeff. C. Davis's divisions across the Tennessee to strengthen Buell, who was moving northward through middle Tennessee, to meet Bragg. One of these divisions garrisoned Nashville while the other marched with Buell after Bragg into Kentucky.

In the early days of September, after the disaster of the "Second Bull Run," the friends of the Union watched with almost breathless anxiety the advance of Lee into Maryland, of Bragg into Kentucky, and the hurrying of the Army of the Potomac northward from Washington, to get between Lee and the cities of Washington, Baltimore, and Philadelphia. The suspense lest McClellan should not be in time to head off Lee—lest Buell should not arrive in time to prevent Bragg from taking Louisville or assaulting Cincinnati, was fearful.

At this time I was stationed at Corinth with the "Army of the Mississippi," having succeeded General Pope in that command on the 11th of June. We were in the District of West Tennessee, commanded by General Grant. Under the idea that I would reënforce Buell, General Sterling Price, who, during July and August, had been on the Mobile and Ohio railway near Guntown and Baldwyn, Miss., with 15,000 to 20,000 men, moved up to Iuka about the 12th of September, intending to follow me; and, as he reported, "finding that General Rosecrans had not crossed the Tennessee River," he "concluded to withdraw from Iuka toward my [his] old encampment." His "withdrawal" was after the hot battle of Iuka on September 19th, two days after the battle of Antietam which had caused Lee's "withdrawal" from Maryland.

During the month of August General Price had been conferring with General Van Dorn, commanding all the Confederate troops in Mississippi except Price's, to form a combined movement to expel the Union forces from northern Mississippi and western Tennessee, and to plant their flags on the banks of the Lower Ohio, while Bragg was to do the like on that river in Kentucky. General Earl Van Dorn, an able and enterprising commander, after disposing his forces to hold the Mississippi from Grand Gulf up toward Memphis, late in September, with Lovell's division, a little over 8000 men, came up to Ripley, Mississippi, where, on the 28th of September, he was joined by General Price, with Hébert's and Maury's divisions, numbering 13,863 effective infantry, artillery, and cavalry.

This concentration, following the precipitate "withdrawal" of Price from Iuka, portended mischief to the Union forces in west Tennessee, numbering some forty to fifty thousand effectives, scattered over the district occupying the vicinity of the Memphis and Charleston railway from Iuka to Memphis, a stretch of about a hundred and fifteen miles, and located at interior positions on the Ohio and Mississippi from Paducah to Columbus, and at Jackson, Bethel, and other places on the Mississippi Central and Mobile and Ohio railways.

The military features of west Tennessee and northern Mississippi will be readily comprehended by the reader who will examine a map of that region

PROVOST-MARSHAL'S OFFICE, CORINTH. FROM A WAR-TIME PHOTOGRAPH.

and notice: (1) That the Memphis and Charleston railway runs not far from the dividing lines between the States, with a southerly bend from Memphis eastward toward Corinth, whence it extends eastwardly through Iuka, crosses Bear River and follows the Tuscumbia Valley on the south side of that east and west reach of the Tennessee to Decatur. Thence the road crosses to the north side of this river and unites with the Nashville and Chattanooga road at Stevenson *en route* for Chattanooga. (2) That the Mobile and Ohio railway, from Columbus on the Mississippi, runs considerably east of south, passes through Jackson, Tennessee, Bethel, Corinth, Tupelo, and Baldwyn, Mississippi, and thence to Mobile, Alabama. (3) That the Mississippi Central, leaving the Mobile and Ohio at Jackson, Tennessee, runs nearly south, passing by Bolivar and Grand Junction, Tennessee, and Holly Springs, Grenada, etc., to Jackson, Mississippi. All this region of west Tennessee and the adjoining counties of Mississippi, although here and there dotted with clearings, farms, settlements, and little villages, is heavily wooded. Its surface consists of low, rolling, oak ridges of diluvial clays, with intervening crooked drainages traversing narrow, bushy, and sometimes swampy, bottoms. The streams are sluggish and not easily fordable, on account of their miry beds and steep, muddy, clay banks. Water in dry seasons is never abundant, and in many places is only reached by bore-wells of 100 to 300 feet in depth, whence it is hoisted by rope and pulley carrying water-buckets of galvanized iron pipes from 4 to 6 inches in diameter, and 4 to 5 feet long, with valves at the lower end. These matters are of controlling importance in moving and handling troops in that region. Men and animals need hard ground to move on, and must have drinking-water.

The strategic importance of Corinth, where the Mobile and Ohio crosses the Memphis and Charleston, ninety-three miles east of Memphis, results from its control of movements either way over these railways, and the fact that it is not far from Hamburg, Eastport, and Pittsburg Landing on the Tennessee River, to which points good freight steamers can ascend at the lowest stages of water. Corinth is mainly on low, flat ground, along the Mobile and Ohio railway, and flanked by low, rolling ridges, except the cleared patches, covered with oaks and undergrowth for miles in all directions. With few clearings, outside of those made by the Confederate troops in obtaining fuel during their wintering in 1861–2, the country around Corinth, in all directions, was densely wooded.

While General Halleck was advancing on Corinth, the Confederates had extended a line of light defensive works from the Memphis and Charleston road on the west, about two and a half miles from the town, all the way round by the north and east to the same railway east. When the Union forces took possession, General Halleck ordered a defensive line to be constructed about a mile and a half from the town, extending from the Memphis and Charleston railway on the west around southerly to cover the Union front in that direction. After the departure of General Buell's command toward Chattanooga this work was continued, although we had no forces to man it adequately, and it was too far away to afford protection to our stores at Corinth. During August I used to go over from my camp at Clear Creek to General Grant's headquarters at Corinth, and after the usual greetings would ask: "How are you getting along with the line?" He would say: "Well, pretty slowly, but they are doing good work." I said to him: "General, the line isn't worth much to us, because it is too long. We cannot occupy it." He answered, "What would you do?" I said, "I would have made the depots outside of the town north of the Memphis and Charleston road between the town and the brick church, and would have inclosed them by field-works, running tracks in. Now, as the depot houses are at the cross-road, the best thing we can do is to run a line of light works around in the neighborhood of the college up on the knoll." So, one day, after dining with General Grant, he proposed that we go up together and take Captain Frederick E. Prime with us, and he gave orders to commence a line of breastworks that would include the college grounds. This was before the battle of Iuka. After Iuka I was ordered to command the district, and General Grant moved his headquarters to Jackson, Tennessee. Pursuant to this order, on the 26th of September I repaired to Corinth, where I found the only defensive works available consisted of the open batteries Robinett, Williams, Phillips, Tannrath, and Lothrop, established by Captain Prime on the College Hill line. I immediately

CORONA COLLEGE, CORINTH. FROM A WAR-TIME PHOTOGRAPH.

ordered them to be connected by breastworks, and the front to the west and north to be covered by such an abatis as the remaining timber on the ground could furnish. I employed colored engineer troops organized into squads of twenty-five each, headed by a man detailed from the line or the quartermaster's department, and commanded by Captain William B. Gaw, a competent engineer. I also ordered an extension of the line of redoubts to cover the north front of the town, one of which, Battery Powell, was nearly completed before the stirring events of the attack. No rifle-pits were constructed between Powell and the central part covering the northwest front of the town, which was perfectly open north-east and south-east, with nothing but the distant, old Confederate works between it and the country.

To add to these embarrassments in preparing the place to resist a sudden attack, Grant, the general commanding, had retired fifty-eight miles north to Jackson, on the Mobile and Ohio railway, with all the knowledge of the country acquired during the four months in which his headquarters were at Corinth, and I, the new commander, could not find even the vestige of a map of the country to guide me in these defensive preparations.

BREVET MAJOR-GENERAL THOMAS A. DAVIES.
FROM A PHOTOGRAPH.

During the 27th, 28th, 29th, and 30th of September, the breastworks were completed joining the lunettes from College Hill on the left. A thin abatis made from the scattering trees, which had been left standing along the west and north fronts, covered the line between Robinett and the Mobile and Ohio; thence to Battery Powell the line was mostly open and without rifle-pits.

To meet emergencies, Hamilton's and Stanley's divisions, which had been watching to the south and south-west from near Jacinto to Rienzi, were closed in toward Corinth within short call.

RAILWAY STATION AND TISHOMINGO HOTEL, CORINTH. FROM A WAR-TIME PHOTOGRAPH.

On the 28th I telegraphed to General Grant at Columbus, Kentucky, confirmation of my report of Price's movement to Ripley, adding that I should move Stanley's division to Rienzi, and thence to Kossuth, unless he had other views. Two days later I again telegraphed to General Grant that there were no signs of the enemy at Hatchie Crossing, and that my reason for proposing to put Stanley at or near Kossuth was that he would cover nearly all the Hatchie Crossing, as far as Pocahontas, except against heavy forces, and that Hamilton would then move at least one brigade, from Rienzi. I asked that a sharp lookout be kept in the direction of Bolivar. October 1st, I telegraphed General Grant that we were satisfied there was no enemy for three miles beyond Hatchie; also, that prisoners reported that General John C. Breckinridge, of Van Dorn's command, had gone to Kentucky with three Kentucky regiments, leaving his division under the command of General Albert Rust. The combined forces under Van Dorn and Price were reported to be encamped on the Pocahontas road, and to number forty thousand.∫

Amid the numberless rumors and uncertainties besetting me at Corinth during the five days between September 26th, when I assumed command, and October 1st, how gratifying would have been the knowledge of the following facts, taken from Van Dorn's report, dated Holly Springs, October 20th, 1862:

"Surveying the whole field of operations before me, . . . the conclusion forced itself irresistibly upon my mind that the taking of Corinth was a condition precedent to the accomplishment of anything of importance in west Tennessee. To take Memphis would be to destroy an immense amount of property without any adequate military advantage, even admitting that it could be held without heavy guns against the enemy's gun and mortar boats. The line of fortifications around Bolivar is intersected by the Hatchie River, rendering it impossible to take the place by quick assault. . . . It was clear to my mind that if a successful attack could be made upon Corinth from the west and north-west, the forces there driven back on the Ten-

∫ In fact about 22,000, as stated by Van Dorn in the report quoted. And see "With Price East of the Mississippi," by Colonel Thomas L. Snead, p. 726.— EDITORS.

nessee and cut off, Bolivar and Jackson would easily fall, and then, upon the arrival of the exchanged prisoners of war, west Tennessee would soon be in our possession, and communication with General Bragg effected through middle Tennessee. . . .

"I determined to attempt Corinth. I had a reasonable hope of success. Field returns at Ripley showed my strength to be about 22,000 men. Rosecrans at Corinth had about 15,000, with about 8000 additional men at outposts, from 12 to 15 miles distant. I might surprise him and carry the place before these troops could be brought in. . . . It was necessary that this blow should be sudden and decisive. . . .

"The troops were in fine spirits, and the whole Army of West Tennessee seemed eager to emulate the armies of the Potomac and of Kentucky. No army ever marched to battle with prouder steps, more hopeful countenances, or with more courage than marched the Army of West Tennessee out of Ripley on the morning of September 29th, on its way to Corinth."

But of all this I knew nothing. With only McKean's and Davies's divisions, not ten thousand men, at Corinth on the 26th of September, by October 1st I had gradually drawn in pretty close Stanley's and Hamilton's divisions. They had been kept watching to the south and south-west of Corinth.

Our forces when concentrated would make about 16,000 effective infantry and artillery for defense, with 2500 cavalry for outposts and reconnoitering.

On October 2d, while Van Dorn was at Pocahontas, General Hurlbut telegraphed the information, from an intelligent Union man of Grand Junction, that "Price, Van Dorn, and Villepigue were at Pocahontas, and the talk was that they would attack Bolivar." Evidence arriving thick and fast showed that the enemy was moving, but whether on Corinth or Bolivar, or whether, passing between, they would strike and capture Jackson, was not yet clear to any of us. I knew that the enemy intended a strong movement, and I thought they must have the impression that our defensive works at Corinth would be pretty formidable. I doubted if they would venture to bring their force against our command behind defensive works. I therefore said: The enemy may threaten us and strike across our line entirely, get on the road between us and Jackson and advance upon that place, the capture of which would compel us to get out of our lines; or he may come in by the road from Tupelo so as to interpose his force between us and Danville. But all the time I inclined to the belief that it would not be for his interest to do that. I thought that perhaps he would cross the Memphis and Charleston road and, going over to the Mobile and Ohio road, force us to move out and fight him in the open country.

October 2d, I sent out a cavalry detachment to reconnoiter in the direction of Pocahontas. They found the enemy's infantry coming close in, and that night some of our detachment were surprised, and their horses and a few of the men were captured. Those that escaped reported the enemy there in force. This was still consistent with the theory that the enemy wished to cross the Memphis and Charleston road, go north of us, strike the Mobile and Ohio road and manœuvre us out of our position.

To be prepared for whatever they might do, I sent Oliver's brigade of McKean's division out to Chewalla, ten miles north-west in Tennessee. On the morning of the 3d the enemy's advance came to Chewalla, and Oliver's brigade fell back fighting. I sent orders to the brigade commander to make a stiff resistance, and see what effect it would have, still thinking that the attack was probably a mask for their movement for the north. I ordered Stanley to move in close to town near the middle line of works, called the "Halleck line," and to wait for further developments.

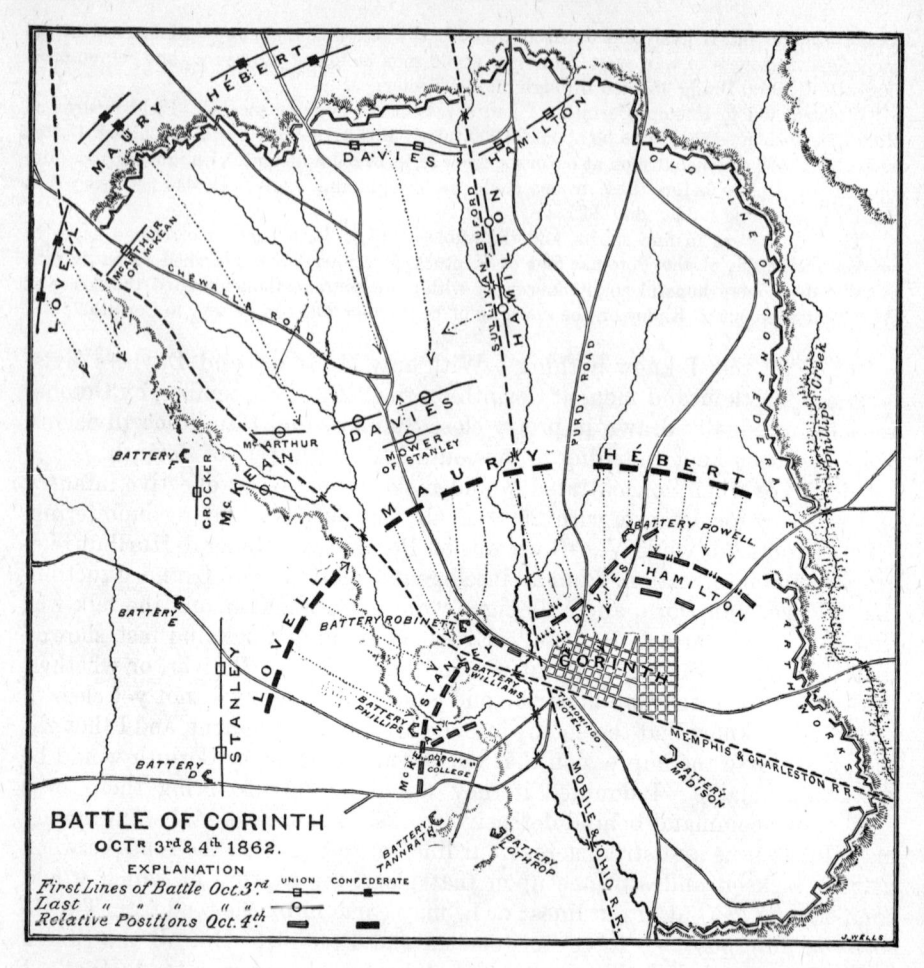

An order dated 1:30 A. M., October 3d, had set all the troops in motion. The impression that the enemy *might* find it better to strike a point on our line of communication and compel us to get out of our works to fight him or, if he should attempt Corinth, that he would do it, if possible, by the north and east, where the immediate vicinage was open and the place without defenses of any kind, governed these preliminary dispositions of my troops. The controlling idea was to prevent surprise, to test by adequate resistance any attacking force, and, finding it formidable, to receive it behind the inner line that had been preparing from College Hill around by Robinett.

To meet all probable contingencies, 9 o'clock on the morning of the 3d found my troops disposed as follows: Hamilton's division, about 3700 strong, on the

Purdy road north of the town, to meet any attempt from the north; Davies's division, 3204 strong, between the Memphis and Charleston and Mobile and Ohio railways, north-west of the town; McKean's division, 5315 strong, to the left of Davies's and in rear of the old Halleck line of batteries; and Stanley's division, 3500 strong, mainly in reserve on the extreme left, looking toward the Kossuth road.

Thus in front of those wooded western approaches, the Union troops, on the morning of October 3d, waited for what might happen, wholly ignorant of what Van Dorn was doing at Chewalla, ten miles away through thick forests. Of this General Van Dorn says:

"At daybreak on the 3d, the march was resumed . . . Lovell's division, in front, kept the road on the south side of the Memphis and Charleston railroad. Price, after marching on the same road about five miles, turned to the left, crossing the railroad, and formed line of battle in front of the outer line of intrenchments and about three miles from Corinth."

The intrenchments referred to were old Confederate works, which I had no idea of using except as a cover for a heavy skirmish line, to compel the enemy to develop his force, and to show whether he was making a demonstration to cover a movement of his force around to the north of Corinth. During the morning this skirmish work was well and gallantly accomplished by Davies's division, aided by McArthur with his brigade, and by Crocker, who moved up toward what the Confederate commander deemed the main line of the Union forces for the defense of Corinth. Upon this position moved three brigades of Lovell's division,—Villepigue's, Bowen's, and Rust's,—in line, with reserves in rear of each; Jackson's cavalry was on the right *en échelon*, the left flank on the Charleston railroad; Price's corps of two divisions was on the left of Lovell.

Thus the Confederate general proceeded, until, "at 10 o'clock, all the Union skirmishers were driven into the old intrenchments," and a part of the opposing forces were in line of battle confronting each other. There was a belt of fallen timber about four hundred yards wide between them, which must be crossed by the Confederate forces before they could drive this

VIEW ON THE RAILWAY, LOOKING NORTH-WEST FROM THE CORINTH DEPOT.
FROM A WAR-TIME PHOTOGRAPH.

stubborn force of Davies's, sent to compel the enemy to show his hand. Van Dorn says: "The attack was commenced on the right by Lovell's division and gradually extended to the left, and by 1:30 P. M. the whole line of outer works was carried, several pieces [two] of artillery being taken."

Finding that the resistance made by Oliver's little command on the Chewalla road early in the morning was not stiff enough to demonstrate the enemy's object, I had ordered McArthur's brigade from McKean's division to go to Oliver's assistance. It was done with a will. McArthur's Scotch blood rose, and the enemy being in fighting force, he fought him with the stubborn ferocity of an action on the main line of battle, instead of the resistance of a developing force.

The same remark applies to the fighting of Davies's division, and as they were pushed and called for reënforcements, orders were sent to fall back slowly and stubbornly. The Confederates, elated at securing these old outworks, pushed in toward our main line, in front of which the fighting in the afternoon was so hot that McKean was ordered to send further help over to the fighting troops, and Stanley to send "a brigade through the woods by the shortest cut" to help Davies, whose division covered itself with glory, having Brigadier-General Hackleman killed, Brigadier-General Oglesby desperately wounded, with nearly twenty-five per cent. of its strength put out of the fight. Watching intently every movement which would throw light on the enemy's intentions, soon after midday I decided that it was a main attack of the enemy. Hamilton's division had been sent up the railroad as far as the old Confederate works in the morning, and formed the right of our line. At 1 o'clock his division was still there watching against attack from the north. When the enemy prepared to make the attack on our first real line of battle, word was sent up to Hamilton to advise us if any Confederate force had gotten through, on the Mobile and Ohio road. At 3 o'clock when the fighting began and became very heavy, Stanley was ordered to move up from his position and succor McKean's and Davies's divisions that had been doing heavy fighting. Colonel Ducat, acting chief of staff, was sent to direct General Hamilton to file by fours to the left, and march down until the head of his column was opposite the right of Davies's, then to face his brigades south-westerly, and move down in that direction. The enemy's left did not much overpass the right of Davies, and but few troops were on the line of the old Confederate works. Hence Hamilton's movement, the brigades advancing *en échelon*, would enable the right of Buford's brigade to far out-lap the enemy's left, and pass toward the enemy's rear with little or no opposition, while the other brigade could press back the enemy's left, and by its simple advance drive him in and attack his rear.

Hamilton told Colonel Ducat that he wanted a more positive and definite order before he made the attack. Ducat explained the condition of the battle and urged an immediate movement, but was obliged to return to me for an order fitted to the situation. I sent the following:

"HEADQUARTERS, ARMY OF THE MISSISSIPPI, October 3d, 1862. BRIGADIER-GENERAL HAMILTON, Commanding Third Division: Rest your left on General Davies and swing round your

MEMPHIS AND CHARLESTON RAILROAD, LOOKING TOWARD CORINTH—REMAINS OF FORT WILLIAMS ON THE RIGHT. FROM A PHOTOGRAPH TAKEN IN 1884.

right and attack the enemy on their left flank, reënforced on your right and center. Be careful not to get under Davies's guns. Keep your troops well in hand. Get well this way. Do not extend to your right too much. It looks as if it would be well to occupy the ridge where your skirmishers were when Colonel Ducat left, by artillery, well supported, but this may be farther to right than would be safe. Use your discretion. Opposite your center might be better now for your artillery. If you see your chance, attack fiercely.—W. S. ROSECRANS, Brigadier-General."

I added a sketch of the line on a bit of paper. The delay thus caused enabled the enemy to overpass the right of Davies so far that while Ducat was returning he was fired on by the enemy's skirmishers, who had reached open ground over the railway between Hamilton and Corinth. Two orderlies sent on the same errand afterward were killed on the way. Upon the receipt of these explanations Hamilton put his division in motion, but by sunset he only reached a point opposite the enemy's left; and after moving down a short distance Sullivan's brigade, facing to the west, crossed the narrow flats flanking the railway, went over into the thickets, and had a fierce fight with the enemy's left, creating a great commotion. Buford's brigade had started in too far to the west and had to rectify its position; so that Hamilton's division thus far had only given the enemy a terrific scare, and a sharp fight with one brigade. Had the movement been executed promptly after 3 o'clock, we should have crushed the enemy's right and rear. Hamilton's excuse that he could not understand the order shows that even in the rush of battle it may be necessary to put orders in writing, or to have subordinate commanders who instinctively know or are anxious to seek the key of the battle and hasten to its roar.✝

At nightfall of the 3d it was evident that, unless the enemy should withdraw, he was where I wished him to be—between the two railroad lines

✝ See General Charles S. Hamilton's statements, p. 758.—EDITORS.

and to the south of them—for the inevitable contest of the morrow. Van Dorn says:

"I had been in hopes that one day's operations would end the contest and decide who should be the victors on this bloody field; but a ten miles' march over a parched country on dusty roads without water, getting into line of battle in forests with undergrowth, and the more than equal activity and determined courage displayed by the enemy, commanded by one of the ablest generals of the United States army, who threw all possible obstacles in our way that an active mind could suggest, prolonged the battle until I saw with regret the sun sink behind the horizon as the last shot of our sharp-shooters followed the retreating foe into their innermost lines. One hour more of daylight and victory would have soothed our grief for the loss of the gallant dead who sleep on that lost but not dishonored field. The army slept on its arms within six hundred yards of Corinth, victorious so far."

Alas, how uncertain are our best conclusions! General Van Dorn, in his subsequent report as above, bewails the lack of one hour of daylight at the close of October 3d, 1862. I bewailed that lack of daylight, which would have brought Hamilton's fresh and gallant division on the Confederate left and rear. That hour of daylight was not to be had; and while the regretful Confederate general lay down in his bivouac, I assembled my four division commanders, McKean, Davies, Stanley, and Hamilton, at my headquarters and arranged the dispositions for the fight of the next day. McKean's division was to hold the left, the chief point being College Hill, keeping his troops well under cover. Stanley was to support the line on either side of Battery Robinett, a little three-gun redan with a ditch five feet deep. Davies was to extend from Stanley's right north-easterly across the flat to Battery Powell, a similar redan on the ridge east of the Purdy road. Hamilton was to be on Davies's right with a brigade, and the rest in reserve on the common east of the low ridge and out of sight from the west. Colonel J. K. Mizner with his cavalry was to watch and guard our flanks and rear from the enemy, and well and effectively did his four gallant regiments perform that duty. As the troops had been on the move since the night of October 2d, and had fought all day of the 3d (which was so excessively hot that we were obliged to send water around in wagons), it became my duty to visit their lines and see that the weary troops were surely in position.

BRIGADIER-GENERAL PLEASANT A. HACKLEMAN, KILLED AT CORINTH. FROM A STEEL ENGRAVING.

I returned to my tent at three o'clock in the morning of October 4th, after having seen everything accomplished and the new line in order. It was about a mile in extent and close to the edge of the north side of the town. About 4 o'clock I lay down. At half-past 4 the enemy opened with a six-gun battery. Our batteries, replying, soon silenced it, but I had no time for breakfast. The troops got very little. They had not been allowed to build fires during the night, and were too tired to intrench.

The morning opened clear and soon grew to be hot. It must have been ninety-four degrees in the shade. The enemy began to extend his infantry line across the north of the town. I visited the lines and gave orders to our skirmishers to fall back the moment it was seen that the enemy was developing a line of battle. About 8 o'clock his left, having crossed the Mobile and Ohio railroad, got into position behind a spur of table land, to reach which they had moved by the flank for about half a mile. When they began to advance in line of battle they were not over three hundred yards distant.

I told McKean on the left to be very watchful of his front lest the enemy should turn his left, and directed General Stanley to hold the reserve of his command ready either to help north of the town or to aid McKean if required. I visited Battery Robinett and directed the chief of artillery, Colonel Lothrop, to see to the reserve artillery, some batteries of which were parked in the public square of the town; then the line of Davies's division, which was in nearly open ground, with a few logs, here and there, for breastworks, and then on his extreme right Sweeny's brigade, which had no cover save a slight ridge, on the south-west slope of which, near the crest, the men were lying down. Riding along this line, I observed the Confederate forces emerging from the woods west of the railroad and crossing the open ground toward the Purdy road. Our troops lying on the ground could see the flags of the enemy and the glint of the sunlight on their bayonets. It was about 9 o'clock in the morning. The air was still and fiercely hot. Van Dorn says the Confederate preparations for the morning were:

"That Hébert, on the left, should mask part of his own division on the left, placing Cabell's brigade *en échelon* on the left — Cabell having been detached from Maury's division for that purpose, move Armstrong's cavalry brigade across the Mobile and Ohio road, and, if possible, to get some of his artillery in position across the road. In this order of battle, Hébert was to attack, swinging his left flank toward Corinth, and advance down the Purdy ridge. On the right, Lovell, with two brigades in line of battle and one in reserve, with Jackson's cavalry to the right, was ordered to await the attack on his left, feeling his way with sharp-shooters until Hébert was heavily engaged with the enemy. Maury was to move at the same time quickly to the front directly at Corinth; Jackson to burn the railroad bridge over the Tuscumbia during the night."

The left of General Van Dorn's attack was to have begun earlier, but the accident of Hébert's sickness prevented. The Confederates, from behind a spur of the Purdy ridge, advanced splendidly to the attack. The unfavorable line occupied by Davies's division made the resistance on that front inadequate. The troops gave way; the enemy pursued; but the cross-fire from the Union batteries on our right soon thinned their ranks. Their front line was broken, and the heads of their columns melted away. Some of the enemy's scattered line got into the edge of the town; a few into the reserve artillery, which led to the impression that they had captured forty pieces of artillery. But they were soon driven out by Stanley's reserve, and fled, taking nothing away.

At this time, while going to order Hamilton's division into action on the enemy's left, I saw the L-shaped porch of a large cottage packed full of

THE DEFENSE OF BATTERY ROBINETT. FROM A WAR-TIME SKETCH.

43D OHIO.    63D OHIO.    27TH OHIO.

Captain George A. Williams, 1st U. S. Infantry, who commanded the siege artillery, says in his report:

"About 9:30 or 10 A. M. the enemy were observed in the woods north of the town forming in line, and they soon made their appearance, charging toward the town. As soon as our troops were out of the line of fire of my battery, we opened upon them with two 30-pounder Parrott guns and one 8-inch howitzer, which enfiladed their line (aided by Maurice's battery and one gun on the right of Battery Robinett, which bore on that part of the town), and continued our fire until the enemy were repulsed and had regained the wood.

"During the time the enemy were being repulsed from the town my attention was drawn to the left side of the battery by the firing from Battery Robinett, where I saw a column advancing to storm it. After advancing a short distance they were repulsed, but immediately re-formed, and, storming the work, gained the ditch, but were repulsed. During this charge eight of the enemy, having placed a handkerchief on a bayonet and calling to the men in the battery not to shoot them, surrendered, and were allowed to come into the fort.

"They then re-formed, and, re-storming, carried the ditch and the outside of the work, the supports having fallen a short distance to the rear in slight disorder. The men of the 1st U. S. Infantry, after having been driven from their guns (they manned the siege guns), resorted to their muskets, and were firing from the inside of the embrasures at the enemy on the outside, a distance of about ten feet intervening; but the rebels having gained the top of the work, our men fell back into the angle of the fort, as they had been directed to do in such an emergency. Two shells were thrown from Battery Williams into Battery Robinett, one bursting on the top of it and the other near the right edge. In the meanwhile the 11th Missouri Volunteers (in reserve) changed front, and, aided by the 43d and 63d Ohio Volunteers with the 27th Ohio Volunteers on their right, gallantly stormed up to the right and left of the battery, driving the enemy before them."— EDITORS.

Confederates. I ordered Lieutenant Lorenzo D. Immell, with two field-pieces, to give them grape and canister. After one round, only the dead and dying were left on the porch. Reaching Hamilton's division I ordered him to send Sullivan's brigade forward. It moved in line of battle in open ground a little to the left of Battery Powell. Before its splendid advance the scattered enemy, who were endeavoring to form a line of battle, about 1 P. M. gave way and went back into the woods, from which they never again advanced.

Meanwhile there had been terrific fighting at Battery Robinett. The roar of artillery and musketry for two or three hours was incessant. Clouds of smoke filled the air and obscured the sun. I witnessed the first charge of the enemy on this part of the line before I went over to Hamilton. The first repulse I did not see because the contestants were clouded in smoke. It was an assault in column. There were three or four assaulting columns of regiments, probably a hundred yards apart. The enemy's left-hand column had tried to make its way down into the low ground to the right of Robinett, but did not make much progress. The other two assaulting columns fared better, because they were on the ridge where the fallen timber was scarcer. I ordered the 27th Ohio and 11th Missouri to kneel in rear of the right of Robinett, so as to get out of range of the enemy's fire, and the moment he had exhausted himself to charge with the bayonet [see p. 759]. The third assault was made just as I was seeing Sullivan into the fight. I saw the enemy come upon the ridge while Battery Robinett was belching its fire at them. After the charge had failed I saw the 27th Ohio and the 11th Missouri chasing them with bayonets.

The head of the enemy's main column reached within a few feet of Battery Robinett, and Colonel Rogers, who was leading it, colors in hand, dismounted, planted a flag-staff on the bank of the ditch, and fell there, shot by one of our drummer-boys, who, with a pistol, was helping to defend Robinett. I was told that Colonel Rogers was the fifth standard-bearer who had fallen in that last desperate charge. It was about as good fighting on the part of the Confederates as I ever saw. The columns were plowed through and through by our shot, but they steadily closed up and moved forward until they were forced back.

Just after this last assault I heard for the first time the word "ranch." Passing over the field on our left, among the dead and dying, I saw leaning against the root of a tree a wounded lieutenant of an Arkansas regiment who had been shot through the foot. As I offered him some water he said, "Thank you, General; one of your men just gave me some." I said,

THE GROUND IN FRONT OF BATTERY ROBINETT. FROM A PHOTOGRAPH TAKEN AFTER THE BATTLE.

GRAVE OF COLONEL WILLIAM P. ROGERS, LOOKING TOWARD CORINTH FROM THE EMBANKMENT OF FORT ROBINETT. FROM A PHOTOGRAPH TAKEN IN 1884.

"Whose troops are you?" He replied, "Cabell's." I said, "It was pretty hot fighting here." He answered, "Yes, General, you licked us good, *but we gave you the best we had in the ranch.*"

Before the enemy's first assault on Robinett, I inspected the woods toward our left where I knew Lovell's division to be. I said to Colonel Joseph A. Mower, afterward commander of the Seventeenth Army Corps, and familiarly known as "Fighting Joe Mower": "Colonel, take the men now on the skirmish line, and find out what Lovell is doing." He replied, "Very well, General." As he was turning away I added, "Feel them, but don't get into their fingers." He answered significantly: "*I'll feel them!*" Before I left my position Mower had entered the woods, and soon I heard a tremendous crash of musketry in that direction. His skirmishers fell back into the fallen timber, and the adjutant reported to me: "General, I think the enemy have captured Colonel Mower; I think he is killed." Five hours later when we captured the enemy's field-hospitals, we found that Colonel Mower had been shot in the back of the neck and taken prisoner. Expressing my joy at his safety, he showed that he knew he had been unjustly reported to me the day before as intoxicated, by saying: "Yes, General, but if they had reported me for being 'shot in the neck' to-day instead of yesterday, it would have been correct."

About 2 o'clock we found that the enemy did not intend to make another attack. Faint from exhaustion I sought the shade of a tree, from which point I saw three bursts of smoke and said to my staff, "They have blown up some ammunition wagons, and are going to retreat. We must push them." I was all the more certain of this, because, having failed, a good commander like Van Dorn would use the utmost dispatch in putting the forests between him and his pursuing foe, as well as to escape the dangers to him which might arise from troops coming from Bolivar.

Even at this distant time memory lingers on the numerous incidents of distinguished bravery displayed by officers and men who fought splendidly on the first day, when we did not know what the enemy was going to do. Staff as well as line officers distinguished themselves while in action. The first day my presence was required on the main line, and the fighting in front of that did not so much come under my eye, but on the second day I was everywhere on the line of battle. Temple Clark of my staff was shot through the breast. My *sabretasche* strap was cut by a bullet, and my gloves were stained with the blood of a staff-officer wounded at my side. An alarm spread that I was killed, but it was soon stopped by my appearance on the field.

Satisfied that the enemy was retreating, I ordered Sullivan's command to push him with a heavy skirmish line, and to keep constantly feeling them. I rode along the lines of the commands, told them that, having been moving and fighting for three days and two nights, I knew they required rest, but that they could not rest longer than was absolutely

COLONEL WILLIAM P. ROGERS, C. S. A., KILLED IN LEADING THE ASSAULT UPON FORT ROBINETT. FROM A PHOTOGRAPH.

necessary. I directed them to proceed to their camps, provide five days' rations, take some needed rest, and be ready early next morning for the pursuit.

General McPherson, sent from Jackson with five good regiments to help us, arrived and bivouacked in the public square a little before sunset. Our pursuit of the enemy was immediate and vigorous, but the darkness of the night and the roughness of the country, covered with woods and thickets, made movement impracticable by night and slow and difficult by day. General McPherson's brigade of fresh troops with a battery was ordered to start at daylight and follow the enemy over the Chewalla road, and Stanley's and Davies's divisions to support him. McArthur, with all of McKean's division except Crocker's brigade, and with a good battery and a battalion of cavalry, took the route south of the railroad toward Pocahontas; McKean followed on this route with the rest of his division and Ingersoll's cavalry; Hamilton followed McKean with his entire force.

The enemy took the road to Davis's Bridge on the Hatchie, by way of Pocahontas. Fortunately General Hurlbut, finding that he was not going to be attacked at Bolivar, had been looking in our direction with a view of succoring us, and now met the enemy at that point [Hatchie Bridge]. General Ord, arriving there from Jackson, Tennessee, assumed command and drove back

GROUP OF UNION SOLDIERS AT CORINTH. FROM A WAR-TIME PHOTOGRAPH.

the head of the enemy's column. This was a critical time for the Confederate forces; but the reader will note that a retreating force, knowing where it has to go and having to look for nothing except an attack on its rear, always moves with more freedom than a pursuing force. This is especially so where the country is covered with woods and thickets, and the roads are narrow. Advancing forces always have to feel their way for fear of being ambushed.

The speed made by our forces from Corinth during the 5th was not to my liking, but with such a commander as McPherson in the advance, I could not doubt that it was all that was possible. On the 6th better progress was made. From Jonesborough, on October 7th, I telegraphed General Grant:

"Do not, I entreat you, call Hurlbut back; let him send away his wounded. It surely is easier to move the sick and wounded than to remove both. I propose to push the enemy, so that we need but the most trifling guards behind us. Our advance is beyond Ruckersville. Hamilton will seize the Hatchie crossing on the Ripley road to-night. A very intelligent, honest young Irishman, an ambulance driver, deserted from the rebels, says that they wished to go together to railroad near Tupelo, where they will meet the nine thousand exchanged prisoners, but he says they are much scattered and demoralized. They have much artillery."

From the same place, at midnight, after learning from the front that McPherson was in Ripley, I telegraphed General Grant as follows:

"GENERAL: Yours 8:30 P. M. received. Our troops occupy Ripley. I most deeply dissent from your views as to the manner of pursuing. We have defeated, routed, and demoralized the army which holds the Lower Mississippi Valley. We have the two railroads leading down toward the Gulf through the most productive parts of the State, into which we can now pursue them with safety. The effect of our return to old position will be to pen them up in the only corn country they have west of Alabama, including the Tuscumbia Valley, and to permit them to recruit their forces, advance and occupy their old ground, reducing us to the occupation of a defensive position, barren and worthless, with a long front, over which they can harass us until bad weather prevents an effectual advance except on the railroads, when time, fortifications, and rolling stock will again render them superior to us. Our force, including what you have with Hurlbut, will garrison Corinth and Jackson, and enables us to push them. Our advance will cover even Holly Springs, which would be ours when we want it. All that is needful is to continue pursuing and whip them. We have whipped, and should now push them to the wall and capture all the rolling stock of their railroads. Bragg's army alone, west of the Alabama River, and occupying Mobile, could repair the damage we have it in our power to do them. If, after considering these matters, you still consider the order for my return to Corinth expedient, I will obey it and abandon the chief fruits of a victory, but, I beseech you, bend everything to push them while they are broken and hungry, weary and ill-supplied. Draw everything possible from Memphis to help move on Holly Springs, and let us concentrate. Appeal to the governors of the States to rush down some twenty or thirty new regiments to hold our rear, and we can make a triumph of our start."

As it was, Grant telegraphed to Halleck at 9 A. M. the next day, October 8th:

"Rosecrans has followed rebels to Ripley. Troops from Bolivar will

QUARTERS AT CORINTH OCCUPIED BY THE 52D ILLINOIS VOLUNTEERS DURING THE WINTER OF 1862-3. FROM A WAR-TIME PHOTOGRAPH.

occupy Grand Junction to-morrow, with reënforcements rapidly sent on from the new levies. I can take everything on the Mississippi Central road. I ordered Rosecrans back last night, but he was so averse to returning that I have directed him to remain still until you can be heard from."

Again on the same day, October 8th, Grant telegraphed to Halleck:

"Before telegraphing you this morning for reënforcements to follow up our victories I ordered General Rosecrans to return. He showed such reluctance that I consented to allow him to remain until you could be heard from if further reënforcements could be had. On reflection I deem it idle to pursue further without more preparation, and have for the third time ordered his return."

This was early in October. The weather was cool, and the roads in prime order. The country along the Mississippi Central to Grenada, and especially below that place, was a corn country — a rich farming country — and the corn was ripe. If Grant had not stopped us, we could have gone to Vicksburg. My judgment was to go on, and with the help suggested we could have done so. Under the pressure of a victorious force the enemy were experiencing all the weakening effects of a retreating army, whose means of supplies and munitions are always difficult to keep in order. We had Sherman at Memphis with two divisions, and we had Hurlbut at Bolivar with one division and John A. Logan at Jackson, Tennessee, with six regiments. With these there was nothing to save Mississippi from our grasp. We were about six days' march from Vicksburg, and Grant could have put his force through to it with my column as the center one of pursuit. Confederate officers told me afterward that they never were so scared in their lives as they were after the defeat before Corinth.

I have thus given the facts of the fight at Corinth, the immediate pursuit, the causes of the return, and, as well, the differing views of the Federal commanders in regard to the situation. Let the judgments of the future be formed upon the words of impartial history.

In a general order announcing the results of the battle to my command, I stated that we killed and buried 1423 officers and men of the enemy, including some of their most distinguished officers. Their wounded at the usual rate would exceed 5000. We took 2268 prisoners, among whom were 137 field-officers, captains, and subalterns.↓ We captured 3300 stand of small-arms, 14 stand of colors, 2 pieces of artillery, and a large quantity of equipments. We pursued his retreating column forty miles with all arms, and with cavalry sixty miles. Our loss was 355 killed, 1841 wounded, 324 captured or missing.

In closing his report General Van Dorn said:

"A hand-to-hand contest was being enacted in the very yard of General Rosecrans's headquarters and in the streets of the town. The heavy guns were silenced, and all seemed to be about ended when a heavy fire from fresh troops from Iuka, Burnsville, and Rienzi, who had succeeded in reaching Corinth, poured into our thinned ranks. Exhausted from loss of sleep, wearied from hard marching and fighting, companies and regiments without officers, our troops — let no one censure them — gave way. The day was lost. . . . The attempt at Corinth has failed, and in consequence I am condemned and have been superseded in my command. In my zeal for my country I may have ventured too far without adequate means, and I bow to the opinion of the people whom I serve. Yet I feel that if the spirits of the gallant dead, who now lie beneath the batteries of Corinth, see and judge the motives of men, they do not rebuke me, for there is no sting in my conscience, nor does retrospection admonish me of error or of a reckless disregard of their valued lives." ▶

And General Price says in his report:

"The history of this war contains no bloodier page, perhaps, than that which will record this fiercely contested battle. The strongest expressions fall short of my admiration of the gallant conduct of the officers and men under my command. Words cannot add luster to the fame they have acquired through deeds of noble daring which, living through future time, will shed about every man, officer and soldier, who stood to his arms through this struggle, a halo of glory as imperishable as it is brilliant. They have won to their sisters and daughters the dis-

↓ The official Confederate reports make their loss 505 killed, 2150 wounded, 2183 missing.— EDITORS.

▶ The charges against General Van Dorn (of neglect of duty and of cruel and improper treatment of his officers and soldiers) were investigated by a Court of Inquiry, which unanimously voted them disproved.— EDITORS.

tinguished honor, set before them by a general of their love and admiration upon the event of an impending battle upon the same field, of the proud exclamation, ' My brother, father, was at the great battle of Corinth.'"¶

¶ Reference is doubtless made here to the address of General Albert Sidney Johnston to the soldiers of the Army of the Mississippi on the eve of the battle of Shiloh, April 3d, 1862.—EDITORS.

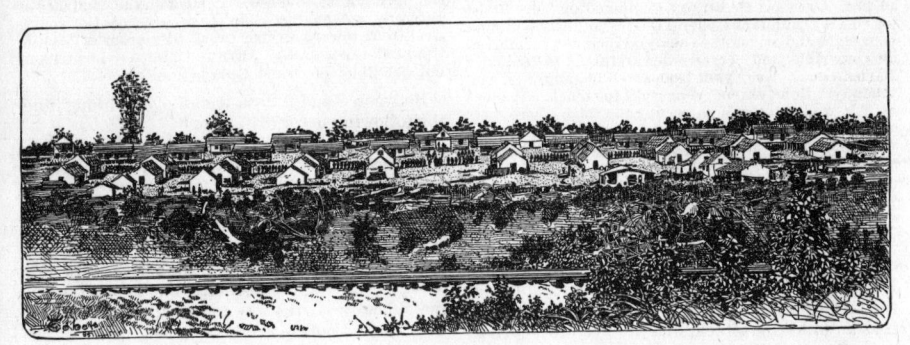

CAMP OF THE 57TH ILLINOIS INFANTRY AT CORINTH. FROM A WAR-TIME PHOTOGRAPH.

## HAMILTON'S DIVISION AT CORINTH.

### BY CHARLES S. HAMILTON, MAJOR-GENERAL, U. S. V.

THE following order, issued about 9 A. M. on the first day of the battle of Corinth, fixed the position of my division:

"CORINTH, Oct. 3d, 1862. BRIGADIER-GENERAL HAMILTON, Commanding Third Division. GENERAL: The general commanding directs that you cover with your division the Purdy road, from the swamp on the railroad to where the road runs through the rebel works. By command of MAJOR-GENERAL ROSECRANS.— GODDARD, A. A. A. General.

"P. S. You may perhaps have to move farther out, as Davies does not find good ground until he gets near the old rebel works, and he proposes to swing his right still farther around. By order of MAJOR-GENERAL ROSECRANS.— GODDARD, A. A. A. General."

Again at 2 P. M. the same day the following circular was sent to both Hamilton and Davies:

"For fear of a misunderstanding in relation to my orders, I wish it distinctly understood that the extreme position is not to be taken until driven to it. By order of MAJOR-GENERAL ROSECRANS.— S. C. LYFORD, Acting Aide-de-Camp."

The extreme position mentioned was not understood by either Davies or myself, but probably meant an advanced position. But how we could be driven to it by an enemy in our front is difficult to understand. Just following the circular, this order was received by me:

"The general commanding desires me to say to you not to be in a hurry to show yourself. Keep well covered and conceal your strength. The enemy will doubtless feel your position, but do not allow this to hasten your movements.— S. C. LYFORD, Acting Aide-de-Camp."

About 3:30 P. M. the following was received:

"GENERAL HAMILTON: Davies, it appears, has fallen behind the works, his left being pressed in. If this movement continues until he gets well drawn in, you will make a flank movement, if your front is not attacked, falling to the left of Davies when the enemy gets sufficiently well in so as to have full sweep, holding a couple of regiments looking well to the Purdy road. Examine and reconnoiter the ground for making this movement. By order of MAJOR-GENERAL ROSECRANS.— H. G. KENNETT, Colonel and Chief of Staff."

On the back of this order I indorsed the following:

"Respectfully returned. I cannot understand it.— C. S. HAMILTON, Brigadier-General."

Rosecrans returned it to me indorsed as follows:

"Ducat has been sent to explain it. W. S. ROSECRANS, Major-General.— S. C. LYFORD, Acting Aide-de-Camp."

Now bearing in mind that Davies's division was to the left and in front of mine, if this order meant anything it was that my division should abandon its position on the right of the army entirely, and pass either to the rear or front of Davies in order to reach the place indicated, and would therefore have destroyed every possible chance of attacking the enemy in the flank, and would also have left the right of Davies's exposed, and the way into Corinth open to the enemy. Now this order, which is the one Rosecrans claims as his order to attack the enemy, was given as follows in his article on this engagement, in "The Century" for October, 1886 [see p. 746]:

"Colonel Ducat, acting chief-of-staff, was sent with an order to General Hamilton, to file by fours to the left and march down until the head of his column was opposite Davies's right. He was ordered then to face his brigade west-south-west and to move down in a south-westerly direction."

The order, as I have given it, is an exact copy of the original now in my possession, and General Rosecrans's statement of it in "The Century" was made from a defective memory after twenty-three years had elapsed.

At 5 P. M. I received the following order:

"HEADQUARTERS, ARMY OF THE MISSISSIPPI, October 3d, 1862. GENERAL HAMILTON, Commanding Third Division: Rest your left on General Davies, and swing around your right and attack the enemy on their left, reënforced on your right and center. Be careful not to get under Davies's guns. Keep your troops well in hand. Get well this way. Don't extend your right too much. It looks as if it would be well to occupy the ridge where your skirmishers were when Colonel Ducat left, by artillery well supported, but this may be farther to right than would be safe. Use your discretion. Opposite your center might be better now for your artillery. If you see your chance attack fiercely.—W. S. ROSECRANS, Brigadier-General."

As a simple order to attack the enemy in flank could have reached me by courier from General Rosecrans, any time after 2 P. M., in 15 minutes, the verbosity of the above is apparent. I construed it as an order for attack, and at once proceeded to carry it out. Sullivan's brigade of my division had been ordered some time previously to move toward the enemy's left in preparation for an attack, and Buford's brigade was now ordered down on Sullivan's right to support him.

The brigades were some distance apart, and having been concealed in the woods had not been discovered by the enemy. The moment that Buford began to move a detached force of the enemy was seen some distance in his front. They opened on him with a single piece of artillery, and he, taking it for granted he was beset by the enemy in force, moved to his front to drive them out of the way. In thus moving he went almost in an opposite direction to the one necessary to support Sullivan. I sent an officer with a positive order to change his course. His reply was, "Tell General Hamilton, the enemy is in my front and I am going to fight him." Meantime his brigade had been moving toward what he supposed to be the enemy, and was a half mile from Sullivan. I sent a second order to change his course instantly, and move to Sullivan's support. This order he obeyed, first detaching the 4th Minnesota regiment, under Colonel J. B. Sanborn, to attack the enemy. He then moved down to the position indicated, but, meantime, a precious hour had been lost, the sun had gone down, and the attack having to be made through a forest of dense undergrowth, it was too late to execute the flank movement with any chance of success. The enemy's fire on Davies's division had ceased. Waiting a few moments in expectation of its renewal, night closed down upon us, and the battle for the day was over.

General Rosecrans first intended the troops to pass the night in the position now held, as shown by the following order, received about 7:30 P. M.:

"HEADQUARTERS, ARMY OF THE MISSISSIPPI, October 3d, 1862, 7 P. M. GENERAL HAMILTON: Throw out promptly vedettes, grand guards, scouts, and a line of skirmishers in rear of abatis on your front and flanks. Pick up all the prisoners you can. Get all the information possible, which report promptly and often to these headquarters. Furnish brigade commanders with a copy of this order as soon as possible. During the night and coming daylight, much will depend on the vigilance of outposts and guards. Our cavalry is on the south-west front toward Bridge Creek. By order of MAJOR-GENERAL ROSECRANS.—ARTHUR C. DUCAT, Lieutenant-Colonel, Chief of Grand Guards and Outposts."

Between 8 and 9 P. M. a staff-officer brought me the following order:

"Place your batteries on the Purdy road at 10 P. M. and play them two hours in a north-west direction with shot and shell, where the enemy is massed, and at midnight attack them with your whole division with the bayonet. —W. S. ROSECRANS, Major-General." ☆

I was astounded, and turning to the officer said: "Tell General Rosecrans I cannot execute that order till I see him personally, and explain to him the difficulties in the way and what the result must be if carried out." An hour passed, when the officer who brought the order returned, bringing General Rosecrans with him. General John B. Sanborn, of Minnesota, and others heard the following conversation which then took place:

General ROSECRANS [savagely]: "General Hamilton, what do you mean by disobeying my order to attack the enemy?"

General HAMILTON: "General Rosecrans, I am ready to execute your order, but there is too much at stake here to be risked by a night attack. The ground between us and the enemy is a dense forest, with a thick undergrowth in which the troops cannot move ten minutes without breaking their formation. It is dark in the forest— too dark to distinguish friend from foe. If my division is once disorganized it cannot be re-formed until daylight comes. We are ignorant of the enemy's exact position and must feel around in the darkness of the forest to find him. Let me say that your lines are too long. My division is not in supporting distance of any other division, and when the town is assaulted in the morning your army will be cut in two and destroyed. Davies's division has withdrawn so far that the skirmishers of the enemy occupy his last position in line. Your position is a false one. The troops should be withdrawn and placed within the earth-works of the town. Place them within the fortifications and in support of each other. It is a strong position and insures a victory. But as we are now you cannot make a strong defense, and the battle which is certain for the morning will surely be a defeat for us."

General ROSECRANS [after a few moments of reflection without reply]: "Hamilton, you are right. Place your division as you suggest, and the others shall be placed accordingly."

The change of my division was accomplished by 3 A. M., and the troops sought their rest on the morrow's battle-field, full of hope and sure of victory. Thus closed the operations of the day. And thus was brought about the change that led to victory on the following day, but from that time to this no public writing or utterance on the part of General Rosecrans has ever acknowledged the services so rendered.

☆ The "Official Records" do not contain this order or any allusion to the subject of it.—EDITORS.

## AN ORDER TO CHARGE AT CORINTH.

BY DAVID S. STANLEY, MAJOR-GENERAL, U. S. V.

An assertion made by General Rosecrans in "The Century" magazine for October, 1886, is misleading. The statement [see p. 751] is as follows:

"I ordered the 27th Ohio and the 11th Missouri to kneel in rear of the right of Robinett so as to get out of the range of the enemy's fire, and the moment he had exhausted himself to charge with the bayonet."

The lapse of a quarter of a century has certainly made the memory of the worthy general treacherous, for at the time that his memory causes him to say that he gave this order, I saw him a quarter of a mile away trying to rally Davies's troops to resist the advancing forces of the Confederates, and I consider it impossible for the two regiments to have heard any order from him above the rifle's rattle and the cannon's roar at such a distance. I cannot say what General Rosecrans may have said to these regiments about using the bayonet when visiting my lines that morning before the occurrence mentioned, but I do know that I posted them myself, and that Colonel J. W. Fuller, 27th Ohio, commander of the brigade during the heat of the battle, gave the order for his own and the 11th Missouri regiments to charge with the bayonet.

SAN ANTONIO, TEXAS, January 19th, 1888.

## THE OPPOSING FORCES AT CORINTH, MISS.

### October 3d and 4th, 1862.

The composition, losses, and strength of each army as here stated give the gist of all the data obtainable in the Official Records. K stands for killed; w for wounded; m w for mortally wounded; m for captured or missing; c for captured.

### THE UNION FORCES.

ARMY OF THE MISSISSIPPI.—Major-General William S. Rosecrans.

SECOND DIVISION, Brig.-Gen. David S. Stanley. Staff loss: w, 1.
*First Brigade,* Col. John W. Fuller: 27th Ohio, Maj. Zephaniah S. Spaulding; 39th Ohio, Col. A. W. Gilbert, Lieut.-Col. Edward F. Noyes; 43d Ohio, Col. J. L. Kirby Smith (m w), Lieut.-Col. Wager Swayne; 63d Ohio, Col. John W. Sprague; Jenks's Co., Ill. Cav., Capt. Albert Jenks; 3d Mich. Battery, Lieut. Carl A. Lamberg; 8th Wis. Battery (section), Lieut. John D. McLean; F, 2d U. S. Art'y, Capt. Thomas D. Maurice. Brigade loss: k, 65; w, 255; m, 11 = 321. *Second Brigade,* Col. Joseph A. Mower (w): 26th Ill., Maj. Robert A. Gillmore; 47th Ill., Col. William A. Thrush (k), Capt. Harman Andrews (w), Capt. Samuel R. Baker; 5th Minn., Col. Lucius F. Hubbard; 11th Mo., Maj. Andrew J. Weber; 8th Wis., Lieut.-Col. George W. Robbins (w), Maj. John W. Jefferson (w), Capt. William B. Britton; 2d Iowa Battery, Capt Nelson T. Spoor. Brigade loss: k, 48; w, 248; m, 26 = 322.
THIRD DIVISION, Brig.-Gen. Charles S. Hamilton.
*Escort:* C, 5th Mo. Cavalry.
*First Brigade,* Brig.-Gen. Napoleon B. Buford: 48th Ind., Lieut. Col. De Witt C. Rugg (w), Lieut. James W. Archer; 59th Ind., Col. Jesse I. Alexander; 5th Iowa, Col. Charles L. Matthies; 4th Minn., Col. John B. Sanborn; 26th Mo., Lieut.-Col. John H. Holman (w); M, 1st Mo. Art'y, Lieut. Junius W. MacMurray; 11th Ohio Battery, Lieut. Henry M. Neil. Brigade loss: k, 7; w, 48 = 55. *Second Brigade,* Brig.-Gen. Jeremiah C. Sullivan, Col. Samuel A. Holmes: 56th Ill., Lieut.-Col. Green B. Raum; 10th Iowa, Maj. Nathaniel McCalla; 17th Iowa, Maj. Jabez Banbury; 10th Mo., Col. Samuel A. Holmes, Maj. Leonidas Horney; E, 24th Mo., Capt. Lafayette M. Rice; 80th Ohio, Maj. Richard Lanning (k), Capt. David Skeels; 6th Wis. Battery, Capt. Henry Dillon; 12th Wis. Battery, Lieut. Lorenzo D. Immell. Brigade loss: k, 34; w, 227; m, 15 = 276.
CAVALRY DIVISION, Col. John K. Mizner.
(Division organized into two brigades, Col. Edward Hatch commanding the First and Col. Albert L. Lee the Second.) 7th Ill., Lieut.-Col. Edward Prince; 11th Ill., Col. Robert G. Ingersoll; 2d Iowa, Maj. Datus E. Coon; 7th Kan., Lieut.-Col. T. P. Herrick; 3d Mich., Capt. Lyman G. Willcox; 5th Ohio (4 co's), Capt. Joseph C. Smith. Division loss: k, 5; w, 17; m, 14 = 36.
UNATTACHED: 64th Ill. (Yates's Sharp-shooters), Capt. John Morrill; 1st U. S. (6 co's — siege artillery), Capt. G. A. Williams. Unattached loss: k, 16; w, 53; m, 15 = 84.
ARMY OF WEST TENNESSEE.
SECOND DIVISION, Brig.-Gen. Thomas A. Davies.
*First Brigade,* Brig.-Gen. Pleasant A. Hackleman (k), Col. Thomas W. Sweeny: 52d Ill., Col.Thomas W. Sweeny, Lieut. Col. John S. Wilcox; 2d Iowa, Col. James Baker (m w), Lieut.-Col. Noah W. Mills (m w), Maj. James B. Weaver; 7th Iowa, Col. Elliott W. Rice; Union Brigade (composed of detachments of 58th Ill., and 8th, 12th, and 14th Iowa), Lieut.-Col. John P. Coulter. Brigade loss: k, 49; w, 318; m, 36 = 403. *Second Brigade,* Brig.-Gen. Richard J. Oglesby (w), Col. August Mersy: 9th Ill., Col. August Mersy; 12th Ill., Col. Augustus L. Chetlain; 22d Ohio, Maj. Oliver Wood; 81st Ohio, Col. Thomas Morton. Brigade loss: k, 38; w, 222; m, 73 = 333. *Third Brigade,* Col. Silas D. Baldwin (w), Col. John V. Du Bois: 7th Ill., Col. Andrew J. Babcock; 50th Ill., Lieut.-Col. William Swarthout; 57th Ill., Lieut.-Col. Frederick J. Hurlbut, Maj. Eric Forsse. Brigade loss: k, 21; w, 115; m, 46 = 182. *Artillery,* Maj. George H. Stone: D, 1st Mo., Capt. Henry Richardson; H, 1st Mo., Capt. Frederick Welker; I, 1st Mo., Lieut. Charles H. Thurber; K, 1st Mo., Lieut. Charles Green. Artillery loss: k, 6; w, 29 = 35. *Unattached:* 14th Mo. (Western Sharp-shooters), Col. Patrick E. Burke. Loss: k, 6; w, 14; m, 3 = 23.
SIXTH DIVISION, Brig.-Gen. Thomas J. McKean.
*First Brigade,* Col. Benjamin Allen, Brig.-Gen. John McArthur: 21st Mo., Col. David Moore, Maj. Edwin Moore; 16th Wis., Maj. Thomas Reynolds; 17th Wis., Col. John L. Doran. Brigade loss: k, 11; w, 67; m, 23 = 101. *Second Brigade,* Col. John M. Oliver: Indpt. Co., Ill. Cav., Capt. William Ford; 15th Mich., Lieut.-Col. John McDermott; 18th Mo. (4 co's), Capt. Jacob R. Ault; 14th Wis., Col. John Hancock; 18th Wis., Col. Gabriel Bouck. Brigade loss: k, 45; w, 108; m, 38 = 191. *Third Brigade,* Col. Marcellus M. Crocker: 11th Iowa, Lieut.-Col. William Hall; 13th Iowa, Lieut.-Col. John Shane; 15th Iowa, Lieut.-Col. William W. Belknap, Col. Hugh T. Reid; 16th Iowa, Lieut.-Col. Addison H. Sanders (w), Maj. William Purcell. Brigade loss: k, 14; w, 111; m, 24 = 149. *Artillery,* Capt. Andrew Hickenlooper: F, 2d Ill., Lieut. J. W. Mitchell; 1st Minn., Lieut. G. F. Cooke; 3d Ohio (section), Capt. Emil Munch, Sergt. Sylvanus Clark; 5th Ohio, Lieut. B. S.

Matson; 10th Ohio, Capt. H. B. White. Artillery loss: w, 8.

Total Union loss: killed, 355; wounded, 1841; captured or missing, 324 = 2520.

The effective strength of Rosecrans's command is not specifically stated in the "Official Records." According to the return for September 30th, 1862, his "aggregate present for duty" was 23,077 (Vol. XVII., Pt. II., p. 246). Probably not less than twenty thousand participated in the battle. On page 172, Vol. XVII., Pt. I., General Rosecrans estimates the Confederate strength at nearly forty thousand and says that was almost double his own numbers.

## THE CONFEDERATE FORCES.

ARMY OF WEST TENNESSEE.—Major-General Earl Van Dorn.

PRICE'S CORPS OR ARMY OF THE WEST.—Major-General Sterling Price.

FIRST DIVISION, Brig.-Gen. Louis Hébert, Brig.-Gen. Martin E. Green.

*First Brigade*, Col. Elijah Gates: 16th Ark., ——; 2d Mo., Col. Francis M. Cockrell; 3d Mo., Col. James A. Pritchard (w); 5th Mo., ——; 1st Mo. Cav. (dismounted), Lieut.-Col. W. D. Maupin; Mo. Battery, Captain William Wade. Brigade loss: k, 53; w, 332; m, 92 = 477. *Second Brigade*, Col. W. Bruce Colbert: 14th Ark., ——; 17th Ark., Lieut.-Col. John Griffith; 3d La., ——; 40th Miss., ——; 1st Tex. Legion, Lieut.-Col. E. R. Hawkins. 3d Tex. Cav. (dismounted), ——; Clark's (Mo.) Battery, Lieut. J. L. Faris; St. Louis (Mo.) Battery, Capt. William E. Dawson. Brigade loss: k, 11; w, 129; m, 132 = 272. *Third Brigade*, Brig.-Gen. Martin E. Green, Col. W. H. Moore (w): 7th Miss. Battalion, Lieut.-Col. J. S. Terral (w); 43d Miss., Col. W. H. Moore; 4th Mo., Col. A. MacFarlane; 6th Mo., Col. Eugene Erwin (w); 3d Mo. Cav., (dismounted), ——; Mo. Battery, Capt. Henry Guibor; Mo. Battery, Capt. John C. Landis. Brigade loss: k, 77; w, 369; m, 302 = 748. *Fourth Brigade*, Col. John D. Martin (m w), Col. Robert McLain (w); 37th Ala.; 36th Miss., Col. W. W. Witherspoon; 37th Miss., Col. Robert McLain; 38th Miss., Col. F. W. Adams. (Battery attached to this brigade not identified.) Brigade loss: k, 41; w, 203 = 244.

MAURY'S DIVISION, Brig.-Gen. Dabney H. Maury.

*Moore's Brigade*, Brig.-Gen. John C. Moore: 42d Ala., Col. John W. Portis; 15th Ark., Lieut.-Col. Squire Boone; 23d Ark., Lieut.-Col. A. A. Pennington; 35th Miss., Col. William S. Barry; 2d Tex., Col. W. P. Rogers (k); Mo. Battery, Capt. H. M. Bledsoe. Brigade loss: k, 53; w, 230; m, 1012 = 1295.

*Cabell's Brigade*, Brig.-Gen. William L. Cabell: 18th Ark., Col. John N. Daly (m w); 19th Ark., Col. T. P. Dockery; 20th Ark., Col. H. P. Johnson (k); 21st Ark., Col. Jordan E. Cravens; Ark. Battalion (Jones's), ——; Ark. Battalion (Rapley's), Capt. James A. Ashford; Ark. (Appeal) Battery, Lieut. William N. Hogg. Brigade loss: k, 98; w, 323; m, 214 = 635. *Phifer's Brigade*, Brig.-Gen. C. W. Phifer: 3d Ark. Cav. (dismounted), ——; 6th Tex. Cav. (dismounted), Col. L. S. Ross; 9th Tex. Cav. (dismounted), ——; Stirman's Sharp-shooters, Col. Ras. Stirman: Ark. Battery (McNally's), Lieut. Frank A. Moore. Brigade loss: k, 94; w, 273; m, 200 = 567. *Cavalry* (composition probably incomplete), Brig.-Gen. Frank C. Armstrong: 2d Ark., Col. W. F. Slemons; Miss. Reg't, Col. Wirt Adams; 2d Mo., Col. Robert McCulloch. Cavalry loss: w, 2; m, 9 = 11. *Reserve Artillery:* Tenn. Battery (Hoxton's), Lieut. Thomas F. Tobin (c); Ala. Battery, Capt. Henry H. Sengstak. Artillery loss: k, 1; w, 4; m, 14 = 19.

DISTRICT OF THE MISSISSIPPI.

FIRST DIVISION, Maj.-Gen. Mansfield Lovell.

*First Brigade*, Brig.-Gen. Albert Rust: 4th Ala., Battalion, Maj. —— Gibson; 31st Ala., ——; 35th Ala., Capt. A. E. Ashford; 9th Ark., Col. Isaac L. Dunlop; 3d Ky., Col. A. P. Thompson; 7th Ky., Col. Ed. Crossland; Miss. (Hudson), Battery, Lieut. John R. Sweaney. Brigade loss: k, 25; w, 117; m, 83 = 225. *Second Brigade* (composition not fully reported), Brig.-Gen. J. B. Villepigue: 33d Miss., Col. D. W. Hurst; 39th Miss., Col. W. B. Shelby. Brigade loss: k, 21; w, 76; m, 71 = 168. *Third Brigade*, Brig.-Gen. John S. Bowen: 6th Miss., Col. Robert Lowry; 15th Miss., Col. M. Farrell; 22d Miss., Capt. J. D. Lester; Miss. Battalion, Capt. C. K. Caruthers; 1st Mo., Lieut.-Col. A. C. Riley; La. (Watson) Battery, Capt. A. A. Bursley. Brigade loss: k, 28; w, 92; m, 40 = 160. *Cavalry Brigade*, Col. W. H. Jackson: 1st Miss., Lieut.-Col. F. A. Montgomery; 7th Tenn., Lieut.-Col. J. G. Stocks. Brigade loss: k, 1. *Unattached:* La. Zouave Battalion, Maj. St. L. Dupiere. Loss: k, 2; m, 14 = 16. Total Confederate loss (including Hatchie Bridge, Oct. 5th): killed, 505; wounded, 2150; captured or missing, 2183 = 4838. General Van Dorn says ("Official Records," Vol. XVII., Pt. I., p. 378): "Field returns at Ripley showed my strength to be about 22,000 men." It is estimated that at least 20,000 were brought into action at Corinth.

MONUMENT IN THE NATIONAL CEMETERY, CORINTH. FROM A PHOTOGRAPH TAKEN IN 1884.

END OF VOLUME II.